EDUCATION IN THE UNITED STATES
A DOCUMENTARY HISTORY

SOL COHEN is Associate Professor of Education in the
Graduate School of Education at the University of
California, Los Angeles. He received his Ph.D. in 1964
from Columbia University where he was a Romiett
Stevens Scholar and Alumni Fellow at Teachers
College. He is the author of *Progressive and Urban
School Reform* (1965) and has contributed numerous
articles to scholarly journals and encyclopedias.
Professor Cohen has also been a Visiting Scholar at
the University of London Institute of Education.

EDUCATION IN THE UNITED STATES
A DOCUMENTARY HISTORY

Edited by
SOL COHEN

UNIVERSITY OF
CALIFORNIA
LOS ANGELES

VOLUME 3

Random House New York

Reference Series Editors:

Fred L. Israel
William P. Hansen

Acknowledgments for use of material covered by
Copyright Conventions appear on pages 3395–99.

Art spots courtesy of Dover Pictorial Archives

FIRST EDITION

9 8 7 6 5 4 3 2 1

Education in the United States: A Documentary
History *is now exclusively published and distributed
by* Greenwood Press, Inc.
51 Riverside Avenue
Westport, Ct. 06880
ISBN 0-313-20141-2 SET
0-313-20142-0 v.1
0-313-20143-9 v.2
0-313-20144-7 v.3
0-313-20145-5 v. 4
0-313-20146-3 v.5

Designed by Marsha Picker
for computer typesetting by Volt Information Sciences, Inc.

VOLUME III
CONTENTS

THE
PROFESSION
OF EDUCATION

Old-Time Schools and Teachers

THE NEW ENGLAND DISTRICT SCHOOL AS IT WAS (c. 1810–18)   From
Warren Burton, *The District School as It Was, by One Who Went to It,* Clifton Johnson,
ed. (Boston, 1897), pp. 56–61.

There, the class have read; but they have something else to do before
they take their seats. "Shut your books," says he who has been hearing them read.
What makes this row of little countenances brighten up so suddenly, especially the
upper end of it? What wooden faces and leaden eyes, two minutes ago! The reading
was nothing to them,—those select sentences and maxims in Perry's spelling-book
which are tucked in between the fables. It is all as dull as a dirge to those life-loving
boys and girls. They almost drowsed while they stood up in their places. But they
are fully awake now. They are going to spell. But this in itself is the driest exercise
to prepare for, and the driest to perform, of the whole round. The child cares no
more in his heart about the arrangement of vowels and consonants in the
orthography of words, than he does how many chips lie one above another at the
school-house wood-pile. But he does care whether he is at the head or foot of his
class; whether the money dangles from his own neck or another's. This is the secret
of this interest in spelling. Emulation is awakened, ambition roused. There is
something like the tug of strength in the wrestle, something of the alternation of
hope and fear in a game of chance. There has been a special preparation for the
trial. Observe this class any day, half an hour before they are called up to read.
What a flitting from top to bottom of the spelling column, and what a flutter of lips
and hissing of utterance! Now the eye twinkles on the page to catch a word, and
now it is fixed on the empty air, while the orthography is syllabled over and over
again in mind, until at length it is syllabled on the memory. But the time of trial has
come; they have only to read first. "The third class may come and read." "O dear, I
haven't got my spelling lesson," mutters Charlotte to herself. She has just begun the
art of writing this winter, and she lingered a little too long at her hooks and
trammels. The lesson seems to her to have as many again hard words in it as
common. What a flutter she is in! She got up above George in the forenoon, and
she would not get down again for anything. She is as slow in coming from her seat
as she possibly can be and keep moving. She makes a chink in her book with her
finger, and every now and then, during the reading exercise, steals a glance at a
difficult word.

But the reading is over, and what a brightening up, as was said before, with the
exception, perhaps, of two or three idle or stupid boys at that less honorable
extremity of the class called the foot! That boy at the head—no, it was a boy; but

THE
PROFESSION
OF EDUCATION

1283

Harriet has at length got above him; and, when girls once get to the head, get them away from it if you can. Once put the "pride of place" into their hearts, and how they will queen it! Then they are more sensitive regarding anything that might lower them in the eyes of others, and seem the least like disgrace. I have known a little girl to cry the half of one day, and look melancholy the whole of the next, on losing her place at the head. Girls are more likely to arrive at and keep the first place in the class, in consequence of a little more help from mother nature than boys get. I believe that they generally have a memory more fitted for catching and holding words and other signs addressed to the eye, than the other sex. That girl at the head has studied her spelling lesson, until she is as confident of every word as the unerring Perry himself. She can spell every word in the column, in the order it stands, without the master's "putting it out," she has been over it so many times. "Now, Mr. James, get up again if you can," thinks Harriet. I pity you, poor girl; for James has an ally that will blow over your proud castle in the air. Old Boreas, the king of the winds, will order out a snow-storm by and by, to block up the roads, so that none but booted and weather-proof males can get to school; and you, Miss, must lose a day or two, and then find yourself at the foot with those blockhead boys who always abide there. But let it not be thought that all those foot lads are deficient in intellect. Look at them when the master's back is turned, and you will see mischievous ingenuity enough to convince you that they might surpass even James and Harriet, had some other faculties been called into exercise besides the mere memory of verbalities.

The most extraordinary spelling, and indeed reading machine, in our school, was a boy whom I shall call Memorus Wordwell. He was mighty and wonderful in the acquisition and remembrance of words,—of signs without the ideas signified. The alphabet he acquired at home before he was two years old. What exultation of parents, what exclamation from admiring visitors! "There was never anything like it." He had almost accomplished his Abs before he was thought old enough for school. At an earlier age than usual, however, he was sent; and then he went from *Ache* to *Abomination* in half the summers and winters it took the rest of us to go over the same space. Astonishing how quickly he mastered column after column, section after section, of obstinate orthographies. Those martial terms I have just used, together with our hero's celerity, put me in mind of Cæsar. So I will quote him. Memorus might have said in respect to the host of the spellingbook, "I came, I saw, I conquered." He generally stood at the head of a class, each one of whom was two years his elder. Poor creatures! they studied hard, some of them, but it did no good: Memorus Wordwell was born to be above them, as some men are said to have been "born to command." At the public examination of his first winter, the people of the district, and even the minister, thought it marvelous that such monstrous great words should be mastered by "such a leetle mite of a boy!" Memorus was mighty also in saying those after spelling matters—the Key, the Abbreviations, the Punctuation, &c. These things were deemed of great account to be laid up in remembrance, although they were all very imperfectly understood, and some of them not understood at all.

Punctuation—how many hours, days, and even weeks, have I tugged away to lift, as it were, to roll up into the store-house of my memory, the many long, heavy sentences comprehended under this title! Only survey (we use this word when speaking of considerable space and bulk)—only survey the first sentence, a transcript of which I will endeavor to locate in these narrow bounds. I would have my readers of the rising generation know what mighty labors we little creatures of five, six, and seven years old were set to perform:—

"Punctuation is the art of pointing, or of dividing a discourse into periods by points, expressing the pauses to be made in the reading thereof, and regulating the cadence or elevation of the voice."

There, I have labored weeks on that; for I always had the lamentable defect of mind not to be able to commit to memory what I did not understand. My teachers never aided me with the least explanation of the above-copied sentence, nor of other reading of a similar character, which was likewise to be committed to memory.

REGULATIONS OF THE SCHOOLS OF PROVIDENCE, RHODE ISLAND
(1820)   From *Centennial Report of the School Committee, 1899–1900*, pp. 42–43, as quoted in Ellwood P. Cubberley, ed., *Readings in the History of Education* (Boston, 1920), pp. 548–49.

Regulations for the Instruction and Government of the Publick Schools in the Town of Providence

The Publick Schools are established for the general benefit of the community; And all children, of both sexes, having attained the age of six years, shall be received therein and faithfully instructed, without preference or partiality.

The Instruction shall be uniform in the several schools, and shall consist of spelling, Reading, the use of Capital letters and Punctuation, Writing, English Grammar & Arithmetick.

The Pronunciation shall be uniform in the several schools & the standard shall be the Critical Pronouncing Dictionary of John Walker.

The following Books, and none others, shall be used in the several schools, viz: Alden's Spelling Book, first & second part, New Testament, American Preceptor, Murray's Sequel to the English Reader, Murray's Abridgement of English Grammar and Dabols Arithmetick.

The scholars shall be put in separate classes according to their several improvements, each sex by itself.

The Schools are statedly to begin and end as follows: From the first Monday in October to the first Monday in May to begin at 9 o'clock A.M. and end at 12 ock. M.: and half past one ock. P.M. & end at half past four ock. P.M. From the first Monday in May to the first Monday in October, to begin at 8 ock. A.M. & end at 11 ock. A.M.; And at 2 ock. P.M. and end at 5 ock. P.M.

The Scholars shall be excused from attending the schools on Saturdays, on Christmas day, on the 4th day of July, on public Fasts and Thanksgiving, on the last Monday in April, on the day of Regimental Training; on the day succeeding each quarterly visitation and during the whole of Commencement Week. But on no other days shall the Preceptors dismiss the Schools without permission obtained from the Town Council.

As Discipline and Good Government are absolutely necessary to improvement it is indispensible that the scholars should implicitly obey the Regulations of the Schools.

The good morals of the Youth being essential to their own comfort & to their progress in useful knowledge, they are strictly enjoined to avoid idleness and profaneness, falsehood and deceitfulness, and every other wicked & disgraceful practice; and to conduct themselves in a sober, orderly & decent manner both in & out of school. If any scholar should prove disobedient & refractory, after all reasonable means used by the Preceptor to bring him or her to a just sense of duty, such offender shall be suspended from attendance & instruction in any School, until the next visitation of the committee. Each Scholar shall be punctual in attendance at the appointed hour and be as constant as possible in daily attendance and all excuses for absence shall be by note, from the Parent or Guardian of the scholar.

It shall be the duty of the Preceptors to report at each quarterly visitation the names of those scholars who have been grossly negligent in attending School or inattentive to their Studies.

It is recommended to the Preceptors, as far as practicable, to exclude corporal punishment from the schools, and particularly that they never permit it to be inflicted by their ushers in their presence, or at any time by a scholar.

That they inculcate upon the scholars the necessity of good behaviour during their absence from school. That they endeavor to convince the children by their treatment that they feel a parental affection for them, and never make dismission from school at an early hour a reward for good conduct or diligence, but endeavor to teach the scholars to consider being at school as a privilege & dismission from it as a punishment.

That they endeavor to impress on the minds of the scholars a sense of the Being & Providence of God & their obligations to love & reverence Him,—their duty to their parents & preceptors, the beauty & excellency of truth, justice & mutual love, tenderness to brute creatures, the happy tendency of self government and obedience to the dictates of reason & religion; the observance of the Sabbath as a sacred institution, the duty which they owe to their country & the necessity of a strict obedience to its Laws, and that they caution them against the prevailing vices.

JAMES G. CARTER CRITICISES THE COMMON SCHOOLS OF MASSACHUSETTS (1826)   From James G. Carter, *Essays On Popular Education* . . ., (Boston, 1826), pp. 34–37, 40–41.

Before we attempt, however, to take a single step towards reform let us see what we have to amend. Unless faults can be shown to exist in the organization of our system of popular education, and great ones; it will do but little good to recommend improvements. For it is with communities as with individuals; and "no one," says Fisher Ames, "is less likely to improve, than the coxcomb, who fancies he has already learned out." The pride, which we of New England have been accustomed to feel and, perhaps, to manifest, in our free schools, as the best in the country, and in the world, has not improved their condition. But, on the contrary, the great complacency with which we contemplate this institution is a most effectual bar to all improvements in it. The time has come, when we owe it to our country and ourselves to speak the whole truth in this matter, even though it disturb our self-satisfaction a little.

It will be convenient to point out the faults of the public provisions for popular education under the two following heads; first, the "Summer Free Schools," which are, generally, taught in the country towns for a few months in the warm season of the year by females; and second, the "Winter Free Schools," which are taught by men, commonly, for a shorter period, during the cold season. Children of both sexes of from four to ten or twelve years, usually attend these primary summer schools, and females often to a much later age. This is a very interesting period of human life. No one, who has reflected much upon the subject of early discipline; no one, I trust, who has even followed me through the preceding essays, can doubt, that it is one of the most important parts, if not the very most important part of our lives, as it regards the influence of education in its widest sense. It is important as it regards the development of the powers of the body, or physical education. Because the parts of the body, the limbs, the muscles, the organs, or whatever are the technical names for them, now assume a firmness and consistency in discharging their proper functions, or they become distorted and enfeebled; and these habits, thus early contracted, became a part of ourselves and are as abiding as our lives. Yet what has been done in this branch of education? Nothing at all, absolutely nothing at all, even in our best schools. This period is vitally important as it regards the cultivation of the heart and its affections. What has been done here? Chance and ill-directed efforts make up all the education, which we have received or are giving to our children in the schools in this department. Finally, it is important to us, as it regards the discipline of the head, the development of the understanding and its faculties. What have we done in this department? We have done something, indeed, and think that we have done much. We have done, and we continue to do, *more* than we do *well*. We resort to many expedients and apply many means, without distinctly understanding, either what we wish to attain, whether it be possible to attain it, or if so, the adaptation of our means to its attainment. Success here, therefore, if the best possible results have ever been gained in any instance, has been more the result of chance than of skill.

To whom do we assign the business of governing and instructing our children from four to twelve years of age? Who take upon themselves the trust of forming those principles and habits, which are to be strengthened and confirmed in manhood, and make our innocent little ones through life, happy or miserable in themselves, and the blessings or the curses of society? To analyze, in detail, the habits, which are formed and confirmed in these first schools, to trace the abiding influence of good ones, or to describe the inveteracy of bad ones, would lead me from my present purpose. But are these interesting years of life and these important branches of education committed to those, who understand their importance or their influence upon the future character? Are they committed to those, who would know what to do, to discharge their high trust successfully if they did, indeed, understand their importance? I think not. And I am persuaded, that all, who have reflected but for a moment upon the age, the acquirement, and the experience of those who assume to conduct this branch of education, must have come to the same conclusion.

The teachers of the primary summer schools have rarely had any education beyond what they have acquired in the very schools where they begin to teach. Their attainments, therefore, to say the least, are usually *very moderate*. But this is not the worst of it. They are often very young, they are constantly changing their employment, and consequently can have but little experience; and what is worse than all, they never have had any direct preparation for their profession. This is the only service, in which we venture to employ young, and often, ignorant persons, without some previous instruction in their appropriate duties. We require experience in all those, whom we employ to perform the slightest mechanical labour for us. We would not buy a coat or a hat of one, who should undertake to make them without a previous apprenticeship. Nor would any one have the hardihood to offer to us the result of his first essay in manufacturing either of these articles. We do not even send an old shoe to be mended, except it be to a workman of whose skill we have had ample proof. Yet we commit our children to be educated to those, who know nothing, absolutely nothing, of the complicated and difficult duties assigned to them. Shall we trust the developement of the delicate bodies, the susceptible hearts, and the tender minds of our little children to those who have no knowledge of their nature? Can they, can these rude hands finish the workmanship of the Almighty? No language can express the astonishment, which a moments reflection on this subject excites in me.

But I must return to the examination of the qualifications of the female teachers of the primary summer schools, from which purpose I have unconsciously a little departed to indulge in a general remark. They are a class of teachers unknown in our laws regulating the schools unless it be by some latitude of construction. No standard of attainments is fixed, at which they must arrive before they assume the business of instruction. So that any one *keeps school*, which is a very different thing from *teaching school*, who wishes to do it, and can persuade, by herself, or her friends, a small district to employ her. And this is not a very difficult matter, especially when the remuneration for the employment is so very trifling. The farce of an examination and a certificate from the minister of the town, for it is a perfect farce, amounts to no efficient check upon the obtrusions of ignorance and inexperience. As no standard is fixed by law, each minister makes a standard for himself, and alters it as often as the peculiar circumstances of the case require. And there will always be enough of peculiar circumstances to render a refusal inexpedient.

Let those, who are conversant with the manner in which these schools are managed, say, whether this description of them undervalues their character and efficacy. Let those, who conduct them, pause and consider whether all is well, and whether there are not abuses and perversions in them, which call loudly for attention and reformation. Compare the acquirements, the experience, the knowledge of teaching possessed by these instructers, not one with another, for the standard is much too low; but with what they might be, under more favorable circumstances and with proper preparation. Compare the improvement made in these little nurseries of piety and religion, of knowledge and rational liberty, not one with another, for the progress in all of them is much too slow; but with what the infant mind and heart are capable of, at this early age, under the most favourable auspices. And there can be no doubt, that all will arrive at the same conclusions, a dissatisfaction with the condition of these schools; and an astonishment, that the public have been so long contented with so small results from means, which all will acknowledge capable of doing so much. . . .

The young man, who lays down his axe and aspires to take up the "rod" and rule in a village school, has, usually, in common with other young men, a degree of dignity and self-complacency, which it is dangerous to the extent of his power to disturb. And when he comes to his minister, sustained by his own influence in the parish, and that of a respectable father and perhaps a large family of friends, and asks of him the legal approbation for a teacher, it is a pretty delicate matter to refuse it. A firm and conscientious refusal of approbation to a school-master, has led, in more instances than one, to a firm and conscientious refusal to hear the minister preach. And, by the parish difficulties growing out of so small an affair, he has found himself at last "unsettled" and thrown with his family, perhaps in his old age, upon the world to seek and gain his subsistence as he may. This is truly martyrdom. And martyrs in ordinary times are rare. Even good men can make peace with their consciences on better terms. So much for the literary qualifications of instructers.

It is the intention of the school-law to secure good, moral characters in the public instructers by requiring the approbation, as to this qualification, of the selectmen of the town, where the school is to be taught. No doubt selectmen are as good judges of morality as any body of men, which could readily be appealed to. But either we are a very moral people, or they are not very discriminating; for instances are rare, indeed, of refusal of their approbation on this ground. If a young man be moral enough to keep out of the State-Prison, he will find no difficulty in getting approbation for a school-master. These things ought not to be so. Both the moral and the intellectual character of the rising generation are influenced more by their instructers, during the period of from four to twelve years of age, than by any cause so entirely within our control. It becomes then of momentous concern to the community, in a moral and religious, as well as in political point of view, that this influence should be the greatest and the best possible. That it is not now so, every one, I trust, who has followed me through my preceding essays, is convinced. And if something be not done, and that speedily, to improve the condition of the free schools, and especially the primary *summer schools,* they will not only fail of their happiest influence, but in a short time of all influence which will be worth estimating.

If the policy of the legislature, in regard to free schools, for the last twenty years be not changed, the institution, which has been the glory of New England will, in twenty years more, be extinct. If the State continue to relieve themselves of the trouble of providing for the instruction of the whole people, and to shift the responsibility upon the towns, and the towns upon the districts, and the districts upon individuals, each will take care of himself and his own family as he is able, and as he appreciates the blessing of a good education. The rich will, as a class, have much better instruction than they now have, while the poor will have much worse or none at all. The academies and private schools will be carried to much greater perfection than they have been, while the public free schools will become stationary or retrograde; till at length, they will be thrown for support upon the gratuitous, and of course capricious and uncertain efforts of individuals; and then, like the lower schools of the crowded cities of Europe, they will soon degenerate into mere mechanical establishments, such as the famous *seminaries* of London, Birmingham, and Manchester of which we hear so much lately, not for rational moral and intellectual instruction of human beings, but for training young animals to march, sing, and draw figures in sand,—establishments, in which the power of one man is so prodigiously multiplied, that he can overlook, direct and control the intellectual exercises of a thousand! And this wretched mockery of education, they must be right glad to accept as a charity, instead of inheriting as their birthright as good instruction as the country affords.

A DAME SCHOOL IN BEVERLY, MASSACHUSETTS (c. 1830) From Lucy
Larcom, *A New England Girlhood*, (Boston, 1889), pp. 42-45.

Aunt Hannah used her kitchen or her sitting-room for a schoolroom, as
best suited her convenience. We were delighted observers of her culinary operations
and other employments. If a baby's head nodded, a little bed was made for it on a
soft "comforter" in the corner, where it had its nap out undisturbed. But this did
not often happen; there were so many interesting things going on that we seldom
became sleepy.

Aunt Hannah was very kind and motherly, but she kept us in fear of her ferule,
which indicated to us a possibility of smarting palms. This ferule was shaped much
like the stick with which she stirred her hasty pudding for dinner,—I thought it was
the same,—and I found myself caught in a whirlwind of family laughter by reporting
at home that "Aunt Hannah punished the scholars with the pudding-stick."

There was one colored boy in school, who did not sit on a bench, like the rest,
but on a block of wood that looked like a backlog turned endwise. Aunt Hannah
often called him a "blockhead," and I supposed it was because he sat on that block.
Sometimes, in his absence, a boy was made to sit in his place for punishment for
being a "blockhead" too, as I imagined. I hoped I should never be put there. Stupid
little girls received a different treatment,—an occasional rap on the head with the
teacher's thimble; accompanied with a half-whispered, impatient ejaculation, which
sounded very much like "Numskull!" I think this was a rare occurrence, however,
for she was a good-natured, much-enduring woman.

One of our greatest school pleasures was to watch Aunt Hannah spinning on her
flax-wheel, wetting her thumb and forefinger at her lips to twist the thread, keeping
time, meanwhile, to some quaint old tune with her foot upon the treadle.

A verse of one of her hymns, which I never heard anybody else sing, resounds in
the farthest corner of my memory yet:—

> "Whither goest thou, pilgrim stranger,
> Wandering through this lowly vale?
> Knowest thou not 't is full of danger?
> And will not thy courage fail?"

Then a little pause, and the refrain of the answer broke in with a change, quick
and jubilant, the treadle moving more rapidly, also:—

> "No, I'm bound for the kingdom!
> Will you go to glory with me?
> Hallelujah! Praise the Lord!"

I began to go to school when I was about two years old, as other children about
us did. The mothers of those large families had to resort to some means of keeping
their little ones out of mischief, while they attended to their domestic duties. Not
much more than that sort of temporary guardianship was expected of the good
dame who had us in charge.

But I learned my letters in a few days, standing at Aunt Hannah's knee while she pointed them out in the spelling-book with a pin, skipping over the "a b abs" into words of one or two syllables, thence taking a flying leap into the New Testament, in which there is concurrent family testimony that I was reading at the age of two years and a half. Certain it is that a few passages in the Bible, whenever I read them now, do not fail to bring before me a vision of Aunt Hannah's somewhat sternly smiling lips, with her spectacles just above them, far down on her nose, encouraging me to pronounce the hard words. I think she tried to choose for me the least difficult verses, or perhaps those of which she was herself especially fond. Those which I distinctly recall are the Beatitudes, the Twenty-third Psalm, parts of the first and fourteenth chapters of the Gospel of St. John, and the thirteenth chapter of the First Epistle to the Corinthians.

I liked to say over the "Blesseds,"—the shortest ones best,—about the meek and the pure in heart; and the two "In the beginnings," both in Genesis and John. Every child's earliest and proudest Scriptural conquest in school was, almost as a matter of course, the first verse in the Bible.

But the passage which I learned first, and most delighted to repeat after Aunt Hannah,—I think it must have been her favorite too,—was, "Let not your heart be troubled. In my Father's house are many mansions."

The Voice in the Book seemed so tender! Somebody was speaking who had a heart, and who knew that even a little child's heart was sometimes troubled. And it was a Voice that called us somewhere; to the Father's house, with its many mansions, so sunshiny and so large.

HENRY BARNARD ON THE PLIGHT OF THE TEACHING PROFESSION

(1839)   From *First Annual Report of the Board of Commissioners of Common Schools in Connecticut,* together with the *First Annual Report of the Secretary of the Board,* May, 1839 (Hartford, 1839), pp. 37–38.

Most of the teachers employed the past winter, have not taught the same schools two successive seasons. Out of 1292 teachers returned, but 341 have taught the same school before. Omitting those who are engaged for the whole year, as permanent teachers, the number is less than 240. And these were not engaged in the summer, but only for the winter. In this single fact is found an explanation of many of the acknowledged defects in our schools.

In the first place, nearly one month of the school is practically lost in the time consumed by the teacher in getting acquainted with the temper, wants, dispositions, and previous progress of his various pupils, with a view to their proper classification, and to the adaptation of his own peculiar modes of government and instruction. By the time the school is in good progress, the scholars begin to drop away, the school money is exhausted, and the school dismissed. After a vacation of unnecessary length, as far as the recreation and relief of the children are concerned, the summer school commences with reduced numbers, under a less vigilant supervision, with a poorly compensated teacher, to go through the same course as before; and so on from year to year. The loss of time consequent on the change of

THE PROFESSION OF EDUCATION

teachers, and the long intermission between the two seasons of schooling, not only retards the progress of the school, but leads to the breaking up of regular habits of study, which will be felt in the whole future life.

In the second place, it leads to the perpetual and expensive change of school books, so much complained of, and so justly complained of, by parents. Every teacher has his favorite text books, and is naturally desirous of introducing them wherever he goes. And as there is no system adopted in relation to this subject in any society, he usually succeeds in introducing more or less of them in every school. The money now expended in the purchase of new books, caused by the change of teachers, would go far to continue the same teacher another month in the same school. Thus the district might practically gain, without any additional expense, two months schooling each year by employing the same teacher year after year.

In the third place, this practice excludes from our common schools nearly all those who have decided to make teaching a profession and drives them, almost as a matter of course, into private schools or academies. Out of the 1292 teachers employed, only 100 have been engaged in teaching for more than 10 years; and of this number a large proportion have only taught in the winter.

WALT WHITMAN DESCRIBES "THE WHIP" IN THE SCHOOLS OF BROOKLYN (1845)   From *Brooklyn Evening Star,* October 22, 1845.

The Whip in Schools

We wish our Brooklyn teachers could have had the pleasure, as we had, of hearing Horace Mann's address on Education the other night, at the Tabernacle in New York. It embodied nearly all the philosophy which modern thinkers and writers have settled to be philosophy on the subject—and treated with great clearness and no little severity the old fallacies that unfortunately are by no means yet completely routed from among us. "They who expel wrong doing by means of physical chastisement," said Mr. Mann, "cast out devils, through Beelzebub, the prince of devils!" Are not some of our Brooklyn teachers a little too profuse of this satanic power?

It is with no unkind spirit that we affirm—and call all good and sound modern reasoners on the subject to back us—that the instructor who uses the lash in his school at all, is unworthy to hold the power he does hold. That he has found no other means—that he ever brings himself into a predicament where the honor of his *authority* demands the use of the rod—that he has not been forearmed with some escape which, in emergency, will enable him to avoid such a use—that he can bethink him of no better and easier, and gentle and more humane plan to ensure obedience than thrashing, proves him fit perhaps for dog-whipper, or menagerie-tamer, but not for the holy office of fashioning an immortal human soul.

Do we speak strongly on this subject! Ah, we know how much need there is of it! Of the thousands of bright hearted, and red-cheeked young creatures who are gathered together in this country in schools, and drilled by the sound of whistles, the tinkle of bells, and the dread of ratans, to go through certain evolutions with the limbs, and speak by rote certain lessons with the voice—we feel how much more could be made of them under a milder and truer system. How many noble spirited boys are beaten into sullen and spiteful endurance of what there is no earthly need—sharp taunts, blows, and frowning looks! Awake! parent and teacher, to higher ideas for your kind, in the young freshness wherewith God has formed them, than to suppose there are not a hundred better ways of drawing out what is good, and repelling what is bad, in them, than the ferrule and the rod!

As a general thing the faults of our public schools system are—crowding too many students together, insufficiency of books, and their cost being taxed directly on the pupil—and the flogging system, which in a portion of the schools still holds its wretched sway. With pride we unite in the numerous commendations of the grand free school system of this State—with its twelve thousand seminaries, and its twenty thousand teachers, to whom each child, rich or poor, can come without money and without price! But we are none the less aware that the prodigious sum—hundreds of thousands of dollars—annually expended on these schools, might be expended to more profit. We have by no means ascended to the height of the great argument of education. The monotonous *old* still resists the fresh philosophical *new*. Form and precedent often are more thought of than reality. What are mere "order" or "learning lessons," or all the routine of the simple *outside* of school-keeping?—Absolutely nothing, in themselves; and only valuable, as far as they help the higher objects of educating the child. To teach the child *book grammar* is nothing; to teach him by example, by practice, by thoroughly clarifying the principles of correct syntax, *how to talk and write harmoniously,* is every thing. To put him through the arithmetic is not much; to make him able to compare, calculate, and quickly seize the bearings of a practical figure-question such as occurs in business every hour, is a good deal. Mere atlas geography is a sham, too, unless the learner have the position of places in his mind, and *know* the direction, distances, bearings, etc., of the countries, seas, cities, rivers and mountains, whose names (as our miserable school geographies give them,) he runs over so glibly. We care very little indeed for—what is the pride of many teachers' hearts—the military discipline of their schools, and the slavish obedience of their pupils to the imperial nod or waved hand of the master. As to the flogging plan, it is the most wretched item yet left of the ignorance and inefficiency of school-keeping. It has surrounded the office, (properly one of the noblest on earth,) with a character of contemptibleness and petty malignance, that will stick to it as long as whipping sticks among teachers' habits. What nobleness can reside in a man who catches boys by the collar and cuffs their ears? What elevation or dignity of character can even a child's elastic thoughts connect with one who cuts him over the back with a ratan or makes him hold out his hand to receive the whack of a ferule? For teachers' own sakes—for the true height and majesty of their office, hardly second to the priesthood—they should one and all unite in precluding this petty and foolish punishment—this degrader and bringerdown of their high standing. As things are, the word school-teacher is identified with a dozen unpleasant and ridiculous associations—a sour face, a whip, hard knuckles snapped on tender heads, no gentle, fatherly kindness, no inciting of young ambition in its noble phases, none of the beautifiers of authority, but all that is small, ludicrous, and in after life productive of indignation. We have reason to think that the flogging system still prevails in several of our Brooklyn schools to quite a wretched extent. In the school in Baltic st. under a former management, forty children in the boys' department were thrashed in the course of one morning! and in the female department a little girl was so cut and marked with the ratan over back, neck and shoulders, for some trifling offence, that the livid marks remained there for several days! This is a pretty fact for the character of our public seminaries! Justice to the mass of the teachers, however, demands that they should not be confounded with these ultra and repulsive cases. In general, doubtless, they whip with moderation—if that word may be applied to such a punishment at all. Nor do we mean to impugn the motives altogether. *They* think they are doing right. So did the Spanish torturers in Peru—inquisitors in Spain—and the learned doctors who denounced Jenner.

SCHOOL SUPERINTENDENT OF ALLEGHANY COUNTY, NEW YORK STATE, EVALUATES THE TEACHERS OF HIS COUNTY (1843) From New York State, Department of Public Instruction, *Annual Report of the Superintendent* of Common Schools . . . 1843 (Albany, 1843), pp. 77–80.

I have found them from first rate down to the lowest grade, whose services do more hurt than good, who communicate more error than truth, and who would establish more bad habits in the practice of scholars in a single term of four months than a thorough and competent instructor would break up in eight. I have found ladies and gentlemen engaged in the responsible business of directing the youthful mind in our common schools, whose only ambition seemed to be to shine in their profession, and benefit their juvenile charge all in their power; who would scorn alike the sneers of those engaged in private schools, and the contempt of those who consider the district school fit only for the instruction of the very lowest grade of community, whose *breath* is *contagion*, and whose *touch* is immediate *moral death*. The class of teachers to which I now refer, have established themselves in the estimation of the friends of popular education, by a course of well doing, and a strict attention to all the means within their reach intended to elevate the condition and character of district schools. They are systematic and thorough in every department of their labors. . . I believe that about one-sixth of all the teachers whose schools I have visited will rank in the first class, and their labors and persevering efforts do honor to the profession.

The next class I shall mention is more numerous than the former, and who appear to enter upon the business of teaching with high expectation and flattering prospects. For a time they go on with all that ardor and ambition peculiar to the character of the young, infusing all the energy of soul they possess into the feelings of their scholars, and drawing into requisition every power within their reach for the attainment of their high object. After pursuing this course for a time, they grow tired of the labor it imposes, and begin to relax in their exertions to do all in their power to elevate the standard of district schools; they begin to descend from the elevation they have gained, lose their influence over their pupils, their respect and subordination; their systematic course is in some measure abandoned; they have not that decision of purpose with which they set out; they become peevish and fretful, easily thrown out of a train of good humor, and are exposed to the mercy of their scholars, who, when they perceive they can make them appear ridiculous, will seek every pretext to harrass and irritate their feelings. This class, I am sorry to say, are much more numerous than the one before mentioned, and can be denominated no higher than second rate teachers.

A third class are those who enter upon the business of teaching for the purpose of raising a sum of money in a given time, which they could not do in any other business in which they could find employment. They enter not upon the discharge of these vast responsibilities because they love to teach, or because they have any desire to see the rising generation growing up with that knowledge so necessary to fit them for the transaction of business, and for usefulness in the community in which they may be placed, but for the pecuniary benefit derived from the employment. They have no desire so to manage their schools as to gain employment in that district again, for they wish to form new acquaintances, and therefore prefer to stay but one term in a place. It matters not with them whether they communicate ideas of those placed under their charge or not; whether their pupils have an understanding of what they are required to commit to memory, or whether they repeat their lessons parrot-like, without knowing what they mean . . .

Another, and the last class of teachers I will mention, are those who, to gain a notoriety, which is beyond their reach by any other means, thrust themselves upon the notice of the public to be employed in giving a proper turn to the youthful mind. They are such as have no definite ideas of the business they are about to engage in, or of those things they are required to teach. They enter their schools without seeing any thing clearly. Their minds are confused, and they know not what to do, how to act, or what to expect. They know not where to begin, or how to proceed after having begun. If called upon to explain the principle upon which any rule in arithmetic is founded, they are utterly at a loss to know what is meant by the question. It has never once entered their heads that the rules of arithmetic are founded upon any principles whatever. In the examination of a teacher, whose school I visited last winter, I asked him why he carried one for every ten in addition of whole numbers. "Because figures *decrease* from the right hand to the left in a tenfold proportion." "But, sir, you *cannot* mean '*decrease*' can you?" *Sartin*, I mean decrease, and that is what the *rule says*; for I have larnt it by heart." He could recite as he had learned them the tables of weights and measures in arithmetic; but could not answer one question in ten when asked promiscuously. I desired him to tell what part of speech is "*wise*" in the following example: "Into the will and arbitration *wise* of the Supreme." After looking at it for some time with a vacant stare, he replied, "I don't git hold of the meanin of the author in that place, and don't know what part of speech *wise* is. I never studied grammar only about tu weeks, and I don't pretend to understand it perfectly; but I reckoned how I understood it well enough to keep the school in this deestrick." I asked him to spell *potato*, and tell me which syllable had the full or primary accent? He spelled the word, and said "the full accent is on the last syllable." I then pronounced the word with the accent agreeably to his notion, and asked him if it was right? He thought not. He then said "it is the first;" but after making a practical application of accent to the first syllable, he perceived he was mistaken, and said "it is the second." I asked him which is the most northeastern State? He did "not know sartin, but he bleaved it was Ohio or Indiana." He was a most wretched reader and worse speller . . This is an extreme case of the class of teachers I am now describing. How do many of them manage the affairs of their schools? After spending, perhaps, fifteen or twenty minutes in trying to produce silence in the school, a class is called upon to read. "Toe that crack," says the teacher to the children who are called upon to read. But instead of "toeing the crack," some face to the north, some to the south, some to the east, and some to the west. "Now stand up straight and speak up loud and distinct." The teacher, or rather the apology for one, takes a book to see if any mistakes are made by any in the class. Whilst the one at the head is reading, a boy presents his writing book for a copy. He at once lays aside the reading book and begins to write the copy. Whilst doing this, another bawls out, "will you mend my pen." Willing to accommodate all, he leaves the copy and takes the pen; and before he finishes that, another "wants a sum done;" another, "can't find a name on the map." All these calls are attended to forthwith by the teacher, and all of them unfinished, to attend to something else. Thus, perhaps, from twenty to forty minutes have been spent, the class has become tired of reading, and some one calls out, "haint we read fur enough;" "I don't know," says the teacher, "how fur have you read?" "Six chapters;" "Wal, you have read fur enough, you needent read no furder, go long to your seats and *set* still, and tend to your studies."

WALT WHITMAN ON THE FAULTS OF THE PUBLIC SCHOOLS (1847)
From Walt Whitman, "Free Seminaries of Brooklyn," *Brooklyn Eagle*, February 4, 1847.

As a general thing the faults of our public schools system are—crowding too many students together, insufficiency of books, and their cost being taxed directly on the pupil—and the flogging system, which in a portion of the schools still holds its wretched sway. With pride we unite in the numerous commendations of the grand free school system of this State—with its twelve thousand seminaries, and its twenty thousand teachers, to whom each child, rich or poor, can come without money and without price! But we are none the less aware that the prodigious sum— hundreds of thousands of dollars—annually expended on these schools, might be expended to more profit. We have by no means ascended to the height of the great argument of education. The monotonous *old* still resists the fresh philosophical *new*. Form and precedent often are more thought of than reality. What are mere "order" or "learning lessons," or all the routine of the simple *outside* of school-keeping!— Absolutely nothing, in themselves; and only valuable, as far as they help the higher objects of educating the child. To teach the child *book grammar* is nothing; to teach him by example, by practice, by thoroughly clarifying the principles of correct syntax, *how to talk and write harmoniously,* is every thing. To put him through the arithmetic is not much; to make him able to compare, calculate, and quickly seize the bearings of a practical figure-question such as occurs in business every hour, is a good deal. Mere atlas geography is a sham, too, unless the learner have the position of places in his mind, and *know* the direction, distances, bearings, etc., of the countries, seas, cities, rivers and mountains, whose names (as our miserable school geographies give them,) he runs over so glibly. We care very little indeed for—what is the pride of many teachers' hearts—the military discipline of their schools, and the slavish obedience of their pupils to the imperial nod or waved hand of the master. As to the flogging plan, it is the most wretched item yet left of the ignorance and inefficiency of school-keeping. It has surrounded the office, (properly one of the noblest on earth,) with a character of contemptibleness and petty malignance, that will stick to it as long as whipping sticks among teachers' habits. What nobleness can reside in a man who catches boys by the collar and cuffs their ears? What elevation or dignity of character can even a child's elastic thoughts connect with one who cuts him over the back with a ratan or makes him hold out his hand to receive the whack of a ferule? For teachers' own sakes—for the true height and majesty of their office, hardly second to the priesthood—they should one and all unite in precluding this petty and foolish punishment—this degrader and bringerdown of their high standing. As things are, the word school-teacher is identified with a dozen unpleasant and ridiculous associations—a sour face, a whip, hard knuckles snapped on tender heads, no gentle, fatherly kindness, no inciting of young ambition in its noble phases, none of the beautifiers of authority, but all that is small, ludicrous, and in after life productive of indignation. We have reason to think that the flogging system still prevails in several of our Brooklyn schools to quite a wretched extent. In the school in Baltic St. under a former management, forty children in the boys' department were thrashed in the course of one morning! and in the female department a little girl was so cut and marked with the ratan over back, neck and shoulders, for some trifling offence, that the livid marks remained there for several days! This is a pretty fact for the character of our public seminaries! Justice to the mass of the teachers, however, demands that they should not be confounded with these ultra and repulsive cases. In general, doubtless, they whip with moderation—if that word may be applied to such a punishment at all. Nor do we mean to impugn their motives altogether. *They* think they are doing right. So did the Spanish torturers in Peru—inquisitors in Spain—and the learned doctors who denounced Jenner.

DESCRIPTION OF A DISTRICT SCHOOL IN UNION COUNTY, PENNSYLVANIA (1857) From *Pennsylvania School Journal*, vol. V, pp. 11–12.

Sir: In accordance with the instructions of the Department, I have the honor of submitting the following Report:

The School-House

The situation of the house is such, that with a little trouble and expense it can be made to look quite beautiful. But, as it is, there is no fence around the house; there is no playground except the highway; and a few old oak trees in the rear (in a field, where, of course, the pupils are not permitted to enter) are all that is near to remind a person of shade trees. There is no house, shed, or any thing of the kind in which to put the wood, coal, &c., used for warming the house. There is no privy, and it is deplorable that that part is nearly always neglected in building school-houses. The house is twenty-four feet long and twenty-two wide, with a ceiling eight and a half feet high. It is of brick, and was built about four years ago. There is a small wood stove in the house. In cold weather it is impossible to get the house comfortable, but with a large coal stove this might easily be done. There is no arrangement at all for ventilation, not even a trap-door in the ceiling.

School Furniture

The number of desks is sufficient to accommodate forty-eight pupils. They are of different heights; the lower are placed nearest the platform occupied by the teacher, and those that are higher, back farther. They are arranged in tiers, fronting toward the south, with an aisle between each tier. There are five tiers, and two pupils can set at each desk in three of them, but the desks in the tiers along the walls are calculated for one pupil only. The desks intended for the *smaller pupils*, are high enough for the *tallest*. They are made of white pine boards, planed smooth, but they are not painted. They have no lids, but there is a board under them where the scholar can keep his books, &c. The teacher's desk is situated at the south end of the house, on a small platform which is about eight inches high. The blackboard is about ten feet in length, and three in width, and is nailed to the wall behind the teacher's desk. There is not a map, globe, chart, or anything of the kind belonging to the school furniture. At the distance of six feet from the floor there is a strip of board nailed to each wall, in which nails are driven and on these nails the hats, cloaks, shawls, &c., are hung. This is a poor arrangement, for the scholars must always get on the benches with their feet when they wish to hang up their clothes, and then do the same to get them again.

The School

This is not a graded school, but all lawful scholars are admitted. The whole number of scholars last winter was forty-five, while the average per day was only twenty-one. The scholars are well-classified. The branches taught are, Reading, Writing, Orthography, Spelling, Arithmetic written and mental, English Grammar, Geography, Music and Book-keeping. The books used, are Porter's Rhetorical Reader, Sander's Readers Nos. 1 and 2, Sander's Spelling Book: (one of the scholars had Adam's Arithmetic, and another had Greenleaf's), Davie's Arithmetic, Colburn's Mental Arithmetic, Smith's English Grammar, Morse's Geography, and Crittenden's Book-keeping.—The New Testament is also used daily, but not as a text book. The punishments are not corporal.—Government is maintained chiefly by appealing to the nobler natures of the pupils, and to their sense of duty. Three intermissions are given each day. First one commencing at 10 1/2 o'clock A.M., and lasting 20 minutes—that is, the boys have ten minutes, and the girls ten; second, there is an intermission at noon of one hour; and third, commencing at 2 1/2 o'clock, P.M., twenty minutes more are given. The attention paid to study by the pupils is not as great as it should be; still some of them made a good degree of advancement, but the degree of advancement of the majority of the pupils is poor, considering what it might have been, had they been more careful to improve their privileges. Their attendance is regular during the latter part of December, the month of January, and part of February, but the rest of the time, it is very irregular.

The Teacher

The teacher of this school is nineteen years of age, and was educated principally at Mifflinburg Academy. He has been teaching school three winters. He does not know yet whether he will be a permanent teacher or not. The School and Schoolmaster, Page's Theory and Practice of Teaching, the Pennsylvania School Journal, and the New York Teacher, are the principal educational books and periodicals he has read.

At the close of the term, there was an examination and exhibition, and the number of visitors on that occasion was quite large. The visits of the Directors were not very frequent. During the five months that I taught, only one Director visited the school, and he was there only twice. The President of the Board and the Secretary were on the way to visit the school at one time, but it so happened that there was no school on that day. Most of the parents visited the school once, and some of them twice, but I had to invite some of them pretty often before they did so.

ADVENTURES OF A HOOSIER SCHOOLMASTER (1871) From Edward Eggleston, *The Hoosier Schoolmaster* (New York, 1871), pp. 1–3, 10–12.

"Want to be a school-master, do you? You? Well, what would *you* do in Flat Crick deestrick, *I'd* like to know? Why, the boys have driv off the last two, and licked the one afore them like blazes. You might teach a summer school, when nothin' but children come. But I 'low it takes a right smart *man* to be school-master in Flat Crick in the winter. They'd pitch you out of doors, sonny, neck and heels, afore Christmas."

The young man, who had walked ten miles to get the school in this district, and who had been mentally reviewing his learning at every step he took, trembling lest the committee should find that he did not know enough, was not a little taken aback at this greeting from "old Jack Means," who was the first trustee that he lighted on. The impression made by these ominous remarks was emphasized by the glances which he received from Jack Means' two sons. The older one eyed him from the top of his brawny shoulders with that amiable look which a big dog turns on a little one before shaking him. Ralph Hartsook had never thought of being measured by the standard of muscle. This notion of beating education into young savages in spite of themselves, dashed his ardor.

He had walked right to where Jack Means was at work shaving shingles in his own front yard. While Mr. Means was making the speech which we have set down above, and punctuating it with expectorations, a large brindle bull-dog had been sniffing at Ralph's heels, and a girl in a new linsey-woolsey dress, standing by the door, had nearly giggled her head off at the delightful prospect of seeing a new school-teacher eaten up by the ferocious brute.

Between the disheartening words of the old man, the immense muscles of the young man who was to be his rebellious pupil, the jaws of the ugly bull-dog, and the heartless giggle of the girl, Ralph had a delightful sense of having precipitated himself into a den of wild beasts. Faint with weariness and discouragement, and shivering with fear, he sat down on a wheelbarrow.

"You, Bull!" said the old man to the dog, which was showing more and more a disposition to make a meal of the incipient pedagogue, "you, Bull! git aout, you pup!" The dog walked sullenly off, but not until he had given Ralph a look full of promise of what he meant to do when he got a good chance. Ralph wished himself back in the village of Lewisburg, whence he had come.

THE
PROFESSION
OF EDUCATION

1299

"You see," continued Mr. Means, spitting in a meditative sort of a way, "you see, we a'n't none of your saft sort in these diggins. It takes a *man* to boss this deestrick. Howsumdever, ef you think you kin trust your hide in Flat Crick school-house I ha'n't got no 'bjection. But ef you git licked don't come on us. Flat Crick don't pay no 'nsurance, you bet! Any other trustees? Wal, yes. But as I pay the most taxes, t'others just let me run the thing. You can begin right off a Monday. They a'n't been no other applications. You see it takes some grit to apply for this school. The last master had a black eye for a month. But, as I said, you can jist roll up and wade in. I 'low you've got pluck, may be, and that goes for a heap sight more'n sinnoo with boys. Walk in, and stay over Sunday with me. You'll hev to board roun', and I guess you better begin here."

Ralph did not go in, but sat out on the wheelbarrow, watching the old man shave shingles, while the boys split the blocks and chopped wood. Bull smelled of the newcomer again in an ugly way, and got a good kick from the older son for his pains. But out of one of his red eyes the dog warned the young school-master that he should yet suffer for all kicks received on his account.

"Ef Bull once takes a holt, heaven and yarth can't make him let go," said the older son to Ralph, by way of comfort.

* * *

There was a moment of utter stillness. But the magnetism of Ralph's eye was too much for Bill Means. The request was so polite, the master's look was so innocent and yet so determined. Bill often wondered afterward that he had not "fit" rather than obeyed the request. But somehow he put the dog out. He was partly surprised, partly inveigled, partly awed into doing just what he had not intended to do. In the week that followed, Bill had to fight half a dozen boys for calling him "Puppy Means." Bill said he wished he'd a licked the master on the spot. 'Twould a saved five fights out of the six.

And all that day and the next, the bull-dog in the master's eye was a terror to evil-doers. At the close of school on the second day Bud was heard to give it as his opinion that "the master wouldn't be much in a tussle, but he had a heap of thunder and lightning in him." Did he inflict corporal punishment? inquires some philanthropic friend. Would you inflict corporal punishment if you were tiger-trainer in Van Amburgh's happy family? If you had been among the human bears on Flat Creek you would have used the rod also. But poor Ralph could never satisfy his constituency.

"Don't believe he'll do," was Mr. Pete Jones's comment to Mr. Means. "Don't thrash enough. Boys won't larn 'less you thrash 'em, says I. Leastways, mine won't. Lay it on good, is what I says to a master. Lay it on good. Don't do no harm. Lickin' and larnin' goes together. No lickin', no larnin', says I. Lickin' and larnin', lickin' and larnin', is the good ole way."

THE SCHOOLHOUSE AT PRAIRIE VIEW, KANSAS (c. 1880) From Marshall
A. Barber, *The Schoolhouse at Prairie View* (Lawrence, Kans., 1953), pp. 11–13.

Our schoolhouse was the one-room-and-hall kind common in that region. Inside, most of the space was occupied by the schoolroom with well-windowed sides but with the rear wall blank. There were two doors leading into the narrow windowless hall but only one from the hall to the exterior of the building. The schoolroom had a low platform in front and on it a desk or table for the teacher. Facing him sat the pupils of all sizes, the smaller ones in front—presumably because they were a restless lot and needed the most watching. Behind them sat the larger pupils, the largest ones occupying the coveted seat against the blank wall. The boys sat on one side of the room and the girls on the other; sometimes a brother and a sister were allowed to share the same seat, probably to allow them to look over some of the books together and thus spare the expense of two sets. In the kindergarten latitude sat the big iron stove. On very cold days we could drag up benches and all sit near its red-hot flanks. It was a smelly kind. We once had a school stove which burned clean logs like our home fires, but it was early displaced by one addicted to a dirty soft coal.

Our desks were of different sizes and probably designed to fit different sizes of pupil, but there was a greater variety in stature among the children than among the desks. At one time we had plain wooden desks which did not fold up to protect the books. We just stuck them into a sort of shelf under the top. Later we got a patent collapsing kind whose top folded down and shut the books, slates, and sometimes less lawful articles into a compact, rectangular, vertical mass. This kind of furniture was especially prone to get out of order and need replacement—maybe the crafty salesman counted on that. The desks had a well for ink, and only the boldest boys ventured to carve names or figures on their shiny tops.

One felt much freer with the old kind of desk which was sometimes elaborately sculptured. They were not only rich in initials and names but were sometimes carved to represent whole biographies. The top of a desk might represent the farm of a mythical "S" (maybe of Mr. Schnaik the bachelor). Here he had built his house and here his barn. Here was a path which led to his well; here he had dug his well. This scheme was not so elaborate as that of a certain Buddhist temple in Java, where the illiterate can follow every detail of the life of his saint, but perhaps it contained the germ of the same idea—the transmission of knowledge without the tedious process of reading. As I remember, these wooden histories were favorites with some of the German children, who sometimes found reading English a bit difficult.

When the new furniture came in, some of the old longer benches were retained. I am sure we had none so primitive as those consisting of a half-log with the flat side smoothed to make a seat and the legs stuck into the rounded belly, reminiscent of those stiff-legged quadrupeds whose pictures used to stray into the margins of children's copybooks. We had a smooth hard kind, made entirely of boards with a broad support over which the seat board projected, the whole end effect suggesting to me the teacher's frown overhanging the rest of his face.

We also had a much longer bench, often put into the corners of the room and used for recitations. I associate reading and history with a long bench placed in the northwest corner of the room. For arithmetic when one stood at the blackboard or for oral spelling we did not need recitation benches, but I have a vague association of these benches with mental arithmetic; maybe the hardness of the bench was associated in my mind with the hardness of the problem—I was not good at arithmetic.

The rest of the furniture of the room was mostly attached to the front wall. There was a broad blackboard in front with a trough below it for pointers, erasers, chalk, and such chalk-dust as was not absorbed by our lungs. That trough was a good place for switches too, but maybe I imagine the switches through the association of chalk and the punishment of sin. Chalk, especially the longer pieces, was a commodity not to be taken from the schoolroom; it was public property and not replaceable without paying out school money. On the broad blackboard all writing was erasable, but just above it we had a narrower sort where the letters of the alphabet were permanently written. And it was so beautifully done, almost (I thought) as if Mr. Spencer himself had deigned to visit our school and write those letters as an everlasting model. I used to gaze at those wavy, shaded capitals for hours, I think. It was my first clear impression of the unattainable.

Much of the remainder of the front wall was covered with maps. I presume many countries were hung there, but, curiously, all I can clearly remember was one impressive word, "Mediterranean."

The Normal School

JAMES CARTER'S PLAN FOR A TEACHER-TRAINING SEMINARY
(1825)   From "Outline of an Institution for the Education of Teachers," *Essays on Popular Education* . . . (Boston, 1826), pp. 47–51.

If a seminary for the purpose of educating teachers scientifically be essential in order to give the greatest efficacy to our system of popular education; then, in the progress of the discussion, the three following questions arise in the order in which they are stated. By whom should the proposed institution be established? What would be its leading features? And what would be some of the peculiar advantages to the public, which would result from it. To answer these several questions at length would require a book; while I have, at present, only leisure to prepare one or two newspaper-essays. A few hints, therefore, upon the above three topics are all that I dare profess to give, and more than I fear I can give, either to my own satisfaction or that of those readers, who may have become interested in the subject.

The institution from its peculiar purpose must necessarily be both literary and scientific in its character. And although, with its design constantly in view, we could not reasonably expect it to add, directly, much to the stock of what is now called literature, or to enlarge much the boundaries of what is now called science; yet, from the very nature of the subject to which it wuld be devoted, and upon which it would be employed, it must in its progress create a kind of literature of its own, and open a new science somewhat peculiar to itself—the science of the developement of the infant mind, and the science of communicating knowledge from one mind to another while in a different stage of maturity. The tendency of the inquiries which must be carried on, and the discoveries which would be constantly made, in a seminary for this new purpose, would be to give efficacy to the pursuits of other literary and scientific institutions. Its influence, therefore, though indirect, would be not the less powerful upon the cause of literature and the sciences generally. These remarks may seem to anticipate another part of my subject; but they are introduced here, to show, that a seminary for the education of teachers, would stand, at least, on as favourable a footing in relation to the public as other literary and scientific institutions. It seems now to be believed that the Legislature of the State are the rightful proprietors of all public institutions for the diffusion of knowledge. And if they are of any, they certainly ought to be of one for such a purpose. Because there are none in which the public would be more deeply interested. There are none, which would tend so much to diffuse knowledge among the whole mass of the people. And this, as has been before remarked, is a solemn duty enjoined upon our

THE PROFESSION OF EDUCATION

1303

government by the constitution, under which they are organized, and from which they derive their authority. Besides it is the first impulse of every government, operating as quickly and as steadily as instinct, to provide for its own preservation. And it seems to be conceded on all hands, by the friends as well as the enemies of freedom, that a government like our own can only exist among a people generally enlightened; the only question as to the permanency of free institutions being, whether it be possible to make and to keep the *whole* population of a nation so well educated as the existence of such institutions supposes and requires.

Our government, therefore, are urged by every motive, which the constitution can enjoin or self-preservation suggest to see to it, that knowledge is generally diffused among the people. Upon this subject of popular education, a *free* government must be *arbitrary*. For its existence depends upon it. The more ignorant and degraded people are, the less do they feel the want of instruction, and the less will they seek it. And these are the classes of a community, which always increase the fastest up to the very point, where the means of subsistence fail. So that if any one class of men, however small, be suffered as a body, to remain in ignorance, and to allow their families to grow up without instruction, they will increase in a greater ratio compared with their numbers, than the more enlightened classes, till they have a preponderance of physical power. And when this preponderance becomes overwhelming, what hinders a revolution, and an arbitrary government, by which the mind of a few can control the physical strength of the many.

If this reasoning be correct, a free government must look to it betimes, that popular ignorance does not gain upon them. If it do, there is a thistle in the vineyard of the republic, which will grow and spread itself in every direction, till it cannot be eradicated. The ignorant must be allured to learn, by every motive which can be offered to them. And if they will not thus be allured, they must be taken by the strong arm of government and brought out, willing or unwilling, and made to learn, at least, enough to make them peaceable and good citizens. It would be well, indeed, if the possibility could be held out to all of successfully aspiring to responsible stations in society. A faint hope is better than despair. And though only one chance in a thousand be favourable, even that is worth something to stimulate the young to greater efforts to become worthy of distinction. The few, who under all the disadvantages, which adverse circumstances impose, can find their way by untired perseverance to places of trust and influence in the republic, serve to give identity of feeling, of purpose and pursuit to the whole. They harmonise and bind together all those different and distant classes of the community, between which fretful jealousies naturally subsist.

These are hints, only, at an argument, perhaps unintelligible ones, to establish the principle, that free governments are the proprietors of all literary and scientific institutions so far as they have the tendency to diffuse knowledge generally among the people. The free schools of Massachusetts, as the most efficient means of accomplishing that object, should therefore be the property and the peculiar care of government. An argument will, at once, be drawn from these principles why they should assume the direction of the schools, so far as to ensure to the people over whom they are appointed to preside, competent teachers of them. And as this is the main purpose of the proposed institution, the reasoning seems to be conclusive, why they should be its proprietor, or, at least, its patron and protector.

An institution for the education of teachers, as has been before intimated, would form a part, and a very important part of the free school system. It would be, moreover, precisely that portion of the system, which should be under the direction of the State whether the others are or not. Because we should thus secure at once, an uniform, intelligent and independent tribunal for decisions on the qualifications of teachers. Because we should thus relieve the clergy of an invidious task, and ensure to the public competent teachers, if such could be found or prepared. An institution for this purpose would become by its influence on society, and particularly on the young, an engine to sway the public sentiment, the public morals, and the public religion, more powerful than any other in the possession of government. It should, therefore, be responsible immediately to them. And they should, carefully, overlook it; and prevent its being perverted to other purposes, directly or indirectly, than those for which it is designed. It should be emphatically the State's institution. And its results would soon make it the State's favourite and pride, among other literary and scientific institutions. The Legislature of the State should, therefore, establish and build it up, without waiting for individuals at great private sacrifices to accomplish the work. Such would be the influence of an institution for the education of teachers; and such is the growing conviction of the strength of early associations and habits, that it cannot be long before the work will be begun in some form. If it be not undertaken by the public and for public purposes, it will be undertaken by individuals for private purposes.

The people of Massachusetts are able and willing, yea, more than willing, they are anxious to do something more for popular education, for the diffusion of knowledge generally. The only questions with them are how and where can means be applied to the purpose to the greatest advantage. It may safely be submitted, by the friends of the free schools, to a republican people and their republican government, which institutions on comparison most deserve the public bounty; those whose advantages can be enjoyed but by a few, or those which are open to the whole population; those which have for their main objects good that is remote, or those, whose happy influences are felt, at once, through the whole community. Which institutions deserve the first consideration, and the most anxious attention of a popular government, those, which will place a few scholars and philologists upon a level with the Germans in a knowledge of Greek accents; or those which will put our whole people upon the level of enlightened men in their practical knowledge of common things. These objects may all be important to us. But the former will be provided for by individuals; the latter are the peculiar care of government.

The next question, mentioned above, as arising in the progress of this discussion, was, what would be the leading features of an institution for the education of teachers. If the institution were to be founded by the State, upon a large scale, the following parts would seem to be obviously essential. 1. An appropriate library with a philosophical apparatus. 2. A Principal and assistant Professors in the different departments. 3. A school for children of different ages, embracing both those desiring a general education, and those designed particularly for teachers. 4. A Board of Commissioners, or an enlightened body of men representing the interests and wishes of the public.

THOMAS H. GALLAUDET CALLS FOR SEMINARIES FOR TEACHERS

(1825)   From the *Connecticut Observer,* Jan. 4, 1825, as quoted in *American Annals of Education,* vol. I, (January, 1831), pp. 25–26.

No important result can be attained with regard to the accomplishment of any object which affects the temporal or eternal wellbeing of our species, without enlisting an entire devotedness to it of intelligence, zeal, fidelity, industry, integrity, and practical exertion. What is it that has furnished us with able divines, lawyers, and physicians? The undivided consecration of the talents and efforts of intelligent and upright individuals to these professions. How have these talents been matured, and these efforts been trained, to their beneficial results? *By a diligent course of preparation, and a long discipline in the school of experience.* We have our theological, law, and medical institutions, in which our young men are fitted for the pursuit of these respective professions, by deriving benefit from the various sources of information which libraries, lectures, and experiments afford. Unaided by such auxiliaries, genius, however brilliant; invention, however prolific; observation, however acute; ingenuity, however ready; and perseverance, however indefatigable, have to grope their way, through a long and tiresome process, to the attainment of results which a little acquaintance with the labors of others in the same track of effort, would render a thousand times more easy, rapid, and delightful. *Experience is the storehouse of knowledge.* Now why should not this experience be resorted to as an auxiliary in the education of youth? Why not make this department of human exertion *a profession,* as well as those of divinity, law, and medicine? Why not have an *Institution for the training up of Instructors,* for their sphere of labor, as well as institutions to prepare young men for the duties of the divine, the lawyer, or the physician?

Can a subject of more interest present itself to the consideration of the public? Does not the future improvement of our species, to which the philanthropist and the Christian look forward with such anticipations, depend on plans which are adopted for the development and cultivation of the intellectual and moral powers of man? Must not these plans begin with infancy and childhood? Do not the attainments of the pupil depend upon the talents, the fidelity, and the integrity of those by whom he is taught? How will he learn to think, to speak, to read, and to write with accuracy unless his instructors are able to teach him? Shall their ability depend upon their individual experience and attainments? You do not do this in the case of a divine, a lawyer, or a physician. Why not, then, require in the instructors of youth, to whom you commit the training up of your offspring, an adequate preparation for their most important and responsible employment? . . .

Let the same provision, then, be made for giving success to this department of effort that is so liberally made for all others. Let an institution be established in every state, for the express purpose of training up young men for the profession of instructors of youth in the common branches of an English education. Let it be so well endowed, by the liberality of the public, or of individuals, as to have two or three professors, men of talents and habits adapted to the pursuit, who should devote their lives to the object of the "Theory and Practice of the Education of Youth," and who should prepare and deliver, and print, a course of lectures on the subject.

Let the institution be furnished with a *library,* which shall contain all the works, theoretical and practical, in all languages, that can be obtained on the subject of education, and also with all the apparatus that modern ingenuity has devised for this purpose; such as maps, charts, globes, orreries, etc.

Let there be connected with the institution a school, smaller or larger, as circumstances might dictate, in which the theories of the professors might be reduced to practice, and from which daily experience would derive a thousand useful instructions.

To such an institution let young men resort who are ready to devote themselves to the business of instructors of youth. Let them attend a regular course of lectures on the subject of education; read the best works; take their turns in the instruction of the experimental school; and, after thus becoming qualified for their office, leave the Institution with a suitable certificate or diploma, recommending them to the confidence of the public.

*   *   *

WALTER R. JOHNSON CALLS FOR SCHOOLS FOR TEACHERS
(**1825**)   From *Observations on the Improvement of Seminaries of Learning In The United States* (Philadelphia, 1825), pp. 8–18.

If internal improvements of any kind or for any purpose be desirable, a point which none seem disposed to contest, they can in no respect be more advantageous than when applied to meliorate the social condition, by curing those most distressing maladies, ignorance and moral degradation. Without the removal of these evils, the physical resources of a country may be developed to any extent we please, and poverty and distress be still stalking abroad in their most hideous deformity. The means and incitements to the indulgence of brutal appetites are increased, without any corresponding increase in the high moral restraints upon meanness and sensuality. Why, amidst all these changes, at which we have just glanced, should no change, no improvement, be deemed necessary in the means and institutions of learning?

The expedients for accomplishing this universal improvement in the *internal man* must, however, be eminently practical—intelligible to ordinary capacities—not too fanciful, complicated, and expensive for a whole community, nor too humble and inefficient for any part. They ought not to perpetuate invidious distinctions of rich and poor, much less to create them. Schools and instructors, with whom the rich may be satisfied, ought to be provided for all classes. Ours ought not to be a system of *poor schools* in any sense; means ought therefore to be devised to make them all good. The practice of most of the States of the Union is in favour of a gradation of institutions, beginning with the common schools and ending with the universities. It is not our purpose at present to discuss either the absolute or relative value of these different classes of seminaries, (believing them *all* useful and necessary in due proportion,) but to offer some suggestions for the improvement of them all. This end is proposed to be accomplished by the introduction of a class of schools hitherto unknown in our country, but for which the public exigencies seem loudly to call, and those are *schools for teachers*. This plan is not offered as in itself a novelty; it has long been in successful operation in some countries on the continent of Europe, particularly in Germany, (a region to which modern learning owes more than the learned are all willing to acknowledge,) and there its beneficial influence is seen in every aspect of society. Some, we are aware, will be ready to object that we have hitherto been supplied, *without* such establishments, with as many teachers as could find employment, and with more than ever *deserved* it. True; and this is precisely the reason for founding institutions which shall afford a supply of *such as may deserve* the public confidence.

It is believed that the demand for good instructors is increasing in our country, in a ratio far exceeding that of the augmentation of our population. This belief is founded upon the consideration that many of the States, which have hitherto been destitute of school systems, are now forming plans for the general or universal diffusion of knowledge: that higher institutions, as well as common schools, are in all parts of the Union becoming the objects of favour and attention, to a degree heretofore unequalled: that in seminaries of every grade, the number of branches expected to be taught, is much greater than formerly: that in every quarter it is beginning to be understood, that under free political institutions, the cause of good learning is the foundation of success to all other good causes, and that as the public become enlightened on the subject, they are also becoming better qualified to distinguish the able from the imbecile, and those who act from principle from those who follow caprice or sordid interest alone. It is daily made more and more evident, even to those who reflect but little, that every man is not by nature an instructer; a truth which seems to have been overlooked by those who have been ready to employ the weak, untaught, and inexperienced for those offices in which eminent abilities, thorough instruction, and experience are of the utmost importance. Besides, the qualifications of instructers must bear some proportion to the attainments required of their pupils in after life, by the circumstances in which they are to be placed. Adverting, then, to the qualifications *now* demanded of those who are to fill stations of public trust, or to occupy a distinguished rank in the affairs of private life, we may be further convinced of the increasing demand for superior talents and high attainments, in those who are to form the character of our youthful citizens. Not only are our executive and legislative offices, in conformity with the public wishes, filled with the most eminent scholars of our country; not only do the bar, the bench, and the pulpit demand, as heretofore, the best talents of the community, but our army and navy also are beginning to make high intellectual attainments their principal passports to honour and promotion. Agriculture, manufactures, and commerce, are calling to their aid men of science, intelligence, and liberality of mind; and the impulse given to physical improvements, implies the future demand for a large amount of energetic mental powers. To be ignorant of the rudiments of education, is at present regarded by persons of all ranks, and even of all complexions, as a serious misfortune; and in some parts of our country, as a heavy, positive reproach, to be covered neither by graces of person, respectability of parentage, nor splendour of fortune. Neither the sons nor the daughters of America feel that they have discharged their duty, either to themselves or to their country, until they have redeemed from a state of waste some good portion of that intellectual inheritance which has fallen to their share. Accordingly, we find that in districts of country where yesterday, the first crash of the falling forest was heard, to-day the voice of science rises from the walls of her neat and classic habitation; and where within the memory of the present generation the shrieking matron was torn from her infant daughter by the ruthless savage, that daughter is *now*, amidst scenes of comfort and elegance, storing her mind with every solid and useful accomplishment, and *possibly* finds by her side, the daughter of that very savage, an ardent but generous rival in the same ennobling employment.

These facts of themselves suggest, that a larger number than heretofore of persons able and willing to devote superior powers to the development of mind and the communication of knowledge, must be employed in these responsible offices. Instead, then, of being regarded as surprising, that a project of this kind should be suggested at all, we ought, perhaps, under a view of all the circumstances, to think it remarkable that it has not been done sooner: that while every other profession has its appropriate schools for preparation, *that* on which the usefulness and respectability of all others essentially depend, is left to the will of chance, or *"to take care of itself."* We have theological seminaries—law schools—medical colleges—military academies—institutes for mechanics—and colleges of Pharmacy for apothecaries; but no shadow of an appropriate institution to qualify persons for discharging with ability and success, the duties of *instruction,* either in these professional seminaries, or in any other. Men have been apparently presumed to be qualified to *teach,* from the moment that they passed the period of ordinary pupilage;—a supposition, which with few exceptions, must, of course, lead only to disappointment and mortification. It has often been asked why men will not devote themselves *permanently* to the profession of teaching. Among other reasons, much weight is, no doubt, to be attached to this want of preparation, and to the discouragements and perplexities encountered in blindly attempting to hit upon the right course of procedure. Many persons, we have reason to believe, commence the business of instructing, not only with few of the qualifications for communicating knowledge, but even without any fixed plan of proceeding, or any definite ideas of the peculiar duties and difficulties of the employment. With such persons, the operation is altogether *tentative*—a system of temporary expedients—or, no system at all. They begin *somehow*—follow one course for a time, then drop it for another, which (finding it equally unsuitable) they abandon for some new project, that change or caprice brings in their way, or, which is perhaps more common, after having found their good intentions unappreciated, and their labours unrewarded, they abandon in disgust both the plan and the profession together. And happy will it be, if in this unprofitable course of groping in the dark, they have done nothing worse than to fail in attaining the object of their pursuit;—happy if they have not wasted their health, impaired their mental energies, diminished their social propensities, and lost their relish for the refinements of literature and the researches of science.—To obviate in some degree these difficulties, to render his duties less irksome to the teacher, and more profitable to the pupil—to give to our institutions of learning (already the subjects of much applause) a still higher character, and thereby to subserve the interests of our country and of humanity, it is proposed to afford, by the institutions in question, an opportunity, to those who are designed for teachers, of making themselves theoretically and practically acquainted with the duties which they will be called upon to discharge, *before* they enter upon the performance of their trusts. In order, however, to afford illustrations of the principles of education, it is indispensable that *practice* should be added to precept, and that too, in situations favourable to the operation of those causes which display both the powers of the mind, and the peculiarities of the several departments of science and art. The school for teachers, then, ought not to be an insulated establishment, but to be connected with some institution, where an extensive range in the sciences is taken, and where pupils of different classes are pursuing the various departments of education adapted to their respective ages. The practice of superintending, of arranging into classes, instructing and governing, ought to form *one* part of the duty of the young teacher. The attending of lectures on the science of mental development, and the various collateral topics should constitute another. An extensive course of reading and study of authors who have written with ability and practical good sense on the subject, would be necessary, in order to expand the mind, and free it from those prejudices which, on this subject, are apt to adhere even to persons who fancy themselves farthest removed from their influence. The present is not an age when narrow prejudices of any kind can be expected to enjoy toleration and support; and least of all, can such favour be expected for the prejudices of instructers, who, from the very relation in which they stand to their pupils, ought to be foremost in eradicating the absurd notions which a false estimate of things, and a wrong application of terms, have implanted in the mind. That this is not at present the characteristic of instructers, there is but too much reason to fear; and that the course here recommended would beget a more liberal spirit, there is every reason to hope. That class of prejudices, in particular, which arises from a disposition to form or adopt fanciful theories not reducible to practice, would be corrected by reading the kind of authors here recommended; and the same effect would be insured by adhering, in the choice of lecturers, to those, who, added to a truly philosophical character, have possessed an extensive *experience* in the duties of instruction. Should it be necessary, there might also be provision for the pursuit of other sciences in addition to that of teaching, by those who are preparing for that office. A perfect plan for the education of teachers and professors would require that the institution, with which the school for teachers is proposed to be connected, should embrace a complete circle of the Sciences and Arts, and that a professor should be appointed to lecture on the mode of teaching in each separate department. But besides that few, if any institutions of our country extend to so great a number of objects, there would be an insuperable obstacle to the execution of such a plan, in the *expense* which must necessarily be incurred—an expense, which no authority short of the highest legislative body in the nation would, perhaps, feel itself adequate to meet—and *that* body has hitherto shown an aversion to extend its interpretation of "the general welfare" so far as to embrace the trifling subject of educating the sons and daughters of a republic.

ANNOUNCEMENT OF A SCHOOL FOR TEACHERS IN OHIO (1833) From
American Annals of Education (December, 1833), p. 595.

The School Examiners for the County of Portage, Ohio, held a meeting at Ravenna, on the 23rd of October last, at which several resolutions were passed expressive of their regret at the present low condition of common schools, and of their determination to make efforts to improve them by the introduction of approved books and apparatus, and by an increased attention to the qualifications of candidates who should present themselves for school teaching. One of these resolutions was to establish a preparatory school for teachers of common schools in the county; and several gentlemen having proposed to locate it for the present at Cuyahoga Falls, it was proposed to recommend to those who were expecting to teach the ensuing winter, to avail themselves of this opportunity for improving themselves in their profession. The school was to be opened on the 11th of November.

The first term is intended as an experiment, and will be short; but the Committee hope for encouragement to pursue a more extended and useful course later. For the present the course will be confined to evening lectures, and daily examinations and exercises in the several branches already taught or proposed to be taught in the schools, including the use of Holbrook's and other school apparatus; and to the discussion of a series of questions respecting proper management and discipline.

HORACE MANN ON THE REQUISITES OF THE TEACHER (1840) From
Fourth Annual Report of the Secretary of the Board of Education, as quoted in *Life and Works of Horace Mann* (Boston, 1891), vol. III, pp. 57–70.

A brief consideration of a few of the qualifications essential to those who undertake the momentous task of training the children of the State, will help us to decide the question, whether the complaints of the committees, in regard to the incompetency of teachers, are captious and unfounded; or whether they proceed from enlightened conceptions of the nature of their duties and office, and therefore require measures to supply the deficiency.

1st. *Knowledge of Common-School Studies.*—Teachers should have a perfect knowledge of the rudimental branches which are required by law to be taught in our schools. They should understand, not only the rules, which have been prepared as guides for the unlearned, but also the principles on which the rules are founded,—those principles which lie beneath the rules, and supersede them in practice; and from which, should the rules be lost, they could be framed anew. Teachers should be able to teach *subjects,* not manuals merely.

However much other knowledge a teacher may possess, it is no equivalent for a mastership in the rudiments. It is not more true in architecture, than in education, that the value of the work, in every upper layer, depends upon the solidity of all beneath it. The leading, prevailing defect in the intellectual department of our schools, is a want of thoroughness,—a proneness to be satisfied with a verbal memory of rules, instead of a comprehension of principles,—with a knowledge of the names of things, instead of a knowledge of the things themselves;—or, if some knowledge of the things is gained, it is too apt to be a knowledge of them as isolated facts, and unaccompanied by a knowledge of the relations, which subsist between them, and bind them into a scientific whole. That knowledge is hardly worthy of the name, which stops with things, as individuals, without understanding the relations, existing between them. The latter constitutes indefinitely the greater part of all human knowledge.

2nd. *Aptness to Teach.*—The next principal qualification in a teacher is the *art of teaching.* This is happily expressed in the common phrase, *aptness to teach,* which in a few words, comprehends many particulars. The ability to acquire, and the ability to impart, are wholly different talents. The former may exist in the most liberal measure, without the latter. It was a remark of Lord Bacon, that "the art of well-delivering the knowledge we possess is among the secrets, left to be discovered by future generations." Dr. Watts says, "there are some very learned men, who know much themselves, but who have not the talent of communicating their knowledge." Indeed, this fact is not now questioned by any intelligent educationist. Hence we account for the frequent complaints of the committees, that those teachers who had sustained an examination, in an acceptable manner, failed in the school room, through a want of facility in communicating what they knew. The ability to acquire is the power of understanding the subject-matter of investigation. Aptness to teach involves the power of perceiving how far a scholar understands the subject-matter to be learned, and what, in the natural order, is the next step he is to take. It involves the power of discovering and of solving at the time, the exact difficulty, by which the learner is embarrassed. The removal of a slight impediment, the drawing aside of the thinnest veil, which happens to divert his steps, or obscure his vision, is worth more to him, than volumes of lore on collateral subjects. How much does the pupil comprehend of the subject? What should his next step be? Is his mind looking towards a truth or an error? The answer to these questions must be intuitive, in the person who is apt to teach. As a dramatic writer throws himself, successively, into the characters of the drama he is composing, that he may express the ideas and emotions, peculiar to each; so the mind of a teacher should migrate, as it were, into those of his pupils, to discover what they know and feel and need; and then, supplying from his own stock, what they require, he should reduce it to such a form, and bring it within such a distance, that they can reach out and seize and appropriate it. He should never forget that intellectual truths are naturally adapted to give intellectual pleasure; and that, by leading the minds of his pupils onward to such a position in relation to these truths, that they themselves can discover them, he secures to them the natural reward of a new pleasure with every new discovery, which is one of the strongest, as well as most appropriate incitements to future exertion.

Aptness to teach includes the presentation of the different parts of a subject, in a natural order. If a child is told that the globe is about twenty-five thousand miles in circumference, before he has any conception of the length of a mile, or of the number of units in a thousand, the statement is not only utterly useless as an act of instruction, but is will probably prevent him, ever afterwards, from gaining an adequate idea of the subject. The novelty will be gone, and yet the fact unknown. Besides, a systematic acquisition of a subject knits all parts of it together, so that they will be longer retained and more easily recalled. To acquire a few of the facts, gives us fragments only;—and even to master all the facts, but to obtain them promiscuously, leaves what is acquired so unconnected and loose, that any part of it may be jostled out of its place and lost, or remain only to mislead.

Aptness to teach, in fine, embraces a knowledge of methods and processes. These are indefinitely various. Some are adapted to accomplish their object in an easy and natural manner; others in a toilsome and circuitous one;—others, again, may accomplish the object at which they aim, with certainty and despatch, but secure it by inflicting deep and lasting injuries upon the social and moral sentiments. We are struck with surprise, on learning, that, but a few centuries since, the feudal barons of Scotland, in running out the lines around their extensive domains, used to take a party of boys, and whip them, at the different posts and land-marks, in order to give them a retentive memory, as witnesses, in case of future litigation or dispute. Though this might give them a vivid recollection of localities, yet it would hardly improve their ideas of justice, or propitiate them to bear true testimony in favor of the chastiser. But do not those, who have no aptness to teach, sometimes accomplish their objects by a kindred method?

He who is apt to teach is acquainted, not only with common methods for common minds, but with peculiar methods for pupils of peculiar dispositions and temperaments; and he is acquainted with the principles of all methods, whereby he can vary his plan, according to any difference of circumstances. The statement has been sometimes made, that it is the object of Normal Schools to subject all teachers to one, inflexible, immutable course of instruction. Nothing could be more erroneous, for one of the great objects is, to give them a knowledge of modes, as various as the diversity of cases that may arise,—that like a skilful pilot, they may not only see the haven for which they are to steer, but know every bend in the channel that leads to it. No one is so poor in resources for difficult emergencies as they may arise, as he whose knowledge of methods is limited to the one in which he happened to be instructed. It is in this way that rude nations go on for indefinite periods, imitating what they have seen, and teaching only as they were taught.

3d. *Management, Government, and Discipline of a School.*—Experience has also proved, that there is no necessary connection between literary competency, aptness to teach, and the power to manage and govern a school successfully. They are independent qualifications; yet a marked deficiency in any one of the three, renders the others nearly valueless. In regard to the ordinary management or administration of a school, how much judgment is demanded in the organization of classes, so that no scholar shall either be clogged and retarded, or hurried forward with injudicious speed, by being matched with an unequal yoke-fellow. Great discretion is necessary in the assignment of lessons, in order to avoid, on the one hand, such shortness in the tasks, as allows time to be idle; and, on the other, such over-assignments, as render thoroughness and accuracy impracticable, and thereby so habituate the pupil to mistakes and imperfections, that he cares little or nothing about committing them. Lessons, as far as it is possible, should be so adjusted to the capacity of the scholar, that there should be no failure in a recitation, not occasioned by culpable neglect. The sense of shame, or of regret for ignorance, can never be made exquisitely keen, if the lessons given are so long, or so difficult, as to make failures frequent. When "bad marks," as they are called, against a scholar, become common, they not only lose their salutary force, but every addition to them debases his character, and carries him through a regular course of training, which prepares him to follow in the footsteps of those convicts, who are so often condemned, that at length they care nothing for the ignominy of the sentence. Yet all this may be the legitimate consequence of being unequally mated, or injudiciously tasked. It is a sad sight in any school, to see a pupil marked for a deficiency, without any blush of shame, or sign of guilt; and it is never done with impunity to his moral character.

The preservation of order, together with the proper dispatch of business, requires a mean, between the too much and the too little, in all the evolutions of the school, which it is difficult to hit. When classes leave their seats for the recitation-stand, and return to them again, or when the different sexes have a recess, or the hour of intermission arrives;—if there be not some order and succession of movement, the school will be temporarily converted into a promiscuous rabble, giving both the temptation and the opportunity for committing every species of indecorum and aggression. In order to prevent confusion, on the other hand, the operations of the school may be conducted with such military formality and procrastination;—the second scholar not being allowed to leave his seat, until the first has reached the door, or the place of recitation, and each being made to walk on tiptoe to secure silence,—that a substantial part of every school session will be wasted, in the wearisome pursuit of an object worth nothing when obtained.

When we reflect, how many things are to be done each half day, and how short a time is allotted for their performance, the necessity of system in regard to all the operations of the school, will be apparent. System compacts labor; and when the hand is to be turned to an almost endless variety of particulars, if system does not preside over the whole series of movements, the time allotted to each will be spent in getting ready to perform it. With lessons to set; with so many classes to hear; with difficulties to explain; with the studious to be assisted; the idle to be spurred; the transgressors to be admonished or corrected; with the goers and comers to observe;—with all these things to be done, no considerable progress can be made, if one part of the wheel is not coming up to the work, while another is going down. And if order do not pervade the school, as a whole, and in all its parts, all is lost; and this is a very difficult thing;—for it seems as though the school were only a point, rescued out of a chaos that still encompasses it, and is ready, on the first opportunity, to break in and reoccupy its ancient possession. As it is utterly impracticable for any committee to prepare a code of regulations coextensive with all the details, which belong to the management of a school, it must be left with the teacher; and hence the necessity of skill in this item of the long list of his qualifications.

The government and discipline of a school demands qualities still more rare, because the consequences of error, in these, are still more disastrous. What caution, wisdom, uprightness, and sometimes, even intrepidity, are necessary in the administration of punishment. After all other means have been tried, and tried in vain, the chastisement of pupils found to be otherwise incorrigible, is still upheld by law, and sanctioned by public opinion. But it is the last resort, the ultimate resource, acknowledged, on all hands, to be a relic of barbarism, and yet authorized, because the community, although they feel it to be a great evil, have not yet devised and applied an antidote. Through an ignorance of the laws of health, a parent may so corrupt the constitution of his child, as to render poison a necessary medicine; and through an ignorance of the laws of mind, he may do the same thing in regard to punishment. When the arts of health and of education are understood, neither poison nor punishment will need to be used, unless in most extraordinary cases. . . .

4th. *Good Behavior.*—In two words, the statute opens, to all teachers, an extensive field of duty, by ordaining that all the youth in the schools shall be taught *"good behavior."* The framers of the law were aware, how rapidly good or bad manners mature into good or bad morals; they saw that good manners have not only the negative virtue of restraining from vice, but the positive one of leading, by imperceptible gradations, towards the practice of almost all the social virtues. The effects of civility or discourtesy, of gentlemanly or ungentlemanly deportment, are not periodical or occasional, merely, but of constant recurrence; and all the members of society have a direct interest in the manners of each of its individuals; because each one is a radiating point,—the centre of a circle, which he fills with pleasure or annoyance, not only for those who voluntarily enter it, but for those also, who, in the promiscuous movements of society, are caught within its circumference. Good behavior includes the elements of that equity, benevolence, conscience, which, in their great combinations, the moralist treats of in his books of ethics, and the legislator enjoins in his codes of law. The school room and its play-ground, next to the family table, are the places, where the selfish propensities come into most direct collision with social duties. Here, then, a right direction should be given to the growing mind. The surrounding influences, which are incorporated into its new thoughts and feelings, and make part of their substance, are too minute and subtile to be received in masses, like nourishment;—they are rather imbibed into the system, unconsciously, by every act of respiration, and are constantly insinuating themselves into it, through all the avenues of the senses. If, then, the manners of the teacher are to be imitated by his pupils—if he is the glass, at which they "do dress themselves," how strong is the necessity, that he should understand those nameless and innumerable practices, in regard to deportment, dress, conversation, and all personal habits, that constitute the difference between a gentleman and a clown. We can bear some oddity, or eccentricity in a friend whom we admire for his talents, or revere for his virtues; but it becomes quite a different thing, when the oddity, or the eccentricity, is to be a pattern or model, from which fifty or a hundred children are to form their manners. It was well remarked, by the ablest British traveller who has ever visited this country, that amongst us, "every male above twenty-one years of age, claims to be a sovereign. He is, therefore, *bound to be a gentleman.*"

5th. *Morals.*—On the indispensable, all-controlling requisite of moral character, I have but a single suggestion to make, in addition to those admirable views on this subject, which are scattered up and down through the committees' reports. This suggestion relates to the responsibility resting on those individuals, who give letters of recommendation, or certificates of character, to candidates for schools. . . . In the contemplation of the law, the school committee are sentinels stationed at the door of every schoolhouse in the State, to see that no teacher ever crosses its threshold, who is not clothed, from the crown of his head to the sole of his foot, in garments of virtue; and they are the enemies of the human race,—not of contemporaries only, but of posterity,—who, from any private or sinister motive, strive to put these sentinels to sleep, in order that one, who is profane, or intemperate, or addicted to low associations, or branded with the stigma of any vice, may elude the vigilance of the watchmen, and be installed over the pure minds of the young, as their guide and exemplar. If none but teachers of pure tastes, of good manners, of exemplary morals, had ever gained admission into our schools, neither the school rooms, nor their appurtenances would have been polluted, as some of them now are, with such ribald inscriptions, and with the carvings os such obscene emblems, as would make a heathen blush. Every person, therefore, who endorses another's character, as one befitting a school teacher, stands before the public as his moral bondsman and sponsor, and should be held to a rigid accountability.

HORACE MANN ON THE EMPLOYMENT OF FEMALE TEACHERS

(**1844**) From *Eighth Annual Report of the Secretary of the Board of Education,* as quoted in *Life and Works of Horace Mann* (Boston, 1891), vol. III, pp. 426–29.

One of the most extraordinary changes which have taken place in our schools, during the last seven years, consists in the great proportionate increase in the number of female teachers employed.

In 1837, the number of male teachers in all our public schools, including
summer and winter terms, was,...2370
Of females 3591
In the school year 1843–4, it was,—males,...2529
Females...4581
Increase in the number of male teachers 159
   "   "   "   female   "   "   990
During the same time, the number of schools, in the State, has increased
only.. 418

    This change in public sentiment, in regard to the employment of female
teachers, I believe to be in accordance with the dictates of the soundest philosophy.
Is not woman destined to conduct the rising generation, of both sexes, at least
through all the primary stages of education? Has not the Author of nature pre-
adapted her, by constitution, and faculty, and temperament, for this noble work?
What station of beneficent labor can she aspire to, more honorable, or more
congenial to every pure and generous impulse? In the great system of society, what
other part can she act, so intimately connected with the refinement and purification
of the race? How otherwise can she so well vindicate her right to an exalted station
in the scale of being; and cause that shameful sentence of degradation by which she
has so long been dishonored, to be repealed? Four fifths of all the women who have
ever lived, have been the slaves of man,—the menials in his household, the drudges
in his field, the instruments of his pleasure; or, at best, the gilded toys of his leisure
days in court or palace. She has been outlawed from honorable service, and almost
incapacitated, by her servile condition, for the highest aspirations after usefulness
and renown. But a noble revenge awaits her. By a manifestation of the superiority of
moral power, she can triumph over that physical power which has hitherto
subjected her to bondage. She can bless those by whom she has been wronged. By
refining the tastes and sentiments of man, she can change the objects of his
ambition; and, with changed objects of ambition, the fields of honorable exertion
can be divided between the sexes. By inspiring nobler desires for nobler objects, she
can break down the ascendency of those selfish motives that have sought their
gratification in her submission and inferiority. All this she can do, more rapidly, and
more effectually than it can ever be done in any other way, unless through miracles,
by training the young to juster notions of honor and duty, and to a higher
appreciation of the true dignity and destiny of the race.
    The more extensive employment of females for educating the young, will be the
addition of a new and mighty power to the forces of civilization. It is a power, also,
which, heretofore, to a very great extent, has been unappropriated; which has been
allowed, in the administration of the affairs of men, to run to waste. Hence it will
be an addition to one of the grandest spheres of human usefulness, without any
subtraction from other departments;—a gain without a loss. For all females,—the
great majority,—who are destined, in the course of Providence, to sustain maternal
relations, no occupation or apprenticeship can be so serviceable; but, in this
connection, it is not unworthy of notice, that, according to the census of
Massachusetts, there are almost eight thousand more females than males belonging
to the State.
    But if a female is to assume the performance of a teacher's duties, she must be
endowed with high qualifications. If devoid of mental superiority, then she
inevitably falls back into that barbarian relation, where physical strength measures
itself against physical strength. In that contest, she can never hope to succeed; or, if

she succeeds, it will be only as an Amazon, and not as a personification of moral power. Opportunities, therefore, should be everywhere opened for the fit qualification of female teachers; and all females possessing in an eminent degree, the appropriate natural endowments, should be encouraged to qualify themselves for this sacred work. Those who have worthily improved such opportunities, should be rewarded with social distinction and generous emoluments. Society cannot do less than this, on its own account, for those who are improving its condition; though for the actors themselves, in this beneficent work, the highest rewards must forever remain where God and nature have irrevocably placed them—in the consciousness of well-doing.

Could public opinion, on this one subject, be rectified, and brought into harmony with the great law of Christian duty and love, there are thousands of females amongst us, who now spend lives of frivolity, of unbroken wearisomeness and worthlessness, who would rejoice to exchange their days of painful idleness for such ennobling occupations; and who, in addition to the immediate rewards of well-doing, would see, in the distant prospect, the consolations of a life well spent, instead of the pangs of remorse for a frivolous and wasted existence.

HENRY BARNARD ON THE ADVANTAGES OF WOMEN AS TEACHERS

(1839)   From Connecticut Board of Commissioners of Common Schools, *First Annual Report of the Secretary* (Hartford, Conn., 1839), pp. 38–39.

The average rate of wages for male teachers is $15.48 per month, exclusive of board; for female teachers, $8.33. This includes the very liberal salaries paid in some of our large cities and districts, for teachers permanently engaged. Leaving them out of the estimate, the average rate will be somewhat reduced.

It is time for every friend of improvement in our common schools to protest against the inadequate and disproportionate compensation paid to female teachers. I have no hesitation in saying, that in the schools which I have visited, the female teachers were as well qualified, as devoted to their duties, and really advanced their pupils as far as the same number of male teachers. Let but a more generous appreciation of the value of their services as teachers, especially in the primary departments, prevail—let the system be so far modified as to admit of their being employed more extensively than now, not only in the summer, but the winter schools, and, as far as possible for the year round, and a new and happy impulse would not only be felt, in the more thorough intellectual training of youth, but in the improved manners and morals of society. As it is now, that class of females best qualified, by having enjoyed the advantages of superior and expensive schools, cannot be induced to enter the common schools as teachers, on account of the inadequate compensation, and the unnecessary difficulties and inconveniences connected with the employment. If the State would but furnish an opportunity for a numerous and most deserving class of young females, who are forced by their necessities into the corrupted atmosphere and unhealthy employments of our workshops and factories, to prepare themselves for teaching, and then remove the obstacles in the way of their being employed to the best advantage, an untold amount of female talent and usefulness, now in part wasted, or if employed even at better compensation, at least to a far less useful purpose, would be enlisted in the so much needed work of molding the childhood and youth of this State and nation.

This is a field in which practical and immediate improvement can be made. Fitted by nature, education, and the circumstances of society with us, for teachers, our law should be framed, so as to encourage and admit of their more general and permanent employment. Schools of a higher grade than the common district school as it exists, should be established, as well for other purposes, but especially with a view of adapting the studies there to the better education of females than can now be given. This is one of the most serious deficiencies of common school instruction. It is not adapted to form and cultivate a sufficiently high standard of female character. This want can be supplied, and is in some measure supplied, to the daughters of the wealthy, by our many excellent, but expensive female seminaries. But these are practically closed to two thirds of the community.

THE SUPERIORITY OF WOMEN AS TEACHERS (1846)   From Catherine E. Beecher, *The Evils Suffered by American Women and American Children: The Causes and the Remedy* (New York, 1846), pp. 9–10.

Now, without expressing any opinion as to the influence, on health and morals, of taking women away from domestic habits and pursuits, to labor with men in shops and mills, I simply ask if it would not be *better* to put the thousands of men who are keeping school for young children into the mills, and employ the women to train the children?

Wherever education is most prosperous, there woman is employed more than man. In Massachusetts, where education is highest, five out of seven of the teachers are women; while in Kentucky, where education is so much lower, five out of six of the teachers are men.

Another cause of depression to our sex is found in the fact that there is no profession for women of education and high position, which, like law, medicine, and theology, opens the way to competence, influence, and honor, and presents motives for exertion. Woman ought never to be led to married life except under the promptings of pure affection. To marry for an establishment, for a position, or for something to do, is a deplorable wrong. But how many women, for want of a high and honorable profession to engage their time, are led to this melancholy course. This is not so because Providence has not provided an ample place for such a profession for woman, but because custom or prejudice, or a low estimate of its honorable character, prevents her from entering it. *The education of children, that is the true and noble profession of a woman—that* is what is worthy the noblest powers and affections of the noblest minds.

Another cause which deeply affects the best interests of our sex is the contempt, or utter neglect and indifference, which has befallen this only noble profession open to woman. There is no employment, however disagreeable or however wicked, which custom and fashion cannot render elegant, interesting, and enthusiastically sought. A striking proof of this is seen in the military profession. This is the profession of *killing our fellow-creatures,* and is attended with everything low, brutal, unchristian, and disgusting; and yet what halos of glory have been hung around it, and how the young, and generous, and enthusiastic have been drawn into it! If one-half the poetry, fiction, oratory, and taste thus misemployed had been used to embellish and elevate the employment of training the mind of childhood, in what an altered position should we find this noblest of all professions!

As it is, the employment of teaching children is regarded as the most wearying drudgery, and few resort to it except from necessity; and one very reasonable cause of this aversion is the utter neglect of any arrangements for *preparing* teachers for this arduous and difficult profession. The mind of a young child is like a curious instrument, capable of exquisite harmony when touched by a skillful hand, but sending forth only annoying harshness when unskillfully addressed. To a teacher is committed a collection of these delicate contrivances; and, without experience, without instruction, it is required not only that each one should be tuned aright, but that all be combined in excellent harmony: as if a young girl were sent into a splendid orchestra, all ignorant and unskillful, and required to draw melody from each instrument, and then to combine the whole in faultless harmony. And in each case there are, here and there, individual minds, who, without instruction, are gifted by nature with aptness and skill in managing the music either of matter or of mind; but that does not lessen the folly, in either case, of expecting the whole profession, either of music or of teaching, to be pursued without preparatory training.

HENRY BARNARD ON THE SIGNIFICANCE OF SCHOOL GRADING

(**1845**)   From *Report of the Condition and Improvement of the Public Schools of Rhode Island, 1845* (Providence, 1845), as quoted in John J. Brubacher, ed., *Henry Barnard on Education* (New York, 1931), pp. 78–87.

Something should be done to reduce the multiplicity and variety of cares and duties which press at one and the same time, upon the attention of the teacher, and to introduce more of system and permanency into the arrangement of classes and studies in all the schools. No matter whether the school be large or small, there will be found collected into one apartment, under one teacher, children of both sexes, and of every age from four years and under, to sixteen years and upwards.

This variety of age calls for a multiplicity of studies, from the alphabet to the highest branches ever pursued in well regulated academies. The different studies require at least a corresponding number of classes; and in most schools the number of classes actually required, is more than doubled by the diversity of books, and of different editions of the same book, in which the same studies are pursued by different scholars. The number of classes are again increased by the differing attainments of scholars in the same study, arising out of differences in school attendance, parental cooperation, individual capacity and habits of attention. Each class requires a separate recitation, and in those studies, such as arithmetic and penmanship, in which no classification is attempted, the teacher will be obliged to give individual assistance to as many scholars as may be pursuing them, which is never less than one-half of the whole school. With so many causes at work to prevent the teacher from acting on any considerable number at a time, he is obliged to carry forward his school by individual recitations and assistance. Out of one hundred and sixty schools, from which information on this point was obtained, in 1844, there were fifty schools containing more than seventy scholars, in which the number of distinct recitations, including the classes in reading and spelling, and excluding the attention given to pupils in arithmetic and penmanship, averaged as high as twenty-three in each half day; there were one hundred and ten, numbering over fifty scholars, in which the average exceeded seventeen. The amount of time in a half-day's session, which can be made available for purposes of recitation, in most schools, with the utmost diligence on the part of the teacher, does not exceed one hundred and fifty minutes, and much of this is lost in calling and dismissing the classes, and in beginning and ending the lessons, so that an equitable distribution of the teacher's time and attention, gives but a small fragment to each class, and still less to each individual. The disadvantages under which pupils and teachers labor, in consequence of this state of things, are great and manifold.

There is a large amount of physical suffering and discomfort, as well as great hindrance in the proper arrangement of scholars and classes, caused by crowding the older and younger pupils into the same school-room, without seats and furniture appropriate to either; and the greatest amount of suffering and discomfort falls upon the young, who are least able to bear it, and who in consequence, acquire a distaste to study and the school-room.

The work of education going on in such schools, cannot be appropriate and progressive. There cannot be a regular course of discipline and instruction, adapted to the age and proficiency of pupils—a series of processes, each adapted to certain periods in the development of the mind and character, the first intended to be followed by a second and the second by a third,—the latter always depending on the earlier, and all intended to be conducted on the same general principles, and by methods varying with the work to be done, and the progress already made.

With the older and younger pupils in the same room, there cannot be a system of discipline which shall be equally well adapted to both classes. If it secures the cheerful obedience and subordination of the older, it will press with unwise severity upon the younger pupils. If it be adapted to the physical wants, and peculiar temperaments of the young, it will endanger the good order, and habits of study, of the more advanced pupils, by the frequent change of posture and position, and other indulgences which it permits and requires of the former.

With studies ranging from the alphabet and the simplest rudiments of knowledge, to the higher branches of an English education, a variety of methods of instruction and illustration is called for, which are seldom found together, or in an equal degree, in the same teacher, and which can never be pursued with equal success in the same school-room. The elementary principles of knowledge, to be made intelligible and interesting to the young, must be presented by a large use of the oral and simultaneous methods. The higher branches, especially all mathematical subjects, require patient application and habits of abstraction, on the part of the older pupils, which can with difficulty, if at all, be attained by many pupils, amid a multiplicity of distracting exercises, movements and sounds. The recitations of this class of pupils, to be profitable and satisfactory, must be conducted in a manner which requires time, discussion and explanation, and the undivided attention of both pupils and teacher.

From the number of class and individual recitations, to be attended to during each half day, these exercises are brief, hurried and of little practical value. They consist, for the most part, of senseless repetitions of the words of a book. Instead of being the time and place where the real business of teaching is done, where the ploughshare of interrogation is driven down into the acquirements of each pupil, and his ability to comprehend clearly, remember accurately, discriminate wisely, and reason closely, is cultivated and tested—where the difficult principles of each lesson are developed and illustrated, and additional information imparted, and the mind of the teacher brought in direct contact with the mind of each pupil, to arouse, interest and direct its opening powers—instead of all this and more, the brief period passed in recitation, consists, on the part of the teacher, of hearing each individual and class in regular order, and quick succession, repeat words from a book; and on the part of the pupils, of *saying their lessons,* as the operation is significantly described by most teachers, when they summon the class to the stand. In the mean time the order of the school must be maintained, and the general business must be going forward. Little children without any authorized employment for their eyes and hands, and ever active curiosity, must be made to sit still, while every muscle is aching from suppressed activity; pens must be mended, copies set, arithmetical difficulties solved, excuses for tardiness or absence received, questions answered, whisperings allowed or suppressed, and more or less of extempore discipline administered. Were it not a most ruinous waste of precious time, did it not involve the deadening, crushing, disturbing, dwarfing of immortal faculties and noble sensibilities, were it not an utter perversion of the noble objects for which schools are instituted, it would be difficult to conceive of a more diverting farce than an ordinary session of a large public school, whose chaotic and discordant elements had not been reduced to a system by a proper classification. The teacher, at least the conscientious teacher, thinks it anything but a farce to him. Compelled to hurry from one study to another, the most diverse, from one class to another, requiring a knowledge of methods altogether distinct, from one recitation to another, equally brief and unsatisfactory, one requiring a liveliness of manner, which he does not feel and cannot assume, and the other closeness of attention and abstraction of thought, which he cannot give amid the multiplicity and variety of cares, from one case of discipline to another, pressing on him at the same time, he goes through the same circuit day after day, with a dizzy brain and aching heart, and brings his school to a close with a feeling, that with all his diligence and fidelity, he has accomplished but little good.

Among these conditions of success in the operation of a system of public schools, is such a classification of the scholars as shall bring a larger number of similar age and attainments, at all times, and in every stage of their advancement, under teachers of the right qualifications, and enable these teachers to act upon numbers at once, for years in succession, and carry them all forward effectually together, in a regular course of instruction.

The great principle to be regarded in the classification, either of the schools of a town or district, or of scholars in the same school, is equality of attainments, which will generally include those of the same age. Those who have gone over substantially the same ground, or reached or nearly reached the same point of attainment in several studies, should be put together, and constitute, whenever their numbers will authorize it, one school. These again should be arranged in different classes, for it is seldom practicable, even if it were ever desirable, to have but one class in every study in the same grade of school. Even in very large districts, where the scholars are promoted from a school of a lower grade to one of a higher, after being found qualified in certain studies, it is seldom that any considerable number will have reached a common standard of scholarship in all their studies. The same pupil will have made very different progress in different branches. He will stand higher in one and lower in another. By arranging scholars of the same general division in different classes, no pupil need be detained by companions who have made, or can make less progress, or be hurried over lessons and subjects in a superficial manner, to accommodate the more rapid advancement of others. Although equality of attainment, should be regarded as the general principle, some regard should be paid to age, and other circumstances. A large boy of sixteen, from the deficiency of his early education, which may be his misfortune and not his fault, ought not to be put into a school or class of little children, although their attainments may be in advance of his. This step would mortify and discourage him. In such extreme cases, that arrangement will be best which will give the individual the greatest chance of improvement, with the least discomfort to himself, and hindrance to others. Great disparity of age in the same class, at the same school, is unfavorable to uniform and efficient discipline, and the adaptation of methods of teaching, and of motives to application and obedience. Some regard, too, should be had to the preferences of individuals, especially among the older pupils, and their probable destination in life. The mind comes into the requisitions of study more readily, and works with higher results, when led onward by the heart; and the utility of any branch of study, its relations to future success in life, once clearly apprehended, becomes a powerful motive to effort.

Each class in a school should be as large as is consistent with thoroughness and minuteness of individual examination, and practicable, without bringing together individuals of diverse capacity, knowledge and habits of study. A good teacher can teach a class of forty with as much ease as a class of ten, and with far more profit to each individual, than if the same amount of time was divided up among four classes, each containing one fourth of the whole number. When the class is large, there is a spirit, a glow, a struggle which can never be infused or called forth in a small class. Whatever time is spent upon a few, which could have been as profitably spent on a larger number who were not thus benefited. The recitations of a large class must be more varied, both as to order, and methods, so as to reach those whose attention would wander if not under the pressure of constant excitement, or might become slothful from inaction or a sense of security. Some studies will admit of a larger number in a class than others.

The number of classes for recitation in the same apartment, by one teacher, should be small. This will facilitate the proper division of labor in instruction, and allow more time for each class. The teacher entrusted with the care of but few studies, and few recitations, can have no excuse but indolence, or the want of capacity, if he does not master these branches thoroughly, and soon acquire the most skilful and varied methods of teaching them. His attention will not be distracted by a multiplicity and variety of cares, pressing upon him at the same time. This principle does not require that every school should be small, but that each teacher should have a small number of studies and classes to superintend.

In a large school, properly classified, a division of labor can be introduced in the department of government, as well as in that of instruction. By assigning the different studies to a sufficient number of assistants, in separate classrooms, each well qualified to teach the branches assigned, the principal teacher may be selected with special reference to his ability in arranging the studies, and order of exercises of the school, in administering its discipline, in adapting moral instruction to individual scholars, and superintending the operations of each class-room, so as to secure the harmonious action and progress of every department. The talents and tact required for these and similar duties, are more rarely found than the skill and attainments required to teach successfully a particular study. When found, the influence of such a principal, possessing in a high degree, the executive talent spoken of, will be felt through every class, and by every subordinate teacher, giving tone and efficiency to the whole school.

Every class should have its appropriate time for study and recitation, and this distribution of time should not be postponed, abridged or prolonged, except from absolute necessity. The punctuality and precision is agreeable to children, is the only way in which justice can be done to each class, and is highly beneficial in its operation on each individual, and the whole school.

The classification of a school, and the character of the recitations of each class, and especially of such recitations as are in the nature of a review of the ground gone over the previous week, month, or term, should be entered in a book, to be preserved from term to term, and year to year. With such a record, there need not be so much time lost in organizing a school, whenever there is a change of teachers, and there never should be for an hour, the perfect chaos into which almost every school is thrown on the opening of a new administration.

To what extent the gradation of schools shall be carried, in any town or district, and to what limit the number of classes in any school can be reduced, will depend on the compactness, number, and other circumstances of the population, in that town or district, and the number and age of the pupils, and the studies and methods of instruction in that school. A regular gradation of schools might embrace Primary, Secondary and High Schools, with Intermediate Schools, or departments, between each grade, and Supplementary Schools, to meet the wants of a class of pupils not provided for in either of the above grades.

HENRY BARNARD ON THE CERTIFICATION OF TEACHERS (1852)   From State of Connecticut, *Seventh Annual Report of the Secretary of the Board of Education* (1852), pp. 46–48.

The certificate or diploma of a school teacher should be worth something to him, and be at the same time an evidence to parents and local committees who may not have the requisite time and qualifications to examine and judge for themselves of the fitness of a person to classify, teach and govern a school. It should, therefore, be granted by a committee, composed of one or more persons competent to judge, from having a practical and familiar knowledge of the subjects and points to which an examination should be directed, and above all, of what constitutes aptness to teach, and good methods of classification, instruction and discipline. The person or committee should be so appointed and occupy such a local position as to remove the granting, withholding or annulling of a certificate above all suspicion of partiality or all fears of personal consequences. A diploma should mark the grade of school which the holder, after due examination, is judged qualified to teach, and for this purpose, there should be a classification of diplomas. The first granted, and the only one which should be granted to a candidate who has not had at the time some experience as an assistant in the practical duties of teaching, should entitle the holder to teach in the particular school for which he has, or is about to apply, and which should be specified in the diploma. Before granting such a diploma, the circumstances of the school should be known to the person or board granting the same. After a successful trial for one term in this school, an indorsement on the back of the certificate to this effect, might give that certificate currency in all the districts of the town, where committees and parents could themselves know or judge of his attainments, character and skill as a teacher. A diploma of the second degree should not be granted until after a more rigorous and extended examination of the candidate has been held, and the evidence of at least one year of successful teaching can be adduced. This examination should cover all the studies pursued in common schools, of every grade, except in public high schools, in cities and large villages. This certificate should be good for any town in the county for which it is granted. After three years of successful teaching, teachers who have received the first and second certificates, may apply for the third, which should be granted only by a board composed of the inspectors or examiners in two or more counties. This certificate, until annulled, should exempt the holder from all local and annual examinations, and be good for every school, so far as entitling the holder to be paid out of any public funds. Every certificate should be based on satisfactory evidence of good moral character, and unexceptionable conduct, and every teacher who proves himself unworthy of the profession by criminal or immoral acts, should have his certificate publicly annulled. The great object is to prevent incompetent persons from gaining admission into the profession, and exclude such as prove themselves unworthy of its honors and compensation. Every board of examination should be composed of working school men, of persons who have been practical teachers, or shown their interest in the improvement of schools, and the advancement of the profession by their works. Every examination should be conducted both by oral and written questions and answers, should be held only at regular periods, which should be designated in the law, and the examination papers, and record of the doings of every meeting should be properly kept and preserved. The names of the successful candidates for certificates of the second and third degree, should be published annually, in the Report of the State Superintendent, as well as the names of those teachers whose certificates have been annulled for criminal or immoral conduct. A portion of the public school money in each town should be paid directly to the teacher, according to the grade of certificate he may hold.

TEACHER TRAINING AT PHILLIPS ANDOVER ACADEMY (1834)   From *American Annals of Education* (June 1834), p. 288.

We have insisted upon no point more earnestly, or with more confidence, than the *necessity of a professional education for teachers,* as indispensable to the permanent improvement of our schools. We are rejoiced to learn that the Trustees of Phillips' Academy have resolved to place the Seminary at Andover on a broader and more permanent basis for the accomplishment of this object. They have been urged to this measure by the success of the plan thus far, and the numerous calls for teachers from the destitute portions of our country. In addition to the large building and apparatus already used for this purpose, a farm for manual labor, lodging houses, and a hall for boarding have been provided as a means of diminishing the expenses of students. It is confidently believed that many young men, well qualified for the office, are ready to devote themselves to the business of teaching as a profession, provided they can receive a little aid in addition to the means of support now offered.

SAMUEL READ HALL'S TEACHER-TRAINING COURSE AT PHILLIPS ANDOVER ACADEMY (1837)   From *American Journal of Education*, vol. V, p. 379.

In the TEACHER'S DEPARTMENT are *three classes*. The course of study can be accomplished in three years. But, as the middle and senior classes are expected to be absent to enable them to teach during the winter term, the course requires three and a half years. The regular time for admission is at the commencement of the summer term. Candidates for admission to the junior class must be prepared to pass a satisfactory examination on the sounds of English letters, rules of spelling, reading, geography, first principles of etymology and syntax, intellectual arithmetic, history of the United States, ground rules of written arithmetic, and fractions. The year is divided into three terms, and the following studies are pursued at each:

JUNIOR CLASS

First Term.—English Grammar; Intellectual Arithmetic. *reviewed;* History of the United States, *reviewed.*

Second Term.—Written Arithmetic; Geography, ancient and modern; History of England.

Third Term.—Written Arithmetic, *finished;* Linear Drawing; Construction of Maps; Use of Globes; Book-keeping.

MIDDLE CLASS

First Term.—Algebra; Euclid; Rhetoric.

Second Term.—Algebra, *finished;* Trigonometry; Chemistry.

Third Term.—Chemistry, *finished;* Surveying; Spherical Geometry. Conic Sections.

SENIOR CLASS

First Term.—Natural Philosophy; Logic; Civil Engineering.

Second Term.—Natural Theology; Evidences of Christianity; Moral Philosophy; Astronomy.

Third Term.—Political Economy; Intellectual Philosophy; Art of Teaching.

All the members of the junior class attend to the *"Political Class Book"* on Saturdays, and declamation and composition on Wednesdays, throughout the year. The middle and senior classes write compositions on subjects connected with the art of teaching.

THE PROFESSION OF EDUCATION

Lectures are given, accompanied with illustrations and experiments, on the most important studies; particularly, natural philosophy, chemistry, and school keeping. Each one who finishes the course will have attended more than fifty lectures on the latter subject.

DONATION OF A PHILANTHROPIST (EDMUND DWIGHT) FOR NORMAL SCHOOLS IN MASSACHUSETTS (1837)   From Mary Peabody Mann, *Life of Horace Mann* (Boston, 1865), p. 101.

To the President of the Senate and the Speaker of the House of Representatives

GENTLEMEN,—Private munificence has placed at my disposal the sum of $10,000 to promote the cause of popular education in Massachusetts.

The condition is, that the Commonwealth will contribute the same amount from unappropriated funds in aid of the same cause; both sums to be drawn upon equally as needed, and to be disbursed, under the direction of the Board of Education, in qualifying teachers for our common schools.

As the proposal contemplates that the State in its collective capacity shall do no more than is here proffered to be done from private means, and as, with a high and enlightened disregard of all local, party, and sectional views, it comprehends the whole of the rising generation in its philanthropic plan, I cannot refrain from earnestly soliciting for it the favorable regards of the Legislature.

Very respectfully,
HORACE MANN,
Secretary of the Board of Education.

THE MASSACHUSETTS BOARD OF EDUCATION RECOMMENDS THE ESTABLISHMENT OF STATE NORMAL SCHOOLS (1838)   From "First Annual Report of the Board of Education, 1838," as quoted in Mary P. Mann, *Life and Works of Horace Mann* (Boston, 1891), vol. II, pp. 376–78.

The subject of the education of teachers has been more than once brought before the Legislature, and is of the very highest importance in connection with the improvement of our schools. That there are all degrees of skill and success on the part of teachers, is matter of too familiar observation to need repetition; and that these must depend, in no small degree, on the experience of the teacher, and in his formation under a good discipline and method of instruction in early life, may be admitted without derogating, in any measure, from the importance of natural gifts and aptitude, in fitting men for this as for the other duties of society. Nor can it be deemed unsafe to insist that, while occupations requiring a very humble degree of intellectual effort and attainment demand a long-continued training, it cannot be that the arduous and manifold duties of the instructor of youth should be as well performed without as with a specific preparation for them. In fact, it must be admitted, as the voice of reason and experience, that institutions for the formation of teachers must be established among us, before the all-important work of forming the minds of our children can be performed in the best possible manner, and with the greatest attainable success.

No one who has been the witness of the ease and effect with which instruction is imparted by one teacher, and the tedious pains-taking and unsatisfactory progress which mark the labors of another of equal ability and knowledge, and operating on materials equally good, can entertain a doubt that there is a mastery in teaching as in every other art. Nor is it less obvious that, within reasonable limits, this skill and this mastery may themselves be made the subjects of instruction, and be communicated to others.

We are not left to the deductions of reason on this subject. In those foreign countries, where the greatest attention has been paid to the work of education, schools for teachers have formed an important feature in their systems, and with the happiest result. The art of imparting instruction has been found, like every other art, to improve by cultivation in institutions established for that specific object. New importance has been attached to the calling of the instructor by public opinion, from the circumstance that his vocation has been deemed one requiring systematic preparation and culture. Whatever tends to degrade the profession of the teacher, in his own mind or that of the public, of course impairs his usefulness; and this result must follow from regarding instruction as a business which in itself requires no previous training.

The duties which devolve upon the teachers even of our Common Schools, particularly when attended by large numbers of both sexes, and of advanced years for learners (as is often the case), are various, and difficult of performance. For their faithful execution, no degree of talent and qualification is too great; and when we reflect that in the nature of things only a moderate portion of both can, in ordinary cases, be expected, for the slender compensation afforded the teacher, we gain a new view of the necessity of bringing to his duties the advantage of previous training in the best mode of discharging them.

A very considerable part of the benefit, which those who attend our schools might derive from them, is unquestionably lost for want of mere skill in the business of instruction, on the part of the teacher. This falls with especial hardship on that part of our youthful population, who are able to enjoy, but for a small portion of the year, the advantage of the schools. For them it is of peculiar importance, that, from the moment of entering the school, every hour should be employed to the greatest advantage, and every facility in imparting knowledge, and every means of awakening and guiding the mind, be put into instant operation: and where this is done, two months of schooling would be as valuable as a year passed under a teacher destitute of experience and skill. The Board cannot but express the sanguine hope, that the time is not far distant, when the resources of public or private liberality will be applied in Massachusetts for the foundation of an institution for the formation of teachers, in which the present existing defect will be amply supplied.

THE FIRST TERM OF CYRUS PIERCE, FIRST PRINCIPAL OF THE LEXINGTON, MASSACHUSETTS, NORMAL SCHOOL (1839)

From *The Journal of Cyrus Pierce, July 3, 1839–March 12, 1841,* as quoted in Arthur O. Norton, ed., *The First State Normal School in America: The Journals of Cyrus Pierce and Mary Swift* (Cambridge, Mass., 1926), pp. 3–9.

The First Term, July 3–October 1, 1839

Lexington July 3d 1839

This Day the Normal School, the first in the Country, commenced.

Three Pupils Misses Hawkins, Smith & Damon were examined by the Board of Visitors—viz Messrs. Sparks, Rantoul & Putnam, & admitted—

July 8 Monday School opened this day with 3 pupils Hawkins, Smith & Stowe—one Miss Rolph added during the day Exercises Conversation—Grammar & Arithmetic. Three of the Scholars promise well.

[*July*] 9—This [day] Misses Stodder & Damon came into School as pupils

[*July*] 10—This Day Mary Swift of Nantucket joined the School—making 7 scholars in all. Our Exercises thus far have been chiefly in Grammar, Reading Geography and Arithmetic. Some of the Pupils not yet provided with Books—Exercises consisting chiefly of conversation and Interrogatories.

July 15 2d Week. This day held a session in the upper room. Hitherto the sessions have been in the sitting room—School visited by Mr Sparks—

July 17 Almira Locke was examined & admitted—

[*July*] 22. An order of Exercise has been decided upon for the School-Room, and some Rules for the regulation of the House. The Studies for this week, and time indefinite, are to be The Common branches, Algebra, Nat. Philosophy, Physiology, Mental Philosophy, Book-Keeping, Moral Philosophy, & Geometry.

[*July*] 23 Miss Margaret O'Connor entered the School.

[*July*] 26. Mr Chamberlain brought up the Apparatus—which has been purchased for the use of the School—The Library has been set up—The School-rooms & the Entries have been painted, & the Building now is nearly put in order for the School—The Grounds around the Building are not yet prepared—and the Sleeping apartments still need further accommodations.

July 29 Two Scholars absent this day, Misses O'Connor & Smith—The former had leave of absence to go home last Friday 26th Ins.—The latter is reported sick. The School this day visited by Messrs Rantoul and Woodbury. The Former one of the Board of Visiters—who was pleased to express a decided Satisfaction in the appearance of the School.

[*July*] 30 Miss O'Connor this day returned and took her seat in School.

Aug. 5 The Apparatus and the Principal part of the Library have been received and set up. The Order of Exercises has been adopted, as well as a System of Rules for the Regulation of the House and the government of the School. For a few days past the School has been going on more orderly and systematically and the pupils have made progress, and the Prospect seems more encouraging than at first.

On the 2d Aug. we had a very pleasant visit from Prof. S. H. Newman, who gave some very excellent Advice to the pupils; and which was listened to with great apparent Satisfaction.

Some of the Regulations of the School do not yet receive quite that attention and respect which satisfy me. This point must be attended to.

Aug. This day School visited by Miss Stowe sister of my pupil. Spent the morning in a kind of Moral and religious lecture to the Pupils in connexion with the Reading in the Scriptures. The subject of the Remarks was Herod's Oath & Treatment of John the Baptist;—The Nature of Promises and the influence of early and parental Education. The Scholars seemed attentive, & the Lecture, I think, was useful.

Aug. 9 Set up the Clock in the Room—Had a visit from Mr. Wood, former teacher of the Coffin School, Nantucket.

Aug. 10. Delivered a Lecture—The Scholars wrote Composition. School has made some progress this week.

[*Aug.*] *12* Several Scholars absent this day in the afternoon because of the rain. This I was sorry to see. It augurs ill. It is a poor compliment to their interest and zeal in the business for which they came hither. Judging from this example, we may expect to have much absence from bad weather. But I shall take occasion to remark upon it.

[*Aug.*] *13* After hearing the lessons this morning, I remarked the absence of yesterday, I hope in such a way as to do good.

Some of my pupils last sabbath asked the privilege of walking to W. Cambridge. This I thought an unwise project; but reluctantly consented. One made a visit home; the others, accompanied her. When the young ladies returned, I believed they in the retrospect, thought much of the Plan as I did in prospect. I think such a thing will not be likely to take place again.

[*Aug.*] *15* Many of my pupils absent this day

[*Aug.*] *16* This commenced a new-mode of Recitation by the scholars giving abstracts of lessons *written* out. I also this day committed the hearing of the Morning Lesson to Miss Swift. Both experiments quite as satisfactory as I expected—Yesterday, I received a visit from Dr. Ware Jr and Rev. Mr. Putnam—of Roxbury; they did not, however go into school

[*Aug.*] *19* The Scholars for 2 or 3 days past have been giving written abstracts of their Physiological Lessons as a *mode* of *Reciting.* The Success has been somewhat various. On the whole, I am inclined to regard it a good variety of the modes of Recitation.

Aug. 23 During this week the N[ormal] School has been visited by Miss Stodder of Boston, Miss Starbuck and Mrs Swain of Nantucket. The Exercises have not been quite so promptly and well recited as they have been during some of the preceding weeks; but on the whole, I am not certain that they have not made as much progress. The Scholars all continue to seem pleasant; industrious, interested and happy. Miss (*sic*) has been unwell during most of the time; and this morning, in company with her sister, she left for Boston.

[*Aug.*] *27* Very warm weather for several days—and several of the pupils have been so unwell as to be detained from school.—I think the scholars have not been much habituated to hard close and methodical studying. There is great deficiency among them in knowledge of the Common Branches. With two or three exceptions, most that are in school I think will need nearly all of the first year to fit themselves thoroughly. Reading, Spelling, Grammar, Arithmetic Geography all need attention.

[*Aug.*] Tomorrow and next day I shall hold no session purposing in company with some of my Scholars to attend Commencement at Cambridge—

[*Aug.*] *28–29* School suspended—I attended Commencement at Cambridge with some of the pupils;—which as it was new & interesting so I hope it may prove beneficial to them—Miss Parks examined and admitted into School.

Sept 2d Miss Sarah E. Locke examined and admitted into School.

[*Sept.*] 5 This morning I recited the lessons to the Class—or rather I delivered a short familiar Lecture to them instead of the recitation—I think, it may be advantageous to a school for Teachers to recite [to] their classes rather than classes to their Teachers. If it has no other effect, it diversifies the modes of operation.

I am having the chambers of the School-house, and the School-rooms better prepared for ventilation. Also a small Wood-shed is building. I am not certain how this last step will meet the views of the Board of Visitors; but I trust they will think of it as I do.

School visited the 3d Inst. by Rev. Mr. Damon of West-Cambridge.

[*Sept.*] 9 The School now consists of twelve Scholars—They seem industrious & interested; and nearly every one of *fair* capacity. But many of them are yet backward; and I apprehend it will require more than one year's Instruction to qualify them to teach. They want language—they want the power of generalization, and of communication. But I think in all things they are gaining ground, and I feel encouraged. Misses Smith, Stodder, Damon, Haskell, Stowe & Swift give quite as much promise at present as any of them.

[*Sept.*] 11 This began a Course of Experimental Lectures—Explained the Barometer and Thermometer—also the suction and forcing pumps—experimented with each—experiment in Refraction—all successful. This day commenced a New Exercise; styled 'Conversational Exercise'. Each scholar relates a story, anecdote or fact—in her own language. It was quite a hopeful beginning.

[*Sept.*] 12. School this day visited by Mr. Mann who spent the day with us. The School did well—Mr. M. was pleased to express much gratification in visit—the state of prospect of the school; and we all felt benefited and cheered by his presence. This Visit will make quite an Epoch in our history.

[*Sept.*] 13–14 No School—on the 13th the Principal attended the county Convention at Concord—as the Annual Address of the Secretary of the Board of Education was delivered—On the 14—went to Boston to procure stoves for the rooms.

[*Sept.*] 15. School came together rather thin—2 or 3 absent—Recitations pretty good—some improvement in reading.

[*Sept.*] 17.—Much as yesterday—

[*Sept.*] 18 This was our day for conversations. The Exercise pretty successful—I think it will prove beneficial if [it] is properly attended to—and preparations be well made.—Many of the Scholars want the power of language—I [think] this will aid them. Each one is expected to relate a story, an anecdote, a piece of history, a Biography in good style. A second familiar Lecture in Nat. Phi. was given—

[*Sept.*] 21. The week, which now closes has been, on the whole; a quiet, pleasant, and satisfactory [one].—Most of the pupils need most of their time for the common Branches—There is great deficiency in Reading and Spelling. I mentioned to them it is in contemplation, soon to get up a model School. This will be composed of children of the village and town from the age from 6 to 10—to be taught by the best Scholars of the N[ormal] School—under the supervision of the principal.—I hope to have it in operation in 2 or three weeks.

I must try to awaken more freedom of *Inquiry* and discussion. I think, the exercise is a valuable one.

23d Sept. A fair and pleasant day—School-Exercises successful. All pupils present except Miss Hawkins.

[*Sept.*] 25. This day the School-Exercises were a little out of their usual course. A Review in Nat. History, and Moral Philosophy. Besides Physiology, Conversational Exercise and Physiological Discussion.

In Moral Philosophy—the Exercises consisting of partly original thoughts and partly Extracts & Condensations were read. Some of them were very successful.

Yesterday the school was visited by four strangers—In the Evening there was a meeting of sundry citizens, in the Baptist Meeting-House; to consider the subject of a Model School to be connected with the Normal School—Not many present—some progress made. The project seems to meet the views of people well—The meeting stands adjourned at the East Village.

[*Sept.*] 26—This day's business was somewhat retarded by cold; the room not yet supplied with the means of having a fire—Scholars read abstracts of their Physiological Lessons, which were very good. The Principal delivered a familiar experimental Lecture in Natural Philosophy.

[*Sept.*] 28. School visited this day by Messrs Dr Webb of Boston and Gen. Wadsworth of Geneseo N.Y.—Put up my stoves in School-room.

[*Sept.*] 30 Had a fire in the School-room.

Oct. 1 School this day visited by Dr. Howe Principal of the Blind Institution S.B. [*i.e.*, South Boston] and one of the female teachers in said Institution.

This day my first quarter closes. (12 Scholars)

In review of the Term I feel encouraged. The numbers have been much fewer than I anticipated; but in regard to most of those who have attended, I believe they have made a good beginning & will make teachers. Few of them think of staying more than one year; all of which with great diligence, will be required to prepare them to teach in the *Common* Branches.—It seems to be a general impression in the minds of those with whom I converse that the next term the school will be filled up. I hope it may be so—I think there will be an addition. The Rooms will accommodate about 90. It is in contemplation to unite a Model School with the Normal School: Some of the incipient steps toward this have already been taken. It will be composed of children selected from those of the vicinity—of the age from 6 to 10 inclusive; to commence next term Oct. 21. This, I think, may awaken some additional interest. There are several mistakes—erroneous opinions prevailing in regard to the school, which I trust (*sic*) have operated and do operate, to its prejudice: These time, and the activity of the friends of the Institution must correct.

Oct. 9 During the Vacation, which commenced on the 2d Inst. Proposals have been made to the Inhabitants of this village and the town to furnish 30 children from 6 to 10 to form a Model School to be connected with the Normal School, to be under the Supervision of the Principal & to be taught by the Pupils of the Normal School. The Proposition meets with a flattering reception from the Inhabitants, and there is encouraging prospect that the School will go into operation at the Commencement of next term—Five children are to be taken from each District—If the more remote districts do not avail themselves of the overture, then a greater number is to be taken from the Centre School District.

THE FIRST TERM OF A STUDENT AT THE LEXINGTON,
MASSACHUSETTS, NORMAL SCHOOL (1839)   From *The Journal of Mary Swift,*
as quoted in Arthur O. Norton, ed., *The First State Normal School in America: The Journals
of Cyrus Pierce and Mary Swift* (Cambridge, Mass., 1926), pp. 81–87.

The First Term, August 1—October 1, 1839

Agreeably to the wishes of our teacher, Mr Peirce, I have purchased this
book, which is to contain an account of the business of the school, & of the studies
In which we are engaged.

This morn we were favored with a visit from Professor Newman, who is going
to teach the Normal School, at Barre in Worcester County.—At the close of the
school, he addressed the scholars. Some of his ideas upon the subject, were the
following; he said that when the students in medicine were attending a course of
lectures, they took notes & were enabled in doubtful cases, to recur to these &
derive instruction from them in practise. Many acquired great facility in this; so that
they could take the great part of every lecture. As we were studying a profession,
we could adopt that plan, & we should find that we should be able to recall past
events much more easily, by having written notes. By writing abstracts we should
acquire a better use of language & make the ideas contained in the works our own,
so that, when we were required to write Composition, we need not be obliged to
say that we had no ideas. He commended the spirit of inquiry which seemed to
pervade the school, & said that it created a much greater interest in our studies.—
The business of teaching, he said, was regarded as very laborious, but if the teacher
attended to the normal and intellectual education of his pupil, he would find the
drudgery greatly lessened. Instead of doing this, many thought the business of
teaching consisted only in instructing the pupils in Reading, Writing, & Calculation,
& this is the cause of the low standing of our Common Schools at the present
time.—He had several children & there was a public school near his house, but he
had never sent them. He feared that they would be injured by the company of the
scholars. It is the business of the teacher to remove this impression concerning
public schools, by elevating their moral standards; and to do this the teacher must
think seriously upon the subject, and influence the pupils both by example and
precept.——

*   *   *

After writing the above abstract the remaining time on Saturday morning was
occupied by Mr P— in delivering a lecture to the pupils.—The subject of which was
Normal Schools, their origin & the expectations of the Board of Education & of the
Friends of Education in general. When our forefathers first came to this country, (he
said) they saw the necessity of schools, and established those which we call
Grammar Schools. As the population became more numerous, the demand for
public schools increased, and various kinds have been instituted, from the High
Schools down to the Infant Schools. A better idea of the number of these schools,
can be formed, by considering that nineteen-twentieths of the children in the United
States, receive their Education from them.—As our commerce increased, and the
tide of emigration flowed more rapidly, the people found it necessary to do

something for the support of the government, and knowing that it must devolve upon the rising generations, they turned their attention to the subject of Education. It was discussed freely, and Periodical Journals were established devoted to the subject.—Finally, the Board of Education was formed. While we were thus rousing to activity on this side of the Atlantic, our intercourse with the inhabitants of the other world became more frequent, and we learned that the people of Prussia under their despotic government, had advanced farther than we, notwithstanding the celebrity which we had acquired. They had established Normal Schools; and it was expected that teachers should be prepared for their work, as much as those of any other profession. The legislature of Massachusetts were awakened, and by the assistance of private munificence, the school, whose advantages we now enjoy, was established. To us, therefore, all the friends of Education turn, anxious for the success of the first effort to establish such schools. For this success, we shall depend, chiefly, on three particulars: 1st on interesting you in the studies to which you attend & in the daily remarks; 2nd on the course of lectures to be given & 3d on the Model School.—

Monday 5th Aug. This morn the Natural Philosophy lesson was unprepared, owing to a misunderstanding among the pupils. Accordingly, the time was occupied in a review of the part which we had gone over. The lesson in Physiology was well recited, & was very interesting.—That in Intellectual Philosophy was not quite prepared.—In the afternoon, our first lesson was in Arithmetic. The subjects were the proof of Multiplication, by casting out the nines and Division. Both were satisfactorily explained, and the processes made perfectly intelligible.—We recited our first lesson in Wayland's Moral Philosophy. It was a new study and the class found it difficult to remember. Mr P. seemed pretty well satisfied, & foretold the same improvement in this, as in other recitations.—The Lesson in Geography was omitted for want of time.—

Tuesday 6th This day passes very much like its predecessor, & a particular description of it will be superfluous. The lessons were, generally, well recited in the morning. In the afternoon the lesson in Grammar was upon the subject of Tenses. Mr P. read over the portion in Peirce's Grammar on the subject of the verb, which part of speech he calls *asserters.* His names of the tenses seemed to [be] more appropriate than those employed by many grammarians. The lessons in Wayland's Science was omitted & after copying some problems on the globe school was dismissed.—

Wednesday 7th—Mr Peirce read the story of the daughter of Herodias, and the parable of the five loaves and two fishes.

After reading, he remarked that it was not his intention to make any observations, which should affect, at all, the sentiments which individuals might hold with regard to religious subjects. But that the portion which he had read, was so fruitful of instructive matter, that he did not feel that he could pass it by silently.— He then commented upon the influence which old people exerted over young, as instanced in the story mentioned, where the daughter of Her—was told by her mother to demand the head of John the Baptist. He said that the person who had wicked parents was much to be pitied, on account of this influence, and the person having wise parents, was proportionably blessed.—Few stories in the Bible were so full of interest as this, & it was especially so to the young of the same sex. The question arising from this, would be, ought Herod to have considered himself bound by his oath to perform this?—If for example she had asked him to have sent her to the moon, he would have refused, giving as an excuse his physical inability. For the reason of moral inability, he could have declined her last request.—The manner in which a promise is taken, should depend on the spirit in which it is made.—

The exercises of the forenoon were similar to those of the two past.——

Thursday, [8th] The lessons for this morn were N. Philosophy, Physiology, N. History. The subjects of the first were Light & Refraction. Our teacher explained the rule, that the intensity of light diminished as the square of the distance increased, in such a manner as to make it much more clear than it has been before in my mind.— The lesson in Physiology was very practical, & he made some remarks in connection with it, upon tightness of dress, apparently, thinking that it was the fashion at the present time to dress tightly. He has not probably heard that the wisdom or some other good quality of the age has substituted the reverse fashion for the time present.—The lesson in N. History treated of the divisions of animals into warm & cold blooded & of other minor divisions.—In the P.M., we read in Abbott's Teacher, & copied some more Problems upon the Globe, which occupied nearly all the time. After that, we punctuated some sentences and school—closed.—

Friday. [9th] The morning passed like the preceding—Philosophy lesson upon the refraction and reflection of light, and the reason of the appearance of the rainbow. Physiology, upon the efficacy of the warm bath, its superiority of this over the cold for most people, and especially invalids. Natural History, upon the Classification of Animals, and their division into Genera, Orders, and Species. Recited the first lesson in Political Economy, from the work by Professor Newman.—At noon, received letters from home, and returning to dinner, found Mr Wood with Mr P. in the sitting room. He spent the afternoon in school. The time was devoted to Reading, Orthoëpy, and Music. Reading exercise was principally an illustration of the divisions and subdivisions which the teacher should make, in order to bring the subject down to the comprehension of the pupils.—The example given was the manner of ascertaining the longitude of a place, by noticing the eclipses of Jupiter's satellites.—After tea, took a short walk in company with Mr & Mrs Peirce & Mr Wood. The former related some anecdotes concerning the former owners of the house now occupied by their descendant, Miss Clark, and concerning the old tree in front of it.——

Saturday. [10th] After reading a portion in the Scriptures, Mr Peirce proceeded to give a Second lecture to the pupils.—The object of the lecture was, to show what the teacher is to do. The two grand divisions of the teachers work, are 1st, the discipline of the faculties, 2nd, the communication of instruction.—These appear to be synonymous, but the difference between them, may be made apparent by an example. Take the case of the lecturer; he understands his subject fully, and communicates facts to his hearers.—He, perhaps, carries most of the hearers along with him. They hear and understand, but it is without any exercise of the faculties of the mind. It is thus with the scholar; the teacher may talk upon his studies, and impart knowledge, but his faculties will remain unimproved.

HORACE MANN'S DEDICATION OF THE STATE NORMAL SCHOOL AT BRIDGEWATER, MASSACHUSETTS (1846)   From "Address, August 19, 1846," as quoted in *Life and Works of Horace Mann* (Boston, 1891), p. 218.

Mr. President, I consider this event as marking an era in the progress of education,—which, as we all know, is the progress of civilization,—on this western continent and throughout the world. It is the completion of the first Normal School-house ever erected in Massachusetts,—in the Union,—in this hemisphere. It belongs to that class of events which may happen once, but are incapable of being repeated.

I believe Normal Schools to be a new instrumentality in the advancement of the race. I believe that, without them, Free Schools themselves would be shorn of their strength and their healing power, and would at length become mere charity schools, and thus die out in fact and in form. Neither the art of printing, nor the trial by jury, nor a free press, nor free suffrage, can long exist, to any beneficial and salutary purpose, without schools for the training of teachers; for, if the character and qualifications of teachers be allowed to degenerate, the Free Schools will become pauper schools, and the pauper schools will produce pauper souls, and the free press will become a false and licentious press, and ignorant voters will become venal voters, and through the medium and guise of republican forms, an oligarchy of profligate and flagitious men will govern the land; nay, the universal diffusion and ultimate triumph of all-glorious Christianity itself must await the time when knowledge shall be diffused among men through the instrumentality of good schools. Coiled up in the institution, as in a spring, there is a vigor whose uncoiling may wheel the spheres.

REGULATIONS OF THE MASSACHUSETTS STATE NORMAL SCHOOLS (1846)   From Massachusetts Board of Education, *Tenth Annual Report . . . of the Secretary of the Board* (Boston, 1847), pp. 218–22.

Among the standing regulations adopted by the Board, for the government of the State Normal Schools, are the following:—most of which were adopted in the beginning and have been constantly in force,—only a few modifications, and those very slight ones, having since been introduced.

ADMISSION

As a prerequisite to admission, candidates must declare it to be their intention to qualify themselves to become school teachers. If they belong to the State, or have an intention and a reasonable expectation of keeping school in the State, tuition is gratuitous. Otherwise, a tuition-fee is charged, which is intended to be about the same as is usually charged at good academies in the same neighborhood. If pupils, after having completed a course of study at the State Normal Schools, immediately engage in school keeping, but leave the State, or enter a private school or an academy, they are considered as having waived the privilege growing out of their declared intention to keep a Common School in Massachusetts, and are held bound in honor to pay a tuition-fee for their instruction.

If males, pupils must have attained the age of seventeen years complete, and of sixteen, if females; and they must be free from any disease or infirmity, which would unfit them for the office of school teachers.

They must undergo an examination, and prove themselves to be well versed in orthography, reading, writing, English grammar, geography and arithmetic.

They must furnish satisfactory evidence of good intellectual capacity and of high moral character and principles.

Examinations for admission take place at the commencement of each term, of which there are three in a year.

TERM OF STUDY

At West Newton and Bridgewater, the minimum of the term of study is one year, and this must be in consecutive terms of the schools. In regard to the School at Westfield, owing to the unwillingness of the pupils in that section of the State, to remain at the school, even for so short a time as one year, the rule requiring a year's residence has been from time to time suspended. It is found to be universally true, that those applicants whose qualifications are best, are desirous to remain at the school longest.

COURSE OF STUDY

The studies first to be attended to in the State Normal Schools, are those which the law requires to be taught in the district schools, namely, orthography, reading, writing, English grammar, geography and arithmetic. When these are mastered, those of a higher order will be progressively taken.

For those who wish to remain at the school more than one year, and for all belonging to the school, so far as their previous attainments will permit, the following course is arranged:

1. Orthography, reading, grammar, composition, rhetoric and logic.

2. Writing, drawing.

3. Arithmetic, mental and written, algebra, geometry, book-keeping, navigation, surveying.

4. Geography, ancient and modern, with chronology, statistics and general history.

5. Human Physiology, and hygiene or the Laws of Health.

6. Mental Philosophy.

7. Music.

8. Constitution and History of Massachusetts and of the United States.

9. Natural Philosophy and Astronomy.

10. Natural History.

11. The Principles of piety and morality, common to all sects of Christians.

12. The Science and Art of Teaching with reference to all the above named studies.

A portion of the Scriptures shall be read daily, in every State Normal School.

Each Normal School is under the immediate inspection of a Board of Visiters, who are in all cases to be members of the Board of Education, except that the Secretary of the Board may be appointed as one of the visiters of each school.

The Board appoints one Principal Instructer for each school, who is responsible for its government and instruction, subject to the rules of the Board, and the supervision of the Visiters. The Visiters of the respective schools appoint the assistant instructers thereof.

To each Normal School, an Experimental or Model School is attached. This School is under the control of the Principal of the Normal School. The pupils of the Normal School assist in teaching it. Here, the knowledge which they acquire in the science of teaching, is practically applied. The art is made to grow out of the science, instead of being empirical. The Principal of the Normal School inspects the Model School more or less, daily. He observes the manner in which his own pupils exemplify, in practice, the principles he has taught them. Sometimes, all the pupils of the Normal School, together with the Principal, visit the Model School in a body, to observe the manner in which the teachers of the latter, for the time being, conduct the recitations or exercises. Then, returning to their own schoolroom, in company with the assistant teachers themselves, who have been the objects of inspection, each one is called upon to deliver his views, whether commendatory or otherwise, respecting the manner in which the work has been performed. At this amicable exposition of merits and defects, the Principal of the Normal School presides. After all others have presented their views, he delivers his own; and thus his pupils, at the threshold of their practice, have an opportunity to acquire confidence in a good course, of which they might otherwise entertain doubts, and to rectify errors which otherwise would fossilize into habit.

The salaries of the teachers of the State Normal Schools are paid by the State.

THE AUTHORITY OF THE TEACHER IN MASSACHUSETTS (1846) From Massachusetts, Board of Education, *Tenth Annual Report . . . of the Secretary of the Board* (Boston, 1847), pp. 188–90.

---

131. Before leaving those provisions which the law has made for the *internal* management and regulation of the schools, it is necessary to say a few words respecting the authority of teachers.

Until a Public School teacher has received a certificate of qualification from the committee of the town where he keeps, it is at least questionable whether he has any authority at all as a teacher, and whether he would have any right to enforce commands, openly and contumaciously resisted. But, having a legal certificate in his possession, he has an indisputable right to repress disobedience to his orders, and to enforce compliance with all lawful commands. For this purpose, he may, in the last

THE
PROFESSION
OF EDUCATION

1337

resort, appeal to physical force, and inflict any bodily chastisement, not unsuitable to the age, sex or condition of the offender. The circumstances which justify an appeal to this ultimate remedy must, in the first instance, be decided upon by the teacher himself; but this decision is always liable to be appealed from, and the soundness of the discretion used, to be readjudicated, by a court and jury of the country. It is true, there is no statutory provision in our law empowering teachers to inflict blows; but the reason of this omission was, not because it was intended not to confer the power, but because the power was so universally known and recognized, as to supersede the necessity of conferring it. There is not a law book in the English language, which treats of the relative rights and duties of parents and children, of master and apprentice, or master and servant, or teacher and pupil, which does not recognize in the former, in certain supposable cases, a right to inflict personal chastisement upon the latter; and there is not a court of record either in England or America in which this right has ever been denied or questioned, while it has been affirmed in innumerable instances. In all the legal adjudications that have ever been made, no question has ever been raised as to the abstract right. The only questions have been, either as to the sufficiency of the circumstances, alleged and proved, to justify its use; or whether the punishment, considering the nature and circumstances of the offence, has not been excessive.

132. But pupils have rights as well as teachers. They have as valid a right to immunity from punishment, when they have committed no offence; they have as valid a right to exemption from severity or frequency of punishment, when their offences have been slight, or far between, as the teacher has to inflict punishment at all.

133. Teachers have a right to expel *temporarily,* from school; committees have a right to expel, permanently, from school,—that is, during their continuance in office. If teachers have occasion to suspend or expel a scholar from school, the sentence should not cover a longer period of time, than would be sufficient for convening the committee, in order to lay the case before them. (See Report made by the Committee on Education to the House of Representatives, Feb. 8, 1841; cited at length in the Common School Journal, vol. 3, p. 65.)

134. The question is not without some practical difficulty, how far the school committee and teachers may exercise authority over school children, before the hour when the school begins, or after the hour when it closes, or outside of the schoolhouse door or yard. On the one hand, there is certainly some limit to the jurisdiction of the committee and teachers, out of school hours and out of the schoolhouse; and, on the other hand, it is equally plain, if their jurisdiction does not commence until the minute for opening the school has arrived, nor until the pupil has passed within the door of the schoolroom, that all the authority left to them, in regard to some of the most sacred objects for which our schools were instituted, would be but of little avail. To what purpose would the teacher prohibit profane or obscene language among his scholars, within the schoolroom and during school hours, if they could indulge it with impunity and to any extent of wantonness, as soon as the hour for dismissing the school should arrive? To what purpose would he forbid quarrelling and fighting among the scholars, at recess, if they could engage in single combat, or marshal themselves into hostile parties for a general encounter, within the precincts of the schoolhouse, and within the next five minutes after the school should be closed? And to what purpose would he repress insolence to himself, if a scholar, as soon as he had passed the threshold might shake his fist in the teacher's face, and challenge him to personal combat? These considerations would seem to show that there must be a portion of time, both before the school

commences and after it has closed, and also a portion of space between the door of the schoolhouse and that of the paternal mansion, where the jurisdiction of the parent, on one side, and of the committee and teachers, on the other, is concurrent. Many of the towns in the Commonwealth have acted in accordance with these views, and have framed regulations for the government of the scholars, both before and after school hours, and while going to and returning from the school. The same principle of necessity, by virtue of which this jurisdiction, out of school hours and beyond school premises, is claimed, defines its extent and affixes its limit. It is claimed, because the great objects of discipline and of moral culture would be frustrated without it. When not essential, therefore, to the attainment of these objects, it should be forborne.

A NEW JERSEY TEACHER'S CONTRACT (1841)   From David Murray, *History of Education in New Jersey* (Washington, D.C., 1889), p. 141.

Joseph Thompson hereby agrees to teach a common English day school for the term of thirteen weeks of five days in each week (or an equivalent) in the Center schoolhouse, being District No. 8, of Bridgewater, to which is attached a part of Readington Township. He will give instruction to all the youth of the district that may be placed under his care in some or all of the following branches, as their capacities may reach, viz: Orthography, reading, writing, arithmetic, English grammar, geography, history, composition, and bookkeeping by single entry. And we, the trustees of said school, do hereby agree to furnish said teacher with fuel and all necessaries for the comfort and convenience of said school, and at the expiration of the term pay to him or his order in compensation for his services the sum of sixty-five dollars. The said teacher shall have the privilege of instructing his own children in said school and not be required to pay any proportional part of the above sum. All pupils which do not belong in the district and attend this school to learn any of the above-named branches, one half of their schooling shall belong to the teacher, and the other half to go into the funds of the school. The excess of charge for higher branches (if any are taught) shall belong exclusively to the teacher. If circumstances should occur to render it necessary to discontinue the school before the expiration of the term, a majority of the trustees or the teacher may discontinue, and he receive pay for the time then taught.

In witness whereof the parties have to these presents interchangeably set their hands this thirtieth day of October, in the year of our Lord 1841.

> JOSEPH THOMPSON, *Teacher.*
> ABRAHAM A. AMERMAN,
> PETER Q. BROKAW,
> ABRAHAM AMERMAN,
> *Trustees.*

FIRST ANNUAL REPORT OF THE NEW BRITAIN, CONNECTICUT, STATE NORMAL SCHOOL (1850)

From Henry Barnard, ed., *Normal Schools, and Other Institutions, Agencies, and Means Designed for the Professional Education of Teachers* (Hartford, Conn., 1851), pp. 47–50.

The State Normal School or "Seminary for the training of teachers in the art of teaching and governing the Common Schools" of Connecticut was established by act of the legislature, May session, 1849, and the sum of eleven thousand dollars was appropriated for its support for a period of at least four years.

The sum appropriated for the support of the school is derived not from the income of the School Fund, or any of the ordinary resources of the Treasury, but from a bonus of ten thousand dollars paid by the State Bank, at Hartford, and of $1,000 paid by the Deep River Bank, for their respective charters. No part of this sum can be expended in any building or fixtures for the school, or for the compensation of the trustees.

The entire management of the Institution as to the application of the funds, the location of the school, the regulation of the studies and exercises, and the granting of diplomas, is committed to a Board of Trustees, consisting of the Superintendent of Common Schools, ex officio, and one member for each of the eight counties of the state, appointed by the Legislature, two in each year, and to hold their office for the term of four years, and serve without compensation. The Board must submit an annual report as to their own doings, and the progress and condition of the seminary.

The Normal School was located permanently in New Britain, on the 1st of February, 1850, after full consideration of the claims and offers of other towns, on account of the central position of the town in the state, and its accessibility from every section by railroad; and also in consideration of the liberal offer on the part of its citizens to provide a suitable building, apparatus, and library, to the value of $16,000 for the use of the Normal School, and to place all the schools of the village under the management of the Principal of the Normal School, as Schools of Practice.

The Building provided for the accommodation of the Normal School, and the Schools of Practice, when completed will contain three large study-halls, with nine class-rooms attached, a hall for lectures and exhibitions, a laboratory for chemical and philosophical experiments, an office for the Principal and trustees, a room for the library, and suitable accommodations for apparatus, clothes, furnaces, fuel &c. The entire building will be fitted up and furnished in the most substantial manner, and with special reference to the health, comfort and successful labor of pupils and teachers. In addition to the Normal School building, there are three houses located in different parts of the village for the accommodation of the primary schools belonging to the Schools of Practice.

The immediate charge of the Normal School and Schools of Practice, is committed to Rev. T. D. P. Stone, Associate Principal, to whom all communications relating to the schools can be addressed.

The school was opened for the reception of pupils on Wednesday, the 15th of May, 1850, and the first term closed on Tuesday, October 1st. The number of pupils in attendance during the term was sixty-seven; thirty males, and thirty-seven females.

The second term will commence on Wednesday, the 4th of December, 1850, and continue till the third Wednesday in April, 1851, divided into two sessions as given below.

Terms and Vacations

The year is divided into two terms, Summer and Winter, each term consisting of two sessions.

The first session of the winter term commences on the first Wednesday of December, and continues fourteen weeks. The second session of the winter term commences on the third Wednesday of March, and continues six weeks.

The first session of the summer term commences on the third Wednesday of May, and continues twelve weeks. The second session of the summer term commences on the third Wednesday of August, and continues six weeks.

To accommodate pupils already engaged in teaching, the short session of each term will, as far as shall be found practicable, be devoted to a review of the studies pursued in the district schools in the season of the year immediately following, and to a course of familiar lectures on the classification, instruction and discipline of such schools.

Admission of Pupils

The highest number of pupils which can be received in any one term, is two hundred and twenty.

Each school society is entitled to have one pupil in the school; and no society can have more than one in any term, so long as there are applicants from any society, at the time unrepresented. Until the whole number of pupils in actual attendance shall reach the highest number fixed by law, the Principal is authorized to receive all applicants who may present themselves, duly recommended by the visitors of any school society.

Any person, either male or female, may apply to the school visitors of any school society for admission to the school, who will make a written declaration, that their object in so applying is to qualify himself (or herself) for the employment of a common school teacher, and that it is his (or her) intention to engage in that employment, in this state.

The school visitors are authorized to forward to the Superintendent of Common Schools, in any year, the names of four persons, two of each sex, who shall have applied as above, for admission to the school, and who shall have been found on examination by them, "possessed of the qualifications required of teachers of common schools in this state," and whom they "shall recommend to the trustees as suitable persons, by their age, character, talents, and attainments, to be received as pupils in the Normal School."

Applicants duly recommended by the school visitors, can forward their certificate directly to the Associate Principal of the Normal School at New Britain, who will inform them of the time when they must report themselves to be admitted to any vacant places in the school.

Persons duly recommended, and informed of their admission, must report themselves within the first week of the term for which they are admitted, or their places will be considered as vacated.

Any persons, once regularly admitted to the Normal School, can remain connected with the same for three years, and will not lose their places, by temporary absence in teaching common schools in the state—such experience, in connection with the instruction of the Institution, being considered a desirable part of a teacher's training.

Studies

The course of instruction will embrace: 1. A thorough review of the studies pursued in the lowest grade of common schools. 2. An acquaintance with such studies as are embraced in the highest grade of common schools, authorized by law, and which will render the teaching of the elementary branch more thorough and interesting. 3. The art of teaching and its methods, including the history and progress of education, the philosophy of teaching and discipline, as drawn from the nature of the juvenile mind, and the application of those principles under the ordinary conditions of our common schools.

The members of the school will be arranged in three classes—Junior, Middle and Senior. All pupils on being admitted to the school, will be ranked in the *Junior Class*, until their familiarity with the studies of the lowest grade of common schools have been satisfactorily tested. The *Middle Class* will embrace those who are pursuing the branches usually taught in Public High Schools. The *Senior Class* will comprise those who are familiar with the studies of the Junior and Middle Classes, or who are possessed of an amount of experience in active and successful teaching, which can be regarded as a practical equivalent. All the studies of the school will be conducted in reference to their being taught again in common schools.

Practice in the Art of Teaching and Governing Schools

The several schools of the first school district, comprising the village of New Britain, are placed by a vote of the District, under the instruction and discipline of the Associate Principal, as Model Schools and Schools of Practice, for the Normal School. These schools embrace about four hundred children, and are classified into three Primary, one Intermediate and one High School. The course of instruction embraces all the studies pursued in any grade of common schools in Connecticut. The instruction of these schools will be given by pupils of the Normal School, under the constant oversight of the Associate Principal and Professors.

Text Books

A Library of the best text books, in the various studies pursued in the schools, is commenced, and already numbers upward of four thousand volumes. Pupils are supplied with text books in such studies as they may be engaged, at a charge, barely sufficient to keep the books in good condition, and supply such as may be injured or lost. Arrangements have also been made to furnish teachers who wish to own a set of text books at the publishers' lowest wholesale price.

*   *   *

Apparatus

The sum of one thousand dollars is appropriated for the purchase of apparatus, which will be procured from time to time, as the wants of the school may require. As far as practicable, such articles of apparatus will be used in the class-rooms of the Normal School, as can be readily made by teachers themselves, or conveniently procured at low prices, and be made useful in the instruction of District Schools.

Library

The school is already furnished with the best works on the Theory and Practice of Education, which the Normal pupils are expected to read, and on several of which they are examined. The library will be supplied with Encyclopedias, Dictionaries, and other books of reference, to which free access will be given to members of the school.

Board

Normal pupils must board and lodge in such families, and under such regulations, as are approved by the Associate Principal.

The price of board, including room, fuel, lights and washing, in private families, ranges from $2.00 to $2.50 per week. Persons, expecting to join the school, should signify their intention to the Associate Principal, as early as practicable, before the commencement of a term, that there may be no disappointment in the place and price of board.

Discipline

The discipline of the institution is committed to the Associate Principal, who is authorized to secure the highest point of order and behavior by all suitable means, even to a temporary suspension of a pupil from the schools. The age of the pupils, the objects which bring them to a Normal School, and the spirit of the institution itself, will, it is believed, dispense with the necessity of a code of rules. The members are expected to exemplify in their own conduct, the order, punctuality, and neatness of good scholars, and exhibit in all their relations, Christian courtesy, kindness and fidelity.

Examination and Inspection

The school will be visited each term by a committee of the trustees, who will report on the results of their examination to the Board.

There will be an examination at the close of each term, before the whole Board, and at the close of the summer term, the examination will be public, and will be followed by an exhibition.

The school is at all times open to inspection, and school visitors, teachers, and the friends of education generally in the state are cordially invited to visit it at their convenience.

Diploma

The time required to complete the course of instruction and practice, which shall be deemed by the trustees a suitable preparation for the business of teaching, and entitle any applicant to a Diploma of the Normal School, will depend on the age, attainments, mental discipline, moral character, and evidence of practical tact in instruction and government of each applicant.

No diploma will be given to any person who does not rank in the Senior Class, and has not given evidence of possessing some practical talent as a teacher in the Schools of Practice, or in the District Schools of the state.

AN ACCOUNT OF THE NEW YORK STATE NORMAL SCHOOL AT ALBANY (1850)   From New York State Normal School, *Annual Circular of the Executive Committee, 1850,* as quoted in Henry Barnard, ed., *Normal Schools . . .* (Hartford, Conn., 1851), pp. 245–49.

Each county in the state is entitled to send to the school a number of pupils, (either male or female,) equal to twice the number of members of the Assembly in such county. The pupils are appointed by the county and town superintendents at a meeting called by the county superintendent for that purpose. This meeting should be held and the appointment made at least two weeks before the commencement of each term, or as soon as information is received as to the number of vacancies. A list of the vacancies for each term will be published in the District School Journal, as early as the number of such vacancies can be ascertained, usually before the close of the former term.

Pupils once admitted to the school will hve the right to remain until they graduate; unless they forfeit that right by voluntarily vacating their place, or by improper conduct.

Persons failing to receive appointments from their respective counties, should, after obtaining testimonials of a good moral character, present themselves the first day of the term, for examination by the Faculty. If such examination is satisfactory, they will receive an appointment from the Executive Committee, without regard to the particular county, provided any vacancies exist. In such case the pupil will receive mileage.

By an act of the Legislature, passed April 11, 1849, "every teacher shall be deemed a qualified teacher, who shall have in possession a Diploma from the State Normal School."

Qualifications of Applicants

Females sent to the school must be sixteen years of age, and males eighteen.

The superintendents, in making their appointments, are urged to pay no regard to the political opinions of applicants. The selections should be made with reference to the *moral worth* and abilities of the candidates. Decided preference ought to be given to those, who, in the judgment of the superintendents, give the highest promise of becoming the most efficient teachers of common schools. It is also desirable that those only should be appointed who have already a good knowledge of the common branches of study, and *who intend to remain in the school until they graduate.*

Entrance

All the pupils, on entering the school, are required to sign the following declaration:

'*We the subscribers hereby* DECLARE, *that it is our intention to devote ourselves to the business of teaching district schools, and that our sole object in resorting to this Normal School is the better to prepare ourselves for that important duty.*'

As this should be signed in good faith on the part of the pupils, they should be made acquainted with its import before they are appointed. It is expected of the superintendents, that they shall select such as will sacredly fulfill their engagements in this particular.

Pupils on entering the school are subjected to a thorough examination, and are classified according to their previous attainments. The time required to accomplish the course will depend upon the attainments and talents of the pupil, varying from *one* to *four* terms. *Very few*, however, can expect to graduate in one term.

Privileges of the Pupils

All pupils receive their tuition free. They are also furnished with the use of text-books without charge; though if they already own the books of the course, they would do well to bring them, together with such other books for reference as they may possess. Moreover, they draw a small sum from the fund for the support of the school, to defray in part their expenses.

It is proposed to apportion the sum of $1,700 among the 256 pupils, who may compose the school during the next term. 1. Each pupil shall receive three cents a mile on the distance from his county town to the city of Albany. 2. The remainder of the $1,700 shall then be divided equally among the students in attendance.

The following list will show how much a student from each county will receive, during the ensuing term:

Albany, $2.41; Allegany, $10.09; Broome, $6.76; Cattaraugus, $11.17; Cayuga, $7.09; Chatauqua, $12.49; Chemung, $8.35; Chenango, $5.41; Clinton, $7.27; Columbia, $3.28; Cortland, $6.67; Delaware, $4.72; Dutchess, $4.66; Erie, $10.93; Essex, $6.19; Franklin, $8.77; Fulton, $3.76; Genesee, $9.73; Greene, $3.43; Hamilton, $4.87; Herkimer, $4.81; Jefferson, $7.21; Kings, $6.97; Lewis, $6.28; Livingston, $9.19; Madison, $5.44; Monroe, $8.98; Montgomery, $3.61; New-York, $6.85; Niagara, $10.72; Oneida, $5.29; Onondaga, $6.40; Ontario, $8.26; Orange, $5.44; Orleans, $10.12; Oswego, $7.21; Otsego, $4.39; Putnam, $5.59; Queens, $7.63; Rensselaer, $2.59; Richmond, $7.32; Rockland, $6.07; Saratoga, $4.78; Schenectady, $2.86; Schoharie, $3.07; Seneca, $7.54; St. Lawrence, $8.59; Steuben, $8.89; Suffolk, $9.16; Sullivan, $5.80; Tioga, $7.42; Tompkins, $7.31; Ulster, $4.15;

Warren, $4.27; Washington, $3.85; Wayne, $7.84; Westchester, $6.46; Wyoming, $9.85; Yates, $7.96.

It is proper to state, that if the number of pupils is less than 256, the sum to be received will be proportionately increased. The above schedule shows, therefore, the minimum sum to be received by each pupil. His apportionment cannot be less than as above stated, and it may be more.

This money will be paid at the *close of the term.*

Apparatus

A well assorted apparatus has been procured sufficiently extensive to illustrate all the important principles in Natural Philosophy, Chemistry, and Human Physiology. Extraordinary facilities for the study of Physiology are afforded by the Museum of the Medical College, which is open at all hours for visitors.

Library

Besides an abundant supply of text-books upon all the branches of the course of study, a well-selected miscellaneous library has been procured, to which all the pupils may have access free of charge. In the selection of this library, particular care has been exercised to procure most of the recent works upon Education, as well as several valuable standard works upon the Natural Sciences, History, Mathematics, &c. The State library is also freely accessible to all.

Terms and Vacations

The year is divided into two terms, so as to bring the vacations into April and October, the months for holding the Teachers' Institutes. This also enables the pupils to take advantage of the cheapness of traveling by the various means of water communication in the State, in going to and from the school.

The SUMMER TERM commences on the first Monday in May, and continues twenty weeks, with an intermission of one week from the first of July.

The WINTER TERM commences on the first Monday in November, and continues twenty-two weeks, with an intermission from Christmas to New Year's day inclusive.

Prompt Attendance

As the school will open on Monday, it would be for the advantage of the pupils, if they should reach Albany by the Thursday or Friday preceding the day of opening. The Faculty can then aid them in securing suitable places for boarding.

As the examinations of the pupils preparatory for classification will commence on the first day of the term, it is exceedingly important that all the pupils should report themselves on the first morning. Those who arrive a day after the time, will subject not only the teachers to much trouble, but themselves also to the rigors of a private examination. After the first week, no student, except for the strongest reasons, shall be allowed to enter the school.

Price of Board

The price of board in respectable families, varies from $1.50 to $2.00, exclusive of washing. Young gentlemen by taking a room and boarding themselves, have sustained themselves at a lower rate. This can better be done in the summer term.

The ladies and gentlemen are not allowed to board in the same families. Particular care is taken to be assured of the respectability of the families who propose to take boarders, before they are recommended to the pupils.

Experimental School

Two spacious rooms in the building are appropriated to the accommodation of the two departments of this school. These two departments are under the immediate supervision of the Permanent Teacher, who is a graduate of the Normal School.

The object of this school is to afford each Normal Pupil an opportunity of practising the methods of instruction and discipline inculcated at the Normal School, as well as to ascertain his 'aptness to teach,' and to discharge the various other duties pertaining to the teacher's responsible office. Each member of the graduating class is required to spend at least two weeks in this department.

In the experimental School there are ninety-three pupils between the ages of six and sixteen years. FIFTY-EIGHT of these are free pupils. The free seats will be hereafter given exclusively to fatherless children, residing in the city of Albany. This is in consideration of an appropriation by the city to defray in part the expense of fitting up one of the rooms of the school. The remaining THIRTY-FIVE pupils are charged $20 per year for tuition and use of books. This charge is made merely to defray the expense of sustaining the school."

Course of Study

The following is the course of study for the School; and a thorough acquaintance with the whole of it, on the part of the male pupils, is made a condition for graduating.

The School is divided into three classes, JUNIORS, MIDDLES AND SENIORS. These classes are arranged in divisions to suit the convenience of recitation.

JUNIORS

Reading and Elocution.
Spelling.
Orthography, ...Normal Chart.
Writing.
Geography and Outline Maps,
 (with Map Drawing,) ....Mitchell.
Drawing, (begun.)
Intellectual Arithmetic,...Colburn.
Elementary Arithmetic, ...Perkins.
English Grammar, (begun.)..Brown.
History of United States,...Willson.
Higher Arithmetic, (begun,)...Perkins.
Elementary Algebra, (begun,) ....Perkins.

Reading and Elocution.
Spelling.
Orthography, ...Normal Chart.
Writing.
Geography and Outline Maps,
 (with Map Drawing,) ....Mitchell
Drawing.
Intellectual Arithmetic, ...Colburn.
English Grammar, ...Brown.
History of United States, ...Willson.
Higher Arithmetic, ...Perkins.
Elementary Algebra, ...Perkins.
Human Physiology, ...Cutter.
Geometry, (begun,) ....Perkins.
Perspective Drawing, ...Lectures.
Mathematical Geography and Use of Globes.

The division of this class composed of the Juniors of the former term, will not be required to review such studies as they have already completed.

Higher Algebra, Chaps. VII. and VIII, (omitting Multinomial Theorem and
 Recurring Series,) ....Perkins.
Geometry, Six Books, ...Perkins' Elements.
Plane Trigonometry, as contained in ....Davies' Legendre.
Land Surveying, ...Davies
Natural Philosophy, ...Olmstead.
Chemistry, with (Experimental Lectures,) ....Silliman.
Intellectual Philosophy, ...Abercrombie.
Moral Philosophy, ...Wayland, abridged.
Rhetoric ....Lectures.
Constitutional Law, with select parts of the Statutes of this state, most intimately
 connected with the rights and duties of citizens, ...Young's Science of
 Government, Revised Statutes.
Art of Teaching, ...Lectures, Theory and Practice of Teaching, and Experimental
 School.
Elements of Astronomy, ...Lectures.

Lessons in Vocal Music, to be given to all.

The same course of study, omitting the Higher Algebra, Plane Trigonometry and Surveying, must be attained by females as a condition of graduating.

Any of the pupils who desire further to pursue mathematics, can be allowed to do so after completing the above course of study.

ESTABLISHMENT OF A NORMAL SCHOOL IN SOUTH CAROLINA

(1857) From *The Statutes at Large of South Carolina,* vol. XII, pp. 516–17.

Whereas it is necessary to any system of public education that provision should be made for the training of teachers in Normal Schools; and whereas it is desirable to establish such schools in different parts of the State; and whereas the Commissioners of Free Schools of the Parishes of St. Philip and St. Michaels have offered to conduct such a school if the State will authorize and assist the same:

I. *Be it therefore enacted* By the Senate and House of Representatives, now met and sitting in General Assembly, and by the authority of the same, That the Commissioners of Free Schools for the Parishes of St. Philip and St. Michaels are authorized to establish and conduct a Normal School for the training of female teachers for the State at large, in connection with a Female High School for the said Parishes, and for that purpose to erect and furnish a suitable building; and that whenever ten thousand dollars shall have been subscribed by the citizens of the said Parishes for the erection and furnishing of the said building, the State will subscribe an equal amount, and will pay the same in portions equal to the portions paid by the said citizens.

II. The State will also contribute annually, for five years, the sum of five thousand dollars, for the support of the said school: *Provided,* That at least an equal amount shall also be contributed by the inhabitants of the said Parishes annually, for the same purpose, either by assessment or contribution.

III. The said Commissioners shall receive into the said school, free of any charge for tuition, female pupils from every part of the State, not exceeding fifteen to each Congressional District, for the purpose of being trained as teachers: *Provided,* That such applicants shall have the qualifications, and shall stand the examinations required of other applicants of equal grade.

IV. The said Commissioners shall have power to conduct the said school, and to make such regulations for its government as they may deem best suited to its beneficial operations, and shall report its condition and expenses annually, with their usual report, to the General Assembly.

THE CHARACTERISTICS OF NORMAL SCHOOLS (1865)   From Richard

Edwards, "Normal Schools in the United States," National Teachers' Association *Lectures and Proceedings* (1865), pp. 277–82.

We say, then, most emphatically, that Normal Schools, with their distinctive characteristics, should be established and maintained in each State at public expense.

And what are these distinctive characteristics? Wherein and how does a Normal School differ from any other well-conducted institution, in which the same subjects in the main are taught?

First, we answer, it differs in its aim. Using, to a great extent, the same instruments as other schools, namely, treatises upon science and language, it nevertheless uses them for purposes very diverse. In an ordinary school, the treatise on arithmetic is put into the hands of the student in order that he may *learn arithmetic;* in the Normal School, the same book is used to enable him to learn *how to teach* arithmetic. In the ordinary school, the youth reads his Cicero with the purpose of learning the structure, vocabulary, and power of the Latin language; the normal student pores over the same author that he may adjust in his mind a method by which he may most successfully teach others these things. Both use the same materials, acquire, to some extent, the same knowledge, but aiming all the while at different ends. Of course it is clear that one of these objects must pre-suppose the accomplishment of the other. The proper work of the Normal School can not be performed unless the mastery of the subjects has first been obtained.

*   *   *

. . . To the ordinary student, arithmetic is associated, it may be, with severe efforts at mastering its principles; with perseverance and success, or irresolution and failure. But to him who is preparing to teach, it recalls the points most difficult of *explanation,* and the minds most difficult to reach. His constant question is, not "How can I master this principle or process?" but "How will this point seem to my pupils?" To one it is an end. His concern with it ceases when, obedient to his will, its principles come at call, and appear before his mind luminous and clear. To the other, it is a means to the training of mind. It is not enough for him that his eye can take in the whole field and scan the relation of the parts. He must see that, as an instrument, it does the work—accomplishes the result set for it. To him the study must culminate in an increase of intellectual and moral power somewhere. He must see, as the result of it all, a well-developed, symmetrical, human soul!

In these schools the whole animus of both teacher and pupil is this idea of future teaching. Every plan is made to conform to it. Every measure proposed is tried by this as a test. There is no other aim or purpose to claim any share of the mental energy of either. It is the Alpha and Omega of schemes of study and modes of thought.

And is this distinct and separate aim in the preparatory seminary of any value to the novice? Will he be likely, on account of this, to make a better teacher than he would without it—his training, in all other respects, being the same? In answer to this question we say, most emphatically, Yes! And in so saying we doubtless express the conviction of every educator who has given the subject much thought. May we not say that if every scrap of educational literature were to be blotted out; if Comenius were to be forgotten with all his works; if Roger Ascham were to fade out from the literary horizon; if Pestalozzi were to become as a myth; if the educational utterances of Socrates, Plato, and Quintilian were to be eliminated from the sun of human knowledge; if Horace Mann, with the thoughts and the inspiration he has left us, were to vanish from book and from memory; if all this were to happen, and if nothing were to be left the teacher and pupil in the Normal School but their own thought and their unaided efforts, may we not even then say that these institutions, by the mere force of the fact that their aim is what it is, would be not only useful but necessary—ay, all the more necessary on account of these very circumstances? Shall we not, therefore, concede that the difference in aim between the normal and ordinary school makes one of the distinctive and essential characteristics of the former, and that this difference is of itself sufficient to establish its claim to separate support?

*   *   *

It has been sometimes intimated that this pretended science of education is a myth—that the talk about it is of little account. It has been charged, perhaps not altogether generously, that its advocates and professors are more enthusiastic than wise—that they are either intentional deceivers of the public, or unwitting deceivers of themselves—that, in short, the whole matter is a sort of well-intentioned imposture. Now we are free to confess that some of the talk aforesaid has been a trifle unsubstantial—that an occasional apostle has appeared with more zeal than knowledge—that some of the professors, it is barely possible, have chipped the shell a little prematurely. But it is not, I trust, necessary, at this late day, to assure you that there is here as noble a science as ever engaged the thought of man. There are immutable principles here, that ought to be studied and comprehended by every young person entering upon the work of teaching. There is, in the nature of things, a foundation for a profession of teachers. Compare the science of education with other sciences in this respect. Take the science of Medicine. Have we not well-defined, universally acknowledged, practically important principles as well in the Teachers' College as the College of Physicians? and as the science of medicine now is, with its various schools and numerous isms, have we not about as many of them that are universally acknowledged? Or take the clerical profession, including all the denominations considered respectable, and are there not as many useful and important points, upon which we teachers are all agreed, as there are among the ministers? In truth, the science of education is now, in some respects, in the most satisfactory condition. Its conclusions have not crystallized into such rigid forms that there is no room for further discussion. Its principles are sufficiently well-established to serve as guides to the thoughtful inquirer, but not sufficiently limited to cramp his faculties or repress his thought.

Here then we have the second distinctive characteristic of the Normal School—that it instructs its pupils in the Science of Education and Art of Teaching.

Another essential requisite in a Normal School is, that it gives its pupils an opportunity of some kind for practice in teaching, under the supervision and subject to the criticism of experienced and skillful instructors. This is accomplished in various ways; by exercises in conducting the regular classes of the Normal School; by classes of normal pupils assuming for the time the character of children, and receiving instruction and answering questions as they think children would; and by a separate school of children in which the novice is intrusted with the charge of a class, either permanently or for a stated period, as a week or two weeks, as the case may be. There seem to be different opinions as to which of these is the best and most efficient method. The Model or Experimental School has been objected to because it interferes with the daily drill of the normal student in his classes, and also because the children taught by these students are supposed not to be so well taught as they would be by instructors of more experience. But I think both these evils may be entirely avoided—the first, by a proper distribution of the time for study and for teaching, and the second, by an adequate supervision of the pupil-teachers, added to the responsibility imposed upon them by continuing the same class, under the same teacher, during a term of school, and subjecting it at the close of that term to such an examination as is usual in the case of regular teachers. The school for practice is unquestionably essential to the complete idea of a Normal School. When the young practitioner is dealing with children, he encounters the reality of his work. The actual difficulties of his employment are before him. There is no make-believe. He is never in doubt as to whether his methods are such as to instruct and interest children, for the children are there, and he can see for himself, and all others can do the same, whether they are instructed and interested, or not. Every question he asks, every suggestion he makes, is tested on the spot by the proper and natural test. But it is said that more skill is necessary to teach a class of adults personating children, than to teach an equal number of actual little ones, and that, therefore, this practice is of more value than the other. This statement may be true in respect to the difficulty, and if we knew that every additional degree of difficulty adds strength to the mind overcoming it, we might allow that higher results might be gained in this way than by the other. But this assumption is not true. It is more difficult to calculate an eclipse than to ascertain the value of ten pounds of sugar at twenty cents a pound, and what a vast increase of mental strength is acquired in passing from the latter to the former. But it is also more difficult to shoot pigeons with a sixty-four pounder than with a common fowling-piece, and most difficult of all to see any advantage that is likely to come from the attempt. Increasing the difficulty of an undertaking does not necessarily improve its effect. Unnatural methods of accomplishing results are difficult, and certainly not to be commended on that or any other account.

Again we mention as a distinctive characteristic of Normal Schools that they beget an *esprit du corps,* and kindle a glowing enthusiasm among their pupils. They tend to exalt the business of teaching. They show it up in its nobler instead of its meaner colors. By infusing an element of philosophy into the very work of instruction, they dignify every step of it. Under this influence the work of primary instruction becomes the worthiest of the whole task, because, considered with respect to the child's wants, it is the most important. It takes profounder insight into the child's nature to lay aright the foundations of his culture in the primary

Westfield State Normal School, Westfield, Mass., c. 1848.

school, than to help him at any other stage of his progress, because the primary teacher must see the end from the very beginning. His plans for the future must embrace the child's entire career. No partial view of the field is sufficient. This the Normal School brings into view and insists upon. Admit this truth and you at once exalt the work of elementary instruction into a dignified science, into something worth the study of any mind. Make the excellence of teaching to depend upon *what* you teach, and there is little to arouse the enthusiasm of some of our number, for a knowledge of the alphabet and abs can hardly be considered as bestowing much dignity on one.

Normal Schools, then, should be reestablished and maintained by State authority. For this we urge the consideration that they are needed to promote the success of the common schools, and that they are eminently adapted to this purpose. This adaptation we have tried to prove from the distinguishing characteristics of these institutions. These characteristics are that they have in view the special object of preparing teachers, that this is their entire aim and end; that they foster a professional spirit and generate professional enthusiasm; that they give instruction in the science and art of teaching; and that just now, as our country is situated, they are specially needed in order to extend the influence of free schools all over the region lately blasted by slavery. Any one of these characteristics is sufficient vindication of these institutions. Taken together, they form an argument in behalf of normal schools irresistable and imposing. May these institutions continue to grow in usefulness and in public favor until they have achieved results worthy of the confidence they solicit.

Books on Teaching

ADVICE TO MOTHERS (1831)   From Lydia Maria Child, *The Mother's Book* (Boston, 1831), pp. 22–29.

The good old fashioned maxim that "example is better than precept," is the best thing to begin with. The great difficulty in education is that we give *rules* instead of inspiring *sentiments*. The simple fact that your child never saw you angry, that your voice is always gentle, and the expression of your face always kind, is worth a thousand times more than all the rules you can give him about not beating his dog, pinching his brother, &c. It is in vain to load the understanding with rules, if the affections are not pure. In the first place, it is not possible to make rules enough to apply to all manner of cases; and if it were possible, a child would soon forget them. But if you inspire him with right *feelings*, they will govern his *actions*. All our thoughts and actions come from our affections; if we love what is good, we shall think and do what is good. Children are not so much influenced by what we say and do in particular reference to them, as by the general effect of our characters and conversation. They are in a great degree creatures of imitation. If they see a mother fond of finery, they become fond of finery; if they see her selfish, it makes them selfish; if they see her extremely anxious for the attention of wealthy people, they learn to think wealth is the only good.

Those whose early influence is what it should be, will find their children easy to manage, as they grow older.

An infant's wants should be attended to without waiting for him to cry. At first, a babe cries merely from a sensation of suffering—because food, warmth, or other comforts necessary to his young existence, are withheld; but when he finds crying is the only means of attracting attention, he soon gets in the habit of crying for everything. To avoid this, his wants should be attended to, whether he demand it or not. Food, sleep, and necessary comforts should be supplied to him at such times as the experience of his mother may dictate. If he has been sitting on the floor, playing quietly by himself a good while, take him up and amuse him, if you can spare time, without waiting for weariness to render him fretful. Who can blame a child for fretting and screaming, if experience has taught him that he cannot get his wants attended to in any other manner?

Young children should never be made to cry by plaguing them, for the sake of fun; it makes them seriously unhappy for the time, and has an injurious effect upon their dispositions. When in any little trouble, they should be helped as quick as possible. When their feet are caught in the rounds of a chair, or their playthings entangled, or when any other of the thousand and one afflictions of baby-hood occur, it is an easy thing to teach them to wait by saying, "Stop a minute, and I will come to you." But do not say this, to put them off; attend to them as quick as your employments will permit; they will then wait patiently should another disaster occur. Children, who have entire confidence that the simple truth is always spoken to them, are rarely troublesome.

A silent influence, which they do not perceive, is better for young children than direct rules and prohibitions. For instance, should a child be in ill humor, without any apparent cause (as will sometimes happen)—should he push down his play-things, and then cry because he has injured them—chase the kitten, and then cry because she has run out of his reach—it is injurious to take any direct notice of it, by saying, "How cross you are today, James. What a naughty boy you are. I don't love you today." This, in all probability, will make matters worse. The better way is to draw off his attention to pleasant thoughts by saying, "I am going in the garden"— or, "I am going out to see the calf. Does James want to go with me?" If, in the capriciousness of his humor, he says he does not want to go, do not urge him: make preparations to go, and he will soon be inclined to follow. A few flowers, or a little pleasant talk about the calf, will, in all probability produce entire forgetfulness of his troubles. If the employment suggested to him combine usefulness with pleasure,—such as feeding the chickens, shelling peas for dinner, &c, so much the better. The habit of assisting others, excites the benevolent affections, and lays the foundation of industry.

When a little child has been playing, and perhaps quarrelling, out of doors, and comes in with his face all of a blaze, sobbing and crying, it is an excellent plan to take him by the hand and say, "What is the matter, my dear boy? Tell me what is the matter. But, how dirty your face is! Let me wash your face nicely, and wipe it dry, and then you shall sit in my lap and tell me all about it." If he is washed gently, the sensation will be pleasant and refreshing, and by the time the operation is finished, his attention will be drawn off from his vexations; his temper will be cooled, as well as his face. Then seat him in your lap, encourage him to tell you all about his troubles, comb his hair gently in the meantime, and in a few minutes the vexation of his little spirit will be entirely soothed. This secret of calling off the attention by little kind offices is very valuable to those who have the care of invalids, or young children. Bathing the hands and feet, or combing the hair gently, will sometimes put a sick person to sleep when they can obtain rest in no other way.

*　　*　　*

By such expedients as I have mentioned, ill-humor and discontent are driven away by the influence of kindness and cheerfulness; "evil is overcome with good." Whipping and scolding could not have produced quiet so soon; and if they could, the child's temper would have been injured in the process.

I have said that example and silent influence were better than direct rules and commands. Nevertheless, there are cases where rules must be made; and children must be taught to obey implicitly. For instance, a child must be expressly forbidden to play with fire, to climb upon the tables, &c. But whenever it is possible, restraint should be invisible.

The first and most important step in management is, that whatever a mother says, always *must* be done. For this reason, do not require too much; and on no account allow your child to do at one time, what you have forbidden him at another. Sometimes when a woman feels easy and good-natured, and does not expect any company, she will allow her children to go to the table and take lumps of sugar; but should visitors be in the room, or she out of humor with the occurrences of the day, she will perhaps scold, or strike them for the self same trick. How can a mother expect obedience to commands so selfish and capricious? What inferences will a child draw from such conduct? You may smile at the idea that very young children draw inferences; but it is a fact, that they do draw inferences—and very just ones too. We mistake, when we trust too much to children's not thinking, or observing. They are shrewd reasoners in all cases where their little interests are concerned. They know a mother's ruling passion; they soon discover her weak side, and learn how to attack it most successfully . . .

The necessity of obedience early instilled is the foundation of all good management. If children see you governed by a real wish for their good, rather than by your own selfishness, or capricious freaks, they will easily acquire this excellent habit. Wilful disobedience should never go unpunished. If a little child disobeys you from mere forgetfulness and frolic, it is best to take no notice of it; for his intention is not bad, and authority has greater effect when used sparingly, and on few occasions. Should he forget the same injunction again, look at him very seriously, and tell him that if he forgets again, you shall be obliged to punish him. Should he commit the offence the third time, take from him the means of committing it; for instance, if you tell him not to tear his picturebook, and he does tear it, take it away from him. Perhaps he will pout and show ill humor;—will push off with his little chair, and say "I don't love you, mother."—If so, take no notice. Do not laugh, for that would irritate him, without performing the least use; do not seem offended with him, for that will awaken a love of power in his little mind. It excites very bad feelings in a child, to see that he can vex a parent, and make her lose her self-command. In spite of his displeasure, therefore, continue your employment tranquilly, as if nothing had happened. If his ill humor continue, however, and show itself in annoyances to you, and others around him, you should take him by the hand, look very seriously in his face, and say, "James, you are such a naughty boy, that I must punish you. I am very sorry to punish you; but I must, that you may remember to be good next time." This should be done with perfect calmness, and a look of regret. When a child is punished in anger, he learns to consider it a species of revenge; when he is punished in sorrow, he believes that it is done for his good.

The punishment for such peevishness as I have mentioned should be being tied in an armchair, or something of that simple nature. I do not approve of shutting the little offender in the closet. The sudden transition from light to darkness affects him with an undefined species of horror, even if he has been kept perfectly free from frightful stories. A very young child will become quite cold in a few minutes, at midsummer, if shut in a dark closet.

If the culprit is obstinate, and tries to seem as if he did not care for his punishment, let him remain in confinement till he gets very tired; but in the meanwhile be perfectly calm yourself, and follow your usual occupations. You can judge by his actions, and the expression of his countenance, whether his feelings begin to soften. Seize a favorable moment, and ask him if he is sorry he has been so naughty; if he says "yes," let him throw himself into your arms, kiss him, and tell him you hope he will never be naughty again; for if he is, you must punish him, and it makes you very sorry to punish him. Here is the key to all good management: always punish a child for wilfully disobeying you in the most trifling particular; but never punish him in anger.

Having adverted in the preceding Lecture, to certain existing evils, unfriendly to the character and usefulness of common schools, I shall, in this, call your attention to *the requisite qualifications of an instructer*. This subject is of high importance. All who possess the requisite *literary* attainments, are not qualified to assume the direction of a school. Many entirely fail of usefulness, though possessed of highly cultivated minds. Other things are required in the character of a good school-master. Among these, *common sense* is the first. This is a qualification exceedingly important, as in teaching school one has constant occasion for its exercise. Many, by no means deficient in intellect, are not persons of *common* sense. I mean by the term, that faculty by which things are seen as they are. It implies judgment and discrimination, and a proper sense of propriety in regard to the common affairs of life. It leads us to form judicious plans of action, and to be governed by our circumstances, in the way which men in general will approve. It is the exercise of reason, uninfluenced by passion or prejudice. It is in man nearly what instinct is in brutes. Very different from genius or talent, as they are commonly defined, it is better than either. Never blazing forth with the splendor of noon, but it shines with a constant and useful light.

2. *Uniformity of temper* is another important trait in the character of an instructer. Where this is wanting, it is hardly possible to govern or to teach with success. He, whose temper is constantly varying, can never be uniform in his estimation of things around him. Objects change in their appearance as his passions change. What appears right in any given hour may seem wrong in the next. What appears desirable to-day, may be beheld with aversion tomorrow. An uneven temper, in any situation of life, subjects one to many inconveniences. But when placed in a situation where his every action is observed and where his authority, must be in constant exercise, the man who labors under this malady is especially unfortunate. It is impossible for him to gain and preserve respect among his pupils. No one who comes under the rule of a person of uneven temper, can know what to expect or how to act.

3. A capacity to *understand and discriminate character*, is highly important to him who engages in teaching. The dispositions of children are so various, the treatment and government of parents so dissimilar, that the most diversified modes of governing and teaching need to be employed. The instructer who is not able to discriminate, but considers all alike, and treats all alike, does injury to many. The least expression of disapprobation to one is often more than the severest reproof to another; a word of encouragement will be sufficient to excite attention in some, while others will require to be urged, by every motive that can be placed before them. All the varying shades of disposition and capacity should be quickly learned by the instructer, that he may benefit all and do injustice to none. Without this, well meant efforts may prove hurtful, because ill-directed, and the desired object may be defeated, by the very means used to obtain it.

4. Teachers should possess much *decision of character*. In every situation of life this trait is important, but in none more so, than in that of which I am treating. The little world, by which he is surrounded, is a miniature of the older community. Children have their aversions and partialities, their hopes and fears, their plans,

schemes, propensities and desires. These are often in collision with each other and not unfrequently in collision with the laws of the school, and in opposition to the best interest of themselves. Amidst all these, the instructer should be able to pursue a uniform course. He ought not to be easily swayed from what he considers right. If easily led from his purpose, or induced to vary from established rules, his school must become a scene of disorder. Without decision, the teacher loses the confidence and respect of his pupils. I would not say, that, if, convinced of having committed an error, or of having given a wrong judgment, you should persist in the wrong. But I would say, it should be known as one of your first principles in school-keeping, that what is required must be complied with in every case, unless cause can be shown why the rule ought, in a given instance, to be dispensed with. There should *then* be a frank and easy compliance with the reasonable wish of the scholar. In a word, without decision of purpose in a teacher, his scholars can never be brought under the kind of discipline, which is requisite for his own ease and convenience, or for the improvement in knowledge, of those placed under him.

5. A schoolmaster ought to be *affectionate.* The human heart is so constituted, that it cannot resist the influence of kindness. When affectionate intercourse is the offspring of those kind feelings which arise from true benevolence, it will have an influence on all around. It leads to ease in behavior, and genuine politeness of manners. It is especially desirable in those who are surrounded by the young. Affectionate parents usually see their children exhibit similar feelings. Instructers who cultivate affection, will generally excite the same in their scholars. No object is more important than to gain the love and good will of those we are to teach. In no way is this more easily accomplished than by a kind interest manifested in their welfare; an interest which is exhibited by actions as well as words. This cannot fail of being attended with desirable results.

6. A just *moral discernment,* is of pre-eminent importance in the character of an instructer. Unless governed by a consideration of his moral obligation, he is but poorly qualified to discharge the duties which devolve upon him. He is himself a moral agent, and accountable to himself, to his employers, to his country and to his God, for the faithful discharge of duty. If he have no moral sensibility, no fear of disobeying the laws of God, no regard for the institutions of our holy religion, how can he be expected to lead his pupils in the way that they should go? The cultivation of virtuous propensities is more important to children than even their intellectual culture. The *virtuous* man, though illiterate, will be happy, while the learned, if *vicious,* must be miserable in proportion to his attainments. The remark of the ancient philosopher, that 'boys ought to be taught that which they will most need to practise when they come to be men,' is most true. To cultivate virtuous habits, and awaken virtuous principles;—to excite a sense of duty to God and of dependence on Him, should be the first objects of the teacher. If he permits his scholars to indulge in vicious habits—if he regard nothing as sin, but that which is a transgression of the laws of the school, if he suffer lying, profaneness, or other crimes, to pass unnoticed and unpunished, he is doing an injury for which he can in no way make amends. An instructer without moral feeling, not only brings ruin to the children placed under his care, but does injury to their parents, to the neighborhood, to the town and, doubtless, to other generations. The moral character of instructers should be considered a subject of very high importance; and let every one, who knows himself to be immoral, renounce at once the thought of such an employment, while he continues to disregard the laws of God, and the happiness of his fellow men. Genuine piety is highly desirable in every one

entrusted with the care and instruction of the young; but morality, at least should be *required,* in every candidate for that important trust.

7. Passing over many topics connected with those already mentioned, I shall now remark on the necessary literary qualifications of a schoolmaster. It will at once be apparent that no one is qualified for this business, who has not a thorough knowledge of the branches required to be taught in common schools. These are Reading, Spelling, Writing, Grammar, Arithmetic, Geography, and in some states the History of the United States. All these branches are necessary, to enable individuals to perform the common business and common duties of life. The four first are requisite in writing a letter on business or to a friend. The fifth is required in the business transactions of every day. The two last are necessary to enable every one to understand what he reads in the common newspapers, or in almost every book which comes within his reach. Of each of these branches, the instructer should certainly have a thorough knowledge; for he ought to have a full knowledge of what he is to teach. As he is to lay the *foundation* of an education, he should be well acquainted with the first principles of science. Of the letters of the alphabet such disposition is made, as to produce an immense number of words, to each of which a distinct meaning is given. 'The nature and power of letters, and just method of spelling words,' should be very distinctly understood. If there be defect in *knowledge* here, there must be a defect in teaching. A man cannot be expected to teach that which he does not know himself. Among all the defects I have witnessed in the literary qualification of instructers, the most common, by far the most common, have been here. Among a great number, both of males and females, I have found *very few* who possessed the requisite knowledge of the nature and power of letters, and rules of spelling. The defect originates in the fact, that these subjects are neglected after childhood, and much that is learned then is subsequently forgotten. Teachers, afterwards, especially of academies, presume that these subjects are familiar, and seldom make the inquiry of scholars, whether they have sufficient knowledge on these points. As a considerable part of every school is composed of those who are learning to spell and read, much importance is attached to the requisite qualifications of the teacher, to lay a proper foundation for subsequent attainments.

DAVID P. PAGE ON TEACHING (1847)   From David P. Page, *Theory and Practice of Teaching, or, The Motives and Methods of Good School-Keeping* (New York, 1847), pp. 22–24, 39–43, 47.

Those who are beginning the study of education should be reminded that the field of inquiry is a vast one, and that if they would attain the highest professional standing, they must pursue this subject in its three main phases—the practical, the scientific, and the historical. If the time for preparation is short, a beginning should be made in becoming acquainted with the best current methods of organizing, governing, and instructing a school. Then should follow a study of the science of education, to the end that the teacher may interpret the lessons of daily experience, and thus be helped to grow into higher and higher degrees of competence; and, finally, for giving breadth of view, for taking full advantage of all past experience and experiments, and for gaining that inspiration which comes from retracing the long line of an illustrious professional ancestry, there should be a study of the history of education.

All who propose to teach need to recollect that the very basis of fitness for teaching, so far as it can be gained from study, is a broad and accurate scholarship. To be a teacher, one must first of all be a scholar. So much stress is now placed on method, and the theory of teaching, that there is great danger of forgetting the supreme importance of scholarship and culture. For these there is no substitute; and any scheme of professional study that is pursued at the expense of scholarship and culture, is essentially bad. To be open-minded, magnanimous, and manly; to have a love for the scholarly vocation, and a wide and easy range of intellectual vision, are of infinitely greater worth to the teacher than any authorized set of technical rules and principles. Well would it be for both teachers and taught, if all who read this book were to be inspired by Plato's ideal of the cultured man: "A lover, not of a part of wisdom, but of the whole; who has a taste for every sort of knowledge and is curious to learn, and is never satisfied; who has magnificence of mind, and is the spectator of all time and all existence; who is harmoniously constituted; of a well-proportioned and gracious mind, whose own nature will move spontaneously towards the true being of every thing; who has a good memory, and is quick to learn, noble, gracious, the friend of truth, justice, courage, temperance."

*   *   *

Chapter III
Personal Habits of the Teacher

The importance of correct habits to any individual cannot be overrated. The influence of the teacher is so great upon the children under his care, either for good or evil, that it is of the utmost importance to them as well as to himself that his habits should be unexceptionable. It is the teacher's sphere to *improve* the community in which he moves, not only in learning, but in morals and manners; *in every thing* that is "lovely and of good report." This he may do partly by precept,—but very much by example. *He teaches, wherever he is.* His manners, his appearance, his character, are all the subject of observation, and to a great extent of imitation, by the young in his district. He is observed not only in the school, but in the family, in the social gathering, and in the religious meeting. How desirable then that he should be a *model* in all things!

Man has been said to be a "bundle of habits;" and it has been as pithily remarked—"Happy is the man whose habits are his friends." It were well if all persons, before they become teachers, would attend carefully to the formation of their personal habits. This, unhappily, is not always done,—and therefore I shall make no apology for introducing in this place some very plain remarks on what I deem the essentials among the habits of the teacher.

1. NEATNESS

This implies cleanliness of the person. If some who assume to teach were not proverbial for their slovenliness, I would not dwell on this point. On this point, however, I must be allowed great plainness of speech, even at the expense of incurring the charge of excessive nicety; for it is by attending to a *few little things* that one becomes a strictly neat person. The morning ablution, then, should never be omitted, and the comb for the hair and brush for the clothes should always be called into requisition before the teacher presents himself to the family, or to his school. Every teacher would very much promote his own health by washing the whole surface of the body every morning in cold water. This is now done by very many of the most enlightened teachers, as well as others. When physiology is better understood, this practice will be far more general. To no class of persons is it more essential than to the teacher; for on account of his confinement, often in an unventilated room, with half a hundred children during the day, very much more is demanded of the exhalents in him than in others. His only safety is in a healthy action of the skin.

The *teeth* should be attended to. A brush and clean water have saved many a set of teeth. It is bad enough to witness the deplorable neglect of these important organs so prevalent in the community; but it is extremely mortifying to see a filthy set of teeth in the mouth of the teacher of our youth. The *nails*, too, I am sorry to say, are often neglected by some of our teachers, till their *ebony tips* are any thing but ornamental. This matter is made worse, when, in the presence of the family or of the school, the penknife is brought into requisition to remove that which should have received attention at the time of washing in the morning. The *teacher* should remember that it is a *vulgar* habit to pare or clean the nails while in the presence of others, and especially during conversation with them.

The teacher should be neat in his *dress*. I do not urge that his dress should be expensive. His income ordinarily will not admit of this. He may wear a very plain dress; nor should it be any way singular in its fashion. All I ask is, that his clothing should be in good taste, and *always clean*. A slovenly dress, covered with dust, or spotted with grease, is never so much out of its proper place, as when it clothes the teacher.

While upon this subject I may be indulged in a word or two upon the use of tobacco by the teacher. It is quite a puzzle to me to tell why any man but a Turk, who may lawfully dream away half his existence over the fumes of this filthy narcotic, should ever use it. Even if there were nothing wrong in the use of unnatural stimulants themselves, the filthiness of tobacco is enough to condemn it among teachers, especially in the form of chewing. It is certainly worth while to ask whether there is not some moral delinquency in teaching this practice to the young, while it is admitted, by nearly all who have fallen into the habit, to be an evil, and one from which they would desire to be delivered. At any rate, I hope the time is coming, when the good taste of teachers, and a regard for personal neatness and the comfort of others, shall present motives sufficiently strong to induce them to break away from a practice at once so unreasonable and so disgusting.

2. ORDER

In this place I refer to that system and regularity so desirable in every teacher. He should practise it in his room at his boarding-house. Every thing should have its place. His books, his clothing, should all be arranged with regard to this principle. The same habit should go with him to the school-room. His desk there should be a pattern of orderly arrangement. Practising this himself, he may with propriety insist upon it in his pupils. It is of great moment to the teacher, that, when he demands order and arrangment among his pupils, they cannot appeal to any breach of it in his own practice.

The teacher should ever be courteous, both in his language and in his manners. *Courtesy of language* may imply a freedom from all *coarseness*. There is a kind of communication, used among boatmen and hangers-on at bar-rooms, which should find no place in the teacher's vocabulary. All vulgar jesting, all double-entendres, all low allusions, should be forever excluded from his mouth. And profanity,—can it be necessary that I should speak of this as among the habits of the teacher? Yes, it is even so. Such is the want of moral sense in the community, that men are still employed in some districts, whose ordinary conversation is poisoned with the breath of blasphemy; ay, and even the walls of the school-room resound to undisguised oaths! I cannot find words to express my astonishment at the indifference of parents, or at the recklessness of teachers, wherever I know such cases to exist.

Speaking of the *language* of the teacher, I might urge also that it should be both *pure* and *accurate*. Pure as distinguished from all those cant phrases and provincialisms which amuse the vulgar in certain localities; and accurate as to the terms used to express his meaning. As the *teacher teaches* in this, as in every thing, by example as well as by precept, he should be very careful to acquire an unexceptionable use of our language, and never deviate from it in the hearing of his pupils or elsewhere.

JACOB ABBOTT ON THE GOVERNMENT OF A CLASSROOM (1856) From Jacob Abbott, *The Teacher: Moral Influences Employed in the Instruction and Government of the Young* (New York, 1856), pp. 36–37, 58–62, 71–72.

The objects, then, to be aimed at in the general arrangements of school are twofold:

1. That the teacher may be left uninterrupted, to attend to one thing at a time.

2. That the individual scholars may have constant employment, and such an amount and such kinds of study as shall be suited to the circumstances and capacities of each.

I shall examine each in their order.

1. The following are the principal things which, in a vast number of schools, are all the time pressing upon the teacher; or, rather, they are the things which must every where press upon the teacher, except so far as, by the skill of his arrangements, he contrives to remove them.

1. Giving leave to whisper or to leave seats.
2. Distributing and changing pens.
3. Answering questions in regard to studies.
4. Hearing recitations.
5. Watching the behavior of the scholars.
6. Administering reproof and punishment for offenses as they occur.

A pretty large number of objects of attention and care, one would say, to be pressing upon the mind of the teacher at one and the same time—and *all the time* too! Hundreds and hundreds of teachers in every part of our country, there is no doubt, have all these crowding upon them from morning to night, with no cessation, except perhaps some accidental and momentary respite. During the winter months, while the principal common schools in our country are in operation, it is sad to reflect how many teachers come home every evening with bewildered and aching heads, having been vainly trying all day to do six things at a time, while He who made the human mind has determined that it shall do but one. How many become discouraged and disheartened by what they consider the unavoidable trials of a teacher's life, and give up in despair, just because their faculties will not sustain a six-fold task. There are multitudes who, in early life, attempted teaching, and, after having been worried, almost to distraction, by the simultaneous pressure of these multifarious cares, gave up the employment in disgust, and now unceasingly wonder how any body can like teaching. I know multitudes of persons to whom the above description will exactly apply.

I once heard a teacher who had been very successful, even in large schools, say that he could hear two classes recite, mend pens, and watch his school all at the same time, and that without any distraction of mind or any unusual fatigue. Of course the recitation in such a case must be from memory. There are very few minds, however, which can thus perform triple or quadruple work, and probably none which can safely be tasked so severely. For my part, I can do but one thing at a time; and I have no question that the true policy for all is to learn not *to do every thing at once,* but so to classify and arrange their work that *they shall have but one thing at once to do.* Instead of vainly attempting to attend simultaneously to a dozen things, they should so plan their work that only *one* will demand attention.

*   *   *

We come now to one of the most important subjects which present themselves to the teacher's attention in settling the principles upon which he shall govern his school. I mean the degree of influence which the boys themselves shall have in the management of its affairs. Shall the government of school be a *monarchy* or a *republic?* To this question, after much inquiry and many experiments, I answer, a monarchy; an absolute, unlimited monarchy; the teacher possessing exclusive power as far as the pupils are concerned, though strictly responsible to the committee or to the trustees under whom he holds his office.

While, however, it is thus distinctly understood that the power of the teacher is supreme, that all the power rests in him, and that he alone is responsible for its exercise, there ought to be a very free and continual *delegation* of power to the pupils. As much business as is possible should be committed to them. They should be interested as much as possible in the affairs of the school, and led to take an active part in carrying them forward; though they should, all the time, distinctly understand that it is only *delegated* power which they exercise, and that the teacher can, at any time, revoke what he has granted, and alter or annul at pleasure any of their decisions. By this plan we have the responsibility resting where it ought to rest, and yet the boys are trained to business, and led to take an active interest in the welfare of the school. Trust is reposed in them, which may be greater or less, as they are able to bear. All the good effects of reposing trust and confidence, and committing the management of important business to the pupils will be secured, without the dangers which would result from the entire surrender of the management of the institution into their hands.

There have been, in several cases, experiments made with reference to ascertaining how far a government strictly republican would be admissible in a school. A very fair experiment of this kind was made some years since at the Gardiner Lyceum, in Maine. At the time of its establishment, nothing was said of the mode of government which it was intended to adopt. For some time the attention of the instructors was occupied in arranging the course of study, and attending to the other concerns of the institution; and, in the infant state of the Lyceum, few cases of discipline occured, and no regular system of government was necessary.

Before long, however, complaints were made that the students at the Lyceum were guilty of breaking windows in an old building used as a town-house. The principal called the students together, mentioned the reports, and said that he did not know, and did not wish to know who were the guilty individuals. It was necessary, however, that the thing should be examined into, and that restitution should be made, and, relying on their faithfulness and ability, he should leave them to manage the business alone. For this purpose, he nominated one of the students as judge, some others as jurymen, and appointed the other officers necessary in the same manner. He told them that, in order to give them time to make a thorough investigation, they were excused from farther exercises during the day.

The principal then left them, and they entered on the trial. The result was that they discovered the guilty individuals, ascertained the amount of mischief done by each, and sent to the selectmen a message, by which they agreed to pay a sum equal to three times the value of the injury sustained.

The students were soon after informed that this mode of bringing offenders to justice would hereafter be always pursued, and arrangements were made for organizing a *regular republican government* among the young men. By this government all laws which related to the internal police of the institution were to be made, all officers were appointed, and all criminal cases were to be tried. The students finding the part of a judge too difficult for them to sustain, one of the professors was appointed to hold that office, and, for similar reasons, another of the professors was made president of the legislative assembly. The principal was the executive, with power to *pardon*, but not to *sentence*, or even *accuse*.

Some time after this a student was indicted for profane swearing; he was tried, convicted, and punished. After this he evinced a strong hostility to the government. He made great exertions to bring it into contempt, and when the next trial came on, he endeavored to persuade the witnesses that giving evidence was dishonorable, and he so far succeeded that the defendant was acquitted for want of evidence, when it was generally understood that there was proof of his guilt, which would have been satisfactory if it could have been brought forward. For some time after this the prospect was rather unfavorable, though many of the students themselves opposed with great earnestness these efforts, and were much alarmed lest they should lose their free government through the perverseness of one of their number. The attorney general, at this juncture, conceived the idea of indicting the individual alluded to for an attempt to overturn the government. He obtained the approbation of the principal, and the grand jury found a bill. The court, as the case was so important, invited some of the trustees, who were in town, to attend the trial. The parent of the defendant was also informed of the circumstances and requested to be present, and he accordingly attended. The prisoner was tried, found guilty, and sentenced, if I mistake not, to expulsion. At his earnest request, however, to be permitted to remain in the Lyceum and redeem his character, he was pardoned and restored, and from that time he became perfectly exemplary in his conduct and character. After this occurrence the system went on in successful operation for some time.

The legislative power was vested in the hands of a general committee, consisting of eight or ten, chosen by the students from their own number. They met about once a week to transact such business as appointing officers, making and repealing regulations, and inquiring into the state of the Lyceum. The instructors had a negative upon all their proceedings, but no direct and positive power. They could pardon, but they could assign no punishments, nor make laws inflicting any.

Now such a plan as this may succeed for a short time, and under very favorable circumstances; and the circumstance which it is chiefly important should be favorable is, that the man who is called to preside over such an association should possess such talents of *generalship* that he can really manage the institution *himself*, while the power is *nominally* and *apparently* in the hands of the boys. Should this not be the case, or should the teacher, from any cause, lose his personal influence in the school, so that the institution should really be surrendered into the hands of the pupils, things must be on a very unstable footing. And, accordingly, where such a plan has been adopted, it has, I believe, in every instance, been ultimately abandoned.

Real self-government is an experiment sufficiently hazardous among men, though Providence, in making a daily supply of food necessary for every human being, has imposed a most powerful check upon the tendency to anarchy and confusion. Let the populace of Paris or of London materially interrupt the order and break in upon the arrangements of the community, and in eight-and-forty hours nearly the whole of the mighty mass will be in the hands of the devourer, hunger, and they will be soon brought to submission. On the other hand, a month's anarchy and confusion in a college or an academy would be delight to half the students, or else times have greatly changed since I was within college walls.

Although it is thus evident that the important concerns of a literary institution can not be safely committed into the hands of the students, very great benefits will result from calling upon them to act upon and to decide questions relative to the school within such limits and under such restrictions as are safe and proper. Such a practice will assist the teacher very much if he manages it with any degree of dexterity; for it will interest his pupils in the success of the school, and secure, to a very considerable extent, their cooperation in the government of it. It will teach them self-control and self-government, and will accustom them to submit to the majority—that lesson which, of all others, it is important for a republican to learn.

In endeavoring to interest the pupils of a school in the work of co-operating with the teacher in its administration, no little dexterity will be necessary at the outset. In all probability, the formal announcement of this principle, and the endeavor to introduce it by a sudden revolution, would totally fail. Boys, like men, must be gradually prepared for power, and they must exercise it only so far as they are prepared. This, however, can very easily be done. The teacher should say nothing of his general design, but, when some suitable opportunity presents, he should endeavor to lead his pupils to co-operate with him in some particular instance.

There are dangers, however. What useful practice has not its dangers? One of these is, that the teacher will allow these arrangements to take up too much time. He must guard against this. I have found from experience that fifteen minutes each day, with a school of 135, is enough. This ought never to be exceeded.

Another danger is, that the boys will be so engaged in the duties of their *offices* as to neglect their *studies*. This would be, and ought to be, fatal to the whole plan. This danger may be avoided in the following manner. State publicly that you will not appoint any to office who are not good scholars, always punctual, and always prepared; and when any boy who holds an office is going behindhand in his studies, say to him kindly, "You have not time to get your lessons, and I am afraid it is owing to the fact that you spend so much time in helping me. Now if you wish to resign your office, so as to have more time for your lessons, you can. In fact, I think you ought to do it. You may try it for a day or two, and I will notice how you recite, and then we can decide."

Such a communication will generally be found to have a powerful effect. If it does not remedy the evil, the resignation must be insisted on. A few cases of this kind will effectually remove the evil I am considering.

*　　*　　*

The principles, then, which this chapter has been intended to establish, are simply these: in making your general arrangements, look carefully over your ground, consider all the objects which you have to accomplish, and the proper degree of time and attention which each deserves. Then act upon system. Let the mass of particulars which would otherwise crowd upon you in promiscuous confusion be arranged and classified. Let each be assigned to its proper time and place, so that your time may be your own, under your own command, and not, as is too often the case, at the mercy of the thousand accidental circumstances which may occur.

In a word, be, in the government of your school, yourself supreme, and let your supremacy be that of authority; but delegate power, as freely as possible, to those under your care. Show them that you are desirous of reposing trust in them just so far as they show themselves capable of exercising it. Thus interest them in your plans, and make them feel that they participate in the honor or the disgrace of success or failure.

I have gone much into detail in this chapter, proposing definite measures by which the principles I have recommended may be carried into effect. I wish, however, that it may be distinctly understood that all I contend for is the principles themselves, no matter what the particular measures are by which they are secured. Every good school must be systematic, but all need not be on precisely the same system. As this work is intended almost exclusively for beginners, much detail has been admitted, and many of the specific measures here proposed may perhaps be safely adopted where no others are established. There may also, perhaps, be cases where teachers, whose schools are already in successful operation, may ingraft upon their own plans some things which are here proposed. If they should attempt it, it must be done cautiously and gradually. There is no other way by which they can be safely introduced, or even introduced at all. This is a point of so much importance, that I must devote a paragraph to it before closing the chapter.

JACOB ABBOTT ON HOW TO MANAGE THE YOUNG (1872)   From Jacob
Abbott, *Gentle Measures in the Management and Training of the Young* (New York, 1872),
pp. 14–15.

The Three Modes of Management

It is not impossible that in the minds of some persons the idea of
employing gentle measures in the management and training of children may seem to
imply the abandonment of the principle of *authority*, as the basis of the parental
government, and the substitution of some weak and inefficient system of artifice and
manœuvring in its place. To suppose that the object of this work is to aid in
effecting such a substitute as that, is entirely to mistake its nature and design. The
only government of the parent over the child that is worthy of the name is one of
authority—complete, absolute, unquestioned *authority*. The object of this work is,
accordingly, not to show how the gentle methods which will be brought to view can
be employed as a substitute for such authority, but how they can be made to aid in
establishing and maintaining it.

THREE METHODS

There are three different modes of management customarily employed by parents as
means of inducing their children to comply with their requirements. They are,
1. Government by Manœuvring and Artifice.
2. By Reason and Affection.
3. By Authority.

*   *   *

GOVERNING BY AUTHORITY

3. By the third method the mother secures the compliance of the child by a direct
exercise of authority. She says to her—the circumstances of the case being still
supposed to be the same—
"Mary, your father and I are going out to ride this afternoon, and I am sorry, for
your sake, that we can not take you with us."
"Why can't you take me?" asks Mary.
"I can not tell you why, now," replies the mother, "but perhaps I will explain it
to you after I come home. I think there *is* a good reason, and, at any rate, I have
decided that you are not to go. If you are a good girl, and do not make any
difficulty, you can have your little chair out upon the front door-step, and can see
the chaise come to the door, and see your father and me get in and drive away; and
you can wave your handkerchief to us for a good-bye."
Then, if she observes any expression of discontent or insubmission in Mary's
countenance, the mother would add,
"If you should *not* be a good girl, but should show signs of making us any
trouble, I shall have to send you out somewhere to the back part of the house until
we are gone."
But this last supposition is almost always unnecessary; for if Mary has been
habitually managed on this principle she will *not* make any trouble. She will

THE
PROFESSION
OF EDUCATION

1367

perceive at once that the question is settled—settled irrevocably—and especially that it is entirely beyond the power of any demonstrations of insubmission or rebellion that she can make to change it. She will acquiesce at once. She may be sorry that she can not go, but she will make no resistance. Those children only attempt to carry their points by noisy and violent demonstrations who find, by experience, that such measures are usually successful. A child, even, who has become once accustomed to them, will soon drop them if she finds, owing to a change in the system of management, that they now never succeed. And a child who never, from the beginning, finds any efficiency in them, never learns to employ them at all.

CONCLUSION

Of the three methods of managing children exemplified in this chapter, the last is the only one which can be followed either with comfort to the parent or safety to the child; and to show how this method can be brought effectually into operation by gentle measures is the object of this book. It is indeed, true that the importance of tact and skill in the training of the young, and of cultivating their reason, and securing their affection, can not be overrated. But the influences secured by these means form, at the best, but a sandy foundation for filial obedience to rest upon. The child is not to be made to comply with the requirements of his parents by being artfully inveigled into compliance, nor is his obedience to rest on his love for father and mother, and his unwillingness to displease them, nor on his conviction of the rightfulness and reasonableness of their commands, but on simple *submission to authority*—that absolute and almost unlimited authority which all parents are commissioned by God and nature to exercise over their offspring during the period while the offspring remain dependent upon their care.

WARREN BURTON ON TEACHING INFANTS IN THE HOME (1865)
From Warren Burton, *The Culture of the Observing Faculties in the Family and the School* (New York, 1865), pp. 9–13, 32–35.

The Beginning

The intellectual development of the human being begins as soon as he can open his eyes and put forth his hands—as soon as his senses come in contact with the material world. From this time onward he is continually gaining knowledge, and preparing for his future of usefulness and enjoyment. It is said that all the simple elements of knowledge and the best part of man's education are obtained before he is seven years of age. These foundations are mainly laid at home. The work is, or should be, under the supervision of the parents. This education, however, goes on, whether they attend to it or not. Indeed the child will be continually educating himself. It may be truly said that the first and the most important part of man's intellectual culture, as things have been, is self-culture. Now this fostering from kindly nature, this forth-putting and forth-grasping of the infant faculties, may be greatly assisted by the parents and other older members of the family, if they did but think of it, and would but give themselves to it. Help in this primary home institution is as valuable as in the public seminaries to which the mind is afterward introduced. In the majority of homes, however, this assistance is casually and poorly rendered. It is because parents have the notion that they have nothing to do with intellectual development. This, they suppose, belongs only to the school. If a child asks a question about any thing new to his curiosity, he may be kindly answered. If he persistently puts many questions, he is patiently borne with, or perhaps hastily hushed or snapped off. The parents have not the least suspicion that, in replying to such questions, they are really exercising tutorships and professorships as important, to say the least, as any in college. Indeed, it may be affirmed with absolute truth, that, as schools have generally been conducted, especially for little children, the education mostly stops at the school threshold; at least it begins to be exceedingly hindered, as will plainly appear.

Knowledge Without Books

Just watch a babe, and see what Nature, or rather his own divinely devised constitution, prompts him to do, and let us gather useful hints from the observation. As soon as there is any visual discernment, there is a separation of one thing from another, and the reception of distinct ideas. The little one leaves the maternal lap— for what? to work, and to get knowledge to prepare him for more and more work. He creeps about the room, not only for the pleasure of muscular action, but to seek for new objects to his curiosity; hunting for prey, if we may so speak, as food to his awakened and craving perceptions. Everything he gets hold of is a subject of interest—a fund of entertainment; and, though his mother perhaps thinks not of it, it is a source of most valuable instruction. We can not just yet say of him that "he who runs may read," but we may say that he who creeps can—can read the great book of perceptible and practical knowledge, which is open boundlessly before him, just as fast and far as he can get at it. Toeing and kneeing it along, he lays hold of every thing within the touch and the crook of his fingers. Why? he wants knowledge, and he will have it. First the thing—the individual—it is separate from some other things he perceives, and he wants to know about it as another and distinct object. The several perceptive powers then come into action: finding out the various qualities—figure, color, size, weight—as they are peculiar to each individual thing. Thus the child ranges through the room; and when, in due time he mounts to the top of his feet, he runs about the house, and soon out of doors, and then round about the premises, all the time after knowledge—knowledge of objects, qualities, operations, uses. Before the little looker and hunter is four years old, he is acquainted with hundreds of things—perhaps we might say thousands, He knows nothing about the book, it may be, but is he deficient in language? By no means; objects are distinguished by names; qualities by appropiate terms. What riches of language are his, even now, though he may never have been at school, and can not read a word! All this time he has been in training for the duties and enjoyments of maturer life. He has been studying the Creator's perfect works, and unconsciously finding the steps which lead up to the Most Wise and Most Loving. He has been acquainted himself with the things also made by human hands, and examining the materials of which they are composed. This is in preparation for the time when he himself will make similar things, and will need accurate knowledge of fabrics and materials as to qualities and fitness for specific purposes.

Nay, farther, our little beginner at life is something more than a learner—he is a maker. He is at his mechanics, too. See him putting this thing with that in rude efforts at construction . . .

*　　*　　*

The Object Game

As a mutual benefit and pleasure indeed, let parent and child have a sort of game at finding objects. It may be called "the thing game," or, if you please, "the object game." The wall, ceiling, window, floor, carpet, table, chairs, and so on, will probably first strike attention, and be named. Soon all the prominent objects of the room will be exhausted. Then there will be a scramble for something more. Objects will be discovered which otherwise would not have met the eye, or been thought of. The head of a nail, a shred of cloth, the minutest thread, or any particle of matter; a spot or mark on the furniture or wall, or any thing else—any thing which may bear a name, will be detected one after another; and he is the victor who shall find the minutest or most out-of-the-way thing to which may be put a name, or the last thing to be found. At another time the same game may be played with objects in the yard, or any where around the house, or as far away as the sight can reach from door or window. Different apartments in the house may be made the scene of the game. If the time be the dark evening or a winter's cold day, let the trial be who shall call to recollection the most objects in some other room in the house, or in the more distant shed or barn. What an inventory will thus be made of the implements and various goods of the household! You might go farther and call to recollection what may have been noticed in a neighbor's domicile, or any where else. Thus, in mere exciting pastime, you will develop in your child and in yourselves the central and most important faculty of the intellect. You will all be trained to keep your eyes open, to look, to see, and to separate one thing from another, and thus to obtain knowledge of new and distinct things wherever you go. How keen at catching objects at a glance will you become, if you only try! You know how the sailor will discover a ship at the distant horizon when it seems but a speck, but which the undisciplined passenger could not possibly perceive. It is because he has been for years searching the ocean's surface for any object which may break the blank uninformity, and especially for his eye's love—a sail. His success at such perception is a matter of discipline and use. Just so the sight of children might be trained to acuteness of observation among the objects on the land, if parents would set themselves and their children about it. Of course, as was intimated before, there will be differences in accomplishment according to differences in organic constitution.

Qualities: Form

Next after individualizing the world of matter around comes the learning of the forms of things. These forms can be seen by the eye in the light—can be felt by the hand in the dark: they are the objects of two senses. Soon will the child learn the ideas and the names, long and short, square and round. Indeed, you may cheaply provide blocks exhibiting all the various geometrical figures, and the child in due time (for I would force nothing) might learn the various geometrical names. At his impressible age, it will be as easy for him to fasten on his memory a scientific term as any other word, if there is only a real visible object under it. How easily, then, will he learn whether any object his sense falls on is most like a square, triangle, cube, parallelogram, sphere, cone, pyramid, or any thing else! I need not here run through the several geometrical figures and names. You may easily get a book and look at them, and the advantage to yourselves and children will amply repay the trouble.

Size and Measurement

To proceed with qualities: next comes the size of things. The child soon perceives this, without you telling him that one object is larger or smaller than another. All he wants from you are words to designate differences in dimension. Yes, he does want, or rather need something else. He needs training to accuracy in discriminating the size and bulk of different things.

19th Century Schoolbooks

SELECTION FROM A SIMPLIFIED HISTORY TEXT-BOOK FOR
AMERICAN YOUTH (1802)   From Preface to *The Columbian Reading Book or
Historical Preceptor,* 2d ed. (New Brunswick, N.J., 1802), pp. 8-9.

Address to Parents
and those entrusted with the Education of Youth

To most of the books used in schools for exercising children in reading, it may be justly objected, that they are either far beyond the capacity of those for whom they are intended, or elso so dry and insipid as to increase the difficulties incident to the acquisition of learning.

It appears as irrational to put an elegant didactic essay into the hands of a child of eight or ten years of age, as to clothe an infant with the armour of a giant. The one is as ill calculated to comprehend the profound reasoning of such a production, as the other is to support the cumbersome defence that would suit a Garagantua. Yet many of the reading books used in our schools, are formed principally of the elegant and playful productions of Addison, the profound reasonings of Johnson, or the sober and convincing arguments of Knox.

From a consideration of this circumstance, it occurred to the compiler, that a reading book might be framed in such a manner as to obviate those objections, by collecting together short and agreeable stories, calculated to invite to virtue, or deter from vice. That the plan is perfect, he does not pretend. It may be improved in a future edition. Such as it is, he unhesitatingly submits it to the judgment of a candid public.

*   *   *

V. Wonderful Effect of Filial Affection

A woman of illustrious birth had been condemned to be strangled. The Roman praetor delivered her up to the triumvir, who caused her to be carried to prison, in order to be put to death. The jailor who was ordered to execute her, was struck with compassion, and could not resolve to kill her. He chose therefore to let her die of hunger. Besides which, he suffered her daughter to see her in prison; taking care, however, that she brought her nothing to eat. As this continued many days, he was surprised that the prisoner lived so long without eating; and suspecting the daughter, upon watching her, he discovered that she nourished her mother with her own milk. Amazed at so pious, and at the same time so ingenious an invention, he told the fact to the triumvir, and the triumvir to the praetor, who believed the thing merited relating to the assembly of the people. The criminal was pardoned; a decree was passed that the mother and daughter should be subsisted for the rest of their lives at the expense of the public, and that a temple sacred to piety should be erected near the prison.

*　　*　　*

VI. Brotherly Love

The king of Cucho had three sons; and like many other parents, having most affection for the youngest, some days before his death declared him his successor, to the exclusion of his brethen. This proceeding was the more extraordinary as it was contrary to the laws of the kingdom. The people therefore, thought that after the death of the king, they might without any crime raise the eldest son to the throne. This design was universally approved of: but the new king, calling to mind his father's last words, rejected the offer, and taking the crown, placed it on the head of his youngest brother, publicly declaring, that he renounced it, and thought himself unworthy of it, as he was excluded by his father's will, and his father could not now retract what he had done. His brother, being affected with such a generous action, instantly intreated him not to oppose the inclination of the people, who desired him for their ruler. He urged, that he alone was the lawful successor to the crown, and that their father could not infringe the laws of the kingdom; that he had been betrayed by an extravagant fondness; and that, in a word, the people had the power of redressing any breach in the established law. Nothing, however, was capable of persuading his brother to accept of the crown. There was a glorious contest between the two princes; and as they perceived that the dispute would be endless, they retired from court: thus each having both conquered and been vanquished, they went to end their days together in peaceful solitude, and left the kingdom to their other brother.

THREE BOYS DISCUSS A "CHOICE OF BUSINESS FOR LIFE" (1807)

From "Dialogue on the Choice of Business for Life," as quoted in Caleb Bingham, *The Columbian Orator . . .* (Hartford, 1807), pp. 150–53.

Enter EDWARD, CHARLEY, and THOMAS

Edward. It appears to me high time for us to choose our business for life. Our academical studies will soon be completed; and I wish to look a little forward. What say you? am I right?

Charley. It may be well for you: poor men's sons must look out for themselves. My father is able to support me at my ease; and my mamma says she would rather see me laid in a coffin than shut up in a study, spoiling my eyes and racking my brains, plodding over your nonsensical minister, doctor, and lawyer books; and I am sure she would never have me confined behind a counter, or a merchant's desk. She intends I shall be brought up a gentleman. My mother is of noble blood, and she don't intend that I shall disgrace it.

Edw. Pray, master Charley, who was the father of your noble-blooded mother?

Char. A gentleman, I'd have you to know.

Edw. Yes, a gentleman cobler, to my knowledge.

Char. Aye, he followed that business, to be sure, sometimes, to stop the clamour of the vulgar. Then poor people could not bear to see a rich man living at his ease, or give a nobleman his title. But times are altering for the better, my mamma says: the rich begin to govern now. We shall soon live in style, and wear titles here as well as in England. She intends to send over and get my coat of arms, and she hopes to add a title to them.

Edw. High style! titles! and coats of arms! fine things in America, to be sure! Well, after all, I can't really disapprove of your mamma's plan. A lapstone, an awl, and shoe-hammer will make a fine picture, and may appear as well in your mother's parlour, as in her father's shop: and the title of cobler, or shoe-maker would well become her darling Charley.

Char. I will not be insulted on account of my grandfather's employment, I'll have you to know! I have heard my mother say, her father was grandson of an aunt of 'squire Thorn, who once had a horse that run a race with the famous horse of a cousin of the Duke of Bedford, of—.

Edw. Quite enough! I am fully convinced of the justice of your claim to the title of Duke, or whatever you please. About as much merit in it, I perceive, as in your father's title to his estate. Ten thousands dollars drawn in a lottery! already two thirds spent. A title to nobility derived from the grandson of an aunt of 'quire Thorn, from 'squire Thorn's horse, or perhaps from some monkey, that has been a favorite playmate with the prince of Wales. These are to be the support of your ease and honor through life. Well, I believe there is no need of your troubling yourself about your future employment: that is already determined. Depend upon it, you will repent of your folly, or scratch a poor man's head as long as you live. I advise you to set about the former, in order to avoid the latter.

Char. I did not come to you for advice. I'll not bear your insults, or disgrace myself with your company any longer. My parents shall teach you better manners.

[*Exit Charley*]

Thomas. I pity the vanity and weakness of this poor lad. But reflection and experience will teach him the fallacy of his hopes.

Edw. Poor child; he does not know that his lottery money is almost gone; that his father's house is mortgaged for more than it is worth; and that the only care of his parents is to keep up the appearance of present grandeur, at the expense of future shame. Happy for us, that we are not deluded with such deceitful hopes.

Tho. My parents were poor; not proud. They experienced the want of learning; but were resolved their children should share the benefit of a goood education. I am the fourth son, who owe the debt of filial gratitude. All but myself are well settled in business, and doing honor to themselves and their parents. If I fall short of their example, I shall be most ungrateful.

Edw. I have neither father nor mother to excite my gratitude, or stimulate my exertions. But I wish to behave in such a manner, that if my parents could look down and observe my actions, they might approve my conduct. Of my family, neither root nor branch remains: all have paid the debt of nature. They left a name for honesty; and I esteem that higher than a pretended title to greatness. They have left me a small farm, which, though not enough for my support, will with my own industry, be sufficient. For employment, to pass away the winter season, I have determined upon keeping a school for my neighbours' children.

Tho. I heartily approve of your determination. Our mother Earth rewards, with peace and plenty, those, who cultivate her face; but loads, with anxious cares, those, who dig her bowels for treasure. The life you contemplate is favorable to the enjoyment of social happiness, improvement of the mind, and security of virtue; and the task of training the tender mind is an employment, that ought to meet the encouragement, the gratitude of every parent, and the respect of every child.

Edw. I am pleased that you approve my choice. Will you frankly tell me your own?

Tho. I will: my intention is to follow the inclination of my kind parents. It is their desire that I should be a preacher. Their other sons have taken to other callings; and they wish to see one of their children in the desk. If their prayers are answered, I shall be fitted for the important task. To my youth, it appears formidable; but others, with less advantages, have succeeded, and been blessings to society, and an honor to their profession.

Edw. You have chosen the better part. Whatever the licentious may say to the contrary, the happiness of society must rest on the principles of virtue and religion; and the pulpit must be the nursery, where they are cultivated.

Tho. "—The pulpit;

And I name it, fill'd with solemn awe,
Must stand acknowledg'd, while the world shall stand,
The most important and effectual guard,
Support and ornament of virtue's cause.
There stands the messenger of truth. There stands
The legate of the skies: his theme divine,
His office sacred, his credentials clear.
By him the violated law speaks out
Its thunders, and by him, in strains as sweet
As angels use, the gospel whispers peace."

My heart glows with the subject; and if my abilities could equal my zeal, I could at least hope to realize the sublime character so beautifully drawn by Cowper.

Edw. It is a laudable ambition to aim at eminence in religion, and excellence in virtue.

LINDLEY MURRAY, NEW ENGLISH READER FOR YOUNG PERSONS

(1823)   From Preface to *The English Reader . . . Selected from the Best Writers* (Cooperstown, N.Y., 1829), preface.

Preface

Many selections of excellent matter have been made for the benefit of young persons. Performances of this kind are of so great utility, that fresh productions of them, and new attempts to improve the young mind, will scarcely be deemed superfluous, if the writer make his compilation instructive and interesting, and sufficiently distinct from others.

The present work, as the title expresses, aims at the attainment of three objects: to improve youth in the art of reading; to meliorate their language and sentiments; and to inculcate some of the most important principles of piety and virtue.

The pieces selected, not only give exercise to a great variety of emotions, and the correspondent tones and variations of voice, but contain sentences and members of sentences, which are diversified, proportioned, and pointed with accuracy. Exercises of this nature are, it is presumed, well calculated to teach youth to read with propriety and effect. A selection of sentences, in which variety and proportion, with exact punctuation, have been carefully observed, in all their parts as well as with respect to one another, will probably have a much greater effect, in properly teaching the art of reading, than is commonly imagined. In such constructions, everything is accommodated to the understanding and the voice; and the common difficulties in learning to read well are obviated. When the learner has acquired a habit of reading such sentences, with justness and facility, he will readily apply that habit, and the improvements he has made, to sentences more complicated and irregular, and of a construction entirely different.

The language of the pieces chosen for this collection has been carefully regarded. Purity, propriety, perspicuity, and, in may instances, elegance of diction, distinguish them. They are extracted from the works of the most correct and elegant writers. From the sources whence the sentiments are drawn, the reader may expect to find them connected and regular, sufficiently important and impressive, and divested of everything that is either trite or eccentric. The frequent perusal of such composition naturally tends to infuse a taste for this species of excellence; and to produce a habit of thinking, and of composing, with judgment and accuracy.

That this collection may also serve the purpose of promoting piety and virtue, the Compiler has introduced many extracts, which place religion in the most amiable light; and which recommend a great variety of moral duties, by the excellence of their nature, and the happy effects they produce. These subjects are exhibited in a style and manner which are calculated to arrest the attention of youth; and to make strong and durable impressions on their minds.

The Compiler has been careful to avoid every expression and sentiment, that might gratify a corrupt mind, or, in the least degree, offend the eye or ear of innocence. This he conceives to be peculiarly incumbent on every person who writes for the benefit of youth. It would indeed be a great and happy improvement in education, if no writings were allowed to come under their notice, but such as are perfectly innocent; and if on all proper occasions, they were encouraged to peruse those which tend to inspire a due reverence for virtue, and an abhorrence of

EDUCATION IN THE UNITED STATES

1376

vice, as well as to animate them with sentiments of piety and goodness. Such impressions deeply engraven on their minds, and connected with all their attainments, could scarcely fail of attending them through life, and of producing a solidity of principle and character, that would be able to resist the danger arising from future intercourse with the world.

The Author has endeavoured to relieve the grave and serious parts of his collection, by the occasional admission of pieces which amuse as well as instruct. If, however, any of his readers should think it contains too great a proportion of the former, it may be some apology to observe, that in the existing publications designed for the perusal of young persons, the preponderance is greatly on the side of gay and amusing productions. Too much attention may be paid to this medium of improvement. When the imagination, of youth especially, is much entertained, the sober dictates of the understanding are regarded with indifference; and the influence of good affections is either feeble, or transient. A temperate use of such entertainment seems therefore requisite, to afford proper scope for the operations of the understanding and the heart.

The reader will perceive, that the Compiler has been solicitous to recommend to young persons, the perusal of the sacred Scriptures, by interspersing through his work some of the most beautiful and interesting passages of those invaluable writings. To excite an early taste and veneration for this great rule of life, is a point of so high importance, as to warrant the attempt to promote it on every proper occasion.

To improve the young mind, and to afford some assistance to tutors, in the arduous and important work of education, were the motives which led to this production. If the Author should be so successful as to accomplish these ends, even in a small degree, he will think that his time and pains have been well employed, and will deem himself amply rewarded.

LESSONS IN DOMESTIC ECONOMY FROM THE AMERICAN SPELLING BOOK (1831) From Noah Webster, *The American Spelling Book* (Middletown, Conn., 1831), pp. 163–65.

Additional Lessons.
Domestic Economy,
Or, the History of Thrifty and Unthrifty

There is a great difference among men, in their ability to gain property; but a still greater difference in their power of using it to advantage. Two men may acquire the same amount of money, in a given time; yet one will prove to be a poor man, while the other becomes rich. A chief and essential difference in the management of property, is, that one man spends only the *interest* of his money, while another spends the *principal*.

I know a farmer by the name of *Thrifty*, who manages his affairs in this manner: He rises early in the morning, looks to the condition of his house, barn, homelot, and stock—sees that his cattle, horses and hogs are fed; examines the tools to see whether they are all in good order for the workmen—takes care that breakfast is ready in due season, and begins work in the cool of the day—When in the field, he keeps steadily at work, though not so violently as to fatigue and exhaust the body—nor does he stop to tell or hear long stories—When the labor of the day is past, he takes refreshment, and goes to rest at an early hour—In this manner he earns and gains money.

When *Thrifty* has acquired a little property, he does not spend it or let it slip from him, without use or benefit. He pays his taxes and debts when due or called for, so that he has not officers' fees to pay, nor expenses of courts. He does not frequent the tavern, and drink up all his earnings in liquor that does him no good. He puts his money to use, that is, he buys more land, or stock, or lends his money at interest—in short, he makes his money produce some profit or income. These savings and profits, though small by themselves, amount in a year to a considerable sum, and in a few years they swell to an estate—Thrifty becomes a wealthy farmer, with several hundred acres of land, and a hundred head of cattle.

Very different is the management of UNTHRIFTY: He lies in bed till a late hour in the morning—then rises, and goes to the bottle for a dram, or to the tavern for a glass of bitters—Thus he spends six cents before breakfast, for a dram that makes him dull and heavy all day. He gets his breakfast late, when he ought to be at work. When he supposes he is ready to begin the work of the day, he finds he has not the necessary tools, or some of them are out of order,—the plow-share is to be sent half a mile to a blacksmith to be mended; a tooth or two in a rake or the handle of a hoe is broke; or a sythe or an ax is to be ground.—Now, he is in a great hurry, he bustles about to make preparation for work—and what is done in a hurry is ill done—he loses a part of the day in getting ready—and perhaps the time of his workmen. At ten or eleven o'clock, he is ready to go to work—then comes a boy and tells him, the sheep have escaped from the pasture—or the cows have got among his corn—or the hogs into the garden—He frets and storms, and runs to drive them out—a half hour or more time is lost in driving the cattle from mischief, and repairing a poor old broken fence—a fence that answers no purpose but to lull him into security, and teach his horses and cattle to be unruly—After all this bustle, the fatigue of which is worse than common labor, *Unthrifty* is ready to begin a day's work at twelve o'clock.—Thus half his time is lost in supplying defects, which proceed from want of foresight and good management. His small crops are damaged or destroyed by unruly cattle.—His barn is open and leaky, and what little he gathers, is injured by the rain and snow.—His house is in a like condition—the shingles and clapboards fall off and let in the water, which causes the timber, floors and furniture to decay—and exposed to inclemencies of weather, his wife and children fall sick—their time is lost, and the mischief closes with a ruinous train of expenses for medicines and physicians.—After dragging out some years of disappointment, misery and poverty, the lawyer and the sheriff sweep away the scanty remains of his estate. This is the history of UNTHRIFTY—his principal is spent—he has no interest.

Not unlike this, is the history of the Grog-drinker. This man wonders why he does not thrive in the world; he cannot see the reason why his neighbor *Temperance* should be more prosperous than himself—but in truth, he makes no calculations. Ten cents a day for grog, is a small sum, he thinks, which can hurt no man! But let us make an estimate—arithmetic is very useful for a man who ventures to spend small sums every day. Ten cents a day amount in a year to thirty-six dollars and a half—a sum sufficient to buy a good farm-horse! This surely is no small sum for a farmer or mechanic—But in ten years, this sum amounts to three hundred and sixty-five dollars, besides interest in the mean time! What an amount is this for drams and bitters in ten years! it is money enough to build a small house! But look at the amount in thirty years!—One thousand and ninety-five dollars!—What a vast sum to run down one man's throat . . .

GOOD PRONUNCIATION WITH MORAL LESSONS FROM THE AMERICAN SPELLING BOOK (1831) From Noah Webster, *The American Spelling Book* (Middletown, Conn., 1831), pp. 53–57.

Table XIII

LESSONS OF EASY WORDS, TO TEACH CHILDREN TO READ, AND TO KNOW THEIR DUTY

Lesson I

No man may put off the law of God:
My joy is in his law all the day.
O may I not go in the way of sin!
Let me not go in the way of ill men.

II

A bad man is a foe to the law:
It is his joy to do ill.
All men go out of the way.
Who can say he has no sin?

III

The way of man is ill.
My son, do as you are bid:
But if you are bid, do no ill.
See not my sin, and let me not go to the pit.

IV

Rest in the Lord, and mind his word.
My son, hold fast the law that is good.
You must not tell a lie, nor do hurt.
We must let no man hurt us.

V

Do as well as you can, and do no harm.
Mark the man that doth well, and do so too.
Help such as want help, and be kind.
Let your sins past put you in mind to mend.

VI

I will not walk with bad men, that I may not be cast off with them.
I will love the law and keep it.
I will walk with the just and do good.

VII

This life is not long; but the life to come has no end.
We must pray for them that hate us.
We must love them that love not us.
We must do as we like to be done to.

VIII

A bad life will make a bad end.
He must live well that will die well.
He doth live ill that doth not mend.
In time to come we must do no ill.

IX

No man can say that he has done no ill.
For all men have gone out of the way.
There is none that doeth good; no, not one.
If I have done harm, I must do it no more.

X

Sin will lead us to pain and wo.
Love that which is good, and shun vice.
Hate no man, but love both friends and foes.
A bad man can take no rest, day nor night.

XI

He who came to save us, will wash us from all sin; I will be glad in his name.

A good boy will do all that is just; he will flee from vice; he will do good, and walk in the way of life.

Love not the world, nor the things that are in the world; for they are sin.

I will not fear what flesh can do to me; for my trust is in him who made the world.

He is nigh to them that pray to him, and praise his name.

XII

Be a good child; mind your book; love your school, and strive to learn.

Tell no tales; call no ill names; you must not lie, nor swear, nor cheat, nor steal.

Play not with bad boys; use no ill words at play; spend your time well; live in peace, and shun all strife. This is the way to make good men love you, and save your soul from pain and woe.

XIII

A good child will not lie, swear, nor steal.—He will be good at home, and ask to read his book; when he gets up he will wash his hands and face clean; he will comb his hair, and make haste to school; he will not play by the way, as bad boys do.

XIV

When good boys and girls are at school, they will mind their books, and try to learn to spell and read well, and not play in the time of school.

SELECTION FROM McGUFFEY'S SECOND ECLECTIC READER

(1879)   From William Holmes McGuffey, *McGuffey's Second Eclectic Reader, Revised* (Cincinnati, 1879), pp. 11–12.

---

news′pā per	cold	ôr′der	sēem	through
stŏck′ings	chăt	sto′ry	light	Hăr′ry
brănch′es	kĭss	bûrns	Mrs.	e vĕnts′
an ŏth′er	Mr.	stōōl	lămp	mĕnds

Evening at Home

1. It is winter. The cold wind whistles through the branches of the trees.

2. Mr. Brown has done his day's work, and his children, Harry and Kate, have come home from school. They learned their lessons well to-day, and both feel happy.

3. Tea is over. Mrs. Brown has put the little sitting-room in order. The fire burns brightly. One lamp gives light enough for all. On the stool is a basket of fine apples. They seem to say, "Won't you have one?"

4. Harry and Kate read a story in a new book. The father reads his newspaper, and the mother mends Harry's stockings.

5. By and by, they will tell one another what they have been reading about, and will have a chat over the events of the day.

6. Harry and Kate's bed-time will come first. I think I see them kiss their dear father and mother a sweet good-night.

7. Do you not wish that every boy and girl could have a home like this?

LESSONS IN ARTICULATION AND PRONUNCIATION FROM McGUFFEY'S THIRD ECLECTIC READER (1848) From William Holmes McGuffey, *McGuffey's Newly Revised Third Eclectic Reader* (Cincinnati, 1848), pp. 10–11.

Articulation

To TEACHERS.—An eminent orator being asked, what was the first requisite in a public speaker, replied;—ENUNCIATION. Being asked what was the quality second in importance, he again replied;—ENUNCIATION. The question being repeated as to the third essential qualification, he still answered;—ENUNCIATION. In other words, this quality is of so great importance in public speaking, in *reading*, and in conversation, that all other excellencies dwindle into comparative insignificance. Nothing, indeed, can compensate for an indistinct and deficient utterance.

This will appear evident, if we reflect, for a moment, upon the use of language. Words are useful only as conductors of ideas, and these ideas cannot be comprehended, until the words which convey them are clearly appreciated, and these words cannot be thus appreciated, unless uttered with a sufficient degree of distinctness, force, and accuracy.

That there is a great and general defect in early education, in this particular, all who are acquainted with the subject, will bear testimony. The remedy can only be applied where the evil commences. There is no inherent difficulty in this part of education, any more than in other departments. The faculty of articulating distinctly, and of pronouncing correctly, may be acquired with as much certainty as that of spelling. All that is necessary for this purpose, is that the same degree of attention should be devoted to it.

This is pre-eminently a branch, which can be taught only by example. The teacher's voice must be the model, and the pupil must imitate him, and practice, in this way, must be persevered in, until the object is accomplished. It will require persevering and laborious exertion, both on the part of the teacher and on that of the pupil, but their efforts will, in the end, be richly rewarded.

Nothing more is intended in these remarks, than to throw out a few hints for the consideration of teachers. With this view, also, exercises are subjoined, intended to illustrate some of the more common errors into which learners are liable to fall, and to exhibit the best methods for practice in articulation.

In practicing upon these exercises, and others of a similar nature, the pupil should be made to see in what consists the common error, and then directed to pronounce the word with distinctness and force, giving to each letter its full and appropriate sound.

In correcting errors of this kind, it is important to guard against any change in the accent, and to avoid giving, in pronunciation, any undue prominence to the syllable corrected.

Exercises in Articulation and Pronunciation

N. B. The letters placed in *italics,* in these exercises, are *not silent letters,* but are italicized, to point them out as the letters which are apt to be badly articulated or pronounced, whereas, they should receive their full and proper sound.

EXERCISE I

In the following, and similar words, the letter *a* is often indistinctly articulated, or improperly sounded; as, fat'l for fat*a*l; thus, "That is a fat'l mistake," for "That is a fat*a*l mistake;" or "He 'pears well," or "He *u*ppears well," for "He *a*ppears well."

Incorrect.		Correct.	Incorrect.		Correct.
fa-t'l	*for*	fa-t*a*l.	sep-*er*-ate	*for*	sep-*a*-rate.
met'l	"	met-*a*l.	tem-per-*u*nce	"	tem-per-*a*nce.
mu-si-c'l	"	mu-sic-*a*l.	fur-ther-*u*nce	"	fur-ther-*a*nce.
cap-i-t'l	"	cap-i-t*a*l.	*u*p-pear	"	*a*p-pear.
nu-mer-i-c'l	"	nu-mer-ic-*a*l.	*u*p-prove	"	*a*p-prove.
crit-i-c*u*l	"	crit-ic-*a*l.	*u*p-ply	"	*a*p-ply.
prin-ci-p*u*l	"	prin-ci-p*a*l.	tem-per-*it*	"	tem-per-*a*te.
fes-ti-v*u*l	"	fes-ti-v*a*l.	mod-er-*it*	"	mod-er-*a*te.
test'ment	"	test-*a*-ment.	in-ti-m*it*	"	in-ti-m*a*te.
firm'ment	"	firm-*a*-ment.	a-mal-*gur*-mate	"	a-mal-g*a*-mate.

EXERCISE II

In the following words, and those of a similar character, the *e* is often omitted or improperly sounded; as ev'ry for ev*e*ry; mom*u*nt for mom*e*nt; thus; "Ev'ry mom*u*nt is precious," for "Ev*e*ry mom*e*nt is precious."

Incorrect.		Correct.	Incorrect.		Correct.
ev'ry	*for*	ev-*e*r-y.	sev'ral	*for*	sev-*e*r-al.
b'lief	"	be-lief.	c'leb-ri-ty	"	c*e*-leb-ri-ty.
pr'vail	"	pr*e*-vail.	'spy	"	*e*s-py.
pr'dict	"	pr*e*-dict.	'special	"	*e*s-pe-cial.
trav'ler	"	trav-*e*l-er.	ev-i-d*u*nce.	"	ev-i-d*e*nce.
mur-d'rer	"	mur-d*e*r-er.	prov-i-d*u*nce.	"	prov-i-d*e*nce.
flut'ring	"	flut-t*e*r-ing.	si-l*u*nt	"	si-l*e*nt.
in-t'rest-ing	"	in-t*e*r-est-ing.	test-a-m*u*nt	"	test-a-ment.
tel'scope	"	tel-*e*-scope.	mon-u-m*u*nt	"	mon-u-ment.

LESSON FROM McGUFFEY'S THIRD ECLECTIC READER (1848)

From William Holmes McGuffey, *McGuffey's Newly Revised Third Eclectic Reader* (Cincinnati, 1848), pp. 32–34.

Lesson V

WORDS TO BE SPELLED AND DEFINED

A-light'-ed, got off, descended from.

O-ver-take', to come up with.

Clev'-er-ly, handsomely, skillfully.

Shel'-ter, that which protects.

O-bli -ging, kind, ready to assist.

Phi-los'-o-pher, a man learned in science, *here used figuratively for* a contented person.

Con-tent -ed, quiet, satisfied.

The Little Philosopher

RULE.—This kind of composition is called *Dialogue*. It should be read with the same tone, and in the same manner, that we use in conversation.

Mr. Lenox was one morning riding by himself; he alighted from his horse to look at something on the roadside; the horse got loose and ran away from him. Mr. Lenox ran after him, but could not overtake him. A little boy, at work in a field, heard the horse; and, as soon as he saw him running from his master, ran very quickly to the middle of the road, and catching him by the bridle, stopped him, till Mr. Lenox came up.

Mr. Lenox. Thank you, my good boy, you have caught my horse very cleverly. What shall I give you for your trouble?

Boy. I want nothing, sir.

Mr. L. Do you want nothing? So much the better for you. Few men can say as much. But what were you doing in the field?

B. I was rooting up weeds, and tending the sheep that were feeding on turnips.

Mr. L. Do you like to work?

B. Yes, sir, very well, this fine weather.

Mr. L. But would you not rather play?

B. This is not hard work; it is almost as good as play.

Mr. L. Who set you to work?

B. My father, sir.

Mr. L. What is your name?

B. Peter Hurdle, sir.

Mr. L. How old are you?

B. Eight years old, next June.

Mr. L. How long have you been out in this field?

B. Ever since six o'clock this morning.

Mr. L. Are you not hungry?

B. Yes, sir, but I shall go to dinner soon.

Mr. L. If you had sixpence now, what would you do with it?

B. I do not know, sir. I never had so much in my life.

Mr. L. Have you no play things?

B. Play things? what are they?

Mr. L. Such as nine-pins, marbles, tops, and wooden horses.

B. No, sir. Tom and I play at foot-ball in winter, and I have a jumping-rope. I had a hoop, but it is broken.

Mr. L. Do you want nothing else?

B. I have hardly time to play with what I have. I have to drive the cows, and to run of errands, and to ride the horses to the fields, and that is as good as play.

Mr. L. You could get apples and cakes, if you had money, you know.

B. I can have apples at home. As for cake, I do not want that; my mother makes me a pie now and then, which is as good.

Mr. L. Would you not like a knife to cut sticks?

B. I have one; here it is; brother Tom gave it to me.

Mr. L. Your shoes are full of holes. Don't you want a new pair?

B. I have a better pair for Sundays.

Mr. L. But these let in water.

B. I don't mind that, sir.

Mr. L. Your hat is all torn, too.

B. I have a better hat at home.

Mr. L. What do you do when it rains?

B. If it rains very hard when I am in the field, I get under the tree for shelter.

Mr. L. What do you do, if you are hungry before it is time to go home?

B. I sometimes eat a raw turnip.

Mr. L. But if there are none?

B. Then I do as well as I can without. I work on, and never think of it.

Mr. L. Why, my little fellow, you are quite a *philosopher,* but I am sure you do not know what that means.

B. No, sir. I hope it means no harm.

Mr. L. No, no! Were you ever at school?

B. No, sir; but father means to send me next winter.

Mr. L. You will want books then.

B. Yes, sir, the boys all have an Eclectic spelling book and Reader, and a Testament.

Mr. L. Then I will give them to you; tell your father so, and that it is because you are an obliging, contented little boy.

B. I will, sir, Thank you.

Mr. L. Good by, Peter.

B. Good morning, sir.

QUESTIONS

What service did this little boy perform for the gentleman? Would he take any pay for it? What did the gentleman think of the boy? What do you suppose made him so contented with his condition? Why should we always be contented with such things as we have? What note is that which is placed after all the questions in this lesson? What stop is that after the last word "sir?"

What nouns are there in the first sentence of this lesson? In what number is each? What is the plural number of each?

ARTICULATION

Be careful to utter *g* distinctly. Morn-ing, not *morn-in:* ri-ding not *ri-din:* run-ning, not *run-nin:* catch-ing, not *catch-in:* noth-ing, not *noth-in:* root-ing, not *root-in:* tend-ing, not *tend-in:* feed-ing, not *feed-in:* spell-ing, not *spell-in.*

TO TEACHERS

The amount of instruction derived from reading exercises, may be increased by introducing, occasionally, questions upon *grammatical construction*. These will assist the pupil in understanding the lesson, and afford valuable *practice* in parsing, and will add interest and variety to the recitation. A few questions are appended to some of the lessons in this book, as specimens of the kind of examination which, it is believed, will be found interesting and instructive.

LESSONS IN SPEECH FROM McGUFFEY'S NEW FOURTH ECLECTIC READER (1867)   From William Holmes McGuffey. *McGuffey's New Fourth Eclectic Reader* (Cincinnati, 1867), pp. 28–29.

TS FINAL

Incorrect.		*Correct.*	*Incorrect.*		*Correct.*
Hoce	*for*	hos*ts*.	sec's	*for*	sec*ts*.
boce	"	bos*ts*.	bus	"	bus*ts*.
tes	"	tes*ts*.	cense	"	cen*ts*.
lif's	"	lif*ts*.	tense	"	ten*ts*.
tuff's	"	tuf*ts*.	ob-jec's	"	ob-jec*ts*.
ac's	"	ac*ts*.	re-spec's	"	re-spec*ts*.

Exercise VI

SENTENCES like the following may be often read with great advantage, for the purpose of acquiring distinctness and precision in articulation.

This *act*, more than all other *acts*, laid the *ax* at the root of the evil. It is *false* to say he had no other *faults*.

The *hosts* still stand in strangest plight. That la*st* still night. That la*sts* till night. On *either* side *an* ocean exists. On neither side *a* notion exists.

Among the rugged rocks the restless ranger ran. I said *pop-u-lar*, not pop'lar. I said *pre-vail*, not pr'vail. I said *be-hold*, not b'hold.

Thinkst thou so meanly of my *Phocion? Henceforth* look *to* your *hearths.* Canst thou *minister* to a *mind* diseased? A thousand *shrieks* for hopeless mercy call.

The preceding exercises have been prepared with much care, and, it is believed, will be found very useful in aiding the teacher and pupil in this much-neglected department of education. It must be borne in mind that very much depends upon the teacher; that unremitting attention on his part is absolutely necessary; that his voice must be the model for the pupil; and that repeated and persevering practice is necessary, but will, with great certainty, produce the desired result.

Bad habits in articulation are almost always formed in early childhood, and *very young* children may be made to understand and profit by instruction on the subject. But, once more, let it be remembered that everything in this matter depends upon the teacher.

Accent

Accent, marked thus ('), is an increased force of voice upon some one syllable of a word; as,

Col′o-ny, bot′a-ny; re-mem′ber, im-port′ant; rec-ol-lect′, rep-re-sent′.

In the words *col′o-ny* and *bot′a-ny,* the *first* syllable is accented. In the words *re-mem′ber* and *im-port′ant,* the *second* syllable is accented. In the words *rec-ol-lect′* and *rep-re-sent′,* the *third* syllable is accented.

Inflection

Is an upward or downward slide of the voice.

The rising inflection, marked thus (′) is an *upward* slide of the voice.

EXAMPLES

Has he come ?	. . . . To be read thus:	Has he come?
Has he gone′?	. . . .	Has he gone?
Are you sick ?	. . . .	Are you sick?
Will you go ?	. . . .	Will you go?
Are they here′?	. . . .	Are they here?

The falling inflection, marked thus (ˋ), is a *downward* slide of the voice.

EXAMPLES

They are here	. . . . To be read thus:	They are here.
He has goneˋ	. . . .	He has gone.
He has comeˋ	. . . .	He has come.
I will goˋ	. . . .	I will go.
I am well	. . . .	I am well.

THE
PROFESSION
OF EDUCATION

1387

SELECTION FROM McGUFFEY'S FIFTH ECLECTIC READER

(1879)   From William Holmes McGuffey, *McGuffey's Fifth Eclectic Reader, Revised* (Cincinnati, 1879), pp. 51–55.

I. The Good Reader

1. It is told of Frederick the Great, King of Prussia, that, as he was seated one day in his private room, a written petition was brought to him with the request that it should be immediately read. The King had just returned from hunting, and the glare of the sun, or some other cause, had so dazzled his eyes that he found it difficult to make out a single word of the writing.

2. His private secretary happened to be absent; and the soldier who brought the petition could not read. There was a page, or favorite boy-servant, waiting in the hall, and upon him the king called. The page was a son of one of the noblemen of the court, but proved to be a very poor reader.

3. In the first place, he did not articulate distinctly. He huddled his words together in the utterance, as if they were syllables of one long word, which he must get through with as speedily as possible. His pronunciation was bad, and he did not modulate his voice so as to bring out the meaning of what he read. Every sentence was uttered with a dismal monotony of voice, as if it did not differ in any respect from that which preceded it.

4. "Stop!" said the King, impatiently. "Is it an auctioneer's list of goods to be sold that you are hurrying over? Send your companion to me." Another page who stood at the door now entered, and to him the King gave the petition. The second page began by hemming and clearing his throat in such an affected manner that the King jokingly asked him if he had not slept in the public garden, with the gate open, the night before.

5. The second page had a good share of self-conceit, however, and so was not greatly confused by the King's jest. He determined that he would avoid the mistake which his comrade had made. So he commenced reading the petition slowly and with great formality, emphasizing every word, and prolonging the articulation of every syllable. But his manner was so tedious that the King cried out, "Stop! are you reciting a lesson in the elementary sounds? Out of the room! But no: stay! Send me that little girl who is sitting there by the fountain."

6. The girl thus pointed out by the King was a daughter of one of the laborers employed by the royal gardener: and she had come to help her father weed the flower-beds. It chanced that, like many of the poor people in Prussia, she had received a good education. She was somewhat alarmed when she found herself in the King's presence, but took courage when the King told her that he only wanted her to read for him, as his eyes were weak.

7. Now, Ernestine (for this was the name of the little girl) was fond of reading aloud, and often many of the neighbors would assemble at her father's house to hear her; those who could not read themselves would come to her, also, with their letters from distant friends or children, and she thus formed the habit of reading various sorts of hand-writing promptly and well.

8. The King gave her the petition, and she rapidly glanced through the opening lines to get some idea of what it was about. As she read, her eyes began to glisten, and her breast to heave. "What is the matter?" asked the King; "don't you know

how to read?" "Oh, yes! sire," she replied, addressing him with the title usually applied to him: "I will now read it, if you please."

9. The two pages were about to leave the room. "Remain," said the King. The little girl began to read the petition. It was from a poor widow, whose only son had been drafted to serve in the army, although his health was delicate and his pursuits had been such as to unfit him for military life. His father had been killed in battle, and the son had a strong desire to become a portrait-painter.

10. The writer told her story in a simple, concise manner, that carried to the heart a belief of its truth; and Ernestine read it with so much feeling, and with an articulation so just, in tones so pure and distinct, that when she had finished, the King, into whose eyes the tears had started, exclaimed, "Oh! now I understand what it is all about; but I might never have known, certainly I never should have felt, its meaning had I trusted to these young gentlemen, whom I now dismiss from my service for one year, advising them to occupy the time in learning to read."

11. "As for you, my young lady," continued the King, "I know you will ask no better reward for your trouble than the pleasure of carrying to this poor widow my order for her son's immediate discharge. Let me see if you can write as well as you can read. Take this pen, and write as I dictate." He then dictated an order, which Ernestine wrote, and he signed. Calling one of his guards, he bade him go with the girl and see that the order was obeyed.

12. How much happiness was Ernestine the means of bestowing through her good elocution, united to the happy circumstance that brought it to the knowledge of the King! First, there were her poor neighbors, to whom she could give instruction and entertainment. Then, there was the poor widow who sent the petition, and who not only regained her son, but received through Ernestine an order for him to paint the King's likeness; so that the poor boy soon rose to great distinction, and had more orders than he could attend to. Words could not express his gratitude, and that of his mother, to the little girl.

13. And Ernestine had, moreover, the satisfaction of aiding her father to rise in the world, so that he became the King's chief gardener. The King did not forget her, but had her well educated at his own expense. As for the two pages, she was indirectly the means of doing them good, also; for, ashamed of their bad reading, they commenced studying in earnest, till they overcame the faults that had offended the King. Both finally rose to distinction, one as a lawyer, and the other as a statesman; and they owed their advancement in life chiefly to their good elocution.

DEFINITIONS

1. Pe-tĭ tion, *a formal request.* 3. Ar-tĭc ū-lāte, *to utter the elementary sounds.* Mŏd ū-lāte, *to vary or inflect.* Mo-nŏt o-ny, *lack of variety.* 4. Af-fĕct ed, *unnatural and silly.* 9. Drăft ed, *selected by lot.* 10. Con-çĭse, *brief and full of meaning.* 11. Dis-chàrge, *release.* Dĭc tāte, *to utter so that another may write down.* 12. Distĭnc tion, *honorable and notable position.* Ex-prĕss, *to make known the feelings of.*

NOTES

Frederick II. of Prussia (*b.* 1712, *d.* 1786), or Frederick the Great, as he was called, was one of the greatest of German rulers. He was distinguished for his military exploits, for his wise and just government, and for his literary attainments. He wrote many able works in the French language. Many pleasant anecdotes are told of this king, of which the one given in the lesson is a fair sample.

**LESSON IN VOICE AND GESTURE FROM McGUFFEY'S SIXTH
ECLECTIC READER (1867)**   From William Holmes McGuffey, *McGuffey's New Sixth
Eclectic Reader* (Cincinnati, 1867), pp. 57–59.

VI. Gesture

It is not designed, in this book, to give a minute system of rules and instructions on the subject of Gesture. That would be a difficult task without the assistance of plates; and even with their aid, any directions must be very imperfect, without the example and illustrations of the living teacher, as the speaking model. It will be sufficient to give some general hints by means of which the student may form rules, or pursue a discipline for himself.

Gesture is that part of the speaker's manner which pertains to his attitude, to the use and carriage of his person, and the movement of his limbs in delivery.

Every person, in beginning to speak, feels the natural embarrassment resulting from his new position. The novelty of the situation destroys his self-possession, and, with the loss of that, he becomes awkward, his arms and hands hang clumsily, and now, for the first time, seem to him worse than superflous members. This embarrassment will be overcome gradually, as the speaker becomes faimiliar with his position; and it is sometimes overcome at once, by a powerful exercise of the attention upon the matter of the speech. When that fills and possesses the mind, the orator insensibly takes the attitude which is becoming, and, at least, easy and natural, if not graceful.

*   *   *

1st. The first general direction that should be given to the speaker is, that he should stand erect and firm, and in that posture which gives an expanded chest and full play to the organs of respiration and utterance.

2d. Let the attitude be such that it can be shifted with ease, and without shuffling and hitching the limbs. The student will find, by trial, that no attitude is so favorable to this end, as that in which the weight of the body is thrown upon one leg, leaving the other free to be advanced or thrown back, as fatigue or the proper action of delivery may require.

The student, who has any regard to grace or elegance, will of course avoid all the gross faults which are so common among public speakers, such as resting one foot upon a stool or bench, or throwing the body lazily forward upon the support of the rostrum.

3d. Next to attitude, come the movements of the person and limbs. In these, two objects are to be observed, and, if possible, combined, viz., *propriety* and *grace.* There is expression in the extended arm, the clinched hand, the open palm, and the smiting of the breast. But let no gesture be made that is not in harmony with the thought or sentiment that is uttered; for it is this harmony which constitutes propriety. As far as possible, let there be a correspondence between the style of action and the train of thought. Where the thought flows on calmly and sweetly, let there be the same graceful and easy flow of gesture and action. Where the style is sharp and abrupt, there is propriety in the quick, short, and abrupt gesticulation.

Especially avoid that ungraceful sawing of the air with the arms, into which an ill-regulated fervor betrays many young speakers.

What is called a *graceful manner,* can only be attained by those who have some natural advantages of person. So far as it is in the reach of study or practice, it seems to depend chiefly upon the general cultivation of manners, implying freedom from all embarrassments, and entire self-possession. The whole secret of acquiring a graceful style of gesture, we apprehend, lies in the habitual practice, not only when speaking, but at all times, of free and graceful movements of the limbs.

There is no limb nor feature, which the accomplished speaker will not employ with effect, in the course of a various and animated delivery. But the arms are the chief reliance of the orator in gesture; and it will not be amiss to give a hint or two in reference to their proper use.

And *first;—*It is not an uncommon fault to use one arm exclusively, and to give that a uniform movement. Such movement may, sometimes, have grown habitual from one's profession or employment. But in learners, also, there is often a predisposition to this fault.

*Secondly;—*It is not unusual to see a speaker use only the lower half of his arm. This always gives a stiff and constrained manner to delivery. Let the whole arm move, and let the movement be free and flowing.

*Thirdly;—*As a general rule, let the hand be open, with the fingers slightly curved. It then seems liberal, communicative, and candid; and, in some degree, gives that expression to the style of delivery. Of course, there are passages which require the clinched hand, the pointed finger, &c.; but these are used to give a particular expression.

*Fourthly;—*In the movements of the arm, study variety and the grace of curved lines.

When a gesture is made with one arm only, the *eye* should be cast in the direction of that arm; not *at* it, but *over* it.

All speakers employ, more or less, the motions of the head. In reference to that member, we make but one observation. Avoid the continuous bobbing and shaking of the head, which is so conspicuous in the action of many ambitious public speakers.

The beauty and force of all gesture consist in its timely, judicious, and natural employment, when it can serve to illustrate the meaning, or give emphasis to the force of an important passage. The usual fault of young speakers is too much action. To emphasize all parts alike, is equivalent to no emphasis; and by employing forcible festures on unimportant passages, we diminish our power to render other parts impressive.

THE LESSON OF AMERICAN HISTORY (1859)   From John Bonner, *A Child's History of the United States* (New York, 1859), vol. II, pp. 319–20.

I have tried to recount how a few straggling bands of poor wanderers, seeking a scanty living on the wild sea-coast of America, have grown to be one of the greatest nations of the earth. It is a beautiful and a wonderful subject to write about, and I wish, for your sake, that I had written the story with more skill.

No other people, since the world began, ever grew out of so small a beginning to so towering a height of power and prosperity in so short a time. If you seek to know why your countrymen have outstripped all the nations of the earth in this respect, the reason is easily found. The founders of this nation were honest, true men. They were sincere in all they said, upright in all their acts. They feared God and obeyed the laws. They wrought constantly and vigorously at the work they had to do, and strove to live at peace with their neighbors. When they were attacked they fought like men, and, defeated or victorious, would not have peace till their point was gained. Above all, they insisted, from the very first, on being free themselves, and securing freedom for you, their children.

If you follow the example they set, and love truth, honor, religion, and freedom as deeply, and, if need be, defend them as stoutly as they did, the time is not far distant when this country will as far excel other countries in power, wealth, numbers, intelligence, and every good thing, as other countries excelled it before Columbus sailed away from Spain to discover the New World.

THE RISE OF HARRY WALTON (1874)   From Horatio Alger, *Risen From the Ranks; or Harry Walton's Success* (New York, 1874), pp. vii–viii, 9–17, 343–349

Preface

"RISEN FROM THE RANKS" contains the further history of Harry Walton, who was first introduced to the public in the pages of "Bound to Rise." Those who are interested in learning how far he made good the promise of his boyhood, may here find their curiosity gratified. For the benefit of those who may only read the present volume, a synopsis of Harry's previous life is given in the first chapter.

In describing Harry's rise from the ranks I have studiously avoided the extraordinary incidents and pieces of good luck, which the story writer has always at command, being desirous of presenting my hero's career as one which may be imitated by the thousands of boys similarly placed, who, like him, are anxious to rise from the ranks. It is my hope that this story, suggested in part by the career of an eminent American editor, may afford encouragement to such boys, and teach them that "where there is a will there is always a way."

Chapter I

"I am sorry to part with you, Harry," said Professor Henderson. "You have been a very satisfactory and efficient assistant, and I shall miss you."

"Thank you, sir," said Harry. "I have tried to be faithful to your interests."

"You have been so," said the Professor emphatically. "I have had perfect confidence in you, and this has relieved me of a great deal of anxiety. It would have been very easy for one in your position to cheat me out of a considerable sum of money."

"It was no credit to me to resist such a temptation as that," said Harry.

"I am glad to hear you say so, but it shows your inexperience nevertheless. Money is the great tempter nowadays. Consider how many defalcations and breaches of trust we read of daily in confidential positions, and we are forced to conclude that honesty is a rarer virtue than we like to think it. I have every reason to believe that my assistant last winter purloined, at the least, a hundred dollars, but I was unable to prove it, and submitted to the loss. It may be the same next winter. Can't I induce you to change your resolution, and remain in my employ? I will advance your pay."

"Thank you, Professor Henderson," said Harry gratefully. "I appreciate your offer, even if I do not accept it. But I have made up my mind to learn the printing business."

"You are to enter the office of the 'Centreville Gazette,' I believe."

"Yes, sir."

"How much pay will you get?"

"I shall receive my board the first month, and for the next six months have agreed to take two dollars a week and board."

"That won't pay your expenses."

"It *must*," said Harry, firmly.

"You have laid up some money while with me, haven't you!"

"Yes, sir; I have fifty dollars in my pocket-book, besides having given eighty dollars at home."

"That is doing well, but you won't be able to lay up anything for the next year."

"Perhaps not in money, but I shall be gaining the knowledge of a good trade."

"And you like that better than remaining with me, and learning my business?"

"Yes, sir."

"Well, perhaps you are right. I don't fancy being a magician myself; but I am too old to change. I like moving round, and I make a good living for my family. Besides I contribute to the innocent amusement of the public, and earn my money fairly."

"I agree with you, sir," said Harry. "I think yours is a useful employment, but it would not suit everybody. Ever since I read the life of Benjamin Franklin, I have wanted to learn to be a printer."

"It is an excellent business, no doubt, and if you have made up your mind I will not dissuade you. When you have a paper of your own, you can give your old friend, Professor Henderson, an occasional puff."

"I shall be glad to do that," said Harry, smiling, "but I shall have to wait some time first."

"How old are you now?"

"Sixteen."

"Then you may qualify yourself for an editor in five or six years. I advise you to try it at any rate. The editor in America is a man of influence."

"I do look forward to it," said Harry, seriously. "I should not be satisfied to remain a journeyman all my life, nor even the half of it."

"I sympathize with your ambition, Harry," said the Professor, earnestly, "and I wish you the best success. Let me hear from you occasionally."

"I should be very glad to write you, sir."

"I see the stage is at the door, and I must bid you good-by. When you have a vacation, if you get a chance to come our way, Mrs. Henderson and myself will be glad to receive a visit from you. Good-by!" And with a hearty shake of the hand, Professor Henderson bade farewell to his late assistant.

Those who have read "Bound to Rise," and are thus familiar with Harry Walton's early history, will need no explanation of the preceding conversation. But for the benefit of new readers, I will recapitulate briefly the leading events in the history of the boy of sixteen who is to be our hero.

Harry Walton was the oldest son of a poor New Hampshire farmer, who found great difficulty in wresting from his few sterile acres a living for his family. Nearly a year before, he had lost his only cow by a prevalent disease, and being without money, was compelled to buy another of Squire Green, a rich but mean neighbor, on a six months' note, on very unfavorable terms. As it required great economy to make both ends meet, there seemed no possible chance of his being able to meet the note at maturity. Beside, Mr. Walton was to forfeit ten dollars if he did not have the principal and interest ready for Squire Green. The hard-hearted creditor was mean enough to take advantage of his poor neighbor's necessities, and there was not the slightest chance of his receding from his unreasonable demand. Under these circumstances Harry, the oldest boy, asked his father's permission to go out into the world and earn his own living. He hoped not only to do this, but to save something toward paying his father's note. His ambition had been kindled by reading the life of Benjamin Franklin, which had been awarded to him as a school prize. He did not expect to emulate Franklin, but he thought that by imitating him he might attain an honorable position in the community.

Harry's request was not at first favorably received. To send a boy out into the world to earn his own living is a hazardous experiment, and fathers are less sanguine than their sons. Their experience suggests difficulties and obstacles of which the inexperienced youth knows and possesses nothing. But in the present case Mr. Walton reflected that the little farming town in which he lived offered small inducements for a boy to remain there, unless he was content to be a farmer, and this required capital. His farm was too small for himself, and of course he could not give Harry a part when he came of age. On the whole, therefore, Harry's plan of becoming a mechanic seemed not so bad a one after all. So permission was accorded, and our hero, with his little bundle of clothes, left the paternal roof, and went out in quest of employment.

After some adventures Harry obtained employment in a shoe-shop as pegger. A few weeks sufficed to make him a good workman, and he was then able to earn three dollars a week and board. Out of this sum he hoped to save enough to pay the note held by Squire Green against his father, but there were two unforeseen obstacles. He had the misfortune to lose his pocket-book, which was picked up by an unprincipled young man, by name Luke Harrison, also a shoemaker, who was always in pecuniary difficulties, though he earned much higher wages than Harry. Luke was unable to resist the temptation, and appropriated the money to his own use. This Harry ascertained after a while, but thus far had succeeded in obtaining the restitution of but a small portion of his hard-earned savings. The second obstacle was a sudden depression in the shoe trade which threw him out of work. More than most occupations the shoe business is liable to these sudden fluctuations and suspensions, and the most industrious and ambitious workman is often compelled to spend in his enforced weeks of idleness all that he had been able to save when employed, and thus at the end of the year finds himself, through no fault of his own, no better off than at the beginning. Finding himself out of work, our hero visited other shoe establishments in the hope of employment. But his search was in vain. Chance in this emergency made him acquainted with Professor Henderson, a well-known magician and conjurer, whose custom it was to travel, through the fall and winter, from town to town, giving public exhibitions of his skill. He was in want of an assistant, to sell tickets and help him generally, and he offered the position to our hero, at a salary of five dollars a week. It is needless to say that the position was gladly accepted. It was not the business that Harry preferred, but he reasoned justly that it was honorable, and was far better than remaining idle. He found Professor Henderson as he called himself, a considerate and agreeable employer, and as may be inferred from the conversation with which this chapter begins, his services were very satisfactory. At the close of the six months, he had the satisfaction of paying the note which his father had given, and so of disappointing the selfish schemes of the grasping creditor.

This was not all. He met with an adventure while travelling for the Professor, in which a highwayman who undertook to rob him, came off second best, and he was thus enabled to add fifty dollars to his savings. His financial condition at the opening of the present story has already been set forth.

Though I have necessarily omitted many interesting details, to be found in "Bound to Rise," I have given the reader all the information required to enable him to understand the narrative of Harry's subsequent fortunes.

*   *   *

Conclusion

I have thus traced in detail the steps by which Harry Walton ascended from the condition of a poor farmer's son to the influential position of editor of a weekly newspaper. I call to mind now, however, that he is no longer a boy, and his future career will be of less interest to my young readers. Yet I hope they may be interested to hear, though not in detail, by what successive steps he rose still higher in position and influence.

Harry was approaching his twenty-first birthday when he was waited upon by a deputation of citizens from a neighboring town, inviting him to deliver a Fourth of July oration. He was at first disposed, out of modesty, to decline; but, on consultation with Ferguson, decided to accept and do his best. He was ambitious to produce a good impression, and his experience in the Debating Society gave him a moderate degree of confidence and self-reliance. When the time came he fully satisfied public expectation. I do not say that his oration was a model of eloquence, for that could not have been expected of one whose advantages had been limited, and one for whom I have never claimed extraordinary genius. But it certainly was well written and well delivered, and very creditable to the young orator. The favor with which it was received may have had something to do in influencing the people of Centreville to nominate and elect him to the New Hampshire Legislature a few months later.

He entered that body, the youngest member in it. But his long connection with a Debating Society, and the experience he had gained in parliamentary proceedings, enabled him at once to become a useful working member. He was successively re-elected for several years, during which he showed such practical ability that he obtained a State reputation. At twenty-eight he received a nomination for Congress, and was elected by a close vote. During all this time he remained in charge of the Centreville "Gazette," but of course had long relinquished the task of a compositor into his brother's hands. He had no foolish ideas about this work being beneath him; but he felt that he could employ his time more profitably in other ways. Under his judicious management, the "Gazette" attained a circulation and influence that it had never before reached. The income derived from it was double that which it yielded in the days of his predecessor; and both he and Ferguson were enabled to lay by a few hundred dollars every year. But Harry had never sought wealth. He was content with a comfortable support and a competence. He liked influence and the popular respect, and he was gratified by the important trusts which he received. He was ambitious, but it was a creditable and honorable ambition. He sought to promote the public welfare, and advance the public interests, both as a speaker and as a writer; and though sometimes misrepresented, the people on the whole did him justice.

A few weeks after he had taken his seat in Congress, a young man was ushered into his private room. Looking up, he saw a man of about his own age, dressed with some attempt at style, but on the whole wearing a look of faded gentility.

"Mr. Walton," said the visitor, with some hesitation.

"That is my name. Won't you take a seat?"

The visitor sat down, but appeared ill at ease. He nervously fumbled at his hat, and did not speak.

"Can I do anything for you?" asked Harry, at length.

"I see you don't know me," said the stranger.

"I can't say I recall your features; but then I see a great many persons."

"I went to school at the Prescott Academy, when you were in the office of the Centreville 'Gazette.' "

Harry looked more closely, and exclaimed, in astonished recognition, "Fitzgerald Fletcher!"

"Yes," said the other, flushing with mortification, "I am Fitzgerald Fletcher."

"I am glad to see you," said Harry, cordially, forgetting the old antagonism that had existed between them.

He rose and offered his hand, which Fletcher took with an air of relief, for he had felt uncertain of his reception.

"You have prospered wonderfully," said Fletcher, with a shade of envy.

"Yes," said Harry, smiling. "I was a printer's devil when you knew me; but I never meant to stay in that position. I have risen from the ranks."

"I haven't," said Fletcher, bitterly.

"Have you been unfortunate? Tell me about it, if you don't mind," said Harry, sympathetically.

"My father failed three years ago," said Fletcher, "and I found myself adrift with nothing to do, and no money to fall back upon. I have drifted about since then; but now I am out of employment. I came to you to-day to see if you will exert your influence to get me a government clerkship, even of the lowest class. You may rest assured, Mr. Walton, that I need it."

Was this the proud Fitzgerald Fletcher, suing, for the means of supporting himself, to one whom, as a boy, he had despised and looked down upon? Surely, the world is full of strange changes and mutations of fortune. Here was a chance for Harry to triumph over his old enemy; but he never thought of doing it. Instead, he was filled with sympathy for one who, unlike himself, had gone down in the social scale, and he cordially promised to see what he could do for Fletcher, and that without delay.

On inquiry, he found Fletcher was qualified to discharge the duties of a clerk, and secured his appointment to a clerkship in the Treasury Department, on a salary of twelve hundred dollars a year. It was an income which Fletcher would once have regarded as wholly insufficient for his needs; but adversity had made him humble, and he thankfully accepted it. He holds the position still, discharging the duties satisfactorily. He is glad to claim the Hon. Harry Walton among his acquaintances, and never sneers at him now as a "printer's devil."

Oscar Vincent spent several years abroad, after graduation, acting as foreign correspondent of his father's paper. He is now his father's junior partner, and is not only respected for his ability, but a general favorite in society, on account of his sunny disposition and cordial good nature. He keeps up his intimacy with Harry Walton. Indeed, there is good reason for this, since Harry, four years since, married his sister Maud, and the two friends are brothers-in-law.

Harry's parents are still living, no longer weighed down by poverty, as when we first made their acquaintance. The legacy which came so opportunely improved their condition, and provided them with comforts to which they had long been strangers. But their chief satisfaction comes from Harry's unlooked-for success in life. Their past life of poverty and privation is all forgotten in their gratitude for this great happiness.

The next and concluding volume of this series will be
HERBERT CARTER'S LEGACY.

Beginnings of Professionalization

STATE TEACHERS' ASSOCIATIONS CALL FOR THE ORGANIZATION OF
A NATIONAL TEACHERS' ASSOCIATION (1857) From Edgar B. Wesley, *NEA:
The First Hundred Years* (New York, 1957), pp. 21–22.

TO THE TEACHERS OF THE UNITED STATES:

The eminent success which has attended the establishment and operations of the several teachers' associations in the states of this country is the source of mutual congratulations among all friends of popular education. To the direct agency and the diffused influence of these associations, more, perhaps than to any other cause, are due the manifest improvement of schools in all their relations, the rapid intellectual and social elevation of teachers as a class, and the vast development of public interest in all that concerns the education of the young.

That the state associations have already accomplished great good, and that they are destined to exert a still broader and more beneficent influence, no wise observer will deny.

Believing that what has been accomplished for the states by state associations may be done for the whole country by a National Association, we, the undersigned, invite our fellow-teachers throughout the United States to assemble in Philadelphia on the 26th day of August next, for the purpose of organizing a National Teachers' Association.

We cordially extend this invitation to all practical teachers in the North, the South, the East, and the West, who are willing to unite in a general effort to promote the general welfare of our country by concentrating the wisdom and power of numerous minds, and distributing among all the accumulated experiences of all; who are ready to devote their energies and their means to advance the dignity, respectability, and usefulness of their calling; and who, in fine, believe that the time has come when the teachers of the nation should gather into one great educational brotherhood.

As the permanent success of any association depends very much upon the auspices attending its establishment, and the character of the organic laws it adopts, it is hoped that all parts of the Union will be largely represented at the inauguration of the proposed enterprise.

ORGANIZATION OF THE NATIONAL TEACHERS' ASSOCIATION

(**1857**)   From *American Journal of Education*, vol. XIV. p. 17.

Philadelphia, August 26, 1857.
To the Teachers of the United States.

The eminent success which has attended the establishment and operations of the several State Teachers' Associations in this country, is the source of mutual congratulations among all friends of Popular Education. To the direct agency, and the diffused influence of these Associations, more, perhaps, than to any other cause, are due the manifest improvement of schools in all their relations, the rapid intellectual and social elevation of teachers as a class, and the vast development of public interest in all that concerns the education of the young.

That the State Associations have already accomplished great good, and that they are destined to exert a still broader and more beneficent influence, no wise observer will deny.

Believing that what has been done for States by State Associations may be done for the whole country by a National Association, we, the undersigned, invite our fellow-teachers throughout the United States to assemble in Philadelphia, on the 26th day of August next, for the purpose of organizing a NATIONAL TEACHERS' ASSOCIATION.

We cordially extend this invitation to all *practical teachers* in the North, the South, the East, and the West, who are willing to unite in a general effort to promote the educational welfare of our country, by concentrating the wisdom and power of numerous minds, and by distributing among all the accumulated experiences of all, who are ready to devote their energies and contribute of their means to advance the dignity, respectability, and usefulness of their calling; and who, in fine, believe that the time has come when the teachers of the nation should gather into one great Educational Brotherhood.

As the permanent success of any association depends very much upon the auspices attending its establishment, and the character of the organic laws it adopts, it is hoped that all parts of the Union will be largely represented at the inauguration of the proposed enterprise.

T. W. Valentine, *President New York State Teachers' Association.*
D. B. Hagar, *President Massachusetts Teachers' Association.*
W. T. Lucky, *President Missouri Teachers' Association.*

AN ADDRESS TO THE ORGANIZING CONVENTION OF THE NATIONAL TEACHERS' ASSOCIATION (1857) From William Russell, "National Organization of Teachers," as quoted in National Education Association, *Proceedings of the Nineteenth Annual Meeting* (Washington, D.C., 1952), pp.435–39.

Fellow teachers: We are met on a great occasion. For the first time in the history of our country, the teachers of youth have assembled as a distinct professional body, representing its peculiar relations to all parts of our great national union of states. The event is a most auspicious one, as regards the intellectual and moral interest of the whole community of which, as citizens, we are members; and, to ourselves, professionally and individually, it opens a view of extended usefulness, in efficient action, such as never yet has been disclosed to us.

We meet not as merely a company of friends and wellwishers to education, one of the great common interests of humanity, in which we are happy to cooperate with philanthropic minds and hearts of every class and calling; but we have at length recognized our peculiar duty to come forward and take our own appropriate place as the immediate agents and appointed organs of whatever measures are best adapted to promote the highest interests of society, by the wider diffusion of whatever benefits are included in the whole range of human culture. In stepping forward to take the professional position now universally accorded to us, we do so in no exclusive or selfish spirit. We are, in fact, only complying with the virtual invitation given us, by all who feel an interest in the advancement of education, to assume, in regular form, the acknowledged responsibilities of our office, as guardians of the mental welfare of the youth of our country, responsible to the whole community for the fidelity and efficiency with which we discharge our trust. The liberal measures recently adopted in so many of our states for the establishment of permanent systems of public education; the generous recognition, now so general, of the value of the teacher's office and his daily labors; the warm reception offered to every form of teachers associations—from those which represent whole states down to the local gatherings in our towns and villages—all intimate the universal readiness of society to welcome the formation of a yet more extensive professional union of teachers—of one coextensive with our national interests and relations.

We meet the invitation, not as a mere professional recognition, entitling us to withdraw from the ground which we have hitherto occupied, in common with friends of education, whether of the learned professions or of other occupations, in the promotion of its interests, and, by an exclusive organization, to cut ourselves off from all communication beyond the limited sphere of a close corporation. It is in no such spirit that we would act. But we do feel that there is a duty devolving on us, as teachers, which we desire to fulfill. We feel that, as a professional body, we are distinctly called on to form a national organization, that we may be the better enabled to meet the continually enlarging demands of our vocation for higher personal attainments in the individual and for more ample qualifications adequately to fill the daily widening sphere of professional action.

We wish, as teachers, to reap whatever benefits our medical brethren derive from their national association, in opportunities of communication for mutual aid and counsel. We desire to see annually a professional gathering, such as may fairly represent the instructors of every grade of schools and higher institutions, thruout the United States. We hope to see a numerous delegation, at such meetings, from every educating state in the Union, of the men who, in their respective state associations of teachers, are already responding to the manifest demand for distinct appropriate professional action, on the part of those on whom devolves the immediate practical business of instruction.

Teaching is, in our day, an occupation lacking neither honor or emolument. Those who pursue this employment are in duty bound to recognize the position which is so liberally assigned them. The vocation is well entitled to all the aid and support which an acknowledged professional rank can confer upon it. The personal interest of every individual who pursues the calling, or who means to adopt it, is concerned in every measure which tends to elevate its character or extend its usefulness. Every teacher who respects himself, and whose heart is in his work, will respond, we think, with alacrity to the call which the establishment of such an association as we propose makes upon him for his best efforts in its aid.

From the formation of a *national* association of teachers, we expect great *national* benefits:

1. As regards *wider* and *juster views of education,* and *corresponding methods of instruction.*

In a progressive community like ours, amid the vast and rapid developments of science by which our times are characterized, and the universal craving for yet better modes of human culture, to imagine that we have already attained to perfection in our modes of education, would be absurd. The statistics of society proclaim the falsity of such an opinion. The daily records of our race tell too plainly the sad story of our deficiencies and our failures, in the prevalent feeble organizations of body, and the imperfect health, which we still owe to our culpable neglect of proper educational training, by which physical vigor and efficiency might be, in great measure, secured to every human being. The teacher, in our large cities, at least, daily finds himself compelled to limit his intellectual requirements to the condition of many minds incapable of sustaining lengthened or vigorous application, or of retaining the rudimental germs which it is his desire to implant. Of our acknowledged defective moral education, it is unnecessary to speak. Thruout our country, the parent is appealing to the teacher, and the teacher to the parent, for efficient effort which may bring about a better state of things. Who will venture, in such circumstances, the assertion that we are already perfect?

The whole ground of education needs a thoro survey and revision, with a view to much more extensive changes and reforms than have yet been attempted. The cry for more healthful, more invigorating, more inspiring, more effective modes of culture, comes up from all classes of society, on behalf of the young who are its treasured hope. A truer and deeper investigation is everywhere needed in regard to the constitution, the capabilities, and the wants of man, equally in his temporal and his eternal relations.

Adverting thus to the acknowledged need of a renovation in the form and character of education, we would not be understood as desiring the indiscriminate subversion of existing modes of culture, or of the institutions to which we have been so largely indebted for whatever degree of mental attainment has character-ized the past, or benefits the present. It belongs to others than teachers to propose those rash and headlong changes, unsanctioned by true philosophy or stable theory, which have demolished without reconstructing, and whose toppling fabrics have served the sole purpose of forming the sepulchral monuments of "zeal without knowledge."

No: one of the surest and best results of a great national association of teachers, will be the careful retention of all unquestionable good residuum gained by the sure filtration of experience; another will be the building up, to yet nobler heights of beneficial influence, the high places of all true learning. Room can be made for the cultivation of all invigorating and purfying influences in human development, without the sacrifice of one valuable acquisition; or, rather, with the addition of many, which a more genial nurture will certainly introduce. But it is high time that the broad experience and observation of teachers, the tried servants of humanity, in all the relations of culture, should unite to claim a hearing on the great subject of their daily duties and endeavors; and that their voice should have its weight in the adoption of the successive steps which the ceaseless advances of knowledge will always require at the hands of education. A harmonious cooperation of educational skill with scientific progress and parental interests, may thus be fully secured for the enlargement and fertilizing of the whole field of mental and moral culture.

A professional association, founded on the broad basis which we now contemplate, will necessarily give unity and effect to communications expressing the views and bearing the sanction of such a body; and instructors thruout our country will thus have an opportunity of contributing more widely, and more effectively, to the furtherance of whatever good is embraced in the whole range of education, whether in its immediate or its remotest results.

2. From the establishment of a national society of teachers, we may justly expect a large amount of *professional benefit to its members.* Fellow teachers! we are not assembled to boast of the dignity of our vocation, or of the intellectual eminence of those who pursue it; but rather, in the spirit of faithful and earnest endeavor, to do what we can to render ourselves, individually and collectively, more worthy of its honors, by becoming more capable of fulfilling its duties.

Contemplating then, in this sober light, the aggregate of such learning and skill as the annual communications of a national reunion of teachers must contribute to our advancement individually, in professional qualifications, we may well congratulate one another on the advantages anticipated as accruing from such occasions. Nor need these advantages be temporary or evanescent. A national association of teachers will necessarily give rise to an appropriate organ of communication between its members themselves, and the community in general. By this means, the fruits of the maturest minds in the ranks of our profession, in the ample discussion of the great primary questions of education, may be daily reaped by the youngest of our corps, while the zeal and enthusiasm, and the ardent aspirations of the youngest, may communicate life and fire to all.

But it is not merely in our professional relations that a national association will benefit us. It will be an invaluable aid to us, as students of the sciences which we teach. We arrogate nothing for our profession, when we say that it includes among its members men of the highest attainments—not to say eminence—in the various departments of science and literature. Their communications with us will be instruction of the highest order, to which it will be a peculiar privilege to listen. If there be any doubt on this point, in any mind, we will verify our assertion by pointing to such men as Agassiz and Guyot, who, in the true spirit of the teacher's vocation, have, for years, so generously dispensed the rich fruits of their own surpassing attainments for the benefit of their fellow teachers, thruout their adopted country. Passing by, however, those luminaries of the upper sphere of science, have we not many in all parts of the Union, who, in comparison of such names, would not be unwilling to be ranked but as among the "lesser lights," and who have no ambition beyond that of contributing their silent personal endeavor to the advancement of knowledge and to the instruction of youth, yet have minds fraught with untold wealth of acquirement, which they would readily lend for the profit and pleasure of others less amply furnished?

But to return to our strictly professional relations. Education is now studied both as a science and as an art. We have among us already, not only those who, by extensive acquirements, and professional skill, and special study, are amply competent to guide the minds of others in the path of philosophical investigation of the principles of education, and to exhibit, in actual application, the methods of instruction which spring from such principles; we have, already, the products of such minds, nurtured and matured in wellendowed and wellconducted professional seminaries, established by enlightened legislation, for the express purpose of furnishing such products in the persons of welltrained, capable, enlightened and successful teachers, of both sexes. With the aid of such minds, in addition to that of the many widely known individuals who have made a lifetime's business of education, and daily live amid an atmosphere of grateful feeling, emanating from the surrounding hearts of more than one generation which their labors have enlightened and elevated—with such aid to rely on, can we be accounted rash if we feel that we are ready to meet the exigency of our time which calls us to unite, under the sanction of our free political institutions, for the establishment of a professional society dedicated to the effective advancement of education by its own executive agents.

Other associations of a more general character, which are nobly engaged in promoting the interests of education, we recognize with respect and gratitude. Many of us have helped to found and maintain these; and the thought of superceding or impairing them is the last that would enter our minds. But in our individual capacity as teachers, and in our relations as—many, perhaps most of us— members of state associations of teachers, we feel that the time is fully come when our own professional interests, and the educational progress of our country, demand the institution of a strictly professional association of teachers, embracing in its scope and design all who are engaged in our occupation thruout the United States, and having for its aim a faithful and persevering endeavor to enlarge the views, unite the hearts, strengthen the hands, and promote the interests of all its members.

The annual meetings of such an association as we contemplate, would form a most attractive scene, not only as one of extensive fellowship and sympathy in common labors and common interests, but one of peculiar and elevated intellectual advancement and gratification. At one hour we might enjoy an enlightened exposition or discussion of a great principle of education, in which we might be benefitted by all the lights of philosophic theory, verified and attested by practical experience. At another, we might experience similar benefit from the statement and illustration of methods and subjects of instruction. Again, we might have opportunity of listening to vital suggestions on moral culture, on appropriate physical exercise and training, on the control and direction of schools, on the classification of pupils, on motives to application, on cooperation with parental influence, on the teacher's position in society, and in short, on every topic of importance usually advanced at our teachers meetings—but with this superior advantage, that we should hear the results of experience and observation from a much wider circle than in the case of associations of more limited range of action.

CALL FOR THE ESTABLISHMENT OF A NATIONAL BUREAU OF
EDUCATION (1866)   From U.S. Bureau of Education, *Annual Report of the
Commissioner of Education, 1892–1893* (Washington, D.C.,1895), pp. 1290–91.

*I. Memorial of the National Association of State and City School Superintendents
to the Senate and House of Representatives of the United States,
February 10, 1866*

At a meeting of the National Association of State and City School Superintendents, recently held in the city of Washington, D. C., the undersigned were appointed a committee to memorialize Congress for the establishment of a national bureau of education.

It was the unanimous opinion of the association that the interests of education would be greatly promoted by the organization of such a bureau at the present time; that it would render needed assistance in the establishment of school systems where they do not now exist, and that it would also prove a potent means for improving and vitalizing existing systems. This it could accomplish—

(1) By securing greater uniformity and accuracy in school statistics, and so interpreting them that they may be more widely available and reliable as educational tests and measures.

(2) By bringing together the results of *school systems* in different communities, States, and countries, and determining their comparative value.

(3) By collecting the results of all important experiments in new and special methods of *school instruction and management,* and making them the common property of school officers and teachers throughout the country.

(4) By diffusing among the people information respecting the school laws of the different States; the various modes of providing and disbursing school funds; the different classes of school officers and their relative duties; the qualifications required of teachers, the modes of their examination, and the agencies provided for their special training; the best methods of classifying and grading schools; improved plans of schoolhouses, together with modes of heating and ventilation, etc., information now obtained only by a few persons and at great expense, but which is of the highest value to all intrusted with the management of schools.

(5) By aiding communities and States in the organization of school systems in which mischievous errors shall be avoided and vital agencies and well-tried improvements be included.

(6) By the general diffusion of correct ideas respecting the value of education as a quickener of intellectual activities; as a moral renovator; as a multiplier of industry and a consequent producer of wealth; and, finally, as the strength and shield of civil liberty.

In the opinion of your memorialists, it is not possible to measure the influence which the faithful performance of these duties by a national bureau would exert upon the cause of education throughout the country; and few persons who have not been intrusted with the management of school systems can fully realize how widespread and urgent is the demand for such assistance, Indeed, the very existence of the association which your memorialists represent is itself positive proof of a demand for a natural channel of communication between the school officers of different States. Millions of dollars have been thrown away in fruitless experiments, or in stolid plodding, for the want of it.

Your memorialists would also submit that the assistance and encouragement of the General Government are needed to secure the adoption of school systems throughout the country. An ignorant people have no inward impulse to lead them to self-education. Just where education is most needed, there it is always least appreciated and valued. It is, indeed, a law of educational progress that its impulse and stimulus come from without. Hence it is that Adam Smith and other writers on political economy expressly except education from the operation of the general law of supply and demand. They teach, correctly, that the demand for education must be awakened by external influences and agencies.

This law is illustrated by the fact that entire school systems, both in this and in other countries, have been lifted up, as it were bodily, by just such influences as a national bureau of education would exert upon the schools of the several States; and this, too, without its being invested with any official control of the school authorities therein. Indeed, the highest value of such a bureau would be its quickening and informing influence, rather than its authoritative and direct control. The true function of such a bureau is not to direct officially in the school affairs in the States, but rather to cooperate with and assist them in the great work of establishing and maintaining systems of public instruction. All experience teaches that the nearer the responsibility of supporting and directing schools is brought to those immediately benefited by them, the greater their vital power and efficiency.

Your memorialists beg permission to suggest one other special duty which should be intrusted to the national bureau, and which of itself will justify its creation, viz, an investigation of the management and results of the frequent munificent grants of land made by Congress for the promotion of general and special education. It is estimated that these grants, if they had been properly managed, would now present an aggregate educational fund of about $500,000,000. If your memorialists are not misinformed, Congress has no official information whatever respecting the manner in which these trusts have been managed.

In conclusion, your memorialists beg leave to express their earnest belief that universal education, next to universal liberty, is a matter of deep national concern. Our experiment of republican institutions is not upon the scale of a petty municipality or State, but it covers half a continent, and embraces people of widely diverse interests and conditions, but who are to continue "one and inseparable." Every condition of our perpetuity and progress as a nation adds emphasis to the remark of Montesquieu, that "it is in a republican government that the *whole power of education is required*."

It is an imperative necessity of the American Republic that the common school be planted on every square mile of its peopled territory, and that the instruction therein imparted be carried to the highest point of efficiency. The creation of a bureau of education by Congress would be a practical recognition of this great

truth. It would impart to the cause of education a dignity and importance which would surely widen its influence and enhance its success.

All of which is respectfully submitted.

E. E. WHITE,
State Commissioner of Common
Schools of Ohio.

NEWTON BATEMAN
State Superintendent of Public
Instruction, Illinois.

J. S. ADAMS,
Secretary State Board of Education,
Vermont.

WASHINGTON, D. C., February 10, 1866.

AN ACT TO ESTABLISH A UNITED STATES BUREAU OF EDUCATION

(**1867**)   From U.S. Bureau of Education, *Report of the Commissioner of Education, 1892–1893* (Washington, D.C., 1895), pp. 1291–92.

B*e it enacted by the Senate and House of Representatives of the United States of America in Congress assembled,* That there shall be established at the city of Washington a department of education for the purpose of collecting such statistics and facts as shall show the condition and progress of education in the several States and Territories, and of diffusing such information respecting the organization and management of schools and school systems, and methods of teaching, as shall aid the people of the United States in the establishment and maintenance of efficient school systems, and otherwise promote the cause of education throughout the country.

SEC. 2. *And be it further enacted,* That there shall be appointed by the President, by and with the advice and consent of the Senate, a commissioner of education, who shall be intrusted with the management of the department herein established, and who shall receive a salary of four thousand dollars per annum, and who shall have authority to appoint one chief clerk of his department, who shall receive a salary of two thousand dollars per annum, and one desk clerk who shall receive a salary of eighteen hundred dollars per annum, and one clerk who shall receive a salary of sixteen hundred dollars per annum, which said clerks shall be subject to the appointing and removing power of the commissioner of education.

SEC. 3. *And be it further enacted,* That it shall be the duty of the commissioner of education to present annually to Congress a report embodying the results of his investigations and labors, together with a statement of such facts and recommendations as will, in his judgment, subserve the purpose for which the department is established. In the first report made by the commissioner of education under this act there shall be presented a statement of the several grants of land made by Congress to promote education, and the manner in which these several trusts have been managed, the amount of funds arising therefrom, and the annual proceeds of the same, as far as the same can be determined.

SEC. 4. *And be it further enacted,* That the Commissioner of Public Buildings is hereby authorized and directed to furnish proper offices for the use of the department herein established.

The following year this Department was reduced to the rank of a Bureau.

SEC. 516. There shall be in the Department of the Interior a Bureau called the Office of Education, the purpose and duties of which shall be to collect statistics and facts showing the condition and progress of education in the several States and Territories, and to diffuse such information respecting the organization and management of schools and school systems, and methods of teaching, as shall aid the people of the United States in the establishment and maintenance of efficient school systems, and otherwise promote the cause of education throughout the country.

SEC. 517. The management of the Office of Education shall, subject to the direction of the Secretary of the Interior, be intrusted to a Commissioner of Education, who shall be appointed by the President, by and with the advice and consent of the Senate, and shall be entitled to a salary of $3,000 a year.

SEC. 518. The Commissioner of Education shall present annually to Congress a report embodying the results of his investigations and labors, together with a statement of such facts and recommendations as will, in his judgement, subserve the purpose for which the office is established.

SEC. 519. The Chief of Engineers shall furnish proper offices for the use of the Office of Education.

FIRST ANNUAL REPORT OF U.S. COMMISSIONER OF EDUCATION
JOHN EATON (1870) From U.S. Bureau of Education, *Annual Report of the Commissioner of Education, 1870* (Washington, D.C., 1871), pp. 5, 79-80.

DEPARTMENT OF THE INTERIOR, BUREAU OF EDUCATION,
Washington, D. C., October 27, 1870.

SIR: Less than eight months have elapsed since I entered upon the duties of this office. I found that the entire working force of this Bureau at that time consisted of two clerks, at a salary of $1,200 each, and that the rooms assigned to its use were so crowded with books, pamphlets, and desk as to be wholly unfit for successful clerical work.

The aid you were able to afford me, by the detail of an additional clerk, was of great service. The efficiency of the office was further increased by the favorable action of Congress in passing the law of July 12, 1870, allowing three clerks, one at $1,800, one at $1,600, and one at $1,400, and a messenger at $840, and also making an appropriation of $3,000 for additional work in compiling statistics and preparing reports.

Since September the work has been greatly facilitated by the transfer of the office to the more ample quarters supplied by your order. The office had already experienced various vicissitudes of fortune. First established as an independent Department, it was afterward reduced to an office in the Interior Department, where now the law styles it a Bureau. The salary of the Commissioner, originally $4,000, had been diminished to $3,000. The compensation of the clerical force had suffered a corresponding reduction. In addition to the difficulties and limitations in the office itself, I was at once made conscious of most serious obstacles, arising not only from a general misapprehension with regard to the character and objects, but from a failure to see any necessity for the existence, of the Bureau.

The idea of national attention to education, as well as to agriculture, had been urged in vain by Washington and his compeers, and repeated from time to time by many of our most patriotic statesmen, until finally the special action of a convention of school superintendents, in a well-considered memorial to Congress, led to the enactment of a law, approved March 2, 1867, establishing a Department of Education "for the purpose of collecting such statistics and facts as shall show the condition and progress of education in the several States and Territories, and of diffusing such information respecting the organization and management of school systems and methods of teaching as shall aid the people of the United States in the establishment and maintenance of efficient school systems, and otherwise promote the cause of education throughout the country."

*   *   *

Relation of the National Government to Education

What is now presented as the annual report can be considered only as an initiative effort, either in respect to the body of the information or the tables included. The relation of the National Government to education with many is not recognized because their attention has not been directed to it. There are, however, certain things which the National Government may and should do in this relation, so palpable that their statement is sufficient to secure almost universal assent:

1. It may do all things required for education in the Territories. 2. It may do all things required for education in the District of Columbia. 3. It may also do all things required by its treaties with and its obligations to the Indians. 4. The National Government may also do all that its international relations require in regard to education. 5. The National Government may use either the public domain or the money received from its sale for the benefit of education. 6. The National Government may know all about education in the country, and may communicate of what it knows at the discretion of Congress and the Executive. 7. The Government should provide a national educational office and an officer, and furnish him clerks, and all means for the fulfillment of the national educational obligations.

Recommendations

The present opportunities of this Bureau are utterly inadequate to the proper discharge of these duties. I, therefore, recommend—

First. An increase of the clerical force of this Bureau, to enable it to extend, subdivide, and systematize its work, so that its correspondence, domestic and foreign, and the collection of statistics, may each be in charge of a person specially fitted for the same.

Second. That appropriate quarters be furnished, so that the plan of making and preserving a collection of educational works, reports, pamphlets, apparatus, maps, &c., may be carried out with facility.

Third. That increased means be furnished for the publication of facts, statistics, and discussions, to meet the constantly increasing demand.

Fourth. That the educational facts necessary for the information of Congress be required by law to be reported through this Bureau in regard to the District of Columbia and the Territories, and all national expenditures in aid of education.

Fifth. In view of the specially limited financial resources and the great amount of ignorance in portions of our country, and the immediate necessity for adequate instrumentalities and opportunities for elementary education to the people of those sections, and the anxieties awakened by impending Asiatic immigration, that the net income from the sale of the public lands be divided annually *pro rata* among the people in the respective States, Territories, and the District of Columbia.

Conclusion

My sense of the incompleteness of this report is most painful. Should it prove the beginning of something which shall grow satisfactorily toward perfection, this labor, I shall hope, will not be in vain.

For whatever value it has I am specially indebted to the very competent labor of those who have assisted me in its preparation, who have not made the customary office hours the limit of their endeavors, but have willingly done their utmost in the work assigned to them.

The courtesy and energy with which the Public Printing Office is conducted secure its issue promptly, in spite of the delays in furnishing manuscript, incident to my want of clerical force, in connection with the other annual executive reports. For statistical matter I am especially indebted to General Francis A. Walker, Superintendent of the Census; Hon. Edward Young, Superintendent of the Bureau of Statistics; and to the Commissioner of Internal Revenue.

Whatever measure of success the office has been able to attain since I entered upon these duties, I should be wanting in common honesty not to acknowledge that it is largely due to your thorough appreciation and prompt consideration of the subjects and duties in hand, and the uniform sympathy and coöperation of the President.

I have the honor to be, sir, very respectfully, your obedient servant,

JOHN EATON, JR,
Commissioner.

Hon. J. D. COX,
Secretary of the Interior.

THE UNITED STATES COMMISSIONER OF EDUCATION DESCRIBES THE RELATION BETWEEN THE GOVERNMENT AND PUBLIC EDUCATION (1871)

From John Eaton, "The Relation of the National Government to Public Education," National Teachers' Association, *Addresses and Journal of Proceedings of the Tenth Annual Meeting, 1871*, pp. 115-126.

. . . Another view under the fact of this relation of the National government to public education should not here escape us. It is directly connected with the late rebellion and its suppression. It is becoming so fashionable in certain quarters, when any allusion, good or evil, is made to those events, to cry out

"Let the dead past bury its dead,"

that the question arises whether there is not abroad a spirit which would bury in oblivion all memories of patriotic sacrifices, and plunge on into the darkness of the future, unmindful of past lessons, the inviting subject of some other calamity, if possible more dire and admonitory. But whatever others may do, the educators of the rising generation must secure the full import of the catastrophe which has overpast carrying with it nine billions of treasure and a million of lives.

How promptly as a class, though in the usages of nations exempt from military service as a profession, these patriotic teachers came forward, leaving their fields of usefulness at home to offer their superior skill to the service of their country, and, if need be, lay down their lives a sacrifice for its preservation, the memorials scattered through the wide land will never fail to tell. From their experience as a class they have reason to appreciate the struggle; from the superior intelligence of their profession they are under special obligations to understand it. It should not be forgotten here that the sentiments which struggled for the overthrow of the Union had been the subjects of misguided instruction, poisoning specially for a generation the channels of thought among the people of a large section of the country. On the other hand, the sentiments which sustained the Union existed, nay, were strong, clear and active, only to the extent that patriotic teachers and educational instrumentalities had made them so. Some one in 1861 fitly observed—"the plantation system and the school district system have come to a crisis."

The intelligence, the character, the philanthropic and christian principles with regard to man, which they had inculcated, not only inspired the national army in its purely military efforts, but gave rise among friends at home, and those in warlike array on the tented field, to those christian charities, finding expression in ways unnumbered and undescribed, toward the disabled soldier and escaping slave, which cast a halo round the conflict with more in it of heaven than of earth. I can not pause here to even allude to the work of the Sanitary and Christian Commissions, amounting in the aggregate to $20,000,000 of expenditure.

Christian endeavors at home and in the field were aroused, not only for the liberty of the slave and his protection from physical suffering, but the spirit which had made so prominent, in certain minds, from the earliest colonial date, the public welfare and the associated ideas of man's privileges, rights and equalities by nature, irrespective of all adventitious circumstances, moved the nobler hearts in the army and navy to labors for colored enlistment, industry, observance of family rights, property rights and duties as citizens, and sent among them willing and heroic teachers, often from the best schools at home, resulting in dotting the Atlantic coast and the Mississippi Valley, within the regions of the rebellion, with a new civilization, holding in germ, under national defenses and by national powers the ideas and institutions which are to repossess and become universal throughout the area shadowed by slavery. Freedman's organizations sprang up through the loyal sections and became active. In the language of the great War Minister, "the sentiment of the country adopted the ex-slaves as the nation's wards."

The national mind, through the movements of the army, became specially cognizant also of another class, in the regions swept over by our forces, ignorant and terribly degraded, described in the South by various designations, but generally known as "poor whites." Many of them and others fleeing from the calamities of the war had received food, clothing, medical attention and shelter from the national government.

Vast tracts of land had also been abandoned by the owners and naturally came under the national supervision. Congress, pervaded by the sentiment of the country respecting these two classes of persons, put the three great special facts together, and established in March, 1865, at the close of the war, the Bureau of Refugees, Freedmen and Abandoned Lands. The christian hero, General O. O. Howard, was designated as its chief. His reports show a total expenditure from January 1, 1865, to August 1, 1869, of $11,249,028.19. Much of this amount was of course expended for physical relief, but the zealous and philanthropic chief of the Bureau deeply felt that in the temporary relief provided by Government, it could not but be intended by the nation that there should be appropriate endeavors to prepare these people for all the amenities and responsibilities of citizenship. He therefore centralized the educational supervision which he found, continued and pushed forward the methods of educational aid in existence, till in 1869 he reports 114,522 colored people under instruction. It will be observed that most of this effort has been directed to the improvement of the colored race, for obvious reasons. So great has been their avidity for knowledge that they have seized every opportunity for education, and General Howard is of the opinion that probably 250,000 colored adults and children have received instruction during the year 1869. Over thirty higher institutions of learning have been brought into existence through the aid of the Bureau.

*   *   *

I remark some things that the National Government may not do in its relation to public education. Thus far we have noticed only the fact of this relation as it has been recognized and acted upon under the constitutional powers given Congress, before the recent great grants of power to protect the liberty, the citizenship, and the right to vote of every male citizen in the country. The theory of our government has proceeded on the supposition that no protection is like that assured by universal education in intelligence and virtue. The occasions which have rendered necessary barriers so strong as the new constitutional bulwarks against the reflow of the waves of evil must be great, and clearly impose a struggle of no small moment upon those who are in those communities to sustain faithfully their sentiment and action to the National Government. Their demand for educational aid, and elsewhere the conviction of its necessity, are uniting under the new grants of power to Congress to demand further national action.

1. I mention, therefore, first under this head, that the national government can and should seek to do nothing in violation of constitutional law. . . .

2. I observe again, under this head, that nothing should be done calculated to decrease local or individual effort for education. It is *of* the individual and *by* the

individual, but it is *for* all men. Whatever comes to any one's education from his relations to others, must after all be determined by what he does. The first formal relation outside of the child is the family. A still larger relation is represented by the Church, the School, or the State. The individuality of each of these is pre-eminently American, and is deeply rooted in the National Constitution. . . .

3. Again, the national government in its relation to public education may not suffer either the local or general prevalence of ignorance, that shall result in the destruction of the principles of liberty by the centralization of power. It is incompatible with the genius of our government to tolerate other than Indian barbarism within its limits. If, in any part, disorder reigns, a remedy must be found; there can be no greater cause for the development of such a condition of things than ignorance. Writers of every age have used the strongest terms at their command to characterize it. Adam Smith likened ignorance, spread through the lower classes and neglected by the state, to a leprosy, and says "where the duty of education is neglected the State is in danger of falling into terrible disorder."

*   *   *

I next mention some things which the National Government *may* do in this relation.

1. It may do all things required for education in the territories.
2. It may do all things required for education in the District of Columbia.
3. It may also do all things required by its treaties with and its obligations to the Indians. . . .
4. The National Government may also do all that its international relations require in regard to education.

Probably a Diogenes could not find a citizen of this country who does not believe in the American mission. Fair Columbia is not for herself alone, but was sent for the benefit of others. We have seen that education, directly or indirectly, is one of the first functions of government with respect to its own citizens. Basing his abstract ideas of government on reason and conscience, the American naturally applies the principle of all nations, and acts accordingly. Our fathers, "out of a decent respect to the opinion of mankind, declared the causes which impelled them to the separation;" our statesmen have ever sought to infuse into international law principles of rectitude; the growth of the nation, and especially its triumphant deliverance from its recent perils, have steadily advanced it toward pre-eminence among nations. The leading statesmen of the most advanced powers of Europe, as Dr. Hoyt observes, have come to accept it as a settled maxim of government that the enlightenment of the people and national prosperity are not accidentally coincident, but necessarily so, sustaining to each other the relation of cause and effect. They therefore seek the key to the secret of American progress in our methods of training youth. England, France, Germany send out their commissioners to examine and report. How long shall it be true, as recently affirmed on the floor of Congress by the Hon. G. F. Hoar, "that the only respectable accounts of public instruction in this country have been prepared by foreign governments?" Certainly, whatever excellence is attained in our system of education no American would withhold from any quarter of the globe. How can the Yankee nation preserve its character for universality without doing and being prepared to do all that may be fit to disseminate knowledge of whatever is excellent in the culture of any of its people? To respond to every call, whether it comes as recently from Hungary, with regard to our city schools, or from France, with regard to teaching of drawing and design, or from England, with regard to military training, or from the remote colonies of Victoria and South Australia, or from the teachers of the Netherlands seeking American educational statistics and information? . . .

Does not the Nation, moreover, owe it, not only to the children but to their teachers, that no improvement should be made in any quarter of the globe without the full benefits of it being secured for them? What valuable information and powerful impulses have been brought to us from educational efforts in Europe? What other instrumentality can so fitly as the nation secure these, communicate and scatter them abroad? . . .

5. The National Government may call all persons or States to account for whatever has been intrusted to them by it for educational purposes. This is only the declaration of the principle founded in nature and embodied in our national compact. A very considerable portion of the permanent school fund of the country, and in some instances the total amount, has been received from the United States, either in land grants or the surplus distributed from the treasury. In several of the Southern States, one of the first indications of their separation from the responsibilities of the Union was the waste of these funds for war purposes. Indeed, at the last session of Congress facts that were becoming known with regard to the Agricultural College land grants, were prompting the committee on education and labor unanimously to seek a remedy of the evils, even though it should be through an absolute revocation of the grants. No one familiar with incitements to human accountability can doubt, that had the national government, from the first donation of aid, simply required a report of the management of all grants, bestowed and deposits made, there would have been much better use made of them and vastly greater benefits accrued to her youth and citizens.

6. The National Government may use either the public domain or the money received from its sale for the benefit of education.

Senator Willey, of West Virginia, introduced a bill for this purpose during the last session of Congress, and in his speech in its support observed, that "it had been ascertained that the net balance from the land sales for the year ending June 30, 1869, was $3,919,070, which divided among the States according to the provisions of his bill would give to each congressional district the sum of about $10,600."

Suppose either the lands or the money from their sale be given with a condition that some specified amount be raised by local (city, county or state) taxation, and that the schools be conducted in accordance with approved principles of organization, maintained by the people and directed by officers of their choosing; what a stimulus would be communicated throughout the whole country to educational endeavor? Great as is the direct advantage from the $90,000 annually distributed from the Peabody fund, far greater good will result from the conditions on which it is distributed by the trustees through Dr. Sears, that wise and skillful educator.

7. The National Government may know all about education in the country, and may communicate of what it knows at the discretion of Congress and the Executive. . . .

8. The National Government may make laws for these several purposes, and the Federal Courts may adjudicate questions under them.

9. In accordance with these laws, plainly the Government should provide a national educational office and officer, and furnish him clerks, and all means for the fulfillment of the national educational obligations.

10. The Government may take, as has been established, by legislative and

executive action, and by the decision of the courts, such exceptional action as exceptional circumstances may require, (a), for the public welfare, (b), for the assurance of a Republican form of government, (c), for the protection of the liberty of those lately slaves, (d), for the security of their citizenship, (e), for the free exercise of the right to vote, (f), for the equality of all men before the law, and (g), for the fitting of any citizen for any responsibility the nation may impose on him.

PRESIDENT JAMES B. ANGELL RECOMMENDS COURSES IN PEDAGOGY AT THE UNIVERSITY OF MICHIGAN (1874) From "Report to the Board of Regents, 1874," as quoted in B. A. Hinsdale, *History of the University of Michigan* (Ann Arbor, Mich., 1906), p. 83.

It cannot be doubted that some instruction in Pedagogics would be very helpful to our Senior class. Many of them are called directly from the University to the management of large schools, some of them to the superintendency of the schools of a town. The whole work of organizing schools, the management of primary and grammar schools, the art of teaching and governing a school,—of all this it is desirable that they know something before they go to their new duties. Experience alone can thoroughly train them. But some familiar lectures on these topics would be of essential service to them.

THE UNIVERSITY OF MICHIGAN ESTABLISHES A CHAIR IN THE "HISTORY, THEORY AND ART OF EDUCATION" (1879) From Editorial, "Teaching How to Teach," *Harper's Weekly*, July 26, 1879, p. 583.

The University of Michigan is one of the most progressive as well as efficient of our great schools of learning, and adapts itself with singular facility to the situation in a rapidly developing country. It was, we believe, the first of our larger universities to adopt the elective system of study, and its spirit has been always hospitable and generous. The most striking fact in its recent annals is the establishment of a chair of the history, theory, and art of education. The value of such a chair is seen at once from the fact that the public schools of Michigan generally fall under the control of the graduates of the university. The State Normal School is engaged in the same general work, but upon another plane. In a society like ours, whose security depends upon educated intelligence, there is no more important function and service than that of teaching the teachers. The art of the teacher is that of effectively communicating knowledge. But this can be taught, like every art and science, only by those who are especially fitted for the work; and the University of Michigan is fortunate in finding for its new chair apparently the very man to fill it.

The authorities of the university have invited to the new professorship the late Superintendent of the Public Schools of Adrian, Professor Payne. He has been twenty-one years continuously in the public school service of the State, and his admirable influence has been gladly and generally acknowledged. But his efficient administration has only deepened his interest in the philosophic principles of his profession, and his views were fully set forth in a course of lectures delivered last year in the Normal Department of Adrian College, which have commanded the interested attention of "educators" as an admirable exposition of the subject. He is now called to the first chair of the kind established in this country, and the University of Michigan again justifies its position as the head of the educational system of the State.

This action will promote the highest interests of education, not only by tempting future teachers to the training of the university, but by apprising the public that teaching is itself an art, and that the knowledge how to teach may make all the difference between school money well or uselessly spent in the community. Both the educational and charitable systems of Michigan have an enviable reputation, and the good example again set by its university will be doubtless heeded and followed elsewhere.

PROFESSOR OF EDUCATION AT THE UNIVERSITY OF MICHIGAN JUSTIFIES EDUCATION AS A UNIVERSITY COURSE OF STUDY

(1889)   From B. A. Hinsdale, "Pedagogical Chairs in Colleges and Universities," National Education Association *Journal of Addresses and Proceedings* (Topeka, Kans. 1889), pp. 560–64.

By common consent the university has two great functions. One of these is research, the discovery of truth; the other is instruction, the practice of the art of teaching—that is, the university first finds out truth, and then gives it forth. The two interact. Furthermore, the university not only practices research, but it makes research itself the object of study and investigation. Science becomes reflective, and lays bare all her processes and methods. Why, then, should it not investigate and teach its other function, viz., that of teaching? Why should an institution that exists for the sake of investigating the arts and sciences, leave its own peculiar art neglected and despised?

But education is much more than a great and difficult art; it is a noble science. Back of its methods, processes, and systems, are facts, ideas, principles, and theories—in fact, whole systems of philosophy. As Rosenkranz remarks, pedagogy cannot be deduced from a single principle with such strictness as logic and ethics, but is a mixed science, like medicine, deriving its presuppositions from other sciences, as physiology, psychology, logic, aesthetics, ethics, and sociology. It is therefore conditioned upon some of the noblest of the sciences, especially those of the moral group. The very fact that it is a mixed science adds to its difficulty, and emphasizes the demand for its cultivation. It is hard to see how the university, whose admitted function is education, can pass by the science of education without discrediting its own work and virtually denying its own name. To practice the art

THE
PROFESSION
OF EDUCATION

1415

and refuse to cultivate or teach the science of teaching, is little better than rank empiricism.

The last argument derives additional strength from the peculiar stage of education upon which the foremost nations and countries have now entered. Education has at last reached the reflective or scientific stage. Throwing off the clutch of the empiricist, she has ascended to her long-vacant seat in the family of sciences. Evidences of this art are the increased attention paid to education by text-writers on psychology and ethics, the later pedagogical literature, and the more systematic and rational methods of instruction in schools, and the rapidly-increasing facilities for teaching educational science. Thus the very existence of the chair is a proof of its usefulness and its necessity. On this ground alone—indeed, on the narrower ground of endowing research alone—the chair can be fully vindicated.

Again, education has a history. In the very broadest sense, the field of educational history is the field of human culture; and even when limited, as before, to the conscious work of teachers in schools, it still presents whole series of facts, problems and lessons of the greatest interest and importance. Before the pedagogist lies the whole field of school-life, from the simple prophets' and priests' schools of early times to the highly-developed schools and school systems of Europe and America. While education belongs to general history, the study of which is pursued for its culture value, it has been almost wholly neglected. The writer and lecturer on general history do indeed touch the education of the ancients, and make mention of the mediæval universities; they pay some small attention to the marvelous educational development of modern times; but they lay much more emphasis on subjects of far inferior interest. But education should be made the subject of special historical study as much as religion, art, or politics. Were it as throughly investigated as the Polytechnic School of Munich investigates engineering (maintaining forty-five distinct courses of lectures in that science), the history of education alone would tax the resources of the most learned and laborious professor. It is not contended that the chair of pedagogy can at present cultivate this field as carefully as this allusion may imply; but certainly here are topics of the greatest interest and importance, that demand admission to the university list on an equal footing with other subjects of historical investigation. So long as the history of education is a means of education, so long will it continue a proper university study.

Thus far the argument has been theoretical, resting on the need of investigating the science, art and history of teaching, and on their educational value. But the practical phases of the subject must also be presented.

1. Even if the work done by the pedagogical chair should pay no immediate attention to the preparation of teachers, it could not fail to be of much practical value. The scientific study and teaching of a science and an art in their purely theoretical aspects always promote the practice of the art; and the presence in every university in the land of a pedagogical professor, thoroughly devoted to his chair, could not fail to quicken interest in the subject, and to promote the teaching art.

2. While it is a serious error to hold the university merely as a place of instruction and to overlook research—an error that is only too common in the United States—instruction is still one of its grand functions. It is engaged in teaching the highest branches of knowledge. Its professors hold their chairs by reason of their professional ability, as well as by reason of their learning. Where,

then, may the science, the history, and art of teaching be so properly taught as where the art flourishes in its highest forms?

3. The conditions of pedagogical study existing in the university are the best that can be imagined. First, the university offers the student a varied curriculum from which to choose collateral studies. Secondly, it illustrates teaching in all the branches of liberal, and in many branches of technical study, Thirdly, the library, which furnishes an extensive apparatus for general as well as special study, is an invaluable facility. Fourthly, the university is the home of liberal studies; its traditions and associations are conductive to cultivation, and the student in residence finds himself in the midst of a learned and cultivated society.

The last of these points is deserving of a more elaborate statement. It is well known that special schools tend at once to depth and narrowness: intention is secured at the expense of extension. This is necessary to a degree; but if the process is carried too far, mischievous results follow. Hence the advantage of uniting the professional school with the school of liberal studies; an advantage greater now than ever before, because scholars, men of science and teachers are pushing specialization to its extreme limits. We should not be surprised, therefore, to find all the writers who have touched the topic laying much stress on the advantage to the student of receiving his pedagogical instruction in unacademical institutions, Professor Laurie insists that the teachers of the secondary schools of Scotland need professional preparation as well as university training. "Where shall they get this?" he asks. "They might be required to combine attendance at a training college with attendance at the university for a degree; but this, though it might serve as a provisional arrangement, would not secure the end we seek. And why should not this arrangement secure the end we seek? For this reason, and for no other, that a specialist training college does not answer the same purpose as a university. The broader culture, the purer air, the higher aims of the latter give to it an educational influence which specialist colleges can never exercise."

Whether academical teaching should be furnished in a normal school, is a question often discussed. That question does not come within the range of this paper; but the observation may be made that such instruction must be defended theoretically, if at all, on the ground of its liberalizing and strengthening tendencies.

4. It is a function of the university to furnish society with teachers. Research, teaching, and the preparation of teachers, are the three great duties that it owes society. The preparation of teachers for primary and grammar schools, and possibly for the lower classes of high schools, may be left to normal and training schools. But high schools and other secondary schools must receive their character from teachers of a higher grade of scholarship, It is the favorite conceit of some public-school men that the public schools are fully adequate to create their own teachers, unless it be in some of the more special lines of high school study and instruction; even the superintendents, they hold, should "come up from the ranks"; but no man who understands the tendencies and effects of specialization, particularly the results of breeding in-and-in, will for a moment favor such a narrow policy. The public schools have done an invaluable work in furnishing teachers to society; but it is a weighty fact that no schools more need to be kept in vital relation with the schools of higher instruction.

5. The chair of pedagogy and the teaching profession need the strength and

dignity that university recognition will give them. Such recognition will be the strongest testimony that the university can bear to the public of the estimate in which it holds the art that it exists to practice. In that way, too, it will most strongly impress its students with the estimate in which it holds the teacher's calling. When our aspiring young men and women see accomplished professors of the science, history and art of teaching in the colleges and universities of the land, vying with the professors of philosophy, ethics, jurisprudence, political economy, and history, in the exposition of their favorite subjects, they will form a higher conception of the teacher's work. This argument also has been urged with much force by writers on education. Professor Laurie, for example, says that the teaching profession of Scotland, almost with one voice, hailed the action of the trustees of the Bell fund, who established the Bell chairs at St. Andrews and Edinburgh. The feeling was, they "have conferred honor on a department of work that Dr. Bell delighted to honor. They have unquestionably done very much to promote education in Scotland, not only by raising the work of the school-master in public estimation, but also by attracting public attention to education as being not merely a question of machinery for the institution of schools (essential through this undoubtedly is), but a question of principles and methods—in brief, of philosophy." He says, further, that the institution of the Edinburgh chair increased the importance of the teaching body, gave it academical standing, and made it possible for the first time to institute in the universities a faculty of education, like the faculties of law, medicine, and theology.

CHARLES KENDALL ADAMS ON "THE TEACHING OF PEDAGOGY IN COLLEGES AND UNIVERSITIES" (1888) From New England Association of Colleges and Preparatory Schools, *Addresses And Proceedings, 1888,* pp. 26–29.

W e spend enormous sums in large and well-arranged school buildings and elegant furniture and expensive school books and then frustrate the purpose of them all by not having the one thing, compared with which, all the other things are as nothing, namely, A GOOD SCHOOL.

How is a change for the better to be brought about? In no other way than by a change of public opinion. This is, of course, the manner in which all reforms in a government like ours must proceed, and a radical change in this respect is absolutely necessary. There is in the public mind no general idea that our schools are inferior. Mr. Matthew Arnold, whose professional office it was to study educational systems, told the people of Europe in his report of 1868, that they had nothing to learn from American methods; and just after the Educational Exhibition in Philadelphia, in 1876, one of our oldest and wisest state superintendents declared that we had more to learn from Sweden and Russia in regard to methods of instruction than Sweden and Russia had to learn from us. But these were simply individual voices, and the prevailing belief in our country has been that, on the whole, so far from having any reason to be dissatisfied, we should be proud of our great and glorious system of free schools, and should abundantly thank God that we are not as other men are.

But then we may ask, in turn, How is this absurd popular optimism to be changed for the better? In no way, I answer, so readily, so rapidly, and so effectively, as by raising up and putting into positions of influence as large a class as possible of teachers who know what education is in those countries of the world where it has been most successful. And this brings me, after what I fear you will think a long wandering, to the subject of the systematic teaching of pedagogy in our schools and colleges.

In every college class there are certain ones who intend to be teachers; and as graduates from college they are to take positions to exert whatever influence can be exerted in behalf of the best educational methods. In all of our towns, it is, after all, the superintendents and teachers who exert the greatest influence in the formation of public opinion concerning our schools. It is, therefore, of great, I will say of unspeakable, importance, that this class of teachers should know what the world has to teach as to this art of teaching, which, as we have seen, in one country does so much, and in another does so little. It is certain, moreover, that much can be learned; for the study is not one of exceptional difficulty. The literature, especially in French and German, is abundant; and if this is well at the command of the teacher, there will be no difficulty in bringing to the class a mass of most valuable and helpful information.

Instruction in this subject, it seems to me, should consist of no less than four somewhat distinct parts; and these may well form four courses of instruction extending through the collegiate year. As to the order in which the student should take these courses, there may be some differences of opinion; but the courses themselves may be roughly described as follows:

1. The History of Education; ancient, medieval, and modern. While the enterprising teacher will depend chiefly upon lectures for giving life and inspiration to this course, some text-book, probably Compayré's "History of Pedagogy," should be required of the class at the recitations and examinations.

2. The Philosophy of Education. Analysis and discussion of the several theories that have prevailed, and that now prevail, in regard to the development of the human mind. This will involve, of course, a consideration of the educational values of different studies, and of their effects on the growing mind. More psychological than any of the others, this course will depend for its success upon the philosophical bent and skill of the teacher. But the successful study and teaching of pedagogy, as a science, must rest very largely upon a psychological basis; and hence the best teachers have always laid considerable stress on this method. Paulsen, at Berlin, and Hall, at Johns Hopkins, were both teachers of philosophy as well as pedagogy in its more restricted sense. Payne, formerly of Michigan, but now of Tennessee, has given such a course with most satisfactory results.

3. Methods in the School Room. This is the practical side of the work, and should embrace a discussion of such questions as the art of teaching and governing; methods of most successfully imparting instruction; general school-room practice; general school management; the art of grading and arranging courses of study, and perhaps, the conducting of school institutes. This course, like the first, though dependent chiefly on the lectures of the Professor, should be accompanied with the careful use of some text-book, say Fitch's admirable "Lectures on Teaching."

4. The Teachers' Seminary. Here should be freely examined and discussed the most obscure and difficult problems that confront the teacher. A comparative study of educational systems may well form a part of the work here carried on. There

should be the utmost freedom between Professor and student; indeed, in every respect, the meeting should have the informality of personal conference, rather than the formality of any approach to official relations.

Then, in addition to these courses, there may well be given by professors in the leading departments of the college or university courses designed exclusively to instruct how to teach young pupils the subject in hand. This is done in some of the universities of this country, as well as in many of the universities of Continental Europe. In the German universities it is carried not only into a theoretical discussion of what ought to be done, but also into the practical work of actual instruction. Some years ago I accompanied a class with Professor Masius, to one of the city schools of Leipzig, to witness an exercise of this kind. One of the Seminary students was put in charge of the class for the lesson of the hour, and the work was all done in the presence of the Professor and of the other members of the Seminary. Each of the members received practice of this kind, and the work of each was subjected to searching review and criticism by the other members and by the Professor, at the next meeting. The spirit of the exercise throughout was that of men who were putting the finishing touches to work in preparation for a profession of which they were proud, and to which their lives were henceforth with enthusiasm to be devoted. These, and such as these, are the men who teach the boys of Germany during all of the school days between nine and eighteen.

That in our own country we can at present have teachers thus trained and equipped to teach our boys during their grammar school days seems indeed too much to hope. Before that happy day comes, public opinion must undergo a revolution. But, until then, let us restrain all vain boasting; and, so far as is possible, bear ourselves with becoming humility. But in the meanwhile, be it long or be it short, what more promising method is there of changing public opinion than by the professional teaching of pedagogy in our colleges and universities?

HISTORICAL SKETCH OF THE FOUNDING OF TEACHERS COLLEGE, COLUMBIA UNIVERSITY (c. 1887) From Walter L. Hervey, "Historical Sketch of Teachers College From Its Foundation to 1897," *Teachers College Record*, Vol. I, pp. 12–17, 19–21.

The story of how Teachers College came to be, how it grew, and how it reached its present form, has never been fully told; and though the time is not yet ripe for telling it fully, I have undertaken, at the request of the Dean of the College, to trace the main lines of growth, materially and educationally, from the inception of the work to the close of the year 1896–97.

Teachers College is the product of an interesting evolution in which it is possible to distinguish two main streams of influence. The first of these was purely philanthropic in its nature; the second, purely educational. One emanated from the hearts of a group of generous and devoted men and women, desirous of promoting practical measures of social helpfulness; the other had its rise in the clear and far-seeing vision of President Barnard, of Columbia College, who may justly be called the Father of the movement in this community for the higher study of education.

Until the two were joined, the first was perhaps more deed than idea; the second, idea rather than deed. How each of these streams ran its independent course, until it became joined with the other, naturally forms the first chapter in the story of how there came to be such an institution as Teachers College.

Under an "Act for the incorporation of benevolent, charitable, scientific, and missionary purposes," the progenitor on the philanthropic side received its charter in the year 1880. The purpose of this movement was to promote the domestic industrial arts among the laboring classes, to diffuse true principles and correct methods, and to establish a centre of reference and consultation. From its four annual reports, we learn that it enjoyed an income varying from $551.48 to $994.50 per year; that in one year nine hundred young girls in New York and its vicinity alone were taught the elements of house-keeping and home-making, and that from the first the importance of the training of teachers was appreciated. The Association issued important publications, and conducted a wide correspondence that resulted in promoting the cause not only in many parts of this country but in Europe, China, Japan, and India. But the energy and ambition of the leaders of this movement were not satisfied by these results. They believed that they were called to a broader work.

Accordingly, on March 31, 1884, the old organization was dissolved, and the new work was launched under the name of the Industrial Education Association, the aims of which were:

I. To promote special training of both sexes in any of those industries which affect the house and home directly or indirectly, and which will enable those receiving it to become self-supporting.

II. To select, prepare, and publish such books and pamphlets as shall conduce to an increased knowledge of these subjects.

III. To study, devise, and introduce methods and systems of domestic and industrial training into schools.

IV. To form special classes for technical training.

V. To train teachers, who shall be able and ready to assist in the work, whenever a favorable opening occurs.

In order to fortify themselves in the pursuit of these broader aims, and to guard their work from degenerating into a manual training school, the Trustees of the Association, in December, 1886, appointed a Committee to outline the policy of the Association. The report of that Committee, which was later adopted, was called not inaptly the Articles of Faith of the Association. This declaration of principles, which has been stated by a high authority to be "one of the most enlightened, forceful, and concise statements of the principles underlying manual training that has ever been published," is here given in full.

The Association holds:

I. That the complete development of all the faculties can be reached only through a system of education which combines the training found in the usual course of study with the elements of manual training.

II. That the current system trains the memory too largely, the reasoning powers less, the eye and hand too little.

III. That industrial training, to have its fullest value, must be an integral part of general education. While valuable in some measure alone, it is alone little better than manual training as leading to the learning of trades.

IV. That it is not the aim of the Association to teach trades. That boys and girls will, if educated according to the system which it advocates, be better able to take up the study of any particular trade, it recognizes as one of the results of the system. It is the development of all the faculties which it holds to be the essential aim of the system.

V. That the fact is generally recognized, among those best informed on the subject of education, that the kindergarten system produces the best results with young children. The Association claims that the system which combines industrial training with the usual and necessary branches is nothing more than a development of the kindergarten theory; a system found wise for young children, modified and adapted to children of more mature growth.

VI. That, as children, wherever found, possess the same faculties and develop the same characteristics, this system should be introduced into all classes and grades of schools, the private as well as the public, and not alone in the primary public schools, but in all those of more advanced grades.

VII. That this system tends to the development of certain moral qualities, as well as to the development of the intellectual faculties.

VIII. That the various occupations which are by this system given to children render study less irksome than any system can in which the exercise of the faculty of memory is alone involved.

IX. That there exists in this country a wide-spread disinclination for manual labor which the present system of education seems powerless to overcome. There is a wide range of occupations which boys and girls might with advantage enter were it not that they are prevented from so doing by a false view of the dignity of labor. The Association holds that one of the results of this system of education will be to destroy a prejudice which in a measure arises from a want of familiarity with hand work.

X. That the first and last object of the Association, the main reason for its existence, is the creation of a public interest in this system and a public belief in its value.

In adopting this platform, the founders of the movement sharply differentiated their work from all similar undertakings. They believed, with Washington Gladden, "that there is an industrial training, which is neither technical nor professional, which is calculated to make better men and better citizens of the pupils, no matter what calling they may afterward follow; which affects directly, and in a most salutary manner, the mind and character of the pupil, and which will be of constant service to him through all his life, whether he be wage-earner or trader, teacher, or clergyman." Thus, in espousing the cause of practical education, the Industrial Education Association did not establish a trade school. This purpose its founders disclaimed explicitly and once for all. "The training of the eye and of the hand," said they, with Dr. Gladden, are "important and essential elements in all good education." With General Francis A. Walker, they held that "the use of tools and the teaching of cooking and sewing are as truly educational as any of the familiar features of the public school; they supply desirable elements which can be obtained as well from no other source; they are not only compatible with the integrity and dignity of the school system, but they promise greatly to increase the general interest in the schools, if not to become the very salvation of the school system itself"; and they placed on the title page of the first report of the Association, though without appreciating their full import at the time, these words of Baron Humboldt: "Whatever we wish to see introduced into the life of a nation must be first introduced into the life of its schools."

The support which this new enterprise received from the people of New York was generous beyond the expectations of its founders. Its annual budget grew in four years from $2015.52 to $38,702.81. Its lines of work multiplied. It enlisted a notable company of fellow-workers, including such names as President F. A. P. Barnard, General Alexander S. Webb, President Daniel C. Gilman, Mr. William E. Dodge, Mr. William F. Bridge, Mr. William A. Potter, Mrs. Peter M. Bryson, the

Hon. Seth Low, and corresponding members from many cities both in this country, in England, and on the continent of Europe. The following paragraph from the first report of the Association suggests the nature and value of the work done:

> Not only has the Association accomplished much practical work, but, by means of private interest, and through the public press, it has presented its objects, tested the sympathy of the community with its purposes, deepened the conviction of their importance, and received the approval of many thoughtful men and women.

A phase of the work, which is especially interesting in view of the recent vacation-school movement, is thus described in the third report of the Association:

> During the summer of 1887, vacation work was undertaken in the tenement districts of the City, at Staten Island and Oyster Bay. While a Vacation School is too short-lived to afford valuable educational results, the benefit is obvious of substituting healthful and interesting occupation for the demoralizing influences to which the children of the poor are subjected during the long vacation. It must be remembered that in these schools the attendance is not compulsory, and the discipline of the ordinary school impossible. Something finer is reached, where boys and girls submit cheerfully to necessary restraint for the sake of the interest which the work inspires. In the three schools held in the City in July and August, over four hundred pupils were instructed in drawing, modelling, construction, wood-carving, sewing, and cooking.

Those familiar with the work of the Association at this period will also remember the Children's Exhibition, held under the auspices of the Association in the spring of 1887. The plan was undertaken with a view of showing the public what advances had already been achieved in the direction of incorporating manual training in the school curriculum. The invitations to participate in the exhibition, extended by the Association to cities where manual training had already been introduced, met with a hearty response. Exhibits came from points as remote as St. Paul and St. Louis, and from many cities and towns nearer at hand. And though the exhibits were crude, the sight of work done by the children's hands, as a part of regular school work, was something new; to the seven thousand parents, teachers, and children who visited the exhibition during the week in which it was held, it was a surprise and a revelation. The interest of the public was reflected in the columns of the press, which contained full accounts both of the Children's Exhibition and of the Association under whose auspices it was undertaken. This was altogether the most brilliant event in the history of the Association.

The affairs of the Industrial Education Association had now reached a critical point. Apparently, the Association had scored a brilliant success; but the Trustees perceived that, in spite of large numbers and rapid growth, their work was still falling short of the effectiveness it must attain. For, while it was clear that they had succeeded in arousing and educating public sentiment in favor of manual training in the schools, it was equally clear that they had by so doing created a demand for trained teachers, to meet which there was an inadequate supply. The question arose, where and by whom were these teachers to be trained? Manifestly, said they, this training should and must be done by the Association, and they straightway proceeded to organize such normal classes as their facilities permitted. This was no sooner done than it became evident that such a scheme must assume the proportions of a training college, and must be placed under the guidance of a trained and expert educator. Search was at once begun for the right man for the place, and this man was found in the person of Dr. Nicholas Murray Butler, who became President of the Association, and at once began the work of organizing the new training college.

Meanwhile, the building occupied by the Association had become outgrown, and in the fall of 1887 the building at No. 9 University Place—then "New No. 9" but in later years known as "Old No. 9"—was leased for a term of years, having been previously altered and equipped for the purposes of the Association. Here the work of promoting the cause was carried forward on a broader basis and in more effective ways. Two main lines of work were distinguishable in the Association proper: on the one hand, the education of the public, by lectures, publications, and "object lessons" in the new education; and, on the other hand, the instruction of pupils in drawing, carpentry, sewing, cooking, kindergarten, and domestic training. The Association at its height had under instruction during a single year 4383 pupils, some taught within the building itself, the remainder in "outside classes," taught by a staff of teachers employed for the purpose. Courses of public lectures on educational subjects were offered, an educational museum established, a library for teachers founded, and the entire work of the Association thrown open to visitors, many hundreds of whom, from all parts of the Union, and from foreign countries, came for light and help. Two publications, entitled "Educational Leaflets" and "Educational Monographs," were issued by the Association, and did effective pioneer service.

In his first report to the Trustees of the Association, President Butler could truly say that "a platform of humanitarianism had been exchanged for one of educational reform and advancement." The change came naturally, and, though the result of a long development, swiftly. And the change was complete. The College, which was at first one of the departments of the Association, soon absorbed the Association into itself, and became its legal successor with a charter of its own.

But, in order to understand the nature of the development which now took place, it is necessary to go back and trace in outline the growth of that idea which was destined to have such a potent moulding influence on the future of this work; for it must not be forgotten that while the work of the Industrial Association had become avowedly educational, the future scope and quality of that work were as yet undefined, and the nature of the case demanded that this definition should not be left to chance but should be worked out according to an idea. This idea, as the event proved, was nothing less than that of the higher study of education and the higher training of the teacher.

*   *   *

If, on the one hand, it was a good thing for the training of teachers that the Industrial Education Association thus aided in realizing the idea of a teachers' college, it must on the other hand always be accounted a most happy circumstance for the Association itself that when its Trustees were seeking an executive able to develop their work on broader lines, their choice fell, not on a specialist in manual training, but on one "who had determined to bring about the university study of education, and the higher training of teachers, through an institution especially organized for the purpose, if it were within the bounds of possibility to do so."

Under the name, "College for the Training of Teachers," the work of training teachers was begun in the fall of 1887 as one of the two departments of the Industrial Education Association, the other branch of the work being concerned with the creation of a public interest in manual training as an intellectual discipline, and involving the publication of information bearing upon that subject. The College began with a faculty of five teachers, viz.: in the departments of History and Institutes of Education, Mechanical Drawing and Wood-working, Domestic Economy, Kindergarten Methods, and Industrial Art. The departments of Natural Science and Methods of Teaching were a part of the original scheme, but the professors in these departments were not appointed until the year following. The original course of study of the College occupied two years, and included psychology, the history and science of education, methods of teaching, observation and practice in model school, school organization and administration in the United States, England, France, and Germany, the theory and practice of the kindergarten, natural science including the construction of simple illustrative apparatus, history, and the subjects included under the term manual training, viz.: industrial art, domestic economy, mechanical drawing, and wood-working. Applicants for admission to the junior class were examined in the following subjects: arithmetic, plane geometry, United States history, geography, elementary science, English composition, and the correction of specimens of bad English. Certificates were accepted in lieu of examination. The College opened with 18 students in the junior class and 86 special students; in 1888–1889 there were 50 candidates for diploma and 161 special students; in 1889–1890, 50 candidates for diploma and certificates and 123 special students; in 1890–1891, 89 candidates for diploma and certificates and 93 special students.

The founding of Teachers College which thus took place was, from more than one point of view, a remarkable event. It was, in the first place, a radical departure. The central thought in the Industrial Education Association had been manual training and its propaganda. The central idea of the College was the training of teachers, and its central department was the department of education. The Industrial Education Association, in so far as it had trained teachers at all, had trained teachers having manual training as a specialty. The College undertook to train teachers able to teach manual training in connection with other subjects as a part of regular school work; it thus proposed to work within the schools, not outside of the schools. A school of observation and practice which should be complete, and should illustrate the teaching of every subject from kindergarten to college, was an integral part of the original plan. It thus appears that the College was from its inception an educational institution to be sharply distinguished from all institutions similar to it in general aim, but lacking its distinctive feature. It is a remarkable fact that while the College has experienced many changes, and has in each year of its existence made adaptations more or less radical, there has been absolutely no change in the original plan and scope of the institution as conceived and outlined by its first President. The original idea of the College was so broad and practicable that it not only utilized much of the work that had gone before, but it led naturally and by processes of growth to all the developments and affiliations that have come since. With the founding of Teachers College, and its successful administration and steady growth during the first four years of its existence, closes the first chapter of the present sketch,—a chapter which illustrates as happily as anything I know how a work that has life in it will grow, and how an idea that has life in itself will appropriate existing materials and mould them to s own uses.

WILLIAM JAMES ON THE MENTAL LIFE OF CHILDREN (1892)   From
William James, *Talks to Teachers on Psychology: And to Students on Some of Life's Ideals*
(New York, 1899), pp. 15–20, 24–29, 196.

Lecture II

"THE STREAM OF CONSCIOUSNESS"

I said a few minutes ago that the most general elements and workings of the mind are all that the teacher absolutely needs to be acquainted with for his purposes.

Now the *immediate* fact which psychology, the science of mind, has to study is also the most general fact. It is the fact that in each of us, when awake (and often when asleep), *some kind of consciousness is always going on.* There is a stream, a succession of states, or waves, or fields (or of whatever you please to call them), of knowledge, of feeling, of desire, of deliberation, etc., that constantly pass and repass, and that constitute our inner life. The existence of this stream is the primal fact, the nature and origin of it form the essential problem, of our science. So far as we class the states or fields of consciousness, write down their several natures, analyze their contents into elements, or trace their habits of succession, we are on the descriptive or analytic level. So far as we ask where they come from or why they are just what they are, we are on the explanatory level.

In these talks with you, I shall entirely neglect the questions that come up on the explanatory level. It must be frankly confessed that in no fundamental sense do we know where our successive fields of consciousness come from, or why they have the precise inner constitution which they do have. They certainly follow or accompany our brain states, and of course their special forms are determined by our past experiences and education. But, if we ask just *how* the brain conditions them, we have not the remotest inkling of an answer to give; and, if we ask just how the education moulds the brain, we can speak but in the most abstract, general, and conjectural terms. On the other hand, if we should say that they are due to a spiritual being called our Soul, which reacts on our brain states by these peculiar forms of spiritual energy, our words would be familiar enough, it is true; but I think you will agree that they would offer little genuine explanatory meaning. The truth is that we really *do not know* the answers to the problems on the explanatory level, even though in some directions of inquiry there may be promising speculations to be found. For our present purposes I shall therefore dismiss them entirely, and turn to mere description. This state of things was what I had in mind when, a moment ago, I said there was no "new psychology" worthy of the name.

We have thus fields of consciousness,—that is the first general fact; and the second general fact is that the concrete fields are always complex. They contain sensations of our bodies and of the objects around us, memories of past experiences and thoughts of distant things, feelings of satisfaction and dissatisfaction, desires and aversions, and other emotional conditions, together with determinations of the will, in every variety of permutation and combination.

In most of our concrete states of consciousness all these different classes of ingredients are found simultaneously present to some degree, though the relative proportion they bear to one another is very shifting. One state will seem to be composed of hardly anything but sensations, another of hardly anything but memories, etc. But around the sensation, if one consider carefully, there will always be some fringe of thought or will, and around the memory some margin or penumbra of emotion or sensation.

In most of our fields of consciousness there is a core of sensation that is very pronounced. You, for example, now, although you are also thinking and feeling, are getting through your eyes sensations of my face and figure, and through your ears sensations of my voice. The sensations are the *centre* or *focus*, the thoughts and feelings the *margin*, of your actually present conscious field.

On the other hand, some object of thought, some distant image, may have become the focus of your mental attention even while I am speaking,—your mind, in short, may have wandered from the lecture; and, in that case, the sensations of my face and voice, although not absolutely vanishing from your conscious field, may have taken up there a very faint and marginal place.

Again, to take another sort of variation, some feeling connected with your own body may have passed from a marginal to a focal place, even while I speak.

The expressions "focal object" and "marginal object," which we owe to Mr. Lloyd Morgan, require, I think, no further explanation. The distinction they embody is a very important one, and they are the first technical terms which I shall ask you to remember.

In the successive mutations of our fields of consciousness, the process by which one dissolves into another is often very gradual, and all sorts of inner rearrangements of contents occur. Sometimes the focus remains but little changed, while the margin alters rapidly. Sometimes the focus alters, and the margin stays. Sometimes focus and margin change places. Sometimes, again, abrupt alterations of the whole field occur. There can seldom be a sharp description. All we know is that, for the most part, each field has a sort of practical unity for its possessor, and that from this practical point of view we can class a field with other fields similar to it, by calling it a state of emotion, of perplexity, of sensation, of abstract thought, of volition, and the like.

*　　*　　*

Vague and hazy as such an account of our stream of consciousness may be, it is at least secure from positive error and free from admixture of conjecture or hypothesis. An influential school of psychology, seeking to avoid haziness of outline, has tried to make things appear more exact and scientific by making the analysis more sharp. The various fields of consciousness, according to this school, result from a definite number of perfectly definite elementary mental states, mechanically associated into a mosaic or chemically combined. According to some thinkers,— Spencer, for example, or Taine,—these resolve themselves at last into little elementary psychic particles or atoms of "mind-stuff," out of which all the more immediately known mental states are said to be built up. Locke introduced this theory in a somewhat vague form. Simple "ideas" of sensation and reflection, as he called them, were for him the bricks of which our mental architecture is built up. If I ever have to refer to this theory again, I shall refer to it as the theory of "ideas." But I shall try to steer clear of it altogether. Whether it be true or false, it is at any rate only conjectural; and, for your practical purposes as teachers, the more unpretending conception of the stream of consciousness, with its total waves or fields incessantly changing, will amply suffice.

Lecture III

"THE CHILD AS A BEHAVING ORGANISM"

* * *

I shall ask you now—not meaning at all thereby to close the theoretic question, but merely because it seems to me the point of view likely to be of greatest practical use to you as teachers—to adopt with me, in this course of lectures, the biological conception, as thus expressed, and to lay your own emphasis on the fact that man, whatever else he may be, is primarily a practical being, whose mind is given him to aid in adapting him to this world's life.

In the learning of all matters, we have to start with some one deep aspect of the question, abstracting it as if it were the only aspect; and then we gradually correct ourselves by adding those neglected other features which complete the case. No one believes more strongly than I do that what our senses know as "this world" is only one portion of our mind's total environment and object. Yet, because it is the primal portion, it is the *sine qua non* of all the rest. If you grasp the facts about it firmly, you may proceed to higher regions undisturbed. As our time must be so short together, I prefer being elementary and fundamental to being complete, so I propose to you to hold fast to the ultra-simple point of view.

The reasons why I call it so fundamental can be easily told.

First, human and animal psychology thereby become less discontinuous. I know that to some of you this will hardly seem an attractive reason, but there are others whom it will affect.

Second, mental action is conditioned by brain action, and runs parallel therewith. But the brain, so far as we understand it, is given us for practical behavior. Every current that runs into it from skin or eye or ear runs out again into muscles, glands, or viscera, and helps to adapt the animal to the environment from which the current came. It therefore generalizes and simplifies our view to treat the brain life and the mental life as having one fundamental kind of purpose.

Third, those very functions of the mind that do not refer directly to this world's environment, the ethical utopias, æsthetic visions, insights into eternal truth, and fanciful logical combinations, could never be carried on at all by a human individual, unless the mind that produced them in him were also able to produce more practically useful products. The latter are thus the more essential, or at least the more primordial results.

Fourth, the inessential "unpractical" activities are themselves far more connected with our behavior and our adaptation to the environment than at first sight might appear. No truth, however abstract, is ever perceived, that will not probably at some time influence our earthly action. You must remember that, when I talk of action here, I mean action in the widest sense. I mean speech, I mean writing, I mean yeses and noes, and tendencies "from" things and tendencies "toward" things, and emotional determinations; and I mean them in the future as well as in the immediate present. As I talk here, and you listen, it might seem as if no action followed. You might call it a purely theoretic process, with no practical result. But it *must* have a practical result. It cannot take place at all and leave your conduct unaffected. If not to-day, then on some far future day, you will answer some question differently by reason of what you are thinking now. Some of you will be led by my words into new veins of inquiry, into reading special books. These will develop your opinion, whether for or against. That opinion will in turn be expressed, will receive criticism from others in your environment, and will affect your standing in their eyes. We cannot escape our destiny, which is practical; and even our most theoretic faculties contribute to its working out.

These few reasons will perhaps smooth the way for you to acquiescence in my proposal. As teachers, I sincerely think it will be a sufficient conception for you to adopt of the youthful psychological phenomena handed over to your inspection if you consider them from the point of view of their relation to the future conduct of their possessor. Sufficient at any rate as a first conception and as a main conception. You should regard your professional task as if it consisted chiefly and essentially in *training the pupil to behavior;* taking behavior, not in the narrow sense of his manners, but in the very widest possible sense, as including every possible sort of fit reaction on the circumstances into which he may find himself. . . .

✳   ✳   ✳

Lecture V

"THE NECESSITY OF REACTIONS"

If all this be true, then immediately one general aphorism emerges which ought by logical right to dominate the entire conduct of the teacher in the classroom.

No reception without reaction, no impression without correlative expression,— this is the great maxim which the teacher ought never to forget.

An impression which simply flows in at the pupil's eyes or ears, and in no way modifies his active life, is an impression gone to waste. It is physiologically incomplete. It leaves no fruits behind it in the way of capacity acquired. Even as mere impression, it fails to produce its proper effect upon the memory; for, to remain fully among the acquisitions of this latter faculty, it must be wrought into the whole cycle of our operations. Its *motor consequences* are what clinch it. Some effect due to it in the way of an activity must return to the mind in the form of the *sensation of having acted,* and connect itself with the impression. The most durable impressions are those on account of which we speak or act, or else are inwardly convulsed.

The older pedagogic method of learning things by rote, and reciting them parrot-like in the schoolroom, rested on the truth that a thing merely read or heard, and never verbally reproduced, contracts the weakest possible adhesion in the mind. Verbal recitation or reproduction is thus a higher important kind of reactive behavior on our impressions; and it is to be feared that, in the reaction against the old parrot-recitations as the beginning and end of instruction, the extreme value of verbal recitation as an element of complete training may nowadays be too much forgotten.

When we turn to modern pedagogics, we see how enormously the field of reactive conduct has been extended by the introduction of all those methods of concrete object teaching which are the glory of our contemporary schools. Verbal reactions, useful as they are, are insufficient. The pupil's words may be right, but the conceptions corresponding to them are often direfully wrong. In a modern school, therefore, they form only a small part of what the pupil is required to do. He must keep notebooks, make drawings, plans, and maps, take measurements, enter the laboratory and perform experiments, consult authorities, and write essays. He must do in his fashion what is often laughed at by outsiders when it appears in prospectuses under the title of "original work," but what is really the only possible training for the doing of original work thereafter. The most colossal improvement which recent years have seen in secondary education lies in the introduction of the manual training schools; not because they will give us a people more handy and practical for domestic life and better skilled in trades, but because they will give us citizens with an entirely different intellectual fibre. Laboratory work and shop work engender a habit of observation, a knowledge of the difference between accuracy and vagueness, and an insight into nature's complexity and into the inadequacy of all abstract verbal accounts of real phenomena, which once wrought into the mind, remain there as lifelong possessions. They confer precision; because, if you are *doing* a thing, you must do it definitely right or definitely wrong. They give honesty; for, when you express yourself by making things, and not by using words, it becomes impossible to dissimulate your vagueness or ignorance by ambiguity. They beget a habit of self-reliance; they keep the interest and attention always cheerfully engaged, and reduce the teacher's disciplinary functions to a minimum.

Of the various systems of manual training, so far as woodwork is concerned, the Swedish Sloyd system, if I may have an opinion on such matters, seems to me by far the best, psychologically considered. Manual training methods, fortunately, are being slowly but surely introduced into all our large cities . . .

No impression without expression, then,—that is the first pedagogic fruit of our evolutionary conception of the mind as something instrumental to adaptive behavior. But a word may be said in continuation. The expression itself comes back to us, as I intimated a moment ago, in the form of a still farther impression,—the impression, namely, of what we have done. We thus receive sensible news of our behavior and its results. We hear the words we have spoken, feel our own blow as we give it, or read in the bystander's eyes the success or failure of our conduct. Now this return wave of impression pertains to the completeness of the whole experience, and a word about its importance in the schoolroom may not be out of place.

It would seem only natural to say that, since after acting we normally get some return impression of result, it must be well to let the pupil get such a return impression in every possible case. Nevertheless, in schools where examination marks and "standing" and other returns of result are concealed, the pupil is frustrated of this natural termination of the cycle of his activities, and often suffers from the sense of incompleteness and uncertainty; and there are persons who defend this system as encouraging the pupil to work for the work's sake, and not for extraneous reward. Of course, here as elsewhere, concrete experience must prevail over psychological deduction. But, so far as our psychological deduction goes, it would suggest that the pupil's eagerness to know how well he does is in the line of his normal completeness of function, and should never be balked except for very definite reasons indeed.

❉   ❉   ❉

I have now ended these talks. If to some of you the things I have said seem obvious or trivial, it is possible that they may appear less so when, in the course of a year or two, you find yourselves noticing and apperceiving events in the schoolroom a little differently, in consequence of some of the conceptions I have tried to make more clear. I cannot but think that to apperceive your pupil as a little sensitive, impulsive, associative, and reactive organism, partly fated and partly free, will lead to a better intelligence of all his ways. Understand him, then, as such a subtle little piece of machinery. And if, in addition, you can also see him *sub specie boni*, and love him as well, you will be in the best possible position for becoming perfect teachers.

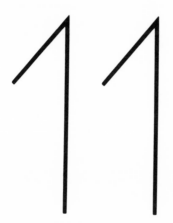

11

HIGHER
EDUCATION

The Old-Time College

STUDENT REGULATIONS AT SOUTH CAROLINA COLLEGE (1807)   From Edwin L. Green, *A History of the University of South Carolina* (Columbia, S.C., 1916), pp. 220–22.

1. If any student shall be guilty of any blasphemy, robbery, dueling, fornication, forgery, or any such atrocious crime, he shall be expelled.

2. All the students are strictly forbidden to play at cards, or any unlawful game; to use profane or obscene language; to strike or insult any person; to associate with persons of known bad character; to visit taverns without liberty; to appear in indecent dress, or in woman's apparel; to lie, steal, get drunk, or be guilty of other gross immoralities. If any student shall transgress in any of these respects, he shall be admonished, suspended, degraded or expelled, as the case may require.

3. No student may keep in his room any kind of firearms or gun powder; nor fire any in or near the College, in any manner whatever; and any student who shall violate this law, shall be liable to admonition, suspension or expulsion.

Rutgers' College (constructed 1811), New Brunswick, N.J., c. 1840.

4. If any student shall wilfully insult or strike any of the officers of the College, he shall be suspended or expelled.

5. All the students are strictly forbidden to play on any instrument of music in the hours of study, and also on Sunday; and shall abstain from their usual diversions and exercises on those days.

6. If any student shall refuse to open the door of his room, when required to do it by one of the Faculty, he shall be liable to public admonition; and the Faculty, when they shall think it necessary may break open any room in the College at the expense of those by whom they are refused admittance.

7. If any student shall refuse to give evidence respecting the violation of any of the laws of the College, when required by the Faculty, he shall be admonished or suspended.

8. No student is permitted to make a practice of entertaining company in his room, especially in the hours of study.

9. All students are strictly forbidden, without previous liberty obtained of a member of the Faculty, to bring any spiritous liquor into the College; and if any student, by bringing spiritous liquor into the College, shall be the occasion of riotous conduct or tumult, he shall be liable to admonition or suspension.

10. No student shall make any festival entertainment in the College, or in the town of Columbia, or take part in any thing of the kind, without liberty previously obtained of the President.

11. All the students are required to be particularly careful respecting fire, especially when they are obliged to go from their rooms; or in carrying it through the entries; and they are strictly forbidden to smoke segars or pipes in any part of the College, except their own rooms.

12. If any students shall enter into a combination to oppose the authority of the Faculty, or to impede the operation of the laws, they shall be punished by admonition, suspension or expulsion; and if any student shall express a determination not to submit to the laws, he shall be immediately suspended from the College; and be reported to the trustees.

DANIEL WEBSTER ARGUES THE DARTMOUTH COLLEGE CASE

(1819)   From "The Trustees of *Dartmouth College* vs. *Woodward*," *Reports of Cases Argued and Decided in the Supreme Court of the United States* (Newark, N.J., 1882), vol. IV, pp. 598–600.

If it could be made to appear that the trustees and the president and professors held their offices and franchises during the pleasure of the legislature, and that the property holden belonged to the state, then, indeed, the legislature have done no more than they had a right to do. But this is not so. The charter is a charter of privileges and immunities; and these are holden by the trustees expressly against the state forever. It is admitted that the state, by its courts of law, can enforce the will of the donor, and compel a faithful execution of the trust. The plaintiffs claim no exemption from legal responsibility. They hold themselves at all times answerable to the law of the land for their conduct in the trust committed to them. They ask only to hold the property of which they are owners, and the franchises which belong to them, until they shall be found, by due course and process of law, to have forfeited them. It can make no difference whether the legislature exercise the power it has assumed, by removing the trustees and the president and professors, directly, and by name, or by appointing others to expel them. The principal is the same, and in point of fact, the result has been the same. If the entire franchise cannot be taken away, neither can it be essentially impaired. If the trustees are legal owners of the property, they are sole owners. If they are visitors, they are sole visitors. No one will be found to say, that if the legislature may do what it has done, it may not do anything and every thing which it may choose to do, relative to the property of the corporation, and the privileges of its members and officers.

If the view which has been taken of this question be at all correct, this was an eleemosynary corporation; a private charity. The property was private property. The trustees were visitors, and their right to hold the charter, administer the funds, and visit and govern the college, was a franchise and privilege, solemnly granted to them. The use being public, in no way diminishes their legal estate in the property, or their title to the franchise. There is no principle, nor any case, which declares that a gift to such a corporation is a gift to the public. The acts in question violate property. They take away privileges, immunities, and franchises. They deny to the trustees the protection of the law; and they are retrospective in their operation. In all which respects, they are against the constitution of New Hampshire.

2. The plaintiffs contend, in the second place, that the acts in question are

repugnant to the 10th section of the 1st article of the Constitution of the United States. The material words of that section are: "No state shall pass any bill of attainder, *ex post facto* law, or law impairing the obligation of contracts."

*　　*　　*

There are, in this case, all the essential constituent parts of a contract. There is something to be contracted about; there are parties, and there are plain terms in which the agreement of the parties, on the subject of the contract, is expressed. There are mutual considerations and inducements. The charter recites, that the founder, on his part, has agreed to establish his seminary in New Hampshire, and to enlarge it, beyond its original design, among other things, for the benefit of that province; and thereupon a charter is given to him and his associates, designated by himself, promising and assuring to them, under the plighted faith of the state, the right of governing the college, and administering its concerns, in the manner provided in the charter. There is a complete and perfect grant to them of all the power of superintendence, visitation, and government. Is not this a contract? If lands or money had been granted to him and his associates, for the same purposes, such grant could not be rescinded. And is there any difference, in legal contemplation, between a grant of corporate franchises and a grant of tangible property? No such difference is recognized in any decided case, nor does it exist in the common apprehension of mankind.

It is therefore contended, that this case falls within the true meaning of this provision of the constitution, as expounded in the decisions of this court; that the charter of 1769 is a contract, a stipulation, or agreement; mutual in its considerations, express and formal in its terms, and of a most binding and solemn nature. That the acts in question impair this contract, has already been sufficiently shown. . . .

The case before the court is not of ordinary importance, nor of every-day occurrence. It affects not this college only, but every college, and all the literary institutions of the country. They have flourished, hitherto, and have become in a high degree respectable and useful to the community. They have all a common principle of existence—the inviolability of their charters. It will be a dangerous, a most dangerous experiment, to hold these institutions subject to the rise and fall of popular parties, and the fluctuations of political opinions. If the franchise may be at any time taken away, or impaired, the property also may be taken away, or its use perverted. Benefactors will have no certainty of effecting the object of their bounty; and learned men will be deterred from devoting themselves to the service of such institutions, from the precarious title of their officers. Colleges and halls will be deserted by all better spirits, and become a theatre for the contention of politics. Party and faction will be cherished in the places consecrated to piety and learning. These consequences are neither remote nor possible only. They are certain and immediate.

When the court in North Carolina declared the law of the state, which repealed a grant to its university, unconstitutional and void, the legislature had the candor and the wisdom to repeal the law. This example, so honorable to the state which exhibited it, is most fit to be followed on this occasion. And there is good reason to hope that a state which has hitherto been so much distinguished for temperate councils, cautious legislation, and regard to law, will not fail to adopt a course which will accord with her highest and best interest, and, in no small degree, elevate her reputation. It was for many obvious reasons most anxiously desired that the question of the power of the legislature over this charter should have been finally decided in the state court. An earnest hope was entertained that the judges of that court might have viewed the case in a light favorable to the rights of the trustees. That hope has failed. It is here that those rights are now to be maintained, or they are prostrated forever. *Omnia alia perfugia bonorum, subsidia, consilia, auxilia, jura ceciderunt. Quem enim alium appellem? quem obtestor? quem implorem? Nisi hoc loco, nisi apud vos, nisi per vos, judices, salutem nostram, quae spe exigua extremaque pendet, temerimus; nihil est praeterea quo confugere possimus.*

This, Sir, is my case! It is the case, not merely of that humble institution, it is the case of every College in the land. It is more. It is the case of every Eleemosynary Institution throughout our country—of all those great charities founded by the piety of our ancestors to alleviate human misery, and scatter blessings along the pathway of life. It is more! It is, in some sense, the case of every man among us who has property of which he may be stripped, for the question is simply this: Shall our State Legislatures be allowed to take *that* which is not their own, to turn it from its original use, and apply it to such ends or purposes as they, in their discretion, shall see fit!

Sir, you may destroy this little Institution; it is weak; it is in your hands! I know it is one of the lesser lights in the literary horizon of our country. You may put it out. But, if you do so, you must carry through your work! You must extinguish, one after another, all those greater lights of science which, for more than a century, have thrown their radiance over our land!

It is, Sir, as I have said, a small College. And yet, *there are those who love it—.*

Sir, I know not how others may feel . . . but, for myself, when I see my alma mater surrounded, like Caesar in the senate house, by those who are reiterating stab after stab, I would not, for this right hand, have her turn to me, and say, *Et tu quoque mi fili! And thou too, my son!*

CHIEF JUSTICE JOHN MARSHALL'S OPINION IN THE DARTMOUTH COLLEGE CASE (1819)   From *Trustees of* Dartmouth College *vs.* Woodward, *4 Wheaton 624* (1819).

Feb. 2d, 1819

The opinion of the Court was delivered by Mr. Chief Justice MARSHALL.

This is an action of trover, brought by the trustees of Dartmouth College against William H. Woodward, in the State Court of New Hampshire, for the book of records, corporate seal, and other corporate property, to which the plaintiffs allege themselves to be entitled. . . .

The title of the plaintiffs originates in a charter dated the 13th day of December, in the year 1769, incorporating twelve persons therein mentioned, by the name of "The Trustees of Dartmouth College," granting to them and their successors the usual corporate privileges and powers, and authorizing the trustees, who are to govern the college, to fill up all vacancies which may be created in their own body.

The defendant claims under three acts of the legislature of New Hampshire, the most material of which was passed on the 27th of June, 1816, and is entitled, "an act to amend the charter, and enlarge and improve the corporation of Dartmouth College." Among other alterations in the charter, this act increases the number of trustees to twenty-one, gives the appointment of the additional members to the executive of the state, and creates a board of overseers, with power to inspect and control the most important acts of the trustees. This board consists of twenty-five persons. The president of the senate, the speaker of the house of representatives, of New Hampshire, and the Governor and Lieutenant-Governor of Vermont, for the time being, are to be members *ex officio*. The board is to be completed by the Governor and council of New Hampshire, who are also empowered to fill all vacancies which may occur. The acts of the 18th and 26th of December are supplemental to that of the 27th of June, and are principally intended to carry that act into effect.

The majority of the trustees of the college have refused to accept this amended charter, and have brought this suit for the corporate property, which is in possession of a person holding by virtue of the acts which have been stated.

It can require no argument to prove that the circumstances of this case constitute a contract. An application is made to the crown for a charter to incorporate a religious and literary institution. In the application, it is stated that large contributions have been made for the object, which will be conferred on the corporation as soon as it shall be created. The charter is granted, and on its faith the property is conveyed. Surely in this transaction every ingredient of a complete and legitimate contract is to be found.

The points for consideration are:

1. Is this contract protected by the constitution of the United States?
2. Is it impaired by the acts under which the defendant holds?

*　　*　　*

The parties in this case differ less on general principles, less on the true construction of the constitution in the abstract, than on the application of those principles to this case, and on the true construction of the charter of 1769. This is the point on which the cause essentially depends. If the act of incorporation be a grant of political power, if it create a civil institution to be employed in the administration of the government, or if the funds of the college be public property, or if the state of New Hampshire, as a government, be alone interested in its transactions, the subject is one in which the legislature of the state may act according to its own judgment, unrestrained by any limitation of its power imposed by the constitution of the United States.

*　　*　　*

Dartmouth College is really endowed by private individuals, who have bestowed their funds for the propogation of the Christian religion among the Indians, and for the promotion of piety and learning generally. From these funds the salaries of the tutors are drawn; and these salaries lessen the expense of education to the students. It is, then, an eleemosynary, and, as far as respects its funds, a private corporation.

Do its objects stamp on it a different character? Are the trustees and professors public officers, invested with any portion of political power, partaking in any degree in the administration of civil government, and performing duties which flow from the sovereign authority?

That education is an object of national concern, and a proper subject of legislation, all admit. That there may be an institution founded by government, and placed entirely under its immediate control, the officers of which would be public officers, amenable exclusively to government, none will deny. But is Dartmouth College such an institution? Is education altogether in the hands of government? Does every teacher of youth become a public officer, and do donations for the purpose of education necessarily become public property, so far that the will of the legislature, not the will of the donor, becomes the law of the donation? These questions are of serious moment to society, and deserve to be well considered.

Doctor [Eleazar] Wheelock, as the keeper of his charity-school, instructing the Indians in the art of reading, and in our holy religion; sustaining them at his own expense, and on the voluntary contributions of the charitable, could scarcely be considered as a public officer, exercising any portion of those duties which belong to government; nor could the legislature have supposed that his private funds, or those given by others, were subject to legislative management, because they were applied to the purposes of education. When, afterwards, his school was enlarged, and the liberal contributions made in England, and in America, enabled him to extend his cares to the education of the youth of his own country, no change was wrought in his own character, or in the nature of his duties. . . .

A corporation is an artificial being, invisible, intangible, and existing only in contemplation of law. Being the mere creature of law, it possesses only those properties which the charter of its creation confers upon it, either expressly or as incidental to its very existence. These are such as are supposed best calculated to effect the object for which it was created. Among the most important are immortality, and, if the expression may be allowed, individuality; properties by which a perpetual succession of many persons are considered as the same, and may act as a single individual. They enable a corporation to manage its own affairs, and to hold property without the perplexing intricacies, the hazardous and endless necessity, of perpetual conveyances for the purpose of transmitting it from hand to hand. It is chiefly for the purpose of clothing bodies of men, in succession, with these qualities and capacities, that corporations were invented, and are in use. By these means, a perpetual succession of individuals are capable of acting for the promotion of the particular object, like one immortal being. But this being does not share in the civil government of the country, unless that be the purpose for which it was created. Its immortality no more confers on it political power, or a political character, than immortality would confer such power or character on a natural person. It is no more a state instrument than a natural person exercising the same powers would be. If, then, a natural person, employed by individuals in the education of youth, or for the government of a seminary in which youth is educated, would not become a public officer, or be considered as a member of the civil government, how is it that this artificial being, created by law, for the purpose of being employed by the same individuals for the same purposes, should become a part of the civil government of the country? Is it because its existence, its capacities, its powers, are given by law? Because the government has given it the power to take and to hold property in a particular form, and for particular purposes, has the government a consequent right substantially to change that form, or to vary the purposes to which the property is to be applied? This principle has never been asserted or recognized, and is supported by no authority. Can it derive aid from reason?

The objects for which a corporation is created are universally such as the government wishes to promote. They are deemed beneficial to the country; and this benefit constitutes the consideration, and, in most cases, the sole consideration of the grant. In most eleemosynary institutions, the object would be difficult, perhaps unattainable, without the aid of a charter of incorporation. Charitable, or public-spirited individuals, desirous of making permanent appropriations for charitable or other useful purposes, find it impossible to effect their design securely, and certainly, without an incorporating act. They apply to the government, state their beneficent object, and offer to advance the money necessary for its accomplishment, provided the government will confer on the instrument which is to execute their designs the capacity to execute them. The proposition is considered and approved. The benefit to the public is considered as an ample compensation for the faculty it confers, and the corporation is created. If the advantages to the public constitute a full compensation for the faculty it gives, there can be no reason for exacting a further compensation, by claiming a right to exercise over this artificial being a power which changes its nature, and touches the fund, for the security and application of which it was created. . . .

From this review of the charter, it appears that Dartmouth College is an eleemosynary institution, incorporated for the purpose of perpetuating the application of the bounty of the donors, to the specified objects of that bounty; that its trustees or governors were originally named by the founder, and invested with the power of perpetuating themselves; that they are not public officers, nor is it a civil institution, participating in the administration of government; but a charity school, or a seminary of education, incorporated for the preservation of its property, and the perpetual application of that property to the objects of its creation. . . .

Almost all eleemosynary corporations, those which are created for the promotion of religion, of charity, or of education, are of the same character. The law of this case is the law of all. In every literary or charitable institution, unless the objects of the bounty be themselves incorporated, the whole legal interest is in trustees, and can be asserted only by them. The donors or claimants of the bounty, if they can appear in court at all, can appear only to complain of the trustees. In all other situations, they are identified with, and personated by, the trustees; and their rights are to be defended and maintained by them. Religion, Charity, and Education, are, in the law of England, legatees or donees, capable of receiving bequests or donations in this form. They appear in court, and claim or defend by the corporation. Are they of so little estimation in the United States that contracts for their benefit must be excluded from the protection of words which, in their natural import, include them? Or do such contracts so necessarily require new-modeling by the authority of the legislature that the ordinary rules of construction must be disregarded in order to leave them exposed to legislative alteration?

All feel that these objects are not deemed unimportant in the United States. The interest which this case has excited proves that they are not. The framers of the constitution did not deem them unworthy of its care and protection. They have, though in a different mode, manifested their respect for science, by reserving to the government of the Union the power "to promote the progress of science and useful arts, by securing for limited times to authors and inventors the exclusive right to their respective writings and discoveries." They have so far withdrawn science, and the useful arts, from the action of the state governments. Why, then, should they be supposed so regardless of contracts made for the advancement of literature as to intend to exclude them from provisions made for the security of ordinary contracts between man and man? No reason for making this supposition is perceived.

If the insignificance of the object does not require that we should exclude contracts respecting it from the protection of the constitution, neither, as we conceive, is the policy of leaving them subject to legislative alteration so apparent as to require a forced construction of that instrument in order to effect it. These eleemosynary institutions do not fill the place, which would otherwise be occupied by government, but that which would otherwise remain vacant. They are complete acquisitions to literature. They are donations to education; donations which any government must be disposed rather to encourage than to discountenance. It requires no very critical examination of the human mind to enable us to determine that one great inducement to these gifts is the conviction felt by the giver, that the disposition he makes of them is immutable. It is probable that no man ever was, and that no man ever will be, the founder of a college, believing at the time that an act of incorporation constitutes no security for the institution; believing that it is immediately to be deemed a public institution, whose funds are to be governed and applied, not by the will of the donor, but by the will of the legislature. All such gifts are made in the pleasing, perhaps delusive hope, that the charity will flow forever in the channel which the givers have marked out for it. If every man finds in his own bosom strong evidence of the universality of this sentiment, there can be but little reason to imagine that the framers of our constitution were strangers to it, and that, feeling the necessity and policy of giving permanence and security to contracts, of withdrawing them from the influence of legislative bodies, whose fluctuating policy, and repeated interferences, produced the most perplexing and injurious embarrassments, they still deemed it necessary to leave these contracts subject to those interferences.

DEFENSE OF THE CLASSICS: THE YALE REPORT (1828)   From "Original Papers in Relation to a Course of Liberal Education," *American Journal of Science and Arts*, vol. XV, pp. 297–303, 308–13, 315, 317–20, 340.

At a Meeting of the President and Fellows of Yale College, Sept 11th, 1827, the Following Resolution Was Passed

That His Excellency Governor Tomlinson, Rev. President Day, Rev. Dr. Chapin, Hon. Noyes Darling, and Rev. Abel McEwen, be a committee to inquire into the expediency of so altering the regular course of instruction in this college, as to leave out of said course the study of the *dead languages*, substituting other studies therefor; and either requiring a competent knowledge of said languages, as a condition of admittance into the college, or providing instruction in the same, for such as shall choose to study them after admittance; and that the said committee be requested to report at the next annual meeting of this corporation.

This committee, at their first meeting in April, 1828, after taking into consideration the case referred to them, requested the Faculty of the college to express their views on the subject of the resolution.

The expediency of retaining the ancient languages, as an essential part of our course of instruction, is so obviously connected with the object and plan of education in the college, that justice could not be done to the particular subject of inquiry in the resolution, without a brief statement of the nature and arrangement of the various branches of the whole system. The report of the faculty was accordingly made out in *two parts;* one containing a summary view of the plan of education in the college; the other, an inquiry into the expediency of insisting on the study of the ancient languages.

*   *   *

The guardians of the college appear to have ever acted upon the principle, that it ought not to be stationary, but continually advancing. Some alteration has accordingly been proposed, almost every year, from its first establishment. It is with no small surprise, therefore, we occasionally hear the suggestion, that our system is unalterable; that colleges were originally planned, in the days of monkish ignorance; and that "by being immovably moored to the same station, they serve only to measure the rapid current of improvement which is passing by them."

How opposite to all this, is the real state of facts, in this and the other seminaries in the United States. Nothing is more common, than to hear those who revisit the college, after a few years absence, express their surprise at the changes which have been made since they were graduated. Not only the course of studies, and the modes of instruction, have been greatly varied; but whole sciences have, for the first time, been introduced; chemistry, mineralogy, geology, political economy, &c. By raising the qualifications for admission, the standard of attainment has been elevated. Alterations so extensive and frequent, satisfactorily prove, that if those who are intrusted with the superintendence of the institution, still firmly adhere to some of its original features, it is from a higher principle, than a blind opposition to salutary reform. Improvements, we trust, will continue to be made, as rapidly as they can be, without hazarding the loss of what has been already attained.

But perhaps the time has come, when we ought to pause, and inquire, whether it will be sufficient to make *gradual* changes, as heretofore; and whether the whole system is not rather to be broken up, and a better one substituted in its stead. From different quarters, we have heard the suggestion, that our colleges must be *new-modelled;* that they are not adapted to the spirit and wants of the age; that they will soon be deserted, unless they are better accommodated to the business character of the nation. As this point may have an important bearing upon the question immediately before the committee, we would ask their indulgence, while we attempt to explain, at some length, the nature and object of the present plan of education at the college.

We shall in vain attempt to decide on the expediency of retaining or altering our present course of instruction, unless we have a distinct apprehension of the *object* of a collegiate education. A plan of study may be well adapted to a particular purpose, though it may be very unsuitable for a different one. Universities, colleges, academical, and professional seminaries, ought not to be all constituted upon the same model; but should be so varied as to attain the ends which they have severally in view.

What then is the appropriate object of a college? It is not necessary here to determine what it is which, in every case, entitles an institution to the *name* of a college. But if we have not greatly misapprehended the design of the patrons and guardians of this college, its object is to LAY THE FOUNDATION OF A SUPERIOR EDUCATION: and this is to be done, at a period of life when a substitute must be provided for *parental superintendence*. The ground work of a thorough education, must be broad, and deep, and solid. For a partial or superficial education, the support may be of looser materials, and more hastily laid.

The two great points to be gained in intellectual culture, are the *discipline* and the *furniture* of the mind; expanding its powers, and storing it with knowledge. The former of these is, perhaps, the more important of the two. A commanding object, therefore, in a collegiate course, should be, to call into daily and vigorous exercise the faculties of the student. Those branches of study should be prescribed, and those modes of instruction adopted, which are best calculated to teach the art of fixing the attention, directing the train of thought, analyzing a subject proposed for investigation; following, with accurate discrimination, the course of argument; balancing nicely the evidence presented to the judgment; awakening, elevating, and controlling the imagination; arranging, with skill, the treasures which memory gathers; rousing and guiding the powers of genius. All this is not to be effected by a light and hasty course of study; by reading a few books, hearing a few lectures, and spending some months at a literary institution. The habits of thinking are to be formed, by long continued and close application. The mines of science must be penetrated far below the surface, before they will disclose their treasures. If a dexterous performance of the manual operations, in many of the mechanical arts, requires an apprenticeship, with diligent attention for years; much more does the training of the powers of the mind demand vigorous, and steady, and systematic effort.

In laying the foundation of a thorough education, it is necessary that *all* the important mental faculties be brought into exercise. It is not sufficient that one or two be cultivated, while others are neglected. A costly edifice ought not to be left to rest upon a single pillar. When certain mental endowments receive a much higher culture than others, there is a distortion in the intellectual character. The mind never attains its full perfection, unless its various powers are so trained as to give them the fair proportions which nature designed. If the student exercises his reasoning powers only, he will be deficient in imagination and taste, in fervid and impressive eloquence. If he confines his attention to demonstrative evidence, he will be unfitted to decide correctly, in cases of probability. If he relies principally on his memory, his powers of invention will be impaired by disuse. In the course of instruction in this college, it has been an object to maintain such a proportion between the different branches of literature and science, as to form in the student a proper *balance* of character. From the pure mathematics, he learns the art of demonstrative reasoning. In attending to the physical sciences, he becomes familiar with facts, with the process of induction, and the varieties of probable evidence. In ancient literature, he finds some of the most finished models of taste. By English reading, he learns the powers of the language in which he is to speak and write. By logic and mental philosophy, he is taught the art of thinking; by rhetoric and oratory, the art of speaking. By frequent exercise on written composition, he acquires copiousness and accuracy of expression. By extemporaneous discussion, he becomes prompt, and fluent, and animated. It is a point of high importance, that eloquence and solid learning should go together; that he who has accumulated the richest treasures of thought, should possess the highest powers of oratory. To what purpose has a man become deeply learned, if he has no faculty of communicating his knowledge? And of what use is a display of rhetorical elegance, from one who knows little or nothing which is worth communicating? Est enim scientia comprehendenda rerum plurimarum, sine qua verborum volubilitas inanis atque irridenda est. Cic. Our course, therefore, aims at a union of science with literature; of solid attainment with skill in the art of persuasion.

No one feature in a system of intellectual education, is of greater moment than such an arrangement of duties and motives, as will most effectually throw the student upon the *resources of his own mind*. Without this, the whole apparatus of libraries, and instruments, and specimens, and lectures, and teachers, will be insufficient to secure distinguished excellence. The scholar must form himself, by his own exertions. The advantages furnished by a residence at a college, can do little more than stimulate and aid his personal efforts. The *inventive* powers are especially to be called into vigorous exercise. However abundant may be the acquisition of the student, if he has no talent at forming new combinations of thought, he will be dull and inefficient. The sublimest efforts of genius consist in the creations of the imagination, the discoveries of the intellect, the conquests by which the dominions of science are extended. But the culture of the inventive faculties is not the *only* object of a liberal education. The most gifted understanding cannot greatly enlarge the amount of science to which the wisdom of ages has contributed. If it were possible for a youth to have his faculties in the highest state of cultivation, without any of the knowledge which is derived from others, he would be but poorly fitted for the business of life. To the discipline of the mind, therefore, is to be added instruction. The analytic method must be combined with the synthetic. Analysis is most efficacious in directing the powers of invention; but is far too slow in its progress to teach, within a moderate space of time, the circle of the sciences.

In our arrangements for the communication of knowledge, as well as in intellectual discipline, such branches are to be taught as will produce a proper symmetry and balance of character. We doubt whether the powers of the mind can be developed, in their fairest proportions, by studying languages alone, or mathematics alone, or natural or political science alone. As the bodily frame is brought to its highest perfection, not by one simple and uniform motion, but by a variety of exercises; so the mental faculties are expanded, and invigorated, and adapted to each other, by familiarity with different departments of science.

A most important feature in the colleges of this country is, that the students are generally of an age which requires, that a substitute be provided for *parental superintendence*. When removed from under the roof of their parents, and exposed to the untried scenes of temptation, it is necessary that some faithful and affectionate guardian take them by the hand, and guide their steps. This consideration determines the *kind* of government which ought to be maintained in our colleges. As it is a substitute for the regulations of a family, it should approach as near to the character of parental control as the circumstances of the case will admit. It should be founded on mutual affection and confidence. It should aim to effect its purpose, principally by kind and persuasive influence; not wholly or chiefly by restraint and terror. Still, punishment may sometimes be necessary. There may be perverse members of a college, as well as of a family. There may be those whom nothing but the arm of law can reach.

The parental character of college government, requires that the students should be so collected together, as to constitute one family; that the intercourse between them and their instructers may be frequent and familiar. This renders it necessary that suitable *buildings* be provided, for the residence of the students:—we speak now of colleges in the country, the members of which are mostly gathered from a distance.

*　*　*

The collegiate course of study, of which we have now given a summary view, we hope may be carefully distinguished from several *other* objects and plans, with which it has been too often confounded. It is far from embracing *every thing* which the student will ever have occasion to learn. The object is not to *finish* his education; but to lay the foundation, and to advance as far in rearing the superstructure, as the short period of his residence here will admit. If he acquires here a thorough knowledge of the principles of science, he may then, in a great measure, educate himself. He has, at least, been taught *how* to learn. With the aid of books, and means of observation, he may be constantly advancing in knowledge. Wherever he goes, into whatever company he falls, he has those general views, on every topic of interest, which will enable him to understand, to digest, and to form a correct opinion, on the statements and discussions which he hears. There are many things important to be known, which are not taught in colleges, because they may be learned any where. The knowledge, though indispensable, comes to us as freely, in the way of our business, as our necessary supplies of light, and air, and water.

The course of instruction which is given to the undergraduates in the college, is not designed to include *professional* studies. Our object is not to teach that which is peculiar to any one of the professions; but to lay the foundation which is common to them all. There are separate schools for medicine, law, and theology, connected with the college, as well as in various parts of the country; which are open for the reception of all who are prepared to enter upon the appropriate studies of their several professions. With these, the academical course is not intended to interfere.

But why, it may be asked, should a student waste his time upon studies which have no immediate connection with his future profession? Will chemistry enable him to plead at the bar, or conic sections qualify him for preaching, or astronomy aid him in the practice of physic? Why should not his attention be confined to the subject which is to occupy the labors of his life? In answer to this, it may be observed, that there is no science which does not contribute its aid to professional skill. "Every thing throws light upon every thing." The great object of a collegiate education, preparatory to the study of a profession, is to give that expansion and balance of the mental powers, those liberal and comprehensive views, and those fine proportions of character, which are not to be found in him whose ideas are always confined to one particular channel. When a man has entered upon the practice of his profession, the energies of his mind must be given, principally, to its appropriate duties. But if his thoughts never range on other subjects, if he never looks abroad on the ample domains of literature and science, there will be a narrowness in his habits of thinking, a peculiarity of character, which will be sure to mark him as a man of limited views and attainments. Should he be distinguished in his profession, his ignorance on other subjects, and the defects of his education, will be the more exposed to public observation. On the other hand, he who is not only eminent in professional life, but has also a mind richly stored with general knowledge, has an elevation and dignity of character, which gives him a commanding influence in society, and a widely extended sphere of usefulness. His situation enables him to diffuse the light of science among all classes of the community. Is a man to have no other object, than to obtain a *living* by professional pursuits? Has he not duties to perform to his family, to his fellow citizens, to his country; duties which require various and extensive intellectual furniture?

Professional studies are designedly excluded from the course of instruction at college, to leave room for those literary and scientific acquisitions which, if not commenced there, will, in most cases, never be made. They will not grow up spontaneously, amid the bustle of business. We are not here speaking of those giant minds which, by their native energy, break through the obstructions of a defective education, and cut their own path to distinction. These are honorable exceptions to the general law; not examples for common imitation. Franklins and Marshalls are not found in sufficient numbers to fill a college. And even Franklin would not have been what he was, if there had been no colleges in the country. When an elevated standard of education is maintained, by the higher literary institutions, men of superior powers, who have not had access to these, are stimulated to aim at a similar elevation, by their own efforts, and by aid of the light which is thus shining around them.

As our course of instruction is not intended to complete an education, in theological, medical, or legal science; neither does it include all the minute details of *mercantile, mechanical,* or *agricultural* concerns. These can never be effectually learned except in the very circumstances in which they are to be practised. The young merchant must be trained in the counting room, the mechanic, in the workshop, the farmer, in the field. But we have, on our premises, no experimental farm or retail shop; no cotton or iron manufactory; no hatter's, or silver-smith's, or coach-maker's establishment. For what purpose, then, it will be asked, are young men who are destined to these occupations, ever sent to a college? They should not be sent, as we think, with an expectation of *finishing* their education at the college; but with a view of laying a thorough foundation in the principles of science, preparatory to the study of the practical arts. As every thing cannot be learned in four years, either theory or practice must be, in a measure at least, postponed to a future opportunity. But if the scientific theory of the arts is *ever* to be acquired, it is unquestionably first in order of time. The corner stone must be laid, before the superstructure is erected. If suitable arrangements were made, the details of mercantile, mechanical, and agricultural education, might be taught at the college, to *resident graduates.* Practical skill would then be grounded upon scientific information.

The question may be asked, What is a young man fitted for, when he takes his degree? Does he come forth from the college qualified for business? We answer, no,—if he stops here. His education is begun, but not completed. Is the college to be reproached for not accomplishing that which it has never undertaken to perform? Do we complain of the mason, who has lad the foundation of a house, that he has done nothing to purpose; that he has not finished the building; that the product of his labor is not habitable; and that, therefore, there is nothing practical in what he has done? Do we say of the planter, who has raised a crop of cotton, that he has done nothing practical, because he has not given to his product the form of wearing apparel?

In education, as well as in morals, we often hear the suggestion, that principles are of no consequence, provided the practice is right. Why waste on theories, the time which is wanted for acquiring practical arts? We are aware, that some operations may be performed, by those who have little or no knowledge of the principles on which they depend. The mariner may set his sails to the wind, without understanding the laws of the decomposition of forces; the carpenter may square his framework, without a knowledge of Euclid's Elements; the dyer may set his colors, without being indoctrinated in the principles of chemistry. But the labors of such an one, are confined to the narrow path marked out to him by others. He needs the constant superintendence of men of more enlarged and scientific information. If he ventures beyond his prescribed rule, he works at random, with no established principles to guide him. By long continued practice, he may have attained a good degree of manual dexterity. But the arranging of plans of business, the new combinations of mechanical processes, the discoveries and improvements in the arts, must generally come from minds more highly and systematically cultivated. There is a fertility in scientific principles, of which the mere artist has no apprehension. A single general law may include a thousand or ten thousand particular cases; each one of which is as difficult to be learned or remembered, as the law which explains them all. Men of mere practical detail are wanted, in considerable numbers, to fill the subordinate places in mechanical establishments; but the higher stations require enlightened and comprehensive views.

We are far from believing that theory *alone*, should be taught in a college. It cannot be effectually taught, except in connection with practical illustrations. These are necessary in exciting an interest in theoretical instructions; and especially important in showing the application of principles. It is our aim therefore, while engaged in scientific investigations, to blend with them, as far as possible, practical illustrations and experiments. Of what use are all the sublime discoveries which have immortalized the names of Newton, Archimedes, and others; if the principles which they have unfolded, are never to be taught to those who can reduce them to practice? Why do we bestow such exalted encomiums on inventive genius, if the results of original investigations, are to be confined to a few scientific men, and not diffused among those who are engaged in the active duties of life? To bring down the principles of science to their practical application by the laboring classes, is the office of men of superior education. It is the separation of theory and practice, which has brought reproach upon both. Their union alone can elevate them to their true dignity and value. The man of science is often disposed to assume an air of superiority, when he looks upon the narrow and partial views of the mere artisan. The latter in return laughs at the practical blunders of the former. The defects in the education of both classes would be remedied, by giving them a knowledge of scientific principles, preparatory to practice.

We are aware that a thorough education is not within the reach of all. Many, for want of time and pecuniary resources, must be content with a partial course. A defective education is better than none. If a youth can afford to devote only two or three years, to a scientific and professional education, it will be proper for him to make a selection of a few of the most important branches, and give his attention exclusively to these. But this is an imperfection, arising from the necessity of the case. A partial course of study, must inevitably give a partial education.

This, we are well convinced, is far preferable to a *superficial* education. Of all the plans of instruction which have been offered to the public, that is the most preposterous, which supposes to teach almost every thing in a short time. In this way, nothing is effectually taught. The pupil is hurried over the surface so rapidly, that scarce a trace of his steps remains, when he has finished his course. What he has learned, or thinks he has learned, is just sufficient to inflate his vanity, to expose him to public observation, and to draw on him the ridicule of men of sound judgment and science. A partial education is often expedient; a superficial one, never. Whatever a young man undertakes to learn, however little it may be, he ought to learn it so effectually, that it may be of some practical use to him. If there is any way in which every thing worth knowing may be taught in four years, we are free to acknowledge, that we are not in possession of the secret.

But why, it is asked, should *all* the students in a college be required to tread in the *same steps?* Why should not each one be allowed to select those branches of study which are most to his taste, which are best adapted to his peculiar talents, and which are most nearly connected with his intended profession? To this we answer, that our prescribed course contains those subjects only which ought to be understood, as we think, by every one who aims at a thorough education. They are not the peculiarities of any profession or art. These are to be learned in the professional and practical schools. But the principles of science, are the common foundation of all high intellectual attainments. As in our primary schools, reading, writing, and arithmetic are taught to all, however different their prospects; so in a college, all should be instructed in those branches of knowledge, of which no one destined to the higher walks of life ought to be ignorant. What subject which is now studied here, could be set aside, without evidently marring the system. Not to speak particularly, in this place, of the ancient languages; who that aims at a well proportioned and superior education will remain ignorant of the elements of the various branches of the mathematics, or of history and antiquities, or of rhetoric and oratory, or natural philosophy, or astronomy, or chemistry, or mineralogy, or geology, or political economy, or mental and moral philosophy?

It is sometimes thought that a student ought not to be urged to the study of that for which he has *no taste or capacity*. But how is he to know, whether he has a taste or capacity for a science, before he has even entered upon its elementary truths? If he is really destitute of talent sufficient for these common departments of education, he is destined for some narrow sphere of action.

*   *   *

The Universities on the continent of Europe, especially in Germany, have of late gained the notice and respect of men of information in this country. They are upon a broad and liberal scale, affording very great facilities for a finished education. But we doubt whether they are models to be copied in every feature, by our American colleges. We hope at least, that this college may be spared the mortification of a ludicrous attempt to imitate them, while it is unprovided with the resources necessary to execute the purpose. . . .

*   *   *

One of the pleas frequently urged in favor of a partial education, is the alleged *want of time* for a more enlarged course. We are well aware, as we have already observed, that a thorough education cannot be begun and finished in four years. But if three years immediately preceding the age of twenty-one be allowed for the study of a profession, there is abundant time previous to this for the attainment of all which is now required for admission into the college, in addition to the course prescribed for the undergraduates. Though the limit of age for admission is fixed by our laws at fourteen, yet how often have we been pressed to dispense with the rule, in behalf of some youth who has completed his preparation at an earlier period; and who, if compelled to wait till he has attained the requisite age, "is in danger of being ruined for want of employment?" May we not expect, that this plea will be urged with still greater earnestness, when the present improved methods of instruction in the elementary and preparatory schools, are more and more accelerating the early progress of the pupil?

But suppose it should happen that the student, in consequence of commencing his studies at a later period, should be delayed a little longer, before entering upon the duties of his profession; is this a sacrifice worthy to be compared with the immense difference between the value of a limited and a thorough education? Is a young man's pushing forward into business, so indispensable to his future welfare, that rather than suspend it for a single year, he must forego all the advantage of superior intellectual discipline and attainments?

We well know that the whole population of the country can never enjoy the benefit of a thorough course of education. A large portion must be content with the very limited instruction in our primary schools. Others may be able to add to this the privilege of a few months at an academy. Others still, with higher aims and more ample means, may afford to spend two or three years, in attending upon a partial course of study, in some institution which furnishes instruction in any branch or branches selected by the pupil or his parents.

The question is then presented, whether the college shall have all the variety of classes and departments which are found in academies; or whether it shall confine itself to the single object of a well proportioned and thorough course of study. It is said that the public demand, that the doors should be thrown open to all; that education ought to be so modified, and varied, as to adapt it to the exigencies of the country, and the prospects of different individuals; that the instruction given to those who are destined to be merchants, or manufacturers, or agriculturalists, should have a special reference to their respective professional pursuits.

The public are undoubtedly right, in demanding that there should be appropriate courses of education, accessible to all classes of youth. And we rejoice at the prospect of ample provision for this purpose, in the improvement of our academies, and the establishment of commercial high-schools, gymnasia, lycea, agricultural seminaries, &c. But do the public insist, that every college shall become a high-school, gymnasium, lyceum, and academy? Why should we interefere with these valuable institutions? Why wish to take their business out of their hands? The college has its appropriate object, and they have theirs. What advantage would be gained by attempting to blend them all in one? When in almost all our schools, and academies, and professional seminaries, the standard of education has been enlarged and elevated, is this a time for the college to *lower* its standard? Shall we fall back, and abandon the ground which, for thirty years past, we have been striving so hard to gain? Are those who are seeking only a partial education to be admitted into the college, merely for the purpose of associating its *name* with theirs? of carrying away with them a collegiate *diploma*, without incurring the fearful hazard of being overeducated? Why is a degree from a college more highly prized, than a certificate from an academy, if the former is not a voucher of a superior education? When the course of instruction in the one, is reduced to the level of that in the other; to be graduated at either, will be equally honorable. What is the characteristic difference between a college and an academy? Not that the former teaches more branches than the latter. There are many academies in the country, whose scheme of studies, at least upon paper, is more various than that of the colleges. But while an academy teaches a little of every thing, the college, by directing its efforts to one uniform course, aims at doing its work with greater precision, and economy of time; just as the merchant who deals in a single class of commodities, or a manufacturer who produces but one kind of fabrics, executes his business more perfectly, than he whose attention and skill are divided among a multitude of objects.

If our treasury were overflowing, it we had a *surplus fund*, requiring us to look out for some new object on which to expend it, there might perhaps be no harm in establishing a department for a brief and rapid course of study, so far connected with the college, as to be under the superintendence of the same board of trust. But it ought to be as distinct from the four classes of undergraduates, as is the medical or law school. All the means which are now applied to the proper collegiate department, are barely sufficient, or rather are insufficient, for the object in view. No portion of our resources, or strength, or labor, can be diverted to other purposes, without impairing the education which we are attempting to give. A London university, commencing with a capital of several hundred thousand dollars, and aiming to provide a system of instruction for the youth in a city whose population is more than a million, may well establish its higher and inferior courses, its scientific and practical departments, its professional, mercantile, and mechanical institutions. But shall a college, with an income of two or three thousand a year from funds, affect to be at once a London university? Should we *ever* become such an institution, our present undergraduate course, ought still to constitute one distinct branch of the complicated system of arrangements.

But might we not, by making the college more accessible to different descriptions of persons, enlarge our *numbers,* and in that way, increase our income? This might be the operation of the measure, for a very short time, while a degree from the college should retain its present value in public estimation; a value depending entirely upon the character of the education which we give. But the moment it is understood that the institution has descended to an inferior standard of attainment, its reputation will sink to a corresponding level. After we shall have become a college in *name only,* and in reality nothing more than an academy; or half college, and half academy; what will induce parents in various and distant parts of the country, to send us their sons, when they have academies enough in their own neighborhood? There is no magical influence in an act of incorporation, to give celebrity to a literary institution, which does not command respect for itself, by the elevated rank of its education. When the college has lost its hold on the public confidence, by depressing its standard of merit, by substituting a partial, for a thorough education, we may expect that it will be deserted by that class of persons who have hitherto been drawn here by high expectations and purposes. Even if we should *not* immediately suffer in point of *numbers,* yet we shall exchange the best portion of our students, for others of inferior aims and attainments.

As long as we can maintain an elevated character, we need be under no apprehension with respect to numbers. Without character, it will be in vain to think of retaining them. It is a hazardous experiment, to act upon the plan of gaining numbers first, and character afterwards. . . .

No question has engaged the attention of the faculty more constantly, than how the course of education in the college might be improved, and rendered more practically useful. Free communications have at all times been held between the faculty and the corporation, on subjects connected with the instruction of the college. When the aid of the corporation has been thought necessary, it has been asked; and by this course of proceeding, the interests of the institution have been regularly advanced. No remark is more frequently made by those, who visit the college after the absence of some years, than that changes have been made for the better; and those who make the fullest investigation, are the most ready to approve what they find. The charge, therefore, that the college is stationary, that no efforts are made to accommodate it to the wants of the age, that all exertions are for the purpose of perpetuating abuses, and that the college is much the same as it was at the time of its foundation, are wholly gratuitous. The changes in the country, during the last century, have not been greater than the changes in the college. These remarks have been limited to Yale College, as its history is here best known; no doubt, other colleges alluded to in the above quotations, might defend themselves with equal success.

RELIGIOUS REVIVAL AT DENISON COLLEGE (1840)   From G. Wallace Chessman, *Denison: The Story of an Ohio College* (Granville, Ohio, 1957), pp. 81-82.

It had been wild excitement, and we had gone to chapel simply because it was duty, when in the dull routine, "Little Kerr" [John Kerr], who was sitting back by the chimney, rose and asked us to pray for him! We were amazed; we were not ready, but we had to work immediately, ready or not. In a little while seven or eight of as wild boys as were in the college, broke down, and sobbing, begged us to pray for them. And the next night the chapel was full and many more begging for the prayers of Christians, and the following night a similar scene. On Saturday morning we told the faculty that we had all we could do. Sent a carriage down for the dear old Doctor [Going]. He sat for an hour perhaps, looking on this exciting scene; and then the good man kneeled down and went way up yonder, along a Highway that he had travelled over so many years, and begged in tones wonderfully tender for a blessing from the King who sat at the head of that Highway to rest upon these young men. That body of students sat with bowed heads and hearts thoroughly subdued. The stillness of death for a few moments after the prayer prevailed in the room, and then Albert Baldwin struck up in his beautiful tenor voice, "Go to Dark Gethsemane," and that was too much. The student at my right side fell helpless to his seat before we got through the first verse, the one on my left hand held on till we were in the second verse, then he, too, gave it up, and went down. We staid in that room until 2 p.m. before we went to dinner.

A PLEA FOR COLLEGES IN THE WEST (1844)   From Truman M. Post, "Plea for Western Colleges," as quoted in *The First Report of the Society for the Promotion of Collegiate and Theological Education at the West* (New York, 1844), pp. 25–28.

The considerations advanced in my last article go to show, that Colleges are a necessity of every extensive community, marked by nature as a social unity. We are now to look at some reasons why they are peculiarly needed at the West. First, then, we find such a reason in the fact that Rome is at this time making unprecedented efforts to garrison this valley with her seminaries of education. She claims already to have within it between fifteen and twenty colleges and theological schools; and this number is rapidly increasing. To these permanency is ensured by the steadfastness of her policy, the constancy of her receipts from Catholic Europe, yearly increasing under the stimulating reports of her missionaries, and by her exacting despotism, moral if not ecclesiastic, over the earnings of her poor in this country. They are among the enduring formative forces in western society; and the causes which sustain them, will constantly add to their number. These institutions, together with numerous grades, under the conduct of their Jesuits and various religious orders, are offering (what professes to be) education almost as a gratuity, in many places in the West. Whatever other qualities her education may lack, we may be sure it will not want a subtle and intense proselytism, addressing not the reason but the senses, the taste, the imagination, and the passions; applying itself diversely to the fears of the timid, the enthusiasm of the ardent, the credulity of the simple, the affections of the young, and to that trashy sentiment and mawkish charity to which all principles are the same. Now the policy of Rome in playing upon all these elements through her educational enginery, is steadfast and profoundly sagacious. Her aim, in effect, is at the whole educational interest. The college is naturally the heart of the whole. The lower departments necessarily draw life from that. If Rome then grasps the college in the system of Western education, she virtually grasps the common school; she distils out the heart of the whole, if not a putrid superstition, at least that covert infidelity of which she is still more prolific.

Now a system so deep and so persistent, must be met by a correspondent depth and persistency of policy. Protestantism can no more counteract it by temporary and spasmodic efforts, than she could stop the Mississippi with a whirlwind. She can encounter it only by a system of permanent and efficient Protestant colleges. And this for two reasons. First, the Catholic seminaries in this country seem to meet a great and deeply felt social want, and can be displaced only by a supply for this want from another quarter. And secondly, in the nature of things, a college alone can counteract a college. The college acts upon the public mind in a manner so peculiar, through such ages and classes, and through influences so various and subtle, so constant, noiseless and profound, that it can be successfully combated only by a similar institution. Place efficient Protestant colleges in the proximity of the Catholic, and the latter will wither. For all purposes of severe intellectual discipline or masculine reason, their education is soon found to be a sham. A spiritual despotism dare not, cannot, teach true history or a free and manly philosophy. Again, other facts, which constitute a peculiar necessity for colleges in the West, are found in the circumstances and character of its population. First, the West is in its formative state. Never will impressions be made so easily and so enduringly for good or evil. Never will it be so important that its architect-minds— its plastic forces—should be endued with a broad and liberal intelligence. According to the elements now thrown in, it will soon permanently crystalize into dark and unshapely forms, or into order and beauty.

Another peculiar demand for colleges, may be found in the immense rapidity of our growth, and in the character of that growth, being a representative of almost every clime, opinion, sect, language, and social institute, not only of this country but of Christian Europe. Never was a more intense power of intellectual and moral fusion requisite to prevent the utter disorganization of society. Never was a people put to such a perilous proof of its power of assimilation, or required to incorporate with itself so rapidly such vast masses. We have in this fact, as well as in that of the Catholic aggression, dangers and trials put upon us, which our fathers never knew. Society here is new yet vast, and with all its forces in insulation or antagonism. Never was a community in more urgent need of those institutions, whose province it is profoundly to penetrate a people with a burning intelligence that shall fuse it into a unity with those great principles which are the organic life and binding forces of all society.

Again, in consequence of the incoherency of this element in a population thus heterogeneous, and broken off from the fixtures of old communities, without time to form new ones, all the social forces are shifting and mutable, and yield like the particles of liquid to the last force impressed. This quality of western society, combined with the bold, prompt, energetic and adventurous temperament impressed generally on it by common influences in the life of the emigrant, exposes it to vehement and brief excitements, to epidemic delusion and agitation. Upon this sea of incoherent and vehement mind, every wind of opinion has been let loose, and is struggling for the mastery; and the mass heaves restlessly to and fro under the thousand different forces impressed. The West is, therefore, peculiarly perturbed with demagoguism and popular agitation, not only in politics, but in religion, and all social interests. Amid these shifting social elements, we want principles of stability, we want a system of permanent forces, we want deep, strong and constant influences, that shall take from the changefulness and excitability of the western mind, by giving it the tranquillity of depth, and shall protect it from delusive and fitful impulses, by enduing it with a calm, profound and pure reason.

Thus, while society with us has on the one hand to contend against a masked and political spiritual despotism entrenching itself in the educational interest, and on the other against a demagogic agitation, urged on too often by avarice, or ruffianism, or faction, or a sophistical but specious skepticism, or by fanatical or superstitious or shallow religionisms and socialisms of every hue, we find our defence against both to be the same, a thorough popular enlightenment and belief, anchored by permanent institutions gradually pervading the mass with great and tranquil and guardian truths, and adjusting the system to the fixed laws of intellectual and moral gravitation. It may perhaps be asked, "Why not, in such a community, immediately proceed by opposing to agitation for evil, agitation for good?" This may at times be expedient, but cannot be relied on permanently. First, because popular agitation, unless based on deep-wrought intellectual convictions, can only palliate, it cannot cure any evil. In the second place, in the germ of popular agitation, a freedom from the restraints of conscience and truth and honor, often gives a decisive advantage, and agitating movements springing forth immediately from the people to be moved, and possessing a quiet sympathy with its feeling, and a shrewd tact in dealing with its passions and prejudices, must ever out-general any counter-movement originating from a different source. Especially, movements of this kind from abroad are liable to find themselves forestalled—the popular ear and mind preoccupied—arguments closed—opposing tracts already in the hands of the people—and the Bible itself, under their elected interpreters, made to preach another gospel.

The above exigencies of Western society cannot be met without colleges. I am far from undervaluing over [other?] movements of Christian philanthropy towards the country. I am most grateful for them. I bless God for his Word broad-cast by the American Bible Society amid this people; I am thankful for the interest the American Tract Society are directing hitherward, and hail with pleasure all the living truth and hallowed thought brought by it into contact with the popular mind. The attitude and history of the American Home Missionary Society in relation to the West, fill my mind with a sentiment of moral sublimity, and give it rank among the noblest and most sagacious schemes in the records of Christian benevolence. It will stand in history invested, to a great extent, with the moral grandeur of a civilizer and evangelizer of a new empire. But these are far from excluding the scheme of colleges. The permanency of their benefits can be grounded only on a thorough and liberal popular enlightenment. The educational interest, then, must underlie them all. But the only way in which the East can lay a controlling grasp on this, is by the establishment among us of permanent educational institutions. In a population, one tenth at least of which cannot read, it is plain that education is an essential prerequisite to bringing a large class—and that most necessary to be reached—within the influence of truth through the press. And no system of foreign supply of ministers, teachers or educated men, can obviate the necessity of institutions that shall constantly send forth those that shall be the educators of this people, in the school, the pulpit, the legislature, and the various departments of social life. Artifical irrigation cannot take the place of living waters. We are grateful for streams from abroad, but we feel there is need of opening fountains of life in the bosom of the people itself. The supplies from abroad we cannot rely on long. They are every day becoming more inadequate in numbers, and must to some extent be deficient in adaptation to our wants; a deficiency that often for years, sometimes for life, shuts one out from the people.

The common exigencies, then, of every extensive society, require colleges within itself. The peculiar evils to which that of the West is exposed, obviously cannot be permanently and successfully met by other means. The question then recurs in every aspect of this subject, Will the East assist the West in establishing a Protestant system of home education, or will she leave her to grapple single-handed with Romanism, and the other peculiar dangers to which she is exposed, in addition to the necessities that cluster around every infant community, or will she attempt by palliatives addressed to the symptoms, to heal a disease seated in the heart? A dangerous malady is on the patient. The peril is imminent and requires promptitude. Shall remedies be adapted to the disease or the symptoms? or, with such fearful chances against it, shall the patient be abandoned to the conflict betwixt nature and death? Let the East remember the life thus hazarded involves her own—it is to her the brand of Meleager.

EDUCATION AT HOBART COLLEGE (1849) From *Selected Chapters from the Autobiography of Andrew D. White* (Ithaca, N.Y., 1939). pp. 15–19.

It was in the autumn of 1849 that I went into residence at the little college and was assigned a very unprepossessing room in a very ugly barrack. Entering my new quarters I soon discovered about me various cabalistic signs, some of them evidently made by heating large iron keys, and pressing them against the woodwork. On inquiring I found that the room had been occupied some years before by no less a personage than Philip Spencer, a member of the famous Spencer family of Albany, who, having passed some years at this little college, and never having been able to get out of the freshman class, had gone to another institution of about the same grade, had there founded a Greek letter fraternity which is now widely spread among American universities, and then, through the influence of his father, who was Secretary of War, had been placed as a midshipman under Commodore McKenzie on the brig-of-war *Somers*. On the coast of Africa a mutiny was discovered, and as, on examination, young Spencer was found at the head of it, and papers discovered in his cabin revealed the plan of seizing the ship and using it in a career of piracy, the young man, in spite of his connection with a member of the Cabinet, was hanged at the yard-arm with two of his associates.

The most curious relic of him at the college was preserved in the library of the Hermean Society. It was a copy of "The Pirates' Own Book": a glorification of the exploits of "Blackbeard" and other great freebooters, profusely adorned with illustrations of their joys and triumphs. This volume bore on the fly-leaf the words, "Presented to the Hermean Society by Philip Spencer," and was in those days shown as a great curiosity.

The college was at its lowest ebb; of discipline there was none; there were about forty students, the majority of them, sons of wealthy churchmen, showing no inclination to work and much tendency to dissipation. The authorities of the college could not afford to expel or even offend a student, for its endowment was so small that it must have all the instruction fees possible, and must keep on good terms with the wealthy fathers of its scapegrace students. The scapegraces soon found this out, and the result was a little pandemonium. Only about a dozen of our number studied at all; the rest, by translations, promptings, and evasions escaped without labor. I have had to do since, as student, professor, or lecturer, with some half-dozen large universities at home and abroad, and in all of these together have not seen so much carousing and wild dissipation as I then saw in this little "Church college" of which the especial boast was that, owing to the small number of its students, it was "able to exercise a direct Christian influence upon every young man committed to its care."

The evidences of this Christian influence were not clear. The president of the college, Dr. Benjamin Hale, was a clergyman of the highest character; a good scholar, an excellent preacher, and a wise administrator; but his stature was very small, his girth very large, and his hair very yellow. When, then, on the thirteenth day of the month, there was read at chapel from the Psalter the words, "And there was little Benjamin, their ruler," very irreverent demonstrations were often made by the students, presumably engaged in worship; demonstrations so mortifying, indeed, that at last the president frequently substituted for the regular Psalms of the day one of the beautiful "Selections" of Psalms which the American Episcopal Church has so wisely incorporated into its prayerbook.

But this was by no means the worst indignity which these youth "under direct Christian influence" perpetrated upon their reverend instructors. It was my privilege to behold a professor, an excellent clergyman, seeking to quell hideous riot in a student's room, buried under a heap of carpets, mattresses, counterpanes, and blankets; to see another clerical professor forced to retire through the panel of a door under a shower of lexicons, boots, and brushes, and to see even the president himself, on one occasion, obliged to leave his lecture-room by a ladder from a window, and, on another, kept at bay by a shower of beer-bottles.

One favorite occupation was rolling cannon-balls along the corridors at midnight, with frightful din and much damage: a tutor, having one night been successful in catching and confiscating two of these, pounced from his door the next night upon a third; but this having been heated nearly to redness and launched from a shovel, the results was that he wore bandages upon his hands for many days.

Most ingenious were the methods for "training freshmen,"—one of the mildest being the administration of soot and water by a hose-pipe thrust through the broken panel of a door. Among general freaks I remember seeing a horse turned into the chapel, and a stuffed wolf, dressed in a surplice, placed upon the roof of that sacred edifice.

But the most elaborate thing of the kind I ever saw was the breaking up of a

"Second Adventist" meeting by a score of student roysterers. An itinerant fanatic had taken an old wooden meeting-house in the lower part of the town, had set up on either side of the pulpit large canvas representations of the man of brass with feet of clay, and other portentous characters of the prophecies, and then challenged the clergy to meet him in public debate. At the appointed time a body of college youth appeared, most sober in habit and demure in manner, having at their head "Bill" Howell of Black Rock and "Tom" Clark of Manlius, the two wildest miscreants in the sophomore class, each over six feet tall, the latter dressed as a respectable farmer, and the former as a country clergyman, wearing a dress-coat, a white cravat, a tall black hat wrapped in crape, leaning on a heavy ivory-knobbed cane, and carrying ostentatiously a Greek Testament. These disguised malefactors, having taken their seats in the gallery directly facing the pulpit, the lecturer expressed his "satisfaction at seeing clergymen present," and began his demonstrations. For about five minutes all went well; then "Bill" Howell solemnly arose and, in a snuffling voice, asked permission to submit a few texts from scripture. Permission being granted, he put on a huge pair of goggles, solemnly opened his Greek Testament, read emphatically the first passage which attracted his attention and impressively asked the lecturer what he had to say to it. At this, the lecturer, greatly puzzled, asked what the reverend gentleman was reading. Upon this Howell read in New Testament Greek another utterly irrelevant passage. In reply the lecturer said, rather roughly, "If you will speak English I will answer you." At this Howell said with the most humble suavity, "Do I understand that the distinguished gentleman does not recognize what I have been reading?" The preacher answered, "I don't understand any such gibberish; speak English." Thereupon Howell threw back his long black hair and launched forth into eloquent denunciation as follows: "Sir, is it possible that you come here to interpret to us the Holy Bible and do not recognize the language in which that blessed book was written? Sir, do you dare to call the very words of the Almighty 'gibberish?' " At this all was let loose; some students put asafetida on the atove; others threw pigeonshot against the ceiling and windows, making a most appalling din, and one wretch put in deadly work with a syringe thrust through the canvas representation of the man of brass with feet of clay. But, alas, Constable John Dey had recognized Howell and Clark, even amid their disguises. He had dealt with them too often before. The next tableau showed them, with their tall hats crushed over their heads, belaboring John Dey and his myrmidons, and presently, with half a dozen other ingenuous youth, they were haled to the office of justice. The young judge who officiated on this occasion was none other than a personage who will be mentioned with great respect more than once in these reminiscences,—Charles James Folger,—afterward my colleague in the State Senate, Chief Justice of the State and Secretary of the Treasury of the United States. He had met Howell often, for they were members of the same Greek letter fraternity,—the thrice illustrious Sigma Phi,—and, only a few days before, Howell had presented me to him; but there was no fraternal bond visible now; justice was sternly implacable, and good round fines were imposed upon all the culprits caught.

The philosophy of all this waywardness and dissipation was very simple. There was no other outlet for the animal spirits of these youth. Athletics were unknown; there was no gymnasium, no ball-playing, and, though the college was situated on the shore of one of the most beautiful lakes in the world, no boating. As regards my own personal relation to this condition of things I have pictured, it was more that of a good-natured spectator than of an active accomplice. My nearest friends were in the thick of it, but my tastes kept me out of most of it. I was fond of books, and, in the little student's library in my college building I reveled. Moreover, I then began to accumulate for myself the library which has since grown to such large proportions. Still the whole life of the place became more and more unsatisfactory to me, and I determined, at any cost, to escape from it and find some seat of learning where there was less frolic and more study.

LETTER DISCUSSING AMERICAN SCIENCE IN THE MID-NINETEENTH CENTURY (1850)   From Joseph Goldmark to Professor Gabriel Gustav Valentin, September 6, 1850, as quoted in Morris U. Schappes, ed., *A Documentary History of the Jews in the United States, 1654–1875* (New York, 1950), pp. 302–6.

New York, September 6, 1850

Dear Friend,

I have just come from New Haven, where, because of the meeting of the American Association for the Advancement of Science, I had a favorable opportunity to see Prof. Agassiz sooner than would have been the case if I had gone to Cambridge, which I should probably have been able to visit next month. New Haven is a very friendly, quiet university town situated on Long Island Sound, inhabited by pious Puritans, where theaters are banned by law as irreligious institutions and where Sunday boredom has set up headquarters. If I were a European reactionary and C. Vogt fell into my hands, his death sentence would be exile for a Sunday to New Haven; to be sure Vogt would be right in saying that the punishment would be more easily bearable in my company, but that would not be part of the plan. If I spoke of the appearance of a university town, you must not imagine the venerable picture of a German alma mater. Except for the noise of the students and the Philistinism, the schools here have nothing in common with the German ones. The position of the teachers, the manner of instruction are as different as day and night. In all of the United States there are no real state universities. All such institutions are private. Only a few receive occasional grants from their particular states. Most are established by the endowments of rich private individuals and are supported in addition by student fees. Many are simply private business enterprises, such as Crosby College here. Several professors, licensed by the state, provide the necessary buildings and apparatus and open classes. Every newly entering professor contributes his quota to the common capital, and any one leaving takes his share out. Pensions and appointments for life are quite unknown in the United States. Agassiz is appointed for only five years. But as a rule the professors remain until advanced old age because the prosperity of the institution is bound up with their fame and learning. At the endowed universities there are regular salaries that are not very high. Thus Agassiz himself has an annual salary of only $1500. At many others, income is dependent on the number of students; at Crosby College here that would amount to about $2000. In addition, the more famous professors have a considerable and easy source of income from their public lectures, which are very well attended. You see, it is customary throughout the Union for the more notable scholars to visit the larger cities and give popular scientific lectures, both at the invitation of the numerous scientific societies and clubs, as well as on their own. Thus Agassiz when he came here gave six lectures that brought in $2000. His annual income is increased by such lectures to $4000. A third very considerable source of income for the medical professors is their practice as consulting physicians, which takes little time and is very lucrative, if one has acquired some reputation. Instruction itself is extremely superficial. The first introduction consists in visiting patients at the side of a practicing physician. Then the student, who usually has had no previous scientific trainging, takes a two semester course, of four months each, in anatomy, chemistry, pharmacy, therapy, and surgery, and after an easy examination gets his doctor's degree, which, however, is not necessary for practising, since anyone, without the slightest medical knowledge, may assume the title of doctor and begin practising. Here in New York there are three medical schools: the medical faculty of the university where the professor of chemistry will now lecture on physiology too; Crosby College, where so far as I know physiology is not yet taught at all; and the recently established New York Medical College, from the program of which you will see that there is already talk of physiology, organic chemistry, and microscopy, but whether much of that is taught seems very doubtful. Nevertheless there are very capable specialists: for example, the anatomist Knight in New Haven, the operating surgeon Mott here, who was the first one to tie up the anonyma, and the outstanding mineralogist Dana. These men, however, acquired their knowledge in Europe. There is precious little to be found in the way of thorough general scientific, not to speak of philosophical, education. All philosophy here consists of theological controversies, which are quite the equal in absurdity of the old Talmudic *midrashim,* and with which Agassiz had to contend on account of his attacks on the Biblical story of creation. On the other hand, there are in most states very well organized secondary schools—"free schools, free academies"— supported at public expense, where the students are provided free of charge with all necessary books and writing materials.

In regard to appointment to higher academic positions, there prevail here, as in Europe, private considerations, family connections, and national pride. The direct invitation of European teachers, without their previous personal presence, is something quite rare. Nevertheless, European and particularly German science is being more and more recognized here, and its representatives are highly regarded and very welcome, because the American knows very well that the rapid growth of the country can only be ascribed to intellectual activity. Therefore he respects every intellectual power and seeks to acquire it for his advantage. I am firmly convinced that Liebig, who according to the local papers is to come here to give lectures, will receive the most splendid offers, while it would be unlikely that an invitation would be sent to him in Europe. So to form any judgment from these facts in regard to your request, it would be about as follows: it is true, as Agassiz told me too, that you cannot expect an immediate *direct* invitation, still less an advance appointment with pay; however, that you will quite certainly find a very fine position, when you have become personally known to the professors and influential men here, and to the lay public through the press and some lectures. In my opinion it would thus be best to continue your study of English through the winter, finish the next summer semester as early as possible, and come here immediately, alone. By steam ship these days it is a pleasure trip of eleven days, and from Bern to this country in the first cabin, the cost is no more than $200, at the rate of two florins, 30 kreuzer. During the two vacation months you will then have time to become acquainted with the country and its conditions, to give lectures in several large cities, to become acquainted with the academic world at the meeting of American natural scientists which will take place next spring in Cincinnati and in Albany in the fall, and to determine, after some choice, the place of your professional activity, which will not be at all difficult, in view of the considerable number of medical schools. The pecuniary advantages will probably be the same everywhere, consisting of an annual income of at least $4000 from courses and lectures, which could be considerably raised by a consultation practise (and I can see no real reason for its being less), while household expenses here in New York would amount to $1500 or at most $1800, for food is cheaper here than in Vienna and only rooms and clothing are more expensive. A decent place to live costs from $300 to $350.

In regard to your future position and effectiveness, I feel I must not hide the fact that you will have to descend quite far to the students' level of comprehension in order to raise it gradually, as Agassiz had to also; but that you will find a very wide field of activity and without doubt every recognition. There is not a single important physiologist in America, and very few biologists. The difficulties of lecturing in a foreign language are soon overcome after a short sojourn in the country. Agassiz read his first lectures here out of notebooks and even after having been here four years he speaks very correctly, to be sure, but still with an obvious German accent. However, this has only made his lectures all the more piquant and popular. Agassiz was indeed the center of this year's meeting; he towered far above all other members, he was tirelessly engaged all day as a member of nearly every committee of the conference, yet he gave several lectures at every session, always in free, fluent language. He is known and highly regarded throughout the Union partly for his lectures and partly through the exceedingly powerful press. From his experience, it is evident that one can expect the usually meagre resources for scientific work to become more adequate. He was asked why he did not use the university library. When he answered that there was nothing usable in it, the librarian asked him for a list of desirable books. Agassiz refused, with the comment that he would prepare the list as soon as the necessary money was made available; whereupon the book-dealer was ordered immediately to supply $3000 worth of books of Prof. Agassiz's selection. There is quite a lack of scientific periodicals and inexpensive instruments. The analytical laboratory in New Haven gets all its pure chemicals and its apparatus from Europe.

There is nothing to report about the scientific or intellectual life in general of the Germans here (New York numbers 80,000 of them, and about 25,000 Jews). There is a society of German doctors, the purpose of which is supposed to be the furthering of science; its accomplishments up to now, however, have been nil. In its meetings the members exchange their practical experiences as to the native disposition, (genius epid.) and its possible gastric-catarrhic-bilious pathological character. In Philadelphia at present a German medical periodical is being published, whose main weakness is its lack of competent collaborators.

About the bonds of the United States I can tell you only what I have learned from the papers. There are United States bonds and bonds of the individual states. Both yield 6 percent and have a definite date of maturity, at the end of which they are redeemed at their face value. Those are higher which have a later date of maturity. Those that fall in 1868 are now 116-116 1/2 and are very much desired in Europe because they are more secure than all the European issues. In case you want to buy any, one of my acquaintances has offered to buy them and to send them to his banker in Paris, where you can get them. But he wants a guaranty that you will be certain to take them in Paris.

I should have liked very much to enclose a clipping of the death of poor Prof. Webster, but the weight of the letter makes it impossible. He admitted the murder but to the very end denied premeditation.

Finally, one request with which I burden you because I see in the note from

Agassiz the possibility of its rapid realization. The acquisition of European scientific publications is made difficult here for private individuals through tariff, slow transportation, and high prices. (Institutions do not have to pay import duties.) It would therefore be very desirable if you would kindly send me Oesterlein's "Manual of Materia Medica," 3rd edition, and Wunderlich's "Special Pathology and Therapy," so far as it has appeared, through H. Major of Neufchatel, whom Prof. Agassiz is expecting here at the end of October.

And now adieu, with best wishes for your health and happiness, let me know any questions of detail that you still want answered by your friend

Goldmark.

HENRY ADAMS DESCRIBES HIS EDUCATION AT HARVARD (1854-58)

From Henry Adams, *The Education of Henry Adams* (New York, 1931), pp. 54–56, 59–69.

One day in June, 1854, young Adams walked for the last time down the steps of Mr. Dixwell's school in Boylston Place, and felt no sensation but one of unqualified joy that this experience was ended. Never before or afterwards in his life did he close a period so long as four years without some sensation of loss—some sentiment of habit—but school was what in after life he commonly heard his friends denounce as an intolerable bore. He was born too old for it. The same thing could be said of most New England boys. Mentally they never were boys. Their education as men should have begun at ten years old. They were fully five years more mature than the English or European boy for whom schools were made. For the purposes of future advancement, as afterwards appeared, these first six years of a possible education were wasted in doing imperfectly what might have been done perfectly in one, and in any case would have had small value. The next regular step was Harvard College. He was more than glad to go. For generation after generation, Adamses and Brookses and Boylstons and Gorhams had gone to Harvard College, and although none of them, as far as known, had ever done any good there, or thought himself the better for it, custom, social ties, convenience, and, above all, economy, kept each generation in the track. Any other education would have required a serious effort, but no one took Harvard College seriously. All went there because their friends went there, and the College was their ideal of social self-respect.

Harvard College, as far as it educated at all, was a mild and liberal school, which sent young men into the world with all they needed to make respectable citizens, and something of what they wanted to make useful ones. Leaders of men it never tried to make. Its ideals were altogether different. The Unitarian clergy had given to the College a character of moderation, balance, judgment, restraint, what the French called *mesure;* excellent traits, which the College attained with singular success, so that its graduates could commonly be recognized by the stamp, but such a type of character rarely lent itself to autobiography. In effect, the school created a type but not a will. Four years of Harvard College, if successful, resulted in an autobiographical blank, a mind on which only a water-mark had been stamped.

The stamp, as such things went, was a good one. The chief wonder of education is that it does not ruin everybody concerned in it, teachers and taught. Sometimes in after life, Adams debated whether in fact it had not ruined him and most of his companions, but, disappointment apart, Harvard College was probably less hurtful than any other university then in existence. It taught little, and that little ill, but it left the mind open, free from bias, ignorant of facts, but docile. The graduate had few strong prejudices. He knew little, but his mind remained supple, ready to receive knowledge.

What caused the boy most disappointment was the little he got from his mates. Speaking exactly, he got less than nothing, a result common enough in education. Yet the College Catalogue for the years 1854 to 1861 shows a list of names rather distinguished in their time. Alexander Agassiz and Phillips Brooks led it; H. H. Richardson and O. W. Holmes helped to close it. As a rule the most promising of all die early, and never get their names into a Dictionary of Contemporaries, which seems to be the only popular standard of success. Many died in the war. Adams knew them all, more or less; he felt as much regard, and quite as much respect for them then, as he did after they won great names and were objects of a vastly wider respect; but, as help towards education, he got nothing whatever from them or they from him until long after they had left college. Possibly the fault was his, but one would like to know how many others shared it. Accident counts for much in companionship as in marriage. Life offers perhaps only a score of possible companions, and it is mere chance whether they meet as early as school or college, but it is more than a chance that boys brought up together under like conditions have nothing to give each other. The Class of 1858, to which Henry Adams belonged, was a typical collection of young New Englanders, quietly penetrating and aggressively commonplace; free from meannesses, jealousies, intrigues, enthusiasms, and passions; not exceptionally quick; not consciously sceptical; singularly indifferent to display, artifice, florid expression, but not hostile to it when it amused them; distrustful of themselves, but little disposed to trust any one else; with not much humor of their own, but full of readiness to enjoy the humor of others; negative to a degree that in the long run became positive and triumphant. Not harsh in manners or judgment, rather liberal and open-minded, they were still as a body the most formidable critics one would care to meet, in a long life exposed to criticism. They never flattered, seldom praised; free from vanity, they were not intolerant of it; but they were objectiveness itself; their attitude was a law of nature; their judgment beyond appeal, not an act either of intellect or emotion or of will, but a sort of gravitation.

This was Harvard College incarnate, but even for Harvard College, the Class of 1858 was somewhat extreme. Of unity this band of nearly one hundred young men had no keen sense, but they had equally little energy of repulsion. They were pleasant to live with, and above the average of students—German, French, English, or what not—but chiefly because each individual appeared satisfied to stand alone. It seemed a sign of force; yet to stand alone is quite natural when one has no passions; still easier when one has no pains.

*　　*　　*

If the student got little from his mates, he got little more from his masters. The four years passed at college were, for his purposes, wasted. Harvard College was a good school, but at bottom what the boy disliked most was any school at all. He did not want to be one in a hundred—one per cent of an education. He regarded himself as the only person for whom his education had value, and he wanted the whole of it.

He got barely half of an average. Long afterwards, when the devious path of life led him back to teach in his turn what no student naturally cared or needed to know, he diverted some dreary hours of faculty-meetings by looking up his record in the class-lists, and found himself graded precisely in the middle. In the one branch he most needed—mathematics—barring the few first scholars, failure was so nearly universal that no attempt at grading could have had value, and whether he stood fortieth or ninetieth must have been an accident or the personal favor of the professor. Here his education failed lamentably. At best he could never have been a mathematician; at worst he would never have cared to be one; but he needed to read mathematics, like any other universal language, and he never reached the alphabet.

Beyond two or three Greek plays, the student got nothing from the ancient languages. Beyond some incoherent theories of free-trade and protection, he got little from Political Economy. He could not afterwards remember to have heard the name of Karl Marx mentioned, or the title of "Capital." He was equally ignorant of Auguste Comte. These were the two writers of his time who most influenced its thought. The bit of practical teaching he afterwards reviewed with most curiosity was the course in Chemistry, which taught him a number of theories that befogged his mind for a lifetime. The only teaching that appealed to his imagination was a course of lectures by Louis Agassiz on the Glacial Period and Palaeontology, which had more influence on his curiosity than the rest of the college instruction altogether. The entire work of the four years could have been easily put into the work of any four months in after life.

Harvard College was a negative force, and negative forces have value. Slowly it weakened the violent political bias of childhood, not by putting interests in its place, but by mental habits which had no bias at all. It would also have weakened the literary bias, if Adams had been capable of finding other amusement, but the climate kept him steady to desultory and useless reading, till he had run through libraries of volumes which he forgot even to their title-pages. Rather by instinct than by guidance, he turned to writing, and his professors or tutors occasionally gave his English composition a hesitating approval; but in that branch as in all the rest, even when he made a long struggle for recognition, he never convinced his teachers that his abilities, at their best, warranted placing him on the rank-list, among the first third of his class. Instructors generally reach a fairly accurate gauge of their scholars' powers. Henry Adams himself held the opinion that his instructors were very nearly right, and when he became a professor in his turn, and made mortifying mistakes in ranking his scholars, he still obstinately insisted that on the whole, he was not far wrong. Student or professor, he accepted the negative standard because it was the standard of the school.

He never knew what other students thought of it, or what they thought they gained from it; nor would their opinion have much affected his. From the first, he wanted to be done with it, and stood watching vaguely for a path and a direction. The world outside seemed large, but the paths that led into it were not many and lay mostly through Boston, where he did not want to go. As it happened, by pure chance, the first door of escape that seemed to offer a hope led into Germany, and James Russell Lowell opened it.

Lowell, on succeeding Longfellow as Professor of Belles-Lettres, had duly gone to Germany, and had brought back whatever he found to bring. The literary world then agreed that truth survived in Germany alone, and Carlyle, Matthew Arnold, Renan, Emerson, with scores of popular followers, taught the German faith. The literary world had revolted against the yoke of coming capitalism—its money-lenders, its bank directors, and its railway magnates. Thackeray and Dickens followed Balzac in scratching and biting the unfortunate middle class with savage ill-temper, much as the middle class had scratched and bitten the Church and Court for a hundred years before. The middle class had the power, and held its coal and iron well in hand, but the satirists and idealists seized the press, and as they were agreed that the Second Empire was a disgrace to France and a danger to England, they turned to Germany because at that moment Germany was neither economical nor military, and a hundred years behind western Europe in the simplicity of its standard. German thought, method, honesty, and even taste, became the standards of scholarship. Goethe was raised to the rank of Shakespeare—Kant ranked as a law-giver above Plato. All serious scholars were obliged to become German, for German thought was revolutionizing criticism. Lowell had followed the rest, not very enthusiastically, but with sufficient conviction, and invited his scholars to join him. Adams was glad to accept the invitation, rather for the sake of cultivating Lowell than Germany, but still in perfect good faith. It was the first serious attempt he had made to direct his own education, and he was sure of getting some education out of it; not perhaps anything that he expected, but at least a path.

Singularly circuitous and excessively wasteful of energy the path proved to be, but the student could never see what other was open to him. He could have done no better had he foreseen every stage of his coming life, and he would probably have done worse. The preliminary step was pure gain. James Russell Lowell had brought back from Germany the only new and valuable part of its universities, the habit of allowing students to read with him privately in his study. Adams asked the privilege, and used it to read a little, and to talk a great deal, for the personal contact pleased and flattered him, as that of older men ought to flatter and please the young even when they altogether exaggerate its value. Lowell was a new element in the boy's life. As practical a New Englander as any, he leaned towards the Concord faith rather than towards Boston where he properly belonged; for Concord, in the dark days of 1856, glowed with pure light. Adams approached it in much the same spirit as he would have entered a Gothic Cathedral, for he well knew that the priests regarded him as only a worm. To the Concord Church all Adamses were minds of dust and emptiness, devoid of feeling, poetry or imagination; little higher than the common scourings of State Street; politicians of doubtful honesty; natures of narrow scope; and already, at eighteen years old, Henry had begun to feel uncertainty about so many matters more important than Adamses that his mind rebelled against no discipline merely personal, and he was ready to admit his unworthiness if only he might penetrate the shrine. The influence of Harvard College was beginning to have its effect. He was slipping away from fixed principles; from Mount Vernon Street; from Quincy; from the eighteenth century; and his first steps led toward Concord.

He never reached Concord, and to Concord Church he, like the rest of mankind who accepted a material universe, remained always an insect, or something much lower—a man. It was surely no fault of his that the universe seemed to him real; perhaps—as Mr. Emerson justly said—it was so; in spite of the long-continued effort of a lifetime, he perpetually fell back into the heresy that if anything universal was unreal, it was himself and not the appearances; it was the poet and not the banker; it was his own thought, not the thing that moved it. He did not lack the wish to be transcendental. Concord seemed to him, at one time, more real than Quincy; yet in truth Russell Lowell was as little transcendental as Beacon Street. From him the boy got no revolutionary thought whatever—objective or subjective as they used to call it—but he got good-humored encouragement to do what amused him, which consisted in passing two years in Europe after finishing the four years of Cambridge.

The result seemed small in proportion to the effort, but it was the only positive result he could ever trace to the influence of Harvard College, and he had grave doubts whether Harvard College influenced even that. Negative results in plenty he could trace, but he tended towards negation on his own account, as one side of the New England mind had always done, and even there he could never feel sure that Harvard College had more than reflected a weakness. In his opinion the education was not serious, but in truth hardly any Boston student took it seriously, and none of them seemed sure that President Walker himself, or President Felton after him, took it more seriously than the students. For them all, the college offered chiefly advantages vulgarly called social, rather than mental.

Unluckily for this particular boy, social advantages were his only capital in life. Of money he had not much, of mind not more, but he could be quite certain that, barring his own faults, his social position would never be questioned. What he needed was a career in which social position had value. Never in his life would he have to explain who he was; never would he have need of acquaintance to strengthen his social standing; but he needed greatly some one to show him how to use the acquaintance he cared to make. He made no acquaintance in college which proved to have the smallest use in after life. All his Boston friends he knew before, or would have known in any case, and contact of Bostonian with Bostonian was the last education these young men needed. Cordial and intimate as their college relations were, they all flew off in different directions the moment they took their degrees. Harvard College remained a tie, indeed, but a tie little stronger than Beacon Street and not so strong as State Street. Strangers might perhaps gain something from the college if they were hard pressed for social connections. A student like H. H. Richardson, who came from far away New Orleans, and had his career before him to chase rather than to guide, might make valuable friendships at college. Certainly Adams made no acquaintance there that he valued in after life so much as Richardson, but still more certainly the college relation had little to do with the later friendship. Life is a narrow valley, and the roads run close together. Adams would have attached himself to Richardson in any case, as he attached himself to John LaFarge or Augustus St. Gaudens or Clarence King or John Hay, none of whom were at Harvard College. The valley of life grew more and more narrow with years, and certain men with common tastes were bound to come together. Adams knew only that he would have felt himself on a more equal footing with them had he been less ignorant, and had he not thrown away ten years of early life in acquiring what he might have acquired in one.

Socially or intellectually, the college was for him negative and in some ways mischievous. The most tolerant man of the world could not see good in the lower habits of the students, but the vices were less harmful than the virtues. The habit of drinking—though the mere recollection of it made him doubt his own veracity, so fantastic it seemed in later life—may have done no great or permanent harm; but the habit of looking at life as a social relation—an affair of society—did no good. It cultivated a weakness which needed no cultivation. If it had helped to make men of the world, or give the manners and instincts of any profession—such as temper, patience, courtesy, or a faculty of profiting by the social defects of opponents—it would have been education better worth having than mathematics or languages; but so far as it helped to make anything, it helped only to make the college standard permanent through life. The Bostonian educated at Harvard College remained a collegian, if he stuck only to what the college gave him. If parents went on, generation after generation, sending their children to Harvard College for the sake of its social advantages, they perpetuated an inferior social type, quite as ill-fitted as the Oxford type for success in the next generation.

Luckily the old social standard of the college, as President Walker or James Russell Lowell still showed it, was admirable, and if it had little practical value or personal influence on the mass of students, at least it preserved the tradition for those who liked it. The Harvard graduate was neither American nor European, nor even wholly Yankee; his admirers were few, and his critics many; perhaps his worst weakness was his self-criticism and self-consciousness; but his ambitions, social or intellectual, were not necessarily cheap even though they might be negative. Afraid of serious risks, and still more afraid of personal ridicule, he seldom made a great failure of life, and nearly always led a life more or less worth living. So Henry Adams, well aware that he could not succeed as a scholar, and finding his social position beyond improvement or need of effort, betook himself to the single ambition which otherwise would scarcely have seemed a true outcome of the college, though it was the last remnant of the old Unitarian supremacy. He took to the pen. He wrote.

The College Magazine printed his work, and the College Societies listened to his addresses. Lavish of praise the readers were not; the audiences, too, listened in silence; but this was all the encouragement any Harvard collegian had a reasonable hope to receive; grave silence was a form of patience that meant possible future acceptance; and Henry Adams went on writing. No one cared enough to criticise, except himself who soon began to suffer from reaching his own limits. He found that he could not be this—or that—or the other; always precisely the things he wanted to be. He had not wit or scope or force. Judges always ranked him beneath a rival, if he had any; and he believed the judges were right. His work seemed to him thin, commonplace, feeble. At times he felt his own weakness so fatally that he could not go on; when he had nothing to say, he could not say it, and he found that he had very little to say at best. Much that he then wrote must be still in existence in print or manuscript, though he never cared to see it again, for he felt no doubt that it was in reality just what he thought it. At best it showed only a feeling for form; an instinct of exclusion. Nothing shocked—not even its weakness.

Inevitably an effort leads to an ambition—creates it—and at that time the ambition of the literary student, which almost took place of the regular prizes of scholarship, was that of being chosen as the representative of his class—the Class Orator—at the close of their course. This was political as well as literary success, and precisely the sort of eighteenth-century combination that fascinated an eighteenth-century boy. The idea lurked in his mind, at first as a dream, in no way serious or even possible for he stood outside the number of what were known as popular men. Year by year, his position seemed to improve, or perhaps his rivals disappeared, until at last, to his own great astonishment, he found himself a candidate. The habits of the college permitted no active candidacy; he and his rivals had not a word to say for or against themselves, and he was never even consulted on the subject; he was not present at any of the proceedings, and how it happened he never could quite divine, but it did happen, that one evening on returning from Boston he received notice of his election, after a very close contest, as Class Orator over the head of the first scholar, who was undoubtedly a better orator and a more popular man. In politics the success of the poorer candidate is common enough, and Henry Adams was a fairly trained politician, but he never understood how he managed to defeat not only a more capable but a more popular rival.

To him the election seemed a miracle. This was no mock-modesty; his head was as clear as it ever was in an indifferent canvass, and he knew his rivals and their following as well as he knew himself. What he did not know, even after four years of education, was Harvard College. What he could never measure was the bewildering impersonality of the men, who, at twenty years old, seemed to set no value either on official or personal standards. Here were nearly a hundred young men who had lived together intimately during four of the most impressionable years of life, and who, not only once but again and again, in different ways, deliberately, seriously, dispassionately, chose as their representatives precisely those of their companions who seemed least to represent them. As far as these Orators and Marshals had any position at all in a collegiate sense, it was that of indifference to the college. Henry Adams never professed the smallest faith in universities of any kind, either as boy or man, nor had he the faintest admiration for the university graduate, either in Europe or in America; as a collegian he was only known apart from his fellows by his habit of standing outside the college; and yet the singular fact remained that this commonplace body of young men chose him repeatedly to express his and their commonplaces. Secretly, of course, the successful candidate flattered himself—and them—with the hope that they might perhaps not be so commonplace as they thought themselves; but this was only another proof that all were identical. They saw in him a representative—the kind of representative they wanted—and he saw in them the most formidable array of judges he could ever meet, like so many mirrors of himself, an infinite reflection of his own shortcomings.

All the same, the choice was flattering; so flattering that it actually shocked his vanity; and would have shocked it more, if possible, had he known that it was to be the only flattery of the sort he was ever to receive. The function of Class Day was, in the eyes of nine-tenths of the students, altogether the most important of the college, and the figure of the Orator was the most conspicuous in the function. Unlike the Orators at regular Commencements, the Class Day Orator stood alone, or had only the Poet for rival. Crowded into the large church, the students, their families, friends, aunts, uncles and chaperones, attended all the girls of sixteen or twenty who wanted to show their summer dresses or fresh complexions, and there, for an hour or two, in a heat that might have melted bronze, they listened to an Orator and a Poet in clergyman's gowns, reciting such platitudes as their own experience and their mild censors permitted them to utter. What Henry Adams said in his Class Oration of 1858 he soon forgot to the last word, nor had it the least value for education; but he naturally remembered what was said of it. He remembered especially one of his eminent uncles or relations remarking that, as the work of so young a man, the oration was singularly wanting in enthusiasm. The young man—always in search of education—asked himself whether, setting rhetoric aside, this absence of enthusiasm was a defect or a merit, since, in either case, it was all that Harvard College taught, and all that the hundred young men, whom he was trying to represent, expressed. Another comment threw more light on the effect of the college education. One of the elderly gentlemen noticed the orator's "perfect self-possession." Self-possession indeed! If Harvard College gave nothing else, it gave calm. For four years each student had been obliged to figure daily before dozens of young men who knew each other to the last fibre. One had done little but read papers to Societies, or act comedy in the Hasty Pudding, not to speak of all sorts of regular exercises, and no audience in future life would ever be so intimately and terribly intelligent as these. Three-fourths of the graduates would rather have addressed the Council of Trent or the British Parliament than have acted Sir Anthony Absolute or Dr. Ollapod before a gala audience of the Hasty Pudding. Self-possession was the strongest part of Harvard College, which certainly taught men to stand alone, so that nothing seemed stranger to its graduates than the paroxysms of terror before the public which often overcame the graduates of European universities. Whether this was, or was not, education, Henry Adams never knew. He was ready to stand up before any audience in America or Europe, with nerves rather steadier for the excitement, but whether he should ever have anything to say, remained to be proved. As yet he knew nothing. Education had not begun.

A "PRAYER FOR COLLEGES" (1855)   From W. S. Tyler, *Prayer for Colleges. A Premium Essay, Written For "The Society for the Promotion of Collegiate and Theological Education at the West"* (New York, 1855), pp. 103–12, 117–20.

The necessity for a well-educated ministry of the gospel has never been so generally and powerfully felt any where else as in our own country; and this feeling has been the leading motive in the establishment of by far the larger part of American colleges. "Dreading to leave an illiterate ministry to the churches, when our ministers shall lie in the dust"—such is the language in which the founders of Harvard College describe their own motives in that far-seeing and self-denying enterprise, which they undertook just as soon as they had provided comfortable houses for themselves, and selected convenient places for the worship of God. And sixty years later, Cotton Mather says: "Our fathers saw that without a college to train an able and learned ministry, the church in New England must have been less than a business of an age,—must soon have come to nothing." "Pro Christo et Ecclesia"—*for Christ and the Church*—is to this day the motto of Harvard College, though sadly fallen, alas! from the truth as it is in Jesus.

Yale College, as we have already mentioned, was founded by ministers. It was also founded chiefly for the education of ministers for the colony of Connecticut. It originated, as they tell us, in their sincere regard and zeal for upholding the Protestant religion by a succession of learned and orthodox men.

"Princeton College was founded by the Synod of New York for the purpose of supplying the church with learned and able preachers of the Word." And its paramount religious design and spirit are well expressed in the language of President Witherspoon: "Cursed be all that learning that is contrary to the cross of Christ; cursed be all that learning that is not coincident with the cross of Christ; cursed be all that learning that is not subservient to the cross of Christ."

"Dartmouth College was originated in the warmest spirit, and established in the most elevated principles of Christian piety."

Amherst College grew out of a charity school, which was established for the education of indigent young men for the ministerial and the missionary work. It was born of the prayers, and baptized with the tears, of holy men; and, as in the early history of Harvard, the colonists contributed of their deep poverty, "one bringing a piece of cotton stuff, valued at nine shillings; another, a pewter pot of the same value; a third, a fruit-dish, a spoon, and a large and small salt-cellar;" so, in the founding of Amherst College, the friends of learning and religion in the vicinity brought in the materials, and built up the walls with their own hands, while those at a distance gave in money, or the fruit of their labors, whatever they could spare, which might conduce to the endowment of the institution, and the maintenance of its officers and students. Such self-denials and sacrifices, as were made by the founders of these, and, indeed, most of our colleges, could have proceeded only from religious motives,—only from hearts overflowing with love to Christ and his church. Amherst College was one of the *earliest* institutions that grew up under the influence of the foreign missionary enterprise, and the new impulse which was thus given to all benevolent efforts; and it is, in its character and history a type of a new class of colleges which have sprung up, particularly in the new States, and which may be called emphatically, both as regards their origin and influence, Missionary Colleges.

"Western Reserve College was founded by domestic missionaries, and designed to furnish pastors for the infant churches on the Reserve. Illinois College originated in the union of two independent movements; the one emanating from Home Missionary operations in Illinois, the other from a Society of Inquiry respecting Missions at Yale College. The site of Wabash College was dedicated to God in prayer by its founders kneeling upon the snow in the primeval forest. Marietta College was founded mainly to meet demands for competent teachers and ministers of the gospel."

In fact, nearly all of those institutions which have lived and prospered, and exerted a decided influence, even in our literary and political history, were established by evangelical Christians; and have been taught, for the most part, by evangelical ministers, with a direct and special reference to supplying these churches, and the country and the world, with a learned and pious evangelical ministry. Institutions established by worldly men, for mere worldly objects, have not prospered. Infidelity or irreligion, or no religion, may have founded them, but it could not sustain them; and it has been found necessary to transfer them to the hands of religious guardians and teachers, in order to save them from utter extinction. They have been planned by the wisdom of political sages, and fostered by the wealth and power of the State, but they could not be well managed and governed without the sanctions of religion. They have not won the confidence of parents and guardians, for even irreligious parents do not generally want their children educated in infidelity or impiety; and Christianity, though hated in itself, has been welcomed as a necessary means; though excluded by statutes and constitutions, it has, sooner or later, been admitted to a practical and controlling influence. The history of the University of Virginia, the University of South Carolina, Transylvania University, Dickinson College, Girard College, and, to some extent, Harvard College, had we time to give it, would furnish a satisfactory demonstration of these statements. Baptists and Methodists, Congregationalists and Presbyterians,[1] all the evangelical Protestant sects, have their prosperous literary institutions in almost every State of the Union; but infidelity has yet to make its first successful enterprise of this sort; and State policy, State patronage, exclusive of religious influence, cannot show a single flourishing college from the Atlantic and the Great Lakes to the Pacific and the Gulf of Mexico.

These are remarkable facts, especially when considered in connection with the voluntary system, and the entire civil and religious liberty of the American people. A wealthy and powerful establishment,—a church wedded to the State, and enriched by State patronage through successive centuries, we might well suppose, could secure such results. A rich and lordly hierarchy, lording it over the consciences and

[1] Much the larger number by these last-named denominations. Of the 120 colleges in the United States, 13 are Baptist, 13 Methodist and Episcopalian, and the rest, for the most part, under Congregational and Presbyterian influence.

the estates of the whole people, we should think, might build religious colleges by scores in every part of the country, or might subsidize existing literary institutions, and make them subservient to their views of religion. But that the free voluntary movements of so many different denominations of Christians should have reared a hundred and twenty colleges in different parts of these United States,—many of them in the very infancy of the States, or Provinces, and all within little more than two hundred years after the first settlement of the country; and furnished them with such a succession of learned and pious teachers, and brought them so completely under the controlling influence of a practical Christianity,—this is truly remarkable. It shows that Christianity, with all its divisions and corruptions, still possesses a vital energy, and is still guided and guarded by Him who has all wisdom and all power. It shows that the church is still self-denying in her spirit, and far-reaching in her plans; for nothing but self-denying charity, and far-reaching sagacity, will plant colleges in a new country, when there is a present demand for the necessities of life, rather than for high mental culture. It shows that there is a natural and mutual affinity between religion and learning; that each alternately seeks the alliance and support of the other, while both are left to the freest action and development. It shows that the American people are imbued with a deep, practical conviction that the college was in its origin, and is in its nature, a religious institution; and must be so, if it would realize its proper literary and political ends. Above all, it proves, as we cannot but believe, and would acknowledge with devout gratitude, that the providence of God has watched over our beloved country in all its history, and guarded it against the dangers to which a youthful and free people are most exposed, as if he intended, in spite of adverse agencies, to preserve this goodly land as a heritage for himself.

The college, then, is the daughter of the church, cherished by her with all a mother's love and care, and self-denial. Has the daughter done any thing in return for the mother? Surely she were an unnatural child if she has made no return of filial love and service to her, to whom she owes all that she has, and all that she is, even to her very existence.

Is it nothing to the church that the system of popular education, the preparation of text-books, the examination and direction of teachers, and, to so great an extent, the education of the teachers themselves, is in the hands of men who have been trained by Christian scholars in Christian colleges? Is it a small thing for the church, that colleges established by herself, and conducted by her ablest and best men, give tone, in so great a measure, to the literature of the country, and control the reading of the people, not only in books of history and philosophy, and poetry and belles-lettres, but in those magazines and newspapers, which now occupy more and more the pens of our most thoughtful, learned and elegant writers? Is it of little or no consequence to the church that men educated at Christian colleges have, to so great an extent, filled the office of presidents, and governors, and judges, and other civil magistrates in our country, and are also extending their influence every day more widely among the people through the popularization of learning, and those countless applications of science to common life, which are pouring wealth into the bosom of the church for her enterprises of benevolence? Is it nothing to the church, that so many of our lawyers and physicians, and other men of influence in the community, have been taught in college to recognize the divine origin of Christianity, to respect the institutions of religion, and to carry more or less of Christian principles and a Christian spirit with them into the higher walks of life?

The men for all our benevolent enterprises must come from the colleges, and will carry through life very much of the character and spirit they had when in college. Students give more *money* for benevolent objects, in proportion to their means, than almost any other community. This may not be so with all colleges and higher seminaries, but we know it is so in more than one. We have seen the poor student throw his last quarter into the contribution box, saying (with a sublime faith, not perhaps to be imitated by all, but worthy of universal admiration), "There is all the money I have in the world. I will have that safe."

But money is the smallest contribution which is made by students in college to the cause of Christian charity. They have first given themselves to the Lord and to his work, wherever and whatever it may be. With a faith, like that of Abraham, they have been willing to leave their country, not knowing whither they go, while with a love, like that of Christ, they have offered up themselves on the altar of reconciliation between God and their fellow-men.

The commencement of the new era of benevolence,—the era of Missionary and Bible, and Tract and Education Societies—was marked by the establishment of an unusual number, we might almost say, a new kind of colleges; and they in turn have sustained and furthered the various forms of associated benevolence, with unwonted zeal and devotion. At the same time (to their honor be it said, as well as in truth and justice), some of the older institutions have caught not a little of the new spirit, and lavished the accumulated treasures of their wisdom and their influence in the support of those moral and religious enterprises which are the glory of the age.

Those revivals of religion, which so illustrate and bless our times, have prevailed in colleges with greater frequency and power than in any other communities; and who can calculate the good influences, direct and indirect, which revivals in colleges have exerted on the churches? How many ministers and magistrates, professional men and men of influence, have *there been born* into the kingdom of Christ; and how many more *re*-converted, so that, like Peter, they could strengthen their brethren? How many, while members of college, have caught the spirit of revivals and of missions, and carried it home to the church to which they belong, and with the characteristic ardor and *strength of young men* in a course of education, diffused it through the place of their nativity? And when such men have been settled in the ministry, their own churches have been revival churches, and missionary churches; the life of the communities around them, and the light of this dark world. It has been estimated that one revival of religion, which took place in Yale College, under the presidency of Dr. Dwight, raised up ministers who were instrumental of the conversion of fifty thousand souls in one generation.

Thus, it appears that marked eras in the history of the church have usually been marked eras in the history of colleges, from the establishment of the first seminary in the early Christian church to the foundation of the last college in our western wilderness. The progress of the churches has been *registered,* so to speak, and their attainments have been secured and perpetuated by the colleges, while, in turn, every new wave of thought, and tide of feeling in the colleges, has had its corresponding wave and tide in the churches. The stream will not permanently rise higher than the fountain. The fountain determines the quality, as well as the height of the stream. The college and the church are alternately or mutually fountain and stream. More frequently the impulse originates in the college. It was so in the Reformation. It was so with the Oxford heresy. The Unitarian defection in New England originated perhaps with the churches, or rather with their pastors, but it has been perpetuated by Harvard College. The tide rose in the churches till it burst open the gates and inundated the college, but now it has turned, and is flowing back, more gradually, but not less powerfully, and even more effectively, from the college into the churches and the community. Let all our colleges become like Harvard, and Unitarianism would overflow the country. Or let them become such schools of infidelity as Jefferson and Girard would fain have established; and, unless they are abandoned and their gates closed, the next generation will forsake the religion of their fathers, and the churches will be deserted by the people. Or let our ministers and men of influence be uneducated, or half educated, and errors and heresies will spring up like thorns and briers in a neglected field; for it is men who are untaught in history (especially the history of doctrines), and undisciplined in their mental and moral faculties, whose minds have been the hot-beds of theological error in every age of the church. To pray for the colleges, then, is to pray for the churches, for an educated and devoted ministry,—for a pure and Protestant Christianity—for foreign and home missions,—for evangelical revivals of religion; in a word, for churches, that shall live and work, and propagate a sound faith, lively hope and impartial charity through the world.

DEFENSE OF THE OLD-TIME COLLEGE BY PRESIDENT NOAH PORTER OF YALE (1870)   From Noah Porter, *The American Colleges and the American Public* (New Haven, 1870), pp. 40–42, 63–64, 71–72, 92–93, 101–4, 122, 126–29, 139–40, 172–78, 206.

$\mathbf{W}$e contend not only that the colleges have judged rightly in giving to the study of language the prominence which it receives, and that the Greek and Latin deserve the special preëminence which has been assigned them, but that there are peculiar reasons why they should be even more thoroughly and earnestly cultivated than they have been.

Our first position is, that for the years appropriated to school and college training, there is no study which is so well adapted to mental discipline as the study of language. We argue this from the fact that language is the chief instrument of intelligence. It is thought made visible and clear, not merely to the person to whom thoughts are to be conveyed, but to the person who thinks for and by himself. The earliest discriminations and memories to which to which we are tasked by nature are those which are involved in the mastery of our mother tongue. It is true the observation required for the education of the eye and the ear and in the control and discipline of the body, involves a multitude of "object lessons," and imposes much "object teaching," but it can scarcely be contended that this discipline of the senses requires either the *culture* or the *discipline* of the intellect, in the same sense as does that attention to language which is required in learning to speak and write the language which is first acquired. We assume, because it is not necessary to prove, that the most conspicuously intellectual of the various intellectual acts of infancy and childhood are exercised upon language. The slowness and difficulty with which some children learn to use language is correctly taken as an infallible sign of some defect or late development of intellectual power. Nor should it be overlooked that the most important part of the knowledge which we acquire is gained through words spoken or written, and that the study of nature itself must be prosecuted to a large extent through books. Natural history, with its curious facts and nice discriminations, geography with its descriptions of mountains and rivers, of distant and unseen lands, and romance with its fairy tales, so exciting and so dear to the child, all presuppose and exercise the same knowledge. The world of words is, in its way, as important and as real to the child as the world of things; and most of the intellectual relations of either things or thoughts can only be discerned by first apprehending and attending to the relations of words. The world of words is not to him, as is often charged, a world of dead and dry abstractions, but it is the realm in which the imagination weaves its subtle creations, and disports itself in the delights of its never wearied romancing.

As school-life begins and advances, the intellect is tasked and disciplined by special classes of studies, the object of which is to train the intellectual power, and to furnish it with facts and truths. The mind is constrained to reflection and analysis. From acquisition, observation and memory, it proceeds to be trained to the independent judgments of science. What shall be the subject matter upon which its essays are employed? Nature directs, and the experience of many generations has confirmed the wisdom of her intimations, that language is the appropriate sphere of these essays. The mind is not sufficiently matured to study nature in a scientific way. Of *natural history* the mind at this period is capable, but not of the *sciences of nature*. The *facts* of natural history, the experiments of physics and chemistry, do not discipline the youth enough; the *science* of these facts involves a training and progress which the intellect has not yet attained. The mathematics present a most important field, but this field is peculiar and unique. For the sphere and materials of what we call intellectual training we are shut up to the study of language; not exclusively, indeed, for, as we shall show in its place, facts and imaginations should both instruct and relieve the excessive and one-sided strain which the discipline of language involves; but if there is to be discipline in the eminent sense, it must be effected by means of the study of language. Whatever substitute be devised, it will fail of imparting that peculiar intellectual facility and power which this study secures.

Assuming that the study of language is the most efficient instrument of discipline, we assert that the study of the classical languages should be universally preferred to any other as a means of discipline in every course of liberal education, and should continue to be made prominent and necessary in the American colleges.

*　　*　　*

We contend that the American colleges have been in the right in requiring a prescribed course of study as the condition for a degree. In support of this opinion we shall offer no extended argument in addition to those we have already presented, but shall occupy ourselves chiefly with the arguments that are urged against it. If the considerations already urged are admitted to be pertinent and convincing, our argument is complete. If it be conceded that the studies which have been usually prescribed in the American colleges are the best fitted to impart a liberal culture, then it follows that the practice of these colleges in making them the ordinary conditions for the first degree is well grounded and ought to be adhered to. If our argument concerning the theory of the curriculum of studies is valid, then these studies ought to be prescribed. There is not a single study that is superfluous. Not one should be displaced, because not one can be spared. The theory of this curriculum has been to provide for all those studies which could properly find a place in a system of liberal culture, or should enter into the scheme of a complete and generous education. The end has not been to train men for the learned professions as such, but to train for that position in life which many others besides professional men should aim to occupy. For such a position the curriculum has been arranged, not by theorists in education, nor by the traditional adherents to an hereditary system made sacred by hallowed associations, but under the just demands of public life as tested by long experience and confirmed in the success of many generations. In this curriculum the study of the ancient languages has been prominent as training to the power of subtle analysis; the mathematics, as strengthening to continuity and rigor of attention, to sharp and bold discrimination; physics, to give power over nature,—real power, as we wield and apply her forces, and intellectual, as we interpret her secrets, predict her phenomena, enforce her laws, and re-create her universe; psychology, that we may know ourselves and so understand the instrument by which we know at all; ethics, that we may rightly direct the springs of action and subject the individual will to the consecrating law of duty; political science, that we may know the state as to the grounds and limits of its authority; the science of religion, that we may justify our faith to the disciplined and instructed reason; history, that we may trace the development of man and the moral purposes of God; logic, rhetoric, and literature, that the powers thus enriched and thus trained may express themselves aptly and skillfully by writing and in speech.

* * *

For the more advanced students of a college, and even for the students of professional schools, instruction by lecturing should be sparingly applied. It should never supersede the independent reading of the student nor the task-work of individual acquisition and thought. For pupils who are less advanced it should be employed very rarely, and only for the purposes of rousing the attention, stimulating the zeal, and gathering into brief and comprehensive statements the most general views of the topic or author which is studied. The chief occupation of such students should be to commit to memory, and to master by thought, the words and principles which the text-books present for study. The use of a text-book is, however, in no sense degrading to the instructor, nor does it preclude him from giving instruction in the amplest variety and the most effective manner. The teacher is not necessarily degraded to the position of a mere examiner of his pupils' work or a hearer of recitations. On the contrary, he enjoys special advantages for the most effective teaching, viz., teaching by the Socratic method.

* * *

The consideration of the common life of the college is essential to a just estimate of its importance. Without it the college can neither be understood nor appreciated. It is a true and pregnant saying, "You send your child to the schoolmaster, but 'tis the schoolboys who educate him." The studies, the systems and methods of teaching, the knowledge and skill of the instructors, do not constitute the whole of the educating influences of the college. Often they do not furnish half of those influences which are most efficient, which are longest remembered, or which are most highly valued. It is true that without the first the second could not be exerted, for they could not exist. The more obvious and essential elements of the college also exert upon its common life a positive and formative influence. They do not merely serve as the necessary nucleus around which the crystalline material is gathered in bright and beauteous order, but they act as living germs which shoot vitalizing influences through the organized body. But they are not themselves the whole of the body, nor do they include all the forces which it has at command. Very many even of those college graduates who have turned to the best account all the resources which their *alma mater* could furnish, feel themselves quite as much indebted to the educating influences of its community for the awakening and direction of their energies, as to their studies or their instructors. The examples of successful effort which are constantly present, the inspiration that may be derived from the striking achievements witnessed in others, the kind words of a classmate or a college-mate, the encouragement spoken at a critical moment, the prevailing estimate of literary and artistic tastes above the vulgar aspirations after wealth and power which is inwrought into the very fibres of the soul of every genuine college alumnus, his pronounced aversion to all sorts of Philistinism—the inbreathing for years of a stimulating atmosphere that is fragrant with "sweetness" and pervaded by "light;" these,—together with the warmth of college friendships, the earnestness of college rivalries, the revelations of character, the manifestations of growth, the issues of villainy and passion in retribution and shame, the rewards of perseverance and fidelity in triumph and honor—all make the college world to the student to be full of excitement in its progress and to abound in the warmest recollections in the retrospect. The men whom the student knew so thoroughly in college become ever afterwards the representatives and types of all other men; the incidents which there occurred are examples of all other events; its loves and its hatreds, its triumphs and defeats are those by which he ever afterwards reads and interprets society and literature, politics and history.

The intellectual stimulus and education which are furnished by the college community are of a kind which neither circumstances nor instructors can impart. They are eminently a self-education. Most of the efforts at self-improvement which are prompted by the independent movements of one's fellows are zealously prosecuted because they are self-enforced. They fall in with the voluntary activities of awakening manhood and of dawning responsibility. They train to the dignity and duty of self-culture. The studies which they directly foster and inspire are preëminently literary and rhetorical studies, because these studies are more dependent on individual tastes and individual culture, and from their very nature cannot be successfully prescribed nor enforced in the regular curriculum. Studies and ambitions of this sort are indeed not unfrequently irregular, desultory, and unwise. They often interfere very seriously with the thorough mastery of the curriculum of the college. Excessive attention to them sometimes weakens the intellectual energies, induces bad intellectual habits, depraves the taste, and perverts the judgment. But with all these abatements, the intellectual excitement and guidance which are indirectly furnished from the community of fellow students are to many a man the influences of all others which leave the strongest impression, because it is with these that he connects the first consciousness of awakening power, the earliest sense of independent activity and the beginnings of a steady course of self-culture. Some book recommended by a fellow student, some incident casually occurring in the varied course of college experience, some conversation of a wise and faithful adviser, some achievement of a classmate or friend, is remembered as a starting or turning point in the intellectual life.

Nor are the social influences less important in the formation of the character and the furnishing of the man with the beginnings of all kinds of practical knowledge. It may be said that the college world is a narrow and peculiar world, is artificial and factitious in many of its workings, is greatly unlike the larger and freer world of mankind, and is therefore incapable of serving as a preparation for the actual life for which it must so soon be exchanged. Whatever may be its disadvantages in these respects, the advantages which it brings are manifold. The intimacies are most unreserved, the opportunities for the study and interpretation of character are various and long continued. It is at this period of life that the man is, if ever, proverbially frank and transparent, open and fearless. During its progress the character rapidly undergoes many transformations, which are open to the inspection of one's fellows and are often forced upon their attention. The leisure and curiosity of this morning of life, together with the zest with which its novel experiences of research and discovery are enjoyed, all contribute to give energy and interest to this study of character.

This study of character must involve the constant exercise of ethical judgments and the training of the moral powers. That there are peculiar exposures and dangers of a practical sort from this excited and onesided life in an isolated and self-sufficing community, cannot be denied. That not a few are misled by its special temptations, not merely nor chiefly to vices and prodigalities of a grosser sort, but to a refined and subtle insensibility to good that is more insidious and not less really evil, will be confessed by many. That the moral powers often become paralyzed in some of their functions and incapable either of right judgments or active feelings on certain classes of ethical questions, is one of those ever recurring enigmas and scandals that puzzle and offend the looker-on. To the guardian and instructor of one or many victims of these abnormal ethical paroxysms, the question will often present itself whether he ought to be more vexed or amused at these instances of suspended animation in the conscience. And yet with all these biasing and perverting influences, it is found to be true that the observations and experiences of college life are often eminently effective in educating and quickening the conscience and in awakening and directing the moral faculty. The failures and derelictions of college life, and even the occasional paralysis of the conscience of which we have spoken, may serve most important uses as warnings from similar repetitions. The moral lessons of college life are indeed sometimes learned at a painful and bitter cost. But similar experiences are not uncommon with youth in every situation of life. Perhaps under no circumstances can they be made with a more wholesome and permanent ethical effect.

The religious influences of this common life should not be omitted. We suppose that the college is a truly Christian institution, so far as the instructions and the faith of its teachers are concerned. There are not a few reasons why the public life of such an institution should be favorable to earnest religious thought and a positive religious faith. The life of the student is necessarily intellectual and reflective; whatever subjects are studied, the study of them involves intellectual effort and studious attention. During the period of college life the earnest mind often encounters those questionings which require a decided answer, and it awakes to thoughts which cannot be repressed. It is haunted by the presence of mysterious realities which cannot be dismissed. The prospect of coming manhood with the responsibilities of individual character and of independent life, at once sobers and elevates. It often happens that many nearly allied as friends and classmates, are moved to similar earnest emotions and to like searching inquiries. The common sympathies of a familiar circle thus occupied quicken the better emotions and favor the happiest results. The temptations in college to sensualism and to unbelief are manifold; but so are the influences which favor an earnest and zealous Christian life. The number of those is not small who look back to the common life of the college as the beginning or the helper of the higher life of the Christian. Were the religious influences that proceed from the colleges of this country to be withdrawn or sensibly diminished, it would seem that the Gospel itself might almost cease to be acknowledged,—so manifold are the relations of each generation of college students to the faith and life of the whole Christian Church.

The effect of these varied intellectual, social, ethical, and religious influences are so powerful and salutary that it may well be questioned whether the education which they impart does not of itself more than repay the time and money which it costs, even to those idlers at college who derive from their residence little or nothing more than these accidental or incidental advantages. The constant companionship with the members of a community professedly devoted to intellectual pursuits and elevated by literary tastes, the constantly renewed interest in those incidents which will ever break forth from its exuberant and irrepressible life, the pressure of its necessary restraints, the countless lessons of good which cannot be unheeded even by the most thoughtless and perverse, elevate the life of the merest laggard and drone at college immeasurably above the life of the luxurious do-nothing who haunts the saloons, promenades the streets, and lounges at the concerts and theatres of a large city, or who drones away the animal, most likely the sensual, life of a rich man's son in the country.

Such idlers sometimes awake to manliness and to duty when they leave college. However heavy may be the burden which they carry through life as the result of folly and waste, they rarely fail to have stored up an abundant stock of rich experiences as well as of pleasant recollections. To many who persistently neglect the college studies, the college life is anything rather than a total loss. Even those who sink downward with no recovery, find their descent retarded by the associations of dignity and self-respect with which their previous access to culture has enriched them.

*   *   *

The consideration of the American colleges as communities has brought us to the question of their religious character. This includes several subordinate questions, such as, whether they ought to be placed under a positive religious influence, and to what extent and in what manner this influence may properly be exercised. These questions, and many others which arise under this comprehensive topic, are from the nature of the subject not easily answered, and in the present state of opinion are involved in somewhat serious complications.

We may as well say, at the outset, that the view which any man, otherwise well-informed, will take of this subject, must necessarily vary with the views which he takes of religion itself, as to its essential nature and authority, its evidence, and its relation to man's responsibility and destiny. It will vary also with the views which he takes of Christianity; according as he regards it as supernaturally given and historically true, or as he believes it to be of human origination, and, therefore, so far as its miracles and the claims and conceptions of its central personages are concerned, as more or less historically erroneous. It will vary also according as his views are more or less enlarged of its relations to human culture, and of its friendliness to the highest forms of human development.

The position which we occupy is that "the Christian faith is the perfection of human reason;" that supernatural and historical Christianity is the only Christianity which is worth defending or which is capable of being defended on the grounds of reason or history; and that such a Christianity, when interpreted by enlightened judgment, as to its truths and its precepts, is not only friendly to the highest forms of culture, but is an essential condition of the same.

There are not a few at the present time who do not agree with us in this position. More than a few, we fear, of those interested in the higher education of the country, so far hesitate to receive any positive form of religion as to assume in all their reasonings, that the claims of supernatural Christianity are more likely than otherwise to be set aside in the progress of historical and scientific investigation, and that it is therefore inconsistent as well as impolitic for the universities and colleges of the country to be very positively committed to the support of these claims. Such a recognition of Christianity, in their view, hinders the freedom of investigation and of teaching, and is inconsistent with that tolerance among scholars which is required by the spirit of the age. They might repel the charge of being anti-religious or atheistic or even anti-Christian in their own faith, but they reason that for a college to recognize the Christian faith in its teachings is to commit itself to an implied bondage of opinion, which cannot but constrain the freedom of its spirit, or which must, at least, make it unwisely intolerant. We cannot accept this position or the inferences to which it leads.

NOAH PORTER ON THE ELEMENTS OF MORAL SCIENCE (1885) From
Noah Porter, *The Elements of Moral Science* (New York, 1885), pp. 1–3, 7, 11–13.

---

1. MORAL SCIENCE is the science of duty; i.e., the science which defines, regulates, and enforces duty. This definition is preliminary and inadequate, as every definition must be which is given at the beginning of a treatise. A satisfactory and adequate definition of any science can only be attained by an exhaustive discussion of the subject-matter of which it treats. For this reason it should be looked for at the end, rather than at the beginning, of our inquiries. . . .

As a science, Moral Science proposes to give the results of careful observations, subtile and exhaustive analyses, clear and complete definitions, verified inductions, logical deductions, in the form of a consistent, articulated, and finished system.

The scientific knowledge of duty at which we aim, also supposes that there is a so-called popular knowledge which is already possessed and made secure (cf. *The Human Intellect,* §435). Duty is a subject-matter which all men acknowledge and believe in, and of which all men think more or less. All men adopt principles of duty which are more or less correct and comprehensive. All men accept rules of duty for themselves and others which are more or less satisfying and sacred. The transition from common to scientific knowledge may be less abrupt in this than in many other cases; but it does not follow, for this reason, that it is less desirable to effect it. It may be even more important, because of the greater liability of men to careless thinking and investigation in the treatment of themes with which they imagine themselves to be familiar.

Every science is also capable of being applied as an art to some kind of activity for which it furnishes the rules. This is conspicuously true of logic and æsthetics, which, by means of scientific analyses, devise and justify practical rules for the direction of our thinking and reasoning, and the exercise and improvement of our sense of the beautiful and sublime. In a certain sense, both logic and æsthetics present rules for right conduct; but this is pre-eminently true of Moral Science, inasmuch as it assumes the control of every description of human activity, so far as it can be modified by the human will under the influence of the highest motives. The results of its scientific knowledge can be applied to the direction of human conduct and the improvement of human character, to the well-being of the individual and the community, in almost every conceivable variety of circumstances. Moral Science, as a system of well-grounded rules of human character and conduct, is justly esteemed one of the most important of studies, for the simple reason that questions of duty present themselves to all men, in all circumstances; and the consequences of correctly answering these questions are of the utmost practical importance.

2. Duty is the subject-matter of Moral Science. *But what is duty?* We reply in general, and provisionally, Duty in the concrete is an action, or collection of actions, which ought to be done: in the abstract, it is the quality or relation which is common to and distinguishes such actions.

We do not undertake at present to enumerate or designate these actions. We give no definition or theory of the quality which belongs to them. We do not assert that this is the only relation or property which belongs to the acts in question: we simply recognize it as the one quality, among others, which is designated by the term "duty" in every action which is owed or due, and which may be claimed or enforced.

The term "action," as used in the foregoing definition, is obviously not limited to corporeal or external actions, as a word or blow, or even a gesture or look, nor indeed to any bodily movement or effect whatever, independently of the intentions; but it also includes the inner activities, as a wish, or desire, or purpose, whether these are, or are not, made manifest by word or deed.

Nor is the term, when thus applied, limited to single and transient states. It may also be applied to those continued or permanently active conditions of the man which we call his *character,* his *disposition,* and *habits,* so far as these admit the relation of moral obligation or moral quality. In Moral Science psychical activities and states are esteemed of no less consequence than any other, if, indeed, they do not constitute its proper sphere.

*   *   *

6. The importance and dignity of this study will appear from the following considerations:—

(1) Duty is a legitimate and worthy object of scientific inquiry. Truths of duty constantly present themselves for man's assent and faith. The precepts of duty perpetually require his obedience or sacrifice. Motives of duty never cease to inspire his love and devotion. Questions of duty every day task his understanding, or distract his conscience.

Duty, moreover, is esteemed by most men to be of the highest consequence. It excites the warmest emotions of hope or fear, of love or hate, of self-complacence or remorse. It exacts the most costly sacrifices of wealth, of the good opinion of others, and of life itself. So far as duty is capable of scientific analysis and justification, in order that our doubts may be resolved, our inquiries answered, our zeal rekindled, or our actions guided, it deserves to be investigated with a thorough and patient scientific spirit.

(2) The science of duty is necessary as a preparation for professional and public life. The principles and rules of duty are fertile and never-failing themes for discussion by educated men. They will never cease to be enforced upon the attention of men in public life by their fellows and by public men upon their generation. Every man whom we shall meet in life will have some claim to urge or some demand to assert. Every social organization, from the family of the household to the great family of mankind, asserts rights which can only be responded to by some duty acknowledged or disowned. Every community and association has its code of duty, and its tribunal at which its laws are enforced, its rewards are allotted, or its penalties are exacted. Every form of civil government supposes manifold duties to be owed and confessed by its citizens. Even those movements which seem to be anti-social, and destructive of social order, are aroused by appeals to some sense of duty or some claim of right. They more commonly profess to be pre-eminently ethical in their reasonings and appeals. Combinations, strikes, seditions, and revolutions are usually aroused by some real or imagined violation of rights. They are kindled by some professed call of duty, or are justified by some actual or fancied wrong. Judicial tribunals of every grade are constantly trying questions which concern the rights and the consequent duties of men. The argument of every lawyer, the charge of every judge, the verdict of every jury, the sentence of every culprit, supposes some principle in Moral Science either asserted or derived, some rule of Ethics that is obeyed or dishonored, some sensibility to right or wrong that is followed or offended, some obligation that is acknowledged or violated.

Every educated man who assumes the function of teaching or leading his fellow-men finds that one of his principal functions is to discuss and enforce propositions of duty. Clergymen, jurists, publicists, political leaders, teachers, writers, and journalists are, by the nature of their office, expounders of Moral Science. It is true, they may seem to themselves and to others to have no faith in duty. They may think themselves successful in their doubts and denials in respect to its reality; but such denials and questionings only respect certain of its forms and relations. They may reduce duty to very narrow limits, and derive it from a very ignoble origin, and enforce it by very unworthy motives; but no man in public life, no teacher or leader of men, would ever think of denying every form of duty, or cease to use the nomenclature of Ethics. For these reasons a scientific knowledge of the foundations and precepts of duty would seem to be a necessary prerequisite for the discharge of the special functions of most of the leaders of society, and masters of the opinions of their fellow-men. Every such person holds and expounds a true or a false, a profound or superficial, theory of morals.

(3) The study of Moral Science is practically useful. Its natural and almost necessary tendency is to lead men to think of duty, and consequently to believe in duty. If duty is the solid and sacred thing which it claims to be, then it will bear the closest scrutiny. Not only will it endure this, but the more thoroughly it is examined, the more solid will be its grounds, and the more binding its claims. It is true, speculative studies have their exposures. Science may be pursued in a narrow or a dishonest spirit, and seem to lead to superficial and dangerous conclusions; but the legitimate ends and efforts of science are truth, made more evident to the

inquirer in proportion to the fidelity of his researchers and the breadth of his views. The worst of all possible scepticisms in the thinking man is the distrust of thorough and bold investigation. The most dangerous enemy of duty is the man who dissuades from an exhaustive examination of its grounds and claims in the light of scientific insight and with the widest possible range of inquiry. No man is so faithless to duty in fact, whatever his intentions may be, as he who loses faith in its capacity to meet and endure the severest scrutiny of scientific thought.

Moreover, the scientific study of duty must keep pace with the attention given to the scientific investigation of other forms of truth. A man who has been trained to scientific habits in any department of thought, or upon whatever subject-matter, will of course apply these habits in all his thinking. He will require that every conclusion which he accepts shall have been viewed in its scientific relations—more or less profoundly. He must justify to his reflective and matured reason every truth and fact which is liable to be called in question. There may be facts and principles, indeed, which he does not need thus to examine and justify; but this is not true of the facts and rules of duty. These he must either recieve or deny, he must either apply or neglect them, and he must do both intelligently.

The College Reform Movement

ACT ESTABLISHING A MILITARY ACADEMY AT WEST POINT
(1802)   From U.S. Congress, *Debates and Proceedings, 7th Congress* (December 7,
1801–March 3, 1803), p. 1312.

Sec. 26. *And be it further enacted,* That the President of the United States is hereby authorized and empowered, when he shall deem it expedient, to organize and establish a corps of engineers, to consist of one engineer, with the pay, rank, and emoluments of a major; two assistant engineers, with the pay, rank, and emoluments of captains; two other assistant engineers, with the pay, rank, and emoluments of first lieutenants; two other assistant engineers, with the pay, rank, and emoluments of second lieutenants; and ten cadets, with the pay of sixteen dollars per month, and two rations per day; and the President of the United States is, in like manner, authorized, when he shall deem it proper, to make such promotions in the said corps, with a view to particular merit, and without regard to rank, so as not to exceed one colonel, one lieutenant colonel, two majors, four captains, four first lieutenants, four second lieutenants, and so as that the number of the whole corps shall, at no time, exceed twenty officers and cadets.

Sec. 27. *And be it further enacted,* That the said corps when so organized shall be stationed at West Point, in the State of New York, and shall constitute a military academy; and the engineers, assistant engineers, and cadets of the said corps, shall be subject, at all times, to do duty in such places, and on such service, as the President of the United States shall direct.

Sec. 28. *And be it further enacted,* That the principal engineer, and in his absence the next in rank, shall have the superintendence of the said military academy, under the direction of the President of the United States; and the Secretary of War is hereby authorized, at the public expense, under such regulations as shall be directed by the President of the United States, to procure the necessary books, implements, and apparatus, for the use and benefit of the said institution.

Sec. 29. *And be it further enacted,* That so much of any act or acts, now in force, as comes within the purview of this act, shall be and the same is hereby, repealed; saving, nevertheless, such parts thereof as relate to the enlistments or term or service of any of the troops, which, by this act, are continued on the present military establishment of the United States.

Approved, March 16, 1802.

HIGHER
EDUCATION

ESTABLISHMENT OF THE "CATHOLEPISTEMIAD OR UNIVERSITY OF MICHIGANIA"(1817)

From Frank E. Robbins, ed., *Records of the University of Michigan, 1817–1837* (Ann Arbor, Mich., 1935), pp. 3–6.

AN ACT TO ESTABLISH THE CATHOLEPISTEMIAD, OR UNIVERSITY, OF MICHIGANIA

Be it enacted by the Governor and the Judges of the Territory of Michigan that there shall be in the said Territory a *catholepistemiad,* or university, denominated the *catholepistemiad,* or university, of Michigania. The *catholepistemiad,* or university of Michigania shall be composed of thirteen *didaxiim* or professorships: first, a *didaxia* or professorship, of *catholepistemia,* or universal science, the *didactor* or professor, of which shall be president of the institution; second, a *didaxia,* or professorship, of *anthropoglossica,* or literature, embracing all the *epistemiim,* or sciences, relative to language; third, a *didaxia,* or professorship, of *mathematica,* or mathematics; fourth, a *didaxia,* or professorship, of *physiognostica,* or natural history; fifth, a *didaxia,* or professorship, of *physiosophica,* or natural philosophy; sixth, a *didaxia,* or professorship, of *astronomia,* or astronomy; seventh, a *didaxia,* or professorship, of *chymia,* or chemistry; eight, a *didaxia,* or professorship, of *iatrica,* or medical sciences; ninth, a *didaxia,* or professorship, of *aeconomica,* or economical sciences; tenth, a *didaxia,* or professorship, of *ethica,* or ethica[*l*] sciences; eleventh, a *didaxia,* or professorship, of *polemitactica,* or military sciences; twelfth, a *didaxia,* or professorship, of *diegetica,* or historical sciences; and, thirteenth, a *didaxi*[*a*] or professorship of *ennaeica,* or intellectual sciences, embracing all the *epistemiim,* or sciences, relative to the minds of animals, to the human mind, to spiritual existences, to the deity, and to religion, the *didactor,* or professor, of which shall be vice-presiden[t] of the institution. The *didactors,* or professors, shall be appointed and commissioned by the Governor. There shall be paid, from the treasury of Michigan, in quarterly payments, to the president of the institution, to the vice-president, and to each *didactor,* or professor, an annual salary, to be, from time to time, ascertained by law. More than one *didaxia,* or professorship, may be conferred upon the same person. The president and *didactors,* or professors, or a majority of them, assembled, shall have power to regulate all the concer[ns] of the institution, to enact laws for that pu[r] pose, to sue, to be sued, to acquire, to hol[d] and to aliene, property, real, mixed, and personal, to make, to sue, and to alter, a seal, to establish colleges, academies, schools, libraries, musaeums, athenaeums, botanic gardens, laboratories, and other useful literary and scientific institutions, consonant to the laws of the United States of America and of Michigan, and to appoint officers, instructors and instructrixes, in, among, and throughout, the various counties, cities, towns, townships, and other geographical divisions, of Michigan. Their name and stile as a corporation shall be "The *catholepistemiad,* or university, of Michigania," To every subordinate instructor, and instructrix, appointed by the *catholepistemiad,* or university, there shall be paid, from the treasury of Michigan, in quarterly payments, an annual salary, to be, from time to time, ascertained by law. The existing public taxes are hereby increased fifteen per cent; and, from the proceeds of the present, and of all future public taxes, fifteen per cent are appropriated for the benefit of the *catholepistemiad,* or university. The treasurer of Michigan shall keep a separate account of the university fund. The *catholepistemiad,* or university, may propose and draw four successive lotteries, deducting from the prizes in the same fifteen per cent for the benefit of the institution. The proceeds of the preceding sources of revenue, and of all subsequent, shall be applied in the fir[st] instance, to the acquisition of suitable land[s] and buildings, and books, libraries, and apparatus, and afterwards to such purposes as shall be, from time to time, by law directed. The *honorarium* for a course of lectures sh[all] not exceed fifteen dollars, for classical instruction ten dollars a quarter, and for ordinary instruction six dollars a quarter. If the judges of the court of any county, or a majority of them, shall certify that the parent, or guardian, of any person has not adequate means to defray the expense of the suitable instruction, and that the sam[e] ought to be a public charge, the *honorarium* shall be paid from the Treasury of Michigan. An annual report of the state, concerns, and transactions, of the institution shall be laid before the legislative power for the time being. This law, or any part of it, may be repealed by the legislative power for the time being.

   Made, adopted, and published, from the laws of seven of the original states, to wit the states of Connecticut, Massachusetts, New-Jersey, New-York, Ohio, Pennsylvania, and Virginia, as far as necessary and suitable to the circumstances of Michigan; at the City of Detroit, on Tuesday the twenty sixth day of August, in the year one thousand eight hundred seventeen.

WILLIAM WOODBRIDGE
Secy of Michigan, and at present Acting Governour thereof

A. B. WOODWARD
Presiding Judge of the Supreme Court of the Territory of Michigan
JOHN GRIFFIN
One of the Judges of the Territory of Michigan

JEFFERSON CRITICIZES THE FASHIONABLE LEARNING OF THE DAY

(**1814**)   Letter from Thomas Jefferson to John Adams, July 15, 1814, in Paul Leicester Ford, ed., *The Writings of Thomas Jefferson* (Washington, D.C., 1905), vol. IX, pp. 462–465.

Monticello, July 5, 1814

. . . I am just returned from one of my long absences, having been at my other home for five weeks past. Having more leisure there than here for reading, I amused myself with reading seriously Plato's Republic. I am wrong, however, in calling it amusement, for it was the heaviest taskwork I ever went through. I had occasionally before taken up some of his other works, but scarcely ever had patience to go through a whole dialogue. While wading through the whimsies, the puerilities, and unintelligible jargon of this work, I laid it down often to ask myself how it could have been, that the world should have so long consented to give reputation to such nonsense as this? How the *soi-disant* Christian world, indeed, should have done it, is a piece of historical curiosity. But how could the Roman good sense do it? And particularly, how could Cicero bestow such eulogies on Plato! Although Cicero did not wield the dense logic of Demosthenes, yet he was able, learned, laborious,

HIGHER
EDUCATION

1483

practised in the business of the world, and honest. He could not be the dupe of mere style, of which he was himself the first master in the world. With the moderns, I think, it is rather a matter of fashion and authority. Education is chiefly in the hands of persons who, from their profession, have an interest in the reputation and the dreams of Plato. They give the tone while at school, and few in their after years have occasion to revise their college opinions. But fashion and authority apart, and bringing Plato the test of reason, take from him his sophisms, futilities and incomprehensibilities, and what remains? In truth, he is one of the race of genuine sophists, who has escaped the oblivion of his brethren, first, by the elegance of his diction, but chiefly, by the adoption and incorporation of his whimsies into the body of artificial Christianity. His foggy mind is forever presenting the semblances of objects which, half seen through a mist, can be defined neither in form nor dimensions. Yet this, which should have consigned him to early oblivion, really procured him immortality of fame and reverence. The Christian priesthood, finding the doctrines of Christ levelled to every understanding, and too plain to need explanation, saw in the mysticism of Plato materials with which they might build up an artificial system, which might, from its indistinctness, admit everlasting controversy, give employment for their order, and introduce it to profit, power and pre-eminence. The doctrines which flowed from the lips of Jesus himself are within the comprehension of a child; but thousands of volumes have not yet explained the Platonisms engrafted on them; and for this obvious reason, that nonsense can never be explained. Their purposes, however, are answered. Plato is canonized; and it is now deemed as impious to question his merits as those of an Apostle of Jesus. He is peculiarly appealed to as an advocate of the immortality of the soul; and yet I will venture to say, that were there no better arguments than his in proof of it, not a man in the world would believe it. It is fortunate for us, that Platonic republicanism has not obtained the same favor as Platonic Christianity; or we should now have been all living, men, women and children, pell mell together, like beasts of the field or forest. Yet "Plato is a great philosopher," said La Fontaine. But, says Fontenelle, "Do you find his ideas very clear?" "Oh no! he is of an obscurity impenetrable." "Do you not find him full of contradictions?" "Certainly," replied La Fontaine, "he is but a sophist." Yet immediately after he exclaims again, "Oh, Plato was a great philosopher." Socrates had reason, indeed, to complain of the misrepresentations of Plato; for in truth, his dialogues are libels of Socrates.

But why am I dosing you with these antediluvian topics? Because I am glad to have some one to whom they are familiar, and who will not receive them as if dropped from the moon. Our post-revolutionary youth are born under happier stars than you and I were. They acquire all learning in their mother's womb, and bring it into the world ready made. The information of books is no longer necessary; and all knowledge which is not innate, is in contempt, or neglect at least. Every folly must run its round; and so, I suppose, must that of self-learning and self-sufficiency; of rejecting the knowledge acquired in past ages, and starting on the new ground of intuition. When sobered by experience, I hope our successors will turn their attention to the advantages of education. I mean of education on the broad scale, and not that of the petty *academies*, as they call themselves, which are starting up in every neighborhood, and where one or two men, possessing Latin and sometimes Greek, a knowledge of the globes, and the first six books of Euclid, imagine and communicate this as the sum of science. They commit their pupils to the theatre of the world, with just taste enough of learning to be alienated from industrious pursuits, and not enough to do service in the ranks of science. We have some exceptions, indeed. I presented one to you lately, and we have some others. But the terms I use are general truths. I hope the necessity will, at length, be seen of establishing institutions here, as in Europe, where every branch of science, useful at this day, may be taught in its highest degree. Have you ever turned your thoughts to the plan of such an institution? I mean to a specification of the particular sciences of real use in human affairs, and how they might be so grouped as to require so many professors only as might bring them within the views of a just but enlightened economy? I should be happy in a communication of your ideas on this problem, either loose or digested. But to avoid my being run away with by another subject, and adding to the length and ennui of the present letter, I will here present to Mrs. Adams and yourself, the assurance of my constant and sincere friendship and respect.

PLAN FOR REFORMING THE UNIVERSITY OF VIRGINIA: THE
ROCKFISH GAP REPORT (1818)   From Nathaniel Francis Cabell, ed., *Early History of the University of Virginia* . . . (Richmond, 1856), pp. 432–43.

Report of the Commissioners Appointed to Fix the Site
of the University of Virginia, &c.

The Commissioners for the University of Virginia, having met, as by law required, at the tavern, in Rockfish Gap, on the Blue Ridge, on the first day of August, of this present year, 1818; and having formed a board, proceeded on that day to the discharge of the duties assigned to them by the act of the Legislature, entitled "An act, appropriating part of the revenue of the literary fund, and for other purposes;" and having continued their proceedings by adjournment, from day to day, to Tuesday, the 4th day of August, have agreed to a report on the several matters with which they were charged, which report they now respectfully address and submit to the Legislature of the State.

The first duty enjoined on them, was to enquire and report a site, in some convenient and proper part of the State, for an university, to be called the "University of Virginia." . . . the Board, after full enquiry, and impartial and mature consideration, are of opinion, that the central point of the white population of the State is nearer to the Central College than to either Lexington or Staunton, by great and important differences; and all other circumstances of the place in general being favorable to it, as a position for an university, they do report the Central College, in Albemarle, to be a convenient and proper part of the State for the University of Virginia.

2. The Board having thus agreed on a proper site for the University, to be reported to the Legislature, proceed to the second of the duties assigned to them— that of proposing a plan for its buildings—and they are of opinion that it should consist of distinct houses or pavilions, arranged at proper distances on each side of a lawn of a proper breadth, and of indefinite extent, in one direction, at least; in each of which should be a lecturing room, with from two to four apartments, for the accommodation of a professor and his family; that these pavilions should be united by a range of dormitories, sufficient each for the accommodation of two students

HIGHER
EDUCATION

only, this provision being deemed advantageous to morals, to order, and to uninterrupted study; and that a passage of some kind, under cover from the weather, should give a communication along the whole range. It is supposed that such pavilions, on an average of the larger and smaller, will cost each about $5,000; each dormitory about $350, and hotels of a single room, for a refectory, and two rooms for the tenant, necessary for dieting the students, will cost about $3500 each. The number of these pavilions will depend on the number of professors, and that of the dormitories and hotels on the number of students to be lodged and dieted. The advantages of this plan are: greater security against fire and infection; tranquillity and comfort to the professors and their families thus insulated; retirement to the students; and the admission of enlargement to any degree to which the institution may extend in future times. It is supposed probable, that a building of somewhat more size in the middle of the grounds may be called for in time, in which may be rooms for religious worship, under such impartial regulations as the Visitors shall prescribe, for public examinations, for a library, for the schools of music, drawing, and other associated purposes.

3, 4. In proceeding to the third and fourth duties prescribed by the Legislature, of reporting "the branches of learning, which should be taught in the University, and the number and description of the professorships they will require," the Commissioners were first to consider at what point it was understood that university education should commence? Certainly not with the alphabet, for reasons of expediency and impracticability, as well from the obvious sense of the Legislature, who, in the same act, make other provision for the primary instruction of the poor children, expecting, doubtless, that in other cases it would be provided by the parent, or become, perhaps, subject of future and further attention of the Legislature. The objects of this primary education determine its character and limits. These objects would be,

To give to every citizen the information he needs for the transaction of his own business;

To enable him to calculate for himself, and to express and preserve his ideas, his contracts and accounts, in writing;

To improve, by reading, his morals and faculties;

To understand his duties to his neighbors and country, and to discharge with competence the functions confided to him by either;

To know his rights; to exercise with order and justice those he retains; to choose with discretion the fiduciary of those he delegates; and to notice their conduct with diligence, with candor, and judgment;

And, in general, to observe with intelligence and faithfulness all the social relations under which he shall be placed.

To instruct the mass of our citizens in these, their rights, interests and duties, as men and citizens, being then the objects of education in the primary schools, whether private or public, in them should be taught reading, writing and numerical arithmetic, the elements of mensuration (useful in so many callings,) and the outlines of geography and history. And this brings us to the point at which are to commence the higher branches of education, of which the Legislature require the development; those, for example, which are,

To form the statesmen, legislators and judges, on whom public prosperity and individual happiness are so much to depend;

To expound the principles and structure of government, the laws which regulate the intercourse of nations, those formed municipally for our own government, and a sound spirit of legislation, which, banishing all arbitrary and unnecessary restraint on individual action, shall leave us free to do whatever does not violate the equal rights of another;

To harmonize and promote the interests of agriculture, manufactures and commerce, and by well informed views of political economy to give a free scope to the public industry;

To develop the reasoning faculties of our youth, enlarge their minds, cultivate their morals, and instill into them the precepts of virtue and order;

To enlighten them with mathematical and physical sciences, which advance the arts, and administer to the health, the subsistence, and comforts of human life;

And, generally, to form them to habits of reflection and correct action, rendering them examples of virtue to others, and of happiness within themselves.

These are the objects of that higher grade of education, the benefits and blessings of which the Legislature now propose to provide for the good and ornament of their country, the gratification and happiness of their fellow-citizens, of the parent especially, and his progeny, on which all his affections are concentrated.

In entering on this field, the Commissioners are aware that they have to encounter much difference of opinion as to the extent which it is expedient that this institution should occupy. Some good men, and even of respectable information, consider the learned sciences as useless acquirements; some think that they do not better the condition of man; and others that education, like private and individual concerns, should be left to private individual effort; not reflecting that an establishment embracing all the sciences which may be useful and even necessary in the various vocations of life, with the buildings and apparatus belonging to each, are far beyond the reach of individual means, and must either derive existence from public patronage, or not exist at all. This would leave us, then, without those callings which depend on education, or send us to other countries to seek the instruction they require. But the Commissioners are happy in considering the statute under which they are assembled as proof that the Legislature is far from the abandonment of objects so interesting. They are sensible that the advantages of well-directed education, moral, political and economical, are truly above all estimate. Education generates habits of application, of order, and the love of virtue; and controls, by the force of habit, any innate obliquities in our moral organization. We should be far, too, from the discouraging persuasion that man is fixed, by the law of his nature, at a given point; that his improvement is a chimera, and the hope delusive of rendering ourselves wiser, happier or better than our forefathers were. As well might it be urged that the wild and uncultivated tree, hitherto yielding sour and bitter fruit only, can never be made to yield better; yet we know that the grafting art implants a new tree on the savage stock, producing what is most estimable both in kind and degree. Education, in like manner, engrafts a new man on the native stock, and improves what in his nature was vicious and perverse into qualities of virtue and social worth. And it cannot be but that each generation succeeding to the knowledge acquired by all those who preceded it, adding to it their own acquisitions and discoveries, and handing the mass down for successive and constant accumulation, must advance the knowledge and well-being of mankind, not *infinitely*, as some have said, but *indefinitely*, and to a term which no one can fix and foresee. Indeed, we need look back half a century, to times which many now living remember well, and see the wonderful advances in the sciences and arts which have been made within that period.

*   *   *

Encouraged, therefore, by the sentiments of the Legislature, manifested in this statute, we present the following tabular statements of the branches of learning which we think should be taught in the University, forming them into groups, each of which are within the powers of a single professor:

    I.   Languages, ancient:
        Latin,
        Greek,
        Hebrew.

    II.   Languages, modern:
        French,
        Spanish,
        Italian,
        German,
        Anglo-Saxon.

    III.   Mathematics, pure:
        Algebra,
        Fluxions,
        Geometry, Elementary,
                      Transcendental.
        Architecture, Military.
                     Naval.

    IV.   Physico-Mathematics:
        Mechanics,
        Statics,
        Dynamics,
        Pneumatics,
        Acoustics,
        Optics,
        Astronomy,
        Geography.

    V.   Physics, or Natural Philosophy:
        Chemistry,
        Mineralogy.

    VI.   Botany,
        Zoology.

    VII.   Anatomy,
        Medicine.

    VIII.   Government,
        Political Economy,
        Law of Nature and Nations,
        History, being interwoven with Politics and Law.

    IX.   Law, municipal.

    X.   Ideology,
        General Grammar,
        Ethics,

Rhetoric,
Belles Lettres, and the fine arts.

*   *   *

Some articles in this distribution of sciences will need observation. A professor is proposed for ancient languages, the Latin, Greek, and Hebrew, particularly; but these languages being the foundation common to all the sciences, it is difficult to foresee what may be the extent of this school. At the same time, no greater obstruction to industrious study could be proposed than the presence, the intrusions and the noisy turbulence of a multitude of small boys; and if they are to be placed here for the rudiments of the languages, they may be so numerous that its character and value as an University will be merged in those of a Grammar school. It is, therefore, greatly to be wished, that preliminary schools, either on private or public establishment, could be distributed in districts through the State, as preparatory to the entrance of students into the University. The tender age at which this part of education commences, generally about the tenth year, would weigh heavily with parents in sending their sons to a school so distant as the central establishment would be from most of them. Districts of such extent as that every parent should be within a day's journey of his son at school, would be desirable in cases of sickness, and convenient for supplying their ordinary wants, and might be made to lessen sensibly the expense of this part of their education. And where a sparse population would not, within such a compass, furnish subjects sufficient to maintain a school, a competent enlargement of district must, of necessity, there be submitted to. At these district schools or colleges, boys should be rendered able to read the easier authors, Latin and Greek. This would be useful and sufficient for many not intended for an University education. At these, too, might be taught English grammar, the higher branches of numerical arithmetic, the geometry of straight lines and of the circle, the elements of navigation, and geography to a sufficient degree, and thus afford to greater numbers the means of being qualified for the various vocations of life, needing more instruction than merely menial or praedial labor, and the same advantages to youths whose education may have been neglected until too late to lay a foundation in the learned languages. These institutions, intermediate between the primary schools and University, might then be the passage of entrance for youths into the University, where their classical learning might be critically completed, by a study of the authors of highest degree; and it is at this stage only that they should be received at the University. Giving then a portion of their time to a finished knowledge of the Latin and Greek, the rest might be appropriated to the modern languages, or to the commencement of the course of science for which they should be destined. This would generally be about the fifteenth year of their age, when they might go with more safety and contentment to that distance from their parents. Until this preparatory provision shall be made, either the University will be overwhelmed with the grammar school, or a separate establishment, under one or more ushers, for its lower classes, will be advisable, at a mile or two distant from the general one; where, too, may be exercised the stricter government necessary for young boys, but unsuitable for youths arrived at years of discretion.

The considerations which have governed the specification of languages to be taught by the professor of modern languages were, that the French is the language of general intercourse among nations, and as a depository of human science, is unsurpassed by any other language, living or dead; that the Spanish is highly interesting to us, as the language spoken by so great a portion of the inhabitants of our continents, with whom we shall probably have great intercourse ere long, and is that also in which is written the greater part of the earlier history of America. The Italian abounds with works of very superior order, valuable for their matter, and still more distinguished as models of the finest taste in style and composition. And the German now stands in a line with that of the most learned nations in richness of erudition and advance in the sciences. It is too of common descent with the language of our own country, a branch of the same original Gothic stock, and furnishes valuable illustrations for us. But in this point of view, the Anglo-Saxon is of peculiar value. We have placed it among the modern languages, because it is in fact that which we speak, in the earliest form in which we have knowledge of it. It has been undergoing, with time, those gradual changes which all languages, ancient and modern, have experienced; and even now needs only to be printed in the modern character and orthography to be intelligible, in a considerable degree, to an English reader. It has this value, too, above the Greek and Latin, that while it gives the radix of the mass of our language, they explain its innovations only. Obvious proofs of this have been presented to the modern reader in the disquisitions of Horn Tooke; and Fortescue Aland has well explained the great instruction which may be derived from it to a full understanding of our ancient common law, on which, as a stock, our whole system of law is engrafted. It will form the first link in the chain of an historical review of our language through all its successive changes to the present day, will constitute the foundation of that critical instruction in it which ought to be found in a seminary of general learning, and thus reward amply the few weeks of attention which would alone be requisite for its attainment; a language already fraught with all the eminent science of our parent country, the future vehicle of whatever we may ourselves achieve, and destined to occupy so much space on the globe, claims distinguished attention in American education.

Medicine, where fully taught, is usually subdivided into several professorships, but this cannot well be without the accessory of an hospital, where the student can have the benefit of attending clinical lectures, and of assisting at operations of surgery. With this accessory, the seat of our University is not yet prepared, either by its population or by the numbers of poor who would leave their own houses, and accept of the charities of an hospital. For the present, therefore, we propose but a single professor for both medicine and anatomy. By him the medical science may be taught, with a history and explanations of all its successive theories from Hippocrates to the present day; and anatomy may be fully treated. Vegetable pharmacy will make a part of the botanical course, and mineral and chemical pharmacy of those of mineralogy and chemistry. This degree of medical information is such as the mass of scientific students would wish to possess, as enabling them in their course through life, to estimate with satisfaction the extent and limits of the aid to human life and health, which they may understandingly expect from that art; and it constitutes such a foundation for those intended for the profession, that the finishing course of practice at the bed-sides of the sick, and at the operations of surgery in a hospital, can neither be long nor expensive. To seek this finishing elsewhere, must therefore be submitted to for a while.

In conformity with the principles of our Constitution, which places all sects of religion on an equal footing, with the jealousies of the different sects in guarding that equality from encroachment and surprise, and with the sentiments of the Legislature in favor of freedom of religion, manifested on former occasions, we have proposed no professor of divinity; and the rather as the proofs of the being of a God, the creator, preserver, and supreme ruler of the universe, the author of all the relations of morality, and of the laws and obligations these infer, will be within the province of the professor of ethics; to which adding the developments of these moral obligations, of those in which all sects agree, with a knowledge of the languages, Hebrew, Greek, and Latin, a basis will be formed common to all sects. Proceeding thus far without offence to the Constitution, we have thought it proper at this point to leave every sect to provide, as they think fittest, the means of further instruction in their own peculiar tenets.

We are further of opinion, that after declaring by law that certain sciences shall be taught in the University, fixing the number of professors they require, which we think should, at present, be ten, limiting (except as to the professors who shall be first engaged in each branch,) a maximum for their salaries, (which should be a certain but moderate subsistence, to be made up by liberal tuition fees, as an excitement to assiduity), it will be best to leave to the discretion of the visitors, the grouping of these sciences together, according to the accidental qualifications of the professors; and the introduction also of other branches of science, when enabled by private donations, or by public provision, and called for by the increase of population, or other change of circumstances; to establish beginnings, in short, to be developed by time, as those who come after us shall find expedient. They will be more advanced than we are in science and in useful arts, and will know best what will suit the circumstances of their day.

We have proposed no formal provision for the gymnastics of the school, although a proper object of attention for every institution of youth. These exercises with ancient nations, constituted the principal part of the education of their youth. Their arms and mode of warfare rendered them severe in the extreme; ours, on the same correct principle, should be adapted to our arms and warfare; and the manual exercise, military manoeuvres, and tactics generally, should be the frequent exercise of the students, in their hours of recreation. It is at that age of aptness, docility, and emulation of the practices of manhood, that such things are soonest learnt and longest remembered. The use of tools too in the manual arts is worthy of encouragement, by facilitating to such as choose it, an admission into the neighboring workshops. To these should be added the arts which embellish life, dancing, music, and drawing; the last more especially, as an important part of military education. These innocent arts furnish amusement and happiness to those who, having time on their hands, might less inoffensively employ it. Needing, at the same time, no regular incorporation with the institution, they may be left to accessory teachers, who will be paid by the individuals employing them, the University only providing proper apartments for their exercise.

The fifth duty prescribed to the Commissioners, is to propose such general provisions as may be properly enacted by the Legislature, for the better organizing and governing the University.

In the education of youth, provision is to be made for, 1, tuition; 2, diet; 3, lodging; 4, government; and 5, honorary excitements. The first of these constitutes the proper functions of the professors; 2, the dieting of the students should be left to private boarding houses of their own choice, and at their own expense; to be regulated by the Visitors from time to time, the house only being provided by the University within its own precincts, and thereby of course subjected to the general regimen, moral or sumptuary, which they shall prescribe. 3. They should be lodged in dormitories, making a part of the general system of buildings. 4. The best mode of government for youth, in large collections, is certainly a desideratum not yet attained with us.

GEORGE TICKNOR ON A PLAN OF REFORM AT HARVARD (1825) From
George Ticknor, *Remarks on Changes Lately Proposed or Adopted in Harvard University* (Boston, 1825), pp. 35–41.

The report of Mr Lowell, and that of Mr Justice Story, were both discussed together, in January last, with great thoroughness; and the result was, that Mr Justice Story's report, which contemplated much larger changes than Mr Lowell's, prevailed by a great majority, and was sent to the corporation, with a request, that they would embody in it such parts of Mr Lowell's as were not inconsistent with its general design, and report the whole to the Overseers, in the shape of some settled system for the management and instruction of the College.

This was done in June last, and, having been sanctioned by the Overseers, is now before the public in a code of Laws, called "Statutes and Laws of the University in Cambridge, Massachusetts," embraced in about forty pages and an hundred and fiftythree separate regulations, which, on account of the important changes it proposes, and the influence they may be likely to exercise, it is proposed now partly to examine.

*　　*　　*

A *third* important change, and one which may be useful in many colleges, is that introduced by the fiftyeighth, sixtieth and sixtythird sections of the new laws, which provide, that the instruction given at College shall be given by *departments;* and that the students shall, to a certain degree, have a choice in the studies they are to pursue. For the branches of knowledge professed at Cambridge, which were originally few and humble, are now grown to be so numerous and important, and may be so easily extended, that the old principle of requiring every student to pass through the hands of every instructer can no longer be wisely applied, since the time for the whole academic life has not been protracted. That this would probably be the result at some time or other, may have been foreseen from the very first; for it is apparent, that, if all the students were destined to pass in all future time, through the hands of every teacher, and the circumstances of the college should occasion a large increase in the number of teachers, then, at some time or other, there must be more teachers than the system could employ, and the students must be permitted, at least within certain limits, to choose their studies; or else the appropriate benefit to be derived from the increase of instructers must be lost. That Cambridge is already arrived at this result, is evident from the fact gathered out of official documents, that four teachers give just about three quarters of the whole instruction received by undergraduates, while the remaining quarter part is distributed among eleven; and that, even on this arrangement, unequal and disproportionate as it is, it has been necessary in more than one branch, either to leave a choice or to exact nothing at all. Such a system, of course, neither gives employment to all the talent it pays for among the instructers, nor such a beneficial choice to the students, as will enable them to derive the benefit they ought to derive from any one branch.

These evils, it is apparent, may be avoided by a judicious and effective division of the instruction given at any large college, into separate departments, while some advantages may be gained which are now, perhaps, nowhere enjoyed. For, in the first place, the teacher at the head of one of these departments, would be to a considerable degree responsible for its management and success, for the character and faithfulness of the instructers associated, with him, and for the progress of the students entering it, as he would now have an opportunity to exercise a constant supervision over the whole, and better means to turn the capacity of each individual, however humble or elevated, to the best account. In the next place, such an arrangement ought to lead to another improvement; for it would permit each department to be so adjusted, as that each individual devoting himself to its studies, should, according to his capacity, possess himself of an entire subject, rather than to be merely examined, as he has been, in certain books, and so left; for it is of little consequence, that a young man should recite the Collectanea, if he fail to learn Greek, or recite Brown's Philosophy with verbal exactness, if he fail to strengthen his intellectual faculties for purposes of reasoning, or do not gain an useful knowledge of metaphysics. Yet those faults are certainly obvious enough at all our colleges, as well as at Cambridge; for we believe, that every where the division of studies is made by *books* rather than by the *purposes* for which those books should be read and studied. Finally, such a choice of studies, as is implied by the division into departments, would much increase the interest of the students in their occupations, and tend to make the knowledge they acquire more valuable for their future purposes in life. And, why should not the unused means of the College be employed? And why should not the student or his friends determine in a greater or less degree, what studies he shall pursue, since more may be offered to him than it is possible he should pursue profitably? It were to be wished, indeed, that the choice could be left without limitation, and that the period passed at College could be thus more intimately connected with the remainder of life, and rendered more directly useful to it; but this, perhaps, is not yet possible with us, though it is actually doing in the University of Virginia, and will soon, it is to be hoped, be considered indispensable in all our more advanced colleges.

A *fourth* important change is made by the sixtyfirst section of the new Laws, and provides that the divisions of the classes for recitation and teaching shall be made according to proficiency; and that each division thus made shall be carried forward as rapidly as may be found consistent with a thorough knowledge of its subjects and studies. This may be regarded, as the broad corner stone for beneficial changes in all our colleges; and as a change to which all must come so fast as their means will permit them. For it is a plain injustice, which nothing but the necessity of the case can excuse, to give a young man of high powers and active industry no more and no other means of improvement than are given to the idlest and dullest in a class of sixty or seventy. Every student has a right not only to hasten forward as fast and as far as his talents and industry will carry him without any limit or hindrance whatsoever; but if the institution, where he is educated, possess the means, he may claim and the community may claim for him, that he should be helped forward with appropriate instruction at every step of his progress. It is a right, which all enjoy in good preparatory schools before they resort to college; and it is a right of which no man will permit himself to be easily defeated, when he is afterwards entering into his profession or into the business and interests of the world.

The benefits from such a change are apparent. The time of all the students may be better filled up; and all may be appropriately assisted and excited with instructers in every part of their studies. Discipline may be improved and made easier, for the best moral discipline of students is that which is laid in the careful and wise occupation of all their time and powers; and the healthiest reward for exertion may be offered to all, since all will feel that acknowledged, open progress, which was the motive that governed their best efforts at school, and which is the motive, that will vindicate its power again as soon as they emerge into the cares and struggles of life.

But besides these great advantages, the number of students that would recite together, being small, and those being associated for instruction in each branch, who from talent and industry belong together, the recitations, instead of being dull examinations restricted to a given book, may be made interesting as sources of instruction on the subject itself; the mind of the teacher being made to act directly on the minds of his pupils in familiar teaching and illustration, for which, under the present awkward division into alphabetical classes, no opportunity exists.

Moreover, with a division of the students according to proficiency, it will be more difficult to organise extensive combinations or rebellions, which now arise almost entirely from their arrangement into large classes; an arrangement, which makes no distinction between the industrious and the idle, the dull and those of uncommon talent, the orderly and the turbulent; but which often gives most influence to those who employ their time and powers chiefly in acquiring and using it badly. Now, on the present plan, if faithfully executed, no such division of classes can exist as has heretofore been recognised; and precisely the same individuals will, probably, be seldom brought together in two branches of instruction. The intelligent and laborious, therefore, standing by themselves and united among themselves in the respective departments and divisions, will not come into subjection to an unworthy majority as they often do now at all our colleges; while, at the same time, these who would recite together in one branch, as for instance mathematics, being little likely to meet in exactly the same relations for their exercises in Greek or Latin, the very principle on which combinations and rebellions are now organised would be almost entirely unfelt.

INNOVATION AT OBERLIN COLLEGE (1834) From *American Annals of Education*, vol. III, p. 429.

The Founding

We have lately received a notice of another institution with the same general object in view, in a select colony about to be established under the name of Oberlin, in Loraine County, Ohio. It is intended, ultimately, to embrace all grades of instruction from the Infant School to the Theological Seminary, with the great object of preparing teachers and pastors for the great basin of the Mississippi. Its plan is founded on sound principles of education. It is also to embrace the plan of manual labor, and from the favorable circumstances of its situation and privileges, its founders feel themselves authorized to state that a donation of $150, expended in establishing the literary and manual labor departments, will secure the education of one student annually for active usefulness, without any more labor than his own welfare demands.

Report on the First Year

From a recent circular we learn the following additional particulars as to Oberlin Collegiate Institute.

The system embraces instruction in every department, from the Infant School to a Collegiate and Theological course. Physical and moral education are to receive particular attention. The institution was opened in December last, and has sixty students; about forty in the academic, and twenty in the primary department. All of them, whether male or female, rich or poor, are required to labor four hours daily. Male students are to be employed in agriculture, gardening, and some of the mechanic arts; females in housekeeping, useful needle-work, the manufacture of wool, the culture of silk, certain appropriate parts of gardening, &c. The Institution has 500 acres of good land, of which, though a complete forest a year ago, about 30 acres are now cleared and sown with wheat. They have also a steam mill, and a saw mill, in operation. During the present year it is contemplated to add 50 acres to the cleared land, to erect a flouring mill, a shingle machine, turning lathe, a work shop, and an extensive boarding house (which, together with the present buildings, will accommodate about 150 students), with furniture, farming mechanic, and scientific apparatus; and begin a library.

During the winter months the young men are at liberty to engage as agents, school teachers, or in any other occupation they may select. The expenses of students in the seminary for board at the table spread only with vegetable food, are 80 cents a week, and 92 cents a week for the same with animal food twice a day. Tuition is from 15 to 35 cents a week. The avails of the students' labors have thus far varied from 1 to 8 cents an hour; the average has been 5 cents. A majority of the male students have, by their four hours daily labor, paid their board, fuel, lights, washing and mending, and some even more; and this without any interference with their progress in their studies.

FAVORABLE IMPRESSIONS OF COEDUCATION AT OBERLIN COLLEGE

(1836)   From Anonymous letter dated September 1, 1836, *New York Evangelist,* October 1, 1836, as quoted in Robert S. Fletcher, *A History of Oberlin College* (Oberlin, Ohio, 1943), pp. 381–82.

In regard to bringing both sexes into the same table—and also in calling in the aid of the female scholars to perform all the labor for themselves and for others,—I will give you my impressions as I have received them, by spending two days in the place, and enjoying every facility both for inquiry and observation, which I could desire.

The rooms for the young ladies are entirely distinct from the young men, and no young man is allowed to enter them. They have also a pleasant room for meetings and visits among themselves, devoted exclusively to their use. At the tables in the dining hall, there are about four young men to one young lady, and these are seated, usually, on one side of the table, 2 or 3 together, at regular intervals. Here they

HIGHER
EDUCATION

1495

perform the same services for those within reach, as they would in a private family—and results have been happy.

All the grossness and vulgarity so often witnessed in college commons is here excluded—and the matron informed me that if some new comers happened to manifest a disposition to coarseness, when placed beyond the immediate eye of the young ladies, the stationing of one or two of the most discreet near them, never failed at once to suppress it.

AN OBERLIN COMMITTEE'S REPORT ON SOME EVILS OF COEDUCATION (1845)   From "Report on Educating the Sexes Together," as quoted in Robert S. Fletcher, *A History of Oberlin College* (Oberlin, Ohio, 1943), pp. 377–78.

Evils

1. A tendency to spend too much time & to be too much engrossed in each others society. This tendency makes it necessary to adopt specific rules respecting calls, visits, late hours, study hours, walking out in the evening, rides into the country &c &c.

These rules are imposed with more strictness upon the young ladies than upon the young men. The latter often resist their action upon the young ladies, speak of these regulations with contempt, the results of which are very unhappy, & obedience on the part of the young ladies is secured with great difficulty.

2. A second great evil is early matrimonial engagements. These result sometimes in violation of this engagement; and usually in a great absorption of time & thought, in a decline of piety, distaste for study, & impaired usefulness.

A SYMPATHETIC DESCRIPTION OF COEDUCATION AT OBERLIN COLLEGE (1854)   From *Oberlin Evangelist,* June 7, 1854, as quoted in Robert S. Fletcher, *A History of Oberlin College* (Oberlin, Ohio, 1943), vol. I, p. 379.

We take it the golden mean lies in so shaping the association of young gentlemen with young ladies as to make its general tone elevated and pure; the topics of conversation solid, not vapid; more sensible than sentimental; and drawn from the realms of literature, science and morals, rather than from the limbo of Vanity. Similar studies, common recitations, the daily measuring of mental strength, conduce greatly to the practical impression on each sex that the other are to be held and deemed as intellectual and social beings. The relation of beau and belle is in good measure displaced by the more healthful one of fellow-student. The idea that the young lady is a toy or a plaything is very thoroughly exploded by the practical working of intellectual competition on the college race ground,—to say nothing of the influence of that higher nobler Christian life, in which united efforts for the salvation of souls deeply engross the heart.

ANTIOCH COLLEGE CATALOGUE (1854)   From George Allen Hubbell, *Horace Mann in Ohio* (New York, 1900), pp. 57–62.

---

1. Faculty of Antioch College

Hon. Horace Mann, LL. D., President and Professor of Political Economy, Intellectual and Moral Philosophy, Constitutional Law and Natural Theology.

Rev. W. H. Doherty, A. M., Professor of Rhetoric, Logic and Belles-Lettres.

Ira W. Allen, A. M., Professor of Mathematics, Astronomy and Civil Engineering.

Rev. Thomas Holmes, A. M., Professor of Greek Language and Literature.

C. S. Pennell, A. M., Professor of Latin Language and Literature.

Miss R. M. Pennell, Professor of Physical Geography, Drawing, Natural History, Civil History and Didactics.

——— ———, Professor of Mineralogy and Geology.

——— ———, Professor of Modern Languages.

Rev. A. L. McKinney, Principal of Preparatory Department.

A preparatory school will be connected with the College which will be under the general supervision and regulation of the President. At this school pupils will be fitted for admission to the freshman class. The instruction will not be confined to the course preparatory to College; but will embrace the branches usually taught in high schools and academies. All pupils of this school, if sufficiently advanced to be benefited by the lectures delivered in the College, will be allowed to attend them.

No person under twelve years of age will be admitted into the preparatory school.

Requisites for Admission

Candidates for admission to the Freshman Class will be examined in the following studies: English Grammar, Outlines of Ancient and Modern Geography, History, Miss Peabody's Polish-American system of Chronology, Worcester's Elements, Arithmetic, Algebra, Loomis's Elements or its equivalent, Geometry, Loomis's first Five Books or first Four of Davies' Legendre, Latin, Bullion's Grammar, Bullion's Reader, Bullion's Cæsar's Commentaries, two books, Bullion's Vergil's Aeneid, first six books, with prosody and scanning, Bullion's Cicero's Orations, four against Cataline and the one for the Poet Archeas, Bullion's Sallust's Cataline's Conspiracy, Bullion's Latin Composition, Bullion's Grammar, Bullion's Reader. Greek, Gospel according to John, Greek Composition.

Undergraduate Course, Freshman Class

Algebra: Loomis's.
Latin: Lincoln's Selections from Livy, first three books with Latin Composition.
Greek: Anabasis, first four books with Greek composition.
Elective Studies: Drawing and Designing.

SECOND TERM

English language and elocution.
Geometry continued, Loomis's.
Greek: Homer's Iliad, first five books with Greek composition.
Elective: Jahn's Hebrew Commonwealth, and Sismondi's Decline and Fall of Rome for the first 1000 years after Christ.

THIRD TERM

Trigonometry, Plain and Spherical, Loomis's.
Human Physiology alternating with Latin and Greek.
Latin: Livy continued, 21st book; Horace, Schmitz's & Zumpt's, continued; Odes commenced; Latin Composition continued.
Elective: Botany, Gray's Botanical Text Book.

Sophomore Class

FIRST TERM

Mensuration, surveying and navigation.
Latin: Horace, Art of Poetry, Satires and Epistles.
Rhetoric and Belles-Lettres.
Elective: Didactics, the theory and art of teaching. Porter and Emerson's School and School Master. Page's Theory and Practice of Teaching.

SECOND TERM

Analytical Geometry, Loomis's.
Latin: De Senectute and Amicitia.
Greek: Longinus on the Sublime.
Elective: Hallam's Middle Ages and Bancroft's United States.

THIRD TERM

Differential and Integral Calculus, or the Acts of the Apostles of the New Testament, at the option of the student.
Latin: Germania and Agricola of Tacitus (Tyler's edition preferred), and one play of Plautus or Terence.
French: Grammar and Translation.
Elective: Didactics or the Theory and Art of Teaching continued.

Junior Class

FIRST TERM

Physical Geography: Guyot and Mrs. Somerville's.
Chemistry.
Natural Philosophy, Mechanics.
Elective: French continued, with conversation and composition.

SECOND TERM

Civil Engineering.
Chemistry as Applied to Agriculture and the Arts.
German: Pronunciation, Grammar and Translation.
Elective: French continued.

THIRD TERM

Logic and Belles-Lettres.
Zoology: Agassiz and Gould's.
Natural Philosophy: Physics.
Elective: German continued with conversation and composition.

Senior Class

FIRST TERM

Political Economy.
Astronomy.
Geology and Mineralogy.

SECOND TERM

Intellectual Philosophy.
Rhetoric, Logic and Belles-Lettres.
Evidences of Christianity.
History of Civilization, Guizot.
Natural Theology.

THIRD TERM

Constitutional Law.
Moral Philosophy.
Rhetoric: Exercises and English composition will be required weekly during the whole course. Lectures during the whole course will be given by professors in their respective departments.

There will be extensive and daily oral instruction. Teaching from text books alone is like administering the same prescription to all the patients in the hospital ward; but oral instruction is mingling the cup of healing for each individual case.

For admission to any advanced class the applicant must submit to an examination in the studies of the previous class or classes; excepting in the case of those who choose the elective studies, who may be examined in the previous elective studies instead of those for which the electives were taken.

Applicants able to join any class will be admitted for periods less than a full course.

All students will be required to attend public religious services twice every Sabbath, provided there are churches in this vicinity where they can conscientiously worship.

Terms, &c.

The first term of the College will open ten weeks after the Wednesday next preceding the fourth of July, and will continue thirteen weeks.

The second term will open one week from the close of the first, and will continue thirteen weeks.

The third term will open two weeks from the close of the second, and will continue thirteen weeks to commencement.

The exercises of commencement will take place on the Wednesday next preceding the fourth of July.

Owing to the unfinished state of the buildings the college will not be opened during the present year (1853), until the first Wednesday in October. On that day the Preparatory School will be opened for the admission of pupils; applicants for admission to the Freshman Class will be examined, and should a sufficient number present themselves and pass the examination in all the studies required for admission to the Sophomore Class, such a class will be also formed, but neither the Junior nor the Senior Class.

This being the first presentation of Antioch College to the notice of the public, a brief statement respecting its location, its origin and its objects may be expected.

Antioch College was incorporated in 1852. It is situated at Yellow Springs, Greene County, Ohio, a spot widely celebrated for the beauty of its scenery, the healthfulness of its climate, and the medical and restorative character of the waters from which it takes its name.

Yellow Springs is on a railroad connecting Cincinnati and Sandusky, midway between Xenia and Springfield, and only nine miles from either. It is 74 miles N. N. E. from Cincinnati, and easily accessible by railroad and steamboat from all the great towns and cities of the western states. The college edifices consist of one main building and two dormitory buildings. The former is in the shape of a cross, 170 feet long and 110 feet wide. This structure is designed for chapel library, lecture room, laboratory, recitation rooms, etc., etc. The dormitory buildings stand back from the main building, one on the north, and the other on the south side. The dimensions are 39 feet by 160 feet, four stories high. All front the east. They are situated in a beautiful enclosure, 20 acres in extent, and are surrounded by a street seventy-five feet in width.

The leading minds under whose auspices and by whose patronage Antioch College was founded, long ago called themselves "Christians," not invidiously, but devoutly, and in honor of the author and finisher of their faith; and they have now selected a name by which to designate their institution at once scriptural and commemorative because "the disciples were called Christians first at Antioch."

In some particulars of its aim and scope this college differs from most of the higher literary institutions of the country. It recognizes the claims of the female sex to equal opportunities of education with the male, and these opportunities it designs to confer. Its founders believe that labors and expenditures for the higher education of men will tend indirectly to elevate the character of women; but they are certain that all wise efforts for the improved education of women will speed the elevation of the whole human race.

It is designed in this college not only to give marked attention to the study of the laws of human health and life, but to train up the pupils in a systematic observance of them. As one may learn the most beautiful theory of ethics and religion and yet remain in his sins; so one may commit to memory all the laws pertaining to hygiene and longevity and yet bring a life tormented by repulsive diseases to an early and painful death. But both knowledge and observance, both theory and practice of the physiological laws for four, or a half dozen years, can hardly fail to add the abiding strength of reason to the quick instinct of self-preservation in intercepting and resisting the strength of appetite. The best knowledge is no match for bad habits. But true knowledge and virtuous habits will say to the demons of appetite and sensuality, "Get ye behind me."

The college is designed to occupy no ground of opposition or envious rivalry toward any of the literary institutions of the country. It abjures all emulation save that which provokes to good works. It will rejoice to co-operate with others in imparting that kind of knowledge which shall be known for its cubical rather than for its superficial contents. Not any branch of the industry of this great country, nor any one of its numerous administrations can ever be creditably and prosperously carried on, unless it shall be founded upon the laws of nature, of political economy and of the human mind. Also so of our literature. If it is to live it must be founded upon the laws of human brotherhood. The literature of a country will never become Christianized until its literary men are so.

The college will exert no sectarian influence over its pupils. On this point its patrons and administrators occupy a ground somewhat peculiar. The "Christian Connection" adopt no government-made or man-made creed or confession of faith. They take the Bible as their rule of faith and practice, and in the true Protestant spirit allow liberty of interpretation. Until two men are alike in all respects they cannot believe alike in all respects; and as no two men ever were alike in all respects, no two men ever believed alike in all respects, however many times they may have signed, rehearsed or sworn to the same articles of belief.

According to the momentous saying of the Saviour, so wise that an angel may be instructed by it and yet so simple that a child can understand it, "The tree is known by its fruit," the "Christian Connection" hold that a man is to be known by his life; and therefore the Christian character is the true test of Christian fellowship among men. Hence they are led to withhold regard from dogmatic or polemic theology in the education of youth, and to bestow their confidence upon the acted religious life rather than professed religious faith. True faith lives in works. "With the heart, man believeth unto righteousness." "He that doeth righteousness is righteous."

The deepest convictions as well as their liveliest affections urge them to put forth all sympathies and efforts to turn the thankful heart to duty, rather than to doctrinate the youthful intellect into dogmas; and hence the public at large have the security of their press and the pledge of their promises that the new college will not be a proselyting institution. In the psalm which shall arise from this temple founded by so many sacrifices and thus far watched over by so many vigils and supplications, whatever earthly harmonies may mingle into the strain, its key-note is to be pitched after that grand master tone of love to God and love to man which was first struck by the angels who hymned the advent of the Saviour upon earth and which is yet to be sounded over all the world and through the ages of eternity.

PRESIDENT FRANCIS WAYLAND OF BROWN UNIVERSITY CALLS FOR REFORM OF AMERICAN COLLEGES (1842)   From Francis Wayland, *Thoughts on the Present Collegiate System in the United States* (Boston, 1842), pp. 11–17, 40–41, 108–12.

It has been said that the course of study in our colleges was formed in a remote age, and that it is adapted only to a state of society very different from our own. Specially has it been urged that the study of the *classics* is at best but useless, that it has no relation to our present duties and every day engagements, and that the time devoted to it had much better be employed upon the study of the Modern Languages. Besides, it has been said that our collegiate course should extend its benefits to merchants, manufacturers, and every class of citizens. These persons desire the honors of a degree as much as others. They do not however wish to waste their time in the study of the classics, and therefore the studies required of the candidate for a degree should be accommodated so as to meet these their reasonable wishes. It was predicted that as soon as this change should be made, our colleges would be crowded with those who were anxious to avail themselves of these advantages and to obtain the honor of a degree.

In obedience with these suggestions a change was made some years since in the studies of some of our colleges. Both a classical and scientific course were established, the first requiring the study of the Learned and the other substituting in their room the Modern languages. Teachers were engaged, classes were divided, each student had his option, and all who wished were invited to become candidates for a degree upon these modified conditions. But what was the result? No one came to accept of what was thus freely offered. The system dragged for a few years, and then perished from mere inanition.

Very much the same course has been pursued in regard to the higher mathematics. The same objections were made to this branch of a liberal education, and it has been proposed to substitute in their place the study of history or of natural science. To a considerable degree this experiment has been combined with the other, and with very much the same result. The colleges so far as I know, which have obeyed the suggestions of the public, have failed to find themselves sustained by the public. The means which it was supposed would increase the number of students in fact diminished it, and thus things gradually after every variety of trial have generally tended to their original constitution. So much easier is it to discover faults than to amend them; to point out evils than to remove them. And thus have we been taught that the public does not always know what it wants, and that it is not always wise to take it at its word.

But as the number of students in most of our colleges was commonly much less than could be desired, and as colleges have steadily continued to multiply, it was next supposed that the reason why they were not more numerously attended was the high price of tuition. The price of a collegiate education, however, it may be remarked in passing, has always been exceedingly low in this country. It is, and has long been much less than that of private tuition; and the officers of colleges are always remunerated at a much lower rate than other professional men. Still it was believed that collegiate education would be in a more prosperous condition if tuition could be much more nearly given away. When the number of students in a college began to diminish so that the pittance granted to instructors could no more be doled out, an effort was next made to raise additional funds for the support of instructors. This fund has sometimes been used for the endowment of professorships, and sometimes for the general reduction of tuition or for the support of indigent students. Very large sums have been from time to time appropriated to this purpose. This of course will partly remedy the evil. When a valuable consideration is to be given away, it is not generally difficult to find persons willing to accept of it.

In this manner there is no doubt that a college may be supported. If after buildings have been erected, and a considerable amount of funds invested, and the teachers remunerated at the lowest possible rate, pupils cannot be attracted in sufficient numbers to support the establishment, we may yet be allowed to draw upon the charities of the public to make up the deficiency, the system may doubtless be sustained. And this is I believe at present the very general condition of colleges among us. I doubt whether any one could attract a respectable number of pupils, however large its endowments and however great its advantages, did it charge for tuition the fees which would be requisite to remunerate its officers at the rate ordinarily received by other professional men. In some of our colleges education is given away to every person who enters the plea of indigence. Others are in possession of funds appropriated to a considerable amount to this purpose. In most of them, candidates for the ministry are educated gratuitously or at a great reduction from the ordinary charge for tuition. In this manner collegiate education has come to be considered to a very great extent a matter of charity; and the founding of a college consists not so much in providing means for higher education and thus elevating the general standard of intellectual attainment, as the collecting of funds for eleemosynary distribution, by which those who desire to pursue the course which we have marked out may be enabled to do so at the least possible cost.

Now I cannot but look at this as an unnatural state of things. Let a man reflect upon the wages of labor in this country, at the ease with which industrious men in every occupation arrive at competence, let him pass through our streets and enter our houses and inspect our modes of living and he will surely say that a very large portion of our people are able to meet the expenses of bestowing upon their children as good an education as they can receive with advantage. There does not appear from our outward circumstances any reason why a man should not pay a fair price for the education of his son just as he pays a fair price for the education of his daughter; or for the furniture, the carpets, the pianos, the mirrors of his parlor, or the implements, the stock, and the acres of his farm. Nor can it be said that as a people we are unaware of the advantages of knowledge. In all our cities and towns, the private instructor is liberally paid. There are certainly all the elements in existence out of which must arise a strong desire for the intellectual improvement of our offspring. And yet while this is the fact we find all around us very large investments made for the purposes of public education, the interest of their investments is bestowed upon the public, and yet we cannot induce men to pursue a collegiate course unless we offer it vastly below its cost, if we do not give it away altogether.

From the preceding facts I think we are warranted in coming to the following conclusions. First, that there is in this country a very general willingness both in the public and on the part of individuals to furnish all the necessary means for the improvement of collegiate education. Second, that the present system of collegiate education does not meet the wants of the public. The evidence of this is seen in the fact that change after change has been suggested in the system without however any decided result, and still more from the fact that although this kind of education is afforded at a lower price than any other, we cannot support our present institutions without giving a large portion of our education away. Third, that this state of things is neither owing to the poverty of our people nor to their indifference to the subject of education. Our citizens seem really more willing to educate other men's sons than their own, to provide the means of education rather than to avail themselves of them after they have been provided. Now, do not these facts indicate the necessity of some change in our educational system. A liberal education is certainly a valuable consideration. Can it not be made to recommend itself; so that he who wishes to obtain it shall also be willing to pay for it? Cannot this general impression in favor of education be turned to some practical account, so that the system may be able to take care of itself?

*　　*　　*

There are three modes in which our present system might be modified.

First, the number of studies pursued during the College course, might be limited in such manner that whatever is taught may be taught thoroughly. The College would in this case be open only for persons who are candidates for degrees. The standard of attainment may be as high as is considered desirable. The difference aimed at would be this, that, instead of learning *many* things *imperfectly*, we should learn a *smaller* number of things *well*. I am sure that every man in active life would, on retrospection, wish that his education had been thus conducted. By learning one science well, we learn *how to study*, and how to master a subject. Having made this attainment in one study, we readily apply it to all other studies. We acquire the habit of thoroughness, and carry it to all other matters of inquiry. The course of study at West Point Academy is very limited, but the sciences pursued are carried much farther than in other institutions in our country; and it is owing to this that the reputation of the institution is so deservedly high. The English University course is, in respect to the number of branches pursued, limited, and yet it is remarkably successful in developing the powers of the mind. Observe the maturity and vigor which the young men there frequently obtain. They sometimes go from the University, as for instance, Pitt, Fox, and Canning, directly to the House of Commons, and are competent at once, to take an important part in the labors of that august assembly. And yet more, I apprehend that the acquisition of the habit of thoroughness is the true method of arriving at the most extensive attainments. A few years since I had the pleasure of meeting one of the most learned German scholars who has visited this country. I asked him how it was that his countrymen were able, at so early an age, to obtain the mastership of so many languages. He replied "I began the study of Latin at an early age. Every book that I studied I was made thoroughly acquainted with. I was taught to read and re-read, translate forwards and backwards, trace out every word and know every thing about it.

Before I left a book it became as familiar to me as if written in German. *After this I never had any difficulty with any other language."*

2. But secondly. Suppose a course so limited does not find favor, and it be contended that as the branches of knowledge are multiplied, a greater number must be included in the course of liberal education. If this be thought preferable, let us do this. But let us not attempt impossibilities, nor let us be contented with superficial education. Let us extend the term. It was originally in fact, seven years. Let us make it five, or six. If the requirements of admission were greater, and the College course increased by the addition of one or two years, a great gain would be made to the cause of education. I think that there is but small fear of our doing too much, if we only do it well.

3. The third plan would be to make a College more nearly to resemble a real University; that is, to make it a place of education in all the most important branches of human learning. This might properly include instruction in all professional, as well as ante-professional science. It should comprize teaching in Latin, Greek, French, German, and Hebrew languages. Mathematics, Mechanics, and all the branches of Natural Philosophy, Moral Philosophy, Intellectual Philosophy, Physical Science in all its departments, Rhetoric and its kindred literature, History, as well as instruction in Law and Medicine.

Of these branches, those might be selected which should be required of the candidate for the degree of Bachelor of Arts, and his graduation might depend not on time of residence, but on proficiency to be determined by examination. Another course embracing other studies might be made requisite to the obtaining of another degree. If one is Bachelor of Arts, the other might be Bachelor of Science, or of Literature. And still more, in order to bring the whole course of study within the scope of University stimulants, the degree of Master of Arts, instead of being conferred without additional attainment, as it is at present, might be conferred only on those who have pursued successfully the whole circle of study marked out for the candidates for both degrees. The degree of Master of Arts would then designate a degree of positive attainment, and would be a valuable and efficient testimonial. As it is now, to all practical purposes, we throw this degree away. It exerts no power of motive whatever. The best and the worst scholars are equally entitled to it on the third year after graduation. It might be made, as it seems to me, to subserve a valuable purpose in a system of education. A still further modification of the studies taught in a College will be suggested on a subsequent page.

It may be a question which of these plans is best suited to the purposes of our country. Either would I think be preferable to our present system. One may answer better in one place and another in another. I merely suggest these as topics for consideration to those who are interested in the cause of Collegiate education. I am desirous at least of laying the case before the visitors and officers of Colleges among us for candid consideration. If they should contribute in even so small a degree to direct the public attention to the points to be aimed at, or even to be avoided, I shall receive a full reward. In this country, if a movement can only be but commenced in the right direction, it will soon make ample progress. I say a movement in the right direction, for I have no idea that any change of value can be made instantaneously. If however the learned and able and self-sacrificing men who are now engaged in the profession of teaching can be led to act wisely and in concert on this subject, and the public can be brought into harmony with their action, I believe that a mighty impulse might be communicated to the cause of education among us.

FRANCIS WAYLAND'S PROPOSAL FOR THE REFORM OF BROWN
UNIVERSITY (1850)   From Francis Wayland, *Report to the Corporation of Brown University, on Changes in the System of Collegiate Education* (Providence, 1850), pp. 50–61, 74–76.

If it be the fact that our colleges cannot sustain themselves, but are obliged to make repeated calls upon the benevolence of the community, not because the community is poor and education inordinately expensive, but because, instead of attempting to furnish scientific and literary instruction to every class of our people, they have furnished it only to a single class, and that by far the least numerous; if they are furnishing an education for which there is no remunerative, but even at the present low prices, a decreasing demand; if they are, not by intention, but practically, excluding the vastly larger portion of the community from advantages in which they would willingly participate, and are thus accomplishing but a fraction of the good which is manifestly within their power, then it would seem that relief must be expected from a radical change of the system of collegiate instruction. We must carefully survey the wants of the various classes of the community in our own vicinity, and adapt our courses of instruction, not for the benefit of one class, but for the benefit of all classes. The demand for general education in our country is pressing and universal. The want of that science, which alone can lay the foundation of eminent success in the useful arts, is extensively felt. The proportion of our young men who are devoting themselves to the productive professions, is great and annually increasing. They all need such an education as our colleges, with some modifications in their present system, could very easily supply. Is there not reason to believe that, if such an education were furnished, they would cheerfully avail themselves of it?

Were an institution established with the intention of adapting its instruction to the wants of the whole community, its arrangements would be made in harmony with the following principles.

1. The present system of adjusting collegiate study to a fixed term of four years, or to any other term, must be abandoned, and every student be allowed, within limits to be determined by statute, to carry on, at the same time, a greater or less number of courses as he may choose.

2. The time allotted to each particular course of instruction would be determined by the nature of the course itself, and not by its supposed relation to the wants of any particular profession.

3. The various courses should be so arranged, that, in so far as it is practicable, every student might study what he chose, all that he chose, and nothing but what he chose. The Faculty, however, at the request of a parent or guardian, should have authority to assign to any student, such courses as they might deem for his advantage.

4. Every course of instruction, after it has been commenced, should be continued without interruption until it is completed.

5. In addition to the present courses of instruction, such should be established as the wants of the various classes of the community require.

6. Every student attending any particular course, should be at liberty to attend any other that he may desire.

7. It would be required that no student be admitted as a candidate for a degree, unless he had honorably sustained his examination in such studies as may be

ordained by the corporation; but no student would be under any obligation to proceed to a degree, unless he chose.

8. Every student would be entitled to a certificate of such proficiency as he may have made in every course that he has pursued.

The courses of instruction to be pursued in this institution might be as follows:

1. A course of instruction in Latin, occupying two years.
2. A course of instruction in Greek, occupying two years.
3. A course of instruction in three Modern Languages.
4. A course of instruction in Pure Mathematics, two years.
5. A course of instruction in Mechanics, Optics, and Astronomy, either with or without Mathematical Demonstrations, 1 1/2 years.
6. A course of instruction in Chemistry, Physiology and Geology, 1 1/2 years.
7. A course of instruction in the English Language and Rhetoric, one year.
8. A course of instruction in Moral and Intellectual Philosophy, one year.
9. A course of instruction in Political Economy, one term.
10. A course of instruction in History, one term.
11. A course of instruction in the Science of Teaching.
12. A course of instruction on the Principles of Agriculture.
13. A course of instruction on the Application of Chemistry to the Arts.
14. A course of instruction on the Application of Science to the Arts.
15. A course of instruction in the Science of Law.

Some of these courses would require a lesson or lecture every working day of the week, others only two or three in the week. Any professor might be allowed to conduct the studies of more than one course, if he could do it with advantage to the institution.

Should this idea be adopted, and the instruction given in this college be arranged on these principles, it would be seen that opportunity would be afforded to modify it as as [sic] experience should prove desirable. Some courses may be abridged or abolished, and others added or extended. The object of the change would be to adapt the institution to the wants, not of a class, but of the whole community. It by no means is to be taken for granted, in a country like our own, that every college is to teach the same studies, and to the same extent. It would be far better that each should consult the wants of its own locality, and do that best, for which it possessed the greatest facilities. Here would arise opportunity for diversified forms of excellence; the knowledge most wanted would the more easily become diffused, and the general progress of science would receive an important impulse from every institution of learning in our land.

It may be proper here to indicate the manner in which, as your committee believes, the plan proposed would relieve the embarrassments of the institution.

In explaining their views on this part of the subject, it is not pretended, that with any plan that can be devised, in the present condition of New England, this can be wholly a self-supporting institution. Education is afforded at all our colleges so far below cost, that, at cost price, it is doubtful whether it could be disposed of. The college is far from supporting itself now. Unless it receives some aid, it cannot be carried on. The inquiry which we have felt it to be our duty to make, has been this: In what manner, at the least expense to its friends, can it be put in a condition to support itself? It has seemed to your committee, that in no other way can this result be arrived at, than by extending its advantages to every class of the community, and thus increasing the number of its pupils. The more it can do for itself, the less need its friends do for it.

That such a change as is here proposed, would add to the number of its pupils, seems to your committee probable, for several reasons.

1. The course of instruction will, it is hoped, present a better preparation for the learned professions, than that pursued at present. There is no reason, therefore, why this class of pupils should be diminished.

2. Opportunity would be afforded to those who wished to pursue a more generous course of professional education, to remain in college profitably for five or six years, instead of four, as at present.

3. Many young men who intend to enter the professions, are unwilling or unable to spend four years in the preparatory studies of college. They would, however, cheerfully spend one or two years in such study, if they were allowed to select such branches of science as they chose. This class would probably form an important addition to our numbers, and we should thus, in some degree, improve the education of a large portion of all the professions.

4. If we except the ancient languages, there are but few of the studies now pursued in college, which, if well taught, would not be attractive to young men preparing for any of the active departments of life. If these several courses were so arranged as to be easily accessible to intelligent young men of all classes, it may reasonably be expected that many will desire to spend a term, a year, or two years, under our instruction.

5. It is not probable that the courses of instruction in agriculture, or chemistry, or science applied to the arts, will, of necessity, occupy all the time of the student. Many of these persons will probably desire to avail themselves of the advantages so easily placed in their power. Another source of demand for the courses in general science would thus be created.

FRANCIS WAYLAND ON HIGHER EDUCATION AND DEMOCRACY

(**1855**)   From Francis Wayland, *The Education Demanded by the People of the United States* (Boston, 1855), pp. 24–27.

We have a population increasing in wealth with a rapidity wholly unprecedented. The intellect of this people is aroused to action by the means universally provided for common school education. This awakened intellect is stimulated to uncommon activity by the legitimate effects of the democratic principle. Now, can a philanthropist, a patriot, or a statesman, hesitate for a moment, when he is called upon to determine the principles by which the higher education of such a people should be governed?

Shall we, having educated the whole people up to a certain point, giving to all equal advantages for self-development, then reverse our whole system, and bestow the advantages of higher education only upon a few? Shall we say that the lawyer, and physician, and clergyman, need a knowledge of principles in order to pursue their callings with success, while the farmer, the mechanic, the manufacturer, and the merchant require no knowledge of the laws upon which the success of every operation which they perform depends? Shall we say that we need a literary class of men, and for the education of these we will make ample provision, while for all the rest it makes no manner of difference whether they be thoughtful, independent and self-reliant, or nothing but mere hewers of wood and drawers of water? Shall we say that intellect is to be cultivated and talent developed in one direction alone, or developed in every possible direction? I cannot conceive it possible for American citizens to hold any divided opinion on this subject. He would certainly be a rare man who would openly contend for such a distinction as these questions suppose. We are all equal. We are all left each one for himself to work out his own destiny, and to make provision for those that shall come after him. Every one needs knowledge, knowledge of the laws which shall command success in his own avocation. Every one needs that knowledge which shall enable him to form correct judgments, and all men need it equally. Wherever a provision is made for education by private munificence, all men may reasonably expect to share it without distinction; where provision is made by the public, they may rightfully demand it. Nothing can be conceived of, more diametrically opposed to the first principles of our government, than to impose a tax upon the whole, and then appropriate it to the benefit of a part.

But it will, I presume, be answered, that I am contending where there is no adversary; that all our institutions of learning are equally open for all, and that all men may avail themselves of their advantages if they be so disposed. All this I grant. But I ask, for whom were our present systems of collegiate education devised?—for the few or for the many? They were originally designed exclusively for the clergy, and in the fatherland they have been perpetuated for the clergy and the aristocracy. They are, in this country, devised mainly for the professions, and their success is measured by their results upon the professions. The learning which they cultivate is in kind and amount measured by the demands of the professions. But I ask, as I have done before, have not the mechanic and the merchant, the farmer and the manufacturer, as much need of knowledge, each in his own profession, as the lawyer, the minister, and the physician? Have they not as just a claim on the money taken from their own earnings, as those classes which have been so exclusively favored? May they not then justly demand that not only education in higher knowledge shall be provided for them, but that it shall be education of which they may profitably avail themselves; so that they may enter upon their career in life, under as favorable auspices as those who prefer what are sometimes called literary professions?

It would seem then that, in devising a system of higher education for our country, we should commence with the self-evident maxim, that we are to labor not for the benefit of one but of all; not for a caste, or a clique, but for the whole community. Proceeding upon this ground, we should provide the instruction needed by every class of our fellow-citizens. Wherever an institution is established in any part of our country, our first inquiry should be, what is the kind of knowledge (in addition to that demanded for all) which this portion of our people needs, in order to perfect them in their professions, give them power over principles, enable them to develop their intellectual resources and employ their talents to the greatest advantage for themselves and for the country? This knowledge, whatever it may be, should be provided as liberally for one class as for another. Whatever is thus taught, however, should be taught, not only with the design of increasing knowledge, but also of giving strength, enlargement and skill to the original faculties of the soul. When a system of education formed on these principles shall pervade this country, we may be able to present to the world the legitimate results of free institutions; by pursuing any other career we may render them a shame and a by-word.

HENRY TAPPAN'S IDEA OF A UNIVERSITY (1852)   From *A Discourse*
Delivered by Henry P. Tappan . . . on the Occasion of His Inauguration as Chancellor of
the University of Michigan, December 21, 1852 (Detroit, 1852), pp. 25, 28–31, 36–41,
50–52.

It is demonstrable that a system of public education can not only never be
complete, but that it can never work with unjarring, noiseless wheels, in the due co-
ordination of its parts, without a fully developed University at the lead of the
movement. This alone can set the standard of education and define the boundaries
of the primary and the intermediate schools; this alone can afford the requisite
stimulus to educational efforts, by showing every student the place where all his
wants and aspirations can be met; as a beating heart sending its currents of life
through the whole, and maintaining the perfection of the organism by visiting the
minutest parts.

*   *   *

The Primary School, the Intermediate School, and the University, now stand
before us clearly defined; and these three constitute the educational system founded
alike upon philosophy and experience. The Primary has connected with it, as its
necessary adjunct, the Normal School. The Intermediate has connected with it,
special schools for the arts of industry, where the University is not contemplated.
And the University crowns the whole.

Would I bring before you the most perfect exemplification of this system, I
should refer to Prussia. Prussia occupies a portion of the earth's surface two fifths
larger than the State of Michigan, but by no means equal to it in soil and natural
resources generally. It has fifteen millions of inhabitants. For these, are provided
seven Universities. In 1835 the number of gymnasia or intermediate schools was one
hundred and twenty-four, containing about twenty five thousand scholars; and the
number of Primary Schools about twenty two thousand, in which two millions of
children of both sexes were receiving an education. The largest University is that of
Berlin, in which, in 1850, were one hundred and sixty five Professors and teachers,
and eighteen hundred and fifty students. Of the students, one hundred and eighty
four were matriculated in theology, five hundred and seventy in law, and two
hundred and twenty three in medicine, and three hundred and twenty-five in
philosophy, or general science and literature. Besides these, five hundred and fifty-
seven not matriculated, were pursuing studies in special departments.

The primary schools have for their scope intellectual, moral and physical
development. They embrace the following branches: 1.—Religion and morality,
established on the positive truths of Christianity; 2.—The German language; 3.—The
elements of Geometry and general principles of drawing; 4.—Calculation and
applied Arithmetic; 5.—The elements of physics, of general history, and of the
history of Prussia; 6.—Singing; 7.—Writing; 8.—Gymnastic exercises; 9.—The more
simple manual labours, and some instruction in the relative country occupations.

The Burgher School is a higher form of the primary, established in the towns,
and affords a more advanced education.

The Seminaries for Primary Instructors, or normal schools embrace the
following branches: 1.—Biblical history, the study of the Bible, and Christian

doctrine and morals; 2.—The German language in its etymology, grammar, and use in speaking and composition; 3.—Mathematics; 4.—History; 5.—Geography and geology; 6.—Natural history and physics; 7.—Music in theory and practice; 8.— Drawing; 9.—Penmanship; 10.—Pedagogy or the art of education, conjoined with practice; 11.—Elements of horticulture; 12.—Gymnastics.

Pedagogy is a department of Literature which in Germany is cultivated to an extent almost equal to any other. In 1830, there were published five hundred and one works of this class; in 1831, four hundred and fifty-two were published; and in 1832, five hundred and twenty six were published. Of these, twenty were journals supported by subscribers.

The course of study in the Gymnasium may be represented by that of our Academy and College combined.

The Primary School embraces a wider range of studies than our Primary School. The Student remains in the Gymnasium until he has completed his eighteenth year. He can then enter the University, provided he is prepared to undergo the examination. It not unfrequently happens that two or three years longer are required.

In the University, the course in Theology is usually completed in three years; the course in Law, in two years; and the course in Medicine in four years. The course in Philosophy or general Science and Literature is extended at the pleasure of the Student.

A Student pursuing any one of these courses may avail himself of the others according to his ability and inclination.

Such is a very brief outline of the Prussian system. Its completeness and thoroughness are evident to every one. The education of man, whether we consider his capabilities, the duties which he is called to perform, or his ultimate destinies, is a mighty affair, and therefore demands a mighty provision. It is the highest work of society.

Now, in persuing the work to which I have already referred—"The system of public Instruction and Primary School Law of Michigan"—I was delighted to find the following statement by the Honorable Superintendent of Public Instruction:— "The SYSTEM OF PUBLIC INSTRUCTION which was intended to be established by the framers of the constitution, the conception of the office, its province, its powers and duties were derived from Prussia. That system consisted of three degrees. Primary instruction corresponding to our district schools; secondary instruction, communicated in schools call Gymnasia; and the highest instruction, communicated in Universities. The superintendence of this entire system, which was formed in 1819, was entrusted to a Minister of State, called the Minister of Public Instruction, and embraced every thing which belonged to the moral and intellectual advancement of the people. The system of Michigan was intended to embrace all institutions which had for their object the instruction of youth, comprising the education of the primary, the intermediate class of schools, however denominated, and the University."

And the first Superintendent, Mr. Pierce, in speaking of the Primary School system of this State refers also to the Prussian system as the model.

I have not, therefore, been travelling out of the record in giving an exposition of the Prussian system as a just and adequate exemplification of what is meant by a System of Public Instruction. I have indeed taken high ground as to education, but I have done no violence to public sentiment. I have only been reiterating and expounding the thoughts and words of the men who laid the foundations of the educational system of Michigan, of the men who have been, and are now, its acknowledged supporters.

One half of the work is done when we have laid down a principle, and adopted a model. How can we vacillate now? How can we be looking about for expedients? Our way lies right before us.

*   *   *

And now we come, last of all, to enquire into the condition of the University. The first question which here arises is, whether the University as far as developed conforms to the English, or to the Prussian model? Like most of the similar institutions of our country, it is of a mixed character. In many things, like them, it conforms to the English model. In the Literary and Scientific course, like the English colleges, it has adopted the term of four years, with four classes named like theirs, and closing with a Commencement celebration, and the conferring of the degree of Bachelor of Arts. But, on the other hand, in common again with several institutions in the United States, it has recognized several Faculties each connected with a distinct department. In this respect, in common with them, it departs from the English model; for, at Oxford and Cambridge we do not find one college devoted to literature, science and the arts, another to theology, another to law, and another to medicine; but, we find, only, a congeries of colleges, each being a classical and scientific school. In our distinct departments and faculties, therefore, we have followed the Prussian model. But do we closely conform to the Prussian model? No, we do not. Wherein do we differ from it? Let me tell you. And now I speak in reference to all the institutions of the land which have constituted dstinct departments and faculties, in reference to Harvard and Yale, for example, as well as in reference to the University of Michigan.

First; in the Department of Literature, Science and the Arts, called, also, the Academic, and the Undergraduate Department, the course universally adopted corresponds not at all to that of the Prussian Universities; but, whether we consider the age of admission, the studies pursued, the method of instruction, and the term of study, is very similar to that of the Prussian Gymnasia. Thus in our so called Universities we have, often, only the Gymnastic course, and omit the higher and proper University course, altogether.

Secondly; in institutions which, like Yale and Harvard, introduce a course distinct from the Undergraduate, and which take some aspects of a proper University course, attendance upon the undergraduate course is not insisted upon as a prerequisite. In Prussia, on the contrary, a course of at least four years at the Gymnasium is necessary for an introduction into the University.

Thirdly; in respect to the three departments of Theology, Law, and Medicine, the usage, in our country, is to require the undergraduate course or an equivalent thereto, for the first, but not for the two last; while in Prussia, Theology, Law, and Medicine, alike, require the previous course of the Gymnasium.

You perceive, therefore, that the Prussian system is philosophic in its principles, consistent and proportionate in its parts, and thorough in its methods and discipline: while ours is mixed and vacillating, and consequently imperfect.

You will naturally, ask me, at this point, what I would propose for the improvement of our system?

The answer is attended with difficulties. I would answer neither rashly, nor dogmatically, nor in general and indefinite terms. I would give an honest, candid, and fearless answer, and according to my best judgment, holding myself ready to be corrected. We have a common interest at stake. There are no other motives that should influence us than the most enlightened, patriotic, and humane. In this free country, let every man speak his mind freely, and with a true heart.

I propose then, generally, that you follow out the principles you have adopted, and perfect, manfully, your system of education according to these principles. Dare to be in advance of the whole country, if need be. And this is the way in which I would carry out these principles:

First, let the Primary Schools be enlarged and perfected in their discipline and courses of study, according to the Prussian model. This will most effectually be done by means of the Union and Normal Schools. The union of districts will enable you to concentrate your resources for employing better teachers, and introducing higher branches of study. You will observe that in Prussia the Primary Schools carry forward the pupil until he is prepared for the Gymnasium. In our Union Schools, as in the Burgher Department of the Prussian Schools, we may introduce the study of the classics; and thus we shall want no other preparatory schools for either the classical or scientific departments of our colleges, taking them as equivalent to the Gymnasia. The multiplication of Union Schools appears to me, therefore, essential to our system.

The Normal School is connected immediately with the interests of the whole Primary School System, as our great resource for competent teachers.

Now, when we come to consider particularly the University, we find there existing as yet in the Department of Science, Literature, and the Arts, only, the College or Gymnasium. According to the practice of our country, we have connected our Gymnasium with our University, and placed it under the same faculty. Our organization is a University organization, by departments and faculties. Our course of instruction, also, is carried on by Masters of Arts or Professors in full, and not by mere Baccalaureate tutors and fellows, as in the English Colleges. But before the University course proper could be developed, it was necessary that the Professors should give instruction in the Gymnastic course.

No exception can be taken to this: University Professors may instruct in a Gymnasium, if they please: They are called, imperatively, to do so while, as yet, University students do not present themselves, and Gymnasia alone exist. And thus we might have many Gymnasia under the shadow of the University, ordered by University Professors. This, indeed, would be in accordance with old usage, since, in Paris, for example, instruction in the Colleges was given by University Professors, at the very time, that in England the University and its Professors were laid aside for the Colleges and their tutors.

Most of the higher institutions of our country are organized in some respect as Universities; but there are some of them which as yet have not only created but one faculty, but continue, also, from year to year to confine their instructions in this faculty to the Gymnastic or Collegiate course. Sometimes a struggle is made to advance beyond this by occasional lectures. But as these lectures are given to the undergraduates, the University does not in this make its appearance.

In the Literary and Scientific department of the University of Michigan, we find ourselves, at the present moment, in just this condition: We are a University Faculty giving instruction in a College or Gymnasium.

Now, our first object will be to perfect this Gymnasium. To this end, we propose to establish a Scientific course parallel to the classical course. In this scientific course a more extended study of the Mathematics will be substituted for the Greek and Latin. There will be comprised in it, besides other branches, Civil Engineering,

Astronomy with the use of an Observatory, and the application of Chemistry and other Sciences to Agriculture and the industrial arts, generally. The entire course will run through four years, in which the Students will be distributed into four classes similarly to the classical course: and in both courses, instead of the old names of *Freshman, Sophomore, Junior,* and *Senior* borrowed from the English colleges, we will take the designations employed in the institutions of the Continent of Europe, of *First, Second, Third,* and *Fourth.*

Students who pursue the full Scientific course, and pass the regular Examinations, we shall graduate as *Bachelors of Science*—borrowing a title here from the French Colleges, as the Lawrence Scientific School of Harvard, and the University of Rochester have done before us—in distinction from the *Bachelors of Arts* in the Classical course.

But, in addition to this, we shall allow Students to select special courses, and give them, at their departure, certificates of their proficiency. The school of civil Engineering, and the school of Agriculture and Mechanics will belong to these special courses.

We shall thus make our College or Gymnasium an Institution where the youth of our State can freely enter to prepare themselves for professional study, for the higher pursuits of Science and Literature, or for the pursuits of business life.

By establishing the scientific course in distinction from the classical, we do not intend to do any discredit to classical learning, or to imply ought in opposition to those who advocate its surpassing value and importance to general and finished Scholarship.

*   *   *

I know that the scheme proposed is on a large scale. But let no man call it visionary. Nothing is visionary that can be sustained by facts and examples. What I have laid before you is in accordance with the oldest experience in education. It is now a familiar and general fact on the Continent of Europe. It exists in France; it exists in Germany. Why may it not exist in America—why may it not exist in the State of Michigan?

It is worthy of our political institutions. Because, it is found amid monarchies and aristocracies, it is not therefore monarchical and aristocratical. Science is found there also. Protestantism is found there also. The Universities of Germany and France are the seats of liberal principles. In Germany the students and professors of the Universities have more than once been the objects of governmental persecution on account of their democratic tendencies. Do we not acknowledge that the universal diffusion of knowledge is the foundation of our hopes that our free institutions will be preserved and perpetuated? And if we demand knowledge in the lower degrees, do we fear it in the higher? Is it our doctrine that perfected knowledge prepares mankind for despotism? Is it not rather our doctrine, that a free people cannot know too much, and that the more we know, the more strongly shall we lay hold upon freedom? The clearer, the more perfect the element of light, the better we shall see.

This University belongs to the people. Their votes elect the Regents who have the supervision over all its interests and movements. Its advantages are freely thrown open to the people. The son of the poorest man can enter here as freely and independently, as the richest. Education levels all artificial distinctions, and creates only that aristocracy which all men acknowledge, and which the God of the universe sanctions, the aristocracy of intellectual and moral worth. It creates such aristocrats as Clay, Webster, Cass and Pierce, men of the Constitution, men of the people, the glorious dead! the honored living!

But, it is often said, we are a young people, the nations of Europe are old: the European Universities are the growth of centuries. In opposition to this I would state that the most eminent Universities of Germany are of modern growth.—The University of Berlin, for example, was founded in 1810, and in 1826 when it was scarcely older than the University of Michigan is now, it contained sixteen hundred and forty-two matriculated students. I know the wide difference between an old and a new State as to the resources which foster such an institution; but, nevertheless, it proves that a great University may be of rapid growth.

Let me remind you, too, that it is not in accordance with the spirit of our country to let improvements grow slowly. This great State is the growth of a quarter of a century.—In our industrial arts and improvements we are not willing to fall behind Europe according to the ratio of our respective ages. We aim not merely to equal, but even to surpass the old nations of the world, in our manufactures, our steamboats, and our railroads. We level the forest in a day, lay down our tracks, and startle the old world with the sound of our engines. Our steamers outspeed their's across the ocean. Our yachts win the royal prize over the ancient ship builders in the sight of the Majesty of England. The Autocrat of Russia employs our engineers to make his railroads; and his steamers are built on our shores.

Shall we be behind then only in the great matter of Education? Can we not build up Universities too? Shall we apply to the cultivation of Mind a principle of slow progression which we scorn to apply to anything else? Let it not be my countrymen—let it not be. Arouse thy energies young State of Michigan! Giant of the West! holding the great lakes in the hollow of thine hands; bearing on thy bosom, deep engraven, the memorials of thy glorious deeds; looking with eyes of light upon all thy brothers around thee, and inspiring them with thy majesty and beauty; speak out with thy strong and melodious voice the decree that here a new Athens shall arise with its schools of Philosophy and Art, and its Acropolis crowned with another Parthenon more glorious than that of old because illumined with the true light from heaven!

DETROIT FREE PRESS ATTACKS HENRY TAPPAN (1853)   From an editorial,
Detroit Free Press, December 28, 1853.

The State University

PRESIDENT TAPPAN'S idea of a University is grand—imposing! The German University at Berlin is his model, and he would bring the Wolverine institution up to the Berlin standard with all possible haste. He has a similar idea of cities and towns, though he don't say so in this report. He thinks no city should be without its heaven-pointing monuments and great public works. He conceives that it is a mistake of the Americans that they build warehouses and neglect monuments. He wants to know what will be thought of our country, by future generations, when our structure shall have crumbled, if there shall be no silent, gloomy monuments found, overlooking the general wreck of matter? With a far-stretching vision, he sees America reduced to Egyptian decay, and he is of opinion that we ought to write the history of our rise and progress upon tall monuments for the especial edification of generations that will be yet unborn half a dozen centuries hence! Something akin to this is his notion of institutions of learning.

> One thing is certain, that whether we consider the resources of the State of Michigan and its rapidly advancing greatness, or, its position in reference to surrounding States, we shall neither be true to our own trust, nor shall we pursue a wise policy, if we make our calculations upon a diminuitive scale. Divine Providence has afforded us a great opportunity, and given us indications *which seem almost like a positive command.* To embrace the opportunity, to obey the indications, is the true way of success.

This looks very well on paper to one who has little sense of the ludicrous and the bombastic.—With proper management and steady perseverance—such perseverance as has, after the lapse of a century and a half, made Yale what it is—the University of Michigan can be made one of the first institutions of learning in the country. There is such a thing, especially in educational matters, as going too fast as well as too slow; and often the one is more fatal than the other. A wise statesman makes haste slowly.

*   *   *

To what extent the people of Michigan will feel inclined to maintain a grand Prussian University at Ann Arbor by direct appropriations from the public treasury is a pretty grave question. We have no hesitation in saying, in the outset, as one of the people, that we are hostile to any such use of money that is drawn from the pockets of the whole people. If the permanent endowment of the University is not sufficient to support it, it must tax the recipients of its benefits to make up the deficiency. . . .

HENRY TAPPAN ON THE DEMOCRATIC CHARACTER OF THE UNIVERSITY OF MICHIGAN (1855) From Henry P. Tappan, *Seventh Annual Report of the Board of Regents of the University of Michigan,* as quoted in *Annual Report of the Superintendant of Instruction of the State of Michigan for 1855,* pp. 111–12.

The Popular Character of the University

By this we mean its adaptation to the people at large.

It is a prevailing opinion that the Common School is the most popular of all our institutions of learning. This would be true, did the Common School meet all the educational wants of the people, and were it the only one open to them. But it certainly cannot be true, merely, because the Common School is the *lowest* grade of education, unless we adopt the monstrous principle that the people are entitled only to the lowest grade.

All civilized countries, and especially those which have popular forms of government—where the people have alike the sovereign power, and are alike eligible to civil offices—require a great number of highly educated men. Indeed, the more widely the higher degrees of education are diffused, the better. But, where the high institutions of learning are so constituted as to be accessible only to the rich, and to privileged classes, they cannot be popular institutions.

Now the University of Michigan is popular, in the strictest sense, whether we consider its courses of study, or the fact that it is freely opened to all the people, without distinction. If any wish to give their sons a classical education, with a view of introducing them into the learned professions, they find here the requisite course of study.

If any wish to give their sons a purely scientific education, or to introduce them to branches connected with the mechanic arts, with manufactures, with commerce, with agriculture, or with civil engineering, the requisite courses are all here provided.

The University thus meets the wants of the people, in all the higher degrees of education.

In the next place, the University having been endowed by the General Government, affords education without money, and without price. There is no young man so poor, that industry, diligence, and perseverance will not enable him to get an education here.

The present condition of the University confirms this view of its character. While the sons of the rich, and of men of more or less property; and, in larger proportion, the sons of substantial farmers, mechanics, and merchants, are educated here; there is also a very considerable number of young men dependent entirely upon their own exertions—young men who, accustomed to labor on the farm, or in the mechanic's shop, have become smitten with the love of knowledge, and are manfully working their way through to a liberal education, by appropriating a portion of their time to the field or the workshop.

I could mention many noble instances of this kind. Some of our best scholars, and who give the fairest promise of taking a high position in after life, belong to this class.

ANDREW D. WHITE REMINISCES ABOUT HENRY TAPPAN AND THE UNIVERSITY OF MICHIGAN From *Selected Chapters From The Autobiography of Andrew D. White* (Ithaca, 1939). pp. 65–68.

The features which mainly distinguished the University of Michigan from the leading institutions of the East were that it was utterly unsectarian, that various courses of instruction were established, and that options were allowed between them. On these accounts that university holds a most important place in the history of American higher education; for it stands practically at the beginning of the transition from the old sectarian college to the modern university, and from the simple, single, cast-iron course to the form which we now know, in which various courses are presented, with free choice between them. The number of students was about five hundred, and the faculty corresponded to these in numbers. Now that the university includes over four thousand students, with a faculty in proportion, those seem the days of small things; but to me at that period it was all very grand. It seemed marvelous that there were then very nearly as many students at the University of Michigan as at Yale; and, as a rule, they were students worth teaching—hardy, vigorous, shrewd, broad, with faith in the greatness of the country and enthusiasm regarding the nation's future. It may be granted that there was, in many of them, a lack of elegance, but there was neither languor nor cynicism. One seemed, among them, to breathe a purer, stronger air. Over the whole institution Dr. Tappan presided, and his influence, both upon faculty and students, was, in the main, excellent. He sympathized heartily with the work of every professor, allowed to each great liberty, yet conducted the whole toward the one great end of developing a university more and more worthy of our country. His main qualities were of the best. Nothing could be better than his discussion of great questions of public policy and of education. One of the noblest orations I ever heard was an offhand speech of his on receiving for the university museum a cast of the Laocoon from the senior class; yet this speech was made without preparation, and in the midst of engrossing labor. He often showed, not only the higher qualities required in a position like his, but a remarkable shrewdness and tact in dealing with lesser questions. Typical was one example, which taught me much when, in after years, I was called to similar duties at Cornell. The present tower and chime of the University of Michigan did not then exist; between the two main buildings on the university grounds there was simply a wooden column, bearing a bell of moderate size, which was rung at every lecture-hour by the principal janitor. One cold winter night those of us living in the immediate neighborhood heard the sound of axe-strokes. Presently there came a crash, and all was still. Next morning, at the hour for chapel, no bell was rung; it was found that the column had been cut down and the bell carried off. A president of less shrewdness would have declaimed to the students on the enormity of such a procedure, and have accentuated his eloquence with threats. Not so Dr. Tappan. At the close of the morning prayers he addressed the students humorously. There was a great attendance, for all wished to know how he would deal with the affair. Nothing could be better than his matter and manner. He spoke somewhat on this wise: "Gentlemen, there has doubtless been a mistake in the theory of some of you regarding the college bell. It would seem that some have believed that if the bell were destroyed, time would cease, and university exercises would be suspended. But, my friends, time goes on as ever, without the bell as with it; lectures and exercises of every sort continue, of course, as usual. The only thing which has occurred is that some of you have thought it best to dispense with the aid in keeping time which the regents of the university have so kindly given you. Knowing that large numbers of you were not yet provided with watches, the regents very thoughtfully provided the bell, and a man to ring it for you at the proper hours and they will doubtless be pleased to learn that you at last feel able to dispense with it, and save them the expense of maintaining it. You are trying an interesting experiment. In most of the leading European universities, students get along perfectly without a bell; why should we not? In the interests of the finances of the university, I am glad to see you trying this experiment, and will only suggest that it be tried thoroughly. Of course the rolls will be called in the lecture-rooms promptly, as usual, and you will, of course, be present. If the experiment succeeds, it will enable us to dispense with a university bell forever; but if, after a suitable time, you decide that it is better to have the bell back again to remind you of the hours, and if you will make a proper request to the regents through me, I trust that they will allow you to restore it to its former position."

The students were greatly amused to see the matter taken in this way. They laughingly acknowledged themselves outwitted, and greeted the doctor's speech with applause. All of the faculty entered into the spirit of the matter; rolls were called perhaps rather more promptly than formerly, and students not present were marked rather more mercilessly than of old. There was evidently much reluctance on their part to ask for excuses, in view of the fact that they had themselves abolished the bell which had enabled them to keep the time; and one morning, about a month or six weeks later, after chapel, a big jolly student rose and asked permission to make a motion. This motion was that the president of the university be requested to allow the students to restore the bell to its former position. The proposal was graciously received by the doctor, put by him after the usual parliamentary manner, carried unanimously, and, a few mornings later, the bell was found in its old place on a new column, was rung as usual, and matters went on after the old fashion.

Every winter Dr. Tappan went before the legislature to plead the cause of the university, and to ask for appropriations. He was always heard with pleasure, since he was an excellent speaker; but certain things militated against him. First of all, he had much to say of the excellent models furnished by the great German universities, and especially by those of Prussia. This gave demagogues in the legislature, anxious to make a reputation in buncombe, a great chance. . . .

*   *   *

Though many good things may be justly said for the University of Virginia, the real beginning of a university in the United States, in the modern sense, was made by Dr. Tappan and his colleagues at Ann Arbor. Its only defects seemed to me that it included no technical side, and did not yet admit women. As to the first of these defects, the State had separated the agricultural college from the university, placing it in what, at that period, was a remote swamp near the State Capitol, and had as yet done nothing toward providing for other technical branches. As to the second, though a few of us favored the admission of women, President Tappan opposed it; and, probably, in view of the condition of the university and of public opinion at that time, his opposition was wise.

The Emerging University

JONATHAN BALDWIN TURNER'S PLAN FOR AN INDUSTRIAL
UNIVERSITY (1851)   From "Plan for an Industrial University, for the State of Illinois,"
as quoted in Jonathan B. Turner, *Industrial Universities for the People* . . . (Chicago,
1854), pp. 18-26.

All civilized society is, necessarily, divided into two distinct cooperative, not antagonistic, classes:—a small class, whose proper business it is to teach the true principles of religion, law, medicine, science, art, and literature; and a much larger class, who are engaged in some form of labor in agriculture, commerce, and the arts. For the sake of convenience, we will designate the former the PROFESSIONAL, and the latter the INDUSTRIAL class; not implying that each may not be equally industrious: the one in their intellectual, the other in their industrial pursuits. Probably, in no case would society ever need more than five men out of one hundred in the professional class, leaving ninety-five in every hundred in the industrial; and so long as so many of our ordinary teachers and public men are taken from the industrial class, as there are at present, and probably will be for generations to come, we do not really need over one professional man for every hundred, leaving ninety-nine in the industrial class.

The vast difference, in the practical means, of an APPROPRIATE LIBERAL EDUCATION, suited to their wants and their destiny, which these two classes enjoy, and ever have enjoyed the world over, must have arrested the attention of every thinking man. True, the same general abstract science exists in the world for both classes alike, but the means of bringing this abstract truth into effectual contact with the daily business and pursuits of the one class does exist, while in the other case it does not exist, and never can, till it is new created.

The one class have schools, seminaries, colleges, universities, apparatus, professors, and multitudinous appliances for educating and training them for months and years, for the peculiar profession which is to be the business of their life; and they have already created, each class for its own use, a vast and voluminous literature, that would well nigh sink a whole navy of ships.

But where are the universities, the apparatus, the professors, and the literature, specifically adapted to any one of the industrial classes? Echo answers, where? In other words, society has become, long since, wise enough to know that its TEACHERS need to be educated; but it has not yet become wise enough to know that its WORKERS need education just as much. In these remarks I have not forgotten that our common schools are equally adapted and applied to all classes; but reading, writing, &c., are, properly, no more education than gathering seed is agriculture, or cutting ship-timber navigation. They are the mere rudiments, as they are called, or means, the mere instrument of an after education, and if not so used they are, and can be, of little more use to the possessor than an axe in the garret or a ship rotting upon the stocks.

Nor am I unmindful of the efforts of the monarchs and aristocrats of the old world in founding schools for the "fifteenth cousins" of their order, in hopes of training them into a sort of *genteel farmers,* or rather *overseers* of farmers; nor yet, of the several "back fires" (as the Prairie Farmer significantly designates them) set by some of our older professional institutions, to keep the rising and blazing thought of the industrial masses from burning too furiously. They have hauled a canoe alongside of their huge professional steamships, and invited all the farmers and mechanics of the State to jump on board and sail with them; but the difficulty is, they will not embark. But we thank them even for this pains and courtesy. It shows that their hearts are yearning toward us, notwithstanding the ludicrous awkwardness of their first endeavors to save us.

But an answer to two simple questions will perhaps sufficiently indicate our ideas of the whole subject, though that answer, on the present occasion, must necessarily be confined to a bare outline. The first question, then, is this:

I. What Do the Industrial Classes Want?
II. How Can That Want Be Supplied?

The first question may be answered in few words. They want, and they ought to have, the same facilities for understanding the true philosophy—the science and the art of their several pursuits, (their life-business,) and of efficiently applying existing knowledge thereto and widening its domain, which the professional classes have long enjoyed in their pursuits. Their first labor is, therefore, to supply a vacuum from fountains already full, and bring the living waters of knowledge within their own reach. Their second is, to help fill the fountains with still greater supplies. They desire to depress no institution, no class whatever; they only wish to elevate themselves and their pursuits to a position in society to which all men acknowledge they are justly entitled, and to which they also desire to see them aspire.

II. How Then Can That Want Be Supplied?

In answering this question, I shall endeavor to present, with all possible frankness and clearness, the outline of impressions and convictions that have been gradually deepening in my own mind, for the past twenty years, and let them pass for whatever the true friends of the cause may think them worth.

And I answer, first, negatively, that this want cannot be supplied by any of the existing institutions for the professional classes, nor by any incidental appendage attached to them as a mere secondary department.

These institutions were designed and adapted to meet the wants of the professional classes, as such—especially the clerical order; and they are no more suited to the real wants of the industrial class than the institution we propose for them, would be suited to the professional class.

Their whole spirit and aim is, or should be, literary and intellectual—not practical and industrial; to make men of books and ready speech—not men of work, and industrial, silent thought.—But, the very best classical scholars are often the very worst practical reasoners; and that they should be made workers is contrary to the nature of things—the fixed laws of God. The whole interest, business, and destiny for life of the two classes, run in opposite lines; and that the same course of study should be equally well adapted to both, is as utterly impossible as that the same pursuits and habits should equally concern and befit both classes.

The industrial classes know and feel this, and therefore they do not, and will not, patronize these institutions, only so far forth as they desire to make professional men for public use. As a general fact, their own multitudes do, and *will forever,* stand aloof from them; and, while they desire to foster and cherish them for their own appropriate uses, they know that they do not, and cannot, fill the sphere of their own urgent industrial wants. They need a similar system of *liberal education* for their own class, and adapted to their own pursuits; to create for them an INDUSTRIAL LITERATURE, adapted to their professional wants, to raise up for them *teachers* and *lecturers,* for subordinate institutes, and to elevate them, their pursuits, and their posterity to that relative position in human society for which God designed them.

The whole history of education, both in Protestant and Catholic countries, shows that we must begin with the higher institutions, or we can never succeed with the lower; for the plain reason, that neither knowledge nor water will run up hill. No people ever had, or ever can have, any system of common schools and lower seminaries worth anything, until they first founded their higher institutions and fountains of knowledge from which they could draw supplies of teachers, &c., for the lower. We would begin, therefore, where all experience and common sense show that we must begin, if we would effect anything worthy of an effort.

In this view of the case, the first thing wanted in this process is a NATIONAL INSTITUTE OF SCIENCE, to operate as the great central luminary of the national mind, from which all minor institutions should derive light and heat, and toward which they should, also, reflect back their own. This primary want is already, I trust, supplied by the Smithsonian Institute, endowed by James Smithson, and incorporated by the U. S. Congress, at Washington, D. C.

To co-operate with this noble Institute, and enable the industrial classes to realize its benefits in practical life, we need a *University for the Industrial Classes* in each of the States, with their consequent subordinate institutes, lyceums, and high schools, in each of the counties and towns.

The objects of these institutes should be to apply existing knowledge directly and efficiently to all practical pursuits and professions in life, and to extend the boundaries of our present knowledge in all possible practical directions.

Plan for the State University

There should be connected with such an institution, in this State, a sufficient quantity of land of variable soil and aspect, for all its needful annual experiments and processes in the great interests of Agriculture and Horticulture.

Buildings of appropriate size and construction for all its ordinary and special uses; a complete philosophical, chemical, anatomical, and industrial apparatus; a general cabinet, embracing everything that relates to, illustrates or facilitates any one of the industrial arts; especially all sorts of animals, birds, reptiles, insects, trees, shrubs, and plants found in this State and adjacent States.

Instruction should be constantly given in the anatomy and physiology, the nature, instincts, and habits of animals, insects, trees, and plants; their laws of propagation, primogeniture, growth, and decay, disease and health, life and death, on the nature, composition, adaptation, and regeneration of soils; on the nature, strength, durability, preservation, perfection, composition, cost, use, and manufacture of all materials of art and trade; on political, financial, domestic, and manual economy, (or the saving of labor of the hand,) in all industrial processes; on the true principles of national, constitutional, and civil law; and the true theory and art of governing and controlling, or directing the labor of men in the State, the family, shop, and farm; on the laws of vicinage, or the laws of courtesy and comity between neighbors, as such, and on the principles of health and disease in the human subject, so far at least as is needful for household safety; on the laws of trade and commerce, ethical, conventional, and practical; on book-keeping and accounts; and, in short, in all those studies and sciences, of whatever sort, which tend to throw light upon any art of employment, which any student may desire to master, or upon any duty he may be called to perform; or which may tend to secure his moral, civil, social, and industrial perfection, as a man.

No species of knowledge should be excluded, practical or theoretical; unless, indeed, those specimens of "organized ignorance" found in the creeds of party politicians and sectarian ecclesiastics should be mistaken by some for a species of knowledge.

Whether a distinct classical department should be added or not, would depend on expediency. It might be deemed best to leave that department to existing colleges as their more appropriate work, and to form some practical and economical connection with them for that purpose; or it might be best to attach a classical department in due time to the institution itself.

To facilitate the increase and practical application and diffusion of knowledge, the professors should conduct, each in his own department, a continued series of *annual experiments*.

*   *   *

The APPARATUS required for such a work is obvious. There should be grounds devoted to a botanical and common garden, to orchards and fruit yards, to appropriate lawns and promenades, in which the beautiful art of landscape gardening could be appropriately applied and illustrated, to all varieties of pasture, meadow, and tillage needful for the successful prosecution of the needful annual experiments. And on these grounds should be collected and exhibited a sample of every variety of domestic animal, and of every tree, plant, and vegetable that can minister to the health, wealth, or taste and comfort of the people of the State; their nature, habits, merits, production, improvement, culture, diseases, and accidents thoroughly scrutinized, tested, and made known to the students and to the people of the State.

There should, also, be erected a sufficient number of buildings and out-buildings for all the purposes above indicated, and a REPOSITORY, in which all the ordinary tools and implements of the institution should be kept, and models of all other useful implements and machines from time to time collected, and tested as they are proffered to public use. At first it would be for the interest of inventors and vendors to make such deposits. But should similar institutions be adopted in other States, the general government ought to create in each State a general patent office, attached to the Universities, similar to the existing deposits at Washington, thus rendering this department of mechanical art and skill more accessible to the great mass of the people of the Union.

I should have said, also, that a suitable industrial library should be at once procured, did not all the world know such a thing to be impossible, and that one of the first and most important duties of the professors of such institutions will be to begin to create, at this late hour, a proper practical literature, and series of text books for the industrial classes.

As regard the PROFESSORS, they should, of course, not only be men of the most eminent practical ability in their several departments, but their connexion with the institution should be rendered so fixed and stable, as to enable them to carry through such designs as they may form, or all the peculiar benefits of the system would be lost.

Instruction, by lectures or otherwise, should be given mostly in the coldest months of the year; leaving the professors to prosecute their investigations, and the students their necessary labor, either at home or on the premises, during the warmer months.

The institution should be open to all classes of students above a fixed age, and for any length of time, whether three months or seven years, and each taught in those particular branches of art which he wishes to pursue, and to any extent, more or less. And all should pay their tuition and board bills, in whole or in part, either in money or necessary work on the premises—regard being had to the ability of each.

Among those who labor, medals and testimonials of merit should be given to those who perform their task with most promptitude, energy, care, and skill; and all who prove indolent or ungovernable, excluded at first from all part in labor, and speedily, if not thoroughly reformed, from the institution itself; and here again let the law of nature instead of the law of rakes and dandies be regarded, and the true impression ever made on the mind of all around, that WORK ALONE IS HONORABLE, and indolence certain disgrace if not ruin.

At some convenient season of the year, the Commencement, or ANNUAL FAIR of the University, should be holden through a succession of days. On this occasion the doors of the institution, with all its treasures of art and resources of knowledge, should be thrown open to all classes, and as many other objects of agricultural or mechanical skill, gathered from the whole State, as possible, and presented by the people for inspection and premium on the best of each kind; judgment being rendered, in all cases, by a committee wholly disconnected with the institution. On this occasion, all the professors, and as many of the pupils as are sufficiently advanced, should be constantly engaged in lecturing and explaining the divers objects and interests of their departments. In short, this occasion should be made the great annual GALA-DAY of the Institution, and of all the industrial classes, and all other classes in the State, for the exhibition of their products and their skill, and for the vigorous and powerful diffusion of practical knowledge in their ranks, and a more intense enthusiasm in its extension and pursuit.

As matters now are, the world has never adopted any efficient means for the application and diffusiion of even the practical knowledge which does exist. True, we have fairly got the primer, the spelling book, and the newspaper abroad in the world, and we think that we have done wonders; and so, comparatively, we have. But if this is a wonder, there are still not only wonders, but, to most minds, inconceivable miracles, from new and unknown worlds of light, soon to burst forth upon the industrial mind of the world.

Here, then, is a general, though very incomplete outline of what such an institution should endeavor to become. Let the reader contemplate it as it will appear when generations have perfected it, in all it magnificence and glory; in its means of good to man, to *all men* of *all classes;* in its power to evolve and diffuse practical knowledge and skill, true taste, love of industry, and sound morality—not only through its apparatus, experiments, instructions, and annual lectures and reports, but through its thousands of graduates, in every pursuit in life, teaching and lecturing in all our towns and villages; and then let him seriously ask himself, is not such an object worthy of at least an effort, and worthy of a state which God himself, in the very act of creation, designed to be the first agricultural and commercial State on the face of the globe?

Who should set the world so glorious an example of educating their sons worthily of their heritage, their duty, and their destiny, if not the people of such a State? In our country, we have no aristocracy, with the inalienable wealth of ages and constant leisure and means to perform all manner of useful experiments for their own amusement; but we must create our nobility for this purpose, as we elect our rulers, from our own ranks, to aid and serve, not to domineer over and control us. And this done, we will not only beat England, and beat the world in yachts, and locks, and reapers, but in all else that contributes to the well being and true glory of man.

RECOMMENDATIONS OF THE ILLINOIS STATE LEGISLATURE FOR THE ESTABLISHMENT OF A SYSTEM OF INDUSTRIAL UNIVERSITIES

(1854) From Edmund J. James, *The Origin of the Land-Grant Act of 1862 and Some Account of Its Author, Jonathan B. Turner* (Urbana, Ill., 1910), pp. 16–17.

Whereas, the spirit and progress of this age and country demand the culture of the highest order of intellectual attainment in theoretic and industrial science; and

Whereas, it is impossible that our commerce and prosperity will continue to increase without calling into requisition all the elements of internal thrift arising from the labors of the farmer, the mechanic, and the manufacturer, by every fostering effort within the reach of the government; and

Whereas, a system of Industrial Universities, liberally endowed in each state of the union, co-operative with each other, and with the Smithsonian Institute of Washington, would develop a more liberal and practical education among the people, tend to more intellectualize the rising generation and eminently conduct to the virtue, intelligence and true glory of our common country; therefore be it

Resolved, by the House of Representatives, the Senate concurring herein, That our Senators in Congress be instructed, and our Representatives be requested, to use their best exertions to procure the passage of a law of Congress donating to each state in the Union an amount of public lands not less in value than five hundred thousand dollars, for the liberal endowment of a system of Industrial Universities, one in each state of the Union, to co-operate with each other, and with the Smithsonian Institute at Washington, for the more liberal and practical education of our industrial classes and their teachers; a liberal and varied education, adapted to the manifold wants of a practical and enterprising people, and a provision for such educational facilities being in manifest concurrence with the intimation of the popular will, it urgently demands the united efforts of our strength.

Resolved, That the Governor is hereby authorized to forward a copy of the foregoing resolutions to our Senators and Representatives in Congress, and to the Executive and Legislature of each of our sister States, inviting them to co-operate with us in this meritorious enterprise.

PRESIDENT BUCHANAN'S VETO OF THE FIRST MORRILL BILL

(1859)   From James D. Richardson, ed., *A Compilation of the Messages and Papers of the Presidents* (Washington, D.C., 1897), vol. V, pp. 543–47.

Washington City, February 24, 1859.

To the House of Representatives of the United States:

I return with my objections to the House of Representatives, in which it originated, the bill entitled "An act donating public lands to the several States and Territories which may provide colleges for the benefit of agriculture and mechanic arts," presented to me on the 18th instant.

This bill makes a donation to the several States of 20,000 acres of the public lands for each Senator and Representative in the present Congress, and also an additional donation of 20,000 acres for each additional Representative to which any State may be entitled under the census of 1860.

According to a report from the Interior Department, based upon the present number of Senators and Representatives, the lands given to the States amount to 6,060,000 acres, and their value, at the minimum Government price of $1.25 per acre, to $7,575,000.

The object of this gift, as stated by the bill, is "the endowment, support, and maintenance of at least one college (in each State) where the leading object shall be, without excluding other scientific or classical studies, to teach such branches of learning as are related to agriculture and the mechanic arts, as the legislatures of the States may respectively prescribe, in order to promote the liberal and practical education of the industrial classes in the several pursuits and professions in life."

As there does not appear from the bill to be any beneficiaries in existence to which this endowment can be applied, each State is required "to provide, within five years at least, not less than one college, or the grant to said State shall cease." In that event the "said State shall be bound to pay the United States the amount received of any lands previously sold, and that the title to purchasers under the State shall be valid."

The grant in land itself is confined to such States as have public lands within their limits worth $1.25 per acre in the opinion of the governor. For the remaining States the Secretary of the Interior is directed to issue "land scrip to the amount of their distributive shares in acres under the provisions of this act, said scrip to be sold by said States, and the proceeds thereof applied to the uses and purposes prescribed in this act, and for no other use or purpose whatsoever." The lands are granted and the scrip is to be issued "in sections or subdivisions of sections of not less than one-quarter of a section."

According to an estimate from the Interior Department, the number of acres which will probably be accepted by States having public lands within their own limits will not exceed 580,000 acres (and it may be much less), leaving a balance of

5,480,000 acres to be provided for by scrip. These grants of land and land scrip to each of the thirty-three States are made upon certain conditions, the principal of which is that if the fund shall be lost or diminished on account of unfortunate investments or otherwise the deficiency shall be replaced and made good by the respective States.

I shall now proceed to state my objections to this bill. I deem it to be both inexpedient and unconstitutional.

1. This bill has been passed at a period when we can with great difficulty raise sufficient revenue to sustain the expenses of the Government. Should it become a law the Treasury will be deprived of the whole, or nearly the whole, of our income from the sale of public lands, which for the next fiscal year has been estimated at $5,000,000.

*   *   *

3. This bill, should it become a law, will operate greatly to the injury of the new States. The progress of settlements and the increase of an industrious population owning an interest in the soil they cultivate are the causes which will build them up into great and flourishing commonwealths. Nothing could be more prejudicial to their interests than for wealthy individuals to acquire large tracts of the public land and hold them for speculative purposes. The low price to which this land scrip will probably be reduced will tempt speculators to buy it in large amounts and locate it on the best lands belonging to the Government. The eventual consequence must be that the men who desire to cultivate the soil will be compelled to purchase these very lands at rates much higher than the price at which they could be obtained from the Government.

4. It is extremely doubtful, to say the least, whether this bill would contribute to the advancement of agriculture and the mechanic arts—objects the dignity and value of which can not be too highly appreciated.

The Federal Government, which makes the donation, has confessedly no constitutional power to follow it into the States and enforce the application of the fund to the intended objects. As donors we shall possess no control over our own gift after it shall have passed from our hands. It is true that the State legislatures are required to stipulate that they will faithfully execute the trust in the manner prescribed by the bill. But should they fail to do this, what would be the consequence? The Federal Government has no power, and ought to have no power, to compel the execution of the trust. It would be in as helpless a condition as if, even in this, the time of great need, we were to demand any portion of the many millions of surplus revenue deposited with the States for safe-keeping under the act of 1836.

5. This bill will injuriously interfere with existing colleges in the different States, in many of which agriculture is taught as a science and in all of which it ought to be so taught. These institutions of learning have grown up with the growth of the country, under the fostering care of the States and the munificence of individuals, to meet the advancing demands for education. They have proved great blessings to the people. Many, indeed most, of them are poor and sustain themselves with difficulty. What the effect will be on these institutions of creating an indefinite number of rival colleges sustained by the endowment of the Federal Government it is not difficult to determine.

THE MORRILL (LAND-GRANT) ACT (1862)   From George P. Sanger, ed., *The Statutes at Large, Treaties, and Proclamations, of the United States of America* (Boston, 1863), vol. XII, pp. 503-5.

An Act Donating Public Lands to the Several States and Territories Which May Provide Colleges for the Benefit of Agriculture and the Mechanic Arts

Be it enacted by the Senate and House of Representatives of the United States of America in Congress assembled, That there be granted to the several States, for the purposes hereinafter mentioned, an amount of public land, to be apportioned to each State a quantity equal to thirty thousand acres for each senator and representative in Congress to which the States are respectively entitled by the apportionment under the census of eighteen hundred and sixty: *Provided*, That no mineral lands shall be selected or purchased under the provisions of this act.

SEC. 2. *And be it further enacted.* That the land aforesaid, after being surveyed, shall be apportioned to the several States in sections or subdivisions of sections, not less than one quarter of a section; and whenever there are public lands in a State subject to sale at private entry at one dollar and twenty-five cents per acre, the quantity to which said State shall be entitled shall be selected from such lands within the limits of such State, and the Secretary of the Interior is hereby directed to issue to each of the States in which there is not the quantity of public lands subject to sale at private entry at one dollar and twenty-five cents per acre, to which said State may be entitled under the provisions of this act, land scrip to the amount in acres for the deficiency of its distributive share; said scrip to be sold by said States and the proceeds thereof applied to the uses and purposes prescribed in this act, and for no other use or purpose whatsoever: *Provided*, That in no case shall any State to which land scrip may thus be issued be allowed to locate the same within the limits of any other State, or of any Territory of the United States, but their assignees may thus locate said land scrip upon any of the unappropriated lands of the United States subject to sale at private entry at one dollar and twenty-five cents, or less, per acre: *And provided further*, That not more than one million acres shall be located by such assignees in any one of the States: *And provided further*, That no such location shall be made before one year from the passage of this act.

SEC. 3. *And be it further enacted*, That all the expenses of management, superintendence, and taxes from date of selection of said lands, previous to their sales, and all expenses incurred in the management and disbursement of the moneys which may be received therefrom, shall be paid by the States to which they may belong, out of the treasury of said States, so that the entire proceeds of the sale of said lands shall be applied without any diminution whatever to the purposes hereinafter mentioned.

SEC. 4. *And be it further enacted*, That all moneys derived from the sale of the lands aforesaid by the State to which the lands are apportioned, and from the sales of land scrip hereinbefore provided for, shall be invested in stocks of the United States, or of the States, or some other safe stocks, yielding not less than five per centum upon the par value of said stocks; and that the moneys so invested shall constitute a perpetual fund, the capital of which shall remain forever undiminished, (except so far as may be provided in section fifth of this act,) and the interest of which shall be inviolably appropriated, by each State which may take and claim the benefit of this act, to the endowment, support, and maintenance of at least one college where the leading object shall be, without excluding other scientific and classical studies, and including military tactics, to teach such branches of learning as are related to agriculture and the mechanic arts, in such manner as the legislatures of the States may respectively prescribe, in order to promote the liberal and practical education of the industrial classes in the several pursuits and professions in life.

SEC. 5. *And be it further enacted,* That the grant of land and land scrip hereby authorized shall be made on the following conditions, to which, as well as to the provisions hereinbefore contained, the previous assent of the several States shall be signified by legislative acts:

First. If any portion of the fund invested, as provided by the foregoing section, or any portion of the interest thereon, shall, by any action or contingency be diminished or lost, it shall be replaced by the State to which it belongs, so that the capital of the fund shall remain forever undiminished; and the annual interest shall be regularly applied without diminution to the purposes mentioned in the fourth section of this act, except that a sum, not exceeding ten per centum upon the amount received by any State under the provisions of this act, may be expended for the purchase of lands for sites or experimental farms, whenever authorized by the respective legislatures of said States.

Second. No portion of said fund, nor the interest thereon, shall be applied, directly or indirectly, under any pretense whatever, to the purchase, erection, preservation, or repair of any building or buildings.

Third. Any State which may take and claim the benefit of the provisions of this act shall provide, within five years, at least not less than one college, as described in the fourth section of this act, or the grant to such State shall cease; and said State shall be bound to pay the United States the amount received of any lands previously sold, and that the title to purchasers under the State shall be valid.

Fourth. An annual report shall be made regarding the progress of each college, recording any improvements and experiments made, with their costs and results, and such other matters, including State industrial and economical statistics, as may be supposed useful; one copy of which shall be transmitted by mail free, by each, to all the other colleges which may be endowed under the provisions of this act, and also one copy to Secretary of the Interior.

Fifth. When lands shall be selected from those which have been raised to double the minimum price, in consequence of railroad grants, they shall be computed to the States at the maximum price, and the number of acres proportionally diminished.

Sixth. No State while in a condition of rebellion or insurrection against the government of the United States shall be entitled to the benefit of this act.

Seventh. No State shall be entitled to the benefits of this act unless it shall express its acceptance thereof by its legislature within two years from the date of its approval by the President.

SEC. 6. *And be it further enacted,* That land scrip issued under the provisions of this act shall not be subject to location until after the first day of January, one thousand eight hundred and sixty-three.

SEC. 7. *And be it further enacted,* That the land officers shall receive the same fees for locating land scrip issued under the provisons of this act as is now allowed for the location of military bounty land warrants under existing laws: *Provided,* their maximum compensation shall not be thereby increased.

SEC. 8. *And be it further enacted,* That the Governors of the several States to which scrip shall be issued under this act shall be required to report annually to Congress all sales made of such scrip until the whole shall be disposed of, the amount received for the same, and what appropriation has been made of the proceeds. Approved, July 2, 1862.

REVEREND HORACE BUSHNELL ON THE NEED FOR A COLLEGE IN CALIFORNIA (1858)   From Horace Bushnell, *California: Its Characteristics and Prospects* (San Francisco, 1858), pp. 3–4, 14–16.

Whoever wishes, for health's sake or for any other reason, to change the sceneries or the objects and associations of his life, should set off, not for Europe, but for California. And this the more certainly, if he is a loving and sharp observer of nature; for nature meets us here in mood entirely new; so that we have even to make her acquaintance over again, going back, as it were, to be started in a fresh childhood. All our common, or previously formed impressions, calculations and weather-wisdoms are at fault. We find that we really understand nothing and have everything to learn. We begin to imagine, for example, that her way is to be thus, or thus; or that her operations are to be solved in this, or that manner, but we very soon discover that it will not hold. Our guess must be given up and we must try again. A person who is at all curious in the study of natural phenomena, will be held in a puzzle thus for whole months, and will nearly complete the cycle of the year, before he seems to himself to have come into any real understanding with the new world he is in; just as if he were sent on a visit to Jupiter, and wanted to sail round the sun with him, for at least once, and feel out his year, before he can be sure that he understands a single day.

California being to this extent a new world, having its own combinations, characters, and colors, it is not to be supposed that we can make any reader acquainted with it by words of description. The most we can hope to accomplish is, that by giving some notes on its physical and social characteristics, we may excite a more curious and possibly a more intelligent interest in California life, and the certainly great scenes preparing to be revealed in that far off, outside, isolated state of the Republic. It is not to be supposed that every particular representation or suggestion we may offer will be verified by the experiments and exact observations of science, or by the tests of moral and economical statistics; we only look on with our mere eyes, giving our impressions, and venturing what guesses and possible applications may occur to us.

The first and most difficult thing to apprehend respecting California is the climate, upon which, of course, depend the advantages of health and physical development, the growths and their conditions and kinds, and the *modus operandi*, or general cast, of the seasons. But this, again, is scarcely possible, without dismissing, first of all, the word *climate*, and substituting the plural climates. For it cannot be said of California, as of New England, or the Middle States, that it has a climate. On the contrary, it has a great multitude of them, curiously pitched together, at short distances, one from another, defying too, not seldom, our most accepted notions of the effects of latitude and altitude and the defences of mountain ranges. The only way, therefore, is to dismiss generalities, cease to look for a climate, and find, if we can, by what process the combinations and varieties are made; for when we get hold of the manner and going on of cause, all the varieties are easily reducible.

*   *   *

There remains a single topic to which, in the conclusion of our article, already too far extended, we must briefly refer, viz: to the effort now on foot to establish a College or University in California. The heaviest detraction, after all, from the future prospects of California, is in the fact that so many only go thither as adventurers, not meaning to stay, and that so many, often the most prosperous, are continually returning. And they do it in great part, because they cannot educate their families there, as their means allow them to desire. In the first place, many never take out their families for this reason, and in the next place, when they have done it, and their sons are grown up to the age of which they begin to want the best advantages, they return with them, and are so lost to the State as a family; for the distance, and the moral perils of a separation from parents are so great, that there is no alternative but a reemigration. This begets an unsettled feeling in those who remain, which makes them careless often of the good of the State, and besides it carries off a large per centage of the wealth created; for the families that return are commonly such as have been most successful, and all which they have gained they carry with them. And the probability is, that if the contemplated railroad were built across the continent, (which it will not be for a long time to come,) it would scarcely help them at all, but might rather hasten them in this losing process.

What they want, therefore, at this time, above all things else, is a good College, or University. Such an institution would do more to consolidate and settle their State, and to settle the confidence of their future, than even the railroad itself. There are no five States together, in our western world, which, if they had none at all, would want an institution of this kind so much as California. For the supply of this want, some of their best and ablest men are preparing. They have had a charter for three years, organizing the "College of California." Their Board of Trustees contains a representation of all the Christian denominations, who are united in cordiality and good understanding. They are said lately to have fixed on their site— on the eastern side of the Bay, opposite San Francisco. They have had a preparatory school for three years past, under the tuition of Rev. Henry Durant, an accomplished scholar and a Christian, and the design is to organize a Freshman Class the coming autumn.

What then is now wanted is the endowment, and for this everything is ready. To obtain this endowment in California, except in part, will now be impossible. Much of the wealth is not in the right hands; and where it is not, where there is every disposition to aid, the possibility is very much reduced by the heavy loads of debt, which many who ought to be rich are required just now to carry. When money will bring three per cent. per month, year by year, on perfect security, the lending party is not likely to put much of it in a College, and the borrowing party still less. Are there no great men in the East, no millionaires or less in computation, who will be induced to look at such an opportunity? Had we the fortune of but half a million in our editorial hands, we are quite sure of this, that whoever might want to assume the endowment of such an institution would have to be very quick in his action, or he would lose the chance. What an opportunity for a man of fortune, who has no object in life, no family to provide for, or none but such as are already rich enough, and who would be greatly more ennobled, by his name and example, as the founder of such an institution, than by all his property without a name. How many such too, are there, who are really meaning, when they die, to accomplish some great work with their money! Why not do it when they are living, and have a satisfaction of a consciousness enriched, and a heart enlarged by their beneficence? To have one's name on such an institution as this, connected with the great history, and with all the learning, and all the most forward influences of this New World on the Pacific, is a thought which might quicken the blood even of a man most sluggish and dull. For it is to win a greater honor, by many times, than the President of our great Republic. That is an honor, which, as the line grows longer, loses more and more its significance, till finally, it will signify as little to have been one of the Presidents as to have been one of the Doges of Venice. But the other, like the names of Harvard and Yale, will brighten and gather to itself a greater weight and power, as long as the tongue itself may exist. And the satisfaction one may have in this honor is sublimely justified in the fact, that he is not merely to be known, or mentioned in the future ages of the world—that might be a very common ambition, for who is there who does even naturally desire as much?—but is permitted to know that his name is to be a power, and to work for all the coming ages, growing brighter and doing more good than he himself while living. That is a legitimate and glorious ambition—the highest that a mortal can cherish. The Trustees, in the Appeal they published a year ago, placed the subject thus:

"Could some rich citizen, who can do it without injury to himself, step forward at this time of our beginning, and set his name upon the institution itself, by the side of a Harvard or a Yale, by subscribing a large part of the proposed endowment; giving us an opportunity, assisted by his beginning and example, to carry up the subscription even to the highest point we have named, he would be enriched by the sense of his munificence, as no man ever was or can be by the count of his money. We have no delicacy in respect to the customary honors conferred by universities, when they set the names of the benefactors on the halls, libraries and professorships endowed by their munificence; or when they drop the dry, impersonal name of their charter for one that represents the public spirit, and the living heart of a living man who could be more than rich, the patron of learning, the benefactor and father of coming ages. There are monuments that may well provoke a degree of ambition; not even an Egyptian pyramid raised over a man's ashes could so far ennoble him, as to have the learning and science of long ages and eternal realms of history superscribed to his name. And yet this better kind of monument is itself a power so beneficent, that he ought, even as duty, to desire it, and for no false modesty decline it. Such monuments are not like those of stone or brass, which simply stand doing nothing; they are monuments eternally fruitful, showing to men's eyes and ears what belongs to wealth, and what the founders of the times gone by have set as examples of beneficence."

THE ORGANIC ACT: AN ACT CREATING THE UNIVERSITY OF
CALIFORNIA (1868)   From *California Statutes, 1867–1868,* pp. 248–52.

T*he People of the State of California, represented in Senate and Assembly, do enact as follows:*

SECTION 1. A State University is hereby created, pursuant to the requirements of Section four, Article nine, of the Constitution of the State of California, and in order to devote to the largest purposes of education the benefaction made to the State of California under and by the provisions of an Act of Congress passed July second, eighteen hundred and sixty-two, entitled an Act donating land to the several States and Territories which may provide colleges for the benefit of agriculture and the mechanic arts. The said University shall be called the University of California, and shall be located upon the grounds heretofore donated to the State of California by the President and Board of Trustees of the College of California. The said University shall be under the charge and control of a Board of Directors, to be known and styled "the Regents of the University of California." The University shall have for its design, to provide instruction and complete education in all the departments of science, literature, art, industrial and professional pursuits, and general education, and also special courses of instruction for the professions of agriculture, the mechanic arts, mining, military science, civil engineering, law, medicine and commerce, and shall consist of various colleges, namely:

First—Colleges of Arts.

Second—A College of Letters.

Third—Such professional and other colleges as may be added thereto or connected therewith.

SEC. 2. Each full course of instruction shall consist of its appropriate studies, and shall continue for at least four years, and the Faculty, instructors and body of students in each course shall constitute a college, to be designated by its appropriate name. For this purpose there shall be organized as soon as the means appropriated therefor shall permit—

First—The following Colleges of Arts: A State College of Agriculture; a State College of Mechanic Arts; a State College of Mines; a State College of Civil Engineering; and such other Colleges of Arts as the Board of Regents may be able and find it expedient to establish.

Second—A State College of Letters.

Third—Colleges of Medicine, Law and other like professional colleges.

SEC. 3. A proper degree of each college shall be conferred at the end of the course upon such students as, having completed the same, shall, at the annual examination, be found proficient therein; but each college shall also have a partial course for those who may not desire to pursue a full course therein; and any resident of California, of the age of fourteen years or upwards, of approved moral character, shall have the right to enter himself in the University as a student at large, and receive tuition in any branch or branches of instruction at the time when the same are given in their regular course, on such terms as the Board of Regents may prescribe. The said Board of Regents shall endeavor so to arrange the several courses of instruction that the students of the different colleges and the students at large may be largely brought into social contact and intercourse with each other by attending the same lectures and branches of instruction.

HIGHER
EDUCATION

1533

SEC. 4. The College of Agriculture shall be first established; but in selecting the professors and instructors for the said College of Agriculture, the Regents shall, so far as in their power, select persons possessing such acquirements in their several vocations as will enable them to discharge the duties of professors in the several colleges of Mechanic Arts, of Mines and of Civil Engineering, and in such other colleges as may be hereafter established. As soon as practicable a system of moderate manual labor shall be established in connection with the Agricultural College, and upon its agricultural and ornamental grounds, having for its object practical education in agriculture, landscape gardening, the health of the students, and to afford them an opportunity by their earnings of defraying a portion of the expenses of their education. These advantages shall be open in the first instance to students in the College of Agriculture, who shall be entitled to a preference in that behalf.

SEC. 5. The College of Mechanic Arts shall be next established; and in organizing this, or any other college, the same regard hereinbefore indicated shall be had for the general requirements of each professor and instructor, so that he may be able to give general and special instruction in as many classes and courses of instruction as possible; and inasmuch as the original donation, out of which the plan of a State University has had its rise, was made to the State by virtue of the aforesaid Act of Congress entitled an Act donating land to the several States and Territories which may provide colleges for the benefit of agriculture and the mechanic arts, approved July second, eighteen hundred and sixty-two, the said Board of Regents shall always bear in mind that the College of Agriculture and the College of Mechanic Arts are an especial object of their care and superintendence, and that they shall be considered and treated as entitled primarily to the use of the funds donated for their establishment and maintenance by the said Act of Congress.

SEC. 6. The College of Mines and the College of Civil Engineering shall be next established, and such other Colleges of Arts as the Board of Regents may be able to establish with the means in their possession or under their control; and in order to fulfill the requirements of the said Act of Congress, all able-bodied male students of the University, whether pursuing full or partial courses in any college, or as students at large, shall receive instruction and discipline in military tactics in such manner and to such extent as the Regents shall prescribe, the requisite arms for which shall be furnished by the State.

SEC. 7. The Board of Regents, having in regard the said donation already made to the State by the President and Board of Trustees of the College of California, and their proposition to surrender all their property to the State for the benefit of the State University, and to become disincorporate and go out of existence as soon as the State shall organize the University, by adding a Classical College to the College of Arts, shall, as soon as they deem it practicable, establish a College of Letters. The College of Letters shall be co-existent with the aforesaid Colleges of Arts, and shall embrace a liberal course of instruction in language, literature and philosophy, together with such courses or parts of courses in the aforesaid Colleges of Arts as the authorities of the University shall prescribe. The degree of Bachelor of Arts, upon due examination, and afterwards the degree of Master of Arts, in usual course, shall be conferred upon the graduates of this college. But the provisions herein and hereinbefore contained regarding the order in which the said colleges shall be organized shall not be construed as directing or permitting the organization of any of the specified colleges to be unnecessarily delayed, but only as indicating the order in which said colleges shall be organized, beginning with the College of Agriculture and adding in succession to the body of instructors in that and the other colleges such other instructors as may be necessary to organize the other colleges successively in the order above indicated. Only the first year's course of instruction shall be provided for in each college at first, the other successive years courses being added in each year as the students advance to the same, until the full course in each college is established; *provided*, however, that the Board of Regents may organize at once the full course of the College of Letters, if in their judgment it is expedient so to do in order to allow the College of California to immediately convey the residue of its property to the State for the benefit of the University, and to become disincorporate and go out of existence, pursuant to its proposition to that effect.

SEC. 8. The Board of Regents may affiliate with the University, and make an integral part of the same, and incorporate therewith, any incorporated College of Medicine or of Law, or other special course of instruction now existing, or which may hereafter be created, upon such terms as to the respective corporations may be deemed expedient; and such college or colleges so affiliated shall retain the control of their own property, with their own Boards of Trustees, and their own Faculties and Presidents of the same, respectively, and the students of those colleges, recommended by the respective Faculties thereof, shall receive from the University the degree of those colleges; *provided*, however, that the President of the University shall be, ex officio, a member of the Faculty of each and every college of the University, and President of such Faculty.

SEC. 9. The examinations for degrees shall be annual, and the Board of Regents shall take measures to make such examinations thorough and complete. Students who shall have passed not less than a full year as resident students in any college, academy or school in this State, and, after examination by the respective Faculty of such college, academy or school, are recommended by such Faculty as proficient candidates for any degree in any regular course of the University, shall be entitled to be examined therefor at the annual examination; and, on passing such examination, shall receive such degree for that course, and the diploma of the University therefor, and shall rank and be considered in all respects as graduates of the University. All students of the University who have been resident students thereof for not less than one year, and all graduates of the University in any course, may present themselves for examination in any other course, or courses, at the annual examinations, and on passing such examination shall receive the degree and diploma of that course. Upon such examinations each professor and instructor of that course shall cast one vote upon each application for recommendation to the Board of Regents for a degree, and the votes shall be by ballot. In case the College of California shall surrender its property to the University, and said donation shall be accepted by the Board of Regents, and said College of California shall thereafter become disincorporate in pursuance of its proposition heretofore made to that effect, the graduates and those who shall have received the degrees of that college shall receive the degrees from the University, and be considered in all respects graduates of the same. And the last above expressed provisions shall apply to the previous graduates of any incorporated College of Medicine, Law, or other professional college which shall become affiliated with the University, as herein otherwise provided. The Board of Regents shall also confer certificates of proficiency in any branch of study upon such students of the University as, upon examination, shall be found entitled to the same. The style of diplomas and degrees shall be: "University of California, College of Agriculture;" or, with the name of the other respective college; but honorary degrees for the higher degrees, not lower than that of Master of Arts, may be conferred, with the designation of the University alone, upon persons distinguished in literature, science and art.

SEC. 10. Scholarships may be established in the University by the State, associations or individuals, for the purpose of affording tuition in any course of the University, free from the ordinary charges, to any scholar in the public schools of the State who shall distinguish himself in study, according to the recommendation of his teachers, and shall pass the previous examination required for the grade at which he wishes to enter the University, or for the purpose of private benefaction; *provided,* that the said scholarships shall be approved and accepted by the Board of Regents.

SEC. 11. The general government and superintendence of the University shall vest in a Board of Regents, to be denominated the "Regents of the University of California," who shall become incorporated under the general laws of the State of California by that corporate name and style. The said Board shall consist of twenty-two members, all of whom shall be citizens and permanent residents of the State of California, . . .

*   *   *

DESCRIPTION OF EARLY DAYS AT THE UNIVERSITY OF CALIFORNIA, BERKELEY (1869)   From William Dallan Armes, ed., *Autobiography of Joseph Le Conte* (New York, 1903), pp. 243, 251, 252.

The University . . . was opened on the twentieth of September, 1869, when I entered on my duties. Eleven students were inherited from the College of California;—twenty-five entered the freshman class, and one or two enrolled as special students, a total of about thirty-eight.—

The University of California received from the College of California not only the buildings in Oakland—, but also a magnificent tract of land some five miles to the north, which it had acquired as a site for new buildings. While the laboratories and recitation halls were building in Berkeley, as the new site was christened, the University used the old buildings in Oakland. In June, 1873, two of the new buildings were completed and the commencement exercises were held in Berkeley. During the rest of that year and the whole of the next the University was literally on wheels. There were no accommodations at Berkeley, so students and faculty went out from Oakland in the morning and came back in the afternoon, a horsecar line having been built for the express purpose.

The side of the University is certainly one of the most beautiful in the world. Behind the Berkeley hills, with their softly rounded forms mantled with green, rise to a height of over two thousand feet within the distance of a mile; in front the ground slopes gently to the noble San Francisco Bay, with its bold islands.

COMPARISON OF THE GERMAN AND THE AMERICAN UNIVERSITY

(1872–73)   From James Morgan Hart, *German Universities: A Narrative of Personal Experience* (New York, 1874), pp. 249–61, 264–65, 267–68.

I revisited Germany in 1872–3. In that time I studied at Leipsic, Marburg, and Berlin, and passed a summer at Vienna. Brought thus in contact with professors, students and men of letters in the great German centers of thought, I had ample opportunity of reviewing and modifying early impressions, and of judging the university system as a whole. I venture to offer these remarks, then, as the result of recent comparative investigation.

The first question that suggests itself is naturally this,

I. WHAT IS A UNIVERSITY?

To the German mind the collective idea of a university implies a *Zweck*, an object of study, and two *Bedingungen*, or conditions. The object is *Wissenschaft*; the conditions are *Lehrfreiheit* and *Lernfreiheit*. By *Wissenschaft* the Germans mean knowledge in the most exalted sense of that term, namely, the ardent, methodical, independent search after truth in any and all of its forms, but wholly irrespective of utilitarian application. *Lehrfreiheit* means that the one who teaches, the professor or *Privatdocent*, is free to teach what he chooses, as he chooses. *Lernfreiheit* or the freedom of learning, denotes the emancipation of the student from *Schulzwang*, compulsory drill by recitation.

If the object of an institution is anything else than knowledge as above defined, or if either freedom of teaching or freedom of learning is wanting, that institution, no matter how richly endowed, no matter how numerous its students, no matter how imposing its buildings, is not, in the eye of a German, a *university*. On the other hand, a small, out-of-the-way place like Rostock, with only thirty-four professors and docents, and one hundred and thirty-five students, is nevertheless as truly a university as Leipsic, where the numbers are one hundred and fifty and three thousand respectively, because Rostock aims at theoretical knowledge and meets the requirements of free teaching and free study. The difference is one of size, not of species.

If we examine the list of lectures and hours of universities like Leipsic, Berlin, and Vienna, we shall be overwhelmed, at first sight, with the amount and the variety of literary and scientific labor announced. The field seems boundless. All that human ingenuity can suggest is apparently represented. On examining more closely, however, we shall find that this seemingly boundless field has its limits, which are very closely traced and which are not exceeded. Strange as it may sound to the American, who is accustomed to gauge spiritual greatness by big numbers and extravagant pretensions, a German university, even the greatest, perceives what it can do and what it *can not do*.

It is not a place "where any man can study anything." Its elevated character makes it all the more modest. It contents itself with the theoretical, and leaves to other institutions the practical and the technical. The list of studies and hours for Leipsic in the semester 1872–3 fills thirty octavo pages. In all that list we shall discover scarcely one course of work that can be called in strictness practical. A German university has one and only one object: to train thinkers. It does not aim at producing poets, painters, sculptors, engineers, miners, architects, bankers,

HIGHER
EDUCATION

1537

manufacturers. For these, the places of instruction are the Art Schools of Dresden, Munich, Düsseldorf, the Commercial Schools at Bremen, Hamburg, Berlin, Frankfort, the Polytechnicums at Hanover, Frankenberg, Stuttgart, etc. Even in the professions themselves, theory and practice are carefully distinguished, and the former alone is considered as falling legitimately within the sphere of university instruction. Taking up the four faculties in order: theology, law, medicine, philosophy, and watching them at work, we shall perceive that the evident tendency of their method is to produce theologians rather than pastors, jurists rather than lawyers, theorizers in medicine rather than practitioners, investigators, scholars, speculative thinkers rather than technologists and school-teachers. Yet every pastor, lawyer, doctor, teacher, botanist, geologist has passed through the university course. What is meant, then, by the assertion that the university gives only theoretical training? Do not the practical men in all the professions receive their professional outfit at the university and can receive it nowhere else? The seeming discrepancy is to be explained only by considering the university as a permanent, self-supporting institution, a world in itself, existing for itself, rather than a mere ladder by which to ascend from a lower to a higher plane. Self-supporting, I mean, of course, in the sense that the university is a detached organism assimilating and growing in accordance with its own laws. In a pecuniary sense, it is wholly or almost wholly dependent upon state subvention. The distinction, subtle as it may appear, is essential in forming a just conception of the character of university work. The university supplies itself with its educational staff exclusively from its own graduate members, who pass their entire lives within its precincts. The professors, assistant-professors, docents whose names one reads in the catalogue of Berlin or Leipsic or Heidelberg are one and all, with scarcely an exception, men who started in life as theoreticians and never made the effort to become practitioners. To them the university was not a mere preparatory school, where they might remain long enough to get their theoretical training, and then turn their backs upon it forever. On the contrary, it was an end, a career in itself. They have always been university men, and never expect to become anything else. In this place I must guard against being misunderstood. The reader would receive a very unfair impression of Göttingen, for instance, if he were to infer, from what has been said, that the Göttingen faculty is made up exclusively of Göttingen graduates. Quite the reverse is the case. Probably two thirds come from elsewhere. As a rule, the young *Privatdocent* receives his first call as professor from a university where he has not been known as a student. There exists in this respect complete parity among the German institutions of learning. The feeling which prompts an American college to prefer its own graduates for professors is something quite unknown in Germany. I leave it to the reader's judgement to decide which of the two systems is better: that of liberal selection, or that of "Breeding-in." When I speak of a university as recruiting exclusively from its graduates, I mean neither Berlin nor Leipsic nor Heidelberg in particular, but the twenty universities of the German empire regarded as one body, the members of which are perfectly co-ordinate. Professors and docents, and even students, pass from one to another with a restlessness, we might say, that would be surprising in America, but which is looked upon in Germany as a matter of course. It is the exception, not the rule, when a man passes his entire career as instructor in one place. The key-note of the system is simply this. To those who are connected with the university in any instructional capacity whatever, it is an end and not a means, a life and not a phase of life, a career and not a discipline. The professors are not selected from among the leading lawyers, pastors, doctors, teachers, scientists of the country or province. When a chair already existing becomes vacant, or a new chair is created, and the question of filling it comes up, the Senatus Academicus does not scrutinize the bench or the bar or the gymnasium for an available man. It endeavors to ascertain who is the most promising *Privatdocent*, either in its own midst or at some other seat of learning, the young man who has made his mark by recent publications or discoveries. The newly organized university of Strassburg is a signal instance in point. Within two years after the close of the French war, Strassburg was opened with a full corps of instructors in all the departments. The total number at present is eighty. Yet of these eighty not one, so far as I can ascertain, is what might be called a practitioner. They are all full or half-professors or docents called from other institutions of learning. One who is familiar with the muster-roll of the universities can resolve the Strassburg list into its elements, saying: This man came from Berlin, that one from Vienna, that one from Würzburg, and so on. The reader will probably say? Is not this the case in America also? Are not our college professors all college graduates? To which the answer must be: Not in the same way, not to the same extent. How many of our college professors have been professors, and nothing else? How many have qualified themselves directly for the respective chairs which they occupy, by a life of special study? How many of them formed the resolve while still students, to lead a college life forever, to devote themselves exclusively to instructing others in turn, either at their own Alma Mater or at some other college? I do not have in view such institutions as Yale or Harvard, old, well endowed, fed from the rich soil of New England culture. I mean the typical American college as it exists in the Middle, Southern, and Western States. How many of the professors have been in business, or tried their skill at farming, engineering, journalism? Has or has not the professor of Latin served an apprenticeship as mathematical tutor, or kept a boarding school for young ladies? How few of the hundreds and thousands of men, from New York to San Francisco, calling themselves professors, can say with a comfortable degree of pride: I selected my specialty in youth, I have pursued it without intermission, without deviation ever since, and I have produced such and such tangible evidences of my industry as a specialist.

No, the reader may rest assured that the character and atmosphere of a German university differ radically from the character and atmosphere of the typical American college. It is a difference of kind, not merely of degree. Comparisons, according to the popular adage, are odious. Yet even at the risk of giving offense, I take the liberty of drawing a comparison that may serve, perhaps, to throw some light on this vital point. At all events, the comparison shall be a just one. Marburg, in Hesse, has at present 430 students; Princeton, my Alma Mater, has 420. The numbers, then, are almost identical. Each is located in a small country town. Yet Princeton has, all told, not more than 18 professors and tutors; Marburg has 62. Among them are men renowned throughout the world for their original investigations. The same might be said, indeed, of the Princeton faculty, but only with grave restrictions. No one professor at Princeton has the opportunity of working either himself or his students up to his or their full capacity. The instruction goes by routine, each professor contributing his quota to the supposed general development of all the students in a body. At Marburg there is the fourfold division of faculties; there are students pursuing theology, law, medicine, classic philology, modern philology, the natural sciences, history, orientalia. Each instructor has his select band of disciples, upon whom he acts and who re-act upon him. There is the same quiet, scholarly atmosphere, the same disregard for bread-and-butter study, the same breadth of culture, depth of insight, liberality of opinion and freedom of conduct, that one finds in the most favored circles of Leipsic, Berlin, Heidelberg, or Vienna.

During every hour of the two months that I passed at Marburg, I was made to feel that a German university, however humble, is a world in and for itself; that its aim is not to turn out clever, pushing, ambitious graduates, but to engender culture.

This condition is both cause and effect. Many of the students who attend the university do so simply with a view to becoming in time professors. The entire *personnel* of the faculty is thus a close corporation, a spiritual order perpetuating itself after the fashion of the Roman Catholic hierarchy. Inasmuch as every professional man and every schoolteacher of the higher grades has to pass through the university, it follows that the shaping of the intellectual interests of the country is in the hands of a select few, who are highly educated, perfectly homogeneous in character and sympathies, utterly indifferent to the turmoils and ambitions of the outer-world, who regulate their own lives and mould the dispositions of those dependent upon them according to the principles of abstract truth. The quality of university education, then, is determined by its object, and that object is to train not merely skillful practitioners, *but also future professors.* In fact, the needs of the former class are subordinated to the needs of the latter. In this respect, the faculty acts, unconsciously, in accordance with the promptings of the instinct of self-preservation. If thorough scientific culture is an essential element in national life, it must be maintained at every cost. The slightest flaw in the continuity of spiritual descent would be as dangerous as a break in the apostolic succession of the church. Every inducement, therefore, must be held out to young men to qualify themselves in season for succeeding to their present instructors. The lectures and other instruction must be adapted to train and stimulate *Privat-docenten,* for they are the ones who are to seize and wear the mantles of the translated Elijahs. For every professor dead or removed, there must be one or two instantly ready to fill his place.

This is not the *avowed* object of the university course. One might pass many years in Germany without perceiving it stated so bluntly. Yet I am persuaded that it is at bottom the determining factor in the constitution of university life. It will explain to us many incidental features for which there is elsewhere no analogy; for instance, the sovereign contempt that all German students evince for everything that savors of "bread-and-butter." The students have caught, in this respect, the tone of their instructors. Even such of them as have no intention of becoming *Privat-docenten* pass three and four years of their life in generous devotion to study pure and simple, without casting a single forward glance to future "business." All thought of practical life is kept in abeyance. The future practitioners and the future theoreticians sit side by side on the same bench, fight on the same *Mensur,* drink at the same *Kneipe,* hear the same lectures, use the same books, have every sentiment in common; hence the perfect *rapport* that exists in Germany between the lawyer and the jurist, the pastor and the theologian, the practicing doctor and the speculative pathologist, the gymnasial teacher of Latin and Greek and the professed philologist. Hence the celerity with which innovating ideas spread in Germany. . . .

To repeat, the university instruction of Germany does not attempt to train successful practical men, unless it be indirectly, by giving its students a profound insight into the principles of the science, and then turning them adrift to deduce the practice as well as they can from the carefully inculcated theory. Its chief task, that to which all its energies are directed, is the development of great thinkers, men who will extend the boundaries of knowledge.

Viewed from this point, then, the two conditions, *Lehrfreiheit* and *Lernfreiheit,* are not only natural and proper, but are absolutely essential. Were the object of higher education merely to train "useful and honorable members of society," to use the conventional phrase of the panegyrists of the American system, the German universities might possibly change their character. In place of professors free to impart the choicest results of their investigations, they might substitute pedagogues with text-books and class-books, noting down the relative merits and demerits of daily recitations. In place of students free to attend or to stay away, free to agree with the professor or to differ, free to read what they choose and to study after their own fashion, they might create a set of undergraduates reciting glibly from set lessons and regarding each circumvention of the teacher as so much clear gain. . . . The professor has but one aim in life: scholarly renown. To effect this, he must have the liberty of selecting his studies and pushing them to their extreme limits. The student has but one desire: to assimilate his instructor's learning, and, if possible, to add to it. He must, therefore, be his own master. He must be free to accept and reject, to judge and prove all things for himself, to train himself step by step for grappling with the great problems of nature and history. Accountable only to himself for his opinions and mode of living, he shakes off spiritual bondage and become an independent thinker. He *must* think for himself, for there is no one set over him as spiritual adviser and guide, prescribing the work for each day and each hour, telling him what he is to believe and what to disbelieve, and marking him up or down accordingly.

The universities occupy, then, an impregnable position. Recruiting their tuitional forces (*Lehrkräfte*) from among themselves, they are independent of the outer world.

✻   ✻   ✻

II. PROFESSORS

The character of the German professor will be best understood by first disposing of the preliminary question: What is he not?

The professor is not a teacher, in the English sense of the term; he is a specialist. He is not responsible for the success of his hearers. He is responsible only for the quality of his instruction. His duty begins and ends with himself.

No man can become a professor in a German university without having given evidence, in one way or another, that he has pursued a certain line of study, and produced results worthy to be called novel and important. In other words, to become a professor, he must first have been a special investigator. Professional chairs are not conferred "on general principles," or because the candidate is "a good teacher," or "well qualified to govern the young." Neither is there such springing about from one department of study to another as we observe in America. . . .

The chief attraction in the professorial career, however, is the nature of the work itself. No human lot, it is true, is without its trials. The life of a professor is anything but a bed of roses. It means severe intellectual toil from morning till evening, from manhood to declining years. But there is a freedom about it that is inexpressibly fascinating. The professor is his own master. His time is not wasted in cudgeling the wits of refractory or listless reciters. His temper is not ruffled by the freaks or the downright insults of mutinous youths. He lectures upon his chosen subject, comments upon his favorite Greek or Roman or early German or Sanscrit author, expounds some recently discovered mathematical theorem, discusses one or another of the grave problems of history or morals, and is accountable only to his own conscience of what is true and what is false. He lectures only to those who are willing and able to hear. He is sustained by the consciousness that his words are not scattered by the wayside, but that they fall upon soil prepared to receive them, and will bring forth new fruit in turn. His relation with his hearers is that of one gentleman speaking to another.

DESCRIPTION OF EARLY DAYS AT CORNELL (c. 1860)   From *Selected Chapters from the Autobiography of Andrew D. White* (Ithaca, N.Y., 1939), pp. 78–79, 83–84, 93, 115–17, 121–27.

Recalled to Syracuse after five years in Michigan, my old desire to see a university rising in the State of New York was stronger than ever. Michigan had shown me some of my ideals made real; why might not our own much greater commonwealth be similarly blessed?

The first thing was to devise a plan for a suitable faculty. As I felt that this must not demand too large an outlay, I drew up a scheme providing for a few resident teachers supported by endowments, and for a body of nonresident professors or lecturers supported by fees. These lecturers were to be chosen from the most eminent professors in the existing colleges and from the best men then in the public-lecture field; and my confidant in the matter was George William Curtis, who entered into it heartily, and who afterward, in his speech at my inauguration as president of Cornell, referred to it in a way which touched me deeply.

The next thing was to decide upon a site. It must naturally be in the central part of the State; and, rather curiously, that which I then most coveted, frequently visited, walked about, and inspected was the rising ground southeast of Syracuse since selected by the Methodists for their institution which takes its name from that city.

My next effort was to make a beginning of an endowment, and for this purpose I sought to convert Gerrit Smith. He was, for those days, enormously wealthy. His property, which was estimated at from two to three millions of dollars, he used munificently; and his dear friend and mine, Samuel Joseph May, had told me that it was not too much to hope that Mr. Smith might do something for the improvement of higher instruction. To him, therefore, I wrote, proposing that if he would contribute an equal sum to a university at Syracuse, I would give to it one half of my own property. In his answer he gave reasons why he could not join in the plan, and my scheme seemed no nearer reality than my former air-castles. It seemed, indeed, to have faded away like

"The baseless fabric of a vision"

and to have left

"Not a wrack behind"—

when all its main features were made real in a way and by means utterly unexpected; for now began the train of events which led to my acquaintance, friendship, and close alliance with the man through whom my plans became a reality, larger and better than any ever seen in my dreams—Ezra Cornell.

. . . I was one day going down from the State Capitol, when Mr. Cornell joined me

EDUCATION
IN THE
UNITED STATES

1542

and began conversation. He was, as usual, austere and reserved in appearance; but I had already found that below this appearance there was a warm heart and noble purpose. No observant associate could fail to notice that the only measures in the legislature which he cared for were those proposing some substantial good to the State or nation, and that he despised all political wrangling and partizan jugglery.

On this occasion, after some little general talk, he quietly said, "I have about half a million dollars more than my family will need: what is the best thing I can do with it for the State?" I answered: "Mr. Cornell, the two things most worthy of aid in any country are charity and education; but, in our country, the charities appeal to everybody. Any one can understand the importance of them, and the worthy poor or unfortunate are sure to be taken care of. As to education, the lower grades will always be cared for in the public schools by the State; but the institutions of the highest grade, without which the lower can never be thoroughly good, can be appreciated by only a few. The policy of our State is to leave this part of the system to individuals; it seems to me, then, that if you have half a million to give, the best thing you can do with it is to establish or strengthen some institution for higher instruction." I then went on to show him the need of a larger institution for such instruction than the State then had; that such a college or university worthy of the State would require far more in the way of faculty and equipment than most men supposed; that the time had come when scientific and technical education must be provided for in such an institution; and that education in history and literature should be the bloom of the whole growth.

He listened attentively, but said little. The matter seemed to end there; but not long afterward he came to me and said: "I agree with you that the land-grant fund ought to be kept together, and that there should be a new institution fitted to the present needs of the State and the country. I am ready to pledge to such an institution a site and five hundred thousand dollars as an addition to the land-grant endowment, instead of three hundred thousand, as I proposed at Rochester."

As may well be imagined, I hailed this proposal joyfully, and soon sketched out a bill embodying his purpose so far as education was concerned. But here I wish to say that, while Mr. Cornell urged Ithaca as the site of the proposed institution, he never showed any wish to give his own name to it. The suggestion to that effect was mine. He at first doubted the policy of it; but, on my insisting that it was in accordance with time-honored American usage, as shown by the namees of Harvard, Yale, Dartmouth, Amherst, Bowdoin, Brown, Williams, and the like, he yielded.

✻   ✻   ✻

Mr. Cornell had asked me, from time to time, whether I could suggest any person for the presidency of the university. I mentioned various persons, and presented the arguments in their favor. One day he said to me quietly that he also had a candidate; I asked him who it was, and he said that he preferred to keep the matter to himself until the next meeting of the trustees. Nothing more passed between us on that subject. I had no inkling of his purpose, but thought it most likely that his candidate was a Western gentleman whose claims had been strongly pressed upon him. When the trustees came together, and the subject was brought up, I presented the merits of various gentlemen, especially of one already at the head of an important college in the State, who, I thought, would give us success. Upon this, Mr. Cornell rose, and, in a very simple but earnest speech, presented my name. It was entirely unexpected by me, and I endeavored to show the trustees that it was impossible for me to take the place in view of other duties; that it needed a man of more robust health, of greater age, and of wider reputation in the State. But Mr. Cornell quietly persisted, our colleagues declared themselves unanimously of his opinion, and, with many misgivings, I gave a provisional acceptance.

*   *   *

Although my formal election to the university presidency did not take place until 1867, the duties implied by that office had already been discharged by me during two years.

While Mr. Cornell devoted himself to the financial questions arising from the new foundation, he intrusted all other questions to me. Indeed, my duties may be said to have begun when, as chairman of the Committee on Education in the State Senate, I resisted all efforts to divide the land-grant fund between the People's College and the State Agricultural College; to have been continued when I opposed the frittering away of the entire grant among more than twenty small sectarian colleges; and to have taken a more direct form when I drafted the educational clauses of the university charter and advocated it before the legislature and in the press. This advocacy was by no means a light task. The influential men who flocked to Albany, seeking to divide the fund among various sects and localities, used arguments often plausible and sometime forcible. These I dealt with on various occasions, but especially in a speech before the State Senate in 1865, in which was shown the character of the interested opposition, the farcical equipment of the People's College, the failure of the State Agricultural College, the inadequacy of the sectarian colleges, even though they called themselves universities; and I did all in my power to communicate to my colleagues something of my own enthusiasm for a university suitably endowed, free from sectarian trammels, centrally situated, and organized to meet fully the wants of the State as regarded advanced education, general and technical.

Three points I endeavored especially to impress upon them in this speech. First, that while, as regards primary education, the policy of the State should be diffusion of resources, it should be, as regards university education, concentration of resources. Secondly, that sectarian colleges could not do the work required. Thirdly, that any institution for higher education in the State must form an integral part of the whole system of public instruction; that the university should not be isolated from the school system, as were the existing colleges, but that it should have a living connection with the system, should push its roots down into it and through it, drawing life from it and sending life back into it. Mr. Cornell accepted this view at once. Mr. Horace Greeley, who, up to that time, had supported the People's College, was favorably impressed by it, and, more than anything else, it won for us his support. To insure this vital connection of the proposed university with the school system, I provided in the charter for four "State scholarships" in each of the one hundred and twenty-eight Assembly districts. These scholarships were to be awarded to the best scholars in the public schools of each district, after due examination, one each year; each scholarship entitling the holder to free instruction in the university for four years. Thus the university and the schools were bound closely together by the constant and living tie of five hundred and twelve students. As the number of Assembly districts under the new constitution was made, some years later, one hundred and fifty, the number of these competitive free scholarships is now six hundred. They have served their purpose well. Thirty years of this connection have greatly uplifted the whole school system of the State, and made the university a life-giving power in it; while this uplifting of the school system has enabled the university steadily to raise and improve its own standard of instruction.

*   *   *

Just previously to my election to the university presidency I had presented a "plan of organization," which, having been accepted and printed by the trustees, formed the mold for the main features of the new institution; and early among my duties came the selection and nomination of professors. In these days one is able to choose from a large body of young men holding fellowships in the various larger universities of the United States; but then, with the possible exception of two or three at Harvard, there was not a fellowship, so far as I can remember, in the whole country. The choosing of professors was immeasurably more difficult than at present. With reference to this point, a very eminent graduate of Harvard then volunteered to me some advice, which at first sight looked sound, but which I soon found to be inapplicable. He said: "You must secure at any cost the foremost men in the United States in every department. In this way alone can a real university be created." Trying the Socratic method upon him, I asked, in reply, "How are we to get such men? The foremost man in American science is undoubtedly Agassiz, but he has refused all offers of high position at Paris made him by the French Emperor. The main objects of his life are the creation of his great museum at Harvard and his investigations and instruction in connection with it; he has declared that he has 'no time to waste in making money!' What sum or what inducement of any sort can transfer him from Harvard to a new institution on the distant hills of central New York? So, too, with the most eminent men at the other universities. What sum will draw them to us from Harvard, Yale, Columbia, the University of Virginia, and the University of Michigan? An endowment twice as large as ours would be unavailing." Therefore it was that I broached, as a practical measure, in my "plan of organization," the system which I had discussed tentatively with George William Curtis several years before, and to which he referred afterward in his speech at the opening of the university at Ithaca. This was to take into our confidence the leading professors in the more important institutions of learning, and to secure from them, not the ordinary, conventional paper testimonials, but confidential information as to their young men likely to do the best work in various fields, to call these young men to our resident professorships, and then to call the most eminent men we could obtain for non-resident professorships or lectureships. This idea was carried out to the letter. The most eminent men in various universities gave us confidential advice; and thus it was that I was enabled to secure a number of bright, active, energetic young men as our resident professors, mingling with them two or three older men, whose experience and developed judgment seemed necessary in the ordinary conduct of our affairs.

As to the other part of the plan, I secured Agassiz, Lowell, Curtis, Bayard Taylor, Goldwin Smith, Theodore Dwight, George W. Greene, John Stanton Gould, and at a later period Froude, Freeman, and others, as non-resident professors and lecturers. Of the final working of this system I shall speak later.

CHARLES W. ELIOT'S INAUGURAL ADDRESS AS PRESIDENT OF
HARVARD (1869)   From Charles W. Eliot, *Educational Reform: Essays and Addresses*
(New York, 1898), pp. 1–6, 10–18, 30–38.

The endless controversies whether language, philosophy, mathematics, or
science supplies the best mental training, whether general education should be
chiefly literary or chiefly scientific, have no practical lesson for us to-day. This
University recognizes no real antagonism between literature and science, and
consents to no such narrow alternatives as mathematics or classics, science or
metaphysics. We would have them all, and at their best. To observe keenly, to
reason soundly, and to imagine vividly are operations as essential as that of clear
and forcible expression; and to develop one of these faculties, it is not necessary to
repress and dwarf the others. A university is not closely concerned with the
applications of knowledge, until its general education branches into professional.
Poetry and philosophy and science do indeed conspire to promote the material
welfare of mankind; but science no more than poetry finds its best warrant in its
utility. Truth and right are above utility in all realms of thought and action.

It were a bitter mockery to suggest that any subject whatever should be taught
less than it now is in American colleges. The only conceivable aim of a college
government in our day is to broaden, deepen, and invigorate American teaching in
all branches of learning. It will be generations before the best of American
institutions of education will get growth enough to bear pruning. The descendants
of the Pilgrim Fathers are still very thankful for the parched corn of learning.

Recent discussions have added pitifully little to the world's stock of wisdom
about the staple of education. Who blows to-day such a ringing trumpet-call to the
study of language as Luther blew? Hardly a significant word has been added in two
centuries to Milton's description of the unprofitable way to study languages. Would
any young American learn how to profit by travel, that foolish beginning but
excellent sequel to education, he can find no apter advice than Bacon's. The
practice of England and America is literally centuries behind the precept of the best
thinkers upon education. A striking illustration may be found in the prevailing
neglect of the systematic study of the English language. How lamentably true to-day
are these words of Locke: "If any one among us have a facility or purity more than
ordinary in his mother-tongue, it is owing to chance, or his genius, or anything
rather than to his education or any care of his teacher."

The best result of the discussion which has raged so long about the relative
educational value of the main branches of learning is the conviction that there is
room for them all in a sound scheme, provided that right methods of teaching be
employed. It is not because of the limitation of their faculties that boys of eighteen
come to college, having mastered nothing but a few score pages of Latin and Greek,
and the bare elements of mathematics. Not nature, but an unintelligent system of
instruction from the primary school through the college, is responsible for the fact
that many college graduates have so inadequate a conception of what is meant by
scientific observation, reasoning, and proof. It is possible for the young to get actual
experience of all the principal methods of thought. There is a method of thought in
language, and a method in mathematics, and another of natural and physical
science, and another of faith. With wise direction, even a child would drink at all

these springs. The actual problem to be solved is not what to teach, but how to teach. . . .

*   *   *

With good methods, we may confidently hope to give young men of twenty to twenty-five an accurate general knowledge of all the main subjects of human interest, besides a minute and thorough knowledge of the one subject which each may select as his principal occupation in life. To think this impossible is to despair of mankind; for unless a general acquaintance with many branches of knowledge, good so far as it goes, be attainable by great numbers of men, there can be no such thing as an intelligent public opinion; and in the modern world the intelligence of public opinion is the one indispensable condition of social progress.

What has been said of needed reformation in methods of teaching the subjects which have already been nominally admitted to the American curriculum applies not only to the university, but to the preparatory schools of every grade down to the primary. The American college is obliged to supplement the American school. Whatever elementary instruction the schools fail to give, the college must supply. The improvement of the schools has of late years permitted the college to advance the grade of its teaching, and adapt the methods of its later years to men instead of boys. This improvement of the college reacts upon the schools to their advantage; and this action and reaction will be continuous. A university is not built in the air, but on social and literary foundations which preceding generations have bequeathed. If the whole structure needs rebuilding, it must be rebuilt from the foundation. Hence, sudden reconstruction is impossible in our high places of education. Such inducements as the College can offer for enriching and enlarging the course of study pursued in preparatory schools, the Faculty has recently decided to give. The requirements in Latin and Greek grammar are to be set at a thorough knowledge of forms and general principles; the lists of classical authors accepted as equivalents for the regular standards are to be enlarged; an acquaintance with physical geography is to be required; the study of elementary mechanics is to be recommended, and prizes are to be offered for reading aloud, and for the critical analysis of passages from English authors. At the same time the University will take to heart the counsel which it gives to others.

In every department of learning the University would search out by trial and reflection the best methods of instruction. The University believes in the thorough study of language. It contends for all languages—Oriental, Greek, Latin, Romance, German, and especially for the mother-tongue; seeing in them all one institution, one history, one means of discipline, one department of learning. In teaching languages, it is for this American generation to invent, or to accept from abroad, better tools than the old; to devise, or to transplant from Europe, prompter and more comprehensive methods than the prevailing; and to command more intelligent labor, in order to gather rapidly and surely the best fruit of that culture and have time for other harvests.

The University recognizes the natural and physical sciences as indispensable branches of education, and has long acted upon this opinion; but it would have science taught in a rational way, objects and instruments in hand—not from books merely, not through the memory chiefly, but by the seeing eye and the informing fingers. Some of the scientific scoffers at gerund grinding and nonsense verses might well look at home; the prevailing methods of teaching science, the world over, are, on the whole, less intelligent than the methods of teaching language. The University would have scientific studies in school and college and professional school develop and discipline those powers of the mind by which science has been created and is daily nourished—the powers of observation, the inductive faculty, the sober imagination, the sincere and proportionate judgment. A student in the elements gets no such training by studying even a good text-book, though he really master it, nor yet by sitting at the feet of the most admirable lecturer.

If there be any subject which seems fixed and settled in its educational aspects, it is the mathematics; yet there is no department of the University which has been, during the last fifteen years, in such a state of vigorous experiment upon methods and appliances of teaching as the mathematical department. It would be well if the primary schools had as much faith in the possibility of improving their way of teaching multiplication.

The important place which history, and mental, moral, and political philosophy, should hold in any broad scheme of education is recognized of all; but none know so well how crude are the prevailing methods of teaching these subjects as those who teach them best. They cannot be taught from books alone, but must be vivified and illustrated by teachers of active, comprehensive, and judicial mind. To learn by rote a list of dates is not to study history. Mr. Emerson says that history is biography. In a deep sense this is true. Certainly, the best way to impart the facts of history to the young is through the quick interest they take in the lives of the men and women who fill great historical scenes or epitomize epochs. From the centers so established, their interest may be spread over great areas. For the young especially, it is better to enter with intense sympathy into the great moments of history, than to stretch a thin attention through its weary centuries.

Philosophical subjects should never be taught with authority. They are not established sciences; they are full of disputed matters, open questions, and bottomless speculations. It is not the function of the teacher to settle philosophical and political controversies for the pupil, or even to recommend to him any one set of opinions as better than another. Exposition, not imposition, of opinions is the professor's part. The student should be made acquainted with all sides of these controversies, with the salient points of each system; he should be shown what is still in force of institutions or philosophies mainly outgrown, and what is new in those now in vogue. The very word "education" is a standing protest against dogmatic teaching. The notion that education consists in the authoritative inculcation of what the teacher deems true may be logical and appropriate in a convent, or a seminary for priests, but it is intolerable in universities and public schools, from primary to professional. The worthy fruit of academic culture is an open mind, trained to careful thinking, instructed in the methods of philosophic investigation, acquainted in a general way with the accumulated thought of past generations, and penetrated with humility. It is thus that the university in our day serves Christ and the church.

*   *   *

The rigorous examination for admission has one good effect throughout the college course: it prevents a waste of instruction upon incompetent persons. A school with a low standard for admission and a high standard of graduation, like West Point, is obliged to dismiss a large proportion of its students by the way. Hence much individual distress, and a great waste of resources, both public and private. But, on the other hand, it must not be supposed that every student who enters Harvard College necessarily graduates. Strict annual examinations are to be passed. More than a fourth of those who enter the College fail to take their degree.

* * *

Only a few years ago, all students who graduated at this College passed through one uniform curriculum. Every man studied the same subjects in the same proportions, without regard to his natural bent or preference. The individual student had no choice of either subjects or teachers. This system is still the prevailing system among American colleges, and finds vigorous defenders. It has the merit of simplicity. So had the school methods of our grandfathers—one primer, one catechism, one rod for all children. On the whole, a single common course of studies, tolerably well selected to meet the average needs, seems to most Americans a very proper and natural thing, even for grown men.

* * *

In education, the individual traits of different minds have not been sufficiently attended to. Through all the period of boyhood the school studies should be representative; all the main fields of knowledge should be entered upon. But the young man of nineteen or twenty ought to know what he likes best and is most fit for. If his previous training has been sufficiently wide, he will know by that time whether he is most apt at language or philosophy or natural science or mathematics. If he feels no loves, he will at least have his hates. At that age the teacher may wisely abandon the school-dame's practice of giving a copy of nothing but zeros to the child who alleges that he cannot make that figure. When the revelation of his own peculiar taste and capacity comes to a young man, let him reverently give it welcome, thank God, and take courage. Thereafter he knows his way to happy, enthusiastic work, and, God willing, to usefulness and success. The civilization of a people may be inferred from the variety of its tools. There are thousands of years between the stone hatchet and the machine-shop. As tools multiply, each is more ingeniously adapted to its own exclusive purpose. So with the men that make the State. For the individual, concentration, and the highest development of his own peculiar faculty, is the only prudence. But for the State, it is variety, not uniformity, of intellectual product, which is needful.

These principles are the justification of the system of elective studies which has been gradually developed in this College during the past forty years. At present the Freshman year is the only one in which there is a fixed course prescribed for all. In the other three years, more than half the time allotted to study is filled with subjects chosen by each student from lists which comprise six studies in the Sophomore year, nine in the Junior year, and eleven in the Senior year. The range of elective studies is large, though there are some striking deficiencies. The liberty of choice of subject is wide, but yet has very rigid limits. There is a certain framework which must be filled; and about half the material of the filling is prescribed. The choice offered to the student does not lie between liberal studies and professional or utilitarian studies. All the studies which are open to him are liberal and disciplinary, not narrow or special. Under this system the College does not demand, it is true, one invariable set of studies of every candidate for the first degree in Arts; but its requisitions for this degree are nevertheless high and inflexible, being nothing less than four years devoted to liberal culture.

It has been alleged that the elective system must weaken the bond which unites members of the same class. This is true; but in view of another much more efficient cause of the diminution of class intimacy, the point is not very significant. The increased size of the college classes inevitably works a great change in this respect. One hundred and fifty young men cannot be so intimate with each other as fifty used to be. This increase is progressive. Taken in connection with the rising average age of the students, it would compel the adoption of methods of instruction different from the old, if there were no better motive for such change. The elective system fosters scholarship, because it gives free play to natural preferences and inborn aptitudes, makes possible enthusiasm for a chosen work, relieves the professor and the ardent disciple of the presence of a body of students who are compelled to an unwelcome task, and enlarges instruction by substituting many and various lessons given to small, lively classes, for a few lessons many times repeated to different sections of a numerous class. The College therefore proposes to persevere in its efforts to establish, improve, and extend the elective system. Its administrative difficulties, which seem formidable at first, vanish before a brief experience.

There has been much discussion about the comparative merits of lectures and recitations. Both are useful—lectures, for inspiration, guidance, and the comprehensive methodizing which only one who has a view of the whole field can rightly contrive; recitations, for securing and testifying a thorough mastery on the part of the pupil of the treatise or author in hand, for conversational comment and amplification, for emulation and competition. Recitations alone readily degenerate into dusty repetitions, and lectures alone are too often a useless expenditure of force. The lecturer pumps laboriously into sieves. The water may be wholesome, but it runs through. A mind must work to grow. Just as far, however, as the student can be relied on to master and appreciate his author without the aid of frequent questioning and repetitions, so far is it possible to dispense with recitations. Accordingly, in the later College years there is a decided tendency to diminish the number of recitations, the faithfulness of the student being tested by periodical examinations. This tendency is in a right direction, if prudently controlled.

The discussion about lectures and recitations has brought out some strong opinions about text-books and their use. Impatience with text-books and manuals is very natural in both teachers and taught. These books are indeed, for the most part, very imperfect, and stand in constant need of correction by the well-informed teacher. Stereotyping, in its present undeveloped condition, is in part to blame for their most exasperating defects. To make the metal plates keep pace with the progress of learning is costly. The manifest deficiencies of text-books must not, however, drive us into a too sweeping condemnation of their use. It is a rare teacher who is superior to all manuals in his subject. Scientific manuals are, as a rule, much worse than those upon language, literature, or philosophy; yet the main improvement in medical education in this country during the last twenty years has been the addition of systematic recitations from text-books to the lectures which were formerly the principal means of theoretical instruction. The training of a medical student, inadequate as it is, offers the best example we have of the methods and fruits of an education mainly scientific. The transformation which the average student of a good medical school undergoes in three years is strong testimony to the efficiency of the training he receives.

We come now to the heart of the University—the Corporation. This board holds the funds, makes appointments, fixes salaries, and has, by right, the initiative in all changes of the organic law of the University. Such an executive board must be small to be efficient. It must always contain men of sound judgment in finance; and literature and the learned professions should be adequately represented in it. The Corporation should also be but slowly renewed; for it is of the utmost consequence to the University that the Government should have a steady aim, and a prevailing spirit which is independent of individuals and transmissible from generation to generation. And what should this spirit be? First, it should be a catholic spirit. A university must be indigenous; it must be rich; but, above all, it must be free. The winnowing breeze of freedom must blow through all its chambers. It takes a hurricane to blow wheat away. An atmosphere of intellectual freedom is the native air of literature and science. This University aspires to serve the nation by training men to intellectual honesty and independence of mind. The Corporation demands of all its teachers that they be grave, reverent, and high-minded; but it leaves them, like their pupils, free. A university is built, not by a sect, but by a nation.

Secondly, the actuating spirit of the Corporation must be a spirit of fidelity—fidelity to the many and various trusts reposed in them by the hundreds of persons who, out of their penury or their abundance, have given money to the President and Fellows of Harvard College in the beautiful hope of doing some perpetual good upon this earth. The Corporation has constantly done its utmost to make this hope a living fact. One hundred and ninety-nine years ago, William Pennoyer gave the rents of certain estates in the county of Norfolk, England, that "two fellows and two scholars forever should be educated, brought up, and maintained" in this College. The income from this bequest has never failed, and to-day one of the four Pennoyer scholarships is held by a lineal descendant of William Pennoyer's brother Robert. So a lineal descendant of Governor Danforth takes this year the income of the property which Danforth bequeathed to the College in 1699. The Corporation have been as faithful in the greater things as in the less. They have been greatly blessed in one respect: in the whole life of the Corporation, seven generations of men, nothing has ever been lost by malfeasance of officers or servants. A reputation for scrupulous fidelity to all trusts is the most precious possession of the Corporation. That safe, the College might lose everything else and yet survive; that lost beyond repair, and the days of the College would be numbered. Testators look first to the trustworthiness and permanence of the body which is to dispense their benefactions. The Corporation thankfully receive all gifts which may advance learning; but they believe that the interests of the University may be most effectually promoted by not restricting too narrowly the use to which a gift may be applied. Whenever the giver desires it, the Corporation will agree to keep any fund separately invested under the name of the giver, and to apply the whole proceeds of such investment to any object the giver may designate. By such special investment, however, the insurance which results from the absorption of a specific gift in the general funds is lost. A fund invested by itself may be impaired or lost by a single error of judgment in investing. The change of such loss is small in any one generation, but appreciable in centuries. Such general designations as salaries, books, dormitories, public buildings, scholarships graduate or undergraduate, scientific collections, and expenses of experimental laboratories, are of permanent significance and effect; while experience proves that too specific and minute directions concerning the application of funds must often fail of fulfilment, simply in consequence of the changing needs and habits of successive generations.

Again, the Corporation should always be filled with the spirit of enterprise. An institution like this College is getting decrepit when it sits down contentedly on its mortgages. On its invested funds the Corporation should be always seeking how safely to make a quarter of a per cent. more. A quarter of one per cent. means a new professorship. It should be always pushing after more professorships, better professors, more land and buildings, and better apparatus. It should be eager, sleepless, and untiring, never wasting a moment in counting laurels won, ever prompt to welcome and apply the liberality of the community, and liking no prospect so well as that of difficulties to be overcome and labors to be done in the cause of learning and public virtue.

You recognize, gentlemen, the picture which I have drawn in thus delineating the true spirit of the Corporation of this College. I have described the noble quintessence of the New England character—that character which has made us a free and enlightened people; that character which, please God, shall yet do a great work in the world for the lifting up of humanity.

Apart from the responsibility which rests upon the Corporation, its actual labors are far heavier than the community imagines. The business of the University has greatly increased in volume and complexity during the past twenty years, and the drafts made upon the time and thought of every member of the Corporation are heavy indeed. The high honors of the function are in these days most generously earned.

The President of the University is primarily an executive officer; but, being a member of both governing boards and of all the faculties, he has also the influence in their debates to which his more or less perfect intimacy with the University and greater or less personal weight may happen to entitle him. An administrative officer who undertakes to do everything himself will do but little, and that little ill. The President's first duty is that of supervision. He should know what each officer's and servant's work is, and how it is done. But the days are past in which the President could be called on to decide everything from the purchase of a door-mat to the appointment of a professor. The principle of divided and subordinate responsibilities, which rules in government bureaus, in manufactories, and all great companies, which makes a modern army a possibility, must be applied in the University. The President should be able to discern the practical essence of complicated and long-drawn discussions. He must often pick out that promising part of theory which ought to be tested by experiment, and must decide how many of things desirable are also attainable, and what one of many projects is ripest for execution. He must watch and look before—watch, to seize opportunities to get money, to secure eminent teachers and scholars, and to influence public opinion toward the advancement of learning; and look before, to anticipate the due effect on the University of the fluctuations of public opinion on educational problems; of the progress of the institutions which feed the University; of the changing condition of the professions which the University supplies; of the rise of new professions; of the gradual alteration of social and religious habits in the community. The University must accommodate itself promptly to significant changes in the character of the people for whom it exists. The institutions of higher education in any nation are always a faithful mirror in which are sharply reflected the national history and character. In this mobile nation the action and reaction between the University and society at large are more sensitive and rapid than in stiffer communities. The President, therefore, must not need to see a house built before he can comprehend the plan of it. He can profit by a wide intercourse with all sorts of men, and by every real discussion on education, legislation, and sociology.

The most important function of the President is that of advising the Corporation concerning appointments, particularly about appointments of young men who have not had time and opportunity to approve themselves to the public. It is in discharging this duty that the President holds the future of the University in his hands. He cannot do it well unless he have insight, unless he be able to recognize, at times beneath some crusts, the real gentleman and the natural teacher. This is the one oppressive responsibility of the President: all other cares are light beside it. To see every day the evil fruit of a bad appointment must be the cruelest of official torments. Fortunately, the good effect of a judicious appointment is also inestimable; and here, as everywhere, good is more penetrating and diffusive than evil.

It is imperative that the statutes which define the President's duties should be recast, and the customs of the College be somewhat modified, in order that lesser duties may not crowd out the greater. But, however important the functions of the President, it must not be forgotten that he is emphatically a constitutional executive. It is his character and his judgment which are of importance, not his opinions. He is the executive officer of deliberative bodies, in which decisions are reached after discussion by a majority vote. Those decisions bind him. He cannot force his own opinions upon anybody. A university is the last place in the world for a dictator. Learning is always republican. It has idols, but not masters.

What can the community do for the University? It can love, honor, and cherish it. Love it and honor it. The University is upheld by this public affection and respect. In the loyalty of her children she finds strength and courage. The Corporation, the Overseers, and the several faculties need to feel that the leaders of public opinion, and especially the sons of the College, are at their back, always ready to give them a generous and intelligent support. Therefore we welcome the Chief Magistrate of the Commonwealth, the Senators, Judges, and other dignitaries of the State, who by their presence at this ancient ceremonial bear witness to the pride which Massachusetts feels in her eldest university. Therefore we rejoice in the presence of this throng of the Alumni testifying their devotion to the College which through all changes, is still their home. Cherish it. This University, though rich among American colleges, is very poor in comparison with the great universities of Europe. The wants of the American community have far outgrown the capacity of the University to supply them. We must try to satisfy the cravings of the select few as well as the needs of the average many. We cannot afford to neglect the Fine Arts. We need groves and meadows as well as barracks; and soon there will be no chance to get them in this expanding city. But, above all, we need professorships, books, and apparatus, that teaching and scholarship may abound.

And what will the University do for the community? First, it will make a rich return of learning, poetry, and piety. Secondly, it will foster the sense of public duty—that great virtue which makes republics possible. The founding of Harvard College was an heroic act of public spirit. For more than a century the breath of life was kept in it by the public spirit of the Province and of its private benefactors. In the last fifty years the public spirit of the friends of the College has quadrupled its endowments. And how have the young men nurtured here in successive generations repaid the founders for their pious care? Have they honored freedom and loved their country? For answer we appeal to the records of the national service; to the lists of the Senate, the cabinet, and the diplomatic service, and to the rolls of the army and navy. Honored men, here present, illustrate before the world the public quality of the graduates of this College. Theirs is no mercenary service. Other fields of labor attract them more and would reward them better; but they are filled with the noble ambition to deserve well of the republic. There have been doubts, in times yet recent, whether culture were not selfish; whether men of refined tastes and manners could really love Liberty, and be ready to endure hardness for her sake; whether, in short, gentlemen would in this century prove as loyal to noble ideas as in other times they had been to kings. In yonder old playground, fit spot whereon to commemorate the manliness which there was nurtured, shall soon rise a noble monument which for generations will give convincing answer to such shallow doubts; for over its gates will be written: "In memory of the sons of Harvard who died for their country." The future of the University will not be unworthy of its past.

CHARLES W. ELIOT DEFENDS THE ELECTIVE SYSTEM AT HARVARD

(1885)   From Charles W. Eliot, "Liberty in Education," in *Educational Reform: Essays and Addresses* (New York, 1898), pp. 125–33, 138–42, 145.

How to transform a college with one uniform curriculum into a university without any prescribed course of study at all is a problem which more and more claims the attention of all thoughtful friends of American learning and education. To-night I hope to convince you that a university of liberal arts and sciences must give its students three things:

I. Freedom in choice of studies.

II. Opportunity to win academic distinction in single subjects or special lines of study.

III. A discipline which distinctly imposes on each individual the responsibility of forming his own habits and guiding his own conduct.

These three subjects I shall take up in succession, the first of them taking the greater part of the time allotted me.

I. Of freedom in choice of studies.

Let me first present what I may call a mechanical argument on this subject. A college with a prescribed curriculum must provide, say, sixteen hours a week of instruction for each class, or sixty-four hours a week in all for the four classes, without allowing for repetitions of lectures or lessons. Six or eight teachers can easily give all the instruction needed in such a college, if no repetitions are necessary. If the classes are so large that they need to be divided into two or more sections, more teachers must be employed. If a few extra or optional studies, outside of the curriculum, are provided, a further addition to the number of teachers must be made. Twenty teachers would, however, be a liberal allowance for any college of this type; and accordingly there are hundreds of American colleges at this moment with less than twenty teachers all told. Under the prescribed system it would be impossible for such a college to find work for more teachers, if it had them. Now there are eighty teachers employed this year in Harvard College exclusive of laboratory assistants; and these eighty teachers give about four hundred and twenty-five hours of public instruction a week without any repetitions, not counting the very important instruction which many of them give in laboratories. It is impossible for any undergraduate in his four years to take more than a tenth part of the instruction given by the College; and since four fifths of this instruction is of a higher grade than any which can be given in a college with a prescribed curriculum, a diligent student would need about forty years to cover the present field; and during those years the field would enlarge quite beyond his powers of occupation.

Since the student cannot take the whole of the instruction offered, it seems to be necessary to allow him to take a part. A college must either limit closely its teaching, or provide some mode of selecting studies for the individual student. The limitation of teaching is an intolerable alternative for any institution which aspires to become a university; for a university must try to teach every subject, above the grade of its admission requirements, for which there is any demand; and to teach it thoroughly enough to carry the advanced student to the confines of present knowledge, and make him capable of original research. These are the only limits which a university can properly set to its instruction—except indeed those rigorous limits which poverty imposes. The other alternative is selection or election of studies.

The elective system at Harvard has been sixty years in developing, and during fourteen of these years—from 1846 to 1860—the presidents and the majority of the faculty were not in favor of it; but they could find no way of escape from the dilemma which I have set before you. They could not deliberately reduce the amount of instruction offered, and election of studies in some degree was the inevitable alternative.

The practical question then is, At what age, and at what stage of his educational progress, can an American boy be offered free choice of studies? or, in other words, At what age can an American boy best go to a free university? Before answering this question I will ask your attention to four preliminary observations.

1. The European boy goes to free universities at various ages from seventeen to twenty; and the American boy is decidely more mature and more capable of taking care of himself than the European boy of like age.

2. The change from school to university ought to be made as soon as it would be better for the youth to associate with older students under a discipline suited to their age, than with younger pupils under a discipline suited to theirs—as soon, in short, as it would be better for the youth to be the youngest student in a university than the oldest boy in a school. The school might still do much for the youth; the university may as yet be somewhat too free for him: there must be a balancing of advantages against disadvantages; but the wise decision is to withdraw him betimes from a discipline which he is outgrowing, and put him under a discipline which he is to grow up to. When we think of putting a boy into college, our imaginations are apt to dwell upon the occasional and exceptional evil influences to which his new freedom will expose him, more than upon those habitual and prevailing influences of college companionship which will nourish his manliness and develop his virtue; just as we are apt to think of heredity chiefly as a means of transmitting vices and diseases, whereas it is normally the means of transmitting and accumulating infinitely various virtues and serviceable capacities.

3. A young man is much affected by the expections which his elders entertain of him. If they expect him to behave like a child, his lingering childishness will oftener rule his actions; if they expect him to behave like a man, his incipient manhood will oftener assert itself. The pretended parental or sham monastic regime of the common American college seems to me to bring out the childishness rather than the manliness of the average student; as is evidenced by the pranks he plays, the secret societies in which he rejoices, and the barbarous or silly customs which he accepts and transmits. The conservative argument is: a college must deal with the student as he is; he will be what he has been, namely, a thoughtless, aimless, lazy, and possibly vicious boy; therefore a policy which gives him liberty is impracticable. The progressive argument is: adapt college policy to the best students, and not to the worst; improve the policy, and in time the evil fruits of a mistaken policy will

disappear. I would only urge at this point that a far-seeing educational policy must be based upon potentialities as well as actualities, upon things which may be reasonably hoped for, planned, and aimed at, as well as upon things which are.

4. The condition of secondary education is an important factor in our problem. It is desirable that the young men who are to enjoy university freedom should have already received at school a substantial training, in which the four great subdivisions of elementary knowledge—languages, history, mathematics, and natural science—were all adequately represented; but it must be admitted that this desirable training is now given in very few schools, and that in many parts of the country there are not secondary schools enough of even tolerable quality. For this condition of secondary education the colleges are in part responsible; for they have produced few good teachers, except for the ancient languages; and they have required for admission to college hardly anything but the elements of Greek, Latin, and mathematics. But how should this condition of things affect the policy of an institution which sees its way to obtain a reasonable number of tolerably prepared students? Shall we stop trying to create a university because the condition of secondary education in the country at large is unsatisfactory? The difficulty with that policy of inaction is that the reform and development of secondary education depend upon the right organization and conduct of universities. It is the old problem: Which was first created, an egg or a hen? In considering the relation of college life to school life, many people are confused by a misleading metaphor—that of building. They say to themselves: on weak foundations no strong superstructure can be built; schools lay the foundations on which the university must build; therefore, if preparatory schools fail to do good work, no proper university work can subsequently be done. The analogy seems perfect, but has this fatal defect: education is a vital process, not a mechanical one. Let us, therefore, use an illustration drawn from a vital function, that of nutrition. A child has had poor milk as an infant, and is not well developed; therefore, when its teeth are cut, and it is ready for bread, meat, and oatmeal, you are to hold back this substantial diet, and give it the sweetened milk and water, and Mellin's Food, which would have suited it when a baby. The mental food of a boy has not been as nourishing and abundant as it should have been at school; therefore when he goes to college or university his diet must be that which he should have had at school, but missed. Education involves growth or development from within in every part; and metaphors drawn from the process of laying one stone upon another are not useful in educational discussions. Harvard College now finds itself able to get nearly three hundred tolerably prepared students every year from one hundred or more schools and private tutors scattered over the country; and she is only just beginning to reap the fruit of the changes in her own policy and discipline which the past eighteen years have wrought. Schools follow universities, and will be what universities make them.

With these preliminary suggestions I proceed to answer the question, At what age can an American boy best go to a university where choice of studies is free? and to defend my answer. I believe the normal age under reasonably favorable conditions to be eighteen. In the first place, I hold that the temperament, physical constitution, mental aptitudes, and moral quality of a boy are well determined by the time he is eighteen years old. The potential man is already revealed. His capacities and incapacities will be perfectly visible to his teacher, or to any observant and intimate friend, provided that his studies at school have been fairly representative. If his historical studies have been limited to primers of Greek, Roman, and American history, his taste and capacity for historical study will not be known either to his teacher or to himself; if he has had no opportunity to study natural science, his powers in that direction will be quite unproved; but if the school course has been reasonably comprehensive, there need be no doubt as to the most profitable direction of his subsequent studies. The boy's future will depend greatly upon the influences, happy or unhappy, to which he is subjected; but given all favorable influences, his possibilities are essentially determined. The most fortunate intellectual influences will be within his reach, if he has liberty to choose the mental food which he can best assimilate. Secondly, at eighteen the American boy has passed the age when a compulsory external discipline is useful. Motives and inducements may be set vividly before him; he may be told that he must do so and so in order to win something which he desires or values; prizes and rewards near or remote may be held out to him; but he cannot be driven to any useful exercise of his mind. *Thirdly,* a well-instructed youth of eighteen can select for himself—not for any other boy, or for the fictitious universal boy, but for himself alone—a better course of study than any college faculty, or any wise man who does not know him and his ancestors and his previous life, can possibly select for him. In choosing his course he will naturally seek aid from teachers and friends who have intimate knowledge of him, and he will act under the dominion of that intense conservatism which fortunately actuates civilized man in the whole matter of education, and under various other safeguards which nature and not arbitrary regulation provides. When a young man whom I never saw before asks me what studies he had better take in college, I am quite helpless, until he tells me what he likes and what he dislikes to study, what kinds of exertion are pleasurable to him, what sports he cares for, what reading interests him, what his parents and grandparents were in the world, and what he means to be. In short, I can only show him how to think out the problem for himself with such lights as he has and nobody else can have. The proposition that a boy of eighteen can choose his own studies, with the natural helps, more satisfactorily than anybody else can choose them for him, seems at first sight absurd; but I believe it to be founded upon the nature of things, and it is also for me a clear result of observation.

✻　✻　✻

Before I leave the subject of election of studies, let me point out that there is not a university of competent resources upon the continent of Europe in which complete freedom of studies has not long prevailed; and that Oxford and Cambridge have recently provided an almost complete liberty for their students. In our own country respectable colleges now offer a considerable proportion of elective studies, and as a rule the greater their resources in teachers, collections, and money, the more liberal their application of the elective principle. Many colleges, however, still seem to have but a halting faith in the efficacy of the principle, and our educated public has but just begun to appreciate its importance. So fast as American institutions acquire the resources and powers of European universities, they will adopt the methods proper to universities wherever situate. At present our best colleges fall very far short of European standards in respect to number of teachers, and consequently in respect to amplitude of teaching.

As yet we have no university in America—only aspirants to that eminence. All the more important is it that we should understand the conditions under which a university can be developed—the most indispensable of which is freedom in choice of studies.

PRESIDENT JAMES McCOSH OF PRINCETON ATTACKS HARVARD'S "NEW DEPARTURE" (1885)   From James McCosh, *The New Departure in College Education, Being a Reply to President Eliot's Defense of it in New York* (New York, 1885), pp. 1–23.

I was told by the Nineteenth Century Club that the President of Harvard was to advocate what was called his "new departure," and I was invited to criticize it. I have noticed with considerable anxiety that departure as going on for years past without parents or the public noticing it. I am glad that things have come to a crisis. Fathers and mothers and the friends of education will now know what is proposed, what is in fact going on, and will have to decide forthwith whether they are to fall in with and encourage it, or are to oppose it.

I asked first what the question was. President Eliot has shaped it as follows: "IN A UNIVERSITY THE STUDENT MUST CHOOSE HIS STUDIES AND GOVERN HIMSELF." I saw at once that the question thus announced was large and loose, vague and ambiguous, plausible to the ear, but with no definite meaning. But it commits its author to a positive position and gives me room to defend a great and good cause. The form is showy but I can expose it; I can prick the bubble so that all may know how little matter is inside.

On the one hand I am sorry that the defence of solid and high education should have devolved on me rather than on some more gifted advocate. But on the other hand I feel it to be a privilege that I am invited to oppose proposals which are fitted, without the people as yet seeing it, to throw back in America (as Bacon expresses it) "The Advancement of Learning."

I will not allow any one (without protest) to charge me with being antiquated, or old-fashioned, or behind the age—I may be an old man but I cherish a youthful spirit. For sixteen years I was a professor in the youngest and one of the most advanced universities in Great Britain, and I have now been sixteen years in an American college, and in both I have labored to elevate the scholarship. I act on the principle that every new branch of what has shown itself to be true learning is to be introduced into a college. My friends in America have encouraged me by generously giving me millions of money to carry out this idea. I am as much in favor of progress as President Eliot, but I go on in a different, I believe a better way. I adopt the new, I retain what is good in the old. I am disappointed, I am grieved when I find another course pursued which allows, which encourages, which tempts young men in their caprice to choose easy subjects, and which are not fitted to enlarge or refine the mind, to produce scholars, or to send forth the great body of the students as educated gentlemen.

Freedom is the catch-word of this new departure. It is a precious and an attractive word. But, O Liberty! what crimes and cruelties have been perpetrated in thy name! It is a bid for popularity. An entering Freshman will be apt to cheer when he hears it—the prospect is so pleasant. The leader in this departure will have many followers. The student infers from the language that he can study what he pleases. I can tell you what he will possibly or probably choose. Those who are in the secrets of colleges know how skilful certain students are in choosing their subjects. They can choose the branches which will cost them least study, and put themselves under the popular professors who give them the highest grades with the least labor. I once told a student in an advanced stage of his course, "If you had shown as much skill in pursuing your studies as in choosing the easiest subjects you would have been the first man in your class." I am for freedom quite as much as Dr. Eliot is, but it is for freedom regulated by law. I am for liberty but not licentiousness, which always ends in servitude.

I am to follow the President of Harvard in the three roads which he has taken; placing positions of mine face to face with his:

I. *FREEDOM IN CHOOSING STUDIES*
II. *FREEDOM IN CHOOSING SPECIALTIES*
III. *FREEDOM IN GOVERNMENT*

I

Freedom in Choosing Studies.—I am for freedom, but it must be within carefully defined limits. First, a young man should be free to enter a university or not to enter it. He is to be free to choose his department in that university, say Law or Medicine, or the Academic terminating in the Bachelor or Master's Degree. But, having made his choice, is he to have all possible freedom ever after? At this point the most liberal advocate of liberty will be obliged to tell the student, "We are now required to lay some restraints upon you," and the youth finds his liberty is at an end. He has to take certain studies and give a certain amount of time to them, say, according to the Harvard model, to select four topics. He goes in for Medicine: he may make his quartette Physical Geography, which tells what climate is; and Art, which teaches us to paint the human frame; and Music, which improves the voice; and Lectures on the Drama, which show us how to assume noble attitudes. These seem more agreeable to him than Anatomy and Physiology, than Surgery and Materia Medica, which present corpses and unpleasant odors. I tell you that, though this youth should get a diploma written on parchment, I would not, however ill, call him in to prescribe to me, as I might not be quite sure whether his medicines would kill me or cure me. Or the intention of the youth is Engineering in order to make or drive a steam engine, and he does not take Mathematics, or Mechanics, or Graphics, or Geodesy; but as unlimited choice is given him, he prefers drawing and field work—when the weather is fine, and two departments of gymnastics—now so well taught in our colleges—namely, boxing and wrestling. I tell you I am not to travel by the railway he has constructed. But he has a higher aim: he is to take a course in the Liberal Arts and expects a Master's Degree; but Greek and Mathematics and Physics and Mental Philosophy are all old and waxing older, and he takes French to enable him to travel in Europe, and Lectures on Goethe to make him a German scholar, and a Pictorial History of the age of Louis XIV., and of the Theatre in ancient and modern times. This is a good year's work, and he can take a like course in each of the four years; and if he be in Yale or Princeton College, he will in Spring and Fall substitute Base Ball and Foot Ball, and exhibit feats more wonderful than were ever performed in the two classical countries, Greece and Rome, at their famous Olympian Games and Bull Fights.

I have presented this designedly rude picture to show that there must be some limits put to the freedom of choice in studies. The able leader of the new departure, with the responsibilities of a great College upon him, and the frank and honest gentleman, who has such a dread of a Fetish—the creature of his own imagination—will be ready to admit that in every department of a University there should be a well considered and a well devised curriculum of study. It is one of the highest and most important functions of the governing bodies to construct such a scheme. It should have in it two essential powers or properties.

First, there should be branches required of all students who pursue the full

HIGHER EDUCATION

1559

course and seek a degree. This is done in such departments as Engineering and Medicine and should be done in Arts. The obligatory branches should be wisely selected. They should all be fitted to enlarge or refine the mind. They should be fundamental, as forming the basis on which other knowledge is built. They should be disciplinary, as training the mind for further pursuits. Most of them should have stood the test of time and reared scholars in ages past. There will be found to be a wonderful agreement among educated men of high tastes as to what these should be.

*   *   *

We in Princeton believe in a Trinity of studies: in Language and Literature, in Science, and in Philosophy. Every educated man should know so much of each of these. Without this, man's varied faculties are not trained, his nature is not fully developed and may become malformed.

A college should give what is best to its students, and it should not tempt them to what is lower when the higher can be had. Harvard boasts that it gives two hundred choices to its students, younger and older.[1] I confess that I have had some difficulty in understanding her catalogue. I would rather study the whole Cosmos. It has a great many perplexities, which I can compare only to the cycles, epicycles, eccentricities of the old astronomy, so much more complex than that of Newton. An examination of students upon it would be a better test of a clear head than some of their subjects, such as "French Plays and Novels." As I understand it, one seeking a degree, may, in his free will choose the following course:

In Sophomore Year—

   1. French Literature of the Seventeenth Century.

   2. Mediaeval and Modern European History.

   3. Elementary Course in Fine Art, with collateral instruction in Water-coloring.

   4. Counterpoint (in music).

In Junior Year—

   1. French Literature of the Eighteenth Century.

   2. Early Mediaeval History.

   3. Botany.

   4. History of Music.

In Senior Year—

   1. French Literature of the Nineteenth Century.

   2. Elementary Spanish.

   3. Greek Art.

   4. Free Thematic Music.[2]

---

[1] In Princeton we have nearly all the branches taught in Harvard, but we do not subdivide and scatter them as they do; we put them under compacted heads. In his address to the Johns Hopkins University, Dr. Eliot refers to the supposed deficiency in teaching history in Princeton. In reply I have to state that we have a small examination on the subject for entrance; that in the Sophomore year we use one of Freeman's textbooks to give an elementary view of universal history; that in the Junior and Senior the Professor of the Philosophy of History gives a historical and critical survey of the science and methods of history. More particularly each Professor is expected to give a history of his own branch, and so we have histories of Politics, of Philosophy, of Greece, of Rome, of the literature of Germany and of France, etc. I do not agree with Mr. J. S. Mill that history cannot be taught in college (it would take forty years and more to go over all history); but I think the numerous narrative histories of epochs is just a let-off to easy-going students from the studies which require thought.

There are twenty such dilettanti courses which may be taken in Harvard. I cannot allow that this is an advance in scholarship. If this be the modern education, I hold that the old is better. I would rather send a young man, in whom I was interested, to one of the old-fashioned colleges of the country, where he would be constrained to study Latin, Greek, Mathematics, Rhetoric, Physics, Logic, Ethics, and Political Economy, and I am persuaded that his mind would thereby be better trained and he himself prepared to do higher and more important work in life. From the close of Freshman year on it is perfectly practicable for a student to pass through Harvard and receive the degree of Bachelor of Arts, without taking any course in Latin, Greek, Mathematics, Chemistry, Physics, Astronomy, Geology, Logic, Psychology, Ethics, Political Economy, German, or even English! (If, as President Eliot insists, a knowledge of our mother-tongue is the true basis of culture, what is to be said of this?)

Secondly. It should be an essential feature of the course for a degree, that the attendance of the student on lectures and recitations should be obligatory. This is a very important matter. The student may have freedom in his choice, but having made his election he should be bound to attend on the instruction imparted.

✻   ✻   ✻

II

Specialties in Study.—Men have special talents, and so they should have special studies provided for them. They are to have special vocations in life, and college youth should so far be prepared for them. Every student should have Obligatory studies, but he should also be allowed Elective studies. The branches of knowledge are now so numerous and literature is so wide and varied, that no one can master it all; should he try to do so, he would only be "a jack of all trades and a master of none."

The student should have two kinds of electives provided for him. He may be allowed to take subjects which could not be required of all, such, for example, as Sanscrit, Anglo-Saxon, the Semitic Tongues, and in science, Histology and Physical Geography. No college should make these obligatory, and yet considerable numbers of students would prize them much and get great benefit from them, to fit them for their further study and life-work. Or, the student, after taking certain elementary branches, should have higher forms of the same provided for him, and be encouraged to take them. Of all the rudimentary branches or cardinal studies, there should be a course or courses required of all in order to make them educated gentlemen, but there should be advanced courses—Electives, to produce high scholars in all branches, literary, linguistic, scientific, philosophic. All students should know several of the highest languages, ancient and modern, but there should be advanced linguistic studies, and especially a science of Comparative Language. I defy you to make all master Quaternions, or Quantics, or Functions, but these should be in the college for a select few. All should be taught the fundamental laws of the human mind, but there should also be a number entering into the depths and climbing the heights, of the Greek, the Scotch, and the German philosophies.

[2]In the debate we were told that this is a deep study; then the Degree of Master of Music (M.M.) should be given to it but not M.A.

I hold that in a college with the variety there should be a unity. The circle of the sciences should have a wide circumference but also a fixed centre.

III

Self Government.—I hold that in a college, as in a country, there should be government; there should be care over the students, with inducements to good conduct, and temptations removed, and restraints on vice. There should be moral teaching; I believe also religious teaching—the rights of conscience being always carefully preserved. But one part of this instruction should be to inculcate independence, independence in thinking, independence in action and self-control. The student should be taught to think for himself, to act for himself. If he does not acquire this spirit, no external authority will be able to guide and restrain him. I abhor the plan of secretly watching students, of peeping through windows at night, and listening through key-holes. Under the *spy* system, the students will always beat their tutors. The tricky fellows will escape, while only the simple will be caught.

✻ ✻ ✻

It is time that fathers and mothers should know what it is proposed to do with their sons at college. The college authorities are in no way to interfere with them. They are to teach them Music and Art, and French Plays and Novels, but there is no course in the Scriptures—in their poetry, their morality, their spirituality. The President of Harvard recommends that all colleges should be in great cities. Students are to be placed in the midst of saloons, and gambling-houses, and temples of Venus, but meanwhile no officer of the college is to preach to them, to deal with them. Suppose that under temptation the son falls. I can conceive a father saying to the head of the institution, "I sent my son to you believing that man is made in the image of God, you taught him that he is an upper brute, and he has certainly become so; I sent him to you pure, and last night he was carried to my door drunk. Curse ye this college; 'curse ye bitterly,' for you took no pains to allure him to good, to admonish, to pray for him." I was once addressed by a mother in very nearly these words. I was able to show that her son had come to us a polluted boy from an ungodly school, and that we had dealt with him kindly, warned him solemnly, disciplined him, given notice of his conduct to his mother, and prayed for him. Had I not been able to say this conscientiously I believe I would that day have given in my resignation of the office I hold, and retired to a wilderness to take charge of myself, feeling that I was not competent to take care of others.

It is a serious matter what we are to do to provide religious studies in our colleges. Professor Huxley knows that there is little or nothing in our ordinary school books to mould and form the character of children, and so, as member of the London School Board, he votes for the reading of the Scriptures in the schools, not that he believes them, but because they are fitted to sway the mind,—which I remark they are able to do, because they are divine. Everybody knows that science alone is not fit to form or guard morality; and Herbert Spencer is very anxious about this transition period, when the old has passed away (so he thinks) and the new morality is not yet published. Emerson stood up manfully for the retention of prayers in Harvard University. Are we now in our colleges to give up preaching? to give up Bible instruction? to give up prayers? But I am on the borders of the religious question, on which I now formally propose that *This club should have another meeting, in which President Eliot will defend the new departure in the religion of colleges, and I engage with God's help to meet him.*

In closing, I have to confess that I regard this new departure with deep anxiety. The scholarship of America is not yet equal to that of Germany or Great Britain. Some of us are anxious to raise it up to the standard of Europe. We are discouraged by this plan of Harvard to allow and encourage its students to take branches in which there is so little to promote high intellectual culture. We know what a galaxy of great men appeared in Harvard an age ago, under the old training. I know that it is keenly discussed, within the college itself, whether there is anything in the present and coming modes of dissipated instruction to rear men of the like intellectual calibres. Has there been of late any great poem, any great scientific discovery, any great history, any great philosophic work, by the young men of Cambridge? I observe that the literary journals, for which our young writers prepare articles, have now fixed their seat in New York rather than Boston.

The wise leaders of the new departure do not propose to fight against religion. They do not fight with it, but they are quite willing to let it die out, to die in dignity. They have put severe learning on a sliding scale, not it may be in order to a sudden fall, but insensibly to go down to the level of those boys who do not wish to think deeply or study hard. I am glad things have come to a crisis. Let parents know it, let the churches know it, let all America know it, let scholars in Europe know it, let the world know it—for what is done in Harvard has influence over the world. But some timid people will say, "Tell it not in the lands whence our pious fathers came that the college whose motto is *Pro Christo et Ecclesia* teaches no religion to its pupils. Tell it not in Berlin or Oxford that the once most illustrious university in America no longer requires its graduates to know the most perfect language, the grandest literature, the most elevated thinking of all antiquity.

*   *   *

Tell it not in Paris, tell it not in Cambridge in England, tell it not in Dublin, that Cambridge in America does not make mathematics obligatory on its students. Let not Edinburgh and Scotland and the Puritans in England know that a student may pass through the once Puritan College of America without having taken a single class of philosophy or a lesson in religion. But whatever others may do, *I say, I say*, let Europe know in all its universities—I wish my voice could reach them all—that in a distinguished college in America a graduate need no longer take what the ages have esteemed the highest department of learning; and I believe that such an expression of feeling will be called forth, that if we cannot avert the evil in Harvard we may arrest it in the other colleges of the country.

DANIEL COIT GILMAN ON THE NATURE AND FUNCTION OF A
UNIVERSITY (1876) From "The Johns Hopkins University in Its Beginning: An
Inaugural Address, Baltimore, 1876," as quoted in *University Problems* (New York, 1898),
pp. 13-14, 18-20.

The institutions which are founded in modern society for the promotion of superior education may be grouped in five classes: 1. Universities; 2. Learned Societies; 3. Colleges; 4. Technical Schools; 5. Museums (including literary and scientific collections). It is important that the fundamental ideas of these various institutions should be borne in mind.

The University is a place for the advance and special education of youth who have been prepared for its freedom by the discipline of a lower school. Its form varies in different countries. Oxford and Cambridge universities are unlike the Scotch, and still more unlike the Queen's University in Ireland; the university of France has no counterpart in Germany; the typical German universities differ much from one another. But while forms and methods vary, the freedom to investigate, the obligation to teach, and the careful bestowal of academic honors are always understood to be among the university functions. The pupils are supposed to be wise enough to select, and mature enough to follow, the courses they pursue.

The Academy, or Learned Society (of which the Institute of France, with its five academies, and the Royal Society of London, are typical examples), is an association of learned men, selected for their real or reputed merits, who assemble for mutual instruction and attrition, and who publish from time to time the papers they have received and the proceedings in which they have engaged. The University is also an association of learned men, but the bond which holds them together differs essentially from that of the Academy. In the universities teaching is essential, research important; in academies of science research is indispensable, tuition rarely thought of.

The College implies, as a general rule, restriction rather than freedom; tutorial rather than professorial guidance; residence within appointed bounds; the chapel, the dining-hall, and the daily inspection. The College theoretically stands *in loco parentis;* it does not afford a very wide scope; it gives a liberal and substantial foundation on which the university instruction may be wisely built.

The Technical Schools present the idea of preparation for a specific calling, rather than the notion of a liberal culture. . . .

*　　*　　*

The schedule will include twelve points on which there seems to be a general agreement.

1. All sciences are worthy of promotion; or, in other words, it is useless to dispute whether literature or science should receive more attention, or whether there is any essential difference between the old and the new education.

2. Religion has nothing to fear from science, and science need not be afraid of religion. Religion claims to interpret the word of God, and science to reveal the laws of God. The interpreters may blunder, but truths are immutable, eternal, and never in conflict.

3. Remote utility is quite as worthy to be thought of as immediate advantage.

Those ventures are not always the most sagacious that expect a return on the morrow. It sometimes pays to send our argosies across the seas, to make investments with an eye to slow but sure returns. So is it always in the promotion of science.

4. As it is impossible for any university to encourage with equal freedom all branches of learning, a selection must be made by enlightened governors, and that selection must depend on the requirements and deficiencies of a given people in a given period. There is no absolute standard of preference. What is more important at one time or in one place may be less needed elsewhere and otherwise.

5. Individual students cannot pursue all branches of learning, and just be allowed to select under the guidance of those who are appointed to counsel them. Nor can able professors be governed by routine. Teachers and pupils must be allowed great freedom in their method of work. Recitations, lectures, examinations, laboratories, libraries, field exercises, and travels are all legitimate means of culture.

6. The best scholars will almost invariably be those who make special attainments on the foundation of a broad and liberal culture.

7. The best teachers are usually those who are free, competent, and willing to make original researches in the library and the laboratory.

8. The best investigators are usually those who have also the responsibilities of instruction, gaining thus the incitement of colleagues, the encouragement of pupils, and the observation of the public.

9. Universities should bestow their honors sparingly, their benefits most freely.

10. A university cannot be created in a day; it is a slow growth. The University of Berlin has been quoted as a proof of the contrary. That was indeed a quick success, but in an old, compact country, crowded with learned men eager to assemble at the Prussian court. It was a change of base rather than a sudden development.

11. The object of the university is to develop character—to make men. It misses its aim if it produces learned pedants, or simple artisans, or cunning sophists, or pretentious practitioners. Its purport is not so much to impart knowledge to the pupils, as to whet the appetite, exhibit methods, develop powers, strengthen judgment, and invigorate the intellectual and moral forces. It should prepare for the service of society a class of students who will be wise, thoughtful, and progressive guides in whatever department of work or thought they may be engaged.

12. Universities easily fall into ruts. Almost every epoch requires a fresh start.

If these twelve points are conceded, our task is simplified, though it is still difficult. It is to apply these principles to Baltimore in 1876.

We are trying to do this with no controversy as to the relative importance of letters and science, the conflicts of religion and science, or the relation of abstractions and utilities; our simple aim is to make scholars, strong, useful, and true.

DANIEL COIT GILMAN ON THE BUSINESS OF A UNIVERSITY

(1885)   From Daniel Coit Gilman, *The Benefits Which Society Derives from Universities, an Address* (Baltimore. 1885), pp. 16–19.

First, it is the business of a university to advance knowledge; every professor must be a student. No history is so remote that it may be neglected; no law of mathematics is so hidden that it may not be sought out; no problem in respect to physics is so difficult that it must be shunned. No love of ease, no dread of labor, no fear of consequences, no desire for wealth will divert a band of well chosen professors from uniting their forces in the prosecution of study. Rather let me say that there are heroes and martyrs, prophets and apostles of learning as there are of religion. To the claims of duty, to the responsibilities of station, to the voices of enlightened conscience such men respond, and they throw their hearts into their work with as much devotion, and as little selfishness, as it is possible for human nature to exhibit. By their labors, knowledge has been accumulated, intellectual capital has been acquired. In these processes of investigation the leading universities of the world have always been engaged.

This is what laboratories, museums and libraries signify. Nothing is foreign to their purpose, and those who work in them are animated by the firm belief that the advancement of knowledge in any direction contributes to the welfare of man. Nor is research restricted to material things; the scholars of a university are equally interested in all that pertains to the nature of man, the growth of society, the study of language, and the establishment of the principles of intellectual and moral conduct.

2. Universities are conservative. They encourage the study of the history, the philosophy, the poetry, the drama, the politics, the religion, in fine, the experience of antecedent ages. Successors of the ancient monasteries, they keep alive in our day the knowledge of ancient languages and art, enrich the literature of our mother tongue, hold up to us the highest standards of excellence in writing and enable us to share in the thoughts of the noblest of our race. Let me especially remind you that to the universities men turn instinctively for light on the interpretation of the Scriptures. When new manuscripts are discovered, or new versions are proposed, or new monuments are unearthed, it is to the universities, where the knowledge of ancient and remote tongues has been cherished, that the religious world looks for enlightenment and guidance. Their dominant influence is highly spiritualizing; I would even go farther and say that it is truly religious. I am not unmindful that within the academic circles men are found whose spiritual insight is but dim,—so it is in all other circles,—but I assert without fear of contradiction, that the influence of study is, on the whole, favorable to the growth of spiritual life, to the development of uprightness, unselfishness and faith, or, in other words, it is opposed to epicureanism and materialism. In belief, there are tides as there are in the ocean, ebb and flow, ebb and flow; but the great ocean is there, with its deep mysteries, unchanging amid all superficial changes. Faith, with all its fluctuations, is as permanently operative in human thought as Knowledge.

3. Universities are refining. They are constantly, by laborious processes, by intricate systems of coöperation, and by ingenious methods, engaged in eliminating human errors and in submitting all inherited possessions to those processes which remove the dross and perpetuate the gold. No truth which has once been discovered is allowed to perish,—but the incrustations which cover it are removed. It is the

universities which edit, interpret, translate and reiterate the acquisitions of former generations both of literature and science. Their revelation of error is sometimes welcomed but it is generally opposed; nevertheless the process goes on, indifferent alike to plaudits or reproaches. If their lessons are hard to the beginners, they lead the persevering to high enjoyment.

4. Universities distribute knowledge. The scholar does but half his duty who simply acquires knowledge. He must share his possessions with others. This is done in the first place by the instruction of pupils. Experience has certainly demonstrated that with rare exceptions, those men are most learned who produce most. The process of acquiring seems to be promoted by that of imparting. The investigator who is surrounded by a bright circle of friendly inquisitors and critics, finds his best powers developed by this influence. Next to its visible circle of pupils, the university should impart its acquisitions to the world of scholars. Learned publications are therefore to be encouraged. But beyond these formal and well recognized means of communicating knowledge, universities have innumerable less obvious, but not less useful opportunities of conveying their benefits to the outside world.

INCORPORATION OF THE UNIVERSITY OF CHICAGO (1890) From Edward C. Elliott, ed., *Charters and Basic Laws of Selected American Universities and Colleges* (New York, 1934), pp. 105–6.

State of Illinois
County of Cook   ss.
To the Honorable Isaac N. Pearson, Secretary of State:

We, the undersigned, John D. Rockefeller, E. Nelson Blake, Marshall Field, Fred. T. Gates, Francis E. Hinckley, and Thomas W. Goodspeed, citizens of the United States, desiring to associate ourselves for the lawful purposes hereinafter stated, and for the purpose of forming a corporation (not for pecuniary profit), under the provisions of the Act of the General Assembly of the State of Illinois, entitled, "An Act concerning Corporations," approved April 18, 1872, and of the several acts amendatory thereof, do hereby state and certify as follows, to wit:

1. The name by which said corporation shall be known in law is
"THE UNIVERSITY OF CHICAGO."

2. The particular objects for which said corporation is formed are to provide, impart, and furnish opportunities for all departments of higher education to persons of both sexes on equal terms; to establish, conduct, and maintain one or more academies, preparatory schools, or departments, such academies, preparatory schools, or departments to be located in the city of Chicago or elsewhere as may be deemed advisable; to establish, maintain, and conduct manual-training schools in connection with such preparatory departments; to establish and maintain one or more colleges, and to provide instruction in all collegiate studies; to establish and maintain a university, in which may be taught all branches of higher learning, and which may comprise and embrace separate departments for literature, law, medicine, music, technology, the various branches of science, both abstract and

applied, the cultivation of the fine arts, and all other branches of professional or technical education which may properly be included within the purposes and objects of a university, and to provide and maintain courses of instruction in each and all of said departments; to prescribe the courses of study, employ professors, instructors, and teachers, and to maintain and control the government and discipline in said University, and in each of the several departments thereof, and in each of the several academies, preparatory schools, or other institutions subordinate thereto, and to fix the rates of tuition, and the qualifications for admission to the University and its various departments; to receive, hold, invest, and disburse all moneys and property, or the income thereof, which may be vested in or intrusted to care of the said corporation, whether by gift, grant, bequest, devise, or otherwise, for educational purposes; to act as trustee for persons desiring to give or provide moneys or property, or the income thereof, for any one or more of the departments of said University, and for any of the objects aforesaid, or for any educational purpose; to grant such literary honors and degrees as are usually granted by like institutions, and to give suitable diplomas; and generally to pursue and promote all or any of the objects above named, and to do all and every of the things necessary or pertaining to the accomplishment of said objects or either of them.

DANIEL COIT GILMAN ON ACADEMIC FREEDOM (1875)   From Daniel Coit Gilman to Reverdy Johnson, January 30, 1875, as quoted in Hugh Hawkins, *Pioneer: A History of the Johns Hopkins University, 1874–1889* (Ithaca, N.Y., 1960), pp. 22–23.

The institution we are about to organize would not be worthy the name of a University, if it were to be devoted to any other purpose than the discovery and promulgation of the truth; and it would be ignoble in the extreme if the resources which have been given by the Founder without restrictions should be limited to the maintenance of ecclesiastical differences or perverted to the promotion of political strife.

As the spirit of the University should be that of intellectual freedom in the pursuit of truth and of the broadest charity toward those from whom we differ in opinion it is certain that sectarian and partisan preferences should have no control in the selection of teachers, and should not be apparent in their official work.

NOAH PORTER'S OBJECTIONS TO WILLIAM GRAHAM SUMNER'S USE OF HERBERT SPENCER IN UNDERGRADUATE CLASSES (1879) From
Noah Porter to William Graham Sumner, December 6, 1879, as quoted in Harris E. Starr, *William Graham Sumner* (New York, 1925), pp. 346–47.

MY DEAR PROF. SUMNER:

The use of Spencer's 'Study of Sociology' as a textbook has made a great deal of talk and is likely to make still more. When the subject has been brought to my notice I have been able to reply that I have used his First Principles and his Psychology in my graduate classes with very great advantage. I cannot, however, think that this is or ought to be satisfactory, for the reason that the capacity of an undergraduate student when introduced to the elements of a science, to discriminate between the valid and the invalid is much below that of a graduate. A much more cogent reason is that the book itself is written very largely in a pamphleteering style, which is very unlike most of Spencer's more solid treatises. The freedom and unfairness with which it attacks every Theistic Philosophy of society and of history, and the cool and yet sarcastic effrontery with which he assumes that material elements and laws are the only forces and laws which any scientific man can recognize, seem to me to condemn the book as a textbook for a miscellaneous class in an undergraduate course. I ought to have examined the book sooner, but I feel assured that the use of the book will bring intellectual and moral harm to the students, however you may strive to neutralize or counteract its influence, and that the use of it will inevitably and reasonably work serious havoc to the reputation of the college. Having these opinions, I can do nothing else than express them, and as I am presumed to authorize the use of every textbook, I must formally object to the use of this.

Faithfully yours,
N. Porter

THE REGENTS OF THE UNIVERSITY OF WISCONSIN ON ACADEMIC FREEDOM (1894) From "Report of the Investigating Committee," in *Papers* of the
Board of Regents, University of Wisconsin, September 18, 1894, as quoted in Merle Curti and Vernon Carstensen, *The University of Wisconsin, 1848–1925* (Madison, Wis., 1949), vol. I, p. 525.

As Regents of the University with over a hundred instructors supported by nearly two millions of people who hold a vast diversity of views regarding the great questions which at present agitate the human mind, we could not for a moment think of recommending the dismissal or even the criticism of a teacher even if some of his opinion should, in some quarters, be regarded as visionary. Such a course would be equivalent to saying that no professor should teach anything which is not accepted by everybody as true. This would cut our curriculum down to very small proportions. We cannot for a moment believe that knowledge has reached its final goal, or that the present condition of society is perfect. We must, therefore, welcome from our teachers such discussions as shall suggest the means and prepare the way by which knowledge may be extended, present evils . . . removed, and others prevented.

We feel that we would be unworthy [of] the position we hold if we did not believe in progress in all departments of knowledge. In all lines of academic investigation it is of the utmost importance that the investigator should be absolutely free to follow the indications of truth wherever they may lead.

Whatever may be the limitations which trammel inquiry elsewhere we believe the great state University of Wisconsin should ever encourage that continual and fearless sifting and winnowing by which alone the truth can be found.

Education of Women

NOAH WEBSTER'S IDEAL YOUNG LADY (1804)   From Noah Webster, *An American Selection . . .* (Boston, 1804), pp. 34–35.

1. Sophia is not a beauty, but in her presence beauties are discontented with themselves. At first, she scarcely appeared pretty; but the more she is beheld, the more agreeable she appears. She gains when others lose, and what she gains she never loses. She is equalled by none in a sweet expression of countenance; and without dazzling beholders she interests them.

2. She loves dress, and is a good judge of it; despises finery, but dresses with peculiar grace, mixing simplicity with elegance. Ignorant she is of what colors are in fashion; but knows well what suits her complexion. She covers her beauties; but so slightly, or rather artfully, as to give play to the imagination. She prepares herself for managing a family of her own by managing that of her father.

3. Cookery is familiar to her, with the price and quality of provisions; and she is a ready accountant. Her chief view, however, is to serve her mother, and lighten her cares. She holds cleanness and neatness to be indispensable in a woman; and that a slattern is disgusting, especially if beautiful.

4. The attention given to externals, does not make her overlook her more material duties. Sophia's understanding is solid, without being profound. Her sensibility is too great for a perfect equality of temper; but her sweetness renders that inequality harmless. A harsh word does not make her angry; but her heart swells, and she retires to disburden it by weeping.

5. Recalled by her father and mother; she comes at the instant, wiping her eyes and appearing cheerful. She suffers with patience any wrong done her; but is impatient to repair any wrong she has done, and does it so cordially, as to make it appear meritorious. If she happen to disoblige a companion, her joy and her caresses, when restored to favor, shew the burthen that lay upon her good heart.

6. The love of virtue is Sophia's ruling passion. She loves it, because no other thing is so lovely. She loves it, because it is the glory of the female sex: She loves it as the only road to happiness, misery being the sure attendant of a woman without virtue: She loves it as dear to her respectable father and tender mother. These sentiments inspire her with a degree of enthusiam, that elevates her soul and subdues every irregular appetite.

7. Of the absent she never talks but with circumspection, her female acquaintance especially. She has remarked, that what renders women prone to detraction, is talking of their own sex; and that they are more equitable with respect to the men.

Sophia therefore never talks of women, but to express the good she knows of them: Of others she says nothing.

8. Without much knowledge of the world, she is attentive, obliging, and graceful in all she does. A good disposition does more for her than much art does for others. She possesses a degree of politeness which, void of ceremony, proceeds from a desire to please, and which consequently never fails to please.

ANNOUNCEMENT OF THE OPENING OF A FEMALE ACADEMY IN WARRENTON, NORTH CAROLINA (1808)   From *Raleigh Register,* August 25, 1808.

In conformity to the wishes of some respectable Patrons in this place and its vicinity, I purpose to open an Institution for Female Improvement, on the first day of January next. The course of Instruction intended to be pursued, is the result of observation and some experience, and will be adopted to the varied dispositions of genius of my Pupils, not losing sight of systematic Arrangement and Progression. My object not merely to impart words and exhibit things, but chiefly to form the mind to the labour of thinking upon and understanding what is taught.—Whether my plan is judicious, a short experience will decide; and by the event I am content to be judged. The domestic arrangement for an efficient accommodation of my Scholars, will be an object of primary concern, and placed under the immediate inspection of Mrs. Mordecai—believing it to be no small part of Education bestowed on Females, to cultivate a *Taste* for neatness in their Persons and propriety of Manners: they will be placed under a superintendence calculated as much as possible to alleviate the solicitude of Parents.—In my Seminary will be taught the English Language, grammatically, *Spelling,* Reading, Writing, Arithmetic, Composition, History, Geography and use of the Globes. The plain and ornamental branches of Needle Work—Drawing, Vocal and Instrumental Music, by an approved Master of distinguished talents and correct deportment.

Terms:—For Board, Washing, Lodging and Tuition (Drawing and Music excepted) $105 per annum. An additional change will be made for necessary Books, Paper, Quills and Ink.

Warrenton, Aug. 18, 1808.

Jacob Mordecai.

Whitworth Female College, Brookhaven, Miss., c. 1881.

A SATIRE ON A COLLEGE FOR WOMEN IN KENTUCKY (1835) From
Springfield (Mass.) *Republican and Journal,* March 14, 1835.

College for Ladies.—The Kentucky Legislature has conferred upon Messrs. Van Doren's Institute for Young Ladies, in Lexington, the chartered rights and standing of a College, by the name of Van Doren's College for young Ladies. By the power granted by the Board of Trustees and the Faculty of the College, we understand from the Daily Reporter, that a Diploma and the honorary degree of M.P.L. (Mistress of Polite Literature) will be conferred upon those young ladies who complete the prescribed course of studies; and that the same honor may be conferred upon other distinguished ladies in our country; and also, that the honorary degree of M.M. (Mistress of Music,) and M.I. (Mistress of Instruction,) may be conferred by this College upon suitable candidates.

Female Degrees.—Yesterday we gave some accounts of the degrees conferred in the Young Ladies College in Kentucky.—In addition to those, we would recommend the following, which we think will be of more use—namely—M.P.M. (Mistress of Pudding Making,) M.D.N. (Mistress of the Darning Needle,) M.S.B. (Mistress of the Scrubbing Brush,) and especially M.C.S. (Mistress of Common Sense.) But, in order to fit the girls for those degrees, it will be necessary to organize a new department— and we recommend to the faculty of the institute to apply to the Legislature immediately for an enlargement of its powers, to enable it to confer these new and more useful degrees—and we furthermore recommend to them to procure some well qualified Professors, from among the farmers' wives, and especially from some of the best regulated kitchens, to teach the young ladies the useful art of house-wifery. When they have done this in the proper manner to fit them for taking charge of the family, and making their husband's fireside comfortable, then let the degrees we have recommended, be conferred, in course; and then, in due season, if they succeed according to their merits, they will attain to the honorary degree, to which, we dare say, they are all looking forward, namely, that of R.W. (the Respectable Wife) H.H. (Of a Happy Husband;) and M.W.R.F. (Mother of a Well Regulated Family.)

EMMA WILLARD ON THE EDUCATION OF WOMEN (1819) From Emma
Willard, *An Address to the Public; Particularly to the Members of the Legislature of New-York, Proposing a Plan for Improving Female Education,* in Anna C. Brackett, ed., *Woman and the Higher Education* (New York, 1893), pp. 1–4, 18–26, 41–44.

The object of this Address, is to convince the public, that a reform, with respect to female education, is necessary; that it cannot be effected by individual exertion, but that it requires the aid of the legislature: and further, by shewing the justice, the policy, and the magnanimity of such an undertaking, to persuade that body, to endow a seminary for females, as the commencement of such reformation.

The idea of a college for males, will naturally be associated with that of a seminary, instituted and endowed by the public; and the absurdity of sending ladies

HIGHER
EDUCATION

1573

to college, may, at first thought, strike everyone, to whom this subject shall be proposed. I therefore hasten to observe, that the seminary here recommended, will be as different from those appropriated to the other sex, as the female character and duties are from the male.—The business of the husbandman is not to waste his endeavours, in seeking to make his orchard attain the strength and majesty of his forest, but to rear each, to the perfection of its nature.

That the improvement of female education will be considered by our enlightened citizens as a subject of importance, the liberality with which they part with their property to educate their daughters, is a sufficient evidence; and why should they not, when assembled in the legislature, act in concert to effect the noble object, which, though dear to them individually, cannot be accomplished by their unconnected exertions.

* * *

If the improvement of the American female character, and that alone, could be effected by public liberality, employed in giving better means of instruction; such improvement of one half of society, and that half, which barbarous and despotic nations have ever degraded, would of itself be an object, worthy of the most liberal government on earth; but if the female character be raised, it must inevitably raise that of the other sex: and thus does the plan proposed, offer, as the object of legislative bounty, to elevate the whole character of the community.

As evidence, that this statement does not exaggerate the female influence in society, our sex need but be considered, in the single relation of mothers. In this character, we have the charge of the whole mass of individuals, who are to compose the succeeding generation: during that period of youth, when the pliant mind takes any direction, to which it is steadily guided by a forming hand. How important a power is given by this charge! yet, little do too many of my sex know how, either to appreciate or improve it. Unprovided with the means of acquiring that knowledge, which flows liberally to the other sex—having our time of education devoted to frivolous acquirements, how should we understand the nature of the mind, so as to be aware of the importance of those early impressions, which we make upon the minds of our children?—or how should we be able to form enlarged and correct views, either of the character, to which we ought to mould them, or of the means most proper to form them aright?

Considered in this point of view, were the interests of male education alone to be consulted, that of females becomes of sufficient importance to engage the public attention. Would we rear the human plant to its perfection, we must first fertilize the soil which produces it. If it acquire its first bent and texture upon a barren plain, it will avail comparatively little, should it be afterwards transplanted to a garden.

In the arrangement of my remarks, I shall pursue the following order.

I. Treat of the defects of the present mode of female education, and their causes.

II. Consider the principles, by which education should be regulated.

III. Sketch a plan of a female seminary.

IV. Shew the benefits which society would receive from such seminaries.

From considering the deficiencies in boarding schools, much may be learned, with regard to what would be needed, for the prosperity and usefulness of a public seminary for females.

I. There would be needed a building, with commodious rooms for lodging and recitation, apartments for the reception of apparatus, and for the accommodation of the domestic department.

II. A library, containing books on the various subjects in which the pupils were to receive instruction; musical instruments, some good paintings, to form the taste and serve as models for the execution of those who were to be instructed in that art; maps, globes, and a small collection of philosophical apparatus.

III. A judicious board of trust, competent and desirous to promote its interests, would in a female, as in a male literary institution, be the corner stone of its prosperity. On this board it would depend to provide,

IV. Suitable instruction. This article may be subdivided under four heads.

1. Religious and Moral.
2. Literary.
3. Domestic.
4. Ornamental.

1. RELIGIOUS AND MORAL. A regular attention to religious duties would, of course be required of the pupils by the laws of the institution. The trustees would be careful to appoint no instructors, who would not teach religion and morality, both by their example, and by leading the minds of the pupils to perceive, that these constitute the true end of all education. It would be desirable, that the young ladies should spend a part of their Sabbaths in hearing discourses relative to the peculiar duties of their sex. The evidences of Christianity, and moral philosophy, would constitute a part of their studies.

2. LITERARY INSTRUCTION. To make an exact enumeration of the branches of literature, which might be taught, would be impossible, unless the time of the pupils' continuance at the seminary, and the requisites for entrance, were previously fixed. Such an enumeration would be tedious, nor do I conceive that it would be at all promotive of my object. The difficulty complained of, is not, that we are at a loss what sciences we ought to learn, but that we have not proper advantages to learn any. Many writers have given us excellent advice with regard to what we should be taught, but no legislature has provided us the means of instruction. Not however, to pass lightly over this fundamental part of education, I will mention one or two of the less obvious branches of science, which, I conceive should engage the youthful attention of my sex.

It is highly important, that females should be conversant with those studies, which will lead them to understand the operations of the human mind. The chief use to which the philosophy of the mind can be applied, is to regulate education by its rules. The ductile mind of the child is intrusted to the mother: and she ought to have every possible assistance, in acquiring a knowledge of this noble material, on which it is her business to operate, that she may best understand how to mould it to its most excellent form.

Natural philosophy has not often been taught to our sex. Yet why should we be kept in ignorance of the great machinery of nature, and left to the vulgar notion, that nothing is curious but what deviates from her common course? If mothers were acquainted with this science, they would communicate very many of its principles to their children in early youth. From the bursting of an egg buried in the fire, I

HIGHER EDUCATION

1575

have heard an intelligent mother, lead her prattling inquirer, to understand the cause of the earthquake. But how often does the mother, from ignorance on this subject, give her child the most erroneous and contracted views of the causes of natural phenomena; views, which, though he may afterwards learn to be false, are yet, from the laws of association, ever ready to return, unless the active powers of the mind are continually upon the alert to keep them out. A knowledge of natural philosophy is calculated to heighten the moral taste, by bringing to view the majesty and beauty of order and design; and to enliven piety, by enabling the mind more clearly to perceive, throughout the manifold works of God, that wisdom, in which he hath made them all.

In some of the sciences proper for our sex, the books, written for the other, would need alteration; because, in some they presuppose more knowledge than female pupils would possess; in others, they have parts not particularly interesting to our sex, and omit subjects immediately relating to their pursuits. There would likewise be needed, for a female seminary, some works, which I believe are no where extant, such as a systematic treatise on housewifery.

3. DOMESTIC INSTRUCTION should be considered important in a female seminary. It is the duty of our sex to regulate the internal concerns of every family; and unless they be properly qualified to discharge this duty, whatever may be their literary or ornamental attainments, they cannot be expected to make either good wives, good mothers, or good mistresses of families: and if they are none of these, they must be bad members of society; for it is by promoting or destroying the comfort and prosperity of their own families, that females serve or injure the community. To superintend the domestic department, there should be a respectable lady, experienced in the best methods of housewifery, and acquainted with propriety of dress and manners. Under her tuition the pupils ought to be placed for a certain length of time every morning. A spirit of neatness and order should here be treated as a virtue, and the contrary, if excessive and incorrigible, be punished with expulsion. There might be a gradation of employment in the domestic department, according to the length of time the pupils had remained at the institution. The older scholars might then assist the superintendent in instructing the younger, and the whole be so arranged, that each pupil might have advantages to become a good domestic manager by the time she has completed her studies.

This plan would afford a healthy exercise. It would prevent that estrangement from domestic duties, which would be likely to take place in a length of time devoted to study, with those, to whom they were previously familiar; and would accustom those to them, who, from ignorance, might otherwise put at hazard their own happiness, and the prosperity of their families.

These objects might doubtless be effected by a scheme of domestic instruction; and probably others of no inconsiderable importance. It is believed, that housewifery might be greatly improved, by being taught, not only in practice, but in theory. Why may it not be reduced to a system, as well as other arts? There are right ways of performing its various operations; and there are reasons why those ways are right; and why may not rules be formed, their reasons collected; and the whole be digested into a system to guide the learner's practice?

It is obvious, that theory alone, can never make a good artist; and it is equally obvious, that practice unaided by theory, can never correct errors, but must establish them. If I should perform anything in a wrong manner all my life, and teach my children to perform it in the same manner, still, through my life and theirs, it would be wrong. Without alteration there can be no improvement; but how are we to alter, so as to improve, if we are ignorant of the principles of our art, with which we should compare our practice, and by which we should regulate it?

In the present state of things, it is not to be expected, that any material improvements in housewifery should be made. There being no uniformity of method, prevailing among different housewives, of course, the communications from one to another, are not much more likely to improve the art, than a communication, between two mechanics of different trades, would be, to improve each in his respective occupation. But should a system of principles be philosophically arranged, and taught, both in theory and by practice, to a large number of females, whose minds were expanded and strengthened by a course of literary instruction, those among them, of an investigating turn, would, when they commenced housekeepers, consider their domestic operations as a series of experiments, which either proved or refuted the system previously taught. They would then converse together like those, who practise a common art, and improve each other by their observations and experiments; and they would also be capable of improving the system, by detecting its errors, and by making additions of new principles and better modes of practice.

4. The ORNAMENTAL branches, which I should recommend for a female seminary, are drawing and painting, elegant penmanship, music, and the grace of motion. Needle-work is not here mentioned. The best style of useful needle-work should either be taught in the domestic department, or made a qualification for entrance; and I consider that useful, which may contribute to the decoration of a lady's person, or the convenience and neatness of her family. But the use of the needle, for other purposes than these, as it affords little to assist in the formation of the character, I should regard as a waste of time.

The grace of motion, must be learnt chiefly from instruction in dancing. Other advantages besides that of a graceful carriage, might be derived from such instruction, if the lessons were judiciously timed. Exercise is needful to the health, and recreation to the cheerfulness and contentment of youth. Female youth could not be allowed to range unrestrained, to seek amusement for themselves. If it was entirely prohibited, they would be driven to seek it by stealth; which would lead them to many improprieties of conduct, and would have a pernicious effect upon their general character, by inducing a habit of treading forbidden paths. The alternative that remains is to provide them with proper recreation, which, after the confinement of the day, they might enjoy under the eye of their instructors. Dancing is exactly suited to this purpose, as also to that of exercise; for perhaps in no way, can so much healthy exercise be taken in so short a time. It has besides, this advantage over other amusements, that it affords nothing to excite the bad passions; but, on the contrary, its effects are, to soften the mind, to banish its animosities, and to open it to social impressions.

It may be said, that dancing would dissipate the attention, and estrange it from study. Balls would doubtless have this effect; but let dancing be practised everyday, by youth of the same sex, without change of place, dress, or company, and under the eye of those, whom they are accustomed to obey, and it would excite no more emotion, than any other exercise or amusement, but in degree, as it is of itself more pleasant. But it must ever be a grateful exercise to youth, as it is one, to which nature herself prompts them, at the sound of animating music.

It has been doubted, whether painting and music should be taught to young ladies, because much time is requisite to bring them to any considerable degree of perfection, and they are not immediately useful. Though these objections have weight, yet they are founded on too limited a view of the objects of education. They leave out the important consideration of forming the character. I should not consider it an essential point, that the music of a lady's piano should rival that of her master's; or that her drawing room should be decorated with her own paintings, rather than those of others; but it is the intrinsic advantage, which she might derive from the refinement of herself, that would induce me to recommend to her, an attention to these elegant pursuits. The harmony of sound, has a tendency to produce a correspondent harmony of soul; and that art, which obliges us to study nature, in order to imitate her, often enkindles the latent spark of taste—of sensibility for her beauties, till it glows to adoration for their author, and a refined love of all his works.

V. There would be needed, for a female, as well as for a male seminary, a system of laws and regulations, so arranged, that both the instructors and pupils would know their duty; and thus, the whole business, move with regularity and uniformity.

The laws of the institution would be chiefly directed, to regulate the pupil's qualifications for entrance, the kind and order of their studies, their behaviour while at the institution, the term allotted for the completion of their studies, the punishments to be inflicted on offenders, and the rewards or honours, to be bestowed on the virtuous and diligent.

The direct rewards or honors, used to stimulate the ambition of students in colleges, are first, the certificate or diploma, which each receives, who passes successfully through the term allotted to his collegiate studies; and secondly, the appointments to perform certain parts in public exhibitions, which are bestowed by the faculty, as rewards for superior scholarship. The first of these modes is admissible into a female seminary; the second is not; as public speaking forms no part of female education. The want of this mode, might, however, be supplied by examinations judiciously conducted. The leisure and inclination of both instructors and scholars, would combine to produce a thorough preparation for these; for neither would have any other public test of the success of their labors. Persons of both sexes would attend. The less entertaining parts, might be enlivened by interludes, where the pupils in painting and music, would display their several improvements. Such examinations, would stimulate the instructors to give their scholars more attention, by which the leading facts and principles of their studies, would be clearly understood, and better remembered. The ambition excited among the pupils, would operate, without placing the instructors under the necessity of making distinctions among them, which are so apt to be considered as invidious; and which are, in our male seminaries, such fruitful sources of disaffection.

Perhaps the term allotted for the routine of study at the seminary, might be three years. The pupils, probably, would not be fitted to enter, till about the age of fourteen. Whether they attended to all, or any of the ornamental branches, should be left optional with the parents or guardians. Those who were to be instructed in them, should be entered for a longer term, but if this was a subject of previous calculation, no confusion would arise from it. The routine of the exercises being established by the laws of the institution, would be uniform, and publicly known; and those who were previously acquainted with the branches first taught, might enter the higher classes; nor would those who entered the lowest, be obliged to remain during the three years. Thus the term of remaining at the institutions, might be either one, two, three, four, or more years; and that, without interfering with the regularity and uniformity of its proceedings.

The writer has now given a sketch of her plan. She has by no means expressed all the ideas, which occurred to her concerning it. She wished to be as concise as possible, and yet afford conviction, that it is practicable, to organize a system of female education, which shall possess the permanency, uniformity of operation, and respectability of our male institutions; and yet differ from them, so as to be adapted, to that difference of character, and duties, to which early instruction should form the softer sex.

It now remains, to enquire more particularly, what would be the benefits resulting from such a system.

Benefits of Female Seminaries

In inquiring, concerning the benefits of the plan proposed, I shall proceed upon the supposition, that female seminaries will be patronized throughout our country.

Nor is this altogether a visionary supposition. If one seminary should be well organized, its advantages would be found so great, that others would soon be instituted; and, that sufficient patronage can be found to put one in operation, may be presumed from its reasonableness, and from the public opinion, with regard to the present mode of female education. It is from an intimate acquaintance, with those parts of our country, whose education is said to flourish most, that the writer has drawn her picture of the present state of female instruction; and she knows, that she is not alone, in perceiving or deploring its faults. Her sentiments are shared by many an enlightened parent of a daughter, who has received a boarding school education. Counting on the promise of her childhood, the father had anticipated her maturity, as combining what is excellent in mind, with what is elegant in manners. He spared no expense that education might realize to him, the image of his imagination. His daughter returned from her boarding school,[1] improved in fashionable airs, and expert in manufacturing fashionable toys; but, in her conversation, he sought in vain, for that refined and fertile mind, which he had fondly expected. Aware that his disappointment has its source in a defective education, he looks with anxiety on his other daughters, whose minds, like lovely buds, are beginning to open. Where shall he find a genial soil, in which he may place them to expand? Shall he provide them male instructors? Then the graces of their persons and manners, and whatever forms the distinguishing charm of the feminine character, they cannot be expected to acquire.—Shall he give them a private tutoress? She will have been educated at the boarding school, and his daughters will have the faults of its instruction second-handed. Such is now the dilemma of many parents; and it is one, from which they cannot be extricated by their individual exertions. May not then the only plan, which promises to relieve them, expect their vigorous support.

Let us now proceed to inquire, what benefits would result from the establishment of female seminaries.

They would constitute a grade of public education, superior to any yet known in the history of our sex; and through them, the lower grades of female instruction might be controlled. The influence of public seminaries, over these, would operate in two ways; first, by requiring certain qualifications for entrance; and secondly, by furnishing instructresses, initiated in their modes of teaching, and imbued with their maxims.

Female seminaries might be expected to have important and happy effects, on common schools in general; and in the manner of operating on these, would probably place the business of teaching children, in hands now nearly useless to society; and take it from those, whose services the state wants in many other ways.

That nature designed for our sex the care of children, she has made manifest, by mental, as well as physical indications. She has given us, in a greater degree than men, the gentle arts of insinuation, to soften their minds, and fit them to receive impressions; a greater quickness of invention to vary modes of teaching to different dispositions; and more patience to make repeated efforts. There are many females of ability, to whom the business of instructing children is highly acceptable, and, who would devote all their faculties to their occupation. They would have no higher pecuniary object to engage their attention, and their reputation as instructors they would consider as important; whereas, whenever able and enterprizing men, engage in this business, they consider it, merely as a temporary employment, to further some other object, to the attainment of which, their best thoughts and calculations are all directed. If then women were properly fitted by instruction, they would be likely to teach children better than the other sex; they could afford to do it cheaper; and those men who would otherwise be engaged in this employment, might be at liberty to add to the wealth of the nation, by any of those thousand occupations, from which women are necessarily debarred.

CATHERINE BEECHER ON THE PURPOSE OF HARTFORD FEMALE SEMINARY (1829) From "Suggestions Respecting Improvements in Education . . ." in Willystine Goodsell, *Pioneers of Women's Education in the United States* (New York, 1931), pp. 146–48, 155–57.

Most of the defects which are continually discovered and lamented in present systems of education may be traced, either directly or indirectly to the fact, that the *formation of the minds of children has not been made a profession securing wealth, influence, or honour*, to those who enter it.

The three professions of law, divinity, and medicine, present a reasonable prospect of reputation, influence and emolument to active and cultivated minds. The mercantile, manufacturing and mechanical professions present a hope of gaining at least that *wealth* which can so readily purchase estimation and influence. But the profession of a *teacher* has not offered any such stimulus.

It has been looked upon as the resource of poverty, or as a drudgery suited only to inferior minds and far beneath the aims of the intellectual aspirant for fame and influence, or of the active competitor for wealth and distinction. The consequence of this has been, as a general fact, that this profession has never, until very recently, commanded, or secured the effort of *gifted minds.* . . .

It is to *mothers,* and to *teachers,* that the world is to look for the character which is to be enstamped on each succeeding generation, for it is to them that the great business of education is almost exclusively committed. And will it not appear by examination that neither mothers nor teachers have ever been properly educated for their profession. What is *the profession* of a *Woman?* Is it not to form immortal minds, and to watch, to nurse, and to rear the bodily system, so fearfully and wonderfully made, and upon the order and regulation of which, the health and well-being of the mind so greatly depends?

But let most of our sex upon whom these arduous duties devolve, be asked; have you ever devoted any time and study, in the course of your education, to any preparation for these duties? Have you been taught any thing of the structure, the nature, and the laws of the body, which you inhabit? Were you ever taught to understand the operation of diet, air, exercise and modes of dress upon the human frame? Have the causes which are continually operating to prevent good health, and the modes by which it might be perfected and preserved ever been made the subject of any *instruction?* Perhaps almost every voice would respond, no; we have attended to almost everything more than to this; we have been taught more concerning the structure of the earth; the laws of the heavenly bodies; the habits and formation of plants; the philosophy of languages; more of *almost any thing,* than the structure of the human frame and the laws of health and reason. But is it not the business, the *profession* of a woman to guard the health and form the physical habits of the young? And is not the cradle of infancy and the chamber of sickness sacred to woman alone? And ought she not to know at least some of the *general principles* of that perfect and wonderful piece of mechanism committed to her preservation and care?

The *restoration* of health is the physician's profession, but the *preservation* of it falls to other hands, and it is believed that the time will come, when woman will be taught to understand something respecting the construction of the human frame; the physiological results which will naturally follow from restricted exercise, unhealthy modes of dress, improper diet, and many other causes, which are continually operating to destroy the health and life of the young.

Again let our sex be asked respecting the instruction they have received in the course of their education, on that still more arduous and difficult department of their profession, which relates to the *intellect* and the *moral susceptibilities.* Have you been taught the powers and faculties of the human mind, and the laws by which it is regulated? Have you studied how to direct its several faculties; how to restore those that are overgrown, and strengthen and mature those that are deficient? Have you been taught the best modes of *communicating* knowledge as well as of *acquiring* it? Have you learned the best mode of correcting bad *moral* habits and forming good ones? Have you made it an object to find how a selfish disposition may be made generous; how a reserved temper may be made open and frank; how pettishness and ill humor may be changed to cheerfulness and kindness? Has any woman studied her profession in this respect? It is feared the same answer must be returned, if not from all, at least from most of our sex. No; we have acquired wisdom from the observation and experience of others, on almost *all other* subjects, but the philosophy of the direction and control of the human mind has not been an object of thought or study. And thus it appears that tho' it is woman's *express business* to rear the body, and form the mind, there is scarcely anything to which her attention has been less directed. . . .

If all females were not only well educated themselves, but were prepared to communicate in an easy manner their stores of knowledge to others; if they not only knew how to regulate their own minds, tempers and habits, but how to effect improvements in those around them, the face of society would speedily be changed. The time *may* come when the world will look back with wonder to behold how much time and effort have been given to the mere cultivation of the memory, and how little mankind have been aware of what every teacher, parent, and friend could accomplish in forming the social, intellectual and moral character of those by whom they are surrounded. . . .

Another fundamental difficulty in education, has resulted from the fact that the great principle of the *Division* of *Labour,* which ensures improvement and success in all the several arts and sciences has never until very recently, and only in a few instances, been introduced into *school education.*

THE COURSE OF STUDY AT THE HARTFORD (CONNECTICUT) FEMALE SEMINARY (1831)   From Hartford Female Seminary, *Annual Catalogue* (Hartford, Conn., 1831).

Course of Study

In order to enter any higher class, the pupil must have recited all the lessons of the branches required from the previous classes, to one of the teachers, either during the term, or at the closing examination.

Studies of the Primary Class

Reading, Writing, Spelling, and Composition. Introductory Course in Botany, Mineralogy, Geology, and Natural History. First Course in Geography. First Course in Arithmetic. First Book in Geometry, with Holbrook's introductory work. First Book of History. First Course in Grammar. First Course in Mental Philosophy.

Studies of the Junior Class

Second Course in Grammar, Geography, and Arithmetic. Ancient Geography. Ancient and Modern History with Bostwick's Charts. The 2*d,* 3*rd,* and 4*th* Books of Euclid's Geometry. Comstock's Chemistry and Natural Philosophy. Finish Mental Philosophy. Astronomy. Composition. Reading, Writing, and Spelling for all who are deficient.

Studies of Senior Class

Review Mental Philosophy. The 5*th* and 6*th* Books and the Supplements in Geometry. The whole of Day's Algebra. Paley's Theology. Sullivan's Political Class Book. Butler's Analogy. Latin. Composition.

If the pupils have a knowledge of Geography, Grammar, and Arithmetic, as not to need the *first course,* they are required only to study the second course.

The time required to complete this course depends upon the age, talents, and previous habits of the pupil, and still more upon the amount of attention given to Composition and Reading. No young lady, of good talents, could complete the course and *read all that is deemed necessary,* and spend as much time as is demanded to *learn to compose well* short of *three years,* and with young scholars commencing at twelve, it would demand four or five years.

MARY LYON SKETCHES A FEMALE SEMINARY FOR TEACHERS

(1832) From "New England Female Seminary for Teachers," as quoted in Edward Hitchcock, *The Power of Christian Benevolence Illustrated in the Life and Labors of Mary Lyon* (Northhampton, 1852), pp. 164–67.

Several friends of education and of evangelical religion are considering the expediency of attempting to raise funds to found a permanent female seminary in New England.

General Object

The main object of the proposed institution will be to prepare young ladies of mature minds for active usefulness, expecially to become teachers.

Character

1. Its religious character is to be strictly evangelical.
2. Its literary character is to be of a high order.

Location

This has not yet been selected. An attempt will be made to embrace as many of the following requisites as possible in the location:
   1. That it be central for New England.
   2. That it be surrounded by a community marked for intelligence and public spirit.
   3. That a liberal proportion of the funds be raised by the town and its immediate vicinity.
   4. That the particular spot be healthy and pleasant, a little removed from public business, and so situated as to be free from all other encumbrances.

Funds

The amount of funds should be sufficient to furnish the following accommodations:—
   1. Several acres of land.
   2. Buildings sufficiently capacious to furnish from one hundred to two hundred pupils with accommodations for school and boarding.
   3. Furniture.
   4. An ample library and apparatus.

HIGHER EDUCATION

1583

Domestic Arrangements

It is proposed that the domestic department should be under the direct superintendence of such persons as are qualified for the trust. In order to give as much independence and facility to the trustees as possible, in organizing the establishment, and in order to avoid difficulties in filling offices from time to time, it is proposed that all the furniture should be owned by the corporation.

Boarding-house

The plan which has been proposed for the buildings is suited,

1. To give to the young ladies superior privileges, both for retirement and for social intercourse, and in an eminent degree to promote health, comfort, and domestic happiness, and intellectual, moral, and religious improvement.

2. To furnish each member with a small chamber, exclusively her own. The great advantages of such a privilege can scarcely be realized, except by those who have often felt that they would give up almost any of their common comforts, for the sake of such retirement as can be enjoyed only in a separate apartment. To persons of reflection, the advantages will doubtless appear much greater than the extra expense, especially when it is considered that this institution is not designed for younger misses, but especially for the benefit of ladies of mature age.

Family Discipline

The family discipline is to be entirely distinct from the domestic concerns. This, together with the general improvement of the pupils out of school, is to be committed directly to the teachers. The family discipline should be very systematic, but of a kind adapted to the age of its members. The whole should resemble a well-regulated voluntary association, where the officers and members are all faithful to their trust.

The plan which has been proposed for buildings is particularly suited to promote family discipline, and to render it at once easy, systematic, and pleasant to all.

1. It is such that the whole family will naturally and necessarily be arranged in a convenient number of sections, each of which can be easily directed by an appropriate head.

2. It is such as to bring all the young ladies under a direct and natural supervision. This will tend at once to secure order and propriety, and at the same time to exclude all necessity of anything like apparent watchfulness or nice inspection, even if the age and character of the members of the institution should not render every thing of the kind needless.

Specific Objects to Be Accomplished

1. To increase the number of well-qualified female teachers. The present want of such teachers is well known to all particularly engaged in the cause of education. This deficiency is the occasion of placing many of our schools under the care of those who are not competent to the undertaking.

2. To induce many who have already become teachers, to make further

improvement in their education. This institution will furnish such ladies with a full course of instruction, and with society adapted to their age and character, and will give them a more suitable and pleasant home than can now be found connected with any of our female seminaries.

3. To exert an influence in bringing as much of the labor of instruction into the hands of ladies as propriety will admit. This seems important, on account of the many public demands on the time of benevolent, educated gentlemen, and the comparatively few demands on the time of benevolent, educated ladies.

4. To lead the way toward the establishment of permanent female seminaries in our land. That there are no female seminaries of this character is, we believe, a fact. Those which appear to have the strongest claim to such a standing are so dependent on their present teachers, and their funds and accommodations are to such an extent the property of private individuals, that it would not be safe to predict even their existence the next century.

MARY LYON ON THE PRINCIPLES AND PRACTICES OF MOUNT HOLYOKE FEMALE SEMINARY (1837)   From Edward Hitchcock, *The Power of Christian Benevolence Illustrated in the Life and Labors of Mary Lyon* (Northampton, 1851), pp. 295-98, 300-304.

This institution is established at South Hadley, Massachusetts. It is to be principally devoted to the preparing of female teachers. At the same time, it will qualify ladies for other spheres of usefulness. The design is to give a solid, extensive, and well-balanced English education, connected with that general improvement, that moral culture, and those enlarged views of duty, which will prepare ladies to be educators of children and youth, rather than to fit them to be mere teachers, as the term has been technically applied. Such an education is needed by every female who takes the charge of a school, and sustains the responsibility of guiding the whole course and of forming the entire character of those committed to her care. And when she has done with the business of teaching in a regular school, she will not give up her profession; she will still need the same well-balanced education at the head of her own family and in guiding her own household.

1. This institution professes to be founded on the high principle of enlarged Christian benevolence. In its plans and in its appeals it seeks no support from local or private interest. It is designed entirely for the public good, and the trustees would adopt no measures not in accordance with this design. It is sacredly consecrated to the great Head of the church, and they would not seek for human approbation by any means which will not be well pleasing in his sight.

2. The institution is designed to be permanent. The permanency of an institution may be considered as consisting of two particulars—first, its perpetual vitality, and second, its continual prosperity and usefulness. The first is to be secured in the same manner that the principle of perpetual life in our higher institutions for young men has been effectually preserved. A fund is to be committed to an independent, self-perpetuating board of trustees, known to the churches as faithful, responsible men; not as a proprietary investment, but as a free offering, leaving

HIGHER EDUCATION

1585

them no way for an honorable retreat from their trust, and binding them with solemn responsibilities to hundreds and thousands of donors, who have committed their sacred charities to their conscientious fidelity. Give to a literary institution, on this principle, an amount of property sufficient to be viewed as an object of great importance, and it is almost impossible to extinguish its vital life by means of adversity. How firmly have our colleges stood amidst the clashing elements around us, and the continual overturnings which are taking place in the midst of us!

The usefulness of this institution, like all others, must depend on its character. This may be very good for a time, where there is no principle of perpetual life, as is the case with some of our most distinguished female seminaries. Amidst all their prosperity, they have no solid foundation, and in themselves no sure principle of continued existence. Could we secure to our public institutions the continued labors of the same teachers through an antediluvial life, the preservation of the vital principle would be a subject of much less consequence. But in view of the present shortened life of man, rendered shorter still by disease and premature decay, and in view of the many changes which are ever breaking in upon the continued services of those to whose care these institutions are committed, every reflecting mind must regard it as of the very first importance to secure to them this principle, especially to a public seminary for the raising up of female teachers.

3. The institution is to be entirely for an older class of young ladies. The general system for family arrangements, for social improvement, for the division of time, for organizing and regulating the school, and the requirements for entrance, will be adapted throughout to young ladies of adult age and of mature character. Any provision in an institution like this for younger misses must be a public loss far greater than the individual good. Their exclusion from the institution will produce a state of society among the members exceedingly pleasant and profitable to those whose great desire is to be prepared to use all their talents in behalf of the cause of education, and of the Redeemer's kingdom; and it will secure for their improvement the entire labors of the teachers, without an interruption from the care and government of pupils too immature to take care of themselves.

4. The young ladies are to take a part in the domestic work of the family. This also is to be on the principle of equality. All are to take part, not as a servile labor, for which they are to receive a small weekly remuneration, but as a gratuitous service to the institution of which they are members, designed for its improvement and elevation. The first object of this arrangement is, to give to the institution a greater degree of independence. The arrangements for boarding all the pupils in the establishment will give to us an independence with regard to private families in the neighborhood, without which it would be difficult, if not impossible, to secure its perpetual prosperity. The arrangements for the domestic work will, in a great measure, relieve it from another source of depressing dependence—a dependence on the will of hired domestics, to which many a family in New England is subject.

The other object of this arrangement is to promote the health, the improvement, and the happiness of the pupils; their health, by its furnishing them with a little daily exercise of the best kind; their improvement, by its tending to preserve their interest in domestic pursuits; and their happiness, by its relieving them from that servile dependence on common domestics, to which young ladies, as mere boarders in a large establishment, are often subject, to their great inconvenience. The adoption of a feature like this, is an institution which aims to be better endowed than any other existing female seminary in the country, must give it an attitude of noble independence, which can scarcely fail to exert an elevating influence on its members.

*   *   *

*Tendencies of the Principles Embraced and the
System Adopted in the Mount Holyoke
Female Seminary*

The enterprise of founding this seminary was commenced nearly five years ago. More than three years were occupied in preparing the way, in raising the funds, and in erecting the building now occupied. It was ready for the reception of scholars November 8, 1837.

The original plan was to provide for two hundred. Only the first building has yet been erected. This can accommodate only ninety. Though it is a noble edifice, and well adapted to its end, it is but a beginning. Full one half of the funds must yet be raised. In order to finish the plan, at least twenty thousand dollars more will be needed for the buildings, besides perhaps five thousand dollars or more for furniture, library, and apparatus.

This seminary is specific in its character, and, of course, does not provide for the entire education of a young lady. Such a provision may be found expedient in foreign countries, where all systems can be brought under the rigid rules of monarchy, without being subject to the continual encroachments and changes necessarily resulting from a free government. But in our country it is doubted whether female seminaries generally can attain a high standard of excellence till they become more specific and less mixed in their character.

1. RELIGIOUS CULTURE

This lies at the foundation of that female character which the founders of this seminary have contemplated. Without this, their efforts would entirely fail of their design. This institution has been for the Lord, that it might be peculiarly his own. It has been solemnly and publicly dedicated to his service. It has been embalmed by prayer in many hearts, and consecrated around many a family altar. The donors and benefactors of this institution, with its trustees and teachers, have felt a united obligation to seek, in behalf of this beloved seminary, "first the kingdom of God and his righteousness." Endeavors have been made to raise the funds and to lay the whole foundation on Christian principles, to organize a school and form a family that from day to day might illustrate the precepts and spirit of the gospel. Public worship, the Bible lesson, and other appropriate duties of the Sabbath, a regular observance of secret devotion, suitable attention to religious instruction and social prayer meetings, and the maintaining of a consistent Christian deportment, are considered the most important objects of regard, for both teachers and scholars. The friends of this seminary have sought that this might be a spot where souls shall be born of God, and where much shall be done for maturing and elevating Christian character. The smiles of Providence and the influences of the Holy Spirit have encouraged them to hope that their desires will not be in vain.

2. CULTIVATION OF BENEVOLENCE

This is implied in the last particular, but it needs special care in a lady's education. While many of the present active generation are fixed in their habits, and will never rise above the standard of benevolence already adopted, the eye of hope rests with anxious solicitude on the next generation. But who shall take all the little ones, and by precept, and still more by example, enforce on them the sentiments of benevolence, and, aided by the Holy Spirit, train them up from their infancy for the service of the Redeemer? Is there not here an appropriate sphere for the efforts of women, through whose moulding hands all our children and youth must inevitably pass?

How important, then, is it that the education of a female should be conducted on strictly benevolent principles! and how important that this spirit should be the presiding genius in every female school! Should it not be so incorporated with its nature, and so wrought into its very existence, that it cannot prosper without it? Such a school the friends of this seminary have sought to furnish. They would have the spirit of benevolence manifest in all its principles, and in the manner of conferring its privileges, in the mutual duties it requires of its members, and in the claims it makes on them to devote their future lives to doing good.

3. INTELLECTUAL CULTURE

This trait of character is of inestimable value to a lady who desires to be useful. A thorough and well-balanced intellectual education will be to her a valuable auxiliary in every department of duty.

This seminary has peculiar advantages for gaining a high intellectual standard. The age required for admission will secure to the pupils, as a whole, greater mental power, and the attainments required for admission will secure to the institution a higher standard of scholarship.

4. PHYSICAL CULTURE

The value of health to a lady is inestimable. Her appropriate duties are so numerous and varied, and so constant in their demands, and so imperious in the moment of their calls, as will render this treasure to her above price. How difficult is it for her to perform all her duties faithfully and successfully, unless she possesses at all times a calm mind, an even temper, a cheerful heart, and a happy face! But a feeble system and a nervous frame are often the direct antagonists of these indispensable traits in a lady's character. A gentleman may possibly live and do some good without much health; but what can a lady do, unless she takes the attitude of an invalid, and seeks to do good principally by patience and submission? If a gentleman cannot do his work in one hour, he may perhaps do it in another, but a lady's duties often allow of no compromise in hours. If a gentleman is annoyed and vexed with the nervousness of his feeble frame, he may perhaps use it to some advantage, as he attempts to move the world by his pen, or by his voice. But a lady cannot make such a use of this infirmity in her influence over her children and family—an influence which must be all times under the control of gentleness and equanimity. Much has been said on this subject, but enough has not been *done,* in our systems of education, to promote the health of young ladies. This is an object of special regard in this seminary.

The time is all regularly and systematically divided. The hours for rising and retiring are early. The food is plain and simple, but well prepared, and from the best materials. No article of second quality of the *kind* is ever purchased for the family, and no standard of cooking is allowed but that of doing everything as well as it can be done. The day is so divided that the lessons can be well learned, and ample time allowed for sleep; the hour for exercise in the domestic department can be secured without interruption, and a half hour in the morning and evening for secret devotion, also half an hour for vocal music, and twenty minutes for calisthenics. Besides, there are the leisure hours, in which much is done of sewing, knitting, and ornamental needlework; and much is enjoyed in social intercourse, in walking, and in botanical excursions. This institution presupposes a good degree of health and correct habits. But little can be done in this seminary, or any other, for those whose constitution is already impaired, or whose physical habits, up to the age of sixteen, are particularly defective. This institution professes to make no remarkable physical renovations. But it is believed that a young lady who is fitted for the system, and who can voluntarily and cheerfully adopt it as her own, will find this place favorable for preserving unimpaired the health she brings with her, and for promoting and establishing the good physical habits already acquired.

5. SOCIAL AND DOMESTIC CHARACTER

The excellence of the female character in this respect consists principally in a preparation to be happy herself in her social and domestic relations, and to make all others happy around her. All her duties, of whatever kind, are in an important sense social and domestic. They are retired and private and not public, like those of the other sex. Whatever she does beyond her own family should be but another application and illustration of social and domestic excellence. She may occupy the place of an important teacher, but her most vigorous labors should be modest and unobtrusive. She may go on a foreign mission, but she will there find a retired spot, where, away from the public gaze, she may wear out or lay down a valuable life. She may promote the interests of the Sabbath school, or be an angel of mercy to the poor and afflicted; she may seek in various ways to increase the spirit of benevolence and the zeal for the cause of missions; and she may labor for the salvation of souls; but her work is to be done by the whisper of her still and gentle voice, by the silent step of her unwearied feet, and by the power of her uniform and consistent example.

DESCRIPTION OF MOUNT HOLYOKE FEMALE SEMINARY (1874) From Mary O. Nutting, "Mount Holyoke," as quoted in Anna C. Brackett, *The Education of American Girls* (New York, 1874), pp. 318–20.

The Mount Holyoke Female Seminary was opened in 1837. During the thirty-six years ending July 3, 1873, it has graduated one thousand four hundred and fifty-five young women. Its founder aimed to provide a permanent institution, where the best advantages should be offered at a moderate expense, and whose entire culture should tend to produce, not only thorough students and skilful teachers, but earnest, efficient, Christian women. Accordingly, its course of study has always given prominence to the solid rather than to the showy, omitting mostly what are termed ornamental branches, and devoting the more time to studies which give mental discipline. There is no preparatory department. In order to enter, pupils are required to pass examination in English Grammar and Analysis, Modern Geography,

History of the United States, Mental and Written Arithmetic, Elementary Algebra, Physical Geography, Latin Grammar and Latin Reader. The course of study was originally arranged for three years, but since 1862 requires four. No pupils are received under sixteen years of age, and none are admitted to the senior class under eighteen, while the majority are considerably older. The age at the time of graduating averages something over twenty-one years. None are received as day-scholars.

The amount of intellectual labor required is about six hours a day; that is, two recitations of forty-five minutes each, and four hours and a half spent in study. As a rule, only two studies are pursued at a time. There are but four recitation days in the week, a fifth being devoted to composition and general business. The day of recreation is Wednesday, an arrangement which is somewhat unusual, and might not be convenient for schools composed in part of day-scholars. Here, however, the holiday interposed in the middle of the week serves to lessen the danger of too protracted application to study, and makes the last two recitation days as easy as the first.

The health of the pupils is under the care of the lady physician residing in the family. She is assisted by a teacher who superintends the diet and nursing of invalids. Besides the frequent suggestions in regard to the care of health, which the Principal addresses to the school, special instructions are given by the physician to her classes in physiology. The pupils are particularly cautioned against exposure of health by insufficient protection of the person from cold or dampness, by running up or down stairs, or by sleeping in unventilated rooms. All are required to retire before ten P.M., and advised to choose an earlier hour as far as practicable. Daily outdoor exercise, for at least half an hour, is required, except when inclement weather or ill-health may prevent. Light gymnastics are practised by all except individuals who have been permanently excused by the physician. All are directed, however, to abstain from gymnastics at certain periods, as well as from long walks, or severe physical exertion of any kind. It has not been found that regular and moderate study at such times is injurious to girls in ordinary health. The pupil is always excused from lessons if she finds herself unable to study, which of course may often be the case with those of delicate and excitable temperament, or unsound health.

It is generally known that the ordinary housework of the seminary family is performed by the young ladies, under the supervision of the teachers and matrons. But so many erroneous ideas have prevailed in regard to the amount of labor required of each pupil, that it seems necessary here to repeat explanations often given before.

Each young lady spends, upon an average, one hour a day in domestic work. The length of time varies a little, according to the kind of work; the more laborious or less agreeable tasks being proportionately shorter than the light and easy ones. The time occupied varies thus from forty-five to seventy minutes a day. On the Sabbath, only about half an hour's work is required, while on Wednesday an additional half hour is necessary. Usually one keeps the same work for a term or more, unless some interference with recitations, or other personal reason, makes a change advisable. Pupils are excused from their domestic work whenever their health requires it, the place being temporarily supplied from a sort of reserve corps, who have no regular places of their own.

The benefit to the health, of having a little daily exercise in doing housework, was one of several considerations in view of which this plan was originally adopted. This opinion is supported by long experience, and has also the sanction of high medical authority. Dr. Nathan Allen of Lowell remarks in his essay upon *Physical Degeneracy*, page 16, "No kind of exercise or work whatever is so well calculated to improve the constitution and health of females as domestic labor. By its lightness, repetition, and variety, it is peculiarly adapted to call into wholesome exercise all the muscles and organs of the body, producing an exuberance of health, vigor of frame, power of endurance, and elasticity of spirits; and to all these advantages are to be added the best possible domestic habits, and a sure and enduring foundation for the highest moral and intellectual culture."

Pupils often remark a decided improvement in their health under the combined influences of moderate and systematic mental labor, judicious exercise, both out of doors and within, and regular hours for eating and sleeping. It should not be forgotten, however, that among any three hundred girls, there will be many slight ailments in the course of a year, if not some cases of serious illness. Being at best inexperienced, as well as excitable and impulsive, girls are liable to expose their health in a thousand ways, notwithstanding all that careful mothers or teachers can do. Mere physical robustness is of far less account in carrying one through an extended course of study than prudence and good sense. Many a girl possessing these traits, though naturally delicate, has not only completed the Holyoke course with honor, but has found herself all the better able to meet the duties of more laborious years, on account of the systematic habits and practical efficiency acquired here. It is much better not to begin the course earlier than eighteen, on account of the greater maturity then to be expected, not only of the physical constitution, but also of the judgment, on which the preservation of health so largely depends.

DESCRIPTION OF THE ALBANY FEMALE ACADEMY (1836) From *Circular and Catalogue of the Albany Female Academy, 1836* (Albany, 1836). pp. 2–5.

Location

This Institution is situated in North Pearl-street, between Maiden-Lane and Steuben-street.

A board of thirteen Trustees, elected annually by the stockholders, according to the provisions of the charter, have the general management of the affairs of the academy.

System of Instruction

The Institution is divided into six departments, exclusive of the classes composed of those scholars from each of the higher departments, who are pursuing the study of the French and Spanish Languages, Natural History, Chemistry, and Botany.

In the Sixth Department, the rudiments of education are commenced. The books used are, Worcester's Primer of the English Language, Gallaudet's Picture Defining and Reading Book, Webster's Spelling-Book, Barber's First Book on Elocution, Olney's Easy Reader, the New-Testament, Smith's Geography, Emerson's and

Smith's Introductory Arithmetics. This department is furnished with Holbrook's apparatus for primary schools.

In the Fifth Department, regular instruction in writing commenced, Colburn's First Lessons and Smith's Geography, Hart's Geography, Smith's Intellectual and Practical Grammar, Irving's Catechisms of the History of Various Nations, Trimmer's Elements of Natural History, and Barber's First Book. As an exercise in the definition and use of words, and the structure of language, the pupils are daily required to incorporate in sentences, to be written by them, words given to them by their teachers.

In the Fourth Department, the studies of the fifth reviewed. The Malte Brun Geography and Atlas by Goodrich, Worcester's General History and Chart, History of N.Y., Gleig's Bible History, Biblical Literature and Chart, History of U. S., Smith's Productive Grammar and Parker's Composition. In this department, Smith's Arithmetic commenced; exercises in composition in the journal and letter form.

In each of these three departments is a library, carefully selected with reference to the capacities and attainments of the pupils, and to be used by them at intervals during the hours of study.

In the Third Department, Parker's Composition, and Smith's Arithmetic concluded, History of New-York, and the other studies of the fourth reviewed; Goodrich's History of the United States, with Emerson's Questions, Robbins' General History, History of England, Ancient Geography, Newman's Rhetoric, Barber's Grammar of Elocution, and Blake's Natural Philosophy; composition in written Essays.

In the Second Department, Ancient Geography, Blake's Natural Philosophy concluded, and the other studies of the third reviewed; N. American Arithmetic (Third Part), Barber's Grammar of Elocution, Ancient and Modern Geography, with construction of Maps, and use of the Globes, Chemistry, Watts on the Mind, Algebra, Physiology, Critical Readings in the English Classics, Principles of Teaching, and Smellie's Philosophy of Natural History; composition in written Essays.

In the First Department, the studies of the second and third continued as exercises; Blair's Lectures on Rhetoric, Moral Philosophy, Alexander's Evidences of Christianity, Paley's Natural Theology, Arnott's Natural Philosophy, first and second volumes, Geometry, Trigonometry, Logic, Astronomy, Bigelow's Technology, History of Literature, Constitutional Law, Select parts of the English Classics, Kames' Elements of Criticism, Butler's Analogy, Mental Philosophy, Moral Philosophy, Linear Drawing, Geology, Mineralogy, Natural History, and Botany. In this department, critical attention is paid to composition, in which there are frequent exercises.

In addition to the recitations in the books above specified, the scholars in each department are exercised in Orthography, Reading, Parsing and Writing.

The Institution is designed to be useful and practical. The studies pursued, and the arrangement of the departments, are believed particularly to contribute to this end; and from the experience of many years, and from the proficiency of the great number of young ladies who have passed examination from time to time, the Trustees flatter themselves that such have been the results of the plan.

It is the design to teach the science itself, and to regard the text book as the basis of the instruction to be communicated. The students are required to give extemporaneous illustrations of every important principle in the science under consideration, and also to give a general as well as a particular analysis of the author.

The general direction of the Institution is committed to a Principal; besides, to each department there is attached a permanent teacher; and whenever the number of pupils renders it expedient, the department is divided, and a teacher appointed to each division. The teachers of Penmanship devote their time to the departments in rotation. Lectures are given in the winter terms on Chemistry and Experimental Philosophy; in the summer terms, on Botany and Geology, by the Professor of Chemistry and Natural Philosophy, and on Biblical Antiquities, by the President.

Instruction in Rhetoric and Composition, and in Sacred Music, is given by the respective Professors of these branches.

Of the present Principal, Mr. ALONZO CRITTENTON, A.M. who has had the charge of the Academy for several years, the Trustees can speak in the highest terms, both as a qualified teacher, and as a gentleman entirely devoted to the interests of the Institution, and to the advancement of the young ladies committed to his charge. They are enabled to say, with a proper estimate of the importance of the trust, that there are few who combine, in so many respects, the qualifications of an able, faithful and efficient teacher.

Visitation

The Board of Trustees is arranged into three committees, which in turn visit the Academy and examine the progress and deportment of the pupils, at least once in four weeks, and the result of their observations is reported at each monthly meeting of the Board.

Library, &c.

The proprietors of this Institution have for twenty years constantly endeavored to afford every facility to the youthful mind, in the pursuit of knowledge, and the Academy has been furnished with Maps, Charts, Globes, Models, a very superior Chemical and Philosophical Apparatus, and an extensive Library. It contains also cabinets of specimens for illustration in the studies of Natural History, Mineralogy, and Botany.

The increased facilities for obtaining instruction in every branch of science, furnished by means of these illustrations, are too obvious to require more than a brief notice.

The books of the Library have been selected with reference to the course of studies pursued in the Academy, as well as to general information: and while the Library is at all times open to the scholars, it is intended not only that the books shall be read by them, but that they shall afford the instructors means for opening before the minds of their pupils the whole field of knowledge. The effect of this, it is anticipated, will be to prepare them for future usefulness, and to teach them to investigate for themselves.

Period of Study and Price of Tuition

The Academical year commences on the first of September, and is divided into four terms, commencing respectively on the 1st of September, 23rd of November, 15th of February, and the 8th of May.

There are two examinations in each year, one in February and one in July.

A vacation of six weeks follows the examination in July, and a vacation of one week the close of the quarter ending the first of May.

The price of Tuition in the Sixth or lowest Department is $3 per quarter; in the Fifth, $4; in the Fourth, $5; in the Third, $6; in the Second, $7; and in the First, $8 per quarter.

An extra charge of $5 per quarter is made for the study of French or Spanish.

Premiums

At the close of the examination in February, a public annunciation of the names of young ladies who have distinguished themselves is made. At the close of the examination in July, premiums are awarded for proficiency in the various branches of study, to the pupils in the lower departments; and to those in the higher, testimonials signed by the several members of the Board. Gold medals are also given to the writers of the three best original essays; the relative merit of which is decided by a committee of gentlemen selected by the trustees; and a gold medal to the best scholar in Mathematics,—a donation having been made for this purpose by a friend of the Academy.

As the course of instruction is designed to embrace all the various branches of a complete system of female education, those who have passed through the course, and made such attainments as to justify the distinction, will receive a diploma, bearing the seal of the Institution, being the highest honor conferred.

Boarding, &c.

The Trustees have made ample arrangements for the accommodation of pupils from a distance, in two establishments connected with the families respectively of the Principal and Professor of Chemistry. The expense incurred by a young lady, for board and tuition, including all the studies taught at the Academy, will not exceed $225 per annum. Every facility will be afforded, in these establishments, for acquiring a knowledge of Music, Drawing, or any of the ornamental branches of female education, at a moderate additional charge.

Application for admission may be made to the Principal, at the Academy, or at his residence; or to either of the Trustees.

For more particular inquiries, reference is made to Chancellor Kent, of the city of New-York, Rev. Dr. Ludlow, Provost of the University of Pennsylvania, Rev. Dr. Ferris, New-York, who, during their residence in Albany, have successively presided over the Institution; to Benjamin F. Butler, Attorney-General of the U.S., Washington City, Hon. Jacob Sutherland, Geneva, N.Y., and J. T. Norton, Esq., Farmington, Conn., late Trustees, or to either of the Trustees.

N. B. If parents should desire it, facilities will be afforded for the instruction of their daughters in the Latin and Greek languages.

CHARLES W. ELIOT ON THE EDUCATION OF WOMEN (1869) From
Inaugural Address of President Charles W. Eliot, October 19, 1869, as quoted in Samuel Eliot Morrison. *The Development of Harvard University . . . 1869–1929* (Cambridge, Mass., 1930), pp. lxx–lxxi.

The attitude of the University in the prevailing discussions touching the education and fit employments of women demands brief explanation. America is the natural arena for these debates; for here the female sex has a better past and a better present than elsewhere. Americans, as a rule, hate disabilities of all sorts, whether religious, political, or social. Equality between the sexes, without privilege or oppression on either side, is the happy custom of American homes. While this great discussion is going on, it is the duty of the University to maintin a cautious and expectant policy. The Corporation will not receive women students into the College proper, nor into any school whose discipline requires residence near the school. The difficulties involved in a common residence of hundreds of young men and women of immature character and marriageable age are very grave. The necessary police regulations are exceedingly burdensome. The Corporation are not influenced to this decision, however, by any crude notions about the innate capacities of women. The world knows next to nothing about the natural mental capacities of the female sex. Only after generations of civil freedom and social equality will it be possible to obtain the data necessary for an adequate discussion of woman's natural tendencies, tastes, and capabilities. Again, the Corporation do not find it necessary to entertain a confident opinion upon the fitness or unfitness of women for professional pursuits. It is not the business of the University to decide this mooted point. In this country the University does not undertake to protect the community against incompetent lawyers, ministers, or doctors. The community must protect itself by refusing to employ such. Practical, not theoretical, considerations determine the policy of the University. Upon a matter concerning which prejudices are deep, and opinion inflammable, and experience scanty, only one course is prudent or justifiable when such great interests are at stake—that of cautious and well-considered experiment. The practical problem is to devise a safe, promising, and instructive experiment. Such an experiment the Corporation have meant to try in opening the newly established University Courses of Instruction to competent women. In these courses the University offers to young women who have been to good schools as many years as they wish of liberal culture in studies which have no direct professional value, to be sure, but which enrich and enlarge both intellect and character. The University hopes thus to contribute to the intellectual emancipation of women. It hopes to prepare some women better than they would otherwise have been prepared for the profession of teaching, the one learned profession to which women have already acquired a clear title. It hopes that the proffer of this higher instruction will have some reflex influence upon schools for girls—to discourage superficiality, and to promote substantial education.

EDWARD CLARKE ON SEX DIFFERENCES IN EDUCATION (1874) From Edward H. Clarke, *Sex in Education; or, a Fair Chance for Girls* (Boston, 1874), pp. 11–19, 22–23.

It is idle to say that what is right for man is wrong for women. Pure reason, abstract right and wrong, have nothing to do with sex: they neither recognize nor know it. They teach that what is right or wrong for man is equally right and wrong for woman. Both sexes are bound by the same code of morals; both are amenable to the same divine law. Both have a right to do the best they can; or, to speak more justly, both should feel the duty, and have the opportunity, to do their best. Each must justify its existence by becoming a complete development of manhood and womanhood; and each should refuse whatever limits or dwarfs that development.

The problem of women's sphere, to use the modern phrase, is not to be solved by applying to it abstract principles of right and wrong. Its solution must be obtained from physiology, not from ethics or metaphysics. The question must be submitted to Agassiz and Huxley, not to Kant or Calvin, to Church or Pope. Without denying the self-evident proposition, that whatever a woman can do, she has a right to do, the question at once arises, What can she do? And this includes the further question, What can she best do? A girl can hold a plough, and ply a needle, after a fashion. If she can do both better than a man, she ought to be both farmer and seamstress; but if, on the whole, her husband can hold best the plough, and she ply best the needle, they should divide the labor. He should be master of the plough, and she mistress of the loom. The *quæstio vexata* of woman's sphere will be decided by her organization. This limits her power, and reveals her divinely-appointed tasks, just as man's organization limits his power, and reveals his work. In the development of the organization is to be found the way of strength and power for both sexes. Limitation or abortion of development leads both to weakness and failure.

Neither is there any such thing as inferiority or superiority in this matter. Man is not superior to woman, nor woman to man. The relation of the sexes is one of equality, not of better and worse, or of higher and lower. By this it is not intended to say that the sexes are the same. They are different, widely different from each other, and so different that each can do, in certain directions, what the other cannot; and in other directions, where both can do the same things, one sex, as a rule, can do them better than the other; and in still other matters they seem to be so nearly alike, that they can interchange labor without perceptible difference. All this is so well known, that it would be useless to refer to it, were it not that much of the discussion of the irrepressible woman-question, and many of the efforts for bettering her education and widening her sphere, seem to ignore any differences of the sexes; seem to treat her as if she were identical with man, and to be trained in precisely the same way; as if her organization, and consequently her function, were masculine, not feminine. There are those who write and act as if their object were to assimilate woman as much as possible to man, by dropping all that is distinctively feminine out of her, and putting into her as large an amount of masculineness as possible. These persons tacitly admit the error just alluded to, that woman is inferior to man, and strive to get rid of the inferiority by making her a man. There may be some subtle physiological basis for such views—some strange quality of brain; for some who hold and advocate them are of those, who, having missed the symmetry and organic balance that harmonious development yields, have drifted into an hermaphroditic condition. One of this class, who was glad to have escaped the chains of matrimony, but knew the value and lamented the loss of maternity, wished she had been born a widow with two children. These misconceptions arise from mistaking differences of organization and function for difference of position in the scale of being, which is equivalent to saying that man is rated higher in the divine order because he has more muscle, and woman lower because she has more fat. The loftiest ideal of humanity, rejecting all comparisons of inferiority and superiority between the sexes, demands that each shall be perfect in its kind, and not be hindered in its best work. The lily is not inferior to the rose, nor the oak superior to the clover: yet the glory of the lily is one, and the glory of the oak is another; and the use of the oak is not the use of the clover. That is poor horticulture which would train them all alike.

When Col. Higginson asked, not long ago, in one of his charming essays, that almost persuade the reader, "Ought women to learn the alphabet?" and added, "Give woman, if you dare, the alphabet, then summon her to the career," his physiology was not equal to his wit. Women will learn the alphabet at any rate; and man will be powerless to prevent them, should he undertake so ungracious a task. The real question is not, *Shall* women learn the alphabet? but *How* shall they learn it? In this case, how is more important than ought or shall. The principle and duty are not denied. The method is not so plain.

The fact that women have often equalled and sometimes excelled men in physical labor, intellectual effort, and lofty heroism, is sufficient proof that women have muscle, mind, and soul, as well as men; but it is not proof that they have had, or should have, the same kind of training; nor is it any proof that they are destined for the same career as men. The presumption is, that if woman, subjected to a masculine training, arranged for the development of a masculine organization, can equal man, she ought to excel him if educated by a feminine training, arranged to develop a feminine organization. Indeed, I have somewhere encountered an author who boldly affirms the superiority of women to all existences on this planet, because of the complexity of their organization. Without undertaking to indorse such an opinion, it may be affirmed, that an appropriate method of education for girls—one that should not ignore the mechanism of their bodies or blight any of their vital organs—would yield a better result than the world has yet seen.

Gail Hamilton's statement is true, that, "a girl can go to school, pursue all the studies which Dr. Todd enumerates, except *ad infinitum;* know them, not as well as a chemist knows chemistry or a botanist botany, but as well as they are known by boys of her age and training, as well, indeed, as they are known by many college-taught men, enough, at least, to be a solace and a resource to her; then graduate before she is eighteen, and come out of school as healthy, as fresh, as eager, as she went in."[1] But it is not true that she can do all this, and retain uninjured health and a future secure from neuralgia, uterine disease, hysteria, and other derangements of the nervous system, if she follows the same method that boys are trained in. Boys must study and work in a boy's way, and girls in a girl's way. They may study the same books, and attain an equal result, but should not follow the same method. Mary can master Virgil and Euclid as well as George; but both will be dwarfed,—defrauded of their rightful attainment,—if both are confined to the same methods. It is said that Elena Cornaro, the accomplished professor of six languages, whose

HIGHER
EDUCATION

[1]Woman's Wrongs, p. 59.

statue adorns and honors Padua, was educated like a boy. This means that she was initiated into, and mastered, the studies that were considered to be the peculiar dower of men. It does not mean that her life was a man's life, her way of study a man's way of study, or that, in acquiring six languages, she ignored her own organization. Women who choose to do so can master the humanities and the mathematics, encounter the labor of the law and the pulpit, endure the hardness of physic and the conflicts of politics; but they must do it all in woman's way, not in man's way. In all their work they must respect their own organization, and remain women, not strive to be men, or they will ignominiously fail. For both sexes, there is no exception to the law, that their greatest power and largest attainment lie in the perfect development of their organization. "Woman," says a late writer, "must be regarded as woman, not as a nondescript animal, with greater or less capacity for assimilation to man." If we would give our girls a fair chance, and see them become and do their best by reaching after and attaining an ideal beauty and power, which shall be a crown of glory and a tower of strength to the republic, we must look after their complete development as women. Wherein they are men, they should be educated as men; wherein they are women, they should be educated as women. The physiological motto is, Educate a man for manhood, a woman for womanhood, both for humanity. In this lies the hope of the race.

✳   ✳   ✳

[I] am always . . . surprised . . . by crowds of pale, bloodless female faces, that suggest consumption, scrofula, anemia, and neuralgia. To a large extent, our present system of educating girls is the cause of this pallor and weakness. How our schools, through their methods of education, contribute to this unfortunate result, and how our colleges that have undertaken to educate girls like boys, that is, in the same way, have succeeded in intensifying the evils of the schools, will be pointed out in another place.

It has just been said that the educational methods of our schools and colleges for girls are, to a large extent, the cause of "the thousand ills" that beset American women. Let it be remembered that this is not asserting that such methods of education are the sole cause of female weaknesses, but only that they are one cause, and one of the most important causes of it. An immense loss of female power may be fairly charged to irrational cooking and indigestible diet. We live in the zone of perpetual pie and doughnut; and our girls revel in those unassimilable abominations. Much also may be credited to artificial deformities strapped to the spine, or piled on the head, much to corsets and skirts, and as much to the omission of clothing where it is needed as to excess where the body does not require it; but, after the amplest allowance for these as causes of weakness, there remains a large margin of disease unaccounted for. Those grievous maladies which torture a woman's earthly existence, called leucorrhoea, amenorrhoea, dysmenorrhoea, chronic and acute ovaritis, prolapsus uteri, hysteria, neuralgia, and the like, are indirectly affected by food, clothing, and exercise; they are directly and largely affected by the causes that will be presently pointed out, and which arise from a neglect of the peculiarities of a woman's organization. The regimen of our schools fosters this neglect.

THOUGHTS ON THE SEX EDUCATION OF AMERICAN GIRLS

(1874)   From Anna C. Brackett, "The Education of American Girls," as quoted in Anna C. Brackett, ed., *The Education of American Girls* (New York, 1874), pp. 62–67.

We send children to school—or rather we begin voluntarily to teach them, too early by several years, and the only result is that the brain is "too early over-strained, and in consequence of such precocious and excessive action, the foundation for a morbid excitation of the whole nervous system is laid in earliest childhood." As far as the home-life fosters this over-activity, that is, before the time of school life, I think it will be readily acknowledged that this showing-off process is applied with greater force to girls than to boys. The boy is left more to his own devices, but the girl must be made to contribute more to the general amusement of the family, and she must learn "to make herself useful." It is true that to be of service to others, in a rational sense, should be her ruling motive of action, but one may, perhaps, question whether such early expectation, in such ways, be not, at least, "penny wise and pound foolish." To this cause may be attributed a great part of the failure in the health at the last special time of development.

As to the mental progress made, John Stuart Mill may, as he says, have entered life "a quarter of a century in advance of his contemporaries," but was he a quarter of a century ahead of others of his own age when he left it? The question is at least suggestive of the truth.

But, with the development of the organs which are so indissolubly associated with the deepest feelings and with the mental powers, there is also a corresponding mental development. Not only does "the blood rush more vigorously, the muscular strength become more easily roused into activity, but an indefinable impulse takes possession of the whole being," and a great excitation of the imagination also is perceivable. Just here, then, the educator recognizes a duty. This increased force, which we could not prevent if we would, and would not if we could, must be guided into rational channels—and here I have to speak of a branch of the subject which is not often considered. I mean the duty of the mother, who is in this department the proper educator, to speak earnestly, fully, and plainly to the girl of the mysterious process of reproduction. Rosenkranz says, somewhere, that when any nation has advanced far enough in culture to inquire whether it is fit for freedom, the question is already answered; and in the same way, when a girl, in her thought, has arrived at the point of asking earnest questions on this subject on this subject, she is fit to be answered. But just here let me call attention to the infinite importance, in this part of education, of perfect confidence and freedom between mother and daughter, and to the equally important fact, that this confidence which does exist at the beginning of life, if once lost, can never fully be restored. If there is a shade of reserve on the part of the girl, it will manifest itself just here and now. Instead of seeking the information which she really desires, at its only proper source, at that source whence she would receive it pure, and invested with a feeling of reverence and sanctity, of which she could never divest herself, she seeks it elsewhere. She picks it up piece-meal in surreptitious and clandestine ways, as if it were some horrible mystery which must, from its very nature, be covered up from the light of day. She talks it over with her young companions in secrecy, and the charm of mystery keeps her thoughts unduly brooding upon the subject.

In old times, and even now, in other countries, the danger was not, is not, so great. Foreign girls have a much closer supervision exercised over them, and their life in the nursery is far less nerve-stimulating than that of American children. They do not ask questions so early as the American girl, and when they do, they have at hand not nearly so many sources of information. If this all-necessary love and confidence is unbroken, and if the mother have been so educated herself, that she recognizes the importance of the moment, and has the requisite knowledge, there is no danger at all. The occasion is seized, and her womanly, "clear, and dignified statement, destroys all the false halo with which the youthful fancy is so prone to surround the process of reproduction, and, at this time, the fancy is very active with relation to whatever pertains to it."

I do not for one moment forget that I am speaking of physical education. The physical consequences of mistakes on this point are decided. By the continual dwelling of the imagination on this subject—of the imagination, I say, for there can be no thought where there is no clearness—the blood is diverted to these organs, and hence, "the brain and spinal cord, which develop so rapidly at this period, are not led to a proper strength. The easily-moulded material is perverted to the newly-aroused reproductive organs," and the preternatural activity thus produced is physical disease.

But more than this: I should be fairly accused of quitting the physical for the moral side of education here, if it were not that I am now upon ground, where, more than on any other, body and soul, matter and spirit, touch each other, and it is very difficult, if not impossible, to draw the dividing line. the inter-action of the two upon each other here becomes so rapid and intense, that one scarcely knows the relation of cause and effect. I repeat—more than this: The patched and medley knowledge of the young girl to whom her mother does not speak, comes to her garbled and confused, the sacred seal of modesty torn off, soiled with the touch of vulgar hands, defaced by the coarse jests of polite society, its sanctity forever missed. The temple has been invaded, its white floors trodden by feet from muddy alleys, the gods thrown down. Is not the temple as much ruined when this profanation has been accomplished, as if the walls had fallen? I will not be misunderstood as doubting, for one moment, the purity of soul of American girls as a whole; but I assert, that the result of which I have spoken is terribly common in our large cities, and that it is much more likely to be common in America than in any other country, from the effect of our climate, our free institutions, and the almost universal diffusion of printed matter.

The remedy lies alone in the hands of the mother, and, where a girl is away from her mother, in the hands of her woman guardian, whoever she may be. When our women are better educated, there will be less prudery and more real modesty. When the minds of our girls and women are kept busy on other things, they will have no time for this most dangerous brooding. Most truly does Schiller say: *"In müssiger Weile schafft der böse Geist,"* and he spares neither body nor soul.

It is always asserted that woman makes and rules society. When our women are better educated themselves, their righteous indignation will banish forever from all conversation in which they have a part, the fashionable jests on subjects which do not admit of jest, and the *doubles entendres* whose power to excite a smile consists in their vulgar and profane suggestions. They are as common in companies of average women as in companies of average men, and they evidence thoughts, and are themselves as much coarser and lower than the outspoken utterances of Shakspeare's ideal women—whom they assume to criticise and condemn—as the smooth and subtle rhymes of Swinburne and Joaquin Miller are below the poetry of Chaucer and Spenser.

Closely connected with this part of my subject is that of the reading in which girls are passively allowed to indulge. How large a proportion of mothers and guardians exercise anything which can be called watchful care as to what books and papers the children shall read; and yet the booksellers' shelves groan under the weight of the most dissipating, weakening, and insidious books that can possibly be imagined; and newspapers which ought never to enter any decent house, lie on the tables of many a family sitting-room. Any one who will take the trouble to examine the records of any large circulating library, will be astounded at the immense demand which there is for these average novels. And in our parlors and chambers to-day, myriads of little girls are curled up in corners, poring over such reading— stories of complicated modern society, the very worst kind of reading for a child— stories "whose exciting pages delight in painting the love of the sexes for each other, and its sensual phases." And the mothers do not know what they are reading; and the children answer, when asked what they read, "Oh, anything that comes along."

How find a remedy for this evil? How stem this tide of insidious poison that is sapping the strength of body and mind? How, but by educating their taste till they shall not desire such trash, and shall only be disgusted with it, if by chance it fall under their eyes? How, but by giving their minds steady and regular work? If the work be intermittent, it will, under the general principles laid down in the remarks on exercise, not only be, from that fact, injurious to the brain, but it will afford, at the most susceptible period of life, leisure for reveries which can lead only to evil, moral and physical. But give our girls steady and regular work of muscle and brain, a rational system of exercise for both, so that the "motor and nervous systems may weary themselves in action, and may be desirous of rest," and evil will be not only prevented, but cured, if existing.

Even if these trashy books, which we find everywhere, not excepting the Sunday-school libraries, be not actually exciting and immoral in tone and sentiment, they are so vapid, so utterly without purpose or object, so devoid of any healthy vigor and life, that they are simply dissipating to the power of thought, and hence weakening to the will. No one needs to be told how great is the influence of the will over physical health, and any weakening of it tends inevitably to a slackening of all the vital forces, by which alone we preserve health, or even life itself.

All such books can be kept out of a house, and their entrance should be guarded against far more vigorously than we oppose the entrance of noxious gases, or even of draughts of pure air. Some of us, many of us, have reason to be grateful that in our fathers' houses no such books were to be found. Poets were there, novelists were there in abundance, but of such poisonous and weakening literature, no trace; and as we are grateful to our parents for the care and simple regimen which preserved our physical health for us, we thank them also for the care which kept out of our way the mental food which they knew to be injurious, and for which they themselves had been too well educated to have any taste.

The possession, through the instrumentality of education, of simple and healthy appetite and taste, physical and mental, is the most valuable gift that the father, that the mother, can give their children, a gift in comparison with which a legacy of millions of dollars sinks into utter insignificance. And a tithe of the thought and care which are expended in accumulating and investing property on the part of the one, a tithe of the care and thought used on dress on the part of the other, would serve to secure it!

The exclusively American habit of taking young girls to fashionable resorts for the summer should also be alluded to here. No custom could be more injurious than this in the influences of food, clothing and sleep, which it almost inevitably brings;

and added to these, girls in idleness, and left to amuse themselves, are often in such places thrown into contact with persons of both sexes, whose conversation is the worst possible in its effect on mind and body.

But, according to the general principle of education, we must not repress imagination in one direction without furnishing it some rational food in another; for education, as has been said, consists not in destroying but in training the natural man, and any system which aims at destroying any natural impulse only defeats its own end. For this purpose, and at this period of life, it were well to draw the imagination to "the enjoyment of the beautiful through an actual contemplation of it, and for this purpose the study of painting and sculpture is of pre-eminent value. . . . Through their means the allurement which the wholly or especially the half-undraped form has for us, becomes softened and purified. The enjoyment of beauty itself is the enjoyment of something divine; and it is only through a coarse, indecent, and already infected imagination, belonging to a general sensuality, that it degenerates into excitement."

WILLIAM JAMES ON THE MENTAL HEALTH OF GIRL STUDENTS (c. 1895)   From William James, *Talks to Teachers on Psychology: And to Students on Some of Life's Ideals* (New York, 1899), pp. 218-23, 227-28.

Even now in New York they have formed a society for the improvement of our national vocalization, and one perceives its machinations already in the shape of various newspaper paragraphs intended to stir up dissatisfaction with the awful thing that it is. And, better still than that, because more radical and general, is the gospel of relaxation, as one may call it, preached by Miss Annie Payson Call, of Boston, in her admirable little volume called 'Power through Repose,' a book that ought to be in the hands of every teacher and student in America of either sex. You need only be followers, then, on a path already opened up by others. But of one thing be confident: others still will follow you.

And this brings me to one more application of psychology to practical life, to which I will call attention briefly, and then close. If one's example of easy and calm ways is to be effectively contagious, one feels by instinct that the less voluntarily one aims at getting imitated, the more unconscious one keeps in the matter, the more likely one is to succeed. *Become the imitable thing,* and you may then discharge your minds of all responsibility for the imitation. The laws of social nature will take care of that result. Now the psychological principle on which this precept reposes is a law of very deep and wide-spread importance in the conduct of our lives, and at the same time a law which we Americans most grievously neglect. Stated technically, the law is this: that *strong feeling about one's self tends to arrest the free association of one's objective ideas and motor processes.* We get the extreme example of this in the mental disease called melancholia.

A melancholic patient is filled through and through with intensely painful emotion about himself. He is threatened, he is guilty, he is doomed, he is annihilated, he is lost. His mind is fixed as if in a cramp on these feelings of his own situation, and in all the books on insanity you may read that the usual varied flow of his thoughts has ceased. His associative processes, to use the technical phrase, are inhibited; and his ideas stand stock-still, shut up to their one monotonous function of reiterating inwardly the fact of the man's desperate estate. And this inhibitive influence is not due to the mere fact that his emotion is *painful*. Joyous emotions about the self also stop the association of our ideas. A saint in ecstasy is as motionless and irresponsive and one-idea'd as a melancholiac. And, without going as far as ecstatic saints, we know how in every one a great or sudden pleasure may paralyze the flow of thought. Ask young people returning from a party or a spectacle, and all excited about it, what it was. "Oh, it was *fine!* it was *fine!* it was *fine!*" is all the information you are likely to receive until the excitement has calmed down. Probably every one of my hearers has been made temporarily half-idiotic by some great success or piece of good fortune. "*Good!* GOOD! GOOD!" is all we can at such times say to ourselves until we smile at our own very foolishness.

Now from all this we can draw an extremely practical conclusion. If, namely, we wish our trains of ideation and volition to be copious and varied and effective, we must form the habit of freeing them from the inhibitive influence of reflection upon them, of egoistic preoccupation about their results. Such a habit, like other habits, can be formed. Prudence and duty and self-regard, emotions of ambition and emotions of anxiety, have, of course, a needful part to play in our lives. But confine them as far as possible to the occasions when you are making your general resolutions and deciding on your plans of campaign, and keep them out of the details. When once a decision is reached and execution is the order of the day, dismiss absolutely all responsibility and care about the outcome. *Unclamp*, in a word, your intellectual and practical machinery, and let it run free; and the service it will do you will be twice as good. Who are the scholars who get 'rattled' in the recitation-room? Those who think of the possibilities of failure and feel the great importance of the act. Who are those who do recite well? Often those who are most indifferent. *Their* ideas reel themselves out of their memory of their own accord. Why do we hear the complaint so often that social life in New England is either less rich and expressive or more fatiguing than it is in some other parts of the world? To what is the fact, if fact it be, due unless to the over-active conscience of the people, afraid of either saying something too trivial and obvious, or something insincere, or something unworthy of one's interlocutor, or something in some way or other not adequate to the occasion? How can conversation possible steer itself through such a sea of responsibilities and inhibitions as this? On the other hand, conversation does flourish and society is refreshing, and neither dull on the one hand nor exhausting from its effort on the other, wherever people forget their scruples and take the brakes off their hearts, and let their tongues wag as automatically and irresponsibly as they will.

They talk much in pedagogic circles to-day about the duty of the teacher to prepare for every lesson in advance. To some extent this is useful. But we Yankees are assuredly not those to whom such a general doctrine should be preached. We are only too careful as it is. The advice I should give to most teachers would be in the words of one who is herself an admirable teacher. Prepare yourself in the *subject so well that it shall be always on tap:* then in the class-room trust your spontaneity and fling away all further care.

My advice to students, especially to girl-students, would be somewhat similar. Just as a bicycle-chain may be too tight, so may one's carefulness and conscientiousness be so intense as to hinder the running of one's mind. Take, for example, periods when there are many successive days of examination impending. One ounce of good nervous tone in an examination is worth many pounds of anxious study for it in advance. If you want really to do your best in an examination, fling away the book the day before, say to yourself, "I won't waste another minute on this miserable thing, and I don't care an iota whether I succeed or not." Say this sincerely, and feel it; and go out and play, or go to bed and sleep, and I am sure the results next day will encourage you to use the method permanently. I have heard this advice given to a student by Miss Call, whose book on muscular relaxation I quoted a moment ago. In her later book, entitled 'As a Matter of Course,' the gospel of moral relaxation, of dropping things from the mind, and not 'caring,' is preached with equal success. Not only our preachers, but our friends the theosophists and mind-curers of various religious sects are also harping on this string. And with the doctors, the Delsarteans, the various mind-curing sects, and such writers as Mr. Dresser, Prentice Mulford, Mr. Horace Fletcher, and Mr. Trine to help, and the whole band of schoolteachers and magazine-readers chiming in, it really looks as if a good start might be made in the direction of changing our American mental habit into something more indifferent and strong.

* * *

The need of feeling responsible all the livelong day has been preached long enough in our New England. Long enough exclusively, at any rate,—and long enough to the female sex. What our girl-students and woman-teachers most need nowadays is not the exacerbation, but rather the toning-down or their moral tensions. Even now I fear that some one of my fair hearers may be making an undying resolve to become strenuously relaxed, cost what it will, for the remainder of her life. It is needless to say that that is not the way to do it. The way to do it, paradoxical as it may seem, is genuinely not to care whether you are doing it or not. Then, possibly, by the grace of God, you may all at once find that you *are* doing it, and, having learned what the trick feels like, you may (again by the grace of God) be enabled to go on.

And that something like this may be the happy experience of all my hearers is, in closing, my most earnest wish.

Adult Education

JOSIAH HOLBROOK'S PROPOSAL FOR A CONSTITUTION FOR THE AMERICAN LYCEUM (1828)   From *American Journal of Education*, vol. III, p. 503.

American Lyceum. The undersigned agree to associate under the name ————, Branch of the American Lyceum, and adopt the following articles for their constitution.

Article 1. The objects of the lyceum are the improvements of its members in useful knowledge, and the advancement of popular education, by introducing uniformity and improvements in common schools, by becoming auxiliary to a board of education.

Article 2. To effect these objects, they will procure a cabinet, consisting of books, apparatus for illustrating the sciences, and a collection of minerals, and will hold meetings for discussions, dissertations, illustrating the sciences, or other exercises which shall be thought expedient.

Article 3. Any person may be a member of the lyceum, by paying into the treasury annually, 2 dollars; and 20 dollars paid at any one time will entitle a person, his or her heirs, or assigns, to membership forever. Persons under 18 years of age will be entitled to all the privileges of the society, except of voting, for one-half of the annual sum above named.

Article 4. The officers of this branch of the lyceum shall be a president, vice-president, treasurer, recording and corresponding secretaries, 3 or 5 curators, and 3 delegates, to be appointed by ballot on the first Wednesday of September annually.

Article 5. The president, vice-president, treasurer, and secretaries will perform the duties usually implied in those offices. The curators will have charge of the cabinet and all other property of the lyceum not appertaining to the treasury, and will be the general agents to do any business for the society under their direction. The delegates will meet delegates from branches of the lyceum in this country semiannually, to adopt regulations for their general and mutual benefit, or to take measures to introduce uniformity and improvements into common schools, and to diffuse useful and practical knowledge generally through the community, particularly to form and aid a board of education.

Article 6. To raise the standard of common education, and to benefit the juvenile members of the lyceum, a portion of the books procured shall be fitted to young minds; and teachers of schools may be permitted to use for the benefit of their pupils who are members of the lyceum, the apparatus and minerals under such restrictions as the association shall prescribe.

Article 7. The president or any five members will have power at any time to call

HIGHER
EDUCATION

1605

a special meeting, which meeting shall be legal, if notice shall be given according to the direction in the By-Laws.

Article 8. The lyceum will have power to adopt such regulations and by-laws as shall be necessary for the management and use of the cabinet, for holding meetings, or otherwise for their interest.

Article 9. The foregoing articles may be altered or amended by vote of two-thirds present, at any legal meetings; said alteration or amendment having been proposed at a meeting, not less than four weeks previous to the one at which it is acted upon.

ABOUT CHAUTAUQUA (1885)   From Smiley Raymond, *About Chautauqua: As an Idea, as a Power, and as a Place* (Toledo, 1885), pp. 1, 12–13, 18, 33.

I.—As an Idea

The application of the Chautauqua Idea has produced an educational movement, which combines sacred and secular knowledge. It takes the teachings and doctrines of the Holy Bible as the corner-stone, while it seeks to establish the relation of Christianity, and of culture, as they should appear in individual and in national life.

This Idea has taken captive the hearts of many thousand pilgrims, who for twelve consecutive summers have journeyed to Chautauqua, as ancient pilgrims went to Mecca, for a knowledge of the truth and for inspiration.

All persons are concerned in that which shapes the life, the destiny and the greatness of the nation of which they form a part. This great movement, which has caused from every direction of the wide world the inquiry—What is this Chautauqua? is a plan by which men and women, boys and girls, may learn the truths which Christianity has nourished, that they may enter into sympathy with those things that are pleasing to God, in order that the best, grandest and noblest of all ideas may have expression in their thoughts, their writings, and in their literature, thus pervading their homes, so that the national life will be rich in all that constitutes the best in human history.

*   *   *

Chautauqua assumes a positive attitude toward all true science and good literature, and seeks, by all its teachings, to bring about the threefold piety of the heart, the intellect, and the will.

Chautauqua emphasizes the belief that there is no divorcement between religion and culture, and seeks to inculcate this fact to the masses of the people of our beloved land, and desires that education only, which is pervaded by the Christian spirit that regards all men as brothers. The whole aim of the leaders and teachers is to secure for men and women the highest development of "soulhood" of which they are capable. They regard science and philosophy as incomplete unless they center in

Christ; therefore comes their belief that no education is complete that is not a Christian education.

Many persons inclined to be critical have asked—Why do Chautauqua leaders say so much about teaching the Bible, and have its doctrines so prominent? Chautauqua teachers answer—"Heaven and earth shall pass away," but these records of divine revelation shall not pass away, but are for direction, and all must possess themselves of the great truths therein contained in order to become educated.

It is pleasant to know that some of the most distinguished educators and literary men of our own times were consulted, and that they most heartily approved this new way of instruction before it was given to the public. William Cullen Bryant endorsed and gave it his strong commendation in a letter written by his own hand, less than a month before his death. The religious teachings of the divine book which were to be so conspicuous did not meet with one objection from our great poet, for there was no antagonism in his heart between Science and Revelation.

The fact that the great portion of the mental food of the present time—as science, history, poetry, morals, essay, and fiction—is prepared by writers who have long since ceased to believe, has compelled leaders in educational interests to consider the momentous question. Although true that there never was a period when the sacred volume, which embodies the world's faith and salvation, had so wide a distribution or was wielding so mighty an influence upon the world's civilization and progress, yet Chautauqua teachers must exalt the Bible in order to show those who are weak in faith, that Science and Religion are not two separate departments, not even two phases of the same truth. For Science has a broader realm in the unseen than in the seen, in the source of power than in the outcome of power, in the sublime laws of spirit than in the laws of matter, and Religion sheds its beautiful light over all the stages of life, till whether we eat or whether we drink, we may do all for the glory of God. Science and Religion make common confession, that the great object of life is to learn and to grow, and Chautauqua teaches that both will come to see that the best possible means for the attainment of this end is a personal relation to that Teacher who is the Way, the Truth, and the Life.

The scientific department of this great movement discusses secular science with the Bible in hand. It studies natural science from the standpoint of faith in God's word, which is opened out and expounded by leaders in Science who, revering Nature, also bow before the God of Revelation.

II.—As a Power

Often has the question, What does the success of Chautauqua mean? been answered by persons who know it well, and the reply from each is in word-pictures that express enthusiasm. In its first year the London *Times* remarked that never since the days of Queen Elizabeth had there been such a revival of learning in the world's history. And now all creeds, as well as countries, are represented in its membership. The results for good are already unbounded. There is not in this world another such scheme for the purpose of educating the human soul! No school, college, university or church has ever held forth such an opportunity for true, grand, harmonious culture.

Chautauqua has been more potent in uniting the people of our own country than any other influence. At this center the most prominent educators of the South, besides men and women of literary culture, also statesmen and Governors, have occupied the platform and sat in the assembly and mingled their voices in praise and prayer with our own, and the most intimate friendships are sought.

*   *   *

III.—As a Place

Chautauqua is the original recreative and educational summer resort on Chautauqua Lake.

Chautauqua is the center of an elegant and literary social life.

Chautauqua is the first of many similar movements in all parts of the land, and the one from which they have received their idea and inspiration.

Chautauqua is the seat of the world-wide "C. L. S. C." (the Chautauqua Literary and Scientific Circle), which enrolls more than one hundred thousand readers, and provides more than thirty distinct courses of reading and study for persons of all ages and degrees of culture.

Chautauqua is a place of rest and recreation; with grounds, high, dry, perfectly drained, clean, delightful; with three lovely natural plateaus rising from the lakeside to an elevation among the very highest on the lake.

Chautauqua is the name of the town where the wonderful Assembly that has been described, annually convenes. It is situated in the western part of the grand old State of New York, on the west shore of a lake having the same Indian name. Its site is a charming and well-wooded plateau, which slopes by terraces down to the edge of the water. The terraces are natural, and rise in succession to the height of one hundred and twenty-five feet, thereby giving a most delightful outlook down, and across the lake.

PRESIDENT WILLIAM RAINEY HARPER OF THE UNIVERSITY OF CHICAGO DESCRIBES THE CORRESPONDENCE SYSTEM OF TEACHING
(**1886**)   From William Rainey Harper, "On Teaching By Correspondence," in John H. Vincent, ed. *The Chautauqua Movement* (Boston, 1886), pp. 77–83.

Four questions may be considered: (1) What *is* the correspondence-system of teaching? (2) What disadvantages attend this system, as compared with oral teaching? (3) What advantages, if any, does the correspondence-system have over oral teaching? (4) What results have thus far been accomplished in the line of teaching by correspondence? In the statements made, special reference is had to the teaching of languages.

I. What Is the Correspondence-System?

A brief explanation of the plan of study by correspondence is first in order.

1. An *instruction-sheet* is mailed to the student each week. This instruction-sheet (a) assigns the tasks which are to be performed—e.g., the chapters of the text to be translated, the sections in the grammar to be learned; (b) indicates an order of work which the student is required to follow; (c) offers suggestions on points in the lesson which are liable to be misunderstood; (d) furnishes special assistance wherever such assistance is deemed necessary; (e) marks out a specified amount of review-work; (f) contains an examination-paper which the student, after having prepared the lesson, is required to write out. The instruction-sheet is intended, therefore, to guide and help the student just as an oral teacher would guide and help him.

2. The *examination-paper* is so constructed, that, in order to its preparation for criticism, one must have prepared before hand most thoroughly the lesson on which it is based. An examination-paper on Caesar, for example, requires of the student (a) the translation of certain chapters into English; (b) the translation into Latin of a list of English sentences based on the Latin which has just been translated; (c) the explanation of the more important constructions, with the grammatical reference for each construction; (d) the placing of forms; (e) the change to "direct discourse" of a corresponding passage in "indirect discourse"; (f) the explanation of geographical and historical allusions; (g) the statement of grammatical principles, etc., etc.

3. In the *recitation-paper* submitted to the instructor, besides writing out the matter called for in the *examination-paper*, the student asks such questions, and notes such difficulties, as may have presented themselves to him in his study of the lesson. This recitation-paper is promptly returned with all errors corrected, and questions answered; and with special suggestions, suited to each individual case.

In this manner each lesson of the course is assigned and studied; and the results of the study submitted to the instructor for correction, criticism, and suggestion.

From this it will be seen that the correspondence-teacher must be painstaking, patient, sympathetic, and *alive;* and that the correspondence-pupil must be earnest, ambitious, appreciative, and likewise *alive.* Whatever a *dead* teacher may accomplish in the classroom, he can do nothing by correspondence; and if a student lacking the qualities just named undertake work by correspondence, one of two things will happen: either he will acquire these qualities, and succeed; or he will remain as he was at the beginning, and fail. The man who does the work at all, must do it well.

II. The Disadvantages under Which the Correspondence-Student Works

There are, I frankly confess, some disadvantages under which the correspondence-student works, and it is only fair to consider them.

1. The personal magnetism of an instructor is often felt by pupils for years after they have ceased to come in contact with him. Some teachers—and it is an occasion of regret that the number of such is not larger—exert upon the students an influence for good which cannot be estimated. Such influence the correspondence-student does not feel; such stimulus he does not receive.

2. In the recitation-room, there is a certain class-spirit, and a certain spirit of

emulation, which tend to elevate the student, to quicken and to dignify him. This, of course, is for the most part lacking in the correspondence-work.

3. An earnest, conscientious teacher, in whatever department he may work, will unconsciously furnish information, impart methods of work, let drop suggestions, which are not to be found in text-books. Under the inspiration of the class-room he will lead his pupils by paths which he himself never trod before. All this, the correspondence-student loses.

4. Ordinarily the student makes one hundred and sixty to one hundred and eighty recitations in a given study during the year. The correspondence-student makes but forty.

5. There is a drudgery in the work of writing out long lessons, which some regard as almost unendurable. This is in sharp contrast with the freedom and pleasure with which others make an oral recitation.

6. There is necessarily a large amount of irregularity in the correspondence-work. The interruptions are, in the very nature of the case, quite numerous; and after such interruptions there inevitably comes discouragement. This is a most serious difficulty.

7. The correspondence-student is not under the eye of an instructor; the temptation to be dishonest is always at hand. He is more likely to use illegitimate helps, and to misuse legitimate ones, than is he who must produce the results of his work in the presence of his comrades and at a moment's notice.

8. Whatever the common opinion may be, the requirements of the correspondence-system are of so exacting and rigid a nature as to prevent some from completing the work, who would certainly be able to pass through the course of study in many of our so-called colleges. This may or may not be a disadvantage of the correspondence-system, according to the point of view taken.

These difficulties, it is true, exist; but some things may be said, which will, at least slightly, modify their force.

1. If personal stimulus furnished by the teacher is absolutely necessary to good results on the part of the student, then two-thirds of the oral instruction given is valueless; for it is safe to assert that two out of three teachers exert no such influence upon their pupils, their work being purely mechanical.

2. Is it true that this personal magnetism, this personal influence, cannot be conveyed by writing? Have words spoken, or words written, produced the greater effect? Have not many of us received greater inspiration from personal letters than from words uttered by mouth? Are there not among our best friends those whom we have never seen, whose voice we have never heard, whose words have reached us only by letter?

In my experience with students by correspondence, brief as it has been, I can refer to hundreds of men who have acknowledged the stimulus and inspiration received by letters in the course of their study.

3. Class-spirit is not wholly lacking. The student knows that he is a member of a class which probably numbers hundreds, the members of which live in every State and Territory and even in foreign lands. Is there not inspiration in this fact? He knows, also, that every recitation-paper is graded, that his progress is very closely watched, that his classmates are pushing on notwithstanding difficulties and obstacles as great as he is called to meet. Is there not stimulus in all this?

4. Only forty recitations a year are required; yet each of these forty demands the preparation and the work of three or four oral recitations; and were the number less than forty, and the amount accomplished less, the fact that the student prepares his

lesson knowing that he must *recite the whole of it*, and that he must recite it by writing, goes far to make up in quality what perhaps in quantity might be lacking.

5. The drudgery is very great, but not so great as many imagine. Besides, those to whom the work seems so onerous are those of whom such work as a matter of discipline should be required.

6. While in correspondence-work it is true that interruptions and consequent discouragements are more likely to occur, it is equally true (a) that this evil is largely mitigated by the fact that the average correspondence-student is thirty years of age, and therefore old enough to overcome the bad effect of such interruptions; (b) that a rigid system of reviews helps greatly, also, to counterbalance this evil; and (c) that, while work lost from sickness or other cause is never really made up in the ordinary class, in the correspondence-class no work is lost, the student being required to begin at the point reached when the interruption took place.

7. After all, dishonesty in correspondence-work is more easily detected than in an oral recitation. And, besides, what is easier than so to construct the examination-paper, in each case, that at least in a large portion of the work no direct aid may possibly be obtained?

8. It is proper in this connection to consider the following points: (a) No one has ever thought of substituting the correspondence-system for the oral; the latter is conceded to be superior, and only those are advised to study by correspondence who cannot in any way obtain oral instruction. (b) The fact that the large proportion of correspondence-students are voluntary workers removes many difficulties which under other circumstances might exist. (c) What the student loses in his correspond-ence-work, he may easily gain by attending Summer Schools, which, indeed, are intended to supplement the correspondence-work.

III. What Advantages Does the Correspondence-System Have?

While it is freely conceded that there are disadvantages attending the correspond-ence-system, it is confidently claimed that this sytem has some advantages over other systems. Our space will scarcely permit any thing more than a bare mention of these:

1. By the correspondence-student, compelled to express every thought *in writing*, there is gained what the student reciting orally does not so easily acquire— the habit of *exact statement*.

2. Of the correspondence-student, compelled to state *in writing* his conception of a principle, or his translation of a paragraph, there is demanded a greater *accuracy of knowledge* than is necessary for an ordinary oral recitation.

3. While each student, in an oral recitation, recites only one-tenth, one-thirtieth, or one-sixtieth of the lesson assigned, each correspondence-student recites the entire lesson, however long it may be. In four oral recitations, each student in a class of thirty recites eight minutes: in the preparation of a single recitation-paper, the correspondence-student spends at least two hours, aside from the previous work of preparing the lesson. The oral student must recite rapidly, often hurriedly: the correspondence-student works out his recitation-paper slowly, thoughtfully.

4. The correspondence-student, given all *necessary* assistance, but compelled to obtain every thing else for himself, or write out his questions and wait for the written answer, is led to investigate, to be independent in his study, and to have a confidence in the results of his own investigation which the student who has constant recourse to his instructor does not have.

5. If a written examination is a more thorough test of a student's knowledge of a given subject, surely a written recitation is not, in respect to *thoroughness*, inferior to an oral one. The correspondence-system requires of its students more thorough preparation of the lesson assigned, a more thorough recitation of it, and, in a word, a more thorough knowledge of the subject treated of in that lesson.

6. A prime requisite in good teaching is the ability to assign the proper lesson. Many excellent teachers fail at this point. The lesson is too long, or too short; the ground to be covered is not definitely indicated; the method of work is not clearly stated, etc., etc. The correspondence-lesson, since it is generally in printed form, is prepared with the greatest care. No part of it is given out hurriedly. It is the result of hours of careful study and calculation. If it is too long to be prepared within six days, the student is allowed a longer time; if it can be prepared within a less time, the student can take up the next lesson. Nothing could be more definite than this lesson, for it is assigned with a minuteness of detail which to some doubtless seems superfluous, but which in the case of others is absolutely essential.

7. Finally, whatever may be the relative merits of the two systems, it is clear to every one who thinks, that there are thousands of men and women unable to avail themselves of oral assistance, who, nevertheless, are eager to study. It is surely an advantage of the correspondence-system, that it can aid this large class, who otherwise would have no help, and would make no progress.

These are some of the advantages of the correspondence-system. But is any one to suppose that there exists, in the mind of those especially interested in this system, a desire to have it take the place of oral instruction? Is the one in any sense a rival of the other? I wish here to record, in answer to these questions, a most emphatic *No*. What is the fact? *Only those persons are encouraged to study by correspondence, or, indeed, admitted to such study, who because of age, poverty, occupation, situation, or some other good reason, cannot avail themselves of oral instruction.* Away, therefore, with all baseless and foolish prejudice in this matter! The correspondence-system would not, if it could, supplant oral instruction, or be regarded as its substitute. There is a field for each which the other cannot fill. Let each do its proper work.

IV. What Has Been Accomplished Thus Far in the Line of Correspondence-Work?

In the strict sense of the term, the correspondence-system has been in use only four or five years. This time has been sufficient, however, to enable us to note a few practical results:

1. It has already helped thousands of men toward a knowledge of certain subjects, which otherwise they would not have had.

2. There are to-day many thousands of men already convinced of the feasibility of the system, who are but waiting for the moment to arrive at which they shall begin. Educators in all lines are beginning to appreciate the possibilities of this system.

3. Institutions have been established, chief among which stands the Chautauqua College of Liberal Arts, through whose influence the system will be more fully developed, and rendered capable of accomplishing still greater good.

I venture, in closing this very brief and imperfect presentation, to make two statements; one an assertion based on large experience, the other a prediction based on strong conviction:

1. The student who has prepared a certain number of lessons in the correspondence-school knows more of the subject treated in those lessons, and knows it better, than the student who has covered the same ground in the class-room.

2. The day is coming when the work done by correspondence will be greater in amount than that done in the class-rooms of our academies and colleges; when the students who shall recite by correspondence will far outnumber those who make oral recitations.

SOME CONSIDERATIONS CONCERNING THE VALUE OF UNIVERSITY EXTENSION (1893)

From Edmund S. James. "Some General Considerations Concerning University Extension," as quoted in George F. James, ed., *Handbook of University Extension* (Philadelphia, 1893), pp. vii–xii.

The movement for popular education known as University Extension should be a matter of profound interest to every American. It has a message for men and women alike; for the educated as well as for the uneducated; for the rich no less than for the poor. It seems likely to prove one of the great organizing and initiating forces so necessary and as yet unfortunately so rare in the educational and social life of the United States.

University Extension is a widening of the doors of the college and university so as to take in classes of people who are not now directly benefited by the higher institutions of learning; it brings to busy people at their homes the opportunity of securing university aid and direction in carrying on their studies while engaged in the round of daily toil; it renders possible a much better utilization of existing educational facilities.

If University Extension did nothing more than this; if it simply made the higher learning possible to those who are thirsting for it, who for any reason have not been able to share it in their youth or have fallen out of contact with it in their advancing age, it would still be a movement in which every thoughtful student of human progress would be interested. But it means vastly more than this. It begets and feeds an interest in higher things, which but for it would never be awakened. It stirs many a mind from a weak and slothful intellectual lethargy into a new and strong activity, with all the countless and widening circles of influence which such an awakening on the part of even one mind begets. It puts new and worthy objects of thought into the lives of people who have been content to live on in intellectual sloth and barrenness. It turns the current of thought and discussion in whole communities from the every-day gossip and tittle-tattle of small social cliques and circles into the great and broad stream of human history and science. It sets them to talking about Shakespeare, and Milton, and Copernicus, and Napoleon, and Bismarck, and Gladstone, instead of about their neighbors; it leads them to think of the possibility of public reforms and improvements instead of giving all their time to a discussion of the weather and its influence on their crops or investments; as Mr. W. T. Harris so neatly says of the great newspaper, at the very worst it replaces village gossip with world gossip to the immense advantage of the community. The reflex action of such increased intellectual activity on the individual and community is simply marvelous and constitutes a service which would alone justify the existence of the great agitation.

But these are not by any means the only services which this great movement performs, or at least may perform, for our American society. It would be difficult, if not impossible, to formulate in one sentence all the purposes of such a many-sided agency as this; but the English Extension workers have given us one statement which is full of insight into the deeper nature of this great subject. The purpose of the Extension movement, they tell us, is to make education, i. e., self-culture, one of the serious and permanent interests of human life. It is to be put side by side with religion, with business, with politics, with amusement, as one of the great categories of human existence. The individual shall give time from day to day, year in and year out, to this subject as religiously as he does to his spiritual relations. It would be considered ridiculous for a man to propose to devote two or three or four years to religious observances, study and reflection with the idea of dispensing with the necessity of ever thinking of them again. It is not less ridiculous for a man to drop the process of systematic self-culture after leaving school or college. From this point of view University Extension has a distinct mission, viz., to preach the doctrine of the duty of systematic self-culture—a duty resting on every man and woman alike. It should not be content with merely ministering to the wants of those who are already alive to their needs; but it should leave no stone unturned to bring home to the conscience, as well as the consciousness of every man, the obligation resting upon him to take up and pursue a course of education lasting as long as his life.

University Extension offers, furthermore, an opportunity—such as the world has never before seen—to preach a sound doctrine to the masses as to their duty to take up and care for the educational interests of the community. The welfare of American education depends in a peculiar way upon public interest in its purpose and instrumentalities. In European countries the ministry of education is charged with the special function of canvassing from time to time the educational needs of the people and of taking stock of the educational agencies; and if it appear that there is a need which is not provided for by an existing educational institution, it becomes the duty of the ministry to provide for the establishment of such an institution. In this country we have no corresponding system of ascertaining and providing for public educational wants. We must depend entirely upon the more or less accidental consciousness of a need on the part of the community and the possibility of arousing the people to action. As a result, our educational system, with all its excellencies, shows serious faults—of omission as well as of commission— which could be easily remedied if public attention could be attracted and enlightened. The University Extension movement offers an excellent opportunity to do this work. The public comes to hear of Shakespeare, or history, or economics; they are glad to remain to hear of education. The Extension lecturer who misses this opportunity, either through wilfulness or ignorance, has not only failed to utilize one of the most efficient means of interesting the public in the movement, but he has become untrue to one of its highest functions.

There is still another educational function performed by the Extension movement which is of immense importance, and that is the education of the general public as to the functions and organization of our colleges and universities. In the United States, as in England, one of our fundamental defects is our indifference to science, an indifference which Matthew Arnold has excellently characterized in his various educational essays and reports. It is difficult, even in our best and richest institutions, to secure the application of their funds for the promotion of advanced scholarship and learning as distinct from elementary teaching, while in the less favorably situated colleges and universities almost nothing is done for the advancement of science. Professors and students alike spend their time and energy in mastering the facts contained in printed books, without ever making one honest effort to widen the sphere of human knowledge. This condition is not likely to improve until there is a more general appreciation on the part of the public of the value of science—knowledge systematically pursued and prized in and for itself—and until the community recognizes the cultivation of science as a chief end of our university system. The University Extension lecturer has a magnificent opportunity to impress this idea upon the public mind and to arouse its interest and enthusiasm in the work of our higher institutions of learning. The colleges and universities of America perform a function as vital to our national welfare as do our railroads, our courts of justice, our army or our navy. But the average American citizen does not realize this fact. He thinks of the university as an institution which serves the purposes of a few classes in our society. The future lawyer, clergyman, physician or teacher may find it worth while to go to college; but neither the college nor university has a message for any one else. University Extension offers an opportunity to correct this false notion, and there is no doubt whatever that the result of the University Extension movement will be to bring students, public sympathy and support, private gifts and benefactions to the work of higher education.

Finally, there is another great function which University Extension may perform for our American society, and which it is already performing in England to a limited though growing extent, and that is its work in the direction of social reform. This educational means offers an opportunity to preach to the public in a convincing form and relation the great doctrine of a higher and nobler life. By its appeal to all classes, by its emphasis of the elements which should be of common interest to all intelligent people, it is a powerful, practical force in the direction of a higher and nobler social form. Our modern industry, our social tendencies and even our education, while they have given the death blow to the class and caste system of the last century, are all steadily working in the direction of building up new class distinctions—erecting new barriers between individuals, communities and orders of society against which even the strong tendencies of modern religious and philanthropic effort have hard work to make headway. University Extension comes as a powerful ally of all those forces which tell for the common brotherhood of man. It is a part of its very nature to bring men and women of all classes and ages and religious faiths nearer together, for it emphasizes those things which are of interest to men as men. The great underlying truths of natural science, the course of human history, the beauties of literature, the science of society and government are all subjects which may and do bring men together, and differences of opinion in the realm of politics and history give way before the common desire to learn the truth of these things.

University Extension has proved one of the most powerful social solvents. It has succeeded when all other agencies have failed in uniting in one common effort the Jew, the Roman Catholic, the Protestant—whether Episcopalian, Methodist, Baptist or Presbyterian. It has brought together in one undertaking the laborer and employer, the rich and poor, the professional man and mechanic, and has demonstrated in a new and convincing way that the interest in higher things and capacity for their enjoyment is by no means limited to the college graduate, or to the male sex, or to the well-to-do. The elevating, unifying, conciliating, educating influences of our modern society are not by any means so numerous that we can affort to dispense with any single one in the great and trying times of social reform toward which we are rapidly drifting.

12

THE
MINORITIES

Negroes—the South

ACCOUNT OF THE BREAKING UP OF A SLAVE FAMILY (c. 1800) From
Walter Fisher, ed., *Father Henson's Story of His Own Life* (New York, 1962), pp. 11-13.

Common as are slave-auctions in the southern states, and naturally as a slave may look forward to the time when he will be put up on the block, still the full misery of the event—of the scenes which precede and succeed it—is never understood till the actual experience comes. The first sad announcement that the sale is to be; the knowledge that all ties of the past are to be sundered; the frantic terror at the idea of being sent "down south"; the almost certainty that one member of a family will be torn from another; the anxious scanning of purchasers' faces; the agony at parting, often forever, with husband, wife, child—these must be seen and felt to be fully understood. Young as I was then, the iron entered into my soul. The remembrance of the breaking up of McPherson's estate is photographed in its minutest features in my mind. The crowd collected round the stand, the huddling group of negroes, the examination of muscle, teeth, the exhibition of agility, the look of the auctioneer, the agony of my mother—I can shut my eyes and see them all.

My brothers and sisters were bid off first, and one by one, while my mother, paralyzed by grief, held me by the hand. Her turn came, and she was bought by Isaac Riley of Montgomery county. Then I was offered to the assembled purchasers. My mother, half distracted with the thought of parting forever from all her children, pushed through the crowd, while the bidding for me was going on, to the spot where Riley was standing. She fell at his feet, and clung to his knees, entreating him in tones that a mother only could command, to buy her *baby* as well as herself, and spare to her one, at least, of her little ones. Will it, can it be believed that this man, thus appealed to, was capable not merely of turning a deaf ear to her supplication, but of disengaging himself from her with such violent blows and kicks, as to reduce her to the necessity of creeping out of his reach, and mingling the groan of bodily suffering with the sob of a breaking heart? As she crawled away from the brutal man I heard her sob out, "Oh, Lord Jesus, how long, how long shall I suffer this way!" I must have been then between five and six years old. I seem to see and hear my poor weeping mother now. This was one of my earliest observations of men; an experience which I only shared with thousands of my race, the bitterness of which to any individual who suffers it cannot be diminished by the frequency of its recurrence, while it is dark enough to overshadow the whole after-life with something blacker than a funeral pall.

EDUCATION
IN THE
UNITED STATES

ANNOUNCEMENT OF THE OPENING OF A NEGRO SCHOOL IN RALEIGH, NORTH CAROLINA (1808) From *Raleigh Register,* August 20, 1808.

John Chaves takes this method of informing his Employers, and the Citizens of Raleigh in general, that the present Quarter of his School will end the 15th of September, and the next will commence on the 19th. He will, at the same time, open an Evening School for the purpose of instructing Children of Colour, as he intends, for the accommodation of some of his employers, to exclude all Children of Colour from his Day School.

The Evening School will commence at an hour by Sun. When the white children leave the House, those of colour will take their places, and continue until ten o'clock.

The terms of teaching the white children will be as usual, two and a half dollars per quarter; these of colour, one dollar and three quarters. In both cases, the whole of the money to be paid in advance to Mr. Benjamin S. King. Those who produce Certificates from him of their having paid the money, will be admitted.

Those who think proper to put their Children under his care, may rely upon the strictest attention being paid, not only to their Education, but to their Morals, which he deems an *important* part of Education.

Aug. 23, 1808.

He hopes to have a better School House by the commencement of the next quarter.

Negro cabin in Virginia, c. 1848.

**MISSISSIPPI LAW FORBIDDING EDUCATION OF SLAVES OR FREE
NEGROES (1823)** From *Laws of the State of Mississippi. Passed at the Sixth Session
of the General Assembly* (Jackson, Miss., 1823), p. 60.

All meetings or assemblies of slaves, or free negroes, or mulattoes, mixing
and associating with such slaves above the number of five, at any place of public
resort, or at any meetinghouse or houses, in the night, or at any school or schools,
for teaching them reading or writing, either in the day or night, under whatsoever
pretext, shall be deemed and considered an unlawful assembly, and any justice of the
peace of the country or corporation wherein such assemblage shall be, either from
his own knowledge, or the information of others, of such unlawful assemblage or
meeting, may issue his warrant, directed to any sworn officer or officers, authorising
him or them to enter the house or houses where such unlawful assemblages or
meetings may be, for the purpose of apprehending or dispersing such slaves, free
negroes or mulattoes, and to inflict corporal punishment on the offender or
offenders, at the discretion of any such justice of the peace, not exceeding thirty-
nine lashes.

**LOUISIANA LAW PROHIBITING THE TEACHING OF SLAVES
(1830)** From *A New Digest of the Statute Laws of Louisiana* (Baton Rouge, 1841), vol.
I, pp. 271–72.

That all persons who shall teach, or permit or cause to be taught, any
slave in this State, to read or write, shall, upon conviction thereof, before any court
of competent jurisdiction, be imprisoned, not more than one month nor more than
twelve months.

THE TARBOROUGH (N.C.) FREE PRESS ON THE OPENING OF A SCHOOL FOR NEGRO GIRLS IN BALTIMORE (1830) From *Tarborough* (N. C.) *Free Press*, February 5, 1830.

A school for the education of girls of color has been established in Baltimore, under the direction of a religious society of colored women, established in June last, who devote themselves to religious duties, and to the christian education of their own color. Besides the care bestowed upon their religious education, the pupils are taught English, French, cyphering and writing, sewing in all its branches, embroidery, washing and ironing. Boarding & tuition, $48 per year.

NORTH CAROLINA LAW PROHIBITING THE TEACHING OF SLAVES (1831) From *Acts Passed by the General Assembly of the State of North Carolina at the Session of 1830–1831* (Raleigh, N.C., 1831), p. 11.

An Act to Prevent All Persons from Teaching Slaves to Read or Write, the Use of Figures Excepted

Whereas the teaching of slaves to read and write, has a tendency to excite dissatisfaction in their minds, and to produce insurrection and rebellion, to the manifest injury of the citizens of this State: Therefore,

Be it enacted by the General Assembly of the State of North Carolina, and it is hereby enacted by the authority of the same, That any free person, who shall hereafter teach, or attempt to teach, any slave within the State to read or write, the use of figures excepted, or shall give or sell to such slave or slaves any books or pamphlets, shall be liable to indictment in any court of record in this State having jurisdiction thereof, and upon conviction, shall, at the discretion of the court, if a white man or woman, be fined not less than one hundred dollars, nor more than two hundred dollars, or imprisoned; and if a free person of color, shall be fined, imprisoned, or whipped, at the discretion of the court, not exceeding thirty nine lashes, nor less then twenty lashes.

II. *Be it further enacted,* That if any slave shall hereafter teach, or attempt to teach, any other slave to read or write, the use of figures excepted, he or she may be carried before any justice of the peace, and on conviction thereof, shall be sentenced to receive thirty nine lashes on his or her bare back.

III. *Be it further enacted,* That the judges of the Superior Courts and the justices of the County Courts shall give this act in charge to the grand juries of their respective counties.

VIRGINIA LAW PROHIBITING THE TEACHING OF SLAVES (1831)   From
Acts Passed at a General Assembly of the Commonwealth of Virginia, 1830–31 (Richmond, 1831), pp. 107–8.

5. *Be it further enacted,* That if any white person or persons assemble with free negroes or mulattoes, at any school-house, church, meeting-house, or other place for the purpose of instructing such free negroes or mulattoes to read or write, such person or persons shall, on conviction thereof, be fined in a sum not exceeding fifty dollars, and moreover may be imprisoned at the discretion of the jury, not exceeding two months.

6. *Be it further enacted,* That if any white person, for pay or compensation, shall assemble with any slaves for the purpose of teaching and shall teach any slave to read or write, such person, or any white person or persons contracting with such teacher, so to act, who shall offend as aforesaid, shall, for such offence, be fined at the discretion of a jury, in a sum not less than ten, not exceeding one hundred dollars, to be recovered on any information or indictment.

ALABAMA LAW PROHIBITING THE TEACHING OF SLAVES (1832)   From
Acts Passed at the Thirteenth Annual Session of the General Assembly of Alabama, 1831–32 (Montgomery, Ala., 1832), p. 16.

Sec. 10. *And be it further enacted,* That any person or persons who shall endeavor or attempt to teach any free person of color, or slave to spell, read, or write, shall upon conviction thereof by indictment, be fined in a sum not less than two hundred and fifty dollars nor more than five hundred dollars.

Pen and Ink

SOUTH CAROLINA LAW FORBIDDING THE TEACHING OF SLAVES
(1834)   From *The Statutes at Large of South Carolina* (1840), vol. VII, p. 468.

I. *Be it enacted,* by the honorable the Senate and House of Representatives, now met and sitting in General Assembly, and by the authority of the same, If any person shall hereafter teach any slave to read or write, or shall aid or assist in teaching any slave to read or write, or cause or procure any slave to be taught to read or write, such person, if a free white person, upon conviction thereof, shall, for each and every offence against this Act, be fined not exceeding one hundred dollars, and imprisoned not more than six months; or if a free person of color, shall be whipped, not exceeding fifty lashes, and fined not exceeding fifty dollars, at the discretion of the court of magistrates and freeholders before which such free person of color is tried; and if a slave, to be whipped at the discretion of the court, not exceeding fifty lashes; the informer to be entitled to one half of the fine, and to be a competent witness. And if any free person of color or slave shall keep any school, or other place of instruction for teaching any slave or free person of color to read or write, such free person of color or slave shall be liable to the same fine, imprisonment and corporal punishment, as are by this act imposed and inflicted on free persons of color and slaves for teaching slaves to read or write.

FREDERICK DOUGLASS DESCRIBES HIS SELF-EDUCATION (c. 1830)   From *The Life and Times of Frederick Douglass, from 1817 to 1882, Written by Himself* (London, 1882), pp. 51–53, 54–57.

The frequent hearing of my mistress reading the Bible aloud, for she often read aloud when her husband was absent, awakened my curiousity in respect to this *mystery* of reading, and roused in me the desire to learn. Up to this time I had known nothing whatever of this wonderful art, and my ignorance and inexperience of what it could do for me, as well as my confidence in my mistress, emboldened me to ask her to teach me to read. With an unconsciousness and inexperience equal to my own, she readily consented, and in an incredibly short time, by her kind assistance, I had mastered the alphabet and could spell words of three or four letters. My mistress seemed almost as proud of my progress as if I had been her own child, and supposing that her husband would be as well pleased, she made no secret of what she was doing for me. Indeed, she exultingly told him of the aptness of her pupil, and of her intention to persevere in teaching me, as she felt it her duty to do, at least to read the Bible. And here arose the first dark cloud over my Baltimore prospects, the precursor of chilling blasts and drenching storms. Master Hugh was astounded beyond measure, and probably for the first time, proceeded to unfold to his wife the true philosophy of the slave system, and the peculiar rules necessary in the nature of the case to be observed in the management of human chattels. Of course he forbade her to give me any further instruction, telling her in the first place that to do so was unlawful, as it was also unsafe, "for," said he, "if you give a nigger an inch he will take an ell. Learning will spoil the best nigger in the world. If he learns to read the Bible it will for ever unfit him to be a slave. He should know nothing but the will of his master, and learn to obey it. As to himself, learning will do him no good, but a great deal of harm, making him disconsolate and unhappy. If you teach him how to read, he'll want to know how to write, and this accomplished, he'll be running away with himself." Such was the tenor of Master Hugh's oracular exposition, and it must be confessed that he very clearly comprehended the nature and the requirements of the relation of master and slave. His discourse was the first decidedly anti-slavery lecture to which it had been my lot to listen. Mrs. Auld evidently felt the force of what he said, and like an obedient wife, began to shape her course in the direction indicated by him. The effect of his words *on me* was neither slight nor transitory. His iron sentences, cold and harsh, sunk like heavy weights deep into my heart, and stirred up within me a rebellion not soon to be allayed. This was a new and special revelation, dispelling a painful mystery against which my youthful understanding had struggled, and struggled in vain, to wit, the white man's power to perpetuate the enslavement of the black man. "Very well," thought I. "Knowledge unfits a child to be a slave." I instinctively assented to the proposition, and from that moment I understood the direct pathway from slavery to freedom. It was just what I needed, and it came to me at a time and from a source whence I least expected it. Of course I was greatly saddened at the thought of losing the assistance of my kind mistress, but the information so instantly derived, to some extent compensated me for the loss I had sustained in this direction. Wise as Mr. Auld was, he underrated my comprehension, and had little idea of the use to which I was capable of putting the impressive lesson he was giving to his wife. He wanted me to be a slave; I had already voted against that on the home plantation of Col. Lloyd. That which he most loved I most hated; and the very determination which he expressed to keep me in ignorance, only rendered me the more resolute to seek intelligence. In learning to read, therefore, I am not sure that I do not owe quite as much to the opposition of my master as to the kindly assistance of my amiable mistress. I acknowledge the benefit rendered me by the one, and by the other, believing that but for my mistress I might have grown up in ignorance.

*   *   *

I lived in the family of Mr. Auld, at Baltimore, seven years, during which time, as the almanac makers say of the weather, my condition was variable. The most interesting feature of my history here, was my learning to read and write under somewhat marked disadvantages. In attaining this knowledge I was compelled to resort to indirections by no means congenial to my nature, and which were really humiliating to my sense of candour and uprightness. My mistress, checked in her benevolent designs toward me, not only ceased instructing me herself, but set her face as a flint against my learning to read by any means. It is due to her to say, however, that she did not adopt this course in all its stringency at first. She either thought it unnecessary, or she lacked the depravity needed to make herself forget at once my human nature. She was, as I have said, naturally a kind and tender-hearted woman, and in the humanity of her heart and the simplicity of her mind, she set out, when I first went to live with her, to treat me as she supposed one human being ought to treat another.

Nature never intended that men and women should be either slaves or slaveholders, and nothing but rigid training, long persisted in, can perfect the character of the one or the other. Mrs. Auld was singularly deficient in the qualities of a slave-holder. It was no easy matter for her to think or to feel that the curly-headed boy, who stood by her side, and even leaned on her lap, who was loved by little Tommy, and who loved little Tommy in turn, sustained to her only the relation of a chattel. I was more than that; she felt me to be more than that. I could talk and sing; I could laugh and weep; I could reason and remember; I could love and hate. I was human, and she, dear lady, knew and felt me to be so. How could she then treat me as a brute, without a mighty struggle with all the noblest powers of her soul? That struggle came, and the will and power of the husband was victorious. Her noble soul was overcome, and he who wrought the wrong was injured in the fall, no less than the rest of the household. When I went into that household, it was the abode of happiness and contentment. The wife and mistress there was a model of affection and tenderness. Her fervent piety and watchful uprightness made it impossible to see her without thinking and feeling, "that woman is a Christian." There was no sorrow nor suffering for which she had not a tear, and there was no innocent joy for which she had not a smile. She had bread for the hungry, clothes for the naked, and comfort for every mourner who came within her reach. But slavery soon proved its ability to divest her of these excellent qualities, and her home of its early happiness. Conscience cannot stand much violence. Once thoroughly injured, who is he who can repair the damage? If it be broken toward the slave on Sunday, it will be toward the master on Monday. It cannot long endure such shocks. It must stand unharmed, or it does not stand at all. As my condition in the family waxed bad, that of the family waxed no better. The first step in the wrong direction was the violence done to nature and to conscience, in arresting the benevolence that would have enlightened my young mind. In ceasing to instruct me, my mistress had to seek to justify herself to herself; and once consenting to take sides in such a debate, she was compelled to hold her position. One needs little knowledge of moral philosophy to see where she inevitably landed. She finally became even more violent in her opposition to my learning to read, than was Mr. Auld himself. Nothing now appeared to make her more angry than seeing me, seated in some nook or corner, quietly reading a book or newspaper. She would rush at me with the utmost fury, and snatch the book or paper from my hand, with something of the wrath and consternation which a traitor might be supposed to feel on being discovered in a plot by some dangerous spy. The conviction once thoroughly established in her mind, that education and slavery were incompatible with each other, I was most narrowly watched in all my movements. If I remained in a separate room from the family for any considerable time, I was sure to be suspected of having a book, and was at once called to give an account of myself. But this was too late: the first and never-to-be-retraced step had been taken. Teaching me the alphabet had been the "inch" given, I was now waiting only for the opportunity to "take the ell."

Filled with the determination to learn to read at any cost, I hit upon many expedients to accomplish that much desired end. The plan which I mainly adopted, and the one which was most successful, was that of using my young white playmates, whom I met in the streets, as teachers. I used to carry almost constantly a copy of Webster's spelling-book in my pocket, and when sent on errands, or when play-time was allowed me, I would step aside with my young friends and take a lesson in spelling. I am greatly indebted to these boys—Gustavus Dorgan, Joseph Bailey, Charles Farity, and William Cosdry.

Although slavery was a delicate subject, and very cautiously talked about among grown-up people in Maryland, I frequently talked about it, and that very freely, with the white boys. I would sometimes say to them, while seated on a curbstone or a cellar door, "I wish I could be free, as you will be when you get to be men." "You will be free, you know, as soon as you are twenty-one, and can go where you like, but I am a slave for life. Have I not as good a right to be free as you have?" Words like these, I observed, always troubled them; and I had no small satisfaction in drawing out from them, as I occasionally did, that fresh and bitter condemnation of slavery which ever springs from natures unseared and unperverted. Of all consciences, let me have those to deal with, which have not been seared and bewildered with the cares and perplexities of life. I do not remember ever to have met with a *boy* while I was in slavery, who defended the system; but I do remember many times, when I was consoled by them, and by them encouraged to hope that something would yet occur by which I would be made free. Over and over again, they have told me that "they believed that I had as good a right to be free as they had," and that "they did not believe God ever made any one to be a slave." It is easily seen that such little conversations with my playfellows had no tendency to weaken my love of liberty, nor to render me contented as a slave.

When I was about thirteen years old, and had succeeded in learning to read, every increase of knowledge, especially anything respecting the Free States, was an additional weight to the almost intolerable burden of my thought—"*I am a slave for life.*" To my bondage I could see no end. It was a terrible reality, and I shall never be able to tell how sadly that thought chafed my young spirit. Fortunately, or unfortunately, I had earned a little money in blacking boots for some gentlemen, with which I purchased of Mr. Knight, on Thames street, what was then a very popular school-book, viz., "The Columbian Orator," for which I paid fifty cents. I was led to buy this book by hearing some little boys say they were going to learn some pieces out of it for recitation. This volume was indeed a rich treasure, and every opportunity afforded me, for a time, was spent in diligently perusing it. Among much other interesting matter, that which I read again and again, with unflagging satisfaction, was a short dialogue between a master and his slave. The slave is represented as having been recaptured in a second attempt to run away; and the master opens the dialogue with an upbraiding speech, charging the slave with ingratitude, and demanding to know what he has to say in his own defence. Thus upbraided, and thus called upon to reply, the slave rejoins that he knows how little anything that he can say will avail, seeing that he is completely in the hands of his owner; and with noble resolution, calmly says, "I submit to my fate." Touched by the slave's answer, the master insists upon his further speaking, and recapitulates the many acts of kindness which he has performed toward the slave, and tells him he is permitted to speak for himself. Thus invited, the quondam slave makes a spirited defence of himself, and thereafter the whole argument for and against slavery is brought out. The master is vanquished at every turn in the argument, and appreciating the fact, he generously and meekly emancipates the slave, with his best wishes for his prosperity.

RECOLLECTIONS OF A NEGRO TEACHER IN THE DEEP SOUTH (c. 1835) From Daniel Alexander Payne, *Recollections of Seventy Years* (Nashville, 1888), pp. 18–25.

I resolved to devote every moment of leisure to the study of books, and every cent to the purchase of them. I raised money by making tables, benches, clothes-horses, and "corset-bones," which I sold on Saturday night in the public market. During my apprenticeship I would eat my meals in a few minutes and spend the remainder of the hour allowed me at breakfast and dinner in reading. After the day's work was done I perused my books till nearly twelve o'clock; and then, keeping a tinder-box, flint, steel, and candle at my bedside, I would awake at four, strike a light, and study till six, when my daily labors began. Thus I went on reading book after book, drawing pictures with crayon, and now and then composing verses. In my nineteenth year I forsook the carpenter's trade for the life of an educator.

*   *   *

My first school was opened in 1829 in a house on Tradd Street occupied by one Cæsar Wright. It consisted of his three children, for each of whom he paid me fifty cents a month. I also taught three adult slaves at night, at the same price, thus making my monthly income from teaching only three dollars. This was not sufficient to feed me, but a slave-woman, Mrs. Eleanor Parker, supplied many of my wants. I was happy in my humble employment, but at the end of the year I was so discouraged at the financial result, and by the remarks expressed by envious persons, that I decided to seek some other employment which would yield better pay.

At this juncture a wealthy slave-holder arrived in Charleston, *en route* to the West Indies for his health. Knowing that British law emancipated every slave that put his foot on British soil, he desired to obtain the services of a free young man of color sufficiently intelligent to do his out-of-door business. I was commended to him, and called upon him at the Planters' Hotel. Among the inducements he offered he said: "If you will go with me, the knowledge that you will acquire of men and things will be of far more value to you than the wages I will pay you. Do you know what makes the difference between the master and the slave? *Nothing but superior knowledge.*"

This statement was fatal to his desire to obtain my services, for I instantly said to myself: "If it is true that there is nothing but superior knowledge between the master and the slave, I will not go with you, but will rather go and obtain that knowledge which constitutes the master." As I politely took my leave these words passed through my mind:

He that flies his Saviour's cross
Shall meet his Maker's frown.

Then these reflections followed. "In abandoning the school-room am I not fleeing from the cross which the Saviour has imposed upon me? Is not the abandonment of the teacher's work in my case a sin?" The answer was easily found, and I resolved to re-open my school and to inform my patrons to that effect.

On the first of the year 1830 I re-opened my school, which continued to increase in numbers until the room became too small, and I was constrained to procure a more commodious place. This in turn became too small, and one was built for me on Anson Street, by Mr. Robert Howard, in the rear of his yard. This house is still standing (1886). Here I continued to teach until April, 1835.

During the three years of my attendance at the school of Mr. Thomas S. Bonneau I learned how to read, write, and spell; also arithmetic as far as the "Rule of Three." Spelling was a delightful exercise of my boyhood. In this I excelled. Seldom did I lose my place at the head of my class, and he who won it did not occupy it long. History was my great delight. Of geography and map-drawing, English grammar and composition I knew nothing, because they were not taught in any of the schools for colored children. I therefore felt the need of knowledge in these directions; but how was I to obtain it?

I had a geography, but had never seen an atlas, and, what was more, I knew not how or where to get one. Fortunately for me, one day as I was sitting on the piazza endeavoring to learn some lesson, a woman entered the gate and approached me with a book in her hand. Said she: "Don't you want to buy this book?" Taking it, I opened it, and to my great joy I beheld the colored maps of an atlas—the very thing I needed. Said I: "What will you take for it?" The woman had found it on the street, and replied: "Whatever you choose to give." All that I could command at the time was a York shilling (twelve and one-half cents in silver coin), so I gave it to her, and rejoiced over my prize. Immediately I went to work with my geography and atlas, and in about six months was able to construct maps on the Mercator's and globular projection. After I had acquired this ability I introduced geography and map-drawing into my school. At the same time with geography I studied and mastered English grammar. I began with "Murray's Primary Grammar," and committed the entire book to memory, but did not understand it; so I reviewed it. Then light sprung up; still I felt like one in a dungeon who beheld a glimmer of light at a distance, and with steady but cautious footsteps moved toward it, inspired by the hope that I would soon find its source and come out into the full blaze of animated day. I then made a second review of it, and felt conscious of my power to teach it. I therefore added that to my curriculum.

Having now the groundwork, I began to build the superstructure. I commenced with "Playfair's Euclid," and proceeded as far as the first five books. The next thing which arrested my attention was botany. The author and her specimens enchanted me; my progress was rapid, and the study became to me a source of great happiness and an instrument of great usefulness. Descriptive chemistry, natural philosophy, and descriptive astronomy followed in rapid succession.

"Burret's Geography of the Heavens" was my text-book in the last-named science. Stimulated by this interesting guide, I watched the total eclipse of 1832 from its commencement to its completion with my *naked eye;* but I paid dear for my rash experiment. The immediate result was a partial loss of sight. No book could be read for about three weeks. Whenever I opened a book the pages had the appearance of *black sheets.* From this injury I have never fully recovered. Up to that time my eyes were like those of the eagle; ever since they have been growing weaker and weaker.

Then, on a Thursday morning, I bought a Greek grammar, a lexicon, and a Greek Testament. On the same day I mastered the Greek alphabet; on Friday I learned to write them; on Saturday morning I translated the first chapter of Matthew's Gospel from Greek into English. My very soul rejoiced and exulted in this glorious triumph. Next came the Latin and the French. Meanwhile I was pushing my studies in drawing and coloring till I was able to produce a respectable flower, fruit, or animal on paper and on velvet.

My researches in botany gave me a relish for zoology; but as I could never get hold of any work on this science I had to *make books* for myself. This I did by killing such insects, toads, snakes, young alligators, fishes, and young sharks as I could catch. I then cleaned and stuffed those that I could, and hung them upon the walls of my school-room. The following fact will give the index of my methods. I bought a live alligator, made one of my pupils provoke him to bite, and whenever he opened his mouth I discharged a load of shot from a small pistol down his throat. As soon as he was stunned I threw him on his back, cut his throat, ripped open his chest, hung him up and studied his viscera till they ceased to move. The flesh of all that I killed I cooked and tasted. I excepted nothing but the toad and snake. My detestation for these was too intense to allow me to put their flesh into my mouth.

My enthusiasm was the inspiration of my pupils. I used to take my first class of boys into the woods every Saturday in search of insects, reptiles, and plants, and at the end of five years I had accumulated some fine specimens of each of these. I had also taken a fatherless boy to educate gratuitously. This lad's sister one day found a large caterpillar on an elderberry-tree. This worm she sent to me. It was the length and thickness of a large laboring-man's middle finger. It had four rows of horns running the whole length of its body; these horns were made up of golden and ebony-like points; its head was also encircled with a crown of these horns.

Not being able to determine the species or genus of this worm, I took it to Mrs. Ferguson, the sister of Judge Colcox, who was unable to give me any information in regard to it; but she advised me to take it to Dr. Bachman, who was then the most distinguished naturalist in South Carolina. I little knew what that visit was to bring about ultimately.

The Doctor received me kindly, and gave its classification. He also instructed me in its nature and habits, and how to carry it through its different stages of existence. This, however, I preferred him to do, allowing me at the same time to visit his studio and observe the transformations. This request was kindly complied with by the learned divine and naturalist. On my second visit he took me into his garden and showed me his fine collections of flowers. He also exhibited to me his herbarium and his valuable collection of insects from different parts of the world. On my last visit he took me into his parlor and introduced me to his wife and daughters as "the young philosopher." There I sat and conversed with his family as freely as though all were of the same color and equal rank; and by my request his daughter skillfully performed several pieces upon the piano. A remark of his at that visit has occurred to me many times through life. There was upon the center-table, protected by a large glass globe, an artificial tree bearing a collection of beautifully-mounted birds. My attention was drawn to them, and I expressed myself to the effect that he had about him everything to make his home pleasant. His reply was substantially this: "Yes; I feel it my duty to throw around my home every possible attraction for my daughters, so that they may never have occasion to seek elsewhere for forbidden pleasures."

My school increased in popularity, and became the most popular of five which then existed. It numbered about sixty children from most of the leading families of Charleston. But I was not without enemies who endeavored to arrest the progress of my school and destroy my usefulness by such remarks as these: "He is an impostor." "Who ever heard of any one learning such things—such things as he teaches—but men trained in a college." "He must deal with the devil."

Such imputations and slanders availed nothing. They seemed to render me more popular, and at last two of the other school-masters came to me to be taught such sciences as they knew not. It was a happiness for me to assist them, which I did, directing them to the authors and the methods which I had employed. It was also one of my methods in order to interest my pupils to erect several gymnastic instruments, that they might develop their muscular systems and find amusement to break the monotony of the school-room; but in all their sports I led them in person.

Negroes—Reconstruction

LETTERS FROM PORT ROYAL BY "MISSIONARIES" FROM NEW ENGLAND (1862-63)   From Elizabeth W. Pearson, ed., *Letters from Port Royal Written at the Time of the Civil War* (Boston, 1906), pp. 22–25, 60, 149, 208–9.

From H. W.

Pine Grove, April 29 [1862]. Our days pass pretty much after this fashion. Mr. Philbrick gets up about six, calls me, and I obey, having stipulated for a full hour in which to dress. After we get downstairs it takes the united efforts of most of the family to get the breakfast on the table, and we are fortunate if we get up from that meal by half-past eight. It generally consists of hominy, very delicious eaten with either milk, butter, or molasses, corn-cake, or waffles of corn-flour—the best of their kind—concentrated coffee, chocolate, or tea, army bread—when we can get it—crackers, when we can't, and boiled eggs or fried fish, as the case may be. The important operations of dish-washing and arranging the rooms upstairs take longer than you can imagine, and things are not always done when I go to school at ten, which with our simple style of living is rather a nuisance. H. begins to pity the Southern housekeepers. This morning, after making the starch in our little kitchen in the house, she waited about for two hours, before she could get hold of one of the three servants. They were all off at the kitchen, smoking and talking and taking things easy. Joe was nominally cleaning knives, Flora had gone to empty a pail of water, and Sukey had no thought about her starched clothes!

Well, I walk off to school, under the white umbrella if the sun shines, dressed as warmly as I can if it does not. My way lies between a row of large "Heshaberry" trees, as the negroes call them; a corruption, I suppose, of Asia Berry, as it is the "Pride of Asia," in full blossom now, with scent something like our lilac, but more delicate. On each side of these trees are the corn-houses, stables, cotton-houses, and near the house a few cabins for house-servants, and the well. They stretch an eighth of a mile, when a gate (left open) shuts off the nigger-house and field. Another eighth brings me to the cabins, which have trees scattered among them, figs and others. The children begin to gather round me before I get there, with their bow and curtsey and "goo' mornin, Marm," and as I go through the quarters I send them in to wash their hands and faces. The praise-house reached, one of the children rings the bell out of the door to summon all, and they gather quickly, some to be sent off to wash their faces—alas, they cannot change their clothes, which are of the raggedest. But now enough clothes have come to begin to sell, I have to have a better dressèd set before long. I keep them in for about two hours—there are about thirty of the little ones who come in the morning, ten and under; all older are in the field, and come in the afternoon, as they finish work by noon always.

I go back to lunch at half-past twelve, a cold one generally, sometimes a few waffles or some hominy for variety, but crackers, sardines, and blackberries which we have in abundance now, make a refreshing meal, with tea or coffee when we please. Shop has to be tended in the afternoon principally, and I sometimes take a turn at it till I go off at half-past three to school again. We use for shop the little room between Mr. G.'s and the entry, selling out of the window over a box for a counter, to the groups on the porch. It is a funny sight and funny work for us, albeit interesting for they have had no clothes for a year, and buy eagerly. Mr. Philbrick has not been able to let them have any clothing before, as there has only been enough to give a garment to one in ten, and they have been so used to being treated alike that their jealousy is very easily roused, and it is a difficult matter to deal with them. For the same reason the clothes have to be sold, the money going back to the Commission, to be used again for their benefit. It would be very much better if only the goods were sent, for they prefer to make their own clothes and all know how to sew.

These people show their subserviency in the way they put Marm or Sir into their sentences every other word and emphasize it as the one important word, and in always agreeing to everything you say. In school it is rather annoying to have them say, "Yes Marm, 'zackly Marm," before it is possible for an idea to have reached their brains.

Flora, our housemaid, who is a character, has a great deal of dignity and influence among the other negroes, and takes the greatest care of us. She is most jealous for what she considers our interests, and moreover is quite an interpreter, though it is hard enough to understand her sometimes. "Learning" with these people I find means a knowledge of medicine, and a person is valued accordingly. Flora wanted to know how much "learning" Miss Helen[1] had had, and it was a long time before I could make out what she meant.

H. says she never saw me look so well, so you see I thrive in spite of fleas, which have almost flayed me alive. I understand what it means by eels' getting *used* to being skinned.

*   *   *

From W. C. G.

May 30 [1862]. Schools are getting on pretty well, I suppose,—slowly, of course. A few are really bright,—a few really dull; the larger part—like the same proportion of white children—could creep, walk, or trot, according to the regularity with which they are driven, and the time devoted to their books. While we have been living at Pine Grove, there have been five schools daily, teaching about one hundred and forty scholars.

*   *   *

[1]Mrs. Philbrick.

From H. W.

Jan. 27 [1863]. Both schools were very satisfactory. If any one could have looked in, without the children's seeing them, they would have thought we presented quite an ordinary school-like appearance. I have a blackboard with numerals and figures and the second line of the Multiplication Table written on it, all of which the oldest school know tolerably, but they make sorry work trying to copy the figures on their slates. I let them use them every day now, however, for they must learn, by gradually growing familiar with the use of a pencil, not to use it like a hoe. There are furrows in the slates made by their digging in which you might plant benny-seed, if not cotton!

From H. W.

Feb. 22 [1863]. I heard Uncle Sam read the first three chapters of Genesis, which he translated into his own lingo as he went along, calling the subtile serpent the most "amiable" of beasts, and ignoring gender, person, and number in an astonishing manner. He says "Lamb books of Life," and calls the real old Southern aristocracy the gentiles! His vocabulary is an extensive one—I wish his knowledge of the art of cooking were as great!

Feb. 25. I was in full tide with my A B C's when I saw two mounted officers pass the window. They presently appeared at the door of the school-room, one of them with a General's stars, addressing me and asking about the school. But he did not introduce himself, and I was in profound ignorance as to who it might be. They came, apparently, to see the place, and while they walked on the beach I got up what lunch I could. The title had an immense effect upon Robert; when I told Sam I must have the water boiled to give the General some coffee, he opened his eyes as wide as the gate, and Rose, who came to ask for the key of the corn-room for him to feed the horses, was such a comical sight, as she stared with mouth and eyes and then dropped a curtsey in the middle of the room, that if any one had been here I think I should have disgraced myself and snickered! Unfortunately the dignitary did not see her.

Feb. 26. I had scarcely done breakfast when I was called upon to serve in the shop for half a dozen men from the blockading vessel off Otter Island, all negroes. They come every once in a while and buy large amounts of sugar and other little things. They evidently think their patronage of great advantage to us.

Five grown men have come in to swell the evening school. I can't do much for them, as they don't all know their letters, but they have books and I hope the children will help them on out of school.

Have I told you that the path to the beach has been bordered with flowers for several weeks, jonquils and narcissus, so far as I can make out, though unlike any I ever saw before? They are in great profusion, and there are a few snow-drops, very pretty, but a foot or more high, and losing their charm in the height and strength. The jasmine and hawthorn are just coming into blossom, and I see what looks like a peach-tree in full bloom in Sam's yard.

ESTABLISHMENT OF THE FREEDMEN'S BUREAU (1865) From George P. Sanger, ed., *Statutes at Large . . . of the United States* (Boston, 1866), vol. XIII, p. 507.

An Act to establish a Bureau for the Relief of Freedmen and Refugees

Be it enacted, That there is hereby established in the War Department, to continue during the present war of rebellion, and for one year thereafter, a bureau of refugees, freedmen, and abandoned lands, to which shall be committed, as hereinafter provided, the supervision and management of all abandoned lands, and the control of all subjects relating to refugees and freedmen from rebel states, or from any district of country within the territory embraced in the operation of the army, under such rules and regulations as may be prescribed by the head of the bureau and approved by the President. The said bureau shall be under the management and control of a commissioner to be appointed by the President, by and with the advice and consent of the Senate. . . .

Sec. 2. That the Secretary of War may direct such issues of provisions, clothing, and fuel, as he may deem needful for the immediate and temporary shelter and supply of destitute and suffering refugees and freedmen and their wives and children, under such rules and regulations as he may direct.

REPORT OF THE NEW ENGLAND FREEDMEN'S AID SOCIETY ON THE NEGROES' FAITH IN EDUCATION (1865) From Walter L. Fleming, ed., *Documentary History of Reconstruction* (New York, 1966), vol. II, pp. 174–75.

Their belief that reading and writing are to bring with them inestimable advantages, seems, in its universality and intensity, like a mysterious instinct. All who have been among them bear witness to this fact. As respects aptitude to learn, there is similar unanimity of testimony. It cannot be expected that a man or woman whose only school-training heretofore has been that of the plantation-school, or that children whose ancestors have been slaves for generations back, should show the same quickness that the children of New-England parents manifest. The negro adult or child, before he enters the Freedmen's school, has been at a very bad preparatory school. Slave-masters are not good schoolmasters: still,—due allowance made for parentage and training—it is not too much to say, that the aptitude at acquiring the elements of knowledge is, by the testimony of all our teachers, marvelous under the circumstances. They do not write as if they found calls for more patience than is demanded in our ordinary Northern schools. And it is a most significant fact, that the most enthusiastic are not the new teachers, but those who have been at their posts from the beginning. It may be of interest to some, to know that they do not find any difference, in respect to intellect, between those of pure blood and those of mixed blood.

The importance of the work of educating the freedmen, can hardly be exaggerated. Its results will reach into the future. . . . The great mass of white men, who are now disloyal, will remain, for some time to come, disaffected. Black men who are now friendly will remain so. And to them must the country look in a large degree, as a counteracting influence against the evil councils and designs of the white freemen.

A DESCRIPTION OF NEGRO SCHOOLS IN THE SOUTH AFTER THE WAR (1866) From Whitelaw Reid, *After the War: A Southern Tour, May 1, 1865, to May 1, 1866* (New York, 1866), pp. 246–58.

In the good old times, before the advent of Farragut and Butler, the statutes of Louisiana declared teaching slaves to read and write a "crime, having a tendency to excite insubordination among the servile class, and punishable by imprisonment at hard labor for not more than twenty-one years, or by death, at the discretion of the court." When asked, therefore, to visit the negro schools of New Orleans, I was not unduly sanguine in my expectations. Reverend and Lieutenant Wheelock, a keen, practical Yankee preacher, acting as secretary to the "Board of Education for Freedmen," instituted by General Banks, was guide.

The first school-house to which we were conducted was an old store-room, the second story of which has been used as a hall for the Knights of the Golden Circle, and still bore on its walls the symbols of that hollowest and most insolent of Southern humbugs. Rude partitions divided the storeroom, and separated the three different grades of the primary school.

In the first we were received by a coarse, ill-dressed, rude-looking man, who evidently sprang from the poor white trash. Ranged along the wall as we entered were a dozen or more boys, reading as boys do read, in the Third Reader—with many a pause and many a tracing of hard words with a great fore-finger that blurs everything it touches. Among the class was a bright, fair-haired boy, who would have been called handsome anywhere. Seated behind the little desks were some large, coarse girls, seemingly eighteen or twenty years of age, conning their spelling-books. The hot air was languidly stirred by the hot breeze from the street windows, which brought in with it the sound of boys at play on the pavement; and one did not wonder at the noise and general inattention that prevailed.

The next room was ruled by a woman as coarse and slatternly as became the neighbor of the man whose school we had just left. A little fellow made some noise to displease her as we entered, and she bowled him against the wall as one would bowl a ball down a ten-pin ally. Children were at work mumbling over charts hung against the wall, and professing, with much noisy show of industry, to be spelling out simple sentences. But their zeal did not prevent surreptitious pinches, when the slatternly school-mistress's back was turned, nor a trade of "five alleys for a bright-colored glass one," on the sly. I think such scenes are not unknown even in model Northern schools.

The teacher in the third room was as great a contrast to the two we had just seen as was her school to theirs. She was smart, bright, looking for all the world like a Lowell factory girl of the better class; and her pupils, though by no means quite as lambs, were in fine order. Their faces had evidently been washed systematically; long labors had forced upon their comprehension the advantages of clean aprons and pinafores; and they appeared attentive and noisily anxious to learn. This teacher seemed capable of giving an intelligent opinion as to the capacities of her scholars. She had taught at the North, and she saw no difference in the rapidity with which whites and blacks learned to spell and read. There were dull scholars and bright scholars everywhere. Some here were as dull as any she ever saw; others were bright as the brightest. And she called out a little coal-black creature, who had been in school eight days, and was apparently not more than as many years old. The eyes of the little thing sparkled as she began to spell! Eight days ago she had not known her letters. From spelling she went to reading, and was soon found to have mastered every sentence on the charts hung about the walls.

The more advanced scholars were found in the old hall of the K. G. C., up stairs. Here, where once schemes for taking Cuba, or perpetuating slavery in the South, were discussed, forty or fifty boys and girls, lately slaves, stood before the platform where the knights had ranged themselves for initiation, and peacefully recited their lesson in the Fourth Reader! Where once the Knight Commander sat, stalked now a loose-jointed, angular oddity from one of the Middle States—narrow-headed, and with ideas in proportion, which he seemed in nowise fitted to impart. Nigger school-teaching was manifestly not the respectable thing to do in New Orleans; and the Board seemed to have been put to sad straits sometimes for teachers. The reading was bunglingly done, but the teacher didn't read so very much better himself. On spelling the class did better. In geography they had learned by rote the answers to the common questions; and they could point out with considerable accuracy, on the outline maps, New Orleans and Louisiana, and the Mississippi River and the Gulf of Mexico. But one woolly-headed urchin brought his teacher to grief and wrath, by selecting Cuba as the proper location for Iceland; matters were nowise improved by the further transfer of Asia to the exact latitude and longitude of San Francisco. Yet, with all the allowances, it was a fair average school. Boys and girls, ranging in age from twelve to twenty, read the Fourth Reader passably; some of them had a fair conception of geography, and they had even made an entrance on the mysteries of grammar. Arithmetic seemed to be all plain sailing till they reached long division. Here the process became too complicated, and they were sure to blunder in the multiplication of the divisor by the dividend, or to add where they should subtract, or to bring down the wrong figures at the wrong time. Was it the fault of the stupid teacher? or was their previous progress due to their imitative faculties, and did they fail now simply because they had reached a point where reasoning powers of their own were needed? It is the question which touches the marrow of the whole discussion about the average negro capacity; but the time has been too short and the experiments have been too incomplete as yet to furnish satisfactory data for its solution.

The next school to which we were conducted was kept by a middle-aged negro, in gold spectacles, and with amusingly consequential air. His assistant—what would not the Opposition journals have given for such a fact during the late political campaign?—was an English girl, young and lame, who seemed to have gone to work here, "among the niggers," very much as she would have gone to work among the pots and kettles, simply because a living was to be earned, and this way to earn it happened to offer. The negro principal has a short, sharp way of dealing with his pupils; and strap and ferule lay convenient for immediate use beside the books upon his table. He explained that many of his pupils were "contrabans," from the plantations, or negroes that had been "refugeed" from the Red River country; and their experiences in slavery had been such that they knew no motive for obedience but the fear of punishment. "Coax 'em and they'll laugh at you; you've got to knock 'em about, or they won't think you've got any power over 'em." The theory seemed to have made a pretty good school, whether by virtue of the ferule or in spite of it.

The children were having their noon recess when we entered, and the school-room was perfectly quiet. At the sound of the bell they came trooping noisily to the door, and in a few moments the black tide had overflowed all the desks. A Fourth Reader class was called up, which read well—quite as well as the average of such classes anywhere. Now and then one noticed a curious mouthing of the words and a quaint mispronunciation that the forms of the ordinary negro dialect would not account for. In these cases the children were of French parentage, and were learning a language as well as the art of reading. "The children are taught exclusively in English," the Board of Education say sententiously in their report. "Bound by the strong ligament of a common tongue, they will never foster the subtle enmity to national unity that lurks in diversity of speech."

The exercises in arithmetic that followed disclosed the same slower progress in this than in other branches, which had already been observed in the schools previously visited. A few questions of a miscellaneous nature showed that the scholars were by no means destitute of general intelligence; and especially that they had a very keen appreciation of the fact that they had once been slaves, but were so no longer.

We were treated to a special performance before we left—reserved for the closing of the school, except upon grand occasions. An astonishing youth, with wool growing down almost to his eyebrows, beneath which gleamed cunning eyes that alone relieved the face from an expression of utter stupidity, took his place in the aisle in front of the teacher's desk. The hum of the school suddenly hushed, and all eyes were fastened on the droll figure. The woolly head gave a bob forward, while the body seemed to go through contortions caused by some inward pain. As the head ducked down the second time and came up with snapping eyes, the opening of the song was ejected, and the shrill voice was soon drowned in the roar that joined in from the whole open-throated throng.

Such singing may never be heard elsewhere. The nearest approach a Northern reader is ever likely to make to it is when he hears the enthusiastic chorus at some noisy camp-meeting about the time the "power" is supposed to be "coming down, coming down." The song was nothing—a rhyming effort of the gold-spectacled teacher himself, I believe, rudely setting forth the joy of the slaves at the great deliverance, and ending in a refrain of thanks and prayer for "Honest Abe." But the negroes, too, have learned to worship the rising rather than the setting sun. "Honest Abe" was very well in his way; but if the schools were to be continued and the teachers paid, there would be more present need of help from his successor. And so the song had been already patched; and the refrain came thundering in for "Andie J." After all, there is a good deal of human nature in negroes!

Some rickety, tumble-down buildings on an out-of-the-way corner had been secured for another school, which we next visited. A motherly old negress here had her brood of little ones gathered about her, learning in concert the alphabet from the chart which she held in her lap. Up the row and down it she led them with the little pointer, which looked as if it might be chosen a double duty to perform. Now one was singled out to name a letter selected at random from some other chart; then the pointer flitted from top to bottom and back to middle of the alphabet, and the shiny-faced urchins eagerly shouted the responses, or winced as the pointer descended threateningly near some naughty hand that was wandering into foreign pockets.

In another room, a bright, lady-like young quadroon, who was similarly occupied, smiled a pleasant greeting as we entered. She had been at the fair at Pierre Soulé's. With ample means and a pleasant home, she volunteered to do this work of duty to her race; and the neat, orderly school-room, with the quiet ways and clean faces of her little charge[s], not less than their prompt answers, told her success.

In one of the rooms in this building a row of picaninnies, ranging from four to fourteen, stood up to recite in the First Reader. At their head, painfully spelling his way through a sentence as we entered, was an old man of sixty, with white wool and a wrinkled face. He wore a pair of huge brass-rimmed spectacles; but they would not stick on his bulled-shaped head without further contrivance, and so he had tied a bit of packing-cord into the ends of the brass temples, and around his head. I asked the old man what he wanted to learn to read for. "Reckon if it's good for white folks, good for me too."

"But you're so old, uncle, one would think you wouldn't care for such things any more."

"Reckon if it's good for chil'en, can't be bad for old folks."

Subsequent talk showed that the old man had a Bible, and wanted to learn to read it, and, further, that he believed, as soon as he could read, he would be entitled to vote. Precisely what good that would do him he did not seem to understand; but he worked away industriously over his well-thumbed First Reader, and scarcely gave a second look to the visitors, at whom the children were staring with all their eyes. It was a trifling thing, doubtless, and the old man may have been very silly to be thus setting himself to children's tasks, in the simplicity of his desire to learn what he knew white folks had found good for them ; but to me there seemed nothing more touching or suggestive in all the sights of New Orleans.

We saw no other old men in the schools, and few young ones beyond the age of twenty; but the teachers said the cases were quite numerous in which the more intelligent scholars were instructing their parents at home. In all such instances the parents were sure to enforce regular attendance on the part of their children, and the influence of the school became reflex, first on the scholars, from them to the families, thence back to the school again.

The few schools spoken of above may be taken as a fair specimen of the system in operation in New Orleans in June, 1865. It was soon destined to give way to the reaction of public feeling, which already began to influence the affairs of the department. But it has now been carried on for fourteen months. Few, even of the most advanced, had, at the beginning, been able to read the simplest sentence. Now there were classes in geography, grammar, and arithmetic, and a very fair proportion of the fourteen thousand seven hundred and forty-one scholars could read quite intelligently. The gate of knowledge had been opened to them; there was little likelihood that hereafter a General commanding would be able to stop the spread of these dangerous arts of reading and writing, by an official notification that the opening of schools for negro children would be very hazardous and unwise.

* * *

So rapid was the progress that, on the 1st of January, 1865, the scholars had advanced so far as to be thus classified:

Writing on slates, 3,883; writing in copy-books, 1,108; studying grammar, 283; studying geography, 1,338; studying practical arithmetic, 1,223; studying mental arithmetic, 4,628; reading, 7,623; spelling, 8,301; learning the alphabet, 2,103.

And from the beginning of the experiment down to the 1st of June, 1865, there had been a regular increase of eleven hundred and fourteen scholars and fourteen teachers per month. Two thousand new scholars had come into the schools in May alone; in April there had been fifteen hundred. The expense of this entire system was about one-half what it cost to support a single regiment in the field. This expense was to be met by a tax on the property within the lines of military occupation; General Banks's order explaining, for the comfort of dissatisfied tax-payers, that henceforth labor must be educated in the South in order to be valuable, and that if they didn't support the negro schools, they would find it hard to secure negro labor.

Judging, both from personal observation and from the testimony of the teachers and the Board of Education, I should say that the negro pupils are as orderly and as easily governed as any corresponding number of white children, under similar circumstances. There is, I think, a more earnest desire to learn, and a more general opinion that it is a great favor to have the opportunity. There is less destruction of books, less whittling of school furniture, less disposition to set up petty revolts against the teacher's authority. The progress in learning to read is exceptionally rapid. I do not believe that in the best schools at the North they learn the alphabet and First Reader quicker than do the average of these slave children. The negroes are not quicker-witted, but they are more anxious to learn. In writing they make equally rapid progress, and where the teachers are competent they do well in geography. Arithmetic presents the first real obstacles, and arouses painful inquiries as to the actual mental capacity of this long-neglected race.

But, up to this point, the question of negro education is no longer an experiment. In reading and writing I do not hesitate to say that the average progress of the children of plantation hands, as shown in every negro school from Fortress Monroe around to New Orleans, is fully equal to the average progress of white children at the North.

The experiment of high schools is about to be tried among them, under the auspices of a voluntary organization, mainly made up and sustained by themselves. Its constitution was adopted a fortnight or more before our visit, and such men as Thomas J. Durant were uniting with the negroes in an effort to get the enterprise properly started.

On the Sunday after our visit to these schools, we were taken to see a Sunday-school, made up largely of the same scholars, although conducted under the auspices of Mr. Conway, a business-like preacher, in charge of the Freedmen's Bureau in the city. The building into which we were conducted had been, in former times, a medical college. Ranged upon the seats, which arose, amphitheater-like, half-way to the ceiling, sat row after row of closely-crowded, smiling, black-faced, but bright-eyed, Sunday-school scholars, as clean, as smiling, and as prettily dressed as one would see almost anywhere in our Northern rural districts. On the higher benches, where the larger scholars sat, were a few young ladies, tastefully attired in white. At that distance, one had difficulty in seeing that their faces were not of the pure Anglo-Saxon tinge; but, neat and pretty as they looked, they were only niggers, and nigger Sunday-school teachers at that.

A graduate of Amherst met us as we mounted the platform once occupied by the demonstrator of anatomy. He was a sober, sedate figure, in professional black, and, with his dignified ways, might have been taken for a Southern Doctor of

Divinity, if you did not look at his face. That was as black as his coat. His son, a handsome, graceful young fellow (always barring the black face and the kinky wool), took his seat at the piano. The sober representative of Amherst rapped on the table, and tapped the little bell, till the children slowly and gradually mastered the almost irrepressible torrent of whispers and laughter. But the bell-taps sounded clearer and clearer; silence at last reigned. A hymn was read; the young negro at the piano softly touched the keys for a moment, and then the whole rich, joyous nature of the children gushed into a volume of melody that rose and swelled till the very air of the old lecture-room was vocal with praise. It was like listening to the grand peals of Plymouth Church itself.

There followed a little address, with, perhaps, a trifle too much of talk about their liberty, and too little of how it should be made profitable; too much about the prejudices against them, and too little about the means for an improvement which should conquer prejudices; too much about the faults of their masters, and too little about their own. But this seems to be the general strain; and perhaps, after all, it may be necessary, in some such way, to gain the confidence of the children before you can instruct them. Occasional questions kept alive the interest, and the lustily shouted answers showed an intelligence that plainly took in the full meaning of the speech.

"What great man freed you all, and was then taken home?"

Surely, if the murdered President could but have been present, beside his old associate, at that scene, he would have thought the shouts that brought back his name the sweetest praise the lips of mortals ever bore him.

"Are you really free now?"

"Yes,yes."

"What would you do if anybody should now try to take your freedom away?"

It was fine to watch the play of surprise and apprehension across the animated faces. "We'd fight," exclaimed a sturdy fellow, twelve or fourteen years old. "We wouldn't let them," said many more. "The soldiers would stop it," murmured the most. That, alas! seemed still the main hope of these submissive, long-enslaved people. They had not reached—not even the oldest of them—the conception of organized effort to protect themselves. "The soldiers would stop it." That was all.

A GENERAL DESCRIPTION OF THE SCHOOLS UNDER THE SUPERVISION OF THE FREEDMEN'S BUREAU (1870) From U.S. Bureau of Education, *Annual Report of the Commissioner of Education, 1870*, p. 337.

By the courtesy of General O. O. Howard, Commissioner of Refugees, Freedmen and Abandoned Lands, we are enabled to include in this report a summary of the general condition of the schools under his supervision, up to July 1, 1870.

In submitting his tenth and final report, embracing a period of six months preceding the above date, the Commissioner states that, although nominally the report is only for the above named period, it includes two-thirds of the usual school months, and therefore gives substantially the results of the whole year. The long vacation closed on the 31st of October, but the opening of the schools was delayed, in many cases, for the gathering of the crops. After the Christmas holidays all commenced, and by New Years were in full operation.

The reports are not as full as those of the last year, on account of changes in the superintendents; but a much higher average attendance is shown than for the preceding year, with a higher grade of teaching. The aggregate of schools, teachers, and pupils reported remains nearly as large as ever. It would be much larger if the work done by the States themselves were included.

The character of the education of the freedmen is in every respect higher than ever before. "The whole race is recovering from the effects of slavery; in all industrial pursuits, in moral status, and intellectual development even the adult population is rapidly 'marching on.' "

More than 247,000 children gathered in the various classes of schools the last year, "under systematic instruction, have been steadily coming forward to a cultured man and womanhood, and the majority to assume, with credit to themselves, the front rank of this rising people. Their influence will be normal, formative, and enstamp itself upon many generations."

But the report, "though closing an office must not be understood as recording a finished work." "This Bureau has only inaugurated a system of instruction helping its first stages, and which is to be continued and perfected." It is "only a yet pending experiment." "The masses of these people are, after all, still ignorant. Nearly a million and a half of their children have never as yet been under any instruction. Educational associations, unaided by Government will of necessity largely fall off. The States south as a whole awake but slowly to the elevation of their lower classes. No one of them is fully prepared with funds, buildings, teachers, and actual organizations to sustain these schools." "With sorrow we anticipate, if the reports of superintendents can be relied on, the closing of hundreds of our school buildings, sending thousands of children who beg for continued instruction to the streets, or what is far worse to squalid, degraded homes to grow up not as props and pillars of society, but its pests." "The several States will ere long, we hope, come nobly forward, in duty to their children. They cannot afford to leave those in ignorance who are so soon to be upon the stage of action."

CHARLES SUMNER OPPOSES SCHOOL SEGREGATION (1872) From
Congressional Globe, 42d Cong.. 2d Sess. (1871–72). part I. p. 384.

It is easy to see that the separate school founded on an odious discrimination and sometimes offered as an equivalent for the common school is an ill-disguised violation of the principle of Equality, while as a pretended equivalent it is an utter failure and instead of a parent is only a churlish step-mother.

A slight illustration will show how it fails, and here I mention an incident occurring in Washington, but which must repeat itself where ever separation is attempted. Colored children, living near what is called the common school, are driven from its doors, and compelled to walk a considerable distance, often troublesome and in certain conditions of the weather difficult, to attend the separate school. One of these children has suffered from this exposure, and I have myself witnessed the emotion of the parent. This could not have occurred had the child been received at the common school in the neighborhood. Now, it is idle to assert that children compelled to this exceptional journeying to and fro are in the enjoyment of equal rights. The super-added pedestrianism and its attendant discomfort furnish the measure of inequality in one of its forms, increased by the weakness or ill health of the child. What must be the feelings of a colored father or mother daily witnessing this sacrifice to the demon of Caste?

This is an illustration merely, but it shows precisely how impossible it is for a separate school to be the equivalent of the common school. And yet it only touches the evil without exhibiting its proportions. The indignity offered to the colored child is worse than any compulsory exposure, and here not only the child suffers, but the race to which he belongs is blasted and the whole community is hardened in wrong.

The separate school wants the first requisite of the common school, inasmuch as it is not equally open to all; and since this is inconsistent with the declared rule of republican institutions, such a school is not republican in character. Therefore it is not a preparation for the duties of life. The child is not trained in the way he should go; for he is trained under the ban of inequality. How can he grow up to the stature of equal citizenship? He is pinched and dwarfed while the stigma of color is stamped upon him. This is plain oppression, which you, sir, would feel keenly were it directed against you or your child. Surely the race enslaved for generations has suffered enough without being compelled to bear this prolonged proscription. Will not the Republic, redeemed by most costly sacrifice, insist upon justice to the children of the land, making the common school the benign example of republican institutions where merit is the only ground of favor.

Nor is separation without evil to the whites. The prejudice of color is nursed when it should be stifled. The Pharisaism of race becomes an element of character, when like all other Pharisaisms, it should be cast out. Better even than knowledge is a kindly nature and the sentiment of equality. Such should be the constant lesson repeated by the lips and inscribed on the heart; but the school itself must practice the lesson. Children learn by example more than by precept. How precious the example which teaches that all are equal in rights. But this can be only where all commingle in the common school as in common citizenship. There is no separate ballot-box. There should be no separate school. It is not enough that all should be taught alike; they must all be taught together. They are not only to receive equal quantities of knowledge, but all are to receive it in the same way. But they cannot be taught alike unless all are taught together; nor can they receive equal quantities of knowledge in the same way, except at the common school.

The common school is important to all; but to the colored child it is a necessity. Excluded from the common school, he finds himself too frequently without any substitute. Often there is no school. But even where a separate school is planted it is inferior in character. No matter what the temporary disposition, the separate school will not flourish as the common school. It is but an offshoot or sucker without the strength of the parent stem. That the two must differ is seen at once, and that this difference is adverse to the colored child is equally apparent. For him there is no assurance of education except in the common school, where he will be under the safeguard of all. White parents will take care not only that the common school is not neglected, but that its teachers and means of instruction are the best possible, and the colored child will have the benefit of this watchfulness. This decisive consideration completes the irresistible argument for the common school as the equal parent of all without distinction of color.

CONSTITUTIONAL PROVISIONS FOR MIXED SCHOOLS IN LOUISIANA AND SOUTH CAROLINA (1868)   From W. L. Fleming, ed., *Documentary History of Reconstruction* (New York, 1966), p. 32.

[Louisiana] Art. 135. The general assembly shall establish at least one free public school in every parish throughout the State, and shall provide for its support by taxation or otherwise. All children of this State between the years of six and twenty-one shall be admitted to the public schools or other institutions of learning sustained or established by the State in common, without distinction of race, color, or previous condition. There shall be no separate schools or institutions of learning established exclusively for any race by the State of Louisiana. . .

Art. 142. A university shall be established and maintained in the city of New Orleans. It shall be composed of a law, a medical, and a collegiate department, each with appropriate faculties. The general assembly shall provide by law for its organization and maintenance: *Provided*, That all departments of this institution of learning shall be open in common to all students capable of matriculating. No rules or regulations shall be made by the trustees, faculties, or other officers of said institution of learning, nor shall any laws be made by the general assembly violating the letter or spirit of the articles [on education].

*   *   *

[South Carolina] Article X. Sec. 10. All the public schools, colleges, and universities of this State, supported in whole or in part by the public funds, shall be free and open to all the children and youths of the State, without regard to race or color.

DESCRIPTION OF MIXED SCHOOLS IN NEW ORLEANS (1875)   From Eugene Lawrence, "Color in the New Orleans Schools," *Harper's Weekly*, vol. XIX, pp. 147–48.

The Superintendent of the Common Schools of Louisiana, the Hon. William G. Brown, is a colored man of unusual attainments, energy, and refinement. He was born in the British West Indies, where the strife of races has long ceased, and was carefully educated in an English school. Afterward he emigrated to New Orleans, became a public teacher, was then an editor, and next, in 1872, was elected to his present office. Before his election his opponents were accustomed to represent him as "an ignorant, brutal, plantation negro." Since he became State Superintendent the public has discovered, and even some of his former defamers admit, that he is admirably fitted for his difficult position. Fearless, impartial, intelligent, he has given a new impulse to public education in Louisiana, and has been particularly useful in advancing the intellectual welfare of his own race. It is even asserted that the colored children of New Orleans are more intelligent than the white, and the colored schools more zealous in the search for knowledge than those of their former superiors. It is indeed to be hoped that in this generous rivalry the latter will resort to no unscholarly expedients to win the race. But unfortunately for the peace of the schools of New Orleans, a question of color has sprung up, excited by the general violence of political feeling in the city, and even the children of the place have formed their own "White League" to expel all colored pupils from the schools attended by the whites.

This is a plain violation of the law. Like their elder examples at Coushatta or Vicksburg, our young crusaders are too impetuous to await the slow action of legislation, or even to regard that which exists, and have essayed to purge the public schools of every shade of the offensive tinge. The constitution of Louisiana, however, provides that there shall be no distinction of color in the schools, and that they shall be open to all children of proper age. In New Orleans there are over seventy schools, about one-third of which are used almost exclusively by the whites, another third by the colored children, and the remainder by a mixture of all shades and colors, including Indians and even Chinese. Color is not alluded to in the law, nor has it had any practical influence upon the course of education. All classes have united in pleasing themselves as to the choice of the schools where they would educate their children. But the law forbids any teacher from rejecting any scholar who applies for admission, and makes it a misdemeanor to do so, and hence colored parents have the right to send their children to the schools where the purest Caucasian tint is alone supposed to prevail. They have not, however, done so, and have in general preferred the mixed or colored schools, which are said to be better taught and managed than the white. Yet it was reported that the white schools for girls were not altogether free from the obnoxious tinge, and a disorderly band of boys, apparently with no more discretion and common sense than most of the White League leaders of New Orleans, went round from school to school to select and drive out the colored pupils. Rude, careless in dress, sometimes armed with sticks, and possibly knives, like their amiable exemplars, the young "regulators" broke into a number of the female schools, but soon found that they had entered upon a task that might have puzzled the keenest observer. It is sufficient to say that they were baffled at every step. They gave up their crusade in shame. The question of color was one that not even the sharpest inquiry could decide. Indignant parents, noted in the gay society of New Orleans, frowned at the insult that had been put upon their children; young maidens of the purest blood were frequently the objects of the mistaken ardor of the young crusaders, and were forced to prove that they were white. From one school the intruders were expelled by a courageous teacher and the friends of his pupils; and the latest crusade of the White Leaguers in the cause of unmixed schools has ended in general ridicule. It throws new light upon their extreme folly and violence.

Nowhere, indeed, would it be so difficult, so invidious, to establish a government founded upon a distinction of color as in New Orleans. Here all shades and tints are blended in harmonious confusion. The dark bronze of the creole inhabitants, the descendants of French and Spanish blood, is sometimes of a deeper shade than the traits of negro descent. Of these there are every degree and every hue. Even the pure Caucasian, white and red from the misty climate of England, grows tawny and atrabilious beneath the sun, the habits, and the dissipation of New Orleans; and there are persons of negro descent apparently so purely white as to surpass in this particular the emigrants from New York and Connecticut. Color has never, in fact, been a badge of division at New Orleans. There are families of African descent of great respectability and wealth, and some of the most valuable citizens have been of that just now unlucky race, so that when the young White Leaguers penetrated into the female schools to drive out their colored sisters, a series of laughable or painful incidents met them at every step of the inquiry. In one of the schools they ordered an intelligent little girl of about eleven years old to leave at once. Of her guilt there could be no mistake, they thought, for the offensive tinge mantled on her cheek.

"Do you know who I am?" said the young girl with natural indignation.

"No," said the captain of the White League, "nor do I desire to know you. You are a negro, and must leave this school."

"A negro!" cried the young girl, with all the pride of her color swelling at her heart. "I am the daughter of your leader. My name is Miss P———."

They made no further attempt to eject her, and retired in confusion. But they went to other schools and drove out children and even fair young women of sixteen, bathed in tears or glowing with indignation. Their threats and their lifted sticks made resistance impossible. Several Jewish maidens, touched with the olive tint of an Orient clime, it is said, were included among those who were expelled. In fact, the coarse manners and rude conduct of the leaders of the movement toward the gentler sex in their foolish crusade have left them few friends among the mothers of New Orleans. If there is anything particularly noticeable in this whole affair of the White League in Louisiana, both of the young and old, it is the total want of intelligence shown by its leaders. Such dull and half-stupefied intellects, such extreme mental weakness, could only have been brought into public notice by its extraordinary wickedness. The "platform" of the White League of New Orleans, which it has recently published to defend its useless cruelty and bloodshed, reads like the drivel of idiots. It speaks of "brutal violence stalking at midnight in the draggled shroud of judicial authority;" it paints the colored people in language that every one will naturally apply to its own acts alone. It would seem not unlikely that the sensible people of all colors in New Orleans must at last unite to throw off the yoke of stupid violence, and settle its affairs in a way that will be satisfactory to all colors and races, and this is to do justice to all.

Mr. Conway, who from 1868 to 1872 was the able State Superintendent of the Common Schools in Louisiana, and on whom fell the duty of first publishing the order throwing them open to children of all colors, relates that when he had issued it he received many letters threatening his life, commanding him to leave the State, and showing the bitter hostility of a part of the people against the new regulation. But he was not intimidated, and persevered. The law was obeyed. The number of white children attending the schools was soon larger than ever before; the irrational rage of their opponents subsided; all races and classes were mingled in the mixed schools, or divided, according to their tastes or nationality, as they chose; and it was not until the recent foolish outbreak of the White League, young and old, that any danger threatened the course of education in New Orleans. Even General Beauregard in 1873 lent his aid to the extinction of the race-quarrel, and a wiser spirit seemed about to animate the people. Since then a White League of twenty-five hundred men has assumed the control of New Orleans, and nearly completed the ruin of the divided city.

CONSTITUTIONAL PROVISION FOR EDUCATION IN NORTH CAROLINA

(1868, 1876)   From Francis N. Thorpe, ed., *The Federal and State Constitutions* . . . (Washington, D.C., 1909), vol. V, pp. 2817, 2838.

[1868]

ARTICLE IX, SEC. 1. Religion, morality, and knowledge being necessary to good government and happiness of mankind, schools and the means of education shall forever be encouraged.

SEC. 2. The general assembly, at its first session under this constitution, shall provide, by taxation and otherwise, for a general and uniform system of public schools, wherein tuition shall be free of charge to all the children of the state between the ages of six and twenty-one years.

[1876]

ARTICLE IX, SEC. 1. Religion, morality and knowledge being necessary to good government and the happiness of mankind, schools and the means of education shall forever be encouraged.

SEC. 2. The General Assembly, at its first session under this Constitution, shall provide by taxation and otherwise for a general and uniform system of public schools, wherein tuition shall be free of charge to all the children of the State between the ages of six and twenty-one years. And the children of the white race and the children of the colored race shall be taught in separate public schools; but there shall be no discrimination in favor of or to the prejudice of either race.

EDUCATIONAL PROVISIONS IN THE TENNESSEE CONSTITUTION

(1870)   From Francis N. Thorpe, ed., *The Federal and State Constitutions* . . . (Washington, D.C., 1909), vol. VI, p. 3469.

ARTICLE XI, SEC. 12. Education to be cherished; common school fund; poll tax; whites and negroes; colleges, etc., rights of.

Knowledge, learning, and virtue, being essential to the preservation of republican institutions, and the diffusion of the opportunities and advantages of education throughout the different portions of the State, being highly conducive to the promotion of this end, it shall be the duty of the General Assembly, in all future periods of this government, to cherish literature and science. And the fund called the common school fund, and all the lands and proceeds thereof, dividends, stocks, and other property of every description whatever, heretofore by law appropriated, by the General Assembly of this State for the use of common schools, and all such as shall hereafter be appropriated, shall remain a perpetual fund, the principal of which shall never be diminished by legislative appropriations; and the interest thereof shall be inviolably appropriated to the support and encouragement of common schools throughout the State, and for the equal benefit of all the people thereof, and no law shall be made authorizing said fund or any part thereof to be

THE MINORITIES

1647

diverted to any other use than the support and encouragement of common schools. The State taxes derived hereafter from polls shall be appropriated to educational purposes, in such manner as the General Assembly shall, from time to time, direct by law. No school established or aided under this section shall allow white and negro children to be received as scholars together in the same school. The above provisions shall not prevent the Legislature from carrying into effect any laws that have been passed in favor of the colleges, universities, or academies, or from authorizing heirs or distributees to receive and enjoy escheated property under such laws as shall be passed from time to time.

EDUCATIONAL PROVISIONS IN THE ALABAMA CONSTITUTION

(1875)   From U.S. Bureau of Education, *Report of the Commissioner of Education, 1892-1893* (Washington, D.C., 1895), pp. 1373-74.

Constitution of Alabama, 1875

ART. V. (*Executive Department.*) 1. The Executive Department shall consist of a Governor, Secretary of State, State Treasurer, State Auditor, Attorney-General, and Superintendent of Education, and a Sheriff for each county.

ART. XI. (*Taxation.*) 8. At the first session of the General Assembly after the ratification of this Constitution, the salaries of the following officers shall be reduced at least twenty-five percentum, viz: Governor, Secretary of State, State Auditor, State Treasurer, Attorney-General, Superintendent of Education, Judges of the Supreme and Circuit Courts, and Chancellors; and after said reduction the General Assembly shall not have the power to increase the same except by a vote of a majority of all the members elected to each House, taken by yeas and nays, and entered on the journals, *Provided*, this section shall not apply to any of said officers now in office.

ART. XIII. (*Education.*) 1. The General Assembly shall establish, organize and maintain a system of public schools throughout the State for the equal benefit of the children thereof, between the ages of seven and twenty-one years; but separate schools shall be provided for the children of citizens of African descent.

2. The principal of all funds arising from the sale or other disposition of lands or other property, which has been or may hereafter be granted or entrusted to this State, or given by the United States for educational purposes, shall be preserved inviolate and undiminished; and the income arising therefrom shall be faithfully applied to the specific objects of the original grants or appropriations.

3. All lands or other property given by individuals, or appropriated by the State for educational purposes, and all estates of deceased persons, who die without leaving a will or heir, shall be faithfully applied to the maintenance of the public schools.

4. The General Assembly shall also provide for the levying and collection of an annual poll tax, not to exceed one dollar and fifty cents on each poll, which shall be applied to the support of the public schools in the counties in which it is levied and collected.

5. The income arising from the sixteenth section trust fund, the surplus revenue fund, until it is called for by the United States government, and the funds enumerated in sections three and four of this article, with such other moneys, to be not less than one hundred thousand dollars per annum, as the General Assembly shall provide by taxation or otherwise, shall be applied to the support and maintenance of the public schools, and it shall be the duty of the General Assembly to increase, from time to time, the public school fund, as the condition of the Treasury and the resources of the State will admit.

6. Not more than four per cent. of all moneys raised, or which may hereafter be appropriated for the support of public schools, shall be used or expended otherwise than for the payment of teachers, employed in such schools; *Provided,* that the General Assembly may, by a vote of two-thirds of each House, suspend the operation of this section.

7. The supervision of the public schools shall be vested in a Superintendent of Education, whose powers, duties, term of office and compensation shall be fixed by law. The Superintendent of Education shall be elected by the qualified voters of the State in such manner and at such time as shall be provided by law.

8. No money raised for the support of the public schools of the State, shall be appropriated to or used for the support of any sectarian or denominational school.

9. The State University and the Agricultural and Mechanical College shall each be under the management and control of a Board of Trustees. The Board of the University shall consist of two members from the congressional district in which the University is located, and one from each of the other congressional districts in the State. The Board for the Agricultural and Mechanical College shall consist of two members from the congressional district in which the College is located, and one from each of the other congressional districts in the State. Said Trustees shall be appointed by the Governor, by and with the advice and consent of the Senate, and shall hold office for a term of six years, and until their successors shall be appointed and qualified. After the first appointment each Board shall be divided into three classes, as nearly equal as may be. The seats of the first class shall be vacated at the expiration of two years, and those of the second class in four years, and those of the third class at the end of six years from the date of appointment, so that one-third may be chosen biennially. No Trustee shall receive any pay or emolument other than his actual expenses incurred in the discharge of his duties as such.

The Governor shall be *ex-officio* President and the Superintendent of Education *ex-officio* a member of each of said Boards of Trustees.

10. The General Assembly shall have no power to change the location of the State University or the Agricultural and Mechanical College as now established by law, except upon a vote of two-thirds of the General Assembly, taken by yeas and nays and entered upon the journals.

EDUCATIONAL PROVISIONS IN THE VIRGINIA CONSTITUTION

(1878) From Benjamin P. Poore, ed., *The Federal and State Constitutions, Colonial Charters, and Other Organic Laws of the United States* (Washington, D.C., 1878), vol. II, pp. 1967–68.

Article VIII

EDUCATION

SECTION I. The general assembly shall elect, in joint ballot, within thirty days after its organization under this constitution, and every fourth year thereafter, a superintendent of public instruction. He shall have the general supervision of the public free-school interests of the State, and shall report to the general assembly for its consideration within thirty days after his election a plan for a uniform system of public free schools.

SEC. 2. There shall be a board of education, composed of the governor, superintendent of public instruction, and attorney-general, which shall appoint and have power to remove for cause and upon notice to the incumbents, subject to confirmation by the senate, all county superintendents of public free schools. This board shall have, regulated by law, the management and investment of all school-funds, and such supervision of schools of higher grades as the law shall provide.

SEC. 3. The general assembly shall provide by law, at its first session under this constitution, a uniform system of public free schools, and for its gradual, equal, and full introduction into all the counties of the State by the year eighteen hundred and seventy-six, or as much earlier as practicable.

SEC. 4. The general assembly shall have power, after a full introduction of the public free-school system, to make such laws as shall not permit parents and guardians to allow their children to grow up in ignorance and vagrancy.

SEC. 5. The general system shall establish, as soon as practicable, normal schools, and may establish agricultural schools and such grades of schools as shall be for the public good.

SEC. 6. The board of education shall provide for uniformity of text-books, and the furnishing of school-houses with such apparatus and library as may be necessary, under such regulations as may be provided by law.

SEC. 7. The general assembly shall set apart, as a permanent and perpetual "literary fund," the present literary funds of the State, the proceeds of all public lands donated by Congress for public-school purposes, of all escheated property, of all waste and unappropriated lands, of all property accruing to the State by forfeiture, and all fines collected for offences committed against the State, and such other sums as the general assembly may appropriate.

SEC. 8. The general assembly shall apply the annual interest on the literary fund, the capitation-tax provided for by this constitution for public free-school purposes, and an annual tax upon the property of the State of not less than one mill, nor more than five mills, on the dollar, for the equal benefit of all the people of the State, the number of children between the ages of five and twenty-one years in each public free-school district being the basis of such division. Provision shall be made to supply children attending the public free schools with necessary text-books, in cases where the parent or guardian is unable, by reason of poverty, to furnish them. Each county and public free-school district may raise additional sums by a tax on property for the support of public free schools. All unexpended sums of any one year in any public free-school district shall go into the general school-fund for redivision the next year: *Provided,* That any tax authorized by this section to be raised by counties or school districts shall not exceed five mills on a dollar in any one year, and shall not be subject to redivision, as hereinbefore provided in this section.

SEC. 9. The general assembly shall have power to foster all higher grades of schools under its supervision, and to provide for such purpose a permanent educational fund.

SEC. 10. All grants and donations received by the general assembly for educational purposes shall be applied according to the terms prescribed by the donors.

SEC. 11. Each city and county shall be held accountable for the destruction of school property that may take place within its limits by incendiaries or open violence.

SEC. 12. The general assembly shall fix the salaries and prescribe the duties of all school officers, and shall make all needful laws and regulations to carry into effect the public free-school system provided for by this article.

EDUCATIONAL PROVISIONS IN THE SOUTH CAROLINA
CONSTITUTION (1868, 1895)   From Francis N. Thorpe, ed., *The Federal and State Constitutions* . . . (Washington, D.C., 1909), vol. VI, pp. 3300–301, 3338–39.

[1868]
ARTICLE X, SEC. 3. The general assembly shall, as soon as practicable after the adoption of this constitution, provide for a liberal and uniform system of free public schools throughout the State, and shall also make provision for the division of the State into suitable school districts. There shall be kept open, at least six months in each year, one or more schools in each school district.

ARTICLE X, SEC. 10. All the public schools, colleges, and universities of this State, supported in whole or in part by the public funds, shall be free and open to all the children and youths of the State, without regard to race or color.

[1895]
ARTICLE XI, SEC. 5. The General Assembly shall provide for a liberal system of free public schools for all children between the ages of six and twenty-one years, and for the division of the Counties into suitable school districts, as compact in form as practicable, having regard to natural boundaries . . .

ARTICLE XI, SEC. 7. Separate schools shall be provided for children of the white and colored races, and no child of either race shall ever be permitted to attend a school provided for children of the other race.

EDUCATIONAL PROVISIONS IN THE LOUISIANA CONSTITUTION (1864, 1868, 1879, 1898)
From Francis N. Thorpe, ed., *The Federal and State Constitutions* . . . (Washington, D.C., 1909), vol. III, pp. 1446, 1465, 1508, 1575–76.

[1864]

ARTICLE 141. The legislature shall provide for the education of all children of the State, between the ages of six and eighteen years, by maintenance of free public schools by taxation or otherwise.

[1868]

ARTICLE 135. The general assembly shall establish at least one free public school in every parish throughout the State, and shall provide for its support by taxation or otherwise. All children of this State between the years of six and twenty-one shall be admitted to the public schools or other institutions of learning sustained or established by the State in common, without distinction of race, color, or previous condition. There shall be no separate schools or institutions of learning established exclusively for any race by the State of Louisiana.

[1879]

ARTICLE 224. There shall be free public schools established by the General Assembly throughout the State for the education of all children of the State between the ages of six and eighteen years; and the General Assembly shall provide for their establishment, maintenance and support by taxation or otherwise. And all moneys so raised, except the poll tax, shall be distributed to each parish in proportion to the number of children between the ages of six and eighteen years.

[1898]

ARTICLE 248. There shall be free public schools for the white and colored races, separately established by the General Assembly, throughout the State, for the education of all the children of the State between the ages of six and eighteen years; provided, that where kindergarten schools exist, children between the ages of four and six may be admitted into said schools. All funds raised by the State for the support of public schools, except the poll tax, shall be distributed to each parish in proportion to the number of children therein between the ages of six and eighteen years. The General Assembly, at its next session shall provide for the enumeration of educable children.

SAMUEL C. ARMSTRONG ON THE FOUNDING OF HAMPTON
INSTITUTE (1868) From "The Founding of the Hampton Institute," *Old South Leaflets,* no. 149 (Boston, 1904), pp. 523–24.

A day-dream of the Hampton School, nearly as it is, had come to me during the war a few times,—once in camp during the siege of Richmond, and once one beautiful evening on the Gulf of Mexico, while on the wheel-house of the transport steamship "Illinois," *en-route* for Texas with the Twenty-fifth Army Corps (Negro) for frontier duty on the Rio Grande River, whither it had been ordered under General Sheridan, to watch and, if necessary, defeat Maximilian in his attempted conquest of Mexico.

The thing to be done was clear: to train selected Negro youth who should go out and teach and lead their people, first by example by getting land and homes; to give them not a dollar that they could earn for themselves; to teach respect for labor; to replace stupid drudgery with skilled hands; and to these ends, to build up an industrial system, for the sake not only of self-support and intelligent labor, but also for the sake of character. And it seemed equally clear that the people of the country would support a wise work for the freedmen. I think so still.

The missionary plan in Hawaii had not, I thought, considered enough the real needs and weaknesses of the people, whose ignorance alone was not half the trouble. The chief difficulty with them was deficient character, as it is with the Negro. He is what his past has made him. The true basis of work for him and all men is the scientific one,—one recognizing the facts of heredity and surrounding all the facts of the case.

There was no enthusiasm for the manual labor plan. People said, "It has been tried at Oberlin and elsewhere and given up; it won't pay." "Of course," said I, "it cannot pay in a *money* way, but it will pay in a *moral* way, especially with the freedmen. It will make them men and women as nothing else will. It is the only way to make them good Christians."

The school has had, from the first, the good fortune of liberal-minded trustees. They accepted its unformulated, practical plan, when it opened in April, 1868, with two teachers and fifteen pupils, and adopted my formal report of 1870, the year of its incorporation under a special act of the Assembly of Virginia. By this Act of Incorporation the school became independent of any association or sect and of the government. It does work for the state and general government, for which it receives aid, but is not controlled or supported by them.

From the first it has been true to the idea of education by self-help, and I hope it will remain so. Nothing is asked for the student that he can provide by his own labor; but the system that gives him this chance is costly. The student gets nothing but an opportunity to work his way. While the workshops must be made to pay as far as possible, instruction is as important as production.

The Slater Fund has been a great stimulus to technical training. The Negro girl has proved a great success as a teacher. The women of the race deserve as good a chance as the men. So far it has been impossible to supply the demand for Negro teachers. School-houses and salaries, such as they are are ready; but competent teachers are the great and pressing need, and there is no better work for the country than to supply them. But the short public school sessions, of from three to seven months, do not give full support, and skilled labor is the only resource of many teachers for over half the year. As farmers and mechanics, they are nearly as useful as in the school-room. Hence the importance of industrial training.

REPORT OF THE COMMITTEE OF VISITORS TO HAMPTON INSTITUTE
(1873) From M. F. Armstrong and Helen W. Ludlow, *Hampton and Its Students* (New York, 1874), p. 170.

By invitation of the Trustees of the Hampton Normal School, the undersigned attended the Commencement exercises of that institution on Thursday, June 12th, 1873. A detailed report might easily have been provided for, but the end contemplated may perhaps be better served by a general statement of the impressions made upon them.

The location of the institution seemed to us every way most felicitous. The scenery is of a subdued and quiet type, but very charming. The historic associations, both remote and recent, are suggestive and stimulating.

The whole spirit of the institution is at the widest possible remove from every thing extravagant and fanatical. The colored race are not overrated, either morally or intellectually. On the contrary, their characteristic infirmities are distinctly recognized, and diligently combated. Consequently the immediate neighbors of the institution, and the white people of Virginia generally, as they come to understand the matter, are more and more friendly from year to year. Self-interest of course dictates the education of a race which has been so suddenly enfranchised; but along with this there is likewise a great deal of the old Anglo-Saxon love of fair play, and the negroes admit they will have themselves only to blame, if they go to the wall.

The institution is singularly happy in its corps of instructors. General Armstrong has a combination of qualities which fit him admirably for his position. He has great enthusiasm and great enthusiasm and great diligence in his work. The teachers under him are much above the average. The recitations we heard gave proof of very thorough and very skillful drilling. Such eagerness for knowledge, on the part of pupils, we never saw before. It seemed to us like a long thirst just beginning to be satisfied. The five canvas tents upon the lawn looked as gallant as any tent ever did on a battle-field.

But the institution has not yet reached half its proper stature. The new building, whose corner-stone we assisted in laying, is most urgently needed. Men of property can make no better use of it than at Hampton, in strengthening an institution which, though it may have rivals, as we hope it may, is not likely to be surpassed by any similar institution anywhere in the South.

ROSWELL D. HITCHCOCK,
HENRY W. BELLOWS,
WILLIAM I. BUDINGTON,
WILLIAM M. TAYLOR.

New-York, January, 1874.

EXTRACT FROM THE CATALOGUE OF HAMPTON INSTITUTE (1873-74)

From M. F. Armstrong and Helen W. Ludlow. *Hampton and Its Students* (New York, 1874), pp. 167–69.

Instructors and Their Special or Principal Branches of Instruction

S. C. ARMSTRONG, Principal, Moral Science and Civil Government.

J. F. B. MARSHALL, Treasurer and Acting Assistant Principal, Book-keeping.

Academic Department.—JOHN H. LARRY, in charge, Natural Science and Elocution and Drill; MARY F. MACKIE, Mathematics; AMELIA TYLER, Grammar and Composition; ELIZABETH H. BREWER, Ancient History and Physical Geography; MARY HUNGERFORD, Reading and United States History; HELEN W. LUDLOW, English Literature; JULIA E. REMINGTON, Geography and Map Drawing; NATHALIE LORD, Reading; M. C. KIMBER, Writing and Physiology.

Musical Department.—THOMAS P. FENNER, in charge; ETHIE K. FENNER, Assistant.

Girls' Industrial Department.—S. H. FENNER, in charge.

Housework and Boarding Department.—SUSAN P. HARROLS, Matron; C. L. MACKIE, Steward and Hospital Department.

Agriculture Department.—ALBERT HOWE, in charge; GEORGE DIXON, Lecturer on Agriculture.

Mechanical Department.—JOHN H. LARRY, in charge.

Printing-Office.—W. J. BUTTERFIELD, in charge.

Students

Whole number, 226. Young men, 149; young women, 77. Seniors, 27; Middlers, 76 (3 sections); Juniors, 98 (3 sections); Preparatory, 23; Post-Graduates, 2. Average age, 18.

Courses of Study

The courses of study embrace three years, and include—

NORMAL COURSE

Language.—Spelling, Reading, Sentence-Making, English Grammar, Analysis, Rhetoric, Composition, Elocution.

Mathematics.—Mental Arithmetic, Written Arithmetic, Algebra, Geometry, Mathematical Drawing.

History.—History of United States, History of England—Readings from English writers. Universal History.

Natural Science.—Geography—Map-drawing, Physical Geography, Natural History, Natural Philosophy, Physiology, Botany.

Miscellaneous.—Science of Civil Government, Moral Science, Bible Lessons, Drill in Teaching, Principles of Business, Vocal Training, Instrumental Music.

Studies of the Normal Course at discretion. Lectures on the following courses: Formation of Soils, Rotation of Crops, Management of Stock, Fruit Culture, Cultivation of Crops, Drainage, Market Gardening, Meteorology, Practical Instruction in the routine of Farming and Market Gardening.

COMMERCIAL COURSE

Studies of the Normal Course at discretion. Instruction in Book-keeping, Single and Double Entry, in Business Letters, Contracts, Account of Sales, and other Business and Legal Papers, and in Commercial Law. Each student is required to keep his account current with the Institute in proper form.

MECHANICAL COURSE

Studies of the Normal Course at discretion. Practical Instruction in the different varieties of Sewing-Machines in use, in household industries, and in the following: Penmanship, Free Hand Drawing, Mechanical Drawing, Printing.

Lectures are given through the year on Agricultural topics. Arrangements are being made to secure every year the services of leading literary and scientific men in a Lecture Course that shall afford the highest order of entertainment and instruction.

Expenses and Labor

Board, per month	$8 00
Washing and lights, per month,	1 00
Fuel, per month,	75
Use of furniture, per month	25

$10 00

Clothing and books extra, to be paid for in cash.

Able-bodied young men and women over eighteen years of age are expected to pay half in cash and half in work; that is, $5 per month in cash, and to work out the balance. Boys and girls of eighteen years and less are required to pay $6 per month. *Students are held responsible for all balances against them that they may not have worked out.*

The amount of profitable labor being limited, it is desired to extend its advantages as far as possible; hence only those who are absolutely unable to pay any thing in cash are allowed to work out their whole expenses. Young men and women whose parents desire that they shall not be taken out of school to work, may, upon the payment of $10 per month, attend school without interruption, but will nevertheless be required to work on Saturdays, at such hours as may be assigned them. LABOR IS REQUIRED OF ALL, for purposes of discipline and instruction. To this end, day scholars are expected to labor at the rate of an hour per day, at such industries as may be assigned them.

Bills are made out and are payable at the end of the month. The regular cash payment is to be *monthly, in advance.*

The regular annual tuition fee of the institution is seventy dollars. Students are not required to pay this. As the amount has to be secured by the Trustees, by solicitation among the friends of education, students are called upon annually to write letters to their benefactors.

Discipline

Courtesy and mutual forbearance are expected of both pupils and teachers, as indispensable to good discipline.

Every student is by enrollment committed to the discipline and regulations of the school.

Students are subject to suspension or discharge for an unsatisfactory course in respect to study, conduct, or labor.

The use of ardent spirits and tobacco is prohibited. Letter-writing is subject to regulation.

The wardrobes of all students are subject to inspection and regulation by the proper officers.

Students are subject to drill and guard duty. Obedience to the Commandant must be implicit. The rights of students are properly guarded.

Daily Order of Exercises at the H. N. and A. Institute

A.M.—5.00 Rising Bell.
"5.45 Inspection of Men.
"6.00 Breakfast
"6.30 Family Prayers.
"8.00 Inspection of quarters.
"8.30 Opening of school, Roll Call and Exercises.
"8.55 to 10.20 Classes in Reading, Natural Philosophy, Arithmetic, Grammar, Geography, and Book-keeping.
"10.20. to 10.40 Recess.
"10.40 to 12.15 Classes in Writing, Arithmetic, Grammar, History, Algebra, and Elocution.
P.M.-12.15 to 1.30 Dinner and intermission.
"1.30 Roll Call.
"1.40 to 2.50 Classes in Spelling, Arithmetic, Grammar, Geography, Natural Philosophy, History, Civil Government, and Moral Science.
"4.00 Cadet Drill.
"6.00 Supper.
"6.45 Evening Prayers.
"7.15 to 9 Evening Study Hours.
"9.30 Retiring Bell.

BOOKER T. WASHINGTON DESCRIBES HIS EDUCATION (Before 1880)

From *Up From Slavery* (Garden City. N.Y., 1900), pp. 1–3, 27–33, 37, 42–43, 46–48, 51–53.

I was born a slave on a plantation in Franklin County, Virginia. I am not quite sure of the exact place or exact date of my birth, but at any rate I suspect I must have been born somewhere and at some time. As nearly as I have been able to learn, I was born near a cross-roads post-office called Hale's Ford, and the year was 1858 or 1859. I do not know the month or the day. The earliest impressions I can now recall are of the plantation and the slave quarters—the latter being the part of the plantation where the slaves had their cabins.

My life had its beginning in the midst of the most miserable, desolate, and discouraging surroundings. This was so, however, not because my owners were especially cruel, for they were not, as compared with many others. I was born in a typical log cabin, about fourteen by sixteen feet square. In this cabin I lived with my mother and a brother and sister till after the Civil War, when we were all declared free.

Of my ancestry I know almost nothing. In the slave quarters, and even later, I heard whispered conversations among the coloured people of the tortures which the slaves, including, no doubt, my ancestors on my mother's side, suffered in the middle passage of the slave ship while being conveyed from Africa to America. I have been unsuccessful in securing any information that would throw any accurate light upon the history of my family beyond my mother. She, I remember, had a half-brother and a half-sister. In the days of slavery not very much attention was given to family history and family records—that is, black family records. My mother, I suppose, attracted the attention of a purchaser who was afterward my owner and hers. Her addition to the slave family attracted about as much attention as the purchase of a new horse or cow. Of my father I know even less than of my mother. I do not even know his name. I have heard reports to the effect that he was a white man who lived on one of the near-by plantations. Whoever he was, I never heard of his taking the least interest in me or providing in any way for my rearing. But I do not find especial fault with him. He was simply another unfortunate victim of the institution which the Nation unhappily had engrafted upon it at that time.

The cabin was not only our living-place, but was also used as the kitchen for the plantation. My mother was the plantation cook. The cabin was without glass windows; it had only openings in the side which let in the light, and also the cold, chilly air of winter. There was a door to the cabin—that is, something that was called a door—but the uncertain hinges by which it was hung, and the large cracks in it, to say nothing of the fact that it was too small, made the room a very uncomfortable one. In addition to these openings there was, in the lower right-hand corner of the room, the "cat-hole," a contrivance which almost every mansion or cabin in Virginia possessed during the ante-bellum period. The "cat-hole" was a square opening, about seven by eight inches, provided for the purpose of letting the cat pass in and out of the house at will during the night. In the case of our particular cabin I could never understand the necessity for this convenience, since there were at least a half-dozen other places in the cabin that would have accommodated the cats. There was no wooden floor in our cabin, the naked earth being used as a floor.

*   *   *

From the time that I can remember having any thoughts about anything, I recall that I had an intense longing to learn to read. I determined, when quite a small child, that if I accomplished nothing else in life, I would in some way get enough education to enable me to read common books and newspapers. Soon after we got settled in some manner in our own cabin in West Virginia, I induced my mother to get hold of a book for me. How or where she got it I do not know, but in some way she procured an old copy of Webster's "blue-back" spelling book, which contained the alphabet, followed by such meaningless words as "ab," "ba," "ca," "da." I began at once to devour this book, and I think that it was the first one I ever had in my hands. I had learned from somebody that the way to begin to read was to learn the alphabets, so I tried in all the ways I could think of to learn it,—all of course without a teacher, for I could find no one to teach me. At that time there was not a single member of my race anywhere near us who could read, and I was too timid to approach any of the white people. In some way, within a few weeks, I mastered the greater portion of the alphabet. In all my efforts to learn to read my mother shared fully my ambition, and sympathized with me and aided me in every way that she could. Though she was totally ignorant, so fas as mere book knowledge was concerned, she had high ambitions for her children, and a large fund of good, hard, common sense which seemed to enable her to meet and master every situation. If I have done anything in life worth attention, I feel sure that I inherited the disposition from my mother.

In the midst of my struggles and longing for an education, a young coloured boy who had learned to read in the state of Ohio came to Malden. As soon as the coloured people found out that he could read, a newspaper was secured, and at the close of nearly every day's work this young man would be surrounded by a group of men and women who were anxious to hear him read the news contained in the papers. How I used to envy this man! He seemed to me to be the one young man in all the world who ought to be satisfied with his attainments.

About this time the question of having some kind of a school opened for coloured children in the Village began to be discussed by members of the race. As it would be the first school for Negro children that had ever been opened in that part of Virginia, it was, of course, to be a great event, and the discussion excited the widest interest. The most perplexing question was where to find a teacher. The young man from Ohio who had learned to read the papers was considered, but his age was against him. In the midst of the discussion about a teacher, another young coloured man from Ohio, who had been a soldier, in some way found his way into town. It was soon learned that he possessed considerable education, and he was engaged by the coloured people to teach their first school. As yet no free schools had been started for coloured people in that section, hence each family agreed to pay a certain amount per month, with the understanding that the teacher was to "board 'round"—that is, spend a day with each family. This was not bad for the teacher, for each family tried to provide the very best on the day the teacher was to be its guest. I recall that I looked forward with an anxious appetite to the "teacher's day" at our little cabin.

This experience of a whole race beginning to go to school for the first time, presents one of the most interesting studies that has ever occurred in connection with the development of any race. Few people who were not right in the midst of the scenes can form any exact idea of the intense desire which the people of my race showed for an education. As I have started, it was a whole race trying to go to school. Few were too young, and none too old, to make the attempt to learn. As fast as any kind of teachers could be secured, not only were day-schools filled, but night-schools as well. The great ambition of the older people was to try to learn to read the Bible before they died, With this end in view, men and women who were fifty or seventy-five years old would often be found in the night-school. Sunday-schools were formed soon after freedom, but the principal book studied in the Sunday-school was the spelling-book. Day-school, night-school, Sunday-school, were always crowded, and often many had to be turned away for want of room.

The opening of the school in the Kanawha Valley, however, brought to me one of the keenest disappointments that I ever experienced. I had been working in a salt-furnace for several months, and my stepfather had discovered that I had a financial value, and so, when the school opened, he decided that he could not spare me from my work. This decision seemed to cloud my every ambition. The disappointment was made all the more severe by reason of the fact that my place of work was where I could see the happy children passing to and from school, mornings and afternoons. Despite this disappointment, however, I determined that I would learn something anyway. I applied myself with greater earnestness than ever to the mastering of what was in the "blue-back" speller.

My mother sympathized with me in my disappointment, and sought to comfort me in all the ways she could, and to help me find a way to learn. After a while I succeeded in making arrangements with the teacher to give me some lessons at night, after the day's work was done. These night lessons were so welcomed that I think I learned more at night than the other children did during the day. My own experiences in the night-school gave me faith in the night-school idea, with which, in after years, I had to do both at Hampton and Tuskegee. But my boyish heart was still set upon going to the day-school, and I let no opportunity slip to push my case. Finally I won, and was permitted to go to the school in the day for a few months, with the understanding that I was to rise early in the morning and work in the furnace till nine o'clock, and return immediately after school closed in the afternoon for at least two more hours of work.

The schoolhouse was some distance from the furnace, and as I had to work till nine o'clock, and the school opened at nine, I found myself in a difficulty. School would always be begun before I reached it, and sometimes my class had recited. To get around this difficulty I yielded to a temptation for which most people, I suppose, will condemn me; but since it is a fact, I might as well state it. I have great faith in the power and influence of facts. It is seldom that anything is permanently gained by holding back a fact. There was a large clock in a little office in the furnace. This clock, of course, all the hundred or more workmen depended upon to regulate their hours of beginning and ending the day's work. I got the idea that the way for me to reach school on time was to move the clock hands from half-past eight up to the nine o'clock mark. This I found myself doing morning after morning, till the furnace "boss" discovered that something was wrong, and locked the clock in a case. I did not mean to inconvenience any body. I simply meant to reach that schoolhouse in time.

When, however, I found myself at the school for the first time, I also found myself confronted with two other difficulties. In the first place, I found that all of the other children wore hats or caps on their heads, and I had neither hat nor cap. In fact, I do not remember that up to the time of going to school I had ever worn any kind of covering upon my head, nor do I recall that either I or anybody else had even thought anything about the need of covering for my head. But, of course, when

I saw how all the other boys were dressed, I began to feel quite uncomfortable. As usual, I put the case before my mother and she explained to me that she had no money with which to buy a "store hat," which was a rather new institution at that time among the members of my race and was considered quite the thing for young and old to own, but that she would find a way to help me out of the difficulty. She accordingly got two pieces of "homespun" (jeans) and sewed them together, and I was soon the proud possessor of my first cap.

The lesson that my mother taught me in this has always remained with me, and I have tried as best I could to teach it to others. I have always felt proud, whenever I think of the incident, that my mother had strength of character enough not to be led into the temptation of seeming to be that which she was not—of trying to impress my schoolmates and others with the fact that she was able to buy me a "store hat" when she was not. I have always felt proud that she refused to go into debt for that which she did not have the money to pay for. Since that time I have owned many kinds of caps and hats, but never one of which I felt so proud.

The time that I was permitted to attend school during the day was short, and my attendance was irregular. It was not long before I had to stop attending day-school altogether, and devote all of my time again to work. I resorted to the night-school again. In fact, the greater part of the education I secured in my boyhood was gathered through the night-school after my day's work was done. I had difficulty often in securing a satisfactory teacher. Sometimes, after I had secured some one to teach me at night, I would find, much to my disappointment, that the teacher knew but little more than I did. Often I would have to walk several miles at night in order to recite my night-school lessons. There was never a time in my youth, no matter how dark and discouraging the days might be, when one resolve did not continually remain with me, and that was a determination to secure an education at any cost.

*   *   *

One day, while at work in the coal-mine, I happened to overhear two miners talking about a great school for coloured people somewhere in Virginia. This was the first time that I had ever heard anything about any kind of school or college that was more pretentious than the little coloured school in our town.

In the darkness of the mine I noiselessly crept as close as I could to the two men who were talking. I heard one tell the other that not only was the school established for the members of my race, but that opportunities were provided by which poor but worthy students could work out all or a part of the cost of board, and at the same time be taught some trade or industry.

As they went on describing the school, it seemed to me that it must be the greatst place on earth, and not even Heaven presented more attractions for me at that time than did the Hampton Normal and Agricultural Institute in Virginia, about which these men were talking. I resolved at once to go to that school, although I had no idea where it was, or how many miles away, or how I was going to reach it; I remembered only that I was on fire constantly with one ambition, and that was to go to Hampton. This thought was with me day and night.

After hearing of the Hampton Institute, I continued to work for a few months longer in the coal-mine. While at work there, I heard of a vacant position in the household of General Lewis Ruffner, the owner of the salt-furnace and coal-mine. Mrs. Viola Ruffner, the wife of General Ruffner, was a "Yankee" woman from

Vermont. Mrs. Ruffner had a reputation all through the vicinity for being very strict with her servants, and especially with the boys who tried to serve her. Few of them had remained with her more than two or three weeks. They all left with the same excuse: she was too strict. I decided, however, that I would rather try Mrs. Ruffner's house than remain in the coal-mine and so my mother applied to her for the vacant position. I was hired at a salary of $5 per month.

*   *   *

Perhaps the thing that touched and pleased me most in connection with my starting for Hampton was the interest that many of the older coloured people took in the matter. They had spent the best days of their lives in slavery, and hardly expected to live to see the time when they would see a member of their race leave home to attend a boarding-school. Some of these older people would give me a nickel, others a quarter, or a handkerchief.

Finally the great day came, and I started for Hampton. I had only a small cheap satchel that contained what few articles of clothing I could get. My mother at the time was rather weak and broken in health. I hardly expected to see her again, and thus our parting was all the more sad. She, however, was very brave through it all. At that time there were no through trains connecting that part of West Virginia with eastern Virginia. Trains ran only a portion of the way, and the remainder of the distance was travelled by stage-coaches.

The distance from Malden to Hampton is about five hundred miles. I had not been away from home many hours before it began to grow painfully evident that I did not have enough money to pay my fare to Hampton. One experience I shall long remember. I had been travelling over the mountains most of the afternoon in an old-fashioned stage-coach, when, late in the evening, the coach stopped for the night at a common, unpainted house called a hotel. All the other passengers except myself were whites. In my ignorance I supposed that the little hotel existed for the purpose of accommodating the passengers who travelled on the stage-coach. The difference that colour of one's skin would make I had not thought anything about. After all the other passengers had been shown rooms and were getting ready for supper, I shyly presented myself before the man at the desk. It is true I had practically no money in my pocket with which to pay for bed or food, but I had hoped in some way to beg my way into the good graces of the landlord, for at that season in the mountains of Virginia the weather was cold, and I wanted to get indoors for the night. Without asking as to whether I had any money, the man at the desk firmly refused to even consider the matter of providing me with food or lodging. This was my first experience in finding out what the colour of my skin meant. In some way I managed to keep warm by walking about, and so got through the night. My whole soul was so bent upon reaching Hampton that I did not have time to cherish any bitterness toward the hotel-keeper.

By walking, begging rides both in wagons and in the cars, in some way, after a number of days, I reached the city of Richmond, Virginia, about eighty-two miles from Hampton. When I reached there, tired, hungry, and dirty, it was late in the night. I had never been in a large city, and this rather added to my misery. When I reached Richmond, I was completely out of money. I had not a single acquaintance in the place, and being unused to city ways, I did not know where to go. I applied at several places for lodging, but they all wanted money, and that was what I did not have. Knowing nothing else better to do, I walked the streets. In doing this I passed by many food-stands where fried chicken and half-moon apple pies were piled high and made to present a most tempting appearance, At that time it seemed to me that I would have promised all that I expected to possess in the future to have gotten hold of one of those chicken legs or one of those pies. But I could not get either of these, nor anything else to eat.

*   *   *

If the people who gave the money to provide that building could appreciate the influence the sight of it had upon me, as well as upon thousands of other youths, they would feel all the more encouraged to make such gifts. It seemed to me to be the largest and most beautiful building I had ever seen. The sight of it seemed to give me new life. I felt that a new kind of existence had now begun—that life would now have a new meaning. I felt that I had reached the promised land, and I resolved to let no obstacle prevent me from putting forth the highest effort to fit myself to accomplish the most good in the world.

As soon as possible after reaching the grounds of the Hampton Institute, I presented myself before the head teacher for assignment to a class. Having been so long without proper food, a bath and change of clothing, I did not, of course, make a very favourable impression upon her, and I could see at once that there were doubts in her mind about the wisdom of admitting me as a student. I felt that I could hardly blame her if she got the idea that I was a worthless loafer or tramp. For some time she did not refuse to admit me, neither did she decide in my favour, and I continued to linger about her, and to impress her in all the ways I could with my worthiness. In the meantime I saw her admitting other students, and that added greatly to my discomfort, for I felt, deep down in my heart that I could do as well as they; if I could only get a chance to show what was in me.

After some hours had passed, the head teacher said to me: "The adjoining recitation-room needs sweeping. Take the broom and sweep it."

It occurred to me at once that here was my chance. Never did I receive an order with more delight. I knew that I could sweep, for Mrs. Ruffner had thoroughly taught me how to do that when I lived with her.

I swept the recitation-room three times. Then I got a dusting-cloth and I dusted it four times. All the woodwork around the walls, every bench, table, and desk I went over four times with my dusting-cloth. Besides, every piece of furniture had been moved and every closet and corner in the room had been throughly cleaned. I had the feeling that in a large measure my future depended upon the impression I made upon the teacher in the cleaning of that room. When I was through, I reported to the head teacher. She was a "Yankee" woman who knew just where to look for dirt. She went into the room and inspected the floor and closets; then she took her handkerchief and rubbed it on the woodwork about the walls, and over the table and benches. When she was unable to find one bit of dirt on the floor, or a particle of dust on any of the furniture, she quietly remarked, "I guess you will do to enter this institution."

I was one of the happiest souls on earth. The sweeping of that room was my college examination, and never did any youth pass an examination for entrance to Harvard or Yale that gave him more genuine satisfaction. I have passed several examinations since then, but I have always felt that this was the best one I ever passed.

I have spoken of my own experience in entering in the Hampton Institute.

Perhaps few, if any, had anything like the same experience that I had, but about that same period there were hundreds who found their way to Hampton and other institutions after experiencing something of the same difficulties that I went through. The young men and women were determined to secure an education at any cost.

The sweeping of the recitation-room in the manner that I did it seems to have paved the way for me to get through Hampton.

BOOKER T. WASHINGTON ON THE EDUCATIONAL OUTLOOK FOR NEGROES IN THE SOUTH (1885)   From Booker T. Washington, "The Educational Outlook in the South," National Education Association *Journal of Proceedings and Addresses, 1884* (Boston, 1885), pp. 125–30.

Fourteen years ago it is said that Northern teachers in the South for the purpose of teaching colored schools were frightened away by the whites from the town of Tuskegee, Alabama. Four years ago the democratic members of the Alabama Legislature from Tuskegee voluntarily offered and had passed by the General Assembly a bill, appropriating $2000 annually to pay the salaries of teachers in a colored normal school to be located at Tuskegee. At the end of the first session of the school the legislature almost unanimously passed a second bill appropriating an additional $1000 annually, for the same purpose. About one month ago one of the white citizens of Tuskegee who had at first looked on the school in a cold, distant kind of way said to me, "I have just been telling the white people that the negroes are more interested in education than we, and are making more sacrifices to educate themselves." At the end of the first year's work, some of the whites said, "We are glad that the Normal School is here because it draws people and makes labor plentiful." At the close of the second year, several said that the Normal School was beneficial because it increased trade, and at the close of the last session more than one has said that the Normal School is a good institution, it is making the colored people in this State better citizens. From the opening of the school to the present, the white citizens of Tuskegee have been among its warmest friends. They have not only given of their money but they are ever ready to suggest and devise plans to build up the institution. When the school was making an effort to start a brick-yard, but was without means, one of the merchants donated an outfit of tools. Every white minister in the town has visited the school and given encouraging remarks. When the school was raising money to build our present hall, it occurred to one of the teachers that it would be a good idea to call on the white ladies for contributions in the way of cakes, etc., toward a fair. The result was that almost every lady, called on, gave something and the fair was made up almost entirely of articles given by these friends. A former slave-holder working on a negro normal school building under a negro master-carpenter is a picture that the last few years have made possible.

Any movement for the elevation of the Southern negro in order to be successful, must have to a certain extent the co-operation of the Southern whites. They control government and own the property—whatever benefits the black man benefits the white man. The proper education of all the whites will benefit the negro as much as the education of the negro will benefit the whites. The Governor of Alabama would probably count it no disgrace to ride in the same railroad coach with a colored man, but the ignorant white man who curries the Governor's horse would turn up his nose in disgust. The president of a white college in Tuskegee makes a special effort to furnish our young men work that they may be able to remain in school, while the miserable unlettered "brother in white" would say "you can't learn a nigger anything." Brains, property, and character for the Negro will settle the question of civil right. The best course to pursue in regard to the civil rights bill in the South is to let it alone; let it alone and it will settle itself. Good school teachers and plenty of money to pay them will be more potent in settling the race question than many civil rights bills and investigating committees. A young colored physician went into the city of Montgomery, Alabama, a few months ago to practice his profession—he was the first to professionally enter the ex-confederate capital. When his white brother physicians found out by a six days' examination that he had brains enough to pass a better examination, as one of them said, than many of the whites had passed, they gave him a hearty welcome and offered their services to aid him in consultation or in any other way possible—and they are standing manfully up to their promise. Let there be in a community a negro who by virtue of his superior knowledge of the chemistry of the soil, his acquaintance with the most improved tools and best breeds of stock, can raise fifty bushels of corn to the acre while his white neighbor only raise thirty, and the white man will come to the black man to learn. Further, they will sit down on the same train, in the same coach and on the same seat to talk about it. Harmony will come in proportion as the black man gets something that the white man wants, whether it be of brains or of material. Some of the county whites looked at first with disfavor on the establishing of a normal school in Tuskegee. It turned out that there was no brick-yard in the county; merchants and farmers wanted to build, but bricks must be brought from a distance or they must wait for one house to burn down before building another. The normal school with student labor started a brick-yard. Several kilns of bricks were burned; the whites came [for] miles around for bricks. From examining bricks they were led to examine the workings of the school. From the discussion of the brick-yard came the discussion of negro education—and thus many of the "old masters" have been led to see and become interested in negro education. In Tuskegee a negro mechanic manufactures the best tin ware, the best harness, the best boots and shoes, and it is common to see his store crowded with white customers from all over the county. His word or note goes as far as that of the whitest man.

I repeat for emphasis that any work looking towards the permanent improvement of the negro South, must have for one of its aims the fitting of him to live friendly and peaceably with his white neighbors both socially and politically. In spite of all talk of exodus, the negro's home is permanently in the South: for coming to the bread-and-meat side of the question, the white man needs the negro, and the negro needs the white man. His home being permanently in the South it is our duty to help him prepare himself to live there an independent, educated citizen.

In order that there may be the broadest development of the colored man and that he may have an unbounded field in which to labor, the two races must be brought to have faith in each other. The teachings of the negro in various ways for the last twenty years have been rather too much to array him against his white brother than to put the two races in co-operation with each other. Thus, Massachusetts supports the Republican party, because the Republican party supports Massachusetts with a protective tariff, but the negro supports the

Republican party simply because Massachusetts does. When the colored man is educated up to the point of reasoning that Massachusetts and Alabama are a long ways apart and the conditions of life are very different and if free trade enables my white neighbor across the street to buy his plows at a cheaper rate it will enable me to so the same thing, then will he be consulted in governmental questions. More than once have I noticed that when the whites were in favor of prohibition the blacks led even by sober upright ministers voted against it simply because the whites were in favor of it and for that reason the blacks said that they knew it was a "Democratic trick." If the whites vote to levy a tax to build a school-house it is a signal for the blacks to oppose the measure, simply because the whites favor it. I venture the assertion that the sooner the colored man South learns that one political party is not composed of all angels and the other of all devils, and that all his enemies do not live in his town or neighborhood and all his friends in some distant section of the country, the sooner will his educational advantages be enhanced many fold. But matters are gradually changing in this respect. The black man is beginning to find out that there are those even among the Southern whites who desire his elevation. The negro's new faith in the white man is being reciprocated in proportion as the negro is rightly educated. The white brother is beginning to learn by degrees that all negroes are not liars and chicken thieves. A former owner of seventy-five or one hundred slaves and now a large planter and merchant said to me a few days ago, "I can see every day the change that is coming about. I have on one of my plantations a colored man who can read and write and he is the most valuable man on the farm. In the first place I can trust him to keep the time on the others or with any thing else. If a new style of plow or cotton planters is taken on the place he can understand its construction in half the time that any of the others can."

My faith is that reforms in the South are to come from within. Southern people have a good deal of human nature. They like to receive praise of doing good deeds and they don't like to obey orders that come from Washington telling them they must lay aside at once customs that they have followed for centuries, and henceforth there must be but one railroad coach, one hotel, and one school-house for ex-master and ex-slave. In proof of my first assertion, the railroads in Alabama required colored passengers to pay the same fare as the whites, and then compelled the colored to ride in the smoking-car. A committee of leading colored people laid the injustice of the matter before the railroad commissioners of Alabama, who at once ordered that within thirty days every railroad in the State should provide equal, but separate accommodations for both races. Every prominent newspaper in the State pronounced it a just decision. Alabama gives $9000 annually towards the support of colored normal schools, The last legislature increased the annual appropriation for free schools by $100,000, making the total annual appropriation over $500,000, and nearly half of this amount goes to colored schools, and I have the first time to hear of any distinction being made between the races by any State officer in the distribution of this fund. Why, my friends, more pippins are growing in the South than crab-apples, more roses than thorns.

Now, in regard to what I have said about the relations of the two races, there should be no unmanly cowering, or stooping to satisfy unreasonable whims of Southern white men, but it is charity and wisdom to keep in mind the two hundred years' schooling in prejudice against the negro, which ex-slave-holders are called upon to conquer. A certain class of whites South object to the general education of the colored man, on the ground that when he is educated he ceases to do manual labor, and there is no evading the fact that much aid is withheld from negro education in the South, by the States, on these grounds. Just here the great mission of

INDUSTRIAL EDUCATION,

coupled with the mental comes in. "It kills two birds with one stone," viz.: secures the co-operation of the whites and does the best possible thing for the black man. An old colored man in a cotton-field in the middle of July, lifted his eyes towards heaven and said, "De cotton is so grassy, de work is so hard, and de sun am so hot, I believe dis darkey am called to preach." This old man, no doubt, stated the true reason why not a few enter school. Educate the black man, mentally and industrially, and there will be no doubt of his prosperity; for a race who have lived at all, and paid for the last twenty years, twenty-five and thirty per cent. interest on the dollar advanced for food with almost no education, can certainly take care of themselves when educated mentally and industrially.

The Tuskegee Normal School, located in the black belt of Alabama, with an ignorant, degraded negro population of twenty-five thousand within a radius of twenty miles, has a good chance to see the direct needs of the people; and to get a correct idea of their condition one must leave the towns and go far out into the country, miles from any railroad, where the majority of the people live. They need teachers with not only trained heads and hearts, but with trained hands. School-houses are needed in every township and country. The present wrecks of log-cabins and bush harbors, where many of the schools are now taught, must be replaced by comfortable, decent houses. In many school-houses rails are used for seats, and often the fire is on the outside of the house, while teacher and scholars are on the inside. Add to this a teacher who can scarcely write his name, and who is as weak mentally as morally, and you have but a faint idea of the educational condition of many parts of the South. It is the work of Tuskegee to send into these places, teachers who will not stand off and tell the people what to do, or what ought to be done, but to send those who can take hold and show the people *how* to do. The blacksmiths, carpenters, brickmasons, and tinners, who learned their trades in slavery, are dying out, and slavery having taught the colored boy that labor is a disgrace few of their places are being filled. The negro now has a monopoly of the trades in the South, but he can't hold it unless the young men are taught trades while in school. The large number of educated loafers to be seen around the streets of our large cities furnishes another reason in favor of industrial education. Then the proud fop with his beaver hat, kid gloves, and walking cane, who has done no little to injure the cause of education South, by industrial training, would be brought down to something practical and useful. The Tuskegee Normal School, with a farm of 500 acres, carpenter's shop, printing-office, blacksmith shop and brick-yard for boys, and a sewing department, laundry, flower gardening, and practical housekeeping for girls, is trying to do its part towards furnishing industrial training. We ask help for nothing that we can do for ourselves; nothing is bought that the students can produce. The boys raise the vegetables, have done the painting, made the brick, the chairs, the tables, the desks; have built a stable, a carpenter's shop, and a blacksmith's shop. The girls do the entire housekeeping, including the mending, ironing, and washing of the boys' clothes; besides they make many garments to sell.

The majority of the students are poor and able to pay but little cash for board; consequently, the school keeps three points before it. First, to give the student the best mental training; secondly, to furnish him with labor that will be valuable to the school, and that will enable the student to learn something from the labor *per se;* thirdly, to teach the dignity of labor.

DAILY PROGRAM AT TUSKEGEE INSTITUTE (1886)   From Booker T.
Washington, *The Story of My Life and Work: An Autobiography* (Atlanta, 1901), pp. 99–100.

[January, 1886] 5 a.m.; rising bell, 5:50 a.m., warning breakfast bell; 6 a.m., breakfast bell; 6:20 a.m. breakfast over; 6:20 to 6:50 a.m., rooms are cleaned; 6:50, work bell; 7:30, morning study hour; 8:20, morning school bell; 8:25 inspection of young men's toilet in ranks; 8:40, devotional exercises in chapel; 8:55, "5 minutes" with the daily news; 9 a.m., class work begins; 12, class work closes; 12:15 p.m. dinner; 1 p.m., work bell; 1:30 p.m. class work begins; 3:30 p.m., class work ends; 5:30 p.m., bell to "knock off" work; 6 p.m., supper; 7:10 p.m., evening prayers; 7:30 p.m., evening study hours; 8:45 p.m., evening study hour closes; 9:20 p.m., warning retiring bell; 9:30 p.m., retiring bell.

BOOKER T. WASHINGTON DESCRIBES "THE TUSKEGEE IDEA"(c.
1890),   From Emmett J. Scott, ed., *Tuskegee and Its People*, (New York, 1916) pp. 8, 11–12.

Industrial training will be more potent for good to the race when its relation to the other phases of essential education is more clearly understood. There is afloat no end of discussion as to what is the "proper kind of education for the Negro," and much of it is hurtful to the cause it is designed to promote. The danger, at present, that most seriously threatens the success of industrial training, is the ill-advised insistence in certain quarters that this form of education should be offered to the exclusion of all other branches of knowledge. If the idea becomes fixed in the minds of the people that industrial education means class education, that it should be offered to the Negro because he is a Negro, and that the Negro should be confined to this sort of education, then I fear serious injury will be done the cause of hand-training. It should be understood rather that at such institutions as Hampton Institute and Tuskegee Institute, industrial education is not emphasized because colored people are to receive it, but because the ripest educational thought of the world approves it; because the undeveloped material resources of the South make it peculiarly important for both races; and because it should be given in a large measure to any race, regardless of color, which is in the same stage of development as the Negro.

On the other hand, no one understanding the real needs of the race would advocate that industrial education should be given to every Negro to the exclusion of the professions and other branches of learning. It is evident that a race so largely segregated as the Negro is, must have an increasing number of its own professional men and women. . . .

Tuskegee emphasizes industrial training for the Negro, not with the thought that the Negro should be confined to industrialism, the plow, or the hoe, but because the undeveloped material resources of the South offer at this time a field peculiarly advantageous to the worker skilled in agriculture and the industries, and here are found the Negro's most inviting opportunities for taking on the rudimentary elements that ultimately make for a permanently progressive civilization.

The Tuskegee Idea is that correct education begins at the bottom, and expands naturally as the necessities of the people expand. As the race grows in knowledge, experience, culture, taste, and wealth, its wants are bound to become more and more diverse; and to satisfy these wants there will be gradually developed within our own ranks—as had already been true of the whites—a constantly increasing variety of professional and business men and women. Their places in the economic world will be assured and their prosperity guaranteed in proportion to the merit displayed by them in their several callings, for about them will have been established the solid bulwark of an industrial mass to which they may safely look for support. The esthetic demands will be met as the capacity of the race to procure them is enlarged through the processes of sane intellectual advancement. In this cumulative way there will be erected by the Negro, and for the Negro, a complete and indestructible civilization that will be respected by all whose respect is worth the having. There should be no limit placed upon the development of any individual because of color, and let it be understood that no one kind of training can safely be prescribed for any entire race. Care should be taken that racial education be not one-sided for lack of adaptation to person fitness, nor unwieldy through sheer top-heaviness. Education, to fulfil its mission for any people anywhere, should be symmetrical and sensible.

A NEGRO COLLEGE PRESIDENT RECALLS TUSKEGEE AND BOOKER T. WASHINGTON (c.1895)

From Isaac Fisher, "A College President's Story," in Emmett J. Scott, ed., *Tuskegee And Its People* (New York, 1916). pp. 101–10.

I was born January 18, 1877, on a plantation called Perry's place, in East Carroll Parish, Louisiana, and was the sixteenth and last child of my parents. My early childhood was uneventful, save during the year 1882, when, by reason of the breaking of the Mississippi River levee near my home, I was compelled, together with my parents, to live six months in the plantation cottongin, fed by the Federal Government and by the determination never to live so close to the "Big Muddy" again; and during 1886, in which year my mother died.

Up to this latter year my life had been nothing more than that of the average Negro boy on a cotton-farm. While I had been too young to feel the burden of farm-life toil, I had not been spared a realization of the narrowness and the dwarfing tendencies of the lives which the Negro farmers and their families were living, and, in my heart, I cursed the farm and all its environs as being in verity an inferno on earth. A broader knowledge of the causes which operated to produce the cheerless life against which my child-nature rebelled, and a clearer insight into the possibilities of rural life, have altered this early impression; and to-day I find myself thinking some thoughts relative to the life lived near to nature's heart which are not at all complimentary to the bustle and selfishness of city life.

The death of my mother furnished the opportunity to leave the farm and go to a city; and I took advantage of this, going to Vicksburg, Miss., to live with an older sister. I had always desired to go to school, and had spent four terms of six months each in the country school near my home; but for some reason, which I can not now remember, I attended the city school in Vicksburg but one year, after which I was employed as a cake-baker's assistant and bread-wagon driver. A short time before this I was a house-boy in the city. I was, at the time of my employment in the bakery, an omnivorous reader of the newspapers, and, in fact, of all kinds of literature; but my hours of labor at both places were so long and incessant that I found it almost impossible to do any reading during my employment at either place.

Finally I saw and took advantage of an opportunity to secure employment with the drug firm of W. H. Jones & Brother; and I count my work in this store, and with these gentlemen as employers, as the turning-point in my life, because there my work demanded some intelligence above the average. I had some chance to study, and in addition, when it was found by these white men that I loved to read, all magazines, newspapers, and drug journals, not needed by the firm and the physicians whose offices were with them, were given to me. I never make any mention of my life in Vicksburg without mentioning, in particular, Mr. W. H. Jones; for not only was he a kind and considerate employer, but I learned from his actions that a white man could be kind and interested in a Negro—a fact which no amount of reasoning could have driven into my stubborn understanding previous to that time.

There came a time when I learned that at the Tuskegee Institute, in Alabama, any poor Negro boy who was willing to work could pay for all his education in labor. To hear was to act. I wrote to Mr. Washington, asking if my information was correct. The affirmative answer came at once. It was the middle of August, and school began in September, but I determined to be present at the opening of the school year. I was then a boy wearing short trousers, but I immediately set about preparing to deliver a "lecture" to help raise funds for my trip. With a knowledge of the subject, and an assurance which I have never since assumed, I spoke to a large audience in Vicksburg on the question, Will America Absorb the Negro? I settled the question then and there to my own satisfaction, even if I did not convince the nation that my affirmative conclusion was rational. The "lecture" netted me my fare to Tuskegee, with a few dollars over, and brought me from Rev. O. P. Ross, pastor of the African Methodist Episcopal Church in Vicksburg, the offer of a scholarship at Wilberforce College at the expense of his church. I respectfully declined the offer, feeling that I did not want to bind myself to any particular denomination by accepting so great a gift; but I have always felt very kindly toward that church ever since.

My first glimpse of Mr. Washington was had in the depot in Montgomery, Ala., where a friend and I, on our way to Tuskegee, had changed cars for the Tuskegee train. Two gentlemen came into the waiting-room where we were seated, one a man of splendid appearance and address, the other a most ordinary appearing individual, we thought. The latter, addressing us, inquired our destination. Upon being told that we were going to Tuskegee, he remarked that he had heard that Tuskegee was a very hard place—a place where students were given too much work to do, and where the food was very simple and coarse. He was afraid we would not stay there three months. We assured him that we were not afraid of hard work, and meant to finish the course of study at Tuskegee at all hazards. He then left us. Very soon after, the gentleman who had so favorably impressed us, and whom we afterward found to be the capable treasurer of the Tuskegee Institute, Mr. Warren Logan, came back and told us that our interlocutor was none other than the President of the school to which we were going.

Arriving at Tuskegee, I found what it meant to be in a school without a penny, without assurance of help from the outside, and wholly dependent upon one's own resources and labor; and I found further that in the severe, trying process through which Mr. John H. Washington, superintendent of industries, brother of Mr. Booker T. Washington, and familiarly though very respectfully known to the students as "old man John," put all students who offered to work for their education, only the fittest, and the fittest of the fit at that, survived.

I was assigned work with the resident physician, a very efficient woman doctor from Philadelphia; and I have a recollection, by no means dim, that when this good woman made her monthly report to the treasurer, she could write, "Health Department to Isaac Fisher, Dr., $12.50—value received." Every morning before breakfast it was my duty to go to the rooms of six hundred young men to see if any were ill, have those who were, carried to the hospital, report all such to four departments, take meals to those confined in the hospital, attend to all their wants, keep their building heated and supplied with fuel, and— But space will not permit the full catalogue of duties. At the end of such a day's work I would attend the night-school during its session of two hours.

Desiring to learn a trade, I asked permission to enter the printing-office for the next year. This was not granted until it was found that I would not leave the school during the summer, but would remain and work until the beginning of the next school year. Accordingly, when my second year began I entered the printing-office as an apprentice. During that year I suffered actual want and privation in the matter of shoes and clothes; but later came under the notice of Mrs. Booker T. Washington, who made arrangements by which I could procure some of the second-hand clothes and shoes sent from the North to the school for just such cases. At the end of this year my health, as a result of my work in the office, was so poor that the resident physician recommended my removal therefrom. To the surprise of Mr. J. H. Washington, I asked to be transferred to the farm; and I think I proved while working on the school-farm that I was sincere when I said that I would work wherever I was placed.

It was during this summer that Mr. Booker T. Washington showed me that I had come favorably under his notice. At one of the weekly prayer-meetings, conducted by the chaplain, Mr. Penney, and at which Mr. Washington was present, I made some remarks relative to the agnosticism of the late Col. Robert G. Ingersoll. The following day Mr. Washington sent for me, inquired my age and class in the school, and then said some very kind things about the talk which I had made in the prayer-meeting, and made me a conditional promise of his friendship, which, despite my oftproven unworthiness, he has ever since given me in unstinted measure. After that second year my hardships as a "work-student" were practically over.

In my third year I entered the day-school, working one day in every week and every other Saturday, and going to school the remainder of the time. While the school made compulsory the earning of some money on the part of all students, it set no maximum limit on the amounts to be earned. I elected to earn as much as I could under the circumstances, earning, by reason of the many odd jobs which I did, often as much as $20 per month, going to school every day in the meantime. The average amount usually earned is $5 and $6 per month. At one time I worked eight days per month on the farm, sent notes of the school to 127 Negro newspapers, cleaned one laboratory every day, played in both the brass band and the orchestra, blew the bugle for the battalion, and taught two classes in the night-school, for each of which duties I received pay; and even though I broke down under the accumulated strain soon after my graduation, I carried my point and completed the course of study as I had planned.

In my fourth year I won the Trinity Church (Boston) Prize of $25 for oratory; and in my senior year won the Loughridge Book Prize for scholarship, and also the valedictory of my class, graduating in 1898.

I was immediately sent to the Schofield School, a Quaker institution for Negroes in Aiken, S. C., to organize farmers' conferences on the order of those conducted by the Tuskegee Institute, and to serve as a teacher in the school. After one year's service in that position Mr. Washington asked me to accept the position of Assistant Northern Financial Agent for Tuskegee. I accepted, and remained two years in New England, helping to interest friends in my *alma mater*. At my own request I was transferred from the Northern work to the South, being assigned this time to the Negro Conference work in Alabama. Before beginning this work I was married to a Tuskegee girl, Miss Sallie McCann.

Within a few months a principal was needed for the Swayne Public School of Montgomery, Ala., and this in the middle of the school year. Mr. Washington recommended me for the work, and I was elected to the position. At the close of the term I went to New York to study the public-school system of that city as far as possible. While there I was reelected principal of the Swayne School, and a notice of the election reached me one morning. Three hours later I received a letter from secretary of the University of Arkansas (white) informing me that my name had been presented to the board of trustees of that institution, and I had been elected to the presidency of the State Branch Normal College at Pine Bluff, Ark. I was not a candidate for the position, but seeing in it an opportunity for greater usefulness, I accepted the position in my twenty-fifth year, and have just been reelected to serve a third term as president of the school. The Branch Normal College was established in 1875 as one of the Land Grant colleges, and has a property valuation of $100,000.

Over my desk hangs a picture of the Principal of Tuskegee; and in my desk are views of the institution which he has built. But these may be removed. In the book of my memory and in the secret chambers of my heart I have enshrined the two names which, with God and the parents now on the other side of the Great Divide, have shaped and given direction to my whole life—Tuskegee and Booker T. Washington.

BOOKER T. WASHINGTON'S ATLANTA EXPOSITION ADDRESS

(**1895**)   From *The Story of My Life and Work: An Autobiography* (Atlanta, 1901), pp. 137–43.

Mr. President and Gentlemen of the Board of Directors and Citizens:

One third of the population of the South is of the Negro race. No enterprise seeking the material, civil, or moral welfare of this section can disregard this element of our population and reach the highest success. I but convey to you, Mr. President and Directors, the sentiment of the masses of my race when I say that in no way have the value and manhood of the American Negro been more fittingly and generously recognized than by the managers of this magnificent Exposition at every stage of its progress. It is a recognition that will do more to cement the friendship of the two races than any occurrence since the dawn of our freedom.

Not only this, but the opportunity here afforded will awaken among us a new era of industrial progress. Ignorant and inexperienced, it is not strange that in the first years of our new life we began at the top instead of at the bottom; that a seat in Congress or the State Legislature was more sought than real estate or industrial skill; that the political convention or stump speaking had more attractions than starting a dairy farm or truck garden.

A ship lost at sea for many days suddenly sighted a friendly vessel. From the mast of the unfortunate vessel was seen a signal: 'Water, water; we die of thirst!' The answer from the friendly vessel at once came back: 'Cast down your bucket where you are.' A second time the signal, 'Water, water; send us water!' ran up from the distressed vessel, and was answered: 'Cast down your bucket where you are.' And a third and fourth signal for water was answered: 'Cast down your bucket where you are.' The captain of the distressed vessel, at last heeding the injunction, cast down his bucket, and it came up full of fresh, sparkling water from the mouth of the Amazon River. To those of my race who depend on bettering their condition in a foreign land, or who underestimate the importance of cultivating friendly relations with the Southern white man, who is their next door neighbor, I would say: 'Cast down your bucket where you are'—cast it down making friends in every manly way of the people of all races by whom we are surrounded.

Cast it down in agriculture, mechanics, in commerce, in domestic service, and in the professions. And in this condition it is well to bear in mind that whatever other sins the South may be called to bear, when it comes to business, pure and simple, it is in the South that the Negro is given a man's chance in the commercial world, and in nothing is this Exposition more eloquent than in emphasizing this chance. Our greatest danger is, that in the great leap from slavery to freedom we may overlook the fact that the masses of us are to live by the productions of our hands, and fail to keep in mind that we shall prosper in proportion as we learn to dignify and glorify common labor, and put brains and skill into the common occupations of life; shall prosper in proportion as we learn to draw the line between the superficial and the substantial, the ornamental gewgaws of life and the useful. No race can prosper till it learns that there is as much dignity in tilling a field as in writing a poem. It is at the bottom of life we must begin, and not at the top. Nor should we permit our grievances to overshadow our opportunities.

To those of the white race who look to the incoming of those of foreign birth and strange tongue and habits for the prosperity of the South, were I permitted, I would repeat what I say to my own race, 'Cast down your bucket where you are. Cast it down among the 8,000,000 Negroes whose habits you know, whose fidelity and love you have tested in days when to have proved treacherous meant the ruin of your firesides. Cast down your bucket among these people who have, without strikes and labor wars, tilled your fields, cleared your forests, builded your railroads and cities, and brought forth treasures from the bowels of the earth, and helped make possible this magnificent representation of the progress of the South. Casting down your bucket among my people, helping and encouraging them as you are doing on these grounds, and, with education of head, hand and heart, you will find that they will buy your surplus land, make blossom the waste places in your fields, and run your factories. While doing this, you can be sure in the future, as in the past, that you and your families will be surrounded by the most patient, faithful, law-abiding, and unresentful people that the world has seen. As we have proved our loyalty to you in the past, in nursing your children, watching by the sick bed of your mothers and fathers, and often following them with tear-dimmed eyes to their graves, so in the future, in our humble way, we shall stand by you with a devotion that no foreigner can approach, ready to lay down lives, if need be, in defense of yours, interlacing our industrial, commercial, civil, and religious life with yours in a way that shall make the interests of both races one. In all things that are purely social we can be as separate as the fingers, yet one as the hand in all things essential to mutual progress.

There is no defense or security for any of us except in the highest intelligence and development of all. If anywhere there are efforts tending to curtail the fullest growth of the Negro, let these efforts be turned into stimulating, encouraging, and making him the most useful and intelligent citizen. Efforts or means so invested will pay a thousand per cent interest. These efforts will be twice blessed—'Blessing him that gives and him that takes.'

There is no escape through law of man or God from the inevitable:

> 'The laws of changeless justice bind
> Oppressor with oppressed;
> And close as sin and suffering joined
> We march to fate abreast.'

Nearly sixteen millions of hands will aid you in pulling the load upward, or they will pull against you the load downwards. We shall constitute one-third and more of the ignorance and crime of the South, or one-third its intelligence and progress; we shall contribute one-third to the business and industrial prosperity of the South, or we shall prove a veritable body of death, stagnating, depressing, retarding every effort to advance the body politic.

Gentlemen of the Exposition, as we present to you our humble effort at an exhibition of our progress, you must not expect overmuch. Starting thirty years ago with ownership here and there in a few quilts and pumpkins and chickens (gathered from miscellaneous sources), remember the path that has led from these to the invention and production of agricultural implements, buggies, steam engines, newspapers, books, statuary, carving, painting, the management of drug stores and banks, has not been trodden without contact with thorns and thistles. While we take pride in what we exhibit as a result of our independent efforts, we do not for a moment forget that our part in this exhibition would fall far short of your expectations but for the constant help that has come to our educational life, not only from the Southern States, but especially from Northern philanthropists, who have made their gifts a constant stream of blessing and encouragement.

The wisest among my race understand that the agitation of questions of social equality is the extremest folly, and that progress in the enjoyment of all the privileges that will come to us must be the result of severe and constant struggle rather than of artificial forcing. No race that has anything to contribute to the markets of the world is long in any degree ostracized. It is important and right that all privileges of the law be ours, but it is vastly more important that we be prepared for the exercise of those privileges. The opportunity to earn a dollar in a factory just now is worth infinitely more than the opportunity to spend a dollar in an opera house.

In conclusion, may I repeat that nothing in thirty years has given us more hope and encouragement, and drawn us so near to you of the white race, as this opportunity offered by the Exposition; and here bending, as it were, over the altar that represents the results of the struggles of your race and mine, both starting practically empty-handed three decades ago, I pledge that, in your effort to work out the great and intricate problem which God has laid at the doors of the South, you shall have at all times the patient, sympathetic help of my race; only let this be constantly in mind that, while from representations in these buildings of the product of field, of forest, of mine, of factory, letters, and art, much good will come, yet far above and beyond material benefits will be the higher good, that let us pray God will come, in a blotting out of sectional differences and racial animosities and suspicions, in a determination to administer absolute justice, in a willing obedience among all classes to the mandates of law. This, coupled with our material prosperity, will bring into our beloved South a new heaven and a new earth.

BOOKER T. WASHINGTON ADDRESSES HARVARD ON BEING AWARDED AN HONORARY DEGREE (1896) From *The Story of My Life and Work: An Autobiography* (Atlanta, 1901), pp. 180–82.

Mr. President and Gentlemen:
   "It would in some measure relieve my embarrassment if I could, even in a slight degree, feel myself worthy of the great honor which you do me to-day. Why you have called me from the Black Belt of the South, from among my humble people, to share in the honors of this occasion, is not for me to explain; and yet it may not be inappropriate for me to suggest that it seems to me that one of the most vital questions that touch our American life, is how to bring the strong, wealthy and learned into helpful touch with the poorest, most ignorant and humblest, and at the same time make the one appreciate the vitalizing, strengthening influence of the other. How shall we make the mansions on yon Beacon street feel and see the need of the spirits in the lowliest cabin in Alabama cotton fields or Louisiana sugar bottoms? This problem Harvard University is solving, not by bringing itself down, but by bringing the masses up.
   "If through me, an humble representative, seven millions of my people in the South might be permitted to send a message to Harvard—Harvard that offered up on death's altar young Shaw, and Russell, and Lowell, and scores of others, that we might have a free and united country—that message would be, 'Tell them that the sacrifice was not in vain. Tell them that by habits of thrift and economy, by way of the industrial school and college, we are coming. We are crawling up, working up, yea, bursting up. Often through oppression, unjust discrimination and prejudice, but through them all we are coming up, and with proper habits, intelligence and property, there is no power on earth that can permanently stay our progress.'
   "If my life in the past has meant anything in the lifting up of my people and the bringing about of better relations between your race and mine, I assure you from this day it will mean doubly more. In the economy of God there is but one standard

by which an individual can succeed—there is but one for a race. This country demands that every race shall measure itself by the American standard. By it a race must rise or fall, succeed or fail, and in the last analysis mere sentiment counts for little. During the next half century and more, my race must continue passing through the severe American crucible. We are to be tested in our patience, our forbearance, our perseverence, our power to endure wrong, to withstand temptations, to economize, to acquire and use skill; in our ability to compete, to succeed in commerce, to disregard the superficial for the real, the appearance for the substance, to be great and yet small, learned and yet simple, high and yet the servant of all. This, this is the passport to all that is best in the life of our republic, and the Negro must possess it, or be debarred.

"While we are thus being tested, I beg of you to remember that wherever our life touches yours, we help or hinder. Wherever your life touches ours, you make us stronger or weaker. No member of your race in any part of our country can harm the meanest member of mine without the proudest and bluest blood in Massachusetts being degraded. When Mississippi commits crime, New England commits crime, and in so much, lowers the standard of your civilization. There is no escape—man drags man down, or man lifts man up.

"In working out our destiny, while the main burden and center of activity must be with us, we shall need, in a large measure in the years that are to come as we have in the past, the help, the encouragement, the guidance that the strong can give the weak. Thus helped, we of both races in the South, soon shall throw off the shackles of racial and sectional prejudice and rise, as Harvard University has risen and as we all should rise, above the clouds of ignorance, narrowness and selfishness, into that atmosphere, that pure sunshine, where it will be our highest ambition to serve man, our brother, regardless of race or previous condition."

GEORGE PEABODY'S TRUST FUND FOR EDUCATION (1867)   From
J. L. M. Curry, *A Brief Sketch of George Peabody, and a History of the Peabody Education Fund . . .* (Cambridge, Mass., 1898), pp. 19–22.

To Hon. Robert C. Winthrop, of Massachusetts; Hon. Hamilton Fish, of New York; Right Rev. Charles P. McIlvaine, of Ohio; General U. S. Grant, of the United States Army; Hon. William C. Rives, of Virginia; Hon. John H. Clifford, of Massachusetts; Hon. William Aiken, of South Carolina; William M. Evarts, Esq., of New York; Hon. William A. Graham, of North Carolina; Charles Macalester, Esq., of Pennsylvania; George W. Riggs, Esq., of Washington; Samuel Wetmore, Esq., of New York; Edward A. Bradford, Esq., of Louisiana; George N. Eaton, Esq., of Maryland; and George Peabody Russell, Esq., of Massachusetts.

Gentlemen: I beg to address you on a subject which occupied my mind long before I left England; and in regard to which one at least of you (the Hon. Mr. Winthrop, the distinguished and valued friend to whom I am so much indebted for cordial sympathy, careful consideration, and wise counsel in this matter) will remember that I consulted him immediately upon my arrival in May last.

I refer to the educational needs of those portions of our beloved and common country which have suffered from the destructive ravages, and the not less disastrous consequences, of civil war.

With my advancing years, my attachment to my native land has but become more devoted. My hope and faith in its successful and glorious future have grown brighter and stronger; and now, looking forward beyond my stay on earth, as may be permitted to one who has passed the limit of threescore and ten years, I see our country, united and prosperous, emerging from the clouds which still surround her, taking a higher rank among the nations, and becoming richer and more powerful than ever before.

But to make her prosperity more than superficial, her moral and intellectual development should keep pace with her material growth, and, in those portions of our nation to which I have referred, the urgent and pressing physical needs of an almost impoverished people must for some years preclude them from making, by unaided effort, such advances in education, and such progress in the diffusion of knowledge, among all classes, as every lover of his country must earnestly desire.

I feel most deeply, therefore, that it is the duty and privilege of the more favored and wealthy portions of our nation to assist those who are less fortunate; and, with the wish to discharge so far as I may be able my own responsibility in this matter, as well as to gratify my desire to aid those to whom I am bound by so many ties of attachment and regard, I give to you, gentlemen, most of whom have been my personal and special friends, the sum of one million of dollars, to be by you and your successors held in trust, and the income thereof used and applied in your discretion for the promotion and encouragement of intellectual, moral, or industrial education among the young of the more destitute portions of the Southern and Southwestern States of our Union; my purpose being that the benefits intended shall be distributed among the entire population, without other distinction than their needs and the opportunities of usefulness to them.

Besides the income thus derived, I give to you permission to use from the principal sum, within the next two years, an amount not exceeding forty per cent.

In addition to this gift, I place in your hands bonds of the State of Mississippi, issued to the Planters' Bank, and commonly known as Planters' Bank bonds, amounting, with interest, to about eleven hundred thousand dollars, the amount realized by you from which is to be added to and used for the purposes of this Trust.

These bonds were originally issued in payment for stock in that Bank held by the State, and amounted in all to only two millions of dollars. For many years, the State received large dividends from that Bank over and above the interest on these bonds. The State paid the interest without interruption till 1840, since which no interest has been paid, except a payment of about one hundred thousand dollars, which was found in the treasury applicable to the payment of the coupons, and paid by a mandamus of the Supreme Court. The validity of these bonds has never been questioned, and they must not be confounded with another issue of bonds made by the State to the Union Bank, the recognition of which has been a subject of controversy with a portion of the population of Mississippi.

Various acts of the Legislature—viz., of February 28, 1842; February 23, 1844; February 16, 1846; February 28, 1846; March 4, 1848—and the highest judicial tribunal of the State have confirmed their validity; and I have no doubt that at an early day such legislation will be had as to make these bonds available in increasing the usefulness of the present Trust.

Mississippi, though now depressed, is rich in agricultural resources, and cannot long disregard the moral obligation resting upon her to make provision for their payment. In confirmation of what I have said, in regard to the legislative and judicial action concerning the State bonds issued to the Planters' Bank, I herewith place in your hands the documents marked A.

The details and organization of the Trust I leave with you, only requesting that Mr. Winthrop may be chairman, and Governor Fish and Bishop McIlvaine Vice-Chairmen, of your body: and I give to you power to make all necessary by-laws and regulations; to obtain an Act of Incorporation, if any shall be found expedient; to provide for the expenses of the Trustees and of any agents appointed by them; and, generally, to do all such acts as may be necessary for carrying out the provisions of this Trust.

All vacancies occurring in your number by death, resignation, or otherwise, shall be filled by your election as soon as conveniently may be, and having in view an equality of representation so far as regards the Northern and Southern States.

I furthermore give to you the power, in case two-thirds the Trustees shall at any time, after the lapse of thirty years, deem it expedient, to close this Trust, and, of the funds which at that time shall be in the hands of yourselves and your successors, to distribute not less than two-thirds among such educational or literary institutions, or for such educational purposes, as they may determine, in the States for whose benefit the income is now appointed to be used. The remainder may be distributed by the Trustees for educational or literary purposes, wherever they may deem it expedient.

In making this gift, I am aware that the fund derived from it can but aid the States which I wish to benefit in their own exertions to diffuse the blessings of education and morality. But if this endowment shall encourage those now anxious for the light of knowledge, and stimulate to new efforts the many good and noble men who cherish the high purpose of placing our great country foremost, not only in power, but in the intelligence and virtue of her citizens, it will have accomplished all that I can hope.

With reverent recognition of the need of the blessing of Almighty God upon this gift, and with the fervent prayer that under His guidance your counsels may be directed for the highest good of present and future generations in our beloved country, I am, gentlemen, with great respect,

Your humble servant,
George Peabody.

Washington, Feb. 7, 1867.

BARNAS SEARS ON PUBLIC SCHOOL SYSTEMS FOR THE SOUTH

(1869)   From Barnas Sears, "Second Report," in *Reports of the General Agent of the Peabody Educational Fund,* pp. 16–17.

A more serious difficulty arose when reference was made to the gradual introduction of *a system of free schools.* The object itself was generally approved, but the present was regarded as an inauspicious time for inaugurating such a system. One year hence, it was said, when the question of the new constitutions (all of which embrace the subject of public schools) shall have been submitted to the people, and the various Legislatures acting under them, or some other authority, shall have indicated what is to be expected from their legislation, it will be much easier for us to see what action should be taken.

The representations made in reply were that, while all these things are unquestionably true, it is no less true that nearly one-half of the white children in all these States are growing up in ignorance, and have been doing so for eight years; and that, unless something is speedily done to prevent it, a semi-barbarous generation will, in the last quarter of the nineteenth century, control the destinies of a section of the country which needs all the resources of knowledge, science and art to recuperate and fully develop its energies. In such circumstances, it was suggested that provisional arrangements for one year might be made for free schools, and that, at the end of the year, those arrangements might be renewed or modified according to circumstances, and that, without periling any interest, they would prepare the way for whatever improved system of education should hereafter be adopted. So much would, at least, be secured for the present or ensuing year: the youth in the towns aided by us would all be educated; the expense of education to each child would be materially reduced, and the character of the instruction given would, by a more careful selection of teachers and by a better classification of the schools, be greatly improved.

These representations spread out in detail were never made in vain. In all the towns visited in seven States, only one declined accepting our proposals: that is, only one declined making the attempt to raise the amount required as the condition for receiving our contribution.

As to the supposed pecuniary inability of the people to comply with our conditions, it should be said that they are quite as frequently relieved of cost as burdened with it. It now falls upon a few; and they often abound more in the number of their children than in wealth. The expense of the schools being divided among a larger number would be proportionally reduced to each. Three classes of contributors are brought in who paid nothing before, namely: 1. Men of elevated character who either have no children, or who have already educated them. They are among the most ardent friends and liberal supporters of Public Schools. The largest subscriptions, varying from $100 to $500, have come from them. 2. Property-holders who wish to attract men who have families, especially intelligent mechanics from abroad, and thereby increase the value of their property. Most men of this class, though they may have few or no children to send to school, are willing to contribute something to promote the growth and prosperity of their town, whether it be by opening Free Schools, or by building Railroads. 3. Families of moderate means which cannot pay high tuition for a large number of children. These, though they formerly kept their children from school, readily subscribe a reasonable amount in order to send them to a place where they can be educated without receiving their tuition as a charity. When the parents, who now almost single-handed support the Private Schools, have the aid of these three classes of contributors, and that also supplied by the Peabody Fund, they do not in point of fact find any great difficulty in providing the funds necessary for the temporary support of a Free School.

It is surprising to see how theoretical objections vanish when brought to the test of actual experiment. Already the majority of the people demand increased education, and as soon as they perceive the radical difference in point of economy and efficiency between Public and Private Schools, they prefer the former. Whenever this question has arisen in the numerous meetings that have been held, I have only found it necessary to explain the two systems, contrasting them with each other, and there has always been present a sufficient number of clear-headed men to take up the question, and in their advocacy of Free Schools to carry all their friends with them. It may, therefore, be fairly said that it is the deliberate choice of the people, after the subject has been fully discussed, to have Free Schools in which no charge is to be made for tuition.—Before concluding these general remarks, it may be proper to say that the great majority of the thoughtful men, whom I have met, express in the strongest terms their admiration of the system of distribution which you have adopted, especially that feature of it which proposes to help only those who help themselves.

Many applicants for aid have said, even when their petitions are not granted, that while they regretted the result as affecting their own interests, they approved of the principle on which we were acting, and would do the same were they in our place. To my surprise, I even heard the opinion earnestly expressed by several eminent and influential gentlemen, that instead of spending much money on schools in the present unsettled state of affairs, it would be safer and better to put the fund out at interest, and have the more to give when the proper time for action should arrive.

A REPORT TO THE BOARD OF TRUSTEES OF THE SLATER FUND
(1885)   From Atticus G. Haygood, *The Case of the Negro, as to Education in the Southern States; a Report to the Board of Trustees* (Atlanta, 1885), pp. 49–50.

Few things could be more unfortunate for the work this Board has in hand than to enter upon it with the feeling that a very uncertain experiment is to be made. There is no mystery whatever in the education of the negro race; it is a question of money more than anything else. The negro is to be taught the things he needs to know to make him all he is capable of becoming. Money will provide the means and instrumentalities for doing the work; there are capable men and women enough who will work in this field for moderate support. The negro youth needs what the white youth needs—knowledge, industry, morals. The schools at work in the Southern States are teaching him books, they are teaching him sound morals, they are beginning to teach him tool-craft. What he learns of one will help him to learn the others, and learning each he will begin to make greater progress in all good things. Nothing in the history of the educational movement for the uplifting of the negroes is more encouraging than the growing interest in the work that is being manifested by the superior white people of the South. This growing sentiment is recognized by some who have the management of the higher grade schools for colored people in hand; Southern names begin to appear in the lists of trustees and managers. It would be very wise, at this time, to increase their number.

The proof of this growing interest is abundant and conclusive. If the work is ever to be done as the needs of both races require that it be done, then the time must come when Southern white people cordially co-operate in the work. It would be as easy to develop a colony into a great State by immigration alone, in a country without births, as to permanently establish and successfully conduct a great educational work by supplies from abroad. Perhaps it may turn out that one of the best results the John F. Slater Fund can accomplish through its management will be the fostering of interest in the work of educating the negro among those white people whose interest in his right education is greater than that of any other white people—whose interest in making of the negro a good citizen is only less than the interest of the negro himself in his own elevation.

THE GENERAL AGENT OF THE SLATER FUND ON THE DIFFICULTIES CONNECTED WITH THE EDUCATION OF THE NEGRO (1895) From J. L. M. Curry, *Difficulties, Complications, and Limitations Connected with the Education of the Negro* (Baltimore, 1895), pp. 5, 7, 22–23.

Civilization certainly, Christianity probably, has encountered no problem which surpasses in magnitude or complexity the Negro problem. For its solution political remedies, very drastic, have been tried, but have failed utterly. Educational agencies have been very beneficial as a stimulus to self-government and are increasingly hopeful and worthy of wider application, but they do not cure social diseases, moral ills. Much has been written of evolution of man, of human society; and history shows marvellous progress in some races, in some countries, in the bettering of habits and institutions, but his progress is not found, in any equal degree, in the negro race in his native land. What has occured in the United States has been from external causes. Usually, human development has come from voluntary energy, from self-evolved organizations of higher and higher efficiency, from conditions which are principally the handiwork of man himself. With the negro, whatever progress has marked his life as a race in this country has come from without. The great ethical and political revolutions of enlightened nations, through the efforts of successive generations, have not been seen in his history.

*   *   *

Much of the aid lavished upon the negro has been misapplied charity, and like much other alms-giving hurtful to the recipient. Northern philanthropy, "disastrously kind," has often responded with liberality to appeals worse than worthless. Vagabond mendicants have been pampered; schools which were established without any serious need of them have been helped; public school systems, upon which the great mass of children, white and colored, must rely for their education, have been underrated and injured, and schools, of real merit and doing good work, which deserve confidence and contributions, have had assistance, legitimately their due, diverted into improper channels. Reluctantly and by constraint of conscience, this matter is mentioned and this voice of protest and warning raised.

*   *   *

Whatever may be the discouragements and difficulties, and however insufficient may be the school attendance, it is a cheering fact that the schools for the negroes do not encounter the prejudices which were too common a few years ago. In fact, there may almost be said to be coming a time when soon there will be a sustaining public opinion. The struggle of man to throw off fetters and rise into true manhood and save souls from bondage is a most instructive and thrilling spectacle, awakening sympathetic enthusiasm on the part of all who love what is noble. From a magazine for November, I quote what a teacher says: "We are engaged in a life and death struggle to secure protection of life and property against mob violence and lynch law." An official paper of a strong religious organization charges that "incendiary fires and acts of vandalism were instigated *solely* by prejudice against the education of the negroes. If those who go South to teach are obliged to take their lives in their hands and to live in constant fear of personal violence, it will render work, already difficult, exceedingly trying."

Conclusions

I

It follows that in addition to thorough and intelligent training in the discipline of character and virtue, there should be given rigid and continuous attention to domestic and social life, to the refinements and comforts and economies of home.

II

Taught in the economies of wise consumption, the race should be trained to acquire habits of thrift, of saving earnings, of avoiding waste, of accumulating property, of having a stake in good government, in progressive civilization.

III

Besides the rudiments of a good and useful education, there is imperative need of manual training, of the proper cultivation of those faculties or mental qualities of observation, of aiming at and reaching a successful end, and of such facility and skill in tools, in practical industries, as will ensure remunerative employment and give the power which comes from intelligent work.

IV

Clearer and juster ideas of education, moral and intellectual, obtained in cleaner home life and through respected and capable teachers in schools and churches. Ultimate and only sure reliance for the education of the race is to be found in the public schools, organized, controlled, and liberally supported by the State.

V

Between the races occupying the same territory, possessing under the law equal civil rights and privileges, speculative and unattainable standards should be avoided, and questions should be met as they arise, not by Utopian and partial solutions, but by the impartial application of the tests of justice, right, honor, humanity and Christianity.

Whereas the Constitution of the United States as recently amended more completely to carry into effect the great principles for which it was ordained, has recognized the right of large numbers of the people, heretofore excluded, to take part in the government, by whose votes the most important and vital public questions may be determined; and, whereas the education of all the citizens, so as to fit them, as far as possible, for an intelligent participation in public affairs, becomes, therefore, an object of national interest and concern, and indispensable to the general welfare; and, whereas an adequate provision for the education of the people is one of the first and most important duties of government: Therefore, Be it enacted by the Senate and House of Representatives of the United States of America in Congress assembled, that there shall be appointed by the President by and with the advice and consent of the Senate, within and for each State, a State superintendent of national schools, who shall receive a salary of   , and who shall hold office for the term of four years from the date of his appointment, unless sooner removed by the president.

Sec. 2. And be it further enacted, that the State superintendent shall divide his State into as many divisions of convenient size as the number of representatives in Congress to which said State is entitled, witch divisions shall be the same as the districts into which said State shall be divided for the choice of representatives, unless for special reasons it shall seem advisable otherwise to divide the State. The Secretary of the Interior shall appoint for each of said divisions a division inspector of national schools, who shall reside within said division, and who shall hold his office until removed by the Secretary of the Interior and who shall receive a salary of

Sec. 3. And be it further enacted, that said divisions shall be divided by the State superintendent into school districts of convenient size having reference to the number of children dwelling therein, and their convenience in attending school. The Secretary of the Interior shall appoint some suitable person to be local superintendent of national school within each school district. The compensation of said local superintendents shall be fixed by the Secretary of the Interior by such general regulations as he shall prescribe. But no local superintendent shall receive more than at the rate of   The divisions and districts shall be distinguished by such numbers or other names as the Secretary of the Interior shall prescribe. Whenever, in the opinion of the State superintendent, any portion of the territory embraced within any division is so sparsely settled that it is impracticable to establish permanent schools therein, such portion of territory need not be included in any school district.

Sec. 4. And be it further enacted that such number of schools shall be kept in each district as the State superintendent shall direct, Provided, that there shall be opportunity afforded to every child dwelling therein between the ages of   and of   to attend school for at least six months in each year subject to such regulations and restrictions as shall be necessary for the discipline of the schools.

Sec. 5. And be it further enacted, that it shall be the duty of every local Superintendent to select the place for the schoolhouse within his district, which he shall purchase or hire in the name of the United States. No contract for such purchase or hire shall be concluded without the written approbation of the State superintendent. In case no suitable place can be obtained with the consent of the owner the division inspector may appropriate a tract for such purpose, by filing a description of the same, by metes and bounds, in the clerk's office of the district court of the United States wherein the same is situated, together with an estimate of the damages caused to any person by taking the same, which appropriation and estimate shall be first approved by the State superintendent, and shall then be recorded by said clerk in a book to be kept for that purpose. From the date of said filing the title of said tract of land shall vest in the United States. Said division inspector shall cause notice to be given of said appropriation and estimate to all persons known to be interested in the tract appropriated, and shall also cause a copy of said notice to be posted upon said tract, within thirty days from the filing of said appropriation and estimate as aforesaid. Any person interested in said estate, aggrieved by the estimate of his damages, may apply by petition to the district court where in said land is situated, setting forth a description of the land, and the fact that he is so aggrieved; and the judge of said court shall thereupon cause due notice to be given by the petitioner to the State superintendent; and if it shall appear to said court that the petitioner is interested in the land so taken, it shall appoint three disinterested and discreet men to be commissioners to revise the estimate of the damages occasioned to the petitioner as aforesaid, the report of whom, or the majority of whom returned into said court and accepted thereby, shall be final and conclusive between the parties to the matter of said damages. The court may for good cause shown, set aside the report of said commissioners, and recommit the matter to them, or to new commissioners, at its discretion.

Sec. 6. And be it further enacted, that the schoolbooks to be used in all the national schools shall be such as are prescribed by the said superintendent, under the direction of the Commissioner of Education. They shall be furnished by State superintendent to the division inspector, and by the latter to the local superintendent, for the children within his district, and by him distributed to them at cost; Provided, that if any child is unable to pay the cost of the books needed and used by it the same shall be furnished gratuitously.

Sec. 7. And be it further enacted, that it shall be the duty of the local superintendent to provide for the care and protection and repairing of the school houses, and to procure fuel therefor, where necessary. If it shall be necessary to erect a school house in any district, the local superintendent shall contract for the same, the contract therefor to receive the approbation of the State superintendent before it shall be binding.

Sec. 8. And be it further enacted, that the local superintendent shall select and contract with a teacher or teachers for the schools within his district, at a rate and for a period of time to be approved by the State Superintendent.

Sec. 9. And be it further enacted, that the Commissioner of Education shall prescribe forms of registers of the attendance, conduct, age, and other particulars respecting the pupils in each school, and shall furnish blanks for the same. The same shall be kept by the teachers in accordance with the rules prescribed by the Commissioners, and shall be returned to the State superintendent. The State superintendent shall make abstracts of said returns, and return them annually to the Commissioner of Education, at such time as the latter shall prescribe, and shall also make a report stating the condition and means of Education in his State with such suggestions as will seem to him important. In the performance of all the duties provided by this act, the local superintendent shall be subject to the direction of the division inspector, the division inspector to those of the State superintendent, and the State superintendent shall be subject to the directions of the Commissioner of Education.

Sec. 10. And be it further enacted that no books shall be used in any of the national schools, nor shall any instruction be given therein calculated to favor the peculiar tenets of any religious sect.

Sec. 11. And be it further enacted, that it shall be the duty of all instructors of youth to exert their best endeavors to impress on the minds of children and youth committed to their care and instruction, the principles of piety and justice, and a sacred regard for truth, love of their country, of liberty, humanity and universal benevolence, sobriety, industry and frugality, chastity, moderation, and temperance, and those other virtues which are the ornaments of human society and the basis upon which a republican Constitution is founded; and it shall be the duty of such instructors to endeavor to lead their pupils, as their ages and capacities will admit, into a clear understanding of the tendency of the above named virtues, to preserve and perfect a republican Constitution and secure the blessings of liberty, as well as to promote their future happiness, and also to point out to them the evil tendency of the opposite vices.

Sec. 12. And be it further enacted, that it shall be the duty of the division inspector to visit as often as once a year each school in his district, to keep himself informed, as far as may be, of the condition of the schools therein, and exercise a general care and oversight of the same, and to make report of the condition of all schools within his division annually, to the State superintendent.

Sec. 13. And be it further enacted that the Commissioner of Education shall annually report to Congress the condition of the national schools in each State together with such suggestions concerning the same as he shall deem important. He shall also, from time to time, prescribe such rules as he shall think fit for the government of the State and local superintendents and division inspectors in accomplishing the purpose of this act.

Sec. 14. And be it further enacted, that the Secretary of the Treasury shall prescribe such rules, in conformity to law, as shall in his judgment be necessary to provide for the payment of teachers, for land, school houses, and other objects herein provided for; and may require such vouchers from any of the officers herein provided for as may be necessary to insure security in the application of moneys so paid.

Sec. 15. And be it further enacted, that a direct tax of   million dollars is hereby laid upon the United States, and the same shall be apportioned among the States, respectively in the manner following:

Sec. 16. And be it further enacted, that said tax shall be assessed and collected in the mode prescribed for the collection of the direct tax in the forty-fifth chapter of the acts of the first session of the thirty-seventh Congress and the acts in addition thereto; Provided, that the assessors and collectors who are now, or may hereafter be, charged by law with the duty of assessing or collecting the internal revenue shall assess and collect the tax herein provided, and the collection districts for the assessment and collection of the direct tax shall be the same as are now or may thereafter be, established for the assessment and collection of said revenue. The dwelling house and lot of land on which the same stands constituting the homestead of any householder having a family and actually owned by him or her shall be exempted from such tax to the value of one thousand dollars.

Sec. 17. And be it further enacted, that all sums of money assessed and raised in each State by virtue of this act shall be expended therein for the purposes of education, as in this act declared.

Sec. 18. And be it further enacted, that any state may lawfully assume, collect, assess, and pay into the treasury of the United States the direct tax, or its quota thereof, imposed by this act upon such State, according to the provisions of said forty-fifth chapter of the acts of the first session of the thirty-seventh Congress.

Sec. 19. And be it further enacted, that this act shall take effect on the first day of   , eighteen hundred and seventy   . Any state may at its election in lieu of the tax provided for by this act, provide for all the children within its borders between the ages of   and   suitable instruction in reading, writing, orthography, arithmetic, geography, and the history of the United States. If any state shall, before said last named day by a resolve of its legislature, approved by the governor, engage to make such provision, and shall notify the President of the United States thereof, all future proceeding for appointing the officers provided for herein, or for the assessment or collection of aforesaid tax within such State, shall be suspended for twelve months from said date. If, at the expiration of said twelve months, it shall be proved to the satisfaction of the President of the United States that there is established in said State a system of common schools which provides reasonably, for all the children therein who dwell where the population is sufficiently dense to enable schools to be maintained, suitable instruction in the aforesaid branches no further steps shall be taken for the appointment of officers or the assessing of the tax therein; otherwise, he shall proceed to cause said tax to be assessed and said schools to be established within such State forthwith thereafter.

REPRESENTATIVE GILBERT WALKER OF VIRGINIA ON FEDERAL AID TO EDUCATION (1876)   From *Congressional Record*, 44th Cong., 1st Sess., 4:4 (May 29, 1876), pp. 3368–70.

The provisions of the bill before the House are plain and explicit. The great object to be accomplished is clearly stated and the means for its attainment succinctly set forth. Its object is the consecration of the revenue derived from the public lands to the education of the whole people. At the close of each fiscal year the Secretary of the Interior is directed to certify the net amount of the proceeds of the public lands for that year to the Secretary of the Treasury, who shall within one month thereafter apportion the same among the several States and Territories and the District of Columbia on the basis of population, to be applied by the local authorities of such States, Territories, and District, in accordance with their local laws, to the education of all the inhabitants thereof between the ages of five and sixteen years. For the first five years the whole amount of such net proceeds is to be thus apportioned; for the succeeding five years, one-half the other half, and after ten years the whole amount, to be invested in United States bonds, only the interest on which shall be thus apportioned, and the investments thus made to remain as a perpetual fund for the benefit of free education throughout our entire country. During the first ten years the apportionments are to be made on the basis of illiteracy, but forever afterward on that of the whole population. While the bill leaves it optional with each State to accept or reject its distributive share, yet when once accepted it must be faithfully and honestly applied to the purposes therein indicated under the penalty of forfeiting all right to any other apportionments until full compliance be made with the conditions prescribed. No interference with the existing laws for the disposition of the public lands is contemplated, and the percentages reserved to certain States remain undisturbed. These are substantially the main provisions of the bill under consideration, and I trust they may meet with the cordial approbation of every member of this House. No patent is claimed for them as for an original discovery, for the principal ideas involved have been brought to the attention of Congress and the country at different times and in various forms during almost the entire period of our national existence.

While with consummate wisdom and foresight the fathers laid the foundations of the Republic upon the broad and enduring principles of civil and religious liberty, they also fully comprehended the truth that the perpetuity of the superstructure they reared depended "upon the virtue and intelligence of the people." Amid the throes of the Revolution, and while freedom yet hung tremblingly in the balance, a committee of the Virginia Legislature, composed of Thomas Jefferson, Edmund Pendleton, and George Wythe, reported a bill to establish "a complete public free-school system to be supported by taxation." A few years later, in the justly celebrated ordinance of 1787, the National Government declared that—"Religion, morality, and knowledge being necessary to good government and the happiness of mankind, schools and other means of education shall forever be encouraged."

And two years earlier the Congress, in the ordinance for ascertaining the mode of disposing of the western lands belonging to the Government, expressly provided that—"There shall be reserved the lot No. 16 of every township for the maintenance of public schools within said township."

Thus early, in advance even of the formation of the Constitution, was inaugurated that profound and liberal policy which has been uniformly and unvaryingly pursued in the organization of new States from the public domain. Grants of public lands have also been made to some of the other States, and in 1862 there was apportioned to all the States an amount equal to thirty thousand acres for each of their Senators and Representatives respectively in Congress, for the purpose of establishing agricultural and mechanical colleges. In fact, more than forty-seven different acts of Congress appropriating nearly eighty millions of acres of the public lands for educational purposes not only attest the wisdom and uniform liberality of the people, as expressed through their governmental agents, but also conclusively and forever silences all question as to the constitutional power of Congress in the premises.

*　　*　　*

Sir, this Government has never owned a foot of soil that she did not hold for the common use and benefit of all her people. And how has this trust been administered? Has equal and exact justice been meted out to all the members of the Union? Has each received its just and equal proportion of this common fund of all or of the benefits flowing therefrom? In fact, until 1862, has one of the original grantors or one of the original thirteen States received one particle of direct benefit from this great trust fund in accordance with the trust, except generally, from the amounts paid into the Federal Treasury? Yet nearly eighty millions of acres have been given to the new States and Territories for educational purposes and 222,469,337 acres to railroads and for other purposes within the same limits. Really the enormous amount of 301,796,139 acres of the public domain, the common treasure of the whole Union, has been disposed of in vioation [sic] of the nation's trust.

But, sir, I am not here to sing jeremiads over the past, nor yet to harshly criticise the action of Congress in making donations of the public lands to the new States and Territories for educational purposes. The grand results which these donations have enabled the new States to achieve in the cause of education, the magnificent systems of public schools which most of them have thus been enabled to establish, palliate at least, if they do not entirely excuse, the wrong done the older States. Congress did right in making these donations, and its only error consisted in its failure to make equally liberal provision for the older States. This injustice, however, has not been suffered to pass unnoticed. Repeated efforts to have this equity of the older States suitably recognized have from time to time been made, and these efforts will continue to be made until justice shall finally triumph.

*   *   *

To what higher, nobler, or more beneficial purpose could the public domain be devoted than the education, mental and moral elevation of the people? Are not the proceeds of the public lands the common heritage of all the people? Do they not in this respect constitute a peculiar and distinctive fund, differing widely from that received from tariffs and taxation, or any other source, in that they are derived from the common property of all the people instead of from that of the few?

Now, sir, having demonstrated, I trust satisfactorily, not only the constitutionality of this bill, but also that it is grounded upon unquestioned equity, an equity already fully recognized and never in fact denied, I now propose to briefly discuss the necessities which imperatively demand its passage. And, sir, I must confess that I enter upon this discussion with feelings of the profoundest regret. Yes; regret at the existence of terrible and inexorable facts, which have only to be known to fully demonstrate the necessities of our situation.

The census of 1870 disclosed a perfectly appalling amount of illiteracy in this country. About one-fifth of our population or nearly 6,000,000 of our people over ten years of age, could neither read nor write. Of the 8,000,000 of voters who mold our institutions and control our social and political destinies, over 1,600,000 could not even read the ballots they cast. And of the 12,055,443 children of school-age, that is, between the ages of five and eighteen, 5,458,977 or nearly one-half, were growing up in the depths of ignorance, without any school advantages whatever. This is the fearful picture presented by the census of 1870. But a far better and to the ordinary mind a more comprehensive picture was prepared by the Superintendent of the Census, and I trust that every member of this House will take immediate occasion to examine it. It consists of a map of the United States so colored and shaded as to exhibit the relative degree of intelligence of every locality of our country. The higher state of intelligence is naturally illustrated by the lighter color, and this is gradually shaded off into the darkness of ignorance. Sir, there is too much color upon that map, too many intensely dark spots. Promptly pass this bill, however, and our next census will present a more radiant picture, with the darkness gradually but surely receding before the advancing light.

An examination of this map, as well as of the census tables of 1870, discloses the fact that the somber shading of illiteracy obtains at the South in a far greater degree than at the North. While this is readily explainable, and upon grounds which substantially free the South from the charge of neglect or want of appreciation of the inestimable benefits of education, yet the fact exists and cannot be ignored. During the four years of civil year and for several years thereafter, the educational institutions of the South were almost universally closed. While the war prevailed the young men were in the field, and the whole country was too unsettled for the maintenance, to any considerable extent of schools, and after the war poverty, interposed for years insuperable obstacles to educational pusuits. Added to this was the emancipation of the colored race, but few of which had ever enjoyed educational facilities. These people constituted over five-twelfths of the entire population of the eleven southern States in 1870; or, to be more accurate, of a total population of 9,487,386 the colored people numbers 3,939,032. This mass of ignorance was suddenly raised to the dignity and responsibility of citizenship, in the midst of their impoverished and largely bankrupt former owners, with no means of their own and without any provision whatever being made for their education. Of the wisdom, or rather unwisdom of this action, I had occasion some years ago to speak, and I repeat here what I then said as expressive of my present views:

"The war resulted in the emancipation of the negro; but no sooner had the sword been sheathed than the strife was transferred to the forum, and days and months, ay, even years, were spent in efforts to cloth the freedman with rights he could not understand and load him with responsibilities which he was unable to comprehend. Statute after statute was enacted, and the fundamental law of the nation itself repeatedly amended to establish the civil and political rights of the negro; but where in the long catalogue of legislation can be found any provision for his education and elevation even to a partial comprehension of the duties and responsibilities which these rights impose? Why did not the mental and moral necessities of these 'wards of the nation' excite the same paternal solicitude as did their political condition? I shall not pause here, nor is it germane to my present purpose, to answer this very natural inquiry. The facts with which we have alone to deal at the present moment are that, although the negro was emancipated from physical slavery, he was left bound in the more terrible chains of universal ignorance; and that, while the nation invested him with the glorious rights and privileges of American citizenship, it not only failed to make any provision for investing him with a knowledge of the high duties and responsibilities which that citizenship imposes, but left him in the depths of poverty and ignorance, to be educated, if educated at all, by the white people of those States, whom the war had so utterly impoverished that they were unable to educate even themselves.

"That this was unwise, unjust, and impolitic, needs no words from me to demonstrate. In my opinion the Government should not only have provided the means for the education of these new suffragans, but it should have gone further, and aided the people of the South to fulfill this high and holy duty to themselves.

"If it be true that one portion of the body-politic cannot suffer in its mental, moral, or physical condition without injury, more or less, to the whole, and if intelligence and virtue be necessary and desirable in the individual citizen of a republic, then the education of the whole people becomes a matter of public interest and national concern. I am, however, no advocate of a governmental system of education except by the States; but I do advocate the extension to all of the States the policy which has uniformly obtained in the organization of new States. The public lands are the common property of the whole people of the Union, held by it in trust for their benefit and behoof, and if there be reason and sound statesmanship in reserving a portion of this property for educational purposes in the sparsely populated but prosperous new States, do not the same reason and statesmanship in a far higher degree dictate the appropriation of a portion of this property to the education of the larger and poorer populations of the older States of the South?

"But I do not go to the length of urging even this very just and correct view of the subject, based though it may be upon the soundest and most substantial and patriotic reasoning. All I seek and all I demand is equality with all the other States of the Republic in this as in all other respects. I merely advocate the performance of what I believe to be a solemn and imperative duty of the Federal Goverment to the black race and to the people of the whole country, and that duty consists in appropriating the entire proceeds derived from the sales of the public lands to educational purposes. . . ."

I am aware, sir, that it may be urged that the basis upon which the apportionments are to be made under this bill for the first ten years is an invasion of that very equity the existence of which I have been endeavoring to establish, because of the fact that, there being a greater amount of illiteracy at the South than at the North, the Southern States will receive a larger proportion of the fund than the Northern. But suppose this in a measure to be true, is it not of the highest moment to place this fund where it is most needed and "where it will do the most good?" Can the new States, that have already been so richly endowed in violation of this equity, complain and will the wealthy Northern States of the original thirteen object? I apprehend not. All must admit that ignorance is such a curse, wherever existing in the country, that it becomes the common interest of all to utterly obliterate it. The disease which affects one portion of the body-politic casts its baleful influence over the whole.

The pressing need of the South to-day is for educational aid. She has not yet recuperated from the terrible devastations and losses of the war, and while most of the States have inaugurated and maintained good systems of free schools, and have largely reduced the sum total of illiteracy in their midst, yet their means are still too limited and the burdens too great for them to maintain their schools for a sufficient period in each year. They need assistance now. Educate the present generation, and those which succeed it will take care of themselves. Once lift the dark pall of ignorance which overshadows the land and the light of universal intelligence will never again be obscured. The history of education in this country shows that it has never turned backward. Its course has been uniformly upward and onward, constantly increasing in strength and expanding in beneficence. The constitution of the human mind itself is such that the acquisition of knowledge begets a thirst for more, and the cultivation and enlargement of its faculties urges it forward to new attainments and new conquests. Has not intelligence ever been the parent of prosperity and the handmaid of virtue? Does not all history teach that a people's productive power and force depends upon its degree of advancement in knowledge, and that crime everywhere recedes as education advances?

SENATOR HENRY W. BLAIR CALLS FOR FEDERAL AID TO EDUCATION (1882)

From *Congressional Record*, 47th Cong., 1st Sess., June 13, 1882, pp. 4830-31.

It is proper to observe that in the rebel States, where slavery existed in 1860, the valuation then aggregated $2,289,029,642, of which $842,927,400 was in slaves, and proper allowance must be made for this fact in estimating present power to bear taxation. The negroes were then taxed; they were productive as property. Now they require to be educated; then education would have destroyed them as property. They are now doing little more as a totality than to support themselves. Their taxable property is thus far very slight. It has been stated as a matter of pride on this floor that in Georgia colored people are taxed for $6,000,000 of property. The assessed valuation of Georgia is by the last census $239,472,559. What, then, must be the general poverty of the colored people of Georgia, even when of her total population (which is 1,542,180) 725,274 have accumulated $6,000,000, or eight dollars each, of taxable property. And if these things be so in Georgia, what must be the destitution of the colored race elsewhere throughout the South, and how idle to be talking of their educating themselves.

*   *   *

I speak now of the general fact, and I believe that this state of things is but temporary. It will, however, become permanent unless the proper remedy of increased intelligence and well-directed industry is applied. And to this end the means must come largely from without, for they do not exist within these States. In Kentucky and Delaware the negro child is educated only from the taxation of his own race. As a rule he can have no school at all unless from charity.

The country was held together by the strong and bloody embrace of war, but that which the nation might and did do to retain the integrity of its territory and of its laws by the expenditure of brute force will all be lost if for the subjection of seven millions of men by the statutes of the States is to be substituted the thralldom of ignorance and tyranny of an irresponsible suffrage. Secession, and a confederacy founded upon slavery as its chief corner-stone, would be better than the future of the Southern States—better for both races, too—if the nation is to permit one-third, and that the fairest portion of its domain, to become the spawning ground of ignorance, vice, anarchy, and of every crime. The nation as such abolished slavery as a legal institution; but ignorance is slavery, and no matter what is written in your constitutions and your laws slavery will continue until intelligence, the handmaid of liberty, shall have illuminated the whole land with the light of her smile.

Before the war the Southern States were aristocracies, highly educated and disciplined in the science of politics. Hence they preserved order and flourished at home, while they imposed their will upon the nation at large. Now all is changed. The suffrage is universal, and that means universal ruin unless the capacity to use it intelligently is created by universal education. Until the republican constitutions, framed in accordance with the Congressional reconstruction which supplanted the governments initiated by President Johnson, common-school systems, like universal suffrage, were unknown. Hence in a special manner the nation is responsible for the existence and support of those systems as well as for the order of things which made them necessary. That remarkable progress has been made under their influence is true, and that the common school is fast becoming as dear to the masses of the people at the South as elsewhere is also evident.

The nation, through the Freedmen's Bureau, and perhaps to a limited extent in other ways, has expended $5,000,000 for the education of negroes and refugees in the earlier days of reconstruction, while religious charities have founded many special schools which have thus far cost some ten millions more. The Peabody fund has distilled the dews of heaven all over the South; but heavy rains are needed; without them every green thing must wither away.

*   *   *

I have had the honor to introduce a bill (Senate bill 151) appropriating fifteen millions of dollars the first year, fourteen millions the second year, and afterward a sum diminishing one million yearly, until there shall have been ten annual distributions, the last of which would be six millions—it being thought probable that State systems could by that time maintain themselves, or that from the perpetual-fund bill, should that fortunately become a law, all the aid necessary could thereafter be derived. This bill has been reported by the Senate Committee on Education and Labor with its unanimous support so far as the amount appropriated is concerned. I believe that to give a larger sum would induce the people of the States where most of it would be expended to depend too largely upon the national Treasury for the support of their schools, and the result would be waste and inefficiency.

The community must pay to the extent of its ability, or it will lose interest in its schools and its children will not be properly educated, no matter how much money may be received, the burden of raising which the people do not feel. Besides it will be difficult for those portions of the country which are comparatively unused to the practical administration of school systems at once economically and profitably to absorb the full amount which is really needed, and which will be required as greater accommodations, competent teachers in sufficient numbers, and larger attendance of pupils are secured. The proportion of $15,000,000 which this bill would give to the Southern States would prolong their existing schools for at least three months, with present accommodations and teachers, and, in addition, would secure the extension of the school system to such districts and children as are now absolutely without the pale of any educational privileges whatever. In my belief no less sum can possibly do this.

THE BLAIR BILL FOR FEDERAL AID TO EDUCATION IS INTRODUCED INTO THE SENATE (1882)   From *Congressional Record*, 47th Cong., 1st Sess., June 13, 1882, p. 4833.

A bill to aid in the establishment and temporary support of common schools.

Be it enacted by the Senate and House of Representatives of the United States of

America in Congress assembled, That for ten years next after the passage of this act there shall be annually appropriated from the money in the Treasury the following sums, to wit: The first year the sum of $15,000,000, the second year the sum of $14,000,000, the third year the sum of $13,000,000, and thereafter a sum diminished $1,000,000 yearly from the sum last appropriated until ten annual appropriations shall have been made, when all appropriations under this act shall cease; which several sums shall be expended to secure the benefits of common-school education to all the children living in the United States.

SEC. 2. That the instruction in the common schools wherein these moneys shall be expended shall include the art of reading, writing, and speaking the English language, arithmetic, geography, history of the United States, and such other branches of useful knowledge as may be taught under local laws, and may include, whenever practicable, instruction in the arts of industry; which instruction shall be free to all, without distinction of race, nativity, or condition in life: *Provided,* That nothing herein shall deprive children of different races, living in the same community but attending separate schools, from receiving the benefits of this act, the same as though the attendance therein were without distinction of race.

SEC. 3. That such money shall annually be divided among and paid out in the several States and Territories in that proportion which the whole number of persons in each who, being of the age of ten years and over, cannot read and write bears to the whole number of such persons in the United States; and until otherwise provided such computation shall be made according to the official returns of the census of 1880.

SEC. 4. That such moneys shall be expended in each State by the concurrent action; each having a negative upon the other, of the Secretary of the Interior, on the part of the United States, and of the superintendent of public schools, board of education, or other body in which the administration of the public school laws shall be vested, on the part of the several States wherein the expenditures are respectively to be made; and whenever the authorities of the United States and of the State fail to agree as to the distribution, use, and application of the money hereby provided for, or any part thereof, payment thereof, or such part thereof, shall be suspended, and if such disagreement continue throughout the fiscal year for which the same was appropriated, it shall be covered into the Treasury and shall be added to the general appropriation for the next year provided for in the first section of this act.

All sums of money appropriated under the provisions of this act to the use of any Territory shall be applied to the use of schools therein by the Secretary of the Interior, through the commissioner of common schools, whose appointment is hereinafter provided for.

SEC. 5. That the moneys distributed under the provisions of this act shall be used in the school districts of the several States and Territories in such way as to provide for the equalization of school privileges to all the children throughout the State or Territory wherein the expenditure shall be made, thereby giving to each child an opportunity for common-school education; and to this end existing public schools not sectarian in character may be aided, and new ones may be established, as may be deemed best in the several localities.

SEC. 6. That a part of the money apportioned to each State or Territory, not exceeding one-tenth thereof, may yearly be applied to the education of teachers for the common schools therein, which sum may be expended in maintaining institutes or temporary training-schools or in extending opportunities for normal or other instruction to intelligent and suitable persons, of any color, who are without necessary means, and who shall agree, in writing, to qualify themselves and teach in the common schools of such State or Territory at least one year.

SEC. 7. That the design of this act not being to establish an independent system of schools, but rather to aid for the time being in the development and maintenance of the school systems established by local power, and which must eventually be wholly maintained by the States and Territories wherein they exist, it is hereby provided that no part of the money appropriated under this act shall be paid out in any State or Territory which shall not during the first five years of the operation of this act annually expend for the maintenance of common schools, free to all, at least one-third of the sum which shall be allotted to it under the provisions hereof, and during the second five years of its operation a sum at least equal to the whole it shall be entitled to receive under this act; and if such expenditure shall not be shown to the Secretary of the Interior at the end of each fiscal year by each State or Territory, respectively, or by such other evidence as shall be satisfactory to him, then the allotment under this act for each subsequent year so long as there shall be a deficiency of such expenditure by the State or Territory from the proceeds of local funds, whether derived from taxation or otherwise, shall be expended for the support of common schools therein wholly in the discretion of the Secretary, who shall apply the same to the support of existing or to the establishment of new schools in such way as he shall deem best.

SEC. 8. That no part of the money herein provided for shall be used for the erection of school-houses or school-buildings of any description, nor for rent of the same: *Provided, however,* That whenever it shall appear to the Secretary that otherwise any given locality will remain wholly without reasonable common-school advantages he may, in his discretion, from the general fund allotted to the State or Territory, provide schools and for their temporary accommodations by rent or otherwise, in the most economical manner possible: *And provided further,* That in no case shall more than 5 per cent. of such allotment be set apart for or be expended under the provisions of this section.

SEC. 9. That there shall be appointed by the President, by and with the advice and consent of the Senate, a commissioner of common schools in each State and Territory, who shall be a citizen thereof and shall reside therein, and shall perform all such duties as may be assigned to him by the Secretary of the Interior, and who shall be specially charged with all the details of the execution of this act within his jurisdiction, and in co-operation with the State authorities. In the Territories he shall also be charged with the general supervision and control of public education, and shall possess all the powers now vested in Territorial superintendents and boards of education, or by whatever Territorial officers the same may have been hitherto exercised. He shall be paid a salary of not less than three nor more than five thousand dollars, in the discretion of the Secretary of the Interior. He shall annually make full reports of all matters connected with schools in his jurisdiction to the Secretary of the Interior, and particular reports when called upon by the Secretary, and especially of all details in the administration of this act. In addition to his other duties he shall devote himself to the promotion of the general interests of public education in the State or Territory for which he is appointed.

SEC. 10. That any State in which the number of persons ten years of age and upward who cannot read is not over 5 per cent. of the whole population, signifying its desire that the amount allotted to it under the provisions of this act shall be appropriated in any other way for the promotion of common-school education, in its own borders or elsewhere, its allotment shall be paid to such State to be thus appropriated: *Provided,* That its Legislature shall have first considered the question of its appropriation to the general fund for use under the provisions of this act in States and Territories where the proportion of illiterate persons is more than 5 per cent. of the whole population.

SEC. 11. That any State whose illiterate is greater than 5 per cent. of its whole population failing to accept the provisions of this act and to comply with its provisions, so as to be entitled to its allotment from year to year, the sum allotted to such State, subject to the discretionary action of the Secretary of the Interior under the sixth and seventh sections of this act, shall become a part of the fund to be distributed among the States which shall be entitled to their respective allotments, and to the Territories. And any State not accepting the provisions of this act, nor acquiring the right to dispose of its allotment as provided in the preceding section, the same shall become a part of the general fund for like distribution.

SEC. 12. That the District of Columbia shall be entitled to the privileges of a Territory under the provisions of this act, but there shall be no commissioner of common schools appointed for said District, nor shall its existing laws and school authorities be interfered with. The Commissioner of Education shall be charged with the duty of superintending the distribution of its allotment, and shall make full report of his doings to the Secretary of the Interior.

SEC. 13. That the Secretary of the Interior shall be charged with the practical administration of this law through the Bureau of Education, and all moneys paid under its provisions shall be made by the Treasury warrant to the individual performing the service to whom indebtedness shall be due, and who shall be personally entitled to receive the money, or to his agent, duly authorized by him, upon vouchers approved by the State authorities, when under the provisions of this act their approval is necessary, and by the commissioner of common schools for the State or Territory wherein the expenditure shall be made, and by the Secretary of the Interior.

A SOUTHERNER'S CRITICISM OF THE SILENT SOUTH (1885) From George W. Cable, *The Silent South* (New York, 1885), pp. 33–37.

A far pleasanter aspect of our subject shows itself when we turn from courts and prisons to the school-house. And the explanation is simple. Were our educational affairs in the hands of that not high average of the community commonly seen in jury-boxes, with their transient sense of accountability and their crude notions of public interests, there would most likely be no such pleasant contrast. But with us of the South, as elsewhere, there is a fairly honest effort to keep the public-school interests in the hands of the State's most highly trained intelligence. Hence our public educational work is a compromise between the unprogressive prejudices of the general mass of the whites and the progressive intelligence of their best minds. Practically, through the great majority of our higher educational officers, we are fairly converted to the imperative necessity of elevating the colored man intellectually, and are beginning to see very plainly that the whole community is sinned against in every act or attitude of oppression, however gross or however refined.

Yet one thing must be said. I believe it is wise that all have agreed not to handicap education with the race question, but to make a complete surrender of that issue, and let it find adjustment elsewhere first and in the schools last. And yet, in simple truth and justice and in the kindest spirit, we ought to file one exception for that inevitable hour when the whole question must be met. There can be no more real justice in pursuing the freedman's children with humiliating arbitrary distinctions and separations in the school-houses than in putting them upon him in other places. If, growing out of their peculiar mental structure, there are good and just reasons for their isolation, by all means let them be proved and known; but it is simply tyrannous to assume them without proof. I know that just here looms up the huge bugbear of Social Equality. Our eyes are filled with absurd visions of all Shantytown pouring its hordes of unwashed imps into the company and companionship of our own sunny-headed darlings. What utter nonsense! As if our public schools had no gauge of cleanliness, decorum, or moral character! Social Equality! What a godsend it would be if the advocates of the old Southern regime could only see that the color line points straight in the direction of social equality by tending toward the equalization of all whites on one side and of all blacks on the other. We may reach the moon some day, not social equality; but the only class that really effects anything toward it are the makers and holders of arbitrary and artificial social distinctions interfering with society's natural self-distribution. Even the little children everywhere are taught, and begin to learn almost with their A B C, that they will find, and must be guided by, the same variations of the social scale in the public school as out of it; and it is no small mistake to put them or their parents off their guard by this cheap separation on the line of color.

IX. The Question of Instinct

But some will say this is not a purely artificial distinction. We hear much about race instinct. The most of it, I fear, is pure twaddle. It may be there is such a thing. We do not know. It is not proved. And even if it were established, it would not necessarily be a proper moral guide. We subordinate instinct to society's best interests as apprehended in the light of reason. If there is such a thing, it behaves with strange malignity toward the remnants of African blood in individuals principally of our own race, and with singular indulgence to the descendants of—for example—Pocahontas. Of mere race *feeling* we all know there is no scarcity. Who is stranger to it? And as another man's motive of private preference no one has a right to forbid it or require it. But as to its being an instinct, one thing is plain: if there is such an instinct, so far from excusing the malignant indignities practiced in its name, it furnishes their final condemnation; for it stands to reason that just in degree as it is a real thing it will take care of itself.

It has often been seen to do so, whether it is real or imaginary. I have seen in New Orleans a Sunday-school of white children every Sunday afternoon take possession of its two rooms immediately upon their being vacated by a black school of equal or somewhat larger numbers. The teachers of the colored school are both white and black, and among the white teachers are young ladies and gentlemen of the highest social standing. The pupils of the two schools are alike neatly attired, orderly, and in every respect inoffensive to each other. I have seen the two races sitting in the same public high-school and grammar-school rooms, reciting in the same classes and taking recess on the same ground at the same time, without one particle of detriment that any one ever pretended to discover, although the fiercest enemies of the system swarmed about it on every side. And when in the light of these observations I reflect upon the enormous educational task our Southern States have before them, the inadequacy of their own means for performing it, the hoped-for beneficence of the general Government, the sparseness with which so much of our Southern population is distributed over the land, the thousands of school districts where, consequently, the multiplication of schools must involve both increase of expense and reductions of efficiency, I must enter some demurrer to the enforcement of the tyrannous sentiments of the old regime until wise experiments have established better reasons than I have yet heard given.

AN ALABAMA SCHOOLMAN ON THE NEGRO QUESTION (1890) From J. A. B. Lovett, "The Education of the Negro in the South," National Education Association, *Journal of Proceedings and Addresses* (Topeka, Kans., 1890), pp. 502–5.

The following propositions may be relied upon by all who are interested in this discussion as reflecting the views of the intelligent, law-abiding citizens, of Anglo-Saxon blood, in the South:

1. This class of Southern citizens would not, under any circumstances, favor the reenslavement of the colored people. Six millions of slaves at an average of six hundred dollars each, aggregates the enormous sum of three billions six hundred millions of dollars. This was all swept away by the emancipation proclamation, and should the Government propose to return this great loss of property to the Southern people in the persons of the negro population, as slaves, there would be a unanimous Southern voice against the resumption of such a burden.

2. They entertain the kindliest feelings toward the colored population: and, with their counsel and aid, they are ever ready to assist them in the acquisition of property, and to deal fairly with him along the line of his political, legal, and natural rights.

3. They have no fears of any serious or general trouble growing out of the fact of negro suffrage, if not interfered with by a low class of political agitators.

4. Were the question submitted to a vote, I feel quite sure that the representative Southern people would elect the negro to remain on his native heath, if he desired to do so.

With regard to the education of the negro, there is a variety of sentiment among our people. We have those among us who do not warmly favor the education of the masses of either race. This sentiment is shown in the fact that we suffer some opposition to popular education. A class similar to this may be found in all educating countries. We have also those who do not advocate negro education, because they have never become reconciled to negro citizenship. Their neutrality on the subject is about all the opposition that comes from this source; and, if their passiveness is an indication of doubt on the subject, it is plain that the negro gets the benefit of the doubt. But the most formidable opposition we have to negro education, is the positive declaration made by a large and respectable class of citizens that education is a decided detriment to the negro's best interest. It is claimed by these opponents that just as soon as the negro obtains a little learning, he is disposed to abandon manual labor, and seeks to engage in politics, preaching, or teaching. It is also claimed that the educated negro often becomes a firebrand among the more ignorant of his race, and uses his acquired talents in stirring up and perpetuating hatred and strife between the races.

Despite all these various phases of opposition to negro education in the South, their schools are generally well filled with enthusiastic learners, and they are making as fair a headway as their limited facilities will admit. And this very fact shows that the majority of the Southern white people are strongly favorable to negro civilization; for it must be known to those who are familiar with the statistics of Southern education, that our legislators make, substantially, the same provision for the education of the colored children as they do for the whites. Nor do we ever hear of our representatives being arraigned by their constituents for supporting measures which give equal advantages to our colored youth. When this is fairly considerd, in connection with the fact that the negro population contributes a very diminutive per centum of the State appropriations for public education, it will be seen that the white people of the South richly deserve the gratitude of the negro, as well as the commendation of all who are interested in his cause.

Having reviewed the opinions of the white people, North and South, on this question, it is proper that something should be said from the negro's point of view.

For the past several years my official relations in the field of education have been of such a character as to enable me to learn something of the purposes and ambitions of the representative negroes of the South. From various conversations with the most intelligent persons of this race, I have gleaned the following facts:

They believe that the intelligent white people of the South are their best friends. They know they are at liberty to leave the South, but they prefer to remain. They take but little stock in the exodus agitations. They think the time for such a movement is not yet. When the Good Father shall arrange his program of final destiny for the negro, possibly there shall be a great emigration of the race to the land of their fathers. At present the burning bush, the presence of a Moses, the inviting Canaan, are not in sight. However, when this day shall come, if ever it shall, there will be no wicked Southern Pharaoh that will detain the colored man from a brighter inheritance; and there will be no infuriated Southern host to be swallowed up in the angry seas, in the wake of his departure. But there will be, should such an event ever occur, a mighty host of friends to the colored man in the South who would raise their prayers to Almighty God to protect and defend the negro, and make of his race a strong and mighty people.

The intelligent Southern negroes do not think that social equality with the whites is either practicable or desirable; not practicable, because it would be unnatural; not desirable, even on their part, because those who undertake to practice it with them inflict upon them a positive injury. In conversation with a highly-cultivated colored man, not long since, I asked him to give me his views on this subject. His answer was replete with wisdom, and full of good common-sense. He said: "The whites who put themselves on an equal social basis with us come to us in white skins, but their hearts are black—they always lower us in the moral scale."

The intelligent Southern negroes are also opposed to the co-education of the races. They generally have a natural parental feeling toward their children, and they would be unwilling to have their offspring to undergo the unavoidable embarrassments that would surely attend the presence of their children among those of the white race. The negroes in the South, as a rule, are eager to receive enlightenment on all subjects which tend to elevate their race; and, while the great mass of them still remain in gross ignorance for want of better educational facilities, very many of them have achieved phenomenal success in the acquisition of knowledge and culture. Wherever the means of education have been placed before them by conscientious, able and faithful teachers, the colored youth have always been improved thereby. And I am fully persuaded that, while a little learning has a tendency to turn the heads of some, the only philosophical, safe and just course to pursue is to educate the colored people. The citizenship of the negro has been settled by governmental action, and this is not likely to be reversed. He should therefore be given a fair and patient trial on the line of civilization. We should remember that it took the colored man several years to fully comprehend the nature of his freedom from slavery. For a number of years immediately succeeding his emancipation, many thought that their freedom meant entire exemption from all kinds of labor; but their natural wants soon taught them differently, and they returned to the abandoned cotton-fields to earn a livelihood. So in their education; many of them are slow to understand the grand end of civilization which the schools have in view. We must learn to labor and to wait. Those who have closely observed the slow but steady improvement of the negro, where good schools have been in their reach, freely confess that education is elevating them not only intellectually, but morally and civilly.

Negroes—the North

THE "RESOLUTE BENEFICIAL SOCIETY" OPENS A SCHOOL FOR
NEGRO CHILDREN IN WASHINGTON, D.C. (1818)   From *National
Intelligencer,* August 29, 1818.

A School

Founded by an association of free people of color of the city of
Washington, called the "Resolute Beneficial Society," situate near the Eastern
public school, and the dwelling of Mrs. Fenwick, is now open for the reception of
children of free people of color, and others that ladies and gentlemen may think
proper to send to be instructed in reading, writing, arithmetic, English grammar, or
other branches of education, applicable to their capacities, by a steady active and
experienced teacher, whose attention is wholly devoted to the purposes described. It
is presumed, that free colored families will embrace the advantages thus presented
to them, either by subscribing to the funds of the society, or by sending their
children to the school; the terms in either case being remarkably moderate. An
improvement of the intellect and morals of colored youth being the leading object
of this institution, the patronage of benevolent ladies and gentlemen, by donating or
subscription, is humbly solicited in aid of the fund,—the demands thereon being
heavy, and the means at present much too limited. For the satisfaction of the
public, the constitution and articles of association are printed and published. And,
to avoid disagreeable occurrences, no writings are to be done by the teacher for a
slave, neither directly nor indirectly to serve the purposes of a slave, on any account
whatsoever. Further particulars may be known, by applying to any of the
undersigned officers.

> WILLIAM COSTIN, President
> GEORGE HICKS, Vice President.
> JAMES HARRIS, Secretary.
> GEORGE BELL, Treasurer.
> ARCHIBALD JOHNSON, Marshal.
> FRED LEWIS, Chairman of the Com.
> ISAAC JOHNSON   Committee.
> SCIPIO BEENS,

N.B. An evening school will commence on the premises, on the first Monday in
October, and continue throughout the season.

The managers of Sunday schools in the Eastern District, are thus most dutifully
and respectfully informed, that on Sabbath days the school-house belonging to this

society, if required, for the tuition of colored youth, will be uniformly at their service.

OPPOSITION TO A PROPOSED NEGRO COLLEGE IN NEW HAVEN
(**1831**)   From *Niles Weekly Register*, October 1, 1831.

"Negro College"

Our readers, no doubt, will be surprised at the caption of this paragraph, and will wonder what we mean by "Negro College." We will inform them that we mean, without any jesting, to say that there has been an attempt, a serious attempt, to get up an institution in this place for the education of colored men. The blacks for a few years past have been treated with attention and kindness by the inhabitants of this city. Two or three of our citizens have devoted much time and money for bettering their condition, but the zeal of a few has constantly increased, until a project has been brought forward, which if carried into execution would ruin the prosperity of the city. New Haven was fixed upon, by the convention held in Philadelphia some time since, for the location of a black college. Our citizens called a public meeting to take the subject into consideration, and the following resolutions were advocated by *judge Daggett, N. Smith, R. I. Ingersoll* and *I. H. Townsend*, esqrs. and adopted by about 700 freemen. The rev. *S. S. Jocelyn* and three others opposed, and voted against them.

At a city meeting, duly warned and held at the city hall, in the city of New Haven, on Saturday, the 10th day of September, 1831, to take into consideration a project for the establishment in this city a college for the education of *colored youth*, the following preamble and resolutions were unanimously adopted, viz:

Whereas endeavors are now making to establish a college in the city for the education of the colored population of the United States, the West Indies, and other countries adjacent; and in connection with this establishment the immediate abolition of slavery in the United States is not only recommended and encouraged by the advocates of the proposed college, but demanded as a right; and whereas an omission to notice these measures may be construed as implying either indifference to, or approbation of the same:

Resolved: That it is expedient that the sentiments of our citizens should be expressed on these subjects, and that the calling of this meeting by the mayor and aldermen is warmly approved by the citizens of this place.

Resolved, That in as much as slavery does not exist in Connecticut, and wherever permitted in other states, depends on the municipal laws of the state which allows it, and over which neither any other states nor the congress of the United States has any control, that the propagation of sentiments favorable to the immediate emancipation of slaves, in disregard of the civil institutions of the states in which they belong, and as auxiliary thereto, the cotemperaneous founding of colleges for educating colored people, is an unwarrantable and dangerous interference with the internal concerns of the other states, and ought to be discouraged.

And whereas, in the opinion of this meeting, Yale college, the institutions for the education of females, and the other schools already existing in this city, are important to the community and the general interests of science, and as such have been deservedly patronized by the public, and the establishment of a college in the same place to educate the colored population, is incompatible with the prosperity if not the existence of the present institutions of learning, and will be destructive of the best interests of the city. And believing, as we do, that if the establishment of such a college in any part of the country were deemed expedient, it should never be imposed on any community without their consent:

Therefore, resolved, by the mayor, aldermen, common council, and freemen of the city of New Haven, in city meeting assembled, That we will resist the establishment of the proposed college in this place by every lawful means.

And on motion it was voted that the proceedings of this meeting be signed by the mayor, and countersigned by the clerk, and published in all the newspapers of this city.

Dennis Kimberly, mayor

NEGRO PETITION AGAINST SEGREGATED SCHOOLS IN BOSTON

(**1844**)   From *The Liberator,* vol. XIV, p. 103.

Resolved, that, impelled by a deep sense of gratitude, we tender to Dr. H. Storer our unfeigned thanks for his successful efforts in instituting the late investigation of affairs connected with the Smith School, and for his unremitting attention to the same from the commencement to the close.

Resolved, That we present our most grateful acknowledgments to the Hon. John C. Park, for the late voluntary and disinterested devotion of his time and eminent talents in the cause of the wronged and neglected colored children of this city.

Whereas, we, the colored citizens of the city of Boston have recently sent a petition to the School Committee, respectfully praying for the abolition of the separate schools for colored children, and asking for the rights and privileges extended to other citizens in respect to the common school system—viz. the right to send our children to the schools established in the respective districts in which we reside; and

Whereas, the School Committee, at their last meeting, passed a vote stating, in substance, that the prayer of our petition would not be granted, and that the separate schools for colored children would be continued; and

Whereas, we believe, and have the opinion of eminent counsel, that the institution and support of separate schools at the public charge, for any one class of the inhabitants in exclusion of any other class, is contrary to the laws of this Commonwealth; therefore,

Resolved, That we consider the late action of the School Committee, in regard to our petition asking for the entire abolition of separate schools for colored children, as erroneous and unsatisfactory.

Resolved, That while we would not turn aside from our main object, the abolition of the separate colored schools, we cannot allow this occasion to pass without an expression of our surprise and regret at the recent acquittal by the

School Committee of Abner Forbes, Principal of the Smith School, and of our deep conviction that he is totally unworthy of his present responsible station; and that the colored parents of this city are recommended to withdraw their children from the exclusive school established in contravention of that equality of privileges which is the vital principle of the school system of Massachusetts.

Resolved, That a copy of the above preamble and resolutions be sent to the Chairman of the School Committee, with a request that the petition heretofore presented may be reconsidered, and that we be allowed a hearing on said petition before them.

Resolved, That the heartfelt thanks of the colored citizens of Boston are due to Messrs. George S. Hillard and John T. Sargent for the humane and independent stand recently taken by them in the School Committee, in behalf of the rights and welfare of the colored children.

Resolved, That the expression of the sense of this meeting be transmitted to the several gentlemen named in the foregoing resolutions, and be also published in the city papers.

CHARLES SUMNER'S ARGUMENT IN ROBERTS v. CITY OF BOSTON THAT SEPARATE SCHOOLS FOR NEGROES ARE INHERENTLY UNEQUAL (1849)   From *Charles Sumner: His Complete Works* (Boston, 1900), vol. III, pp. 52–54, 70–74, 86–88, 97.

MAY IT PLEASE YOUR HONORS:—

Can any discrimination on account of race or color be made among children entitled to the benefit of our Common Schools under the Constitution and Laws of Massachusetts? This is the question which the Court is now to hear, to consider, and to decide.

Or, stating the question with more detail, and with more particular application to the facts of the present case, are the Committee having superintendence of the Common Schools of Boston intrusted with *power*, under the Constitution and Laws of Massachusetts, to exclude colored children from the schools, and compel them to find education at separate schools, set apart for colored children only, at distances from their homes less convenient than schools open to white children?

This important question arises in an action by a colored child only five years old, who, *by her next friend*, sues the city of Boston for damages on account of a refusal to receive her into one of the Common Schools.

It would be difficult to imagine any case appealing more strongly to your best judgment, whether you regard the parties or the subject. On the one side is the City of Boston, strong in wealth, influence, character; on the other side is a little child, of degraded color, of humble parents, and still within the period of natural infancy, but strong from her very weakness, and from the irrepressible sympathies of good men, which, by a divine compensation, come to succor the weak. This little child asks at your hands her *personal rights*. So doing, she calls upon you to decide a question which concerns the personal rights of other colored children,—which concerns the Constitution and Laws of the Commonwealth,—which concerns that *peculiar institution* of New England, the Common Schools,—which concerns the fundamental principles of human rights,—which concerns the Christian character of this community. Such parties and such interests justly challenge your earnest attention.

Though this discussion is now for the first time brought before a judicial tribunal, it is no stranger to the public. In the School Committee of Boston for five years it has been the occasion of discord. No less than four different reports, two majority and two minority, forming pamphlets, of solid dimensions, devoted to this question, have been made to this Committee, and afterwards published. The opinions of learned counsel have been enlisted. The controversy, leaving these regular channels, overflowed the newspaper press, and numerous articles appeared, espousing opposite sides. At last it has reached this tribunal. It is in your power to make it subside forever.

The Question Stated

Forgetting many of the topics and all of the heats heretofore mingling with the controversy, I shall strive to present the question in its juridical light, as becomes the habits of this tribunal. It is a question of jurisprudence on which you are to give judgment. But I cannot forget that the principles of morals and of natural justice lie at the foundation of all jurisprudence. Nor can any reference to these be inappropriate in a discussion before this Court.

Of Equality I shall speak, not only as a sentiment, but as a principle embodied in the Constitution of Massachusetts, and obligatory upon court and citizen. It will be my duty to show that this principle, after finding its way into our State Constitution, was recognized in legislation and judicial decisions. Considering next the circumstances of this case, it will be easy to show how completely they violate Constitution, legislation, and judicial proceedings,—*first*, by subjecting colored children to inconvenience inconsistent with the requirements of Equality, and, *secondly*, by establishing a system of Caste odious as that of the Hindoos,—leading to the conclusion that the School Committee have no such power as they have exercised, and that it is the duty of the Court to set aside their unjust by-law. In the course of this discussion I shall exhibit the true idea of our Common Schools, and the fallacy of the pretension that any exclusion or discrimination founded on race or color can be consistent with Equal Rights.

In opening this argument, I begin naturally with the fundamental proposition which, when once established, renders the conclusion irresistible. According to the Constitution of Massachusetts, *all men, without distinction of race or color, are equal before the law.* In the statement of this proposition I use language which, though new in our country, has the advantage of precision.

*   *   *

Separate Schools Inconsistent with Equality

It is easy to see that the exclusion of colored children from the Public Schools is a constant inconvenience to them and their parents, which white children and white parents are not obliged to bear. Here the facts are plain and unanswerable, showing a palpable violation of Equality. *The black and white are not equal before the law.* I am at a loss to understand how anybody can assert that they are.

Among the regulations of the Primary School Committee is one to this effect. "Scholars to go to the school nearest their residences. Applicants for admission to our schools (with the exception and provision referred to in the preceding rule) are especially entitled to enter the schools nearest to their places of residence." The exception here is "of those for whom special provision has been made" in separate schools,—that is, colored children.

In this rule—without the unfortunate exception—is part of the beauty so conspicuous in our Common Schools. It is the boast of England, that, through the multitude of courts, justice is brought to every man's door. It may also be the boast of our Common Schools, that, through the multitude of schools, education in Boston is brought to every *white* man's door. But it is not brought to every *black* man's door. He is obliged to go for it, to travel for it, to walk for it,—often a great distance. The facts in the present case are not so strong as those of other cases within my knowledge. But here the little child, only five years old, is compelled, if attending the nearest African School, to go a distance of two thousand one hundred feet from here home, while the nearest Primary School is only nine hundred feet, and, in doing this, she passes by no less than five different Primary Schools, forming part of our Common Schools, and open to white children, all of which are closed to her. Surely this is not *Equality before the Law.*

*　　*　　*

Looking beyond the facts of this case, it is apparent that the inconvenience from the exclusion of colored children is such as to affect seriously the comfort and condition of the African race in Boston. The two Primary Schools open to them are in Belknap Street and Sun Court. I need not add that the whole city is dotted with schools open to white children. Colored parents, anxious for the education of their children, are compelled to live in the neighborhood of the schools, to gather about them,—as in Eastern countries people gather near a fountain or a well. The liberty which belongs to the white man, of choosing his home, is not theirs. Inclination or business or economy may call them to another part of the city; but they are restrained for their children's sake. There is no restraint upon the white man; for he knows, that, wherever in the city inclination or business or economy may call him, there will be a school open to his children near his door. Surely this is not *Equality before the Law.*

*　　*　　*

Separate Schools Are in the Nature of Caste

The separation of children in the Schools, on account of race or color, is in the nature of *Caste,* and, on this account, a violation of Equality. The case shows expressly that the child was excluded from the school nearest to her dwelling—the number in the school at the time warranting her admission—"on the sole ground of color."

*　　*　　*

But it is said that the School Committee, in thus classifying the children, have not violated any principle of Equality, inasmuch as they provide a school with competent instructors for colored children, where they have advantages equal to those provided for white children. It is argued, that, in excluding colored children from Common Schools open to white children, the Committee furnish an *equivalent*.

Here there are several answers. I shall touch them briefly, as they are included in what has been already said.

1. The separate school for colored children is not one of the schools established by the law relating to Public Schools.[1] It is not a Common School. As such it has no legal existence, and therefore cannot be a *legal equivalent*. In addition to what has been already said, bearing on this head, I call attention to one other aspect. It has been decided that a town can execute its power to form School Districts only by geographical divisions of its territory, that there cannot be what I would call a *personal* limitation of a district, and that *certain individuals* cannot be selected and set off by *themselves* into a district.[2] The admitted effect of this decision is to render a separate school for colored children illegal and impossible in towns divided into districts. They are so regarded in Salem, Nantucket, New Bedford, and in other towns of this Commonwealth. The careful opinion of a learned member of this Court, who is not sitting in this case, given while at the bar,[3] and extensively published, is considered as practically settling this point.

But there cannot be one law for the country and another for Boston. It is true that Boston is not divided strictly into geographical districts. In this respect its position is anomalous. But if separate colored schools are illegal and impossible in the country, they must be illegal and impossible in Boston. It is absurd to suppose that this city, failing to establish School Districts, and treating all its territory as a single district, should be able to legalize a Caste school, which otherwise it could not do. Boston cannot do indirectly what other towns cannot do directly. This is the first answer to the allegation of equivalents.

2. The second is that in point of fact the separate school is not an equivalent. We have already seen that it is the occasion of inconvenience to colored children, which would not arise, if they had access to the nearest Common School, besides compelling parents to pay an additional tax, and inflicting upon child and parent the stigma of Caste. Still further,—and this consideration cannot be neglected,—the matters taught in the two schools may be precisely the same, but a school exclusively devoted to one class must differ essentially in spirit and character from that Common School known to the law, where all classes meet together in Equality. It is a mockery to call it an equivalent.

3. But there is yet another answer. Admitting that it is an equivalent, still the colored children cannot be compelled to take it. Their rights are found in Equality before the Law; nor can they be called to renounce one jot of this. They have an equal right with white children to the Common Schools. A separate school, though well endowed, would not secure to them that precise Equality which they would enjoy in the Common Schools. The Jews in Rome are confined to a particular

[1] Revised Statutes, Ch. 23.
[2] Perry *v.* Dover, 12 Pick. R., 213.
[3] Hon. Richard Fletcher.

district called the Ghetto, and in Frankfort to a district known as the Jewish Quarter. It is possible that their accommodations are as good as they would be able to occupy, if left free to choose throughout Rome and Frankfort; but this compulsory segregation from the mass of citizens is of itself an *inequality* which we condemn. It is a vestige of ancient intolerance directed against a despised people. It is of the same character with the separate schools in Boston.

Thus much for the doctrine of Equivalents as a substitute for Equality.

* * *

Evils of Separate Schools

But it is said that these separate schools are for the benefit of both colors, and of the Public Schools. In similar spirit Slavery is sometimes said to be for the benefit of master and slave, and of the country where it exists. There is a mistake in the one case as great as in the other. This is clear. Nothing unjust, nothing ungenerous, can be for the benefit of any person or any thing. From some seeming selfish superiority, or from the gratified vanity of class, short-sighted mortals may hope to draw permanent good; but even-handed justice rebukes these efforts and redresses the wrong. The whites themselves are injured by the separation. Who can doubt this? With the Law as their monitor, they are taught to regard a portion of the human family, children of God, created in his image, coequals in his love, as a separate and degraded class; they are taught practically to deny that grand revelation of Christianity, the Brotherhood of Man. Hearts, while yet tender with childhood, are hardened, and ever afterward testify to this legalized uncharitableness. Nursed in the sentiments of Caste, receiving it with the earliest food of knowledge, they are unable to eradicate it from their natures, and then weakly and impiously charge upon our Heavenly Father the prejudice derived from an unchristian school. Their characters are debased, and they become less fit for the duties of citizenship.

Who can say that this does not injure the blacks? Theirs, in its best estate, is an unhappy lot. A despised class, blasted by prejudice and shut out from various opportunities, they feel this proscription from the Common Schools as a peculiar brand. Beyond this, it deprives them of those healthful, animating influences which would come from participation in the studies of their white brethen. It adds to their discouragements. It widens their separation from the community, and postpones that great day of reconciliation which is yet to come.

The whole system of Common Schools suffers also. It is a narrow perception of their high aim which teaches that they are merely to furnish an equal amount of knowledge to all, and therefore, provided all be taught, it is of little consequence where and in what company. The law contemplates not only that all shall be taught, but that *all* shall be taught *together*. They are not only to receive equal quantities of knowledge, but all are to receive it in the same way. All are to approach the same common fountain together; nor can there be any exclusive source for individual or class. The school is the little world where the child is trained for the larger world of life. It is the microcosm preparatory to the macrocosm, and therefore it must cherish and develop the virtues and the sympathies needed in the larger world. And since, according to our institutions, all classes, without distinction of color, meet in the performance of civil duties, so should they all, without distinction of color, meet in the school, beginning there those relations of Equality which the Constitution and Laws promise to all.

MASSACHUSETTS SUPREME COURT DECISION ON CONSTITUTIONALITY OF SEPARATE SCHOOLS FOR NEGROES IN BOSTON (1849)

From *Sarah C. Roberts* v. *The City of Boston,* 59 Mass. (5 Cushing R.), 204 (1849).

The opinion was delivered at the March term, 1850.

SHAW, C. J. The plaintiff, a colored child of five years of age, has commenced this action, by her father and next friend, against the city of Boston, upon the statute of 1845, *c.* 214, which provides, that any child unlawfully excluded from public school instruction, in this commonwealth, shall recover damages therefor, in an action against the city or town, by which such public school instruction is supported. The question therefore is, whether, upon the facts agreed, the plaintiff has been unlawfully excluded from such instruction.

By the agreed statement of facts, it appears, that the defendants support a class of schools called primary schools, to the number of about one hundred and sixty, designed for the instruction of children of both sexes, who are between the ages of four and seven years. Two of these schools are appropriated by the primary school committee, having charge of that class of schools, to the exclusive instruction of colored children, and the residue to the exclusive instruction of white children.

The plaintiff, by her father, took proper measures to obtain admission into one of these schools appropriated to white children, but pursuant to the regulations of the committee, and in conformity therewith, she was not admitted. Either of the schools appropriated to colored children was open to her; the nearest of which was about a fifth of a mile or seventy rods more distant from her father's house than the nearest primary school. It further appears, by the facts agreed, that the committee having charge of that class of schools had, a short time previously to the plaintiff's application, adopted a resolution, upon a report of a committee, that in the opinion of that board, the continuance of the separate schools for colored children, and the regular attendance of all such children upon the schools, is not only legal and just, but is best adapted to promote the instruction of that class of the population.

The present case does not involve any question in regard to the legality of the Smith school, which is a school of another class, designed for colored children more advanced in age and proficiency; though much of the argument, affecting the legality of the separate primary schools, affects in like manner that school. But the question here is confined to the primary schools alone. The plaintiff had access to a school, set apart for colored children, as well conducted in all respects, and as well fitted, in point of capacity and qualification of the instructors, to advance the education of children under seven years old, as the other primary schools; the objection is, that the schools thus open to the plaintiff are exclusively appropriated to colored children, and are at a greater distance from her home. Under these circumstances, has the plaintiff been unlawfully excluded from public school instruction? Upon the best consideration we have been able to give the subject, the court are all of opinion that she has not.

It will be considered, that this is a question of power, or of the legal authority of the committee intrusted by the city with this department of public instruction; because, if they have the legal authority, the expediency of exercising it in any particular way is exclusively with them.

The great principle, advanced by the learned and eloquent advocate of the plaintiff, is, that by the constitution and laws of Massachusetts, all persons without distinction of age or sex, birth or color, origin or condition, are equal before the law. This, as a broad general principle, such as ought to appear in a declaration of rights, is perfectly sound; it is not only expressed in terms, but pervades and animates the whole spirit of our constitution of free government. But, when this great principle comes to be applied to the actual and various conditions of persons in society, it will not warrant the assertion, that men and women are legally clothed with the same civil and political powers, and that children and adults are legally to have the same functions and be subject to the same treatment; but only that the rights of all, as they are settled and regulated by law, are equally entitled to the paternal consideration and protection of the law, for their maintenance and security. What those rights are, to which individuals, in the infinite variety of circumstances by which they are surrounded in society, are entitled, must depend on laws adapted to their respective relations and conditions.

Conceding, therefore, in the fullest manner, that colored persons, the descendants of Africans, are entitled by law, in this commonwealth, to equal rights, constitutional and political, civil and social, the question then arises, whether the regulation in question, which provides separate schools for colored children, is a violation of any of these rights.

Legal rights must, after all, depend upon the provisions of law; certainly all those rights of individuals which can be asserted and maintained in any judicial tribunal. The proper province of a declaration of rights and constitution of government, after directing its form, regulating its organization and the distribution of its powers, is to declare great principles and fundamental truths, to influence and direct the judgment and conscience of legislators in making laws, rather than to limit and control them by directing what precise laws they shall make. The provision, that it shall be the duty of legislatures and magistrates to cherish the interests of literature and the sciences, especially the university at Cambridge, public schools, and grammar schools, in the towns, is precisely of this character. Had the legislature failed to comply with this injunction, and neglected to provide public schools in the towns, or should they so far fail in their duty as to repeal all laws on the subject, and leave all education to depend on private means, strong and explicit as the direction of the constitution is, it would afford no remedy or redress to the thousands of the rising generation, who now depend on these schools to afford them a most valuable education, and an introduction to useful life.

We must then resort to the law, to ascertain what are the rights of individuals, in regard to the schools. By the Rev. Sts. c. 23, the general system is provided for. This chapter directs what money shall be raised in different towns, according to their population; provides for a power of dividing towns into school districts, leaving it however at the option of the inhabitants to divide the towns into districts, or to administer the system and provide schools, without such division. The latter course has, it is believed, been constantly adopted in Boston, without forming the territory into districts.

The statute, after directing what length of time schools shall be kept in towns of different numbers of inhabitants and families, provides (§10) that the inhabitants shall annually choose, by ballot, a school committee, who shall have the general charge and superintendence of all the public schools in such towns. There being no specific direction how schools shall be organized; how many schools shall be kept; what shall be the qualifications for admission to the schools; the age at which children may enter; the age to which they may continue; these must all be regulated by the committee, under their power of general superintendence.

There is, indeed, a provision (§§5 and 6.) that towns may and in some cases must provide a high school and classical school, for the benefit of all the inhabitants. It is obvious how this clause was introduced; it was to distinguish such classical and high schools, in towns districted, from the district schools. These schools being of a higher character, and designed for pupils of more advanced age and greater proficiency, were intended for the benefit of the whole of the town, and not of particular districts. Still it depends upon the committee, to prescribe the qualifications, and make all the reasonable rules, for organizing such schools and regulating and conducting them.

The power of general superintendence vests a plenary authority in the committee to arrange, classify, and distribute pupils, in such a manner as they think best adapted to their general proficiency and welfare. If it is thought expedient to provide for very young children, it may be, that such schools may be kept exclusively by female teachers, quite adequate to their instruction, and yet whose services may be obtained at a cost much lower than that of more highly-qualified male instructors. So if they should judge it expedient to have a grade of schools for children from seven to ten, and another for those from ten to fourteen, it would seem to be within their authority to establish such schools. So to separate male and female pupils into different schools. It has been found necessary, that is to say, highly expedient, at times, to establish special schools for poor and neglected children, who have passed the age of seven, and have become too old to attend the primary school, and yet have not acquired the rudiments of learning, to enable them to enter the ordinary schools. If a class of youth, of one or both sexes, is found in that condition, and it is expedient to organize them into a separate school, to receive the special training, adapted to their condition, it seems to be within the power of the superintending committee, to provide for the organization of such special school.

A somewhat more specific rule, perhaps, on these subjects, might be beneficially provided by the legislature; but yet, it would probably be quite impracticable to make full and precise laws for this purpose, on account of the different condition of society in different towns. In towns of a large territory, over which the inhabitants are thinly settled, an arrangement of classification going far into detail, providing different schools for pupils of different ages, of each sex, and the like would require the pupils to go such long distances from their homes to the schools, that it would be quite unreasonable. But in Boston, where more than one hundred thousand inhabitants live within a space so small, that it would be scarcely an inconvenience to require a boy of good health to traverse daily the whole extent of it, a system of distribution and classification may be adopted and carried into effect, which may be useful and beneficial in its influence on the character of the schools, and in its adaptation to the improvement and advancement of the great purpose of education, and at the same time practicable and reasonable in its operation.

In the absence of special legislation on this subject, the law has vested the power in the committee to regulate the system of distribution and classification; and when this power is reasonably exercised, without being abused or perverted by colorable pretences, the decision of the committee must be deemed conclusive. The committee, apparently upon great deliberation, have come to the conclusion, that the good of both classes of schools will be best promoted, by maintaining the separate primary schools for colored and for white children, and we can perceive no ground to doubt, that this is the honest result of their experience and judgment.

It is urged, that this maintenance of separate schools tends to deepen and perpetuate the odious distinction of caste, founded in a deep-rooted prejudice in public opinion. This prejudice, if it exists, is not created by law, and probably cannot be changed by law. Whether this distinction and prejudice, existing in the opinion and feelings of the community, would not be as effectually fostered by compelling colored and white children to associate together in the same schools, may well be doubted; at all events, it is a fair and proper question for the committee to consider and decide upon, having in view the best interests of both classes of children placed under their superintendence, and we cannot say, that their decision upon it is not founded on just grounds of reason and experience, and in the results of a discriminating and honest judgment.

The increased distance, to which the plaintiff was obliged to go to school from her father's house, is not such, in our opinion, as to render the regulation in question unreasonable, still less illegal.

On the whole the court are of opinion, that upon the facts stated, the action cannot be maintained.

MASSACHUSETTS LAW ENDING SCHOOL DISCRIMINATION (1855) From *Massachusetts Acts and Resolves,* chap. 256 (1855), pp. 674–75.

Be it enacted by the Senate and House of Representatives, in the General Court assembled, and by the authority of the same, as follows:

SECTION 1. In determining the qualifications of scholars to be admitted into any public school or any district school in the Commonwealth, no distinction shall be made on account of the race, color or religious opinions, of the applicant or scholar.

SEC. 2. Any child who, on account of his race, color or religious opinions, shall be excluded from any public or district school in the Commonwealth, for admission to which he may be otherwise qualified, shall recover damages therefor in an action of tort, to be brought in the name of said child by his guardian or next friend, in any court of competent jurisdiction to try the same, against the city or town by which such school is supported.

SEC. 3. In filing interrogatories for discovery in any such action, the plaintiff may examine any number of the school committee, or any other officer of the defendant city or town, in the same manner as if he were a party to the suit.

SEC. 4. Every person belonging to the school committee, under whose rules or directions any child shall be excluded from such school, and every teacher of any such school, shall, on application by the parent or guardian of any such child, state in writing the grounds and reasons of such exclusion.

SEC. 5. This act shall take effect from and after the first day of September next.

[Approved by the Governor, April 28, 1855.].

PROVISION FOR SCHOOLS FOR NEGRO CHILDREN IN NEW YORK
STATE (1841)   From *Statutes at Large of the State of New York* (Albany, 1841), vol. III, pp. 446–47.

A school for colored children may be established in any city or town of this state, with approbation of the commissioners or town superintendent of such city or town, which shall be under the charge of the trustees of the district in which such school shall be kept; and in places where no school districts exist, or where from any cause it may be expedient, such school may be placed in charge of trustees to be appointed by the commissioners or town superintendent of common schools of the town or city, and if there be none, to be appointed by the state superintendent. Returns shall be made by the trustees of such schools to the town superintendent at the same time and in the same manner as now provided by law in relation to districts; and they shall particularly specify the number of colored children over five and under sixteen years of age, attending such school from different districts, naming such districts respectively, and the number from each. The town superintendent shall apportion and pay over to the trustees of such schools, a portion of the money received by them annually, in the same manner as now provided by law in respect to school districts, allowing to such schools the proper proportion for each child over five and under sixteen years of age, who shall have been instructed in such school at least four months by a teacher duly licensed, and shall deduct such proportion from the amount that would have been apportioned to the district to which such child belongs; and in his report to the state superintendent, the town superintendent shall specially designate the schools for colored children in his town or city.

NEW YORK STATE LAW AUTHORIZING THE ESTABLISHMENT OF SEPARATE SCHOOLS FOR NEGRO CHILDREN (1864)   From *Statutes at Large of the State of New York* (Albany, 1868), p. 357.

1. The school authorities of any city or incorporated village . . . may, when they shall deem it expedient, establish a separate school or separate schools for the instruction of children and youth of African descent, resident therein, and over five and under twenty-one years of age; and such school or schools shall be supported in the same manner and to the same extent as the school or schools supported therein for white children, and they shall be subject to the same rules and regulations, and be furnished with facilities for instruction equal to those furnished to the white schools therein.

2. The trustees of any union school-district, or of any school-district organized under a special act, may, when the inhabitants of any such district shall so determine, by resolution at any annual meeting, or at a special meeting called for that purpose, establish a separate school or separate schools for the instruction of such colored children resident therein, and such schools shall be supported in the

same manner, and receive the same care, and be furnished with the same facilities for instruction, as the white schools therein.

NEW YORK STATE LAW REPEALING DISCRIMINATORY SCHOOL LAW

(1900) From *Laws of the State of New York: Passed at the 123rd Session of the Legislature* (Albany, 1900), vol. II, p. 1173.

Section 1. No person shall be refused admission into or be excluded from any public school in the state of New York on account of race or color.

§ 2. Section twenty-eight, article eleven, title fifteen of chapter five hundred and fifty-six of the laws of eighteen hundred and ninety-four, which reads as follows: "The school authorities of any city or incorporated village the schools of which are or shall be organized under title eight of this act, or under special act, may, when they shall deem it expedient, establish a separate school or separate schools for instruction of children and youth of African descent, resident therein, and over five and under twenty-one years of age; and such school or schools shall be supported in the same manner and to the same extent as the school or schools supported therein for white children and they shall be subject to the same rules and regulations, and be furnished facilities for instruction equal to those furnished to the white schools therein," is hereby repealed.

ILLINOIS SCHOOL SUPERINTENDENT NEWTON BATEMAN ON

SEPARATE SCHOOLS FOR NEGROES (1870) From *Eighth Biennial Report of the Superintendent of Public Instruction of the State of Illinois, 1869–1870* (Springfield, Ill., 1870), pp. 25–29.

The principle, then, is established by this first Section of the 8th Article of the supreme law of the State, that hereafter all the school-going children in Illinois, shall be equally entitled to the benefits of the free public schools, without exception or discrimination. All the youth of the State are, and henceforth shall be, equal before the law, in respect to their claims to a good common school education. Whatever laws the General Assembly may pass in relation to public education, whatever system of common schools may be adopted, must be in harmony with this fundamental principle. And whatever inhibitive or restrictive provisions there may be in any existing school laws, in relation to free schools; whatever therein is incompatible or in conflict with this broad and catholic rule of the fundamental law, is already abrogated by the supreme authority of the Constitution itself, and the school system, in all its parts and operations, must be administered in accordance with the letter and spirit of the new Constitution, which recognizes no distinctions or disabilities among the youth of the State.

Having long waited and watched for this great consummation, and having done what little I could to hasten its coming, I hail it now with unspeakable satisfaction. Of all the wise and noble provisions of the new organic law under which Illinois is henceforth to work out her destiny as a commonwealth, not one is wiser or nobler than that which drops the ballot alike into every hand, and, with impartial justice, dispenses to all alike, the priceless blessings of intellectual improvement and culture. God will smile upon the State that thus remembers the children of a poor and despised race, reaching out to them the helping hand.

But what is the immediate present effect of this declaration of the supreme law, upon the *status* of those most concerned, in respect to education, and upon the powers and duties of school officers?

In my judgment, the right to a good common school education is conferred upon colored children, equally with others, by this section of the 8th Article, *ipso facto;* that the right fully accrued and attached, when the new Constitution went into effect, on the 8th of August 1870; and that since that date, now, and henceforth, school directors, and other boards of education working under the general law, may and should provide for the free education of colored children, as efficiently and thoroughly as for the education of white children. It is not a case for labored interpretation or construction; the language of the supreme law is too explicit to need any studied interpretation, and it is as peremptory as it is clear: "Shall provide a thorough and efficient system of free schools, whereby *all the children* of this state may receive a good common school education." There is no white, no black, no exception, distinction or discrimination in this language. Its scope is co-extensive with the territorial limits of the State and the boon which it provides is for every child in the State. The only question, touching the matter of eligibility, will hereafter be: Is this youth one of the "children of this State," and of lawful school age?

* * *

I am glad to be able to say that there is a general disposition throughout the State, to recognize and give effect to the organic law, at once, in advance of any supplementary or compulsory legislation, in respect to the rights of people of color to the benefits of the system of common schools. Boards of directors have, for the most part, already included colored children in their school arrangements and provisions for the current year, and many hundreds of them are now for the first time in the public schools of the State—either in separate schools or in co-attendance with other children.

* * *

The question whether separate schools shall be provided for colored children, or whether there shall be the same schools for all, is one of very secondary importance, and should never be permitted to disturb the peace and harmony of any school district or community. It was regarded as too trivial a matter for mention, even, in the new Constitution, and, in my estimation, the Legislature would do well to be equally silent on the subject. It is one of those matters which involve no *principle* worth striving about, and which are best left to regulate themselves. All experience demonstrates the folly and futility of undertaking to control a matter of that kind by legislative enactments. The result has always been more mischief than good.

The just principle is established, the franchise is conferred, beyond the reach of even the law-making power, that all the children of the State shall receive a good common school education. The strong arm of the supreme authority is pledged to secure this for every child in the State, white or black. This is the one great fact, the one vital point, in comparison with which all else is trivial and unworthy of contention. What our colored citizens need, what they and their friends have been struggling for, is the means of educating their children; the solid boon of *knowledge-culture;* not the paltry privilege, (if it be such,) the empty name, of sitting in the same seats, or in the same house with white children. This great right to free education they now enjoy, this inestimable boon has been conferred upon them. Let them make the most of it, and become an upright, intelligent, educated people, and all other questions and consequences will take care of themselves. I do not think that our colored citizens can *afford* to make a noise about this thing; it is unworthy of them, and of that honorable pride and self-respect which should animate them in their efforts to advance their race in the higher elements of civilization and power. I know, furthermore, that these are the views entertained by the leading minds among them, many of whom have said to me that they preferred separate schools; that they did not desire, and indeed would not permit their children to go where they were not wanted, and where they would be exposed to unfeeling taunts and insults; that in all places where the old prejudices exist, it would be better, in all respects, for their children to attend separate schools; that they were not beggars for social favors, but merely, as citizens, demanded an equal change with others to educate their children, having no fears that *when educated* they would be able to get on in the world and take care of themselves.

*   *   *

With prudence and common sense, this problem will gradually and safely work out its own solution. *Prejudice* and *cost* will be the two antagonistic forces involved in most instances, and sooner or later the *latter* will be likely to prevail. When the continued indulgence of a mere prejudice is found to be expensive, it is not probable that it will be very long persisted in. The conflict of these two opposing elements will especially appear in districts where there are but a few colored children—not enough for a separate school of reasonable size. There are a great many such districts in the State, having less than half a score, each, of colored children of school age. Now, when it is understood that these *must be provided for*—that they cannot be neglected or ignored—that there is room for them in the schools already established, where they can be educated without a dollar of additional expense, while the opening of separate schools would involve heavy outlays, for sites, buildings, teachers, fuel and all the other necessary accessories, greatly increasing the burdens of taxation, and making the cost, *per capita*, of educating this handful of colored children from five to ten times greater than that of the others—when all this comes to be perceived and reflected upon, and it is considered that the same state of things must continue from year to year, the net value of the caste-feeling that lies at the bottom of it all, will be apt to be very thoughtfully reviewed, and most likely given up. The taxpayers will be comforted by the reflection that it cannot, after all, be a very fearful degradation for them to imitate the example of the Congress of the United States, in each chamber of which a colored man now sits daily side by side with the white members of those august bodies.

In districts having colored children in sufficient numbers for separate schools of economical size, this argument will, of course, be without force, or of very little force, since, in such cases, additional school accommodations must be provided at any rate. In these cases it will be for the directors and people, both white and colored, to decide what course to pursue, and should the preference be for separate schools, such preference, whether wise or otherwise, can at least be indulged without adding to the burdens of taxation. In many such cases it may be that, for the present at least, separate schools will be advisable. They will certainly be advisable where the schools of a district would be broken up or imperilled by pursuing the other course. Wiser counsels are sure to prevail in the end.

A NEGRO CADET ON HIS EXPERIENCES AT WEST POINT (1878) From *The Colored Cadet at West Point: Autobiography of Lieutenant Henry Ossian Flipper, U. S. A.* (New York, 1878), pp. 117–20, 124–27, 138.

"A brave and honorable and courteous man
Will not insult me; and none other can."—*Cowper*.

"How do they treat you?" "How do you get along?" and multitudes of analogous questions have been asked me over and over again. Many have asked them for mere curiosity's sake, and to all such my answers have been as short and abrupt as was consistent with common politeness. I have observed that it is this class of people who start rumors, sometimes harmless, but more often the cause of needless trouble and ill-feeling. I have considered such a class dangerous, and have therefore avoided them as much as it was possible.

*   *   *

On the other hand, many have desired this information for a practical use, and that, too, whether they were prejudiced or not. That is, if friends, they were anxious to know how I fared, whether or not I was to be a success, and if a success to use that fact in the interest of the people; and if enemies, they wanted naturally to know the same things in order to use the knowledge to the injury of the people if I proved a failure.

I have not always been able to distinguish one class from the other, and have therefore been quite reticent about my life and treatment at West Point. I have, too, avoided the newspapers as much as possible. I succeeded in this so well that it was scarcely known that I was at the Academy. Much surprise was manifested when I appeared in Philadelphia at the Centennial. One gentleman said to me in the Government building: "You are quite an exhibition yourself. No one was expecting to see a colored cadet."

There are some, indeed the majority of the corps are such, who treat me on all occasions with proper politeness. They are gentlemen themselves, and treat others as it becomes gentlemen to do. They do not associate, nor do they speak other than officially, except in a few cases. They are perhaps as much prejudiced as the others, but prejudice does not prevent all from being gentlemen. On the other hand, there are some from the very lowest classes of our population. They are uncouth and rough in appearance, have only a rudimentary education, have little or no idea of courtesy, use the very worst language, and in most cases are much inferior to the average negro. What can be expected of such people? They are low, and their conduct must be in keeping with their breeding. I am not at all surprised to find it so. Indeed, in ordinary civil life I should consider such people beneath me in the social scale, should even reckon some of them as roughs, and consequently give them a wide berth.

What surprises me most is the control this class seems to have over the other. It is in this class I have observed most prejudice, and from it, or rather by it, the other becomes tainted. It seems to rule the corps by fear. Indeed, I know there are many who would associate, who would treat me as a brother cadet, were they not held in constant dread of this class. The bullies, the fighting men of the corps are in it. It rules by fear, and whoever disobeys its beck is "cut." The rest of the corps follows like so many menials subject to command. In short, there is a fearful lack of backbone. There is, it seems at first sight, more prejudice at West Point than elsewhere. It is not really so I think.

The officers of the institution have never, so far as I can say, shown any prejudice at all. They have treated me with uniform courtesy and impartiality. The cadets, at least some of them, away from West Point, have also treated me with such gentlemanly propriety. The want of backbone predominates to such an alarming extent at West Point they are afraid to do so there.

*　　*　　*

I have been asked, "What is the general feeling of the corps towards you? Is it a kindly one, or is it an unfriendly one. Do they purposely ill-treat you or do they avoid you merely?" I have found it rather difficult to answer unqualifiedly such questions; and yet I believe, and have always believed, that the general feeling of the corps towards me was a kindly one. This has been manifested in multitudes of ways, on innumerable occasions, and under the most various circumstances. And while there are some who treat me at times in an unbecoming manner, the majority of the corps have ever treated me as I would desire to be treated. I mean, of course, by this assertion that they have treated me as I expected and really desired them to treat me, so long as they were prejudiced. They have held certain opinions more or less prejudicial to me and my interests, but so long as they have not exercised their theories to my displeasure or discomfort, or so long as they have "let me severely alone," I had no just reason for complaint. Again, others, who have no theory of their own, and almost no manliness, have been accustomed "to pick quarrels," or to endeavor to do so, to satisfy I don't know what; and while they have had no real opinions of their own, they have not respected those of others. Their feeling toward me has been any thing but one of justice, and yet at times even they have shown a remarkable tendency to recognize me as having certain rights entitled to their respect, if not their appreciation.

As I have been practically isolated from the cadets, I have had little or no intercourse with them. I have therefore had but little chance to know what was really the feeling of the corps as a unit toward myself. Judging, however, from such evidences as I have, I am forced to conclude that it is as given above, viz., a feeling of kindness, restrained kindness if you please.

*　　*　　*

If I am to stand on any other ground than the one white cadets stand upon, then I don't want the cadetship. If I cannot endure prejudice and persecutions, even if they are offered, then I don't deserve the cadetship, and much less the commission of an army officer. But there is a remedy, a way to root out snobbery and prejudice which but needs adoption to have the desired effect. Of course its adoption by a single person, myself for instance, will not be sufficient to break away all the barriers which prejudice has brought into existence. I am quite confident, however, if adopted by all colored cadets, it will eventually work out the difficult though by no means insoluble problem, and give us further cause for joy and congratulations.

The remedy lies solely in our case with us. We can make our life at West Point what we will. We shall be treated by the cadets as we treat them. Of course some of the cadets are low—they belong to the younger classes—and good treatment cannot be expected of them at West Point nor away from there. The others, presumably gentlemen, will treat everybody else as becomes gentlemen, or at any rate as they themselves are treated. For, as Josh Billings quaintly tells us, "a gentleman kant hide hiz true karakter enny more than a loafer kan."

W. E. B. DU BOIS ON BEING A STUDENT AT HARVARD, 1888-90[1] From W. E. B. Du Bois, "A Negro Student at Harvard at the End of the 19th Century," *Massachusetts Review*, vol. I, pp. 439–44, 447, 452.

Harvard University in 1888 was a great institution of learning. It was 238 years old and on its governing board were Alexander Agassiz, Phillips Brooks, Henry Cabot Lodge and Charles Francis Adams; and a John Quincy Adams, but not the ex-President. Charles William Eliot, a gentleman by training and a scholar by broad study and travel, was president. Among its teachers emeriti were Oliver Wendell Holmes and James Russell Lowell. Among the active teachers were Francis Child, Charles Eliot Norton, Justin Winsor and John Trowbridge; Frank Taussig, Nathaniel Shaler, George Palmer, William James, Francis Peabody, Josiah Royce, Barrett Wendell, Edward Channing and Albert Bushnell Hart. In 1890 arrived a young instructor, George Santayana. Seldom, if ever, has any American University had such a galaxy of great men and fine teachers as Harvard in the decade between 1885 and 1895.

To make my own attitude toward the Harvard of that day clear, it must be remembered that I went to Harvard as a Negro, not simply by birth, but recognizing myself as a member of a segregated caste whose situation I accepted. But I was determined to work from within that caste to find my way out.

The Harvard of which most white students conceived I knew little. I had not even heard of Phi Beta Kappa, and of such important social organizations as the

Hasty Pudding Club, I knew nothing. I was in Harvard for education and not for high marks, except as marks would insure my staying. I did not pick out "snap" courses. I was there to enlarge my grasp of the meaning of the universe. We had had, for instance, no chemical laboratory at Fisk; our mathematics courses were limited. Above all I wanted to study philosophy! I wanted to get hold of the bases of knowledge, and explore foundations and beginnings. I chose, therefore, Palmer's course in ethics, but since Palmer was on sabbatical that year, William James replaced him, and I became a devoted follower of James at the time he was developing his pragmatic philosophy.

Fortunately I did not fall into the mistake of regarding Harvard as the beginning rather than the continuing of my college training. I did not find better teachers at Harvard, but teachers better known, who had had wider facilities for gaining knowledge and lived in a broader atmosphere for approaching truth.

I hoped to pursue philosophy as my life career, with teaching for support. With this program I studied at Harvard from the fall of 1888 to 1890, as undergraduate. I took a varied course in chemistry, geology, social science and philosophy. My salvation here was the type of teacher I met rather than the content of the courses. William James guided me out of the sterilities of scholastic philosophy to realist pragmatism; from Peabody's social reform with a religious tinge I turned to Albert Bushnell Hart to study history with documentary research; and from Taussig, with his reactionary British economics of the Ricardo school, I approached what was later to become sociology. Meantime Karl Marx was mentioned, but only incidentally and as one whose doubtful theories had long since been refuted. Socialism was dismissed as unimportant, as a dream of philanthropy or as a will-o-wisp of hotheads.

When I arrived at Harvard, the question of board and lodging was of first importance. Naturally, I could not afford a room in the college yard in the old and venerable buildings which housed most of the well-to-do students under the magnificent elms. Neither did I think of looking for lodgings among white families, where numbers of the ordinary students lived. I tried to find a colored home, and finally at 20 Flagg Street I came upon the neat home of a colored woman from Nova Scotia, a descendant of those black Jamaican Maroons whom Britain had deported after solemnly promising them peace if they would surrender. For a very reasonable sum I rented the second storey front room and for four years this was my home. I wrote of this abode at the time: "My room is, for a college man's abode, very ordinary indeed. It is quite pleasantly situated—second floor, front, with a bay window and one other window. . . As you enter you will perceive the bed in the opposite corner, small and decorated with floral designs calculated to puzzle a botanist. . . On the left hand is a bureau with a mirror of doubtful accuracy. In front of the bay window is a stand with three shelves of books, and on the left of the bureau is an improvised bookcase made of unpainted boards and uprights, containing most of my library of which I am growing quite proud. Over the heat register, near the door, is a mantle with a plaster of Paris pug-dog and a calendar, and the usual array of odds and ends. . . . On the wall are a few quite ordinary pictures. In this commonplace den I am quite content."

Following the attitudes which I had adopted in the South, I sought no friendships among my white fellow students, nor even acquaintanceships. Of course I wanted friends, but I could not seek them. My class was large—some three hundred students. I doubt if I knew a dozen of them. I did not seek them, and naturally they did not seek me. I made no attempt to contribute to the college periodicals since the editors were not interested in my major interests. But I did have a good singing voice and loved music, so I entered the competition for the Glee Club. I ought to have known that Harvard could not afford to have a Negro on its Glee Club travelling about the country. Quite naturally I was rejected.

I was happy at Harvard, but for unusual reasons. One of these was my acceptance of racial segregation. Had I gone from Great Barrington high school directly to Harvard, I would have sought companionship with my white fellows and been disappointed and embittered by a discovery of social limitations to which I had not been used. But I came by way of Fisk and the South and there I had accepted color caste and embraced eagerly the companionship of those of my own color. This was of course no final solution. Eventually, in mass assault, led by culture we Negroes were going to break down the boundaries of race; but at present we were banded together in a great crusade, and happily so. Indeed, I suspect that the prospect of ultimate full human intercourse, without reservations and annoying distinctions, made me all too willing to consort with my own and to disdain and forget as far as was possible that outer, whiter world.

In general, I asked nothing of Harvard but the tutelage of teachers and the freedom of the laboratory and library. I was quite voluntarily and willingly outside its social life. I sought only such contacts with white teachers as lay directly in the line of my work. I joined certain clubs, like the Philosophical Club; I was a member of the Foxcroft dining club because it was cheap. James and one or two other teachers had me at their homes at meal and reception. I escorted colored girls to various gatherings, and as pretty ones as I could find to the vesper exercises, and later to the class day and commencement social functions. Naturally we attracted attention and the *Crimson* noted my girl friends. Sometimes the shadow of insult fell, as when at one reception a white woman seemed determined to mistake me for a waiter.

In general, I was encased in a completely colored world, self-sufficient and provincial, and ignoring just as far as possible the white world which conditioned it. This was self-protective coloration, with perhaps an inferiority complex, but with belief in the ability and future of black folk.

My friends and companions were drawn mainly from the colored students of Harvard and neighboring institutions, and the colored folk of Boston and surrounding towns. With them I led a happy and inspiring life. There were among them many educated and well-to-do folk, many young people studying or planning to study, many charming young women. We met and ate, danced and argued, and planned a new world.

Towards whites I was not arrogant; I was simply not obsequious, and to a white Harvard student of my day a Negro student who did not seek recognition was trying to be more than a Negro. The same Harvard man had much the same attitude toward Jews and Irishmen.

I was, however, exceptional among Negroes at Harvard in my ideas on voluntary race segregation. They for the most part saw salvation only in integration at the earliest moment and on almost any terms in white culture; I was firm in my criticism of white folk and in my dream of a self-sufficient Negro culture even in America.

This cutting of myself off from my white fellows, or being cut off, did not mean unhappiness or resentment. I was in my early manhood, unusually full of high spirits and humor. I thoroughly enjoyed life. I was conscious of understanding and power, and conceited enough still to imagine, as in high school, that they who did not know me were the losers, not I. On the other hand, I do not think that my white classmates found me personally objectionable. I was clean, not well-dressed but decently clothed. Manners I regarded as more or less superfluous and deliberately cultivated a certain brusquerie. Personal adornment I regarded as pleasant but not important. I was in Harvard, but not of it, and realized all the irony of my singing "Fair Harvard." I sang it because I liked the music, and not from any pride in the pilgrims.

With my colored friends I carried on lively social intercourse, but necessarily one which involved little expenditure of money. I called at their homes and ate at their tables. We danced at private parties. We went on excursions down the Bay. Once, with a group of colored students gathered from surrounding institutions, we gave Aristophanes' *The Birds* in a Boston colored church. The rendition was good, but not outstanding, not quite appreciated by the colored audience, but well worth doing. Even though it worked me near to death, I was proud of it.

Thus the group of professional men, students, white collar workers and upper servants, whose common bond was color of skin in themselves or in their fathers, together with a common history and current experience of discrimination, formed a unit that like many tens of thousands of like units across the nation had or were getting to have a common culture pattern which made them an interlocking mass, so that increasingly a colored person in Boston was more neighbor to a colored person in Chicago than to a white person across the street.

Mrs. Ruffin of Charles Street, Boston, and her daughter Birdie were often hostesses to this colored group. She was widow of the first colored judge appointed in Massachusetts, an aristocratic lady, with olive skin and high piled masses of white hair. Once a Boston white lady said to Mrs. Ruffin ingratiatingly: "I have always been interested in your race." Mrs. Ruffin flared: "Which race?" She began a national organization of colored women and published the *Courant,* a type of small colored weekly paper which was then spreading over the nation. In this I published many of my Harvard daily themes.

Naturally in this close group there grew up among the young people friendships ending in marriages. I myself, outgrowing the youthful attractions of Fisk, began serious dreams of love and marriage. There were, however, still my study plans to hold me back and there were curious other reasons. For instance, it happened that two of the girls whom I particularly liked had what was to me then the insuperable handicap of looking like whites, while they had enough black ancestry to make them "Negroes" in America. I could not let the world even imagine that I had married a white wife. Yet these girls were intelligent and companionable. One went to Vassar College, which then refused entrance to Negroes. Years later when I went there to lecture I remember disagreeing violently with a teacher who thought the girl ought not to have "deceived" the college by graduating before it knew of her Negro descent!

*   *   *

Harvard of this day was a great opportunity for a young man and a young American Negro and I realized it. I formed habits of work rather different from those of most of the other students. I burned no midnight oil. I did my studying in the daytime and had my day parceled out almost to the minute. I spent a great deal of time in the library and did my assignments with thoroughness and with prevision of the kind of work I wanted to do later. From the beginning my relations with most of the teachers at Harvard were pleasant. They were on the whole glad to receive a serious student, to whom extracurricular activities were not of paramount importance, and one who in a general way knew what he wanted.

*   *   *

In June 1890, I received my bachelor's degree from Harvard *cum laude* in philosophy. I was one of the five graduating students selected to speak at commencement.

Indians

FATHER GABRIEL RICHARD PROPOSES A MISSION SCHOOL FOR INDIAN CHILDREN ON THE MICHIGAN FRONTIER (1808) From House Document 540 as quoted in U.S. Congress, Senate, *Inaugural Addresses of the Presidents*, 82nd Cong., 2d Sess. (1952), pp. 121–22.

. . . let us teach them the practice and theory of Agriculture and husbandry. let their time at the schools be properly divided between reading, writing, cyphring &c. and hoeing, gardening, plowing &c. let them make their own clothes, let them learn to build their own houses, let them take care of the sheep which will supply the wool to cloth them. let the young Girls spin that wool, and moove the shuttle. let them meelk the cows, raise a quantity of chiken, &c. &c. let the house where they will be educated, be the deposit of the utensils of agriculture, of tools of various trades, of the spinning-wheels, which are annually distributed to the various Indian Tribes; let it be a rule that such instruments shall be given only to such persons who will know the use of them; let those spinning-wheels or other machines be given as premiums at appointed times in the middle of many Spectators under the shade of trees planted by themselves, at the sound of the Musquetery and martial music executed by their companions of school, &c. Such public exhibitions should certainly excite the ambitions of the children and draw the attention of their parents—let it be—that at the end of their education, one cow, a pair of oxen or a horse, and a farm of so many acres of land more or less in proportion to the progress made by each, be given in reward at the public exhibition.

ACT ESTABLISHING THE "INDIAN CIVILIZATION FUND" (1819) From "An Act Making Provision for the Civilization of the Indian Tribes Adjoining the Frontier Settlements," *Annals of Congress*, 15th Cong., 2d Sess. (1819), vol. XXXIV, p. 2527.

B*e it enacted, etc.*, That, for the purpose of providing against the further decline and final extinction of the Indian tribes, adjoining to the frontier settlements of the United States, and for introducing among them the habits and arts of civilization, the President of the United States shall be, and he is hereby, authorized, in every case where he shall judge improvement in the habits and condition of such

THE
MINORITIES

1723

Indians practicable, and that the means of instruction can be introduced with their own consent, to employ capable persons, of good moral character, to instruct them in the mode of agriculture suited to their situation; and for teaching their children in reading, writing, and arithmetic, and for performing such other duties as may be enjoined, according to such instructions and rules as the President may give and prescribe for the regulation of their conduct, in the discharge of their duties.

And be it further enacted, That the annual sum of ten thousand dollars be, and the same is hereby, appropriated, for the purpose of carrying into effect the provisions of this act; and an account of the expenditure of the money, and proceedings, in execution of the foregoing provisions, shall be laid annually before Congress.

THE WAR DEPARTMENT INVITES THE COOPERATION OF "BENEVOLENT ASSOCIATIONS" IN CIVILIZING THE INDIANS

(1819)   From *The Works of John C. Calhoun* (New York, 1883), vol. V, p. 71.

Sir,—In order to render the sum of $10,000, annually appropriated at the last session of Congress for the civilization of the Indians, as extensively beneficial as possible, the President is of opinion that it ought to be applied in cooperation with the exertions of benevolent associations, or individuals, who may choose to devote their time or means to effect the object contemplated by the act of Congress. But it will be indispensable, in order to apply any portion of the sum appropriated in the manner proposed, that the plan of education, in addition to reading, writing, and arithmetic, should, in the instruction of the boys, extend to the practical knowledge of the mode of agriculture, and of such of the mechanic arts as are suited to the condition of the Indians; and in that of the girls, to spinning, weaving, and sewing. It is also indispensable that the establishment should be fixed within the limits of those Indian nations who border on our settlements. Such associations or individuals who are already actually engaged in educating the Indians, and who may desire the co-operation of the Government, will report to the Department of War, to be laid before the President, the location of the institutions under their superintendence, their funds, the number and kind of teachers, the number of youths of both sexes, the objects which are actually embraced in their plan of education, and the extent of the aid which they require; and such institutions as are formed, but have not gone into actual operation, will report the extent of their funds, the places at which they intend to make their establishments, the whole number of youths of both sexes which they intend to educate, the number and kind of teachers to be employed, the plan of education adopted, and the extent of the aid required.

THE COMMITTEE ON INDIAN AFFAIRS OF THE HOUSE OF
REPRESENTATIVES ON THE CIVILIZATION POLICY (1824)   From *American
State Papers, Indian Affairs* (Washington, 1834), vol. II, pp. 457–59.

The committee have carefully examined the measures which have been adopted for the disbursement of the annual allowance made by this law, and find them very judicious, and such as are best calculated to effectuate the benevolent designs of the Government . . .

From this statement, it will appear that twenty-one schools have been established; all, except three, since the passage of the above law, and principally by the means which it affords. At these schools there are taught more than eight hundred scholars, whose progress in the acquisition of an English education exceeds the most sanguine expectations that had been formed.

Very comfortable school-houses have been erected for the accommodation of the different schools, and, in most cases, convenient dwellings for the teachers.

So far as the committee have been able to ascertain, the plan of education has been very judicious, and no pains seem to have been spared to extend to the Indians the full benefit of the law.

All the schools are increasing; and so urgent is the wish of the Indians to have their children educated, that numerous applications are refused, from the limited means which the schools possess. The time of the children is not wholly devoted to their books while at school; the girls are instructed in such arts as are suited to female industry in civilized life, and the boys are required to devote a part of their time in acquiring a knowledge of husbandry. The advances of males and females in these branches are most satisfactory, and have already had no small influence in inducing their parents to become less fond of an erratic life, and more inclined to have fixed residences, and rely for their support on the cultivation of the ground. Such has been the effect of the above circumstances, combined with some others not more influential, that, at many of the places where schools have been established, the Indians have already constructed comfortable dwellings, and now cultivate farms of considerable extent. They have become the owners of property necessary to agricultural pursuits, and for the conveniences of life.

The committee are aware that very considerable aids have been given by different Christian denominations, all of whom feel a deep interest in the paternal views of the Government. But the committee are well persuaded that, had the Government afforded no pecuniary aid, very few, if any, of the benefits which have been conferred, would have been experienced by the Indians. The annual appropriation of ten thousand dollars has encouraged the benevolent and pious, in many parts of the country, to form associations and collect donations, with the view of aiding the humane purposes of the Government. Hundreds of such associations are now in active operation; and they are much cheered in their exertions by the rapid advances to civilization which the Indians have made.

It requires but little research to convince every candid mind that the prospect of civilizing our Indians was never so promising as at this time. Never were means for the accomplishment of this object so judiciously devised, and so faithfully applied, as provided in the above act, and the auxiliary aids which it has encouraged. It is believed to be an essential part of any plan for Indian civilization, that, with the rudiments of education, the males should be taught the arts of husbandry, and the

THE
MINORITIES

females to perform those domestic duties which peculiarly belong to their stations in civilized life. The attempts which have heretofore been made, many of which have failed, omitted this essential part. Many zealous but enthusiastic persons, who have been most conspicuous in endeavoring to reclaim the Indians, persuaded themselves to believe that, to secure this object, it was only necessary to send missionaries among them to instruct them in the Christian religion. Some of their exertions failed, without producing any salutary effect, because the agents employed were wholly unfitted for the task. Others, though productive of some good effect at first, eventually failed, because to their missionary labors were not added the institutes of education and instruction in agriculture. These are combined in the exertions now making; and, from the good which has been done, the most pleasing anticipations of success are confidently cherished. There are many Indian nations within our boundaries who have experienced no aid from these efforts; being restricted in the means, the benefits are, consequently, limited. But the committee are assured that the continuation of the appropriation, seconded by the liberal and increasing aids which are afforded by voluntary contributions, will gradually, and most effectually, extend the benefits of the law to the remotest tribes who inhabit our extensive domain. This will be a work of time; and, for its accomplishment, great labor and perseverance will be necessary. The progress, however, of this work may be more rapid than any can now venture to anticipate. The instruction and civilization of a few enterprising youths will have an immense influence on the tribes to which they belong. As the means are constantly applied, the numbers reclaimed will increase, and an increase of numbers will insure, in a geometrical proportion, success for the future. It is difficult to say what may not be accomplished under such circumstances. No one will be bold enough to denounce him as a visionary enthusiast, who, under such auspices, will look with great confidence to the entire accomplishment of the object. . . .

[The Indians] understand the motive of the Government, and properly appreciate it. So far as the benefits of this policy are extended, will this feeling be cherished; and it affords the safest guaranty against future wars. To say nothing of the valuable lives which have been lost in the Indian conflicts we have had, how much treasure has been expended in our defence! More money was expended, in protecting the exposed parts of our country from Indian depredations, during the late war, than would be required, if judiciously applied, to secure the great plan of Indian Civilization. . . .

The Indians are not now what they once were. They have partaken of our vices more than our virtues. Such is their condition, at present, that they must be civilized or exterminated; no other alternative exists. He must be worse than savage who can view, with cold indifference, an exterminating policy. All desire their prosperity, and wish to see them brought within the pale of civilization. The means which have been adopted, and of which the law in question is the foundation, seem the most likely to obtain the desired result. They should not, therefore, be abandoned. The passage of this law was called for by many of the people in the most populous and influential sections of our country. Their wishes were made known in language that evinced a deep interest—an interest not produced by a momentary excitement, but the result of much reflection and a high sense of moral duty. It may be said, emphatically, that the passage of this law was called for by a religious community. They were convinced of the correctness of the policy in a political point of view, and, as Christians, they felt the full force of the obligations which duty enjoined. Their zeal was tempered by reason. No fanciful schemes of proselytism seem to have been indulged. They formed a correct estimate of the importance of their undertaking, and pointed to the most judicious means for the accomplishment of their wishes. Since the passage of the law, hundreds and thousands have been encouraged to contribute their mite in aid of the wise policy of the Government. However the various denominations of professing Christians may differ in their creeds and general doctrines, they all unite in their wishes that our Indians may become civilized. That this feeling almost universally prevails, has been declared in language too unequivocal to admit of doubt. It has been seen in their words and in their actions.

Establishments for civilizing the Indians

Stations	Sponsor	Year	Scholars	Annual tuition from U.S.	Missionary families	Total expense, 1833
School at Cornwall, Conn.	Am. Board of Foreign Missions, Boston	1817	35	$1,438	—	—
Brainard, Cherokee nation, Tenn.	Am. Board of Foreign Missions, Boston	1817	84	1,200	42	$ 7,632
Elliot, Choctaw nation	Am. Board of Foreign Missions, Boston	1818	80	1,200	12	9,735
Newell, Choctaw nation	Am. Board of Foreign Missions, Boston	1821	15	350	—	668
Mayhew, Choctaw nation	Am. Board of Foreign Missions, Boston	1822	66	800	10	15,706
Dwight, Cherokees, Ark.	Am. Board of Foreign Missions, Boston	1820	50	600	9	6,241
Ft. Wayne, Ind. and Mich.	Baptist General Convention	1820	40	200	10	3,000
Valley Towns, Cherokees, Tenn.	Baptist General Convention	1820	50	500	26	3,000
Tensawattee, Cherokees, Tenn.	Baptist General Convention	1821	25	250	—	—
Withington, Creek nation	Baptist General Convention	1823	40	600	7	3,000
Oneida nation	Hamilton Baptist Missionary Society	1820	24	500	—	—
Tuscarora nation, N.Y.	United Foreign Missionary Society, N.Y.	1819	45	450	—	—
Seneca nation, N.Y.	United Foreign Missionary Society, N.Y.	1820	31	450	6	2,451
Union, Osages, Ark.	United Foreign Missionary Society, N.Y.	1822	12	250	30	6,700
Harmony, Osages, Mo.	United Foreign Missionary Society, N.Y.	1821	17	250	41	4,680
Wyandots, near Upper Sandusky	Methodist Ohio Conference	1801	60	500	—	1,950
Spring Place, Cherokees, Tenn.	United Brethren	1821	20	300	—	744
Monroe, Chickasaw nation	Synod of S.C. and Ga.	1822	54	500	12	2,675
Charity Hall, Chickasaw nation	Cumberland Missionary Society	1823	21	400	—	608
Ottawa, Miami of the Lake	Western Missionary Society	1823	—	300	21	—
Florissant, Mo.	Catholic Bishop of New Orleans	1823	—	800	—	—

. . . They are taught the first rudiments of education, the duties which appertain a man as a member of civil society, and his accountability as a moral agent. Repeal this law, and these exertions are not only paralyzed, but destroyed. The Indians will see, in such an act, that we feel less for their prosperity than our professions have encouraged them to believe; and such an impression cannot fail to produce the most injurious consequences.

From the various lights in which the committee have viewed the policy of this law, they are convinced that it was founded in justice, and should not be repealed. They therefore submit to the House the following resolution: *Resolved,* That it is inexpedient to repeal the law making an annual appropriation of ten thousand dollars for the civilization of the Indians.

INSTRUCTIONS TO THE SUPERINTENDENT OF THE CHOCTAW ACADEMY (1825)
From U. S. Congress, House, Exec. Doc. 109, *Choctaw Treaty,* 26 Cong., 2 Sess. (Washington, 1841), pp. 23-24.

Dear Sir: You have probably received information that, by the board of managers of the Baptist General Convention, you have been unanimously elected instructor and superintendent of the Choctaw Academy, recently located in your vicinity. I am directed, in behalf of the said board of managers, to present to you an outline of the instructions which they conceive may contribute to the improvement of the Indian youth, to your own comfort and usefulness, and to the consequent prosperity of the whole concern. The board wish you, once in each week (on a Monday or Saturday, as you may find convenient) to review the conduct of the youth, and to offer to them such expressions of approbation or censure as their conduct shall appear to deserve; prohibiting them entirely from the use of ardent spirits, which has, in so many lamentable instances, brought destruction to the health and character of individuals and settlements. They recommend your offering to them frequent and affectionate lectures upon the advantages of temperance, mutual good will, respect for their parents, and upon all other topics which an exalted morality can embrace, especially upon the truth and excellency of the Christian religion, and on the happiness of those who welcome its doctrines, observe its precepts, and live under its blessed influence. It is the desire of the board, and they hereby urge the duty of enjoining a strict observance of the Lord's Day, restraining the pupils from all practices which tend to demoralize the mind, and to produce indifference as to the Divine institutions; to which ends, the requiring of a regular attendance upon the public worship of God on that holy day will be found indispensable.

Convinced of its importance to the success of the institution, the board wishes you to visit the children frequently at their respective dwellings, by night and by day, to prevent any disorders which might arise, and to direct them as to the proper employment of their time; to facilitate which, they request you to see that the buildings be conveniently situated, and sufficiently contiguous to each other. It is wished that you ever exercise especial care in observing that the children are comfortably located, and amply supplied with every thing necessary for their welfare; and, particularly, not to suffer them to be interrupted from their studies by manual labor, excepting making their own fires, and performing such services as may be found necessary to their health, recreation, and improvement. You will consider yourself authorized to receive white children into the school, provided their number shall not exceed that of the Indians, and provided, also, that they shall be subject to the same rules, and be placed in every respect on an equality with them.

THE SUPERINTENDENT OF THE CHOCTAW ACADEMY RECOMMENDS VOCATIONAL EDUCATION FOR INDIAN YOUTH (1832)

Letter from Thomas Henderson to Lewis Cass, in U.S. Congress, House, Exec. Doc. 109, *Choctaw Treaty*, 26 Cong., 2 Sess. (Washington, 1941), pp 66–67.

Dear Sir: I have had it in contemplation for several years, to suggest to the honorable Secretary of War the probable advantage that might result to this institution by having attached to the establishment, at some convenient distance from the academy, a few workshops, embracing the most useful and necessary mechanical arts for the promotion of civilized life: say a blacksmith, shoemaker, and wheelright who understood stocking ploughs; or any other which would seem best calculated to suit the present condition of the Indians.

I have been led to these reflections partly from the nature of the case, as it has been presented to my own mind, and partly from having had some boys in the school whose minds appeared to be turned more upon some kind of work than upon their books; and also from the discovery of a considerable mechanical genius among them, together with a desire, manifested by some of the youths themselves, to become mechanics.

It is very certain (were it even practicable to make good scholars of every youth sent to the institution) that, by their education alone, they cannot all hope to get employment, and be supported in the nation, in its present uncultivated condition; and it is equally certain, that nothing will tend more rapidly to promote civilized habits among that unfortunate race of people (in addition to even a moderate English education) than the encouragement of the mechanical arts. Every person is well apprized that it is not every sprightly boy among our white children that is calculated to become a scholar; and although the progress of students in this school has generally far exceeded our most sanguine expectations, yet, while some take learning kindly, manifesting quite a taste for literary attainments, others, like our own children, discover a different turn of mind.

In such cases, it does appear to me that much more good would result to the different tribes by making mechanics of such youths as either cannot or will not take learning freely, and I would not deprive even the most sprightly from the opportunity of acquiring some mechanical art, when it was desired by them. The more I reflect on this subject the more of its benefits, I think, I have been able to discover; and all to whom I have communicated my views have concurred in opinion with me, that, in addition to an education, nothing could possibly be introduced of more real advantage to the Indians than to have their children instructed in some active employment, by which they will be able to support themselves in future life, and benefit their tribes.

My plan would be to erect shops near to the academy, and have professional mechanics entirely under the direction and control of the superintendent of the institution, so that their whole time should be devoted exclusively in learning the boys the respective arts of each trade. I think, by proper management, the greater part of the students, in nearly the same time now devoted at school, would be sent home with good trades, and a sufficient education for mechanics and farmers. Let such as discover a genius and talent for education be permitted to pursue a regular course to the full extent.

THE MINORITIES

1729

PRESIDENT ANDREW JACKSON'S PLAN FOR REMOVAL OF SOUTHERN
INDIANS (1835) From Fred L. Israel, ed., *The State of the Union Messages of the Presidents, 1790–1966* (New York, 1966), vol. I, pp. 438–40.

The plan of removing the aboriginal people who yet remain within the settled portions of the United States to the country west of the Mississippi River approaches its consummation. It was adopted on the most mature consideration of the condition of this race, and ought to be persisted in till the object is accomplished, and prosecuted with as much vigor as a just regard to their circumstances will permit, and as fast as their consent can be obtained. All preceding experiments for the improvement of the Indians have failed. It seems now to be an established fact that they can not live in contact with a civilized community and prosper. Ages of fruitless endeavors have at length brought us to a knowledge of this principle of intercommunication with them. The past we can not recall, but the future we can provide for. Independently of the treaty stipulations into which we have entered with the various tribes for the usufructuary rights they have ceded to us, no one can doubt the moral duty of the Government of the United States to protect and if possible to preserve and perpetuate the scattered remnants of this race which are left within our borders. In the discharge of this duty an extensive region in the West has been assigned for their permanent residence. It has been divided into districts and allotted among them. Many have already removed and others are preparing to go, and with the exception of two small bands living in Ohio and Indiana, not exceeding 1,500 persons, and of the Cherokees, all the tribes on the east side of the Mississippi, and extending from Lake Michigan to Florida, have entered into engagements which will lead to their transplantation.

The plan for their removal and reestablishment is founded upon the knowledge we have gained of their character and habits, and has been dictated by a spirit of englarged liberality. A territory exceeding in extent that relinquished has been granted to each tribe. Of its climate, fertility, and capacity to support an Indian population the representations are highly favorable. To these districts the Indians are removed at the expense of the United States, and with certain supplies of clothing, arms, ammunition, and other indispensable articles; they are also furnished gratuitously with provisions for the period of a year after their arrival at their new homes. In that time, from the nature of the country and of the products raised by them, they can subsist themselves by agricultural labor, if they choose to resort to that mode of life; if they do not they are upon the skirts of the great prairies, where countless herds of buffalo roam, and a short time suffices to adapt their own habits to the changes which a change of the animals destined for their food may require. Ample arrangements have also been made for the support of schools; in some instances council houses and churches are to be erected, dwellings constructed for the chiefs, and mills for common use. Funds have been set apart for the maintenance of the poor; the most necessary mechanical arts have been introduced, and blacksmiths, gunsmiths, wheelwrights, millwrights, etc., are supported among them. Steel and iron, and sometimes salt, are purchased for them, and plows and other farming utensils, domestic animals, looms, spinning wheels, cards, etc., are presented to them. And besides these beneficial arrangements, annuities are in all cases paid, amounting in some instances to more than $30 for each individual of the tribe, and in all cases sufficiently great, if justly divided and prudently expended, to enable them, in addition to their own exertions, to live comfortably. And as a stimulus for exertion, it is now provided by law that "in all cases of the appointment of interpreters or other persons employed for the benefit of the Indians a preference shall be given to persons of Indian descent, if such can be found who are properly qualified for the discharge of the duties."

Such are the arrangements for the physical comfort and for the moral improvement of the Indians. The necessary measures for their political advancement and for their separation from our citizens have not been neglected. The pledge of the United States has been given by Congress that the country destined for the residence of this people shall be forever "secured and guaranteed to them." A country west of Missouri and Arkansas has been assigned to them, into which the white settlements are not to be pushed. No political communities can be formed in that extensive region, except those which are established by the Indians themselves or by the United States for them and with their concurrence. A barrier has thus been raised for their protection against the encroachment of our citizens, and guarding the Indians as far as possible from those evils which have brought them to their present condition. Summary authority has been given by law to destroy all ardent spirits found in their country, without waiting the doubtful result and slow process of a legal seizure. I consider the absolute and unconditional interdiction of this article among these people as the first and great step in their melioration. Halfway measures will answer no purpose. These can not successfully contend against the cupidity of the seller and the overpowering appetite of the buyer. And the destructive effects of the traffic are marked in every page of the history of our Indian intercourse.

JESUIT MISSIONARY DESCRIBES HOW PLAINS INDIANS EDUCATE THEIR YOUNG (1851)

From Hiram M. Chittenden and Alfred T. Richardson, eds., *Life, Letters and Travels of Father Pierre-Jean De Smet* (New York, 1905). vol. III, pp. 1006–7.

You expect, no doubt, that I will tell you something about the savages of America. Here is how they stand in regard to education, which I know is a matter that interests you. The only school in which the Indian youth learn to form their head and heart, is the example of their elders. They give them no preceptors. In the family, the father has charge of the boys, the mother of the girls, and the old proverb, "like father like son," applies more strictly among the Indians than anywhere else. In general, great attention is paid to the physical development of the children and they are prepared from their tenderest infancy for the hardest kind of life. As soon as the child is born, in whatever season, regardless of the severest cold or the greatest heat, they at once plunge it several times into the water. Then, suitably wrapped up, it is placed and entrusted in the hands of some other nurse than its mother. After the first week the parents take it back, and it is put into the cradle, or *berceau*—a machine that deserves to be patented, and which the little individual does not leave until he is able to walk. This is the simple construction of it—a small hide-covered board, about a foot longer than its little occupant. The child is placed upon it and tied tightly with bandages, beginning with the legs and covering it to the shoulders; they are made tightest about the loins and the pit of the stomach, in order to force out the chest as much as possible. Neatly arranged in this style, the little party occupies a place in the lodge, out of harm's way. When the weather is fine, he is set in the doorway of the lodge. If the nurse goes away, she hangs the cradle to the branch of a tree, where the baby warms himself tranquilly in the sun, or on hot days is in the shade, and is in no danger from dogs, wolves or snakes, which are often plentiful in the neighborhood. When they travel, the cradle is hung from the saddle-bow, where it is out of the rider's way and offers no danger to the little prisoner.

After he has learned to walk, and up to the time when he can provide for his own subsistence, he remains attached to his parents' lodge, doing no hard work. At about the age of twelve, he begins to take care of his father's band of horses, and to handle the bow or fire-arms in the chase. At sixteen or eighteen he is invested with the honors and responsibilities of the warrior; he shares the labors and takes part in all the amusements of the village elders. The girls enjoy no such liberty as do the boys. They are early made to help their mother in all her labors; they cut and bring in firewood, help prepare the food, which is no small matter among the Indians, who often dine six or eight times a day; mend and make shoes and garments, with a very great number of etceteras, and when a girl is of age, her father sells her for a horse or two and she becomes the slave of a man to whom very likely she may never have spoken.

A TREATY MADE WITH THE INDIANS (1851)   From Robert H. Heizer and Alan F. Almquist, *The Other Californians* (Berkeley, Cal., 1971), pp. 221–223.

(J.) Treaty Made and Concluded at the Fork of the Cosumnes River, September 18, 1851, Between O. M. Wozencraft, United States Indian Agent, and the Chiefs, Captains, and Head Men of the Cu-Lu, Yas-si, Etc., Tribes of Indians

A treaty of peace and friendship made and concluded at the fork of Cosumnes river, between the United States Indian Agent, O. M. Wozencraft, of the one part, and the chiefs, captains, and head men of the following tribes, viz: Cu-lu, Yas-si, Loc-lum-ne, and Wo-pum-nes.

Article 1. The several tribes or bands above mentioned do acknowledge the United States to be the sole and absolute sovereign of all the soil and territory ceded to them by a treaty of peace between them and the republic of Mexico.

Art. 2. The said tribes or bands acknowledge themselves jointly and severally under the exclusive jurisdiction, authority and protection of the United States and hereby bind themselves hereafter to refrain from the commission of all acts of hostility and agression towards the government or citizens thereof, and to live on terms of peace and friendship among themselves and with all other Indian tribes which are now or may come under the protection of the United States; and furthermore bind themselves to conform to, and be governed by the laws and regulations of the Indian Bureau, made and provided therefor by the Congress of the United States.

Art. 3. To promote the settlement and improvement of said tribes or bands, it is hereby stipulated and agreed that the following district of country in the State of California shall be and is hereby set apart forever for the sole use and occupancy of the aforesaid tribes of Indians, to wit: commencing at a point on the Cosumnes river, on the western line of the county, running south on and by said line to its terminus, running east on said line twenty-five miles, thence north to the middle fork of the Cosumnes river, down said stream to the place of beginning; to have and to hold the said district of country for the sole use and occupancy of said Indian tribes forever. *Provided,* That there is reserved to the government of the United States the right of way over any portion of said territory, and the right to establish and maintain any military post or posts, public buildings, school-houses, houses for agents, teachers, and such others as they may deem necessary for their use or the protection of the Indians. The said tribes or bands, and each of them, hereby engage that they will never claim any other lands within the boundaries of the United States, nor ever disturb the people of the United States in the free use and enjoyment thereof.

Art. 4. To aid the said tribes or bands in their subsistence, while removing to and making their settlement upon the said reservation, the United States, in addition to the few presents made them at this council, will furnish them, free of charge, with five hundred (500) head of beef cattle, to average in weight five hundred (500) pounds, two hundred (200) sacks of flour, one hundred (100) pounds each, within the term of two years from the date of this treaty.

Art. 5. As early as convenient after the ratification of this treaty by the President and Senate, in consideration of the premises, and with a sincere desire to encourage said tribes in acquiring the arts and habits of civilized life, the United States will also furnish them with the following articles, to be divided among them by the agent, according to their respective numbers and wants, during each of the two years succeeding the said ratification, viz: one pair of strong pantaloons and one red flannel shirt for each man and boy, one linsey gown for each woman and girl, four thousand yards of calico and one thousand yards brown sheeting, forty pounds Scotch thread, two dozen pairs of scissors, eight dozen thimbles, three thousand needles, one two and a half point Mackinaw blanket for each man and woman over fifteen (15) years of age, four thousand pounds of iron and four thousand pounds of steel, and in like manner in the first year, for the permanent use of the said tribes, and as their joint property, viz: seventy-five brood mares and three stallions, three hundred milch cows and eighteen bulls, twelve yoke of work cattle with yokes and chains, twelve work mules or horses, twenty-five ploughs, assorted sizes, two hundred garden or corn hoes, eighty spades, twelve grindstones. Of the stock enumerated above, and the product thereof, no part or portion shall be killed, exchanged,sold, or otherwise parted with, without the consent and direction of the agent.

Art. 6. The United States will also employ and settle among said tribes, at or near their towns or settlements, one practical farmer, who shall superintend all agricultural operations, with two assistants, men of practical knowledge and industrious habits, one carpenter, one wheelwright, one blacksmith, one principal school-teacher, and as many assistant teachers as the President may deem proper to instruct said tribes in reading, writing, &c., and in the domestic arts, upon the manual labor system; all the abovenamed workmen and teachers to be maintained and paid by the United States for the period five years, and as long thereafter as the

President shall deem advisable. The United States will also erect suitable school-houses, shops, and dwellings, for the accommodation of the school teachers and mechanics above specified, and for the protection of the public property.

In testimony whereof, the parties have hereunto signed their names and affixed their seals this eighteenth day of September, in the year of our Lord one thousand eight hundred and fifty-one.

O. M. WOZENCRAFT
United States Indian Agent

For and in behalf of the Cu-lu
    MI-ON-QUISH, his X mark   [SEAL]

For and in behalf of the Yas-si
    SAN-TEA-GO, his X mark   [SEAL]

For and in behalf of the Loc-lum-ne
    POL-TUCK, his X mark   [SEAL]

For and in behalf of the Wo-pum-nes
    HIN-COY-E, his X mark   [SEAL]
    MAT-TAS, his X mark   [SEAL]
    HOL-LOH, his X mark   [SEAL]
    BOY-ER, his X mark   [SEAL]

Signed, sealed and delivered, after being fully explained, in presence of
FLAVEL BELCHER
J. B. MCKINNIE
WILLIAM RHOAD

A REPORT ON BOARDING SCHOOLS FOR INDIANS IN OREGON

(**1867**)   From J. R. Doolittle. *Condition of the Indian Tribes, Report of the Joint Special Committee with Appendix* (Washington, 1867), pp. 3–4.

The schools, provided for at both the Siletz and Grande Ronde, seem to result in but little, if any, practical benefit to the Indians, and this remark applies with equal force to all of the tribes, with two or three exceptions, that I have visited.

There is usually incorporated in Indian treaties a provision that a teacher shall be employed and paid by the government; then follows inadequate appropriations for his services, with, occasionally, some slight provision for school books, and here the government terminates its efforts at educating the Indians, without taking into consideration the fact that a poorly paid teacher and a small supply of books furnish but inadequate means for educational purposes. The consequence is, that there is an occasional spasmodic effort made, when some ill adapted and empty building can be obtained for the purpose, in which to teach a few young Indians the alphabet, and usually before that feat is accomplished the teacher leaves, disgusted with the inadequacy of his compensation, or the appropriations become exhausted, and the school is discontinued, to be resumed again at an interval sufficiently remote to give the pupils ample time to forget the lessons but imperfectly learned under the former teacher.

An institution conducted upon such a plan among white people would seldom become famous for its educational advantages. All experience has demonstrated the impossibility of educating Indian children while they are permitted to consort and associate with their ignorant, barbarous, and superstitious parents. It is admitted by all teachers who have ever made the experiment, that the vicious home influences of the Indian lodge or wigwam during the recess of school hours are more than sufficient to counterbalance and destroy all that is taught to the pupil during the period allotted to study.

The only Indian schools which have attained to any degree of success are those where the means have been supplied to feed, clothe, and lodge the children separate and apart from their parents and members of their tribes. Where the Indian youth is left to the alternate struggle between civilization and barbarism the contest is likely to culminate on the side of his savage instincts. To provide for a school for the education of savages in the usual manner which we have adopted is not only a waste of funds, but a mockery.

Where the government has entered into treaty stipulations for the support of Indian schools, it should redeem the pledge by procuring suitable buildings for the purposes of the school remote from the tribe and its influences. It should board, lodge, and clothe the pupils, and employ suitable persons to instruct them in not only what is taught in books, but in other things pertaining to civilization. When this is done, the Indian who parts with his land under the impression that his offspring is to receive an instalment of civilization and intelligence in return, will not be defrauded by a humbug too transparent to deceive any one except a savage. If it is thought that it will require too great an outlay of money to comply in this manner with our treaty stipulations, it would be better to abolish the farce of our annual meagre appropriations for Indian schools, as, under the present system, the most of those appropriations are wasted without doing the Indians or any one else any good.

GENERAL CONDITION OF EDUCATION AMONG THE INDIANS

(1870)   From *U.S. Bureau of Education, Annual Report of the Commissioner of Education For The Year 1870* (Washington D.C., 1875), pp. 339–42.

The Indian tribes and bands resident within the United States are directly under control of the General Government. Its authority over these scattered communities, within the limits which the policy so long followed in relation to them has assigned, is complete. The General Government is the protector and guardian of this race. They are regarded as its "wards." At least such is the theory. In the progress of the nation changes are rendered necessary in the application of this theory. Learning our duties more clearly through the terrible events of the past decade, we are realizing the mistakes that have been made, as well as the obligations resting upon us.

Nothing seems more settled, as a question of national policy, than the obliteration of such distinctions as excluded from the privileges of citizenship a large body of the people on account of color. How soon the Indian shall become a citizen is a question for others to consider. But the conclusion is inevitable. Either citizenship or extinction seems to be the Indian's destiny.

What, then, is our duty? Clearly to prepare them for an intelligent acceptance of the position. We should be incited to a systematic effort for the education of the Indians in our midst, not alone from a realization of the fact that experience has dearly taught that it is cheaper by far to feed and teach than to fight and slay, but from the higher motive of fitly preparing them for the duties of citizenship. Individual ignorance is a curse. That of communities is a degradation to the people who permit its continuance. We have faced that issue so far as the negro is concerned, recognizing that the millions spent under the supervision of the Freedmen's Bureau have been well invested in preparing the freed people for the citizenship they now so honorably enjoy. The returns it brings are already recognized in the form of permanent peace and national integrity, as well as in moral progress, social order, and material benefit resulting from the stability intelligence gives to general prosperity.

Another problem is before us in this question of Indian education, more difficult in some respects than that which we have partially solved, which lies partially in the character of the people with whom we must deal, but far more in their isolation, peculiar situation, and the system under which they now live. To properly comprehend these difficulties it is necessary to ascertain the facts that bear upon them. In this spirit a careful summary of the reports made to the Commissioner of Indian Affairs, so far as they relate to the question of education, will aid the formation of intelligent judgment. The report for 1869 is our authority in ascertaining not only the wants of the Indians but their own desires, in regard to education. Grouping the various superintendences into geographical divisions for a more convenient presentation of the facts, the first examined will be—

The Indians of the Pacific Coast

In the Territory of Washington the Indians number about 22,000, distributed among more than twenty tribes. Of these only four agencies report schools as in operation. The superintendents uniformly report steady progress by the tribes under the influence of these schools, and the missions attached thereto. In each case there is complaint, however, that their usefulness is impaired through the reduction of appropriations for their maintenance. The character of the Indians at agencies where schools exist is declared to be improving. They are deeply interested in the cause of education. Of the Indians on reservations where no such influences exist, the reports are bad. They are described as lazy and debauched.

The school building on the Chehalis reservation has not been completed for want of funds. Generally it is stated that owing to the inadequate appropriations "some of the schools have suspended, and others have failed to accomplish the good expected of them."

Oregon has an Indian population of about 11,700 souls. Of these all but about 1,200 are located on reservations and under charge of the officers of the Indian

Bureau. There are six schools reported. That for the Umatilla agency as having "a measurable degree of success." The Warm Spring agency asks for another school, the children living too far off to attend the only one in existence. At the Grande Ronde agency there are two schools, one being a manual-labor institution. Only one was in operation, however, "for want of means to carry on both successfully at the same time." The manual-labor school at the Siletz agency has been converted into a day school, "which has had but indifferent success." At the Alsea sub-agency no school is in existence, while at that of Klamath one has recently been established. The testimony is generally in favor of the Indians' desire for education and of the rapid improvement of the children where schools are established.

In California the Indians are variously estimated at from 20,000 to 30,000 souls. Their condition appears to be deplorable. There is no attempt at education, except as far as the Catholic mission efforts are maintained. The Spanish policy, which was also that of Mexico, regarded the Indians as possessing no usufructuary or other rights. It was the policy of conquest, and resulted first in the enslavement and then in the merging of the races. Treaties were, however, made with these Indians by United States commissioners, which were rejected by the Senate on the grounds above stated. Reservations have, however, been selected and most of the tribes gathered thereon. The utter neglect of all school facilities is disgraceful.

Nevada reports about 14,000 Indians, who are generally peaceable. Nothing is said as to education among them. Congress has made appropriations for schools and teachers.

Arizona and New Mexico Indians

Within these Territories the tribes most difficult to civilize or even to keep peaceable are to be found. The Apaches are worse than Ishmaelites; their hand is against every man, but they fail to have the redeeming virtue of hospitality, which is a characteristic of their Bedouin prototype. Yet even the Apaches are not entirely given up by some who have had an opportunity to study them closely. It is estimated that in Arizona there is an Indian population of about 25,000; of these, Colonel Jones, United States Army, considers 16,000 to be peaceable. Hon. Vincent Collyer, Secretary of the Indian Peace Commission, visited this Territory as well as that of New Mexico, and from his report the following facts are gathered:

The Moquis number about 4,000. They live in villages, cultivate the soil, raise sheep, show evidence of civilization, are supposed to be descended from the Aztec race, and are anxious for the establishment of schools in their midst. They live in towns. The Yumas, Chemehuevis, New River, Cocopas, Mohaves, Pimos, Maricopas, and Papagos, are all peaceable tribes, generally devoted to agriculture and stock raising. Like the Moquis, the principal tribes, as the Pimos, desire the establishment of schools and also to be taught the mechanical and industrial arts. Some of the Apache bands are desirous of peace, while with others war will continue, in all probability, until they are exterminated. The most valuable fact with regard to Arizona is the existence of the Moquis and Pimo tribes, with several smaller ones of similar character, to whose facility for acquiring a better civilization and general intelligence every one bears ready witness. The shameful neglect as to education which has hitherto characterized our conduct toward their brethren, the Pueblo Indians of the adjacent Territory, should not be repeated here.

The New Mexico Indians are estimated by the superintendent to number 19,000. Of these, 7,000 are Pueblos. The remainder are Apaches, Utes, and Navajoes. The educational condition of the Indians is on the same footing as the whites. It is summed up in a few words—there is not a public school in the Territory; while, according to the census of 1860, over eighty per cent. of the population (excluding Indians, village or tribal) were wholly illiterate. There are some private schools and three or four free schools, under the Sisters of Charity; but not one supported by taxation or organized under law. The condition of the Pueblos in this respect is worse than when our Army occupied the Territory, more than twenty years ago. Under a system established three centuries since, by the Emperor Charles the Fifth, these Indians were gathered into villages and taught the arts of industry and civilization. They were instructed by the Catholic clergy, and many of the adults at the time of annexation were able to read in Spanish. This is not true of the children and those now growing up. It is eleven years since (1860) any educational appropriation was made for their benefit.

Lieutenant E. Ford, United States Army, till recently acting as their agent, recommends in his last report to the superintendent, that a suitable and commodious building be provided with garden land attached for the purpose of establishing a manual labor school. He proposes to select boys of from ten to twelve years of age. The children so chosen should, in his opinion, be considered wards of the Government, then "fed, clothed, boarded, and educated at public expense, for the space of at least three years, when they should be returned to their respective pueblos. Each year a similar number should be selected in like manner from each pueblo, and placed in the school, so that there would each year be two boys returned to every pueblo with a good rudimentary knowledge of English and Spanish.

"In connection with the school there should be established a blacksmith and wheelwright shop, each under the control of a competent workman, under the direction of the agent. One or more boys, about eighteen years of age, should be selected as apprentices in each shop each year, and the term of apprenticeship should last two years. After the boys have served their apprenticeship at the agency shops, they should be established each in his respective pueblo, with the necessary tools and materials with which to commence life on his own account.   It will be seen that in a few years each pueblo would be furnished with a competent blacksmith and wheelwright, each self-supporting, who would do the work of their respective pueblos, and who would instruct apprentices, so that the shops at the agency could then be dispensed with.

"The expense of carrying this design, or one similar, into execution would be but trifling in comparison to the benefit the Indians would derive from it. The cost of feeding the Navajoes alone for one month would be more than ample to erect the buildings and pay the necessary salaries for one year, while the current expenses of the school and workshops would be very small."

Agent Dennison, speaking of the Utes and Apaches over whom he had control, declares it quite practicable to diffuse "among them the knowledge of agricultural and other industrial pursuits." Agent Labode states that the Apaches under his charge, when on the reservation, showed a "desire to have schools and missionaries." Lieutenant Cooper, agent for Pueblo Indians, says that out of 7,000 "not more than one dozen can read or write." He asks the appropriation of $10,000 for school purposes, and says that the Pueblos "are very anxious for schools." Lieutenant Ford says that "they absolutely *crave* education." The Indians of New Mexico demand immediate care in this particular.

Superintendent Hunt, writes of the Utes in Colorado, that no schools have been established among them. Lieutenant Speer, agent for Uncomparge Utes, says that "many of the chiefs have expressed a willingness for their children to be taught in the schools," and he (the agent) believes the establishment of a school would be of great service. Governor McCook, reporting a visit to certain bands of the Utes, says "that the chiefs all promised to send their children to school." From the Territory of Wyoming no word comes of schools. The Indians are charged with being disorderly and treacherous. In Idaho, the most advanced tribe is the Nez Percés. Their agent says that the "school progressed finely," "the children improved more rapidly than was expected." Some came fifty miles to school. Small-pox breaking out, it was closed until April 1869, when it was resumed with more scholars than before. The school superintendent says: "The Indians seemed very much pleased at the prospect of having a school." Of the Bannacks, Shoshones, and Boise Indians, their agent says: "There is quite a desire among them to cultivate the soil.   They also manifest a great interest in having their children sent to school and educated. No schools have as yet (1869) been established."

In Montana, the superintendent, General Sully, whose experience of Indians is almost unequalled, does not give a satisfactory account of those under his charge. The agent of the Flatheads declares, that to the influence of the Catholic missionaries, and the education they have imparted, is to be attributed the peaceful condition of the tribe. The prosperity of the school is chiefly owing to their care. Major Galbraith, United States Army, who was in charge last year, recommends the establishments of an agricultural school. He says the one now in operation had "been as fruitful in its success as could be reasonably expected, considering the little assistance it has received from the Government." Among the Utah Indians, 19,000 in number, it is reported "No schools have ever been established." The tale is brief and sad.

Thus it will be seen that within the four Territories named, having an Indian population of over 55,000, there are but two schools reported, only one of which is in operation, with about 35 scholars.

Indians of Dakota

In this Territory some of the most important results are being worked out. It is the chief home of the warlike Sioux bands, the most powerful Indian nation now in existence. There are nearly or quite 35,000 Indians within its borders. Governor Burbank's report gives a fair insight into both educational and general work. The former, under date of October 1, 1869, was thus summed up: "There is not a school in operation." The Ponca school had been discontinued from bad management and want of sufficient appropriations. No school yet started among the Yanctons, nor at the Crow, Cheyenne, Grand River, and Upper agencies. These Indians are anxious to improve and adopt the habits of the white man; so says the governor. Captain Clifford, at Fort Berthold, says the Arickarees and Mandan Indians "want schools." Captain Poole, at Whetstone agency, thinks that the erection of a school-house and the establishment of a school "would do much toward elevating the morals of the people, and consequently conduce to peace and quiet." Agent Daniels says of the Sisseton Sioux, that

"Our hope for permanent improvement among these Indians must come from the rising generation, as they are willing and desirous of learning work. They should be taught agricultural and mechanical pursuits, as well as to read and write."

Bishop Whipple, of the Protestant Episcopal Church, writes of a visit to the Sioux, of the Sisseton and Wahpeton bands, that they "received me with great demonstrations of gratitude, and manifested a sincere desire to be guided by my advice. At my first council a Christian man said to me, 'For seven years I have prayed to the Great Spirit that he would save us from death. The sky seemed as if it was iron, and I was afraid he would not hear. I look in your face and see we are saved.' I explained to all the Indians the absolute necessity of a change in their mode of life; that it was the determination of their Great Father and the council at Washington that all Indians whom they aided must live as white men, by the cultivation of the soil. In nearly every instance the Indians consented to have their hair cut and at once adopt the habits of civilization. A system of labor was introduced which required that all who were able to work should do so, and be paid for the same out of the goods and provisions purchased for them. The results have far exceeded my warmest expectations."

William Welsh, esq., of the Indian Peace Commission, strengthens the testimony of the good bishop as to the teachability of the Sioux, in the very interesting accounts he has published of visits to the Brulé, Yancton, and Santee Sioux, as well as to the Poncas and Winnesa Chippewas. In his visit to the Yanctons he found them anxious for schools. The head chief, in responding to Mr. Welsh's talk, said, "They all agreed most cordially in an earnest desire to have schools, and also religious instructors." He pertinently added that "it would be wiser to send teachers than to censure men for following the customs of their fathers." The Brulé, Sioux, and the Poncas plead earnestly for instruction; the latter especially, apparently desiring the establishment of a school more, even, than food, though almost in a starving condition. Mr. Welsh asks the aid of this Bureau in cooperating with Indian agents and their helpers, especially as to the preparation of works of instruction, &c. The same request comes from others. There are no means at this Bureau's disposal for such work.

RICHARD PRATT ON THE FOUNDING OF THE CARLISLE INDIAN SCHOOL (1880)

From Richard Henry Pratt, *Battlefield and Classroom: Four Decades with the American Indian, 1867–1904,* Robert M. Utley, ed. (New Haven, 1964), pp. 213–18.

Three months after reaching Hampton with the Missouri River party, I wrote the Secretary of War saying the young Indians were now "accustomed to their new mode of life and interested in educational pursuits"; that, inasmuch as there was an excellent officer who had had Indian experience already detailed at Hampton under the law authorizing an army officer at each agricultural college receiving government allowance, I was no longer necessary to Hampton and thought I might be ordered to my regiment. Mr. McCrary replied by personal note that he had my letter and would give it consideration and inform me later.

During this time General Armstrong and I had many talks, principally at night, when we walked the Hampton grounds sometimes until the midnight hour. I told the General my dissatisfaction with systems to educate the Negro and Indian in exclusively race schools and especially with educating the two races together. Participation in the best things of our civilization through being environed by them was the essential factor for transforming the Indian. The small number of Indians in the United States, then given as 260,000, rendered their problem a very short one. It was surely only necessary to prove that Indians were like other people and could be as easily educated and developed industrially to secure the general adoption of my views. All immigrants were accepted and naturalized into our citizenship by that route and thus had a full fair chance to become assimilated with our people and our industries. Why not the Indian? The Negro was under great prejudice by his change in the South from slavery to freedom under circumstances destructive to the resources and wealth of the Southern people. He numbered thirty times as many as the Indian and was now a citizen. The fitness he had for that high place he had gained by the training he was given during slavery, which made him individual, English speaking, and capable industrially. This was a lesson which in some way should be applied to the Indian. The thing to be overcome in the Indian's case was a fictitious prejudice on both sides. The method we had adopted of driving the Indians away from our communities and from contact with our people and holding them as prisoners on reservations inevitably aroused a great deal of bitterness on their part. That condition was to be overcome and the Indian, as well as the white man, taught that neither was as bad as the other thought. This lesson could never be learned by the Indian or our people through the indurated system of segregating and reservating the Indians and denying them all chances to see and thus to learn and to prove their qualities through competition. Both the white man and the red man must learn the possibilities of the usefulness the Indian could gain through seeing it demonstrated.

General Armstrong was tenacious of racial education. He secured a contingent gift to Hampton of a plantation of 400 acres in the back bay region four miles from Hampton for the purpose of establishing an Indian school to be a branch of Hampton and proposed to place me in charge of it. I went with him and looked the farm over, but without sympathy for the General's purposes. I pointed out that the woods were full of degraded Negros, left there by the army after the war, that the remoteness from the observation of our best people was a fatal drawback, and would still be using Indian education to further the segregating and reservating process, and I could not undertake it. I said: "You have a good army officer and do not need me in connection with any Indian contingent you may undertake at Hampton. Therefore I must insist that I return to my regiment. I have been absent a long time and there is some army discontent about it and it is proper that I should go back and overcome that."

*   *   *

The General took me on several expeditions to New York and New England to raise money for Hampton. On these trips he would take an Indian or two and a colored student or two, as samples and to speak. They aroused new interest in Hampton and the Indians. Hampton was largely sustained by charity. The American Missionary Association, as I remember, gave $10,000 a year, and the state of Virginia allowed $10,000 from the United States Government appropriation on account of agricultural schools, and for the balance needed for its large enrollment

General Armstrong had to depend upon appeals to the northern public, which had been most responsive to the great needs of the former slaves, but that interest was waning.

The papers told that the army appropriation bill carried a clause providing for "the detail of an Army officer not above the rank of Captain with reference to Indian Education." It was introduced by the member of Congress representing the Hampton district. In the short discussion my name was mentioned. This seemed intended to fix by law my stay at Hampton. I plainly told the General that I could not bring myself to become satisfied with such a detail, and he allowed me to go to Washington and talk with the Secretary of the Interior and the Secretary of War about it.

I went first to Mr. Schurz, then Secretary of the Interior, and asked for a private conference. He took me into his little side office and I told him briefly what I was passing through. I said: "You yourself, sir, are one of the very best examples of what we ought to do for the Indians. You immigrated to America as an individual to escape oppression in your own country. You came into fullest freedom in our country. You associated with our people, the best of them, and through these chances you became an American general during the Civil War, then a United States senator, and are now in the President's cabinet, one of the highest offices in the land. It would have been impossible for you to have accomplished your elevation if, when you came to this country, you had been reservated in any of the solid German communities we have permitted to grow up in some sections of America. The Indians need the chances of participation you have had and they will just as easily become useful citizens. They can only reach this prosperous condition through living among our people. If you insist on my remaining in the Indian school work, give me 300 young Indians and a place in one of our best communities and let me prove it is easy to give Indian youth the English language, education, and industries that it is imperative they have in preparation for citizenship. Carlisle Barracks in Pennsylvania has been abandoned for a number of years. It is in a fine agricultural country and the inhabitants are kindly disposed and long free from the universal border prejudice against the Indians."

He listened until I was through and said, "Have you talked to the Indian Commissioner [Ezra A. Hayt]." I said, "No sir, I came directly to you." He said, "Bring the Commissioner here." I went and told the Commissioner the Secretary wanted him. We walked in silence to the Secretary's office. The Secrétary said, "Have you told Mr. Hayt about it?" I said, "No sir." He said, "Tell him what you told me." I repeated to Mr. Hayt. The Secretary then said, "Mr. Commissioner, what do you think of it?" Mr. Hayt said, "We might find money for 100 or 125 students, but we could not find money for 300." The Secretary then said, "Go over to the War Department and tell Secretary McCrary about it, and if he will give Carlisle Barracks for an Indian school, we will establish one immediately and put you in charge."

I went to the War Department. It was then noon. The Secretary had gone to lunch. I went to Adjutant General [E. D.] Townsend. The General and I had had a number of talks about the Indian prisoners being sent to Florida, and he was gratified that he had selected St. Augustine and Fort Marion as the place for their incarceration and defeated the urgency that they be sent to the Dry Tortugas. I told the General my mission from the Secretary of the Interior and he said, "I suggest that you go to Mr. McCrary's house. Here there will be members of Congress and others waiting to see him and you will get a very brief audience." I went to Mr. McCrary's house. The butler showed me into the parlor and said the family was at the luncheon table. I gave my card and said, "Tell the Secretary I am in no hurry." Mr. McCrary came from the dining room with his napkin in his hand and asked, "What is it, Captain?" I said, "I can wait, Mr. Secretary." He said, "I would rather hear you now." I briefly told him of my interview with Mr. Schurz and Mr. Hayt. He at once said: "When I get back to the office I will look it up and if we can turn over Carlisle Barracks for an Indian school, we will do it immediately. If there are legal objections we will ask Congress to remove them. Come around to the Department about two o'clock."

At the time appointed, I was with the Secretary. He informed me that he had submitted the case to the Judge Advocate General, who reported that government property which had been appropriated for and held in one department had never been transferred to another department without a special act of Congress and that it was his judgment that Carlisle Barracks could not be transferred to the Interior Department without a special act.

Mr. McCrary then sent for one of his men and told him he wanted an act drawn to submit to Congress transferring Carlisle Barracks to the Interior Department for an Indian school, and that I would tell him all about it. We went to his room and he soon wrote the proposed law. The Secretary made some alterations and told the clerk to make two copies. I waited in the Secretary's office and in a little while the copies were brought in. The Secretary then said, "Do you know anybody in the House or Senate?" I said: "I do not. I have barely met Senator Pendleton of Ohio. Mrs. Pendleton visited in Florida while I was there and was greatly interested in the Indians, and we became well acquainted." He said: "That is it. We must have this introduced in both the House and Senate; but first you take it to Mr. Schurz and see if he would like to make changes." He kept one of the copies and gave me the other, which I carried to Mr. Schurz. Mr. Schurz was pleased with it, but suggested slight changes. The law had been drawn for Carlisle Barracks only. Mr. Schurz thought it well to insert "Carlisle Barracks or any other vacant military posts or barracks." As drawn, the law proposed "one Army officer to superintend." He thought it should read "one or more Army officers to superintend." With these alterations, I hurried back to the War Department. Secretary McCrary approved of Secretary Schurz' suggestions, called his assistant, and had him make out three copies, one to be retained in the War Department and two to be used in the House and Senate.

In the meantime, he had written a personal note to the Hon. Thad C. Pound, who was a member of the House Indian Committee and had been lieutenant governor of Wisconsin, asking him to introduce the measure in the House. I took the two copies and hurried over to the Capitol and sent in my card to Governor Pound. He came out and I handed him the Secretary's note and the copy of the proposed bill. He said the House was about to adjourn, but he would get it in the next morning. I then hurried over to the Senate and found that the Senate had just adjourned, at which time the Senate floor is open to others than members of the Senate. I went in and was fortunate enough to meet Mr. Pendleton on the floor just as he was about to leave. He gladly listened to what I said, took the proposed law, and said he would introduce it in the Senate in the morning.

I counted this one of the most eventful days of my life. Being ignorant of the methods and ways of legislating in Washington, I was elated to find that things could be so easily and quickly attended to if you only had best help and directions.

Mr. McCrary had asked me to come to see him in the morning. I did so and he said: "There are two things to be attended to. You had better go to Carlisle, look the barracks over, and make me a report of their adaptability and the changes and repairs needed. I will give an order which will pay your expenses, and will ask General Hancock, in whose department Carlisle Barracks is located, and General Sherman, who command the Army, whether the barracks can be spared. They may have plans that need consideration." He gave the order and I went to Carlisle, found the barracks neglected and much out of repair, hunted up a builder, and we itemized the condition of all the buildings and estimated the cost of temporary repairs, and I returned to Washington and made my report.

Secretary McCrary showed me that General Hancock had approved, saying, "I know of no better place to undertake such an experiment," and General Sherman had "Approved, provided both boys and girls are educated in said school," in his own handwriting.

The Secretary then said: "You had better stop here in Washington and help us lobby the bill through. It is getting towards the end of the session, the bill will be well down on the list, and we will have to push hard if we succeed in getting it before Congress this session. You come and see me daily and I will give you notes to members of the House whom I think will take an interest, and see Mr. Schurz and he will tell you how to work on Senate members." The bill had been introduced in both branches as promised. I then began a daily system of explaining the scheme to members of Congress to secure their interest. This was a novel experience. The notes from Mr. McCrary and Mr. Schurz always obtained a prompt conference. These were generally arranged by sending in my card and meeting senators and House members at the Capitol and sometimes making an evening appointment. Some of the members were cordial and interested, and others bluff, even expressing opposition. In a few days Mr. Pound said the bill had been printed, referred back to the Committee for a report, and asked me to write it. He gave me some instructions as to how to word it and I accordingly drew up a report which he submitted to his Committee. It was accepted by the Committee, and the bill with the report went back to the House, and the report was ordered to be printed. The bill was then before the House but was so far down on the list that it seemed unlikely it would be reached that session. Under the directions of the two Secretaries, I continued to see senators and members of the House, and we got some favorable newspaper notices, but somehow the bill could not be brought before the House for its action.

*   *   *

While lobbying one day, Secretary McCrary said: "General Sherman tells me the people of Carlisle are likely to criticize and petition against the Indian school as they did against the Army. What do you say to that?" I said, "A good way to meet that would be to get them to petition for an Indian school." This pleased the Secretary and he said, "Good! You go to Carlisle and get such a petition." I went and on boarding the waiting Cumberland Valley train at Harrisburg found General Biddle, then treasurer of that road, and told him my mission. I had met him on my previous visit and found him friendly to the intended school. He said, "You go back to your work in Washington, and in a few days I will send the Secretary a petition for the school signed by every man and woman in Carlisle." I got off the Carlisle train and returned to Washington and in a few days the Secretary received an ample petition, which pleased him and satisfied General Sherman.

Congress was about to close when, seeing Secretary McCrary one morning, he seemed especially good natured and said: "Captain, I have discovered a way to handle our case. The bill is before both houses of Congress and has a favorable report in the House. I have talked with the Judge Advocate General about it and since the barracks are not in use, and we have the approval of both the General of the Army and General Hancock commanding the department, I have concluded to turn the barracks over to the Interior Department for an Indian school pending the action of Congress on the bill. Your detail for Indian educational duty is already authorized by an act of Congress."

THE FIRST YEAR OF THE CARLISLE INDIAN SCHOOL (1880)   From
Richard H. Pratt, "First Annual Report of the Carlisle School," as quoted in U.S. Bureau of Indian Affairs, *Annual Report of the Commissioner of Indian Affairs, 1880* (Washington, D.C., 1880), pp. 178–81.

TRAINING SCHOOL FOR YOUTH, CARLISLE BARRACKS,
Carlisle, Pa., October 5, 1880.

SIR: I have the honor to transmit the annual report of this school, required by your letter of July 18, 1880.

In order that the whole number of students, tribes, increase and decrease may be understood, I furnish a tabulated statement.

Under your orders of September 6, 1879, I proceeded to Dakota, and brought from the Rosebud and Pine Ridge Agencies 60 boys and 24 girls. This detachment reached Carlisle October 5, 1879. I then went to the Indian Territory, and brought from the Cheyenne, Kiowa, Pawnee, and other tribes, 38 boys and 14 girls, and returned to Carlisle on the 27th of October. On both of these visits I was accompanied by Miss S. A. Mather, of Saint Augustine, Fla., from whom I received valuable assistance in the care and management of the youth.

With the consent of General Armstrong, I had brought from the Hampton Institute 11 of the young men, who were formerly prisoners under my care, in Florida, and had, at that time, been under the care of the Hampton Institute 18 months. These formed a nucleus for the school, and rendered most valuable assistance in the care and management of the large number of new children, most of whom came directly from the camps.

The school opened on the 1st of November, 1879, with 147 students. On the 6th of November we received 6 Sisseton Sioux and 2 Menomonees. On the 28th of February, 1880, 8 Iowa and Sac and Fox children reached us, under the care of Agent Kent. On the 9th of March a Lipan boy and girl were sent to us by order of the War Department. They had been captured three years previous, by the Fourth Cavalry, in Old Mexico. On the 20th of February 11 Ponca and Nez Percés children were received from Inspector Pollock, and on the 1st of April 10 Kiowa, Comanche, and Wichita children were added to those previously received from that agency. July 31, Rev. Sheldon Jackson brought to us 1 Apache and 10 Pueblo children from New Mexico. September 6, Agent John D. Miles brought to us 41 Cheyenne, Arapaho, and Comanche children from his own and the Kiowa Agencies. This aggregated us 239 children in all.

Our losses have been 28 boys and 9 girls, returned to their agencies. Nine of these were of the former Florida prisoners, who being sufficiently advanced to render good service at their agencies as workers and examples to their people, and being rather old, and some of them heads of families, it was considered best to return them to their tribes, and fill up with children, great numbers of whom were anxious to come.

Of the remaining 19 boys and 9 girls returned, Spotted Tail, because of dissatisfaction on account of the non-employment of his son-in-law, carried away 9 of his own children and relations; 4 of the others were allowed to go home with the chiefs for special reasons, and the remaining 15 were returned because of imperfect physical and mental condition. We have lost by death 6 boys, and have heard of the death of 4 of those returned to their agencies. These changes leave us at the date of this report, October 5, with 196 pupils, 139 of whom are boys and 57 girls.

About one-half of these had received instruction at agency schools; the remainder came to us directly from the camps. Two-thirds are the children of chiefs and head men. About 10 per cent. are mixed blood.

The school work is organized into six graded departments, with additional side recitations. In the educational department the instruction is objective, although object-teaching is subordinate to the study of the language. This is the first point, the mastery of the English language. We begin this study and that of reading by the objective word method. The object or thought is presented first, then language given to express the idea. We use script characters first, reading and writing being taught at the same time by the use of the blackboard. Drill in elementary sounds aids in securing correct pronunciation. Spelling is taught only in this way and by writing. Numbers are taught objectively, as far as the knowledge of language will permit, following Grube's method. Geography is taught by oral lessons and by drawing.

For beginners we use no text-books. Keep's First Lessons for the Deaf and Dumb has been serviceable and suggestive for teachers' use. To a limited extent we have followed this method. We use Webb's Model First Reader and Appleton's Second, Keep's Stories, with questions, and in arithmetic Franklin's Primary. Picture-Teaching, by Janet Byrne, is especially adapted to Indian work, but is expensive. We find pictures and objects of great service, furnishing material for sentence-building and conversations.

The progress in our school-room work is most gratifying. It is not too much to say that these Indian children have advanced as well as other children would have done in the same period. They have been especially forward in arithmetic and in writing, and their correspondence with their parents and friends is becoming a source of great interest and satisfaction.

Industrially, it has been our object to give direction and encouragement to each student of sufficient age in some particular branch. To accomplish this, various branches of the mechanic arts have been established, under competent and practical workmen, and a skilled farmer placed in charge of the agricultural department. The boys desiring to learn trades have generally been allowed to choose. Once placed at a trade they are not changed, except for extraordinary reasons. A number of the boys who have passed the age of maturity, and have expressed a desire to become proficient mechanics, are kept continuously at work, and are given the benefits of a night-school; but the general system has been to work at the trades a day and a half or two days each week and attend school the other days.

Under this system we have a blacksmith and wagon-maker with ten apprentices, a carpenter with seven apprentices, a harness-maker with thirteen apprentices, a tinner with four apprentices, a shoemaker with eight apprentices, and a tailor with three apprentices. There are three boys in the printing office, under competent instruction, and two baking bread. The mechanical branches, except the shoemaker and carpenter, were established last April. All boys not under instruction at trades have been required to work, periodically, under the direction of the farmer. The progress, willingness to work, and desire to learn on the part of the boys in their several occupations have been very satisfactory. Being guided and watched by competent mechanics, the quality of the work turned out challenges comparison.

The carpenters have been kept busy in repairing and remodeling, &c., and in constructing the chapel and an addition to our mess-room. The blacksmith and wagon-maker, in addition to fitting up the shops and getting ready for work, has made a number of plows, harrows, and other agricultural implements; has done all our repairing, horse and mule shoeing, and has constructed one carriage and two spring-wagons suitable for agency use. In the harness-shop the boys have developed a special capacity. We have manufactured 55 double sets of wagon harness and 3 single sets of carriage harness.

In the tin-shop we have manufactured 177 dozen of tinware, consisting of buckets, coffee-pots, teapots, pans, foot-baths, oil-cans, and cups; and in addition have repaired our roofs, spouting, &c., to the extent of about a month's work for the instructor and apprentices. In the shoemaker's shop we have been unable, so far, to do much outside of repairing. We have half-soled and otherwise repaired about 800 pairs of shoes. The tailoring department was only established the 15th of August. Already our boys are able to do all the sewing on a pair of trousers very satisfactorily. Two of the boys in the printing office are able to set type and assist in getting off our school paper, printing lessons, &c., and one of them is so far advanced as to edit and print a very small monthly paper, which he calls "The School News," and which has won many friends for the school. Our bakers make good wholesome bread, in quantities sufficient to supply the school. The products of the farm are given in the general statistics. In all these several branches of labor we have found capacity and industry sufficient to warrant the assertion that the Indian, having equal chances. may take his place and meet successfully the issues of competion with his white neighbor.

The girls have been placed under a system of training in the manufacture and mending of garments, the use of the sewing-machine, laundry work, cooking, and the routine of household duties pertaining to their sex. All of the girls' clothing, and most of the boys' underwear and some of the boys' outer garments, have been manufactured in the industrial room, in all of which the girls have taken part and given very satisfactory evidence of their capacity. About twenty-five of the older girls do effective work on the sewing-machine.

At our recent fair here we placed on exhibition samples of the work of all the departments, all of which attracted much favorable comment. The report of the committee appointed to examine and report on the exhibit made by the school is appended hereto.

Under the authority of the department, last spring I sent two boys and one girl to Lee, Mass., where they were placed in the family of Mr. Hyde for the summer months. Arrangements were made for twenty-five others, through Captain Alvord, of Easthampton, Mass. A misunderstanding having arisen with regard to the ages and probable working qualities of the youth to be sent, I did not send this last party. Five girls and sixteen boys were placed in families in this vicinity for different periods during the summer months. The children have generally given satisfaction. The coming year, with a better understanding of the Indian on the part of the whites, and a better understanding of English and increased desire to work on the part of the Indian, there is reason to believe that all the children we may desire to put out during vacation will find places. This plan is an individualizing process most helpful to the work.

The discipline of the school has been maintained without difficulty, and punishments have been called for but infrequently. When offenses have been serious enough to demand corporal punishment, the cases have generally been submitted to a court of the older pupils, and this has proved a most satisfactory method. No trouble has arisen from the coeducation of the sexes; on the contrary, it has marked advantages.

The boys have been organized into companies as soldiers, and the best material selected for sergeants and corporals. They have been uniformed and drilled in many of the movements of army tactics. This has taught them obedience and cleanliness, and given them a better carriage.

A lady friend in Boston gave us a set of brass instruments. Under the direction of a competent instructor, twelve of the boys have in a little over two months learned to play these instruments so as to give us tolerable music for our parades.

There has been no epidemic, and we have had but very few deaths that could not be traced to hereditary causes or chronic affections.

The good people of the town have given us active sympathy and aid, and have welcomed the children to the different Sunday schools and churches. All of the boys have been divided into classes, and regularly attend the different Sunday schools of the town. This has been an inestimable benefit and a great encouragement to teachers and scholars. Several of our older and more intelligent boys have become members of the Presbyterian Church, and in their daily conduct show a proper regard for their profession. The Episcopal Church has baptized and confirmed most of the Sioux children. The Rev. Dr. Wing, of the Presbyterian Church, and Professor Lippincott, of Dickinson College, have been kind enough to give us regular religious services on Sabbath afternoons.

Numerous letters from many parts of the Indian country, and from parents and relations of the children here, and from other Indians, show that there is an awakening among the Indians in favor of education and industrial training for the young.

I have to acknowledge with gratitude the deep interest and liberal support of the department, the hearty and efficient co-operation of teachers and other employes, and the sympathy and kindness of a multitude of friends all over the country, which, with the blessing of God, have rendered this effort so far a success. With great respect, I am your obedient servant,

R. H. PRATT,
First Lieutenant, in charge.

DESCRIPTION OF THE CARLISLE INDIAN SCHOOL (1880) From U.S. Bureau of Education, *The Indian School at Carlisle Barracks* (Washington, D.C., 1880), pp. 3–5.

Sir: In compliance with your instructions to represent this Office on the visit of inspection to the Indian training school at Carlisle Barracks, Pa., on the 21st instant, I left this city on the evening of the 20th for Harrisburg. The Secretary of the

Interior, Mr. Stickney, of the Board of Indian Commissioners, and others of the party took the same train.

Leaving Harrisburg the next morning, after an early breakfast, Carlisle was reached before 9 o'clock. We were met by carriages from the barracks and were at once conveyed thither.

The barracks stand west of the town, on a well drained piece of land belonging to the Government. A piece of arable land adjoining this property will be leased during the approaching spring for use as a school farm and garden and for the training in the care of stock.

The buildings occupy the sides of a grassy square used for parade ground, &c. One row is occupied by the superintendent and his staff, another by the teachers' and female pupils' dormitories, a third by the boys' dormitories. Other buildings conveniently placed are used as chapel, school-house, refectory, infirmary, gymnasium, stable and coach-house, trade schools, &c. There is ample accommodation for double the actual number of pupils.

Lieutenant Pratt has at present under his charge about 110 boys and 44 girls, from several tribes. It was found impossible to obtain as many girls as boys, because the labor of the girls is so useful under the present ideas and social arrangements of the Indians.

A few of the older pupils had received some instruction and training before coming to this school, e. g., in Florida under Lieutenant Pratt, at Hampton Normal School, and in the mission schools at the tribal agencies. More than a hundred of them, however, were last October utterly without any civilized knowledge or training whatever. "They had never been inside of a school or a house," said one of the employes. They were brought to the barracks filthy, vermin covered, and dressed in their native garb. When they were assigned to their sleeping quarters "they lay down on the veranda, on their bellies, and glared out between the palings of the railing like wild beasts between the bars of their cages." The first thing to do was to clean them thoroughly and to dress them in their new attire. Baths are compulsory thrice a week. The vermin have been suppressed, all the more easily because the boys have allowed their hair to be cut in the fashion of white people. Everything except swallowing, walking, and sleeping had to be taught; the care of person, clothing, furniture, the usages of the table, the carriage of the body, civility, all those things which white children usually learn from their childhood by mere imitation, had to be painfully inculcated and strenuously insisted on. In addition to this, they were to be taught the rudiments of an English school course and the practical use of tools.

*　　*　　*

Three and a half months have passed, and the change is astonishing. The present condition of affairs can be told best by resuming the account of the day's work.

On arriving at the barracks a programme of the morning's inspection was handed to those who wished to know what was to be done. This, in a few words, comprised an examination of (a) the schools, (b) the lodgings, (c) the shops, (d) the table, (e) physical exercise, and (f) the infirmary. It is not necessary to say that a mild, kind, firm, but sympathetic Christian influence pervades the whole atmosphere of the place and every part of the management.

We entered one room after another. The first was one in which a number of the younger children were being exercised in the use of a vocabulary and in the formation of English sentences. On the teacher's desk was a large number of small familiar objects, drinking glasses, balls, cups, &c. The children successively were asked to name an object; the teacher phonetized the name into its sound elements and the children repeated it in the same way. Then the teacher placed one object on the top of another and the child made a sentence on the following model: "The cup is on the book."

In another room a class of boys was reciting a lesson in geography. One boy pointed out and named the continents, another the countries in North America, a third the oceans, a fourth the seas of Europe, and so on.

In another room a lesson in arithmetic was going on; a model of a fence afforded opportunities for questions in multiplication, division, &c. This seemed to me somewhat less satisfactory. A class of larger boys, however, wrote down, at the dictation of Secretary Schurz, a long sum in addition, which was solved with satisfactory speed and correctness.

A number of children in another class were employed in making sentences, which they wrote at once on the blackboard. A child would be told to do something; then another would tell what had been done and write what he said. The writing was very fair.

A class in calisthenics was also seen. The scholars went through a variety of motions intended to develop the chest and arms, following the example set by one of the young ladies of the teaching corps.

The Dormitories

We next visited the quarters assigned to the pupils. Each child has a separate cot bedstead with sheets, blankets, and white counterpane. The lavatories were sufficient and in good order. The number of beds in each room on the boys' side was eleven; this may be thought too many for the size of the room (about 20 feet square it seemed to me); but it was explained that these Indians of their own accord sleep with the windows open all night. Indeed, as one of the employés remarked, "They would never shut even a door if it depended on their sensations." Each room is in charge of an older boy, who is squadmaster, and responsible for the behavior of the others and for the care of the bedding and other furniture.

The Shops

We found some of the girls learning how to sew, others cooking, others mending clothes. Some of the boys were cobbling shoes, some were in the carpenter's shop, where a pinewood table was being finished by one pupil, while another was making tongues and grooves on the edges of boards, apparently for the top of another table; a third was working on table and chair legs. Two other boys were at a blacksmith's forge working away industriously. Three of the older boys had been apprenticed to a wagonmaker in Carlisle; one of these is painting wagons, another is making or putting together the parts of wheels and other woodwork; the third devotes his attention to the iron parts. I understood that these young men propose when they return home to pursue wagonmaking in partnership. The pupils are said to learn the

EDUCATION
IN THE
UNITED STATES

1750

use of tools as readily as white children do. There is a master blacksmith, master carpenter, and a shoemaker in the corps of instruction.

Dinner

At half past twelve we went to the refectory, where the pupils' dinner was in progress. The bill of fare for the day was roast beef, sweet and Irish potatoes, tomatoes, and wheat bread. I tasted each, and found it palatably cooked. All except the very smallest children managed their own knives and forks, of course with varying degrees of skill and grace. I thought the girls in general more successful in this than the boys. The supply seemed abundant and the appetites good. The attendance on the table was done by a detail of girls.

Physical Exercise

In addition to the calisthenics already mentioned and to the drill (which the state of the weather did not permit) the boys are supplied with a good sized and sufficiently appointed gymnasium. I think that an instructor in this branch would prove of great use; and that apparatus such as that devised by McLaren for home gymnastics should be introduced into the rooms of the female pupils.

The personal appearance of the pupils is generally satisfactory; there is some coughing, particularly among the boys, but no more than would be heard among an equal number of white boys. Whenever from admixture of blood the skin was pale enough to show the color of the blood, the cheeks were more or less rosy. Most of them are straight; nearly all walk in the usual ungraceful Indian fashion with no divergence of the toes. The teeth of most seemed in good condition.

The Infirmary

There is only one patient at the present time. Those who had not been vaccinated at the agencies were vaccinated on their reception. There have been two deaths since the opening of the school; in both cases the superintendent objected to the admission of these pupils, but was overruled by various considerations.

Items

Secretary Schurz addressed the pupils in the chapel before dinner. Three of the older pupils, who for the day wore their native garb, performed an Indian dance. This was most humorously varied by the assistance of a little half-breed boy who had a ludicrously droll and acute face. This was greeted with great laughter, even the stoical calm of the Indians breaking down at the sight.

One of the visitors made the following suggestive remark, which seemed to summarize Lieutenant Pratt's ideas: "The design seems to be to suppress or eradicate the Indian's instinct for *de*struction by substituting a love of *con*struction by means of the processes of *in*struction."

I hope that arrangements will be made by which a sufficient number of girls can be educated to supply these young men and boys with wives; this point, which you yourself consider so important, is rendered particularly emphatic to me by what my father told me of marriages between Christian men and heathen women in

Hindustan, and also by personal observations among our southern freed people after the late war.

After a delightful lunch, at which Mrs. Pratt presided with great simplicity and kindness, we bade the Indian Training School farewell.

I reached this city at 9 p. m. Saturday, the 21st instant, after an absence of twenty five hours.

I am, sir, very respectfully, your obedient servant,

CHARLES WARREN,
Chief Clerk

Hon. JOHN EATON,
Commissioner of Education.

PRESIDENT CHESTER ARTHUR ON THE INDIAN PROBLEM (1881)   From President Arthur's First Annual Message, December 6, 1881, as quoted in James D. Richardson, ed., *Messages and Papers of the Presidents* (New York, 1911), vol. VIII, pp. 54–57.

Prominent among the matters which challenge the attention of Congress at its present session is the management of our Indian affairs. While this question has been a cause of trouble and embarrassment from the infancy of the Government, it is but recently that any effort has been made for its solution at once serious, determined, consistent, and promising success.

It has been easier to resort to convenient makeshifts for tiding over temporary difficulties than to grapple with the great permanent problem, and accordingly the easier course has almost invariably been pursued.

It was natural, at a time when the national territory seemed almost illimitable and contained many millions of acres far outside the bounds of civilized settlements, that a policy should have been initiated which more than aught else has been the fruitful source of our Indian complications.

I refer, of course, to the policy of dealing with the various Indian tribes as separate nationalities, of relegating them by treaty stipulations to the occupancy of immense reservations in the West, and of encouraging them to live a savage life, undisturbed by any earnest and well-directed efforts to bring them under the influences of civilization.

The unsatisfactory results which have sprung from this policy are becoming apparent to all.

As the white settlements have crowded the borders of the reservations, the Indians, sometimes contentedly and sometimes against their will, have been transferred to other hunting grounds, from which they have again been dislodged whenever their newfound homes have been desired by the adventurous settlers.

These removals and the frontier collisions by which they have often been preceded have led to frequent and disastrous conflicts between the races.

It is profitless to discuss here which of them has been chiefly responsible for the disturbances whose recital occupies so large a space upon the pages of our history.

We have to deal with the appalling fact that though thousands of lives have been sacrificed and hundreds of millions of dollars expended in the attempt to solve the Indian problem, it has until within the past few years seemed scarcely nearer a solution than it was half a century ago. But the Government has of late been cautiously but steadily feeling its way to the adoption of a policy which has already produced gratifying results, and which, in my judgment, is likely, if Congress and the Executive accord in its support, to relieve us ere long from the difficulties which have hitherto beset us.

For the success of the efforts now making to introduce among the Indians the customs and pursuits of civilized life and gradually to absorb them into the mass of our citizens, sharing their rights and holden to their responsibilities, there is imperative need for legislative action.

My suggestions in that regard will be chiefly such as have been already called to the attention of Congress and have received to some extent its consideration.

First. I recommend the passage of an act making the laws of the various States and Territories applicable to the Indian reservations within their borders and extending the laws of the State of Arkansas to the portion of the Indian Territory not occupied by the Five Civilized Tribes.

The Indian should receive the protection of the law. He should be allowed to maintain in court his rights of person and property. He has repeatedly begged for this privilege. Its exercise would be very valuable to him in his progress toward civilization.

Second. Of even greater important is a measure which has been frequently recommended by my predecessors in office, and in furtherance of which several bills have been from time to time introduced in both Houses of Congress. The enactment of a general law permitting the allotment in severalty, to such Indians, at least, as desire it, of a reasonable quantity of land secured to them by patent, and for their own protection made inalienable for twenty or twenty-five years, is demanded for their present welfare and their permanent advancement.

In return for such considerate action on the part of the Government, there is reason to believe that the Indians in large numbers would be persuaded to sever their tribal relations and to engage at once in agricultural pursuits. Many of them realize the fact that their hunting days are over and that it is now for their best interest to conform their manner of life to the new order of things. By no greater inducement than the assurance of permanent title to the soil can they be led to engage in the occupation of tilling it.

The well-attested reports of their increasing interest in husbandry justify the hope and belief that the enactment of such a statute as I recommend would be at once attended with gratifying results. A resort to the allotment system would have a direct and powerful influence in dissolving the tribal bond, which is so prominent a feature of savage life, and which tends so strongly to perpetuate it.

Third. I advise a liberal appropriation for the support of Indian schools, because of my confident belief that such a course is consistent with the wisest economy. . . .

Even among the most uncultivated Indian tribes there is reported to be a general and urgent desire on the part of the chiefs and older members for the education of their children. It is unfortunate, in view of this fact, that during the past year the means which have been at the command of the Interior Department for the purpose of Indian instruction have proved to be utterly inadequate.

The success of the schools which are in operation at Hampton, Carlisle, and Forest Grove should not only encourage a more generous provision for the support of those institutions, but should prompt the establishment of others of a similar character.

They are doubtless much more potent for good than the day schools upon the reservation, as the pupils are altogether separated from the surroundings of savage life and brought into constant contact with civilization.

There are many other phases of this subject which are of great interest, but which cannot be included within the becoming limits of this communication. They are discussed ably in the reports of the Secretary of the Interior and the Commissioner of Indian Affairs.

GOVERNMENT SCHOOLS FOR INDIANS (1881) From U. S. Bureau of Indian Affairs, *Annual Report of the Commissioner of Indian Affairs, 1881* (Washington, D.C., 1881), pp. 32–34.

Schools for Indians are divided into three classes—day-schools and boarding-schools for Indians in the Indian country, and boarding schools in civilized communities remote from Indian reservations. Although varying greatly in the extent and character of their results, each holds its own important place as a factor in Indian civilization.

In many tribes the less expensive and less aggressive day-school prepares the way for the boarding school, and occupies the field while buildings for boarding pupils are being erected and furnished, or while Congress is discussing the desirability of appropriating funds necessary for their construction. It disarms native prejudice and opposition to education, and awakens a desire for the thorough fundamental teaching which the boarding-school gives. The sending of twenty Pueblo children to Carlisle is the direct result of the inroads made by day-schools on the superstition and prejudice of the most conservative tribe on the continent. In more civilized tribes like those in Michigan and California the government day-school supplies the place of the State common school.

Exclusive of those among the five civilized tribes, the day schools during the past year have numbered 106, and have been attended by 4,221 pupils. Two schools have been opened among the Mission Indians, the first ever given these hard-working, much-abused people by either government or State. Three others will open soon. At Pine Ridge day-schools in the various Indian settlements are having a very good influence, pending the erection of the new boarding-school building; and they will be needed after its completion in order to extend to the 1,400 children of the agency who cannot be accommodated therein some small degree of civilizing influence—an influence which will not be confined to the pupils, but will extend to the families in the vicinity of the schools, whose remoteness from the agency renders it specially important that some civilizing force should be exerted in their midst.

Of the 106 schools one is supported by the State of Pennsylvania, and 28 are located in and supported by the State of New York as part of its common-school system. As a result, of the 1,590 Indian children of school age in that State 1,164 have attended school some portion of the past year, and the average daily attendance has been 625. This provision for Indian schools has been made by New York for twenty years, at an annual expense of about $7,000, and last year the New York Indian agent reported that nearly all the Indians in his agency could read and write. For the support of these schools New York does not depend on the uncertainties of a local tax, but gives to her Indians their *pro rata* share of the State school-tax and of the income of the permanent invested fund of the State.

* * *

Were this example followed by other States—Michigan, Minnesota, Wisconsin, Nebraska, North Carolina, and California, for instance—States which have within their borders considerable numbers of Indians who are semi-civilized and practically self-supporting, the status attained by the next generation would attest both the wisdom of the course pursued and its economy. That it is cheaper for a State to educate her lower classes than to allow them to grow up in ignorance and superstition may be considered a truism, but, so far as it related to Indians, the truth of it needs practical acknowledgement in many localities.

Sixty-eight boarding schools have been in operation during the year; an increase of eight over last year. They have been attended by 3,888 pupils. Of the new schools six have been opened at Colorado River, San Carlos, Pima, Pueblo, Siletz, and Uintah Agencies. They will accommodate 351 pupils, and are the first boarding-schools ever provided for the 27,000 Indians of those agencies who represent a school population of not less than 5,000. A second boarding-school has been given the Omahas, who are waking up to the importance of education, and a boarding-school for boys has been established at Cheyenne River, where a mission school for girls has been in successful operation for several years. Delay in the erection of buildings has prevented the opening of the other five schools referred to in last report.

* * *

The interest, aptness, docilty and progress of the pupils is remarked on by their teachers as being fully equal to that of white children. Their acquirements, of course, are much behind those of white children. The first two school years, at least, must be spent mainly in acquiring the English language and the white man's way of living, lessons which the child of civilized parents learns in the nursery, and in these two branches progress is impeded by the reluctance of Indians to use any but their native tongue, and is seriously interrupted by the annual vacation, which returns the children to the old ways of speech, thought, and life. The interest of parents in education continues to increase, and some schools have been overcrowded.

The agency boarding-school is the object lesson for the reservation. The new methods of thought and life there exemplified, while being wrought into the pupils, are watched by those outside. The parents visit the school, and the pupils take back into their homes new habits and ideas gained in the school-room, sewing-room, kitchen, and farm. Though more or less dissipated in the alien atmosphere of a heathen household, these habits and ideas still have an influence for good, real and valuable, though it cannot always be distinctly traced. The agency school takes the pupils as it finds them; the dull and frail have a chance with the quick-witted and robust; and since Indians are much less willing to send away their daughters than their sons, it furnishes the girls of the tribe almost their only opportunity for acquiring a knowledge of books and of home-making.

But so long as the American people now demand that Indians shall become white men within one generation, the Indian child must have other opportunities and come under other influences than reservations can offer. He must be compelled to adopt the English language, must be so placed that attendance at school shall be regular, and that vacations shall not be periods of retrogression, and must breathe the atmosphere of a civilized instead of a barbarous or semi-barbarous community. Therefore, youth chosen for their intelligence, force of character, and soundness of constitution are sent to Carlisle, Hampton, and Forest Grove to acquire the discipline and training which, on their return, shall serve as a leverage for the uplifting of their people.

RULES FOR INDIAN SCHOOLS (1890)   From "Rules for Indian Schools," U.S. Bureau of Indian Affairs, *Annual Report of the Commissioner of Indian Affairs, 1890* (Washington, D.C., 1890), pp. cxlvi, cl–clii.

The importance attached to the subject of Indian education is set forth in the following letter addressed by the honorable the Secretary of the Interior to each newly appointed Indian agent:

"In connection with your appointment as agent at the ――― agency, I am directed by the President to inform you that the office to which you are appointed is considered one of far more than ordinary importance, both for the interests of the Government and of the Indians who will be brought under your charge and direction; that sobriety and integrity must mark the conduct of everyone connected or associated directly or indirectly with the agency under your charge; that an improved condition in the affairs of the agency will be expected within a reasonable time, both as to methods of doing business and as to the condition of the Indians; that the education and proper training of the Indian children and the agricultural and other industrial pursuits of the adult Indians must receive your constant and careful attention, to the end that they may be advanced in the ways of civilization and to the condition of self-support; and that your commission will be held with the express understanding that you will use your utmost endeavors to further these objects and purposes."

The general purpose of the Government is the preparation of Indian youth for assimilation into the national life by such a course of training as will prepare them for the duties and privileges of American citizenship. This involves the training of the hand in useful industries; the development of the mind in independent and self-directing power of thought; the impartation of useful practical knowledge; the culture of the moral nature, and the formation of character. Skill, intelligence, industry, morality, manhood, and womanhood are the ends aimed at.

Government schools for Indians are divided into five general classes: Reservation day schools, reservation boarding schools of first and second grades, and industrial training schools of first and second grades.

It is the duty and design of the Government to remove, by the shortest method, the ignorance, inability, and fears of the Indians, and to place them on an equality with other races in the United States. In organizing this system of schools, the fact is not overlooked that Indian schools, as such, should be preparatory and temporary; that eventually they will become unnecessary, and a full and free entrance be obtained for Indians into the public school system of the country. To this end all officers and employes of the Indian school service should work.

*   *   *

General Rules

32. Employés are expected to reside in the school buildings when quarters there are provided for them; otherwise, as near to the buildings as practicable. Employés must keep their rooms in order at all times.

33. Employés are not allowed to have pupils in their rooms except by permission of the superintendent for specified reasons.

34. No person, other than an attaché of the school, shall be allowed in any school building later than 9.30 p. m. except by special permission of the superintendent.

35. A retiring bell rung at 9 p. m. (or later during warm weather, if advisable) shall be the signal for absolute quiet in all the dormitories and adjacent rooms.

36. Every night, at irregular periods, some person or persons duly assigned to such duty must "make the rounds," visiting every portion of the school buildings and premises, to guard against fire, prevent intrusion of unauthorized persons, and detect any improper conduct on the part of pupils or others.

37. Social dancing, card playing, gambling, profanity, and smoking are strictly prohibited in the school buildings and on the premises. Pupils are forbidden to carry concealed weapons.

38. There shall be a session of school each evening for reading, study, singing, or other exercises, at the close of which the pupils shall retire in an orderly manner to their dormitories. The employments for Saturday shall be arranged by the superintendent and matron to the best advantage of the school.

39. The Sabbath must be properly observed. There shall be a Sabbath school or some other suitable service every Sunday, which pupils shall be required to attend. The superintendent may require employés to attend and participate in all the above exercises; but any employé declining as a matter of conscience shall be excused from attending and participating in any or all religious exercises.

40. Every school should be carefully graded and pupils should be classified according to their capacity and scholarship and be promoted from grade to grade under such rules as may be prescribed by the superintendent. At the close of each term pupils should be examined in all the studies pursued during the term and promotions should be made on the basis of these examinations. Pupils who have completed the school course should be reported to the Indian Office for promotion to a school of higher grade.[1]

41. All instruction must be in the English language. Pupils must be compelled

[1]It is the purpose of the Indian Office to fill the training schools with pupils taken from the reservation schools, and for some time, until the training schools shall be filled, it will doubtless be necessary to take pupils from reservation schools before they have finished their course in those schools.

to converse with each other in English, and should be properly rebuked or punished for persistent violation of this rule. Every effort should be made to encourage them to abandon their tribal language. To facilitate this work it is essential that all school employes be able to speak English fluently, and that they speak English exclusively to the pupils, and also to each other in the presence of pupils.

42. Instruction in music must be given at all schools. Singing should be a part of the exercises of each school session, and wherever practicable instruction in instrumental music should be given.

43. Except in cases of emergency, pupils shall not be removed from school either by their parents or others, nor shall they be transferred from a Government to a private school without special authority from the Indian Office.

44. The school buildings should be furnished throughout with plain, inexpensive, but substantial furniture. Dormitories or lavatories should be so supplied with necessary toilet articles, such as soap, towels, mirrors, combs, hair, shoe, nail, and tooth brushes, and wisp brooms, as to enable the pupils to form exact habits of personal neatness.

45. Good and healthful provisions must be supplied in abundance; and they must well cooked and properly placed on the table. A regular bill of fare for each day of the week should be prepared and followed. Meals must be served regularly and neatly. Pains should be taken not only to have the food healthful and the table attractive, but to have the bill of fare varied. The school farm and dairy should furnish an ample supply of vegetables, fruits, milk, butter, cottage cheese, curds, eggs, and poultry. Coffee and tea should be furnished sparingly; milk is preferable to either, and children can be taught to use it. Pupils must be required to attend meals promptly after proper attention to toilet, and at least one employé must be in the dining room during each meal to supervise the table manners of the pupils and to see that all leave the table at the same time and in good order.

46. The superintendent will establish a common mess for the employés and may prescribe rules governing the same. Their meals may be prepared by the school cook, if such work will not interfere with the proper discharge of her regular duties, and she shall receive from the members of the mess a fair allowance for the extra duty thus imposed upon her, such allowance to be divided among them pro rata; or they may hire a cook who is not a school employé. The matron, under the direction of the superintendent, may have immediate charge of the employés' mess.

47. So far as practicable, a uniform style of clothing for the school should be adopted. Two plain, substantial suits, with extra pair of trousers for each boy, and three neat, well-made dresses for each girl, if kept mended, ought to suffice for week-day wear for one year. For Sunday wear each pupil should be furnished a better suit. The pupils should also be supplied with underwear adapted to the climate, with night clothes, and with handkerchiefs, and, if the climate requires it, with overcoats and cloaks and with overshoes.

48. The buildings, outhouses, fences, and walks should at all times be kept in thorough repair. Where practicable, the grounds should be ornamented with trees, grass, and flowers.

49. There should be a flag staff at every school, and the American flag should be hoisted, in suitable weather, in the morning and lowered at sunset daily.

50. Special hours should be allotted for recreation. Provision should be made for outdoor sports, and the pupils should be encouraged in daily healthful exercise under the eye of a school employé; simple games should also be devised for indoor amusement. They should be taught the sports and games enjoyed by white youth, such as baseball, hopscotch, croquet, marbles, bean bags, dominoes, checkers,

logomachy, and other word and letter games, and the use of dissected maps, etc. The girls should be instructed in simple fancy work, knitting, netting, crocheting, different kinds of embroidery, etc.

51. Separate play grounds, as well as sitting rooms, must be assigned the boys and the girls. In play and in work, as far as possible, and in all places except the school room and at meals, they must be kept entirely apart. It should be so arranged, however, that at stated times, under suitable supervision, they may enjoy each other's society; and such occasions should be used to teach them to show each other due respect and consideration, to behave without restraint, but without familiarity, and to acquire habits of politeness, refinement, and self-possession.

52. New Year's Day, Franchise Day (February 8), Washington's Birthday (February 22), Arbor Day, Decoration Day (May 30), Fourth of July, Thanksgiving Day, and Christmas, are to be appropriately observed as holidays.

53. Corporal punishment must be resorted to only in cases of grave violations of rules, and in no instances shall any person inflict it except under the direction of the superintendent, to whom all serious questions of discipline must be referred.[2] Employés may correct pupils for slight misdemeanors only.

54. Any pupil twelve years of age or over, guilty of persistently using profane or obscene language; of lewd conduct; stubborn insubordination; lying; fighting; wanton destruction of property; theft; or similar misbehavior, may be punished by the superintendent either by inflicting corporal punishment or imprisonment in the guardhouse; but in no case shall any unusual or cruel or degrading punishment be permitted.

55. A permanent record should be kept on file at each school showing the history of each pupil, giving name, age, sex, height, weight, chest measurements, state of health, residence, names of parents, and of tribe to which the family belongs, time of entering and leaving school, and the advancement made in education. If an English name is given to the pupil, the Indian name of the father should be retained as a surname. (See office circular in regard to names, dated March 19, 1890, of which copy is appended hereto.)

INDUSTRIAL WORK

56. A regular and efficient system of industrial training must be a part of the work of each school. At least half of the time of each boy and girl should be devoted thereto—the work to be of such character that they may be able to apply the knowledge and experience gained, in the locality where they may be expected to reside after leaving school. In pushing forward the school-room training of these boys and girls, teachers, and especially superintendents, must not lose sight of the great necessity for fitting their charges for the every-day life of their after years.

57. A farm and garden, if practicable an orchard also, must be connected with each school, and especial attention must be given to instruction in farming, gardening, dairying, and fruit growing.

58. Every school should have horses, cattle, swine, and poultry, and when practicable, sheep and bees, which the pupils should be taught to care for properly.

[2] In some of the more advanced schools it will be practicable and advisable to have material offenses arbitrated by a school court composed of the advanced students, with school employés added to such court in very aggravated cases. After due investigation, the amount of guilt should be determined and the quantity of punishment fixed by the court, but the approval of the superintendent shall be necessary before the punishment is inflicted, and the superintendent may modify or remit but may not increase the sentence.

The boys should look after the stock and milk the cows, and the girls should see to the poultry and the milk.

59. The farm, garden, stock, dairy, kitchen, and shops should be so managed as to make the school as nearly self-sustaining as practicable, not only because Government resources should be as wisely and carefully utilized as private resources would be, but also because thrift and economy are among the most valuable lessons which can be taught Indians. Waste in any department must not be tolerated.

60. The blacksmith, wheelwright, carpenter, shoemaker, and harness maker trades, being of the most general application, should be taught to a few pupils at every school. Where such mechanics are not provided for the school pupils should, so far as practicable, receive instruction from the agency mechanics.

61. The girls must be systematically trained in every branch of housekeeping and in dairy work; be taught to cut, make, and mend garments for both men and women; and also be taught to nurse and care for the sick. They must be regularly detailed to assist the cook in preparing the food and the laundress in washing and ironing.

62. Special effort must be made to instruct Indian youth in the use and care of tools and implements. They must learn to keep them in order, protect them properly, and use them carefully.

The Evolution of Equal Educational Opportunity for Negroes, Indians, and Chinese in California (1860-90)

CALIFORNIA SCHOOL LAWS (1860-80)   From State of California, *Statutes Passed at the Eleventh Session of the Legislature, 1859–60* (Sacramento, 1860), p. 325.

SEC. 8. Negroes, Mongolians, and Indians, shall not be admitted into the public schools; and, whenever satisfactory evidence is furnished to the Superintendent of Public Instruction to show that said prohibited parties are attending such schools, he may withhold from the district in which such schools are situated all share of the State School Fund; and the Superintendent of Common Schools for the county in which such district is situated shall not draw his warrant in favor of such district, for any expenses incurred, while the prohibited parties aforesaid were attending the public schools therein; *provided,* that the Trustees of any district may establish a separate school for the education of Negroes, Mongolians, and Indians, and use the public school funds for the support of the same.

From State of California, *Statutes Passed at the Fifteenth Session of the Legislature, 1863–64* (Sacramento, 1864), p. 213.

SEC. 13. Section sixty-eight of the aforesaid Act of April sixth, eighteen hundred and sixty-three, is hereby amended so as to read as follows:

Section 68. Negroes, Mongolians, and Indians, shall not be admitted into the Public Schools; *provided,* that upon the application of the parents or Guardians of ten or more such colored children, made in writing to the Trustees of any district, said Trustees shall establish a separate School for the education of Negroes, Mongolians, and Indians, and use the Public School funds for the support of the same; and, *provided,* further, that the Trustees of any School District may establish a separate school, or provide for the education of any less number of Negroes,

THE
MINORITIES

1761

Mongolians and Indians, and use the Public School funds for the support of the same, whenever in their judgment it may be necessary for said Public Schools.

From State of California, *Statutes Passed at the Eighteenth Session of the Legislature, 1869–70* (Sacramento, 1870), p. 398.

SEC. 56. Any Board of Trustees, or Board of Education, by a majority vote, may admit into any public school half-breed Indian children, and Indian children who live in white families or under guardianship of white persons.

SEC. 57. Children of African or Mongolian descent, and Indian children not living under the care of white persons, shall not be admitted into public schools, except as provided in this Act, *provided,* that upon the written application of the parents or guardians of at least ten such children to any Board of Trustees or Board of Education, a separate school shall be established for the education of such children; and the education of a less number may be provided for by the Trustees in any other manner.

SEC. 58. When there shall be in any district any number of children, other than white children, whose education can be provided for in no other way, the Trustees, by a majority vote may permit such children to attend schools for white children, *provided,* that a majority of the parents of the children attending such school make no objection, in writing, to be filed with the Board of Trustees.

SEC. 59. The same laws, rules, and regulations which apply to schools for white children, shall apply to schools for colored children.

From State of California, *Acts Amendatory of the Codes Passed at the Twentieth Session of the Legislature, 1873–74* (Sacramento, 1874), p. 839.

SEC. 56. The education of children of African descent, and Indian children, shall be provided for in separate schools. Upon the written application of the parents or guardians of at least ten such children to any Board of Trustees or Board of Education, a separate school shall be established for the education of such children; and the education of a less number may be provided for by the Trustees, in separate schools, in any other manner.

SEC. 57. The same laws, rules and regulations which apply to schools for white children shall apply to schools for colored children.

From California Department of Public Instruction, *School Law of California, Rules and Regulations of the State Board of Education* (Sacramento, 1880), p. 38.

SEC. 26. Section sixteen hundred and sixty-two of said Code is amended to read as follows:

1662. Every school, unless otherwise provided by law, must be open for the admission of all children between six and twenty-one years of age residing in the district; and the Board of Trustees, or City Board of Education, have power to admit adults and children not residing in the district, whenever good reasons exist therefor. Trustees shall have the power to exclude children of filthy or vicious habits, or children suffering from contagious or infectious deseases.

California, Department of Public Instruction, *School Law of California; Rules and Regulations of the State Board of Education,* . . . (Sacramento, 1885), p. 13.

1662. Every school, unless otherwise provided by law, must be open for the admission of all children between six and twenty-one years of age residing in the district, and the Board of Trustees, or City Board of Education, have power to admit adults and children not residing in the district whenever good reason exists therefor. Trustees shall have the power to exclude children of filthy or vicious habits, or children suffering from contagious or infectious diseases, and also to establish separate schools for children of Mongolian or Chinese descent. When such separate schools are established, Chinese or Mongolian children must not be admitted into any other schools.

CALIFORNIA SUPREME COURT RULES THAT A NEGRO CHILD MAY BE DENIED PERMISSION TO ATTEND PUBLIC SCHOOL WITH WHITE CHILDREN (1874)   From *Ward v. Flood,* 48 Calif. 36 (1874).

The opportunity of instruction at public schools is afforded the youth of the State by the statute of the State, enacted in obedience to the special command of the Constitution of the State, directing that the Legislature shall provide for a system of common schools, by which a school shall be kept up and supported in each district, at least three months in every year, etc. The advantage or benefit thereby vouchsafed to each child, of attending a public school is, therefore, one derived and secured to it under the highest sanction of positive law. It is, therefore, a right—a legal right—as distinctively so as the vested right in property owned is a legal right, and as such it is protected, and entitled to be protected by all the guarantees by which other legal rights are protected and secured to the possessor.

The clause of the Fourteenth Amendment referred to did not create any new or

THE MINORITIES

1763

substantive legal right, or add to or enlarge the general classification of rights of persons or things existing in any State under the laws thereof. It, however, operated upon them as it found them already established, and it declared in substance that, such as they were in each State, they should be held and enjoyed alike by all persons within its jurisdiction. The protection of law is indeed inseparable from the assumed existence of a recognized legal right, through the vindication of which the protection is to operate. To declare, then, that each person within the jurisdiction of the State shall enjoy the equal protection of its laws, is necessarily to declare that the measure of legal rights within the State shall be equal and uniform, and the same for all persons found therein—according to the respective condition of each— each child as all other children—each adult person as all other adult persons. Under the laws of California children or persons between the ages of five and twenty-one years are entitled to receive instruction at the public schools, and the education thus afforded them is a measure of the protection afforded by law to persons of that condition.

The education of youth is emphatically their protection. Ignorance, the lack of mental and moral culture in earlier life, is the recognized parent of vice and crime in after years. Thus it is the acknowledged duty of the parent or guardian, as part of the measure of protection which he owes to the child or ward, to afford him at least a reasonable opportunity for the improvement of his mind and the elevation of his moral condition, and, of this duty, the law took cognizance long before the now recognized interest of society and of the body politic in the education of its members had prompted its embarkation upon a general system of youth. So a ward in chancery, as being entitled to the protection of the Court, was always entitled to be educated under its direction as constituting a most important part of that protection. The public law of the State—both the Constitution and Statute—having established public schools for educational purposes, to be maintained by public authority and at public expense, the youth of the State, are thereby become *pro hac vice* the wards of the State, and under the operations of the constitutional amendment referred to, equally entitled to be educated at the public expense. It would, therefore, not be competent to the Legislature, while providing a system of education for the youth of the State, to exclude the petitioner and those of her race from its benefits, merely because of their African descent, and to have so excluded her would have been to deny to her the equal protection of the laws within the intent and meaning of the Constitution.

But we do not find in the Act of April, 1870, providing for a system of common schools, which is substantially repeated in the Political Code now in force, any legislative attempt in this direction; nor do we discover that the statute is, in any of its provisions, obnoxious to objections of a constitutional character. It provides in substance that schools shall be kept open for the admission of white children, and that the education of children of African descent must be provided for in separate schools.

In short, the policy of separation of races for educational purposes is adopted by the legislative department, and it is in this mere policy that the counsel for the petitioner professes to discern "an odious distinction of caste, founded on a deep-rooted prejudice in public opinion." But it is hardly necessary to remind counsel that we cannot deal here with such matters, and that our duties lie wholly within the much narrower range of determining whether this statute, in whatever motive it originated, denies to the petitioner, in a constitutional sense, the equal protection of the laws; and in the circumstances that the races are separated in the public schools, there is certainly to be found no violation of the constitutional rights of the one race more than of the other, and we see none of either, for each, though separated from the other, is to be educated upon equal terms with that other, and both at the common public expense.

*　　*　　*

We concur in these views, and they are decisive of the present controversy. In order to prevent possible misapprehension, however, we think proper to add that in our opinion, and as the result of the views here announced, the exclusion of colored children from schools where white children attend as pupils, cannot be supported, except under the conditions appearing in the present case; that is, except where separate schools are actually maintained for the education of colored children; and that, unless such separate schools be in fact maintained, all children of the school district, whether white or colored, have an equal right to become pupils at any common school organized under the laws of the State, and have a right to registration and admission as pupils in order of their registration, pursuant to the provisions of subdivision fourteen of section 1,617 of the Political Code.

Writ of mandamus denied.

A U.S. BUREAU OF EDUCATION OFFICIAL ON EDUCATION AND THE CHINESE MIGRATION (1875) From H. N. Day, "The Chinese Migration," as quoted in U.S. Bureau of Education, *Report of the Commissioner of Education for the Year 1870* (Washington, D.C., 1871). pp. 428–30.

II.—Results to Be Arrived At

This incoming element, then, which must either greatly hamper or greatly help our national prosperity, which, perhaps we should say, must either overwhelm and smother, or immeasurably enlarge and enrich our political and social life, is to be controlled, not checked; and we cannot too carefully and steadily keep before us the definite end to which all the particulars of this control should be directed. It is, in a proper sense perhaps of that expression, but a high peculiar sense, to be utilized. It is to be utilized after the laws of its own nature—after the principles of rational freedom in the most exact reciprocity of duty and privilege. It is to be assimilated to our own life and incorporated into it. The thorough Americanization of this new element is the comprehensive result which all political and individual endeavors in regard to them should seek. It is to be assimilated to the highest, completest form of our civilization, as intelligent, free, Christian.

It will prove a terrible pest and bane if it be allowed to have a place in our social system only as a foreign element, as fungous or parasitic, China has never known caste; America knows it no more. The institutions of both countries alike repel and abominate it. Only the greed or the tyranny of individuals, or of communities among us, can, and then only in spite of our fundamental laws and in audacious resistance to them, make a servile class of these immigrants; and the true way to prevent this result is not to stop back the stream, but arrest the iniquity that would poison it. Full and exact equality of social duty and privilege is the fundamental principle of all true and wise policy in the treatment of immigrants to our shores. The indispensable condition of our highest national well-being is the organic membership of all the races, all the kindreds, all the families, all the individuals dwelling among us, so that each shall minister and be ministered to, nourish and be nourished by, all the rest—one common pulsation beating through every element in our system.

Nor need any alarm be taken from outcries against the horrors of "amalgamation" and "miscegenation." These are mere bug-bears, invented by political cunning to frighten silly men, who do not understand that the freedom of our life and institutions assures, in the main, that social connections and alliances will be between parties best suited to each other, and therefore that public morality and decency will not be shocked by unseemly unions. At all events, history shows that whatever evil of this kind may arise, it is sporadic and exceptional, and can only be aggravated by governmental interference.

Chinese civilization has much that is in common to what is peculiar to American as distinguished from European civilization. Its principles of social equality, as before alluded to, its submission to law and authority rather than to hereditary and personal rule, its love of home and family, its requirement of universal education, its enforcement of political responsibility, are true American principles; and fresh importations will but help to overthrow and exterminate what of hostility to the free working of these principles the feudal and out-of-door life of European society has introduced among us. The characteristic vices of Chinese life are rather moral and religious than political, as their superstition, their idolatry, their gambling propensities, their love of opium, which last vice, it should be remarked, is but of recent introduction and of limited extent, forced, in a sense, upon them by foreign cupidity and power against their established laws. These vices are not to be kept out by a futile attempt to stop the providentially-ordered intercourse between nations, but to be cured by suitable moral means. Most certainly it would be very unwise to oppose their spread by closing the channels of intercommunication between members of our own political body. Fusion, rather than fencing and walling into separate fields, is the true result which wisdom prescribes.

This thorough incorporation into our common national life involves some particulars of policy which it may not be amiss to specify.

THE ADOPTION OF THE AMERICAN LANGUAGE

The citizens of this country should speak the same language incorruptly. Diversity of dialects may possibly consist with a certain national unity and integrity; it is certainly ever a hinderance to it. The thoughts and sentiments of a people to be in accord and sympathy, to be healthful and nourishing in the fullest extent, must flow in and out, to and from the different parts, through the channel of a single dialect. A pure, uncorrupt English should be held forth as the indispensable attainment of every American citizen. Any corruption of our noble speech by foreign dialectic intermixtures, any *patois*, should be everywhere and by every means discountenanced and opposed. It is gratifying to learn that the Chinese immigrant shows no proclivity in himself to that miserable jargon called *Pigeon-English*. In North Adams he has nothing of it, knows nothing of it, desires nothing of it.

On the other hand, and positively, no more efficient means of assimilating foreigners to our manners, our institutions, our national life, than the learning, the reading, the speaking our language habitually; than the habitual admission of all thoughts and sentiments, and the habitual utterance of them through the common speech of American life.

In common with the foreign dialect, the foreign dress and all the personal habits which are foreign to our manners should be replaced by such as are properly American. Every conspicuous badge of alienism should be avoided. It is one of the favorable prognostics of the experiment at North Adams that the American dress is adopted, so far as taste and comfort dictate. The fact indicates how far the treatment which the stranger receives at our hands may keep him from that isolation which is betrayed by the foreign dress and speech; how far that isolation, where it exists, is attributable to the social atmosphere into which he is brought.

A thorough American domestication is to be sought. The family life, as has been stated, is the predominant characteristic of the Chinese. The love and reverence paid among them to parents and to ancestors, the religious sentiments that they are trained to cherish toward the home of the family should be provided with the opportunities of gratification. They should be guided and helped to homes in America, where all the sacred relics of the departed may be securely and permanently enshrined, where the strong family feeling may be indulged and cherished. The low, narrow superstition that defies this worthy domestic disposition is to be eliminated by lifting and enlarging the filial sentiment from the earthly to the heavenly Father, so that the piety which rightly and naturally begins, and is fostered toward the natural parent, shall develop into a love and reverence for the eternal and supreme. There will be difficulty in this at the start. Work on railroads and in mines, and first employment in factories and in private households, must, of course, hinder separate establishment in dwellings. But certainly the settling down in families in the midst of native Americans, so that all the neighborhood intercourse of common life shall be in a fully American atmosphere, must have an influence in Americanizing that cannot be too highly estimated.

Most earnestly to be deprecated is the isolation of foreigners, and especially of Chinamen into separate villages, towns, or wards. The testimony is that the Chinaman is not more clannish than other men; but it is purely natural that common origin, common estrangement in regard to the land of their adoption, common dialect, should breed common sympathies, and should draw together. Thorough and complete Americanization is, however, hindered by all such isolation.

As the man is fashioned in the training of the child, and as the spirit of the nation is shaped in the family, it is of the first importance that not only the family life be maintained and protected, but also in order to the completest fusion that this family life be impregnated by the true American spirit, and be shaped after a pure American and Christian pattern. The family spirit which so characterizes the Chinaman should not be eradicated and supplanted, but only elevated and expanded.

In like manner a full initiation into the peculiar social usages and manners of American life, so far, at least, as worthy, is to be desired, as also a free introduction into that vast diversity of our arts and occupations, as likewise into our religious usages and habits. Into this whole social life, this new element may bring in something that will liberalize, expand, enrich, as well as purify and elevate our manners; but it should be carefully grafted into the fundamental principles and spirit of our social order and economy, and not root itself and grow up a distinct and isolated growth.

ADMISSION TO CITIZENSHIP

Finally, on the broadest, surest grounds of a true and wise policy, the Chinaman should be brought to a free participation in our political life. Intelligence and morality, indeed, should be the conditions of political rights and privileges; but such conditions only as are accorded to others should be imposed on him. His wonted training and spirit, as already observed, do not predispose him to seek political privileges, rather to shun them. He, therefore, needs no unusual checks. He is to be nationalized in his feelings and views, his characteristic family spirit being expanded into the proper love of country as the characteristic filial spirit rises and swells into reverence for the Divine Father of all. This is the only safe result for him, as for the country. The sordid calculations of political partisanship will doubtless often prompt to strong opposition to the naturalization of the Chinaman, perhaps sometimes seek to effect it too hastily, and with too much disregard of settled limitations and safeguards. The dangers of the too free admission of foreigners to citizenship will be as much exaggerated in the one case as underrated in the other. The one safe, desirable course is, under suitable limitations and conditions of intelligence, morality, time of residence, and the like, to bring in all that dwell among us into the full exercise of all political rights, and the corresponding participation in all political burdens and responsibilities.

III.—Method of Attainment

To the question, now, how such thorough assimilation of this foreign element to American life after its highest type is best to be accomplished, all the facts in the case point to the answer: *By education under a right popular sentiment.*

This right popular sentiment in regard to the whole Chinese question is indispensable even to much success in any educational effort, for this must itself spring from an enlightened, philanthropic feeling, and be guided and sustained by this feeling, while all educational endeavors may be effectually prostrated by a strong popular sentiment arrayed in hostility, and bent on oppression or extermination. It is most important, therefore, that the public mind be carefully and accurately informed in respect to all the facts and principles involved in this question. It should be lifted above the low, mean selfishness which vitalizes the caste spirit in every form, whether industrial or political. It should be familiarized with the lofty, worthy views that are inspired at once by that superintending providence which has brought the swelling tide of population onward till it has reached our waiting continent, that it may spread over its wastes a reclaiming, regenerating life; and also by that noble spirit of philanthropy which from the first has extended a hand of welcome to all the oppressed and crushed from other lands.

A REPORT ON CHINESE CHILDREN AND THE PUBLIC SCHOOLS OF CALIFORNIA (1885) From "Report of the Special Committee of the Board of Supervisors of San Francisco," as quoted in Willard B. Farwell, *The Chinese at Home and Abroad* (San Francisco, 1884), pp. 58–62.

The Chinese Children and the Public Schools

We have shown that there are 722 children of Chinese parentage in Chinatown. Most if not all of these were born here, and are to all intents and purposes "native Americans." Though "native" they are not "to the manner born," because in every attribute of juvenile life they are Mongolian, as much so as if born in the province of Canton. The very exclusiveness and clannishness of the Chinese has so far preserved these children from contact with the Caucasian race, and not one word of English, or any other language than Chinese, can they articulate. In the drift of life it is quite possible that some of these later on may be brought in their younger years sufficiently in contact with the English-speaking Christian world to imbibe some of its habits and acquire some knowledge of the language.

But what results will follow? Will assimilation begin, and race mixture begin, with a mingling of Caucasian and Mongolian blood, and a new addition be thus made to the strain of American blood mixture to add one more thread to the intricacy of the present race problem that is to be worked out on our shores? To follow this inquiry and to indulge in speculation on this point forms no part of our duty at the present moment, however interesting and important it may be in the broad consideration of the Chinese question.

The point is, what shall we do with these Chinese children born upon our soil, though partaking in no respect of the proclivities and habits of any other known race except those of their own progenitors? And this opens the question that has often been agitated as to their admission to the public schools, and their right, under the law, to share the benefits to be derived from the public school fund. We have shown that there is no distinct line of demarcation—here at least—between domestic life and prostitution. We have shown that the painted harlots of the slums and alleys, the women who are bought and sold to the slavery of prostitution, are surrounded by children in some instances, and intermingle freely with the border class of family life where other children abound. We have shown that to all outward intents and purposes prostitution such as this, and with these surroundings, is a recognized feature of the economy of Mongolian life, in San Francisco at least. What, then, shall be said if the doors of our schoolhouses are to be opened to admit children reared in such an atmosphere? What, indeed, shall be said of the proposition to educate them separate and apart from children of other races, and how can we with consistency deny them this right? Speaking no language but the Chinese, born and nurtured in filth and degradation, it is scarcely probable that any serious attempt could be made to mingle them with the other children of our public schools without kindling a blaze of revolution in our midst. And again, by what right, constitutional or statutory, can we set apart separate schools and a separate fund for their education or maintenance? And yet something must be done with them, some action must be taken to rid them of their race proclivities and habits if we would protect posterity from unlimited evil consequences. Here there may well be a field for true missionary work and a problem that will tax the wisdom and patience of mankind to solve. If the immigration of the race were effectually stopped the riddle would be less intricate to deal with. But if it is to continue, even under the conditions of misnamed "restriction" which at present exist, how to deal with this constantly increasing number of Mongolian children, born and nurtured in such conditions of immorality and degradation, becomes indeed a more serious problem than any which the American people have ever yet been called upon to solve, not excepting the abrogation of African slavery and the horrors which attended its achievement.

If these children could be separated from their parents and scattered among our own people, away from the populous centers, the question involved would be perhaps easy of adjustment. The laws of nature and of men prohibit this, while the laws of morality, and the law of self-protection, must compel our own people to sternly prohibit them from mingling with our children in the public schools, or as companions and playmates. What, then, we again ask, is to be done with the Chinese children, born upon our soil, and that are yet to be born, in a ratio co-equal in its increase with the increase of immigration? To this inquiry there seems to be but one answer. Chinese immigration must stop!—absolutely stop!! For it is beyond the ingenuity of men to deal fairly with this phase of the question, except by a reversal of the laws of nature. And a violent separation of children from parents as fast as they are born, and delivering them over to our own race for education and a new order of life is a proposition not to be thought of. So, then, while the conclusions which your Committee have arrived at as to the best method of dealing with the Chinese here among us, and those which are to come after, as a local remedy for the evils which their presence now inflict upon us, are' in their judgment wise and practical, the real remedy is the eventual stoppage of Chinese immigration, by such absolute, autocratic Congressional legislation as shall make it physically impossible for the Chinamen to land upon our shores, except, perhaps, in a commercial capacity alone, or as a student seeking the advantages of our educational institutions. Such legislation, perhaps, cannot be secured until the Eastern mind is educated on the Chinese question as have been the minds of the people upon this coast. And the best way to accompish that end is to so deal with the Chinese here by local laws, made to be enforced, so as to drive them from our midst to mingle with Eastern communities, and to educate them by contact with their presence, as they have educated us through the same process, up to a realizing sense of the frightfully-disastrous results growing out of their presence among them. Until such results as these can be reached—be it at an early or a late day—what we shall do with the Chinese children is a question that may well rest in abeyance. Meanwhile, guard well the doors of our public schools, that they do not enter. For, however hard and stern such a doctrine may sound, it is but the enforcement of the law of self-preservation, the inculcation of the doctrine of true humanity, and an integral part of the enforcement of the iron rule of right by which we hope presently to prove that we can justly and practically defend ourselves from this invasion of Mongolian barbarism.

CALIFORNIA SUPREME COURT RULING ON THE EXCLUSION OF CHINESE CHILDREN FROM PUBLIC SCHOOLS ATTENDED BY WHITE CHILDREN (1885)   From *Tape* v. *Hurley,* 77 Calif. 473 (1885)

Appeal from a judgment of the Superior Court of the city and county of San Francisco.

The respondent, through her guardian *ad litem,* applied to the appellant Hurley, the principal of one of the public schools of the city and county of San Francisco, for admission therein. The respondent is a Chinese child, and because of this fact Miss Hurley, acting in obedience to a resolution of the board of education of the city and county of San Francisco, refused to admit her as a pupil into the school. A writ of mandate was then sued out against Miss Hurley, A. J. Moulder, superintendent of public instruction, and the members of the board of education, individually. The Superior Court dismissed the writ as to the members of the board of education, and ordered it to issue against Miss Hurley and A. J. Moulder. From such judgment the appeal was taken. The further facts are sufficiently stated in the opinion of the court.

H. G. Platt, for Appellants.

William F. Gibson, and *Sheldon G. Kellogg,* for Respondent.

SHARPSTEIN, J.—The main question in this case is whether a child "between six and twenty-one years of age, of Chinese parentage, but who was born and has always lived in the city and county of San Francisco," is entitled to admission in the public school of the district in which she resides.

The language of the code is as follows:

"Every school, unless otherwise provided by law, must be open for the admission of all children between six and twenty-one years of age residing in the district; and the board of trustees, or city board of education, have power to admit adults and children not residing in the district, whenever good reasons exist therefor. Trustees shall have the power to exclude children of filthy or vicious habits, or children suffering from contagious or infectious diseases." (Political Code, § 1667.)

That is the latest legislative expression on the subject, and was passed as late as 1880. Prior to that time the first clause of the section read, "Every school, unless otherwise provided by special statute, must be open for the admission of all white children between five and twenty-one years of age, residing in the district."

As amended, the clause is broad enough to include all children who are not precluded from entering a public school by some provision of law; and we are not aware of any law which forbids the entrance of children of any race or nationality. The legislature not only declares who shall be admitted, but also who may be excluded, and it does not authorize the exclusion of any one on the ground upon which alone the exclusion of the respondent here is sought to be justified. The vicious, the filthy, and those having contagious or infectious diseases, may be excluded, without regard to their race, color or nationality.

This law must be construed as any other would be construed. "Where a law is plain and unambiguous, whether it be expressed in general or limited terms, *the legislature should be intended to mean what they have plainly expressed,* and consequently, no room is left for construction." (*Fisher* v. *Blight,* 2 Cranch, 358, 399.) "When the law is clear and explicit, and its provisions are susceptible of but one interpretation, its consequences, if evil, can only be avoided by a change of the law itself, to be effected by legislative and not judicial action." (*Bosley v. Mattingly*, 14 B. Mon. 73.) This rule is never controverted or doubted, although perhaps sometimes lost sight of. In this case, if effect be given to the intention of the legislature, as indicated by the clear and unambiguous languaged used by them, respondent here has the same right to enter a public school that any other child has. It is not alleged that she is vicious, or filthy, or that she has a contagious or infectious disease. As the legislature has not denied to the children of any race or nationality the right to enter our public schools, the question whether it might have done so does not arise in this case.

We think the superintendent of schools was improperly joined as a defendant in this action, and that the court properly dismissed the action as to the board of education. In *Ward* v. *Flood*, 48 Cal. 26, the action was against the teacher alone. That it was properly brought, seems to have been conceded.

The board of education has power "to make, establish, and enforce all necessary and proper rules and regulations *not contrary to law*," and none other. (Stats. 1871–2, p. 846.) Teachers cannot justify a violation of law, on the ground that a resolution of the board of education required them to do so.

The judgment must be modified, so as to make the writ run against the defendant Hurley alone.

In other respects it is affirmed.

THORNTON, J., MYRICK, J., MCKEE, J., MCKINSTRY, J., ROSS, J., and MORRISON, C. J., concurred.

CALIFORNIA SUPREME COURT RULING ON EXCLUSION OF NEGRO CHILDREN FROM PUBLIC SCHOOLS ATTENDED BY WHITE CHILDREN (1890)   From *Wysinger* v. *Crookshank*, 82 Calif. 588 (1890).

Appeal from a judgment of the Superior Court of Tulare County. The facts are stated in the opinion.

W. A. Gray, and *Oregon Sanders*, for Appellant.

N. O. Bradley, and *W. B. Wallace*, for Respondent.

FOOTE, C.—This is an application for a writ of mandate to compel the defendant, Crookshank, a teacher of a public school located in the city of Visalia school district, of the county of Tulare, to admit the plaintiff as a scholar. The application was denied, and from the judgment rendered therein, and an order refusing a new trial, this appeal is prosecuted.

The only ground for the refusal of the teacher to admit the applicant to the public school as a pupil is, as stated by the former, that the father of the petitioner, "on October 1, 1888, came to me at the public school in Visalia with a boy about twelve years of age, named Arthur; Wysinger said he had brought his boy to put in school; he said: 'Here is my boy to put in your school.' I told him to take his boy to Mr. McAdams, who taught the colored school. I just assigned him to the colored school. I refused to admit his boy to the public school on Locust Street because he was colored, and because this public colored school was established by the board of education, who had instructed me to send the colored children to that colored school. These were my only reasons for refusing to admit him to the public school on Locust Street."

The boy thus excluded from a public school established for white children is a person of African descent, and both he and his father are colored citizens of the state of California and of the United States.

The sole question to be determined is, whether or not, under the laws of this state touching the education of children in the public schools, it is within the power of the board of education of the city of Visalia, in the county of Tulare, to establish a public school exclusively for such children as the applicant, and to exclude them from the schools established for white children.

At the date of the decision rendered by the appellate court of this state in *Ward* v. *Flood*, 48 Cal. 37, the statute governing the admission of children to public schools ran thus:—

"SEC. 53. Every school, unless otherwise provided by special law, shall be open for the admission of all white children between five and twenty-one years of age, residing in that school district, and the board of trustees or board of education shall have power to admit adults and children not residing in the district, whenever good reasons exist for such exceptions.

*   *   *

"SEC. 56. The education of children of African descent, and Indian children, shall be provided for in separate schools. Upon the written application of the parents or guardians of at least ten such children to any board of trustees or board of education, a separate school shall be established for the education of such children; and the education of a less number may be provided for by the trustees, in separate schools, in any other manner.

"SEC. 57. The same laws, rules, and regulations which apply to schools for white children shall apply to schools for colored children." (Laws 1869–70, p. 838.)

In pursuance of these statutes, the board of education of the city and county of San Francisco adopted a rule which provided that "children of African or Indian descent shall not be admitted into schools for white children; but separate schools shall be provided for them in accordance with the California school law."

It was held in the case *supra* that separate schools for colored children of African descent might be established, and that such establishment was not in conflict with the constitution of the state, nor with the thirteenth and fourteenth amendments to the constitution of the United States; but that the legislature could not exclude children from the benefits of a system of education provided for the youth of the state, merely because such children, so excluded, were of African descent. It was there said, at page 56:—

"In order to prevent possible misapprehension, however, we think proper to add that in our opinion, and as the result of the views here announced, the exclusion of colored children from schools where white children attend as pupils cannot be supported, except under the conditions appearing in the present case; that is, except where separate schools are actually maintained for the education of colored children; and that unless such separate schools be in fact maintained, all children of the school district, whether white or colored, have an equal right to become pupils at any common school organized under the laws of the state, and have a right to registration and admission as pupils in the order of their registration, pursuant to the provisions of subdivision 14 of section 1617 of the Political Code."

If the statutes as they stood when the decision *supra* was made had remained the law of the state at the time when the petitioner made his application, there can be no question but that it might have been lawfully refused, as a separate school, in all respects like the white school in the same district, had been established for children of African descent.

But following this decision, by an act of the legislature, passed April 7, 1880 (Amendments of 1880, p. 47), sections 1669, 1670, 1671 of the Political Code were repealed. They were as follows:—

"SEC. 1669. The education of children of African descent, and Indian children, must be provided for in separate schools; provided, that if the directors or trustees fail to provide such separate schools, then such children must be admitted into the schools for white children.

"SEC. 1670. Upon the written application of the parents or guardians of such children to any board of trustees of board of education, a separate school must be established for the education of such children.

"SEC. 1671. The same laws, rules, and regulations which apply to schools for white children apply to schools for colored children." (Deering's Pol. Code, note at foot of page 290.)

Section 1662 of the Political Code was by the same act amended so as to omit the word "white" before the word "children" as it had stood before that time, and as amended it read:—

"Every school, unless otherwise provided by law, must be open for the admission of all children between six and twenty-one years of age residing in the district; and the board of trustees, or city board of education, have power to admit adults and children not residing in the district whenever good reason exists therefor. Trustees shall have the power to exclude children of filthy and vicious habits, or children suffering from contagious or infectious diseases."

Following the repeal and amendment of the sections *supra*, a Mongolian or Chinese child applied for admission to a public school for white children, established in the city and county of San Francisco; its admission was refused by the teacher of the school, and an application for a writ of mandate was made to compel admission. The appellate court, in *Tape* v. *Hurley*, 66 Cal. 473, speaking by Mr. Justice Sharpstein, held that such Chinese or Mongolian child could not be excluded from a white school. And it was there said, in reference to section 1662 *supra*, as amended by striking out the word "white" before the word "children" (erroneously printed as section 1667 in the opinion):—

"That is the latest legislative expression on the subject, and was passed as late as 1880. Prior to that time the first clause of the section read: 'Every school, unless otherwise provided by special statute, must be open for the admission of all *white* children, between five and twenty-one years of age, residing in the district.'

"As amended, the clause is broad enough to include all children who are not precluded from entering a public school by some provision of law, and we are not aware of any law which forbids the entrance of children of any race or nationality. The legislature not only declares who shall be admitted, but also who may be excluded, and it does not authorize the exclusion of any one on the ground upon which alone the exclusion of the respondent here is sought to be justified. The vicious, the filthy, and those having contagious or infectious diseases may be excluded, without regard to their race, color, or nationality.

"In this case, if effect be given to the intention of the legislature, as indicated by the clear and unambiguous language used by them, respondent here has the same right to enter a public school that any other child has. . . .

"The board of education has power 'to make, establish, and enforce all necessary and proper rules and regulations *not contrary to law*,' and none other. (Stats. 1871–72, p. 846.) Teachers cannot justify a violation of law, on the ground that a resolution of the board of education required them to do so."

After the rendition of the judgment in this case, the legislature in 1885 amended section 1662 of the Political Code so as to add, after the word "diseases," "and also to establish separate schools for children of Mongolian or Chinese descent. When such separate schools are established, Chinese or Mongolian children must not be admitted into any other school." (Deering's Pol. Code, sec. 1662.)

And so the law existed upon the subject at the date of the institution of this action, and so it stands now.

It must appear clear, therefore, that the power to establish separate public schools for children of African descent, and to exclude them from the public schools established for white children, has been taken away from boards of school trustees and board of education, and that the power claimed by the teacher and the board of education of the city of Visalia does not exist.

If it had been intended by the law-making department of the government to invest such board with the power claimed, it would have given it as expressly as it was taken away by the repeal and amendment of the statutes which authorized it, and especially is this plainly to be discerned when section 1662, *supra*, as it now stands, gives the power to establish separate schools for Chinese or Mongolian children, but none other.

The whole policy of the legislative department of the government upon this matter is easily gathered from the course of legislation shown herein, and there can be no doubt but that it was never intended that, as a matter of classification of pupils, the right to establish separate schools for children of African descent, and thereby to exclude them from white schools of the proper district, should be given to such boards under section 1617 of the Political Code, which reads:—

"The powers and duties of trustees of school districts and of boards of education in cities are as follows:—

"1. To prescribe and enforce rules not inconsistent with law, or those prescribed by the state board of education, for their own government and the government of schools."

If the people of the state desire separate schools for citizens of African descent, and Indians, their wish may be accomplished by laws enacted by the law-making department of the government in accordance with existing constitutional provisions. But this course has not been pursued, as the law now stands, and the powers given to boards of education and school trustees, under section 1617 of the Political Code,

do not include the right claimed by the board of education of Visalia.

For these reasons, we advise that the judgment and order be reversed, and the court below directed to issue a mandate compelling the admission of the appellant as prayed for.

BELCHER, C. C., and HAYNE, C., concurred.

**THE
NEW
EDUCATION**

Pestalozzianism or "Object Training"

DESCRIPTION OF THE PESTALOZZIAN DEPARTMENT OF A KENTUCKY SCHOOL (1830)   From *Prospectus of the Rev. Mr. Peer's School . . .* as quoted in Edgar W. Knight and Clifton S. Hall, eds., *Readings in American Educational History* (New York, 1951), p. 487.

In this department, the younger students will have the foundation laid, by constant and appropriate *practice*, of valuable habits such as *observation, analysis, induction*, &c. For the attainment of this, the most important of the two great ends of education, the principles laid down by that revered philanthropist, with whose name we have honoured this branch of our school, are admirably calculated. The following are some of them.

I. "The instruction given should be adapted to the age and capacity of the pupil, so that he will comprehend it easily and perfectly.

II. "A regular and easy progression should be observed, beginning with that which is simple and plain, and proceeding by easy and gradual steps, to that which is complicated and difficult.

III. "In this progress, nothing should be passed, till it is perfectly understood and familiarized, so that it will be retained, both as a useful acquisition in itself, and as a facility to the acquisition of other matters connected with and depending upon it.

IV. "A plan of discipline and excitement should be employed which will produce great ardor and industry of pursuit, and supersede the necessity of coercion by an appeal to force or fear."

Among other things in which our pupils will be *practiced* in conformity with these principles, are elementary Mathematical exercises relating both to number and form, *exact copies of which as used in Pestalozzi's school*, we have been fortunate enough to obtain (together with many valuable directions), from a Swiss gentleman who aided in organizing his institution.

EDWARD SHELDON ON HIS EARLY WORK AT OSWEGO (c. 1853) From Mary Sheldon Barnes, ed., *Autobiography of Edward Austin Sheldon* (New York, 1911), pp. 114–15.

In those early days I attached great importance to written examinations. The last month of each year was devoted to them exclusively. They were designed as a review covering all the work done for the year as a test of its thoroughness. I personally prepared the questions for every grade. I marked the answer to every question, keeping a personal account with each pupil and teacher. The results were all tabulated and printed in the annual reports of the board and sometimes in the daily papers. In this way I kept up a high pressure on the schools. The rivalry and competition were something tremendous. It took me a long time to learn that there was a better way, but at last the lesson was learned. I carried a straight-jacket system of close classification to its highest point of perfection, accompanied by a course of study as precise, definite and exacting as it is possible to make, tested by complete and exhaustive examinations which left no room for doubt as to the thoroughness of the work done. I have good reason for believing that I had organized and perfected the most complete educational machine that was ever constructed. By looking at my watch, I could tell exactly what every teacher in the city was doing.

PESTALOZZIAN METHODS AT OSWEGO (1861) From Oswego, New York, *Annual Report of the Board of Education, for the Year Ending March 31, 1861,* as quoted in Ellwood P. Cubberley, ed., *Readings in Public Education in the United States* (Boston, 1934), pp. 343–45.

The system which we have adopted is justly termed Pestalozzian, for to Pestalozzi, that greatest of all modern reformers in education, may be credited the development, and, in many important points, the origin of those ideas which lie at the basis of this system. It is true that these ideas, and the modes of applying them in the development of the human faculties, have been somewhat modified and improved during the experience of half a century, but they are none the less the real thought and discoveries of this great philosopher. Its principles have become more or less widely diffused, but have been more generally and thoroughly incorporated with the methods of teaching in some of the countries of Europe, than in our own, ... but in no country, perhaps, have these principles been more thoroughly systematized and developed than in a few training colleges in Great Britain. . . . From these institutions have been sent out thousands of teachers thoroughly prepared for the work of primary instruction on these improved principles.

This plan claims to begin where other systems have ever failed to commence, at the beginning, and here, laying surely and firmly the foundation, to proceed carefully and by natural and progressive steps to rear the super-structure, ever adapting the means to the results to be obtained. Following this course, we first begin with things, the qualities of which are cognizable by the senses of the children, and awaken, lead out, and guide the observation and quicken the perception. That the observation may be more accurate, the various senses are carefully cultivated. These are the earliest, and in childhood the most strongly developed of human faculties. This fact must settle, beyond a doubt, the correctness of this mode of procedure. . . .

We begin, then, by presenting simple forms, and the primitive and more distinct colors. Once familiar with these, the children are led to trace them in the objects of nature about them, and lastly to observe their various resultant combinations. In each object their attention is called to the individual characteristics or qualities which, combined, constitute the object, and distinguish it from every other object.

From the concrete they are led to the abstract. Through the medium of things known they are led to the unknown. They are now prepared to form clear conceptions of things they have never seen, through the medium of things they have seen.

It is now a full year since we adopted this system of instruction, and of its superiority over the old methods we can speak with some degree of assurance.

The annual examination of these schools has just closed. The Examining Committee, who had this in charge, have taken special pains to observe carefully the results of this system in awakening mind, quickening thought, perception, and all the early faculties of the child, and they return the most flattering reports of its success as a means of mental development.

Wherever the teachers have caught the spirit of the plan, and have made a practical application of it, the effect is very marked in the awakened and quickened faculties of the children. It was never our pleasure before to witness so much interest in any class exercise. There was no dull routine of questions and monosyllabic answers, no mere recitation of dry and stereotyped formulas, no apparent unloading of the memory, but we seemed as in the presence of so many youthful adventurers fresh from their voyages of discovery, each eager to recount the story of his successes. In their explorations, the fields, the wood, the garden, and the old house, from the cellar to the garret, will testify to their vigilance. The knowledge both of the parents and the teacher is often put to the severest test. They are continually plied with questions too difficult for them to answer.

Teachers say to us now, "We have no longer any dull pupils." All are wide awake. The children say it is "real fun" to go to school now. It is not that the work of the schoolroom is less real and earnest, but that it is better adapted to child nature, and meets the demands of their young life energies. This is what we call education, in its true spirit and purpose.

EDWARD SHELDON ON "OBJECT TEACHING" (1864)   From Edward A. Sheldon, "Object Teaching," *American Journal of Education*, vol. XIV, pp. 93–102.

In opening the discussion on this occasion, on what is sometimes technically called "Object Teaching," I propose first very briefly to state the principles upon which the methods thus indicated are based. Secondly to consider some of the difficulties that lie in the way of the progress of these reformed methods of teaching, and the best way of removing them; and lastly consider the true aim and limit of these methods as applied to the development of the early faculties of childhood.

We assume first that education should embrace the united, harmonious development of the *whole being,* the *moral,* the *physical,* and the *intellectual;* and that no one of these should be urged forward to the neglect or at the expense of the other. We likewise assume that there is a natural order in the evolution of the human faculties, and also of appliances for their development, a knowledge of which is essential to the highest success in education; that the perceptive faculties are the first and most strongly developed and upon them are based all future acquirements; that just in proportion as they are quick and accurate in receiving impressions, will all the future processes of education and outgrowing attainments be easy and rapid, and ever prove unfailing sources of delight; and hence they should be the first to receive distinctive and special culture. To this we may add that childhood has certain marked and distinctive characteristics which should never be lost sight of in all our dealings with children. Among the more prominent of these are activity, love of sympathy, and a desire for constant variety. In the natural order of subjects we recognize as first, mathematics, including a consideration of form, size, and number, second, physics, including objects in nature, their sensible qualities and properties, and third, language, including oral and written expression, reading and spelling.

We have thus stated, as concisely as possible, the very first steps in this natural order, upon which must be based all successful educational efforts; for the limited time allotted to this paper reminds us of the necessity of confining ourselves closely to the point under discussion.

*   *   *

. . . book speculators are continually making use of the term as a catch word, for the purpose of disposing of their wares; thus imposing upon the uninitiated, and bringing into discredit methods of which these books are the farthest possible from being the representatives. In this way old books have received new title pages, and new books with old methods have been christened with the catch word, "Object Lessons," or "On the Object Plan"; and what is lamentable, multitudes know not the difference between the *name* and the *thing.* In this way much mischief has already been done, and much more is yet to be experienced.

Realizing these objections, some have proposed to change the name, substituting a term more comprehensive and less liable to objection. But this change of names will only subject publishers to an additional expense of new title pages, and will not wholly obviate the evils referred to. Our plan would be to drop all specific names, and speak of all improved, natural or philosophical methods of teaching as such, and let the great effort be to infuse right principles into the minds of teachers, to lead them to study the mental, moral and physical constitution of children, and the best method of bringing this treble nature out in harmonious development. In this lies our only hope of any substantial improvement in educational processes.

*   *   *

A common error committed in Object Teaching is in converting exercises that should be strictly for development, into instruction in abstract science. Now the aim of all these early lessons should be to quicken the perceptions, and give them accuracy, awaken thought and cultivate language. To this end the senses must be exercised on the sensible qualities and properties of objects; and when the consideration of these objects goes beyond the reach of the senses, then of course, the exercise ceases to be a development exercise, and becomes either an exercise of the memory or of some of the higher faculties. All these early lessons then should be confined to objects, their parts, qualities and properties that come clearly within the reach of the senses of the children, and no generalizations should include any thing more than such objects and their qualities. Definitions should in no case go beyond the mere description of the actual perceptions of the children. These points we regard of vital importance, and that we may be clearly understood, we will be a little more definite, and indicate just where we would begin, and how far we would go in carrying out the leading exercises employed. In the theory we have presented, these should consist of lessons on Form, Size and Number as belonging to mathematics; of lessons on Objects, Animals, Plants, Color, and Place or Geography, as belonging to Natural History, and lessons on language, including oral and written expression, reading and spelling.

And here I trust I shall be pardoned for presenting my views on these points in nearly the words of a report on this subject presented last week at the Annual meeting of the New York Teachers' Association. In lessons in number the children should be held long and closely to the simple combination of objects, and hence must be confined to numbers that come fairly within the range of the perceptions.

The lessons of Form should be confined to the observation and description of some of the more simple and common forms in nature. Here we must guard against abstractions; the mere memorizing of definitions that go beyond the observations of the children. As we have already said, definitions should be nothing more than mere descriptions, a remark that applies equally to all kindred subjects of instruction. The lessons on Size consist of nothing more than the actual measurement of various objects and distances, and the simple exercise of the judgment in the application of the knowledge thus gained.

In lessons in Color, the children may be led to observe, discriminate and name the leading colors and their tints and shades, and apply them to the description of objects in nature. This will add largely to their stock of language, and greatly aid them in their future lessons. It is worthy of remark just here, that the deficiency in terms to express in our language distinctions in color is one that is deeply felt, and any effort at improvement in this direction should receive our hearty encouragement. Beyond this the children may be indulged in mixing colors, to observe how the various colors are produced from the primaries, and finally their intuitive perceptions of the harmony of colors may be called out. Not that any attempt should be made to teach the scientific law underlying the harmony of colors, but they simply observe that "certain colors look well together."

In lessons on Place or Elementary Geography, the attention of the child is confined to a consideration of that part of the earth which he sees in his daily walks, its physical and industrial features, the various grouping and relation of objects to each other and himself, as a preparation for the consideration of what lies beyond his own immediate neighborhood. In lessons on animals and plants we begin by calling attention to the parts, position, and finally, uses of parts. At the next step, in lessons on animals, the children are led to consider something of characteristics and habits, and *finally* of adaptation of parts to habits. The children are continually exercised in close and accurate observation, by means of specimens or pictures, and to a limited extent from given or tangible facts and phenomena, to draw conclusions, thus calling forth the, as yet, feeble powers of reason. In some of these later lessons some little knowledge of the natural history of the animals considered, is also imparted. All these lessons are given on the more familiar quadrupeds and birds, either those inhabiting the immediate neighborhood, or of which they have been made acquainted by information. Some attention has also been given by the teacher to the order in which these lessons have been presented, grouping together, or rather giving in succession, lessons belonging to the same class or order. Thus far, however, the children have no realizing sense of any such design. After having gone over in this way with a few of the leading types of each order of mammals, they are led to associate in natural groups or orders the animals that have constituted the subjects of these lessons, aided by the knowledge they have acquired of their characteristic parts and habits. These systematic lessons, however, are confined to mammals and birds, as being more familiar to the children. For variety an occasional lesson may be given on a fish, an insect, a reptile, or a shell, those somewhat familiar to the children, but a large proportion of the animals belonging to these and the lower subdivisions of the animal kingdom are farther removed from the child's immediate sphere of observation, and therefore the basis of the classification is less apparent.

In "Lessons on Objects" proper, as distinct from "Lessons on Animals and Plants," the first lessons should be on objects of the most familiar character, and for a long time their attention should only be called to the simple parts and their position. This involves no use of difficult terms, but at the same time cultivates observation and the power of accurate expression. At the next step some of the more simple and common qualities are added. At a further step more occult qualities, requiring more close and careful observation, and such as are brought out by experiment, may be introduced; also, to a limited extent, the adaptation of qualities, material or structure, to use, may be considered. At a still more advanced stage, some information in regard to the objects considered may be brought in, as also a *simple classification* of the objects and qualities considered. In connection with all these lessons, the cultivation of language should be made one of the leading points; commencing with the simplest oral expressions, leading on to written reproductions, and finally to consecutive narrative.

This leads us directly to a consideration of *language,* the subject next in order. It was a favorite maxim of Pestalozzi, that "The *first* object in education must be to lead a child to *observe with accuracy; the second,* to *express with correctness* the result of his observations." Again, "*ideas first,* and language afterward." That there is a natural connection between thought and speech, observation and expression, there can be no reasonable doubt. Who has not observed that children always seek a name for every new object of discovery, and are never satisfied until they receive it? It is, in fact, out of this necessity of our nature, that language has grown up, expanded and enlarged, to keep pace with the growth of ideas. Bacon has well said, "Men believe their reason to be lord over their words; but it often happens too, that words exercise a reciprocal and reactionary power over our intellect. Words, as a Tartar's bow, shoot back upon the understanding of the wisest, and mightily entangle and pervert the judgment."

Again, of what practical advantage would be the careful cultivation of observation, without a corresponding power of expression? Ideas unuttered are valueless to all but their possessor, but well expressed, they are a power to move the world. Like the ripple started on the surface of the placid lake, their influence is felt to the remotest shores of time. Now as observation is cultivated by careful and constant use, so is language by the frequent expression of ideas. But how is the child to acquire this power of language, or what is the process and order of this acquisition? This is an interesting question, and deserves an intelligent answer. Here, as in everything else, we must go back to nature, if we would make no mistakes. Observe then the child in his first utterances. His first efforts at speech are to articulate the names of those persons, objects and actions, bearing the most immediate relation to his desires and necessities; the names of pa and ma, the articles of food and drink, the different members of the household, and familiar objects about him. Next in order come action-words.

Neither name nor action-words are as yet qualified, but these quality words follow slowly along.

The third step is reached before the time of school life begins. However, when the transfer is made from the nursery to the school-room, this vocabulary must be enlarged to keep pace with the growth of ideas. Observing then the order already indicated, we begin with the names of objects, the wholes and their parts. Next come the names of the properties and qualities of objects, proceeding, of course, from the most simple to the more difficult. But is it asked to what extent are these terms to be given? We answer most unhesitatingly, *just so far as the child feels the necessity for their use, and has the power to apply them.* But it is objected that "The use of words can not be long kept up or remembered by the children, that are above the current language of the circle in which they move."

We can say with that assurance that springs from careful observation and experience, that they are governed quite as much in the application of these terms, and consequently in their familiarity with them, by the necessity they experience for their use in the description of objects about them, and in the expression of their perceptions, as by the language of the home circle, or immediate associates. To this may be added the fact that for five hours in the day, and five days in the week, and this for several successive years, they live in the atmosphere of the school-room, where these terms are "current language," and the children from the humblest homes readily incorporate them into their own dialect. Were not these *facts,* there would be poor encouragement for the teacher to labor to improve the diction, manners or morals of the poorer classes.

The success of every good school located in such unfortunate neighborhood, in elevating the children in all these points, is sufficient to substantiate this position. On what other principle can we account for the elevation of successive generations and races of men above their immediate ancestors? And how else can we account for the growth of language? We must depend upon the school to exert a refining, civilizing influence, and that too above and beyond the immediate "circle in which they move." Now in the language of the masses of the people there is a great dearth of terms descriptive of the properties and qualities of objects. How and where is this defect to be remedied? We answer emphatically, by the *cultivation of language in the schools.* We have already stated that language as the expression of ideas, bears an important relation to their development and growth, and therefore that the two should be carried on contemporaneously. We should, therefore, as we proceed with the exercises in developing ideas, give the terms expressive of those ideas, always using, however, those terms which are most simple, and at the same time expressive of the perceptions to be indicated. In all these exercises reference should be had to the mental status of the children; never giving any more than can be readily comprehended and appropriated. In these and all other school exercises, the answers of the children should be incorporated into full and complete expressions. As they advance they will take pleasure in reproducing their object lessons on their slates. This should always be encouraged, and should become a daily and regular exercise.

Where this course is pursued the children will early acquire the power of easy and elegant diction, and readiness in composition.

The subject of reading is one surrounded with many difficulties. These, it is the business of the teacher to so divide and classify as to present but one difficulty at a time, and make the successive steps easy and pleasurable to the child. The difficulties that meet the young learner at the very threshold, are the number of different sounds represented by the same character, the number of different characters representing the same sound, the representation of the same sound sometimes by one character and sometimes by another, and sometimes by a combination of characters, and the frequent use of silent letters. To obviate these difficulties he should not for a long time be confused with more than a single form to a single sound. With twenty-three characters and the same number of sounds a large amount of reading matter, consisting of easy simple words, may be given. It is better to commence with the small forms of the letters, as they are better adapted for general use. When the children become familiar with these, the capitals may be introduced. Gradually new sounds may be brought in, and with them new words. A few words may be learned as words, to enable us to fill up the reading matter. In connection with the Object Lessons, also, new words are being continually learned. By this process, in which the children are able to help themselves at every step of their progress, they ever find fresh delight. By a simple plan of classification, in which words of like anomalies are brought together, and which the children at first dictate themselves, the work of spelling is made one of the most pleasing, and animated exercises in the school-room. These words are both spelled orally and written upon the slate. The plan we have suggested, of which we have been able only to give the merest outline, we have found a very rapid and thorough one in teaching children to read and spell, and in its details strictly Pestalozzian.

We have thus briefly alluded to a few of the leading exercises, and the extent to which they should be employed in the development of the early faculties of childhood, that our position may be definitely understood, and for the reason that we believe them liable to much abuse.

AN "OBJECT" LESSON ON NUMBER (1862)   From Edward A. Sheldon, *Elementary Instruction* (Oswego, 1862), pp. 33–34.

A lesson to develop the perception of the number expressed by the word "three," and to communicate the name of the number.

The following sketch of a lesson will show the plan to be pursued with all numbers as far as ten.

Before commencing a lesson on a number which is new to the children, the teacher should ascertain that they have clear ideas of those on which they have already received instruction. In this instance it is supposed that the number *two* has been the subject of a lesson, and is thoroughly understood, and that the teacher tests this by directing one of the children to bring two pencils, two books, etc., while the others look on observantly, and approve or otherwise, as the case may demand. If the requirements be rigidly met, the class may simultaneously describe the objects as they are presented, saying, "Two pencils," "Two slates," "Two books," etc. Here also the objects should be diverse.

With this attainment made, the class may be led on to the observation of the number Three.

1. The teacher should now add one pencil to the two pencils, one slate to the two slates, or one book to the two books, and as this is done, require the children to say, in each case, "Three pencils," "Three slates," "Three books," etc. As an exercise, groups of *three* of different objects may be placed before the class, and one of the children desired to bring a similar number of the same object, or of some other. When observation has been well exercised by varied examples of this kind, the children may again be told that such a number of any object whatever is called *three* of it, and that the name of that number is THREE.

2. The teacher should then try to discover how far the children are able to connect the word *three* with the corresponding number, by calling on several of them in rotation to bring three pencils, or three books, or three pins—to bring three of their companions to the teacher, to hold up three fingers, or to clap their hands three times, etc.

3. The object of the next exercise is to ascertain whether the children can promptly apply the proper name to the number, when presented to them in different objects. The teacher may hold up three fingers and ask how many are held up, and then take up three pencils and again ask how many there are, or make three strokes upon the slate, and ask how many such a number of anything is said to be.

It may confirm ideas already gained as to the *succession* of numbers, if the children are required to tell, in regular succession, those they have acquired while the succession is *enacted*, as it were, by the teacher. Several sets of objects should be at hand, from each of which the teacher takes at first just one, then a second, then a third; the children saying, as this is done, "One pencil," "Two pencils," "Three pencils"; "One pin," "Two pins," "Three pins," etc.

This should be followed by an exercise in ascending and descending enumeration, thus:

"Now, altogether say with me, *One, Two, Three*; and again *Three, Two, One*. And now say the same without me, for I shall be silent."

In these exercises, which will need frequent repetition, great care must be taken not to perplex the children; the perception of number should be permitted to grow upon them almost without their being conscious of the attainment. It should be attained by simple observation, rather than by a process of reasoning, although it is true that, at a further stage of the child's education, it will be found that all the higher calculations of arithmetical reasoning are, in fact, based upon the knowledge for which it is the aim of these initiatory exercises to prepare.

The Kindergarten

DESCRIPTION OF THE KRAUS-BOELTE SCHOOL IN NEW YORK CITY
(**1872**)   From Henry Barnard, ed., *Papers on Froebel's Kindergarten* (Hartford, Conn.,
1884), pp. 557–58.

Training Class

The instruction given to the Training Class begins in October, and ends in June following—embracing at least five lessons per week, besides the actual practice in the Kindergarten, for all the working portions of one year.

The qualities and qualifications looked for in candidates for the diploma of this class are:

1. A quick and responsive sympathy with children—a real, genuine sympathy, and not simulated.

2. A kind and motherly heart—something which inspires the feeling of sister and mother for children, and makes them happy in their company, and gives a clear insight into child nature and life up to the seventh year.

3. An exact knowledge and spiritual comprehension united with dextrous handling of the Kindergarten material.

4. Sufficient musical knowledge and vocal ability to sing well the little songs and guide the plays.

5. A cheerful humor, that can easily enter into the child's plays, and is not easily disturbed by occasional forwardness, or real shyness.

The object of the course is to give the members of the class a clear conception of Froebel's pedagogic aim in his several gifts and occupations, and to show the deep significance of the child's natural play, and breathe a true spirit into employments which become otherwise incomprehensible mechanism. The characteristic of Froebel's method of occupying children to their own development, lies in permitting them unconsciously to bring forth a product by their own feeble efforts, and thus awaken and develop the germs of the creative spirit to produce individual work, and not mere imitation.

To secure a real fusion of learning, work, and play, the objects are not all ready made, and enough only is said or done, so as to invite some independent mental or muscular energy upon the material. Children's activity must be encouraged, and only so far directed, so as to be saved from destructiveness, and prevented from exhausting itself into languor and thoughtlessness. The danger of the occupations of children degenerating into mere imitation and mechanical routine, must be obviated, by leaving ample scope for exciting and employing the imagination and invention, in their own combination of the material.

Too much is done in our American Kindergartens, and the same defect is noticed in most European institutions, with perfected patterns and elaborated materials; and great efforts are made in this Training Class to teach its members how to vary the exercises, encourage children to devise patterns, and use, modify, and make up the material for themselves, each in his own way. In their published circular Mr. and Mrs. Kraus say:

> "It cannot too often be repeated that the significance of Froebel's system consists in so arranging the gifts and occupations as to encourage and enable the child to transform and recombine the material, and thus strengthen by exercise his bodily and mental faculties. Individuality is thus developed. Froebel gives explanations how to conduct their games: to know them all is quite a study; to apply them well, an art; to understand their full significance, a science. No one can master all these details without deep study, much observation, and thoughtful practice. And when mastered, the Kindergartner deserves a rank and remuneration not now accorded to her."

Nearly two hundred ladies have availed themselves of the opportunities in training which this Seminary has offered, and hold its diploma. Many of them are now teachers of the Kindergarten method in several Normal Schools, Principals of Ladies High Schools, conductors of independent Kindergartens in some of our chief cities, ladies of education from different parts of the country, with their daughters for their own personal culture, sisters of charity and other devoted women, to qualify themselves to conduct asylums, and infant schools for neglected children.

FELIX ADLER ON THE KINDERGARTEN AND WORKINGMAN'S SCHOOL OF THE NEW YORK SOCIETY FOR ETHICAL CULTURE
(1878)   From Henry Barnard, ed., *Papers on Froebel's Kindergarten* (Hartford, Conn., 1884), pp. 687–90.

The Institution

The workingman's School and Free Kindergarten form one institution. The children are admitted at the age of three to the Kindergarten. They are graduated from it at six, and enter the Workingman's School. They remain in the School till they are thirteen or fourteen years of age. Thereafter those who show decided ability receive higher technical instruction. For the others who leave the School proper and are sent to work, a series of evening classes will be opened, in which their industrial and general education will be continued in various directions. This graduate course of the Workingman's School is intended to extend up to the eighteenth or twenty-first year.

The Free Kindergarten

The characteristics of our Free Kindergarten may be briefly summarized as follows:

It is a *Kindergarten*. It has the merits which belong to the Kindergarten system generally. It is a *Free Kindergarten* for the poor, that is, it brings Kindergarten education to the poorest class, who are not able to pay for it themselves. It has the negative advantage of taking little children from the streets, where they would otherwise be exposed to bad companionship and pernicious influences of every kind. If it accomplished nothing more than this, our Kindergarten would be rendering no little service. But it has also the positive merit of placing the poor children under the best educational influence which modern times have devised. It is moreover the first step in a *rational system of education*. Kindergartens exist in great number. But a very large part of their benefits is lost because the rational method which they begin is not followed up in the later education of the child. That our Kindergarten is connected with and followed by a Workingman's School, is one of its characteristics upon which I lay especial stress. Of other features of the Kindergarten, I mention the following:

It has a *Normal Class* attached to it. This was founded by and is in charge of the Principal. The lady pupils of the Normal Class receive instruction gratis in the theory and art of Kindergartning. In return, they devote their service for a year to the Kindergarten, and assist in its practical management. We have thus every year a corps of eight or nine Assistant-Kindergartners supplied to us by the Normal Class.

The Kindergarten has a *Ladies' Committee* directly concerned in the care of it. The ladies are members of the general Executive Committee, but they exercise especial watchfulness over the pupils of the Kindergarten. It is their duty to visit the home of every applicant for admission, in order that we may be sure that only the really poor are taken into our Institution, and we may thus be protected against imposture. The ladies also undertake at least one annual visitation of all the families connected with the Kindergarten, in order to foster healthful relations between the home and School.

Warm Luncheons are provided for the children daily in the Kindergarten. The little children often came to us hungry. We found it difficult to give them instruction on an empty stomach. A Free Kindergarten for the poor must look to the bodily wants of its pupils as well as to their minds. Garments and shoes are also distributed among the children by the Ladies' Committee, whenever cases of great destitution, such as often occur, are reported.

The results already achieved by our Kindergarten work are satisfactory. Children came to us who could not smile; some of them remained for weeks in the Kindergarten before they were seen to smile. In the Kindergarten these sad little faces were gradually changed. The children were taught how to play; they learned how to be joyous. The children came to us unclean in every way; in the Kindergarten they are made clean, and a neat appearance and habits of tidiness are insisted upon. The children's minds were awakened; their faculties—physical and intellectual—were developed. And here, of course, the degree of success achieved in each individual case varied with the natural ability of the pupils. Best of all, a powerful moral influence has been brought to bear on the children of the Kindergarten. Even the fact that they live in a little children's community, and are compelled to submit to the laws of that community, is important. Then, too, direct moral suasion is brought to bear upon the children by their teachers. The faults of each child are studied; obstinacy is checked, selfishness is put to the blush, and, by a firm, yet mild treatment, the character is improved.

The Workingman's School

The school, in which *work* will constitute an essential feature, not for its future productive value, but for its current educative influence, was opened in February, 1880, under the direction of G. Bamberger, a native of Hesse, and trained in the best methods, of which it is the aim of the founders to make this institution a model—"in which the entire system of rational and liberal education for the children of the poorer class might be exhibited from beginning to end." The example, "having once been set, would not be without effect upon the common school system at large," which is thought by the projectors (in the light of an article in Harpers' Magazine for November, 1880), not to be altogether satisfactory, at least for those who are to get their living by the labor of their hands, or to discharge the duties of men and women in American society. Assisted by the munificent gift of $10,000 from Mr. Joseph Seligman, the "United Relief Work" of the Society for Ethical Culture added to the Free Kindergarten, which had already attained to seven classes, the two lower classes of the Workingman's School—composed of twenty-five graduates of the Kindergarten. The Principal (Mr. Bamberger), in his first report at the Class of 1880, makes a statement, of which the following are paragraphs:

> Our School is to consist of eight classes, of which two are now in operation. The scheme of studies will be found appended at the close of the report. It embraces four hours' instruction weekly in the use of tools, and to this I beg leave to call especial attention.
>
> First, we begin industrial instruction at the very earliest age possible. Already in our Kindergarten, we lay the foundation for the system of work instruction that is to follow. In the School proper, then, we seek to bridge over the interval lying between the preparatory Kindergarten training and the specialized instruction of the technical school, utilizing the school age itself for the development of industrial ability. This, however, is only one characteristic feature of our institution. The other, and the capital one, is, that we seek to combine industrial instruction organically with the ordinary branches of instruction, thus using it, not only for the material purpose of creating skill, but also ideally as a factor of mind-education. To our knowledge, such an application of work-instruction has nowhere, as yet, been attempted, either abroad or in this country.
>
> The softest wood is too hard for the delicate fingers of children seven years old, and, moreover, requires the use of heavy and sharp tools, such as are not willingly entrusted to little ones at so tender an age. We finally decided to use clay. Clay, after it has been prepared in a special way for this purpose, is easy to cut and to manipulate, does not stick to the tool, and is not brittle enough to break and crumble. This proved entirely successful.
>
> A complete series of patterns had to be invented which might be worked by young pupils out of this material. Thirty such patterns have been produced, and in them we have the system of elementary industrial exercises, with which we begin.

*   *   *

By means of a simple arrangement the school desks are converted into work-tables. Every child is supplied with a set of cheap and suitable tools. The work lessons occur in the afternoon on two days of the week, and last two hours each time. The pupils are obliged to behave as quietly during work as in the other school hours; only just so much whispering is permitted as is necessary for the requesting and rendering of necessary assistance. We endeavor to give the school-room the air of a well-conducted workshop. Each pupil-workman has his own place and tools, for which he is held responsible so far as possible. All begin work simultaneously, and stop at the same moment.

*   *   *

In this way we endeavor to make work-instruction contribute towards the general development of the child. The hand is educated by the mind, the mind by the hand.

What further advantages does the introduction of this species of work-instruction offer? A great moral advantage, besides the purely intellectual ones. The habit of working together, of living, as it were, together, exercises the best moral influence. At an age when they are most susceptible to educational influences, the children learn to live harmoniously in social groups, and become accustomed to mutual aid and support. No individual can place himself above another; all have similar duties, equal rights, equivalent claims. But, on the other hand, there is no false, artificial equality. The children are taught from the beginning the necessity of subordinating themselves to the more able and skillful, while, warned by their own failures, they learn to sympathize with the weak and helpless.

ELIZABETH PEABODY DESCRIBES THE IDEAL KINDERGARTNER
(1872)   From Elizabeth P. Peabody, *Lectures in the Training Schools for Kindergartners* (Boston, 1893), pp. 1-2, 4-5, 88.

Whoever proposes to become a kindergartner according to the idea of Froebel, must at once dismiss from her mind the notion that it requires less ability and culture to educate children of three, than those of ten or fifteen years of age. It demands more; for, is it not plain that to superintend and guide accurately the *formation* of the human understanding itself, requires a finer ability and a profounder insight than to listen to recitations from books ever so learned and scientific? To form the human understanding is a work of time, demanding a knowledge of the laws of thought, will, and feeling, in their interaction upon the threshold of consciousness, which can be acquired only by the study of children themselves in their every act of life—a study to be pursued in the spirit that reveals what Jesus Christ *meant*, when he said: "He that receiveth a little child in my name, receiveth *me, and Him that sent me;*" "Woe unto him who offends one of these little ones, for their spirits behold the face of my Father who is in heaven."

Not till children who have been themselves educated according to Froebel's principles, grow up, will there be found any adult persons who can keep kindergartens without devoting themselves to a special study of child-nature in the spirit of devout humility. For we are all suffering the ignorance and injury inevitable from having begun our own lives in the confusions of accidental and disorderly impressions, without having had the clue of reason put into our hands by that human providence of education, which, to be true, must reflect point by point the Divine Providence, that according to the revelations of history is educating the whole race, and which may find hints for its procedure in observing the spontaneous play of children fresh from the hands of the Creator. and enjoyment of ever-widening relations to our kind, with the fulfilment of the duties belonging to them. It is the absolute helplessness of the human infant which challenges the maternal instinct to rush to his rescue, lest he should die at once. And to continue to study his manifestations of pleasure and discontent with obedient respectfulness, is the perfection of the maternal nursing. But when the child has got on so far as to know the simplest uses of its own body, and especially after it has learned enough words to express its simplest wants and sensations, even parents seem to think it can get on by itself, so that children from about two to five years of age are left to self-education, as it were; this virtual abandonment being crossed by a capricious and arbitrary handling of them—mind and body—on the part of those around them, which is even worse than the neglect; for when are children more unable, than between three and five years old, to guide their own thoughts and action? How would a garden of flowers fare, to be planted, and then left to grow with so little scientific care taken by the gardener, as is bestowed upon children between one and five years old?

Froebel, in the very word kindergarten, proclaimed that gospel for children which holds within it the promise of the coming of the kingdom, in which God's will is to be done on earth as it is in heaven—a consummation which we daily pray for with our lips, but do not do the first thing to bring about, by educating our children in the way of order, which is no less earth's than "heaven's first law," and makes earth heaven so far as it is fulfilled.

A kindergarten means a guarded company of children, who are to be treated as a gardener treats his plants; that is, in the first place, studied to see what they are, and what conditions they require for the fullest and most beautiful growth; in the second place, put into or supplied with these conditions, with as little handling of their individuality as possible, but with an unceasing genial and provident care to remove all obstructions, and favor all the circumstances of growth. It is because they are living organisms that they are to be *cultivated*—not *drilled* (which is a process only appropriate to insensate stone).

I think there is perhaps no better way of making apparent what this kindergart-ning is, which makes such an importunate demand on your consideration, than to tell you how the idea germinated and grew in the mind of Froebel himself; for thus we shall see that it would be unreasonable to expect that it could be improvised by every teacher; but that here, as elsewhere in human life, God has sent into the world a gifted person to guide his fellows, according to the law enunciated by St. John in the 38th verse of the 4th chapter of his Gospel.

*   *   *

It is because kindergartning is this true education, which is mutual delight to the adult and the child, that I have faith it will prevail, and its prevalence is my hope for humanity. By the infinite mercy of God, no human being is hopeless of redemption into God's perfect image at last; but humanity will not be redeemed as a whole,—will not become the image of God, or live the life of God,—until little children are suffered to go unto Christ while they are yet of the kingdom of heaven, and are blessed from the first and continually, by those who shall take them in their arms to bless them. Those are only perfect kindergartners who are "hidden in Christ," receiving every child in his name, and humbly learning of them the secrets of greatness in the kingdom of heaven, which is to be established on earth.

Kindergartning is not a craft, it is a religion; not an avocation, but a vocation from on High.

ELIZABETH PEABODY ON THE "OCCUPATIONS" OF THE
KINDERGARTEN (1877)   From Elizabeth P. Peabody, *Guide to the Kindergarten . . .*
(New York, 1877), pp. 43–47, 52–53.

Kindergarten Occupations

There is a kind of thing done in Kindergarten, which retains the best characteristics of childish play, and yet assumes the serious form of occupation.

Fancy-work, if Froebel's method be strictly followed, is the best imitation of industry; for it can serve to a perfect intellectual training.

Childish play has all the main characteristics of art, inasmuch as it is the endeavor to "conform the shows of things to the desires of the mind,"—Bacon's definition of poetry. A child at play is histrionic. He personates characters, with costume and mimic gesture. He also undertakes to represent whatever thing interests his mind by embodiment of it in outward form. Advantage is taken of this, by Froebel, to initiate exquisite manipulation, in several different materials; a veritable artistic work, which trains the imagination to use, and develops the understanding to the appreciation of beauty, symmetry, or order,—"Heaven's first law."

Froebel's first two Gifts, as they are called, are a box of colored worsted balls, and a box containing the cube, the sphere, and the cylinder. These two Gifts belong more especially to the nursery series, and were published some years since in Boston, with little books of rhymes, and suggestions for playing with babies.

But they can be used, in some degree, in the Kindergarten: the first, to give lessons on the harmonies of colors; and the second, to call attention to fundamental differences of form.

It is possible, however, to omit these, and begin a Kindergarten with the Third Gift, which is a little wooden box, containing eight cubes of an inch dimension.

The first plays with these blocks, especially if the children are very young, will be to make what Froebel calls forms of life: that is, chairs, tables, columns, walls, tanks, stables, houses, &c. Everybody conversant with children knows how easily they will "make believe," as they call it, all these different forms, out of any materials whatever; and are most amused, when the materials to be transformed by their personifying and symbolizing fancy are few, for so much do children enjoy the exercise of imagination, that they find it more amusing to have simple forms, which they can "make believe,"—first to be one thing, and then another,—than to have elaborately carved columns, and such like materials, for building. There is nothing in life more charming to a spectator, than to see this shaping fancy of children, making everything of nothing, and scorning the bounds of probability, and even of possibility. It is a prophecy of the unending dominion which man was commanded, at his creation, to have over nature; and gives meaning to the parable of the Lord God's bringing all creatures before Adam, that he might give them their names.

Wordsworth felicitously describes, in that ode which he calls "Intimations of Immortality in Childhood," this victorious play of—

"The seer blest,
On whom those truths do rest,
Which we are toiling all our lives to find."

"Behold the child among his new-born blisses;
A six years' darling of a pigmy size;
See where, mid work of his own hand, he lies,
Fretted by sallies of his mother's kisses,
With light upon him from his father's eyes!
See at his feet some little plan or chart,
Some fragment of his dream of human life,
Shaped by himself with newly learned art,—
     A wedding or a festival,
     A mourning or a funeral;
And this hath now his heart,
And unto this he frames his song.
Then he will fit his tongue
To dialogues of business, love, or strife;
     But it will not be long
     Ere this be thrown aside,
     And with new joy and pride,
The little actor cons another part;
Filling from time to time his humourous stage
With all the persons down to palsied age
That life brings with her in her equipage."

That this is a literal picture, every mother knows; and, in this childish play, there is all the subjective part of a genuine work of art; the effort being to dramatize, or embody in form, the inward fancy, no less than in the case of the most mature and successful artist. The child seizes whatever materials are at hand to give objectivity to what is within; and he is only baffled in the effect, because he is not developed enough in understanding, and has not knowledge enough to discover or appreciate means appropriate to his ends. It is for the adult to show him that the universe is a magazine of materials given to the human race, wherewith each is to build an image of God's creative wisdom, into which he shall inwardly grow by the very act of accomplishing this destiny.

As the child is satisfied at first with a symbolical representation of his inward thought, a row of chairs and foot-stools, arranged in a line, makes a railroad to his imagination; and no less a row of cubes, one being piled on another for the engine.

In using the blocks in a Kindergarten, the child at first is left to his own spontaneity, as much as possible; but the teacher is to suggest means of carrying out whatever plan or idea he has. What is cultivating about the exercise is, that the child makes or receives a plan, and then executes it; has a thought, and embodies it in a form.

But something more can be done with the blocks. They can be made symbolical of the personages and objects of a story. Thus even with the eight blocks, five may be a flock of sheep, one the shepherd, one a wolf who is seen in the distance, and who comes to steal a sheep, and one the shepherd's dog who is to defend the sheep against the wolf.

When all the Gifts come to be used, much more complicated dramas may be represented. The teacher should set an example; as, for instance, thus: "I am going to build a light-house, so;" (she piles up some blocks and leaves openings near the top, which she says are "the lantern part where the lights are put;" near the light-house are a number of blocks, rather confusedly laid together, of which she says,) "These are rocks, which are very dangerous for ships, but which are scarcely ever seen, because the water dashes over them, especially when there is a storm, or when the night is dark; and that is the reason the light-house is put here. Whenever sailors see a light-house, they know there is danger where it stands; and so they steer their ships away from the place. Look here! here is a ship" (and she constructs with other blocks something which she calls a ship, or schooner, or sloop, representing respectively the number of masts which characterize each kind of vessel), "and there is a pilot standing upon it who has seen the light-house, and is turning the ship another way."

Having built her story, she will now call upon the children to build something. Some will imitate her; others will have plans of their own. As soon as one has finished, he or she must hold up a hand; and the teacher will call upon as many as there is time for, to explain their constructions. There is no better way for a teacher to learn what is in children, their variety of mental temperament and imagination, than by this playing with blocks. Some will be prosaic and merely imitative; some will show the greatest confusion, and the most fantastic operations of mind; others, the most charming fancies; and others, inventive genius. But there will always be improvement, by continuing the exercise; and it is a great means of development into self-subsistence and continuity of thought.

But to return to Froebel's Third Gift, consisting of eight blocks. In making things with the blocks, a great deal is to be said about setting them accurately upon each other, and upon the squares drawn on the table (if it is so painted). I was both amused and instructed, when I was in Hamburg, by seeing a little table full of children taking a first lesson in making two chairs, by piling three blocks on each other for the back, and putting one in front for the seat; the Kindergartner going round so seriously to see if each block was adjusted exactly, and stood squarely. When, at length, the chairs were done, the children took hold of hands, and recited, simultaneously with the Kindergartner, a verse of poetry; and then sang it. I could not understand the words; but the conversation, while they were making the chairs, had helped the several children's fancy to seat their fathers, mothers, or grandparents, or some other favorite friends, in them; each child having been asked for whom he wished to make his chairs, which developed a good deal of the domestic circumstances. None of the class was more than four years old. But the most important use of the eight blocks is to lead the children through a series of symmetrical forms, which Froebel calls forms of beauty.

As a preparation for this work, the children are questioned, till they understand which is the right, and which the left side of the cube made by the eight blocks; which the front, and which the back side; which the upper, and which the under side; and are able to describe a cube by its dimensions; also to know how to divide the whole cube into two, four, or eight parts; how to divide the length, how the breadth, and how the height, into two parts,—lessons of analysis sufficiently amusing, and giving precision to their use of words.

Dividing the height, they get a simple fundamental form; and the four blocks taken off can be arranged around the others symmetrically.

The great secret of the charm of working out symmetrical forms is, that the mind is created to make, like the divine mind. "God geometrizes," says Plato; and therefore man geometrizes. The generation of forms by crystallization, and by vegetable and animal organization, follows the law of polarity, which is alike the law of the human and the mode of the divine creation. It was amusing to hear a little child cry out, "I cannot find an opposite;" and, when another said, "No matter, take this," reply, "But then it will not make anything."

In going through the series of forms, made first by the eight blocks, then by those of the Fourth Gift, and afterwards by the larger number of the Fifth and Sixth Gifts, the child comes, by being led perpetually to put down *opposites*, in order to make symmetry, to learn the value of the law of polarization, which obtains alike in thought, and in the created universe.

But, besides the boxes of solids, there are boxes of triangles, one of equilateral, one of right angle, and two of isosceles triangles—one acute and one obtuse—affording means for an infinity of forms of beauty; so that this amusement of making symmetrical forms is not exhausted in the whole four years of the Kindergarten course.

The same principle of polarity is brought out in the combination of colors, as well as of forms.

In weaving bookmarks and mats, with strips of different colored papers, the series of forms becomes more attractive by observing the harmonies of color. The children are taught, by the colored balls of the First Gift, to distinguish the primary and secondary colors, and to arrange them harmoniously. Children acquire very soon a very exquisite taste in color, and, if carefully called to attend to harmonies, detect an incongruity at once.

* * *

To make forms from the hint of an engraving, is a little above imitation; and it is to be remembered that we do not wish the children to stop with imitations. Let them go on and invent forms, beautiful vases, pitchers, &c. When they begin to make heads and human figures, a teacher, who understands the principles of drawing, can bring to their notice the proportions of the human figure and face found in nature, which make ideal beauty. Many a heaven-destined sculptor will find himself out, in the Kindergarten.

In Germany, at the quadrennial meetings of the Froebel Union, it is the custom to carry specimens of the children's work in all these kinds. A series of each kind is made up by taking the best work of all the children. The six meetings which have already taken place, have all been signalized by impressing upon the commissioners of education of some State, the value of Froebel's culture to the interests of art,— fine and mechanical,—followed by its adoption. And yet its value to art is of secondary importance to its influence on character, which must needs be lifelong,— leading away from temptation, and delivering from evil, the activity secured to the production of use and beauty.

In America, where the excitements of opportunity are literally infinite, the importance of training the speculative mind and immense energy of the people to law, order, beauty, and love (which are all one in the last analysis), is incalculable; and that it can be done most easily and certainly by beginning with the child's mind while he is still "beholding the face of the Father in heaven" with his heart, no one who has ever faithfully tried Kindergarten culture will doubt.

EMMA MARWEDEL DESCRIBES THOSE WHO CAN BECOME
KINDERGARTNERS (1884) From "Kindergarten Work in California," *San Francisco Herald*, July 1880, as quoted in Henry Barnard, ed., *Papers on Froebel's Kindergarten* (Hartford, Conn., 1884), pp. 671–72.

Only those who—

1. Are able to depend on a healthy, graceful body; a perfectly balanced, serene temper; a *good voice;* a lively, sympathetic countenance; and a loving heart for children.

2. Those who have already not only a good foundation of general knowledge, but who themselves are interested in all questions about causes and effects; able to catch at once the ideas of the child, and to illustrate them in such a manner that they shall instruct and interest the child, sufficiently to make its *own original* representation according to Froebel's laws: dictating to develop the child's own knowledge, leading it to observe and compare for itself, from the general to the special, from the concrete to the abstract, always in direct connection with what is at hand, to make an impression upon the child's senses.

3. Those who have practical ability to learn, and artistic talent to execute Froebel's occupations, and are able to impart them to the child without any mechanical drill (though instruction in order and accuracy in detail are essential), always bearing in mind that *these occupations* are only the *tools* for a systematic educational development of all the faculties born *in* and *with* the child; and that the explanation of *how* and *why* these tools are to be applied, according to obvious laws contain the most important points of the system, and, further, that these laws have to be fully understood in the movement plays and use of the ball, as well as in the weaving and the modeling, so that their profound logical connection, for the rigorous, systematic appliance, may be recognized. This philosophic insight into the depths of the system is needed to mature you to independence of thought and originality in arrangements,—for kindergartnerinen are *nothing* if not original,—and that you may do justice to your individual talents, your own conceptions, your own observation of nature and life, and of their educational relation to the child and its human existence; to be saved from the great danger of debasing the system to a repetition of mere words, phrases, and dead actions, thereby introducing more monotonies, more mechanism, and narrowing influences into this educational training than exists in the ordinary school methods. There never was a more liberal, tolerant leader than Froebel himself, who, in all his works and all his letters, addresses the motherly and individual *natural* teaching power and ingenuity,—the source of his own ideas.

4. Those who are able to observe, to study, and describe, the wonders and the beauty of nature and man, in that elevating, poetical, and moral sense we call *religion*,—a religion which teaches the tender heart of the child what is right and wrong, by filling its sweet mind with taste for beauty; to reject the wrong

instinctively and habitually, unconsciously becoming aware that it is born to serve itself and others, and that life has no other value than what we make of it by our own work, and that each one is responsible to the *whole* of which even the child is a part; every play, every song, every little gift made by the child, being presided over by this spirit.

5. And, finally, all those who are earnestly striving to fulfill these conditions may joyfully enter the glorious field of this educational mission, known under the name of the Kindergarten system. And if ever any earthly work does carry its own reward, it is the teaching and loving of our dear little ones according to Froebel's advice; making the teacher a child among children, and the happiest of all, because she feels that she is a teacher, a mother, and a playmate, all in one! But she must not only be the youngest and the oldest of her circle: she must also unite them. The power she exercises will lead the children, unconsciously, either to wrong habits or right power. Her unworded but powerful example is to impress the young mind with all the higher aims and laws of life.

She has to be true, firm, just, and above all, loving. The few rules, once given, have to be strictly kept; orders, when given, must be fulfilled. She must live *in* all and *for* all, never devoting herself to one while neglecting others. She must hear and see, have an eye for every thing, good and bad. Then the child will feel bound under the spiritual power, which will fill his whole imagination, his faith, his love, his veneration. She will be a teacher who never fails! And this finally is the only key to discipline. Without it all other powers will be powerless.

THE SILVER STREET KINDERGARTEN IN SAN FRANCISCO (1884)   From Emma Warwedel, "Kindergarten Work In California," *San Francisco Herald,* July 1880, as quoted in Henry Barnard, ed., *Papers On Froebel's Kindergarten,* (Hartford, 1884) pp. 667–71.

The history of the Silver street Kindergarten alone would make a volume in itself, so many interesting incidents occur there daily. There is not a phase of human nature the Principal has not seen during the two years she has been in charge. In visiting families, she has been called upon to perform the duties of spiritual counselor, physician, mother, nurse, provider, benefactor, and general guardian; with what success may be learned from scores of parents in the neighborhood who have been raised from squalor, drunkenness, and crime to cleanliness, sobriety, and virtue, and who now speak in terms of enthusiastic and unqualified praise, tinged with reverential awe, of "Miss Kate." The Silver street Kindergarten originated as follows: In July, 1878, Professor Felix Adler, the New York philanthrophist, came to San Francisco and delivered a series of lectures on various topics, in which frequent allusion was made to the astonishing beneficial results, morally, intellectually, and physically, of free kindergartens. On one occasion he said: "If we apply the spirit of preventive charity to our age, we must face the evil of pauperism, the root of which lies in a lack of education of the children. In the United States the social question is not yet acute, as it is in Europe, and we are called upon to prevent it from becoming a menace to our republican institutions by building up a class of voters—inaugurating the Kindergarten system of education, and so save the rising generation from destruction." In private he sought out Solomon Heydenfeldt, S. Nicklesburg, Dr. J. Hirschfelder, and other friends, all of whom he so thoroughly convinced that kindergarten was unapproachable as a moral, benevolent, and educational agency, that they agreed to organize a Kindergarten Society, if meeting with public support and encouragement. Accordingly, they set out to secure subscribers, and in one day they obtained one hundred. This was considered sufficient to form a nucleus, and a card bearing the following call was mailed to each:

> DEAR SIR: A meeting for organization of the Public Kindergarten Society of San Francisco will be held Tuesday evening, July 23d, at 9 o'clock P. M., in the Baldwin Hotel parlors. The assistance and countenance of your presence at this first and most important meeting is especially and earnestly requested. For the Committee,
>
> FELIX ADLER.

Pursuant to this call a meeting was held that evening. The attendance was very large, and Mr. Heydenfeldt was elected Chairman, and Dr. J. Hirschfelder Secretary. The proceedings were characterized by great enthusiasm and unanimity. At another meeting held two days subsequent, the "Public Kindergarten Society of San Francisco" was organized by the election of the following officers: S. Heydenfeldt, President; S. Nicklesburg, Vice-President; Dr. Jos. Hirschfelder, Secretary; Julius Jacobs, Treasurer. Board of Directors—Rev. Horatio Stebbins, John Swett, Frederick Roeding, Mrs. L. Gottig, Mrs. H. Behrendt, Mrs. H. Lessing, Miss E. Marwedel.

So faithfully and well have they discharged their duties that they have been unanimously re-elected every term, and now hold the same positions. The Directors were Schueneman Pott, Mrs. H. Behrendt, Mrs. L. Gottig, afterwards increased by the addition of Mrs. H. Lessing and Miss Marwedel. In June, 1870, another addition was made to the Board, including Rev Dr. Stebbins, John Swett, Professor Hilgard, Dr. Fisk, Fred. Roeding. The directors now stand: Rev. Dr. Stebbins, John Swett, Dr. Fisk, Professor Hilgard, Fred. Roeding, Mrs. L. Gottig, Mrs. H. Behrendt, Mrs. H. Lessing, and Miss E. Marwedel.

A Teacher's Trials and Troubles

On the recommendation of Miss E. Marwedel, Miss Kate Smith, who was then in Santa Barbara, was selected as teacher. Miss Smith experienced great difficulty at first in getting mothers to understand the nature and object of the new school, but succeeded in a remarkably short time. On the opening day, which was the first Monday in September, she had eight pupils, and before the week was out she had over fifty applicants and a full school. The regular attendance now is about forty. The roll numbers fifty. There are several hundred applicants. Many of the children being street Arabs of the wildest type, the prosecution of her multifarious duties were fraught with incalculable vexation and hardships during the opening days. On the first afternoon there were several free fights, resulting in scratched and bleeding noses and faces. During a momentary and ominous silence on the second day that foreboded little good, the electrifying clang of the fire-bell brought every youngster to his or her feet, and pell-mell they rushed in an eager go-as-you-please contest for the scene of the conflagration near by. Miss Smith's warning voice was unheard or unheeded. She called after them in vain, with hands convulsively clasped, great tear drops dewing her eye-lashes, and her countenance wearing a most woe-be-gone expression. She sank upon a settee in despair, deploring from the bottom of her heart that she ever left her peaceful home and school in Santa Barbara. But the little scapegraces all returned and day by day they were gradually weaned from their unruly conduct and taught to find pleasure in obedience, and the musicians of "Sunny Italy" may grind their most heart and ear-piercing strains of unrecognizable operas under the very windows of the schoolhouse without disturbing Miss Smith's equanimity or mental serenity, for not a child will turn its head in that direction. The transformation which takes place in some children is truly marvelous, a fact strikingly illustrated in a most cruel and selfish overgrown boy, about four years old, who was among the first admitted. Both his parents were drunkards, and make a precarious livelihood by retailing liquor. The youth had been raised in the full enjoyment of the concentrated essence of malicious mischief. He had been given up as intractable at home, and so was sent to the Kindergarten, out of the way. Here his worst passions found a wide field of activity. He proved domineering and cruel to his childish associates, whom he viciously attacked on the slightest provocation. Self-willed and rebellious, he would violate every injunction of his teacher, whom he bit, scratched, kicked, and cursed from pure ugliness—often anticipating and violating her wishes with aggravating delight. From his advent he was a terror in the school-room, and was given a wide berth. Within six months he was remolded into an exemplary child, and became a favorite with all. His less robust companions looked up to him for encouragement and assistance, and he was ever ready to lend a helping hand. He grew to fairly worship his teacher, whose hands and clothing he would caress with childish expressions of spontaneous endearment, and found perfect happiness in performing for her any little favors she might ask. All his apples, oranges, sweets, cake, and flowers were brought to her, and he would refuse the use of any till she accepted a portion. He "graduated" last Christmas, and now stands at the head of his class in the primary school. This may be said of nearly every child who has gone from the Kindergarten into the public schools.

One difficulty and source of great annoyance to Miss Smith was that of striving to clean the children and keep them so. If every child required one or two daily washings at her hands, she might as well change the establishment into a bath-house, and devote her energies to ablution. Miss Smith wracked her brain for a remedy. She was well aware that to go and tell a mother that her offspring was too dirty to come to school, would result in an open breach of friendship, if not of the peace. The plan she adopted, and which worked to perfection, was to see the mother and make a friend of her—listen to all her woes, secrets, and gossip, meanwhile, little by little work upon her self-respect and better nature till ultimately, not only the child but the whole family were transformed from mire-wallowers to paragons of cleanliness. After two years' unremitting strife, toil, and trouble, Miss Smith has the rare satisfaction of seeing grand results attend her efforts, and now she has gone East on three months' leave of absence to compare notes with leading minds in the work there. Miss Smith has been materially assisted by the young ladies of the High School Normal class, two or three of whom are in daily attendance in her Kindergarten.

Among the generous-hearted supporters of this institution are Wm. M. Lent, who was the first to avail himself of the privilege of becoming a life member of the Society by payment of $100. His daughter, Miss Fannie, also became a life-member nearly a year ago. Hundreds of ladies and gentlemen who have visited the Kindergarten and examined its method of operation and results, have attested their unqualified belief in the system, and left substantial evidence of the fact in the hands of Dr. Hirschfelder, the Secretary. Mrs. R. Johnson, the almoner of the late Michael Reese, donated the institution $500 last December, and $400 more was realized from the dramatic benefit entertainment already alluded to; yet it requires a large amount of money to continue the successful prosecution of the work, and contributions are always welcome.

Kindergarten Workers

Solomon Heydenfeldt, the President, is an earnest advocate of kindergarten, and has a proposition in mind to lay before the pastors of the various churches with a view to getting them interested in the work in their respective Sunday-schools. He claims that at present only the very poor and very rich may derive benefit from kindergartering, while the great middle class is excluded. He thinks that by a very little effort a kindergarten could be opened in connection with every church and conducted at a trifling expense, till such times as provision can be made for the accommodation of all in the School Department.

Since his identification with the public Kindergarten Society, Rev. Dr. Stebbins has been a most zealous and active member. To his efforts is largely due the favorable action recently taken by the Board of Education, which seems disposed to do what lies in its power towards engrafting the kindergarten system on to that of the public schools. Dr. Stebbins, with Prof. Swett, Dr. Fisk, and Professor Hilgard were appointed by the society a committee to confer with the board upon this subject. The result of the conference was that a special meeting was held in the Board of Supervisors' Chambers, new City Hall, on February 27th, for the purpose of hearing the views of the Committee and their friends. The attendance was one of the largest ever seen there, and included scholars of every profession, educators, philanthropists, and business men. Stirring addresses were made by Dr. Stebbins, Judge Heydenfeldt, Mrs. Sarah B. Cooper, Miss Kate D. Smith, Prof. Swett, John W. Taylor, A. McF. Davis, and others, all of whom testified to the transcendent merits of kindergarten over all other known systems of juvenile training, and strongly urged its adoption by the board. The benevolent side of the question, which is one of its strongest, was not advanced, but only the educational pure and simple.

SUSAN E. BLOW ON THE "GIFTS" OF THE KINDERGARTEN

(1884) From "Some Aspects of the Kindergarten," in Henry Barnard, ed., *Papers on Froebel's Kindergarten* (Hartford, 1884), pp. 600–3.

In what I have to say of Froebel's gifts and occupations I wish to be distinctly understood as stating only their theoretic possibilities. Their adaptations to children of different ages and characters can only be learned by experience. Some of them may be profitably used by the baby in the nursery,—others are valuable in the primary school. Again, the same gift or occupation may be used in different ways to secure different ends. From the blocks the child builds with when he is five years old, he may learn at seven the elements of form and number. The square of paper, which the beginner creases into a salt-cellar or twists into a rooster, the older child uses to produce artistic forms and combinations. In general, there is advance from indefinite impressions to clear perceptions, from vague and half-conscious comparison to sharp distinction and clear analysis, from isolated experiences to connected work and thought, and from a mere general activity to production and creation.

With this general understanding pass we now to a detailed consideration of the gifts and occupations, and of their relationship to each other and to the child.

The First Gift consists of six soft worsted balls of the colors of the rainbow.

The Second Gift consists of a wooden sphere, cube and cylinder.

The Third Gift is a two-inch cube divided equally once in each dimension, producing eight small cubes.

The Fourth Gift is a two-inch cube divided by one vertical and two horizontal cuts into eight rectangular parallelopipeds. Each of these parallelopipeds is two inches long, one inch broad and half an inch thick.

The Fifth Gift is a three-inch cube divided equally twice in each dimension into twenty-seven small cubes. Three of these are divided by one diagonal cut into two triangular parts, and three by two diagonal cuts into four triangular parts.

The Sixth Gift is a cube of three inches divided into twenty-seven parallelopipeds of the same dimensions as those of the Fourth Gift. Three of these are divided lengthwise into square prisms, two inches long, half an inch wide and half an inch thick, and six are divided crosswise into square tablets an inch square and half an inch thick. Thus the gift contains thirty-six pieces.

The Seventh Gift consists of square and triangular tablets. Of the latter there are four kinds, viz.: Equilateral, right and obtuse isosceles and right scalene triangles.

The Eighth Gift is a connected slat,—the Ninth consists of disconnected slats.

The Tenth Gift consists of wooden sticks of various lengths, and the Eleventh Gift of whole and half wire rings of various diameter.

Looking at the gifts as a whole we see at once that their basis is mathematical, and we notice that they illustrate successively the solid, the plane and the line. We perceive, too, that they progress from undivided to divided wholes, and from these to separate and independent elements. Finally, we observe that there is a suggestiveness in the earlier gifts which the later ones lack, while on the other hand the range of the latter far exceeds that of the former. The meaning of these distinctions and connections will grow clear to us as we study the common objects of the varied gifts. These objects are:

I. To aid the mind to abstract the essential qualities of objects by the presentation of striking contrasts.

II. To lead to the classification of external objects by the presentation of typical forms.

III. To illustrate fundamental truths through simple applications.

IV. To stimulate creative activity.

I. We can never recur too often to the history of the race for the interpretation of the individual. So I cannot consider it irrelevant to refer to a recent result of linguistic research which throws into clearer light the trite, yet only vaguely understood, truth that knowledge rests upon comparison, and which strongly confirms the wisdom of Froebel in stimulating comparison by suggesting contrasts.

*   *   *

The order of the Kindergarten gifts follows the order of mental evolution, and at   1803 each stage of the child's growth Froebel presents him with his "objective counterpart." "The child," he says, "develops like all things, according to laws as simple as they are imperative. Of these the simplest and most imperative is that force existing must exert itself—exerting itself it grows strong—strengthening it unfolds—unfolding it represents and creates—representing and creating it lifts itself to consciousness and culminates in insight." This perception of the course of development determines his idea of the stages of early education. It should aim, first, to strengthen the senses and muscles conceived as the tools of the spirit,—second, to prepare for work by technical training, and to aid self-expression by supplying objects which through their indefiniteness may be made widely representative,—third, to provide material adapted to the conscious production of definite things and diminish the suggestiveness of this material in direct ratio to the increase of creative power, and fourth, by analysis of the objects produced, and the method of their production lift the child to conscious communion with his own thought. The first stage of this educational process is realized through the "Songs for Mother and Child,"—the second through the Kindergarten games, the simpler occupations and the first two Gifts,—the third through the exercises with blocks, tablets, slats, sticks and rings, and the work in drawing, folding, cutting, peas work and modeling, and the fourth through the wise appeal of the Kindergartner to the thought of the child as she leads him slowly from the what to the how, and from the how to the why and wherefore of his own action.

The definitely productive exercises begin with the Third Gift. Froebel contends that the proverbial destructiveness of children is a perversion to the faculties of investigation and construction, and that the broken toys strewn over our nursery floors express the mind's impatient protest against finished and complicated things. Unable to rest in externals the child breaks his toys to find out "what is inside," and scornful of what makes no ap ' to his activity he turns from the most elegant playthings to the crude results o.   · own manufacture. What he wants is not something made for him, but material to make something himself. What he needs is an object which he can take to pieces without destroying, and through which he can gratify his instinct to transform and to reconstruct. At the same time the possibilities of the object must not be too varied and it must be suggestive through its limitations. The young mind may be as easily crushed by excess as it is paralyzed by defect. Hence, Froebel's choice of a cube divided into eight smaller cubes. It is easily separated into its elements and easily reconstructed. It is capable of a reasonable number of transformations, and its crude resemblances satisfy the child's crude thought. It offers no variety of form to confuse his mind, but rigidly confines him to vertical and horizontal, to the right angle and the square. Moreover, he can scarcely arrange his blocks in any way without their taking forms which will suggest some object he has seen. If he piles them one above the other a word from mother or Kindergartner enables him to see in the unsought result of his doing a tower, light-house or a lamp post. If he arranges them side by side he is confronted with a wall, if in two parallel rows, behold the railroad! The change of a single block transforms the railroad into a train of cars, and with another movement the cars vanish in a house. Having as it were reached these results accidentally the child next directly aims to reproduce them, and thus through the suggestiveness of his material is helped from an instinctive to a self-directing activity, and from simple energy to definite production. This point once attained he triumphs over more and more complicated material, and constrains an ever increasing variety of elements to obey his thought. With planes and sticks he advances to surface representation, and prepares the way for drawing, and finally begins of himself to form letters and to spell out the names of familiar things. His progress, like that of the race, moves thus from the concrete to the abstract, from the fact to the picture, and from the picture to the sign.

SUSAN BLOW ON THE SYMBOLIC MEANING OF PLAY (1894)   From Susan E. Blow, *Symbolic Education* (New York, 1894), pp. 120–29.

The traditional games handed down from age to age are truer than those of the individual child, because they image a wider life; they are defective, in that they sometimes accentuate vanishing rather than permanent elements of experience, and in that they often reflect not a healthy but a depraved social condition. Thus, among the favorite games of French children is one which represents an interview between a priest and a penitent who, confessing to the grievous offense of stealing a pin, is for punishment commanded to kiss the confessor; the refrain of the song which accompanies the game being, "If penance is so delightful, I'll sin again and again." Another play pictures an interview between a married woman and her lover, the heroine exhorting the hero to fly from her husband, who has broken his promise of going to the country that day. The games of American children are generally of purer moral tone; still, their darling theme is courtship and marriage, and their favorite climax a kiss. Illustrations are superfluous, for we have all seen some eager child turn from "East to West to choose the one she loved the best," and observed the excitement of all the little players at the thrilling moment when the chorus sang:

> "Open the ring to let him in,
> And kiss him as he enters in."

To make explicit the ideal implicit in instinctive play is the aim of Froebel in his Mutter und Kose Lieder. This aim he accomplishes by neglecting the accidental and emphasizing the typical aspects of Nature and of human life. It is not intended that the games suggested by him shall be exclusively played, nor even played at all if others can be found which embody in better poetic form the same universal ideals and aspirations. It is, however, emphatically claimed that Froebel pioneers the effort to transfigure play, and that all future advance must be upon the path which he has broken.

Undoubtedly instinctive and traditional games furnish the material which may be transfigured into truly educative play. The claim that any one person (and that person an old man) could evolve a complete series of games, as the German artist evolved the camel "out of the silent depths of his own moral consciousness," is an absurdity. Froebel never claimed it for himself, nor has any sensible disciple claimed it for him. What he does claim is, that, through insight into the generic ideal, we may select from among traditional games those which will develop the child into its image; that we may reproduce them in a form adequate to their aim; and that we may present them not abstractly and alone, but in a logically related sequence. Thus presented, each game re-enforces all the others, and becomes a vital element in a developing process. Each new generation must add plays imaging the fresh elements of experience, and, finally, each individual child needs dramatic reproduction of the vital and formative facts of his own life.

We count it the highest achievement of literary art so to portray human deeds as to reveal their ethical character. We esteem it a mark of poetic genius to depict nature as the symbol of mind, and to show in "light and skies and mountains the painted vicissitudes of the soul." We reverently study these great works of art in order to clear our spiritual vision and interpret our own fragmentary experience. Need we hesitate, therefore, to admit that the child requires help in his efforts to interpret the life around him, and that, in order to realize its own ideal, play must be purified by rational insight?

It is needless to add that Froebel does not propose to do away with the free play of childhood. For such free play there is plenty of time outside of the three hours spent in the kindergarten. Its importance as a means of preserving intellectual balance and developing individuality can not be too strongly insisted upon. But just as Froebel makes "the archetypes of nature the playthings of the child," and thus introduces a principle of order into his sense-perceptions, so he presents in the kindergarten games the typical aspects of nature and the typical deeds of man, and thus introduces an organizing principle into the imagination.

Having discovered the procreant idea of the kindergarten games, let us now endeavor to trace the genesis of the gifts and occupations. Directing our attention once again to the spontaneous deeds of childhood, we observe that the primitive impulses to express the inner and investigate the outer life manifest themselves in forms other than those thus far considered. Prof. Preyer observes that "the most remarkable day, from a psychogenetic point of view, in the life of an infant is the one in which he first experiences the connection of a movement executed by himself with a sense-impression following upon it." This experience came to his child during the fifth month, when, upon tearing paper into smaller and smaller pieces, he noticed on the one hand the lessening size of the fragments and on the other the noise which accompanied his act. In the thirteenth month he found pleasure in shaking a bunch of keys, and in the fourteenth he deliberately took off and put on the cover of a can seventy-nine times without stopping for a moment's rest. Still later he enjoyed pulling out, emptying, refilling, and pushing in a table-drawer, heaping up and strewing about sand and garden mold, throwing stones into water, and pouring water into and out of bottles, cups, and watering-pots.[1] It is easy to see that each of these occupations was for the young experimenter both a step in the discovery of his own self-hood as a causative energy and a step in the interpretation of external objects.

With increasing consciousness of his own power and increasing knowledge of the properties and adaptations of objects the child begins to exercise a higher form of causative activity. Discerning in objects some ideal possibility, he seeks to make that possibility actual, and the mere exertion of force rises into productive and transforming energy. Observing the various forms in which this productive energy finds expression, we become gradually aware of a fresh parallel between the development of the individual and that of the race. Science has shown that the embryonic period of physical development is a masquerade of long-vanished forms of life. In like manner the children of each new generation seek instinctively to revive the life that is behind them and in their favorite occupations and amusements re-enact the prehistoric experiences of mankind. All children crave living pets, build

[1] Preyer's Development of the Intellect, p. 192.

sand houses, and make caves in the earth; are fond of intertwining bits of straw, paper, or other pliable material; delight in shaping bowls and cups and saucers out of mud; and are inveterate diggers in the ground, even when, as in city streets and alleys, such digging is wholly without result. Can we fail to recognize in these universal cravings the soul echoes of that forgotten past when man began the subjugation of Nature by the taming of wild beasts, the erection of rude shelters, the weaving of garments, and the manufacture of pottery? Can we doubt that the order of history should be the order of education, and that before we teach the child to read and write we should aid his efforts to repeat in outline the earlier stages of human development?

Even more interesting than the reproduction of primitive industries is the struggle of the child's soul to express its own nature in the varied forms of art. To sing, to dance, to hear and repeat simple rhymes are chief delights of all young children; and alliteration, too, has for them a tireless charm. Nor are they less eager to build, draw, paint, and model. To a pathetic experience of Froebel's own childhood, when, with such material as he could pick up, he vainly tried to imitate a Gothic church, may be traced the impulse which bore fruit in the building gifts of the kindergarten. The love of drawing shows itself in many forms. The child draws with his finger in the air, traces outlines in the sand, makes shadow pictures on the wall, blows on the window-pane, and covers its clouded surface with his motley fancies, and even bites his cookies into the forms of men and animals. In like manner his plastic instinct finds satisfaction in shaping figures out of wax, clay, or dough, and, lacking a paint-box, he will find or invent coloring material for himself.

The kindergarten gifts are Froebel's practical response to the cravings of childhood. The six soft balls of the first gift, and the sphere, cube, and cylinder of the second gift, satisfy on the one hand the primitive desire to exert force and cause change, and on the other afford typical experiences of movement, form, color, direction, and position. The care of animals, the cultivation of plants, the building exercises with the third and fourth gifts, the occupations of weaving, folding, cutting, sewing, intertwining, etc., accentuate the educative elements implicit in the industries of aboriginal men; and finally, through the architectural exercises of the fifth and sixth gifts, through the work with tablets, sticks, and rings; through drawing and painting exercises; through peas-work, and through clay and cardboard modeling, the artistic powers of the child are called into happy play, and he becomes, so far as in him lies, an architect, painter, designer, and sculptor. Add to these varied forms of artistic expression the kindergarten games with their dramatic representations, rhythmic movements, poetry and song, and we must, I think, admit that Froebel has in truth provided for what he is fond of calling "the all-sided development" of innate powers.

But, urges the objector, what is there in Froebel's scheme that is new or original? Have not wise mothers always supplied their children with balls and building blocks, encouraged them to roll mud pies, shown them how to fashion simple objects out of paper and cardboard, and taught them the use of needle, scissors, pencil, and knife? Lovers of the kindergarten recognize in all such criticisms testimony to the merit of Froebel's games and occupations, for were these something wholly new under the sun they would, according to all sound psychologic principles, be something wholly wrong. Froebel claims only to do with clear consciousness and persistent purpose what maternal instinct has always blindly and intermittently attempted. He gladly accepts the traditional material, but vitalizes it by giving it a mathematical basis, and by formulating the principles which should govern its use. Through the productive exercises suggested by him, the child achieves a fivefold development. Advancing from the external arrangement of fixed material to technical and artistic processsses, he gains manual dexterity and skill. Rising from mere imitation and production by rule to free creation, he develops originality of thought and power of expression. Receiving from productive activity the incitement of observation, he studies the salient qualities of physical objects and masters thus the alphabet of externality. Energizing to realize in external things his vision of their ideal possibilities, his will power is strengthened, and he becomes a practical force. Last, but not least, through the exertion of causal energy he forms the habit of looking from sensible facts to their producing causes, and of explaining all objects and events through their process of evolution.

Corruptio optimi pessima. It is a sad thing for any one who has mastered Froebel's principles to witness the perverted application so often made of his gifts. In many kindergartens the sole thought seems to be to use these gifts for teaching the elements of form and number; in others, manual dexterity is the one object sought; while in still others the material of the gifts suggests tedious object lessons on wood . . .

Francis W. Parker and the Quincy Methods

THE NEW EDUCATION IN THE PUBLIC SCHOOLS OF QUINCY, MASS.
(1879)   From Charles F. Adams, *The New Departure in the Common Schools of Quincy*
(Boston, 1879), pp. 33–40.

---

*A Paper Prepared for the Association of School
Committees and Superintendents of Norfolk County
at Its Spring Meeting of 1879*

The more than local interest which has of late been evinced in certain changes and, so to speak, experiments, which during the last four years have been made in the common-school course in the town of Quincy, would seem at this time to justify a more particular statement in regard to them. They are not without a general value, as the condition of affairs which preceded and led to them was by no means peculiar to Quincy, and the results reached there, if of value, are easily attainable anywhere. It may perhaps be best to concisely state the object of these changes and experiments in the first place:—it was to secure, if possible, a thoroughly good common-school education at a not unreasonable cost. The two points of excellence and economy were to be kept clearly in view, and neither was to be subordinated to the other.

In presenting to the town their annual report on the condition of its schools in 1873, the Quincy committee took occasion to refer to the state of what they termed "immobility" at which those schools had then arrived. They used the following language:—

> A retrospect of ten years will discover no very remarkable results. Ten years ago, so far as we remember, the children read and wrote and spelled about as well as they do to-day; and the fundamental rules of arithmetic were as thoroughly taught then as now. And at present, as in the past, most of the pupils who have finished the grammar course neither speak nor spell their own language very perfectly, nor read and write it with that elegance which is desirable. This immobility seems to show that a point has been reached which is near the natural term of such force as our present system of schooling is calculated to exert.

useless, however, to look for any steady improvement through the efforts of individual members of the committee. They were busy men, and they were not specialists in education. Committees elected by popular vote and entirely unequal to any sustained effort; and only through a sustained effort can the spirit necessary to any permanent improvement be infused into teachers, and a steady direction given to it.

It was determined, therefore, to ask the town to employ a superintendent of schools, and to put the working-out of the new system in his hands. This was done, and in the Spring of 1875 the necessary authority was obtained. And now the first serious difficulty presented itself in the practical selection of a superintendent; for it is a noticeable fact that, large and costly as the common-school system of this country is and greatly as it stands in need of intelligent direction, not a single step has yet been taken towards giving it such a direction through an educated superintendency. Accordingly, very much as Bentham defined a judge as "an advocate run to seed," the ordinary superintendent is apt to be a grammar school teacher in a similar condition. Where he is not this, he is usually some retired clergyman or local politician out of a job, who has no more idea of the processes of mental development or the science of training than the average schoolmaster has of the object of teaching English grammar. The blind are thus made to lead the blind, and naturally both plunge deeper into the mire. That this should be so is certainly most singular, for the idea of managing a school system as complicated as that of any populous New England town has now become, without the assistance of some trained specialist, is manifestly as absurd as it would be to try to manage a college without a president. Yet the superintendency is not yet recognized as a distinct profession, and, accordingly, trained men not being supplied for it, it has actually fallen into a sort of discredit through the wretched substitutes for trained men to whom towns have in their need been compelled to have recourse.

All this the members of the school committee of Quincy did but dimly appreciate when they determined to try their experiment. They had a definite object in view, in accomplishing which everything depended on their selection of an agent. Their object was to improve the schools while not increasing their cost;—to get one hundred cents worth of value for every dollar of the town's money. According to their own admission in the extract from the report of 1873, which has been quoted, there had been no perceptible improvement during the ten preceding years. Yet during those years the annual cost to the town of educating each child in the public schools had increased from six dollars to fifteen dollars. To secure the services of a better grade of teachers, those qualified to give a direction of their own to their instruction,—men and women of ideas, of individuality, as it is termed,—would have necessitated a general rise of salaries which would have increased the annual cost from fifteen dollars to at least thirty. This was out of the question. The burden on the tax-payer was already heavy enough. Even education can be paid for at too high a price, and it is useless to have model schools if no one but the tax-gatherer can afford to live in the town which supports them. The only other way to improve the system was to concentrate the directing individuality in one man, and trust to him to infuse his spirit into the others. One man the town could afford to pay; twenty men it could not afford to pay. The thing was, with the means at their command,— the salary of an assistant college professor,—to secure the services of that one man.

In this all-important matter, the Quincy committee were as a whole most fortunate. After some desultory discussion of candidates, they chanced across one who had not only himself taught, but in teaching had become possessed with the idea that it was a science, and that he did not understand it. Accordingly he had gone abroad in search of that training which he was unable to get in America, and at a comparatively mature age had made himself master of the modern German theories of common-school education. A self-educated and self-made man, with all the defects as well as the virtues of men of that class, he was now eagerly looking about for an opportunity to put his theories in practice. That opportunity was offered him in Quincy, and under circumstances peculiarly favorable to success. In the first place he found a committee strong in the confidence of the town and holding office with a degree of permanence most unusual, the members of which were in a singularly disgusted and dissatisfied frame of mind. They had reached the conclusion that the whole existing system was wrong,—a system from which the life was gone out. Acting on this conclusion, they had gone to work to remedy matters; but, as usually happens in such cases, they had succeeded only in destroying the old system without developing a new one. They had bitterly attacked the unintelligent instruction they found going on, and they had made school after school go hopelessly to pieces by calling on overgrown children to practically make use of the knowledge they had been so painfully acquiring. When it came, however, to substituting a better method of instruction for that which they condemned, they had their own affairs to attend to, and a few spasmodic, half-matured suggestions of something they did not have time to think out, was all they could do for the discouraged and bewildered teachers. It gradually, therefore, had begun to dawn upon them that they had taken a larger contract on their hands than they had at all intended. A little too much of the innovating, questioning spirit had, in fact, broken down something besides the school system of the town;—it had broken down the committee system as well.

Realizing this,—conscious of the fact that they themselves were unequal to the work before them,—the members of the committee were also sensible enough to know that an agent to be successful must have a chance. He must not be continually hampered and thwarted by unnecessary interference. They were not, as under similar circumstances is too frequently the case, jealous of their little authority. They had no fear of losing their power, and no consequent desire to make a mere huckster of their superintendent by degrading him into a purchasing agent. They listened to his plans as he submitted them, and gave them the best consideration they could; then, once those plans were approved, he had a free field in which to carry them out, with the understanding that by the results, and the results alone, would he be judged.

Meanwhile the members of the committee had ideas of their own, as well as the superintendent. Most fortunately,—for it was a single chance in a hundred that it should so happen, and yet it did so happen,—Mr. Parker, while he brought radical theories of his own to the work in hand, fully entered into and sympathized with the less clearly defined ideas of the committee. There was no conflict. His specialty was primary instruction; the later methods and practical outcome of the system were what they most severely criticised. The result, naturally, was a gradual but complete revolution, than which it may well be questioned whether the common school system of Massachusetts has of late years furnished a more interesting or instructive study.

The essence of the new system was that there was no system about it;—it was marked throughout by intense individuality. The programme found no place anywhere in it; on the contrary, the last new theory, so curiously amplified in some of our larger cities, that vast numbers of children should be taught as trains on railroads are run, on a time-table principle,—that they are here now, that they will be at such another point to-morrow, and at their terminus at such a date;—while a general superintendent sits in his central office and pricks off each step in the advance of the whole line on a chart before him,—this whole theory was emphatically dismissed. In place of it the tentative principle was adopted.

Experiments were to be cautiously tried and results from time to time noted. The revolution, however, was all-pervading. Nothing escaped its influence; it began with the alphabet and extended into the last effort of the grammar school course.

The most noticeable change, however, and that which has excited the most general interest was at the very beginning,—in the primaries. The old "dame school" disappeared at once. In place of it appeared something as different as light from darkness. The alphabet itself was no longer taught. In place of the old, lymphatic, listless "school-marm," pressing into the minds of tired and listless children the mystic significance of certain hieroglyphics by mere force of over-laying, as it were,—instead of this time-honored machine-process, young women, full of life and nervous energy, found themselves surrounded at the blackboard with groups of little ones who were learning how to read almost without knowing it;—learning how to read, in a word, exactly as they had before learned how to speak, not by rule and rote and by piecemeal, but altogether and by practice. The hours of school were kept diversified; the fact was recognized that little children were, after all, little children still, and that long confinement was irksome to them. A play-table and toys were furnished them, and from time to time the exercises were stopped that all might join in physical movement. That this system was harder for the teachers,— calling upon them at all times to actively throw themselves into the instruction of their classes, to interest them and to keep the school-room, as it were, in motion,— all this, goes without saying. But, on the other hand, while more exhausting, it was also far more inspiriting. The drudgery of the alphabet was gone,—so was the listless, drawling instruction;—there was a sense of constant activity in the occupation, which gave to the teacher a consciousness of individuality and a perceptible pride of calling. She felt, in fact, that she was doing something in a new way, and doing it uncommonly well.

The effect produced by this changed school atmosphere on the children was, however, the point of interest. It showed itself in the way least possible to mistake:—going to school ceased to be a home-sick tribulation. That this should be so seems opposed both to child-nature and to all human experience; and yet that it was so admitted of no denial. The children actually went to school without being dragged there. Yet the reason of this was not far to seek. The simple fact was, that they were happier and more amused and better contented at school than at home. The drudgery of the impossible primer no longer made infant life miserable. The alphabet was robbed of its terrors, and stole upon them unawares; while the most confounding thing to the members of the committee was, that in hearing the primaries read not a child among them could repeat its letters, or even knew their names; unless, perchance, to the teacher's increased trouble, they had been taught them at home.

So daring an experiment as this can, however, be tested in but one way:—by its practical results, as proven by the experience of a number of years, and testified to by parents and teachers as well as observed in children. The method has now been four years in use in the schools of Quincy and has ceased to be an experiment; its advantages are questioned by none, least of all by teachers and parents. Among the teachers are those who, having for many years taught class after class in the old way, found themselves called upon to attempt with deep misgiving the new and to them mysterious process. They now join their testimony to the others and confess that, to human beings, even though they be children, the ways of nature are the easier ways. After all the lesson is not a very profound one, and it is strange indeed that it took so long to find it out. A child learns to talk and to walk—the two most difficult things it is called on to learn in its whole life—without any instruction and by simple practice; the process of learning is not painful to it or wearisome to others; on the contrary, it is an amusement to both. Why the same process should not have been pursued in other and less difficult branches of education is not apparent. One thing only is clear: it was not pursued. In place of it an arbitrary system of names and sounds, having no significance in themselves, and of rules and formulas absolutely unintelligible except to the mature intellect, was adopted; and with these, generation after generation of children have been tortured. Only now do we deign in imparting knowledge to give any attention to natural processes, which have forever been going on before our eyes and in our families, and yet we profess to think that there is no science in primary education, and that all that there is to it can be learned in a few hours. The simple fact is, however, that within these few years it required a man of absolute genius to discover how to teach the alphabet.

The new departure, therefore, started with the Quincy primaries, and it left little in them that had not undergone a change. The reorganization was complete. This, however, was entirely the work of Superintendent Parker; the committee simply gave him a free field to experiment in, and the result fully justified them in so doing. Ascending into the several grades of grammar schools the case was somewhat different. The committee there had their own views, and those views were little else than an emphatic protest against the whole present tendency of the educational system of Massachusetts, whether school, academic, or university. If there is one thing which may be considered more characteristic of that system of late years than another, it is its tendency to multiply branches of study. The school year has become one long period of diffusion and cram, the object of which is to successfully pass a stated series of examinations. This leads directly to superficiality. Smatter is the order of the day. To enter college the boy of seventeen must know a little of everything; but it is not necessary for him to know anything well,—not even how to write his own language. From this the vicious system has gone up through the professional, and down through the high, to the very lowest grade of grammar school. No matter whether it can understand it or not, the child must be taught a little of everything; at any rate enough of it to pass an examination. Against this whole theory and system the Quincy school committee resolutely set their faces. They did not believe in it; they would have nothing to do with it. Instead of being multiplied, the number of studies should, they insisted, be reduced. It was impossible to teach everything in a grammar-school course, and for the vast majority of children a thorough grounding in the elements of knowledge was all that could be given. The attempt to give more simply resulted in not giving that. In proof of this the examination papers for admission to high schools were appealed to. These showed the acquirements of the more proficient scholars; for as a rule it is they who go to the high schools. Judging by these papers the graduates of the grammar schools were very far from being proficient in either writing, spelling or grammar. Now, these are things which the common schools can and should give all children, no matter what else is sacrificed. They are not given, however, for the simple reason that to give them requires practice, and the multiplicity of studies forbids practice in any one study. The results of the old system in Quincy, as brought to light through the earlier examinations, have already been referred to; the ridiculous knowledge, for instance, of parts of speech and abstract rules of grammar, acquired in order to be able to parse complicated sentences, but combined with an utter inability to correctly write or decently spell the words of the most ordinary letter.

Under these circumstances the general policy outlined by the committee was sufficiently radical. Its execution was entrusted wholly to the superintendent.

Education was to recur to first principles. Not much was to be attempted; but whatever was attempted was to be thoroughly done, and to be tested by its practical results, and not by its theoretical importance. Above all, the simple comprehensible processes of nature were to be observed. Children were to learn to read and write and cypher as they learned to swim, or to skate, or to play ball.

A DISCIPLE OF FRANCIS W. PARKER ON THE DISTINGUISHING FEATURES OF THE QUINCY SCHOOLS (1885) From Lelia E. Patridge, *The "Quincy Methods" Illustrated* (New York, 1885), pp. xii–xiv.

---

1. The joyous life of the schools and the comradeship of teacher and pupils.
2. By grouping their pupils (in the lower grades) they obtained many of the benefits of individual teaching.
3. The skillful use of a great amount and variety of "Busy-Work."
4. Lessons in subjects not usually taught—Drawing, Modeling, Form, Color, Natural History, etc.
5. The constant use of Drawing as a means of expression.
6. Use of text-books as repositories of knowledge.
7. Amount and variety of Supplementary Reading.
8. Substitution of the expression of original thought on the part of the pupils for the old-fashioned memoriter recitation.
9. Carefully varied programme, *whose order was known only to the teacher.*
10. The atmosphere of happy work which encompassed teachers and pupils.
11. Disorder not worrying the teacher and wasting her time.
12. The confidence, courtesy, and respect characterizing the attitude not only of pupils to teacher, but teacher to pupils.
13. The absence of scolding, snubbing, or spying.
14. The dignity, self-possession, and lack of self-consciousness of pupils.
15. The making of the child the objective point, and not Courses of Study, examinations, or promotions.
16. The great economy, naturalness, and practicability of the devices employed.
17. The marked attention paid to the so-called dull pupils.
18. The evident growth of moral power.
19. The remarkable skill of the teachers evidencing their comprehension of underlying principles.
20. The wonderful originality and individuality of the teachers—none being imitators; the devices used varying from day to day.
21. The high ideal set before the teachers by the Superintendent, and their hearty co-operation with him in striving to attain it.
22. The absence of machinery, and the absolute freedom from any fixed or prescribed mode of work, each teacher being encouraged to invent and try any device not violating fundamental laws.
23. Examinations aimed to test the teacher's power to teach.

24. Examinations such as to test the children's power to do, not their power to memorize.

It was harmonious education;—the moral and physical natures were recognized and trained along with the mental. There was that alternation of action which results in pleasing and useful variety of work and play. There, too, was the unceasing training in good habits, the unremitting exercise of the better nature and the noblest impulses. It was, in brief, child-gardening. Set to tend the human plants placed in the sunshine of their school-rooms, these teachers sought to learn the divine laws which governed their development, and watched each mind to see what helped or hindered growth. Hence the dull children, like backward plants, received most care and pains. It is true that the pupils were taught to read and write, and ultimately to cipher; that is, the form of the work done belonged to the old education, but the ideal being no longer the gaining of skill and knowledge, but the higher one of growth, the spirit in which it was done was of the new. The old order seemed literally to have passed away, and a new atmosphere of enthusiastic but normal activity filled these schools; a new attraction held these happy pupils, self-poised, self-controlled, all in their places without jar or effort.

A SAMPLE "QUINCY" LESSON IN NUMBER (1885)   From Lelia E. Patridge,
The "Quincy Methods" Illustrated (New York, 1885), pp. 54–57, 59.

A Test Lesson in Number
PURPOSE OF THE LESSON

This is one of the first lessons given, and is not intended to teach Number, but to find out what the children already know, of this limitation. It is preparatory to the regular Number Work. It is also a great aid in the first grouping of the new class, for it reveals each child's mental grasp, and quickness of apprehension, in one direction at least.

PREPARATION MADE BY THE TEACHER

However simple this lesson may appear, it has a definite plan, which has been clearly thought out beforehand by the teacher, whose analysis is given here. The objects used have also been thoughtfully chosen, care being taken in their selection not to present too attractive, or unfamiliar things, lest the attention of the pupils be drawn from the idea of Number to the contemplation of the objects themselves.

PREPARATION MADE BY THE PUPILS

Of course no preparation as such has been made by the little children five and six years of age, to whom this lesson is given, and yet in one sense, every limitation of things as to how many, which they have ever made has helped them in this. But henceforth they will continue these limitations consciously, instead of unconsciously, as most of them have previously done.

PLAN OF THE LESSON

1st. Show a number of things, and let the pupils find the same number.

Test. To see if they know the number.

2d. Call for a number of things by name.

Test. To see if they know the name of the number.

3d. Show a number of things, and ask them to tell me how many.

Test. To see if they know both the number and the name of the number.

4th. Take the children out of sight of the objects and then ask them to bring me a number of things.

Test. To see if they can recall both the number and the name of the number.

5th. Incidentally to test at every step their power to separate and combine numbers.

The Lesson

[The teacher seats herself at the end of the number table, which is in the back part of the room, and the children stand around it. On the table are a pile of blocks, a bundle of splints, some horse-chestnuts, some shells, a few spools, a package of toothpicks, a handful of pebbles, a box of beans, a pile of maple leaves, and a bunch of buttercups.]

Teacher [Holding up two maple leaves]. You may find me so many leaves. [Children each take two leaves.]

Teacher. Maggie may tell me what she has.

Maggie. Two.

Teacher. Two what?

Maggie. Two leaves.

Teacher. Tell it to me in a nice little story. [Maggie only stands and stares.]

Teacher. What have you?

Maggie. Two leaves [again].

Teacher. Then tell me that you have two leaves.

Maggie. I have two leaves.

Teacher. I want all the little children to tell me the whole story when I ask you what you have. Somebody else may tell me a story. Johnnie.

Johnnie. I have two leaves.

Teacher. You may all lay your leaves down on the table. [Teacher takes up two horse-chestnuts.] You may all do as I do. What has Jennie?

Jennie. Two horse-chestnuts.

Teacher. Who can tell me the whole story? Carrie, can you?

Carrie. I have two horse-chestnuts.

Teacher. Now put them back on the table. Harry, you may hand me two blocks, and Mary may give me one block. [They do as she tells them.] Can anybody tell me what I have? Susie.

Susie. Three.

Teacher. Three what? I want the whole story.

Susie. Three blocks.

Teacher. Who has three blocks?

Susie. You have.

Teacher. Now who will tell me the whole story? Mary.

Mary. You have three blocks.

Teacher. You may all take two beans. [Teacher waits till they have done so and then says:] You may take enough more to make three. [Two or three reach at once for one more bean, and the rest, all but three, imitate them. These three stand holding their two beans, not knowing what else to do. Teachers says to the three who don't know:] How many beans have you?

Jimmie [answering.] Two.

Teacher. I want you to have three.

[Jimmie reaches out and gets one: the other two have been watching, and now they do the same.][1]

Teacher. Somebody may tell me the story about what you have in your hand.

Theresa. I have three beans.

Teacher. You may put the beans down, and take two pebbles: take enough to make three. [The three before mentioned are the last to get their pebbles, and only do it by watching the rest and imitating.]

Teacher. Timmie [one of the three] may tell me what he has [taking hold of his hand].

Timmie. I have three little stones.

Teacher. [Nodding toward his hand]. Where?

Timmie. In my hand.

Teacher. [Holding up three buttercups.] Carrie may tell me what I have.

Carrie. You have three flowers.

Teacher. What kind of flowers?

Carrie. Yellow flowers.

Teacher. What kind of flowers does Jennie call them?

Jennie. Pretty flowers.

Teacher. What does Johnnie call them?

Johnnie. Buttercups.

[Teacher lays down the buttercups and picks up two spools.]

Teacher. Theresa, tell me what I have.

Theresa. Two spools.

Teacher. Now how many? [Taking up one more.]

Theresa. Three spools.

Teacher. Maggie, tell me what I have?

Maggie. You have three spools.

Teacher. Jennie, what have I?

Jennie. One block.

Teacher [takes up two more]. Now tell me.

Jennie. Three blocks.

Teacher. Timmie, tell me what I have.

Timmie. Two buttercups.

Teacher. Jimmie.

Jimmie. One shell.

✳   ✳   ✳

[1]Evidently three children, Jimmie, Timmie, and Maggie, out of this group of ten, do not know three.

This entire lesson, including the passing out and back to the seats, has taken just seven minutes. The teacher's speech has been brisk, her manner alert, and the children, as a matter of course, have moved and spoken in like fashion, except when they did not know what to do, and then the teacher waited patiently for them. The celerity of action of the lesson is its best point, for next to accuracy, rapidity of calculation is the thing aimed at in all Number Work.

Again, the opportunity this study (Arithmetic) gives for training in expression has not been lost, the teacher having here begun the teaching of correct and concise language. Having the children draw two of the blocks, splints, etc., is a happy device to make a change in the work, and yet keep the idea of number still in their consciousness, thus deepening the impression of this limitation, already made.

FRANCIS W. PARKER ON NATURAL METHODS OF TEACHING

(**1883**)   From Francis W. Parker, *Notes of Talks on Teaching* (New York, 1891), pp. 21–25.

The work of the next hundred years will be to break away from traditional forms and come back to natural methods.

Every act has a motive, and it is the motive which colors, directs, forms the action. Consequently, if we would understand the educational work of to-day, we must know its motive, bearing in mind the fact that due allowance must be made for the stupefying effects of long-established usage. The motive commonly held up is the acquisition of a certain degree of skill and an amount of knowledge. The quantity of skill and knowledge is generally fixed by course of study and the conventional examinations. This is a mistake. In contrast with this false motive of education, to wit, the gaining of skill and knowledge, I place what I firmly believe to be the true motive of all education, which is the harmonious development of the human being, body, mind, and soul. This truth has come to us gradually and in fragments from the great teachers and thinkers of the past. It was two hundred years ago that Comenius said, "Let things that have to be done be learned by doing them." Following this, but broader and deeper in its significance, came Pestalozzi's declaration, "Education is the generation of power." Last of all, summing up the wisdom of those who had preceded him, and embodying it in one grand principle, Froebel announced the true end and aim of all our work—the harmonious growth of the whole being. This is the central point. Every act, thought, plan, method, and question should lead to this. Knowledge and skill are simply the means and not the end, and these are to work toward the symmetrical upbuilding of the whole being. Another name for this symmetrical upbuilding is character, which should be the end and aim of all education. There are two factors in this process: first, the inborn, inherited powers of the mind, and, second, the environment of the mind, which embraces, so far as the teacher is concerned, the subjects taught. The subjects taught, then, are the means of mental development. To aid in the mind's development the teacher must know, first, the means of mental and moral growth, which are found in the subjects taught; and, second, the mental laws by which alone these means can be applied. Knowing the mind and the means, he can work toward the end, which is growth. Method is the adaptation of means of growth to mind to be developed, and natural method is the *exact* adaptation of means of growth to mind to be developed. To acquire a knowledge of the mind and of the means by which the mind may be developed is the study of a lifetime. Let us stand with humility before immensity.

In the beginning, then, the study of methods aside from principles is of little use; therefore, that investigation should lead to a knowledge of principles is all-important. There are two lines of investigation: the direct one is the study of mental laws, or the investigation of the facts out of which the generalization of principles is made. The second, and indirect way, is the study of the application of methods in detail, in order to discover through such details the principles from which they spring. Let no teacher rest satisfied with a study of the mere details of methods, but use them as illustrating and leading back to principles.

Technical Skill

In order to train children how to do, we must be able to do ourselves; hence the great importance of that preparation on the part of a teacher which will result in skill in the technics of school work. First of all, the voice should be trained, for a clear musical voice is one of the teacher's most potent qualifications for success, and cannot be overrated. Drill in phonics is necessary, not only to gain the ability to give the slow pronunciation with ease and with natural inflections, but as an aid to perfect articulation and pronunciation. That every teacher should be an expressive reader is self-evident, but it might not occur to all that to be an eloquent talker is also one of the requisites demanded by the New Methods. Faults of tone, modulation, and manner are propagated by the teacher, as well as false syntax and incorrect pronunciation. Then, too, every teacher should be able to sing, and sing well. Music fills the air with beauty, and in the school-room everything should be quiet and musical, with never a harsh note. Failing in this the school lacks harmony. Writing is the second great means of language expression, and should follow immediately upon talking. A teacher who cannot write well, cannot teach writing well; for the copy on the blackboard should be well nigh perfect. Skill is the expression of power, and drawing is the second best way of expressing thought. Given the skill to draw, and a teacher is never helpless, for then he can teach, even if everything else is taken away. Besides, I see a future in drawing which I see in nothing else in the way of developing the mental powers; hence the demands made upon teachers for knowledge and skill in this art must increase with every year. Moulding in sand is one of the best possible ways to teach geography, and should precede map drawing. Moulding in clay is a valuable means of form teaching, and is also the best of preparations for drawing. Last of all, gymnastics—the training of the whole body—is of the utmost importance, not only to insure symmetrical physical development, but to aid in the establishment of good order. Mental action, as you know, depends largely upon physical conditions, and therefore we should train the body that the mind may act. Believing that the skill of the teacher in these directions measures in a great degree his power to do good work, I have endeavored in this course of lessons to provide you with the best of teachers for these different departments. Now, a word of caution: time and strength are both limited, therefore don't try too much; but that you may become experts in these technical matters, let me add, whatever you do try, be sure to follow it up.

FRANCIS W. PARKER'S TESTIMONIAL TO TEACHING (1889) From "An Autobiographical Sketch of Francis Wayland Parker," as quoted in William M. Giffin, *School Days in the Fifties* (Chicago, 1906), p. 133.

I can say that all my life I have had a perfect passion for teaching school, and I never wavered in it in my life, and never desired to change. I never had anything outside offered me that had any attractions for me, and never desired to go outside of the work, and it was sort of a wonder to me that I did have such a love for it. I remember when I was teaching in the Grammar School in Piscatauquog I had a little garden. Then we lived near the old home where I was born, and I had a little rocky, gravelly garden, that I used to tend and hoe at morning and night, beans and corn, and so on. Of course when I was hoeing I was dreaming and thinking of school. I remember one day I was hoeing beans, and, by the way, I always liked to hoe beans the best, and I remember just where I stood, and I said to myself, "Why do I love to teach school?" and then I looked around on the little growing plants, and I said, "It is because I love to see things grow," and if I should tell any secret of my life, it is the intense desire I have to see growth and improvement in human beings. I think that is the whole secret of my enthusiasm and study, if there be any secret to it,—my intense desire to see the mind and soul grow.

FRANCIS W. PARKER ON THE CHILD AND THE CURRICULUM (1891) From Francis W. Parker, *Talks on Pedagogics: An Outline of the Theory of Concentration* (New York, 1894), pp. 3–4, 16–21.

I propose in this and the following talks to present a general exposition of the theory of CONCENTRATION.

The least that can be said for this theory is that it presents to some extent an outline of a rounded educational doctrine for the study and criticism of teachers.

In the beginning of these discussions, the question of all questions, and indeed the everlasting question, is: what is the being to be educated? What is the child? What is this little lump of flesh, breathing life and singing the song of immortality? The wisdom and philosophy of ages upon ages have asked this question, and still it remains unanswered. It is the central problem of the universe. The child is the climax and culmination of all God's creations, and to answer the question, "What is the child?" is to approach nearer the still greater question, What is the Creator and Giver of Life?

I can answer the question tentatively. It is a question for you and for me, and for the teachers of the present and the future, to answer; and still it will ever remain the unanswered question. We should study the child, as we study all phenomena, by its actions, and by its tendencies to act. The child is born, we are told by scientists, deaf, dumb, and blind, yet, in design, possessing marvellous possibilities for development. It is well for us to stand by the cradle of a little child who has drawn his first breath, and is ready to be acted upon by the external energies which surround him.

*   *   *

To sum up, the subjects of the child's spontaneous study and persistent interest include all the central subjects of study—geography, geology, mineralogy, botany, zoology, anthropology, etc. In fact, the child begins every subject spontaneously and unconsciously. He must begin these subjects, because he lives, and because his environment acts upon him and educates him. Of course, the difference in environment makes a great difference in the child's mental action, the child's individual concepts; still, in all children there are the same spontaneous tendencies. The boy, for instance, on a farm may have a large range of vegetation to study, and the poor little child in the dark city may worship with his whole soul some potted plant and from it draw lessons of inspiration and love. The child studies the clouds, the sky, the stars, the earth, vegetation, animal life, history, every hour of the day. To be sure, he may have more interest in one subject than another, but to him all these subjects are related one to the other, as the cloud is related to rain, and the rain is related to vegetation and soil. It is the tendency of pedantry to search in the far distance for facts and mysteries, but the truth is that the marvellous is close to us, that miracles are of the most common occurrence.

I wish to call your attention to the wonderful powers acquired by the child in the first three years of its life, and the wonderful persistence there is in such acquirement. Take, for instance, the art of locomotion, the creeping and walking. Watch the face of the child standing for the first time upon its little legs, attracted by the outstretched arms of its mother, who stands across the room; look at the mingled courage and fear in the baby's face. He has a great ambition to move, as he has seen others move, upon his two feet. He stretches out his arms, he fears, he takes courage, he moves one foot and is successful, and then the other; he looks at his mother's encouraging smile, takes another step, and then another, until the great feat of walking across the room is accomplished. From the time he first stands upon his feet to the time he runs around with perfect unconsciousness of his power of movement, there takes place a succession of experiments, of trials, and of failures and successes, all guided and controlled by his desire to walk.

More wonderful than learning to walk is the learning to hear language and to talk. In the beginning the child creates his own language of gesture by means of his own body. He hears language, words that are in themselves complex. Oral words act upon his consciousness and are associated by a fixed and everlasting law of the mind. Idioms are acquired by hearing and association, and with it all comes an intense desire to express thought. With his voice he creates at first his own language, which consists of crudely articulate sound, and then follows the acquisition of the vernacular which he hears. It is well for us to consider carefully the processes of learning to talk. The child must learn to hear first; that is, the words must act upon consciousness and their correspondences must be associated with the appropriate activities in consciousness. The idioms must act in the same way and be associated with their appropriate activies or relations of ideas. Then follows the making of oral words. He learns enunciation, or the utterance of single sounds. He learns articulation, or the unity of sounds in words. He learns accent, pronunciation, and syntax, all by hearing language and under the one controlling motive of expressing his own thought. He begins, it is true, with crude utterances, but these utterances are to him the best possible expression of his thought. He learns any language and every language that he hears. If we could understand the psychological mechanical processes by which a child learns his own vernacular from the first step of hearing to the last step by which the sentence is in his power, we should understand the whole theory of learning any language. Those who have tried to speak a foreign language will readily understand something of the struggle the child goes through in order to master one single phonic element. You see that he does all this unconsciously, that all these efforts are natural and to a great degree automatic. He never for a moment thinks of a single sound by itself unless that sound is a whole word. He knows nothing at all of the complex elements of a language, nothing of slow pronunciation, nothing of syntax, still he masters the language by a natural process. This word natural is variously interpreted. It is exceedingly ambiguous, almost as ambiguous as the word "abstract." Still I believe that we can find a scientific definition of the word natural. If the word natural means anything, it means strict conformity to God's laws. That is, a child learns every oral word by the same law under which every oral or written word in any and every language must be learned. The child does not know the law, but he obeys the law by instinct. If the child makes these marvellous acquisitions naturally, in conformity to law, why not have him continue that conformity to law in all his after-acquisitions?

Learning to write is far easier in itself, if we follow the law, than learning to hear language or learning to speak. The great lesson to teachers is, find the law, follow the law; give the child conditions in learning to write like those he has had in learning to speak. Indeed, the conditions can be made far better, for learning to speak is left very much to accident and to desultory instruction, while learning to write may be under the most careful guidance.

It goes without saying that the child is a student of form and color. Everything that enters his brain, as I have already said, must touch the end-organs, and these attributes or objects which touch the end-organs are forms of matter. Froebel, who had such divine insight, understood the great value of the tactual sense. Color is representative in its power. It brings into consciousness the correspondences to forms of external objects.

Not only does the child study form, but he makes intuitively a systematic preparation for the study of number. The child begins with no idea of distance. He grasps for the moon with the same confidence as he does for an object near at hand. The ideas of distance, size, weight, are preparations for number. The child first learns to measure by constantly reaching out his hands, creeping and walking, and after that it measures distance by sight. Not only does it begin to measure and estimate distances, but it judges area and bulk, and compares different sizes, areas, weights, and bulks. The study of weight to him also has its charms, the difference of pressure upon his hand, his own weight in the effort of other children to lift him. He measures force and time in the same unconscious way, the time of sleeping, the time between a promised pleasure and its anticipated realization, and soon he learns to look at the clock to help him out in his judgment. He estimates very carefully the value of a cent and a stick of candy. All these spontaneous activities are in the direction of number study, are mingled with all his activities and are absolutely necessary to his mental and physical action. It is true these measures are very inadequate and imperfect, but they are the beginnings of the power of accurate measuring, the mode of judgment which will end, if he continues to have the right conditions, in exact measuring and weighing, and in accurate knowledge of values.

*   *   *

There is at first a perfect unity of thought and action. Hear the voice and watch the movements of a little child! No dancing teacher, no teacher of elocution, no actor, can ever successfully imitate the voice of the child, or the perfectly unconscious beauty and grace of its movements. Indeed it is the highest aim of artists in acting and elocution to acquire the unconscious grace and power of a child. Listen to the voice of the child,—melodious, harmonious, perfect in emphasis, it is the immediate pulsations of his soul, the instantaneous reflex of his consciousness, with unconsciousness of his body, his organs of expression, his forms of speech. The child, until education intervenes, is a unit of action and expression, and that unity is acquired and maintained by action under a motive with no overpowering consciousness of the means or forms of expression. Must that beautiful unity be broken? Can it be perpetuated and strengthened?

There never was such a thing as a lazy child born on earth. Childhood is full of activities of every kind, stimulated by external energies and shaped by internal power. The child experiments continually until it gains its ends. It will reach hundreds of times for an object, and at last succeed. What modes of expression, excepting speech, does a child acquire in the first years of its life? I should say that all children love music, though there is a vast difference in individual organisms in this as in all other modes of expression. Most children strive to imitate that which they hear in rhythm. Making, or manual work, is really the natural element of the child. I think I can say, without fear of dispute, that a child tries to make everything that he sees made. The little girl wishes to use the scissors, needle and thread. In the kitchen, unless repressed by the mother, she makes cakes and bread. In fact, the whole round of housekeeping in the beginning furnishes countless objects for activity and a desire to imitate. Boys in the shop, or on the farm, strive to do what they see done. They harness each other in teams, they drive the dog and the goat, they make mill-wheels and dams. The tendency to imitate, the desire to make the objects they see made, is intensely strong in every child.

Every child has the artist element born in him; he loves to model objects out of sand and clay. Paint is a perfect delight to children, bright colors charm them. Give the child a paint-brush, and though his expression of thought will be exceedingly crude, it will be very satisfactory to him; he will paint any object with the greatest confidence. It is very interesting to watch the crowd of little children near Lake Chautauqua, as busy as bees and as happy as angels. Let us look at the forms the children make out of the pliable sand. Here are caves where the fairies dwell, mountains, volcanoes, houses where the giants live. All these fantastic forms spring from the brain of the child and are expressed by means of this plastic material. See that little three-year-old girl with the model of a house in her brain: she is now wheeling a wheel-barrow, assisted by a little companion; in the barrow is the wood, and in her brain is the house. Energetic, persistent, happy,—in what direction? In the direction of true growth! The little girl in the kitchen is not happy until she can mould and change the flour into dough, and dough into forms for baking; and here begin her first lessons in chemistry, the wonderful changes which heat brings about. She will dress her doll, working patiently for hours. Inexpert beholders may not know what the crude forms mean, but the child knows and is satisfied,—nay, delighted. Give a child a piece of chalk, and its fancy runs riot: people, horses, houses, sheep, trees, birds, spring up in the brave confidence of childhood. In fact, all the modes of expression are spontaneously and persistently exercised by the child from the beginning except writing. It sings, it makes, it moulds, it paints, it draws, it expresses thought in all the forms of thought-expression, with the one exception.

I have very imperfectly presented, in this brief outline, some of the spontaneous activities of the little child. The more I strive to present them, the more imperfect seems the result, so much lies beyond in the interpretation of the child's instinctive activities, so much seems to exceed all present discovery. The question, my fellow-teachers, is, what should these lessons teach us? The child instinctively begins all subjects known in the curriculum of the university. He begins them because he cannot help it; his very nature impels him. These tendencies, these spontaneous activities of the child spring from the depths of its being, spring from all the past, for the child is the fruit of all the past, and the seed of all the future. These quiet, persistent, powerful tendencies we must examine and continue with the greatest care. The child overcomes great obstacles by persistent energy, always acting with great confidence of himself and his powers. He overcomes these obstacles because his whole being is a unit of action, controlled by one motive. The spontaneous tendencies of the child are the record of inborn divinity; we are here, my fellow-teachers, for one purpose, and that purpose is to understand these tendencies and continue them in all these directions, following nature. First of all, we should recognize the great dignity of the child, the child's divine power and divine possibilities, and then we are to present the conditions for their complete outworking. We are here that the child may take one step higher; we are here to find and present the conditions adapted to the divine nature of the child.

I have tried to show that the whole round of knowledge is begun by the child, and begun because it breathes, because it lives. If the child loves science and history, and studies or attends to them instinctively, then he should go on, and we must know the conditions or subjects and means which should be presented to him for each new demand or need.

I grant that in the past of education attention has been directed too much to dead forms of thought, and for one good reason at least: the sciences are a modern creation of man and have not yet reached the child. Now we have these marvellous subjects presented to us, worked out by great thinkers of the present, and we are to choose whether we will continue the dead formalism that too often leads to pedantry and bigotry, or whether we are to lead the child's soul in that direction which God designed in His creation of the human being.

In conclusion I commend to you, in the words of our greatest American philosopher:

"A babe by its mother lies, bathed in joy;
Glide the hours uncounted; the sun is its toy;
Shines the peace of all being without cloud in its eyes,
And the sum of the world in soft miniature lies."

I commend to you the "sum of the world" for your study, for in this direction lies all the future progress of humanity.

FRANCIS W. PARKER ON THE SCHOOL AND MORAL TRAINING

(1891)   From Francis W. Parker, *Talks on Pedagogics: An Outline of the Theory of Concentration* (New York, 1894), pp. 337-39, 374-75.

School Government and Moral Training

The purpose of a school is educative work. By educative work is meant self-effort in the direction of personal development. School order is that state or condition of a school in which the best educative work is done in the most economical manner. The process of education consists in presenting conditions for educative acts on the part of the individual. Method is the special adaptation of educative conditions to individual needs. Teaching is the presentation of conditions for educative self-effort. Training of the body consists in the presentation of conditions which develop the body, and make it a more efficient means of receiving and manifesting thought.

A school is a community; community life is indispensable to mental and moral growth. If the act of an individual in any way hinder the best work of the community, he is in the wrong. The highest duty of the individual is to contribute all in his power to the best good of all. This principle is the sure guide to all rules and regulations of a school. How much noise shall there be in the school? Just enough to assist each and all to do their best work. How quiet shall it be? Just quiet enough to assist each and all to do their best work. How much whispering? What shall be the rules for coming in and going out? For punctuality? Every rule of a school, in order that it may be of educative influence and be felt to be right by each pupil, consists in carrying out this motto—"Everything to help and nothing to hinder." The first essential rule to true manhood is to feel the dignity of life, and that dignity comes from a sense of responsibility for the conduct of others.

There is but one test, one genuine test, of a school, which may be explained by two questions: First, is every individual in this school doing educative work in the most economical way? Second, is that work the best for the whole, and at the same time the best for each individual? If the answer to these questions is in the affirmative in regard to any school, then it can be said to be in order. The perfect ideal of order is that each and every minute shall be filled with that work which best assists each and all in growth and development.

The initial steps in inducing the government here defined are indeed the most difficult. Children enter school with marked habits of inattention, with a cultivated dislike for work, and frequently with the feeling that the teacher is their natural enemy. The question, then, of first importance is, How can habits of work or self-effort be induced? This question cannot be easily answered, but certain marked factors in it may be mentioned. The highest qualification of a teacher is a dominating love for children, manifested by a strong desire to assist them. The second qualification, an outcome of the first, is that a teacher must be deeply in love with the subjects of study; in other words, must be a persistent, close student of the subjects taught. Third, he must have power and skill in the manifestation of thought. And, fourth, he must have the courage of his convictions.

*   *   *

THE
NEW
EDUCATION

I know that there has been much discussion upon this particular point, and fear has been expressed that there is little or no moral training in our public schools, and a general verdict has been formed that there must be more specific moral training, that text-books with moral precepts and moral directions must be introduced and studied. The solution of this problem is simple and plain: every bit of teaching should be intrinsically moral, and that teaching which has not a moral element in it, that teaching which is not prompted by the highest virtue, is not right teaching, and should be so branded. Special moral training in schools is a suggested remedy for that which need not exist.

The most fruitful cause of all the evils of school life is the *lack of educative work.* Most corporal punishment has its root in the righteous rebellion of children against mind-stupefying and disgusting drudgery. The brightest and best children refuse to toil when they see no reason for it and feel no pleasure in it; rebellion, alas! is their only resource. Prizes, rewards, per-cents, and all the means of stimulating selfishness, and that ambition which ends with self, spring from a profound unbelief that educative work, that right doing, brings its own sweet and sure reward.

Children are lost from total neglect. They cry for bread, and we give them a stone. Their whole nature seeks for the truth, and we give them the lie, in dead forms. The greatest proof of the divinity of the child is that he can meet the ignorant methods of parents and teachers, overcome them, and still persist in goodness. The day is come when the fear of disobedience of a few negatives is not to be the method of the school, when the grand positive precepts of the greatest sermon in the world, the Sermon on the Mount, are to be applied in depth and breadth throughout school life; the centre of that sermon—"Blessed are those who hunger and thirst after righteousness, for they shall be filled." The Saviour said these words because He knew in human souls there is a depth of love and a breadth of desire which, if the right conditions were presented, would be developed into the highest moral and spiritual power.

FRANCIS W. PARKER ON THE CENTRAL SUBJECTS OF STUDY
(**1891**)   From Francis W. Parker, *Talks on Pedagogics: An Outline of the Theory of Concentration* (New York, 1894), pp. 26–27, 43, 46.

Our motive, then, my fellow-teachers, should be to economize educative effort, and with this guide we should seek earnestly for that theory or doctrine of education by the application of which this central aim of education can be best attained. The present trend of study, investigation, and discovery in the science of education is towards the correlation and unification of educative subjects, and their concentration upon human development. All subjects, means, and modes of study are concentrated under this doctrine upon economization of educative efforts. In the unification and correlation of subjects of thought and expression, each subject, means, mode and method finds its absolute and relative educational value, its definite place in the conditions for self-activity and self-effort.

The unification of subjects takes for its hypotheses, first, the unity of the human being in design; second, the unity of the Creator and His creations; and third, that approximating unity of the human being to his Creator is the sublime destiny of man. "For He made man in His own image." "He has crowned him with glory and honor." Unity of body, mind, and soul, unity of educative effort, unity of action, unity of thought, and unity of thought and expression are the aims of the theory of Concentration.

This morning I propose to discuss the unification of the Central Subjects of Study. By central subjects I mean those subjects which lie nearest the truth. All true study is the study of the Creator, through the manifestation of His thought, in the universe and man. The central subjects of study are but the main branches of one subject, and that subject is creation. Creation is eternal; it is the manifestation of invisible, all-efficient power; therefore all study has for its sole aim the knowledge of the invisible. The highest and at the same time the most economical effort of the mind is the effective striving after the truth of creation; this action of the mind may be called intrinsic—it is the shortest line of resistance between the soul and truth. The central subjects of study represent that line, and point in that direction.

* * *

I hold, then, in this brief outline of a vast subject, that all these central subjects of study are in fact one subject. The child begins all these subjects spontaneously, and these tendencies, these spontaneous activities are the indications, positive, of that which should afterwards follow in education.

* * *

I would present, then, the *study of law* as the end and aim of all these central subjects of study. I would lay down the hypothesis, which can scarcely be called a working hypothesis, that there is only one study, and that study is the study of the Infinite, All Efficient Energy, differentiated in its action through bodies of matter of different qualities and properties, first the non-sensient, inorganic matter, and second the sensient, organic matter. The study of law, or the study of differentiated energies acting through matter, is the one unit of investigation. I can assert that, from the beginning, man's growth and development have utterly depended, without variation or shadow of turning, upon his search for God's laws, and his application of them when found, and that there is no other study and no other work of man. We are made in His image, and through the knowledge of His laws and their application we become like unto Him, we approach that image.

All study is a unit; the focus of all efficient energy is the human soul, endowed with reason to know that energy, and the motives to apply it. All acts of consciousness are non-spacial, non-ponderable energy, pure energy, and the human ego infers from the presence of differentiated energies in consciousness, the nature of the matter external to consciousness, the matter through which these energies act. I repeat, my fellow-teachers, that there is but one study in this world of ours, and I can call it, in one breath, the study of law, and the study of God.

FRANCIS W. PARKER ON THE SOCIAL FACTOR IN EDUCATION

(1891)   From Francis W. Parker, *Talks on Pedagogics: An Outline of the Theory of Concentration* (New York, 1894), pp. 420–21, 450–51.

The public school in a republic means that in their early life children of all classes, of all nationalities, of all sects, of rich and poor alike, children of both sexes, shall work together under the highest and best conditions in one community for from eight to twelve years; that they shall have teachers who are trained in the art of all arts—the art of teaching; that in the school, before prejudice has entered their childish souls, before hate has become fixed, before mistrust has become a habit, they shall have influences surrounding them that shall lead to the best work with the best motive of mutual assistance.

Why should boys and girls be taught together from the kindergarten to the university, inclusive? Because they are to live together, to help each other throughout life, and must understand each other. The isolation of sexes in school has begotten mistrust, misunderstanding, false—nay even impure—fancies. The separation of sexes in school is a crime against nature. It is often argued that the sexes differ in intellectual capacity and moral power, and therefore should be separated in education; if this be true, it is all the more reason why they should be together. The strongest factor in education is the reflected light of character upon character.

The social factor in school is the greatest factor of all; it stands higher than subjects of learning, than methods of teaching, than the teacher himself. That which children learn from each other in play or work, though the work be drudgery, is the highest that is ever learned. The young man in the university learns more from his mates, of good or bad, than from his professors. This mingling, fusing, and blending give personal power, and make the public school a tremendous force for the upbuilding of democracy.

*   *   *

Attractive is far more powerful than compulsory education. The common school can be made the best school, in every respect, in the world. Everything is ready to this end, except one thing, and that is the introduction of scientific teaching. The organization is ready, the buildings have been erected, the money is paid: that which awaits is the method of democracy,—that education which shall set the souls of children free.

It is no dream or illusory vision, the realization of a common school, perfect in its appointments, with the means for the highest and best education at hand. All is ready when the people are ready to move, to demand that the methods of quantity shall go, and the methods of quality shall come. Unrealized possibilities of human growth are the infinite line of march.

A school should be a model home, a complete community and embryonic democracy. How? you ask. Again I answer, by putting into every schoolroom an educated, cultured, trained, devoted, child-loving teacher, a teacher imbued with a knowledge of the science of education, and a zealous, enthusiastic applicant of its principles. Where shall we find such teachers? They will spring from the earth and drop from the clouds when they *hear the demand.* We have asked for quantity teachers, and they have come by the tens of thousands. Now, let us demand the *artist teacher*, the teacher trained and skilled in the science of education—a genuine leader of little feet.

Nothing that is good is too good for the child; no thought too deep; no toil too great; no work too arduous: for the welfare of the child means happier homes, better society, a pure ballot and the perpetuity of republican institutions. Not only must the people demand the artist teacher with an authority which will admit no denial, they must also demand that the methods of aristocracy, which have degraded and debased mankind, be totally eliminated from the training of citizens; instead let us have a doctrine of education which means freedom to every child. I commend to your careful study the theory of Concentration, a theory that makes personal liberty the path to universal freedom.

JOSEPH MAYER RICE DESCRIBES THE COOK COUNTY NORMAL
SCHOOL UNDER FRANCIS W. PARKER (1893) From Joseph Mayer Rice, *The Public School System of the United States* (New York, 1893), pp. 209–14.

Of all the schools that I have seen, I know of none that shows so clearly what is implied by an educational ideal as the Cook County Normal School. This school has been for ten years in charge of Colonel Francis W. Parker, who, as is almost too well known to require mention, has done as much if not more than any other single person to spread the doctrine of the new education throughout our country. That the school does not accomplish all that it sets out to do, and that it still has a long road to travel before it will reach perfection, no one feels more keenly than Colonel Parker himself. As in other schools, mistakes are made by pupils in grammar and in spelling, some problems in arithmetic are inaccurately performed, some of the nature-paintings are daubs, some of the color-work is inharmonious, and some of the wood-work made by the children would not command a high price in the market. Indeed, taken all in all, the results as measured on the scale of one hundred are no better and no poorer than those obtained in other progressive American schools.

In one regard, however,—namely, as a source of inspiration to those who desire to enter the profession,—it is almost an ideal. This is true for two reasons: First, the school is almost unique in its suggestiveness, due to the attempt on the part of the teachers to conduct all the work on purely psychological principles, to the completeness of the school from the standpoint of the "all-side" development of the child, and to the manner in which are utilized the opportunities to bring the child into close contact with nature in the beautiful park of twenty acres in which the school is situated. Secondly, Colonel Parker possesses to a remarkable degree the power to inspire his students. Of many institutions it may be said that they are the sources of knowledge, but of few that they are the sources of wisdom. Colonel Parker does not aim to convert his students into storehouses of knowledge, into walking encyclopedias, but rather to impress them with the idea that when they leave the school they will have received but a glimpse of the infinite; and they do feel when they leave him that the development of the human mind is indeed a difficult problem, and that in justice to their pupils they are in duty bound ever to seek such light as will guide them in solving this problem. Colonel Parker sends out into the world no full-grown trees, but only seedlings. In unfavorable soil the seedlings wither or are stunted in their growth; but when the soil in which they are planted is favorable to their growth, they develop into tall and beautiful trees.

The faculty of the normal department of the school is one of the most enthusiastic, earnest, progressive, and thoughtful corps of teachers that may be found anywhere, and they are continually growing. The reason why the results in the primary and grammar grades are not, under these favorable conditions, superior to those obtained in other progressive schools is that it is extremely difficult to find grade teachers equal to the task and to retain the competent ones after they have become imbued with the spirit of the school. The corps of teachers in the elementary department is, therefore, a very unstable one, and it being consequently necessary continually to initiate new teachers into this difficult work, it is natural that imperfections should arise. That it is much more difficult for the grades than it is for the normal department to obtain thorough teachers and to retain them after they have had experience in the school is also natural, when the salaries paid to the grade teachers are only, say, one third as large as those paid to the teachers of the normal department. The great difficulty under which the schools of Quincy, Massachusetts, have been laboring since Colonel Parker made them famous, is that the Quincy teachers are so much in demand that the mere fact of having taught for a year or two at Quincy raises the teachers above the Quincy salaries. Last year as many as one third of the whole number of teachers left the Quincy schools, because higher salaries had been offered to them in other cities.

In the primary and the grammar grades of the school, the work is conducted on the same general lines as those of Minneapolis and La Porte. A great deal of attention is given to the unification of studies, Colonel Parker being a strong advocate of this educational principle; and in his talks to his students he is constantly impressing its value upon their minds. Throughout the school, the curriculum includes the sciences, literature, and the artistic lines of work, such as designing, color-work, and drawing and painting from nature. There is also a complete course in manual training. Language, and to a certain extent arithmetic, are taught incidentally in connection with the other subjects rather than directly, and from the start the pupils are led to illustrate their compositions. In geography the work is made as objective as possible by means of the molding-board, relief maps, pictures, and the magic-lantern, and from time to time the pupils are taken on geographical excursions. In history and in literature the work is in many respects excellent. The courses for the whole school are planned by the members of the normal-school faculty who have special charge of the various subjects throughout the school. In the lowest primary grade, which for many years has been in charge of Miss Griswold, the work appeared to me to be very suggestive, particularly in regard to busy-work. Several groups of children were doing busy-work at the same time, and in no two groups was it alike. In one group the pupils were painting a flower they had just been studying, in another they were writing a story about an animal that had just been utilized in a lesson in reading as well as in number, in a third they were reading silently in their reading-books. In teaching children to read much attention is given to phonics.

In the sciences, the work of the Cook County Normal School is in certain respects unique. Its park of twenty acres affords opportunities for doing ideal work in certain directions, and besides, Mr. Jackman, who has charge of the science department, has given much thought to the methods of teaching the sciences in the elementary schools. He is now laboring hard to solve the difficult problem of how to teach the sciences systematically in these schools. In one portion of the park a rather large plot of ground has been laid out in beds for the cultivation of plants under the supervision of the pupils. This plot has been divided into square rods, one for each grade, each pupil having charge of a certain number of plants of whose growth he keeps a careful record in his note-book. These notes are illustrated with pictures showing the development of the plants at different stages. The park is also utilized for the study of trees. In this study pupils receive the task of observing closely and accurately the development of the foliage of particular trees, and of carefully noting the results of their periodical observations. Some of the drawings and paintings made in their record-books are admirable. I shall publish facsimiles of a few of them in the second part of this volume. Much is also done in the way of studying insects in their natural environment. In the park are two very pretty lakes filled with fishes, the latter being used for the purpose of study. A zoological garden is also found in the park, but at the time of my visit it contained few animals. In addition to the park, the school has a museum containing a large number of stuffed animals, which are taken to the class-rooms when occasion for their use arises. In one of the classrooms a lesson on birds was given during my visit, and it was richly illustrated with stuffed birds of numerous varieties. Besides botany and zoology, physics, chemistry, and geology are studied in all the grades.

THE "ARITHMETIC CREED" OF THE COOK COUNTY TEACHERS'

ASSOCIATION (c. 1900)   From William M. Giffin, *School Days in the Fifties* (Chicago, 1906), pp. 15–16.

ARTICLE I.—All operations which should be taught to children in Number can be performed with numbers of things.

ARTICLE II.—The subjects to be taught in Arithmetic, the terms to be used, and the processes to be employed, shall be determined from the standpoint of the child—not from that of the educated adult.

ARTICLE III.—In determining what shall be taught in Arithmetic, we should be able to show that any topic is: (*a*) practical; that is, that it has to do with the affairs of life; or, (*b*) disciplinary; that is, that it insures mental growth and mental strength.

ARTICLE IV.—We condemn the giving of work in Arithmetic under the name of "Examples," for which conditions stated in problems cannot be made. For instance, complicated examples in complex or compound fractions.

ARTICLE V.—Definition and rule should be required only when the thing to be defined or the process under the rule is thoroughly understood. Hence, definitions and rules should close—not begin—a subject. They should be made by the student.

ARTICLE VI.—Lessons in Arithmetic should *not* be assigned for home study.

ARTICLE VII.—Operations in Arithmetic which have become obsolete, or have never existed elsewhere in the world, should become obsolete in the schoolroom.

ARTICLE VIII.—Problems in Arithmetic should employ the best effort of the pupil, but should never go beyond it. He grows through what he does for himself. The skillful teacher secures and directs his best efforts.

ARTICLE IX.—All that need be taught to children in Arithmetic can be taught under the following subjects: Lines, Area, Volume, Bulk, Time, Weight, Values, and Single Things.

ARTICLE X.—Fundamental operations—four or five, according to your faith. Numbers used to be within the comprehension of pupils. First, *correctness*, then, *rapidity* in work. Use of federal money included in the foregoing.

G. Stanley Hall and the Child Study Movement

G. STANLEY HALL ON THE CONTENTS OF CHILDREN'S MINDS ON ENTERING SCHOOL (1883)   From G. Stanley Hall, "The Contents of Children's Minds," as quoted in *Pedagogical Seminary*, vol. I, pp. 146–51, 154–56.

. . . the writer undertook soon after the opening of the Boston schools in September, 1880, to make out a list of questions suitable for obtaining an inventory of the contents of the minds of children of average intelligence on entering the primary schools of that city. This was made possible by the liberality of Mrs. Quincy Shaw, who detailed four excellent teachers from her comprehensive system of kindergartens to act as special questioners under the writer's direction, and by the co-operation of Miss L. B. Pingree, their superintendent. All the local and many other of the German questions were not suitable to children here, and the task of selecting those that should be so, though perhaps not involving quite so many perplexing considerations as choosing an equally long list of "normal words," was by no means easy. They must not be too familiar nor too hard and remote, but must give free and easy play to thought and memory. But especially, to yield most practical results, they should lie within the range of what children are commonly supposed or at least desired or expected, by teachers and by those who write primary textbooks and prescribe courses of instruction, to know. Many preliminary half-days of questioning small groups of children and receiving suggestions from many sources, and the use of many primers, object-lesson courses, etc., now in use in this country, were necessary before the first provisional list of one hundred and thirty-four questions was printed. The problem first had in mind was strictly practical; viz., what may Boston children be, by their teachers, assumed to know and have seen when they enter school; although other purposes more psychological shaped other questions used later.

The difficulties and sources of possible error in the use of such questions are many. Not only are children prone to imitate others in their answers without stopping to think and give an independent answer of their own, but they often love to seem wise, and, to make themselves interesting, state what seems to interest us without reference to truth, divining the lines of our interest with a subtlety we do not suspect; if absurdities are doubted by the questioner they are sometimes only the more protested by the children; the faculties of some are benumbed and perhaps their tongues tied by bashfulness, while others are careless, listless, inattentive, and answer at random. Again, many questioners are brusque, lacking in sympathy or tact, or real interest or patience in the work, or perhaps regard it as trivial or fruitless. These and many other difficulties seemed best minimized by the following method, which was finally settled upon and, with the co-operation of Mr. E. P. Seaver, superintendent of the Boston schools, put into operation. The four trained and experienced kindergarten teachers were employed by the hour to question three children at a time in the dressing-room of the school by themselves alone, so as not to interrupt the school-work. No constraint was used, and, as several hours were necessary to finish each set, changes and rests were often needful, while by frequent correspondence and by meetings with the writer to discuss details and compare results uniformity of method was sought. The most honest and unembarrassed child's first answer to a direct question, e. g., whether it has seen a cow, sheep, etc., must rarely or never be taken without careful cross-questioning, a stated method of which was developed respecting many objects. If the child says it has seen a cow, but when asked its size points to its own finger-nail or hand and says, *so big*, as not unfrequently occurs, the inference is that it has at most only seen a picture of a cow, and thinks its size reproduced therein, and accordingly he is set down as deficient on that question. If, however, he is correct in size, but calls the color blue, does not know it as the source of milk, or that it has horns or hoofs,—several errors of the latter order were generally allowed. A worm may be said to *swim* on the ground, butchers to kill only the bad animals, etc.; but when hams are said to grow on trees or in the ground, or a hill is described as a *lump* of dirt, or wool as growing on hens, as sometimes occurs, deficiency is obvious. Thus many other visual and other notions that seem to adults so simple that they must be present to the mind with some completeness or not at all, are in a process of gradual acquisition, element by element, in the mind of a child, so that there must sometimes be confessedly a certain degree of arbitrariness in saying, as, except in cases of peculiar uncertainty, the questioners attempted to do, that the child has the concept or does not have it. Men's first names seemed to have designated single striking qualities, but once applied, they become general or specific names according to circumstances. Again, very few children knew that a tree had bark, leaves, trunk, and roots; but very few indeed had not noticed a tree enough for our "pass." Without specifying further details, it may suffice here to say that the child was given the benefit of every doubt and credited with knowledge wherever its ignorance was not so radical as to make a chaos of what instruction and most primary text-books are wont to assume. It is important also to add that the questioners were requested to report manifest gaps in the child's knowledge *in its own words*, reproducing its syntax, pronunciation, etc.

About sixty teachers besides the four examiners made returns from three or more children each. Many of their returns, however, are incomplete, careless, or show internal contradictions, and can be used only indirectly to control results from the other sources. From more than twice that number two hundred of the Boston children were selected as the basis of the following table. For certain questions and for many statistical purposes this number is much too small to yield very valuable results, but where, as in the majority of cases, the averages of these children taken by fifties have varied less than ten per cent., it is safe to infer that the figures have considerable representative worth and far more than they could have if the percentages were small. The precautions that were taken to avoid schools where the children come from homes representing extremes of either culture or ignorance, or to balance deviations from a preliminary conjecture averaged in one direction by like deviations in the other, and also to select from each school-room with the teacher's aid only children of average capacity and to dismiss each child found unresponsive or not acquainted with the English language, give to the percentages, it is believed, a worth which without these and other precautions to this end only far larger numbers could yield.

The following table shows the general results for a number of those questions which admit of categorical answers, only negative results being recorded; the italicized questions in the "miscellaneous" class being based on only from forty to seventy-five children, the rest on two hundred, or in a few cases, on two hundred and fifty.

In 1883, shortly after my own tables, as below, were published, Superintendent I. M. Greenwood of Kansas City tested 678 children of the lowest primary class in that city, of whom 47 were colored, with some of my questions. I here print his percentages in the last two columns. In his state children are admitted to school at six, but his tests were made in March, April, May, or after some seven months more of school life, and probably at greater age.

Name of the Object of Conception.	*Per Cent. of Children Ignorant of it.*		
	In Boston.	*In Kansas City.* *White.*	*Colored.*
Beehive	80.	59.4	66.
Crow	77.	47.3	59.
Bluebird	72.5		
Ant	65.5	21.5	19.1
Squirrel	63.	15.	4.2
Snail	62.		
Robin	60.5	30.6	10.6
Sparrow	57.5		
Sheep	54.	3.5	
Bee	52.	7.27	4.2
Frog	50.	2.7	
Pig	47.5	1.7	
Chicken	33.5	.5	
Worm	22.	.5	
Butterfly	20.5	.5	
Hen	19.	.1	
Cow	18.5	5.2	
Growing wheat	92.5	23.4	66.
Elm tree	91.5	52.4	89.8
Poplar tree	89.		
Willow	89.		
Growing oats	87.5		
Oak tree	87.	62.2	58.6
Pine	87.	65.6	87.2
Maple	83.	31.2	80.8
Growing moss	81.5	30.7	42.5
" strawberries	78.5	26.5	1.1
" clover	74.		
" beans	71.5		
" blueberries	67.5		
" blackberries	66.		
" corn	65.5		

Name of the Object of Conception.	Per Cent. of Children Ignorant of it.		
	In Boston.	In Kansas City. White.	Colored.
Chestnut tree	64.		
Planted a seed	63.		
Peaches on a tree	61.		
Growing potatoes	61.		
" buttercup	55.5		
" rose	54.		
" grapes	53.		
" dandelion	52.		
" cherries	46.		
" pears	32.		
" apples	21.		
Where are the child's ribs	90.5	13.6	6.4
" " " lungs	81.	26.	44.6
" " " heart	80.	18.5	18.1
" " " wrist	70.5	3.	
" " ankles	65.5	14.1	
" " waist	52.5	14.	4.2
" " hips	45.	14.	4.2
" " knuckles	36.	2.9	8.5
" " elbows	25.	1.5	
Knows right and left hand	21.5	1.	10.2
" cheek	18.	.5	
" forehead	15.	.5	
" throat	13.5	1.1	
" knee	7.	1.6	
" stomach	6.	27.2	45.9
Dew	78.	39.1	70.2
What season it is	75.5	31.8	56.1
Seen hail	73.	13.6	18.1
" rainbow	65.	10.3	2.1
" sunrise	56.5	16.6	
" sunset	53.5	19.5	
" clouds	35.	7.3	
" stars	14.	3.	
" moon	7.	26.	53.
Conception of an island	87.5		
" " a beach	55.5		
" " woods	53.5		
" " river	48.		
" " pond	40.		
" " hill	28.		
" " brook	15.		
" " triangle	92.		
" " square	56.		
" " circle	35.		
The number five	28.5		
" " four	17.		
" " three	8.		

Name of the Object of Conception.	Per Cent of Children Ignorant of it.		
	In Boston.	In Kansas City. White.	Colored.
Seen watchmaker at work	68.	30.1	49.7
" file	65.	20.8	36.1
" plough	64.5	13.9	8.5
" spade	62.	7.3	15.
" hoe	61.	5.	10.6
" bricklayer at work	44.5	10.1	2.1
" shoemaker at work	25.	8.7	
" axe	12.	18.4	53.
Knows green by name	15.		
" blue by name	14.		
" yellow by name	13.5		
" red by name	9.		
That leathern things come from animals	93.4	50.8	72.3
Maxim or proverb	91.5		
Origin of cotton things	90.	35.7	15.
What flour is made of	89.	34.7	57.4
Ability to knit	88.		
What bricks are made of	81.1	33.1	53.
Shape of the world	70.3	46.	47.
Origin of woolen things	69.	55.	44.
Never attended kindergarten	67.5		
Never been in bathing	64.5	13.4	
Can tell no rudiment of a story	58.	23.6	12.7
Not know wooden things are from trees	55.	19.3	6.4
Origin of butter	50.5	6.7	
Origin of meat (from animals)	48.	8.3	12.7
Cannot sew	47.5	23.4	
Cannot strike a given musical tone	40.		
Cannot beat time regularly	39.		
Have never saved cents at home	36.	8.2	12.7
Never been in the country	35.5	13.1	19.
Can repeat no verse	28.	20.	42.5
Source of milk	20.5	4.	

Name of the Object of Conception.	Per cent. of ignorance in 150 girls.	Per cent. of ignorance in 150 boys.	Per cent. of ignorance in 50 Irish children.	Per cent. of ignorance in 50 American children.	Per cent. of ignorance in 64 kindergarten children.
Beehive,	81	75	86	70	61
Ant,	59	60	74	38	26
Squirrel,	69	50	66	42	43
Snail,	69	73	92	72	62
Robin,	69	44	64	36	29
Sheep,	67	47	62	40	40
Bee,	46	32	52	32	26
Frog,	53	38	54	35	35

Name of the Object of Conception.	Per cent. of ignorance in 150 girls.	Per cent. of ignorance in 150 boys.	Per cent. of ignorance in 50 Irish children.	Per cent. of ignorance in 50 American children.	Per cent. of ignorance in 64 kindergarten children.
Pig,	45	27	38	26	22
Chicken,	35	21	32	26	22
Worm,	21	17	26	16	9
Butterfly,	14	16	26	8	9
Hen,	15	14	18	2	14
Cow,	18	12	20	6	10
Growing clover,	59	68	84	42	29
" corn,	58	50	60	68	32
" potatoes,	55	54	62	44	34
" buttercup,	50	51	66	40	31
" rose,	48	48	60	42	33
" dandelion,	44	42	62	34	31
" apples,	16	16	18	12	5
Ribs,	88	92	98	82	68
Ankles,	53	52	62	40	38
Waist,	53	52	64	32	36
Hips,	50	47	72	31	24
Knuckles,	27	27	34	12	23
Elbow,	19	32	36	16	12
Right from left hand,	20	8	14	20	4
Wrist,	21	34	44	9	19
Cheek,	10	12	14	14	4
Forehead,	10	11	12	10	7
Throat,	10	18	14	16	14
Knee,	4	5	2	10	2
Dew,	64	63	92	52	57
What season it is,	59	50	68	48	41
Hail,	75	61	84	52	53
Rainbow,	59	61	70	38	38
Sunrise,	71	53	70	36	53
Sunset,	47	49	52	32	29
Star,	15	10	12	4	7
Island,	74	78	84	64	55
Beach,	82	49	60	34	32
Woods,	46	36	46	32	27
River,	38	44	62	12	13
Pond,	31	34	42	24	28
Hill,	23	22	30	12	19
The number five,	26	16	22	24	12
" " four,	15	10	16	14	7
" " three,	7	6	12	8	0

From the above tables it seems not too much also to infer —I. That there is next to nothing of pedagogic value the knowledge of which it is safe to assume at the outset of school-life. Hence the need of objects and the danger of books and word cram. Hence many of the best primary teachers in Germany spend from two to four or even six months in talking of objects and drawing them before any beginning of what we till lately have regarded as primary-school work. II. The best preparation parents can give their children for good school-training is to make them acquainted with natural objects, especially with the sights and sounds of the country, and send to them to good and hygienic, as distinct from the most fashionable, kindergartens. III. Every teacher on starting with a new class or in a new locality, to make sure that his efforts along some lines are not utterly lost, should undertake to explore carefully section by section children's minds with all the tact and and ingenuity he can command and acquire, to determine exactly what is already shown; and every normal-school pupil should undertake work of the same kind as an essential part of his training. IV. The concepts which are the most common in the children of a given locality are the earliest to be acquired, while the rarer ones are later. This order may in teaching generally be assumed as a natural one, e. g. apples first and wheat last (Cf. the first Boston Table above). This order, however, varies very greatly with every change of environment, so that the results of explorations of children's minds in one place cannot be assumed to be valid for those of another save within comparatively few concept-spheres.

The high rate of ignorance indicated in the table may surprise most persons who will be likely to read this report, because the childhood they know will be much above the average of intelligence here sought, and because the few memories of childhood which survive in adult life necessarily bear but slight traces of imperfections and are from many causes illusory. Skeins and spools of thread were said to grow on the sheep's back or on bushes, stockings on trees, butter to come from buttercups, flour to be made of beans, oats to grow on oaks, bread to be swelled yeast, trees to be stuck in the ground by God and to be rootless, meat to be dug from the ground, and potatoes to be picked from the trees. Cheese is squeezed butter, the cow says "bow-wow," the pig purrs or burrows, worms are not distinguished from snakes, moss from the "toad's umbrella," bricks from stones, etc. An oak may be known only as an acorn-tree or a button-tree, a pine only as a needle-tree, a bird's nest only as its bed, etc. So that while no one child has all these misconceptions, none are free from them, and thus the liabilities are great that, in this chaos of half-assimilated impressions, half right, half wrong, some lost link may make utter nonsense or mere verbal cram of the most careful instruction, as in the cases of children referred to above who knew much by rote about a cow, its milk, horns, leather, meat, etc., but yet were sure from the picture-book that it was no bigger than a small mouse.

For 86 per cent. of the above questions the average intelligence of thirty-six country children who were tested ranks higher than that of the city children of the Table, and in many items very greatly. The subject-matter of primers for the latter is in great part still traditionally of country life; hence the danger of unwarranted presupposition is considerable. As our methods of teaching grow natural we realize that city life is unnatural, and that those who grow up without knowing the country are defrauded of that without which childhood can never be complete or normal. On the whole, the material of the city is no doubt inferior in pedagogic value to country experience. A few days in the country at this age has raised the level of many a city child's intelligence more than a term or two of school training could do without it. It is there, too, that the foundations of a love of natural science are best laid.

G. STANLEY HALL ON CHILD STUDY WORK AT CLARK UNIVERSITY
(**1896**)   From G. Stanley Hall, "Some of the Methods and Results of Child Study Work at Clark University," National Education Association *Journal of Addresses and Proceedings, 1896* (Washington, D.C., 1896), pp. 860–62.

Let me first tell you the method we have been using. We have issued syllabi on the different topics, and propose tabulating the answers collected from a large number of individuals. We have issued thirty-two of these syllabi and have sent them sometimes to nearly 1,000 observers each. We have had them reprinted and shall be glad to send them to all who will drop me a postal-card request.

The first investigation undertook the study of anger, on which some thousands of returns have been digested.

The second study was on dolls. Dolls are historically closely connected with idols. The penates, or household gods, shade over into idols. Dolls serve the tremendous purpose of reducing the world to a very petite form, just the size for children to understand. In Russia there has been a doll congress, and official recommendations for the use of dolls. We have found that the doll passion culminates at the age of eight or nine. It begins with rude things, and passes through all the stages of development to the perfect paper or wax creations.

We next studied crying and laughing, two of the most important phenomena of the race. These are the oldest residual phenomena. The noise and laugh of the child take us back to the beginnings of the race. Just as when we laugh and shake we drop back for an instant toward bliss itself and catch a glimpse of paradise lost, so the laughter of children shows us a real paradise set in the midst of civilization. The child repeats and illustrates the history of the race.

Then comes the study of fears. Just think what a chapter that opens. Out of 4,000 people only three were found who had no fears. Thunder and lightning lead all the rest, though less than one-fourth of 1 per cent die of lightning or of thunder either. Aristotle says "Education is to teach us to fear aright." Surely we have not advanced far on the road to wisdom. Fear cramps and arrests more than anything else all influence to good. Perhaps the chief end of education is to banish fear.

We then made a study of common traits and habits. We find that we each have characteristic movements, and these movements which we find in children beginning to write seem to show traces of residual movements going back to an earlier form of life. Just as fear of what has big eyes, fur and teeth, takes us back to the time when man feared animals more than now; so these automatic movements take us back to primitive times. We have thus traces of automatism, just as we have traces of gills, for example, in every human neck.

In the child's attitude toward nature we find something very akin to man's religious development. Every child is born a pagan, a fetish worshipper. Shall we try to stifle this phenomenon? Just as absurd to cut off a tadpole's tail and expect its legs to grow faster. It never falls off but is absorbed. To cut it off dwarfs its hind legs and ties it to an aquatic life. Just so with fetishism. This is the rudimentary organ—the tadpole's tail; cut it off and you dwarf human religion.

Another study was on children's food. We found all the appetites of all the animals. From the time that everything the child gets goes to its mouth, its arms are only tentacles.

Then we grew bold. We issued a year ago last spring two more syllabi, one upon love, the other upon religion.

We then made a special study of the dull child, and of the effect of different environments. We made here twenty-eight classifications. Then we studied old age; then music; then religious phenomena from another standpoint. Then we took up the "only child" and traced the effects of solitude. We even touched upon habit and instinct among the lower animals.

Some of the observers have organized themselves into societies. There are now several societies for studying children in Great Britain; one among the girls at Newnham College; one at Edinburg; one at Dublin.

Now for a few very general remarks about the future of child study. In the first place I believe it will show us the value of individuality. Children are different. As the Irishman said about the ladies, "They are all alike in being different." We must not forget that success in life depends upon the development of each individual in the particular line in which he excels. Every child should be thus developed enough to make a career. Not only because we live under a republican government, but because it is most economical.

In this connection let me say that child study is only one phase of this new movement in psychology; the front that is toward the teacher.

It also goes into physiology and has built up a small literature there; so also into insanity. It takes up the study of mental life in lower animals. Perez studied two cats. I know a friend who is studying a fly. That is a most fascinating study. Another studied the daily life of an amoeba. These are all parts of one great movement.

The child repeats the race. This is a great biological view. We find numerous traces of this in the seventy-two organs of the body, and in many more rudimentary organs. This knowledge has developed since that eventful day when Fritz Muller began his studies on the relations of ontogony and philogomy. Today we take up the literature of the race and use all the traces of archaeology to fill in the gap. Alongside of this we can use the child as embodying at different stages the successive changes of the race. We get evidence of this development in the fossils. We find certain fishes like the fossils. We find the mastodon bearing certain relations to the elephant. We find the series so complete in the batrachian group that we can trace all the stages, including the gradual absorption of gills as it crept out of water.

All of these changes are implanted in the germ-cell by which we repeat in a few days or hours the history of untold ages. It is simply a means of economy. Not that we must pass through all these stages, but it is the *shortest* way to reach this stage of development. Sometimes we find in the course of development rapid leaps. Wherever there have been these rapid leaps there is greatest danger of arrest.

G. STANLEY HALL ON THE RELATION OF CHILD STUDY TO EDUCATION (1900) From "Child-Study and Its Relation to Education," *The Forum*, vol. XXIX, pp. 688–89, 699–702.

Child-study or paidology, often confused with psychogenesis, of which it constitutes a large part, is a new movement which has been well under way hardly a decade. It is already represented by a bibliography of some two thousand titles, including only the books and articles well worth reading, and not comprising the yet larger mass of chaff; by two journals in this country devoted exclusively to it, and by several more which make it a department; by three journals in Germany, two in France, one each in England, Italy, Japan, Russia, and Spain.

Paidology either forms a department, or appears on the programme of most of the leading psychological, philosophical, and educational societies. Its work is supported from the treasury of several of the largest States. Sometimes, as, for example, in New York city, it is a topic in the annual school reports; and expert investigations are paid for out of the municipal treasury. There are several academic chairs devoted mainly or exclusively to it; and I opine that it enters somewhat into the instruction of nearly every course of study that deals with the human mind. There are organizations with which I have been in correspondence in India, South America, Russia, Spain, and Australia; and circles or groups exist in almost every civilized or colonized land.

Studies of child life among the North American Indians, Australian tribes, the Zulus, Chinese, clay-eaters, Kaffirs, Maoris, Arabs, Samoyads, ancient Greeks and Romans, etc., are found in periodicals or publishers' announcements. Child-study forms a section or a part of the work of nearly all the leading women's clubs, summer schools, and organizations of Sunday-school teachers. It is a movement that has been extensively felt in literature, as witness the many books on childhood noticed during the last few years in the journals I edit; and it is even a frequent topic in the daily, weekly, and, especially, the Sunday newspaper press. Teachers of all grades, mothers of all degrees of culture, pupils in colleges and normal schools fill out questionnaires, and perhaps meet to compare results and to report the latest magazine literature upon the subject. I have received some two thousand letters— either unacknowledged or inadequately answered—from all parts of the world, asking how to organize local work, requesting suggestions for reading, or very often seeking advice concerning children. A private secretary devoted solely to this work could do beneficent service; and perhaps a new profession might arise, which might be indicated by some such term as psychic orthopedics or pediatrics.

*   *   *

From this standpoint it is plain that the teacher must know two things: (1) the subject matter to be taught; and (2) the nature and capacity of the minds in which it is to be rooted. The farmer must know soils as well as seeds; the architect, the nature of material as well as ground-plans and elevations; the physician, his patient's history, and perhaps that of his family, and he must know drugs as well—all partial, but helpful, analogies. If logic and the old philosophy of mind have ever helped the teacher, the new genetic conceptions are incalculably more labor-saving in his work.

Let us consider a single representative point. Every one recognizes the importance of interest, how it quickens attention, short-circuits slower processes, and eases the strain of acquisition, and how the teacher who is well informed on the favorite out-of-school amusements and occupations of his pupils, and on the life led by them, and who knows his classes individually and collectively, can shorten the road of learning. To determine and group these interests more fully than ever occurred to Herbart is one of the quests of child-study. One of its goals now near at hand, and which will involve considerable change both in regard to the methods of teaching every subject in the curriculum and the age at which the different subjects can be most profitably taught, is the determination of nascent periods for both mental and muscular work. We shall very soon have curves of the years when many of the chief culture-interests begin to culminate and decline. This will enable us to say definitely which are the premature and which are the belated subjects; *i.e.*, when the matter of school training can be taught without forcing, and without sinning away the sacred hour of maximal receptivity and capacity.

Among the more incidental advantages of the study of children is the new bond which it often establishes between the home and the school. The teacher who no longer regards his pupils as marionettes, to be treated as groups or classes, but as free units, with a bond of sympathy between each of their hearts and his own, desires to know at least something of the home life of each child, and to come to an understanding with parents. Hence, many very different organizations have arisen, from Superintendent Dutton's educational club in Brookline, Massachusetts, to the circles of mothers who meet the teachers weekly after school at Detroit, Michigan. Again, women teachers are increasing, and the method by which they do their best work is to consider individuals and adapt themselves to personal differences. Child study gives sanction to this method, reinforces it, and tends to make the teacher's service of even greater pecuniary value.

Another advantage of interest in child-study is that it helps to break down to some extent the partitions between grades of work, so that the kindergartner and university professor can cooperate in the same task. Best of all, perhaps, it tends to make family life with plenty of children in it more interesting and desirable. Indeed, it is a part of a great culture-movement marked by a new love of the naive, the spontaneous, and the unsophisticated, by a desire to get at what is primitive and original in human nature as it comes fresh from its primal sources. A prevalent theory of art insists that the greatest defect of all art-products is a sign of conscious design, and that the acme of aesthetic enjoyment is reached when it is realized that the poem or picture is a product of unconscious creative force more or less irresistible, and, as with the greatest geniuses, with no thought of effect. Just so in childhood we are coming again to realize that in its fresh thoughts, feelings, and impulses, we have an oracle which declares that the world and human nature are sound to the core.

More yet. There is really no clue by which we can thread our way through all the mazes of culture and the distractions of modern life save by knowing the true nature and needs of childhood and of adolescence. I urge, then, that civilizations, religions, all human institutions, and the schools, are judged truly, or from the standpoint of the philosophy of history, by this one criterion: namely, whether they have offended against these little ones or have helped to bring childhood and adolescence to an ever higher and completer maturity as generations pass by. Childhood is thus our pillar of cloud by day and fire by night. Other oracles may grow dim, but this one will never fail.

Just as at various times in the history of culture man has turned with renewed zest to the old and ultimate humanistic question of what he really is, his place and meaning in the universe, his whence and whither, so now we are asking with unique interest what a child really is. We are slowly awakening to a recognition that children are not like adults, with all the faculties of maturity on a reduced scale, but unique and very different creatures. Their proportions are so different that if head, body, and limbs were each to grow in its original proportion until they reached adult stature, they would be monsters. Adaptable as children are, their ways and thoughts are not as ours; and the adult can no more get back into the child's soul by introspection than he can pass the flaming sword and reclaim his lost Eden. The recollections of our own childhood are the mere flotsam and jetsam of a wrecked stage of development; and the lost points in psychogenesis must be slowly wrought out with toil and patience.

The child's senses, instincts, views of truth, credulity, emotions, and feelings toward objects have very little in common with ours, and indeed are sometimes almost incommensurate; so that we have to explore our way back slowly and tediously, with many an indirect method, if we would solve the great problem that looms before us. The study of a few hundred biographies of great men reveals a large floating body of storiology that is liable to attach itself to the early years of any one who afterwards attains eminence. This has shown that most of the material constituting the records of childhood and even adolescence is nearly as mythic as Niebuhr found the stories of early Roman history to be. This, although perhaps the very least of all the motivations to it, suggests the advisability of a life and health book as one of the inalienable rights of childhood, which children would be the first to claim if they knew enough to make a declaration of their rights.

In some European towns such books are now opened by municipal order, and are kept through required school life. Here all the monthly examinations through all the years are a standing witness of the child's progress and fitness for advancement. The school doctor here records his fears and advice, the parents perhaps add their comments, and, in rare cases, the anthropologist or special student supplements all this; so that on the whole there could hardly be a more useful document for giving each child a serviceable kind of self-knowledge of his own strong and weak points as an aid in the choice of a vocation.

One of the most important themes, both practically and scientifically, is adolescence, the springtime of life, when the emotional nature undergoes nothing less than a regeneration, when the child normally passes from egoism to altruism, and the great subordination of the individual to the race slowly makes itself manifest. This is the most critical period of life, because civilization depends on whether these uncertain final stages, which most differentiate man from animals, shall be completed or arrested. When the nature of this period is understood, and its needs are met, the most radical of all educational changes will be found necessary in the high school and early collegiate years in ways I have elsewhere indicated. Every race, savage and enlightened, has recognized this stage. Indeed, in a sense, education begins here, and widens upward to the university and downward toward the kindergarten, somewhat in proportion as civilization advances.

Regarded from the standpoint of the highest biologic law this adolescent stage is the golden period of life. The faculties of both body and soul here reach their acme. Just as the ape reaches at adolescence that point in his development which is nearest to man, and becomes farther from his as he matures, so the human race grows younger and more adolescent, because at this stage only the bud of the super-man that is to be appears.

G. STANLEY HALL ON THE IDEAL SCHOOL BASED ON CHILD STUDY

(1901)   From G. Stanley Hall, "The Ideal School as Based on Child Study," National Education Association *Journal of Addresses and Proceedings, 1901* (Washington, D.C., 1901), pp. 475–82, 488.

I shall try in this paper to break away from all current practices, traditions, methods, and philosophies, for a brief moment, and ask what education would be if based solely upon a fresh and comprehensive view of the nature and needs of childhood. Hitherto the data for such a construction of the ideal school have been insufficient, and soon they will be too manifold for any one mind to make the attempt; so the moment is opportune. What follows is based almost solely, point by point, upon the study of the stages of child development, and might, perhaps, without presumption be called a first attempt to formulate a practical program of this great movement. In my limited space I can do little more than barely state the conclusions that affect the practical work of teachers.

The school I shall describe exists nowhere, but its methods, unless I err, are valid everywhere. Altho many of its features exist already, and could be pieced together in a mosaic from many lands and ages, it is essentially the school invisible, not made with hands. But, as there is nothing so practical as the truly ideal, altho my school today exists nowhere, it might be organized anywhere tomorrow; and I hope that the most and the least conservative will agree that is is the true goal of all endeavor, and will not differ except as to whether it may be realized at once or only at the end of a long period of labor. I confess that something like this has from the first animated all my own feeble educational endeavors, and that without it I should be without hope and without goal in the world of pedagogy.

Beginning with the deep philosophy often imbedded in words, "school," or "schole," means leisure, exemption from work, the perpetuation of the primaeval paradise created before the struggle for existence began. It stands for the prolongation of human infancy, and the no whit less important prolongation of adolescence. It is sacred to health, growth, and heredity, a pound of which is worth a ton of instruction. The guardians of the young should strive first of all to keep out of nature's way, and to prevent harm, and should merit the proud title of defenders of the happiness and rights of children. They should feel profoundly that childhood, as it comes fresh from the hand of God, is not corrupt, but illustrates the survival of the most consummate thing in the world; they should be convinced that there is nothing else so worthy of love, reverence, and service as the body and soul of the growing child.

Practically, this means that every invasion of this leisure, the provision of a right measure of which is our first duty to youth, has a certain presumption against it, and must justify itself by conclusive reasons. Before we let the pedagog loose upon childhood, not only must each topic in his curriculum give an account of itself, but his inroads must be justified in the case of each child. We must overcome the fetichism of the alphabet, of the multiplication table, of grammars, of scales, and of bibliolatry, and must reflect that but a few generations ago the ancestors of all of us were illiterate; that the invention of Cadmus seemed the sowing of veritable dragon's teeth in the brain; that Charlemagne and many other great men of the world could not read or write; that scholars have argued that Cornelia, Ophelia, Beatrice, and even the blessed mother of our Lord knew nothing of letters. The knights, the elite leaders of the Middle Ages, deemed writing a mere clerk's trick beneath the attention of all those who scorned to muddle their wits with others' ideas, feeling that their own were good enough for them.

Nay more: there are many who ought not to be educated, and who would be better in mind, body, and morals if they knew no school. What shall it profit a child to gain the world of knowledge and lose his own health? Cramming and over-schooling have impaired many a feeble mind, for which, as the proverb says, nothing is so dangerous as ideas too large for it. We are coming to understand the vanity of mere scholarship and erudition, and to know that even ignorance may be a wholesome poultice for weakly souls; while scribes, sophists, scholastics, and pedants suggest how much of the learning of the past is now seen to be vanity, and how incompetent pedagogs have been as guardians of the sacred things of culture. Thus, while I would abate no whit from the praise of learning and education for all who are fit for them, I would bring discrimination down to the very basis of our educational pyramid.

I. The kindergarten age is from two or three to six or seven. Here, before the ideal school can be inaugurated, we need some work of rescue from the symbolists. Now the body needs most attention, and the soul least. The child needs more mother, and less teacher; more of the educated nurse, and less of the metaphysician. We must largely eliminate, and partly reconstruct, the mother-plays, while transforming and vastly enlarging the repertory of the gifts and occupations. We must develop the ideal nursery, playgrounds, and rooms, where light, air, and water are at their best. The influences of the new hygiene have been felt least here, where they are needed most. The neglect of these basal principles suggests that we have still among us those whose practice implies a belief that any old place is good enough to hatch out beautiful souls, provided only Froebelian orthodoxy of doctrine and method is steadfastly maintained. . . .

The kindergarten should fill more of the day, and should strive to kill time. In the Berlin Institute children sleep at noon in a darkened room, with music, crackers, or even bottles, and thus resist man's enemy, fatigue, and restore paradise for themselves. Part of the cult here should be idleness and the intermediate state of reverie. We should have a good excuse to break into these, and at this age children should be carefully shielded from all suspicion of any symbolic sense. Thus in play, and play only, life is made to seem real. Imitation should have a far larger scope. Children should hear far more English and better, and in the later years the ear should be trained for French or German. Color should never be taught as such. The children of the rich, generally prematurely individualized or over-individualized, especially when they are only children, must be disciplined and subordinated; while the children of the poor, usually under-individualized, should be indulged. We should lose no syllable of the precious positive philosophy of Froebel, the deepest of all modern educational thinkers; but we must profoundly reconstruct every practical expression that he attempted of his ideas, and must strive to induce at least a few college-trained men and women to turn their attention to the kindergarten, thus making the training schools feel, what they have hitherto known so little of, the real spirit and influence of modern science. Teachers should study every child, not necessarily by any of the current technical methods. They should learn far more than they can teach, and in place of the shallow manikin child of books they should see, know, and love only the real thing. After this metem-psychosis, the kindergarten should be, and should become, an integral part of every school system.

II. The age of about seven or eight is a transition period of the greatest interest for science. Then most children have less chewing surface by three or four teeth;

there is a year or more of increased danger to the heart; the breath is shorter and fatigue easier; lassitude, nervousness, visual disorders, and cough are somewhat more imminent; and the blood is more often impoverished. The brain has practically finished for life its growth in weight and size; and all work and strain must be reduced. Some important corner in its time of development, not yet fully understood, is turned.

III. At eight or nine there begins a new period, which, for nearly four years, to the dawn of puberty, constitutes a unique stage of life, marked off by many important differences from the period which precedes and that which follows it. During these years there is a decreased rate of growth, so that the body relatively rests; but there is a striking increase of vitality, activity, and power to resist disease. Fatigue, too, is now best resisted, and it is amazing to see how much can be endured. The average child now plays more games, and has more daily activity, in proportion to size and weight, than at any other stage. It would seem, as I have proposed elsewhere with ground for the theory, as tho these four years represented, on the recapitulation theory, a long period in some remote age, well above the simian but mainly before the historic, period, when our early forebears were well adjusted to their environment. Before a higher and much more modern story was added to human nature, the young in warm climates, where most human traits were evolved, became independent of their parents, and broke away to subsist for themselves at an early age. In this age, which will call the juvenile, the individual boy today is a precious key for the construction of a stage in the history of the race otherwise very obscure.

However this may be, child nature suggests very plainly that this period should be mainly devoted to drill, habituation, and mechanism. The age of reason is only dawning, and is not yet much in order; but discipline should be the watchword here. Writing, and even reading, for instance, should be neglected in our system before eight, and previous school work should focus on stories, the study of nature, and education by play and other activities. Now writing and reading should be first taught with stress. Their nascent period is now beginning. If we teach them before, we are apt to make the average child a bad writer for life by precocious overemphasis on the finer muscles. Modern studies show that the zigzag of the eye back and forth along the printed line is as dangerous as is the too early wigwag of the pen. At best the strain laid upon these tiny muscles is dangerous. Too early drill in read-writing is also enormously wasteful, because intensive effort gives facility now in an amazingly short time. Now first the smaller muscles in the average child, so important for mind- and will-training, can bear hard work and much strain. Accuracy, which, when out of its season, is fraught with so many dangers for mind and body, is now in order.

Verbal memory is now at its very best, and should be trained far more than it is. We are now educating the automatic bases of both mind and morals, and habits are never so easily formed or made stable. Manual training and games should be extremely diverse, manifold, and thoro. It is the time to break in the human colt, which is by nature, in some sense, the wildest of all wild animals. If the piano or any other musical instrument is to be learned, this is the time for drill, especially on scales and exercises. An instrumentalist's technique is rarely good if its foundations are not laid in this age. Names, even technical ones, come now. Drawing, too, should now come into prominence, beginning in its large and perfectly free form before writing, and only near the end of the period becoming severely methodic and accurate. Art training should not result in intimidation, but first everything should be drawn—battles, fires, shipwrecks, and railroad accidents, with plenty of human figures and action, and no angles, straight lines, or regular curves, which have come very late in the history of the race. This would make drawing, as it should be, a real expression of the child's soul, and the child should copy what he, and not what the adult, sees.

The mother-tongue will be the vehicle of nearly all the work of this period; but it will be on the short circuit from ear to mouth, which existed for unknown eons before reading and writing, and not chiefly on the long circuit and, biologically, very recent brain-path from eye to hand. Teachers praise written work in home and at school—compositions, essays, class work; but all these appeal to new and undeveloped powers of nerve and muscle. It is because we try to establish good English upon these foundations, so precarious at this stage, that we have so much and so just complaint of bad English. We ruin both handwriting and idiomatic speech by precocity. The child should live in a world of sonorous speech. He should hear and talk for hours each day; and then he would lay foundations for terse and correct English, and would keep read-writing, as it should forever be, subordinate to hearing and speaking. He would write as he speaks, and we should escape the abomination of bookish talk. At this stage written work should be required far less than at present.

Further, to secure these ends, we must first lay stress upon correct spelling— which is, after all, of far less importance than we think—and also upon correct, adult Addisonian syntax. Good grammar is too much to expect yet. We must strive first for utterance and expression, which may be homely, if only vigorous and adequate. Hence, much that we call slang has its place, and is really a revival of English in its most formative stage. The prim proprieties we idolize are not yet, but it is the hour of delight in cogency of expression. We do not yet know what slang to teach, or how to teach it, but we ought to give the best of it an important place. The boy is not totally depraved because he loves the speech of Chimmie Fadden, of Mr. Ade, or of "The Charwoman," because such language is fresh from the mint where all words were made. Our end is the cultivation of expression, which must bring out clearly and strongly what is in the boy's soul. This expression must be of a kind at least no less effective for other boys than for us. A training that gives the power of writing, or even talking, upon any subject or upon none in particular, is bad and vicious. Children have no right to write unless it is upon some subject that they know, and upon which they feel strongly. Theme and composition should be strictly confined to the fields of interest, and then expression will find or make a vent for itself. Moreover, we should not teach language, as such, or apart from objects, acts, and concrete reality-truth. We must burn most of our language books.

At this stage, arithmetic, so greatly overdone in American schools, should be mechanized, with plenty of mental exercises, and later with rules and processes for written work, with only little attempt at explanation. The elements of geometry, especially on the constructive side, and the metric system should come early, and the rudiments of algebra later. This is the stage, too, for beginning one or two foreign languages. These should always first be taught by ear and mouth. The child has a natural desire to express himself in many other vocal forms than the vernacular, for it is the age when all kinds of gibberish, dog Latin, and inventive words culminate. It represents the stage when human speech evolved fastest. If these languages are taught earlier, they jeopardize idiomatic English; if later, they are never pronounced or used with precision, and are not immediate vehicles of thought. Psychology has shown that speech is greatly reinforced by appeals to the eye, not in the form of the written or printed word, but thru pictures, and that even color intensifies the linguistic effect. Many a French or German word that could not otherwise be recalled is reproduced, or first taught more permanently, if the object or picture is shown, or the appropriate action is performed at the same instant. Books should be by no means discarded, but the chief stress should be laid on the oral work and thought. The object should be brought into immediate action without the intervention of the English word.

As to the dead languages, if they are to be taught, Latin should be begun not later than ten or eleven, and Greek never later than twelve or thirteen. Here both object and method are very different. These languages are taught thru English, and the eye-hand circuit should have much more prominence. Word-matching and translation are the goal. The chief reason why the German boy of fifteen or sixteen in *Unter Secunda* does so easily here what seems to us prodigious is because he is taught to study; and the teacher's chief business in class is not to hear recitations, but to study with the boys. One of the best of these teachers told me that the boy should never see a dictionary or even a vocabulary, but the teacher must be a "pony." The pupil should never be brought face to face with an unknown sentence, but everything must be carefully translated for him; he must note all the unknown words from the teacher's lips and all the special grammatical points, so that home study and the first part of the next lesson will be merely repetitions of what the teacher had told and done.

The modern school geography should be reduced to about one-fourth or even one-eighth of its present volume. It is too often a mosaic of geology, topography, physical geography, botany, zoölogy, anthropology, meteorology, and astronomy. The facts of each of these sciences, however, are not taught in their natural or logical order; but the associations are mainly those of place and contiguity, not of similarity and cause. Even in these days of correlation of studies the facts of these sciences are separated from their logical connection with each other; and by the use of a more fortuitous local association the reason is injured. Our geographies do not respect the unity of the child's mind. Their facts are connected neither with each other nor with the nascent stages of growth. The interest in primitive man and animals culminates from nine to ten; that in trade and governmental parts of geography comes from sixteen to twenty. The geographies of the last two or three years have mitigated, but by no means healed, these evils; and, as we speak of Turkey as "the sick man of Europe," we may still speak of geography as the sick subject of our curriculum.

Instead of reverencing this relic of mediaevalism, as its history shows it to be, we should greatly reduce the time given to it, and should first teach *Heimatskunde;* make maps more abundant, but more incidental to every topic, especially history; develop and teach elementary and illustrated anthropology and zoology, broadening to elementary astronomy, geology, meteorology, and botany, taught by and for themselves to bring out their disciplinary value, and so on in ways I have here no space to dwell upon. When we have reduced the enormous time now given in geography, the elements of each of these sciences will be taught in primers—some of which are now begun before the end of this period—which will continue the nature work of the period before seven or eight.

The hand is in a sense never so near the brain as now; knowledge never so strongly tends to become practical; muscular development never so conditions mental. Muscle-training of every kind, from play up to manual work, must now begin. Instead of the Swedish or other curricularized and exactly finished objects made, we should have a curriculum of toys at first and of rude scientific apparatus later, where everything will focus more upon the ulterior use of the object than upon the process of making it. All these things will be chosen from the field of the child's interests.

Singing will be prominent in the ideal school at this age; but far more time will be given to rote singing than to singing from notes, especially at first. The chief aim will be, not to develop the power to read music, important as the place of this is, but to educate the sentiments, and especially to attune them to love of home, nature, fatherland, and religion—the four chief themes of song in all ages, past and present. Music is the language of the feelings, just as speech is of the intellect. It is as absurd to teach notes to children before they can sing well as it would be to teach them reading before they can speak. The object of musical education in the public school is to express and train the emotions, and, thru these, the will and character; to preform joys and conduct, and not to make musicians.

Reason is still very undeveloped. The child's mind is at a stage when there is little in it that has not been brought in by way of sense. We must open wide the eye-gate and the ear-gate. "Show," "demonstrate," and "envisage" should be our watchwords, not "explain." We can easily make casuists and prigs, but we jeopardize thereby the ultimate vigor of reason. Hence we should explain very little. Even with respect to morals and conduct the chief duty of the child at this age is to obey. In most cases to try to explain brings self-consciousness and conceit. This method is the resource of teachers and parents whose personality is deficient in authoritativeness. Obedience should still be a law, if not a passion. If it is lacking, this is due to imperfect character or perverted methods in adults.

In fine, this is the age for training, with plenty of space and time, however, for spontaneity and voluntary action. The good teacher is a true *Pedotrieb*, or boy driver. He needs some method, but much more matter. He or she finds relatively little sentiment, but much selfishness, bound up in the hearts of children at this age. One of the chronic errors of too fond mothers and of modern teachers is to overestimate the capacities of children, especially boys, at this age for sympathy with adult feelings or interests. The world we live in is not theirs. We are "Olympians," and can enforce our will because we are stronger. We must be tolerated and respected, and must be treated with all the forms of respect and obedience that we require; but the interest of children at this age is almost exclusively in each other, and in each other's ways, not in adults. This breaks out suddenly, but just later.

Just before this period ends, boys and girls in the ideal school will be chiefly, tho not exclusively, placed under the care of teachers of their own sex. At the close of this period the ideal child, ideally trained, will be first of all helpful and active in body and mind; will read and write well; will know a great deal about the different aspects of nature in his home environment; will not be bookish, but will already know a few dozen well-chosen books; will understand and read simple French and German; and will perhaps have a good start in Latin and Greek. Some buds of specialization will have begun to bourgeon. This child will be able to play several dozen games; will know something of a number of industries . . .

I have spoken frankly, and have dealt only with general principles over a vast field, far too large to be adequately discussed here. I have carefully avoided all details, altho I have fully worked them out on paper at great length, for each topic to the close of the high-school period or the age of nineteen, when physical growth is essentially completed. This material will soon appear in a volume. The chief petition in my daily prayer now is for a millionaire. With the means at hand, I have no shadow of doubt or fear but that in five years from the date of any adequate gift we shall be able to invite all interested to a system of education, covering this ground, which will be a practical realization of much present prophecy, and which will commend itself even to the most conservative defenders of things as they are and have been, because the best things established will be in it. But it will be essentially pedocentric rather than scholiocentric; it may be a little like the Reformation, which insisted that the sabbath, the Bible, and the church were made for man and not he for them; it will fit both the practices and the results of modern science and psychological study; it will make religion and morals more effective; and, perhaps above all, it will give individuality in the school its full rights as befits a republican form of government, and will contribute something to bring the race to the higher maturity of the superman that is to be, effectiveness in developing which is the highest and final test of art, science, religion, home, state, literature, and every human institution.

CHILD STUDY QUESTIONNAIRE FOR TEACHERS IN MINNESOTA

(1896)   From L. H. Galbreath, "Minnesota Child-Study Association," National Education Association *Journal of Proceedings and Addresses, 1896* (Chicago, 1896), p. 849.

---

1. (a) How long has the study of children, as we understand it, been of interest to you, and what awakened this interest? What factors have led to any change of interest which you may have experienced? To children of what age has your attention been directed? In answering these questions it would be helpful to us if you would name any printed matter, articles, chapters, magazines or books that have been of peculiar stimulus to your interests, and of signal help to you.

(b) Why do you believe in the study of children or why do you not believe in it? (Please answer from personal experience rather than from theoretical reasons.)

(c) What particular phase of study have you found of most interest and what of least? Why?

(d) How has your method of studying children been affected by the new movement and emphasis on child study?

2. (a) If you have pursued recently any special study of children, will you state briefly what your particular objects of study were and by whom they were suggested. How was it carried on and with what results?

(b) What data or conclusions have you, if any, which you could send to the board for analysis and classification?

(c) What defective or exceptional children have you discovered through special study illustrating (1) deficiencies of sense, (2) incomplete and insufficient action of bodily parts, or (3) a lack of vitality and health, which hinders regular work. How did you find them, and what did your discovery lead you to do?

(d) If not described under "c" will you please describe here any devices to test the perception, memory, judgment, feelings or will-power, that you have employed and deem important?

(e) Have you used any special devices or followed any important rule or practice in examining the contents of children's minds, either before or after instruction?

(f) Have you studied the effects of your schoolroom on the respiration, heart action, digestion, muscular vigor, weight or alertness of pupils? If so, what have you found?

(g) If you have attempted to pursue studies outlined by another, with what peculiar difficulties did you meet?

3. (a) What do you desire most from child study and from the State Child Study Association?

(b) What lines of work can be carried on best in local centers?

(c) What helpful suggestions have you to offer as aid to the general work of the state?

WILLIAM JAMES TALKS TO TEACHERS ABOUT CHILD STUDY AND PSYCHOLOGY (1892)   From William James, *Talks to Teachers on Psychology: And to Students on Some of Life's Ideals* (New York, 1899), pp. 3, 5–14.

In the general activity and uprising of ideal interests which every one with an eye for fact can discern all about us in American life, there is perhaps no more promising feature than the fermentation which for a dozen years or more has been going on among the teachers. In whatever sphere of education their functions may lie, there is to be seen among them a really inspiring amount of searching of the heart about the highest concerns of their profession.

✻   ✻   ✻

No one has profited more by the fermentation of which I speak, in pedagogical circles, than we psychologists. The desire of the schoolteachers for a completer professional training, and their aspiration toward the 'professional' spirit in their work, have led them more and more to turn to us for light on fundamental principles. And in these few hours which we are to spend together you look to me, I am sure, for information concerning the mind's operations, which may enable you to labor more easily and effectively in the several schoolrooms over which you preside.

Far be it from me to disclaim for psychology all title to such hopes. Psychology ought certainly to give the teacher radical help. And yet I confess that, acquainted as I am with the height of some of your expectations, I feel a little anxious lest, at the end of these simple talks of mine, not a few of you may experience some disappointment at the net results. In other words, I am not sure that you may not be indulging fancies that are just a shade exaggerated. That would not be altogether astonishing, for we have been having something like a 'boom' in psychology in this country. Laboratories and professorships have been founded, and reviews established. The air has been full of rumors. The editors of educational journals and the arrangers of conventions have had to show themselves enterprising and on a level with the novelties of the day. Some of the professors have not been unwilling to co-operate, and I am not sure even that the publishers have been entirely inert. 'The new psychology' has thus become a term to conjure up portentous ideas withal; and you teachers, docile and receptive and aspiring as many of you are, have been plunged in an atmosphere of vague talk about our science, which to a great extent has been more mystifying than enlightening. Altogether it does seem as if there were a certain fatality of mystification laid upon the teachers of our day. The matter of their profession, compact enough in itself, has to be frothed up for them in journals and institutes, till its outlines often threaten to be lost in a kind of vast uncertainty. Where the disciples are not independent and critical-minded enough (and I think that, if you teachers in the earlier grades have any defect—the slightest touch of a defect in the world—it is that you are a mite too docile), we are pretty sure to miss accuracy and balance and measure in those who get a license to lay down the law to them from above.

As regards this subject of psychology, now, I wish at the very threshold to do what I can to dispel the mystification. So I say at once that in my humble opinion there is no 'new psychology' worthy of the name. There is nothing but the old psychology which began in Locke's time, plus a little physiology of the brain and senses and theory of evolution, and a few refinements of introspective detail, for the most part without adaptation to the teacher's use. It is only the fundamental conceptions of psychology which are of real value to the teacher; and they, apart from the aforesaid theory of evolution, are very far from being new.—I trust that you will see better what I mean by this at the end of all these talks.

I say moreover that you make a great, a very great mistake, if you think that psychology, being the science of the mind's laws, is something from which you can deduce definite programmes and schemes and methods of instruction for immediate schoolroom use. Psychology is a science, and teaching is an art; and sciences never generate arts directly out of themselves. An intermediary inventive mind must make the application, by using its originality.

The science of logic never made a man reason rightly, and the science of ethics (if there be such a thing) never made a man behave rightly. The most such sciences can do is to help us to catch ourselves up and check ourselves, if we start to reason or to behave wrongly; and to criticise ourselves more articulately after we have made mistakes. A science only lays down lines within which the rules of the art must fall, laws which the follower of the art must not transgress; but what particular thing he shall positively do within those lines is left exclusively to his own genius. One genius will do his work well and succeed in one way, while another succeeds as well quite differently; yet neither will transgress the lines.

The art of teaching grew up in the schoolroom, out of inventiveness and sympathetic concrete observation. Even where (as in the case of Herbart) the advancer of the art was also a psychologist, the pedagogies and the psychology ran side by side, and the former was not derived in any sense from the latter. The two were congruent, but neither was subordinate. And so everywhere the teaching must agree with the psychology, but need not necessarily be the only kind of teaching that would so agree; for many diverse methods of teaching may equally well agree with psychological laws.

To know psychology, therefore, is absolutely no guarantee that we shall be good teachers. To advance to that result, we must have an additional endowment altogether, a happy tact and ingenuity to tell us what definite things to say and do when the pupil is before us. That ingenuity in meeting and pursuing the pupil, that tact for the concrete situation, though they are the alpha and omega of the teacher's art, are things to which psychology cannot help us in the least.

The science of psychology, and whatever science of general pedagogics may be based on it, are in fact much like the science of war. Nothing is simpler or more definite than the principles of either. In war, all you have to do is to work your enemy into a position from which the natural obstacles prevent him from escaping if he tries to; then to fall on him in numbers superior to his own, at a moment when you have led him to think you far away; and so, with a minimum of exposure of your own troops, to hack his force to pieces, and take the remainder prisoners. Just so, in teaching, you must simply work your pupil into such a state of interest in what you are going to teach him that every other object of attention is banished from his mind; then reveal it to him so impressively that he will remember the occasion to his dying day; and finally fill him with devouring curiosity to know what the next steps in connection with the subject are. The principles being so plain, there would be nothing but victories for the masters of the science, either on the battlefield or in the schoolroom, if they did not both have to make their application to an incalculable quantity in the shape of the mind of their opponent. The mind of your own enemy, the pupil, is working away from you as keenly and eagerly as is the mind of the commander on the other side from the scientific general. Just what the respective enemies want and think, and what they know and do not know, are as hard things for the teacher as for the general to find out. Divination and perception, not psychological pedagogics or theoretic strategy, are the only helpers here.

But, if the use of psychological principles thus be negative rather than positive, it does not follow that it may not be a great use, all the same. It certainly narrows the path for experiments and trials. We know in advance, if we are psychologists, that certain methods will be wrong, so our psychology saves us from mistakes. It makes us, moreover, more clear as to what we are about. We gain confidence in respect to any method which we are using as soon as we believe that it has theory as well as practice at its back. Most of all, it fructifies our independence, and it reanimates our interest, to see our subject at two different angles,—to get a stereoscopic view, so to speak, of the youthful organism who is our enemy, and, while handling him with all our concrete tact and divination, to be able, at the same time, to represent to ourselves the curious inner elements of his mental machine. Such a complete knowledge as this of the pupil, at once intuitive and analytic, is surely the knowledge at which every teacher ought to aim.

Fortunately for you teachers, the elements of the mental machine can be clearly apprehended, and their workings easily grasped. And, as the most general elements and workings are just those parts of psychology which the teacher finds most directly useful, it follows that the amount of this science which is necessary to all teachers need not be very great. Those who find themselves loving the subject may go as far as they please, and become possibly none the worse teachers for the fact, even though in some of them one might apprehend a little loss of balance from the tendency observable in all of us to overemphasize certain special parts of a subject when we are studying it intensely and abstractly. But for the great majority of you a general view is enough, provided it be a true one; and such a general view, one may say, might almost be written on the palm of one's hand.

Least of all need you, merely *as teachers*, deem it part of your duty to become contributors to psychological science or to make psychological observations in a methodical or responsible manner. I fear that some of the enthusiasts for child-study have thrown a certain burden on you in this way. By all means let child-study go on,—it is refreshing all our sense of the child's life. There are teachers who take a spontaneous delight in filling syllabuses, inscribing observations, compiling statistics, and computing the per cent. Child-study will certainly enrich their lives. And, if its results, as treated statistically, would seem on the whole to have but trifling value, yet the anecdotes and observations of which it in part consists do certainly acquaint us more intimately with our pupils. Our eyes and ears grow quickened to discern in the child before us processes similar to those we have read of as noted in the children,—processes of which we might otherwise have remained inobservant. But, for Heaven's sake, let the rank and file of teachers be passive readers if they so prefer, and feel free not to contribute to the accumulation. Let not the prosecution of it be preached as an imperative duty or imposed by regulation on those to whom it proves an exterminating bore, or who in any way whatever miss in themselves the appropriate vocation for it. I cannot too strongly agree with my colleague, Professor Münsterberg, when he says that the teacher's attitude toward the child, being concrete and ethical, is positively opposed to the psychological observer's, which is abstract and analytic. Although some of us may conjoin the attitudes successfully, in most of us they must conflict.

The worst thing that can happen to a good teacher is to get a bad conscience about her profession because she feels herself hopeless as a psychologist. Our teachers are overworked already. Every one who adds a jot or tittle of unnecessary weight to their burden is a foe of education. A bad conscience increases the weight of every other burden; yet I know that child-study, and other pieces of psychology as well, have been productive of bad conscience in many a really innocent pedagogic breast. I should indeed be glad if this passing word from me might tend to dispel such a bad conscience, if any of you have it; for it is certainly one of those fruits of more or less systematic mystification of which I have already complained. The best teacher may be the poorest contributor of child-study material, and the best contributor may be the poorest teacher. No fact is more palpable than this.

So much for what seems the most reasonable general attitude of the teacher toward the subject which is to occupy our attention.

Manual Training

FRANCIS W. PARKER ON THE BENEFITS OF MANUAL TRAINING
(**1883**)   From Francis W. Parker, *Notes of Talks on Teaching* (New York, 1891),
pp. 179–82.

In my talk upon School Government, I said, that the end and aim of school education, is to train a child to work, to work systematically, to love work, and to put his brains into work. The clearest expression of thought, is expression in the concrete. Working with the hands, is one great means of primary development. It is also one of the very best means of moral training. From the first, every child has an intense desire to express his thought in some other way, than in language. Froebel discovered this, and founded the Kindergarten. No one can deny, that true Kindergarten training is moral training. Ideas and thought come into the mind, demanding expression. The use of that which is expressed, to the child, is the means it gives him to compare his thought, with its concrete expression. The expression of the form made, compared with the ideal, stimulates to further trials. In making and building, is found the best means of training attention.

I wish to make a sharp distinction here, between *real work*, and *drudgery*. Real work is done on real things, producing tangible results, results that are seen and felt. Real work is adapted at every step to the child's power to do. Every struggle brings success, and makes better work possible. Drudgery, on the other hand, is the forced action of the mind upon that which is beyond mental grasp, upon words that cannot be apprehended, upon lessons not understood. Drudgery, consists, mainly, of the monotonous use of the verbal memory. There is no variety; not a bush or shrub along the pathway. This is the kind of study that produces ill-health. It is the straining of the mind upon disliked subjects, with the single motive, to gain applause, rewards, and diplomas. Thousands of nervous, earnest, faithful girls, spurred on by unwise parents, yearly lose their lives, or become hopeless invalids, in this costly and useless struggle. Real work stimulates every activity of mind and body. It furnishes the variety so necessary to interest, and is like true physical development that exercises every muscle and strengthens the whole man. Real work is always interesting, like real play. No matter how earnest the striving may be, it is followed by a glow of genuine pleasurable emotion.

There is great outcry against our schools and colleges, caused by the suspicion that they educate children to be above manual labor. This suspicion is founded upon fact, I am sorry to say; but the statement of the fact is not correct. Children are educated *below* manual labor.

✻   ✻   ✻

The vague, meaningless things they learn, are not adapted to real work; no effectual habits of labor are formed by rote-learning. The student's desire is too often, when he leaves school or college, to get a living by means of empty words. The world has little or no use for such rubbish. That man should gain his bread by the sweat of his brow, is a curse changed to the highest possible blessing. The clergyman, the lawyer, the physician, the teacher, need the benefit of an early training in manual labor, quite as much as the man who is to labor with his hands all his life. Manual labor is the foundation of clear thinking, sound imagination, and good health. There should be no real difference between the methods of our common schools, and the methods of training in manual labor schools. A great mistake has been made in separating them. All school work should be real work. We learn to do by doing. "Satan finds some mischief still, for idle hands to do." The direct influence of real work is, to absorb the attention in the things to be done; leaving no room in the consciousness for idleness, and its consequent vices. Out of real work, the child develops a motive, that directs his life work. Doing work thoroughly, has a great moral influence. One piece of work well done, one subject well mastered, makes the mind far stronger and better, than a smattering of all the branches taught in our schools. School work, and manual labor, have been for a long time divorced; I predict that the time is fast coming, when they will be joined in indissoluble bonds. The time too, is coming, when ministers will urge upon their hearers, the great importance of manual labor, as a means of spiritual growth. At no distant date, industrial rooms will become an indispensable part of every good school; the work of the head, and skill of the hand, will be joined in class-room, and workshop, into one comprehensive method of developing harmoniously the powers of body, mind, and soul. If you would develop morality in the child, train him to work.

THE WORKSHOP AS IDEAL SCHOOL (1886)   From Charles H. Ham, *Mind and Hand: Manual Training the Chief Factor in Education* (New York, 1886), pp. 1–6, 132–33, 144–45.

The Ideal School

The Ideal School is an institution which develops and trains to usefulness the moral, physical, and intellectual powers of man. It is what Comenius called Humanity's workshop, and in America it is becoming the natural center of the Public School system. The building, well-designed for its occupancy, is large, airy, open to the light on every side, amply provided with all appliances requisite for instruction in the arts and sciences, and finished interiorly and exteriorly in the highest style of useful and beautiful architectural effects. The distinguishing characteristic of the Ideal School building is its chimney, which rises far above the roof, from whose tall stack a column of smoke issues, and the hum and whir of machinery is heard, and the heavy thud of the sledgehammer resounding on the anvil, smites the ear.

It is, then, a factory rather than a school?

No. It is a school; the school of the future; the school that is to dignify labor; the school that is to generate power; the school where every sound contributes to the harmony of development, where the brain informs the muscle, where thought directs every blow, where the mind, the eye, and the hand constitute an invincible triple alliance. This is the school that Locke dreamed of, that Bacon wished for, that Rousseau described, and that Comenius, Pestalozzi, and Froebel struggled in vain to establish.

It is, then, science and the arts in apotheosis. For if it be, as claimed, the Ideal school, it is destined to lift the veil from the face of Nature, to reveal her most precious secrets, and to divert to man's use all her treasures.

Yes; it is to other schools what the diamond is to other precious stones—the last analysis of educational thought. It is the philosopher's stone in education; the incarnated dream of the alchemist, which dissolved earth, air, and water into their original elements, and recombined them to compass man's immortality. Through it that which has hitherto been impossible is to become a potential reality.

In this building which resembles a factory or machine-shop an educational revolution is to be wrought. Education is to be rescued from the domination of mediaeval ideas, relieved of the enervating influence of Grecian aestheticism, and confided to the scientific direction of the followers of Bacon, whose philosophy is common sense and its law, progress. The philosophy of Plato left in its wake a long line of abstract propositions, decayed civilizations, and ruined cities, while the philosophy of Bacon, in the language of Macaulay, "has lengthened life; mitigated pain; extinguished diseases; increased the fertility of the soil; given new securities to the mariner; spanned great rivers and estuaries with bridges of form unknown to our fathers; guided the thunderbolt innocuously from heaven to earth; lighted up the night with the splendor of the day; extended the range of the human vision; multiplied the power of the human muscles; accelerated motion; annihilated distance; facilitated intercourse, correspondence, all friendly offices, all dispatch of business; enabled man to descend to the depths of the sea, to soar into the air, to penetrate securely into the noxious recesses of the earth, to traverse the land in cars which whirl along without horses, and the ocean in ships which run ten knots an hour against the wind."

It is this beneficent work of Bacon that the Ideal school is to continue—the work of demonstrating to the world that the most useful thing is the most beautiful thing—discarding Plato, the apostle of idle speculation, and exalting Bacon, the minister of use.

In laying the foundations of education in labor it is dignified and education is ennobled. In such a union there is honor and strength, and long life to our institutions. For the permanence of the civil compact in this country, as in other countries, depends less upon a wide diffusion of unassimilated and undigested intelligence than upon such a thorough, practical education of the masses in the arts and sciences as shall enable them to secure, and qualify them to store up, a fair share of the aggregate produce of labor.

If this school shall appear like a hive of industry, let the reader not be deceived. Its main purpose, intellectual development, is never lost sight of for a moment. It is founded on labor, which, being the most sacred of human functions, is the most useful of educational methods. It is a system of object-teaching—teaching through things instead of through signs of things. It is the embodiment of Bacon's aphorism—"Education is the cultivation of a just and legitimate familiarity betwixt the mind and things." The students draw pictures of things, and then fashion them into things at the forge, the bench, and the turning-lathe; not mainly that they may enter machine-shops, and with greater facility make similar things, but that they may become stronger intellectually and morally; that they may attain a wider range of mental vision, a more varied power of expression, and so be better able to solve the problems of life when they shall enter upon the stage of practical activity.

✳   ✳   ✳

The Ideal school, most precisely representative of the present age—the age of science—is dedicated to a homogeneous system of mental and manual training, to the generation of power, to the development of true manhood. And above all, this school is destined to unite in indissoluble bonds science and art, and so to confer upon labor the highest and justest dignity—that of doing and responsibility. The reason of the degradation of labor was admirably stated by America's most distinguished educational reformer, the late Mr. Horace Mann, who said, "The labor of the world has been performed by ignorant men, by classes doomed to ignorance from sire to son; by the bondmen and bondwomen of the Jews, by the helots of Sparta, by the captives who passed under the Roman yoke, and by the villeins and serfs and slaves of more modern times."

When it shall have been demonstrated that the highest degree of education results from combining manual with intellectual training, the laborer will feel the pride of a genuine triumph; for the consciousness that every thought-impelled blow educates him, and so raises him in the scale of manhood, will nerve his arm, and fire his brain with hope and courage.

THE PROGRAM OF THE MANUAL TRAINING SCHOOL OF WASHINGTON UNIVERSITY, ST. LOUIS (1887) From Calvin M. Woodward, *The Manual Training School* (Boston, 1887), pp. 26–27.

The Daily Program of the Manual Training School

The school-time of the pupils is about equally divided between mental and manual exercises. The daily session begins at 9 A.M., and closes at 3:30 P.M., thirty minutes being allowed for lunch. Each pupil has daily three recitations, one hour of drawing and penmanship, and two hours of shop-practice.

The Course of Instruction

covers three years, and embraces five parallel lines,—three purely intellectual, and two both intellectual and manual,—as follows:—

First, A course of pure mathematics, including arithmetic, algebra, geometry, and plane trigonometry.

Second, A course in science and applied mathematics, including physical geography, botany, natural philosophy, chemistry, mechanics, mensuration, and book-keeping.

Third, A course in language and literature, including English grammar, spelling, composition, literature, history, and the elements of political science and economy. Latin and French are introduced as electives with English or science.

Fourth, A course in penmanship, free-hand and mechanical drawing.

Fifth, A course of tool instruction, including carpentry, wood-turning, molding, brazing, soldering, forging, and bench and machine work in metals.

Students have no option or election as to particular studies, except as regards Latin and French; each must conform to the course as laid down, and take every branch in its order.

A Broader Education

You will see, then, that we have no mean or narrow object. "The education which the manual training school represents is a broader, and not, as the opponents of the new education assert, a narrower education." We put the whole boy to school, not a part of him, and we train him by the most invigorating and logical methods. We believe that mental activity and growth are closely allied to physical activity and growth, and that each is secured more readily and more fully in connection with the other than by itself.

CALVIN M. WOODWARD ON THE FRUITS OF MANUAL TRAINING
(**1887**)   From Calvin M. Woodward, *The Manual Training School* (Boston, 1887), pp. 202–7, 209–12.

The object of this paper is to consider directly the fruits of manual training. By manual training I do not mean merely the training of the hand and arm. If a school should attempt the very narrow task of teaching only the manual details of a particular trade or trades, it would, as Felix Adler says, violate the rights of the children. It would be doing the very thing I have always protested against. That, or very nearly that, is what is done in the great majority of European trade-schools. They have no place in our American system of education.

The word "manual" must, for the present, be the best word to distinguish that peculiar system of liberal education which recognizes the manual as well as the intellectual. I advocate manual training for all children as an element in general education. I care little what tools are used, so long as proper habits (morals) are formed, and provided the windows of the mind are kept open toward the world of *things* and *forces,* physical as well as spiritual.

We do not wish or propose to neglect or underrate literary and scientific culture; we strive to include all the elements in just proportion. When the manual elements which are essential to a liberal education are universally accepted and incorporated into American schools, the word "manual" may very properly be dropped.

I use the word "liberal" in its strict sense of "free." No education can be "free" which leaves the child no choice, or which gives a bias against any honorable occupation; which walls up the avenues of approach to any vocation requiring intelligence and skill. A truly liberal education educates equally for all spheres of usefulness; it furnishes the broad foundation on which to build the superstructure of a happy, useful, and successful life. To be sure, this claim has been made for the old education, but the claim is not allowed. The new education has the missing features all supplied. The old education was like a two-legged stool, it lacked stability; the new education stands squarely on three legs, and it is steady on the roughest ground.

I claim as the fruits of manual training, when combined, as it always should be, with generous mental and moral training, the following:—

1. Larger classes of boys in the grammar and high schools; 2. Better intellectual development; 3. A more wholesome moral education; 4. Sounder judgments of men and things, and of living issues; 5. Better choice of occupations; 6. A higher degree of material success, individual and social; 7. The elevation of many of the occupations from the realm of brute, unintelligent labor, to positions requiring and rewarding cultivation and skill; 8. The solution of "labor" problems. I shall touch briefly on each of these points.

1. Boys Will Stay in School Longer Than They Do Now

Every one knows how classes of boys diminish as they approach and pass through the high school. The deserters scale the walls and break for the shelter of active life. The drill is unattractive, and, so far as they can see, of comparatively little value. There is a wide conviction of the inutility of schooling for the great mass of children beyond the primary grades, and this conviction is not limited to any class or grade of intelligence. Wage-workers we must have, and the graduates of the higher grades are not expected to be wage-workers. According to the report of the president of the Chicago School Board, about one and one-eighth per cent of the boys in the public schools are in the high schools. From his figures it appears, that, if every boy in the Chicago public schools should extend his schooling through a high school, the four classes of the high school would contain some nine thousand boys; in point of fact, they have about four hundred.

* * *

From the observed influence of manual training upon boys, and indirectly upon the parents, I am led to claim, that, when the last year of the grammar and the high schools includes manual training, they will meet a much wider demand; that the education they afford will be really more valuable; and consequently, that the attendance of boys will be more than doubled. Add the manual elements, with their freshness and variety, their delightful shop exercises, their healthy intellectual and moral atmosphere, and the living reality of their work, and *the boys will stay in school.* Such a result would be an unmixed good. I have seen boys doing well in a manual training school who could not have been forced to attend an ordinary school. If the city of Boston shall carry out this year, as I hope it will, Superintendent Seaver's plan for a public manual training school for three hundred boys, there will be, in my judgment, one thousand applications for admission during the first three years.

2. Better Intellectual Development

I am met here with the objection that I am aiming at an impossibility; that, if I attempt to round out education by the introduction of manual training, to develop the creative or executive side, I shall certainly curtail it of elements more valuable still; that the educational cup is now full; and that, if I pour in my gross material notions on one side, some of the most precious intellectual fluid will certainly flow out on the other.

Now, I deny that the introduction of manual training does of necessity force out any essential feature of mental and moral culture. The cup may be, and probably is, full to overflowing; but it is a shrivelled and one-sided cup. It is as sensitive and active in its own defense as are the walls of the stomach, which, when overfed with ill-assorted food, contracts, rebels, and overflows, but which expands and readily digests generous rations of a varied diet.

The education of the hand is the means of more completely and efficaciously educating the brain. Manual dexterity is but the evidence of a certain kind of mental power; and this mental power, coupled with a familiarity with the tools the hands use, is doubtless the only basis of that sound, practical judgment and ready mastery of material forces which always characterize those well fitted for the duties of active, industrial life.

*   *   *

No one can learn from a book the true force of technical terms and definitions, nor the properties of materials. All descriptive words and names must base their meaning upon our own consciousness of the things they signify. The obscurities of the text-books (often doubly obscure from the lack of proper training on the part of the authors, who describe processes they never tried, and objects they never saw) vanish before the steady gaze of a boy whose hands and eyes have assisted in the building of mental images.

Then, again, the habit of clear-headedness, of precision in regard to the minor details of a subject (which is absolutely essential in the shop), an exact and experimental knowledge of the full force of the words and symbols used, stretches with its wholesome influence into the study of words and the structure of language. As Felix Adler says, the doing of one thing well is the beginning of doing all things well. I am a thorough disbeliever in the doctrine that it is ever educationally useful to commit to memory words which are not understood. The memory has its abundant uses, and should be carefully cultivated; but when it usurps the place of the understanding, when it beguiles the mind into the habit of accepting the images of words for the images of the things the words stand for, then the memory becomes a positive hinderance to intellectual development.

3. A More Wholesome Moral Education

The finest fruit of education is character; and the more complete and symmetrical, the more perfectly balanced the education, the choicer the fruit.

To begin with, I have noted the good effect of *occupation*. The program of a manual training school has something to interest and inspire every boy. The daily session is six full hours, but I have never found it too long. The school is not a bore; and holidays, except for the name of the thing, are unpopular. I have been forced to make strict rules to prevent the boys from crowding into the shops and drawing rooms on Saturdays and after school hours. There is little tendency, therefore, to stroll about, looking for excitement. The exercises of the day fill the mind with thoughts pleasant and profitable, at home and at night. A boy's natural passion for handling, fixing, and making things is systematically guided into channels instructive and useful, as parents freely relate.

Again, success in one branch or study (shop exercises are marked like those of the recitation room) encourages effort in others, and the methods of the shop affect the whole school. Gradually the students acquire two most valuable habits, which are certain to influence their whole lives for good; namely, precision and method. As Professor Runkle says, "Whatever cultivates care, close observation, exactness, patience, and method must be valuable training and preparation for all studies and pursuits."

* * *

4. Sounder Judgments of Men and Things

The proverbially poor judgments of scholars have led to the popular belief that theory is one thing and practice a very different thing; that theoretically a thing is one way, practically another. The truth is, that correct theory and practice agree perfectly.

5. Better Choice of Occupations

This point is one of the greatest importance, for out of it are the issues of life. An error here is often fatal. But to choose without knowledge is to draw as in a lottery; and when boys know neither themselves nor the world they are to live in, and when parents do not know their own children, it is more than an even chance that the square plug will get into the round hole.

Parents often complain to me that their sons who have been to school all their lives have no choice of occupation, or that they choose to be accountants or clerks, instead of manufacturers or mechanics. These complaints are invariably unreasonable; for how can one choose at all, or wisely, when he knows so little! Yet their decisions are natural.

I confidently believe that the development of the manual elements in school will prevent those serious errors in the choice of a vocation which too often wreck the fondest hopes. It is not assumed that every boy who enters a manual training school is to be a mechanic; his training leaves him *free*. No pupils were ever more unprejudiced, better prepared to look below the surface, less the victims of a false gentility. Some find that they have no taste for manual arts, and will turn into other paths,—law, medicine, or literature. Great facility in the acquisition and use of language is often accompanied by a lack of either mechanical interest or power. When such a bias is discovered, the lad should unquestionably be sent to his grammar and dictionary rather than to the laboratory or draughting-room. On the other hand, decided aptitude for handicraft is not unfrequently coupled with a strong aversion to, and unfitness for, abstract and theoretical investigations, and especially for committing to memory.

There can be no doubt that, in such cases, more time should be spent in the shop, and less in the lecture and recitation room. Some who develop both natural skill and strong intellectual powers will push on through the polytechnic school into professional life, as engineers and scientists. Others will find their greatest usefulness, as well as highest happiness in some branch of mechanical work, into which they will readily step when they leave school. All will gain intellectually by their experience in contact with things. The grand result will be an increasing interest in manufacturing pursuits, more intelligent mechanics, more successful manufacturers, better lawyers, more skillful physicians, and more useful citizens.

In the past comparatively few of the better educated have sought the manual occupations. The one-sided training of the schools has divided active men into two classes,—those who have sought to live by the work of their own hands, and those who have sought to live by the work of other men's hands.

Hitherto men who have aimed to cultivate their brains have neglected their hands; and those who have labored with their hands have found no opportunity to specially cultivate their brains. The crying demand to-day is for intellectual combined with manual training. It is this want that the manual training school aims to supply.

6. Material Success for the Individual and for the Community

Material success ought not to be the chief object in life, tho it may be sought with honor, and worthily won; in fact, success would appear to be inevitable to one who possesses health and good judgment, and who, having chosen his occupation wisely, follows it faithfully. This point might, then, be granted as a corollary to those already given and without further argument.

Our graduates have been out of school less than a year, but I have seen enough to justify me in saying that their chances of material success are unusually good. As workmen, they will soon step to the front. As employers and manufacturers, they will be self-directing and efficient inspectors; they will be little exposed to the wiles of incompetent workmen.

On the other hand, communities will prosper when their young men prosper. This is the *dynamic age;* the great forces of Nature are being harnessed to do our work, and we are just beginning to learn how to drive. Invention is in its youth, and manual training is the very breath of its nostrils.

Some appear to think that the continued invention of tools and new machines will diminish the demand for men skilled in mechanical matters; but they are clearly wrong. True, they will diminish the demand for *unintelligent* labor,—and some prominent educators, who take ground against manual training, have apparently no idea of labor except unintelligent labor. If there are more machines, there must be more makers, inventors, and directors. Not one useful invention in ten is made by a man who is not a skilled mechanic. But, as I have said, the mechanics have suffered from a one-sided education. They have paid too little attention to science and the graphic arts. Hence every manual pursuit will become elevated in the intellectual scale when mechanics are broadly, liberally trained.

7. The Elevation of Manual Occupations from the Realm of Brute, Unintelligent Labor to a Position Requiring and Rewarding Cultivation and Skill

A brute can exert brute strength: to man alone is it given to invent and use tools. Man subdues Nature and develops art through the instrumentality of tools. To turn a crank, or to carry a hod, one needs only muscular power. But to devise and build the light engine, which, under the direction of a single intelligent master-spirit, shall lift the burden of a hundred men, requires a high degree of intelligence and manual skill. So the hewers of wood and the drawers of water are in this age of invention replaced by saw and planing mills and water-works requiring some of the most elaborate embodiments of thought and skill. Can any one stand beside the modern drawers of water, the mighty engines that day and night draw from the Father of Waters the abundant supply of a hundred thousand St. Louis homes, and not bow before the evidence of "cultured minds and skillful hands," written in unmistakable characters all over the vast machinery?

In like manner every occupation becomes ennobled by the transforming influence of thought and skill. The farmer of old yoked his wife with his cow, and together they dragged the clumsy plow or transported the scanty harvest. Down to fifty years ago the life of a farmer was associated with unceasing, stupefying toil. What will it be when every farmer's boy is properly educated and trained? Farming is rapidly becoming a matter of horse-power, steam-power, and machinery. Who, then, shall follow the farm with honor, pleasure, and success? Evidently only he whose cultivated mind and trained hands make him a master of the tools he must use. With his bench and sharp-edged tools, with his forge and his lathe, and with his chemical laboratory, he will direct and sustain his farm with unparalleled efficiency.

Here is where the influence of manual training will be most beneficial. It will bring the manual occupations a new element, a fairly educated class, which will greatly increase their value, at the same time that it gives them new dignity.

8. The Solution of Labor Problems

Finally, I claim that the manual training school furnishes the solution of the problem of labor *vs.* capital. The new education will give more complete development, versatility, and adaptability to circumstance. No liberally trained workman can be a slave to a method, or depend upon the demand for a particular article or kind of labor. It is only the uneducated, unintelligent mechanic who suffers from the invention of a new tool. The thoroughly trained mechanic enjoys the extraordinary advantage of being able, like the well-taught mathematician, to apply his skill to every problem; with every new tool and new process he rises to new usefulness and worth.

The leaders of mobs are not literate, but they are narrow, the victims of a one-sided education; and their followers are the victims of a double one-sidedness. Give them a liberal training, and you emancipate them alike from the tyranny of unworthy leaders and the slavery of a vocation. The sense of hardship and wrong will never come, and bloody riots will cease, when workingmen shall have such intellectual, mechanical, and moral culture, that new tools, new processes, and new machines will only furnish opportunities for more culture, and add new dignity and respect to their calling.

CALVIN M. WOODWARD ON THE FRUITS OF MANUAL TRAINING

(1892) From Calvin M. Woodward, *Manual Training In Education* (New York, 1892), p. 218.

Note.—In May, 1886, I gave the following brief statement of the fruits of manual training, in the *Journal of Education:* —

The value of manual training, when properly combined with literary, scientific, and mathematical studies, will be shown in various ways.

1. Science and mathematics will profit from a better understanding of forms, materials, and processes, and from the readiness with which their principles may be illustrated.

2. Without shop-work, drawing loses half its value.

3. Correct notions of things, relations, and forces, derived from actual handling and doing, go far toward a just comprehension of language in general; that is, manual training cultivates the mechanical and scientific imagination, and enables one to see the force of metaphors in which physical terms are employed to express metaphysical truths.

4. Manual training will stimulate a love for simplicity of statement, and a disposition to reject fine-sounding words whose meaning is obscure.

5. It will awaken a lively interest in school, and invest dull subjects with new life.

6. It will keep boys and girls out of mischief, both in and out of school.

7. It will keep boys longer at school.

8. It will give boys with strong mechanical aptitudes, and fondness for objective study, an equal chance with those of good memories for language.

9. It will materially aid in the selection of occupations when school-life is over.

10. It will enable an employer of labor to better estimate the comparative value of unskilled and skilled labor, and to exercise a higher consideration for the laboring man.

11. It will raise the standards of attainments in mechanical occupations, and invest them with new dignity and worth.

12. It will increase the bread-winning and home-making power of the average boy, who has his bread to win and his home to make.

13. It will stimulate invention. The age of invention is yet to come, and manual training is the very breath of its nostrils.

14. We shall enjoy the extraordinary advantage of having lawyers, journalists, and politicians with more correct views of social and national conditions and problems.

To the above I will now add:—

15. It will help to prevent the growth of a feeling of contempt for manual occupations and for those who live by manual labor.

16. It will to a certain extent readjust social standards in the interest of true manliness and intrinsic worth.

17. It will accelerate the progress of civilization by greatly diminishing the criminal and pauper classes, which are largely made up of those who are neither willing nor able to earn an honest living.

18. It will show itself in a hundred ways in the future homes of our present pupils: on the one hand, in the convenience and economy of useful appliances; on the other, in evidences of good taste in matters of grace and beauty.

NICHOLAS MURRAY BUTLER ON MANUAL TRAINING (1888) From Nicholas Murray Butler, *The Argument for Manual Training* (New York, 1888), pp. 386–88, 390–95.

In the first place, let me remind you of the distinction already made between the end and the means of education; that the one, the development of the mental faculties, is always the same, but that the second varies according to our knowledge of the child's mind and the changing character of its environment. The manual training which is to be introduced into the school must accord with the end of education and also be abreast of the present requirements of the means of education.

It is objected as to the first that manual training is not mental training, but simply the development of skill in the use of certain implements. This is bad common sense and worse psychology. Manual training is mental training through the hand and eye, just as the study of history is mental training through the memory and other powers. There is something incongruous and almost paradoxical in the fact that while education is professedly based upon psychology, and psychology has ever since Locke been emphasizing the importance of the senses in the development of mental activity, nevertheless sense-training is accorded by a narrow corner in the school-room and even that grudgingly. Industrial education is a protest against this mental oligarchy, the rule of a few faculties. It is a demand for mental democracy, in which each power of mind, even the humblest, shall be permitted to occupy the place that is its due. It is truly and strictly psychological. In view of the prevalent misconception on this point, too much stress cannot be laid upon the fact that manual training, as we use the term, is mental training. What does it matter that the muscles of the arm and hand be well-nourished and perfectly developed, that the nerves be intact and healthy, if the mind that directs, controls, and uses them be wanting? What is it that models the graceful form and strikes the true blow, the muscles or the mind? Do the retina and optic nerves see, or does the mind? It is the mind that feels and fashions, and the mind that sees; the hand and the eye are the instruments which it uses. The argument for manual training returns to this point again, and again, not only because it is essential to a comprehension of what is meant by manual training, but because it furnishes the ground for the contention that manual training should be introduced into the public schools. No one with any appreciation of what our public school system is and why it exists, would for a moment suggest that it be used to train apprentices for any trade or for all trades. It is not the business of the public school to turn out draughtsmen, or carpenters, or metal workers, or cooks, or seamstresses, or modellers. Its aim is to send out boys and girls that are well and harmoniously trained to take their part in life. It is because manual training contributes to this end, that it is advocated. We will all admit, indeed I will distinctly claim, that the boy who has passed through the curriculum which includes manual training will make a better carpenter, a better draughtsman, or a better metalworker than he who has not had the benefit of that training. But it is also true that he will make a better lawyer, a better physician, a better clergyman, a better teacher, a better merchant—should he elect to follow any one of those honorable callings—and all for the same reason; namely, that he is a better equipped and more thoroughly educated man than his fellow in whose preparation manual training is not included. Therefore manual training is in accord with the aim of education.

* * *

Because of this psychological and practical soundness of manual training, the argument in its favor calls for the remodelling of the present curriculum. Manual training cannot be added as an appendix to any other study; it must enter on a plane with the rest. It does not ask admittance as a favor; it demands it as a right. It is suggested that much time now wasted could be saved by better methods of teaching, that logical puzzles over which so much time is now spent be eliminated from arithmetic, that spelling be taught in conjunction with writing, and history with reading. The time thus saved is to be appropriated in about equal parts to drawing and constructive work, both together to occupy from one-quarter to one-third of the pupil's time. Drawing lies at the basis of all manual training, and is to be taught in every grade as a means of expression of thought, only incidentally as an art. The constructive work is to be in material adapted to the child's age and powers. It is at first in paper and pasteboard, then in clay, then in wood, and finally, in the academic grades, in metal. These means are, so far as our present experience goes, the best ones for the training desired. But wider experience and deeper insight may alter or improve them at any time, just as our readers, our spellers, and our arithmetics have been improved.

The curriculum which includes manual training, in addition to meeting the demands of our present knowledge of the pupil's mind and its proper training, is better suited to prepare the child for life than that curriculum which does not include it. The school is to lay the foundation for intelligent citizenship, and as the conditions of intelligent citizenship change with the advance of civilization, the course of study must change in order to adapt itself to these new conditions. No one who can read the lessons of history will assert that the ideally educated man is always the same. Greek education sought beauty, mental and physical; monastic education sought asceticism and a soul dead to the world; Renaissance education sought classical culture and minute acquaintance with the literatures of Greece and Rome; modern education has broadened this conception of culture until it embraces the modern literatures and natural science; common school education in the United States in these closing years of the nineteenth century has broadened its ideal yet further, and is now demanding that the pupil be so trained that the great, busy life of which he is so soon to form a part be not altogether strange to him when he enters it. It demands practicality. It demands reality. It demands that the observation, the judgment, and the executive faculty be trained at school as well as the memory and the reason. Despite the fact that the three former are the most important faculties that the human mind possesses, it is astounding how completely they are overlooked in the ordinary course of study.

* * *

At certain stages of civilization and national development there is a natural training of the expressive or active powers which though desultory, is by no means ineffective. I refer to the training which is the result of an active, out-of-door life, especially in rural districts. The country boy receives his training in the hundred and one small occupations about the farm, and the old-time mechanic's son obtained it in his father's shop. The conditions which once made this natural training available for a large proportion of the rising generation are now altered, and the alteration goes on year by year, with increasing rapidity. We must bear in mind the growth of large cities and our unprecedented commercial and industrial development. The specialization of labor has destroyed one of the above-mentioned possibilities, and the growth of great cities is rapidly removing the other. When our first national census was taken in 1790 only 1/30 of our population lived in cities having more than 8000 inhabitants, and there were only six such cities in the country. At the present time we have over 320 such cities, and their inhabitants number almost 30 per cent of our total population. This fact has a most important bearing on practical life and thus on the public school. We must remember also that between 1850 and 1880 our manufactured product increased in value 550 per cent; and the number of those employed in factories increased 325 per cent. This, when interpreted, means that indefinitely more people than ever before have to employ their observation, their judgment and their executive faculty, and employ them accurately, in the performance of their daily duties. For them, and through them, for all of us, the conditions of practical life have changed and are changing. Has the school responded to the new burdens thus laid upon it? The argument for manual training says no, it has not. A more comprehensive, a broader, a more practical training is necessary.

There is a further argument for manual training, but I have not touched upon it because I desire to discuss the subject from a strictly educational standpoint and according to the requirements of a rigorous pedagogic method. If we permit other than educational considerations to enter into the discussion of questions purely educational, we may be setting a bad precedent. Having premised this, it will not be amiss to refer briefly to the social and economic arguments in favor of manual training.

It is unquestionable that many of our social troubles originate in misunderstandings about labor and in false judgments as to what labor really is. They originate, I take it, from the same misunderstanding that causes the average young man to think it more honorable to add columns of figures for $3.00 a week than to lay bricks for $3.00 a day. Some of us affect to despise manual labor. It must be because we do not understand it. It must be apparent that if manual training is accorded its proper place in education, if we come to see that manual work has in it a valuable disciplinary and educational element, our eyes will be opened as to its real dignity and men will cease to regard it as beneath them and their children. This is what I would call the social argument for manual training. The economic argument is similar. It points out that the vast majority of our public school children must earn their living with their hands, and therefore if the school can aid them in using their hands it is putting just so much bread and butter into their mouths. Now I have no sympathy with the purely utilitarian conception of the school, with what we may call the dollars and cents idea of education. On the contrary I cordially indorse the pungent aphorism of Dr. Munger: "Education is to teach us how to live, not how to make a living." But while standing firmly on the platform, I do say that if the best and most complete education happens to aid a boy in earning his living that is no reason why it should be supplanted by something less thorough and less complete.

OPPOSITION OF ORGANIZED LABOR TO MANUAL TRAINING (1895)
From D. J. O'Donoghue, "Manual vs. Technical Training," *American Federationist*, vol. II,
pp. 82–83.

In view of the marvelously rapid changes which science and invention have succeeded in bringing about in almost all industrial pursuits and methods, mainly within the last fifty years, the artisan, the mechanic, and even the ordinary manual laborer, has been and is obliged to look for and adapt himself to new, and, in most cases, narrower means of securing a living. Almost without exception, the specialist in a given line of business stands first to-day in the chances for employment. The old-time carpenter, tailor, printer—in fact, every tradesman of by-gone days, is being, or is already, driven out of the market. While this change has been going on another factor was operating in a totally different sphere of life. Education was made more general and *a great deal cheaper* than ever before, and, as a necessary consequence, the learned professions ceased to be any longer the specific preserve of the wealthy only. That class of the community, ever sensitive of any encroachment upon what time and favorable circumstances had made to appear as their especial privilege, saw with amazement that the sons of the mechanic and laborer, with a fair field and no favor, were showing themselves the equals always and often the superiors of other competitors in all the branches of higher education. The cry was raised at once, and is as loud now as it ever was, that the professions are being over-crowded. This was and is being heeded, and laws are enacted enabling "the professions" to protect themselves in the many ways that are so familiar to a mechanic or laborer who seeks to educate his son as a lawyer or a doctor. That this may not be too noticeable, certain good people very conveniently discovered that what working people wanted most was a system of manual training in the public schools—that is, a training in tool work as an educational discipline. So persistently and so ably has this system been lauded that to dare offer a contra or deprecatory opinion as to its real object and only demonstrable result is to run the risk of being anathematized.

Theoretically, the advocates of manual training in primary public schools have many honeyed phrases which please the ears of the unthinking, and which they ring in very often when met with the unpalatable and stern logic of fact. Speaking generally, the champions of manual training dilate on the great necessity for a proper training of "the eye and the hand" at one and the same time; that the object is to familiarize children with the use of certain tools, but not to learn them trades; to afford an opportunity of ascertaining the natural trend of the mind of the young pupil as to what trade he would be most likely to excel in, etc., and all for the purpose of fitting him the better to fight the battle of life in due time, and so keep him out of "the learned professions" is always intended, though rarely said.

There is no scarcity in the ranks of any known mechanical calling, nor is it likely there will ever be. More especially is this true of carpentry and iron work, and yet in almost every instance where manual training is part of the primary school system in the countries where that system prevails, a carpenter's bench with certain necessary tools, a forge, a lathe, an anvil and requisite tools, wood carving, and modeling in clay, complete the outfit for training of the pupils. The great bulk of the children of working people in the United States and in Canada leave voluntarily, or are obliged to leave school, before being seventeen years of age. This being true, no thoughtful person will assert that there was more than reasonable time in the

EDUCATION
IN THE
UNITED STATES

1870

previous years to secure a fair and necessary education in the ordinary branches taught in every English school. As a matter of fact, even now too many children are obliged to leave school and fight for a livelihood long before they are grounded in even a fair elementary education, and yet we are told, and many of us are gullible enough to believe, that the time which is now devoted to imparting such an education in our public schools could, with advantage, be reduced so that our children may receive a technical education—and their minds directed away from any higher pursuits! When boys leave school, through any cause, the first thought suggesting itself naturally will be what work or calling to pursue for a living. What, then, will be more natural than that the boy will seek employment in that trade or calling with the use of the tools of which his manual training had made him more or less familiar? A little careful attention on the part of the careful workingman will readily demonstrate that the first aim of the average advocate of manual training in the public schools is that of *utility*, rather than physical or intellectual improvement.

These schools do not turn out trained mechanics—and so much the worse. On the contrary, from the very nature of their limited equipment, these schools only impart a superficial knowledge of certain tools in common use in a few given trades, and the knowledge of each pupil as to these tools, and how best to use them, is in proportion, as a rule, to the time he is able to spend at the school. When finally leaving school, the average pupil will believe he is possessed of much more practical knowledge than is his, and he feels correspondingly elated, but time and bitter experience strikingly demonstrates that he is *only a botch*. Yet he has to live, and very likely the whirligig of time has placed a family of wife and children dependent upon his efforts as well. His employment is intermittent, and when competent men are forced into resistance of outrageous exactions, or to fight for justice, the graduate of the manual training school, if not otherwise employed at the time, will be on hand to replace, for the time being, the other man. Apart from this, having realized his own inferiority as a mechanic, he will be much less independent and, conscious of his own market value, will accept less remuneration for his labor than would a competent mechanic. Hence, he becomes a potent lever in lowering wages. The employer is ever ready to use an incompetent man, and in doing so very often pays more than he knows such a person to be actually worth, in such emergency as a strike, but when the trouble is tided over, out goes the "tool." The world's labor market is always but too well supplied with incapable mechanics— manual training schools are not required to still further augment the glut. Those in ranks of labor who have opportunity of examining the handiwork of pupils of manual training schools, as exemplified in cabinet work, patterns, frames, and various articles of woodwork, in pincers, hammers, nippers, stop-cocks, etc., in ironwork, and in other lines of mechanics, will have no hesitation in asserting that, while the work was of a very inferior character, yet those capable of executing it, such as it was, would find ready employment by any employer whose workmen were "out" through any cause—at least, they would well serve the purpose of "dummies" in the shops to prove that the employer's business was "going on as usual." Is there a union man who does not understand this game?

Herbartianism

THE FIVE STEPS IN THE HERBARTIAN PEDAGOGY (1891) From Charles
De Garmo, *The Essentials of Method* (Boston, 1891), pp. 45–53, 60.

Necessary Stages of Rational Methods:

III

APPERCEPTION OF INDIVIDUAL NOTIONS

12. We have seen how apperception, or the subsumption of new subjects under old predicates, is the condition of understanding. It must at the same time be the condition of all *interest*, for the mind has no interest in that which it does not understand. Not all things understood are interesting, but nothing not understood, in some degree at least, can possibly awaken interest. There are, therefore, two powerful incentives for the teacher to study the conditions of apperception,—the desire to have his pupils comprehend, and the desire to have them interested.

13. It might, at first thought, seem that the native spontaneity of the mind would do all that is necessary to bring up these related conceptions which are to serve as predicates for the new notions acquired through instruction, but reflection will show that this is true to a limited extent only. Who has not seen children completely baffled by some mathematical relation, which a skillful question or two would reveal? Is it not a daily experience of the teacher to find pupils failing to comprehend statements in reading or grammar or number or natural science or geography, simply because their own spontaneity of mind is not sufficient to supply those interpreting ideas, which the teacher might easily cause to appear in consciousness? *It is, therefore, the first great function of the teacher to prepare the way for the rapid and efficient assimilation of that knowledge which the study hour or the recitation period is to furnish.*

14. The teacher's activity in this first great department of education is naturally of two kinds: (1) *The* **preparation** *of the child's mind for a rapid and effective assimilation of new knowledge,* and (2) *The* **presentation** *of the matter of instruction in such order and manner as will best conduce to the most effective assimilation.*

15. From what has been said, it will be seen that this term means that preliminary effort of the teacher, which is designed to prepare the mind of the pupil for a ready apperception, or assimilation, of the new knowledge about to be presented.

16. To understand the real nature of this process, we must recur to the first form of the judgment, or that form in which the subject involves more than is seen in the predicate. The child when he enters school knows many things, has coupled many predicates to many subjects; but neither at this stage nor at any subsequent stage of his education has he coupled to his subjects of knowledge all the predicates involved in them. According to the law of apperception no child can really learn and understand any new knowledge for which he has not a store of related conceptions which can be applied as predicates. It may be, and most probably will be, the case that these needed predicates are held in the child's knowledge only by *implication,* and that it will need a *preparatory effort* on the teacher's part to bring the needed *apperceiving conceptions* to the full consciousness of the pupil. Preparation, therefore, seeks to recall former knowledge, and to bring to consciousness those needed and implied conceptions which through predication should reach out like so many spiritual arms, to embrace and draw into living relations to themselves the new elements of knowledge which it is the business of the hour to cause to appear in the mind of the child.

17. Where, as with small children or in certain kinds of oral work, no lesson for study is assigned, this preparation will take place, in general, at the beginning of each recitation, though it will often happen that a general preparation covering a whole section of a subject may render much preparation on daily subdivisions unnecessary. This matter will be further discussed under the subject of *method-wholes.* In classes where lessons are regularly assigned in text-books, the main part of the preparation should be made when the lesson is assigned for study. A repetition of the same at the beginning of the recitation may be helpful.

The nature and amount of preparation necessary will depend upon the mind of the pupil. In general, one year's work is a preparation for the next; so of the work of each term or month or week or day, and it is on account of the laws of apperception that gaps in education are to be avoided. But this general preparation does not often suffice. Though facts enough to explain the new lesson may have been previously taught, the mind may, on account of forgetfulness, or because it is busied with other things, remain unconscious of them at the time when they are needed to illuminate the new and make it instinct with meaning by supplying the appropriate predicates. Or, if the mind recalls the older and related conceptions, they may yet be dim and weak, or may fail to appear in the best order, or they may be mere feeble general impressions. Under such conditions, it is needful for the teacher to make special effort to put the minds of his pupils into proper relations to the lesson about to be imparted.

These efforts may be considered in the following order:—

(1) A clear and attractive statement of the object of the lesson, or the end to be reached. Thus, for example, the teacher may say, "We have learned that the earth is a great ball or globe which is free in space. We will now consider whether it is at rest or in motion." Or, "We have seen that a fraction is multiplied by multiplying its numerator; let us see if it can be multiplied in any other way." Or, "We have found that the nature of thought gives rise to the subject, the copula, and the predicate, or attribute, of the sentence; let us see, if possible, what property of

thought gives rise to the adjective." But little thought is needed to see that it would be very unpedagogical not to have the pupil understand from the beginning what the aim of the lesson is. In the first place, an attractive or forcible statement of the end to be reached, helps to dispel from the child's mind the distracting thoughts which may be sporting there, and to prepare the way for what the teacher wants to impart. Next, it helps to put the pupil into the frame of mind in which it is desired he should work. It excites expectation, stimulates interest, and allows instruction to begin under favorable conditions. It gives the pupil a favorable impulse towards right willing, and disposes him to self-activity in the solution of the appointed task. But when the end to be reached is not indicated, the danger is that not only the above-mentioned advantages will be sacrificed, but that the pupil, not knowing where he is going, will become confused, especially if he is kept long in the dark. He cannot go forward intelligently, nor can he retrace his steps. His mind is bewildered by perceiving results for which he is no longer able to account. But if he advances with a clear consciousness of the end he is striving to reach, he will not become confused, unless the explanation itself is confusing.

(2) With the purpose or aim of the lesson about to be presented always in view, it is plain that the concepts resulting from the analysis of the present store of knowledge should be derived or developed in unbroken and virtually connected chain from the beginning to the close; for in this way the mind reaches its greatest capability of taking on and assimilating new knowledge. But if the time is spent in recalling past concepts without any regard to their co-ordination and logical connection, or in developing the non-essential, it is plain that the child's mind will not be so ready to apprehend the new lesson in its full significance. The teacher should, therefore, endeavor to discover which of those main concepts, already within the grasp of the child, need to be recalled or derived in order best to master the new lesson. He should then arrange these in their logical order, and proceed to bring them to the child's consciousness in this order. The ease with which this logical arrangement can be secured will depend largely upon the logical arrangement of the subject-matter of the daily lessons. If this is what it should be, but little effort at special arrangement is necessary in the preparation. The more remote the new lesson is from the recent study of the child, the more elaborate must be the preparation. Ordinarily a few sharply put questions will suffice to place the pupils in a frame of mind best adapted to understand the new lesson.

(3) The preparation and the new lesson should not be mixed up together during the preparation, for this is likely to lead to confusion of thought, and may lead to a lack of interest. A foreshadowing of what is to come, however, may secure increased interest and mental activity. If, when a new truth is presented, a pupil discovers that he had dimly foreseen it, his pleasure in the acquisition may be greatly increased thereby. A skillful dramatist never fully reveals his plot ahead of its unfolding, nor does he, on the other hand, ever allow any great but entirely unexpected culmination to occur. Every stage in his drama is a preparation for the next, but not a revelation of it. The revelation of the unknown but not altogether unexpected is a fine art with the dramatist and the novelist, and should be with the teacher.

(4) The preparation should be so extended as to cover the entire matter of the new lesson, or such part of it as may be regarded as a method-whole, in order that time and interest may not be sacrificed by tiresome explanations after the presentation of the new matter has been begun. Wherever much of this appears necessary, it is certain that the preparation has been inadequate, or that the matter is not suited to the present mental acquirements or ability of the pupils.

(5) As to the form of the preparation, it may be remarked that a free exchange

of thought between teacher and pupils in the form of question and answer, or conversation, is the best. Anything that smacks of examination is out of place, since it is destructive of that free movement of thought which is here so desirable; furthermore, it effects no valuable result, besides being deadening to a direct interest in the subject. Pupils delight in an exercise which gives free play to their individuality, nor should this free play of thought be rudely checked, even though matters important only in the eyes of the child should be developed. A skillful teacher can easily guide the free thought of the pupils to the main issue, without checking its spontaneity; besides, the announced purpose of the lesson makes it easy to keep out irrelevant matter.

(6) Repetitions, and even drill upon the main points brought out, may be profitable, but an exhibition of deep earnestness of manner or tone is out of place in the preparation. This should be reserved for a later stage, when it is desired to impress some new truth brought out by the lesson.

When the teacher has done as much as he thinks profitable in way of preparation, he will proceed, as a matter of course, to the presentation of the lesson.

Presentation

18. It is not to be supposed that the child possesses so much knowledge when he enters school that there is involved in it all that he will subsequently need to know, so that a mere analysis of what he now has will reveal all that he should ever have. In this sense Jacotot's dictum, *All is in all,* is false. New knowledge must be imparted. Old predicates must be supplied with new subjects in which the predicates are not already involved. These new predications enrich former ones, so that the subsuming of new subjects under old predicates widens and enriches old conceptions, which in turn extend the significance of subsequent elements of knowledge. Omitting the second, or identical, form of judgment, *A is A,* which as we have seen is valuable only as a mathematical instrument for ascertaining numerical relations, we come to the third form of the judgment, in which the predicate is a broader and deeper term than the subject. The first kind of judgment has been called *analytical,* because an analysis of the subject shows that the predicate was already involved in it. The third, or last, kind of judgment has been called synthetical, because the predicate is something united to the subject,—something which is outside of the subject,—not implied in it. In the word *Carlo* is not involved the idea *dog,* so that the sentence, *Carlo is a dog,* expresses a true synthetic judgment. It is evident, then, that if the child is to learn anything new, the teaching must be of this synthetic, or additive, nature. Without the gaining and assimilating of new facts, or elements of knowledge, there can be but little advance in mental growth. At this stage of our investigation, it is entirely immaterial how these facts are obtained, so that they are *new,* not already involved in what the pupil knows. Facts may, for example, be obtained by induction or by deduction, or they may be gained through a primary use of the senses; they may be learned from a book or from the lips of the teacher. In any case, *presentation* sees that these facts are brought to the consciousness of the pupil in such a way that they may be readily assimilated, or, in other words, be properly understood.

19. An exhaustive treatise on presentation might consider the whole course of development for each branch of study, and also the relations of inter-dependence among the various subjects of the curriculum, because each of these departments of

inquiry has a bearing on the reception and assimilation of knowledge. One large German pedagogical school advocate the presentation of most subjects according to what is called the *historical stages of culture;* this position being taken, on the theory that each child, in its development, passes through all the stages of thought through which the world has passed in its historical development. We should, therefore, say they present to a child of any given age that stage in the development of the subject in which the world was at the time now typically represented by the child. For example, Ziller and his followers recommend the following order of topics for religion and history: first year, "Grimm's Fairy Tales" (Märchen); second year, "Robinson Crusoe;" third year, Bible stories from the time of the patriarchs, "Legends of Thüringia" (Thuringer Sagen); fourth year, Bible stories from the time of the Judges, then of the Kings, "Nibelungen Tales;" fifth year, Bible stories from the time of Christ, History of Henry I., Otto I., Charlemagne; sixth year, Bible stories from the time of Christ continued, Migration of the Nations, Roman Empire and the Pope, the Crusades, The Middle Ages, Rudolph von Hapsburg; seventh year, The Original Congregations or Churches, The Apostle Paul, Discovery of America and its first settlement, History of the Reformation, The Thirty Years' War; eighth year, Instruction in the Catechism, "Frederick the Great," The Napoleonic wars for independence, The Restoration of the German Empire.

This school make religion and history the central subjects for the work of each year, and seek to relate all the other instruction to them. This is the idea of *concentration,* according to which no subject of study should be isolated from the others, but all school study should be related to some common center. Other eminent schoolmen claim that the arrangement and co-ordination of school studies should be quite otherwise. But, however interesting these topics may be in themselves, they lie beyond the range which has been set for this treatise on methods.

*　　*　　*

25. FIXING SERIES IN THE MIND—In order to impress it firmly on the mind, and to secure intimate fusion, or association of its parts, the series arising from each subdivision of the lesson must, without undue haste, be repeated often enough and in enough different ways, so that the members will have sufficient time to become firmly united (Ziller).

Next to the *formation* of the series in instruction comes the need of fixing it in the mind. This, as we have seen, needs time. It needs, also, a constant attention to the matter in hand. *Repetition* gives the *time,* and skill on the part of the teacher will secure the *attention.* Every teacher knows that repetition without attention accomplishes little. One of the chief purposes of *device* in methods is to secure the requisite attention for the mastery of difficult series. Novelty of device is worthy of consideration, for what is new claims the attention of children.

ILLUSTRATION OF AN HERBARTIAN HISTORY LESSON (1891)   From
Charles De Garmo, *The Essentials of Method* (Boston, 1891), pp. 135–36.

History

59. *Course of an oral history lesson in middle and lower classes.*

(A)

(1) PREPARATION.—First observation (inner) and apprehension.

(*a*) Connection with former lessons by means of questions which, reaching back, gather up those points which will serve as transition to, and preparation for, the new lesson.

(*b*) Announcement of the purpose of the lesson.

(*c*) Introductory remarks. These remarks take their rise from the pupil's world of experience. Suppose, for instance, the pupils know the story of the Argonautic expedition, and now come to the journey of Columbus. It is evident that to call the former to mind will increase the interest in the latter. The effort must always be to bridge the gulf which separates the distant deed and its foreign world from the present and the experience of the pupil.

(2) PRESENTATION.—Concrete, vivid narration by the teacher, of the elements of historical life, the stages of the action, and what is characteristic in them. These things must be brought clearly to view in separate subdivisions (method-wholes), that there may be a clear apprehension of the lesson as a whole. For this purpose it is well, at the close of each section, for the teacher, assisted by the pupils, to sum up the chief contents of the section in condensed headings, which are to be drilled upon both now and afterwards. It will be well to have the pupils record these in their note-books.

(B)

(3) FOR GAINING A DEEPER INSIGHT.—(*a*) Placing together of all the written headings, as well as the teacher's whole plan of the lesson, as a guide to the impression upon the mind of all that is to be held.

(*b*) Fuller apprehension of the individual facts by *comparing, uniting, and grouping* the various elements of the given narration.

(*c*) Bringing out of the main points by concentration questions. An example from the seventh grade—Greater method-whole—The Trojan War. Separation into small unities: (1) The inner cause, outer occasion, participants in the war, departure and landing. (2) The battles about Troy. (3) The capture and destruction of the city. Consequences. Suppose the story of the battles has been given. We should ask at the close of the narration concerning the following points: (1) The seat of war (kingdom and city of Priam; plain of Scamander, picture of the city); (2) Actors. Since the Achaian leaders are known from the first section, we have now to do with the increase to the Trojan side, Priam and his house. Parallels: Priam and Agamemnon. (Difference: Priam the ruler of a large empire, and the patriarchal head of a royal family; Agamemnon the military leader of numerous tribes). Hector and Achilles, Menelaus and Paris, Helen and Chalcas, etc. (3) Actions. Pictures of the war. General engagements and duels. Groups of the latter (Battle of Paris and

THE
NEW
EDUCATION

1877

Menelaus, Ajax and Hector, Achilles and Hector). Pictures of cessation from war: Councils (quarrel of Agamemnon and Achilles). Ambassadors. Parting of Hector and Andromache, etc. Special increase of new and unknown elements of historical life, of ethical character (lamentable fate of Hector), etc.

(C)

(4) PRACTICE.—DRILL.—APPLICATION.—Connected recitation of individual points (series formation). Repetition of the condensed headings in connection. Recitation of smaller sections in full and connected form,—all to show an understanding of the whole, which is now deepened and made clear.

A HERBARTIAN'S CORRELATION OF STUDIES WITH THE INTERESTS OF THE CHILD (1895) From Lida Brown McMurry, "Correlation of Studies with the Interests of the Child for the First and Second School Years," *First Yearbook of the Herbart Society for the Scientific Study of Teaching* (Chicago, 1897), pp. 115–17, 133.

Introduction

A correlation of studies to be vitally effective, must be induced by the interests of the child. These interests are determined by the child's nature and by his environment, both of which must be reckoned with constantly in any scheme of correlation.

The center of the child's interests is the home and the little world which lies about the child. Here, before entering school, he spends most of his time playing with toys, with imaginary beings or things, with his pets, or with children. He has a few tasks, perhaps, to perform, but these are for the most part light, and require but little of his time. He is seldom quiet during his waking hours unless listening to stories or watching to see how things are done.

Out-door life is attractive to him. He likes the farm because there is plenty of room there and always something of interest going on. He likes the animals and longs to milk the cows and drive the horses. He is keenly alive to all things doing.

When he enters school the different lines of work must connect closely with these live wires of his interests, if his education, so well begun at home, is to be carried on without a break after he enters school.

It will be noticed that in the following outline the correlation of the different lines of work with one another in the first year is slight. The nature of the child— flitting quickly from one thing to another—suggests that this is in favor of the child. Intensive study has no place here where the child is still spending most of his time getting acquainted with the world; a wide range however, is demanded.

Correlation of the School with the Home—a General Survey of the Whole Network of Relations

The influence of the ideal home upon the school and enrichment of the home life through the school are very prominent during these early years.

The slight tasks which the child has been given to do at home for the purpose of inculcating habits of industry and neatness are continued in the school, each child being responsible for a neat desk, and sharing with the other children the responsibility for a tidy room. Together they keep the books and papers in order on the children's table and care for the plants in the windows. The children who remain at school for lunch eat around a kindergarten table, a teacher presiding at the table. After their lunches are spread out they sing a simple grace and when the meal is over the children clear off the table and brush up the crumbs from the floor before going to their play.

For their construction work they bring from the home wrapping-paper of different colors, wall paper, old seed and furniture catalogs, oat straw, cardboard boxes, pea-pods, and other articles such as every home can furnish. They also gather twigs, burdock burs, wild cucumber pods, wild rose hips, acorns, pebbles, coarse grasses, seeds, flags, and perhaps clay. From these articles, which cost them nothing but the fun of gathering, they learn to make many objects of interest to them, and, because the material is within their reach, they carry on this work at home, answering their own oft-repeated question, "What can I do now, mother?" In making articles at school they are encouraged to think of the home folks. They make holders, table mats, etc., for the mother and paper dolls, balls, harness, and other things for the younger brothers and sisters.

During the Story Hour they are encouraged to tell their classmates good stories which they have learned at home. They are also expected to tell at home the stories which they have learned at school. Poems and songs learned at home and at school are also interchanged. This furnishes the best of motives for oral language.

Nature observation is carried on largely outside of school. The questions raised at school, in regard to their pets, domestic animals, birds, plants, flowers, and the garden, are answered by the children after observing the animals and plants at or near their own homes. They are encouraged by the teacher to provide food for the birds and to furnish them nesting places about their homes. From their home garden they bring plants for the school garden, and the school garden, in turn, furnishes plants for the home garden, vegetables and flowers also.

Games or plays which the child has learned at home, if suitable, he teaches to his classmates, and the many new games which he learns at school are played in the home, so that the distracting, "What can we play, mother?" does not need to be asked.

In written language the children often write riddles which are taken home for the parents to read and guess. They also write short invitations to their school programs to give to their parents.

One day every week, after the children have learned to read fairly well, they bring short stories from home with which they entertain their classmates.

Through parents' meetings the interaction between the home and the school is intelligently established and carried on. The teacher finds out from the parents how much of the school work is really becoming so much a part of the child that he lives it. She also finds what is failing to reach the child, thus enabling her to revise her work to the benefit of the child. The parents, too, learn what they can do at their end of the line to reinforce the work of the school.

*   *   *

Conclusion

Correlation of the child's school life with his home life and the correlation of the different exercises in the school curriculum are worth while, for they unite home and school, give to the child wholesome home occupations, give good motives for work, increase interest in school exercises, promote self-dependence, lead to good habits of thinking, promote thoughtfulness for others, and tend to make school life natural.

FRANK M. McMURRY ON THE DOCTRINE OF CONCENTRATION

(**1895**)   From Frank M. McMurry, "Concentration," *First Yearbook of the Herbart Society for the Scientific Study of Teaching* (Chicago, 1897), p. 28.

Theses

The following are the chief theses maintained in this paper:

I. It is an essential part of good instruction to relate ideas closely and abundantly with one another. The law of apperception demands it. The topic that deals with this matter is properly called concentration, rather than correlation or coordination, of studies.

II. There are at least six weighty arguments in favor of concentration:
   1) It increases strength of character.
   2) It increases the apperceiving power of the mind.
   3) It increases interest in general, especially interest at the beginning of recitations and in review.
   4) It increases thoroughness of knowledge
   5) It saves time and prevents the curriculum from being crowded.
   6) It strengthens memory.

III. Concentration aims at a psychological rather than a philosophical unity of thought.

IV. The studies in the common-school curriculum are by nature closely related to one another.

V. In order that the child may appreciate this relationship, the studies must be carefully arranged with reference to one another. The history of teaching indicates that in making such an arrangement, a center must be chosen about which thoughts shall be associated.

VI. Neither the teacher nor the child can be this desired center: that duty must fall to one of the studies in the curriculum, to which the other studies shall be subordinated.

VII. The unity and individuality of the separate branches need not be destroyed by such subordination.

VIII. Since the development of good character is the primary object of the school, literature and history are the most important subjects of study; hence, they can best form the center for concentration.

IX. History as the central study for the upper grades is abundantly and closely related to other subjects; literature as a center for the lower grades is also probably sufficiently related to secure the proper kind of concentration.

THEORY OF THE RECAPITULATION OF THE RACE (1895)   From C. C. Van Liew, "The Theory of Culture Epochs in the Child and the Race," *First Yearbook of the Herbart Society for the Scientific Study of Education* (Chicago, 1897), pp. 188–91.

I

The child, in attaining a grasp of the social order and civilization into which it is born and the power to adjust itself to that order, *must* pass through those stages of spiritual development that have been essential in the evolution of the race.

This, the so-called theory of the culture epochs, is an application to the psychical development of the child of the theory of recapitulation which the doctrine of evolution regards as established for the physical development of the individual.

The theory may be argued from both the formal and the material points of view.

As to form, the analogy between individual and generic development may be briefly indicated as follows:

II

(*a*) In both child and race, mental development proceeds from absorption in the mass of sense perceptions, through the highly imaginative or mythical and legendary interpretation of phenomena, to the higher historical, philosophic, and scientific interpretation.

(*b*) In both child and race, the development proceeds from the grosser, uncontrolled forms of impulse, through stages of fickleness and caprice, of childish trust in the patriarchal guidance, of rebellion against the law and the lesson of necessary subjection to the law, and of rational insight into the fitness and voluntary self-subjection to the law, or autonomy.

(*c*) Similar lines of comparison may be drawn for the development of the interests and emotions which are, however, very closely associated with and implied in the intellectual and volitional development of the individual and the race.

As to material:

III

The subject matter of development, *i.e.*, the stimulus to development found in both the natural and cultural environment, is very largely the same for the race and for the child, thus giving *occasion* for the parallelism of development.

IV

Education bespeaks for the child a natural development of his powers. In so doing it implies the possibility of a right principle of succession for the materials of instruction and the educative activities.

V

The principles of succession that have thus far been applied may be briefly summed up as (1) the principle of the relative ease of acquisition, which is an imperfect attempt to recognize the limitations which the child places upon the formation of the curriculum, and (2) the principle of the logical unfolding of the subject matter, which recognizes the limitations that the nature of the subject places upon the formation of the curriculum.

VI

Neither of these, alone, can be made the chief principle of succession in the curriculum, for neither adequately meets the requirement of sympathy between the child and the materials that are to stimulate his development at any given stage.

VII

There is need of a more perfect principle of succession, (1) because of the imperfection of the principles stated in thesis V when taken alone, (2) to give unity and purpose to those materials that will best meet the requirements imposed by the child and the aim of instruction, (3) to meet and utilize the child's developing interests and impulses, and (4) to furnish the "leading motive" to the work of concentration.

VIII

The principle that meets these requirements most satisfactorily is that of the culture epochs, since it seeks to recognize the growing interests and powers of the child by introducing organic wholes of subject matter corresponding in general to each successive stage of development, and looking toward the ultimate end of education.

IX

The application of the theory of the culture epochs is limited by the following facts: (1) Each child is born into the world with a constantly increasing store of inheritance, thus shortening, to a slight degree only, the range of recapitulation. (2) Progress in civilization and culture places about each child a somewhat changed environment. Hence, the child finds himself in a *present* environment, the present's expression of past ages, while at the same time following an order of spiritual development that characterized the earlier growth of the race. The modern environment tends, therefore, to hasten the development of the earlier stages, and to render the parallelism of the latter stages less clearly marked.

X

While the Theory of the Culture Epochs is still open to the researches of comparative history and psychology, it is sufficiently well established to admit of application in education, at least along the following lines:

(*a*) It calls for an historical movement in the curriculum, in which the chief theme shall be furnished by history and literature. (Comp. McMurry's Special Method of History and Literature.)

(*b*) It bespeaks for the selection of material in history and literature an emphasis of classic periods and classic products, and their treatment as organic thought wholes. "Periods that no master described, whose spirit no poet breathed, are of little value to education," and "great moral energy is the effect of great scenes and entire unbroken thought masses." (Herbart.)

(*c*) In that the Culture Epochs point to certain prominent phases of growth at different stages in the child's development, they at the same time suggest the most fitting and sympathetic mode of approach to the child.

(*d*) In that the Culture Epochs have distinctly in view the aim of education, in conjunction with the principle of concentration they seek to point all instruction and all school activities toward a fuller and more intelligent grasp of modern social and national order and institutions. Hence they suggest that method of treatment for all the branches of instruction, that shall ultimately place them in the light of their value for human power.

A HERBARTIAN ON THE ELEMENTARY-SCHOOL CURRICULUM

(1895)   From Charles de Garmo, "Most Pressing Problems Concerning the Elementary
Course of Study," *First Yearbook of the Herbart Society for the Scientific Study of Teaching*
(Chicago, 1897), pp. 7–11, 26–27.

During the past forty or fifty years we have had enough to do in the effort to extend the benefits of education to all the people. Public opinion for universal education had to be developed and formulated into laws. The establishment and perfection of the external machinery for such a system was a work of great magnitude. Houses and implements were to be provided; teachers were to be certificated and paid, and to some extent trained for their specific duties.

It is no small task to universalize an idea that affects all the people, especially when that idea is an initial effort of a great nation to determine its welfare and even destiny from within. In all ages men have been governed, for the most part, however, from forces that did not represent their own outflowing thought. But now we have undertaken to determine from the heart of the people, not only our destiny, but also the methods and means whereby we propose to work it out. The greatest agency for this self-evolution of a people is universal education.

Having undertaken, therefore, for the first time in history, this vast enterprise, it is not to be wondered at that our chief efforts in the past have been directed mostly to the perfection of the external machinery necessary for its successful prosecution.

When this pioneer work for the race was being inaugurated, it chanced that it was undertaken by a nation that was still essentially in its pioneer stages of development. We began with the primitive ideas of education that were developed when there were few things to study and but few people to study them. Learning had been confined for the most part to languages, logic, and philosophy, and learners had been restricted to literati, gentlemen, clergymen, and a few professionals. But now a double difficulty confronts us—vast increase in available knowledge and multiplication of learners. Knowledge has been advanced so rapidly, enriched so immensely, and extended in so many directions, that he who still adheres to the ancient course of study, whose strength was its poverty, does so against many urgent protests arising from this growth in knowledge and this extension of education to all children of all classes of men. It is found that the mental food so palatable to gentlemen and literati, and so valuable for professionals, has proved to be neither palatable nor valuable to many of the sons of toil, to whom education traditions are like mythological tales—good enough for idle hours, but of small account in the modern struggle for existence.

One of the problems that has already forced itself upon us, is, therefore, What shall the public school teach? That this problem is already being vigorously attacked, witness the efforts of New England to shorten and enrich the grammar school curriculum, the report of the committee of ten, and the report of the committee of fifteen on elementary education, presented last February before the Department of Superintendence at Cleveland.

Many and various are the schemes for solving the problem. Some would rigorously exclude all the new and cling desperately to the old. Others would discard the old and cling to the new. This is what Professor Stoy used to call *surgical pedagogy*. To reduce weight it amputates limbs. Some advocate the application of the elective system of the university to the elementary and secondary schools. If there is such a wealth of good material, why not let the child choose what he fancies? To such a course many serious objections might be urged. The idea of election in lower schools is apparently based on the doctrine that study of any kind has a disciplinary value for the mind, without much regard to its content. The old idea was that grammar and mathematics are the indispensable disciplines in school training. The new insight appears to be that geography and history, or other studies, will serve the purpose equally well. The validity of this theory is discussed in a very able article by Professor Hinsdale, of the University of Michigan, in a recent number of the *Educational Review*. That article, perhaps, better than anything else of recent origin, brings us down to date on the question of the worth and worthlessness of the idea of formal discipline of the mind by any restricted group of studies.

Some try to meet the new difficulty concerning the curriculum by taking into the course of study all good things; but such efforts defeat themselves so quickly that they may be dismissed at once.

Colonel Parker's most recent and most notable book seeks a solution by basing all concrete study on the central sciences of mineralogy, geology, geography, astronomy, meteorology, biology, zoology, anthropology, ethnology, and history, or, in other words, upon a hierarchy of sciences.

We have, on the other hand, equally earnest attempts to subordinate science studies to the humanities. The monumental work of the late Professor Ziller, of Leipzic, a disciple of Herbart, must ever stand as the prototype for all efforts of this kind.

Finally, men are trying to solve the problem of the curriculum by a rational selection of typical studies in all important departments of learning to the end that a fairly balanced development of mind may be secured for all children and that each individual may find himself in touch with the forces that will determine his destiny, and to the end that he may not wake at the beginning of active life to find himself an adherent of the dust-covered ideals of the past, and quite out of touch with his own most potent environment.

Before discussing in detail the various problems pertaining to the selection, sequence, and articulation of the studies of the curriculum, however, there is an antecedent problem whose solution will in large measure determine their solution. It is to this antecedent problem that attention is now directed.

The Ethical Function of Studies

Before the time when the world decided for universal education it was decided to dissolve the marriage between church and state, thus leaving the divorced pair to quarrel over the control of their child, education. So long as only a few persons were to be educated, the church could fairly hold the field. But when all were to be schooled, only the state had the power and the money to do the work. The result is a general dissatisfaction (sometimes assumed, sometimes expressed, but always earnest and insistent) with the inability of the public school to develop the moral character of the pupil upon the religious basis. The assumption is made, and not always refuted, that virtue to be real must have an ecclesiastical foundation. This, too, is an inherited idea that arose when the world was busily engaged trying to make all men think alike about religion. But the idea is a very potent one with many people and has a certain justification. How has the public school met the criticism? By ignoring it; or by declaring that education is a divided function; one part, the intellectual, belonging to the state, and the other, the moral, as based on religion, belonging to the church. But Herbart and his followers teach that except for the inculcation of dogma and the training in ecclesiastical ceremony, the public school is an adequate agency for the development of moral character. This, if true, is important. Even more than we need to know what to teach do we need to know how to temper our school intellectualism by effective moral training.

What is the new idea that Herbart contributes to the subject of moral training? We have long talked of the liberalizing and humanizing effects of knowledge; as Professor Thomas Metcalf used to say: "Algebra conquers adipose;" and we have long recognized the powerful individual moral influence that a noble character on the part of the teacher has upon the pupil. What more is there? Herbart declares: "Instruction in the studies of the public-school must be made to reveal to the pupil the moral order of the world; and not only must it furnish this moral insight, but it must so touch the heart that a permanent right disposition toward all men, both in their individual and in their organized capacity, may result."

The first implication of such a demand is that the studies must no longer be purely formal or restricted to two or three subjects. Grammar, indeed, investigates the forms of thought and trains to mental acuteness, but it reveals no moral relations; the same is true of number, which is the formal quantitative study of inorganic nature. Both of these subjects are useful and necessary, but in themselves they contribute only very indirectly to any moral insight. But in literature and history and geography we may hear the very heart-beats of the race, as it struggles with temptation or rises on the wings of aspiration. Through science, properly taught, we become aware of our ethical duty toward the lower creation, and we study, moreover, the conditions under which men must meet and strive and live together. All this means that if school studies are to reveal our duties to ourselves and our neighbors, and to sweeten our disposition toward others, they must be full and rich, throbbing with the life of the world, and no longer merely formal, cold, and abstruse. What consequences does this involve for the teacher! He must no longer drag out his weary days on the treadmill of routine, but he must seize the spiritual sense of the English literature, the richest under the sun; he must understand the moral significance of human history as unfolded, not by a machine-made textbook, but by the great masters of language and historical insight; he must read the book of nature in the original, not in translation; he must comprehend the meaning of the civilization about him in its governmental, social, and business aspects. All these things he must know, for how can he make study reveal that of which he himself is unconscious? To reveal the moral order of the world, not alone in its subjective aspects but in all its manifold and far-reaching objective relations, as seen in family, civil, business, and social life is a task that implies not only faith and high purpose, but broad knowledge and deep insight as well.

The second implication contained in the ideal that instruction makes a moral revelation of the world to the pupils is, that the making of the curriculum in all its details is a work of magnitude and importance. The late Dr. Frick, of Halle, in company with a hundred able schoolmen spent eight years in experiment and study upon single studies or groups of studies before he ventured to offer to the world the outlines of an organically developed, well articulated course of study for secondary schools. Professor Rein and his assistants also worked for years upon their *acht Schuljahren,* or course of study for elementary schools. In like manner our principals and teachers must struggle with the outline programs offered by groups of experts like those represented in the report of the committee of ten and that of the committee of fifteen.

A third implication is that moral character can not be glued on to the pupil by any external system of ethical instruction superimposed upon intellectual education, but must grow out of the very heart of studies themselves, through the nature of their content, and by keeping them in close touch with a few fundamental ethical ideals.

In the light of this idea of instruction the moral purposes to be subserved by instruction assume clear outline and definite content. It is assumed that we are all working in the school-room for the uplifting of humanity, and so we are; but in many cases it is the blind leading the blind. Will not the teacher who makes this principle the guide to his study, the high ideal of his teaching, have a new lease of spiritual life? Drudgery and routine we cannot wholly avoid, but they need not be the dominating facts of our teaching experience. They may be transformed by a clearly perceived spiritual purpose, just as love is capable of turning painful labor into joyous service.

In pursuance of this initial purpose of instruction, the Herbartians emphasize first of all the painstaking study of the conditions and development of the child's apprehension, or apperception, as the only reliable guide to the selection of the subject-matter and the methods of presenting it to the child. The same problem is attacked from the physiological side in the child-study so ably and so vigorously represented by President Hall. Those who have read Lange's *Apperception,* translated by the Herbart Club, will understand how completely this idea determines all that the Herbartians do in the way of selecting, articulating, and teaching the various branches of study. The Herbartians do not always agree, but whatever they attempt is always done in the sacred name of the child—his understanding, his sympathies, his interests, his feelings and mental stages, his natural ways of living. With them all educational psychology focuses upon the processes of mental life as exhibited in the child. With the ethical purpose as an end and the apperception of the child as a guide, each of the problems of education is examined, the most important of which will now be considered. . . .

Propositions Deduced from the Foregoing Exposition

1. The highest function of the studies is an ethical revelation of the elements of civilization of the child.

2. Each department of study has a distinct ethical office in fitting the child for life, and should for this reason, if for no other, retain its integrity as a subject of study.

3. The term CORRELATION is universal, and includes both COORDINATION and CONCENTRATION. Concentration subordinates secondary to primary subjects, while coordination associates related subjects, allowing each to retain its integrity as a distinct study, and permitting it to have its own principle of sequence of parts.

4. Objective correlation, as treated in the report of the committee of fifteen, discusses the relative educational value of studies, and involves a consideration of their equivalence. It is made by the philosopher in his study, and does not appeal to the consciousness of the child in the school. It merely determines the function of each study in enabling the child to master his environment, thus giving the reason for its presence in the curriculum; but it determines nothing as to time, amount, sequence of parts, or the relation to other branches that it would have in the recitation.

5. The demands of civilization should take precedence of formal mental discipline as a guide to the selection of studies.

6. The apperception of the child is the basis for those phases of correlation not covered by objective correlation. It determines the position of studies in the curriculum, the principle of sequence to be observed in their progress, and their internal and their external organization, i. e., correlation *within* departments, and correlation *of* departments.

7. The sequence demanded by culture epochs must be recognized, but must be kept in subjection to the demands of the child's environment.

8. Ziller's scheme of concentration, which subordinates all other branches to history and literature, is to be rejected in principle, since his ideal of the ethical value of studies is too subjective, failing to recognize properly the function of the other studies in fitting for the social, political, and economic functions that the individual must perform in a complex civilization.

9. Colonel Parker's plan of concentration gives us our best discussion of the relation of "form" to thought studies, but is open to criticism in that it tends to emphasize nature at the expense of culture subjects, to destroy the identity of departments, and to cause confusion by using too universal a principle as a guide to sequence.

10. The first and most important problem of correlation is organization of parts within each of the departments of study; for, in a last analysis, correlation is important according as it is based upon perceivable and essential causal relations, as opposed to artificial or sentimental ones. Viewed in this way, it must be apparent that, on the whole, the relations that give sequence and coherence to a department of study are more essential and interesting than occasional cross-relations that may be found between different studies.

11. The correlation of departments is useful, however, because of the increased understanding and interest on the part of the child, and because of its value in educating the child to consistent and forceful conduct.

12. Literature is useful in bringing the aesthetic and the intellectual into helpful association.

13. Geography is the most universal, concrete correlating study, and perhaps more than any other may follow the lead of the other branches.

FRANCIS W. PARKER DISCUSSES HERBARTIANISM (1897) From *The First Yearbook of the Herbart Society for the Scientific Study of Teaching* (Chicago, 1897), pp. 153–58.

I am not prepared to discuss the very valuable essay of Dr. Van Liew's, on Culture Epochs. I have read the paper, but have not studied it sufficiently. I trust that this essay will receive such a thorough and careful discussion in the future as it deserves.

EDUCATION
IN THE
UNITED STATES

1888

No subject was ever brought into the American schools that furnishes so much food for thought and such abundant means for discussion as the subject we call "Herbartianism." The distinguished teachers who have spent several years at Jena studying, under the famous Dr. Rein, are, to say the least, full of the subject, full of the doctrine of correlation and concentration. Herbartianism, as I understand it, means earnest and unlimited study of the great subject of education and honest, earnest, fair discussion. The Herbartian doctrine is a working hypothesis to be examined, accepted in part or whole, or to be wholly rejected.

Very much of discussion in the past has been in the air. Discussions have been either vague theories or everlasting denials of any suggestions of progress. The day of pure dogmatism is fast passing away; discipleship, too, has not that hold upon the teachers that it once had. We can point to no one doctrine, or to no one man in the past, that has presented us the whole of truth. We look upon past systems or doctrines as movements toward something higher; nothing is finished nor ever will be finished.

The fundamental good we get out of the past is *direction*. We no doubt get great fundamental principles or direction for action. The final test of a principle or direction is its infinity in application. A method that does not open out a vista of infinity in application is wrong. We can no longer say that this method is right and that is wrong. There is only one method, and that is the economical presentation of conditions for the action of the laws of human growth. There is only one method worth applying, and that is the method of the teacher who studies and understands great fundamental principles and continually applies them; in that application there is everlasting movement toward something higher and better.

We are all ardent admirers of the great Pestalozzi, but it is doubtful whether we would admit him as a teacher in any one of our schools. He was not a psychologist, he was not a philosopher, but he was, indeed, a great lover of humanity. What he formulated was a necessity for his time; what we get from Pestalozzi is his loving, earnest, truthful spirit in its endeavor to find something better for the children, and that, indeed, is what we get from every great teacher of the past.

Dr. Brown has seen fit to condemn Herbart's metaphysics; whose metaphysics of the past shall we not condemn? I never understood that Herbart made any claim to metaphysics. He was a psychologist, he was what the Germans call a Bahnbrecher. He tried to discover a psychology that could be applied in school-room work. He was the founder of rational psychology. Out of Herbartianism has grown the great movement of physiological psychology which is now culminating in child study.

No doubt we can get much from the great philosopher, Hegel. His restatement of the great fundamental principles of Christ so sublimely presented in the "Sermon on the Mount," that self-activity is the fundamental law of growth, is worthy of the attention of every teacher. Herbartianism reaches its object, suggests what shall be done with the child. It may be that I am mistaken, but I have searched diligently to find Hegel applied in the schoolroom. If there is any spot in this country where the Hegelian doctrine has struck the ground, or entered into the life of the children, I wish to be led to that sacred spot that I may worship. No doubt the Herbartian doctrine is full of mistakes and errors; but it proposes to reach the child's mind, proposes to study the nature of that mind, proposes to suggest the best possible methods for mind growth. There are countless theories in vogue, which, as the Germans say, "Schweben in der Luft." They are discussed and rediscussed, over and over again, books are written exposing the theories; but the poor children go on the same weary round of dead-form work. The real test and the true test of a theory is in its practice, in what it gives the child, what it leads the child to do.

We are not here, then, to accept the Herbartian doctrine as the great students of this doctrine present it to us; we are to study it, we are to examine it. As I have already said, it is, no doubt, the best working hypothesis ever presented for the study of teachers.

However, in the study of a doctrine of education, we must also study the history of the people, the nation, out of which the doctrine grew. A reformer can, indeed, get beyond his own age, can get beyond the influence of government and society that presses upon him, and still no doctrine can be studied unless we understand the inner history of the people of which the theory is the outgrowth.

Our friends, the students of Herbart, emphasize the teaching of history and literature as a core, the center, of educational movement. We all agree that there is very much in history and literature. We can also thoroughly understand another very important fact,—that history and literature are a prominent means of adjusting the child to the society, to the state, to the government. Through history and literature a child can be made to believe in his own government and the society in which he is born. If classes exist, through history and literature, he can be made to feel that these classes are the will of God; if there are kings and nobles, he can be made to feel that these kings and nobles are God's anointed. If he is a peasant, he can be made to believe that it is God's will, and can remain all his life a peasant. History and literature, I repeat, are a powerful means of adjusting the child to the exact state of society in which he finds himself. I do not mean to say that history and literature should be used to this end, but I mean to assert that it has been used in Germany to make each German child believe that the Fatherland is the only land, that standing armies are a necessity, that the emperor is God's anointed, and that the establishment of classes is in the line of the highest progressive movement.

Let me illustrate this: I wish to assert here before these students of Herbart what I believe to be a fact—and without understanding this fact and its influence, very little of Herbart can be understood—it is this, that nature study, the study of elementary science in elementary schools, was kept out of the German schools for many years, for fear that the study of nature would lead children to search for the truth themselves, and by that search would be able to understand the nature of the present state of society and government; that they would doubt the infallibility and indestructibility of thrones—in other words, that the rational or reasoning spirit would enter children's minds through the study of nature; and with the French Revolution behind them, the German leaders saw nothing but danger lying in the path of nature study. The instinct of oppression is an acute and sharp one, it scents danger as the hound scents his game, and that danger lay for them in adjusting the child's mind to eternal truth, to God himself. The moment that adjustment takes place, the mind breaks away from the present forms, breaks away from conformity to oppressive government, seeks something higher.

We have the question of the relative place of nature study and the study of history and literature. In the first place, I do not claim,—Mr. Jackman, who is to discuss this question, does not claim,—that nature is the center. I wish to have these words written in Italics, we do not claim that nature is the center, neither do we claim that history and literature are the center, *we do claim that the child is the center,* that this being, this highest creation of God, with its laws of body, mind, and soul, determines in itself, the very nature and condition of its growth. It is not a question, then, with us, who in a loving, true spirit would criticise our friends, the Herbartians, of any subject being the center, but to simply bring to the front this Cinderella of education—nature study. It is to co-ordinate, to give nature study some place, in the curriculum, to make it one of the great means of human development. It may, or may not, equal history and literature, but it is of first importance. Please to understand our position, when I say again, that we do not claim nature as the central study. The study of nature has been the spectre, the horrible spectre, of those who would hold the human mind in subjection both in church and state. You all know with what tremendous opposition the doctrines of

Darwin met; you all know how church and state, with their efficient instrument the pedant, have striven against the onward march of progress, have fought against the search for God's truth in his manifestation of Himself through the universe. We ask for some place, and indeed a great place, for this manifestation of the Eternal One through all His works, and the reason we give for the neglect of science studies in the school, throughout the ages of education, is the awful danger of human progress that confronted those with fixed beliefs and sordid interests.

There is a great study of man, we should call it ethnology, and the study of man is in truth one of the nature studies. History is a report of ethnology, or the development of man from the beginning, a report filled with untruths, a report written by fawners at the foot of thrones, and the obsequious admirers of great generals. The study of history requires the closest investigation. It is, indeed, an all-important study; but ethnology is the central study, let it be understood, and history is the record of ethnology. No one can have a liberal education, or even a movement toward education, without the study of history and literature. It has been a great headlight upon ethnological movements since the beginning. But to say that we make history the center, make the special pleading on the part of dogmatists and vassals the center of a whole system of education, is, to my mind, incorrect—to disdain the direct revelation of God and take up that zigzag, imperfect movement of man.

The great difference between Froebel and Herbart may be found in the difference of appreciation of children and child life. Herbart's greatest mistake was his lack of recognition of the instincts and spontaneous activities of the child. To fail to understand the child is a fundamental failure. To fail to appreciate the action of the child's mind up to the school age, is a great mistake. The child is not born selfish. He is born the bursting bud of the love of God. He should be developed into the full flower and fruit of God's love.

A Critic Speaks

JOSEPH MAYER RICE CRITICIZES MECHANICAL SCHOOLS IN NEW YORK AND ST. LOUIS (1893)   From Joseph Mayer Rice, *The Public-School System of the United States* (New York, 1893), pp. 29–32, 97–98.

The Public-School System of New York City

In describing the schools of our cities, I begin with the discussion of the schools of New York city because they represent a condition that may be regarded, in many respects, as typical of the schools of all of our large cities. They show clearly the elements that lead to an inferior order of schools; and, further, the remedy that I propose for the eradication of their evils is applicable to the school system of every large city.

*   *   *

Now, what is the character of the instruction that will be passed as satisfactory by the superintendents of the public schools of New York city? Surely no one can call me unjust when I answer this question by describing the work of a school whose principal has been marked uniformly "excellent" during the twenty-five years or more that she has held her present position. I cannot say that this school is a typical New York primary school; I shall describe typical work later. But I do most positively assert that the mere fact that a superintendent is permitted to give a school of this nature his warmest indorsement is sufficient to prove that the school system of New York is not conducted for the benefit of the child alone.

The principal of this school has pedagogical views and a maxim peculiarly her own. She believes that when a child enters upon school life his vocabulary is so small that it is practically worthless, and his power to think so feeble that his thoughts are worthless. She is consequently of the opinion that what the child knows and is able to do on coming to school should be entirely disregarded, that he should not be allowed to waste time, either in thinking or in finding his own words to express his thoughts, but that he should be supplied with ready-made thoughts as given in a ready-made vocabulary. She has therefore prepared sets of questions and answers, so that the child may be given in concise form most of the facts prescribed in the course of study for the three years of primary instruction. The instruction throughout the school consists principally of grinding these answers *verbatim* into the minds of the children. The principal's ideal lies in giving each child the ability to answer without hesitation, upon leaving her school, every one of the questions formulated by her. In order to reach the desired end, the school has been converted into the most dehumanizing institution that I have ever laid eyes upon, each child being treated as if he possessed a memory and the faculty of speech, but no individuality, no sensibilities, no soul.

So much concerning the pedagogical views on which this school is conducted; now as to the maxim. This maxim consists of three short words—"Save the minutes." The spirit of the school is, "Do what you like with the child, immobilize him, automatize him, dehumanize him, but save, save the minutes." In many ways the minutes are saved. By giving the child ready-made thoughts, the minutes required in thinking are saved. By giving the child ready-made definitions, the minutes required in formulating them are saved.

∗　　∗　　∗

Everything is prohibited that is of no measurable advantage to the child, such as the movement of the head or a limb, when there is no logical reason why it should be moved at the time. I asked the principal whether the children were not allowed to move their heads. She answered, "Why should they look behind when the teacher is in front of them?"—words too logical to be refuted.

During the recitations many minutes are saved. The principal has indeed solved the problem of how the greatest number of answers may be given in the smallest number of minutes. In the first place, no time is spent in selecting pupils to answer questions, every recitation being started by the first pupil in the class, the children then answering in turn, until all have recited. Secondly, time is economized in the act of rising and sitting during the recitations, the children being so drilled that the child who recites begins to fall back into his seat while uttering the last word of a definition, the next succeeding child beginning his ascent while the one before him is in the act of descending. Indeed, things appear as if the two children occupying adjoining seats were sitting upon the opposite poles of an invisible see-saw, so that the descending child necessarily raises the pupil next to him to his feet. Then, again, the minutes are saved by compelling the children to unload their answers as rapidly as possible, distinctness of utterance being sacrificed to speed, and to scream their answers at the tops of their voices, so that no time may be wasted in repeating words inaudibly uttered. For example, the principal's definition of a note—"A note is a sign representing to the eye the length or duration of time"—is ideally delivered, when it sounds something life "Notsinrepti length d'ration time."

Another way in which time is saved is by compelling the children to stare fixedly at the source whence the wisdom flows. When the teacher is the source of wisdom, all children in the room stare fixedly in the direction of the teacher; when a word on the blackboard is the source of wisdom, all eyes stare fixedly at the point of the blackboard. There is one more peculiarity. When material, of whatever nature, is handed to the children, enough to supply a whole row is given to the end child. The material is then passed along sideways until each child in the row has been supplied. During this procedure the children are compelled to look straight in front of them, and to place their hands sidewise in order to receive the material, without looking whence it comes. The pupils are thus obliged to grope, as if they were blind, for the things passed to them. The principal assured me, however, that to drill the children in this groping is not attended with much difficulty, the pupils in the lowest primary grade—the little five-year-olds—learning to take and pass things like blind people during the first week or two of their school life.

In St. Louis we have an example of how sad the lot of the child may become when the superintendents not only do practically nothing toward raising the standard of the teachers by instructing them in the science of education, but where they do much to depress them by examining their classes and judging them by results alone. This form of supervision results in greater depression in the schools of St. Louis than in the schools thus far discussed, for the reason that in St. Louis supervision is no longer nominal. There are, in that city, four supervising officers to oversee the work of twelve hundred teachers, the superintendents being thus enabled to visit each teacher at more frequent intervals. The consequence is that the teachers at all times labor under a high degree of pressure for results. To secure the desired results is now their aim, and to secure them the children are ever relentlessly pushed. The fact that the child is a child is entirely forgotten, and the characteristic feature of the St. Louis schools—absolute lack of sympathy for the child—ensues. The unkindly spirit of the teacher is strikingly apparent; the pupils, being completely subjugated to her will, are silent and motionless; the spiritual atmosphere of the classroom is damp and chilly.

In one regard the treatment of the children cannot be considered otherwise than barbarous. During several daily recitation periods, each of which is from twenty to twenty-five minutes in duration, the children are obliged to stand on the line, perfectly motionless, their bodies erect, their knees and feet together, the tips of their shoes touching the edge of a board in the floor. The slightest movement on the part of the child attracts the attention of the teacher. The recitation is repeatedly interrupted with cries of "Stand straight," "Don't bend the knees," "Don't lean against the wall," and so on. I heard one teacher ask a little boy: "How can you learn anything with your knees and toes out of order?" The toes appear to play a more important part than the reasoning faculties. The teacher never forgets the toes; every few moments she casts her eyes "toe-ward."

DESCRIPTION OF A PROGRESSIVE PUBLIC SCHOOL SYSTEM IN
INDIANAPOLIS (1893)   From Joseph Mayer Rice, *The Public School System of the United States* (New York, 1893), pp. 101–3.

The scene presented in the Indianapolis classroom differs so widely from that presented in the school-room of St. Louis that it would scarcely appear that these two institutions had anything in common. This striking contrast is due to the fact that the Indianapolis schools abound in the element which in St. Louis is so obviously lacking—consideration for the child, sympathy. The cold, hard, and cruel struggle for results is here unknown. The teacher uses every means at her command to render the life of the child happy and beautiful, without endangering its usefulness..

I entered one of the rooms containing the youngest children at the time of the opening exercises. The scene I encountered was a glimpse of fairyland. I was in a room full of bright and happy children, whose eyes were directed toward the teacher, not because they were forbidden to look in any other direction, but because to them the most attractive object in the room was their teacher. She understood them, sympathized with and loved them, and did all in her power to make them happy. The appearance of the room was charming. The window-sills were filled with plants, and plants were scattered here and there throughout the room. The teacher's desk was strewn with flowers, and upon each of the children's desks flowers had been placed to welcome the little ones to school.

After the children had sung a few little songs, the first lesson of the day was in order. This was a lesson in science; its subject was a flower. It began with the recitation of a poem. The object of introducing these poems into the plant and animal lessons is to inspire the child with love for the beautiful, with love for nature, and with sympathy for all living things. In the lower grades of the schools of Indianapolis much more stress is laid on the life of the plant and the relation of the child to the plant than upon its structure; and the child is taught how to preserve and to protect it rather than how to dissect it, so that lessons upon plants (and animals) partake as much of moral as of science lessons.

Before the teacher endeavored to bring out the points to which she desired to direct the special attention of the class, the children were urged to make their own unaided observations and to express them. As each child was anxious to tell what he had observed in relation to the plant itself, what he otherwise knew of it, how it grew, where it grew, and perhaps some little incident that the flower recalled to him, the class was full of life and enthusiasm. A few minutes sufficed to bring the children to the point beyond which they could not proceed unaided. When this point was reached the teacher came to the rescue, and by careful questioning led the children to observe the particular things to which she had decided to call their attention that morning. Her questions were not put to individual children, but to the whole class, so that every question might serve to set every pupil observing and thinking. That they did observe and think was shown by the number of hands that were raised in answer to every question. In all, fifteen minutes were devoted to this lesson. When the science lesson was over, some of the children were called to the front of the room to read; and silent or busy work was assigned to those remaining at their seats.

The book used during this reading-lesson was the book of nature—the plant they had just been studying. The scene presented by the happy little children each with a flower in his hand, surrounding the teacher, who was smiling upon them, was truly beautiful. For reading-matter the children were called upon for sentences expressing thoughts concerning their flowers. The sentences were written upon the board by the teacher, and when a number of them had been written the pupils began to read them. The children were interested because they all took an active part in the lesson from the beginning to the end. They were all observing, all thinking, they all had something to say and were glad of an opportunity to tell what they had to say. The teacher was fully as enthusiastic as were her pupils, and as much pleased as the children, when bright remarks were made by them. That, in spite of her gentleness, she had them completely under her control, was shown by the fact that they were more than willing to do anything she asked them to do.

How shocked some of our so-called disciplinarians would have been had they witnessed this lesson! The children were expected to talk, and they had much to say; their hands were ever in sight. Our disciplinarian calls the child orderly only when he has nothing to say, when he has no thoughts to express, and when his hands are nowhere in sight. The children's toes were not on the line, but were so arranged that they might be as near their teacher as possible. Some of the little ones even committed the crime of laying their hands on the teacher, and she so far forgot herself as to fondle them in return. Yet the discipline was perfect. What is perfect discipline in the class-room but perfect attention? There was no noise, but there were everywhere signs of life, and such signs of life as become a gathering of young children.

Meanwhile the pupils who had remained at their seats, though practically left to themselves, were far from idle. They had no time for idleness or mischief; they were too deeply absorbed in their work for that. They as well as the others were studying the book of nature, and these little six-year-olds and seven-year-olds were doing thoughtful work even without the aid of the teacher. They were not only reading from their flowers, they were painting them, writing little stories about them, utilizing them for number, form, and color work, and exercising their powers of observation and thought upon them; and, strange to say, every child was doing nearly all of these things at one and the same time.

JOSEPH MAYER RICE CONTRASTS THE OLD EDUCATION WITH THE NEW (1893) From Joseph Mayer Rice, *The Public School System of the United States* (New York, 1893), pp. 19–27.

As my judgment concerning the degree of excellence of a school system is governed by the extent to which the teachers strive to abandon unscientific methods and to regulate their work according to the requirements of the new education, it may be well, before entering on the discussions of the schools of individual cities, to describe what is generally understood by scientific and unscientific schools—by the "old" and the "new" education—as well as to point out wherein they differ.

By an unscientific or mechanical school is meant one that is still conducted on the antiquated notion that the function of the school consists primarily, if not entirely, in crowding into the memory of the child a certain number of cut-and-dried facts—that is, that the school exists simply for the purpose of giving the child a certain amount of information. As, in such schools, the manner in which the mind acquires ideas is naturally disregarded, it follows that the teachers are held responsible for nothing beyond securing certain memoriter results. Consequently, the aim of the instruction is limited mainly to drilling facts into the minds of the children, and to hearing them recite lessons that they have learned by heart from text-books. Such methods are termed antiquated, because they represent instruction as it was before the time of the great educators, when a science of education was unknown. Further, as the manner in which the mind acquires ideas is not taken into account, the teacher makes no attempt to study the needs of the child, and consequently no bond of sympathy forms between the pupil and the teacher. In these schools the attitude of the teacher toward the child is as a rule cold and unsympathetic, and at times actually cruel and barbarous.

The schools conducted on scientific principles differ widely from the mechanical schools. While the aim of the old education is mainly to give the child a certain amount of information, the aim of the new education is to lead the child to observe, to reason, and to acquire manual dexterity as well as to memorize facts—in a word, to develop the child naturally in all his faculties, intellectual, moral, and physical. As in these schools the teacher is guided in her work by the nature of the child mind,—that is, by the laws of mental development,—she is constantly in search of such light as will guide her in giving the child the benefit of what is known of the nature of the mind and its mode of development. We find, therefore, widely distributed among the teachers a truly progressive spirit, much enthusiasm, and a desire to become conversant with the laws of psychology and the principles of education. It is almost exclusively in the cities where the teachers constantly pursue professional studies under the guidance of their superintendents that schools of this order are found.

As it is no longer the text-book or the arbitrary will of the superintendent, but the laws of psychology, that now become the ruling spirit of the school, the order of things becomes reversed and, in consequence, the atmosphere of the school-room entirely changed. The teacher who endeavors to instruct in accordance with the nature of the mind is of necessity obliged to study the child, so that she may understand him and know how to minister to his needs. In this manner a true bond of sympathy forms between the teacher and the child. The attitude of the teacher now changes from that of lord and master to that of friend and guide. She thus ceases to be cold and harsh, and becomes loving and sympathetic. The school-room loses its prison aspect and becomes characteristic of a refined and refining home. Further, when the teacher is guided in her work by the laws of psychology, there is a change in the methods of instruction as well as in the spirit of the classroom. While in the mechanical schools the recitation periods are devoted either to hearing children recite lessons that they have studied by heart, or to drilling the pupils in facts, in the schools conducted on scientific principles such procedures are not tolerated, the teachers being obliged to devote these periods to actual teaching, and—to the best of their ability—in accordance with methods approved by the educational scientists.

It may therefore be seen that the new education recognizes that there are elements aside from measurable results that require consideration in educating the child. The first and foremost among these elements is the child himself. The old system of education thinks only of the results, and with its eye upon the results, forgets the child; while the new system is in large part guided by the fact that the child is a frail and tender, loving and lovable human being. "By their fruits shall ye know them," is a proverb which, though frequently quoted in this connection, does not apply to schools at all, because it leaves out of consideration the fact that the child lives while he is being educated. Who would argue that the steerage is as good as the cabin because the steerage passenger travels as quickly and as safely as the cabin passenger? When natural methods are philosophically applied by the teacher, the child becomes interested in his work, and the school is converted into a house of pleasure. When, on the other hand, the child is taught by mechanical methods, his mental food is given to him in the most indigestible and unpalatable form, in consequence of which he takes no interest in his work, learning becomes a source of drudgery, and the school a house of bondage.

And, further, under the new system elements are brought into play which, by reason of their refining nature, can scarcely fail to exert a favorable influence on the moral character of the child. Among these are—first, the bond of sympathy that forms between the child and the teacher who strives to understand him, to interest him, and to make him happy. The atmosphere of the mechanical school is damp and chilly, while that of the progressive school is glowing with life and warmth. Second, the pursuit of studies that tend to develop the sympathetic and esthetic faculties of the child, among which are, (1) nature studies—the study of plants when regarded from the sympathetic and poetic sides, and the study of animals from the standpoint of sympathy; (2) the purely artistic studies—namely, music, poetry, drawing and painting from nature, the construction of beautiful forms (designing), and work with beautiful colors.

But why do the mechanical schools still exist in an enlightened age and in a country so progressive as ours? It is frequently claimed, in support of the mechanical system, that the old education is more practical than the new. This assertion, however, is made in ignorance of facts. Indeed, facts prove that more is accomplished in a given period by scientific than by mechanical teaching. And, further, that system of education that leads the child to observe and to think, as well as to give him manual dexterity while memorizing facts, is certainly more practical than the education whose aim is limited to leading the pupils to memorize facts. Again, it is claimed that in some localities the old system better answers the needs of the people than the new, and that the system of education must be regulated according to the needs of the individual community. In that case, the old system of education is applicable only to those communities where there is no necessity for the people either to observe or to reason, or to be dexterous in the use of their hands. But where can such a community be found? Again, we all know that in many of our cities the pupils will never receive more than three or four years of schooling, and we all agree that no pains should be spared to give such children at least some knowledge of the three R's before they begin their independent struggle for existence.

If facts should prove that the best results in the three R's are obtained in the primary schools that devote practically all the time to these subjects, and the poorest in the primary schools that spend the most time in leading pupils to observe, to reason, and to use their hands with facility, then the advocates of the reading, writing, and arithmetic schools would still have at least a crutch to lean upon. But it so happens that facts prove the contrary to be true; namely, that the pupils read and write better, and cipher at least as well, in the schools where the work is most thoughtful—that is, where most is done to lead the pupils to acquire ideas by being brought into relation with things instead of words, signs, and symbols. I found, with scarcely an exception, by far the best reading in the schools in which the pupils were taught to read through science lessons, and by far the best—not infrequently incredibly good—results in written language where the children began to express the results of their observations in their own words in writing, as early as the fifth or sixth month of school life. On the other hand, I found the results in reading and in written language almost universally poor in the schools where the reading-matter, at least during the first two years, consisted of nothing but empty words, silly sentences, and baby-trash, and where the time spent in writing was devoted to copying such words and sentences from the blackboard or the reading-book. (But this much need be said here—namely, that unless the teachers be properly prepared for their work, their teaching cannot be scientific. The new education in form without the spirit is a farce, and the spirit of the new education lies in the methods of teaching, and not in the subjects to be taught.

It is not therefore because the old system of education is more practical than the new, or that it better answers the needs of the people, or that it accomplishes more in a given period, that in so many of our cities the science of education is ignored. The real causes for the existence of the mechanical schools at the present stage of civilization are no other than corruption and selfishness on the part of school officials, and unjustifiable ignorance, as well as criminal negligence, on the part of parents. It is in the cities where the school-boards appoint such superintendents as will make able tools, and fail to reelect them when they are conscientious; in cities where it is not merit, but friendship, business, or politics, that determines the appointment and discharge of teachers; in cities where the parents permit the members of the school-board to use their children for selfish purposes, and, with few exceptions, in such cities only, that the science of education does not enter the schools.

In a few instances the antiquated system of education appears to be entirely the result of misdirected and incompetent supervision. When the superintendents fail to instruct and inspire their teachers, or are unable to recognize the difference between scientific and unscientific instruction, the schools are, as a rule, mechanical in spite of honest government. In these cases the teachers are permitted, either through ignorance or carelessness, to fall into ruts out of which they never rise. To divorce the schools from politics does not in itself mean to raise the standard of the schools, but simply to remove the pressure from them so that it becomes possible for them to advance. When schools are no longer under the baneful influence of politics, they become, in nearly every instance, no more and no less than the superintendents make of them. A feature common to all of the purely mechanical schools is the fact that far too little, if anything, is done by their superintendents to inspire and instruct the teachers. In nearly all of them the number of superintendents is too small, more than two hundred teachers being placed in charge of a single supervising officer. Fortunately the schools of many of our cities are now marching along the line of progress; some of these, however, are moving only with the pace of a snail.

JOSEPH MAYER RICE CALLS FOR A NEW SYSTEM OF SCHOOL MANAGEMENT (1893)   From Joseph Mayer Rice, *The Public-School System of the United States* (New York, 1893), pp. 16–19.

Although matters are so thoroughly complicated that the conditions can be in no two cities exactly alike, my observations have nevertheless led me to conclude that when a few fundamental principles are observed in the management of a school system, the development of good schools is almost certain to follow; and on the other hand, that the school evils increase in the same proportion as these laws are ignored. My principal object in following the plan of discussing our schools by cities, will be to show by what concrete examples I have been led to appreciate the fundamental character of these laws. What will be said in criticism of the schools of individual cities, may be regarded therefore in large part as matters incidental to the main issue. As these laws are applicable to the schools of all our cities, my work, although it will touch on the schools of only a few cities, may nevertheless serve as a guide not only to the diagnosis of the standard of the schools of any locality, but also to the study of the causes of their standard, whether high or low, and the remedies suitable to each particular instance.

Although, from what has been mentioned in the foregoing pages, the nature of these laws may be implied, I shall, nevertheless, before proceeding further, state them once more by way of a summary, so that the aim of my future discussions may become perfectly clear. They are three in number:

First. The school system must be absolutely divorced from politics in every sense of the word, in order that the members of the board of education may be free in all of their official acts to do what in their opinion will best serve the interests of the child. In the same proportion as the members of the board allow partizanship or selfishness, of whatever nature, to influence their actions, and particularly in regard to the appointment and discharge of superintendents and teachers, the evils are found to accumulate.

Second. The supervision of the schools must be properly directed and thorough. By properly directed supervision, I understand that form of supervision the principal aim of which is to increase the professional strength of the teachers. The supervision is ideal when the superintendent and his assistants are able educators, who devote their time primarily to educating the teachers in their charge, both by pursuing with them, in teachers' meetings, the study of educational methods and principles, and by aiding them in the class-room in the practical application of the theories discussed at the meetings. Supervision that aims simply to secure results by a periodical examination of classes is productive of as much if not more harm than good, as it is destined to convert both teachers and pupils into automatons.

The third law is implied in the second. It is, namely, that in order that the schools may advance, the teachers must constantly endeavor to grow both in professional and in general intellectual strength. As my remarks will show, by far the most progress has been made in those cities where the teachers themselves are the most earnest students. In whichever light we may regard the matter, it is, after all, the teacher that makes the school. My reasons for laying so much stress on the necessity for securing good school-boards and efficient supervision, have not been because I have lost sight of the fact that the teacher is the most important element, but because I recognize this fact so well. While the teacher makes the school, the superintendent in large part makes the teacher. And as the power to appoint both superintendent and teachers in the vast majority of instances lies in the hands of the board of education, this body is ultimately the strongest factor in making or destroying the schools.

With a knowledge of these principles, the remedies for school evils suggest themselves. Generally speaking, it may be said that one half of the work of placing the schools of any locality upon a healthful foundation has been accomplished when the members of the board of education become endowed with a desire to improve the schools, a desire which, however, must be sufficiently strong to lead them to lay aside all selfishness while legislating for the children intrusted to their care. The remaining half is done when the board appoints a superintendent competent to undertake the task and sufficiently energetic to do all that is required of him, provided, however, that he is given a sufficient amount of independent power to enable him to improve the schools in any manner that may to him seem fit. The board must give to the superintendent the right to select his teachers, retaining in their own hands not more than a veto power, and they must, in addition, give to him an ample number of able assistants. However flagrant the evils in the schools of any city may be, the institutions are not beyond hope. Under a conscientious board and an able staff of superintendents, the striking evils may be in a comparatively small time to a considerable extent eradicated. If parents would but take sufficient interest in the welfare of their children to insist upon securing conscientious boards and able superintendents, the leading educational abuses would soon cease to exist. Until they take an active part in securing such, they must be considered guilty of criminal negligence.

14

THE
EDUCATIONAL
ESTABLISHMENT
SPEAKS

THE THEORY OF AMERICAN EDUCATION AS APPROVED BY
INFLUENTIAL EDUCATORS (1874)   From *A Statement of the Theory of Education in the United States of America as Approved by Many Leading Educators* (Washington, D.C., 1874), pp. 12–16.

The idea of the state and the idea of civil society—the former the idea of the actualization of justice and the latter that of the supply of human wants and necessities through the creation and distribution of wealth—conspire, by general consent, in the production of the American system of public education; and, to its maintenance and support, the property of the community is made to contribute by taxation. Both the preservation of property by the actualization of justice and the increase of property by productive industry are directly conditioned, in a republic, upon the educated intelligence of the people. This is so, especially in that species of incorporeal property of the nature of franchises, such as constitute the basis of those corporate combinations formed for the promotion of manufactures and commerce, the creation of transit-facilities, and the diffusion of information, (patent-rights, charters for railroads, canals, telegraphs, banks of issue, insurance-companies, &c.). These franchises, vested in corporations, incite to the production of wealth to an extraordinary degree, and at the same time make such a demand upon the community for directive intelligence that it may be said that the modern industrial community cannot exist without free popular education carried out in a system of schools ascending from the primary grade to the university. And without a free development of productive industry, enabling the individual to accumulate the wealth necessary for the supply of the necessities of life faster than he consumes them, there is not left the leisure requisite to that cultivation of intelligence needed in the theoretical discussion and comprehension of public affairs; and without such occupation of the individual with public affairs, a democracy could exist only in name.

*   *   *

THE
NEW
EDUCATION

1903

VIII The past and present history of the United States exhibits a process of development comprising three stages:

(a) The settlement of new territory by pioneers and the reduction of the wilderness to an agricultural country.

(b) The rise of commercial towns and the creation of transit-facilities in the new regions.

(c) The development of manufacturing centers and the ascendency of domestic commerce.

In consequence of this constant spectacle of the entire process of founding a civilization and developing it from the rudimentary stages up to the completed type, there is produced a peculiar phase of character in the American people. There is always unlimited opportunity for the individual to build anew his fortunes when disaster has overtaken him in one locality.

As a consequence of the perpetual migration from the older sections of the country to the unoccupied Territories, there are new States in all degrees of formation, and their institutions present earlier phases of realization of the distinctive type than are presented in the mature growth of the system as it exists in

the thickly-settled and older States. Thus States are to be found with little or no provision for education, but they are rudimentary forms of the American State, and are adopting, as rapidly as immigration enables them to do so, the type of educational institutions already defined as the result of the American political and social ideas.

IX The education of the people in schools is a phase of education lying between the earliest period of family-nurture, which is still a concomitant and powerful auxiliary, on the one hand, and the necessary initiation into the specialties of a vocation in practical life on the other. In America, the peculiarities of civil society and the political organization draw the child out of the influence of family-nurture earlier than is common in other countries. The frequent separation of the younger branches of the family from the old stock renders family-influence less powerful in molding character. The consequence of this is the increased importance of the school in an ethical point of view.

X In order to compensate for lack of family-nurture, the school is obliged to lay more stress upon discipline and to make far more prominent the moral phase of education. It is obliged to train the pupil into habits of prompt obedience to his teachers and the practice of self-control in its various forms, in order that he may be prepared for a life wherein there is little police-restraint on the part of the constituted authorities.

XI The school-discipline, in its phase of substitute for the family, uses *corrective* punishment, which presupposes a feeble development of the sense of honor in the child. It is mostly corporal punishment. But in the phase wherein the shcool performs the function of preparing the pupil for the formal government of the state, it uses *retributive* punishment and suspends the pupil from some or all the privileges of the school. In this phase of discipline, a sense of honor is presupposed and strengthened.

XII In commercial cities and towns, the tendency preponderates towards forms of punishment founded on the sense of honor and towards the entire disuse of corporal punishment. This object has been successfully accomplished in New York, Chicago, Syracuse, and some other cities. In the schools of the country, where the agricultural interest prevails, the tendency to the family-form of government is marked.

XIII A further difference between the discipline of city-schools and that of country-schools is founded partly on the fact that the former schools are usually quite large, assembling from three hundred to fifteen hundred pupils in one building, while the latter have commonly less than fifty pupils. In the former, the large numbers admit of good classification; in the latter, classes are quite small, sometimes containing only a single pupil, and the discipline of combination is consequently feebly developed. The commercial tone prevalent in the city tends to develop, in its schools, quick, alert habits and readiness to combine with others in their tasks. Military precision is required in the maneuvering of classes. Great stress is laid upon (1) punctuality, (2) regularity, (3) attention, and (4) silence, as habits necessary through life for successful combination with one's fellow-men in an industrial and commercial civilization.

XIV The course of study is laid down with a view to giving the pupil the readiest and most thorough practical command of those conventionalities of intelligence, those arts and acquirements which are the means of directive power and of further self-education. These preliminary educational accomplishments open at once to the mind of the pupil two opposite directions: *(a)* the immediate mastery over the material world, for the purposes of obtaining food, clothing, and shelter directly; *(b)* the initiation into the means of association with one's fellow-men, the world of humanity.

XV *(a)* The first theoretical study necessary for the mastery over the material world is arithmetic—the quantification of objects as regards numbers.

In American schools, this is looked upon as of so much importance that more time is given to it than to any other study of the course. Its cultivation of the habit of attention and accuracy is especially valued.

After arithmetic follows geography, in a parallel direction, looking towards natural history. Arithmetic is taught from the first entrance into school, while geography is begun as soon as the pupil can read well.

XVI *(b)* The first theoretical study necessary to facilitate combination of man with his fellow-men is reading the printed page. Accordingly, the prevailing custom in American schools is to place a book in the hands of the child when he first enters school and to begin his instruction with teaching him how to read. As soon as he can read, he is able to begin to learn to study books for himself, and thus to acquire stores of knowledge by his own efforts. The art of writing is learned in connection with reading. This culture, in the direction of knowing the feeling, sentiments, and ideas of mankind, is continued throughout the course by a graded series of readers, containing selection of the gems from the literature of the language, both prose and verse. This culture is re-enforced about the fifth year of the course by the study of English grammar, in which, under a thin veil, the pupil learns to discern the categories of the mind and to separate them analytically from modifying surroundings and define them. The common forms of thought and of its expression are thus mastered, and in this way the pupil is to some extent initiated into pure thought and acquires the ability to resolve problems of the material world and of his own life into their radical elements. The study of the history of the United States (and, in most instances, of the national Constitution) carries on this culture by the contemplation of the peculiarities of his nation as exhibited in its historic relations.

XVII The cardinal studies of the "common school" are: (1) reading and writing, (2) grammar, (3) arithmetic, (4) geography; the first two look towards mastery over spiritual combination; the latter two, over material combination. The common school aims to give the pupil the great arts of receiving and communicating intelligence. Drawing and vocal music are taught quite generally and the rudiments of natural science are taught orally in most city-schools. Declamation of oratorical selections is a favorite exercise and is supposed to fit the youth for public and political life. Debating societies are formed for the same purpose.

WILLIAM TORREY HARRIS ON THE VALUE OF THE KINDERGARTEN

(1879)   William Torrey Harris, "The Kindergarten in the Public School System," as quoted in Henry Barnard, ed., *Papers on Froebel's Kindergarten* (Hartford, Conn., 1884), pp. 631, 633, 642.

Kindergartens Prepare for Trades

Here it becomes evident that, if the school is to prepare especially for the arts and trades, it is the kindergarten which is to accomplish the object; for the training of the muscles—if it is to be a training for special skill in manipulation— must be begun in early youth. As age advances, it becomes more difficult to acquire new phases of manual dexterity.

Two weeks' practice of holding objects in his right hand will make the infant, in his first year, right-handed for life. The muscles, yet in a pulpy consistency, are very easily set in any fixed direction. The child trained for one year on Froebel's gifts and occupations will acquire a skillful use of his hands and a habit of accurate measurement of the eye which will be his possession for life.

But the arts and trades are provided for in a still more effective manner by the subsequent gifts. The first group, as we have seen, trains the eye and the sense of touch, and gives a technical acquaintance with solids, and with the elementary operations of arithmetic. The second group frees him from the hard limits which have confined him to the reproduction of forms by mere solids, and enables him to represent by means of light and shade. His activity at each step becomes more purely creative as regards the production of forms, and more rational as regards intellectual comprehension; for he ascends from concrete, particular, tangible objects to abstract general truths and archetypal forms.

*   *   *

Moral Discipline

As regards the claimed transcendence of the system over all others in the way of moral development, I am inclined to grant some degree of superiority to it, but not for intrinsic reasons. It is because the child is then at an age when he is liable to great demoralization at home, and is submitted to a gentle but firm discipline in the kindergarten, that the new education proves of more than ordinary value as a moral discipline. The children of the poor, at the susceptible age of five years, get many lessons on the street that tend to corrupt them. The children of the rich, meeting no wholesome restraint, become self-willed and self-indulgent. The kindergarten may save both classes, and make rational self-control take the place of unrestrained, depraved impulse.

But the kindergarten itself has dangers. The cultivation of self-activity may be excessive, and lead to pertness and conceit. The pupil may get to be irreverent and overbearing—hardened against receiving instruction . . .

THE EDUCATIONAL
ESTABLISHMENT
SPEAKS

Besides the industrial training (through the "gifts and occupations") and the symbolic culture (derived chiefly from the "games"), there is much else, in the kindergarten, which is common to the instruction in the school subsequently, and occupies the same ground. Some disciplines also are much more efficient in the kindergarten, by reason of its peculiar apparatus, than the same are or can be in the common school.

The instruction in manners and polite habits which goes on in all well-conducted kindergartens is of very great value. The child is taught to behave properly at the table, to be clean in his personal habits, to be neat in the arrangement of his apparatus, to practice the etiquette and amenities of polite life. These things are much better provided for in Froebel's system than elsewhere. Moreover, there is a cultivation of imagination and of the inventive power which possesses great significance for the future intellectual growth. The habits of regularity, punctuality, silence, obedience to established rules, self-control, are taught to as great a degree as is desirable for pupils of that age, but not by any means so perfectly as in the ordinary well-conducted primary school. The two kinds of attention that are developed so well in a good school: (1) the attention of each pupil to his own task—so absorbed in it that he is oblivious to the work of the class that is reciting, and (2) the attention of each pupil in the class that is reciting, to the work of pupil reciting—the former being the attention of *industry,* and the latter the attention of *critical observation*—are not developed so well as in the primary school, nor is it to be expected. The freedom from constraint which is essential in the kindergarten, or in any school for pupils of five years of age, allows much interference of each pupil with the work of others, and hence much distraction of attention. It is quite difficult to preserve an exact balance. The teacher of the kindergarten is liable to allow the brisk, strong-willed children to interfere with the others, and occupy their attention too much.

With these suggestions, I leave the subject, believing they are sufficient to justify the directors of our public schools in making the kindergarten a part of our school system. The advantage to the community in utilizing the age from four to six; in training the hand and eye; in developing habits of cleanliness, politeness, self-control, urbanity, industry; in training the mind to understand numbers and geometric forms, to invent combinations of figures and shapes, and to represent them with the pencil—these and other valuable lessons in combination with their fellow-pupils and obedience to the rule of their superiors—above all, the youthful suggestions as to methods of instruction which will come from the kindergarten and penetrate the methods of the other schools—will, I think, ultimately prevail in securing to us the establishment of this beneficent institution in all the city school-systems of our country.

WILLIAM TORREY HARRIS ON THE SCHOOL'S ROLE IN MORAL
EDUCATION (1884)   From William Torrey Harris, "Moral Education in the Common Schools," U.S. Bureau of Education, *Circular of Information*, no. 4 (Washington, D.C., 1888), pp. 81–87, 90–91.

The separation of church and state is an acknowledged principle in our National Government, and its interpretation from generation to generation eliminates with more and more of strictness whatever ceremonies and observances of a religious character still remain attached to secular customs and usages.

Inasmuch as religion, in its definition of what is to be regarded as divine, at the same time furnishes the ultimate and supreme ground of all obligations, it stands in the closest relations to morality, which we may define as the system of duties or obligations that govern the relation of man to himself as individual and as race or social whole.

To the thinking observer nothing can be more obvious than the fact that the institutions of society are created and sustained by the moral activity of man.

The moral training of the young is essential to the preservation of civilization. The so called fabric of society is woven out of moral distinctions and observances. The net-work of habits and usages which makes social combination possible—which enables men to live together as a community—constitutes an ethical system. In that ethical system only is spiritual life possible. Without such a system even the lowest stage of society—that of the mere savage even—could not exist. In proportion to the completeness of development of its ethical system a community rises above barbarism.

It is quite clear that so deep a change in the principle of human government as the separation of church and state involves the most important consequences to the ethical life of our people.

All thoughtful persons look with solicitude on institutions of an educational character in order to discover what means, if any, can remain for moral education after its ecclesiastical foundation has been removed.

It happens quite naturally that some of the best people in the community struggle to retain the ecclesiastical forms and ceremonies in the secular. They find themselves unable to discriminate between the provinces of morality and religion. With them education in morality means education in performing religious rites. But this view certainly does not harmonize with the political conviction of our people. From year to year we see the religious rites and ceremonies set aside in the legislature, the town-meeting, the public assembly, the school. If retained they become empty forms with no appreciable effect.

In this state of affairs we might profitably inquire into the principle which permits institutions to be emancipated from the direct control of the church.

Without entering into this question in its details at the present time, we may remark that the history of Christian civilization shows us a continuous spectacle of the development of institutions into independence. It is a sort of training or nurture of institutions by the church into a degree of maturity in which they come to be able to live and thrive without the support of mere ecclesiastical authority.

But an institution attains its majority only when it has become thoroughly grounded on some fundamental divine principle. The state, for instance, is organized on the principle of justice—the return of each man's deed to himself. On such principle the state may be conducted without fear of collision with the church or other institutions.

The school, too, has certain divine principles which it has borrowed from the church through long centuries of tutelage and perhaps can be conducted by itself without church authority and yet be a positive auxiliary to the church and cause of religion.

The school proposes at first this object, to teach the pupil a knowledge of man and nature—in short, to initiate him into the realm of truth.

Certainly truth is divine, and religion itself is chiefly busied with discovering and interpreting the Divine First Principle of the Universe and his personal relations to men. In so far as truth—real truth, in harmony with the personality of God, and not spurious truth—is taught in the school, it is a positive auxiliary to the church and to religion.

But the intellectual pursuit of truth in the school is conditioned upon a deeper principle. Order is the first law, even of Heaven. The government of human beings in a community is a training for them in the forms of social life. The school must strictly enforce a code of laws. The so-called "discipline" of the school is its primordial condition, and is itself a training in habits essential to life in a social whole, and hence, is itself moral training. Let us study the relation of school-discipline to the development of moral character, and compare its code of duties with the ethical code as a whole.

First let us take an ideal survey of the whole field and see what is desirable before we examine the results of school as actually furnished. One may distinguish moral duties or habits which ought to be taught to youth into three classes:

(a) Mechanical virtues, in which the youth exercises a minimum of moral choice and obeys an external rule prescribed for him. In this, the lowest species of moral discipline, the youth learns self-denial and self-control, and not much besides.

(b) Social duties, those which govern the relation of man to man, and which are the properly called "moral" duties. In this form of moral discipline the youth learns to obey principle rather than the immediate will of another.

(c) Religious duties, or those based on the relation to God as revealed in religion. In these the youth learns the ultimate grounds of obligation and gains both a practical principle for the conduct of life and a theoretic principle on which to base his view of the world. In his religious doctrine man formulates his theory of the origin and destiny of nature and the human race, and at the same time defines his eternal vocation, his fundamental duties. The mere statement of this obvious fact is sufficient to indicate the rank and importance of the religious part of the moral duties.

Turning now to the school, let us take an inventory of its means and appliances for moral education in the line of these several divisions. Let us remember, too, that morality consists in practice rather than in theory and that the school can teach morality only when it trains the will into ethical habits and not when it stops short with inculcating a correct theoretical view of right and wrong, useful as such a view may be.

In the school we note, first, the moral effect of the requirement of implicit obedience; a requirement necessary within the school for its successful administration. The discipline in obedience in its strict form, such as is found in the school-room, has four other applications, which remain valid under all conditions of society:

(a) Obedience towards parents; (b) towards employers, overseers, and supervisors, as regards the details of work; (c) towards the government in its legal constituted authority, civil or military; (d) towards the divine will, howsoever revealed.

In each of these four forms there is and always remains a sphere of greater or less extent, within which implicit obedience is one's duty. In the three first-named this duty is not absolute, but limited; the sphere continually growing narrower with the growth of the individual in wisdom and self-directive power. In the fourth form of obedience to the divine will the individual comes more and more to a personal insight into the necessity of the divine law as revealed in Scripture, in nature, and especially in human life, and through this he is emancipated from the direct personal control of men, even of the wisest and best, and becomes rather a law unto himself. He outgrows mere mechanical obedience, and arrives at a truly moral will in which the law is written on the heart.

Obedience to what is prescribed by authority is obviously a training that fits one for religion, even if religion has no direct part in such training. Hence the school in securing implicit obedience is an auxiliary of the church even when perfectly secular.

The pillars on which school education rest are behavior and scholarship. Deportment, or behavior, comes first as the *sine qua non*. The first requisite of the school is order; each pupil must be taught to conform his behavior to the general standard and repress all that interferes with the function of the school. In the outset, therefore, a whole family of virtues are taught the pupil, and taught him so thoroughly that they become fixed in his character. In the mechanical duties habit is everything, and theory little or nothing. The pupil is taught (a) punctuality; he must be at school in time. Sleep, business, play, indisposition—all must give way to the duty of obedience to this external requirement—to observe the particular moment of time and conform to it.

Punctuality does not end with getting to school, but while in school, it is of equal importance. Combination can not be achieved without it. The pupil must have his lessons ready at the appointed time, must rise from his seat at the tap of the bell, move to line, return; in short, he must go through all the evolutions with this observance of rhythm.

(b) Regularity is the next discipline. Regularity is punctuality reduced to a system. Conformity to the requirements of time in a particular instance is punctuality; made general it becomes regularity.

Combination in school rests on these two virtues. They are the most elementary of the moral code—its alphabet, in short.

This age is often called the age of productive industry—the era of emancipation of man from the drudgery of slavery to his natural wants of food, clothing, and shelter. This emancipation is effected by machinery. Machinery has quadrupled the efficiency of human industry within the past half century. There is one general training especially needed to prepare the generations of men who are to act as directors of machinery and managers of the business that depends upon it—this training is in the habits of punctuality and regularity.

Only by obedience to these abstract external laws of time and place may we achieve a social combination complete enough to free us from thraldom to our physical wants and necessities.

(c) Silence is the third of these semi-mechanical duties. It is the basis for the culture of internality or reflection—the soil in which thought grows. The pupil is therefore taught habits of silence; he learns to restrain his natural animal impulse to prate and chatter. All ascent above his animal nature arises through this ability to hold back the mind from utterance of the immediate impulse. The first impression must be corrected by the second. Combination and generalization are required to reach deep and wide truths, and these depend upon this habit of silence.

This silence in the school-room has a twofold significance—it is necessary in order that there may be no distraction of the attention of others from their work; secondly, it is a direct discipline in the art of combining the diffused and feeble efforts of the pupil himself.

These mechanical duties constitute an elementary training in morals without which it is exceedingly difficult to build any superstructure of moral character whatever.

Moral education, therefore, must begin in merely mechanical obedience and develop gradually out of this stage towards that of individual responsibility.

The higher orders of moral duties fall into two classes—those that relate to the individual himself and those that relate to his fellows.

(a) *Duties to self.*—These are (1) physical, and concern cleanliness, neatness in person and clothing, temperance and moderation in the gratification of the animal appetites and passions.

The school can and does teach cleanliness and neatness, but it has less power over the pupil in regard to temperance. It can teach him self-control and self-sacrifice in the three disciplines already named, punctuality, regularity, and silence, and in so far it may free him from thraldom to the body in other respects. It can and does labor efficiently against obscenity and profanity; that is, immorality in language.

(2) Self-culture. This duty belongs especially to the school. All of its lessons contribute to the pupil's self-culture. By its discipline it gives him control over himself, and ability to combine with his fellow-men; by its instruction it gives him knowledge of the world of nature and man. This duty corresponds nearly to the one named Prudence in ancient ethical systems. The Christian Fathers discuss four cardinal virtues—temperance, prudence, fortitude, and justice. Prudence places the individual above and beyond his present moment, as it were, letting him stand over himself, watching and directing himself. Man is a twofold being, having a particular, special self and a general nature; his ideal self the possibility of perfection. Self-culture stands for the theoretical or intellectual side of this cardinal virtue of prudence, while industry is its practical side.

(3) Industry. This virtue means devotion to one's calling or business. Each one owes it to himself to have some business and to be industrious.

The good school does not tolerate idleness. It has the most efficient means of securing industry from its pupils. Each one has a definite task scrupulously adjusted to his capacity, and he will be held responsible for its performance. Is there any better training yet devised to educate youth into industry and its concomitants of sincerity, earnestness, simplicity, perseverance, patience, faithfulness, and reliability, than the school method of requiring work in definite amounts, at definite times, and of an approved quality?

The pupil has provided for him a business or vocation. By industry and self-sacrifice the pupil is initiated into a third of the cardinal virtues—fortitude.

(b) *Duties to others.*—Duties to self rest on the consciousness of a higher nature in the individual and of the obligation of bringing out and realizing this higher nature. Duties to others recognize this higher ideal nature as something general, and hence as also the true inward self of our fellow-men. This ideal of man we are conscious that we realize only very imperfectly, and yet it is this fact, that we have the possibility of realizing a higher ideal in ourselves, that gives us our value above animals and plants. In our fellow-men we see revelations of this ideal nature that we have not yet realized in ourselves. The experience of each man is a contribution towards our own self-knowledge and vicariously aids us without our being obliged to pay for it in the pain and suffering that the original experience cost. Inasmuch as our ideal can be realized only through this aid from our fellow-men, the virtues that enable us to combine with others and form institutions precede in importance the mechanical virtues.

There are three classes of duties toward others:

(1) Courtesy, including all forms of politeness, good breeding, urbanity, decorum, modesty, respect for public opinion, liberality, magnanimity, etc., described under various names by Aristotle and others after him. The essence of this virtue consists in the resolution to see in others only the ideal of humanity and to ignore any and all defects that may be apparent.

Courtesy in many of its forms is readily taught in the school. Its teaching is often marred by the manner of the teacher, which may be sour and surly, or petulant and fault-finding. The importance of this virtue both to its possessor and to all his fellows demands careful attention on the part of school managers with a view to insure its presence in the school-room.

(2) Justice. This is recognized as the chief in the family of secular virtues. It has several forms or species, as, for example, (a) honesty, fair dealing with others, respect for their rights of person and property and reputation; (b) truth-telling, or honesty in speech—honesty itself being truth-acting. Such names as integrity, uprightness, righteousness, express further distinctions that belong to this staunch virtue.

Justice, while like courtesy in the fact that it looks upon the ideal of the individual, is unlike courtesy in the fact that it looks upon the deed of the individual in a very strict and business-like way, and measures its defects by that high standard. According to the principle of justice, each one receives in proportion to his deeds and not in proportion to his possibilities, wishes, or unrealized aspirations. All individuals are ideally equal in the essence of their humanity; but justice will return upon each the equivalent of his deed only. If it be a crime, justice returns it upon the doer as a limitation of his freedom of person or property.

The school is perhaps more effective in teaching the forms of justice than in teaching those of courtesy. Truth-telling especially receives the full emphasis of all the power of school discipline. Every lesson is an exercise in digging out and closely defining the truth, in extending the realm of clearness and certainty further into the region of ignorance and guesswork. How careful the pupil is compelled to be with his statements in the recitation and how painstaking in his previous preparation!

Justice in discovering the exact performance of each pupil and giving him recognition for it may give place to injustice in case of carelessness on the part of the teacher. Such carelessness may suffer the weeds of lying and deceit to grow up, and it may allow the pupil to gather the fruits of honesty and truth, and thus it may offer a premium for fraud. The school may thus furnish an immoral education, notwithstanding its great opportunities to inculcate this noble virtue of honesty.

The private individual must not be permitted to return the evil deed upon the doer, for that would be revenge, and hence a new crime. All personality and self-interest must be sifted out before justice can be done to the criminal. Hence we have another virtue belonging to this class which is itself an outgrowth of justice—that of respect for law.

(3) Respect for law, as the only means of protecting the innocent and punishing the guilty, is the complement of justice. It looks upon the ideal as realized not in an

individual man, but in an institution represented in the person of an executive officer who is supported with legislative and judicial powers.

WILLIAM TORREY HARRIS ON THE ENDS OF EDUCATION (1885)   From William Torrey Harris, *Compulsory Education In Relation to Crime and Social Morals* (Washington, D.C., 1885), pp. 4–9.

W hat is the training which develops in the child a respect for the social whole, a feeling that society embodies his substantial good,—a feeling of preference for the good of his fellow-man over his own whim or caprice?

Certainly, that training is the training which is given by bringing up the child in the society of others, and causing him to practise perpetually those customs which respect persons and property. A due sense of public opinion, a respect for the ideal standard of right and wrong set up in the community, is the primary requisite.

It is clear that man can live in society and constitute a social whole only so far as individuals are educated out of their natural animal condition, and made to respect social forms more highly than mere animal impulses. Hence, it is clear that society itself rests upon education, in this broad sense of the word.

But what has this to do with school education? Much of the education into a respect for social forms and usages is given by the family, and before the age proper for schooling. Then again, it must be admitted that another part of this education comes later, and is learned in the pursuit of one's vocation in life,—the education that comes from bending one's energies into a special channel for the purpose of earning a living. Another form of education is to be found in the part that one bears in politics, within one's party, or in the exercise of functions conferred by the State, or still farther in the exercise of patriotic feeling. Lastly, there is the Church, which furnishes a form of education most important, because it lays fullest stress on human duty, basing it on divine commands. The Church educates the individual into the sense of his existence as a mere unsubstantial creature when living in neglect of the divine ideal manhood, but as a substantial and eternally blessed life when lived according to the forms prescribed in religion. These forms are forms that respect the welfare of the whole, and measure the conduct of the individual by his preference of that welfare over his own selfish impulses.

The family, the vocation, the State, the Church, are the four great cardinal institutions of education. The school is only a device brought in to re-enforce these substantial institutions; but it is a very important device, notwithstanding its supplementary character. It may re-enforce the family by giving to the youth the command of such conventionalities as reading and writing and moral behavior; or it may re-enforce the vocation by giving instruction in arts and trades or professions; or it may re-enforce the Church as a Sunday-school, giving instruction in religion; the military school or the naval school may re-enforce the education of the State.

Our question deals directly with the education of the school; but we must carefully bear in mind the several educational functions of these institutions, so as not to overestimate the functions of the school or in any way confound its province with what belongs to the great social institutions.

Family education must furnish that indispensable preliminary education in personal habits, such as cleanliness, care of the person and clothing, respectful treatment of elders and superiors, obedience to authority, the sense of shame, religious observances, and the use of the mother tongue. The school must presuppose that these are already taught by the family; but the school must not neglect them, although it does not make them its special aim. The family does more, in fact, than educate the child in those indispensable things just recited. It builds up within the child's mind the structure of his moral character, making for him a second nature of moral habit and custom, whose limits and boundaries he regards as of supreme moment. This second nature, or moral nature, is secured by daily sacrifice; and all forms of education lay stress upon self-sacrifice as the foundation of their disciplines.

This process which we call education is, in short, essentially the shaping of man by habit into an ideal or spiritual type of being,—a realization of what we call human nature in contradistinction to mere animal nature. It is an artificial life, a conventional form of living; but it is far more substantial and divine than the life of the mere animal man. Man as an animal is a savage: as civilized, he is an ethical being, who has set up within himself a system of duties and obligations which he observes at the expense of neglecting the impulses of his merely animal nature.

To what end is all this? Is it not because man, as an individual, wills to combine with his fellow-men in such a way as to avail himself of the united endeavor of all? By the organization of social institutions, he converts a multitude of atomic individuals into a social unity. The individuals do not get lost in this social unity, like the waves of the sea. But the social unity is of that wonderful character that it re-enforces the might of each individual by the might of the whole.

Speaking technically, the individual becomes the species; or, in giving up by self-sacrifice his selfish peculiarities and devoting himself to the service of others, he gains for himself the service of all mankind. The individuals are transmuted into one grand individual, of which each individual is the head, and each individual is also the foot. According to Kant's definition, a living organism is such that every part of it is alike means and end of all the other parts. So, in this social body, every individual human being is alike the means and the end for all others. Hence there is a "Grand Man," as Swedenborgians say.

In the matter of food, clothing, and shelter, the individual toils in his vocation to produce a special product,—something useful to the rest, and demanded in the market of the world. In return for this gift of his day's labor, he is permitted to draw from the market of the world his share of all the productions collected from all climes, brought hither by the commerce of nations. This is a perpetual process of united human endeavor, in which by self-sacrifice the individual re-enforces himself by the race.

So, too, the family, the most embryonic of human institutions,—the family enables the elder to assist the younger, the mature the immature, the well and strong to assist the sick and weak. It equalizes age and bodily condition, re-enforcing each condition by the aid of all others.

The great object, then, of education is the preparation of the individual for a life in institutions, the preparation of each individual for social combination. Education inculcates sacrifice of animal proclivities, in order to secure a higher well-being in the life of the community.

Crime is, therefore, a reaction on the part of the individual against the very object of education. It attacks the necessary forms of social life, and asserts for itself the right to persist in the form of the non-social individual. Society must defend itself, and reduce the rebellious individual to harmony with itself. Inasmuch as the social form is such that the individual who puts it on and becomes a member of the family, the community, or the State, does not act directly for himself, but works for others and accepts the service of others in return for his own deed, so, too, punishment for crime takes on the same form: the criminal is made to receive for his deed an equivalent reflected back from society. As his deed injures society, it is returned upon him by society and injures him. If he attacks his neighbors by personal violence, his deed is made to come back to him by physical constraint or even by violent death on the gallows. If he attacks the property of his fellow-men, he is made to suffer in property, in the possession of personal freedom and the right to the products of his own labor. Thus, society treats the criminal who rebels against it just as though he, the criminal, had intended to do a social deed, and not a selfish one. It is a piece of irony. The State says to the criminal: "Of course, you recognize society, and expect to reap what you sow. You have an undoubted right to possess and enjoy the fruits of your own deeds. I will see that they are returned upon you. Your deed of violence on your neighbor shall therefore return upon you. Whatever you do you shall do to yourself."

Turning now from this view of the general educative character of the institutions of society, and the end and aim of all society to aid the individual by the might of the whole, and from this study of crime, let us define for ourselves the place of the school in education, and try to discover its relation to the prevention of crime.

The school, as we have seen, is a means of education auxiliary to each of the four cardinal institutions; and, as such, the school in all of its forms is ethical and preventive of crime. The ordinary type of school—the so-called "common school"—receives the child from the family at the age of five or six years. It receives him into a social body (for the school is a community), and educates him by "discipline" and "instruction," as they are technically called. By "discipline" is meant the training in behavior, a training of the will, moral training. It consists in imposing upon the child a set of forms of behavior rendered necessary in order to secure concert of action,—such forms as regularity, punctuality, silence, and industry. These are the four cardinal duties of the school pupil. Without them, the school cannot act as a unit, instruction cannot be given in classes, and no good result achieved. We call these duties mechanical duties, but they underlie all higher ethics. Without silence in the school, without self-sacrifice on the part of each pupil, restraining his impulse to prate and chatter and occupy the attention of his fellow-pupils, there could be no work done. Each pupil would interfere with the work of every other pupil; and the result would be chaos or worse,—because anarchy is chaos made active and hostile to heaven's first law.

Order is not only the first celestial law, but it is the first law of all social combination. The school could not possibly undertake a more direct and efficient training of the child for social combination than it does undertake in its four cardinal phases of discipline,—regularity, punctuality, silence, and industry.

Its method of securing these items of discipline may be good, bad, or indifferent, according to the pains it takes to convert external constraint into willing obedience and unconscious habit. The good school unquestionably shows us the constant spectacle of good behavior become or becoming a second nature to the pupils, so that there is a maximum of regularity, punctuality, silence, and industry with a minimum of self-consciousness in regard to it, although there is an insight into the necessity of such conformity to rule, and a conscious conviction in favor of it whenever any untoward occasion brings up the question. Consequently there is a minimum of corporal punishment in the good school. Necessary as it is in dealing with crude depravity, the school must have got far beyond that stage of discipline before it can be called "good."

This training of the will, we observe, is a training of each pupil to behave in such a form of artificial or conventional restraint that he may combine in the best manner with his fellow-pupils, and be in a condition to give to and receive from them school instruction. Is it not clear that, once trained to observe set forms of behavior in the school, it becomes a second nature to observe such forms everywhere, and the individual has solved the problem of life so far as the prevention of crime is concerned?

WILLIAM TORREY HARRIS DESCRIBES THE "FIVE WINDOWS OF THE SOUL" (1898)   From William Torrey Harris, *Psychologic Foundations of Education* (New York, 1898), pp. 321–26.

Psychology of the Course of Study in Schools, Elementary, Secondary, and Higher

§ 208. In the elementary course completed in the first eight years of school life (say from six to fourteen years of age) the pupil has acquired the conventional branches of common English. Reading, writing, arithmetic—the so-called "three R's"—grammar, geography, and United States history, furnish him the necessary disciplines that enable him to take up the rudiments of human experience; they give him a mastery over the technical elements which enter the practical theories of human life.

(*a*) There are five windows of the soul, which open out upon five great divisions of the life of man. Two of these relate to man's comprehension and conquest over Nature, the realm of time and space. Arithmetic furnishes the survey of whatever has the form of time; all series and successions of individuals, all quantitative multiplicity being mastered by the aid of the art of reckoning. Through the geographical window of the soul the survey extends to organic and inorganic Nature. The surface of the earth, its concrete relations to man as his habitat and as the producer of his food, clothing, and shelter, and the means of intercommunication which unite the detached fragments of humanity into one grand man—all these important matters are introduced to the pupil through the study of geography, and spread out as a panorama before the second window of the soul.

(*b*) Three other departments or divisions of human life lie before the view. Human life is revealed in the history—civil, social, and religious—of peoples. The study of the history of one's native country in the elementary school opens the window of the soul which looks out upon the spectacle of the will power of his nation. In the language of a people are revealed the internal logical laws or structural framework of its intellect and the conscious realization of the mind of the race, as they appear in the vocabulary, grammatical laws, or syntax. Grammar opens to the child his view of the inner workings of the mind of the race, and helps him in so far to a comprehension of his own spiritual self. Literature, finally, is the most accessible, as well as the fullest and completest expression of the sentiments, opinions, and convictions of a people; of their ideals, longings, aspirations. The fifth window of the soul looks out upon this revelation of human nature through literature. The study of literature commences with the child's first reader, and continues through his school course, until he learns, by means of the selections from the poets and prose writers in the higher readers, the best and happiest expression for those supreme moments of life felt and described first by men of genius, and left as a rich heritage to all their fellows. Their less gifted brethren may, by the aid of their common mother tongue, participate with them in the enjoyment of their insights.

§ (c) The studies of the school fall naturally into these five co-ordinate groups: first, mathematics and physics; second, biology, including chiefly the plant and the animal; third, literature and art, including chiefly the study of literary works of art; fourth, grammar and the technical and scientific study of language, leading to such branches as logic and psychology; fifth, history and the study of sociological, political, and social institutions. Each one of these groups should be represented in the curriculum of the schools at all times by some topic suited to the age and previous training of the pupil.

209. The first stage of school education is education for culture, and education for the purpose of gaining command of the conventionalities of intelligence. These conventionalities are such arts as reading and writing, the use of figures, technicalities of maps, dictionaries, the art of drawing, and all those semi-mechanical facilities which enable the child to get access to the intellectual conquests of the race. Later on, when the pupil passes out of his elementary studies, which partake more of the nature of practice than of theory, he comes in the secondary school and the college to the study of science and the technique necessary for its preservation and communication. All these things belong to the first stage of school instruction whose aim is culture. On the other hand, post-graduate work and the work of professional schools have not the aim of culture so much as the aim of fitting the person for a special vocation. In the post-graduate work of universities the demand is for original investigation in special fields. In the professional school the student masters the elements of a particular practice, learning its theory and its art.

It is in the first stage, the schools for culture, that these five co-ordinate branches should be represented in a symmetrical manner. On the other hand, a course of university study—that is to say, what is called post-graduate work—and the professional school should be specialized. But specializing should follow a course of study for culture in which the whole of human learning and the whole of the soul has been considered. From the primary school, therefore, on through the academic course of the college there should be symmetry, and the five co-ordinate groups of studies should be represented at each part of the course—at least in each year, although perhaps not throughout each part of the year.

§ 210. All activities of man have a psychological coefficient. There is some special category of the mind employed in each operation. In forming the course of study experience has discovered, one after another, the branches of study needed to open the five windows of the soul. The psychology of education should point out the categories involved in each of these studies, as well as show their objective scope and significance.

*   *   *

(g) School instruction is given to the acquirement of techniques—the technique of reading and writing; of mathematics; of grammar, geography, history, literature, and science in general. One is astonished when he reflects upon it, at first, to see how much is meant by this word *technique*. All products of human reflection are defined and preserved by words used in a technical sense. The words are taken out of their colloquial sense, which is a loose one, except when employed as slang; for slang is a spontaneous effort in popular speech to form technical terms. The technical or conventional use of signs and symbols enables us to write words and to record mathematical calculations; the technical use of words enables us to express clearly and definitely the ideas and relations of all science. Outside of technique all is vague hearsay. The fancy pours into the words it hears such meanings as its feelings prompt. Instead of science there is superstition. The school deals with technique in this broad sense of the word. The mastery of this technique of reading, writing, arithmetic, geography, and history lifts the pupil on to a plane of freedom and self-help hitherto not known to him. He can now by his own effort master for himself the wisdom of the race. By the aid of such instruments as the family education has given him he can not master that wisdom, but only pick up a few of its results, such as the customs of his community preserve. By the process of hearsay and oral inquiry it would take the individual a lifetime to acquire what he can get in six months by aid of the instruments which the school places in his hands; for the school gives the youth the tools of thought.

WILLIAM TORREY HARRIS DEFENDS THE RECITATION IN ELEMENTARY EDUCATION (1900)   From William Torrey Harris, "Elementary Education," as quoted in Nicholas Murray Butler, ed., *Education in the United States* (Albany, 1900), vol. I, pp. 85–91.

With the growth from the rural to the urban condition of population the method of "individual instruction," as it is called, giving it a fine name, has been supplanted by class instruction, which prevails in village and city schools. The individual did not get much instruction under the old plan, for the simple reason that his teacher had only five or ten minutes to examine him on his daily work. In the properly graded school each teacher has two classes, and hears one recite while the other learns a new lesson. Each class is composed of twenty to thirty pupils of nearly the same qualifications as regards the degree of progress made in their studies. The teacher has thirty minutes for a recitation (or "lesson" as called in England), and can go into the merits of the subject and discuss the real thoughts that it involves. The meaning of the words in the book is probed, and the pupil made to explain it in his own language. But besides this all pupils learn more by a class recitation than by an individual recitation. For in the class each can see the lesson reflected in the minds of his fellow-pupils, and understand his teacher's views much better when drawn out in the form of a running commentary on the mistakes of the duller or more indolent pupils. The dull ones are encouraged and awakened to effort by finding themselves able to see the errors and absurdities of fellow-pupils. For no two minds take precisely the same view of a text-book exposition of a topic. One child is impressed by one phase of it, and another by a different phase. In the class recitation each one has his crude and one-sided views corrected more or less by his fellows, some of whom have a better comprehension of this point, and some of that point, in the lesson. He, himself, has some glimpses of the subject that are more adequate than those of his fellows.

The possibilities of a class recitation are, therefore, very great for efficient instruction in the hands of a teacher who understands his business. For he can marshal the crude notions of the members of the class one after another, and turn on them the light of all the critical acumen of the class as a whole, supplemented by his own knowledge and experience. From beginning to end, for thirty minutes, the class recitation is a vigorous training in critical alertness. The pupil afterwards commences the preparation of his next lesson from the book with what are called new "apperceptive" powers, for he finds himself noticing and comprehending many statements and a still greater number of implications of meaning in his lesson that before had not been seen or even suspected. He is armed with a better power of analysis, and can "apperceive," or recognize and identify, more of the items of information, and especially more of the thoughts and reflections, than he was able to see before the discussions that took place in the recitation. He has in a sense gained the points of view of fellow-pupils and teacher, in addition to his own.

It is presupposed that the chief work of the pupil in school is the mastery of text-books containing systematic treatises giving the elements of branches of learning taught in the schools. For in the United States more than in any other country text-book instruction has predominated over oral instruction, its method in this respect being nearly the opposite of the method in vogue in the elementary schools of Germany. The evil of memorizing words without understanding their meaning or verifying the statements made in the text-book is incident to this method and is perhaps the most widely prevalent defect in teaching to be found in the schools of the United States. It is condemned universally, but, nevertheless, practiced. The oral method of Germany escapes this evil almost entirely, but it encounters another evil. The pupil taught by the oral method exclusively is apt to lack power to master the printed page and get out of it the full meaning; he needs the teacher's aid to explain the technical phrases and careful definitions. The American method of text-book instruction throws the child upon the printed page and holds him responsible for its mastery. Hence even in the worst forms of verbal memorizing there is perforce acquired a familiarity with language as it appears to the eye in printed form which gradually becomes more useful for scholarly purposes than the knowledge of speech addressed to the ear. This is the case in all technical, or scientific language, and in all poetry and literary prose; the new words or new shades of meaning require the mind to pause and reflect. This can be done in reading but not in listening to an oral delivery.

In the United States the citizen must learn to help himself in this matter of gaining information, and for this reason he must use his school time to acquire the art of digging knowledge out of books. Hence we may say that a deep instinct or an unconscious need has forced American schools into an excessive use of the text-book method.

In the hands of a trained teacher the good of the method is obtained and the evil avoided. The pupil is taught to assume a critical attitude towards the statements of the book and to test and verify them, or else disprove them by appeal to other authorities, or to actual experiments.

This ideal hovers before all teachers, even the poorest, but it is realized only by the best class of teachers found in the schools of the United States,—a class that is already large and is constantly increasing, thanks to the analytic methods taught in the normal schools. Text-book memorizing is giving place to the method of critical investigation.

This review of methods suggests a good definition of school instruction. It is the process of re-enforcing the sense-perception of the individual pupil by adding the experience of the race as preserved in books, and it is more especially the strengthening of his powers of thought and insight by adding to his own reflections the points of view and the critical observations of books interpreted by his teachers and fellow-pupils.

In the graded school the pupil is held responsible for his work in a way that is impossible in the rural school of sparsely-settled districts. Hence the method of investigation, as above described, is found in the city schools rather than in the rural schools. Where each pupil forms a class by himself, there is too little time for the teacher to ascertain the character of the pupil's understanding of his book. Even if he sees that there has been a step missed somewhere by the child in learning his lesson, he cannot take time to determine precisely what it is. Where the ungraded school makes some attempt at classification of pupils it is obliged to unite into one class say of arithmetic, grammar, or geography, pupils of very different degrees of progress. The consequence is that the most advanced pupils have not enough work assigned them, being held back to the standard of the average. They must "mark time" (or go through the motions of walking without advancing a step) while the rest are coming up. The least advanced find the average lesson rather too much for them, and become discouraged after trying in vain to keep step with their better prepared fellow-pupils. This condition of affairs is to be found in many rural districts even of those states where the advantages of classification are seen and appreciated in city schools, and an effort is in progress to extend those advantages to the rural schools. But the remedy has been, in many cases, worse than the disease. For it has resulted that classification gets in the way of self-help which the bright pupil is capable of, and the best scholars "mark time" listlessly, while the poorest get discouraged, and only the average pupils gain something.

It must be admitted, too, that in many village schools just adopting the system of grading, this evil of holding back the bright pupils and of over-pressure on the dull ones exists, and furnishes just occasion for the criticism which is made against the so-called "machine" character of the American public school. The school that permits such poor classification, or that does not keep up a continual process of readjusting the classification by promoting pupils from lower classes to those above them, certainly has no claim to be ranked with schools organized on a modern ideal.

I have dwelt on this somewhat technical matter because of its importance in understanding the most noteworthy improvements in progress in the schools of the United States. Briefly, the population is rapidly becoming urban, the schools are becoming "graded," the pupils of the lowest year's work placed under one teacher, and those of the next degree of advancement under a second teacher; perhaps from eight to twenty teachers in the same building, thus forming a "union school," as it is called in some sections. Here there is division of labor on the part of teachers, one taking only classes just beginning to learn to read and write, another taking the pupils in a higher grade. The inevitable consequence of such division of labor is increase of skill. The teacher comes to know just what to do in a given case of obstructed progress—just what minute steps of work to introduce—just what thin wedges to lift the pupil over the threshold that holds back the feeble intellect from entering a new and higher degree of human learning.

It will be asked: What proportion of the teachers of cities and villages habitually use this higher method in conducting recitations. According to a careful estimate, at least one-half of them may reasonably claim to have some skill in its use; of the one-half in the elementary schools who use it perhaps two-fifths conduct all their recitations so as to make the work of their pupils help each individual in correcting defects of observation and critical alertness. Perhaps the other three-fifths use the method in teaching some branches, but cling to the old memoriter system for the rest. It may be claimed for graduates of normal schools that a large majority follow the better method.

The complaint urged against the machine character of the modern school has been mentioned. I suppose that this complaint is made quite as often against good schools as against poor ones. But the critical-probing method of conducting a recitation is certainly not machine-like in its effects. It arouses in the most powerful manner the activity of the pupil to think and observe for himself. Machine-like schools do not follow this critical method, but are content with the memoriter system, that prescribes so many pages of the book to be learned verbally, but does not inquire into the pupil's understanding, or "apperception," as the Herbartians call it. It is admitted that about 50 per cent of the teachers actually teaching in the schools of villages and cities use this poor method. But it is certain that their proportion in the corps of teachers is diminishing, thanks to the two causes already alluded to: first, the multiplication of professional schools for the training of teachers; and second, the employment of educational experts as supervisors of schools.

The rural schools, which in the United States enroll one-half of the entire number of school children, certainly lack good class teaching, even when they are so fortunate as to obtain professionally educated teachers, and not five per cent of such schools in the land succeed in procuring better services than the "makeshift" teacher can give. The worst that can be said of these poorly taught schools is that the pupils are either left to help themselves to knowledge by reading their books under the plan of individual instruction, or, in the attempt at classification and grading, the average pupils learn something, while the bright pupils become listless and indolent for want of tasks commensurate with their strength and the backward pupils lose their courage for their want of ability to keep step. Even under these circumstances the great good is accomplished that all the pupils learn the rudiments of reading, writing and arithmetic, and all are made able to become readers of the newspapers, the magazines, and finally of books.

NICHOLAS MURRAY BUTLER ON THE FUNCTION OF THE SECONDARY SCHOOL (1890)   From "An Address Delivered Before the Schoolmasters' Association of New York and Vicinity, March 8, 1890," in *The Meaning of Education and Other Essays and Addresses* (New York, 1898), pp. 154–57, 160–64.

In the past the secondary school in this country has been very often dwarfed in importance and deprived of its proper spontaneity and individuality, because it has permitted itself to settle down to the routine task of preparing pupils for entrance examination to college, fixed and conducted by the college authorities.

Whatever that entrance examination demanded, and in some cases just a trifle more, has been taught; whatever such examination did not call for, no matter how important or valuable it might be for a boy's education, has not been taught. The secondary school has been too largely dominated by the college; and in few cases has that domination been other than unfortunate. As notable instances of the contrary effect may be mentioned the stimulating influence of the more recent regulations regarding entrance examinations adopted by Harvard College, particularly in geometry and in physics, and the novel unity and thoroughness imparted to the instruction in English in the secondary schools by the action of the colleges in uniting with the schools in deciding upon a uniform scheme of requirements for entrance in that subject.

It is neither proper nor dignified for the secondary schools to continue in this condition of dependence upon college entrance examinations. They should be independent and self-centred. By a careful study of the history and principles of education, coupled with the teachings of their own large experience, they should seek to devise that course of study and those methods of instruction that are best suited to the mental, moral, and physical development and culture of the boys and girls committed to their care. Nor need it be feared that in so doing they will interfere in any way with the preparation of their pupils for college work. For in education it is profoundly true that that which is intrinsically the best in any particular stage of development, is also the best preparation for that which comes after.

If the American boy is to obtain his baccalaureate degree at the age of twenty or twenty-one (which is considerably more than a year later than the French boys leave the lycée and the Prussian boys the gymnasium), he must be ready to enter college not later than seventeen; and this can be managed while actually providing for the secondary school a more comprehensive curriculum than at present obtains. Before discussing in detail the composition of such a curriculum, one or two preliminary considerations must be mentioned. They may, however, be dismissed very briefly, since they have so recently been treated with the highest authority by President Eliot. The first of these has to do with the length of the school day and that of the vacations. The former should never be less than five full hours of study and school discipline; the tendency to shorten it any further is irrational and should be checked. A programme arranged on sound educational principles can occupy five hours a day easily enough without in any way impairing the pupil's health or lessening his interest, unless the teacher is peculiarly lacking in mental equipment and professional qualifications. The vacations are now unduly long, and seem to be yielding to a certain strong social pressure to make them even longer.

*　　*　　*

Assuming that more competent teachers are at hand and that a school year of thirty-six weeks of twenty-five hours each is agreed upon, what should be the aim of the instruction in the secondary school and with what curriculum should it endeavor to accomplish it? It should be the aim of the secondary school, I take it, by instruction and discipline to lay the foundation for that cultivation and inspiration that mark the truly educated man. In endeavoring to attain this ideal, the secondary school must not lose sight of the fact that it is educating boys who are to assume the duties and responsibilities of citizenship, and who must, in all probability, pursue a specific calling for the purpose of gaining a livelihood. The fact that the secondary school has also a selective function to perform is often overlooked. Yet this is most important. Secondary school pupils are adolescents, and their tastes and capacities are rapidly forming and finding expression. To afford opportunity for these to develop, and to encourage them to develop along the best and most effective lines, is an obvious duty of the secondary school. Because they are not selective, many secondary courses of study are very ineffective.

To prepare a course of study which shall keep all these points in mind, and at the same time afford the developing intellect of the pupil that exercise of which it is capable, is not an easy task. Indeed, it presents some problems which but a little while ago seemed almost impossible of solution. But patience, wider experience, and a careful study of the surrounding conditions have lessened the difficulties. The chief of these is perhaps that created by the rapid development and present importance of scientific and technical schools. These institutions represent a real and significant movement in modern civilization. They have complicated the question of a curriculum for secondary schools by demanding a preparation quite different from that required for entrance to the average American college. That the problem thus raised belongs to the field of secondary education in general and is not due to conditions prevailing in any one country alone, is shown by the fact that England, Germany, and France have all been brought face to face with it as we have been. In each of these countries much progress towards its solution has been made. In England the so-called "modern side" has been added to the traditional classical course. In France the lycée has its *cours spécial* in which mathematics and the sciences replace Latin and Greek. In Germany the well-established real-gymnasium and real-schule are every year justifying their right to exist on an equal plane with the gymnasium itself. A specially interesting movement in this connection is one in Germany which has for some time past been calling for the establishment of an *Einheitsschule*, in which the main features both of gymnasium and real-schule are to be combined.

The course of study that I would suggest for the typical American secondary school is one in which nine elements are always represented: namely, the mother-tongue, geography and history, natural science, mathematics, Latin, Greek, French and German, drawing and constructive work (manual training), and physical training. It combines some features of the English "modern side" with some of those of the French *cours spécial,* and is not unlike what German students of education have in mind under the name of *Einheitsschule*. It involves beginning the study of one foreign language at ten or eleven years of age, and the elements of algebra and of plane geometry shortly afterward. Ample choice would be permitted to students, provided only that not more than five so-called "book" subjects were carried on at once, that no two new languages were begun at the same time, and that English, geography and history, and natural science were always represented. Pupils of a different temperament, of different points of view, and with different purposes in life would be guided to express and to satisfy themselves to the fullest extent possible. The ability to read intelligently, to write legibly, and to perform understandingly and correctly with integers the four fundamental operations of arithmetic, must be insisted upon at ten years of age.

The growing practice of postponing even this modicum of knowledge until after the tenth year is to be emphatically discouraged. Attention has recently been called to the fact that one of the best-known academies in the United States requires for admission only some knowledge of common school arithmetic, writing, spelling, and the elements of English grammar, and that the average age of pupils on entering is sixteen and one-half years. At this age the French boy is reading Cicero, Virgil, and

Horace, Sophocles and Plato, Shakspere and Tennyson, as well as studying general history, solid geometry, and chemistry. His German contemporary is similarly advanced. It is very evident that at this point there is a tremendous waste in our educational system. It must be remedied and remedied speedily, if our higher education is not to be discredited altogether.

NICHOLAS MURRAY BUTLER DISCUSSES THE "MEANING OF EDUCATION" (1896) From "An Address Delivered Before the Liberal Club of Buffalo, New York, Nov. 19, 1896," in *The Meaning of Education and other Essays and Addresses* (New York, 1898), pp. 16–17, 31–32.

After the child comes into the enjoyment of his physical inheritance, he must be led by the family, the school, and the state into his intellectual or spiritual inheritance. The moment that fact is stated in those terms it becomes absolutely impossible for us ever again to identify education with mere instruction. It becomes absolutely impossible for us any longer to identify education with mere acquisition of learning; and we begin to look upon it as really the vestibule of the highest and the richest type of living. It was the great thought of Plato, that inspired every word he ever wrote and that constitutes an important portion of his legacy to future ages, that life and philosophy are identical; but he used the word philosophy in a sense which was familiar to him and to his time, and for which we might very well substitute, under some of its phases at least, the word education. Life and education are identical, because the period to which we traditionally confine the latter term is merely the period of more formal, definite, determinate adjustment; yet, just so long as life lasts and our impressionability and plasticity remain, we are always adapting ourselves to this environment, gaining power, like Antaeus of old, each time we touch the Mother Earth from which civilization springs.

If education cannot be identified with mere instruction, what is it? What does the term mean? I answer, it must mean a gradual adjustment to the spiritual possessions of the race. Those possessions may be variously classified, but they certainly are at least fivefold. The child is entitled to his scientific inheritance, to his literary inheritance, to his aesthetic inheritance, to his institutional inheritance, and to his religious inheritance. Without them he cannot become a truly educated or a cultivated man.

*　　*　　*

The period of infancy is to be used by civilized men for adaptation along these five lines, in order to introduce the child to his intellectual and spiritual inheritance, just as the shorter period of infancy in the lower animals is used to develop, to adjust, and to co-ordinate those physical actions which constitute the higher instincts, and which require the larger, the more deeply furrowed, and the more complex brain.

That, as it seems to me, is the lesson of biology, of physiology, and of psychology, on the basis of the theory of evolution, regarding the meaning and the place of education in modern life. It gives us a conception of education which must, I am quite sure, raise it above the mechanical, the routine, the purely artificial. We see that this period of preparation is not a period of haphazard action, a period of possible neglect, or a period when time may be frittered away and lost, but that every moment of adjustment is precious and that every new adaptation and correlation is an enrichment not only of the life of the individual but of the life of the race. For now we all understand perfectly well that this long period of infancy and adaptation, this period of plasticity and education, is that which makes progress possible. That is why it is entirely correct to say that each generation is the trustee of civilization. Each generation owes it to itself and to its posterity to protect its culture, to enrich it and to transmit it. The institution that mankind has worked out for that purpose is the institution known as education. When a child has entered into this inheritance, first physical, then scientific, literary, aesthetic, institutional, and religious, then we use the word culture to signify the state that has been attained.

CHARLES W. ELIOT ADVOCATES SHORTENING AND ENRICHING THE GRAMMAR SCHOOL COURSE OF STUDY (1892) From "Shortening and Enriching the Grammar School Course," National Education Association, *Journal of Addresses and Proceedings* (Washington, D.C., 1892), pp. 617–25.

The subject assigned to me is, shortening and enriching the grammar school course.

I. We may properly use the term shortening in either of two senses. In the first place, the number of grades may be reduced from ten to nine and from nine to eight, so that the combined primary and grammar school periods shall end at fourteen or thirteen; or, secondly, the studies of the present course may be reduced in volume or in variety, or in both, so that there shall be room for the introduction of new subjects. I observe that both kinds of shortening have actually been begun in various towns and cities, and I believe that both are desirable, if not universally, at least, in most localities. The argument for the first kind of shortening is a compact and convincing one; averaging the rates of progress of bright children with those of dull children being the great curse of a graded school, it is safer to make the regular programme for eight grades, and lengthen it for the exceptionally slow pupils, than to make it for ten grades and shorten it for the exceptionally quick. In other words, since holding back the capable children is a much greater educational injustice than hurrying the incapable, the programme should be so constructed as to give all possible chances of avoiding the greater evil. Without altering the nominal length of the programme in years, a great shortening of the course can be effected for part of the children, simply by permitting the capable ones to do two years' work in one. I heard a grammar school master testifying a few days ago, in a teacher's meeting, that nearly one-quarter of the pupils in his school (which numbers 650 children) were successfully accomplishing this double task. Such a statement opens a cheerful vista for one who desires to see the grammar school course both shortened and enriched.

With no more words about the first kind of shortening, I turn to the second kind, namely, the desirable reductions in the volume and variety of the present studies. The first great reduction should, I believe, be made in arithmetic. I find that it is very common in programmes of the grades to allot to arithmetic from one-eighth to one-sixth of the whole school-time for nine or ten years. In many towns and cities two arithmetics are used during these years; a small one of perhaps one hundred pages, followed by a larger one of two or three hundred pages. Now the small book ordinarily contains all the arithmetic that anybody needs to know; indeed, much more than most of us ever use. Before a body of experts like this it were superfluous to enlarge on this proposition. On grounds of utility, geometry and physics have stronger claims than any part of arithmetic beyond the elements, and for mental training they are also to be preferred. By the contraction of arithmetic, room is made for algebra and geometry. In a few schools these subjects have already been introduced, with or without mention in the official programmes, and they have proved to be interesting and intelligible to American children of from eleven to thirteen years of age, just as they are to European children. Moreover, the attainments of the pupils in arithmetic are not diminished by the introduction of the new studies, but rather increased. The algebraic way of solving a problem is often more intelligible than the arithmetical, and mensuration is easier when founded on a good knowledge of elementary geometry than it is in the lack of that foundation. The three subjects together are vastly more interesting than arithmetic alone pursued through nine consecutive years. Secondly, language studies, including reading, writing, spelling, grammar and literature, occupy from one-third to two-fifths of most grades' programmes. There is ample room here for the introduction of the optional study of a foreign language, ancient or modern, at the fourth or fifth grade. Here it is to be observed that nothing will be lost to English by the introduction of a foreign language. In many schools the subject of grammar still fills too large a place on the programme, although great improvement has taken place in the treatment of this abstruse subject, which is so unsuitable for children. In the Beginner's Latin Book, by Messrs. Collar & Grant, I noticed, five years ago, an excellent description of the amount of knowledge of English grammar needed by a pupil of ten or twelve years of age about to begin Latin. Of course, the pupil who is not to begin Latin needs no more. All the grammar which the learner needed to know before beginning Latin was "the names and functions of the parts of speech in English, and the meanings of the common grammatical terms, such as subject and predicate, case, tense, voice, declension, conjunction, etc." Manuals have now been prepared in considerable variety for imparting this limited amount of grammatical information by examples and practice rather than by rules and precepts, so that the greater part of the time formerly spent on English grammar can now be saved for more profitable uses. Thirdly, geography is now taught chiefly as a memory study from books and flat atlases, and much time is given to committing to memory masses of facts which cannot be retained, and which are of little value if retained. By grouping physical geography with natural history, and political geography with history, and by providing proper apparatus for teaching geography, time can be saved, and yet a place made for much new and interesting geographical instruction. Fourthly, a small saving of time can be made for useful subjects by striking out the bookkeeping, which, in many towns and cities, is found in the last grade. This subject is doubtless included in the grammar school programme, because it is supposed to be of practical value; but I believe it to be the most useless subject in the entire programme, for the reason that the book-keeping taught is a kind of book-keeping never found in any real business establishment. Every large business has in these days its own forms of accounting and book-keeping, which are, for the most part, peculiar to itself. Almost every large firm or corporation has its own method, with printed headings, schedules, bill-heads, invoices, and duplicating order-books, adapted to its own business, and intended to simplify its accounts and reduce to lowest terms the amount of writing necessary to keep them. What a boy or girl can learn at school which will be useful in after-life in keeping books or accounts for any real business is a good hand-writing, and accuracy in adding, subtracting, multiplying and dividing small numbers. It is a positive injury to a boy to give him the impression that he knows something about bookkeeping, when he has only learned an unreal system which he will never find used in any actual business. At best, book-keeping is not a science, but only an art based on conventions. As trade and industry have been differentiated in the modern world, book-keeping has been differentiated also, and it is, of course, impossible to teach in school the infinite diversities of practice.

II. I have thus indicated in the briefest manner the reductions which may be conveniently made in some of the present subjects in order to effect a shortening of the present grammar school programme. My next topic is diversifying and enriching it. The most complete statement of the new subjects proposed for the grammar school programme is that made by the Association of Colleges in New England at their meeting at Brown University last November. That association then invited the attention of the public to certain changes in the grammar school programme which it recommended for gradual adoption. These changes are five in number:—The first is the introduction of elementary natural history into the earlier years of the programme, to be taught by demonstrations and practical exercises rather than from books. The term natural history was doubtless intended to include botany, zoology, geology and physical geography. Some room for these subjects is already made in most grammar school programmes, and the recommendation of the association refers as much to methods of teaching as to time allotted to the subject. The association recommends that the teaching be demonstrative, and that adequate apparatus be provided for teaching these subjects. There is a lamentable lack of the proper apparatus for teaching geography in the public schools. Indeed, in many schools there is no proper apparatus for teaching geography, or any other natural history subject, to young children. Natural science apparatus has been provided in some exceptional high schools; but as a rule grammar schools are still destitute in this important respect.

The second recommendation is the introduction of elementary physics into the later years of the programme, to be taught by the laboratory method, and to include exact weighing and measuring by the pupils themselves.

The third and fourth recommendations cover the introduction of algebra and geometry at the age of twelve or thirteen.

The fifth is the offering of opportunity to study French or German or Latin, or any two of these languages, from and after the age of ten.

III. Such are in brief the proposals for shortening and enriching the grammar school course. I want to use the rest of the time allotted to me for discussing the objections to these various changes.

The first objection I take up is the objection to a reduction in the time devoted to arithmetic. Many teachers are shocked at the bare idea of reducing the time given to arithmetic, because they believe that arithmetic affords a peculiarly valuable training, first, in reasoning, and secondly, in precision of thought and accuracy of work. They perceive that the greater part of the school programme calls only for memorizing power, and they think that arithmetic develops reasoning power. The fact is, however, that mathematical reasoning is a peculiar form of logic which has very little application to common life, and no application at all in those great fields of human activity where perfect demonstration is not to be obtained. As a rule, neither the biological nor the moral sciences can make use of mathematical reasoning. Moreover, so far as mathematical reasoning is itself concerned, variety of subject is very useful to the pupils. The substitution of algebra and geometry for part of the arithmetic is a clear gain to the pupil so far as acquaintance with the logic of mathematics goes. Again, practice in thinking with accuracy and working with demonstrable precision can be obtained in algebra, geometry and physics just as well as in arithmetic. It is quite unnecessary to adhere to the lowest and least interesting of these exact subjects in order to secure adequate practice in precision of thought and work.

The second objection is that there are children in the grammar schools who are incapable of pursuing these new subjects. Assuming that this allegation is true of some children, I have to remark, first, that we shall not know till we have tried what proportion of children are incapable of pursuing algebra, geometry, physics, and some foreign language by the time they are fourteen years of age. It is a curious fact that we Americans habitually underestimate the capacity of pupils at almost every stage of education from the primary school through the university; the expectation of attainment for the American child, or for the American college student, is much lower than the expectation of attainment for the European. This error has been very grave in its effects on American education all along the line from the primary school through the university, and till within twenty years the effects were nowhere worse than at the college grade. It seems to me probable that the proportion of grammar school children incapable of pursuing geometry, algebra and a foreign language would turn out to be much smaller than we now imagine; but though this proportion should be large, it would not justify the exclusion of all the capable children from opportunities by which they could profit. At the worst this objection can only go to show that it will be necessary to adopt in the grammar schools a flexible instead of a rigid system—some selection or choice of studies instead of a uniform requirement. Those children who are competent to study a foreign language should certainly have the opportunity of doing so at the proper age, that is, not later than ten or eleven years, and those who are competent to begin geometry at twelve and algebra at thirteen should have the chance. If experience shall prove that a considerable proportion of grammar school children are incapable of pursuing the higher studies, that fact will only show that the selection of appropriate studies for children by their teachers should be adopted as a policy by the public grammar school. To discriminate between pupils of different capacity, to select the competent for suitable instruction, and to advance each pupil with appropriate rapidity, will ultimately become, I believe, the most important functions of the public school administrator—those functions in which he or she will be most serviceable to families and to the state.

Another objection to the changes proposed often takes this form—they are said to be aristocratic in tendency. The democratic theory—it is said—implies equality among the children, uniformity of programme, uniform tests for promotion, and no divisions in the same school room according to capacity or merit. I need not say to this audience that these conceptions of true democracy in schools are fallacious and ruinous. Democratic society does not undertake to fly in the face of nature by asserting that all children are equal in capacity, or that all children are alike and should be treated alike. Everybody knows that children are infinitely diverse; that children in the same family even are apt to be very different in disposition, temperament and mental power. Every child is a unique personality. It follows, of course, that uniform programmes and uniform methods of instruction, applied simultaneously to large numbers of children, must be unwise and injurious—an evil always to be struggled against and reformed, so far as the material resources of democratic society will permit. It is for the interest of society, as well as of the individual, that every individual child's peculiar gifts and powers should be developed and trained to the highest degree. Hence, in the public schools of a democracy the aim should be to give the utmost possible amount of individual instruction, to grade according to capacity just as far as the number of teachers and their strength and skill will permit, and to promote pupils not by battalions, but in the most irregular and individual way possible. A few days ago I heard an assistant superintendent in an important city declare that many grammar school teachers in his city objected to any division among the fifty or more pupils in each room, any division, that is, according to the attainments and powers of the individual pupils. They wanted all the pupils in a given room to be in one grade, to move together like soldiers on parade, and to arrive at examination-day having all performed precisely the same tasks, and made the same progress in the same subjects. If that were a true portrait of the city graded school, it would be safe to predict that the urban public school would before long become nothing but a charity-school for the children of the dependent classes. Intelligent Americans will not subject their children to such a discipline, when they once understand what it means. The country district school, in which among forty or fifty pupils there are always ten or a dozen distinct classes at different stages and advancing at different rates of progress, would remain as the only promising type of the free school. Not only is it no serious objection to the new proposals that they must diminish uniformity in schools—it is their strongest recommendation.

THE REPORT OF THE COMMITTEE OF TEN ON SECONDARY-SCHOOL STUDIES (1893)   From *Report of the Committee of Ten on Secondary School Studies,* as quoted in U.S. Department of Education, *Report of the Commissioner of Education for the Year 1892–1893* (Washington. D.C., 1895), vol. II. pp. 1415–17, 1420, 1422–24, 1438–46.

Report of the Committee of Ten on Secondary School Studies to the National Council of Education

The Committee of Ten appointed at the meeting of the National Educational Association at Saratoga on the 9th of July, 1892, have the honor to present the following report:—

At the meeting of the National Council of Education in 1891, a Committee EDUCATION appointed at a previous meeting made a valuable report through their Chairman, IN THE Mr. James H. Baker, then Principal of the Denver High School, on the general UNITED STATES subject of uniformity in school programmes and in requirements for admission to college. The Committee was continued, and was authorized to procure a Confer- 1930 ence on the subject of uniformity during the meeting of the National Council in

1892, the Conference to consist of representatives of leading colleges and secondary schools in different parts of the country. This Conference was duly summoned, and held meetings at Saratoga on July 7th, 8th, and 9th, 1892. There were present between twenty and thirty delegates. Their discussions took a wide range, but resulted in the following specific recommendations, which the Conference sent to the National Council of Education then in session.

1. That it is expedient to hold a conference of school and college teachers of each principal subject which enters into the programmes of secondary schools in the United States and into the requirements for admission to college—as, for example, of Latin, of geometry, or of American history—each conference to consider the proper limits of its subject, the best methods of instruction, the most desirable allotment of time for the subject, and the best methods of testing the pupils' attainments therein, and each conference to represent fairly the different parts of the country.

2. That a Committee be appointed with authority to select the members of these conferences and to arrange their meetings, the results of all the conferences to be reported to this Committee for such action as it may deem appropriate, and to form the basis of a report to be presented to the Council by this Committee.

3. That this Committee consists of the following gentlemen:

CHARLES W. ELIOT, President of Harvard University, Cambridge, Mass., *Chairman.*

WILLIAM T. HARRIS, Commissioner of Education, Washington, D.C.

JAMES B. ANGELL, President of the University of Michigan, Ann Arbor, Mich.

JOHN TETLOW, Head Master of the Girls' High School and the Girls' Latin School, Boston, Mass.

JAMES M. TAYLOR, President of Vassar College, Poughkeepsie, N.Y.

OSCAR D. ROBINSON, Principal of the High School, Albany, N.Y.

JAMES H. BAKER, President of the University of Colorado, Boulder, Colo.

RICHARD H. JESSE, President of the University of Missouri, Columbia, Mo.

JAMES C. MACKENZIE, Head Master of the Lawrenceville School, Lawrenceville, N.J.

HENRY C. KING, Professor in Oberlin College, Oberlin, Ohio.

These recommendations of the Conference were adopted by the National Council of Education on the 9th of July; and the Council communicated the recommendations to the Directors of the National Educational Association, with the further recommendation that an appropriation not exceeding $2500 be made by the Association towards the expenses of these conferences. On the 12th of July the Directors adopted a series of resolutions under which a sum not exceeding $2500 was made available for this undertaking during the academic year 1892–93.

Every gentleman named on the above Committee of Ten accepted his appointment; and the Committee met, with every member present, at Columbia College, New York City, from the 9th to the 11th of November, 1892, inclusive.

In preparation for this meeting, a table had been prepared by means of a prolonged correspondence with the principals of selected secondary schools in various parts of the country, which showed the subjects taught in forty leading secondary schools in the United States, and the total number of recitations, or exercises, allotted to each subject. Nearly two hundred schools were applied to for this information; but it did not prove practicable to obtain within three months verified statements from more than forty schools. This table proved conclusively, first, that the total number of subjects taught in these secondary schools were nearly forty, thirteen of which, however, were found in only a few schools; secondly, that many of these subjects were taught for such short periods that little training could be derived from them; and thirdly, that the time allotted to the same subject in the different schools varied widely. Even for the older subjects, like Latin and algebra, there appeared to be a wide diversity of practice with regard to the time allotted to them. Since this table was comparative in its nature,—that is, permitted comparisions to be made between different schools,—and could be easily misunderstood and misapplied by persons who had small acquaintance with school programmes, it was treated as a confidential document; and was issued at first only to the members of the Committee of Ten and the principals of the schools mentioned in the table. Later, it was sent—still as a confidential paper—to the members of the several conferences organized by the Committee of Ten.

The Committee of Ten, after a preliminary discussion on November 9th, decided on November 10th to organize conferences on the following subjects:— 1. Latin; 2. Greek; 3. English; 4. Other Modern Languages; 5. Mathematics; 6. Physics, Astronomy, and Chemistry; 7. Natural History (Biology, including Botany, Zoölogy, and Physiology); 8. History, Civil Government, and Political Economy; 9. Geography (Physical Geography, Geology, and Meteorology). They also decided that each Conference should consist of ten members. They then proceeded to select the members of each of these Conferences, having regard in the selection to the scholarship and experience of the gentlemen named, to the fair division of the members between colleges on the one hand and schools on the other, and to the proper geographical distribution of the total membership. After selecting ninety members for the nine Conferences, the Committee decided on an additional number of names to be used as substitutes for persons originally chosen who should decline to serve, from two to four substitutes being selected for each Conference. In the selection of substitutes the Committee found it difficult to regard the geographical distribution of the persons selected with as much strictness as in the original selection; and, accordingly, when it became necessary to call on a considerable number of substitutes, the accurate geographical distribution of membership was somewhat impaired. The lists of the members of the several Conferences were finally adopted at a meeting of the Committee on November 11th; and the Chairman and Secretary of the Committee were then empowered to fill any vacancies which might occur.

The Committee next adopted the following list of questions as a guide for the discussions of all the Conferences, and directed that the Conferences be called together on the 28th of December:—

1. In the school course of study extending approximately from the age of six years to eighteen years—a course including the periods of both elementary and secondary instruction—at what age should the study which is the subject of the Conference be first introduced?

2. After it is introduced, how many hours a week for how many years should be devoted to it?

3. How many hours a week for how many years should be devoted to it during the last four years of the complete course; that is, during the ordinary high school period?

4. What topics, or parts, of the subject may reasonably be covered during the whole course?

5. What topics, or parts, of the subject may best be reserved for the last four years?

6. In what form and to what extent should the subject enter into college requirements

for admission? Such questions as the sufficiency of translation at sight as a test of knowledge of a language, or the superiority of a laboratory examination in a scientific subject to a written examination on a text-book, are intended to be suggested under this head by the phrase "in what form."

7. Should the subject be treated differently for pupils who are going to college, for those who are going to a scientific school, and for those who, presumably, are going to neither?

8. At what stage should this differentiation begin, if any be recommended?

9. Can any description be given of the best method of teaching this subject throughout the school course?

10. Can any description be given of the best mode of testing attainments in this subject at college admission examinations?

11. For those cases in which colleges and universities permit a division of the admission examination into a preliminary and a final examination, separated by at least a year, can the best limit between the preliminary and final examinations be approximately defined?

* * *

The ninety members of the Conferences were divided as follows,—forty-seven were in the service of colleges or universities, forty-two in the service of schools, and one was a government official formerly in the service of a university. A considerable number of the college men, however, had also had experience in schools. Each Conference, in accordance with a recommendation of the Committee of Ten, chose its own Chairman and Secretary; and these two officers prepared the report of each Conference. Six of the Chairmen were college men, and three were school men; while of the Secretaries, two were college men and seven school men. The Committee of Ten requested that the reports of the Conferences should be sent to their Chairman by the 1st of April, 1893—three months being thus allowed for the preparation of the reports. Seven Conferences substantially conformed to this request of the Committee; but the reports from the Conferences of Natural History and Geography were delayed until the second week in July. The Committee of Ten, being of course unable to prepare their own report until all the reports of the December Conferences had been received, were prevented from presenting their report, as they had intended, at the Education Congress which met at Chicago July 27th–29th.

All the Conferences sat for three days; their discussions were frank, earnest, and thorough; but in every Conference an extraordinary unity of opinion was arrived at. The nine reports are characterized by an amount of agreement which quite surpasses the most sanguine anticipations. Only two Conferences present minority reports, namely, the Conference of Physics, Astronomy, and Chemistry, and the Conference of Geography; and in the first case, the dissenting opinions touch only two points in the report of the majority, one of which is unimportant. In the great majority of matters brought before each Conference, the decision of the Conference was unanimous. When one considers the different localities, institutions, professional experiences, and personalities represented in each of the Conferences, the unanimity developed is very striking, and should carry great weight.

* * *

Anyone who reads these nine reports consecutively will be struck with the fact that all these bodies of experts desire to have the elements of their several subjects taught earlier than they now are; and that the Conferences on all the subjects except the languages desire to have given in the elementary schools what may be called perspective views, or broad surveys, of their respective subjects—expecting that in later years of the school course parts of these same subjects will be taken up with more amplitude and detail. The Conferences on Latin, Greek, and the Modern Languages agree in desiring to have the study of foreign languages begin at a much earlier age than now,—the Latin Conference suggesting by a reference to European usage that Latin be begun from three to five years earlier than it commonly is now. The Conference on Mathematics wish to have given in elementary schools not only a general survey of arithmetic, but also the elements of algebra, and concrete geometry in connection with drawing. The Conference on Physics, Chemistry, and Astronomy urge that nature studies should constitute an important part of the elementary school course from the very beginning. The Conference on Natural History wish the elements of botany and zoölogy to be taught in the primary schools. The Conference on History wish the systematic study of history to begin as early as the tenth year of age, and the first two years of study to be devoted to mythology and to biography for the illustration of general history as well as of American history. Finally, the Conference on Geography recommend that the earlier course tread broadly of the earth, its environment and inhabitants, extending freely into fields which in later years of study are recognized as belonging to separate sciences.

In thus claiming entrance for their subjects into the earlier years of school attendance, the Conferences on the newer subjects are only seeking an advantage which the oldest subjects have long possessed. The elements of language, number, and geography have long been imparted to young children. As things now are, the high school teacher finds in the pupils fresh from the grammar schools no foundation of elementary mathematical conceptions outside of arithmetic; no acquaintance with algebraic language; and no accurate knowledge of geometrical forms. As to botany, zoölogy, chemistry, and physics, the minds of pupils entering the high school are ordinarily blank on these subjects. When college professors endeavor to teach chemistry, physics, botany, zoölogy, meteorology, or geology to persons of eighteen or twenty years of age, they discover that in most instances new habits of observing, reflecting, and recording have to be painfully acquired by the students,—habits which they should have acquired in early childhood. The college teacher of history finds in like manner that his subject has never taken any serious hold on the minds of pupils fresh from the secondary schools. He finds that they have devoted astonishingly little time to the subject; and that they have acquired no habit of historical investigation, or of the comparative examination of different historical narratives concerning the same periods or events. It is inevitable, therefore, that specialists in any one of the subjects which are pursued in the high schools or colleges should earnestly desire that the minds of young children be stored with some of the elementary facts and principles of their subject; and that all the mental habits, which the adult student will surely need, begin to be formed in the child's mind before the age of fourteen. It follows, as a matter of course, that all the Conferences except the Conference on Greek, make strong suggestions concerning the programmes of primary and grammar schools,—generally with some reference to the subsequent programmes of secondary schools. They desire important changes in the elementary grades; and the changes recommended are all in the direction of increasing simultaneously the interest and the substantial training quality of primary and grammar school studies.

If anyone feels dismayed at the number and variety of the subjects to be opened to children of tender age, let him observe that while these nine Conferences desire each their own subject to be brought into the courses of elementary schools, they all agree that these different subjects should be correlated and associated one with another by the programme and by the actual teaching. If the nine Conferences had sat all together as a single body, instead of sitting as detached and even isolated bodies, they could not have more forcibly expressed their conviction that every subject recommended for introduction into elementary and secondary schools should help every other; and that the teacher of each single subject should feel responsible for the advancement of the pupils in all subjects, and should distinctly contribute to this advancement.

On one very important question of general policy which affects profoundly the preparation of all school programmes, the Committee of Ten and all the Conferences are absolutely unanimous. Among the questions suggested for discussion in each Conference were the following:—

7. Should the subject be treated differently for pupils who are going to college, for those who are going to a scientific school, and for those who, presumably, are going to neither?

8. At what age should this differentiation begin, if any be recommended?

The 7th question is answered unanimously in the negative by the Conferences, and the 8th therefore needs no answer. The Committee of Ten unanimously agree with the Conferences. Ninety-eight teachers, intimately concerned either with the actual work of American secondary schools, or with the results of that work as they appear in students who come to college, unanimously declare that every subject which is taught at all in a secondary school should be taught in the same way and to the same extent to every pupil so long as he pursues it, no matter what the probable destination of the pupil may be, or at what point his education is to cease. Thus, for all pupils who study Latin, or history, or algebra, for example, the allotment of time and the method of instruction in a given school should be the same year by year. Not that all the pupils should pursue every subject for the same number of years; but so long as they do pursue it, they should all be treated alike. It has been a very general custom in American high schools and academies to make up separate courses of study for pupils of supposed different destinations, the proportions of the several studies in the different courses being various. The principle laid down by the Conferences will, if logically carried out, make a great simplification in secondary school programmes. It will lead to each subject's being treated by the school in the same way by the year for all pupils, and this, whether the individual pupil be required to choose between courses which run through several years, or be allowed some choice among subjects year by year.

Persons who read all the appended reports will observe the frequent occurrence of the statement that, in order to introduce the changes recommended, teachers more highly trained will be needed in both the elementary and the secondary schools. There are frequent expressions to the effect that a higher grade of scholarship is needed in teachers of the lower classes, or that the general adoption of some method urged by a Conference must depend upon the better preparation of teachers in the high schools, model schools, normal schools, or colleges in which they are trained. The experienced principal or superintendent in reading the reports will be apt to say to himself,—"This recommendation is sound, but cannot be carried out without teachers who have received a training superior to that of the teachers now at my command." It must be remembered, in connection with these admissions, or expressions of anxiety, that the Conferences were urged by the Committee of Ten to advise the Committee concerning the best possible—almost the ideal—treatment of each subject taught in a secondary school course, without, however, losing sight of the actual condition of American schools, or pushing their recommendations beyond what might reasonably be considered attainable in a moderate number of years. . . .

TABLE III.

1st Secondary School Year

Latin	5 p.
English Literature, 2 p. ⎱	
" Composition, 2 p. ⎰	4 p.
German [or French]	5 p.
Algebra	4 p.
History of Italy, Spain, and France	3 p.
Applied Geography	
(European political—continental	
and oceanic flora and fauna)	4 p.
	——
	25 p.

2nd Secondary School Year

Latin	4 p.
Greek	5 p.
English Literature, 2 p. ⎱	
" Composition, 2 p. ⎰	4 p.
German, continued	4 p.
French, begun	5 p.
Algebra,* 2 p. ⎱	
Geometry, 2 p. ⎰	4 p.
Botany or Zoology	4 p.
English History to 1688	3 p.
	——
	33 p.

*Option of book-keeping and commercial arithmetic.

3rd Secondary School Year

Latin	4 p.
Greek	4 p.
English Literature, 2 p. ⎱	
" Composition, 1 p. ⎬	4 p.
Rhetoric, 1 p. ⎰	
German	4 p.
French	4 p.
Algebra,* 2 p. ⎱	
Geometry, 2 p. ⎰	4 p.
Physics	4 p.
History, English and American	3 p.
Astronomy, 3 p. 1st 1/2 yr. ⎱	
Meteorology, 3 p. 2nd 1/2 yr. ⎰	3 p.
	——
	34 p.

*Option of book-keeping and commercial arithmetic.

4th Secondary School Year

Latin	4 p.
Greek	4 p.
English Literature, 2 p. ⎱	
" Composition, 1 p. ⎬	4 p.
" Grammar, 1 p. ⎰	
German	4 p.
French	4 p.
Trigonometry, ⎱	
Higher Algebra, ⎰	2 p.
Chemistry	4 p.
History (intensive) and	
Civil Government	3 p.
Geology or Physiography, ⎱	
4 p. 1st 1/2 yr. ⎬	4 p.
Anatomy, Physiology, and ⎰	
Hygiene, 4p. 2nd 1/2 yr.	——
	33 p.

The Committee regard Table III not, of course, as a feasible programme, but as the possible source of a great variety of good secondary school programmes. It would be difficult to make a bad programme out of the materials contained in this table, unless indeed the fundamental principles advocated by the Conferences should be neglected. With some reference to Table I, excellent six years' and five years' programmes for secondary schools can readily be constructed by spreading the subjects contained in Table III over six or five years instead of four,—of course with some changes in the time-allotment.

The details of the time-allotment for the several studies which enter into the secondary school programme may seem to some persons mechanical, or even trivial—a technical matter to be dealt with by each superintendent of schools, or by each principal of a secondary school, acting on his own individual experience and judgment; but such is not the opinion of the Committee of Ten. The Committee believe that to establish just proportions between the several subjects, or groups of allied subjects, on which the Conferences were held, it is essential that each principal subject shall be taught thoroughly and extensively, and therefore for an adequate number of periods a week on the school programme. If twice as much time is given in a school to Latin as is given to mathematics, the attainments of the pupils in Latin ought to be twice as great as they are in mathematics, provided that equally good work is done in the two subjects; and Latin will have twice the educational value of mathematics. Again, if in a secondary school Latin is steadily pursued for four years with four or five hours a week devoted to it, that subject will be worth more to the pupil than the sum of half a dozen other subjects, each of which has one sixth of the time allotted to Latin. The good effects of continuous study in one subject will be won for the pupil through the Latin, and they will not be won through the six other subjects among which only so much time as is devoted to the single language has been divided. If every subject studied at all is to be studied thoroughly and consecutively, every subject must receive an adequate time-allotment. If every subject is to provide a substantial mental training, it must have a time-allotment sufficient to produce that fruit. Finally, since selection must be exercised by or on behalf of the individual pupil, all the subjects between which choice is allowed should be approximately equivalent to each other in seriousness, dignity, and efficacy. Therefore they should have approximately equal time-allotments. The Conferences have abundantly shown how every subject which they recommend can be made a serious subject of instruction, well fitted to train the pupil's powers of observation, expression, and reasoning. It remains for makers of school programmes to give every subject the chance of developing a good training capacity by giving it an adequate time-allotment.

The schedule of studies contained in Table III permits flexibility and variety in three respects. First, it is not necessary that any school should teach all the subjects which it contains, or any particular set of subjects. Secondly, it is not necessary that the individual pupil should everywhere and always have the same number of periods of instruction per week. In one school the pupils might have but sixteen periods a week, in another twenty; or in some years of the course the pupils might have more periods a week than in other years. Within the schedule many particular arrangements for the convenience of a school, or for the welfare of an individual pupil would be posssible. Thirdly, it is not necessary that every secondary school should begin its work at the level which is assumed as the starting point of secondary instruction in Tables I, II, and III. If in any community the high school has no such grammar school foundation beneath it as is imagined in Table I it will simply have to begin its work lower down in the table. The sequence of studies recommended by the Conferences would still serve as a guide; but the demarcation between the elementary schools and the high school would occur in that community at a lower point. From this point of view, Tables I, II, and III may be considered to set a standard towards which secondary schools should tend; and not a standard to which they can at once conform.

The adoption of a programme based on Table III would not necessarily change at all the relation of a school to the colleges or universities to which it habitually sends pupils. Any such programme would lend itself either to the examination method of admission to college, or to the certificate method; and it could be slightly modified in such a way as to meet the present admission requirements of any college in the country. Future changes in admission requirements might fairly be made with a view to the capabilities of programmes based on Table III.

As samples of school programmes constructed within the schedules of Table III, the Committee present the following working programmes, which they recommend for trial wherever the secondary school period is limited to four years. All four combined might, of course, be tabulated as one programme with options by subject.

These four programmes taken together use all the subjects mentioned in Table III, and usually, but not always, to about the amounts there indicated. History and English suffer serious contraction in the Classical programme. All four programmes conform to the general recommendations of the Conferences, that is,—they treat each subject in the same way for all pupils with trifling exceptions; they give time enough to each subject to win from it the kind of mental training it is fitted to supply; they put the different principal subjects on an approximate equality so far as time-allotment is concerned; they omit all short information courses; and they make sufficiently continuous the instruction in each of the main lines, namely, language, science, history and mathematics. With slight modifications, they would prepare the pupils for admission to appropriate courses in any American college or university on the existing requirements; and they would also meet the new college requirements which are suggested below.

In preparing these programmes, the Committee were perfectly aware that it is impossible to make a satisfactory secondary school programme, limited to a period of four years, and founded on the present elementary school subjects and methods. In the opinion of the Committee, several subjects now reserved for high schools,— such as algebra, geometry, natural science, and foreign languages,—should be begun earlier than now, and therefore within the schools classified as elementary; or, as an alternative, the secondary school period should be made to begin two years earlier than at present, leaving six years instead of eight for the elementary school period. Under the present organization, elementary subjects and elementary methods are, in the judgment of the Committee, kept in use too long.

The most striking differences in the four programmes will be found, as is intimated in the headings, in the relative amounts of time given to foreign languages. In the Classical programme the foreign languages get a large share of time; in the English programme a small share. In compensation, English and history are more developed in the English programme than in the Classical.

Many teachers will say, at first sight, that physics comes too early in these programmes and Greek too late. One member of the Committee is firmly of the opinion that Greek comes too late. The explanation of the positions assigned to these subjects is that the Committee of Ten attached great importance to two general principles in programme making:—In the first place they endeavored to postpone till the third year the grave choice between the Classical course and the Latin-Scientific. They believed that this bifurcation should occur as late as possible, since the choice between these two roads often determines for life the youth's career. Moreover, they believed that it is possible to make this important decision for a boy on good grounds, only when he has had opportunity to exhibit his quality and discover his tastes by making excursions into all the principal fields of knowledge. The youth who has never studied any but his native language cannot know his own capacity for linguistic acquisition; and the youth who has never made

TABLE IV.

Year	Classical Three foreign languages (one modern)		Latin-Scientific Two foreign languages (one modern)	
I	Latin	5 p.	Latin	5 p.
	English	4 p.	English	4 p.
	Algebra	4 p.	Algebra	4 p.
	History	4 p.	History	4 p.
	Physical Geography	3 p.	Physical Geography	3 p.
		20 p.		20 p.
II	Latin	5 p.	Latin	5 p.
	English	2 p.	English	2 p.
	*German [or French] begun	4 p.	German [or French] begun	4 p.
	Geometry	3 p.	Geometry	3 p.
	Physics	3 p.	Physics	3 p.
	History	3 p.	Botany or Zoölogy	3 p.
		20 p.		20 p.
III	Latin	4 p.	Latin	4 p.
	*Greek	5 p.	English	3 p.
	English	3 p.	German [or French]	4 p.
	German [or French]	4 p.	Mathematics { Algebra 2 } { Geometry 2 }	4 p.
	Mathematics { Algebra 2 } { Geometry 2 }	4 p.	Astronomy 1/2 yr. & Meteorology 1/2 yr.	3 p.
		20 p.	History	2 p.
				20 p.
IV	Latin	4 p.	Latin	4 p.
	Greek	5 p.	English { as in Classical 2 } { additional 2 }	4 p.
	English	2 p.		
	German [or French]	3 p.	German [or French]	3 p.
	Chemistry	3 p.	Chemistry	3 p.
	Trigonometry & Higher Algebra } or } History }	3 p.	Trigonomentry & Higher Algebra } or } History }	3 p.
		20 p.	Geology or Physiography 1/2 yr. and Anatomy, Physiology & Hygiene 1/2 yr. }	3 p.
				20 p.

*In any school in which Greek can be better taught than a modern language, or in which local public opinion or the history of the school makes it desirable to teach Greek in an ample way, Greek may be substituted for German or French in the second year of the Classical programme.

a chemical or physical experiment cannot know whether or not he has a taste for exact science. The wisest teacher, or the most observant parent, can hardly predict with confidence a boy's gift for a subject which he has never touched. In these considerations the Committee found strong reasons for postponing bifurcation, and making the subjects of the first two years as truly representative as possible. Secondly, inasmuch as many boys and girls who begin the secondary school course do not stay in school more than two years, the Committee thought it important to select the studies of the first two years in such a way that linguistic, historical, mathematical, and scientific subjects should all be properly represented. Natural history being represented by physical geography, the Committee wished physics to represent the inorganic sciences of precision. The first two years of any one of the four programmes presented above will, in the judgment of the Committee, be highly profitable by themselves to children who can go no farther.

Although the Committee thought it expedient to include among the four programmes, one which included neither Latin nor Greek, and one which included only one foreign language (which might be either ancient or modern), they desired to affirm explicitly their unanimous opinion that, under existing conditions in the United States as to the training of teachers and the provision of necessary means of instruction, the two programmes called respectively Modern Languages and English must in practice be distinctly inferior to the other two.

In the construction of the sample programmes the Committee adopted twenty as the maximum number of weekly periods, but with two qualifications, namely, that at least five of the twenty periods should be given to unprepared work, and that laboratory subjects should have double periods whenever that prolongation should be possible.

The omission of music, drawing, and elocution from the programmes offered by the Committee was not intended to imply that these subjects ought to receive no systematic attention. It was merely thought best to leave it to local school authorities to determine, without suggestions from the Committee, how these subjects should be introduced into the programmes in addition to the subjects reported on by the Conferences.

The Committee were governed in the construction of the first three programmes by the rule laid down by the language Conferences, namely, that two foreign languages should not be begun at the same time. To obey this rule is to accept strict limitations in the construction of a four years' Classical programme. A five years' or six years' programme can be made much more easily under this restriction. The Committee were anxious to give five weekly periods to every foreign language in the year when it was first attacked; but did not find it possible to do so in every case.

The four programmes can be carried out economically in a single school; because, with a few inevitable exceptions, the several subjects occur simultaneously in at least three programmes and with the same number of weekly periods.

Numerous possible transpositions of subjects will occur to every experienced teacher who examines these specimen programmes. Thus, in some localities it would be better to transpose French and German; the selection and order of science subjects might be varied considerably to suit the needs or circumstances of different schools; and the selection and order of historical subjects admit of large variety.

Many subjects now familiar in secondary school courses of study do not appear in Table III or in the specimen programmes given above; but it must not be supposed that the omitted subjects are necessarily to be neglected. If the recommendations of the Conference were carried out, some of the omitted subjects would be better dealt with under any one of the above programmes than they are now under familiar high school and academy programmes in which they figure as separate subjects. Thus, drawing does not appear as a separate subject in the specimen programmes; but the careful reader of the Conference reports will notice that drawing, both mechanical and freehand, is to be used in the study of history, botany, zoology, astronomy, meteorology, physics, geography, and physiography, and that the kind of drawing recommended by the Conferences is the most useful kind,—namely, that which is applied to recording, describing, and discussing observations. This abundant use of drawing might not prevent the need of some special instruction in drawing, but it ought to diminish the number of periods devoted exclusively to drawing. Again, neither ethics nor economics, neither metaphysics nor aesthetics appear in the programmes; but in the large number of periods devoted to English and history there would be some time for incidental instruction in the elements of these subjects. It is through the reading and writing required of pupils, or recommended to them, that the fundamental ideas on these important topics are to be inculcated. Again, the industrial and commercial subjects do not appear in these programmes; but book-keeping and commercial arithmetic are provided for by the option for algebra designated in Table III; and if it were desired to provide more amply for subjects thought to have practical importance in trade or the useful arts, it would be easy to provide options in such subjects for some of the science contained in the third and fourth years of the "English" programme.

The Committee of Ten think much would be gained if, in addition to the usual programme hours, a portion of Saturday morning should be regularly used for laboratory work in the scientific subjects. Laboratory work requires more consecutive time than the ordinary period of recitation affords; so that an hour and a half is about the shortest advantageous period for a laboratory exercise. The Committee venture to suggest further that, in addition to the regular school sessions in the morning, one afternoon in every week should be used for out-of-door instruction in geography, botany, zoology, and geology, these afternoon and Saturday morning exercises being counted as regular work for the teachers who conduct them. In all laboratory and field work, the Committee believe that it will be found profitable to employ as assistants to the regular teachers,—particularly at the beginning of laboratory and field work in each subject,—recent graduates of the secondary schools who have themselves followed the laboratory and field courses; for at the beginning the pupil will need a large amount of individual instruction in the manipulation of specimens, the use of instruments, and the prompt recording of observations. One teacher without assistants cannot supervise effectively the work of thirty or forty pupils, either in the laboratory or in the field. The laboratory work on Saturday mornings could be maintained throughout the school year; the afternoon excursions would of course be difficult, or impossible, for perhaps a third of the school year.

In general, the Committee of Ten have endeavored to emphasize the principles which should govern all secondary school programmes, and to show how the main recommendations of the several Conferences may be carried out in a variety of feasible programmes.

One of the subjects which the Committee of Ten were directed to consider was requirements for admission to college; and particularly they were expected to report on uniform requirements for admission to colleges, as well as on a uniform secondary school programme. Almost all the Conferences have something to say about the best mode of testing the attainments of candidates at college admission examinations; and some of them, notably the Conferences on History and Geography, make very explicit declarations concerning the nature of college examinations. The improvements desired in the mode of testing the attainments of pupils who have pursued in the secondary schools the various subjects which enter into the course will be found clearly described under each subject in the several Conference reports; but there is a general principle concerning the relation of the secondary schools to colleges which the Committee of Ten, inspired and guided by the Conferences, feel it their duty to set forth with all possible distinctness.

The secondary schools of the United States, taken as a whole, do not exist for the purpose of preparing boys and girls for colleges. Only an insignificant percentage of the graduates of these schools go to colleges or scientific schools. Their main function is to prepare for the duties of life that small proportion of all the children in the country—a proportion small in number, but very important to the welfare of the nation—who show themselves able to profit by an education prolonged to the eighteenth year, and whose parents are able to support them while they remain so long at school. There are, to be sure, a few private or endowed secondary schools in the country, which make it their principal object to prepare students for the colleges and universities; but the number of these schools is relatively small. A secondary school programme intended for national use must therefore be made for those children whose education is not to be pursued beyond the secondary school. The preparation of a few pupils for college or scientific school should in the ordinary secondary school be the incidental, and not the principal object. At the same time, it is obviously desirable that the colleges and scientific schools should be accessible to all boys or girls who have completed creditably the secondary school course. Their parents often do not decide for them, four years before the college age, that they shall go to college, and they themselves may not, perhaps, feel the desire to continue their education until near the end of their school course. In order that any successful graduate of a good secondary school should be free to present himself at the gates of the college or scientific school of his choice, it is necessary that the colleges and scientific schools of the country should accept for admission to appropriate courses of their instruction the attainments of any youth who has passed creditably through a good secondary school course, no matter to what group of subjects he may have mainly devoted himself in the secondary school. As secondary school courses are now too often arranged, this is not a reasonable request to prefer to the colleges and scientific schools; because the pupil may now go through a secondary school course of a very feeble and scrappy nature—studying a little of many subjects and not much of any one, getting, perhaps, a little information in a variety of fields, but nothing which can be called a thorough training. Now the recommendations of the nine Conferences, if well carried out, might fairly be held to make all the main subjects taught in the secondary schools of equal rank for the purposes of admission to college or scientific school. They would all be taught consecutively and thoroughly, and would all be carried on in the same spirit; they would all be used for training the powers of observation, memory, expression, and reasoning; and they would all be good to that end, although differing among themselves in quality and substance. In preparing the programmes of Table IV, the Committee had in mind that the requirements for admission to colleges might, for schools which adopted a programme derived from that table, be simplified to a considerable extent, though not reduced. A college might say,—We will accept for admission any groups of studies taken from the secondary school programme, provided that the sum of the studies in each of the four years amounts to sixteen, or eighteen, or twenty periods a week,—as may be thought best,—and provided, further, that in each year at least four of the subjects presented shall have been pursued at least three periods a week, and that at least three of the subjects shall have been pursued three years or more. For the purposes of this reckoning, natural history, geography, meteorology, and astronomy might be grouped together as one subject. Every youth who entered college would have spent four years in studying a few subjects thoroughly; and, on the theory that all the subjects are to be considered equivalent in educational rank for the purposes of admission to college, it would make no difference which subjects he had chosen from the programme—he would have had four years of strong and effective mental training. The Conferences on Geography and Modern Languages make the most explicit statement to the effect that college requirements for admission should coincide with high-school requirements for graduation. The Conference on English is of opinion "that no student should be admitted to college who shows in his English examination and his other examinations that he is very deficient in ability to write good English." This recommendation suggests that an ample English course in the secondary school should be required of all persons who intend to enter college. It would of course be possible for any college to require for admission any one subject, or any group of subjects, in the table, and the requirements of different colleges, while all kept within the table, might differ in many respects; but the Committee are of opinion that the satisfactory completion of any one of the four years' courses of study embodied in the foregoing programmes should admit to corresponding courses in colleges and scientific schools. They believe that this close articulation between the secondary schools and the higher institutions would be advantageous alike for the schools, the colleges, and the country.

Every reader of this report and of the reports of the nine Conferences will be satisfied that to carry out the improvements proposed more highly trained teachers will be needed than are now ordinarily to be found for the service of the elementary and secondary schools. The Committee of Ten desire to point out some of the means of procuring these better trained teachers. For the further instruction of teachers in actual service, three agencies already in existence may be much better utilized than they now are. The Summer Schools which many universities now maintain might be resorted to by much larger numbers of teachers, particularly if some aid, such as the payment of tuition fees and travelling expenses, should be given to teachers who are willing to devote half of their vacations to study, by the cities and towns which these teachers serve. Secondly, in all the towns and cities in which colleges and universities are planted, these colleges or universities may usefully give stated courses of instruction in the main subjects used in the elementary and secondary schools to teachers employed in those towns and cities. This is a reasonable service which the colleges and universities may render to their own communities. Thirdly, a superintendent who has himself become familiar with the best mode of teaching any one of the subjects which enter in to the school course can always be a very useful instructor for the whole body of teachers under his charge. A real master of any one subject will always have many suggestions to make to teachers of other subjects. The same is true of the principal of a high school, or other leading teacher in a town or city. In every considerable city school system the best teacher in each department of instruction should be enabled to give part of his time to helping the other teachers by inspecting and criticising their work, and showing them, both by precept and example, how to do it better.

In regard to preparing young men and women for the business of teaching, the

1943

country has a right to expect much more than it has yet obtained from the colleges and normal schools. The common expectation of attainment for pupils of the normal schools has been altogether too low the country over. The normal schools, as a class, themselves need better apparatus, libraries, programmes, and teachers. As to the colleges, it is quite as much an enlargement of sympathies as an improvement of apparatus or of teaching that they need. They ought to take more interest than they have heretofore done, not only in the secondary, but in the elementary schools; and they ought to take pains to fit men well for the duties of a school superintendent. They already train a considerable number of the best principals of high schools and academies; but this is not sufficient. They should take an active interest, through their presidents, professors, and other teachers, in improving the schools in their respective localities, and in contributing to the thorough discussion of all questions affecting the welfare of both the elementary and the secondary schools.

Finally, the committee venture to suggest, in the interest of secondary schools, that uniform dates—such as the last Thursday, Friday, and Saturday, or the third Monday, Tuesday, and Wednesday of June and September—be established for the admission examinations of colleges and scientific schools throughout the United States. It is a serious inconvenience for secondary schools which habitually prepare candidates for several different colleges or scientific schools that the admission examinations of different institutions are apt to occur on different dates, sometimes rather widely separated.

The committee also wish to call attention to the service which schools of law, medicine, engineering, and technology, whether connected with universities or not, can render to secondary education by arranging their requirements for admission, as regards selection and range of subjects, in conformity with the courses of study recommended by the committee. By bringing their entrance requirements into close relation with any or all of the programmes recommended for secondary schools, these professional schools can give valuable support to high schools, academies, and preparatory schools.

> CHARLES W. ELIOT.
> WILLIAM T. HARRIS.
> JAMES B. ANGELL.
> JOHN TETLOW.
> JAMES M. TAYLOR.
> OSCAR D. ROBINSON.
> JAMES H. BAKER.
> RICHARD H. JESSE.
> JAMES C. MACKENZIE.
> HENRY C. KING.

December 4, 1893.

THE COMMITTEE OF TEN ON TEACHERS AND TEACHING (1893) From
Report of the Committee of Ten on Secondary School Studies, (Washington, D.C., 1893), pp. 53–55.

Every reader of this report and of the reports of the nine Conferences will be satisfied that to carry out the improvements proposed more highly trained teachers will be needed than are now ordinarily to be found for the service of the elementary and secondary schools. The Committee of Ten desire to point out some of the means of procuring these better trained teachers. For the further instruction of teachers in actual service, three agencies already in existence may be much better utilized than they now are. The Summer Schools which many universities now maintain might be resorted to by much larger number of teachers, particularly if some aid, such as the payment of tuition fees and travelling expenses, should be given to teachers who are willing to devote half of their vacations to study, by the cities and towns which these teachers serve. Secondly, in all the towns and cities in which colleges and universities are planted, these colleges or universities may usefully give stated courses of instruction in the main subjects used in the elementary and secondary schools to teachers employed in those towns and cities. This is a reasonable service which the colleges and universities may render to their own communities. Thirdly, a superintendent who has himself become familiar with the best mode of teaching any one of the subjects which enter into the school course can always be a very useful instructor for the whole body of teachers under his charge. A real master of any one subject will always have many suggestions to make to teachers of other subjects. The same is true of the principal of a high school, or other leading teacher in a town or city. In every considerable city school system the best teacher in each department of instruction should be enabled to give part of his time to helping the other teachers by inspecting and criticising their work, and showing them, both by precept and example, how to do it better.

In regard to preparing young men and women for the business of teaching, the country has a right to expect much more than it has yet obtained from the colleges and normal schools. The common expectation of attainment for pupils of the normal schools has been altogether too low the country over. The normal schools, as a class, themselves need better apparatus, libraries, programmes, and teachers. As to the colleges, it is quite as much an enlargement of sympathies as an improvement of apparatus or of teaching that they need. They ought to take more interest than they have heretofore done, not only in the secondary, but in the elementary schools; and they ought to take pains to fit men well for the duties of a school superintendent. They already train a considerable number of the best principals of high schools and academies; but this is not sufficient. They should take an active interest, through their presidents, professors, and other teachers, in improving the schools in their respective localities, and in contributing to the thorough discussion of all questions affecting the welfare of both the elementary and the secondary schools.

Finally, the Committee venture to suggest, in the interest of secondary schools, that uniform dates—such as the last Thursday, Friday, and Saturday, or the third Monday, Tuesday, and Wednesday of June and September—be established for the admission examinations of colleges and scientific schools throughout the United States. It is a serious inconvenience for secondary schools which habitually prepare candidates for several different colleges or scientific schools that the admission examinations of different institutions are apt to occur on different dates, sometimes rather widely separated.

The Committee also wish to call attention to the service which Schools of Law, Medicine, Engineering, and Technology, whether connected with universities or not, can render to secondary education by arranging their requirements for admission, as regards selection and range of subjects, in conformity with the courses of study recommended by the Committee. By bringing their entrance requirements into close relation with any or all of the programmes recommended for secondary schools, these professional schools can give valuable support to high schools, academies, and preparatory schools.

> CHARLES W. ELIOT,
> WILLIAM T. HARRIS,
> JAMES B. ANGELL,
> JOHN TETLOW,
> JAMES M. TAYLOR,
> OSCAR D. ROBINSON,
> JAMES H. BAKER,
> RICHARD H. JESSE,
> JAMES C. MACKENZIE,
> HENRY C. KING.

G. STANLEY HALL'S CRITICISM OF THE COMMITTEE OF TEN

(**1905**)   From G. Stanley Hall, *Adolescence: Its Psychology and Its Relations to Physiology, Anthropology, Sociology, Sex, Crime, Religion, and Education* (New York, 1905), vol. II. pp. 508–15.

The last decade has witnessed a remarkable new movement on the part of colleges to influence high schools, which began with the Report of the Committee of Ten, printed in 1893. We have also had Reports of the Committee of Seven, Nine, Twelve, Fourteen, Fifteen, besides that of the National Education Association in 1890 on entrance requirements which invoked the aid of the American Historical and Philological Associations. In general these influences have worked from above downward, the dominating influence and the initiative in most cases coming from colleges or universities. That this movement did good for a time no one can deny. It has made many junctures between secondary and higher education; greatly increased the interest of faculties in high schools; given the former fruitful pedagogic themes for their own discussions; brought about a more friendly feeling and better mutual acquaintance; given slow colleges a wholesome stimulus, made school courses richer, given them better logical sequence; detected many weak points; closed many gaps; defined standards of what education means; brought great advantages from uniformity and cooperation, and no doubt, on the whole, has improved the conditions of college entrance examinations and aided in continuity.

One interesting result is the standardizing of high school knowledge, as hardware and even agricultural products, foodstuffs and machines are standardized by sizes, weight, and other measures—six weeks, twelve chapters, four or six hundred pages, forty weeks, eighteen courses, seventy experiments, four hours a week, three and four years of preparatory study, with 3,200 periods, fifteen credits, age eighteen, average mark seventy, so many Latin and Greek words to learn a month, so many minutes of recitation, home work, courses, text-books and examination tests all reduced to arithmetical or quantified dimensions. Knowledge is no longer bullion from the mine, but is minted with a hall-mark of at least some numerical committee. Everything must count and so much, for herein lies its educational value. There is no more wild, free, vigorous growth of the forest, but everything is in pots or rows like a rococo garden. Intellectual pabulum has lost all gamey flavor and is stall-fed or canned. These bales or blocks of condensed and enriched knowledge, which are used to calibrate the youthful mind or test its lifting or carrying power, seem to it stale; the stints become monotonous, mechanical, factory work to the pupil, but to the teacher they acquire an excessive value, as if the world of knowledge had been canonized and certain things set apart as more sacred than other fields of knowledge. Some institutions allow more options between the blocks and assert greater freedom because they offer more patterns and more sizes of essentially the same material. Such scientific goods as can be metered, inspected, and examined by mass methods, tabulated and schematized, always soon seem shopworn to youth who want somewhere room for individuality, if not for distinction, and resist curricularization and, as the French call it, the canalization of knowledge. The pupil is in the age of spontaneous variation which at no period of life is so great. He does not want a standardized, overpeptonized mental diet. It palls on his appetite. He suffers from mental *ennui* and dyspepsia, and this is why so many and an increasing number refuse some of the best prepared courses, like the ducks in James Russell Lowell's story, for which a chemist had demonstrated by long study that celery was the most nutritious of all possible foods, but when his farm was well stocked it was found to be about the only thing "the derned things wouldn't touch," and they pined and died when it was injected with a syringe. As we saw above, truancy is often due to a restlessness which, all unconscious of the cause, is really where the home dietary lacks nutritiousness. To enforce a curriculum without interest suggests the dream of a great Leipzig psychologist who predicted that sometime foods could be prepared so like chyme as to be inserted into the veins through a stop-cock, dispensing with the digestive function of the alimentary canal, and thus the time of eating would be saved and energy set free for a new upward march of culture greater even than that caused by cooking and the control of fire which the legend of Prometheus marks. It is now often painful to set limits to science, and results as surprising as all these may emerge in the future, but they will be different and by yet undiscovered methods. Once beneficent, college entrance requirements, as now enforced in some parts of our country and in some respects, are almost an unmitigated curse to high schools, exploiting them against their normal interests and the purpose of the people who support them, and thus perverting their natural development, enforcing artifacts of both method and matter, and sacrificing the interests of the vast majority who will never go to college.

This invasion and subjection has been rendered plausible even to its victims by three extraordinary fallacies. (*a*) The Committee of Ten "unanimously declare that every subject which is taught at all in a secondary school should be taught in the same way and to the same extent to every pupil so long as he pursues it, no matter what the probable destination of the pupil may be or at what point his education is to cease." This is a masterpiece of college policy. But in the first place this principle does not apply to the great army of incapables, shading down to those who should be in schools for dullards or subnormal children, for whose mental development heredity decrees a slow pace and early arrest, and for whom by general consent both studies and methods must be different. To refuse this concession to the wide range of individual differences is a specious delusion, which in a democracy may be perfectly honest. Difficulties must be omitted, the interest of the hour more appealed to, illustrations multiplied, and different beginnings, means, and goals early sought. Nor does this principle, of course, apply to geniuses. The school is not constructed for such. They go by leaps and find their own way. We must consider, then, only pupils that lie between these extremes. Again, this is unknown in other lands, where it would bring the direst confusion. European systems seem constructed on the converse principle that subjects should be approached in as many different ways as there are ultimate goals, while choices between academic and other careers are made before the teens, and methods and matter in the same topics diverge increasingly up the grades. The courses in English public secondary schools differ as much in method from those of the great endowed fitting schools as they do in matter. So the gymnasia and *Real* schools differ from each other, and both still more from the *Volk* schools, and as do the *lycee* and polytechnic schools in France, while text-books on the same subject are radically different. Besides the distinction between those destined for technical and professional careers and those who study for culture purposes, there are many species and varieties of difference. Again, in the vast number of monotechnic, polytechnic, commercial, and other courses, some of the departments of physics and chemistry, which are of immediate application, are emphasized. The horological school course emphasizes vibrations; the great lithograph school of Vienna lays stress upon light, and that in certain aspects; the schools of telegraphy, upon electricity; those of wine culture, upon the chemistry of fermentation; those of agriculture, upon the practical problems of chemistry involved in fertilization; secondary schools for art, upon the geometry connected with perspective; those for the lower order of engineering, upon mechanics; and so on indefinitely, all selecting those parts and principles, and even sub-aspects and methods, from the fields of these great sciences that lie nearest to and shed most light upon practise, and with comparatively little matter in common with some sciences. With all this precious development the principle of the Committee of Ten would make havoc, lacking as it does all proper conception of the magnitude of each science and its vast variety of approaches. In topics like astronomy and physics, even the question where to begin the mathematical side, how much stress to lay upon it, or whether to omit it entirely, like Tyndall, is largely a problem of destination.

Even in teaching modern languages there are recognized differences of both method and matter, whether the pupil needs to be taught chiefly and first to speak and hear the language or to read and command its literary resources. Geography might almost be called in its best modern development the introduction to various sciences, and I think there is now general agreement that much more stress should be laid upon it for those who finish their education early than for those who continue. So in English, children who leave school early have, as we saw above, an inalienable right to some knowledge, slight though it be, of the general moral lessons of the great masterpieces which those who go on have other means of attaining. Who would say that if a child has six months or one year to learn what the Latin or Greek world really means, he should begin as the pupil would who is to specialize in these topics later? Not only thus does this principle fail to recognize how vast as the mind itself the great departments of knowledge are, but how the pedagogic instinct almost inclines to the belief that there are perhaps almost as many ways of approach to them as there are minds, and that it would not be an insanely wild thesis for those not ignorant of the anthropology of youth to maintain that every individual mind has ideally its own best personal way of approach to every science, because each mind not only has, but is, its own method. There is especially the great fundamental distinction between those approaches that begin with practise, art, skill, and industry or for those who are motor-minded, into whom the great function of the teacher is to instil as much scientific knowledge and as many principles as can be made of practicable service, and the professional and the other culture groups who can follow a logical order. In looking over the text-books for these two kinds of minds or "destinations," one is struck with the very limited amount of subject-matter which is common, and also with the fact that these differences rest on fundamental differences of constitution, and that to force them into one mold would be wasteful, undemocratic, and pedagogically immoral. This principle ignores the fact that the average youth of high school age, and especially in the early teens, has not so far reached the age of reason that logical methods can be made supreme, but that genetic methods which cross-section it must also be largely relied on. Some need far more popular science or can not depart from utilities. But minds destined to high development grasp and follow the order and logic of science far earlier than others. In general the more vigorous and capable of high development is an adolescent mind, the less appeal is needed to this kind of interest—i. e., the smaller the mental area necessary to cultivate, to generate interest in the great spring of mind. The female intellect, in general, is far more in need of this, and develops specialized and abstract interest later than that of the average boy.

(*b*) Closely associated with this is the principle that "all subjects are of equal educational value if taught equally well." This, too, has been reiterated until with some it has almost become a dogma. It is especially startling to those who have accepted the Herbartian view of grades of culture values, for it means that in themselves and when rightly taught, shorthand, Greek, agriculture, mathematics, sewing and surveying, elocution and drawing, the humanities and science, pure and applied knowledge, and all the newest as well as the oldest branches, if taught alike well, have equal educational worth. Here, too, the counter assertion that no two topics have or can ever be given equal culture value is probably somewhat nearer the truth. Were the above precept sound, the supreme desideratum in the world would be good pedagogic methods, for they would be all that is necessary to transform the meanest bread-winning to the best culture topic. A great teacher-scholar has sometimes made the world seem to pivot on a new species or a Greek particle, but this art can never make these themes rank with, e. g., evolution, the renaissance, religion, or mathematics, even if poorly taught. The history of education is rich in warnings, but I can recall no fallacy that so completely evicts content and enthrones form. If true, the greatest educational battles from the Greeks to the present time have been fought for naught, and seas of pedagogic ink will have been spilled in vain.

(*c*) Another related surd that has acquired wide vogue and wrought only mischief is that fitting for college is essentially the same as fitting for life. Indeed, life, it is said, is preparing for an examination. The lawyer crams for his cases; the doctor for his critical trials; the business man for crises. Life itself is an examination. Therefore, that state of man where he is fitting for college is really the best school for life. This involves the colossal assumption that the college has so adjusted itself to the demands of the world as it now is, that the old maxim—*non vitae sed scholae discimus*—presents an antithesis which no longer exists, and the schools and teachers that complain that they must fit for college rather than fit for life are non-suited. This would be true if, e. g., the high school best fitted the vast majority who now leave to do so with least loss and with the greatest advantage at any point during or at the end of the course, for this would, in present conditions, be the greatest good for the greatest number. But this would involve the radical revolution of beginning every topic with its practical, industrial, or applied side, and reserving pure science of every kind till the last. If this be the ideal and ultimate system, colleges are farthest from and will be the last to accept it. Here the counter assertion is that to fit for present entrance examinations involves an at least temporary unfitting for life. It is too sedentary, clerical, bookish, and noetic, and above all, arbitrary and by an alien master who offers at best only a limited range of choices, all of which may fail to appeal to the best powers of youth. Life is not coaching nor cramming, and very few of its tests consist in getting up subjects and writing them, while too many examinations stunt and clog, and if too prolonged, make real life seem tenuous and afar because it lacks the vital element of decision and application.

1949

Again, in one of the most important of recent educational books, Demolins[1] urges that an education which fits for life in existing institutions is bad and must fail because it makes men tuft-hunters, place-seekers, searchers for soft snaps, takes out the blood and iron of their nature, and he demands an education that fits for nothing, for only that is truly liberal, in a way that suggests Lowell's definition of a university as a place where nothing useful is taught. For him it should exhaust all the possibilities of the present and overflow naturally into the future. It is filled with an ideal of what Mr. Kidd called projected efficiency. Its sentiments preform history. Those who escape bondage to past and present alike and who are best fitted for life want, no matter with what degree or at what stage their apprenticeship ends—every man Jack of them—to go out into the world and make careers for themselves. They go West, to the colonies, the slums; devise new enterprises, sometimes almost want to peasantize themselves and fall in love with wheel-grease and the smell of the barnyard; want to sweep the office and run on errands; their instinct to be fundamental impels them to start so low that they can sink no lower, so that every change must be a rise. Academic enervation and anemia is seen when youth desire simply to fit for ready-made positions instead of striking out new ones. Napoleon organized the schools of France to give him civil servants, and the incubus of the French educational system, which all the best teachers of that land now deplore, is that the young baccalaureate and his parents have from the first only a snug little berth in view, and those who fail of this low kind of success eat their hearts out. Their parents, instead of wanting to see them safely housed and married to a dot, should cut the navel-string and toss them out into the current, to sink or swim according to their merit. One college graduate of this mettle wagered that he would start naked in a hotel bathroom and, unaided, pay his way around the world and return in one year with $5,000, and won his wager. With academic wealth comes taste for luxury, enervation, distaste for strenuosity, taste for pemmican courses, the habit of dawdling, and in the end the realizing sense that one has been born just too late and has spent his life in trying to make up the lost quarter of an hour. Education should cease to fit for the past that its graduates should, in Sturm's ideal, be at home if transported to ancient Greece or Rome. Nor should it be content to fit for the present, which will all too soon be an emeritus deity. This enthusiasm for a larger future alone banishes *ennui* and disenchantment. This is fitting for life, but it is not fitting for college or even for present times.

These three so-called principles thus turn out to be only clever recruiting precepts, special pleas of able advocates holding briefs for the college rather than the judicial decisions of educational statesmanship. The strategists of this policy urge that social classes are favored by European schools, and that it is an American idea of unique value that every boy should as long as possible feel that he is on the high road to the bachelor's degree and will reach it, if he does not stop, just as we teach that he may become president, but they ignore the fact that there are as great differences in natural ability as those artificially created in any aristocracy, and that the very life of a republic depends on bringing these out, in learning how to detect betimes, and give the very best training to, those fittest for leadership. If all topics have equal culture value and fit equally well for life and college, every youth would naturally select whatever topics the college suggests, and every teacher would adopt any methods it prescribes, for all other differences are obliterated. The growing preponderance of scholastic topics, the increase of high school classes in the first year, and the augmented subserviency of secondary teachers, who here find the uniformity so dear to the inert mind—because its ready-made scheme, supported by the most respectable pedagogic authority, relieves them from the vaster problems of local and all other adjustments—show the triumphs, and the growing percentages

[1]*Anglo-Saxon Superiority.* London, 1898.

of those who drop out from loss of zest show the havoc wrought by these masterstrokes of college politics. The voters, who have lately so multiplied high schools, were at first pleased with the dignity of the fitting function that seemed to make academic life so accessible, but the people are slower and their interests less enlightened and less sharply defined. Their real voice has not yet been clearly heard, and their unformulated purpose has not yet been accomplished. It is an infinitely greater problem to fit for life than to fit for college, and requires far more thought and a larger accumulation of experiences. It was natural, therefore, that college interests, which are so simple and easy, should be the first on the ground and should come to power. The evils of this dominance are now so great and manifest that they must be transient.

CHARLES W. ELIOT'S RESPONSE TO G. STANLEY HALL (1905) From Charles W. Eliot, "The Fundamental Assumptions in the Report of the Committee of Ten," *Educational Review*, vol. XXX, pp. 325–43.

In the sixteenth chapter of President G. Stanley Hall's large work entitled the *Psychology of adolescence,* that long and interesting chapter which deals with intellectual development and education, the learned author described "three extraordinary fallacies" perpetrated in the Report of the Committee of Ten to the National Council of Education, a report issued in 1893, and apparently accepted with satisfaction by the profession of teaching as a serviceable document at that time and since. These three fallacies are said by President Hall to be "only clever recruiting precepts, special pleas of able advocates holding briefs for the college, rather than the judicial decisions of educational statesmanship." As stated by President Hall they are as follows: (1) "Every subject which is taught at all in a secondary school should be taught in the same way and to the same extent to every pupil so long as he pursues it, no matter what the probable destination of the pupil may be, or at what point his education is to cease." (2) "All subjects are of equal educational value if taught equally well." (3) "Fitting for college is essentially the same as fitting for life." I propose to examine these three principles, which to President Hall seem fallacies, and to consider to what extent each one of them is really affirmed in the Report of the Committee of Ten, hoping to convince you that these principles, within the limitations stated in the Report, far from being fallacies, are sound and permanent educational principles, on which alone a truly democratic school system can be based.

*   *   *

The Committee suggested a list of questions for discussion in each Conference, one of which was the following: "Should the subject be treated differently for pupils who are going to college, for those who are going to a scientific school, and for those who are presumably going to neither?" This question was answered unanimously in the negative by the Conferences, and the Committee of Ten unanimously agreed with the Conferences. These ninety-nine honest and intelligent

THE EDUCATIONAL
ESTABLISHMENT
SPEAKS

1951

teachers, intimately concerned either with the actual work of American secondary schools or with the results of that work as they appear in students who go to college, and fairly representing the profession in the United States, unanimously declared that "every subject which is taught at all in the secondary schools should be taught in the same way and to the same extent to every pupil *so long as he pursues it*, no matter what the probable destination of the pupil may be, or at what point his education is to cease"; and yet President Hall calls this principle, or working rule, an "extraordinary fallacy."

Let us first observe the limitations of this principle. It does not affirm that all pupils should study the same subjects, or that all pupils should pursue a given subject the same length of time. In both these important respects the utmost freedom and variety may exist in any secondary school, and yet this fundamental principle may be strictly observed therein. This freedom and variety are secured by the significant clause—"so long as he pursues it." The affirmation, fairly construed, includes three distinct propositions: (1) there is a best way of beginning and pursuing each subject in its elements, which best way every class that attacks it at all should follow; (2) there are certain topics within each subject which all children who take up the subject may best devote their time to; and (3) these topics can be defined with a good deal of precision and a fair degree of expert consent. Moreover, to give effect to these propositions in any school system there must be some number of week-hours which are to be devoted to it thru some number of months by every pupil who is to study it at all. Evidently the principle under consideration has important applications in program-making and in the quest for desirable uniformity in secondary schools.

It must be borne in mind that the prime object of the appointment of the Committee of Ten was to procure, if possible, a higher degree of uniformity in school programs and in requirements for admission to college than then existed; and it was for the Committee to consider what kind of uniformity was desirable and what was undesirable. Without a program, made by assigning certain studies to certain hours in certain years, no school can do its work. It is well to talk much and strongly, as President Hall does, about individualizing instruction—indeed I have done my share of such talking myself—but every superintendent and principal of the least experience knows that every secondary school must have a program or programs, and that most of the instruction must be addressed to classes and not to individual pupils. Some amount of standardizing, quantifying, calibrating, or schematizing of the subjects to be taught, to use some of President Hall's rather contemptuous words, is absolutely indispensable in every school. The only question is—what shall the amount be? The ninety-nine teachers who constituted the Committee of Ten and its Conferences, said unanimously,—the uniformity should apply to the method of teaching and to the selection of the fundamental topics in each subject which is taught at all in a secondary school, but not to the selection of subjects by the individual pupil, or to the length of time that the individual pupil pursues each subject. The arguments for this limited uniformity are overwhelmingly strong. In the first place, that is the only economical way to use the teaching force in any school. For example, if algebra were taught from the beginning onward, in three or four different ways at different rates to three or four different sets of pupils in the same school, there would inevitably be a great waste of teaching force in the process; and whatever was wasted on algebra would probably be lost to other subjects. Secondly, in democratic society the classification of pupils, according to their so-called probable destinations, should be postponed to the latest possible time of life. It is common in Europe to classify children very early into future peasants, mechanics, trades-people, merchants, and professional people, and to adapt deliberately the education of children from a very early age to this decreed destination. In a democratic society like ours, these early determinations of the career should be avoided as long as possible, particularly in public schools. For example, the point in the program of the public high school at which the pupils who are going to college diverge from the pupils who are not going to college should be placed as late as possible, not in the interest of the college, which President Hall erroneously believes was the governing motive of the Committee of Ten, but in the interest of the pupils whose educational careers and life careers should not be too early determined. President Hall, on the contrary, maintains that the European discriminations according to "ultimate goals" constitute a "precious development." He distinctly expresses approval of the choice "between academic and other careers made before the teens." He likes the differences in both method and matter between the courses in English public secondary schools and those in the great endowed fitting schools,—the first being plebeian, the second aristocratic institutions. The German classification into Gymnasia, Real schools, and Volk schools, and the very different treatment of the pupils in these three sorts of schools command his admiration. In short, he believes that the destinations of the pupils should be settled and taken into account before the teens. Now the American high school is, in the first place, destined for children who have already entered their teens; and, in the next place, it is emphatically a school in which training for power and general cultivation are the fundamental ideas, as distinguished from training in special means of obtaining a predestined sort of livelihood. No one has stated his truth more strongly than President Hall. Thoughtful students of his *Psychology of adolescence* will refuse to believe that the American public intends to have its children sorted before their teens into clerks, watchmakers, lithographers, telegraph operators, masons, teamsters, farm laborers, and so forth, and treated differently in their schools according to these prophecies of their appropriate life careers. Who are to make these prophecies? Can parents? Can teachers? Can university presidents, or even professional students of childhood and adolescence? I have watched many hundreds of successful careers which no one—not even the most intelligent and affectionate parent—could have prophesied of the runners at twelve years of age; and I have always believed that the individual child in a democratic society had a right to do his own prophesying about his own career, guided by his own ambitions and his own capacities, and abating his aspirations only under the irresistible pressure of adverse circumstances. For those children whose parents can afford to keep them at school until they are eighteen years of age, the determination of the specific means of earning the individual's livelihood should be postponed till after graduation at the high school.

Another of President Hall's arguments against the principle under consideration—indeed, he places this argument first in order—is that it "does not apply to the great army of incapables, shading down to those who should be in schools for dullards or abnormal children, for whose mental development heredity decrees a slow pace and early arrest." The fact mentioned in this sentence is correct. The principle does not apply to incapables or abnormal dullards; but when considered as an argument to prove that the principle unanimously accepted by the Committee of Ten and the members of the Conference is a fallacy, this sequence itself will be found to contain several remarkable assumptions. In the first place, it assumes that the incapables or abnormal children may properly be called a "great army." Now, within a population of eighty millions there may possibly be incapables enough to constitute an army, say a hundred thousand, or three hundred thousand strong, in a school population of many millions; but relatively to the total number of school children, the incapables are always but an insignificant proportion; so that any school superintendent or principal who should construct his programs with the incapables chiefly in mind would be a person professionally demented. It would be hard to conceive a more misleading suggestion than is contained in those two short words, "great army." Next, the sentence suggests that the decrees of heredity can be easily read, and are to be accepted without distrust. Now, the plain fact is that heredity seldom gives any certain advice before the teens, and the decrees attributed to it are not only uncertain in themselves till much later in life, but are often attributable to other sources. Again, this sentence states that heredity decrees a slow pace and early arrest, as if these two things—slow pace and early arrest—inevitably belonged together. On the contrary, a slow pace often indicates long profitable continuance. No sensible parents who possess good judgment and adequate resources ever stop the education of their children because the intellectual pace of those children is slow. They persevere, and by perseverance often help their children to win infinite rewards. The early arrest is no more expedient for the slow-witted than for the quick-witted; and the slowness itself is often attributable to the fact that parents and teachers have failed to find out the subject in which the individual child supposed to be slow would prove to be quick. That little clause, "for whose mental development heredity decrees a slow pace and early arrest," is, in my judgment, crammed with educational error and injustice. The early arrest of education for multitudes of children is nowadays recognized as a great evil, which modern public-school systems should contend against in every possible way, and seek remedies for thru evening schools, free lectures, public libraries, and all the other means by which the youth or the adult, who has been compelled to abbreviate his school life, may remedy this defect in later years. It, therefore, is not an evil which democratic society proposes to accept, submit to, and recognize in the construction of its public-school programs. The American teacher does not propose to accept the principle that the child whose education is to be shortest should have the scrappiest and least power-giving course, just because the course is to be short. If the course is to be short, there is all the more reason that its elements and their combination should be the best possible. Then the short course will also be good for the children who are going on longer. On the whole, it seems probable that this first proposition laid down by the Committee of Ten, which President Hall stigmatized as an "extraordinary fallacy," is likely to hold its place firmly in the front rank of American secondary-school policies.

The second fallacy which President Hall attributes to the Committee of Ten he states as follows: "All subjects are of equal educational value if taught equally well." This dogma is nowhere explicitly stated in the Report of the Committee of Ten, but it seems to be implied in some of the opinions expressed by the several Conferences and by the Committee. Here are nine Conferences on nine different subjects, all making strong suggestions concerning the programs of primary and grammar schools, generally with some reference to the subsequent programs of secondary schools. They desire important changes in the elementary grades as well as in the higher grades. The six Conferences on the newer subjects—English; other modern languages; physics, astronomy, and chemistry; natural history; history, civil government, and political economy; and geography—desired to have their respective subjects made as nearly as possible equal to Latin, Greek, and mathematics in weight and influence in the secondary schools, altho they were well aware that educational tradition was adverse to this desire, and that many teachers felt strong distrust of these subjects as disciplinary material. This manifest desire of six

Conferences on comparatively new subjects, felt by experts in the several subjects, and urged in the reports of these Conferences with ingenuity and vigor, is the main foundation for the impression received by some rapid readers of the Report that the Committee of Ten believed one subject of study to be as good as another. The impression was doubtless confirmed by observing that all these bodies of experts desired to have the elements of their several subjects taught earlier than they now are, the Conferences on the newer subjects thus seeking an advantage which the older subjects have long possessed. Furthermore, all the Conferences state that more highly trained teachers are needed in both the elementary and secondary schools, particularly for the newer subjects. These recommendations may seem to imply that "all subjects are of equal educational value if taught equally well," but the abstract doctrine can only be inferred from the Report of the Committee. It is not therein stated or laid down. The doctrine may be inferred from some remarks of the Committee of Ten itself on its tables of the instruction (estimated by the number of weekly periods assigned to each subject) to be given in a secondary school during each year of a four-years' course, for the Committee obviously believed that a selection of studies for the individual pupil would have to be made, at least in the second, third, and fourth years of the secondary-school course, and moreover that different schools would select different subjects to teach, being compelled to omit many good subjects in order to teach thoroly the few that they were prepared to deal with satisfactorily. Such selections, whether for the individual pupil or for the school, imply that many different groups of selected subjects may have equal educational value. The Committee, however, obviously gave great weight to thoroness in any program of study for the individual pupil or for the school; and to attain thoroness in the subjects chosen undoubtedly seemed to them more important than to teach any particular subject or subjects, provided always that every course of study followed in a secondary school should provide excursions into the principal fields of knowledge, such as languages, mathematics, history, and natural science.

*   *   *

It must be remembered that uniformity in requirements for admission to college was one of the topics especially to be studied by this Committee. Accordingly, the Committee prepared four programs, called respectively Classical, Scientific, Modern Languages, and English; and they said of these programs, "The Committee are of opinion that the satisfactory completion of any one of the four-years' courses of study embodied in the foregoing programs should admit to corresponding courses in colleges and scientific schools. They believe that this close articulation between the secondary schools and the higher institutions would be advantageous alike for the schools, the colleges, and the country." This statement is a good interpretation of the meaning of the Committee in saying that "all the subjects are to be considered equivalent in educational rank for the purposes of admission to college." All the opinions expressed by the Committee concerning the equivalence of different studies had an intensely practical bearing, being based on programs for secondary schools and requirements for admission to college, which were necessarily compromises and accommodations to existing conditions. They were not educational dogmas, but practical suggestions to produce smooth action in a complicated educational machine, which has to be mended and improved while incessantly running. It is not in the Report of the Committee of Ten that the phrase "One study is as good as another" occurs, but in the Minority Report signed by President Baker, who thought that doctrine implied in certain passages of the Committee's Report, and felt obliged to protest against it. Yet President Baker carefully adds, "If I rightly understood, the majority of the Committee rejected the theory of equivalence of studies for a general education." He was quite right, and accordingly that doctrine is not found, except in the qualified and limited form, in the Report of the Committee of Ten. President Hall puts within quotation marks the sentence, "All subjects are of equal educational value if taught equally well"; but this sentence cannot have been quoted from the Report of the Committee of Ten.

The Committee's third "extraordinary fallacy" is stated by President Hall in the following form: "Fitting for college is essentially the same as fitting for life," and he calls this proposition a "surd" related to the two preceding fallacies, the term "surd" presumably indicating that the proposition is irrational. This doctrine is nowhere laid down in the Report of the Committee of Ten, or in the reports made by the several Conferences to the Committee. It is nothing but an inference from the unanimously adopted recommendation that every subject which is taught at all in the secondary school should be taught in the same way and to the same extent to every pupil so long as he pursues it; and it is clearly an unjust inference from that proposition, for it takes no account of the indispensable qualification "so long as he pursues it." The Conference on history, civil government, and political economy declared that their interest was chiefly "in the school children who have no expectation of going to college, the larger number of whom will not even enter a high school"; and they added that their "recommendations are in no way directed to building up the colleges or increasing the number of college students." Several other Conferences expressed similar sentiments. Undoubtedly, the Committee and the Conferences all believed that whatever improves the schools must improve the colleges; but the object in view from first to last was the benefit of the school children. President Hall must have been led to attribute this related surd to the Committee of Ten by his own confident belief that the guiding motive of the Committee was the desire to recruit the colleges—a motive, by the way, not vicious in itself, which may have been to some extent in the mind of the National Council of Education when it appointed the Committee of Ten, inasmuch as the Committee was instructed to study uniformity in the requirements for admission to college. That uniformity is primarily in the interest of the secondary schools, but a secondary effect of it might be to recruit more freely the colleges and universities. This secondary effect, however, can hardly be considered an evil.

Let us now examine the doctrine "Fitting for college is essentially the same as fitting for life," altho this doctrine is not found explicitly in the Report of the Committee of Ten. It is certainly the intention of the colleges to fit the young men who come under their care for successful and honorable careers in the real world; and it certainly ought to be true that a young man who pursues a preparatory course of study, which lasts till he is from twenty-one to twenty-three years of age, ought to be better prepared for life than the boy whose preparatory course is ended at eighteen or at fourteen. Whether their preliminary training stop at fourteen, at eighteen, or at twenty-two, all these youths are going out into life, and they are all being fitted for life. If the high school is well planned, it will certainly give its pupils a better preparation for earning a satisfactory livelihood than can by any possibility be procured by the age of fourteen. Clearly, if the high school does not fit a boy for life four years better than the grammar school, the high school is, in some measure, failing to perform its function; and in the same way if the preparation for life obtainable at college is not three or four years better than the preparation obtainable at a high school, the college is in some measure failing to perform its function, and all well-wishers for the community as a whole should go to work to improve the secondary school or the college, or both, and they should never for a moment lose sight of the facts that school and college are both training for life, and that the subsequent life should be larger, more productive, and more enjoyable the longer has been the preparation for it. The proposition that fitting for college at eighteen is different in its essence or main motives from fitting at eighteen for the life of the working world can only be maintained by one who believes that either the work of the secondary school or the work of the college is badly done, altho some diversity may be expedient between the two in the selection of subjects and in their proportions. President Hall seems to believe that the work of both is now badly done, but the work of the secondary school better done, on the whole, relatively to its function, than the work of the college. Hence his dread of any influence over the secondary schools which proceeds from the colleges as they are. Yet President Hall at some moments recognizes the plain fact that the nineteenth-century improvements in education, like those of earlier centuries, did as a matter of fact proceed from above downward, and not from the lower grades of education upward to the higher, and no one has described with more scientific accuracy and fullness or more enthusiam than he the guiding and inspiring function of the university, past, present and future.

It is undoubtedly true that in secondary schools which maintain a variety of programs, each program covering four years, the program which is intended to prepare boys and girls for college is, as a rule, the best and most costly; because it contains the fewest and best taught subjects, the other programs being less substantial and dealing with subjects for which it is harder to obtain competent teachers, such as history, natural history, economics, and civics. This is an unfortunate and unjust traditional condition of things in American secondary schools, and many of the recommendations of the Committee of Ten dealt with remedies for this evil. The preparation for college at eighteen has been a better piece of school work than the preparation for earning a livelihood at eighteen in commercial or industrial employments, and the unanimous effort of educators ought to be towards making one training as good as the other relatively to its object. The clearly expressed opinion of the Committee of Ten was that any one of the four programs they suggested for secondary schools would, in the first place, procure for the youth who followed it a suitable preparation for earning his living to advantage at eighteen, or, in the second place, should admit him to college or scientific school. That is, the youth arrived at eighteen, who had followed any one of the programs recommended by the Committee of Ten, would still hold the option between going to work to earn his living and going to college or scientific school, so far as the preparation afforded by his school course was concerned. That result the Committee undoubtedly thought was both feasible and desirable. To this extent, and only to this extent, is it fair to say that the Committee believed that fitting for college might be the same thing as fitting for life. They obviously believed that not every secondary school subject should be attempted by every boy, or even by every school; but, recognizing that all the subjects taught were really to be dealt with only in their elements, they thought that all pupils who selected a given subject might reasonably be treated in the same manner, so long as they held to that subject,—that is, they were guilty of accepting unanimously President Hall's first "extraordinary fallacy." To this extent they believed that the fitting for college need not be separated from the fitting to earn the livelihood at eighteen. President Hall's real contention, on the contrary, is that the colleges are not fitting for life at all, being too sedentary, clerical, bookish, and arbitrary, and failing to send their students out into the world to make careers for themselves—that, in short, they are suffering from "academic enervation and anaemia." This, of course, is a question of fact, and the public must take their choice among witnesses and testimonies. To my thinking, the American colleges and universities were never before so free, animated, and animating as they have been during the past twenty years, or so abundantly productive of vigorous and serviceable human character, and of fresh knowledge and new applications of knowledge to the advantage of mankind. So far as one can judge from the increasing resort to secondary schools, colleges, and universities, and from the increase of their resources, the American public believes in the higher education more generally and firmly than ever before. President Hall appears to believe not only that the pressure of work in colleges has been reduced, but also that the increase of pressure in the high schools has caused the decrease of pressure in the colleges. I know of no facts which support either of these propositions; but it would certainly be impossible to demonstrate the second. It might be suspected, altho extremely unlikely; but it could not be proved.

In maintaining that the three principles which we have been considering are only "special pleas of able advocates holding briefs for the college," President Hall emphasizes strongly the great differences in natural ability among the children of a democracy, and says that "the very life of a republic depends on bringing these out, on learning how to detect betimes, and give the very best training to, those fittest for leadership." These are sound teachings, not unfamiliar to my own pen for thirty-five years past; but it is strange to see them perverted into an attack on that degree of uniformity in secondary schools which is indispensable to the conduct of any school whatever, and on measures to facilitate the passage of gifted youth from school to college.

With what President Hall maintains concerning the independence and dignity of the secondary school the Committee of Ten and the members of its Conferences would be, I am sure, in cordial agreement. They expressly say that "the secondary schools of the United States, taken as a whole, do not exist for the purpose of preparing boys and girls for colleges. Only an insignificant percentage of the graduates of these schools go to colleges or scientific schools. . . . A secondary-school program intended for national use must therefore be made for those children whose education is not to be pursued beyond the secondary school." But they were engaged in an extremely practical task, and the amount of educational theory or philosophy in their Report is small. The Committee were chiefly concerned to transmit to the public in a clear and forcible way the recommendations made by the Conferences as regards topics, methods, and time-allotment for each subject. The most difficult matter with which the Committee of Ten undertook to deal was the time-allotment on secondary-school programs to each one of the subjects which the Conferences recommended as proper for secondary schools. In recommending time-allotments, and four programs in which the recommended time-allotments were observed, the Committee of Ten made two assumptions of a general character which were indispensable to the solution of that part of their problem. They assumed that subjects deemed important should get a larger number of weekly periods during more months or years than subjects deemed less important; and they also assumed that sufficient schedule time should be assigned to every subject admitted to the program, to bring out the value of that subject as training. The first of these assumptions has generally been acted on in American program-making; but the second has been disregarded in innumerable instances. The Committee also assumed that any large subject like language, mathematics, history, or science, if it is to yield its training value, must be pursued thru several years, and be studied from three to five times a week, and therefore that the individual pupil can advantageously give attention to only a moderate number of subjects. Hence, all the four programs suggested as types by the Committee were intended to secure thoroness, advantageous sequence, and the imparting of power as distinguished from information. The general view of the Committee was clearly stated in the following sentences: "If every subject studied at all is to be studied thoroly and consecutively, every subject must receive an adequate time-allotment. If every subject is to provide a substantial mental training, it must have a time-allotment sufficient to produce that fruit. Finally, since selection must be exercised by, or on behalf of, the individual pupil, all the subjects between which choice is allowed should be approximately equivalent to each other in seriousness, dignity, and efficacy. Therefore they should have approximately equal time-allotments." The reason here given for making approximately equal time-allotments to subjects between which choice is allowed contains the nearest approximation made by the Committee to the theory that "one study is as good as another." It is a reason of large application in any elective *system* of studies, tho not needed when elections can be satisfactorily made without any system or correlation.

One other fundamental assumption ran thru all the work of the Committee—an assumption distinct from, and yet related to the three assumptions which President Hall designates as "extraordinary fallacies." The Committee and all the Conferences believed that every subject they recommended for introduction into elementary and secondary schools should help every other, and that the teacher of each single subject should feel responsible for the advancement of the pupils in all the subjects they respectively study, and should contribute to this advancement; and in this respect the Committee made no distinction between school work and college work, considering the latter only a continuation of the former, since directed to similar ends—namely, training for power and character, for serviceableness and happiness. This sense of continuity thruout the whole course of education the Committee of Ten undoubtedly felt in a high degree. Their own education antedated the epoch of child-study, and of that psychological pedagogy which makes a great deal of certain bodily changes in childhood and youth, and undertakes to mark off the years between birth and maturity into distinct, sharply defined periods, bearing separate names like childhood and adolescence, and to prescribe appropriate pedagogical treatment for each period. They had but an obscure perception of those "stages of development" of which recent pedagogy makes so much, altho they probably recognized some stages in the development of each single individual with wide variations as regards time of occurrence in different individuals; but in general they thought of the expansion of the mind and heart pretty much as they did of the growth of the body, as a continuous series of shaded transitions, liable, to be sure, to occasional accelerations, but in the main a continuous enlargement without breaks or explosions. They were appointed to study in a method prescribed to them certain possible improvements in existing institutions of education, and they discharged this function, it must be confessed, with but scant attention to educational theory, or, indeed, to the physiology and psychology of children. To their minds the best part of their Report was the reports made to the Committee by the nine Conferences they organized, reports which are remarkably free from speculative pedagogy. Nevertheless the Committee believed in 1893 that such portions of educational theory as were implied in their practical suggestions were thoroly sound; and, so far as their chairman knows, observation of the effects of their Report during the past twelve years has only confirmed the Committee in this belief.

REPORT OF THE COMMITTEE OF FIFTEEN ON ELEMENTARY
EDUCATION (1895)   From National Education Association, *Report of the Committee of Fifteen* (Boston, 1895), pp. 3–14, 17–18, 21–23, 25, 35–42, 57–67, 69.

The .undersigned Committee agrees upon the following report, each member reserving for himself the expression of his individual divergence from the opinion of the majority, by a statement appended to his signature, enumerating the points to which exception is taken and the grounds for them.

Correlation of Studies

Your Committee understands by correlation of studies:—

LOGICAL ORDER OF TOPICS AND BRANCHES

First, the arrangement of topics in proper sequence in the course of study, in such a manner that each branch develops in an order suited to the natural and easy progress of the child, and so that each step is taken at the proper time to help his advance to the next step in the same branch, or to the next steps in other related branches of the course of study.

SYMMETRICAL WHOLE OF STUDIES IN THE WORLD OF HUMAN LEARNING

Second, the adjustment of the branches of study in such a manner that the whole course at any given time represents all the great divisions of human learning, as far as is possible at the stage of maturity at which the pupil has arrived, and that each allied group of studies is represented by some one of its branches best adapted for the epoch in question; it being implied that there is an equivalence of studies to a greater or less degree within each group, and that each branch of human learning should be represented by some equivalent study; so that, while no great division is left unrepresented, no group shall have superfluous representatives, and thereby debar other groups from a proper representation.

PSYCHOLOGICAL SYMMETRY–THE WHOLE MIND

Third, the selection and arrangement of the branches and topics within each branch, considered psychologically, with a view to afford the best exercise of the faculties of the mind, and to secure the unfolding of those faculties in their natural order, so that no one faculty is so overcultivated or so neglected as to produce abnormal or one-sided mental development.

CORRELATION OF PUPIL'S COURSE OF STUDY WITH THE WORLD IN WHICH HE LIVES–HIS SPIRITUAL
AND NATURAL ENVIRONMENT

Fourth and chiefly, your Committee understands by correlation of studies the selection and arrangement in orderly sequence of such objects of study as shall give the child an insight into the world that he lives in, and a command over its resources such as is obtained by a helpful co-operation with one's fellows. In a word, the chief consideration to which all others are to be subordinated, in the opinion of your Committee, is this requirement of the civilization into which the child is born, as determining not only what he shall study in school, but what habits and customs he shall be taught in the family before the school age arrives; as well as that he shall acquire a skilled acquaintance with some one of a definite series of trades, professions, or vocations in the years that follow school; and, furthermore, that this question of the relation of the pupil to his civilization determines what political duties he shall assume and what religious faith and spiritual aspirations shall be adopted for the conduct of his life.

To make more clear their reasons for the preference here expressed for the objective and practical basis of selection of topics for the course of study rather than the subjective basis so long favored by educational writers, your Committee would describe the psychological basis, already mentioned, as being merely formal in its character, relating only to the exercise of the so-called mental faculties.

It would furnish a training of spiritual powers analogous to the gymnastic training of the muscles of the body. Gymnastics may develop strength and agility without leading to any skill in trades or useful employment. So an abstract psychological training may develop the will, the intellect, the imagination, or the memory, but without leading to an exercise of acquired power in the interests of civilization. The game of chess would furnish a good course of study for the discipline of the powers of attention and calculation of abstract combinations, but it would give its possessor little or no knowledge of man or nature. The psychological ideal which has prevailed to a large extent in education has, in the old phrenology, and in the recent studies in physiological psychology, sometimes given place to a biological ideal. Instead of the view of mind as made up of faculties like will, intellect, imagination, and emotion, conceived to be all necessary to the soul, if developed in harmony with one another, the concept of nerves or brain-tracts is used as the ultimate regulative principle to determine the selection and arrangement of studies. Each part of the brain is supposed to have its claim on the attention of the educator, and that study is thought to be the most valuable which employs normally the larger number of brain-tracts. This view reaches an extreme in the direction of formal, as opposed to objective or practical grounds for selecting a course of study. While the old psychology with its mental faculties concentrated its attention on the mental processes and neglected the world of existing objects and relations upon which those processes were directed, physiological psychology tends to confine its attention to the physical part of the process, the organic changes in the brain cells and their functions.

Your Committee is of the opinion that psychology of both kinds, physiological and introspective, can hold only a subordinate place in the settlement of questions relating to the correlation of studies. The branches to be studied, and the extent to which they are studied, will be determined mainly by the demands of one's civilization. These will prescribe what is most useful to make the individual acquainted with physical nature and with human nature so as to fit him as an individual to perform his duties in the several institutions—family, civil society, the state, and the Church. But next after this, psychology will furnish important considerations that will largely determine the methods of instruction, the order of taking up the several topics so as to adapt the school work to the growth of the pupil's capacity, and the amount of work so as not to overtax his powers by too much, or arrest the development of strength by too little. A vast number of subordinate details belonging to the pathology of education, such as the hygienic features of school architecture and furniture, programmes, the length of study hours and of class exercises, recreation, and bodily reactions against mental effort, will be finally settled by scientific experiment in the department of physiological psychology.

Inasmuch as your Committee is limited to the consideration of the correlation of studies in the elementary school, it has considered the question of the course of study in general only in so far as this has been found necessary in discussing the grounds for the selection of studies for the period of school education occupying the eight years from six to fourteen years, or the school period between the kindergarten on the one hand and the secondary school on the other. It has not been possible to avoid some inquiry into the true distinction between secondary and elementary studies, since one of the most important questions forced upon the attention of your Committee is that of the abridgment of the elementary course of study from eight or more years to seven or even six years, and the corresponding increase of the time devoted to studies usually assigned to the high school and supposed to belong to the secondary course of study for some intrinsic reason.

The Course of Study—Educational Values

Your Committee would report that it has discussed in detail the several branches of study that have found a place in the curriculum of the elementary school, with a view to discover their educational value for developing and training the faculties of the mind, and more especially for correlating the pupil with his spiritual and natural environment in the world in which he lives.

LANGUAGE STUDIES

There is first to be noted the prominent place of language study that takes the form of reading, penmanship, and grammar in the first eight years' work of the school. It is claimed for the partiality shown to these studies that it is justified by the fact that language is the instrument that makes possible human social organization. It enables each person to communicate his individual experience to his fellows and thus permits each to profit by the experience of all. The written and printed forms of speech preserve human knowledge and make progress in civilization possible. The conclusion is reached that learning to read and write should be the leading study of the pupil in his first four years of school. Reading and writing are not so much ends in themselves as means for the acquirement of all other human learning. This consideration alone would be sufficient to justify their actual place in the work of the elementary school. But these branches require of the learner a difficult process of analysis. The pupil must identify the separate words in the sentence he uses, and in the next place must recognize the separate sounds in each word. It requires a considerable effort for the child or the savage to analyze his sentence into its constituent words, and a still greater effort to discriminate its elementary sounds. Reading, writing, and spelling in their most elementary form, therefore, constitute a severe training in mental analysis for the child of six to ten years of age. We are told that it is far more disciplinary to the mind than any species of observation of differences among material things, because of the fact that the word has a twofold character—addressed to external sense as spoken sound to the ear, or as written and printed words to the eye—but containing a meaning or sense addressed to the understanding and only to be seized by introspection. The pupil must call up the corresponding idea by thought, memory, and imagination, or else the word will cease to be a word and remain only a sound or character.

On the other hand, observation of things and movements does not necessarily involve this twofold act of analysis, introspective and objective, but only the latter—the objective analysis. It is granted that we all have frequent occasion to condemn poor methods of instruction as teaching words rather than things. But we admit that we mean empty sounds or characters rather than true words. Our suggestions for the correct method of teaching amount in this case simply to laying stress on the meaning of the word, and to setting the teaching process on the road of analysis of content rather than form. In the case of words used to store up external observation the teacher is told to repeat and make alive again the act of observation by which the word obtained its original meaning. In the case of a word expressing a relation between facts or events, the pupil is to be taken step by step through the process of reflection by which the idea was built up. Since the word, spoken and written, is the sole instrument by which reason can fix, preserve, and communicate both the data of sense and the relations discovered between them by reflection, no new method in education has been able to supplant in the school the branches, reading and penmanship. But the real improvements in method have led teachers to lay greater and greater stress on the internal factor of the word, on its meaning, and have in manifold ways shown how to repeat the original experiences that gave the meaning to concrete words, and the original comparisons and logical deductions by which the ideas of relations and causal processes arose in the mind and required abstract words to preserve and communicate them.

It has been claimed that it would be better to have first a basis of knowledge of things, and secondarily and subsequently a knowledge of words. But it has been replied to this, that the progress of the child in learning to talk indicates his ascent out of mere impressions into the possession of true knowledge. For he names objects only after he has made some synthesis of his impressions and has formed general ideas. He recognizes the same object under different circumstances of time and place, and also recognizes other objects belonging to the same class by and with names. Hence the use of the word indicates a higher degree of self-activity—the stage of mere impressions without words or signs being a comparatively passive state of mind. What we mean by things first and words afterward, is, therefore, not the apprehension of objects by passive impressions so much as the active investigation and experimenting which come after words are used, and the higher forms of analysis are called into being by that invention of reason known as language, which, as before said, is a synthesis of thing and thought, of outward sign and inward signification.

Rational investigation cannot precede the invention of language any more than blacksmithing can precede the invention of hammers, anvils, and pincers. For language is the necessary tool of thought used in the conduct of the analysis and synthesis of investigation.

Your Committee would sum up these considerations by saying that language rightfully forms the centre of instruction in the elementary school, but that progress in methods of teaching is to be made, as hitherto, chiefly by laying more stress on the internal side of the word, its meaning; using better graded steps to build up the chain of experience or the train of thought that the word expresses.

The first three years' work of the child is occupied mainly with the mastery of the printed and written forms of the words of his colloquial vocabulary; words that he is already familiar enough with as sounds addressed to the ear. He has to become familiar with the new forms addressed to the eye, and it would be an unwise method to require him to learn many new words at the same time that he is learning to recognize his old words in their new shape. But as soon as he has acquired some facility in reading what is printed in the colloquial style, he may go on to selections from standard authors. The literary selections should be graded, and are graded in almost all series of readers used in our elementary schools, in such a way as to bring those containing the fewest words outside of the colloquial vocabulary into the lower books of the series, and increasing the difficulties, step by step, as the pupil grows in maturity. The selections are literary works of art possessing the required organic unity and a proper reflection of this unity in the details, as good works of art must do. But they portray situations of the soul, or scenes of life, or elaborated reflections, of which the child can obtain some grasp through his capacity to feel and think, although in scope and compass they far surpass his range. They are adapted, therefore, to lead him out of and beyond himself, as spiritual guides.

Literary style employs, besides words common to the colloquial vocabulary, words used in a semi-technical sense expressive of fine shades of thought and emotion. The literary work of art furnishes a happy expression for some situation of the soul, or some train of reflection hitherto unutterable in an adequate manner. If the pupil learns this literary production, he finds himself powerfully helped to understand both himself and his fellow-men. The most practical knowledge of all, it will be admitted, is a knowledge of human nature—a knowledge that enables one to combine with his fellow-men, and to share with them the physical and spiritual wealth of the race. Of this high character as humanizing or civilizing, are the favorite works of literature found in the school readers, about one hundred and fifty English and American writers being drawn upon for the material. Such are Shakespeare's speeches of Brutus and Mark Antony, Hamlet's and Macbeth's soliloquies, Milton's L'Allegro and Il Penseroso, Gray's Elegy, Tennyson's Charge of the Light Brigade and Ode on the Death of the Duke of Wellington, Byron's Waterloo, Irving's Rip Van Winkle, Webster's Reply to Hayne, The Trial of Knapp, and Bunker Hill oration, Scott's Lochinvar, Marmion, and Roderick Dhu, Bryant's Thanatopsis, Longfellow's Psalm of Life, Paul Revere, and the Bridge, O'Hara's Bivouac of the Dead, Campbell's Hohenlinden, Collins' How Sleep the Brave, Wolfe's Burial of Sir John Moore, and other fine prose and poetry from Addison, Emerson, Franklin, The Bible, Hawthorne, Walter Scott, Goldsmith, Wordsworth, Swift, Milton, Cooper, Whittier, Lowell, and the rest. The reading and study of fine selections in prose and verse furnish the chief aesthetic training of the elementary school. But this should be re-enforced by some study of photographic or other reproductions of the world's great masterpieces of architecture, sculpture, and painting. The frequent sight of these reproductions is good, the attempt to copy or sketch them with the pencil is better; best of all is an aesthetic lesson their composition, attempting to describe in words the idea of the whole that gives the work its organic unity, and the devices adopted by the artists to reflect this idea in the details and re-enforce its strength. The aesthetic taste of teacher and pupil can be cultivated by such exercises, and once set on the road of development, this taste may improve through life.

A third phase of language study in the elementary school is formal grammar. The works of literary art in the readers, re-enforced as they ought to be by supplementary reading at home of the whole works from which the selections for the school readers are made, will educate the child in the use of a higher and better English style. Technical grammar never can do this. Only familiarity with fine English works will insure one a good and correct style. But grammar is the science of language, and as the first of the seven liberal arts it has long held sway in school as the disciplinary study *par excellence*. A survey of its educational value, subjective and objective, usually produces the conviction that it is to retain the first place in the future. Its chief objective advantage is, that it shows the structure of language, and the logical forms of subject, predicate, and modifier, thus revealing the essential nature of thought itself, the most important of all objects, because it is self-object. On the subjective or psychological side, grammar demonstrates its title to the first place by its use as a discipline in subtle analysis, in logical division and classification, in the art of questioning, and in the mental accomplishment of making exact definitions. Nor is this an empty, formal discipline, for its subject-matter, language, is a product of the reason of a people, not as individuals, but as a social whole, and the vocabulary holds in its store of words the generalized experience of that people, including sensuous observation and reflection, feeling and emotion, instinct and volition.

No formal labor on a great objective field is ever lost wholly, since at the very least it has the merit of familiarizing the pupil with the contents of some one extensive province that borders on his life, and with which he must come into correlation; but it is easy for any special formal discipline, when continued too long, to paralyze or arrest growth at that stage. The overcultivation of the verbal memory tends to arrest the growth of critical attention and reflection. Memory of accessory details too, so much prized in the school, is also cultivated often at the expense of an insight into the organizing principle of the whole and the causal nexus that binds the parts.

✻   ✻   ✻

ARITHMETIC

Side by side with language study is the study of mathematics in the schools, claiming the second place in importance of all studies. It has been pointed out that mathematics concerns the laws of time and space—their structural form, so to speak—and hence that it formulates the logical conditions of all matter both in rest and in motion. Be this as it may, the high position of mathematics as the science of all quantity is universally acknowledged. The elementary branch of mathematics is arithmetic, and this is studied in the primary and grammar schools from six to eight years, or even longer. The relation of arithmetic to the whole field of mathematics has been stated (by Comte, Howison, and others) to be that of the final step in a process of calculation, in which results are stated numerically. There are branches that develop or derive quantitative functions: say geometry for spatial forms, and mechanics for movement and rest and the forces producing them. Other branches transform these quantitative functions into such forms as may be calculated in actual numbers; namely, algebra in its common or lower form, and in its higher form as the differential and integral calculus, and the calculus of variations. Arithmetic evaluates or finds the numerical value for the functions thus deduced and transformed. The educational value of arithmetic is thus indicated both as concerns its psychological side and its objective practical uses in correlating man with the world of nature. In this latter respect as furnishing the key to the outer world in so far as the objects of the latter are a matter of direct enumeration,—capable of being counted,—it is the first great step in the conquest of nature. It is the first tool of thought that man invents in the work of emancipating himself from thraldom to external forces. For by the command of number he learns to divide and conquer. He can proportion one force to another, and concentrate against an obstacle precisely what is needed to overcome it. Number also makes possible all the other sciences of nature which depend on exact measurement and exact record of phenomena as to the following items: order of succession, date, duration, locality, environment, extent of sphere of influence, number of manifestations, number of cases of intermittence. All these can be defined accurately only by means of number. The educational value of a branch of study that furnishes the indispensable first step toward all science of nature is obvious. But psychologically its importance further appears in this, that it begins with an important step in analysis; namely, the detachment of the idea of quantity from the concrete whole, which includes quality as well as quantity. To count, one drops the qualitative and considers only the quantitative aspect.

*   *   *

GEOGRAPHY

The leading branch of the seven liberal arts was grammar, being the first of the *Trivium* (grammar, rhetoric, and logic). Arithmetic, however, led the second division, the *Quadrivium* (arithmetic, geometry, music, and astronomy). We have glanced at the reasons for the place of grammar as leading the humane studies, as well as for the place of arithmetic as leading the nature studies. Following arithmetic, as the second study in importance among the branches that correlate man to nature, is geography. It is interesting to note that the old quadrivium of the Middle Ages included geography, under the title of geometry, as the branch following arithmetic in the enumeration; the subject-matter of their so-called "geometry" being chiefly an abridgment of Pliny's geography, to which were added a few definitions of geometric forms, something like the primary course in geometric solids in our elementary schools. So long as there has been elementary education there has been something of geography included. . . .

*   *   *

HISTORY

The next study, ranked in order of value, for the elementary school is history. But, as will be seen, the value of history, both practically and psychologically, is less in the beginning and greater at the end than geography. For it relates to the institutions of men, and especially to the political state and its evolution.

*   *   *

OTHER BRANCHES

Your Committee has reviewed the staple branches of the elementary course of study in the light of their educational scope and significance. Grammar, literature, arithmetic, geography, and history are the five branches upon which the disciplinary work of the elementary school is concentrated. Inasmuch as reading is the first of the scholastic arts, it is interesting to note that the whole elementary course may be described as an extension of the process of learning the art of reading. First comes the mastering of the colloquial vocabulary in printed and script forms. Next come five incursions into the special vocabularies required *(a)* in literature to express the fine shades of emotion and the more subtle distinctions of thought, *(b)* the technique of arithmetic, *(c)* of geography, *(d)* of grammar, *(e)* of history.

In the serious work of mastering these several technical vocabularies the pupil is assigned daily tasks that he must prepare by independent study. The class exercise or recitation is taken up with examining and criticising the pupil's oral statements of what he has learned, especial care being taken to secure the pupil's explanation of it in his own words. This requires paraphrases and definitions of the new words and phrases used in technical and literary senses, with a view to insure the addition to the mind of the new ideas corresponding to the new words. The misunderstandings are corrected and the pupil set on the way to use more critical alertness in the preparation of his succeeding lessons. The pupil learns as much by the recitations of his fellow-pupils as he learns from the teacher, but not the same things. He sees in the imperfect statements of his classmates that they apprehended the lesson with different presuppositions and consequently have seen some phases of the subject that escaped his observation, while they in turn have missed points which he had noticed quite readily. These different points of view become more or less his own, and he may be said to grow by adding to his own mind the minds of others.

It is clear that there are other branches of instruction that may lay claim to a place in the course of study in the elementary school; for example, the various branches of natural science, vocal music, manual training, physical culture, drawing, etc.

*　　*　　*

Your Committee would mention in this connection instruction in morals and manners, which ought to be given in a brief series of lessons each year with a view to build up in the mind a theory of the conventionalities of polite and pure-minded society. If these lessons are made too long or too numerous, they are apt to become offensive to the child's mind. It is of course understood by your Committee that the substantial moral training of the school is performed by the discipline rather than by the instruction in ethical theory. The child is trained to be regular and punctual, and to restrain his desire to talk and whisper—in these things gaining self-control day by day. The essence of moral behavior is self-control. The school teaches good behavior. The intercourse of a pupil with his fellows without evil words or violent actions is insisted on and secured. The higher moral qualities of truth-telling and sincerity are taught in every class exercise that lays stress on accuracy of statement.

*　　*　　*

The School Programme

In order to find a place in the elementary school for the several branches recommended in this report, it will be necessary to use economically the time allotted for the school term, which is about two hundred days, exclusive of vacations and holidays. Five days per week and five hours of actual school work or a little less per day, after excluding recesses for recreation, give about twenty-five hours per week. There should be, as far as possible, alternation of study-hours and recitations (the word recitation being used in the United States for class exercise or lesson conducted by the teacher and requiring the critical attention of the entire class). Those studies requiring the clearest thought should be taken up, as a usual thing, in the morning session, say arithmetic the second half hour of the morning and grammar the half-hour next succeeding the morning recess for recreation in the open air. By some who are anxious to prevent study at home, or at least to control its amount, it is thought advisable to place the arithmetic lesson after the grammar lesson, so that the study learned at home will be grammar instead of arithmetic. It is found by experience that if mathematical problems are taken home for solution two bad habits arise; namely, in one case, the pupil gets assistance from his parents or others, and thereby loses to some extent his own power of overcoming difficulties by brave and persistent attacks unaided by others; the other evil is a habit of consuming long hours in the preparation of a lesson that should be prepared in thirty minutes, if all the powers of mind are fresh and at command. An average child may spend three hours in the preparation of an arithmetic lesson. Indeed, in repeated efforts to solve one of the so-called "conundrums," a whole family may spend the entire evening. One of the unpleasant results of the next day is that the teacher who conducts the lesson never knows the exact capacity and rate of progress of his pupils; in the recitation he probes the knowledge and preparation of the pupil, plus an unknown amount of preparatory work borrowed from parents and others. He even increases the length of the lessons, and requires more work at home, when the amount already exceeds the unaided capacity of the pupil.

The lessons should be arranged so as to bring in such exercises as furnish relief from intellectual tension between others that make large demands on the thinking powers. Such exercises as singing and calisthenics, writing and drawing, also reading, are of the nature of a relief from those recitations that tax the memory, critical alertness, and introspection, like arithmetic, grammar, and history.

Your Committee has not been able to agree on the question whether pupils who leave school early should have a course of study different from the course of those who are to continue on into secondary and higher work. It is contended, on the one hand, that those who leave early should have a more practical course, and that they should dispense with those studies that seem to be in the nature of preparatory work for secondary and higher education. Such studies as algebra and Latin, for example, should not be taken up unless the pupil expects to pursue the same for a sufficient time to complete the secondary course. It is replied, on the other hand, that it is best to have one course for all, because any school education is at best but an initiation for the pupil into the art of learning, and that wherever he leaves off in his school course he should continue, by the aid of the public library and home study, in the work of mastering science and literature. It is further contended that a brief course in higher studies, like Latin and algebra, instead of being useless, is of more value than any elementary studies that might replace them. The first ten lessons in algebra give the pupil the fundamental idea of the general expression of arithmetical solutions by means of letters and other symbols. Six months' study of it gives him the power to use the method in stating the manifold conditions of a problem in partnership, or in ascertaining a value that depends on several transformations of the data given. It is claimed, indeed, that the first few lessons in any branch are relatively of more educational value than an equal number of subsequent lessons, because the fundamental ideas and principles of the new study are placed at the beginning. In Latin, for instance, the pupil learns in his first week's study the, to him, strange phenomenon of a language that performs by inflections what his own language performs by the use of prepositions and auxiliaries. He is still more surprised to find that the order of words in a sentence is altogether different in Roman usage from that to which he is accustomed. He further begins to recognize in the Latin words many roots or stems which are employed to denote immediate sensuous objects, while they have been adopted into his English tongue to signify fine shades of distinction in thought or feeling. By these three things his powers of observation in matters of language are armed, as it were, with new faculties. Nothing that he has hitherto learned in grammar is so radical and far-reaching as what he learns in his first week's study of Latin. The Latin arrangement of words in a sentence indicates a different order of mental arrangement in the process of apprehension and expression of thought. This arrangement is rendered possible by declensions. This amounts to attaching prepositions to the ends of words, which they thus convert into adjectival or adverbial modifiers; whereas the separate prepositions of the English must indicate by their position in the sentence their grammatical relation. These observations, and the new insight into the etymology of English words having a Latin derivation, are of the nature of mental seeds which will grow and bear fruit throughout life in the better command of one's native tongue. All this will come from a very brief time devoted to Latin in school.

AMOUNT OF TIME FOR EACH BRANCH

Your Committee recommends that an hour of sixty minutes each week be assigned in the programme for each of the following subjects throughout the eight years: physical culture, vocal music, oral lessons in natural science (hygiene to be included among the topics under this head), oral lessons in biography and general history, and that the same amount of time each week shall be devoted to drawing from the second year to the eighth inclusive; to manual training during the seventh and eighth years so as to include sewing and cookery for the girls, and work in wood and iron for the boys.

Your Committee recommends that reading be given at least one lesson each day for the entire eight years, it being understood, however, that there shall be two or more lessons each day in reading in the first and second years, in which the recitation is necessarily very short, because of the inability of the pupil to give continued close attention, and because he has little power of applying himself to the work of preparing lessons by himself. In the first three years the reading should be limited to pieces in the colloquial style, but selections from the classics of the language in prose and in poetry shall be read to the pupil from time to time, and discussions made of such features of the selections read as may interest the pupils. After the third year your Committee believes that the reading lesson should be given to selections from classic authors of English, and that the work of the recitation should be divided between (a) the elocution, (b) the grammatical peculiarities of the language, including spelling, definitions, syntactical construction, punctuation, and figures of prosody, and (c) the literary contents, including the main and accessory ideas, the emotions painted, the deeds described, the devices of style to produce a strong impression on the reader. Your Committee wishes to lay emphasis on the importance of the last item,—that of literary study,—which should consume more and more of the time of the recitation from grade to grade in the period from the fourth to the eighth year. In the fourth year and previously the first item—that of elocution, to secure distinct enunciation and correct pronunciation—should be most prominent. In the fifth and sixth years the second item—that of spelling, defining, and punctuation—should predominate slightly over the other two items. In the years from the fifth to the eighth there should be some reading of entire stories, such as Gulliver's Travels, Robinson Crusoe, Rip Van Winkle, The Lady of the Lake, Hiawatha, and similar stories adapted in style and subject-matter to the capacity of the pupils. An hour should be devoted each week to conversations on the salient points of the story, its literary and ethical bearings.

Your Committee agrees in the opinion that in teaching language care should be taken that the pupil practices much in writing exercises and original compositions. At first the pupil will use only his colloquial vocabulary, but as he gains command of the technical vocabularies of geography, arithmetic, and history, and learns the higher literary vocabulary of his language, he will extend his use of words accordingly. Daily from the first year the child will prepare some lesson or portion of a lesson in writing. Your Committee has included under the head of oral grammar (from the first to the middle of the fifth year) one phase of this written work devoted to the study of the literary form and the technicalities of composition in such exercises as letter writing, written reviews of the several branches studied, reports of the oral lessons in natural science and history, paraphrases of the poems and prose literature of the readers, and finally compositions or written essays on suitable themes assigned by the teacher, but selected from the fields of knowledge studied in school. Care should be taken to criticise all paraphrases of poetry in respect to the good or bad taste shown in the choice of words; parodies should never be permitted.

It is thought by your Committee that the old style of composition writing was too formal. It was kept too far away from the other work of the pupil. Instead of giving a written account of what he had learned in arithmetic, geography, grammar, history, and natural science, the pupil attempted artificial descriptions and reflections on such subjects as "Spring," "Happiness," "Perseverance," "Friendship," or something else outside of the line of his school studies.

Your Committee has already expressed its opinion that a good English style is not to be acquired by the study of grammar so much as by familiarity with great masterpieces of literature. We especially recommend that pupils who have taken up the fourth and fifth readers, containing the selections from great authors, should often be required to make written paraphrases of prose or poetic models of style, using their own vocabulary to express the thoughts so far as possible, and borrowing the *recherche* words and phrases of the author, where their own resources fail them. In this way the pupil learns to see what the great author has done to enrich the language and to furnish adequate means of expression for what could not be presented in words before, or at least not in so happy a manner.

Your Committee believes that every recitation is, in one aspect of it, an attempt to express the thoughts and information of the lesson in the pupil's own words, and thus an initial exercise in composition. The regular weekly written review of the important topics in the several branches studied is a more elaborate exercise in composition, the pupil endeavoring to collect what he knows and to state it systematically and in proper language. The punctuation, spelling, syntax, penmanship, choice of words, and style should not, it is true, be made a matter of criticism in connection with the other lessons, but only in the language lesson proper. But the pupil will learn language, all the same, by the written and oral recitations. The oral grammar lessons, from the first year to the middle of the fifth year, should deal chiefly with the use of language, gradually introducing the grammatical technique as it is needed to describe accurately the correct forms and the usages violated.

Your Committee believes that there is some danger of wasting the time of the pupil in these oral and written language lessons in the first four years by confining the work of the pupil to the expression of ordinary commonplace ideas not related to the subjects of his other lessons, especially when the expression is confined to the colloquial vocabulary. Such training has been severely and justly condemned as teaching what is called prating or gabbling, rather than a noble use of English speech. It is clear that the pupil should have a dignified and worthy subject of composition, and what is so good for his purpose as the themes he has tried to master in his regular lessons? The reading lessons will give matter for literary style, the geography for scientific style, and the arithmetic for a business style; for all styles should be learned.

Your Committee recommends that selected lists of words difficult to spell be made from the reading lessons and mastered by frequent writing and oral spelling during the fourth, fifth, and sixth years.

*   *   *

Methods and Organization

Your Committee is agreed that the time devoted to the elementary school work should not be reduced from eight years, but they have recommended, as herein-before stated, that in the seventh and eighth years a modified form of algebra be introduced in place of advanced arithmetic, and that in the eighth year English grammar yield place to Latin. This makes, in their opinion, a proper transition to the studies of the secondary school and is calculated to assist the pupil materially in his preparation for that work.

THE COMMITTEE OF FIFTEEN ON THE TRAINING OF ELEMENTARY SCHOOL TEACHERS (1895) From H. S. Tarbell, "On the Training of Teachers," as quoted in National Education Association, *Report of the Committee of Fifteen* (Boston, 1895), pp. 95–112.

Conditions for Professional Training—Age and Attainments

It is a widely prevalent doctrine, to which the customs of our best schools conform, that teachers of elementary schools should have a secondary or high school education, and that teachers of high schools should have a collegiate education. Your committee believe that these are the minimum acquirements that can generally be accepted, that the scholarship, culture and power gained by four years of study in advance of the pupils are not too much to be rightfully demanded, and that as a rule no one ought to become a teacher who has not the age and attainments presupposed in the possessor of a high-school diploma. There are differences in high schools, it is true, and a high-school diploma is not a fixed standard of attainment; but in these United States it is one of the most definite and uniform standards that we possess, and varies less than college degrees vary or than elementary schools and local standards of culture vary.

It is, of course, implied in the foregoing remarks that the high school from which the candidate comes is known to be a reputable school, and that its diploma is proof of the completion of a good four-years' course in a creditable manner. If these conditions do not exist, careful examination is the only recourse.

If this condition, high-school graduation or proof by examination of equivalent scholarship, be accepted, the questions of the age and attainment to be reached before entering upon professional study and training are already settled. But if a more definite statement be desired, then it may be said that the candidate for admission to a normal or training school should be eighteen years of age and should have studied English, mathematics, and science to the extent usually pursued in high schools, should be able to write readily, correctly, and methodically upon topics within the teacher's necessary range of thought and conversation, and should have studied, for two or more years, at least one language besides English. Skill in music and drawing is desirable, particularly ability to sketch readily and effectively.

Training Schools

The training of teachers may be done in normal schools, normal classes in academies and high schools, and in city training schools. To all these the general term "training schools" will be applied. Those instructed in these schools will be called pupils while engaged in professional study, and pupil-teachers or teachers-in-training while in practice-teaching preparatory to graduation. Teachers whose work is to be observed by pupil-teachers will be called model-teachers; teachers in charge of pupil-teachers during their practice work will be called critic-teachers. In some institutions model-teachers and critic-teachers are the same persons. The studies usually pursued in academies and high schools will be termed academic, and those post-academic studies to be pursued before or during practice-teaching as a preparation therefor will be termed professional.

Academic Studies

Whether academic studies have any legitimate place in normal or training school is a question much debated. It cannot be supposed that your committee can settle in a paragraph a question upon which many essays have been written, many speeches delivered, and over which much controversy has been waged.

If training schools are to be distinguished from other secondary schools, they must do a work not done in other schools. So far as they teach common branches of study, they are doing what other schools are doing, and have small excuse for existence; but it may be granted that methods can practically be taught only as to subjects, that the study done in professional schools may so treat of the subjects of study, not as objects to be required, but as objects to be presented, that their treatment shall be wholly professional.

One who is to teach a subject needs to know it as a whole, made up of related and subordinate parts, and hence must study it by a method that will give this knowledge. It is not necessary to press the argument that many pupils enter normal and training schools with such slight preparation as to require instruction in academic subjects. The college with a preparatory department is, as a rule, an institution of distinctly lower grade than one without such a department. Academic work in normal schools that is of the nature of preparation for professional work lowers the standard and perhaps the usefulness of such a school; but academic work done as a means of illustrating or enforcing professional truth has its place in a professional school as in effect a part of the professional work. Professional study differs widely from academic study. In the one, a science is studied in its relation to the studying mind; in the other, in reference to its principles and applications. The aim of one kind of study is power to apply; of the other power to present. The tendency of the one is to bring the learner into sympathy with the natural world, of the other with the child world. How much broader becomes the teacher who takes both the academic and the professional view! He who learns that he may know and he who learns that he may teach are standing in quite different mental attitudes. One works for knowledge of subject-matter, the other that his knowledge may have due organization, that he may bring to consciousness the apperceiving ideas by means of which matter and method may be suitably conjoined.

How to study is knowledge indispensable to knowing how to teach. The method of teaching can best be illustrated by teaching. The attitude of a pupil in a training school must be that of a learner whose mental stores are expanding, who faces the great world of knowledge with the purpose to survey a portion of it. If we insist upon a sufficient preparation for admission, the question of what studies to pursue, and especially the controversy between professional and academic work, will be mainly settled.

Professional Work

Professional training comprises two parts: (a) The science of teaching, and (b) the art of teaching.

In the science of teaching are included: (1) Psychology as a basis for principles and methods; (2) Methodology as a guide to instruction; (3) School economy, which adjusts the conditions of work; and (4) History of education, which gives breadth of view.

The art of teaching is best gained: (1) by observation of good teaching; (2) by practice-teaching under criticism.

Relative Time

The existence and importance of each of these elements in the training of teachers are generally acknowledged. Their order and proportionate treatment give rise to differences of opinion. Some would omit the practice work entirely, launching the young teacher upon independent work directly from her pupilage in theory. Others, and much the greater number, advise some preparation in the form of guided experience before the training be considered complete. These vary greatly in their estimate of the proportionate time to be given to practice during training. The answers to the question "What proportion?" which your committee has received range from one-sixteenth to two-thirds as the proportion of time to be given to practice. The greater number, however, advocate a division of time about equal between theory and practice.

The normal schools incline to the smallest proportion for practice-teaching, the city training-schools to the largest. It should be borne in mind, however, that city training-schools are a close continuation, usually, of high schools, and that the the high-school courses give a more uniform and probably a more adequate preparation than the students entering normal schools have usually had. Their facilities for practice-teaching are much greater than normal schools can secure, and for this reason also practice is made relatively more important. As to the relative merits of city training-schools and normal schools, your committee does not desire to express an

THE EDUCATIONAL
ESTABLISHMENT
SPEAKS

1973

opinion; the conditions of education demand the existence of both, and both are necessities of educational advancement. It is important to add, however, that in the judgment of your committee not less than half of the time spent under training by the apprentice-teacher should be given to observation and practice, and that this practice in its conditions should be as similar as possible to the work she will later be required to do independently.

Science of Teaching—Psychology

The laws of apperception teach that one is ready to apprehend new truth most readily when he has already established a considerable and well-arranged body of ideas thereon.

Suggestion, observation, and reflection are each most fruitful when a foundation of antecedent knowledge has been provided. Hence your committee recommends that early in their course of study teachers in training assume as true the well-known facts of psychology and the essential principles of education, and make their later study and practice in the light of these principles. These principles thus become the norm of educational thought, and their truth is continually demonstrated by subsequent experience. From this time theory and practice should proceed together in mutual aid and support.

Most fundamental and important of the professional studies which ought to be pursued by one intending to teach is psychology. This study should be pursued at two periods of the training-school course, the beginning and the end, and its principles should be appealed to daily when not formally studied. The method of study should be both deductive and inductive. The terminology should be early learned from a suitable text-book, and significance given to the terms by introspection, observation, and analysis. Power of introspection should be gained, guidance in observation should be given, and confirmation of psychological principles should be sought on every hand. The habit of thinking analytically and psychologically should be formed by every teacher. At the close of the course a more profound and more completely inductive study of physiological psychology should made. In this way, a tendency to investigate should be encouraged or created.

Study of Children

Modern educational thought emphasizes the opinion that the child, not the subject of study, is the guide to the teacher's efforts. To know the child is of paramount importance. How to know the child must be an important item of instruction to the teacher in training. The child must be studied as to his physical, mental, and moral condition. Is he in good health? Are his senses of sight and hearing normal, or in what degree abnormal? What is his temperment? Which of his faculties seem weak or dormant? Is he eye-minded or ear-minded? What are his powers of attention? What are his likes and dislikes? How far is his moral nature developed and what are its tendencies? By what tests can the degree of difference between bright and dull children be estimated?

To study effectively and observingly these and similar questions respecting children is a high art. No common-sense power of discerning human nature is sufficient; though common sense and sympathy go a long way in such study. Weighing, measuring, elaborate investigation requiring apparatus and laboratory methods, are for experts, not teachers in training. Above all, it must ever be remembered that the child is to be studied as a personality and not as an object to be weighed or analyzed.

Methodology

A part of the work under this head must be a study of the mental and moral effects of different methods of teaching and examination, the relative value of individual and class instruction at different periods of school life and in the study of different branches. The art of questioning is to be studied in its foundation principles and by the illustration of the best examples. Some review of the branches which are to be taught may be made, making the teacher's knowledge of them ready and distinct as to the relations of the several parts of the subject to one another and of the whole to kindred subjects. These and many such subjects should be discussed in the class in pedagogy, investigation should be begun, and the lines on which it can be followed should be distinctly laid down.

The laws of psychology, or the capabilities and methods of mind-activity, are themselves the fundamental laws of teaching, which is the act of exciting normal and profitable mind-action. Beyond these fundamantal laws, the principles of education are to be derived inductively. These inductions when brought to test will be found to be rational inferences from psychological laws and thus founded upon and explained by them.

School Economy

School economy, though a factor of great importance in the teacher's training, can best be studied by the teacher of some maturity and experience, and is of more value in the equipment of secondary than of elementary teachers. Only its outlines and fundamental principles should be studied in the ordinary training-school.

History of Education

Breadth of mind consists in the power to view facts and opinions from the standpoints of others. It is this truth which makes the study of history in a full, appreciative way so influential in giving mental breadth. This general advantage the history of education has in still larger degree, because our interest in the views and experiences of those engaged like us in training the young enables us to enter more fully into their thoughts and purposes than we could into those of the warrior or ruler. From the efforts of the man we imagine his surroundings, which we contrast with our own. To the abstract element of theoretical truth is added the warm human interest we feel in the hero, the generous partisan of truth. The history of education is particularly full of examples of noble purpose, advanced thought, and moral heroism. It is inspiring to fill our minds with these human ideals. We read in the success of the unpractical Pestalozzi the award made to self-sacrifice, sympathy, and enthusiasm expended in giving application to a vital truth.

But with enthusiasm for ideals history gives us caution, warns us against the moving of the pendulum, and gives us points of departure from which to measure progress. It gives us courage to attack difficult problems. It shows which the abiding problems are—those that can be solved only by waiting, and not tossed aside by a supreme effort. It shows us the progress of the race, the changing ideals of the perfect man, and the means by which men have sought to realize these ideals. We can from its study better answer the question, What is education, what may it accomplish, and how may its ideals be realized? It gives the evolution of the present and explains anomalies in our work. And Yet the history of education is not a subject to be treated extensively in a training school. All but the outlines may better be reserved for later professional reading.

Training in Teaching

Training to teach requires (1) schools for observation, and (2) schools for practice.

Of necessity, these schools must be separate in purpose and in organization. A practice-school cannot be a model school, The pupil-teacher should have the opportunity to observe the best models of the teaching art; and the manner, methods, and devices of the model-teacher should be noted, discussed, and referred to the foundation principles on which they rest. Allowable modifications of this observed work may be suggested by the pupil-teacher and approved by the teacher in charge.

There should be selected certain of the best teachers in regular school work, whom the pupil-teachers may be sent to observe. The pupil-teachers should take no part in the school work nor cause any change therein. They should, however, be told in advance by the teacher what purpose she seeks to accomplish This excites expectation and brings into consciousness the apperceiving ideas by which the suggestions of the exercise, as they develop, may be seized and assimilated.

At first these visits should be made in company with their teacher of methods, and the work of a single class in one subject should be first observed. After such visits the teacher of methods in the given subject should discuss with the pupil-teachers the work observed. The pupil-teachers should first describe the work they have seen and specify the excellences noted, and tell why these things are commendable and upon what laws of teaching they are based. Next, the pupil-teachers should question the teacher of methods as to the cause, purpose, or influence of things noted, and matters of doubtful propriety—if there be such—should be considered. Then the teacher in turn should question her pupil-teachers as to matters that seem to have escaped their notice, as to the motive of the model-teacher, as to the reason for the order of treatment, or form of question, wherein lay the merit of her method, the secret of her power. When pupil-teachers have made such observations several times, with several teachers, and in several subjects, the broader investigation may be made as to the organization of one of the model rooms, its daily programme of recitations and of study, the methods of discipline, the relations between pupils and teacher, the "school spirit," the school movements, and class progress. This work should be done before teaching groups or classes of pupils is attempted, and should form an occasional exercise during the period of practice-teaching as a matter of relief and inspiration. If an artist requires the suggestive help of a good example that stirs his own originality, why should not a teacher?

The Practice-School

During the course in methodology certain steps preparatory to practice-teaching may be taken. 1. The pupil-teacher may analyze the topic to be taught, noting essentials and incidentals, seeking the connections of the subject with the mental possessions of the pupils to be considered and the sequences from these points of contact to the knowledge to be gained under instruction. 2. Next, plans of lessons may be prepared and series of questions for teaching the given subjects. 3. Giving lessons to fellow pupil-teachers leads to familiarity with the mechanism of class work, such as calling, directing, and dismissing classes, gives the beginner ease and self-confidence, leads to careful preparation of lessons, gives skill in asking questions, and in the use of apparatus.

The practice-teaching should be in another school, preferably in a different building, and should commence with group-teaching in a recitation-room apart from the schoolroom. Actual teaching of small groups of children gives opportunity for the study of the child-mind in its efforts at reception and assimilation of new ideas, and shows the modifications in lesson plans that must be made to adapt the subject-matter to the child's tastes and activities. But the independent charge for a considerable time of a school-room with a full quota of pupils, the pupil-teacher and the children being much of the time the sole occupants of the room,—in short, the realization of ordinary school conditions, with the opportunity to go for advice to a friendly critic, is the most valuable practice; and no practice short of this can be considered of great value except as preparation for this chief form of preparatory practice. All this work should have its due proportion only, or evil may result. For example, lesson plans tend to formalism, to self-conceit, to work in few and narrow lines, to study of subjects rather than of pupils; lessons to fellow-pupils make one self-conscious, hinder the growth of enthusiasm in work, and are entirely barren if carried beyond a very few exercises; teaching groups of children for considerable time unfits the teacher for the double burden of discipline and instruction, to bear both of which simultaneously and easily is the teacher's greatest difficulty and most essential power.

A critic-teacher should be appointed to the oversight of a schoolroom. The critic may also supervise one or more teachers practicing for brief periods daily with groups of children.

The pupil-teachers are now to emphasize practice rather than theory, to work under the direction of one who regards the interests of the children quite as much as those of the teacher-in-training. The critic must admit the principles of education and general methods taught by the teacher of methodology, but she may have her own devices and even special methods that need not be those of the teacher of methodology. No harm will come to the teachers-in-training if they learn that principles must be assented to by all, but that methods may bear the stamp of the personality of the teacher; that all things must be considered from the point of view of their effect upon the pupils; the critic maintaining the claims of the children, the teacher of methods conforming to the laws of mind and the science of the subject taught. The critics must teach for their pupil-teachers and show in action the justness of their suggestions. In this sense they are model-teachers as well as critics.

The critic should, at the close of school, meet her pupil-teachers for a report of their experiences through the day: What they have attempted, how they have tried to do it, why they did so, and what success they gained. Advice as to overcoming difficulties, encouragement under trial, caution if need be, help for the work of to-morrow, occupy the hour. Above all, the critic should be a true friend, a womanly and cultivated woman, and an inspiring companion, whose presence is helpful to work and improving to personality.

Length of Training-School Course

There are three elements which determine the time to be spent in a training school—the time given to academic studies, the time given to professional studies, and the time given to practice. The sum of these periods will be the time required for the training course. Taking these in the inverse order, let us consider how much time is required for practice work with pupils. The time given to lesson outlines and practice with fellow pupil-teachers may be considered a part of the professional study rather than of practice-teaching. The period of practice with pupils must not be too short, whether we consider the interests of the pupils or of the teachers-in-training. An effort is usually made to counteract the effect upon the children of a succession of crude efforts of teachers beginning practice by strengthening the teaching and supervision through the employment of a considerable number of model and supervisory teachers, and by dividing the pupils into small groups, so that much individual work can be done. These arrangements, while useful for their purpose, destroy to a considerable degree the usual conditions under which school work is to be done, and tend to render the teachers-in-training formal and imitative.

The practice room should be, as far as may be, the ordinary school, with the difficulties and responsibilities that will be met later. The responsibility for order, discipline, progress, records, reports, communication with parents and school authorities, must fall fully upon the young teacher, who has a friendly assistant to whom she can go for advice in the person of a wise and experienced critic, not constantly at hand, but constantly within reach.

Between the critic and the teacher-in-training there should exist the most cordial and familiar relations. These relations are based on the one hand upon an appreciation of wisdom and kindness, on the other, upon an appreciation of sincerity and effort. The growth of such relations, and the fruitage which follows their growth, require time. A half-year is not too long to be allotted for them. During this half-year experience, self-confidence and growth in power have been gained; but the pupil-teacher is still not ready to be set aside to work out her own destiny. At this point she is just ready for marked advance, which should be helped and guided. To remain longer with her critic friend may cause imitation rather than independence, may lead to contentment and cessation of growth. She should now be transferred to the care of a second critic of a different personality, but of equal merit. The new critic is bound by her duty and her ambition to see that the first half year's advancement is maintained in the second. The pupil-teacher finds that excellence is not all upon one model. The value of individuality impresses her. She gains a view of solid principles wrapped in diverse characteristics. Her own individuality rises to new importance, and the elements of a growth not at once to be checked start up within her. For the care of the second critic a second half year must be allowed, which extends the practice work with pupils through an entire school year. For the theoretical work a year is by general experience proven sufficient. The ideal training course is, then, one of two years' length.

Provision for the extended practice which is here recommended can be made only by city training-schools and by normal schools having connection with the schools of a city. To set apart a building of several rooms as a school of practice will answer the purpose only when there are very few teachers in training. In order to give each pupil-teacher a year of practice the number of practice rooms must equal the number of teachers to be graduated annually from the training-school, be the number ten, fifty, or five hundred. In any considerable city a school for practice will not suffice; many schools for practice must be secured. This can be done by selecting one excellent teacher in each of a sufficient number of school buildings, and making her a critic-teacher, giving her charge of two schoolrooms, in each of which is placed a pupil-teacher for training.

This insures that the training shall be done as nearly as may be under ordinary conditions, brings the pupil-teachers at once into the general body of teachers, makes the corps of critics a leaven of zeal, and good teaching scattered among the schools. This body of critics will uplift the schools. More capable in the beginning than the average teacher, led to professional study, ambitious for the best things, they make greater progress than they otherwise would do, and are sufficient in themselves to inspire the general body of teachers. For the sake of the pupil-teachers, and the children, too, this plan is best. Its economy also will readily be apparent. This plan has been tried for several years in the schools of Providence, with results fully equal to those herein claimed.

Tests of Success

The tests of success in practice-teaching are in the main those to be applied to all teaching. Do her pupils grow more honest, industrious, polite? Do they admire their teacher? Does she secure obedience and industry only while demanding it, or has she influence that reaches beyond her presence? Do her pupils think well and talk well? As to the teacher herself: Has she sympathy and tact, self-reliance and originality, breadth and intensity? Is she systematic, direct, and business-like? Is she courteous, neat in person and in work? Has she discernment of character and a just standard of requirement and attainment?

These are some of the questions one must answer before he pronounces any teacher a success or a failure.

Admission to a training school assumes that the pupil has good health, good scholarship, good sense, good ability, and devotion to the work of teaching. If all these continue to be exhibited in satisfactory degree and the pupil goes through the prescribed course of study and practice, the diploma of the school should naturally mark the completion of this work. If it appears on acquaintance that a serious mistake has been made in estimating any of these elements, then, so soon as the mistake is fairly apparent and is probably a permanent condition, the pupil should be requested to withdraw from the work. This is not a case where the wheat and the tares should grow together until the harvest at graduation day or the examinations preceding it. With such a foundation continually maintained, it is the duty of the school to conquer success for each pupil.

Teaching does not require genius. Indeed, genius, in the sense of erratic ability, is out of place in the teacher's chair. Most good teachers at this close of the nineteenth century are made, not born; made from good material well fashioned. There is, however, a possibility that some idiosyncrasy of character, not readily discovered until the test is made, may rise between the prospective teacher and her pupils, making her influence over them small or harmful. Such a defect, if it exists, will appear during the practice-teaching, and the critic will discover it. This defect, on its first discovery, should be plainly pointed out to the teacher-in-training and her efforts should be joined with those of the critic in its removal.

If this effort be a failure and the defect be one likely to harm the pupils hereafter to be taught, then the teacher-in-training should be informed and requested to withdraw from the school. There should be no test at this close of the school course to determine fitness for graduation. Graduation should find the teacher serious in view of her responsibilities, hopeful because she has learned how success is to be attained, inspired with the belief that growth in herself and in her pupils is the great demand and the great reward.

THE COMMITTEE OF FIFTEEN ON THE TRAINING OF HIGH-SCHOOL TEACHERS (1895)   From H. S. Tarbell, "On the Training of Teachers," as quoted in National Education Association, *Report of the Committee of Fifteen* (Boston, 1895), pp. 113–17.

Training of Teachers for Secondary Schools

$\mathbf{P}$erhaps one-sixth of the great body of public school teachers in the United States are engaged in secondary work and in supervision. These are the leading teachers. They give educational tone to communities, as well as inspiration to the body of teachers.

It is of great importance that they be imbued with the professional spirit springing from sound professional culture. The very difficult and responsible positions that they fill demand ripe scholarship, more than ordinary ability, and an intimate knowledge of the period of adolescence, which Rousseau so aptly styles the second birth.

The elementary schools provide for the education of the masses. Our secondary schools educate our social and business leaders. The careers of our college graduates, who mainly fill the important places in professional and political life, are determined largely by the years of secondary training. The college or university gives expansion and finish, the secondary school gives character and direction.

It should not be forgotten that the superintendents of public schools are largely taken from the ranks of secondary teachers, and that the scholarship, qualities, and training required for the one class are nearly equivalent to that demanded for the other.

Our high schools, too, are the source of supply for teachers in elementary schools. Hence the pedagogic influences exerted in the high school should lead to excellence in elementary teaching.

The superintendent who with long foresight looks to the improvement of his schools will labor earnestly to improve and especially to professionalize the teaching in his high school. The management which makes the high school an independent portion of the school system, merely attached and loftily superior, which limits the supervision and influence of the superintendent to the primary and grammar grades, is short-sighted and destructive.

There ought also to be a place and a plan for the training of teachers for normal schools. The great body of normal and training schools in the United States are secondary schools. Those who are to teach in these schools need broad scholarship, thorough understanding of educational problems, and trained experience. To put into these schools teachers whose scholarship is that of the secondary school and whose training is that of the elementary is to narrow and depress, rather than broaden and elevate.

If college graduates are put directly into teaching without special study and training, they will teach as they have been taught. The methods of college professors are not in all cases the best, and, if they were, high school pupils are not to be taught nor disciplined as college students are. High school teaching and discipline can be that neither of the grammar school nor of the college, but is *sui generis*. To recognize this truth and the special differences is vital to success. This recognition comes only from much experience at great loss and partial failure, or by happy intuition not usually to be expected, or by definite instruction and directed practice. Success in teaching depends upon conformity to principles, and these principles are not a part of the mental equipment of every educated person.

These considerations and others are the occasion of a growing conviction, widespread in this land, that secondary teachers should be trained for their work even more carefully than elementary teachers are trained. This conviction is manifested in the efforts to secure normal schools adapted to training teachers for secondary schools, notably in Massachusetts and New York, and in the numerous professorships of pedagogy established in rapidly increasing numbers in our colleges and universities.

The training of teachers for secondary schools is in several essential respects the same as that for teachers of elementary schools. Both demand scholarship, theory, and practice. The degree of scholarship required for secondary teachers is by common consent fixed at a collegiate education. No one—with rare exceptions—should be employed to teach in a high school who has not this fundamental preparation.

It is not necessary to enter in detail into the work of theoretical instruction for secondary teachers. The able men at the head of institutions and departments designed for such work neither need nor desire advice upon this matter. And yet for the purposes of this report it may be allowable to point out a plan for the organization of a secondary training school.

Let it be supposed that two essentials have been found in one locality, (1) a college or university having a department of pedagogy and a department of post-graduate work; (2) a high school, academy, or preparatory school whose managers are willing to employ and pay a number of graduate students to teach under direction for a portion of each day. These two conditions being met, we will suppose that pedagogy is offered as an elective to the college seniors.

Two years of instruction in the science and art of teaching are to be provided; one, mostly theory with some practice, elective during the senior year; the other, mostly practice with some theory, elective for one year as post-graduate work.

During the senior year is to be studied:—

The Science of Teaching

The elements of this science are:—

I. Psychology in its physiological, apperceptive, and experimental features. The period of adolescence here assumes the prominence that childhood has in the psychological study preparatory to teaching in lower schools. This is the period of beginnings, the beginning of a more ambitious and generous life, a life having the future wrapped up in it; a transition period, of mental storm and stress, in which egoism gives way to altruism, romance has charm, and the social, moral, and religious feelings bud and bloom. To guide youth at this formative stage, in which an active fermentation occurs that may give wine or vinegar according to conditions, requires a deep and sympathetic nature, and that knowledge of the changing life which supplies guidance wise and adequate.

II. Methodology: A discussion of the principles of education and of the methods of teaching the studies of the secondary schools.

III. School economy should be studied in a much wider and more thorough way than is required for elementary teachers. The school systems of Germany, France, England, and the leading systems of the United States should also be studied.

IV. History of education, the tracing of modern doctrine back to its sources; those streams of influence now flowing and those that have disappeared in the sands of the centuries.

V. The philosophy of education as a division of an all-involving philosophy of life and thought in which unity is found.

The Art of Teaching

This includes observation and practice. The observation should include the work of different grades and of different localities, with minute and searching comparison and reports upon special topics. How does excellent primary work differ from excellent grammar grade work? How do the standards of excellence differ between grammar grades and high school grades? Between high school and college work? What are the arguments for and against coeducation in secondary schools, as determined by experience? What are the upper and lower limits of secondary education as determined by the nature of the pupil's efforts?

In the college class in pedagogy much more than in the elementary normal school can the class itself be made to afford a means of practice to its members. Quizzes may be conducted by students upon the chapters of the books read or the lectures of the professors. These exercises may have for their object review, or improved statement, or enlarged inference and application, and they afford an ample opportunity to cultivate the art of questioning, skill in which is the teacher's most essential accomplishment.

The head of the department of pedagogy will, of course, present the essential methods of teaching, and the heads of other departments may lecture on methods pertaining to their subject of study; or secondary teachers of known success may still better present the methods now approved in the several departments of secondary work.

THE COMMITTEE OF FIFTEEN ON A STRONG, CENTRALIZED
ORGANIZATION FOR CITY SCHOOL SYSTEMS (1895)   From Andrew S. Draper,
"Organization for City School Systems," National Education Association, *Report of the Committee of Fifteen* (Washington, D.C., 1895), pp. 75–87, 90–92.

It is understood that the committee is to treat of city school systems, which are so large that persons chosen by the people to manage them, and serving without pay, cannot be expected to transact all the business of the system in person, nor to have personal knowledge of all business transactions, and which are so large that one person employed to supervise the instruction cannot be assumed to personally manage or direct all of the details thereof, but must, in each case, act under plans of organization and administration established by law and through assistants or representatives.

The end for which a school system exists is the *instruction of the children*, attaching to the word instruction the meaning it attains in the mind of a well-educated person, if not in the mind of an educational expert.

To secure this end, no plan of organization alone will suffice. Nothing can take the place of a sincere desire for good schools, or a fair knowledge of what good schools are, and what will make them, of a public spirit and a moral sense on the part of the people, which are spontaneous, or which can be appealed to with confidence. Fortunately, the interest which the people have in their own children is so large, and the anxiety of the community for public order and security is so great, that public sentiment may ordinarily be relied upon, or may be aroused to action, to choose proper representatives and take proper measures for the administration of the schools. If, in any case, this is not so, there is little hope of efficient schools. Wherever it *is* so, it alone will not suffice, but proper organization may become the instrument of public sentiment, and develop schools which will be equal to the needs of all, and become the safeguards of citizenship. Efficient schools can be secured only by providing suitable buildings and appliances, and by keeping them in proper order on the one hand, and, on the other hand, by employing, organizing, aiding, and directing teachers, so that the instruction shall have life and power to accomplish the great end for which schools are maintained.

The circumstances of the case naturally and quickly separate the duties of administration into two great departments, one which manages the business affairs, and the other which supervises the instruction. The business affairs of the school system may be transacted by any citizens of common honesty, correct purposes, and of good business experience and sagacity. The instruction will be ineffective and abnormally expensive unless put upon a scientific educational basis and supervised by competent educational experts.

There will be a waste of money and effort and a lack of results, unless the authorities of these two departments are sympathetic with each other; that is, unless, on the one hand, the business management is sound, is appreciative of good teaching, looks upon it as a scientific and professional employment, and is alert to sustain it; and unless, on the other hand, the instructors are competent and self-respecting, know what good business management is, are glad to uphold it, and are able to respect those who are charged with responsibility for it.

To secure efficiency in these departments, there must be adequate authority and quick public accountability. The problem is not merely to secure some good schoolhouses, but good schoolhouses wherever needed, and to avoid the use of all houses which are not suitable for use; it is not to get some good teaching, but to prevent all bad teaching, and to advance all the teaching to the highest possible point of special training, professional spirit, and of life-giving power. All of the business matters must be entrusted to competent business hands and managed upon sound business principles; and all of the instruction must be put upon a professional basis. To insure this, there must be deliberation and wisdom in determining policy, and then the power to do what is determined upon must be present and capable of exercise, and the responsibility for the proper exercise of the power must, in each case, be individual and immediate.

It is imperative that we discriminate between the legislative and executive action in organizing and administering the schools. The influences which enter into legislative action, looking to the general organization and work of the schools, must necessarily and fundamentally flow directly from the people and be widely spread. The greater the number of people, in proportion to the entire population, who can be led to take a positive interest and an active part in securing good schools, the better will the schools be, provided the people can secure the complete execution of their purposes and plans. But experience has clearly shown that many causes intervene to prevent the complete execution of such plans, that all the natural enemies of sound administration scent plenty of plunder and are especially active here, that good school administration requires much strength of character, much business experience, much technical knowledge, and can be only measurably satisfactory when the responsibility is adequate, and the penalties for maladministration are severe. Decentralization in making the plan and determining what shall be done, and centralization in executing the plan and in doing what is to be done, are, perhaps, equally important.

It should be remembered that the character of the school work of a city is not merely a matter of local interest, and that the maintenance of the schools does not rest merely or mainly upon local authority. The people of the municipality, acting, and ordinarily glad to act, but, in any event, being obliged to act, under and pursuant to the law which has been ordained by the sovereign authority of the state, establish and maintain schools. They must have the taxing power which the state alone possesses in order to enable them to proceed at all. They must regard the directions which the state sees fit to give as to the essential character of the schools, when it exercises in their behalf, or when it delegates to them the power of taxation.

The plan should be flexible for good, while inflexible for evil. Meeting essential requirements, the people of the municipality may well be empowered to proceed as much farther as they will in elaborating a system of schools. The higher the plane of average intelligence, and the more generally and the more directly the people act in deciding what shall be done, and the greater the facility and completeness with which the intelligence of the city is able to secure the proper execution of its plans by officers appointed for that purpose, the more elaborate and the more efficient will be the schools, and this should, of course, be provided for.

It is idle to suggest that centering executive functions is unwisely taking power away from the people. The people cannot execute plans themselves. The authority to do it must necessarily be delegated. The question simply is, "Shall it be given to a number of persons, and if so, to how many? Or to only one?" This question is to be decided by experience, and it is, of course, true that experience has not been uniform. But it is doubtless true that the general experience of the communities of the country has shown that where purely executive functions are conferred upon a number of persons jointly, they yield to antagonistic influences and shift the responsibility from one to another; and that centering the responsibility for the proper discharge of executive duties upon a single person, who gets the credit of good work and must bear the disgrace or penalty of bad work, and who can quickly be held accountable for misdeeds and inefficiency, has secured the fullest execution of public plans and the largest results. To call this "centralization," with the meaning which commonly attaches to the word, is inaccurate. Instead of removing the power from the people, it is keeping the power closer to the people, and making it possible for the citizen in his indivdual capacity and for organized bodies of citizens to secure the execution of plans according to the purpose and intent with which those plans were made. Indeed, it is safe to say that experience has shown that this is *the only way* in which to prevent the frequent thwarting of the popular will and the defiance of individuals whose interests are ignored or whose rights are invaded.

*   *   *

The name of the legislative branch of the school government is not material, and the one to which the people are accustomed may well continue to be employed. There is no name more appropriate than the "Board of Education."

The manner of selecting or appointing the members of this legislative body may turn somewhat upon the circumstances of the city. We are strongly of the opinion that in view of the well-known difficulty about securing the attendance of the most interested and intelligent electors at school elections, as well as because of the apparent impossibility of freeing school elections from political or municipal issues, the better manner of elections is by appointment. If the members of the board are appointed, the mayor of the city is likely to be the official to whom the power of appointment may most safely be entrusted. The mayor is not suggested because his office should sustain any relation to the school system, but in spite of the fact that it does not and should not. The school system should be *absolutely emancipated from partisan politics, and completely dissociated from municipal business.* But we think the appointments should be made by some one person, rather than by a board. The mayor is representative of the whole city and all its interests. While not chosen with any reference to the interests of the schools, he may be assumed to have information as to the fitness of citizens for particular responsibilities, and to be desirous of promoting the educational interests of the people. If he is given the power of appointment, he should be particularly enjoined by law to consider the fitness of individuals alone and pay no regard to party affiliations, unless it be to particularly see to it that no one political party has an overwhelming preponderance in the board. The mayor very commonly feels constrained, under the pressure of party expediency, to make so many questionable appointments, that he is only too glad, and particularly so when enjoined by the law, to make very acceptable appointments of members of school boards, in order that he may gratify the better sentiment of the city. We are confident that the problem of getting a representative board of education is not so difficult as many think, if the board is not permitted to make patronage of work and salaried positions at the disposal of the public-school system. Under such circumstances, and more and more so as we have approached such circumstances, appointment in the way we suggest has produced the best school boards in the larger cities of the country.

The members of school boards should be representative of the whole population and of all their common educational interests, and should not be chosen to represent any ward of subdivision of the territory, or any party or element in the political, religious, or social life thereof. Where this principle is not enforced, the members will feel bound to gain what advantage they can for the district or interests they represent; bitter contests will ensue, and the common interests will suffer.

Attempts to eliminate partisanship from school administration, by arraying an equal number of partisans against each other in school boards, do not, at best, lead to an ideal organization. In some instances they have proved fairly successful; in others, very mischievous. The true course is to insist that all who have any share in the management of the schools shall divest themselves of partisanship, whether political or religious, in such management, and give themselves wholly to the high interests entrusted to them. If it be said that this cannot be realized, it may be answered, without admitting it, that even if that were so, it would be no reason why the friends of the schools should not assert the sound principle and secure its enforcement as far as possible. We must certainly give no countenance to make-shifts, which experience has shown to be misleading and expensive. The right must prevail in the end, and the earlier and more strongly it is contended for, the sooner it will prevail.

Relatively small boards are preferable to large ones. In a city of less than a half-million of inhabitants, the number should not exceed nine, and might well not exceed five. In the very largest cities it might be enlarged to fifteen.

The term for which members are appointed should be a reasonably long one, say, five years.

We think it an excellent plan to provide for two branches and sets of powers in the board of education; the one to have the veto power, or, at least, to act as a check upon the acts of the other. This may be accomplished by creating the office of school director and charging the incumbent with executive duties on the business side of the administration, and by giving him the veto power over the acts of the other branch of the board, which may be called the "School Council." Beyond the care and conservation which is ensured by two sets of powers acting against each other, it has the advantage of giving the chief executive officer of the system just as high and good a title as that of members of the board, it is likely to secure a more representative man, and gives him larger prerogatives in the discharge of his executive duties and better standing among the people, particularly among the employees and teachers associated with the public-school system.

If this plan is adopted, the school director should be required to give his entire time to the duties of his position, and be properly compensated therefor. He should be the custodian of all property and should appoint all assistants, janitors, and workmen, authorized by the board, for the care of the same. He should give bond, with sufficient sureties and penalties, for the faithful and proper discharge of all his duties. He should be authorized by law to expend funds, within a fixed limit, for repairs, appliances, and help, without the action of the board. All contracts should be made by him, and should run in his name, and he should be charged with the responsibility of seeing that they are faithfully and completely executed. All contracts involving more than a limited and fixed sum of money should be let upon bids to be advertised for and opened in public. He should have a seat in the board of education; should not vote, but should have the power to veto, either absolutely or conditionally, any of the acts of the board, through a written communication. This officer and the school council should together constitute the board of education.

The board of education should be vested with legislative functions only, and be required to act wholly through formal and recorded resolutions. It should determine and direct the general policy of the school system. Within reasonable limits, as to amount, it should be given power, in its discretion, to levy whatever moneys may be needed for school purposes. It should control the expenditure of all moneys beyond a fixed and limited amount, which may safely and advantageously be left to the discretion of the chief executive business officer. It should authorize, by general resolutions, the appointment of necessary officers and employees in the business department, and the superintendent, assistants, and teachers in the department of instruction, but it should be allowed to make no appointments other than its own clerk. With this necessary exception, single officers should be charged with responsibility for all appointments.

This plan, not in all, but in essential particulars, has been on trial in the city of Cleveland for nearly three years, and has worked with very general acceptability.

If this plan is adopted, the chief executive officer of the system is already provided for and his duties have already been indicated. Otherwise it will be necessary for the board to appoint such an officer. In that event, the law should declare him independent, confer upon him adequate authority for the performance of executive duties, and charge him with responsibility. But we know of no statutory language capable of making an officer appointed by a board, and dependent upon the same board for supplies, independent in fact of the personal wishes of the members of that board. And right here is where the troubles rush in to discredit and damage the school system.

We now come to the subject of paramount importance in making a plan for the school government in a great city, namely, the character of the teaching force and the quality of the instruction. A city school system may be able to withstand some abuses on the business side of its administration and continue to perform its functions with measurable success, but wrongs against the instruction must, in a little time, prove fatal. The strongest language is none too strong here. The safety of the republic, the security of American citizenship, are at stake. Government by the people has no more dangerous pitfall in its road than this, that in the mighty cities of the land the comfortable and intelligent masses, who are discriminating more and more closely about the education of their children, shall become dissatisfied with the social status of the teachers and the quality of the teaching in the common schools. In that event they will educate their children at their own expense, and the public schools will become only good enough for those who can afford no better. The only way to avert this is by maintaining the instruction upon a purely scientific and professional footing. This is entirely practicable, but it involves much care and expense in training teachers, the absolute elimination of favoritism from appointments, the security of the right to advancement after appointment, on the basis of merit, and a general leadership which is kindly, helpful, and stimulating to individuals, which can secure harmonious cooperation from all the members, and lends energy and inspiration to the whole body.

This cannot be secured if there is any lack of authority, and experience amply proves that it will not be secured if there is any division of responsibility. The whole matter of instruction must be placed in the hands of a superintendent of instruction, with independent powers and adequate authority, who is charged with full responsibility.

*   *   *

Moreover, we must consider the alternative. It is not in doubt. All who have had any contact with the subject are familiar with it. It is administration by boards or committees, the members of which are not competent to manage professional matters and develop an expert teaching force. Though necessarily inexperienced, they frequently assume the knowledge of the most experienced. They over-ride and degrade a superintendent, when they have the power to do so, until he becomes their mere factotum. For the sake of harmony and the continuance of his position, he concedes, surrenders, and acquiesces in their acts, while the continually increasing teaching force becomes weaker and weaker, and the work poorer and poorer. If he refuses to do this, they precipitate an open rupture, and turn him out of his position. Then they cloud the issues and shift the responsibility from one to another. There are exceptions, of course, but they do not change the rule.

It will be unprofitable to mince words about this all-important matter. If the course of study for the public schools of a great city is to be determined by laymen, it will not be suited to the needs of a community. If teachers are to be appointed by boards or committees, the members of which are particularly sensitive to the desires of people who have votes or influence, looseness of action is inevitable, and unworthy considerations will frequently prevail. If the action of a board or committee be conditioned upon the recommendation of a superintendent, the plan will not suffice. No one person is stronger than the system of which he is a part. Such a plan results in contests between the board and the superintendents, and such a contest is obviously an unequal one. There is little doubt of the outcome. In recommending for the appointment of teachers, the personal wishes of members of the board, in particular cases, will have to be acquiesced in. If a teacher, no matter how unfit, cannot be dropped from the list without the approval of a board or committee after they have heard from her friends and sympathizers, she will remain indefinitely in the service. This means a low tone in the teaching force and desolation in the work of the schools. If the superintendent accepts the situation, he becomes less and less capable of developing a professional teaching service. If he refuses to accept it, he is very likely to meet humiliation; dismissal is practically inevitable.

The superintendent of instruction should be charged with no duty save the supervision of the instruction, but should be charged with the responsibility of making that professional and scientific, and should be given the position and authority to accomplish that end.

*　　*　　*

In concluding this portion of the report, the committee indicates briefly the principles which must necessarily be observed in framing a plan of organization and government in a large city school system.

First.—The affairs of the schools should not be mixed up with partisan contents or municipal business.

Second.—There should be a sharp distinction between legislative functions and executive duties.

Third.—Legislative functions should be clearly fixed by statute and be exercised by a relatively small board, each member of which board is representative of the whole city. This board, within statutory limitations, should determine the policy of the system, levy taxes, and control the expenditures. It should make no appointments. Every act should be by a recorded resolution. It is preferable that this board be created by appointment rather than election, and that it be constituted of two branches acting against each other.

Fourth.—Administration should be separated into two great independent departments, one of which manages the business interests and the other of which supervises the instruction. Each of these should be wholly directed by a single official, who is vested with ample authority and charged with full responsibility for sound administration.

Fifth.—The chief executive officer on the business side should be charged with the care of all property, and with the duty of keeping it in suitable condition; he should make all agreements and see that they are properly performed; he should appoint all assistants, janitors, and workmen. In a word, he should do all that the law contemplates, and all that the board authorizes, concerning the business affairs of the school system, and when anything goes wrong, he should answer for it. He may be appointed by the board, but we think it preferable that he be chosen in the same way the members of the board are chosen, and be given a veto upon the acts of the board.

Sixth.—The chief executive officer of the department of instruction should be given a long term, and may be appointed by the board. If the board is constituted of two branches, he should be nominated by the business executive and confirmed by the legislative branch. Once appointed, he should be independent. He should appoint all authorized assistants and teachers from an eligible list, to be constituted as provided by law. He should assign to duties and discontinue services for cause at his discretion. He should determine all matters relating to instruction. He should be charged with the responsibility of developing a professional and enthusiastic teaching force and of making all the teaching scientific and forceful. He must perfect the organization of his department, and make and carry out plans to accomplish this. If he cannot do this in a reasonable time, he should be superseded by one who can.